Richard L. Daft

Vanderbilt University

Organization Theory & Design | 12e

CENGAGE
Learning

Australia • Brazil • Mexico • Singapore • United Kingdom • United States

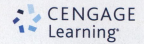
CENGAGE
Learning®

Organization Theory & Design
Twelfth Edition
Richard L. Daft

Vice President, General Manager, Social
 Science & Qualitative Business:
 Erin Joyner

Product Director: Michael Schenk

Senior Product Manager: Scott Person

Content Developer: Suzanne Wilder

Product Assistant: Brian Pierce

Marketing Director: Kristen Hurd

Marketing Manager: Emily Horowitz

Marketing Coordinator: Chris Walz

Art and Cover Direction, Production
 Management, and Composition:
 Lumina Datamatics Inc.

Senior Media Developer: Sally Nieman

Intellectual Property
 Analyst: Diane Garrity

Project Manager: Sarah Shainwald

Manufacturing Planner: Ron Montgomery

Cover Images: Jeffrey Barry/Moment/
 Getty Images, Kjel Larsen/Moment/
 Getty Images

Library of Congress Control Number: 2015933405

ISBN: 978-1-285-86634-5

Cengage Learning
20 Channel Center Street
Boston, MA 02210
USA

Cengage Learning is a leading provider of customized learning solutions
with employees residing in nearly 40 different countries and sales in
more than 125 countries around the world. Find your local representative at **www.cengage.com**.

Cengage Learning products are represented in Canada by
Nelson Education, Ltd.

To learn more about Cengage Learning Solutions, visit **www.cengage.com**

Purchase any of our products at your local college store or at our
preferred online store **www.cengagebrain.com**

Printed in Canada
Print Number: 01   Print Year: 2015

Richard L. Daft, Ph.D., is the Brownlee O. Currey, Jr., Professor of Management in the Owen Graduate School of Management at Vanderbilt University. Professor Daft specializes in the study of organization theory and leadership. Professor Daft is a Fellow of the Academy of Management and has served on the editorial boards of *Academy of Management Journal, Administrative Science Quarterly,* and *Journal of Management Education.* He was the Associate Editor-in-Chief of *Organization Science* and served for three years as Associate Editor of *Administrative Science Quarterly.*

Professor Daft has authored or co-authored 14 books, including *The Executive and the Elephant: A Leader's Guide to Building Inner Excellence* (Jossey-Bass, 2010), *Building Management Skills: An Action-First Approach* (Cengage/South-Western, 2014), *Management* (Cengage/South-Western, 2016), *The Leadership Experience* (Cengage/South-Western, 2015), and *What to Study: Generating and Developing Research Questions* (Sage, 1982). He also published *Fusion Leadership: Unlocking the Subtle Forces That Change People and Organizations* (Berrett-Koehler, 2000) with Robert Lengel. He has authored dozens of scholarly articles, papers, and chapters. His work has been published in *Administrative Science Quarterly, Academy of Management Journal, Academy of Management Review, Organizational Dynamics, Strategic Management Journal, Journal of Management, Accounting Organizations and Society, Management Science, MIS Quarterly, California Management Review,* and *Organizational Behavior Teaching Review.* Professor Daft has been awarded several government research grants to pursue studies of organization design, organizational innovation and change, strategy implementation, and organizational information processing.

Professor Daft is also an active teacher and consultant. He has taught management, leadership, organizational change, organization theory, and organizational behavior. He has been involved in management development and consulting for many companies and government organizations, including the National Academy of Science, Oak Ridge National Laboratory, American Banking Association, AutoZone, Aegis Technology, Bridgestone, Bell Canada, Allstate Insurance, the National Transportation Research Board, the Tennessee Valley Authority (TVA), State Farm Insurance, Tenneco, the U.S. Air Force, the U.S. Army, Eli Lilly, Central Parking System, Entergy Sales and Service, Bristol-Myers Squibb, First American National Bank, and the Vanderbilt University Medical Center.

Brief Contents

Contents

PART 3 Open System Design Elements 139

Contents

PART 4　Internal Design Elements　257

PART 5   Managing Dynamic Processes   383

Integrative Cases   553

My vision for the Twelfth Edition of *Organization Theory and Design* is to integrate current organization design problems with significant ideas and theories in a way that is engaging and enjoyable for students. There is an average of 37 new citations per chapter for new findings and examples that make the Twelfth Edition current and applicable for students. In addition, significant elements of this edition include "Managing by Design Questions" and "How Do You Fit the Design?" boxes, along with updates to every chapter that incorporate the most recent ideas, new case examples, new book reviews, and new end-of-book integrative cases. The research and theories in the field of organization studies are rich and insightful and will help students and managers understand their organizational world and solve real-life problems. My mission is to combine the concepts and models from organizational theory with changing events in the real world to provide the most up-to-date view of organization design available.

Distinguishing Features of the Twelfth Edition

Many students in a typical organization theory course do not have extensive work experience, especially at the middle and upper levels, where organization theory is most applicable. Moreover, word from the field is that many students today often do not read the chapter opening examples or boxed examples, preferring instead to focus on chapter content. To engage students in the world of organizations, the Twelfth Edition uses "Managing by Design Questions" at the start of each chapter. These questions immediately engage students in thinking and expressing their beliefs and opinions about organization design concepts. Another in-chapter feature, "How Do You Fit the Design?" engages students in how their personal style and approach will fit into an organization. Other student experiential activities that engage students in applying chapter concepts include new "BookMarks," new "In Practice" examples, new end-of-chapter cases, and new integrative cases for student analysis. The total set of features substantially expands and improves the book's content and accessibility. These multiple pedagogical devices are used to enhance student involvement in text materials.

How Do You Fit the Design? The "How Do You Fit the Design?" feature presents a short questionnaire in each chapter about the student's own style and preferences to quickly provide feedback about how they fit particular organizations or situations. For example, questionnaire topics include "What Is Your Cultural Intelligence?" "Your Strategy Strength," "Are You Ready to Fill an International Role?" "Corporate Culture Preference," "Is Goal-Setting Your Style?" "Making Important Decisions," and "Personal Networking." These short feedback questionnaires connect the student's personal preferences to chapter material to heighten interest and show the relevance of chapter concepts.

Managing by Design Questions.   Each chapter opens with three short opinion questions that engage students in clarifying their thoughts about upcoming material and concepts. These questions are based on the idea that when students express their opinions first, they are more open to and interested in receiving material that is relevant to the questions. Example questions, which ask students to agree or disagree, include:

> *A certain amount of conflict is good for an organization.*
> *The best measures of business performance are financial.*
> *Savvy organizations should encourage managers to use Twitter.*
> *A CEO's top priority is to make sure the organization is designed correctly.*
> *Managers should use the most objective, rational process possible when making a decision.*

As a follow-up to the three "Managing by Design" questions, each chapter contains three "Assess Your Answer" inserts that allow students to compare their original opinions with the "correct" or most appropriate answers based on chapter concepts. Students learn whether their mental models and beliefs about organizations align with the world of organizations.

BookMarks.   "BookMarks" are short book reviews that reflect current issues of concern for managers working in real-life organizations. These reviews, which represent a unique feature of this text, describe the varied ways companies are dealing with the challenges of today's changing environment. New "BookMarks" in the Twelfth Edition include *Great by Choice: Uncertainty, Chaos, and Luck—Why Some Thrive Despite Them All, Blue Ocean Strategy: How to Create Uncontested Market Space and Make the Competition Irrelevant, Conscious Capitalism: Liberating the Heroic Spirit of Business,* and *Creativity Inc.: Overcoming the Unseen Forces That Stand in the Way of True Inspiration.*

In Practice.   This edition contains many new "In Practice" examples that illustrate theoretical concepts in organizational settings. Many examples are international, and all are based on real organizations. There are 50 new "In Practice" cases used within chapters, including Fujifilm Holding Corporation, Carnival Cruise Lines, Omnicom and Publicis, Amway, Harley Davidson, Morning Star, Valve Software, Amazon, the *Freaky Friday* Management Technique, Bloomberg PLC, Apple, Taco Bell and Frito Lay, L'Oreal, the U.S. Military, Box, BNSF Railway, Toyota Motor Corporation, Royal Dutch Shell PLC, United Health Group, Allegiant Travel, The Vatican, Nike, Richard Ginori, Caesar's Entertainment, International Alliance of Theatrical Stage Employees, Dell, Town of Sandy Springs, Georgia, Panasonic, Zappos, and Narayana Hrudayalaya Hospital.

Manager's Briefcase.   Located in the chapter margins, this feature tells students how to use concepts to analyze cases and manage organizations.

Text Exhibits.   Frequent exhibits are used to help students visualize organizational relationships, and the artwork has been redone to communicate concepts more clearly.

Design Essentials.   This summary and interpretation section tells students how the essential chapter points are important in the broader context of organization theory and design.

Case for Analysis.   These cases are tailored to chapter concepts and provide a vehicle for student analysis and discussion. New cases for analysis include "It Isn't So Simple: Infrastructure Change at Royce Consulting," "The Venable Museum of Art," "CPI Corporation: What Happened?," "AV Corporate: Software Tool Project," "Yahoo: *Get to Work!*," "The Boys Versus Corporate," and "Medici Mediterranean Restaurant."

Integrative Cases.   The integrative cases at the end of the text have been expanded and positioned to encourage student discussion and involvement. The new cases include W. L. Gore—Culture of Innovation, Engro Chemical Pakistan Limited: Restructuring the Marketing Division, Sometimes a Simple Change Isn't So Simple, Rondell Data Corporation, and Disorganization at Semco: Human Resource Practices as a Strategic Advantage. Previous cases that have been retained include IKEA: Scandinavian Style, First Union: An Office Without Walls, Lean Initiatives and Growth at Orlando Metering Company, Costco: Join the Club, The Donor Services Department, Cisco Systems: Evolution of Structure, and Hartland Memorial Hospital.

New Concepts

Many concepts have been added or expanded in this edition. New material has been added on the increasing complexity of the organizational environment, social business, goal conflict and the hybrid organization, big data analytics, the green movement and sustainability, the need for collaboration, social network analysis, quasirationality, manager decision-making biases, stages of disruptive innovation, the smart factory and trends in manufacturing, innovation contests and crowdsourcing, types of resource-dependent relationships, radical decentralization and bossless organization design, conscious capitalism, and global teams as a way to resolve the tension between a need for global uniformity and a need for local responsiveness.

Chapter Organization

Each chapter is highly focused and is organized into a logical framework. Many organization theory textbooks treat material in sequential fashion, such as "Here's View A, Here's View B, Here's View C," and so on. *Organization Theory and Design* shows how they apply in organizations. Moreover, each chapter sticks to the essential point. Students are not introduced to extraneous material or confusing methodological squabbles that occur among organizational researchers. The body of research in most areas points to a major trend, which is reported here. Several chapters develop a framework that organizes major ideas into an overall scheme.

This book has been extensively tested on students. Feedback from students and faculty members has been used in the revision. The combination of organization theory concepts, book reviews, examples of leading organizations, self-insight questionnaires, case illustrations, experiential exercises, and other teaching devices is designed to meet student learning needs, and students have responded favorably.

Supplements

Companion Website.   Access important teaching resources on the companion website. For your convenience, you can download electronic versions of the instructor supplements at the password-protected section of the site, including the Instructor's Manual, Test Bank, and PowerPoint presentations.

To access these additional course materials and companion resources, please visit www.cengagebrain.com. At the CengageBrain.com home page, search for the ISBN of your title (from the back cover of your book) using the search box at the top of the page. This will take you to the product page where free companion resources can be found.

Instructor's Manual.   The Instructor's Manual contains chapter overviews, chapter outlines, lecture enhancements, discussion questions, discussion of activities, discussion of chapter cases, and case notes for integrative cases.

Cognero Test Bank.   The Cognero Test Bank contains easy-to-use test creation software. Instructors can add or edit questions, instructions, and answers and can select questions (randomly or numerically) by previewing them on the screen. Instructors can also create and administer quizzes online.

PowerPoint Lecture Presentation.   The PowerPoint Lecture Presentation enables instructors to customize their own multimedia classroom presentations. Prepared in conjunction with the text and instructor's resource guide, the package contains approximately 150 slides. It includes exhibits from the text as well as outside materials to supplement chapter concepts. Material is organized by chapter and can be modified or expanded for individual classroom use.

Experiential Exercises in Organization Theory and Design, Second Edition.   By H. Eugene Baker III and Steven K. Paulson of the University of North Florida.

Tailored to the table of contents in Daft's *Organization Theory and Design,* Twelfth Edition, the core purpose of *Experiential Exercises in Organization Theory and Design* is to provide courses in organizational theory with a set of classroom exercises that will help students better understand and internalize the basic principles of the course. The chapters of the book cover the most basic and widely covered concepts in the field. Each chapter focuses on a central topic, such as organizational power, production technology, or organizational culture, and provides all necessary materials to fully participate in three different exercises. Some exercises are intended to be completed by individuals, others in groups, and still others can be used either way. The exercises range from instrumentation-based and assessment questionnaires to actual creative production activities.

Acknowledgments

Textbook writing is a team enterprise. The Twelfth Edition has integrated ideas and hard work from many people to whom I am grateful. Reviewers and focus group participants made an especially important contribution. They praised many features, were critical of things that didn't work well, and offered valuable suggestions.

David Ackerman
University of Alaska, Southeast

Kristin Backhaus
SUNY New Paltz

Michael Bourke
Houston Baptist University

Suzanne Clinton
Cameron University

Pat Driscoll
Texas Woman's University

Jo Anne Duffy
Sam Houston State University

Cheryl Duvall
Mercer University

Allen D. Engle, Sr.
Eastern Kentucky University

Patricia Feltes
Missouri State University

Robert Girling
Sonoma State University

Yezdi H. Godiwalla
University of Wisconsin-Whitewater

John A. Gould
University of Maryland

George Griffin
Spring Arbor University

Leda McIntyre Hall
Indiana University, South Bend

Ralph Hanke
Pennsylvania State University

Bruce J. Hanson
Pepperdine University

Thomas Head
Roosevelt University

Patricia Holahan
Stevens Institute of Technology

Jon Kalinowski
Minnesota State University, Mankato

Guiseppe Labianca
Tulane University

Jane Lemaster
University of Texas–Pan American

Kim Lukaszewski
SUNY New Paltz

Steven Maranville
University of Saint Thomas

Rick Martinez
Baylor University

Ann Marie Nagye
Mountain State University

Janet Near
Indiana University

Julie Newcomer
Texas Woman's University

Frank Nolan
Liberty University

Asbjorn Osland
George Fox University

Laynie Pizzolatto
Nicholls State University

Paula Reardon
State University of New York, Delhi

Samantha Rice
Abilene Christian University

Richard Saaverda
University of Michigan

W. Robert Sampson
University of Wisconsin, Eau Claire

Amy Sevier
University of Southern Mississippi

W. Scott Sherman
Pepperdine University

Marjorie Smith
Mountain State University

R. Stephen Smith
Virginia Commonwealth University

Filiz Tabak
Towson University

Thomas Terrell
Coppin State College

Jack Tucci
Southeastern Louisiana University

Renee Tyre
Wilmington University

Isaiah Ugboro
North Carolina A&T State University

Warren Watson
University of North Texas

Richard Weiss
University of Delaware

Judith White
Santa Clara University

Jan Zahrly
University of North Dakota

Among my professional colleagues, I am grateful to my friends and colleagues at Vanderbilt's Owen School—Bruce Barry, Rich Oliver, David Owens, Ty Park, Ranga Ramanujam, and Bart Victor—for their intellectual stimulation and feedback. I also owe a special debt to Dean Eric Johnson and Associate Dean Sal March for providing the time and resources for me to stay current on the organization design literature and develop the revisions for the text.

I want to extend special thanks to my editorial associate, Pat Lane. She skillfully wrote materials on a variety of topics and special features, found resources, and did an outstanding job with the copyedited manuscript and page proofs. Pat's personal enthusiasm and care for the content of this text enabled the Twelfth Edition to continue its high level of excellence. I also thank DeeGee Lester for her work drafting new end-of-chapter and integrative cases. DeeGee's creative writing skills brought to life key organizational issues that students will enjoy discussing and solving.

The team at Cengage Learning also deserves special mention. Scott Person did a great job of designing the project and offering ideas for improvement. Managing Content Developers Suzanne Wilder and Josh Wells were superb to work with and kept the people and project on schedule while solving problems creatively and quickly. Jennifer Ziegler and Joseph Malcolm, Project Managers, provided superb project coordination and used their creativity and management skills to facilitate the book's on-time completion. Emily Horowitz, Marketing Manager; Kristen Hurd, Marketing Director; and Christopher Walz, Marketing Coordinator, offered additional support, creativity, and valuable market expertise.

Finally, I want to acknowledge the love and support of my daughters, Danielle, Amy, Roxanne, Solange, and Elizabeth, and my new grandson, Nelson, who make my life special during our precious time together.

Richard L. Daft
Nashville, Tennessee
January 2015

Introduction to Organizations

1 Organizations and Organization Design

Learning Objectives

After reading this chapter you should be able to:

1. Define an organization and the importance of organizations in society.
2. Identify current challenges that organizations face.
3. Understand how organization design concepts apply to a major company like Xerox.
4. Recognize the structural dimensions of organizations and the contingencies that influence structure.
5. Understand efficiency and effectiveness, and the stakeholder approach to measuring effectiveness.
6. Explain historical perspectives on organizations.
7. Explain the differences in organic and mechanistic organization designs and the contingency factors typically associated with each.
8. Discuss the current trend toward bossless organization design.

Before reading this chapter, please check whether you agree or disagree with each of the following statements:

1 An organization can be understood primarily by understanding the people who make it up.

I AGREE _____   I DISAGREE _____

2 The primary role of managers in business organizations is to achieve maximum efficiency.

I AGREE _____   I DISAGREE _____

3 A CEO's top priority is to make sure the organization is designed correctly.

I AGREE _____   I DISAGREE _____

A Look Inside Xerox Corporation

Everyone has probably used the term *Xerox* to refer to copying pages. Xerox Corporation built its reputation on the copy machine. On the eve of the twenty-first century, Xerox seemed on top of the world, with fast-rising earnings, a soaring stock price, and a new line of computerized copier-printers that were technologically superior to rival products. Less than two years later, however, many considered Xerox a has-been, destined to fade into history. Consider the following events:

- Sales and earnings plummeted as rivals caught up with Xerox's high-end digital machines, offering comparable products at lower prices.
- Xerox's losses for the opening year of the twenty-first century totaled $384 million, and the company continued to bleed red ink. Debt rose to $18 billion.
- The company's stock fell from a high of $64 to less than $4, amid fears that Xerox would file for federal bankruptcy protection. Over an 18-month period, Xerox lost $38 billion in shareholder wealth.
- Twenty-two thousand Xerox workers lost their jobs, further weakening the morale and loyalty of remaining employees. Major customers were alienated, too, by a restructuring that threw salespeople into unfamiliar territories and tied billing up in knots, leading to mass confusion and billing errors.

What Went Wrong?

The company's deterioration is a classic story of organizational mistakes and decline. Although Xerox appeared to fall almost overnight, the organization's problems were connected to a series of organizational blunders over a period of many years.

Xerox was founded in 1906 as the Haloid Company, a photographic supply house that developed the world's first xerographic copier, introduced in 1959. Without a doubt, the 914 copier was a money-making machine. By the time it was retired in the early 1970s, the 914 was the best-selling industrial product of all time, and the new name of the company, Xerox, was listed in the dictionary as a synonym for photocopying. Yet, like many profitable organizations, Xerox became a victim of its own success. Leaders no doubt knew that the company needed to move beyond copiers to sustain its growth, but they found it difficult to look beyond the 70 percent gross profit margins of the 914 copier.

Xerox's Palo Alto Research Center (PARC), established in 1970, became known around the world for innovation—many of the most revolutionary technologies in the computer industry, including the personal computer, graphical user interface, Ethernet, and laser printer, were invented at PARC. But the copier bureaucracy, or *Burox* as it came to be known, blinded Xerox leaders to the enormous potential of these innovations. While Xerox was plodding along selling copy machines, younger, smaller, and hungrier companies were developing PARC technologies into tremendous money-making products and services.

Xerox's market share declined from 95 percent to 13 percent by 1982. And with no new products to make up the difference, the company had to fight hard to cut costs and reclaim market share by committing to Japanese-style techniques and total quality management. Through the strength of his leadership, CEO David Kearns was able to rally the troops and rejuvenate the company by 1990. However, he also set Xerox on a path to future disaster. Seeing a need to diversify, Kearns moved the company into insurance and financial services on a large scale. When he turned leadership over to Paul Allaire in 1990, Xerox's balance sheet was crippled by billions of dollars in insurance liabilities.

Entering the Digital Era

Allaire wisely began a methodical, step-by-step plan for extricating Xerox from the insurance and financial services business. At the same time, he initiated a mixed strategy of cost cutting and new-product introductions to get the stodgy company moving again. Xerox had success with a line of digital presses and new high-speed digital copiers, but it fumbled again by underestimating the threat of the desktop printer.

Desktop printing, combined with the increasing use of the Internet and e-mail, cut heavily into Xerox's sales of copiers. People didn't need to make as many photocopies, but they still needed effective ways to create and share documents. Rebranding Xerox as "The Document Company," Allaire pushed into the digital era, hoping to remake Xerox in the image of the rejuvenated IBM, offering not just "boxes (machines)" but complete document management solutions.

As part of that strategy, Allaire picked Richard Thoman, who was then serving as Louis Gerstner's right-hand man at IBM, as his successor. Thoman came to Xerox as president, chief operating officer, and eventually CEO, amid high hopes that the company could regain the stature of its glory years. Only 13 months later, as revenues and the stock price continued to slide, he was fired by Allaire, who had remained as Xerox's chairman.

The Culture Problem

Allaire and Thoman blamed each other for the failure to successfully implement the digital strategy. Outsiders, however, believe the failure had much more to do with Xerox's dysfunctional culture. The culture was already slow to adapt, and some say that under Allaire it became almost totally paralyzed by politics. Thoman was brought in to shake things up, but when he tried, the old guard rebelled. A management struggle developed, with the outsider Thoman and a few allies on one side lined up against Allaire and his group of insiders who were accustomed to doing things the traditional Xerox way. Recognized for his knowledge, business experience, and intensity, Thoman was also considered to be somewhat haughty and unapproachable. He was never able to exert substantial influence with key managers and employees or to gain the support of board members, who continued to rally behind Allaire.

The failed CEO succession illustrates the massive challenge of reinventing a century-old company. By the time Thoman arrived, Xerox had been going through various rounds of restructuring, cost cutting, rejuvenating, and reinventing for nearly two decades, but little had really changed. Some observers doubted that anyone could fix Xerox because the culture had become too dysfunctional and politicized. "There was always an in-crowd and an out-crowd," says one former executive. "They change the branches, but when you look closely, the same old monkeys are sitting in the trees."

Shaking Up a Century-Old Company

In August 2001, Allaire turned over the CEO reins to Anne Mulcahy, a popular 24-year veteran, who had started at Xerox as a copier saleswoman and worked her way up the hierarchy. Despite her insider status, Mulcahy proved that she was more than willing to challenge the status quo. She surprised skeptical analysts, stockholders, and employees by engineering one of the most extraordinary business turnarounds in recent history.

How did she do it? Few people thought Mulcahy would take the tough actions Xerox needed to survive, but she turned out to be a strong decision maker. She quickly launched a turnaround plan that included massive cost cutting and the closing of several money-losing operations, including the division she had previously headed. She was brutally honest about "the good, the bad, and the ugly" of the company's situation, as one employee put it, but she also showed that she cared about what happened to employees and she gave them hope for a better future. People knew she was working hard to save the company. After major layoffs, Mulcahy walked the halls to tell people she was sorry and let them vent their anger. She personally negotiated the settlement of a long investigation into fraudulent accounting practices, insisting that her personal involvement was necessary to signal a new commitment to ethical business practices. She appealed directly to creditors, begging them not to pull the plug until a new management team could make needed changes.

Mulcahy transferred much of production to outside contractors and refocused Xerox on innovation and service. In addition to introducing new products, Xerox moved into high-growth areas such as document management services,

IT consulting, and digital press technology. A series of small acquisitions enabled the company to enter new markets and expand its base of small and medium-sized business customers.

"We No Longer Make Copiers"

Mulcahy also thought carefully about succession plans, and in 2009 she handed the top job to her second-in-command, Ursula Burns, who became the first African-American woman to head a *Fortune* 500 company. Burns, like Mulcahy, spent decades climbing the ranks at Xerox, actually starting her career there as an intern before earning a master's degree in engineering from Columbia University. Just as Xerox dominated the office of yesterday with its copiers, Burns set a new course to dominate the office of tomorrow. More than half of Xerox's business now comes from services such as running electronic toll solutions on highways and bridges, processing insurance claims, and managing customer call centers. A services deal in trial mode with municipalities in California will give people a ping on their mobile phones saying "There's a parking spot a block over" and then charge the appropriate amount, which enables cities to maximize parking fees during congested parking times. Sophie Vandebroek, Xerox's chief technology officer, got tired of people ignoring the cool new technology at the Xerox booth at career fairs in favor of what was going on at the Google or IBM booths. So, a few years ago, she put up a sign that said "We no longer make copiers." It got plenty of attention from people asking, "So, what *do* you do?"

A decade or so after this American icon almost crashed, Xerox is once again admired in the corporate world. The company was positioned in the "Visionaries" quadrant of Gartner Inc.'s Magic Quadrant for Enterprise Content Management for its ability to deliver content management capabilities, including on-site and cloud-based solutions. Has the "perfect storm" of troubles been replaced with a "perfect dawn"? Burns and her top management team believe Xerox is positioned to be resilient in the face of the current economic slowdown, but in the rapidly changing world of organizations, nothing is ever certain.[1]

Organization Design in Action

Welcome to the real world of organization design. The shifting fortunes of Xerox illustrate organization design in action. Xerox managers were deeply involved in organization design each day of their working lives—but many never realized it. Company managers didn't fully understand how the organization related to the environment or how it should function internally. Organization design gives us the tools to evaluate and understand how and why some organizations grow and succeed while others do not. It helps us explain what happened in the past, as well as what might happen in the future, so that we can manage organizations more effectively. Organization design concepts have enabled Anne Mulcahy and Ursula Burns to analyze and diagnose what is happening and the changes needed to help Xerox keep pace with a fast-changing world. Organization design gives us the tools to explain the decline of Xerox, understand Mulcahy's turnaround, and recognize the steps Burns is taking to keep Xerox competitive.

Similar problems have challenged numerous organizations. Kodak, for example, once ruled the photographic film business but failed to adapt as the business went digital. The company invented one of the first digital cameras and spent hundreds of millions of dollars developing digital technology, but the fear of cannibalizing their lucrative film business paralyzed managers when time came to go to market. Kodak is now struggling to stay alive as it remakes itself into a company that sells printers and ink.[2] Or consider the dramatic organizational missteps illustrated by some U.S. government agencies in recent years. The Secret Service became embroiled in a public relations nightmare when news broke that members of the security team sent to prepare for President Barack Obama's visit to Cartagena, Colombia, engaged in a night of heavy drinking, visited strip clubs, and brought prostitutes to their hotel rooms. Several agents were fired, and director Mark Sullivan and other managers were called before a Senate subcommittee to explain the breakdown in control. The agency was again in trouble in late March 2014 when three agents preparing for Obama's visit to the Netherlands were sent home after one member of the group was found intoxicated and passed out in the hallway of his hotel in Amsterdam.[3] The reputation and effectiveness of the Internal Revenue Service (IRS) was threatened because of a decision to apply additional screening to tax-exempt applications from conservative Tea Party groups. It has long been a practice to give extra scrutiny to certain kinds of groups that present a potential for fraudulent use of tax-exempt status, but critics say the agency went too far in how it applied the practice to conservative political organizations, in some cases delaying applications for years.[4]

Topics

Each of the topics to be covered in this book is illustrated in the opening Xerox case. Indeed, managers at organizations such as Xerox, Kodak, the Secret Service, and the IRS are continually faced with a number of challenges. For example:

- How can the organization adapt to or control such external elements as competitors, customers, government, and creditors in a fast-paced environment?
- What strategic and structural changes are needed to help the organization attain effectiveness?
- How can the organization avoid management ethical lapses that could threaten its viability?
- How can managers cope with the problems of large size and bureaucracy?
- What is the appropriate use of power and politics among managers?
- How should internal conflict and coordination between work units be managed?
- What kind of corporate culture is needed and how can managers shape that culture?
- How much and what type of innovation and change is needed?

These are the topics with which organization design is concerned. Organization design concepts apply to all types of organizations in all industries. Managers at Hyundai, for example, turned the Korean auto manufacturer once known for producing inexpensive no-frills cars with a poor reputation into the world's fourth largest automaker by relentlessly focusing on quality, cost-control, and customer

BRIEFCASE

As an organization manager, keep these guidelines in mind:

Do not ignore the external environment or protect the organization from it. Because the environment is unpredictable, do not expect to achieve complete order and rationality within the organization. Strive for a balance between order and flexibility.

satisfaction. Bob Iger and his top management team revitalized the Walt Disney Company by effectively managing internal conflicts and enhancing coordination both within the company and with outside partners. Managers at high-end cosmetics firm Estée Lauder undertook a major reorganization to improve sales in a weak economy.[5] All of these companies are using concepts based in organization design. Organization design also applies to nonprofit organizations such as the United Way, the American Humane Association, local arts organizations, colleges and universities, and the Make-A-Wish Foundation, which grants wishes to terminally ill children.

Organization design draws lessons from organizations such as Xerox, Walt Disney Company, and United Way and makes those lessons available to students and managers. As our opening example of Xerox shows, even large, successful organizations are vulnerable, lessons are not learned automatically, and organizations are only as strong as their decision makers. Research shows that many new companies don't survive past their fifth birthday, yet some organizations thrive for 50 or even 100 years. This chapter's BookMark examines some characteristics

BOOKMARK 1.0 HAVE YOU READ THIS BOOK?

Great by Choice: Uncertainty, Chaos, and Luck—Why Some Thrive Despite Them All

By Jim Collins and Morten T. Hansen

Jim Collins, the author of the bestseller *Good to Great*, has spent many years looking at companies that perform better than their peers despite periods of instability, uncertainty, and crisis. For his new book *Great by Choice*, Collins teams with management professor Morten Hansen to describe the management actions that contribute to success.

THREE CHARACTERISTICS FOR LONG-TERM SUCCESS

Great by Choice first describes organizations, called 10Xers, that have outperformed their industry averages by at least 10 times over a period of at least 15 years and compares them to similar, less successful companies. The 10Xers include Southwest Airlines, Amgen, Intel, and Progressive Insurance. Managers of 10X companies all share three characteristics:

- *Fanatic Discipline.* The authors use the metaphor of the 20 Mile March, a paced, consistent journey toward goals that requires both the ambition to achieve and the self-control to hold back. 10X managers prefer consistent gains over shoot-for-the moon risks. Andrew Grove at Intel, for example, abandoned the business of making memory chips only after thoroughly learning about the changing technology environment and business environment.
- *Empirical Creativity.* An entire chapter is devoted to the "fire bullets, then cannonballs" approach. Managers in 10X organizations tend to fire bullets to see what

will work and only then bring out the big guns. "After the cannonball hits," they write, "you keep 20 Mile Marching to make the most of your big success."

- *Productive Paranoia.* Herb Kelleher, founder and former CEO of Southwest Airlines, was always preparing for the next recession, even when none was in sight. 10X managers "remain productively paranoid in good times, recognizing that it's what they do before the storm that matters most." They are always building buffers and putting in place shock absorbers to deal with unexpected events.

CONTROL AND DISCIPLINE IN THE FACE OF CHANGE

Change is inevitable and innovation is necessary. The public and the media tend to admire and revere the brash risk-takers, but the organizations that survive over the long term, Collins and Hansen assert, are those that are specific, methodical, and consistent, which they refer to as SMaC. Sometimes, they say, it's better to be "one fad behind." Successful companies prepare rigorously for what they cannot predict, tend to not take excessive risks, and keep comfortable buffers in every area of their business. Managers in these organizations rely on evidence and tend to prefer consistent gains to big winners.

"What's coming next?" the authors ask. "All we know is that no one knows. Yet some companies and leaders navigate this type of world exceptionally well. . . . They build great enterprises that can endure. We do not believe that chaos, uncertainty, and instability are good; companies, leaders, organizations, and societies do not thrive on chaos. But they can thrive in chaos."

Great by Choice, by Jim Collins and Morten T. Hansen, is published by HarperBusiness.

that can help organizations thrive over the long term. Organizations are not static; they continuously adapt to shifts in the external environment. Today, many companies are facing the need to transform themselves into dramatically different organizations because of new challenges in the environment.

Current Challenges

Research into hundreds of organizations provides the knowledge base to make Xerox and other organizations more effective. Challenges organizations face today are different from those of the past, and thus the concept of organizations and organization design is evolving. The world is changing more rapidly than ever before, and managers are responsible for positioning their organizations to adapt to new needs. Some specific challenges today's managers and organizations face are globalization, intense competition, rigorous scrutiny of ethical and green practices, the need for rapid response, and incorporating social business and big data.

Globalization. The cliché that the world is getting smaller is dramatically true for today's organizations. Markets, technologies, and organizations are becoming increasingly interconnected.[6] Today's successful organizations feel "at home" anywhere in the world. Managers who can help their companies develop a global perspective, such as Carlos Ghosn, the Brazilian-Lebanese-French CEO of Japanese automaker Nissan, or Medtronic CEO Omar Ishrak, a Bangladesh native who was educated in the United Kingdom and worked in the United States for nearly two decades, are in high demand.[7]

Companies can locate different parts of the organization wherever it makes the most business sense: top leadership in one country and technical brainpower and production in other locales. Alan Mulally, CEO of U.S.-based Ford Motor Company, spends about a third of his time on matters related to China. Ford was late getting into China and in 2013 had only about 3 percent of the Chinese auto market. Mulally said he planned to build five additional plants in that country, double the number of dealerships, bring 15 new vehicles to China, and launch the Lincoln brand there in 2014. "Clearly this is going to continue to be the highest rate growth for us," Mulally said.[8]

Related trends are *global outsourcing*, or contracting out some functions to organizations in other countries, and *strategic partnering* with foreign firms to gain a global advantage. Cross-border acquisitions and the development of effective business relationships in other countries are vital to many organizations' success. Large multinational corporations are actively searching for managers with strong international experience and the ability to move easily between cultures. Yet doing business on a global scale is not easy. Several garment factory fires in Bangladesh in 2012 and the collapse of another apparel plant in 2013 that killed more than 1,100 workers put the spotlight on poor working conditions in that country. The problem for retailers such as Walmart, H&M, Target, and other big companies that outsource is that similar poor working conditions exist in other low-wage countries such as Pakistan, Cambodia, Indonesia, and Vietnam that produce most of the world's clothing. Both European and American retailers have announced plans aimed at improving safety in overseas factories, but the challenge of monitoring contractors and subcontractors in low-wage countries is a massive one.[9] Apple, Amazon, and other Western companies have also run into problems using overseas contractors to manufacture other types of products.[10]

Intense Competition. The growing global interdependence creates new advantages, but it also means that the environment for companies has become extremely complex and extremely competitive. Customers want low prices for quality goods and services, and the organizations that can meet that demand will win. Outsourcing firms in low-wage countries can often do work for 50 to 60 percent less than companies based in the United States, for instance, so U.S. firms that provide similar services have to search for new ways to compete or go into new lines of business.[11] One entrepreneur with a new type of battery for notebook computers is having the product manufactured by a factory in Shenzhen, China. She wanted to produce it in the United States, but U.S. contract manufacturers wanted millions of dollars up front, a demand not made by any of the manufacturers she met with in China.[12]

In today's weak economy, companies in all industries are feeling pressure to drive down costs and keep prices low, yet at the same time they are compelled to invest in research and development or get left behind in the global drive for innovation. Texas Instruments (TI) recently announced that it is shifting away from the mobile-chip business because of intense competition from smartphone makers' in-house designers. TI is cutting about 1,100 jobs as it refines its focus, which will include developing new embedded processors such as those used in cars and industrial equipment.[13] Or consider McDonald's. Even as managers were seeking ways to expand the menu and draw in new customers, McDonald's labs were testing how to cut the cost of making basic items on the Dollar Menu. With the price of ingredients such as cheese, beef, and buns going up, McDonald's had to cut internal costs or lose money on its dollar-menu products.[14] Auto insurers searched for new ways to compete as drivers faced with steep gas prices looked for ways to cut their transportation costs.[15]

Ethics and the Green Movement. Today's managers face tremendous pressure from the government and the public to hold their organizations and employees to high ethical and professional standards. Following widespread moral lapses and corporate financial scandals, organizations are under scrutiny as never before. A recent survey of Wall Street workers by the law firm Labaton Sucharow found that almost 25 percent of finance professionals say they would cheat to make $10 million if they could get away with it. Moreover, 52 percent believe it is likely that their competitors have engaged in illegal or unethical activity.[16] Big banks such as J.P. Morgan Chase & Company, Bank of America, and Citigroup are spending billions in legal expenses to clean up the mess related to Justice Department investigations of banking-industry activities during the housing downturn and the financial crisis. J.P. Morgan has added 7,000 extra risk-control employees and provided 750,000 hours of training on regulatory and control issues. "Fixing our controls issues is job No. 1," CEO Jamie Dimon said. The bank denies deliberately misleading clients and investors, but Dimon knows he has to prove to regulators and the public that J.P. Morgan is "as adept at maintaining controls as it is in recording profits."[17]

In addition to calls for higher ethical standards, people are demanding a stronger commitment by organizations to social responsibility, particularly when it comes to protecting the natural environment. *Going green* has become a new business imperative, driven by shifting social attitudes, new government policies, climate changes, and the information technology that quickly spreads news of a corporation's negative impact on the environment. Many companies are embracing the philosophy of **sustainability**, which refers to economic development that generates wealth and meets the needs of the current generation while saving the environment so future generations can meet their needs as well.[18] Interface, an Atlanta-based carpet manufacturer, is committed to reducing its use of virgin raw materials and eliminating its impact on the environment by 2020. Currently, 49 percent of Interface's total raw materials are recycled or bio-based. An experimental recycling program called Net-Works in the Philippines allows villagers to dispose of used fishing nets for cash. The nets are baled and sent to a facility that combines them with nylon fluff and other waste materials and makes them into carpet fiber. The program helps the villagers, as well as eliminates a serious hazard for marine life. Interface hopes to expand the program in the Philippines and launch similar efforts in Indonesia and Cameroon.[19]

Speed and Responsiveness. A fourth significant challenge for organizations is to respond quickly and decisively to environmental changes, organizational crises, or shifting customer expectations. For much of the twentieth century, organizations operated in a relatively stable environment, so managers could focus on designing structures and systems that kept the organization running smoothly and efficiently. There was little need to search for new ways to cope with increased competition, volatile environmental shifts, or changing customer demands. Today, new products, new companies, and even entirely new industries rise and fall faster than ever. Studies have found that speed of development contributes to new product success.[20] To retain its status as one of the golf industry's most innovative companies, Callaway Golf introduces seven to eight new products a year, which requires a design process that encourages close coordination between design teams, engineers, manufacturers, marketing staff, and even lawyers, and the sharing of information with partners in the United States, China, Japan, Korea, Mexico, and Taiwan. Collaborative technology gives everyone round-the-clock access to the latest information and documents, eliminating slowdowns created by time zones.[21]

Some companies must be even more nimble. Who ever considered that retailers could accept credit card payments using a smartphone? Who would have thought that musicians would one day not need a record label to make money? Considering the turmoil and flux inherent in today's world, managers and companies need a mindset of continuous reinvention to succeed, which typically means giving people on the front lines the power to experiment and make decisions.[22] General Stanley McChrystal, who ran Joint Special Operations Command in Iraq and Afghanistan and later commanded all U.S. and international forces in Afghanistan before he resigned, explains. "We grew up in the military with this [classic hierarchy]: one person at the top, with two to seven subordinates below that, and two to seven below that, and so on. That's what organizational theory says works." Against Al Qaeda, however, "we had to change our structure, to become a network. We were required to react quickly. Instead of decisions being made by people who were more senior—we found that the wisest decisions were usually made by those closest to the problem."[23]

Social Business and Big Data. Today's realm of the Internet, social networking, blogs, online collaboration, web-based communities, podcasting, mobile devices, Twittering, Facebooking, YouTube-ing, and Skype-ing is radically different from the world many established managers are familiar and comfortable with.[24] The digital revolution has changed everything—not just how we communicate with one another, find information, and share ideas, but also how organizations are designed and managed, how businesses operate, and how employees do their jobs. **Social business**, which refers to using social media technologies for interacting with and facilitating communication and collaboration among employees, customers, and other stakeholders, is one of the most current challenges managers face. **Social media programs**, including a company's online community pages, wikis for virtual collaboration, social media sites such as Facebook or LinkedIn, video channels such as YouTube, microblogging platforms such as Twitter, and company online forums, can improve efficiency, increase productivity, and facilitate faster and smoother operations by improving communication and collaboration within and across firms.[25] In addition, social media technology is being used by companies to build relationships with customers.[26] Dell, for example, launched a social media command room in 2010 to monitor what was being said about the company on social media platforms.[27]

Just as importantly, social media can build stronger, more authentic relationships between managers and employees. Shortly after arriving as the new CEO of MassMutual, Roger Crandall attended the company's biggest sales conference and was asked by an employee with a Flip cam if she could record him at the conference and post the video on the company intranet's community page. "A Week in the Life" was available for the whole company to watch in real time, and "was a great way to create a personal connection," Crandall said.[28] Some managers have begun incorporating video streams into their blogs because they allow them to engage with people in real time on a highly personal level.[29]

Another aspect of the digital revolution is the use of **big data analytics**, which refers to technologies, skills, and processes for searching and examining massive sets of data to uncover hidden patterns and correlations.[30] Facebook, for example, uses the personal data you put on your page and tracks and monitors your online behavior along with everyone else's, then searches through all those data to identify and suggest potential "friends."[31] Amazon.com collects tons of data on customers, including what books they buy, what else they look at, how they navigate through the website, how much they are influenced by promotions and reviews, and so forth. The company uses algorithms that predict and suggest what books a customer might be interested in reading next.[32] However, big data is not just for online companies.[33] Walmart collects more than 2.5 petabytes of data every hour from customer transactions and uses those data to make better decisions (a petabyte is about a million gigabytes or the equivalent of about 20 million filing cabinets full of written data).[34]

Purpose of This Chapter

The purpose of this chapter is to explore the nature of organizations and organization design today. Organization design has developed from the systematic study of organizations by scholars. Concepts are obtained from living, ongoing organizations. Organization theory and design has a practical application, as illustrated by the Xerox case. It helps managers understand, diagnose, and respond to emerging organizational needs and problems.

The next section begins with a formal definition of organization and then explores introductory concepts for describing and analyzing organizations, including various structural dimensions and contingency factors. We introduce the concepts of effectiveness and efficiency and describe the stakeholder approach, which considers what different groups want from the organization. Succeeding sections examine the history of organization design, the distinction between mechanistic and organic designs, organizations as open systems, and how organization theory can help people manage complex organizations in a rapidly changing world. The chapter closes with a brief overview of the themes to be covered in this book.

What Is an Organization?

Organizations are hard to see. We see outcroppings, such as a tall building, a computer workstation, or a friendly employee, but the whole organization is vague and abstract and may be scattered among several locations, even around the world. We know organizations are there because they touch us every day. Indeed, they are so common that we take them for granted. We hardly notice that we are born in a hospital, have our birth records registered in a government agency, are educated in schools and universities, are raised on food produced on corporate farms, are treated by doctors engaged in a joint practice, buy a house built by a construction company and sold by a real estate agency, borrow money from a bank, turn to police and fire departments when trouble erupts, use moving companies to change residences, and receive an array of benefits from various government agencies.[35] Most of us spend many of our waking hours working in an organization of one type or another.

Definition

Organizations as diverse as a bank, a corporate farm, a government agency, and Xerox Corporation have characteristics in common. The definition used in this book to describe organizations is as follows: **organizations** are (1) social entities that (2) are goal-directed, (3) are designed as deliberately structured and coordinated activity systems, and (4) are linked to the external environment.

An organization is a means to an end and it has to be designed to accomplish that end. It might be thought of as a tool or machine to get things done and achieve a specific purpose. The purpose will vary, but the central aspect of an organization is the coordination of people and resources to collectively accomplish desired goals.[36] An organization is not a building or a set of policies and procedures; organizations are made up of people and their relationships with one another. An organization exists when people interact with one another to perform essential functions that help attain goals. Managers and owners deliberately structure organizational resources to achieve the organization's purpose. However, even though work may be structured into separate departments or sets of activities, most organizations today are striving for greater horizontal coordination of work activities, often using teams of employees from different functional areas to work together on projects. Boundaries between departments, as well as those between organizations, are becoming more flexible and diffuse as companies face the need to respond to changes in the external environment more rapidly. An organization cannot exist without interacting with customers, suppliers, competitors, and other elements of the external environment. Today, some companies are even cooperating with their competitors, sharing information and technology to their mutual advantage. Exhibit 1.1 shows the organization as an **open system** that obtains inputs from the external environment, adds value through a transformation process, and discharges products and services back to the environment.

EXHIBIT 1.1
The Organization Is an
Open System

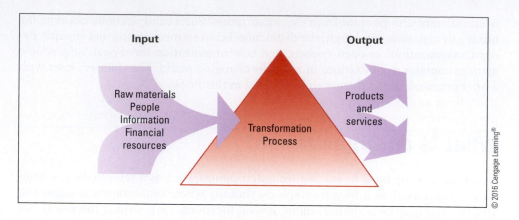

Input

Raw materials
People
Information
Financial
resources

Transformation
Process

Output

Products
and
services

From Multinationals to Nonprofits

Some organizations are large, multinational corporations; others are small, family-owned businesses; and still others are nonprofit organizations or governmental agencies. Some manufacture products such as automobiles, flat-panel televisions, or light bulbs, whereas others provide services such as legal representation, Internet and telecommunications services, mental health resources, or car repair. Later in this text, Chapter 7 will look at the distinctions between manufacturing and service technologies. Chapter 9 discusses size and life cycle and describes some differences between small and large organizations.

Another important distinction is between for-profit businesses and *nonprofit organizations*. All of the topics in this text apply to nonprofit organizations such as the Salvation Army, the World Wildlife Fund, the Save the Children Foundation, and Chicago's La Rabida Hospital, which is dedicated to serving the poor, just as they do to businesses such as Xerox, GameSpot, Sirius XM Radio, and Dunkin' Donuts. However, there are some important distinctions to keep in mind. The primary difference is that managers in businesses direct their activities toward earning money for the company and its owners, whereas managers in nonprofits direct much of their effort toward generating some kind of social impact. The unique characteristics and needs of nonprofit organizations present unique challenges for organizational leaders.[37]

Financial resources for government and charity nonprofits typically come from government appropriations, grants, and donations rather than from the sale of products or services to customers. In businesses, managers focus on improving the organization's products and services to increase sales revenues. In nonprofits, however, services are typically provided to nonpaying clients, and a major problem for many organizations is securing a steady stream of funds to continue operating. Nonprofit managers, committed to serving clients with limited funds, must focus on keeping organizational costs as low as possible and demonstrating a highly efficient use of resources. Moreover, for-profit firms often compete with nonprofits for limited donations through their own philanthropic fundraising efforts.[38]

In addition, many nonprofit organizations, such as hospitals and private universities, do have a "bottom line" in the sense of having to generate enough revenues to cover expenses, buy new equipment, upgrade technology, and so forth, so managers often struggle with the question of what constitutes organizational effectiveness. It is easy to measure dollars and cents, but the metrics of success in nonprofits are much more ambiguous. Managers have to measure intangible goals such as "improve public health," "make a difference in the lives of the disenfranchised," or "enhance appreciation of the arts."

Managers in nonprofit organizations also deal with many diverse stakeholders and must market their services to attract not only clients (customers) but also volunteers and donors. This can sometimes create conflict and power struggles among organizations, as illustrated by the Make-A-Wish Foundation, which has found itself at odds with small, local wish-granting groups as it expands to cities across the United States. The more kids a group can count as helping, the easier it is to raise funds. Local groups don't want Make-A-Wish invading their turf, particularly at a time when charitable donations in general have declined along with the declining economy. Small groups are charging that Make-A-Wish is abusing the power of its national presence to overwhelm or absorb the smaller organizations. "We should not have to compete for children and money," says the director of the Indiana Children's Wish Fund. "They [Make-A-Wish] use all their muscle and money to get what they want."[39]

Thus, the organization design concepts discussed throughout this book, such as dealing with issues of power and conflict, setting goals and measuring effectiveness, coping with environmental uncertainty, implementing effective control mechanisms, and satisfying multiple stakeholders, apply to nonprofit organizations such as the Indiana Children's Wish Fund just as they do to businesses such as Xerox. These concepts and theories are adapted and revised as needed to fit the unique needs and problems of various small, large, profit, or nonprofit organizations.

BRIEFCASE

As an organization manager, keep this guideline in mind:

Consider the needs and interests of all stakeholders when setting goals and designing the organization to achieve effectiveness.

Importance of Organizations

It may seem hard to believe today, but organizations as we know them are relatively recent in the history of humankind. Even in the late nineteenth century there were few organizations of any size or importance—no labor unions, no trade associations, and few large businesses, nonprofit organizations, or governmental agencies. What a change has occurred since then! The development of large organizations transformed all of society, and, indeed, the modern corporation may be the most significant innovation of the past 100 years.[40]

Organizations are all around us and shape our lives in many ways. But what contributions do organizations make? Why are they important? Exhibit 1.2 indicates seven reasons organizations are important to you and to society. First, recall that an organization is a means to an end. Organizations bring together resources to accomplish specific goals. A good example is Northrup Grumman Newport News (formerly Newport News Shipbuilding), which builds nuclear-powered, Nimitz-class aircraft carriers. Putting together an aircraft carrier is an incredibly complex job involving 47,000 tons of precision-welded steel, more than 1 million distinct parts, 900 miles of wire and cable, and more than seven years of hard work by 17,800 employees.[41] How could such a job be accomplished without an organization to acquire and coordinate these varied resources?

Organizations also produce goods and services that customers want at competitive prices. Companies look for innovative ways to produce and distribute desirable goods and services more efficiently. Harley-Davidson once didn't need to worry about efficiency, but the recent recession changed all that. The company's York, Pennsylvania, factory improved efficiency by redesigning the production process.

EXHIBIT 1.2
Importance of
Organizations

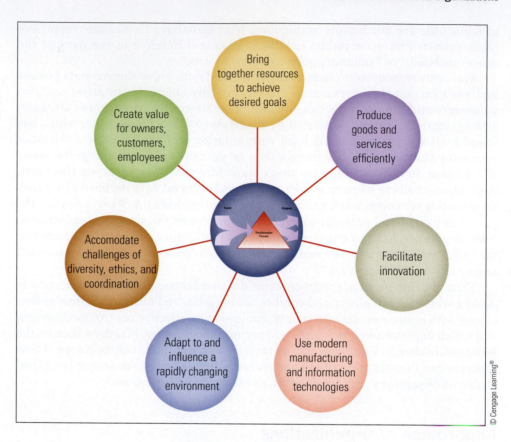

Bring together resources to achieve desired goals

Produce goods and services efficiently

Create value for owners, customers, employees

Facilitate innovation

Accomodate challenges of diversity, ethics, and coordination

Use modern manufacturing and information technologies

Adapt to and influence a rapidly changing environment

© Cengage Learning®

 **IN PRACTICE**

Harley-Davidson

Harley-Davidson has always charged a huge premium for its bikes, and customers were willing to pay the price and wait as long as 18 months to get a bike. It's almost as if inefficiency was part of the charm. But by 2009, the inefficiency wasn't charming anymore. Harley was close to collapse. The stock price had fallen from a high of nearly $75 to $8.

Managers struggled with what to do. For a company with an "American blue-collar, working brand," busting the union or building motorcycles in Mexico would have been catastrophic. They knew the company could compete only by redesigning the production system to increase efficiency. They tore down the existing plant and built a new one, where hundreds of workers, operating in teams of five or six, manually build each motorcycle. It seems like an expensive way to do business, but plant manager Ed Magee points out that there are around 1,200 different configurations and a new bike starts its way through the production line every 80 seconds. Virtually each one is unique, and workers have no idea what's coming 80 seconds later. Unlike robots, human beings can adjust on the fly. For example, one worker noticed that the plastic piece that holds electric parts to the front of a motorcycle wasn't fitting correctly and took a few extra shoves to push into place. He knew those few extra shoves could add up to 2,200 lost bikes a year. With the worker's help, Harley fixed that problem.

Harley's very existence was threatened in 2009, but the York plant recently won an Industry Week Best Plants award. Customer demand is soaring now that people can get a bike within a couple of weeks of ordering rather than waiting a year and a half. Craig Kennison at the research firm Baird said "it's certainly the best turnaround I've ever seen."[42]

Although there are no robots on the main assembly line at Harley, they do perform various peripheral jobs. Managers have combined advanced technology with improved human systems to build motorcycles faster and better. Redesigning organizational structures and management practices can also contribute to increased efficiency. Organizations create a drive for innovation rather than a reliance on standard products and outmoded approaches to management and organization design.

Organizations adapt to and influence a rapidly changing environment. Consider Amazon, which continues to adapt and evolve along with the evolving Internet. Founder and CEO Jeff Bezos continues to push the boundaries of fast shipping, expanding next day and same day shipping service and building new warehouses and distribution centers.[43] Many organizations have entire departments charged with monitoring the external environment and finding ways to adapt to or influence that environment.

Through all of these activities, organizations create value for their owners, customers, and employees. Managers analyze which parts of the operation create value and which parts do not; a company can be profitable only when the value it creates is greater than the cost of resources.

Finally, organizations must cope with and accommodate today's challenges of workforce diversity and growing concerns over ethics and sustainability, as well as find effective ways to motivate employees to work together to accomplish organizational goals.

Dimensions of Organization Design

Organizations shape our lives, and well-informed managers can shape organizations. The first step for understanding organizations is to look at the features that describe specific organizational design traits. These features describe organizations in much the same way that personality and physical traits describe people.

Exhibit 1.3 illustrates two types of interacting features of organizations: structural dimensions and contingency factors. **Structural dimensions** provide labels to describe the internal characteristics of an organization. They create a basis for measuring and comparing organizations. **Contingency factors** encompass larger elements that

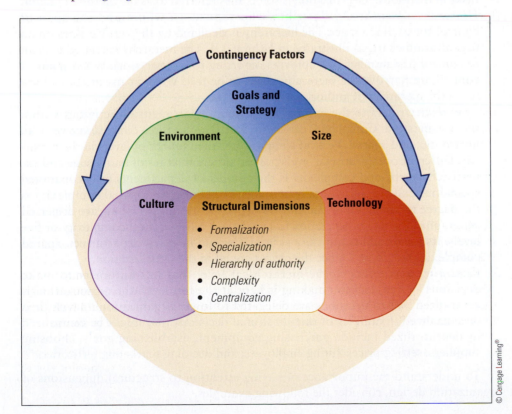

EXHIBIT 1.3

Interacting Structural
Dimensions of Design
and Contingency Factors

© Cengage Learning®

influence structural dimensions, including the organization's size, technology, environment, culture, and goals. Contingency factors describe the organizational setting that influences and shapes the structural dimensions. Contingency factors can be confusing because they represent both the organization and the environment. These factors can be envisioned as a set of overlapping elements that shape an organization's structure and work processes, as illustrated in Exhibit 1.3. To understand and evaluate organizations, one must examine both structural dimensions and contingency factors.[44] These features of organization design interact with one another and can be adjusted to accomplish the purposes listed earlier in Exhibit 1.2.

Structural Dimensions

Key structural dimensions of organizations include formalization, specialization, hierarchy of authority, complexity, and centralization.

1. *Formalization* pertains to the amount of written documentation in the organization. Documentation includes procedures, job descriptions, regulations, and policy manuals. These written documents describe behavior and activities. Formalization is often measured by simply counting the number of pages of documentation within the organization. Large universities, for example, tend to be high on formalization because they have several volumes of written rules for such things as registration, dropping and adding classes, student associations, dormitory governance, and financial assistance. A small, family-owned business, in contrast, may have almost no written rules and would be considered informal.

2. *Specialization* is the degree to which organizational tasks are subdivided into separate jobs. If specialization is extensive, each employee performs only a narrow range of tasks. If specialization is low, employees perform a wide range of tasks in their jobs. Specialization is sometimes referred to as the *division of labor*.

3. *Hierarchy of authority* describes who reports to whom and the span of control for each manager. The hierarchy is depicted by the vertical lines on an organization chart, as illustrated in Exhibit 1.4. The hierarchy is related to *span of control* (the number of employees reporting to a supervisor). When spans of control are narrow, the hierarchy tends to be tall. When spans of control are wide, the hierarchy of authority will be shorter.

4. *Complexity* refers to the number of distinct departments or activities within the organization. Complexity can be measured along three dimensions: vertical, horizontal, and spatial. Vertical complexity is the number of levels in the hierarchy. Different organizational levels possess different stores of knowledge and expertise.[45] Horizontal complexity is the number of departments or occupational specialties existing horizontally across the organization. Spatial complexity is the degree to which an organization's departments and personnel are dispersed geographically. The organization in Exhibit 1.4 has a vertical complexity of five levels. Its horizontal complexity at level 3 would be seven departments. Spatial complexity would be 1 since the offices are all in the same location.

5. *Centralization* refers to the hierarchical level that has authority to make decisions. When decision making is kept at the top level, the organization is centralized. When decisions are delegated to lower organizational levels, it is decentralized. Examples of organizational decisions that might be centralized or decentralized include purchasing equipment, establishing goals, choosing suppliers, setting prices, hiring employees, and deciding marketing territories.

To understand the importance of paying attention to structural dimensions of organization design, consider the following examples.

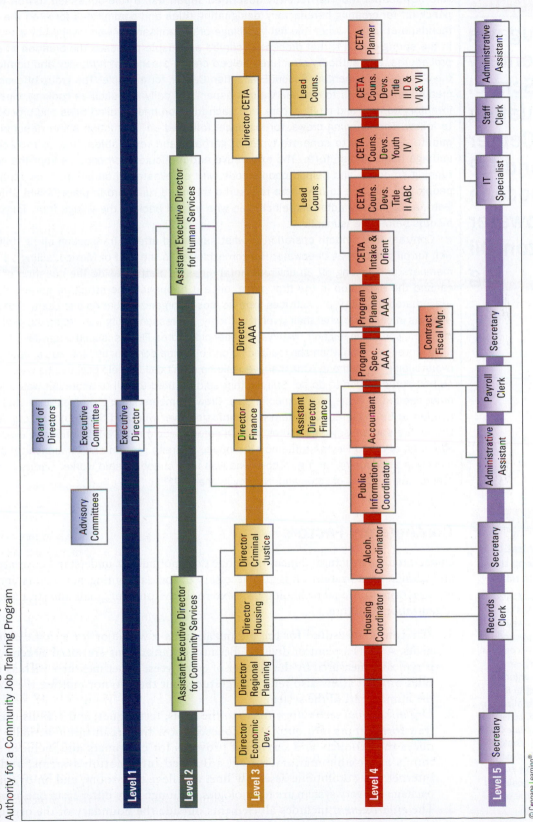

© Cengage Learning®

EXHIBIT 1.4
Organization Chart Illustrating the Hierarchy of
Authority for a Community Job Training Program

☑ **IN PRACTICE**

Shizugawa Elementary School Evacuation Center and BP Transocean Deepwater Horizon Oil Rig

One newspaper reporter recently described Japan as "a rule-obsessed nation with a penchant for creating bureaucracy, designating titles and committees for even the most mundane of tasks." When the fishing village of Minamisanriku was ravaged by a tsunami in the spring of 2011, that propensity served a valuable purpose. The creation of rules, procedures, and authority structures helped create a sense of normalcy and comfort at the Shizugawa Elementary School Evacuation Center, for example. The group of evacuees created six divisions to oversee various aspects of daily life, such as cooking, cleaning, inventory control, and medical care, and each function had detailed rules and procedures to follow. The cleaning crews, for instance, followed an instruction sheet describing in minute detail how to separate types of garbage and recyclables, how to replace the garbage bags, and so forth. The exhaustive and meticulous procedures kept the center running smoothly and helped people cope with a devastating situation. "The Japanese people are the type to feel more reassured the more rules are in place," said Shintaro Goto, a 32-year-old actor and electrician who moved back to the village from Tokyo just months before the tsunami.

Contrast that smooth operation to what happened after a Transocean oil rig drilling a well for oil giant BP at Deepwater Horizon exploded in the Gulf of Mexico, killing 11 crew members and setting off an environmental disaster. Setting aside the question of what caused the explosion in the first place, once it happened the structure aboard the rig exacerbated the situation. Activities were so loosely organized that no one seemed to know who was in charge or what their level of authority and responsibility was. When the explosion occurred, confusion reigned. Twenty-three-year-old Andrea Fleytas issued a mayday (distress signal) over the radio when she realized no one else had done so, but she was chastised for overstepping her authority. One manager said he didn't call for help because he wasn't sure he had authorization to do so. Still another said he tried to call to shore but was told the order needed to come from someone else. Crew members knew the emergency shutdown needed to be triggered, but there was confusion over who had the authority to give the OK. As fire spread, several minutes passed before people received directions to evacuate. Again, an alarmed Fleytas turned on the public address system and announced that the crew was abandoning the rig. "The scene was very chaotic," said worker Carlos Ramos. "There was no chain of command. Nobody in charge."[46]

 BRIEFCASE

As an organization manager, keep these guidelines in mind:

Think of the organization as a means to an end. It is a way to organize people and resources to accomplish a specific purpose. Describe the organization according to its degree of formalization, specialization, centralization, complexity, and hierarchy. Look at contingency factors of size, technology, the environment, goals and strategy, and the organizational culture.

Contingency Factors

Understanding structural dimensions alone does not help us understand or appropriately design organizations. It is also necessary to look at contingency factors, including size, organizational technology, the external environment, goals and strategy, and organizational culture.

1. *Size* can be measured for the organization as a whole or for specific components, such as a plant or division. Because organizations are social systems, size is typically measured by the number of employees. Other measures such as total sales or total assets also reflect magnitude, but they do not indicate the size of the human part of the system.
2. *Organizational technology* refers to the tools, techniques, and actions used to transform inputs into outputs. It concerns how the organization actually produces the products and services it provides for customers and includes such things as flexible manufacturing, advanced information systems, and the Internet. An automobile assembly line, a college classroom, and an overnight package delivery system are technologies, although they differ from one another.
3. The *environment* includes all elements outside the boundary of the organization. Key elements include the industry, government, customers, suppliers, and

the financial community. The environmental elements that affect an organization the most are often other organizations.

4. The organization's *goals and strategy* define the purpose and competitive techniques that set it apart from other organizations. Goals are often written down as an enduring statement of company intent. A strategy is the plan of action that describes resource allocation and activities for dealing with the environment and for reaching the organization's goals. Goals and strategies define the scope of operations and the relationship with employees, customers, and competitors.

5. An organization's *culture* is the underlying set of key values, beliefs, understandings, and norms shared by employees. These underlying values and norms may pertain to ethical behavior, commitment to employees, efficiency, or customer service, and they provide the glue to hold organization members together. An organization's culture is unwritten but can be observed in its stories, slogans, ceremonies, dress, and office layout.

The five structural dimensions and five contingency factors discussed here are interdependent. Certain contingency factors will influence the appropriate degree of specialization, formalization, and so forth for the organization. For example, large organization size, a routine technology, and a stable environment all tend to create an organization that has greater formalization, specialization, and centralization. More detailed relationships among contingency factors and structural dimensions are explored throughout this book.

---

1 **An organization can be understood primarily by understanding the people who make it up.**

   ANSWER: *Disagree.* An organization has distinct characteristics that are independent of the nature of the people who make it up. All the people could be replaced over time while an organization's structural dimensions and contingency factors would remain similar.

ASSESS **YOUR** ANSWER

The organizational features illustrated in Exhibit 1.3 provide a basis for measuring and analyzing characteristics that cannot be seen by the casual observer, and they reveal significant information about an organization. Consider, for example, the dimensions of Valve Software compared with those of Walmart and a governmental agency.

Valve Software Corporation is a leader in the video game industry, with Counter-Strike, Half-Life 2, Left 4 Dead, Portal, and the popular digital distribution platform Steam. In September 2013, the United Kingdom's *WhatCulture* online magazine ranked Gabe Newell, the co-founder of Valve, on its list of the "five richest tech billionaires who dropped out of university." Newell acts as the CEO of Valve, but the company has been "boss free since 1996," as its website proclaims. "It's amazing what creative people can come up with when there's nobody there telling them what to do." Valve's unique organization structure caused a minor media blitz after someone posted the employee handbook online in the spring of 2012, but Valve has been functioning smoothly without bosses since it was founded. Newell and co-founder Mike Harrington, former Microsoft employees, wanted to create a flat, fast organization that allowed employees maximum flexibility. It sounds like a dream for employees, but many people don't adapt to the "no-structure structure" and leave for more traditional jobs. At Valve, everyone has a voice in making important decisions. Any employee can participate in hiring decisions, which are usually made by teams. There are no promotions, only new

☑ **IN PRACTICE**
Valve Software

projects, with someone emerging as the de facto leader. Firings are rare, but teams decide together if someone isn't working out. Team meetings are highly informal and people are invited to share feelings as well as business ideas.

Contrast Valve's approach to that of Walmart, which achieves its competitive edge through internal cost efficiency. A standard formula is used to build each store, with uniform displays and merchandise. Walmart's administrative expenses are the lowest of any chain. The distribution system is a marvel of efficiency. Goods can be delivered to any store in less than two days after an order is placed. Stores are controlled from the top, although store managers have some freedom to adapt to local conditions. Employees follow standard procedures set by management and have little say in decision making. However, performance is typically high, and most employees consider that the company treats them fairly.

An even greater contrast is seen in many government agencies or nonprofit organizations that rely heavily on public funding. Most state humanities and arts agencies, for example, are staffed by a small number of highly trained employees, but workers are overwhelmed with rules and regulations and swamped by paperwork. Employees who have to implement rule changes often don't have time to read the continuous stream of memos and still keep up with their daily work. Employees must require extensive reporting from their clients in order to make regular reports to a variety of state and federal funding sources.[47]

Exhibit 1.5 illustrates several structural dimensions and contingency factors of Valve Software, Walmart, and the state arts agency. Valve is a small organization that ranks very low with respect to formalization and centralization and has a medium degree of specialization. Horizontal collaboration to serve customers with innovative products is emphasized over the vertical hierarchy. Walmart is much more formalized, specialized, and centralized, with a strong vertical hierarchy. Efficiency is more important than new products and services, so most activities are guided by standard regulations. The arts agency, in contrast to the other organizations, reflects its status as a small part of a large government bureaucracy. The agency is overwhelmed with rules and standard procedures. Rules are dictated from the top and communication flows down a strong vertical chain of command.

Structural dimensions and contingency factors can thus tell a lot about an organization and about differences among organizations. These various organization design features are examined in more detail in later chapters to determine the appropriate level of each structural dimension needed to perform effectively based on various contingency factors.

EXHIBIT 1.5
Differing Characteristics of Three Organizations

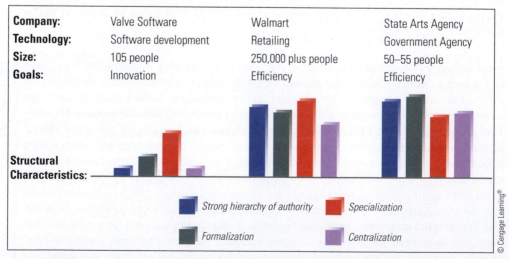

Company:	Valve Software	Walmart	State Arts Agency
Technology:	Software development	Retailing	Government Agency
Size:	105 people	250,000 plus people	50–55 people
Goals:	Innovation	Efficiency	Efficiency

Structural Characteristics:

■ Strong hierarchy of authority   ■ Specialization

■ Formalization   ■ Centralization

© Cengage Learning®

Performance and Effectiveness Outcomes

The whole point of understanding structural dimensions and contingency factors is to design the organization in such a way as to achieve high performance and effectiveness. Managers adjust various aspects of the organization to most efficiently and effectively transform inputs into outputs and provide value. **Efficiency** refers to the amount of resources used to achieve the organization's goals. It is based on the quantity of raw materials, money, and employees necessary to produce a given level of output. **Effectiveness** is a broader term, meaning the degree to which an organization achieves its goals.

To be effective, organizations need clear, focused goals and appropriate strategies for achieving them. The concept of effectiveness, including goals and strategies and various approaches to measuring effectiveness, will be discussed in detail in Chapter 2. Many organizations apply new technology to improve efficiency and effectiveness. A physician's office in Philadelphia increased efficiency by using information technology to reduce paperwork and streamline procedures, enabling the practice to handle more patients with three fewer office employees. The new system improved effectiveness too. Staff can locate information more quickly and make fewer mistakes, leading to a higher quality of care and better customer service.[48]

Achieving effectiveness is not always a simple matter because different people want different things from the organization. For customers, the primary concern is high-quality products and services provided in a timely manner at a reasonable price, whereas employees are mostly concerned with adequate pay, good working conditions, and job satisfaction. Managers carefully balance the needs and interests of various *stakeholders* in setting goals and striving for effectiveness. This is referred to as the **stakeholder approach**, which integrates diverse organizational activities by looking at various organizational stakeholders and what they want from the organization. A **stakeholder** is any group within or outside of the organization that has a stake in the organization's performance. The satisfaction level of each group can be assessed as an indication of the organization's performance and effectiveness.[49] For example, in contrast to the view of government offices as bureaucratic quagmires of inefficiency run by lazy managers, the Hudson Street passport office in lower Manhattan gets glowing reviews on Yelp and other online rating sites. Michael Hoffman, director of the Hudson Street passport office, has a goal of giving customers exactly what they want. Even though he has to deal with some degree of specialization and standardization, he also has discretion in how he manages employees and runs the office. Hoffman has organized the office waiting and work areas in such a way that people and work flow smoothly. He also coaches and supports employees and gives them the resources and discretion to do their jobs without approval from managers when possible. The Hudson Street passport office is a clear example that good organization design and management make a tremendous difference.[50]

2 The primary role of managers in business organizations is to achieve maximum efficiency.

> **ANSWER:** *Disagree.* Efficiency is important, but organizations must respond to a variety of stakeholders, who may want different things from the organization. Managers strive for both efficiency and effectiveness in trying to meet the needs and interests of stakeholders. Effectiveness is often considered more important than efficiency.

ASSESS **YOUR** ANSWER

© Cengage Learning®

EXHIBIT 1.6
Major Stakeholder Groups
and What They Expect

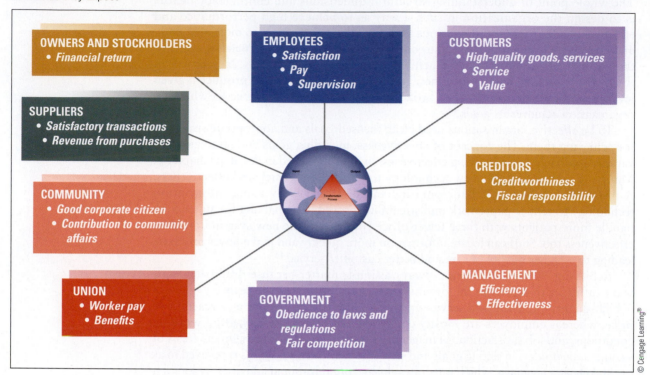

Exhibit 1.6 illustrates various stakeholders and what each group wants from the organization. Stakeholder interests sometimes conflict, and organizations often find it difficult to simultaneously satisfy the demands of all groups. A business might have high customer satisfaction, but the organization might have difficulties with creditors or supplier relationships might be poor. Consider Walmart. Customers love its efficiency and low prices, but the low-cost emphasis has caused friction with suppliers. Some activist groups argue that Walmart's tactics are unethical because they force suppliers to lay off workers, close factories, and outsource to manufacturers from low-wage countries. One supplier said clothing is being sold at Walmart so cheaply that many U.S. companies couldn't compete even if they paid their workers nothing. The challenges of managing such a huge organization have also led to strains in relationships with employees and other stakeholder groups, as evidenced by recent gender discrimination suits and complaints about low wages and poor benefits.[51] The example of Walmart provides a glimpse of how difficult it can be for managers to satisfy multiple stakeholders. In all organizations, managers have to evaluate stakeholder concerns and establish goals that can achieve at least minimal satisfaction for major stakeholder groups.

The Evolution of Organization Design

Organization design is not a collection of facts; it is a way of thinking about organizations and how people and resources are organized to collectively accomplish a specific purpose.[52] Organization design is a way to see and analyze organizations more accurately and deeply than one otherwise could. The way to see and think about organizations is based on patterns and regularities in organizational design and behavior. Organization scholars search for these regularities, define them, measure them, and make them available to the rest of us. The facts from the research are not as important as the general patterns and insights into organizational functioning gained from a comparative study of organizations. Insights from organization design research can help managers improve organizational efficiency and effectiveness, as well as strengthen the quality of organizational life.[53] One area of insight is how organization design and management practices have varied over time in response to changes in the larger society.

Historical Perspectives

You may recall from an earlier management course that the modern era of management theory began with the classical management perspective in the late nineteenth and early twentieth century. The emergence of the factory system during the Industrial Revolution posed problems that earlier organizations had not encountered. As work was performed on a much larger scale by a larger number of workers, people began thinking about how to design and manage work in order to increase productivity and help organizations attain maximum efficiency. The classical perspective, which sought to make organizations run like efficient, well-oiled machines, is associated with the development of hierarchy and bureaucratic organizations and remains the basis of much of modern management theory and practice. In this section, we will examine the classical perspective, with its emphasis on efficiency and organization, as well as other perspectives that emerged to address new concerns, such as employee needs and the role of the environment. Elements of each perspective are still used in organization design, although they have been adapted and revised to meet changing needs. These different perspectives can also be associated with different ways in which managers think about and view the organization, called manager frame of reference. Complete the questionnaire in the "How Do You Fit the Design?" box on page 26 to understand your frame of reference.

Efficiency Is Everything. Pioneered by Frederick Winslow Taylor, **scientific management** emphasizes scientifically determined jobs and management practices as the way to improve efficiency and labor productivity. Taylor proposed that workers "could be retooled like machines, their physical and mental gears recalibrated for better productivity."[54] He insisted that management itself would have to change and emphasized that decisions based on rules of thumb and tradition should be replaced with precise procedures developed after careful study of individual situations.[55] To use this approach, managers develop precise, standard procedures for doing each job, select workers with appropriate abilities, train workers in the standard procedures, carefully plan work, and provide wage incentives to increase output.

Taylor's approach is illustrated by the unloading of iron from railcars and reloading finished steel for the Bethlehem Steel plant in 1898. Taylor calculated that with correct movements, tools, and sequencing, each man was capable of loading 47.5 tons per day instead of the typical 12.5 tons. He also worked out an incentive system that paid each man $1.85 per day for meeting the new standard, an increase from the previous rate of $1.15. Productivity at Bethlehem Steel shot up overnight. These insights helped to establish organizational assumptions that the role of management is to maintain stability and efficiency, with top managers doing the thinking and workers doing what they are told.

HOW DO YOU FIT THE DESIGN?

EVOLUTION OF STYLE

This questionnaire asks you to describe yourself. For each item, give the number "4" to the phrase that best describes you, "3" to the item that is next best, and on down to "1" for the item that is least like you.

1. My strongest skills are:
____ **a.** Analytical skills
____ **b.** Interpersonal skills
____ **c.** Political skills
____ **d.** Flair for drama

2. The best way to describe me is:
____ **a.** Technical expert
____ **b.** Good listener
____ **c.** Skilled negotiator
____ **d.** Inspirational leader

3. What has helped me the most to be successful is my ability to:
____ **a.** Make good decisions
____ **b.** Coach and develop people
____ **c.** Build strong alliances and a power base
____ **d.** Inspire and excite others

4. What people are most likely to notice about me is my:
____ **a.** Attention to detail
____ **b.** Concern for people
____ **c.** Ability to succeed in the face of conflict and opposition
____ **d.** Charisma

5. My most important leadership trait is:
____ **a.** Clear, logical thinking
____ **b.** Caring and support for others
____ **c.** Toughness and aggressiveness
____ **d.** Imagination and creativity

6. I am best described as:
____ **a.** An analyst
____ **b.** A humanist
____ **c.** A politician
____ **d.** A visionary

Scoring: Compute your scores according to the following rater. The higher score represents your way of viewing the organization and will influence your management style.

Structure = 1a + 2a + 3a + 4a + 5a + 6a = _____
Human Resource = 1b + 2b + 3b + 4b + 5b + 6b = _____

Political = 1c + 2c + 3c + 4c + 5c + 6c = _____
Symbolic = 1d + 2d + 3d + 4d + 5d + 6d = _____

Interpretation: Organization managers typically view their world through one or more mental frames of reference. (1) The *structural frame* of reference sees the organization as a machine that can be economically efficient with vertical hierarchy and routine tasks that give a manager the formal authority to achieve goals. This manager way of thinking became strong during the era of scientific management when efficiency was everything. (2) The *human resource frame* sees the organization as its people, with manager emphasis given to support, empowerment, and belonging. This manager way of thinking gained importance after the Hawthorne Studies. (3) The *political frame* sees the organization as a competition for scarce resources to achieve goals, with manager emphasis on building agreement among diverse groups. This manager way of thinking reflects the need for organizations to share information, have a collaborative strategy, and have all parts working together. (4) The *symbolic frame* sees the organization as theater, with manager emphasis on symbols, vision, culture, and inspiration. This manager way of thinking is important for managing an adaptive culture in a learning organization.

Which frame reflects your way of viewing the world? The first two frames of reference—structural and human resource—are important for newer managers at the lower and middle levels of an organization. These two frames usually are mastered first. As managers gain experience and move up the organization, they should acquire political and collaborative skills (Chapter 13) and also learn to use symbols to shape cultural values (Chapter 10). It is important for managers not to be stuck in one way of viewing the organization because their progress may be limited.

Source: Roy G. Williams and Terrence E. Deal, *When Opposites Dance: Balancing the Manager and Leader Within* (Palo Alto, CA: Davies-Black, 2003), pp. 24–28. Reprinted with permission.

The ideas of creating a system for maximum efficiency and organizing work for maximum productivity are deeply embedded in our organizations. A *Harvard Business Review* article discussing innovations that shaped modern management puts scientific management at the top of its list of 12 influential innovations.[56]

How to Get Organized. Another subfield of the classical perspective took a broader look at the organization. Whereas scientific management focused primarily on the technical core—on work performed on the shop floor—**administrative principles** looked at the design and functioning of the organization as a whole. For example, Henri Fayol proposed 14 principles of management, such as "each subordinate receives orders from only one superior" (unity of command) and "similar activities in an organization should be grouped together under one manager" (unity of direction). These principles formed the foundation for modern management practice and organization design.

The scientific management and administrative principles approaches were powerful and gave organizations fundamental new ideas for establishing high productivity and increasing prosperity. Administrative principles in particular contributed to the development of **bureaucratic organizations**, which emphasized designing and managing organizations on an impersonal, rational basis through such elements as clearly defined authority and responsibility, formal recordkeeping, and uniform application of standard rules. Although the term *bureaucracy* has taken on negative connotations in today's organizations, bureaucratic characteristics worked extremely well for the needs of the Industrial Age. One problem with the classical perspective, however, is that it failed to consider the social context and human needs.

What About People? Early work on industrial psychology and human relations received little attention because of the prominence of scientific management. However, a major breakthrough occurred with a series of experiments at a Chicago electric company, which came to be known as the **Hawthorne Studies**. Interpretations of these studies at the time concluded that positive treatment of employees improved their motivation and productivity. The publication of these findings led to a revolution in worker treatment and laid the groundwork for subsequent work examining treatment of workers, leadership, motivation, and human resource management. These human relations and behavioral approaches added new and important contributions to the study of management and organizations.

However, the hierarchical system and bureaucratic approaches that developed during the Industrial Revolution remained the primary approach to organization design and functioning well into the 1980s. In general, this approach worked well for most organizations until the past few decades. During the 1980s, though, it began to cause problems. Increased competition, especially on a global scale, changed the playing field.[57] North American companies had to find a better way.

Can Bureaucracies Be Flexible? The 1980s produced new corporate cultures that valued lean staff, flexibility and learning, rapid response to the customer, engaged employees, and quality products. Organizations began experimenting with teams, flattened hierarchies, and participative management approaches. For example, in 1983, a DuPont plant in Martinsville, Virginia, cut management layers from eight to four and began using teams of production employees to solve problems and take over routine management tasks. The new design led to improved quality, decreased costs, and enhanced innovation, helping the plant be more competitive in a changed environment.[58] Rather than relying on strict rules and hierarchy, managers began looking at the entire organizational system, including the external environment.

Since the 1980s, organizations have undergone even more profound and far-reaching changes. Flexible approaches to organization design have become prevalent. Recent influences on the shifting of organization design include the Internet and other advances in communications and information technology; globalization and the increasing interconnection of organizations; the rising educational level of employees and their growing quality-of-life expectations; and the growth of knowledge- and information-based work as primary organizational activities.[59]

It All Depends: Key Contingencies

Many problems occur when all organizations are treated as similar, which was the case with scientific management and administrative principles that attempted to design all organizations alike. The structures and systems that work in the retail division of a conglomerate will not be appropriate for the manufacturing division. The organization charts and financial procedures that are best for an entrepreneurial Internet firm like Pinterest will not work for a large food processing plant at Kraft or a large nonprofit organization such as the United Way.

A basic premise of this text is that effective organization design means understanding various contingencies and how organizations can be designed to fit contingency factors. **Contingency** means that one thing depends on other things, and for organizations to be effective there must be a "goodness of fit" between their design and various contingency factors.[60] What works in one setting may not work in another setting. There is no "one best way." Contingency theory means *it depends*. For example, a government agency may experience a certain environment, use a routine technology, and desire efficiency. In this situation, a management approach that uses bureaucratic control procedures, a hierarchical structure, and formalized communications would be appropriate. Likewise, a free-flowing design and management processes work best in a high-tech company that faces an uncertain environment with a non-routine technology. The correct approach is contingent on the organization's situation. In the following section, we examine two fundamental approaches to organization design, along with the typical contingency factors associated with each approach.

ASSESS YOUR ANSWER

3 **A CEO's top priority is to make sure the organization is designed correctly.**

ANSWER: *Agree.* Top managers have many responsibilities, but one of the most important is making sure the organization is designed correctly. Organization design organizes and focuses people's work and shapes their response to customers and other stakeholders. Managers consider both structural dimensions and contingency factors as well as make sure the various parts of the organization work together to achieve important goals.

The Contrast of Organic and Mechanistic Designs

Organizations can be categorized along a continuum ranging from a mechanistic design to an organic design. Tom Burns and G. M. Stalker first used the terms *organic* and *mechanistic* to describe two extremes of organization design after observing industrial firms in England.[61] In general, a **mechanistic** design means that the organization is characterized by machine-like standard rules, procedures, and a clear hierarchy of authority. Organizations are highly formalized and are also centralized, with most decisions made at the top. An **organic** design means that the organization is much looser, free-flowing, and adaptive. Rules and regulations often are not written down or, if written down, are flexibly applied. People may have to find their own way through the system to figure out what to do. The hierarchy of authority is looser and not clear-cut. Decision-making authority is decentralized.

Various contingency factors will influence whether an organization is more effective with a primarily mechanistic or a primarily organic design. Exhibit 1.7 summarizes the differences in organic and mechanistic designs based on five elements: structure, tasks, formalization, communication, and hierarchy. The exhibit also lists the typical contingency factors associated with each type of design.

EXHIBIT 1.7

The Contrast of Organic and Mechanistic Designs

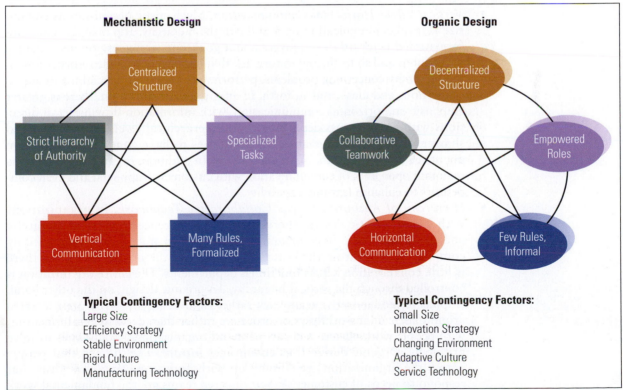

© Cengage Learning®

- *Centralized Versus Decentralized Structure.* Centralization and decentralization pertain to the hierarchical level at which decisions are made. In a mechanistic design, the structure is centralized, whereas an organic design uses decentralized decision making. **Centralization** means that decision authority is located near the top of the organizational hierarchy. Knowledge and control of activities are centralized at the top of the organization, and employees are expected to do as they are told. With **decentralization**, decision-making authority is pushed down to lower organizational levels. In a highly organic organization, knowledge and control of activities are located with employees rather than with supervisors or top executives. People are encouraged to take care of problems by working with one another and with customers, using their discretion to make decisions.

- *Specialized Tasks Versus Empowered Roles.* A **task** is a narrowly defined piece of work assigned to a person. With a mechanistic design, tasks are broken down into specialized, separate parts, as in a machine, with each employee performing activities according to a specific job description. A **role**, in contrast, is a part in a dynamic social system. A role has discretion and responsibility, allowing the person to use his or her judgment and ability to achieve an outcome or meet a goal. In an organization with an organic design, employees play a role in the team or department and roles may be continually redefined or adjusted.

- *Formal Versus Informal Systems.* With a mechanistic design, there are numerous rules, regulations, and standard procedures. Formal systems are in place to manage information, guide communication, and detect deviations from established standards and goals. With an organic design, on the other hand, there are few rules or formal control systems. Communication and information sharing is informal.

- *Vertical Versus Horizontal Communication.* Mechanistic organizations emphasize vertical communication up and down the hierarchy. Top managers pass information downward to employees about goals and strategies, job instructions, procedures, and so forth, and in turn ask that employees provide information up the hierarchy concerning problems, performance reports, financial information, suggestions and ideas, and so forth. In an organic organization, there is greater emphasis on horizontal communication, with information flowing in all directions within and across departments and hierarchical levels. The widespread sharing of information enables all employees to have complete information about the company so they can act quickly. In addition, organic organizations maintain open lines of communication with customers, suppliers, and even competitors to enhance learning capability.

- *Hierarchy of Authority Versus Collaborative Teamwork.* In organizations with a mechanistic design, there is a close adherence to vertical hierarchy and the formal chain of command. Work activities are typically organized by common function from the bottom to the top of the organization and there is little collaboration across functional departments. The entire organization is controlled through the vertical hierarchy. An organic design, on the other hand, emphasizes collaborative teamwork rather than hierarchy. Structure is created around horizontal workflows or processes rather than departmental functions, with people working across department and organizational boundaries to solve problems. Organic design thus encourages *intrapreneurship*, so that people across the organization are coming up with and promoting new ideas that respond to needs of customers.[62] Self-directed teams are the fundamental work unit in highly organic organizations.

Contemporary Design Ideas: Radical Decentralization

To some extent, organizations are still imprinted with the hierarchical, formalized, mechanistic approach that arose in the nineteenth century with Frederick Taylor. Yet current challenges require greater flexibility for most organizations. A few organizations, such as Valve Software, described earlier, have shifted to an extremely organic, "bossless" design. In fact, a few bossless work environments, such as W. L. Gore and the French company FAVI, have existed for decades, but this has become a real trend in recent years. For one thing, how and where work gets done has shifted in big ways because many people can easily work from home or other locations outside a regular office. At Symantec, for example, most employees used to work in cubicles but now many of them work from home or other remote locations scattered all over the world.[63] Even for companies with people working on-site, new technology means that everyone can be wired into the heart of the organization.[64] When everyone has access to the information they need and the training to make good decisions, having layers of managers just eats up costs and slows down response time.

Many bossless companies, such as Valve, Netflix (video streaming and rentals), and Atlassian (enterprise software) are in technology-related industries, but companies as diverse as GE Aviation (aviation manufacturing), W. L. Gore & Associates (best known for Gore-Tex fabrics), Whole Foods (supermarkets), and Semco (diversified manufacturing) have succeeded for years with bossless structures. Morning Star provides one of the most interesting examples of a bossless work environment.

Chris Rufer, founder of Morning Star, the world's largest tomato processor with three factories that produce products for companies such as Heinz and Campbell Soup Company, believes if people can manage the complexities of their own lives without a boss, there is no reason they can't manage themselves in the workplace. Rufer organized Morning Star, where 400 or so employees produce over $700 million a year in revenues, based on the principles of self-management:

IN PRACTICE

Morning Star

- No one has a boss
- Employees negotiate responsibilities with their peers
- Everyone can spend the company's money
- There are no titles or promotions
- Compensation is decided by peers

How does such a system work? As the company grew from the original 24 colleagues (as employees are called) to around 400, problems occurred. Some people had trouble working in an environment with no bosses and no hierarchy. Thus, Rufer created the Morning Star Self-Management Institute to provide training for people in the principles and systems of self-management. Every colleague now goes through training, in groups of 10 to 15 people, to learn how to work effectively as part of a team, how to handle the responsibilities of "planning, organizing, leading, and controlling" that are typically carried out by managers, how to balance freedom and accountability, how to understand and effectively communicate with others, and how to manage conflicts.

Today, every colleague writes a personal mission statement and is responsible for accomplishing it, including obtaining whatever tools and resources are needed. That means anyone can order supplies and equipment, and colleagues are responsible for initiating the hiring process when they need more help. Every year, each individual negotiates a Colleague Letter of Understanding (CLOU) with the people most affected by his or her work. Every CLOU has a clearly defined set of metrics that enables people to track their progress in achieving goals and meeting the needs of colleagues. "Around here," one colleague said, "nobody's your boss and everybody's your boss."[65]

In a bossless work environment such as that at Morning Star, nobody gives orders, and nobody takes them. Accountability is to the customer and the team rather than to a manager. There can be many advantages to a bossless work environment, including increased flexibility, greater employee initiative and commitment, and better, faster decision making.[66] However, bossless work environments also present new challenges. Costs may be lower because of reduced overhead, but money has to be invested in ongoing training and development for employees so they can work effectively within a bossless system and manage themselves. The culture also has to engage employees and support the non-hierarchical environment.

Framework for the Book

How does a course in organization design differ from a course in management or organizational behavior? The answer is related to the concept called *level of analysis*.

Levels of Analysis

Each organization is a system that is composed of various subsystems. Organization systems are nested within systems, and one **level of analysis** has to be chosen as the primary focus. Four levels of analysis normally characterize organizations, as illustrated in Exhibit 1.8. The individual human being is the basic building block of organizations. The human being is to the organization what a cell is to a

EXHIBIT 1.8
Levels of Analysis in
Organizations

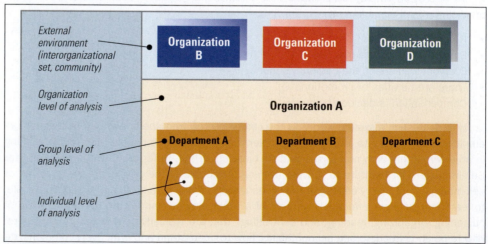

Source: Based on Andrew H. Van De Ven and Diane L. Ferry, *Measuring and Assessing Organizations* (New York: Wiley, 1980), 8; and Richard L. Daft and Richard M. Steers, *Organizations: A Micro/Macro Approach* (Glenview, IL: Scott, Foresman, 1986), 8

biological system. The next higher system level is the group or department. These are collections of individuals who work together to perform group tasks. The next level of analysis is the organization itself. An organization is a collection of groups or departments that combine into the total organization.

Organizations themselves can be grouped together into the next higher level of analysis, which is the interorganizational set and community. The interorganizational set is the group of organizations with which a single organization interacts. Other organizations in the community make up an important part of an organization's environment.

Organization design focuses on the organizational level of analysis, but with concern for groups and the environment. To explain the organization, one should look not only at its characteristics but also at the characteristics of the environment and of the departments and groups that make up the organization. The focus of this book is to help you understand organizations by examining their specific characteristics, the nature of and relationships among groups and departments that make up the organization, and the collection of organizations that make up the environment.

Are individuals included in organization design? Organization design does consider the behavior of individuals, but in the aggregate. People are important, but they are not the primary focus of analysis. Organization design is distinct from organizational behavior.

Organizational behavior is the micro approach to organizations because it focuses on the individuals within organizations as the relevant units of analysis. Organizational behavior examines concepts such as motivation, leadership style, and personality and is concerned with cognitive and emotional differences among people within organizations.

Organization theory and design is a macro examination of organizations because it analyzes the whole organization as a unit. Organization design is concerned with people aggregated into departments and organizations and with the differences in structure and behavior at the organization level of analysis. Organization design might be considered the sociology of organizations, while organizational behavior is the psychology of organizations.

Organization design is directly relevant to top- and middle-management concerns and partly relevant to lower management. Top managers are responsible for the entire organization and must set goals, develop strategy, interpret the external environment, and decide organization structure and design. Middle management is concerned with major departments, such as marketing or research, and must decide how the department relates to the rest of the organization. Middle managers must design their departments to fit work-unit technology and deal with issues of power and politics, intergroup conflict, and information and control systems, each of which is part of organization theory and design. Organization design is only partly concerned with lower management because this level of supervision is concerned with employees who operate machines, create services, or sell goods. Organization design is concerned with the big picture of the organization and its major departments.

As an organization manager, keep this guideline in mind:

Make yourself a competent, influential manager by using the frameworks that organization design provides to interpret and understand the organization around you.

Plan of the Book

The topics within the field of organization design are interrelated. Chapters are presented so that major ideas unfold in logical sequence. The framework that guides the organization of the book is shown in Exhibit 1.9. Part 1 introduces the basic idea of organizations as social systems and the essential concepts of organization design.

EXHIBIT 1.9
Framework for the Book

Part 1 Introduction to Organizations

CHAPTER 1
Organizations and Organization Design

Part 2 Organizational Purpose and Structural Design

CHAPTER 2
Strategy, Organization Design, and Effectiveness

CHAPTER 3
Fundamentals of Organization Structure

Part 3 Open System Design Elements

CHAPTER 4
The External Environment

CHAPTER 5
Interorganizational Relationships

CHAPTER 6
Designing Organizations for the International Environment

Part 4 Internal Design Elements

CHAPTER 7
Manufacturing and Service Technologies

CHAPTER 8
Technology for Control, Social Business, and Big Data

CHAPTER 9
Organizational Size, Life Cycle, and Decline

Part 5 Managing Dynamic Processes

CHAPTER 10
Organizational Culture and Ethical Values

CHAPTER 11
Innovation and Change

CHAPTER 12
Decision-Making Processes

CHAPTER 13
Conflict, Power, and Politics

This discussion provides the groundwork for Part 2, which is about strategic management, goals and effectiveness, and the fundamentals of organization structure. This section examines how managers help the organization achieve its purpose, including the design of an appropriate structure, such as a functional, divisional, matrix, or horizontal structure. Part 3 looks at the various open system elements that influence organization structure and design, including the external environment, interorganizational relationships, and the global environment.

Parts 4 and 5 look at processes inside the organization. Part 4 describes how organization design is related to the contingency factors of manufacturing and service technology, and organizational size and life cycle. Part 5 shifts to dynamic processes that exist within and between major organizational departments and includes topics such as innovation and change, culture and ethical values, decision-making processes, managing intergroup conflict, and power and politics.

Plan of Each Chapter

Each chapter begins with opening questions to immediately engage the student in the chapter content. Theoretical concepts are introduced and explained in the body of the chapter. Several *In Practice* segments are included in each chapter to illustrate the concepts and show how they apply to real organizations. Each chapter also contains a *How Do You Fit the Design?* questionnaire that draws students more deeply into a particular topic and enables them to experience organization design issues in a personal way. A *BookMark* is included in each chapter to present organizational issues that today's managers face in the real world. These short book reviews discuss current concepts and applications to deepen and enrich the student's understanding of organizations. The examples and book reviews illustrate the dramatic changes taking place in management thinking and practice. Key points for designing and managing organizations are highlighted in the *Briefcase* items throughout the chapter. Each chapter closes with a *Design Essentials* section that reviews and explains important theoretical concepts.

Design Essentials

■ Organization design provides tools to understand, design, and manage organizations more effectively, including issues such as how to adapt to a changing environment, cope with increasing size and complexity, manage internal conflict and coordination, and shape the right kind of culture to meet goals.

■ Managers today face new challenges, including globalization, intense competition, rigorous scrutiny of ethical and green practices, the need for rapid response, and incorporating social business and big data.

■ Organizations are open systems that obtain inputs from the external environment, add value through a transformation process, and discharge products and services back to the environment.

■ Organizations are highly important, and managers are responsible for shaping organizations to perform well and meet the needs of society. The structural dimensions of formalization, specialization, hierarchy of authority, complexity, and centralization and the contingency factors of size, organizational technology, environment, goals and strategy, and culture provide labels for measuring and analyzing organizations. These characteristics vary widely from organization to organization. Subsequent chapters provide frameworks for analyzing organizations with these concepts.

■ Many types of organizations exist. One important distinction is between for-profit businesses, in which managers direct their activities toward earning money for the company, and nonprofit organizations, in which managers direct their efforts toward generating some kind of social impact. Managers strive to design organizations to achieve both efficiency and effectiveness. Effectiveness is complex because different stakeholders have different interests and needs that they want satisfied by the organization.

■ Organization design perspectives have varied over time. Managers can understand organizations better by gaining a historical perspective and by understanding the contrast between organic and mechanistic designs.

■ Organization designs fall on a scale ranging from mechanistic to organic. A mechanistic design is characterized by a centralized structure, specialized tasks, formal systems, vertical communication, and a strict hierarchy of authority. An organic design is characterized by a decentralized structure, empowered roles, informal systems, horizontal communication, and collaborative teamwork. Challenges in today's environment are causing many organizations to shift to more organic designs, although mechanistic characteristics are still valuable for some situations.

■ Most concepts in organization theory and design pertain to the top- and middle-management levels of the organization. This book is concerned more with the topics of those levels than with the operational-level topics of supervision and motivation of employees, which are discussed in courses on organizational behavior.

❯❯ KEY CONCEPTS

administrative principles	Hawthorne Studies	scientific management
big data analytics	level of analysis	social business
bureaucratic organizations	mechanistic	social media programs
centralization	open system	stakeholder
contingency factors	organic	stakeholder approach
contingency	organization theory and design	structural dimensions
decentralization	organizational behavior	sustainability
effectiveness	organizations	task
efficiency	role	

❯❯ DISCUSSION QUESTIONS

1. What is the definition of *organization*? Briefly explain each part of the definition as you understand it.
2. Describe some ways in which social business has influenced or affected an organization with which you are familiar, such as your college or university, a local retailer or restaurant, a volunteer organization, a club to which you belong, or even your family. Can you identify both positive and negative aspects of this influence?
3. A handful of companies on the *Fortune* 500 list are more than 100 years old, which is rare. What

organizational characteristics do you think might explain 100-year longevity?
4. Can an organization be efficient without being effective? Can an inefficient organization still be an effective one? Explain your answers.
5. What is the difference between formalization and specialization? Do you think an organization high on one dimension would also be high on the other? Discuss.
6. What does *contingency* mean? What are the implications of contingency theory for managers?

7. What are the primary differences between an organic and a mechanistic organization design? Which type of organization do you think would be easier to manage? Discuss.

8. What does it mean to say an organization is an open system? How is the stakeholder approach related to the concept of open systems?

9. What are some differences one might expect among stakeholder expectations for a nonprofit organization versus a for-profit business? Do you think nonprofit managers have to pay more attention to stakeholders than do business managers? Discuss.

10. Early management theorists believed that organizations should strive to be logical and rational, with a place for everything and everything in its place. Discuss the pros and cons of this approach for today's organizations.

▶️ CHAPTER 1 WORKSHOP   Measuring Dimensions of Organization

Individually or in a small group of two, interview two employees who are in different organizations or who are in the same organization but in different parts and doing different jobs. Ask each person to answer the following questions on a four-point scale from Definitely False, Mostly False, Mostly True, Definitely True. You will be asked to analyze the patterns of scores for the two respondents.

Formalization	Definitely False	Mostly False	Mostly True	Definitely True
1. There is a written description for my job.	——	——	——	——
2. There is a chart showing where people are in the hierarchy.	——	——	——	——
3. There is a written record of each person's job performance.	——	——	——	——
4. There is a written document that tells what to do in a crisis.	——	——	——	——
5. We have written procedures here for most situations.	——	——	——	——

Formalization Score _____. (Sum questions 1 to 5 giving four points for each Definitely True, three points for each Mostly True, two points for each Mostly False, and one point for each Definitely False.

Centralization	Definitely False	Mostly False	Mostly True	Definitely True
6. A person who works in this job cannot expect to make all his or her own decisions.	——	——	——	——
7. Any decision I make has to have my boss's approval.	——	——	——	——
8. Even small matters are typically referred to someone higher up for a decision.	——	——	——	——
9. I participate in the decision to hire staff at my level.	——	——	——	——
10. How things are done here is left up to the person doing the work.	——	——	——	——

Centralization Score _____. (Sum questions 6 to 8, giving four points for each Definitely True, three points for each Mostly True, two points for each Mostly False, and one point for each Definitely False. *Reverse score* items 9 and 10, giving one point for each Definitely True, two points for each Mostly True, three points for each Mostly False, and four points for each Definitely False.)

Technology (Work Variety)	Definitely False	Mostly False	Mostly True	Definitely True
11. My job has new things happening every day.	——	——	——	——
12. One thing around here is the high variety of work.	——	——	——	——
13. There is something different to do here every day.	——	——	——	——
14. The work here is very routine.	——	——	——	——
15. People like me do about the same job in the same way most of the time.	——	——	——	——

Technology Score _____. (Sum questions 11 to 13, giving four points for each Definitely True, three points for each Mostly True, two points for each Mostly False, and one point for each Definitely False. *Reverse score* items 14 and 15, giving one point for each Definitely True, two points for each Mostly True, three points for each Mostly False, and four points for each Definitely False.)

Questions

1. What are the main differences between the three scores for the two people you interviewed?
2. Do you notice any patterns in the three scores, such as a higher score on one characteristic is associated with a higher or lower score on another characteristic?
3. Which of the interviewees seemed more satisfied in their work? Do you think satisfaction is related to their scores on formalization, centralization, and technology? Explain.

CASE FOR ANALYSIS | **It Isn't So Simple: Infrastructure Change at Royce Consulting[67]**

The lights of the city glittered outside Ken Vincent's twelfth-floor office. After nine years of late nights and missed holidays, Ken was in the executive suite with the words "Associate Partner" on the door. Things should be easier now, but the proposed changes at Royce Consulting had been more challenging than he had expected. "I don't understand," he thought. "At Royce Consulting our clients, our people, and our reputation are what count, so why do I feel so much tension from the managers about the changes that are going to be made in the office? We've analyzed why we have to make the changes. Heck, we even got an outside person to help us. The administrative support staff are pleased. So why aren't the managers enthusiastic? We all know what the decision at tomorrow's meeting will be—Go! Then it will all be over. Or will it?" Ken thought as he turned out the lights.

Background

Royce Consulting is an international consulting firm whose clients are large corporations, usually with long-term contracts. Royce employees spend weeks, months, and even years working under contract at the client's site. Royce consultants are employed by a wide range of industries, from manufacturing facilities to utilities to service businesses. The firm has over 160 consulting offices located in 65 countries. At this location Royce employees included 85 staff members, 22 site managers, 9 partners and associate partners, 6 administrative support staff, 1 human resource professional, and 1 financial support person.

For the most part, Royce Consulting hired entry-level staff straight out of college and promoted from within. New hires worked on staff for five or six years; if they did well, they were promoted to manager. Managers were responsible for maintaining client contracts and assisting partners in creating proposals for future engagements. Those who were not promoted after six or seven years generally left the company for other jobs.

Newly promoted managers were assigned an office, a major perquisite of their new status. During the previous year, some new managers had been forced to share an office because of space limitations. To minimize the friction of sharing an office, one of the managers was usually assigned to a long-term project out of town. Thus, practically speaking, each manager had a private office.

Infrastructure and Proposed Changes

Royce was thinking about instituting a hoteling office system—also referred to as a "nonterritorial" or "free-address" office. A hoteling office system makes offices available to managers on a reservation or drop-in basis. Managers are not assigned a permanent office; instead, whatever materials and equipment the manager needs are moved into the temporary office. These are some of the features and advantages of a hoteling office system:

- No permanent office assigned
- Offices are scheduled by reservations
- Long-term scheduling of an office is feasible
- Storage space would be located in a separate file room
- Standard manuals and supplies would be maintained in each office
- Hoteling coordinator is responsible for maintaining offices
- A change in "possession of space"
- Eliminates two or more managers assigned to the same office
- Allows managers to keep the same office if desired
- Managers would have to bring in whatever files they needed for their stay
- Information available would be standardized regardless of office
- Managers do not have to worry about "housekeeping issues"

The other innovation under consideration was an upgrade to state-of-the-art electronic office technology. All managers would receive a new notebook computer with updated communications capability to use Royce's integrated and proprietary software. Also, as part of the electronic office technology, an electronic filing system was considered. The electronic filing system meant information regarding proposals, client records, and promotional materials would be electronically available on the Royce Consulting network.

The administrative support staff had limited experience with many of the application packages used by the managers. While they used word processing extensively, they had little experience with spreadsheets, communications, or graphics packages. The firm had a graphics department and the managers did most of their own work, so the administrative staff did not have to work with those application software packages.

Work Patterns

Royce Consulting was located in a large city in the Midwest. The office was located in the downtown area, but it was easy to get to. Managers assigned to in-town projects often stopped by for a few hours at various times of the day. Managers who were not currently assigned to client projects were expected to be in the office to assist on current projects or work with a partner to develop proposals for new business.

In a consulting firm, managers spend a significant portion of their time at client sites. As a result, the office occupancy rate at Royce Consulting was about 40 to 60 percent. This meant that the firm paid lease costs for offices that were empty approximately half of the time. With the planned growth over the next 10 years, assigning permanent offices to every manager, even in doubled-up arrangements, was judged to be economically unnecessary given the amount of time offices were empty. The proposed changes would require managers and administrative support staff to adjust their work patterns. Additionally, if a hoteling office system was adopted, managers would need to keep their files in a centralized file room.

Organizational Culture

Royce Consulting had a strong organizational culture, and management personnel were highly effective at communicating it to all employees.

Stability of Culture
The culture at Royce Consulting was stable. The leadership of the corporation had a clear picture of who they were and what type of organization they were. Royce Consulting had positioned itself to be a leader in all areas of large business consulting. Royce Consulting's CEO articulated the firm's commitment to being client-centered. Everything that was done at Royce Consulting was because of the client.

Training
New hires at Royce Consulting received extensive training in the culture of the organization and the methodology employed in consulting projects. They began with a structured program of classroom instruction and computer-aided courses covering technologies used in the various industries in which the firm was involved. Royce Consulting recruited top young people who were aggressive and who were willing to do whatever was necessary to get the job done and build a common bond. Among new hires, camaraderie was encouraged along with a level of competition. This kind of behavior continued to be cultivated throughout the training and promotion process.

Work Relationships
Royce Consulting employees had a remarkably similar outlook on the organization. Accepting the culture and norms of the organization was important for each employee. The norms of Royce Consulting revolved around high performance expectations and strong job involvement.

By the time people were made managers, they were aware of what types of behaviors were acceptable. Managers were formally assigned the role of coach to younger staff people, and they modeled acceptable behavior. Behavioral norms included when they came into the office, how late they stayed at the office, and the type of comments they made about others. Managers spent time checking on staff people and talking with them about how they were doing.

The standard for relationships was that of professionalism. Managers knew they had to do what the partners asked and they were to be available at all times. A norms survey and conversations made it clear that people at Royce Consulting were expected to help each other with on-the-job problems, but personal problems were outside the realm of sanctioned relationships. Personal problems were not to interfere with performance on a job. To illustrate, vacations were put on hold and other kinds of commitments were set aside if something was needed at Royce Consulting.

Organizational Values
Three things were of major importance to the organization: its clients, its people, and its reputation. There was a strong client-centered philosophy communicated and practiced. Organization members sought to meet and exceed customer expectations. Putting clients first was stressed. The management of Royce Consulting listened to its clients and made adjustments to satisfy the client.

The reputation of Royce Consulting was important to those leading the organization. They protected and enhanced it by focusing on quality services delivered by quality people. The emphasis on clients, Royce Consulting personnel, and the firm's reputation was cultivated by developing a highly motivated, cohesive, and committed group of employees.

Management Style and Hierarchical Structure

The company organization was characterized by a directive style of management. The partners had the final word on all issues of importance. It was common to hear statements like "Managers are expected to solve problems, and do whatever it takes to finish the job" and "Whatever the partners want, we do." Partners accepted and asked for managers' feedback on projects, but in the final analysis, the partners made the decisions.

Current Situation

Royce Consulting had an aggressive five-year plan that was predicated on a continued increase in business. Increases in the total number of partners, associate partners, managers, and staff were forecast. Additional office space would be required to accommodate the growth in staff; this would increase rental costs at a time when Royce's fixed and variable costs were going up.

The partners, led by managing partner Donald Gray and associate partner Ken Vincent, believed that something had to be done to improve space utilization and the productivity of the managers and administrative personnel. The partners approved a feasibility study of the innovations and their impact on the company.

The ultimate decision makers were the partner group who had the power to approve the concepts and commit the required financial investment. A planning committee consisted of Ken Vincent; the human resources person; the financial officer; and an outside consultant, Mary Schrean.

The Feasibility Study

Within two working days of the initial meeting, all the partners and managers received a memo announcing the hoteling office feasibility study. The memo included a brief description of the concept and stated that it would include an interview with the staff. By this time, partners and managers had already heard about the possible changes and knew that Gray was leaning toward hoteling offices.

Interviews with the Partners

All the partners were interviewed. One similarity in the comments was that they thought the move to hoteling offices was necessary, but they were glad it would not affect them. Three partners expressed concern about managers' acceptance of the change to a hoteling system. The conclusion of each partner was that if Royce Consulting moved to hoteling offices, with or without electronic office technology, the managers would accept the change. The reason given by the partners for such acceptance was that the managers would do what the partners wanted done.

The partners all agreed that productivity could be improved at all levels of the organization: in their own work as well as among the secretaries and the managers.

Partners acknowledged that current levels of information technology at Royce Consulting would not support the move to hoteling offices and that advances in electronic office technology needed to be considered.

Partners viewed all filing issues as secondary to both the office layout change and the proposed technology improvement. What eventually emerged, however, was that ownership and control of files was a major concern, and most partners and managers did not want anything centralized.

Interviews with the Managers

Personal interviews were conducted with all ten managers who were in the office. During the interviews, four of the managers asked Schrean whether the change to hoteling offices was her idea. The managers passed the question off as a joke; however, they expected a response from her. She stated that she was there as an adviser, that she had not generated the idea, and that she would not make the final decision regarding the changes.

The length of time that these managers had been in their current positions ranged from six months to five years. None of them expressed positive feelings about the hoteling system, and all of them referred to how hard they had worked to make manager and gain an office of their own. Eight managers spoke of the status that the office gave them and the convenience of having a permanent place to keep their information and files. Two of the managers said they did not care so much about the status but were concerned about the convenience. One manager said he would come in less frequently if he did not have his own office. The managers believed that a change to hoteling offices would decrease their productivity. Two managers stated that they did not care how much money Royce Consulting would save on lease costs; they wanted to keep their offices.

However, for all the negative comments, all the managers said that they would go along with whatever the partners decided to do. One manager stated that if Royce Consulting stays busy with client projects, having a permanently assigned office was not a big issue.

During the interviews, every manager was enthusiastic and supportive of new productivity tools, particularly the improved electronic office technology. They believed that new computers and integrated software and productivity tools would definitely improve their productivity. Half the managers stated that updated technology would make the change to hoteling offices "a little less terrible," and they wanted their secretaries to have the same software as they did.

The managers' responses to the filing issue varied. The volume of files managers had was in direct proportion to their tenure in that position: The longer a person was a manager, the more files he or she had. In all cases, managers took care of their own files, storing them in their offices and in whatever filing drawers were free.

As part of the process of speaking with managers, their administrative assistants were asked about the proposed changes. Each of the six thought that the electronic office upgrade would benefit the managers, although they were somewhat concerned about what would be expected of them. Regarding the move to hoteling offices, each said that the managers would hate the change, but that they would agree to it if the partners wanted to move in that direction.

Results of the Survey

A survey developed from the interviews was sent to all partners, associate partners, and managers two weeks after the interviews were conducted. The completed survey was returned by 6 of the 9 partners and associate partners and 16 of the 22 managers. This is what the survey showed.

Work Patterns. It was "common knowledge" that managers were out of the office a significant portion of their time, but there were no figures to substantiate this belief, so the respondents were asked to provide data on where they spent their time. The survey results indicated that partners spent 38 percent of their time in the office; 54 percent at client sites; 5 percent at home; and 3 percent in other places, such as airports. Managers reported spending 32 percent of their time in the office, 63 percent at client sites, 4 percent at home, and 1 percent in other places.

For 15 workdays, the planning team also visually checked each of the 15 managers' offices four times each day: at 9 A.M., 11 A.M., 2 P.M., and 4 P.M. These times were selected because initial observations indicated that these were the peak occupancy times. An average of six offices (40 percent of all manager offices) were empty at any given time; in other words, there was a 60 percent occupancy rate.

Alternative Office Layouts. One of the alternatives outlined by the planning committee was a continuation of and expansion of shared offices. Eleven of the managers responding to the survey preferred shared offices to hoteling offices. Occasions when more than one manager was in the shared office at the same time were infrequent. Eight managers reported 0 to 5 office conflicts per month; three managers reported 6 to 10 office conflicts per month. The type of problems encountered with shared offices included not having enough filing space, problems in directing telephone calls, and lack of privacy.

Managers agreed that having a permanently assigned office was an important perquisite. The survey confirmed the information gathered in the interviews about managers' attitudes: All but two managers preferred shared offices over hoteling, and managers believed their productivity would be negatively impacted. The challenges facing Royce Consulting if they move to hoteling offices centered around tradition and managers' expectations, file accessibility and organization, security and privacy issues, unpredictable work schedules, and high-traffic periods.

Control of Personal Files. Because of the comments made during the face-to-face interviews, survey respondents were asked to rank the importance of having personal control of their files. A five-point scale was used, with 5 being "strongly agree" and 1 being "strongly disagree." Here are the responses:

Respondents	Sample	Rank
Partners	6	4.3
Managers:		
0–1 year	5	4.6
2–3 years	5	3.6
4 years	6	4.3

Electronic Technology. Royce Consulting had a basic network system in the office that could not accommodate the current partners and managers working at a remote site. The administrative support staff had a separate network, and the managers and staff could not communicate electronically. Of managers responding to the survey, 95 percent wanted to use the network but only 50 percent could actually do so.

Option Analysis

A financial analysis showed that there were significant cost differences between the options under consideration:

Option 1: Continue private offices with some office sharing

- Lease an additional floor in existing building; annual cost, $360,000
- Build out the additional floor (i.e., construct, furnish, and equip offices and work areas): one-time cost, $600,000

Option 2: Move to hoteling offices with upgraded office technology

- Upgrade office electronic technology: one-time cost, $190,000

Option 1 was expensive because under the terms of the existing lease, Royce had to commit to an entire floor if it wanted additional space. Hoteling offices showed an overall financial advantage of $360,000 per year and a one-time savings of $410,000 over shared or individual offices.

The Challenge

Vincent met with Mary Schrean to discuss the upcoming meeting of partners and managers, where they would present the results of the study and a proposal for action. Included in the report were proposed layouts for both shared and hoteling offices. Vincent and Gray were planning to recommend a hoteling office system, which would include storage areas, state-of-the-art electronic office technology for managers and administrative support staff, and centralized files. The rationale for their decision emphasized the amount of time that managers were out of the office and the high cost of maintaining the status quo and was built around the following points:

1. Royce's business is different: offices are empty from 40 to 60 percent of the time.
2. Real estate costs continue to escalate.
3. Projections indicate there will be increased need for offices and cost-control strategies as the business develops.
4. Royce Consulting plays a leading role in helping organizations implement innovation.

"It's still a go," thought Vincent as he and the others returned from a break. "The cost figures support it and the growth figures support it. It's simple—or is it? The decision is the easy part. What is it about Royce Consulting that will help or hinder its acceptance? In the long run, I hope we strengthen our internal processes and don't hinder our effectiveness by going ahead with these simple changes."

NOTES

1. This case is based on Anthony Bianco and Pamela L. Moore, "Downfall: The Inside Story of the Management Fiasco at Xerox," *Business Week*, March 5, 2001, 82–92; Robert J. Grossman, "HR Woes at Xerox," *HR Magazine*, May 2001, 34–45; Jeremy Kahn, "The Paper Jam from Hell," *Fortune*, November 13, 2000, 141–146; Pamela L. Moore, "She's Here to Fix the Xerox," *Business Week*, August 6, 2001, 47–48; Claudia H. Deutsch, "At Xerox, the Chief Earns (Grudging) Respect," *The New York Times*, June 2, 2002, Section 3, 1, 12; Olga Kharif, "Anne Mulcahy Has Xerox by the Horns," *Business Week Online*, May 29, 2003; Amy Yee, "Xerox Comeback Continues to Thrive," *Financial Times*, January 26, 2005, 30; George Anders, "Corporate News; Business: At Xerox, Jettisoning Dividend Helped Company Out of a Crisis," *The Asian Wall Street Journal*, November 28, 2007, 6; Andrew Davidson, "Xerox Saviour in the Spotlight," *Sunday Times*, June 1, 2008, 6; Betsy Morris, "The Accidental CEO," *Fortune*, June 23, 2003, 58–67; Matt Hartley, "Copy That: Xerox Tries Again to Rebound," *The Globe and Mail*, January 7, 2008, B1; Nanette Byrnes and Roger O. Crockett, "An Historic Succession at Xerox," *Business Week*, June 8, 2009, 18–22; William M. Bulkeley, "Xerox Names Burns Chief as Mulcahy Retires Early," *The Wall Street Journal*, May 22, 2009, B1; Geoff Colvin, "C-Suite Strategies: Ursula Burns Launches Xerox Into the Future," *Fortune*, April 22, 2010, http://money.cnn.com/2010/04/22/news/companies/xerox_ursula_burns.-fortune/ (accessed July 1, 2011); Brian Bergstein, "Q+A Ursula Burns," *MIT Technology Review*, February 20, 2013, http://www.technologyreview.com/featuredstory/511281/xeroxs-ceo-wants-tp-shake-up-the-services-market/ (accessed February 10, 2014); David Zax, "How Xerox Evolved From Copier Company to Creative Powerhouse," *Fast Company*, December 11, 2013, http://www.fastcompany.com/3023240/most-creative-people/dreaming-together-how-xerox-keeps-big-ideas-flowing (accessed February 10, 2014); and "Xerox Positioned in the Visionaries Quadrant of Gartner's 2013 Magic Quadrant for Enterprise Content Management," Press Release, Xerox, October 17, 2013, http://news.xerox.com/news/Xerox-positioned-in-the-Visionaries-Quadrant-of-Gartners-2013-Magic-Quadrant-for-ECM (accessed February 10, 2014).

2. Dana Mattioli, Joann S. Lublin, and Ellen Byron, "Kodak Struggles to Find Its Moment," *The Wall Street Journal*, August 11, 2011, http://online.wsj.com/news/articles/SB10001424053111903454504576488033424421882 (accessed September 24, 2014).

3. Ed O'Keefe, "Lieberman Calls for Wider Inquiry into Secret Service Scandal," *The Washington Post*, April 23, 2012, A3; Laurie Kellman and Alicia A. Caldwell, "Inquiry Hears of Wider Secret Service Misbehavior," *The Salt Lake Tribune*, May 25, 2012; and Evan Perez, "Secret Service Agents Sent Home after One Found Passed Out in Amsterdam," *CNN.com*, March 26, 2014, http://www.cnn.com/2014/03/25/us/secret-service-amsterdam/ (accessed March 26, 2014).

4. Damian Paletta and Dionne Searcey, "Inside IRS Unit Under Fire," *The Wall Street Journal*, May 25, 2013, A1; and Nicholas Confessore, David Kocieniewski, and Michael Luo, "Confusion and Staff Troubles Rife at I.R.S. Office in Ohio," *The New York Times*, May 18, 2013, http://www.nytimes.com/2013/05/19/us/politics/at-irs-unprepared-office-seemed-unclear-about-the-rules.html?pagewanted=all&_r=0 (accessed August 15, 2013).

5. Mike Ramsey and Evan Ramstad, "Once a Global Also-Ran, Hyundai Zooms Forward," *The Wall Street Journal*, July 30, 2011, A1; Richard Siklos, "Bob Iger Rocks Disney," *Fortune*, January 19, 2009, 80–86; Ellen Byron, "Lauder Touts Beauty Bargains," *The Wall Street Journal*, May 5, 2009.

6. Harry G. Barkema, Joel A.C. Baum, and Elizabeth A. Mannix, "Management Challenges in a New Time," *Academy of Management Journal* 45, no. 5 (2002), 916–930.

7. Gregory C. Unruh and Ángel Cabrera, "Join the Global Elite," *Harvard Business Review*, May 2013, 135–139.

8. Mike Ramsey, "Ford's CEO Revs up Auto Maker's China Role," *The Wall Street Journal*, April 16, 2013, B7.

9. Steven Greenhouse and Stephanie Clifford, "U.S. Retailers Offer Safety Plan for Bangladeshi Factories" *The New York Times*, July 10, 2013, http://www.nytimes.com/2013/07/11/business/global/us-retailers-offer-safety-plan-for-bangladeshi-factories.html?pagewanted=all&_r=0 (accessed August 21, 2013); and Kate O'Keeffe and Sun Narin, "H&M Clothes Made in Collapsed Cambodian Factory," *The Wall Street Journal*, May 21, 2013, http://online.wsj.com/article/SB10001

4241278873247870045784970918069 22254.html (accessed August 21, 2013).

10. Vanessa Fuhrmans, "Amazon Acts on German Controversy; Online Retailer Cuts Ties with Security Firm after a Television Documentary on Working Conditions," *The Wall Street Journal*, February 19, 2013, B3; Eva Dou and Paul Mozur, "IPhone-Factory Deaths Dog Apple and Supplier," *The Wall Street Journal Online*, December 11, 2013, http://online.wsj .com/news/articles/SB10001424052702304202204579251913898555706 (accessed February 10, 2014).

11. Keith H. Hammonds, "The New Face of Global Competition," *Fast Company*, February 2003, 90–97; and Pete Engardio, Aaron Bernstein, and Manjeet Kripalani, "Is Your Job Next?" *BusinessWeek*, February 3, 2003, 50–60.

12. Pete Engardio, "Can the U.S. Bring Jobs Back from China?" *BusinessWeek*, June 30, 2008, 38ff.

13. Anna Prior and Don Clark, "Corporate News: Texas Instruments to Cut Jobs," *The Wall Street Journal*, January 22, 2014, B2.

14. Janet Adamy, "McDonald's Tests Changes in $1 Burger as Costs Rise," *The Wall Street Journal*, August 4, 2008, B1.

15. Lavonne Kuykendall, "Auto Insurers Paying Up to Compete for Drivers," *The Wall Street Journal*, April 9, 2008, B5.

16. Reported in Dan Kadlec, "Gordon Gekko Lives: New Evidence That Greed Is Rampant on Wall Street," *Time*, July 17, 2013, http://business.time.com/2013/07/17/gordon-gekko -lives-new-evidence-that-greed-is-rampant-on-wall-street/ (accessed July 19, 2013).

17. Monica Langley and Dan Fitzpatrick, "Embattled J.P. Morgan Bulks Up Overnight," *The Wall Street Journal Online*, September 12, 2013, http://online.wsj.com/news/articles/SB10001424127887324755104579071304170686532 (accessed February 11, 2014).

18. This definition is based on Marc J. Epstein and Marie-Josée Roy, "Improving Sustainability Performance: Specifying, Implementing and Measuring Key Principles," *Journal of General Management* 29, no. 1, (Autumn 2003), 15–31; World Commission on Economic Development, *Our Common Future* (Oxford: Oxford University Press, 1987); and Marc Gunther, "Tree Huggers, Soy Lovers, and Profits," *Fortune*, June 23, 2003, 98–104.

19. Steve Minter, "A Net Gain for Sustainable Manufacturing," *Industry Week*, August 2013, 48.

20. Pinar Cankurtaran, Fred Langerak, and Abbie Giffin, "Consequences of New Product Development Speed: A Meta-Analysis," *Journal of Product Innovation Management* 30, no. 3, (2013), 465–486.

21. Brad Kenney, "Callaway Improves Long Game with Collaborative Tech," *Industry Week*, June 2008, 72.

22. Robert Safian, "Secrets of the Flux Leader," *Fast Company*, November 2012, 96–136.

23. Quoted in Safian, "Secrets of the Flux Leader."

24. This section is based partly on Fahri Karakas, "Welcome to World 2.0: The New Digital Ecosystem," *Journal of Business Strategy* 30, no. 4, (2009), 23–30.

25. Jacques Bughin, Michael Chui, and James Manyika, "Capturing Business Value with Social Technologies," *McKinsey Quarterly*, November 2012, http://www.mckinsey .com/insights/high_tech_telecoms_internet/capturing _business_value_with_social_technologies (accessed September 27, 2013).

26. Roland Deiser and Sylvain Newton, "Six Social-Media Skills Every Leader Needs," *McKinsey Quarterly*, Issue 1, February 2013, http://www.mckinsey.com/insights/high _tech_telecoms_internet/six_social-media_skills_every_leader_ needs (accessed August 21, 2013).

27. Ibid.

28. Leslie Gaines-Ross, "Get Social: A Mandate for New CEOs," *MIT Sloan Management Review*, March 7, 2013, http:// sloanreview.mit.edu/article/get-social-a-mandate-for-new-ceos/ (accessed August 21, 2013).

29. Deiser and Newton, "Six Social Media Skills Every Leader Needs."

30. Darrell K. Rigby, *Management Tools 2013: An Executive's Guide* (Bain & Company 2013), http://www.bain.com/Images /MANAGEMENT_TOOLS_2013_An_Executives_guide .pdf (accessed August 27, 2013); Margaret Rouse, "Big Data Analytics," *TechTarget.com*, January 10, 2012, http:// searchbusinessanalytics.techtarget.com/definition/big-data-analytics (accessed August 27, 2013); and David Kiron, Renee Boucher Ferguson, and Pamela Kirk Prentice, "From Value to Vision: Reimagining the Possible with Data Analytics," *MIT Sloan Management Review Special Report*, March 5, 2013, http://sloanreview.mit.edu/reports/analytics-innovation/ (accessed August 27, 2013).

31. Steve Lohr, "Sure, Big Data Is Great. But So Is Intuition," *The New York Times*, December 29, 2012.

32. Andrew McAfee and Erik Brynjolfsson, "Big Data: The Management Revolution," *Harvard Business Review*, October 2012, 61–68.

33. Lohr, "Sure, Big Data Is Great. But So Is Intuition."

34. McAfee and Brynjolfsson, "Big Data: The Management Revolution."

35. Howard Aldrich, *Organizations and Environments* (Englewood Cliffs, N.J.: Prentice Hall, 1979), 3.

36. Royston Greenwood and Danny Miller, "Tackling Design Anew: Getting Back to the Heart of Organizational Theory," *Academy of Management Perspectives*, November 2010, 78–88.

37. This section is based on Peter F. Drucker, *Managing the Non-Profit Organization: Principles and Practices* (New York: HarperBusiness, 1992); Thomas Wolf, *Managing a Nonprofit Organization* (New York: Fireside/Simon & Schuster, 1990); and Jean Crawford, "Profiling the Non-Profit Leader of Tomorrow," *Ivey Business Journal*, May–June 2010.

38. Christine W. Letts, William P. Ryan, and Allen Grossman, *High Performance Nonprofit Organizations* (New York: John Wiley & Sons, Inc., 1999), 30–35; Crawford, "Profiling the Non-Profit Leader of Tomorrow."

39. Lisa Bannon, "Dream Works: As Make-a-Wish Expands Its Turf, Local Groups Fume," *The Wall Street Journal*, July 8, 2002, A1, A8.

40. Robert N. Stern and Stephen R. Barley, "Organizations and Social Systems: Organization Theory's Neglected Mandate," *Administrative Science Quarterly* 41, (1996), 146–162.

41. Philip Siekman, "Build to Order: One Aircraft Carrier," *Fortune*, July 22, 2002, 180[B]–180[J].

42. Adam Davidson, "Building a Harley Faster," *New York Times Magazine*, January 28, 2014, http://www.nytimes .com/2014/02/02/magazine/building-a-harley-faster.html? _r=0 (accessed February 12, 2014).

43. Lindsey Kratochwill, "02: Amazon: For Speeding Up the Delivery of Change," *Fast Company* (part of the section "The Most Innovative Companies 2013") http://www .fastcompany.com/most-innovative-companies/2013/amazon (accessed February 12, 2014).

44. The discussion of structural dimensions and contingency factors was heavily influenced by Richard H. Hall,

Organizations: Structures, Processes, and Outcomes (Englewood Cliffs, N.J.: Prentice Hall, 1991); D. S. Pugh, "The Measurement of Organization Structures: Does Context Determine Form?" *Organizational Dynamics* 1 (Spring 1973), 19–34; and D. S. Pugh, D. J. Hickson, C. R. Hinings, and C. Turner, "Dimensions of Organization Structure," *Administrative Science Quarterly* 13, (1968), 65–91.

45 This discussion is based in part on Virpi Turkulainen and Mikko Kitokivi, "The Contingent Value of Organizational Integration," *Journal of Organization Design* 2, no. 2, (2013), 31–43.

46. Daisuke Wakabayashi and Toko Sekiguchi, "Disaster in Japan: Evacuees Set Rules to Create Sense of Normalcy," *The Wall Street Journal*, March 26, 2011, A8; Ian Urbina, "In Gulf, It Was Unclear Who Was in Charge of Oil Rig," *The New York Times*, June 6, 2010, A1; Douglas A. Blackmon, Vanessa O'Connell, Alexandra Berzon, and Ana Campoy, "There Was 'Nobody in Charge,'" *The Wall Street Journal*, May 27, 2010, http://online.wsj.com/articles/SB10001424052748704113 504575264721101985024 (accessed September 29, 2014); and Campbell Robertson, "Efforts to Repel Gulf Oil Spill Are Described as Chaotic," *The New York Times*, June 14, 2010, http://www.nytimes.com/2010/06/15/science/earth/15cleanup.html?pagewanted=all (accessed September 29, 2014).

47. "5 Richest Tech Billionaires Who Dropped Out of University," *WhatCulture!*, September 30, 2013, http://whatculture.com/technology/5-richest-tech-billionaires-who-dropped-out-of-university.php (accessed September 30, 2013); "Our People," Valve Website, http://www.valvesoftware.com/company/people.html (accessed September 30, 2013); Claire Suddath, "Why There Are No Bosses at Valve," *Bloomberg Businessweek*, April 27, 2012, www.businessweek.com/articles/2012-04-27/why-there-are-no-bosses-at-valve (accessed August 10, 2012); Rachel Emma Silverman, "Who's the Boss? There Isn't One," *The Wall Street Journal*, June 20, 2012, B1; and Alex Hern, "Valve Software: Free Marketer's Dream, or Nightmare?" *New Statesman*, August 3, 2012, www.newstatesman.com/blogs/economics/2012/08/valve-software-free-marketeers-dream-or-nightmare (accessed August 10, 2012); and John Huey, "Wal-Mart: Will It Take Over the World?" *Fortune*, January 30, 1989, 52–61.

48. Steve Lohr, "Who Pays for Efficiency?" *The New York Times*, June 11, 2007, H1.

49. T. Donaldson and L. E. Preston, "The Stakeholder Theory of the Corporation: Concepts, Evidence, and Implications," *Academy of Management Review* 20, (1995), 65–91; Anne S. Tusi, "A Multiple-Constituency Model of Effectiveness: An Empirical Examination at the Human Resource Sub-unit Level," *Administrative Science Quarterly* 35, (1990), 458–483; Charles Fombrun and Mark Shanley, "What's in a Name? Reputation Building and Corporate Strategy," *Academy of Management Journal* 33, (1990), 233–258; and Terry Connolly, Edward J. Conlon, and Stuart Jay Deutsch, "Organizational Effectiveness: A Multiple-Constituency Approach," *Academy of Management Review* 5, (1980), 211–217.

50. Ray Fisman and Tim Sullivan, "The Most Efficient Office in the World," *Slate*, July 31, 2013, http://www.slate.com/articles/business/the_dismal_science/2013/07/renewing_your_passport_visit_the_incredibly_efficient_new_york_city_passport.html (accessed February 14, 2014).

51. Charles Fishman, "The Wal-Mart You Don't Know—Why Low Prices Have a High Cost," *Fast Company*, December 2003, 68–80.

52. Greenwood and Miller, "Tackling Design Anew."

53. Greenwood and Miller, "Tackling Design Anew"; and Roger L. M. Dunbar and William H. Starbuck, "Learning to Design Organizations and Learning from Designing Them," *Organization Science* 17, no. 2, (March–April 2006), 171–178.

54. Quoted in Cynthia Crossen, "Early Industry Expert Soon Realized a Staff Has Its Own Efficiency," *The Wall Street Journal*, November 6, 2006, B1.

55. Robert Kanigel, *The One Best Way: Frederick Winslow Taylor and the Enigma of Efficiency* (New York: Viking, 1997); Alan Farnham, "The Man Who Changed Work Forever," *Fortune*, July 21, 1997, 114; and Charles D. Wrege and Ann Marie Stoka, "Cooke Creates a Classic: The Story Behind F. W. Taylor's Principles of Scientific Management," *Academy of Management Review*, October 1978, 736–749. For a discussion of the impact of scientific management on American industry, government, and nonprofit organizations, also see Mauro F. Guillèn, "Scientific Management's Lost Aesthetic: Architecture, Organization, and the Taylorized Beauty of the Mechanical," *Administrative Science Quarterly* 42, (1997), 682–715.

56. Gary Hamel, "The Why, What, and How of Management Innovation," *Harvard Business Review*, February 2006, 72–84.

57. Amanda Bennett, *The Death of the Organization Man* (New York: William Morrow, 1990).

58. Ralph Sink, "My Unfashionable Legacy," *Strategy + Business* (Autumn 2007), http://www.strategy-business.com/press/enewsarticle/enews122007?pg=0 (accessed August 7, 2008).

59. Dunbar and Starbuck, "Learning to Design Organizations."

60. Johannes M. Pennings, "Structural Contingency Theory: A Reappraisal," *Research in Organizational Behavior* 14, (1992), 267–309; and Turkulainen and Kitokivi, "The Contingent Value of Organizational Integration."

61. Tom Burns and G. M. Stalker, *The Management of Innovation* (London: Tavistock, 1961).

62. Li-Yun Sun and Wen Pan, "Market Orientation, Intrapreneurship Behavior, and Organizational Performance: Test of a Structural Contingency Model," *Journal of Leadership and Organizational Studies* 18, no. 2, (2011), 274–285.

63. Roxane Divol and Thomas Fleming, "The Evolution of Work: One Company's Story," *McKinsey Quarterly*, Issue 4, (2012), 111–115.

64. Tom Ashbrook, "The Bossless Office," *On Point with Tom Ashbrook* (June 20, 2013, at 11:00 A.M.), http://onpoint.wbur.org.

65. Doug Kirkpatrick, "Self-Management's Success at Morning Star," *T + D*, October 2012, 25–27; and Gary Hamel, "First, Let's Fire All the Managers," *Harvard Business Review*, December 2011, 48–60.

66. Hamel, "First, Let's Fire All the Managers."

67. Presented to and accepted by the Society for Case Research. All rights reserved to the authors and SCR.
This case was prepared by Sally Dresdow of the University of Wisconsin at Green Bay and Joy Benson of the University of Illinois at Springfield and is intended to be used as a basis for class discussion. The views represented here are those of the case authors and do not necessarily reflect the views of the Society for Case Research. The authors' views are based on their own professional judgments. The names of the organization, individuals, and location have been disguised to preserve the organization's request for anonymity.

Organization Purpose and Structural Design

Kjel Larsen/Moment/Getty Images

Strategy, Organization Design, and Effectiveness

Learning Objectives

After reading this chapter you should be able to:

1. Describe the importance of strategy and the strategy process.
2. Understand strategic purpose and operating goals.
3. Explain why goal conflict occurs in organizations and how managers deal with conflicting goals.
4. Know Porter's strategy model and Miles and Snow's strategy typology.
5. Explain how strategy affects organization design.
6. Discuss the goal, resource, internal process, and strategic constituents approaches to measuring effectiveness.
7. Explain the competing values model and how it relates to effectiveness.

MANAGING BY DESIGN QUESTIONS

One of the primary responsibilities of managers is to position their organizations for success by establishing goals and strategies that can keep the organization competitive. Consider the situation at Instagram, where director of operations Emily White has been leading the charge to turn the popular online app into a real business. Instagram, which Facebook acquired for around a billion dollars, hasn't made a cent so far. One problem, White believes, is the lack of a clear mission and goals to guide staff and sell the service to future advertisers. She spent her first two weeks working with co-founder and CEO Kevin Systrom to come up with a short, lofty mission statement: "To capture and share the world's moments." White, Systrom, and the rest of the Instagram team are now formulating a strategy and goals to bring in marketing dollars without alienating loyal Instagram users. Partnerships with other companies are likely to be a big part of the strategy. For example, Levi Strauss & Co. recently kicked off a marketing campaign in which a group of artists on a cross-country train ride will create music and art as they arrive in major cities and upload photos and videos to Instagram.[1]

Instagram probably has a long way to go before it is profitable, but managers know that establishing mission, goals, and strategy is the first step for any business to achieve its purpose. Managers have to know where they want the organization to go before they can take it there. When managers don't have clear goals, or have conflicting goals, the organization finds itself in a difficult position and achieving anything may seem improbable. Consider the faulty early implementation of the Affordable Care Act (ObamaCare). Staff building the federally run insurance exchange HealthCare.gov struggled to develop different parts of the exchange under sometimes conflicting directives from different bosses in different agencies with wildly divergent goals. One person familiar with the development captured the confusion when he said, "It was like building a bridge by starting from both sides of the river. You hoped they met in the middle."[2]

Purpose of This Chapter

Top managers give direction to organizations. They set goals and develop the plans for their organization to attain them. The purpose of this chapter is to help you understand the types of goals that organizations pursue and some of the competitive strategies managers use to reach those goals. We provide an overview of strategic management, examine two significant frameworks for determining strategic action, and look at how strategies affect organization design. The chapter also describes the most popular approaches to measuring the effectiveness of organizational efforts. To manage organizations well, managers need a clear way to measure how effective the organization is in attaining its goals.

The Role of Strategic Direction in Organization Design

The choice of goals and strategy influences how an organization should be designed. An **organizational goal** is a desired state of affairs that the organization attempts to reach.[3] A goal represents a result or end point toward which organizational efforts are directed.

Top executives decide the end purpose the organization will strive for and determine the direction it will take to accomplish it. It is this purpose and direction that shapes how the organization is designed and managed. Indeed, *the primary responsibility of top management is to determine an organization's goals, strategy, and design, thereby adapting the organization to a changing environment.*[4] Middle managers do much the same thing for major departments within the guidelines provided by top management. Exhibit 2.1 illustrates the relationships through which top managers provide direction and then design.

EXHIBIT 2.1

Top Management Role in Organization Direction, Design, and Effectiveness

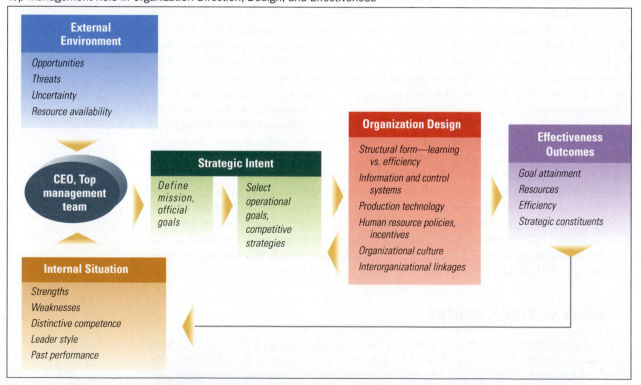

Source: Adapted from Arie Y. Lewin and Carroll U. Stephens, "Individual Properties of the CEO as Determinants of Organization Design," unpublished manuscript, Duke University, 1990; and Arie Y. Lewin and Carroll U. Stephens, "CEO Attributes as Determinants of Organization Design: An Integrated Model," *Organization Studies* 15, no. 2 (1994), 183–212.

The direction-setting process typically begins with an assessment of the opportunities and threats in the external environment, including the amount of change, uncertainty, and resource availability, which we discuss in more detail in Chapter 4. Top managers also assess internal strengths and weaknesses to define the company's distinctive competence compared with other firms in the industry. This competitive analysis of the internal and external environments is one of the central concepts in strategic management.[5]

> **1** **A company's strategic intent or direction reflects managers' systematic analysis of organizational and environmental factors.**
>
> **ANSWER:** *Agree.* The best strategies come from systematic analysis of organizational strengths and weaknesses combined with analysis of opportunities and threats in the environment. Careful study combined with experience enable top managers to decide on specific goals and strategies.

ASSESS **YOUR** ANSWER

The next step is to define and articulate the organization's *strategic intent*, which includes defining an overall mission and official goals based on the correct fit between external opportunities and internal strengths. Leaders then formulate specific operational goals and strategies that define how the organization is to accomplish its overall mission. In Exhibit 2.1, organization design reflects the way goals and strategies are implemented so that the organization's attention and resources are consistently focused toward achieving the mission and goals.

Organization design is the administration and execution of the strategic plan. Managers make decisions about structural form, including whether the organization will be designed primarily for learning and innovation (an organic approach) or to achieve efficiency (a mechanistic approach), as discussed in Chapter 1. Other choices are made about information and control systems, the type of production technology, human resource policies, culture, and linkages to other organizations. Changes in structure, technology, human resource policies, culture, and interorganizational linkages will be discussed in subsequent chapters. Also note the arrow in Exhibit 2.1 running from organization design back to strategic intent. This means that strategies are often made within the current structure of the organization so that current design constrains, or puts limits on, goals and strategy. More often than not, however, the new goals and strategy are selected based on environmental needs and then top managers attempt to redesign the organization to achieve those ends.

Finally, Exhibit 2.1 illustrates how managers evaluate the effectiveness of organizational efforts—that is, the extent to which the organization realizes its goals. This chart reflects the most popular ways of measuring performance, each of which is discussed later in this chapter. It is important to note here that performance measurements feed back into the internal environment so that past performance of the organization is assessed by top managers in setting new goals and strategic direction for the future.

Procter & Gamble (P&G) provides an example of how these ideas translate into organization practice. CEO A. G. Lafley wanted to provide a framework for organizing the discussion about goals and strategic direction so he used the OGSM (Objectives, Goals, Strategies, and Measures) tool illustrated in Exhibit 2.2. Note that a broad objective such as "Be the operating TSR (total shareholder return) leader in North American tissue/towel and value creator for P&G" is translated into more specific goals and strategies, such as "Grow Bounty and Charmin margin."[6]

EXHIBIT 2.2
Procter & Gamble's Framework for Strategy Discussion

OBJECTIVES	STRATEGIES	MEASURES
Improve the lives of families by providing consumer-preferred paper products for kitchen and bathroom Be the operating TSR leader in North American tissue/towel and value creator for P&G	WHERE TO PLAY: • Win in North America • Grow Bounty and Charmin margin of leadership • Win in super market and mass discount channels • Build performance, sensory and value consumer segments	• Operating TSR progress • Share and sales growth progress • Profit growth progress Efficiency measures: • Capital efficiency • Inventory turns

GOALS
Year-on Year operating TSR> XX%
X% annual share and sales growth
X% annual gross & operating profit margin improvement
X% return on capital investments in plant equipment and inventory
	HOW TO WIN:
	1. Be lean
	   • Get plant/equipment capital spend to XX of sales
	   • Reduce inventory by XX%
	2. Be the choice of consumers
	   • Superior base products, prices right
	   • Preferred product formats and designs
	   • Manage category growth
	3. Be the choice of retailers
	   • Improve shelf availability and service
	   • Develop differentiated shopping solutions
	   • Win with the winners
		Consumer preference measures:
		• Weighted purchase intent
		• Trial, purchase and loyalty
		
		Retailer feedback measures:
		• Key business drivers (distribution, share of shelf, share of merchandising, etc.)
		• Preferred vendor

Source: Adapted from A.G. Lafley and Roger Martin, "Instituting a Company-Wide Strategic Conversation at Procter & Gamble," *Strategy & Leadership* 41, no. 4 (2013): 4–9; Table 6.1.

In addition, the chart lists measures that managers will use to determine the success of their efforts. This is the essence of strategic management: setting goals, defining strategies for achieving the goals, and measuring the effectiveness of efforts.

The role of top management is important because managers can interpret the environment differently and develop different goals and strategies. Several years ago, in the midst of a U.S. sales slump, top executives at Walmart tried a new direction. Instead of sticking with goals of strict operational efficiency and everyday low prices, they decided to court upscale customers with remodeled, less cluttered stores, organic foods, and trendy merchandise. Instead of offering everyday low prices, the retailer raised prices on many items and promoted price cuts on select merchandise. Walmart succeeded in meeting its goal of attracting more upscale clientele, but many of its core customers decided they'd start shopping at other discount and dollar store chains. Walmart's sales took a sharp downturn. "I think we tried to stretch the brand a little too far," said William Simon, head of the U.S. division. Now, managers are rethinking goals to try to recapture a winning formula.[7]

The choices top managers make about goals, strategies, and organization design have a tremendous impact on organizational effectiveness. Remember that goals and strategy are not fixed or taken for granted. Top managers and middle managers must select goals for their respective units, and the ability to make good choices largely determines a firm's success. Organization design is used to implement goals and strategy and also determines organization success.

Organizational Purpose

All organizations, including Walmart, Procter & Gamble, Instagram, Google, Harvard University, the Catholic Church, the U.S. Department of Agriculture, the local laundry, and the neighborhood deli, exist for a purpose. This purpose may be referred to as the overall goal, or mission. Different parts of the organization establish their own goals and objectives to help meet the overall goal, mission, or purpose of the organization.

Strategic Intent

Many types of goals exist in organizations, and each type performs a different function. To achieve success, however, organizational goals and strategies are focused with strategic intent. **Strategic intent** means that all the organization's energies and resources are directed toward a focused, unifying, and compelling overall goal.[8] Examples of ambitious goals that demonstrate strategic intent are Microsoft's early goal to "Put a computer on every desk in every home," Komatsu's motto, "Encircle Caterpillar," and Coca-Cola's goal "To put a Coke within 'arm's reach' of every consumer in the world."[9] Strategic intent provides a focus for management action. Three aspects related to strategic intent are the mission, core competence, and competitive advantage.

Mission. The overall goal for an organization is often called the **mission**—the organization's reason for existence. The mission describes the organization's shared values and beliefs and its reason for being. The mission is sometimes called the **official goals**, which refers to the formally stated definition of business scope and outcomes the organization is trying to achieve. Official goal statements typically define business operations and may focus on values, markets, and customers that distinguish the organization. Whether called a mission statement or official goals, the organization's general statement of its purpose and philosophy is often written down in a policy manual or the annual report. Exhibit 2.3 shows the new mission statement for CVS Health. CVS defines its mission (or purpose, as shown in the exhibit) as "Helping people on their path to better health." The statement also defines the company's core values.

One of the primary purposes of a mission statement is to serve as a communication tool.[10] The *mission statement* communicates to current and prospective employees, customers, investors, suppliers, and competitors what the organization stands for and what it is trying to achieve. A mission statement communicates legitimacy to internal and external stakeholders, who may join and be committed to the organization because they identify with its stated purpose and values. Most top leaders want employees, customers, competitors, suppliers, investors, and the local community to look on the organization in a favorable light, and the concept of legitimacy plays a critical role. CVS Caremark recently changed its name to CVS Health and redefined its purpose to reflect a broader health care commitment and the company's vision to "drive innovations needed to shape the future of health."[11] In early 2014, CVS, which provides health clinics as well as

BRIEFCASE

As an organization manager, keep these guidelines in mind:

Establish and communicate organizational mission and goals. Communicate official goals to provide a statement of the organization's mission to external constituents. Communicate operating goals to provide internal direction, guidelines, and standards of performance for employees.

Mission Statement for CVS Health

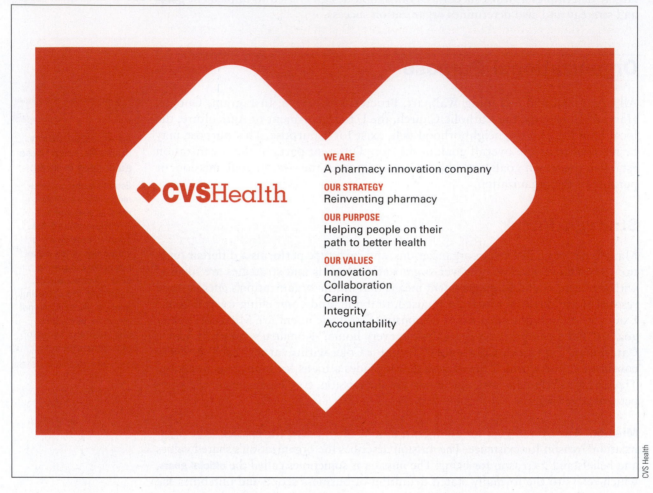

WE ARE
A pharmacy innovation company

OUR STRATEGY
Reinventing pharmacy

OUR PURPOSE
Helping people on their
path to better health

OUR VALUES
Innovation
Collaboration
Caring
Integrity
Accountability

CVS Health

pharmacy and retail sales, announced that it would stop selling cigarettes and other tobacco products by October of that year. For a company involved in promoting health and wellness, managers say, selling tobacco products doesn't make sense and hurts the company's reputation. The decision is expected to cost an estimated $2 billion in sales. Analysts believe other pharmacies involved in providing health care will follow CVS Health's lead because of the need to communicate legitimacy. Companies where managers are sincerely guided by mission statements that focus on a larger social purpose, such as Medtronic's "To restore people to full life and health" or Liberty Mutual's "Helping people live safer, more secure lives," typically attract better employees, have better relationships with external parties, and perform better in the marketplace over the long term.[12]

Competitive Advantage. The overall aim of strategic intent is to help the organization achieve a sustainable competitive advantage. **Competitive advantage** refers to what sets the organization apart from others and provides it with a distinctive edge for meeting customer or client needs in the marketplace. Strategy necessarily changes over time to fit environmental conditions, and good managers pay close attention to trends that might require changes in how the company operates. Managers analyze competitors and the internal and external environments to find potential *competitive openings* and learn what new capabilities the organization needs to gain the upper hand against other companies in the industry.[13] Competitive openings might be thought of as spaces that a company can potentially fill. This chapter's BookMark suggests that instead of trying to compete in crowded markets where companies chew each other up for smaller and smaller chunks of market share (red oceans), smart managers steer their organizations toward vast blue oceans where there is more promise and less competition.

BOOKMARK HAVE YOU READ THIS BOOK?

Blue Ocean Strategy: How to Create Uncontested Market Space and Make the Competition Irrelevant
By W. Chan Kim and Renée Mauborgne

Almost every book or article you read about strategy focuses on how to outpace rivals, beat the competition, and win at the expense of other companies. That's why there are so many managers and companies out there fighting in the "red ocean" of cutthroat and bloody competition. In their popular book *Blue Ocean Strategy*, W. Chan Kim and Renée Mauborgne take a different approach: *Create a new market where there is less competition.* That is the essence of blue ocean strategy.

SOME CLASSIC EXAMPLES OF BLUE OCEAN STRATEGY
Kim and Mauborgne's book is based on more than 15 years of research into 150 strategic moves spanning more than a hundred years and 30 industries. Here are some classic examples of how companies created uncontested market space.

- *The Nintendo Wii.* Rather than battle it out in the red ocean with Sony and Microsoft, Nintendo decided to create a gaming system for a different audience—women, adults, and families. The Wii was low on graphics but high on interactivity, just right for people who didn't normally play video games. The Nintendo Wii invented a new type of gaming.
- *Cirque du Soleil.* This Canadian show cut the expense of a traditional circus—hauling around animals, and so on, and amped up the theatrical aspects of the show, enabling the organization to charge higher prices by appealing to a different market segment where there were no competitors.

- *The New York Public Library (NYPL).* With funding cut by 20 percent and competition intensifying, Paul Holdengräber, Director of Public Programs, made the NYPL one of the hottest venues in town by infusing glamour and theatre into traditional book readings. He brought in poets, politicians, rock stars, and writers to host a dialogue on controversial topics such as obsessions, terrorism, and music downloading. He also moved the events from 6 P.M. to 7 P.M. when more people were free after work.

HOW COMPANIES CREATE BLUE OCEANS
Blue ocean strategy shifts the focus from win-lose to win-win, Kim and Mauborgne say. "New market spaces create a win for companies, societies, employees, and sometimes even for the competition. That's the essence of blue ocean strategy." Moreover, any company can create blue ocean strategies by:

- *Reconstructing market boundaries.* Paul Holdengräber at the NYPL created a blue ocean of new market space by changing the time of events and expanding the topics.
- *Focusing on the big picture, not the numbers.* Cirque du Soleil could have focused on the huge numbers of audience members they were losing by not having animals in the show, but that would have ignored the bigger picture.
- *Reaching beyond existing demand.* When Nintendo created the Wii, there was plenty of demand for games targeted toward male teenagers and young adults, but Nintendo chose to reach beyond that into the blue ocean of untapped customers.

Blue Ocean Strategy, by W. Chan Kim and Renée Mauborgne, is published by Harvard Business School Press.

Core Competence. A company's **core competence** is something the organization does especially well in comparison to its competitors. A core competence may be in the area of superior research and development, expert technological know-how, process efficiency, or exceptional customer service.[14] Mimeo, a printing and copying company, for example, excels with core competencies of superb customer service and the application of technology to ensure internal process efficiency. Mimeo can handle rush jobs that larger companies can't. At Apple, strategy focuses on core competencies of superior design and marketing skills.[15] In each case, managers identified what their company does especially well and built the strategy around it. Amazon has developed a core competence in fast shipping that other retailers are now trying to copy.

IN PRACTICE
Amazon

It's hard to believe Amazon was once a struggling online bookseller. Today, it is "an existential threat" to every retailer, as Fiona Dias, executive vice president of GSI Commerce, put it. Amazon targets customers who want to find good deals and purchase products conveniently over the Internet. Those customers can find just about anything they want on Amazon.com. They will often pay less for it than they would anywhere else. And they can often get it as fast as if they went to the local store.

Amazon wants to provide "premium products at nonpremium prices." To do that, it has developed an extensive network of third-party merchants—partners with whom it maintains close, mutually beneficial relationships, is constantly honing its operational efficiency, and has created one of the most finely tuned distribution systems around. Amazon capitalizes on its core competencies of wide selection, cost efficiency, and slick distribution.

Amazon is already offering same-day delivery in metropolitan areas, and Walmart is aiming to do the same. "Everybody in retail is terrified of Amazon, and they're terrified of losing more wallet share to Amazon," said an analyst with Forrester Research. If Walmart can pull it off, the company would essentially have more than 4,000 Walmart stores as distribution centers, giving it a strong advantage over Amazon. On the other hand, Amazon CEO Jeff Bezos says, "One of the big advantages of Amazon for consumers is that they can get one box with a lot of things in it from different categories." In retail, the shipping wars have just begun.[16]

Operating Goals

The organization's mission and overall goals provide a basis for developing more specific operating goals. **Operating goals** designate the ends sought through the actual operating procedures of the organization and explain what the organization is actually trying to do.[17] Operating goals describe specific measurable outcomes and are often concerned with the short run. Operating goals typically pertain to the primary tasks an organization must perform.[18] Specific goals for each primary task provide direction for the day-to-day decisions and activities within departments. Typical operating goals that define what an organization is trying to accomplish include performance goals, resource goals, market goals, employee development goals, productivity goals, and goals for innovation and change, as illustrated in Exhibit 2.4.

Overall Performance. Profitability reflects the overall performance of for-profit organizations. Profitability may be expressed in terms of net income, earnings per share, or return on investment. Other overall performance goals are growth and output volume. Growth pertains to increases in sales or profits over time. Volume pertains to total sales or the amount of products or services delivered. For example, during the 2013 holiday season, UPS had trouble meeting its performance goals for delivery of packages. While smaller shipping firms were able to adjust during peak demand times by using rented trucks and temporary drivers, large firms like UPS were stuck with unexpected late orders from Amazon, Kohl's, and other partners and were limited in their options for shipping the goods to customers.[19]

Government and nonprofit organizations such as social service agencies or labor unions do not have goals of profitability, but they do have goals that attempt to specify the delivery of services to clients or members within specified expense levels. The Internal Revenue Service has a goal of providing accurate responses to 85 percent of taxpayer questions about new tax laws. Growth and volume goals also may be indicators of overall performance in nonprofit organizations. Expanding their services to new clients is a primary goal for many social service agencies, for example.

Resources. Resource goals pertain to the acquisition of needed material and financial resources from the environment. They may involve obtaining financing for the construction of new plants, finding less expensive sources for raw materials, or hiring top-quality technology graduates. Starbucks recently formed an alliance with India's Tata Group to obtain Indian premium Arabica coffee beans for use in Starbucks stores. Eventually, the alliance will also enable Starbucks to find prime locations for outlets in India, which can also be considered valuable resources.[20] A new resource goal for Walmart is to hire every veteran who wants a job, provided the person left the military in the previous year and did not have a dishonorable discharge. "Let's be clear: Hiring a veteran can be one of the best decisions any of us can make," said William S. Simon, president and CEO of Walmart U.S. "These are leaders with discipline, training, and a passion for service."[21] For nonprofit organizations, resource goals might include recruiting dedicated volunteers and expanding the organization's funding base.

Market. Market goals relate to the market share or market standing desired by the organization. Market goals are largely the responsibility of marketing, sales, and advertising departments. L'Oreal SA, the world's largest cosmetics company, has a

EXHIBIT 2.4
Typical Operating Goals for an Organization

goal of doubling its current clientele, adding one billion consumers by 2020. As one step to achieve the goal, managers are making changes in marketing and selling approaches designed to win over more customers in Brazil. Women there are some of the biggest spenders on beauty products, but L'Oreal has had trouble adapting to the Brazilian market.[22] Market goals can also apply to nonprofit organizations. Cincinnati Children's Hospital Medical Center, not content with a limited regional role in health care, has gained a growing share of the national market by developing expertise in the niche of treating rare and complex conditions and relentlessly focusing on quality.[23]

Employee Development. Employee development pertains to the training, promotion, safety, and growth of employees. It includes both managers and workers. Strong employee development goals are one of the characteristics common to organizations that regularly show up on *Fortune* magazine's list of "100 Best Companies to Work For." Moreover, employee learning goals have been found to be related to higher levels of department performance.[24] Wall Street banks have long been known for encouraging long work hours, but some are now taking a critical look at that hard-charging culture. Bank of America Merrill Lynch, for example, recently issued an internal memo saying junior bankers should have two weekends off a month. To expand employee development, the bank also intends to "make certain that junior bankers work on a wider variety of different assignments . . . and ensure that the development of core skills is an important factor in making staffing assignments."[25]

Productivity. Productivity goals concern the amount of output achieved from available resources. They typically describe the amount of resource inputs required to reach desired outputs and are thus stated in terms of "cost for a unit of production," "units produced per employee," or "resource cost per employee." Illumination Entertainment, the production company behind the hit movie "Hop," has productivity goals that help the company make animated films at about half the cost of those made by larger studios. CEO Christopher Meledandri believes strict cost controls and successful animated films are not mutually exclusive, but it means Illumination's 30 or so employees have to be highly productive.[26]

Innovation and Change. Innovation goals pertain to internal flexibility and readiness to adapt to unexpected changes in the environment. Innovation goals are often defined with respect to the development of specific new services, products, or production processes. Procter & Gamble started a program called Connect + Develop in 2001, with a goal of getting 50 percent of the company's innovation through collaboration with people and organizations outside the company by 2010. The ambitious goal was met and exceeded, resulting in innovations such as Swiffer Dusters, Olay Regenerist, and Mr. Clean Magic Eraser.[27]

Successful organizations use a carefully balanced set of operating goals. Although profitability goals are important, some of today's best companies recognize that a single-minded focus on bottom-line profits may not be the best way to achieve high performance. Innovation and change goals are increasingly important, even though they may initially cause a *decrease* in profits. Employee development goals are critical for helping to maintain a motivated, committed workforce.

Goal Conflict and the Hybrid Organization

Organizations perform many activities and pursue many goals simultaneously to accomplish an overall mission. But who decides what mission and goals to strive for? Pursuing some goals means that others have to be delayed or set aside, which means managers often disagree about priorities. Employee development goals might conflict with productivity goals; goals for innovation might hurt profitability. As one real-life example of goal conflict, Bloomberg News's goals for accurate journalistic reporting sometimes conflict with the business side's goals for sales of financial data terminals.

IN PRACTICE

Bloomberg LP

Most newspapers and magazines have a news side and a business side, and the two often coexist in uneasy tension. The business side managers don't want to run stories critical of major advertisers, for instance. At Bloomberg, the two units got along fairly well in the early years when the news service was too small to anger clients, but that has changed.

Bloomberg's core business is selling financial data terminals, which provide about 85 percent of the company's revenue. However, the company's journalism brings credibility to the organization and the news division has more than doubled in size. Users of the data terminals mostly want short Twitter-like news of market-moving importance, though, not the in-depth articles that journalists want to report.

The potential conflicts are most troubling in China, where financial data revenue has been growing about 45 percent a year. Sales of Bloomberg's data terminals dropped significantly after Bloomberg News's tough reporting about events in China prompted officials to cancel subscriptions. One angry Chinese official said Bloomberg should be publishing only financial news in China, not political news. Editors ordered some stories removed from the company's website, angering Bloomberg journalists. "It's looking increasingly like as a media company, you have a choice in China: You either do news or you do business, but it's hard to do both," said James L. McGregor, a former chief of Dow Jones & Company in China.[28]

Bloomberg and many other media companies represent what is called a hybrid organization. The **hybrid organization** is an organization that mixes value systems and behaviors that represent two different sectors of society, which leads to tensions and conflict within the organization over goals and priorities.[29] The goals and values of the two sides are sometimes mutually exclusive, so managers have to negotiate and come to some agreement on which direction the company will take. Organizations with a social mission, for example, may have to hire business-minded people to sell the organization's services to provide additional income. The business-minded employees stress goals of sales, revenue, and efficiency while public service-minded employees stress goals of sacrifice and meeting social needs. When social welfare organizations have to achieve their social mission through commercial activities, managers are often caught between competing demands of market and social welfare mindsets. One group may champion for-profit priorities and the other champions the contribution to social needs. Another example of a hybrid organization is a biotechnology company that incorporates goals and mindsets of both bias-free scientific research for the sake of new knowledge versus research to develop and market potentially lucrative products. These differences in goal orientation can trigger manipulation, avoidance, or defiance on the part of one side versus the other unless managers can balance the conflicting demands.

One approach to resolving these conflicts is *coalitional management*, which involves building an alliance of people who support a manager's goals and can influence other people to accept and work toward them.[30] Managers talk to people across the organization to find out what challenges and opportunities they face. They learn not only who supports their goals but also who opposes them and why. They don't let conflict over goals simmer and detract from goal accomplishment. It is the job of managers to break down boundaries and get people to negotiate and cooperate across groups and departments to reach agreement and get important goals accomplished. When appropriate, managers may give up on some goals and throw their support behind other managers. Building relationships, discussion, and negotiation are crucial skills for getting things done in hybrid organizations.

The Importance of Goals

Both official goals and operating goals are important for the organization, but they serve very different purposes. Official goals and mission statements describe a value system for the organization and set an overall purpose and vision; operating goals represent the primary tasks of the organization. Official goals legitimize the organization; operating goals are more explicit and well defined.

Operating goals serve several specific purposes, as outlined in Exhibit 2.5. For one thing, goals provide employees with a sense of direction so that they know what they are working toward. This can help to motivate employees toward specific targets and important outcomes. Numerous studies have shown that specific high goals can significantly increase employee performance.[31] A recent study verified that departments perform significantly better when employees are committed to the goals.[32] People like having a focus for their activities and efforts. Jennifer Dulski,

EXHIBIT 2.5
Goal Types and Purposes

Mission, Official Goals
- Communicate purpose and values
- Bestow legitimacy

Operating Goals
- Provide employee direction and motivation
- Offer decision guidelines
- Define standards of performance

© Cengage Learning®

currently president and COO of Change.org, a web platform for social change, talks about how she motivated people at a previous organization. "One quarter we had three big goals. I said, 'If we hit all three, it's the trifecta and we're going to all go to the horse races.' And I gave everybody $50 to bet with at the races. I learned as a teacher that everybody has a little kid inside them, and people really love these fun, silly things. They may not admit they love them, but they do."[33]

Another important purpose of goals is to act as guidelines for employee behavior and decision making. Appropriate goals can act as a set of constraints on individual behavior and actions so that employees behave within boundaries that are acceptable to the organization and larger society.[34] Google uses a system called Objectives and Key Results (OKRs). One manager, for example, established an objective to improve Google Blogger's reputation, and he came up with easily measured results such as "Re-establish leadership by speaking at 3 industry events"; "Regularly participate in Twitter discussions re: Blogger products." Everyone's OKRs are public, from the top leaders on down. These aren't used to determine promotions, but they can be used by employees to keep an eye on what they are accomplishing.

Goals help to define the appropriate decisions concerning organization structure, innovation, employee welfare, or growth. Finally, goals provide a standard for assessment. The level of organizational performance, whether in terms of profits, units produced, degree of employee satisfaction, level of innovation, or number of customer complaints, needs a basis for evaluation. Operating goals provide this standard for measurement.

Two Frameworks for Selecting Strategy and Design

To support and accomplish the organization's strategic intent and keep people focused in the direction determined by organizational mission, vision, and operating goals, managers have to select specific strategy and design options that can help the organization achieve its purpose and goals within its competitive environment. In this section, we examine a couple of practical approaches to selecting strategy and design. The questionnaire in this chapter's "How Do You Fit the Design?" box will give you some insight into your own strategic management competencies.

A **strategy** is a plan for interacting with the competitive environment to achieve organizational goals. Some managers think of goals and strategies as interchangeable, but for our purposes *goals* define where the organization wants to go and *strategies* define how it will get there. For example, a goal might be to achieve 15 percent annual sales growth; strategies to reach that goal might include aggressive advertising to attract new customers, motivating salespeople to increase the average size of customer purchases, and acquiring other businesses that produce similar products. Strategies can include any number of techniques to achieve the goal. The essence of formulating strategies is choosing whether the organization will perform different activities than its competitors or will execute similar activities more efficiently than its competitors do.[35]

Two models for formulating strategies are the Porter model of competitive strategies and the Miles and Snow strategy typology. Each provides a framework for competitive action. After describing the two models, we discuss how the choice of strategies affects organization design.

Porter's Competitive Strategies

Michael E. Porter studied a number of business organizations and proposed that managers can make the organization more profitable and less vulnerable by adopting either a differentiation strategy or a low-cost leadership strategy.[36] Using a low-cost leadership strategy means managers choose to compete through lower costs, whereas with a differentiation strategy the organization competes through the ability to offer unique or distinctive products and services that can command a premium price. These two basic strategies are illustrated in Exhibit 2.6. Moreover, each strategy can vary in scope from broad to narrow.

Differentiation. With a **differentiation strategy** the organization attempts to distinguish its products or services from others in the industry. Managers may use advertising, distinctive product features, exceptional service, or new technology to achieve a product perceived as unique. This strategy usually targets customers who are not particularly concerned with price, so it can be quite profitable.

A differentiation strategy can reduce rivalry with competitors and fight off the threat of substitute products because customers are loyal to the company's brand. However, managers must remember that successful differentiation strategies require a number of costly activities, such as product research and design and extensive advertising. Companies that pursue a differentiation strategy need strong marketing abilities and creative employees who are given the time and resources to seek innovations. One good illustration of a company that benefits from a differentiation strategy is Apple. Apple has never tried to compete on price and likes being perceived as an "elite" brand. The company has built a loyal customer base by providing innovative, stylish products and creating a prestigious image.

EXHIBIT 2.6
Porter's Competitive Strategies

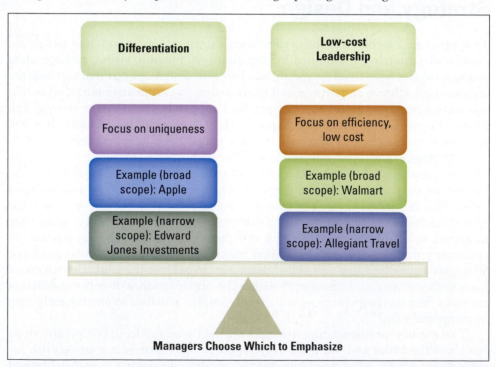

Managers Choose Which to Emphasize

Source: Based on Michael E. Porter, *Competitive Advantage: Creating and Sustaining Superior Performance* (New York: The Free Press, 1988).

Service firms can use a differentiation strategy as well. Trader Joe's, started in 1967 as a typical convenience store, was quickly modified by founder Joe Coulombe into a novel business serving unique food and drink and expanded to 17 stores in southern California. Today, there are more than 370 Trader Joe's nationwide, and people are clamoring for more. But managers are very, very careful about how they expand. TJ's doesn't carry any national brands, but instead offers innovative,

HOW DO YOU FIT THE DESIGN?

YOUR STRATEGY/PERFORMANCE STRENGTH

As a potential manager, what are your strengths concerning strategy formulation and implementation? To find out, think about *how you handle challenges and issues* in your school work or job. Then circle a or b for each of the following items depending on which is more descriptive of your behavior. There are no right or wrong answers. Respond to each item as it best describes how you respond to work situations.

1. When keeping records, I tend to
   a. be very careful about documentation.
   b. be more haphazard about documentation.

2. If I run a group or a project, I
   a. have the general idea and let others figure out how to do the tasks.
   b. try to figure out specific goals, time lines, and expected outcomes.

3. My thinking style could be more accurately described as
   a. linear thinker, going from A to B to C.
   b. thinking like a grasshopper, hopping from one idea to another.

4. In my office or home things are
   a. here and there in various piles.
   b. laid out neatly or at least in reasonable order.

5. I take pride in developing
   a. ways to overcome a barrier to a solution.
   b. new hypotheses about the underlying cause of a problem.

6. I can best help strategy by making sure there is
   a. openness to a wide range of assumptions and ideas.
   b. thoroughness when implementing new ideas.

7. One of my strengths is
   a. commitment to making things work.
   b. commitment to a dream for the future.

8. I am most effective when I emphasize
   a. inventing original solutions.
   b. making practical improvements.

Scoring: For *Strategic Formulator* strength, score one point for each "*a*" answer circled for questions 2, 4, 6, and 8, and for each "*b*" answer circled for questions 1, 3, 5, and 7. For *Strategic Implementer* strength, score one point for each "*b*" answer circled for questions 2, 4, 6, and 8, and for each "*a*" answer circled for questions 1, 3, 5, and 7. Which of your two scores is higher and by how much? The higher score indicates your *Strategy Strength*.

Interpretation: Formulator and Implementer are two important ways managers bring value to strategic management and effectiveness. Managers with implementer strengths tend to work on operating goals and performance to make things more efficient and reliable. Managers with the formulator strength push toward out-of-the-box strategies and like to think about mission, vision, and dramatic breakthroughs. Both styles are essential to strategic management and organizational effectiveness. Strategic formulators often use their skills to create whole new strategies and approaches, and strategic implementers often work with strategic improvements, implementation, and measurement.

If the difference between your two scores is 2 or less, you have a balanced formulator/implementer style and work well in both arenas. If the difference is 4–5, you have a moderately strong style and probably work best in the area of your strength. And if the difference is 7–8, you have a distinctive strength and almost certainly would want to contribute in the area of your strength rather than in the opposite domain.

Source: Adapted from Dorothy Marcic and Joe Seltzer, *Organizational Behavior: Experiences and Cases* (South-Western, 1998), 284–287, and William Miller, *Innovation Styles* (Global Creativity Corporation, 1997).

high quality, health-conscious food and beverage products at modest prices. About 80 percent of products carry TJ's private label, and the company is secretive about who makes products for them. Many TJ's stores carry only about 2,500 items, compared to a traditional supermarket that has more than 40,000, and the selection is constantly changing. What keeps people coming back is the novelty and sense of adventure—you never know what you're going to find—and the friendly service you might expect at the mom-and-pop shop around the corner. Managers evaluate every decision with an eye to how it fits with the goal of maintaining a neighborhood store feel.[37]

Low-Cost Leadership. The **low-cost leadership strategy** tries to increase market share by keeping costs low compared to competitors. With a low-cost leadership strategy, the organization aggressively seeks efficient facilities, pursues cost reductions, and uses tight controls to produce products or services more efficiently than its competitors. Low cost doesn't necessarily mean low price, but in many cases cost leaders provide goods and services to customers at cheaper prices. For example, the CEO of Irish airline Ryanair said of the company's strategy: "It's the oldest, simplest formula: Pile 'em high and sell 'em cheap. . . . We want to be the Walmart of the airline business. Nobody will beat us on price. EVER." Ryanair can offer low fares because it keeps costs at rock bottom, lower than any other airline in Europe. The company's watchword is cheap tickets, not customer care or unique services.[38]

The low-cost leadership strategy is concerned primarily with stability rather than taking risks or seeking new opportunities for innovation and growth. A low-cost leadership position means a company can achieve higher profits than competitors because of its efficiency and lower operating costs. Cost leaders such as Ryanair can undercut competitors' prices and still earn a reasonable profit. In addition, if substitute products or potential new competitors enter the picture, the low-cost producer is in a better position to prevent loss of market share.

Porter found that companies that did not consciously adopt a low-cost or differentiation strategy achieved below-average profits compared to those that used one of the strategies. Many Internet companies have failed because managers did not develop competitive strategies that would distinguish them in the marketplace.[39] On the other hand, Google became highly successful with a coherent differentiation strategy that distinguished it from other search engines.

ASSESS YOUR ANSWER

2 The best business strategy is to make products and services as distinctive as possible to gain an edge in the marketplace.

ANSWER: *Disagree.* Differentiation, making the company's products or services distinctive from others in the market, is one effective strategic approach. A low-cost leadership approach can be equally or even more effective depending on the organization's strengths and the nature of competition in the industry.

Competitive Scope Can Be Broad or Narrow. With either strategy, the scope of competitive action can be either broad or narrow. That is, an organization can choose to compete in many market and customer segments or to focus on a specific market or buyer group. For example, Walmart uses a low-cost leadership strategy and competes in a broad market, selling to many market segments. A good example of a narrowly focused low-cost leadership strategy is Allegiant Travel Company.

"We want to be considered the hometown airline of all the little cities around the country," said Andrew Levy, president of Allegiant Travel Company. Allegiant flies just 64 jets and specializes in flying people from 75 small, underserved cities to 14 warm-weather tourist destinations such as Orlando, Las Vegas, and Honolulu.

Allegiant has achieved the lowest costs, fullest planes, and highest margins in the industry and has been profitable in 39 of its last 41 quarters by serving small cities that competitors don't serve. The focused low-cost leadership strategy means Allegiant faces competition on just 17 of its 203 routes. Managers believe in "attacking niche opportunities." For example, Allegiant moved in when other airlines left the shrinking cities of the Rust Belt and lures Canadian fliers just across the border to fly out of small U.S. airports. The airline has now set its sights on Mexico, hoping to fly middle-class Mexicans from cities such as Zacatecas or Culiacán to tourist destinations such as Las Vegas in the United States.

Allegiant goes to extremes to meet its goals of low cost. It depends largely on word-of-mouth advertising rather than paying travel agents. It offers a no-frills base fare and charges for nearly everything else, from carry-on luggage to water. Managers also say they "only fly when we can make money." The older, used planes the company flies guzzle gas, so they fly only on peak travel days when the flight is nearly full. "On Tuesdays, we look like a bankrupt airline," Levy says, but "who wants to start their vacation on a Tuesday?"[40]

An example of a narrowly focused differentiation strategy is Edward Jones Investments, a St. Louis-based brokerage house. The company concentrates on building its business in rural and small-town America and providing clients with conservative, long-term investment advice. Management scholar and consultant Peter Drucker once said the distinctive safety-first orientation means Edward Jones delivers a product "that no Wall Street house has ever sold before: peace of mind."[41]

Miles and Snow's Strategy Typology

Another strategy typology was developed from the study of business strategies by Raymond Miles and Charles Snow.[42] The Miles and Snow typology is based on the idea that managers seek to formulate strategies that will be congruent with the external environment. Organizations strive for a fit among internal organization characteristics, strategy, and the external environment. The four strategies that can be developed are the prospector, the defender, the analyzer, and the reactor.

Prospector. The **prospector** strategy is to innovate, take risks, seek out new opportunities, and grow. This strategy is suited to a dynamic, growing environment, where creativity is more important than efficiency. Nike, which innovates in both products and internal processes, exemplifies the prospector strategy. For example, the company has introduced a new line of shoes based on designs that can be produced using recycled materials and limited amounts of toxic chemical-based glues.[43]

China's Zhejiang Geely Holding Group is setting a prospector strategy for Volvo Car Corporation after acquiring the global automaker from Ford Motor Company. For many years Volvo focused on stability, seeking to hang on to customers who appreciated the brand's reputation for safe, reliable family vehicles. But Li Shufu, the company's new hard-charging Chinese owner, set a new course for the company, aiming to expand aggressively into the luxury car market and compete head-on with the likes of BMW and Mercedes. Li clashed with Volvo's European CEO, Stefan Jacoby, who wanted to move more slowly away from the company's tradition of modest style, but the two eventually agreed on an ambitious turnaround plan that involves $10 billion in investment over a five-year period and a goal of doubling worldwide sales to 800,000 vehicles by 2020. Li says he wants Volvo to offer innovative, electrifying designs that turn heads and win new customers. China sales are a growing part of the auto business, and Li says Volvo has no future unless it caters to the flashier tastes of emerging rich consumers in that country.[44] Li and Jacoby are continuing to work out their differing visions and management styles, but the prospector strategy to upgrade the product lineup and expand aggressively is on course. Online companies such as Facebook and Google also reflect a prospector strategy.

Defender. The **defender** strategy is almost the opposite of the prospector. Rather than taking risks and seeking out new opportunities, the defender strategy is concerned with stability or even retrenchment. This strategy seeks to hold on to current customers, but it neither innovates nor seeks to grow. The defender is concerned primarily with internal efficiency and control to produce reliable, high-quality products for steady customers. This strategy can be successful when the organization exists in a declining industry or a stable environment. Paramount Pictures has been using a defender strategy for several years.[45] Paramount turns out a steady stream of reliable hits but few blockbusters. Managers shun risk and sometimes turn down potentially high-profile films to keep a lid on costs. This has enabled the company to remain highly profitable while other studios have low returns or actually lose money.

Analyzer. The **analyzer** tries to maintain a stable business while innovating on the periphery. It seems to lie midway between the prospector and the defender. Some products will be targeted at stable environments in which an efficiency strategy designed to keep current customers is used. Others will be targeted at new, more dynamic environments, where growth is possible. The analyzer attempts to balance efficient production for current product or service lines with the creative development of new product lines. Amazon.com provides an example. The company's current strategy is to defend its core business of selling books and other physical goods over the Internet, but also to build a business in digital media, including initiatives such as a digital book service, an online streaming video business, developing original content, and a digital music store to compete with Apple's iTunes.[46]

Reactor. The **reactor** strategy is not really a strategy at all. Rather, reactors respond to environmental threats and opportunities in an ad hoc fashion. With a reactor strategy, top management has not defined a long-range plan or given the organization an explicit mission or goal, so the organization takes whatever actions seem to meet immediate needs. Although the reactor strategy can sometimes be successful, it can also lead to failed companies. Some large, once highly successful companies are struggling because managers failed to adopt a strategy consistent with consumer trends. In recent years managers at the once successful and profitable bookstore Barnes & Noble have been floundering to find the appropriate strategy. The Nook, introduced to compete with the Amazon Kindle, "looked good, worked well, and sold better than Barnes & Noble expected." The problem was, when Apple introduced the iPad, managers at Barnes & Noble reacted by coming out with a competing multifunction device. It was a mistake. The Nook Media business had an operating loss of $475 million for the fiscal year that ended April 2013. "He drank too much of the digital Kool-Aid," said one analyst of Barnes & Noble CEO William Lynch, who has since left the company.[47]

EXHIBIT 2.7
Organization Design
Outcomes of Strategy

Porter's Competitive Strategies	Miles and Snow's Strategy Typology
Strategy: Differentiation	**Strategy:** Prospector
Organization Design:	**Organization Design:**
• Learning orientation; acts in a flexible, loosely knit way, with strong horizontal coordination	• Learning orientation; flexible, fluid, decentralized structure
• Strong capability in research?	• Strong capability in research
• Values and builds in mechanisms for customer intimacy	**Strategy:** Defender
• Rewards employee creativity, risk-taking, and innovation	**Organization Design:**
Strategy: Low-Cost Leadership	• Efficiency orientation; centralized authority; tight cost control
Organization Design:	• Emphasis on production efficiency; low overhead
• Efficiency orientation; strong central authority; tight cost control, with frequent, detailed control reports	• Close supervision; little employee empowerment
• Standard operating procedures	**Strategy:** Analyzer
• Highly efficient procurement and distribution systems	**Organization Design:**
• Close supervision; routine tasks; limited employee empowerment	• Balances efficiency and learning; tight cost control with flexibility and adaptability
	• Efficient production for stable product lines; emphasis on creativity, research, risk-taking for innovation
	Strategy: Reactor
	Organization Design:
	• No clear organizational approach; design characteristics may shift abruptly, depending on current needs

Source: Based on Michael E. Porter, *Competitive Strategy: Techniques for Analyzing Industries and Competitors* (New York: The Free Press, 1980); Michael Treacy and Fred Wiersema, "How Market Leaders Keep Their Edge," *Fortune*, (February 6, 1995), 88–98; Michael Hitt, R. Duane Ireland, and Robert E. Hoskisson, *Strategic Management* (St. Paul, MN.: West, 1995), 100–113; and Raymond E. Miles, Charles C. Snow, Alan D. Meyer, and Henry J. Coleman, Jr., "Organizational Strategy, Structure, and Process," *Academy of Management Review* 3 (1978), 546–562.

The Miles and Snow typology has been widely used, and researchers have tested its validity in a variety of organizations, including hospitals, colleges, banking institutions, industrial products companies, and life insurance firms. In general, researchers have found strong support for the effectiveness of this typology for organization managers in real-world situations.[48]

The ability of managers to devise and maintain a clear competitive strategy is considered one of the defining factors in an organization's success, but many managers struggle with this crucial responsibility.

How Strategies Affect Organization Design

Choice of strategy affects internal organization characteristics. Organization design characteristics need to support the firm's competitive approach. For example, a company wanting to grow and invent new products looks and "feels" different from a company that is focused on maintaining market share for long-established products in a stable industry. Exhibit 2.7 summarizes organization design characteristics associated with the Porter and Miles and Snow strategies.

BRIEFCASE

As an organization manager, keep these guidelines in mind:

Design the organization to support the firm's competitive strategy. With a low-cost leadership or defender strategy, select design characteristics associated with an efficiency orientation. For a differentiation or prospector strategy, on the other hand, choose characteristics that encourage learning, innovation, and adaptation. Use a balanced mixture of characteristics for an analyzer strategy.

With a low-cost leadership strategy, managers take a primarily mechanistic, efficiency approach to organization design, whereas a differentiation strategy calls for a more organic, learning approach. Recall from Chapter 1 that mechanistic organizations designed for efficiency have different characteristics from organic organizations designed for learning. A low-cost leadership strategy (efficiency) is associated with strong, centralized authority and tight control, standard operating procedures, and emphasis on efficient procurement and distribution systems. Employees generally perform routine tasks under close supervision and control and are not empowered to make decisions or take action on their own. A differentiation strategy, on the other hand, requires that employees be constantly experimenting and learning. Structure is fluid and flexible, with strong horizontal coordination. Empowered employees work directly with customers and are rewarded for creativity and risk-taking. The organization values research, creativity, and innovativeness over efficiency and standard procedures.

The prospector strategy requires characteristics similar to a differentiation strategy, and the defender strategy takes an efficiency approach similar to low-cost leadership. Because the analyzer strategy attempts to balance efficiency for stable product lines with flexibility and learning for new products, it is associated with a mix of characteristics, as listed in Exhibit 2.7. With a reactor strategy, managers have left the organization with no direction and no clear approach to design.

Other Contingency Factors Affecting Organization Design

Strategy is one important factor that affects organization design. Ultimately, however, organization design is a result of numerous contingencies, which will be discussed throughout this book. The emphasis given to efficiency and control (mechanistic) versus learning and flexibility (organic) is determined by the contingencies of strategy, environment, size and life cycle, technology, and organizational culture. The organization is designed to "fit" the contingency factors, as illustrated in Exhibit 2.8.

In a stable environment, for example, the organization can have a traditional mechanistic structure that emphasizes vertical control, efficiency, specialization, standard procedures, and centralized decision making. However, a rapidly changing

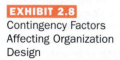
EXHIBIT 2.8
Contingency Factors Affecting Organization Design

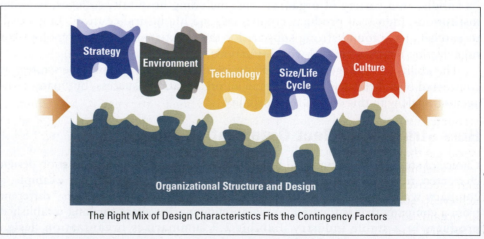
The Right Mix of Design Characteristics Fits the Contingency Factors

© Cengage Learning®

environment may call for a more flexible, organic structure, with strong horizontal coordination and collaboration through teams or other mechanisms. Environment will be discussed in detail in Chapter 4 and Chapter 5. In terms of size and life cycle, young, small organizations are generally informal and have little division of labor, few rules and regulations, and ad hoc budgeting and performance systems. Large organizations such as Coca-Cola, Samsung, or General Electric, on the other hand, have an extensive division of labor, numerous rules and regulations, and standard procedures and systems for budgeting, control, rewards, and innovation. Size and stages of the life cycle will be discussed in Chapter 9.

Design must also fit the workflow technology of the organization. For example, with mass production technology, such as a traditional automobile assembly line, the organization functions best by emphasizing efficiency, formalization, specialization, centralized decision making, and tight control. An e-business, on the other hand, would need to be more informal and flexible. Technology's impact on design will be discussed in detail in Chapter 7 and Chapter 8. A final contingency that affects organization design is corporate culture. An organizational culture that values teamwork, collaboration, creativity, and open communication, for example, would not function well with a tight, vertical structure and strict rules and regulations. The role of culture is discussed in Chapter 10.

One responsibility of managers is to design organizations that fit the contingency factors of strategy, environment, size and life cycle, technology, and culture. Finding the right fit leads to organizational effectiveness, whereas a poor fit can lead to decline or even the demise of the organization.

Assessing Organizational Effectiveness

Understanding organizational goals and strategies, as well as the concept of fitting design to various contingencies, is a first step toward understanding organizational effectiveness. Organizational goals represent the reason for an organization's existence and the outcomes it seeks to achieve. The rest of this chapter explores the topic of effectiveness and how effectiveness is measured in organizations.

Definition

Recall from Chapter 1 that organizational effectiveness is the degree to which an organization realizes its goals. *Effectiveness* is a broad concept. It implicitly takes into consideration a range of variables at both the organizational and departmental levels. Effectiveness evaluates the extent to which multiple goals—whether official or operating—are attained. *Efficiency* is a more limited concept that pertains to the internal workings of the organization. Organizational efficiency is the amount of resources used to produce a unit of output.[49] It can be measured as the ratio of inputs to outputs. If one organization can achieve a given production level with fewer resources than another organization, it would be described as more efficient.[50]

Sometimes efficiency leads to effectiveness, but in other organizations efficiency and effectiveness are not related. An organization may be highly efficient but fail to achieve its goals because it makes a product for which there is no demand. Likewise, an organization may achieve its profit goals but be inefficient. Efforts to increase efficiency, particularly through severe cost cutting, can also sometimes make the organization less effective. For example, one regional fast food chain wanting to increase efficiency decided to reduce food waste by not cooking any food until it was ordered. The move reduced the chain's costs, but it also led to delayed service, irritated customers, and lower sales.[51]

Overall effectiveness is difficult to measure in organizations. Organizations are large, diverse, and fragmented. They perform many activities simultaneously, pursue multiple goals, and generate many outcomes, some intended and some unintended.[52] Managers determine what indicators to measure in order to gauge the effectiveness of their organizations. Four possible approaches to measuring effectiveness are:

- The Goal Approach
- The Resource-Based Approach
- The Internal Process Approach
- The Strategic Constituents Approach

Who Decides?

Key people in charge of the organization, such as top managers or board members, have to make a conscious decision about how they will determine the organization's effectiveness. Just as people determine goals, they also determine when the organization is successful. Organizational effectiveness is a **social construct**, meaning that it is created and defined by an individual or group rather than existing independently in the external world.[53] An analogy from baseball that clarifies the concept is the story of three umpires explaining how they call balls and strikes. The first says, "I call 'em as they are." The second says, "I call 'em as I see 'em." The third takes a social construct approach and says, "They ain't nothin' 'til I call 'em."[54] Similarly, organizational effectiveness is nothing until managers or stakeholders "call it."

An employee might consider the organization is effective if it issues accurate paychecks on time and provides promised benefits. A customer might consider it effective if it provides a good product at a low price. A CEO might consider the organization effective if it is profitable. Effectiveness is always multidimensional, and thus assessments of effectiveness are typically multidimensional as well. Managers in businesses typically use profits and stock performance as indicators of effectiveness, but they also give credence to other measures, such as employee satisfaction, customer loyalty, corporate citizenship, innovativeness, or industry reputation.[55]

Managers often use indicators from more than one of the four approaches (goal, resource, internal process, strategic constituents) when measuring effectiveness. Exhibit 2.9 lists a sample of 15 indicators that managers of large, multinational organizations reported using to assess effectiveness. As you read the descriptions of the four approaches to measuring effectiveness in the following sections, try to decide which approach each of these 15 indicators falls under.[56]

As the items in Exhibit 2.9 reveal, indicators of effectiveness are both quantitative and qualitative, tangible and intangible. An indicator such as achieving sales targets or percentage of market share is easy to measure, but indicators such as employee engagement, quality, or customer satisfaction are less clear-cut and often have to be measured qualitatively.[57] Relying solely on quantitative measurements can give managers a limited or distorted view of effectiveness. Albert Einstein is reported to have kept a sign in his office that read, "Not everything that counts can be counted, and not everything that can be counted counts."[58]

EXHIBIT 2.9

Some Indicators
of Organizational
Effectiveness Reported
by Multinational
Organizations

1. Meeting deadlines; on-time delivery
2. Timely material and equipment acquisition
3. Quality of product or service
4. Customer satisfaction/complaints
5. Market share compared to competitors
6. Employee training and development (number of hours)
7. Staying within budget
8. Shareholder satisfaction
9. Reduction in costs
10. Supply chain delays or improvements
11. Productivity; dollars spent for each unit of output
12. Employee engagement
13. Achieving sales targets
14. Product development cycle time (reduction in cycle time)
15. Number of hours/days and so on to complete tasks

Source: Based on "Table 1; Initial Items Derived from Interviews," in Cristina B. Gibson, Mary E. Zellmer-Bruhn, and Donald P. Schwab, "Team Effectiveness in Multinational Organizations: Evaluation Across Contexts," *Group & Organizational Management* 28, no. 4 (December 2003), 444–474.

Four Effectiveness Approaches

As open systems, organizations bring in resources from the environment, and those resources are transformed into outputs delivered back into the environment, as shown in Exhibit 2.10. In addition, recall from Chapter 1 that organizations interact with a number of stakeholder groups inside and outside the organization. Four key approaches to measuring effectiveness look at different parts of the organization and measure indicators connected with outputs, inputs, internal activities, or key stakeholders, also called strategic constituents.[59]

Goal Approach

The **goal approach** to effectiveness consists of identifying an organization's output goals and assessing how well the organization has attained those goals.[60] This is a logical approach because organizations do try to attain certain levels of output, profit, or client satisfaction. The goal approach measures progress toward the attainment of those goals.

Indicators. The important goals to consider are operating goals, because official goals (mission) tend to be abstract and difficult to measure. Operating goals reflect activities the organization is actually performing.[61]

Indicators tracked with the goal approach include:

- Profitability—the positive gain from business operations or investments after expenses are subtracted
- Market share—the proportion of the market the firm is able to capture relative to competitors

EXHIBIT 2.10

Four Approaches to
Measuring Organizational
Effectiveness

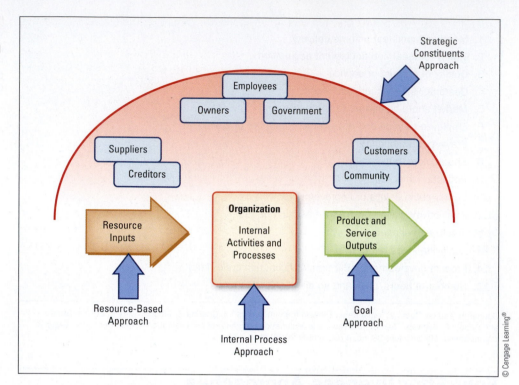

- Growth—the ability of the organization to increase its sales, profits, or client base over time
- Social responsibility—how well the organization serves the interests of society as well as itself
- Product quality—the ability of the organization to achieve high quality in its products or services

Usefulness. The goal approach is used in business organizations because output goals can be readily measured. Some nonprofit organizations that aim to solve social problems also find the goal approach useful. For example, Every Child Succeeds is a public-private partnership funded primarily by United Way that aims to reduce infant mortality and improve maternal health in the area surrounding Cincinnati, Ohio. In the seven Ohio and Kentucky counties around the city, 8.3 out of every 1,000 newborns die before they reach their first birthday, on par with countries such as Lithuania and Brunei. Yet among the mothers enrolled in Every Child Succeeds, that statistic is only 2.8 percent, lower than in virtually every industrialized country. Using a rigorous model of performance measurement based on some of the management practices at P&G, social workers and nurses from 15 participating organizations, including two Cincinnati hospitals and several social service agencies, visit at-risk mothers in their homes and help them stop smoking, learn to eat better, control their diabetes or high blood pressure, and improve their health in other ways. Unlike many social improvement programs, Every Child Succeeds sets and measures a few narrow and specific goals organized under seven focus areas.[62]

In businesses as well as in nonprofit organizations such as Every Child Succeeds, identifying operating goals and measuring effectiveness are not always easy. Two problems that must be resolved are the issues of multiple goals and subjective indicators of goal attainment. Since organizations have multiple and sometimes conflicting goals, effectiveness cannot be assessed by a single indicator. High achievement on one goal might mean low achievement on another. Moreover, there are department goals as well as overall organizational goals. The full assessment of effectiveness should take into consideration several goals simultaneously.

The other issue to resolve with the goal approach is how to identify operating goals for an organization and how to measure goal attainment. For business organizations, there are often objective indicators for certain goals, such as profit or growth. Every Child Succeeds can also use objective indicators for some goals, such as tracking how many infants are immunized or how many clients stop smoking during pregnancy. However, subjective assessment is needed for other goals, such as employee welfare, social responsibility, or client satisfaction. Top managers and other key people on the management team have to clearly identify which goals the organization will measure. Subjective perceptions of goal attainment must be used when quantitative indicators are not available. Managers rely on information from customers, competitors, suppliers, and employees, as well as their own intuition, when considering these goals.

Resource-Based Approach

The **resource-based approach** looks at the input side of the transformation process shown in Exhibit 2.10. It assumes organizations must be successful in obtaining and managing valued resources in order to be effective because strategically valuable resources give an organization a competitive edge.[63] From a resource-based perspective, organizational effectiveness is defined as the ability of the organization, in either absolute or relative terms, to obtain scarce and valued resources and successfully integrate and manage them.[64]

Indicators. Obtaining and successfully managing resources is the criterion by which organizational effectiveness is assessed. In a broad sense, resource indicators of effectiveness encompass the following dimensions:[65]

- Bargaining position—the ability of the organization to obtain from its environment scarce and valued resources, including tangible resources such as a prime location, financing, raw materials, and quality employees, and intangible assets such as a strong brand or superior knowledge
- The abilities of the organization's decision makers to perceive and correctly interpret the real properties of the external environment and supply forces
- The abilities of managers to use tangible (e.g., supplies, people) and intangible (e.g., knowledge, corporate culture) resources and capabilities in day-to-day organizational activities to achieve superior performance
- The ability of the organization to respond to changes in resource sectors of the environment

Usefulness. The resource-based approach is valuable when other indicators of performance are difficult to obtain. In many nonprofit and social welfare organizations, for example, it is hard to measure output goals or internal efficiency. The Shriners Hospitals for Children (SHC) system provides an example. The 22 Shriners Hospitals provide free treatment to thousands of children with orthopedic conditions, burns, spinal cord injuries, and cleft lip and palette conditions. For most

BRIEFCASE

As an organization
manager, keep these
guidelines in mind:

Use the goal approach,
internal process ap-
proach, and resource-
based approach to
obtain specific interpre-
tations of organizational
effectiveness in the
areas of outputs, internal
processes, and inputs.
Assess the satisfaction
of strategic constituents
or use the competing
values model to obtain
a broader picture of
effectiveness.

of its history, the SHC was highly successful in obtaining donations, the main source of funding for the hospitals' operations. However, when the federal government launched a no-cost health insurance program for children of low-income families, Shriners began losing patients to traditional healthcare providers. With a decline in patient registrations, donations began to decline as well. Managers had to search for new ways to respond to the increased competition and obtain needed resources.[66] Many for-profit organizations also use a resource-based approach because resources are critical to competitive success. For example, the British retail firm Marks & Spencer evaluates its effectiveness partly by looking at the company's ability to obtain, manage, and maintain valued resources such as prime locations for stores, a strong brand, quality employees, and effective supplier relationships.[67]

Although the resource-based approach is valuable when other measures of effectiveness are not available, it does have shortcomings. For one thing, the approach only vaguely considers the organization's link to the needs of customers. A superior ability to acquire and use resources is important only if resources and capabilities are used to achieve something that meets a need in the environment. Critics have challenged that the approach assumes stability in the marketplace and fails to adequately consider the changing value of various resources as the competitive environment and customer needs change.[68]

Internal Process Approach

In the **internal process approach**, effectiveness is measured as internal organizational health and efficiency. An effective organization has a smooth, well-oiled internal process. Employees are happy and satisfied. Department activities mesh with one another to ensure high productivity. This approach does not consider the external environment. The important element in effectiveness is what the organization does with the resources it has, as reflected in internal health and efficiency.

Indicators. One indicator of internal process effectiveness is economic efficiency. However, the best-known proponents of an internal process model are from the human relations approach to organizations. Such writers as Chris Argyris, Warren G. Bennis, Rensis Likert, and Richard Beckhard have all worked extensively with human resources in organizations and emphasize the connection between human resources and effectiveness.[69] Results from a study of nearly 200 secondary schools showed that both human resources and employee-oriented processes were important in explaining and promoting effectiveness in those organizations.[70]

Internal process indicators include:[71]

- A strong, adaptive corporate culture and positive work climate
- Confidence and trust between employees and management
- Operational efficiency, such as using minimal resources to achieve outcomes
- Undistorted horizontal and vertical communication
- Growth and development of employees
- Coordination among the organization's parts, with conflicts resolved in the interest of the larger organization

Usefulness. The internal process approach is important because the efficient use of resources and harmonious internal functioning are good ways to assess organizational effectiveness. In the wake of the economic recession, companies such as DuPont, Campbell Soup, and UPS are looking for ways to be more efficient, such as using existing technology to accomplish more with less. At Campbell's Maxton, North Carolina-based factory, hundreds of small changes and improvements, many suggested by employees, have increased operating efficiency to 85 percent of what managers believe is the maximum possible. UPS trucks carry devices that track how many left-turns against traffic its drivers have to make. By helping drivers optimize their routes with fewer left turns, the system will save UPS 1.4 million gallons of fuel per year.[72]

Today, most managers believe that committed, actively involved employees and a positive corporate culture are also important internal measures of effectiveness. The internal process approach also has shortcomings. Total output and the organization's relationship with the external environment are not evaluated. Another problem is that evaluations of internal health and functioning are often subjective because many aspects of inputs and internal processes are not quantifiable. Managers should be aware that this approach alone represents a limited view of organizational effectiveness. Following the merger of Burlington Northern Railroad and the Atchison, Topeka, and Santa Fe Railway, managers at BNSF Railway committed to creating an environment that provided overall organizational effectiveness and they combine an internal process approach to measuring effectiveness with other approaches.

IN PRACTICE

BNSF Railway

When faced with merging two operating systems, management systems, and cultures into one cohesive organization, managers at BNSF knew they could let the culture develop naturally over time or be active participants in creating the culture they wanted. They chose to take a deliberate role in building a positive internal environment.

Indicators of internal effectiveness at BNSF are that people take pride in working at the railway and have opportunities for personal growth and development. Shared values include listening to customers and doing what it takes to meet their expectations. In addition, managers focus employees on continuous improvement and provide a safe working environment.

Managers combine measures of internal process effectiveness with measures of how well BNSF meets goals for 100 percent on-time, damage-free customer service, accurate and timely information about their customer shipments, and giving customers the best value for their transportation dollar. Other goals are for shareholder returns that exceed other railroads and a return on invested capital that is greater than BNSF's cost of capital.

Other stakeholders are considered as well. BNSF considers its ethical and legal commitments to the communities it serves, and well as its sensitivity to the natural environment in evaluating overall effectiveness.[73]

As this example illustrates, many organizations use more than one approach to measuring effectiveness because organizations pursue many different types of activities and serve many different interests.

Strategic Constituents Approach

The strategic constituents approach is related to the stakeholder approach described in Chapter 1. Recall from Exhibit 1.6 that organizations have a variety of internal and external stakeholders that may have competing claims on what they want from the organization. Several important stakeholder groups are also shown at the top of Exhibit 2.10.

In reality, it is unreasonable to assume that all stakeholders can be equally satisfied. The **strategic constituents approach** measures effectiveness by focusing on the satisfaction of key stakeholders, those who are critical to the organization's ability to survive and thrive. The satisfaction of these strategic constituents can be assessed as an indicator of the organization's performance.[74]

Indicators. The initial work on evaluating effectiveness on the basis of strategic constituents looked at 97 small businesses and 7 groups relevant to those organizations. Members of each group were surveyed to determine the perception of effectiveness from each viewpoint.[75] Each constituent group had a different criterion of effectiveness:

Strategic Constituent Group	Effectiveness Criteria
Owners	Financial return
Employees	Pay, good supervision, worker satisfaction
Customers	Quality of goods and services
Creditors	Creditworthiness
Community	Contribution to community affairs
Suppliers	Satisfactory transactions
Government	Obedience to laws and regulations

If an organization fails to meet the needs of several constituent groups, it is probably not meeting its effectiveness goals. Although these seven groups reflect constituents that nearly every organization has to satisfy to some degree, each organization might have a different set of strategic constituents. For example, independent software developers are key to the success of companies such as Facebook even though they are not necessarily customers, suppliers, or owners. CEO Mark Zuckerberg works hard to win over developers. At a developers' conference, he unveiled a technology that lets websites install a Facebook "Like" button for free. Users can click on it to signal their interest in a piece of content. The user's approval then shows up on his or her Facebook page with a link back to the site. The technology will drive traffic from Facebook to other websites, and in turn drive traffic back to Facebook.[76]

Usefulness. Research has shown that the assessment of multiple constituents is an accurate reflection of organizational effectiveness, especially with respect to organizational adaptability.[77] Moreover, both profit and nonprofit organizations care about their reputations and attempt to shape perceptions of their performance.[78] The strategic constituents approach takes a broad view of effectiveness and examines factors in the environment as well as within the organization. It looks at several criteria simultaneously—inputs, internal processes, and outputs—and acknowledges that there is no single measure of effectiveness.

The strategic constituents approach is popular because it is based on the understanding that effectiveness is a complex, multidimensional concept and has no single measure.[79] In the following section, we look at another popular approach that takes a multidimensional, integrated approach to measuring effectiveness.

An Integrated Effectiveness Model

The **competing values model** tries to balance a concern with various parts of the organization rather than focusing on one part. This approach to effectiveness acknowledges that organizations do many things and have many outcomes.[80] It combines several indicators of effectiveness into a single framework.

The model is based on the assumption that there are disagreements and competing viewpoints about what constitutes effectiveness. Managers sometimes disagree over which are the most important goals to pursue and measure. One tragic example of conflicting viewpoints and competing interests comes from NASA. After seven astronauts died in the explosion of the space shuttle Columbia in February 2003, an investigative committee found deep organizational flaws at NASA, including ineffective mechanisms for incorporating dissenting opinions between scheduling managers and safety managers. External pressures to launch on time overrode safety concerns with the Columbia launch.[81] Similarly, Congressional investigations of the 2010 Deepwater Horizon oil rig explosion and oil spill in the Gulf of Mexico found that BP engineers and managers made a number of decisions that were counter to the advice of key contractors, putting goals of cost control and timeliness ahead of concerns over well safety.[82] BP and NASA represent how complex organizations can be, operating not only with different viewpoints internally but also from contractors, government regulators, Congress, and the expectations of the American public.

The competing values model takes into account these complexities. The model was originally developed by Robert Quinn and John Rohrbaugh to combine the diverse indicators of performance used by managers and researchers.[83] Using a comprehensive list of performance indicators, a panel of experts in organizational effectiveness rated the indicators for similarity. Their analysis found underlying dimensions of effectiveness criteria that represented competing management values in organizations.

Indicators. The first value dimension pertains to organizational **focus**, which is whether dominant values concern issues that are *internal* or *external* to the firm. Internal focus reflects a management concern for the well-being and efficiency of employees, and external focus represents an emphasis on the well-being of the organization itself with respect to the environment. The second value dimension pertains to organization **structure** and whether *stability* or *flexibility* is the dominant structural consideration. Stability reflects a management value for efficiency and top-down control, whereas flexibility represents a value for learning and change.

The value dimensions of structure and focus are illustrated in Exhibit 2.11. The combination of dimensions provides four approaches to organizational effectiveness, which, though seemingly different, are closely related. In real organizations, these competing values can and often do exist together. Each approach reflects a different management emphasis with respect to structure and focus.[84]

A combination of external focus and flexible structure leads to an **open systems emphasis**. Management's primary goals are growth and resource acquisition. The organization accomplishes these goals through the subgoals of flexibility, readiness, and a positive external evaluation. The dominant value is establishing a good relationship with the environment to acquire resources and grow. This emphasis is similar in some ways to the resource-based approach described earlier.

The **rational goal emphasis** represents management values of structural control and external focus. The primary goals are productivity, efficiency, and profit. The organization wants to achieve output goals in a controlled way. Subgoals that facilitate these outcomes are internal planning and goal setting, which are rational management tools. The rational goal emphasis is similar to the goal approach described earlier.

The **internal process emphasis** is in the lower-left section of Exhibit 2.11; it reflects the values of internal focus and structural control. The primary outcome is a stable organizational setting that maintains itself in an orderly way. Organizations that are well established in the environment and simply want to maintain their current position would reflect this emphasis. Subgoals include mechanisms for efficient communication, information management, and decision making. Although this part of the competing values model is similar in some ways to the internal process approach described earlier, it is less concerned with human resources than with other internal processes that lead to efficiency.

The **human relations emphasis** incorporates the values of an internal focus and a flexible structure. Here, management concern is for the development of human resources. Employees are given opportunities for autonomy and development. Management works toward the subgoals of cohesion, morale, and training opportunities. Organizations adopting this emphasis are more concerned with employees than with the environment.

The four cells in Exhibit 2.11 represent opposing organizational values. Managers decide which values will take priority in the organization. The way two organizations are mapped onto the four approaches is shown in Exhibit 2.12.[85] Organization A is a young organization concerned with finding a niche and becoming established in the external environment. Primary emphasis is given to flexibility, innovation, the acquisition of resources from the environment, and the satisfaction of external strategic constituents. This organization gives moderate emphasis to human relations and even less emphasis to current productivity and profits. Satisfying and adapting to the environment are more important. The attention given to open systems values means that the internal process emphasis is practically nonexistent. Stability and equilibrium are of little concern.

EXHIBIT 2.11
Four Approaches to
Effectiveness Values

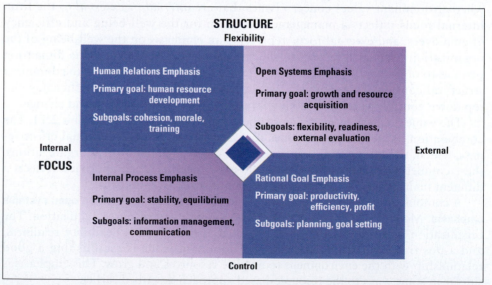

Source: Adapted from Robert E. Quinn and John Rohrbaugh, "A Spatial Model of Effectiveness Criteria: Toward a Competing Values Approach to Organizational Analysis," *Management Science* 29 (1983), 363–377; and Robert E. Quinn and Kim Cameron, "Organizational Life Cycles and Shifting Criteria of Effectiveness: Some Preliminary Evidence," *Management Science* 29 (1983), 33–51.

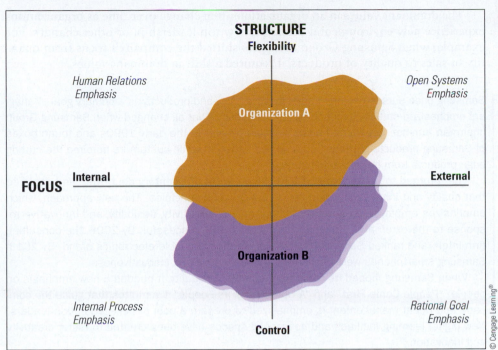

© Cengage Learning®

EXHIBIT 2.12
Effectiveness Values for
Two Organizations

Organization B, in contrast, is an established business in which the dominant value is productivity and profits. This organization is characterized by planning and goal setting. Organization B is a large company that is well established in the environment and is primarily concerned with successful production and profits. Flexibility and human resources are not major concerns. This organization prefers stability and equilibrium to learning and innovation because it wants to maximize the value of its established customers.

3 **The best measures of business performance are financial.**

    ANSWER: *Disagree.* If you can have only one type of measure of business performance, it might have to be financial. But diverse views of performance, such as using the competing values model, have proven to be more effective than financials alone because managers can understand and control the actions that cause business effectiveness. Financial numbers alone provide narrow and limited information.

ASSESS YOUR ANSWER

Usefulness. The competing values model makes two contributions. First, it integrates diverse concepts of effectiveness into a single perspective. It incorporates the ideas of output goals, resource acquisition, and human resource development as goals the organization tries to accomplish. Second, the model calls attention to how effectiveness criteria are socially constructed from management values and shows how opposing values exist at the same time. Managers must decide which values they wish to pursue and which values will receive less emphasis. The four competing values exist simultaneously, but not all will receive equal priority. For example, a new, small organization that concentrates on establishing itself within a competitive environment will give less emphasis to developing employees than to the external environment.

The dominant values in an organization often change over time as organizations experience new environmental demands, new top leadership, or other changes. For example, when Samsung Group managers shifted the company's focus from quantity of sales to quality of products, it required a shift in dominant values.

IN PRACTICE
Samsung Group

Samsung once pursued sales of quantity-driven, low-end products as a primary goal. Managers emphasized stability, productivity, and efficiency. That all changed when Samsung Group chairman Kun-hee Lee visited a Los Angeles retailer in the early 1990s and found boxes of Samsung products gathering dust on back shelves while customers admired the cutting edge products from other manufacturers.

Lee returned to Korea, ordered $50 million worth of inventory destroyed, and declared that quality and innovation would be the new guiding principles. The new approach, which emphasizes employee empowerment and training, creativity, flexibility, and innovative response to the external environment, has been highly successful. By 2006, the consulting firm Interbrand ranked Samsung as the world's most valuable electronics brand. By 2013, Samsung smartphones were challenging Apple for style and innovativeness.

When Samsung flipped its focus from quantity to quality, it needed a new emphasis on people. "People Come First" and "A Company Is Its People" are mottos that guide the company, and talent management is emphasized to prepare a pool of next-generation leaders. New digital learning facilities and networking spaces have been created to foster creativity and innovation.[86]

The effectiveness values that guided Samsung in the past reflected a primarily internal process and rational goal emphasis. Managers valued stability, productivity, efficiency, and steady profits. However chairman Kun-hee Lee saw that profitability would not continue for long unless things changed. He shifted the organization to effectiveness values that reflect a primarily human resource and open systems emphasis. Remember, all organizations are a mix of competing ideas, goals, and values. Goal emphasis and values change over time to meet new needs.

Design Essentials

■ Organizations exist for a purpose. Top managers decide the organization's strategic intent, including a specific mission to be accomplished. The mission statement, or official goals, makes explicit the purpose and direction of an organization. Operating goals designate specific ends sought through actual operating procedures. Official and operating goals are a key element in organizations because they meet these needs—establishing legitimacy with external groups, providing employees with a sense of direction and motivation, and setting standards of performance.

■ Goal conflict is inevitable in organizations and managers sometimes have to negotiate to reach agreement about the important goals to pursue. The hybrid organization means an organization that mixes value systems and behaviors that represent two different sectors of society, which leads to tensions and conflict within the organization over goals and priorities.

■ Two other aspects related to strategic intent are competitive advantage and core competence. Competitive advantage refers to what sets the organization apart from others and provides it with a distinctive edge. A core competence is something the organization does extremely well compared to competitors. Managers look for competitive openings and develop strategies based on their core competencies.

■ Strategies may include any number of techniques to achieve the stated goals. Two models for formulating strategies are Porter's competitive strategies and Miles and Snow's strategy typology. Organization design needs to fit the firm's competitive approach to contribute to organizational effectiveness.

■ Assessing organizational effectiveness reflects the complexity of organizations as a topic of study. Effectiveness is a social construct, meaning that effectiveness criteria are created and decided upon by people. Different people will have different criteria for what makes the organization "effective." Managers have to decide how they will define and measure organizational effectiveness.

■ No easy, simple, guaranteed measure will provide an unequivocal assessment of effectiveness. Organizations must perform diverse activities well—from obtaining resource inputs to delivering outputs—to be successful. Four approaches to measuring effectiveness are the goal approach, resource-based approach, internal process approach, and strategic constituents approach. Effectiveness is multidimensional, so managers typically use indicators from more than one approach and they use qualitative as well as quantitative measures.

■ No approach is suitable for every organization, but each offers some advantages that the others may lack. In addition, the competing values model balances a concern with various parts of the organization rather than focusing on one part. This approach acknowledges different areas of focus (internal, external) and structure (flexibility, stability) and allows managers to choose the values to emphasize.

⟩⟩ KEY CONCEPTS

analyzer	hybrid organization	prospector
competing values model	internal process approach	rational goal emphasis
competitive advantage	internal process emphasis	reactor
core competence	low-cost leadership strategy	resource-based approach
defender	mission	social construct
differentiation strategy	official goals	strategic constituents approach
focus	open systems emphasis	strategic intent
goal approach	operating goals	strategy
human relations emphasis	organizational goal	structure

⟩⟩ DISCUSSION QUESTIONS

1. Discuss the role of top management in setting organizational direction.
2. How might a company's goals for employee development be related to its goals for innovation and change? To goals for productivity? Can you discuss ways these types of goals might conflict in an organization?
3. What is a goal for the class for which you are reading this text? Who established this goal? Discuss how the goal affects your direction and motivation.
4. What is the difference between a goal and a strategy as defined in the text? Identify both a goal and a strategy for a campus or community organization with which you are involved.
5. Discuss the similarities and differences in the strategies described in Porter's competitive strategies and Miles and Snow's typology.

6. Do you believe mission statements and official goal statements provide an organization with genuine legitimacy in the external environment? When a company such as CVS (discussed in the chapter) makes a decision to stop selling cigarettes because that action conflicts with its mission statement, what do you see as the impact on public opinion? On future business? Discuss.
7. Suppose you have been asked to evaluate the effectiveness of the police department in a medium-sized community. Where would you begin, and how would you proceed? What effectiveness approach would you prefer?
8. What are the advantages and disadvantages of the resource-based approach versus the goal approach for measuring organizational effectiveness?

9. What are the similarities and differences between assessing effectiveness on the basis of competing values versus the strategic constituents approach? Explain.

10. A noted organization theorist once said, "Organizational effectiveness can be whatever top management defines it to be." Discuss.

>> CHAPTER 2 WORKSHOP Identify Your Goal Preferences

Assume that you could design the perfect organization that reflected your values. What goals would receive priority in that organization?

Rank order the list of goals below from 1 to 10 to reflect the goals you consider most important to least important in your perfect organization.

Goal	Rank Order from 1 to 10
Employee Development	
Organization Stability	
Market Share Leader	
Creativity-Innovation	
Social Contribution	
High Morale/Satisfaction	
High Productivity	
Rapid Growth/Adaptability	
Profit Maximization	
Within the Law/Ethical	

Questions:

1. Look at the integrated effectiveness model in Exhibit 2.11 and Exhibit 2.12. Allocate each goal above to the quadrant you think it fits. Which quadrant of the model reflects your highest goal values? Which quadrant ranks lowest?

2. Compare your ranking to other students and look for common themes. In what ways are your rankings different?

3. What organizational goals are important to you that are not on the list above? Where would you rank the missing goals?

CASE FOR ANALYSIS | The Venable Museum of Art

Locals referred to it—affectionately or sarcastically—as the "venerable Venable." Housed in the massive Romanesque-style former mansion of Horace and Margaret Venable, the 100-year-old Venable Museum of Art had, by 2010, reached a tipping point of institutional and financial distress. Considered a point of civic and cultural pride, the home and its extensive collection of art had been the generous gift to the city's residents under terms of the legal wills of the childless industrial tycoon and his wife following their deaths in a 1910 motor-car accident.

The museum was established and controlled, as dictated in the will, by a Board of Directors comprised of old-moneyed families, friends of the Venables, whose seats on the board historically passed from one generation to the next. In accordance with Horace and Margaret's desires to make their collections "accessible to all," the museum was, for several decades, free to the public. In its opening

days and weeks, the rarefied opportunity for locals to "see inside the mansion," as much as to see the art, lured scores of visitors who endured long lines to enter the city's most palatial residence. Once the newness had worn off, however, the museum settled into a reputation as the cultural domain of the "la-DE-dah art elite."

Over the decades, the cost of conserving the collection, and the mounting expenses of up-keep for the mansion and the gardens and grounds, spurred the Board to create an annual fund-raising gala that allowed society to admire the art and each other. Later, the necessity of admission fees to the museum added modestly to the overall financial situation, but visitor numbers remained stagnant and the majority of locals never ventured inside. *I always felt like, if I didn't drive up in a Mercedes, the staff didn't care whether or not I came. They were cold to the point of rudeness*, explained one long-time city resident.

Problems at the museum became public knowledge. Hirings and firings occurred at the whim of the Board, and on one occasion, the entire staff was fired without warning. The approaching 2010 centennial was marred by controversy and lawsuits over whether to sell a large portion of the collection in order to keep the museum afloat.

The media and legal commotion over *losing* a collection that a majority of the city's residents had never seen sparked a generous outpouring of private financial support. During the campaign to *Save the Venerable Venable*, the Board, in an effort to impress potential donors, actively sought, and received, the support of an adjacent private university with promises to build a collaborative partnership.

By 2013, with improved financial means to move the museum into a second century, the venerable Board, composed of member names stretching five generations, faced an organizational culture shock and a new and emboldened set of stakeholders. Under pressure to define the future direction of the museum and in preparation for selecting a new director, the Board hired two business students to conduct person-to-person interviews of stakeholders about the future vision and goals for the museum and the relationship of the university to the museum.

Excerpts from some of the more powerful comments by interviewees are listed below:

A major new private donor: *The museum has a reputation as an elitist, unfriendly institution, contrary to the intent of Horace and Margaret Venable. My wife and I gave money with the expectation that the museum would, at last, embrace the vision of its benefactors of bringing the art to everyone. In order to accomplish this, the museum must have an educational component and promote visits from public schools in the area, and particularly serve the inner-city children who don't have access to art and who live within a mile of the museum. The snobbish, elitist atmosphere that extends from the Board through the ranks of the museum staff must be changed.*

A board member: *I've heard rumors that some people want to open this museum to scores of public school tours and after-school programs. I realize that school children need access to art and I sympathize with that need. But this is not a typical museum structure, it's a house that was constructed almost 120 years ago and has a variety of delicate surfaces and structural refinements that must be preserved and treasured for future generations. The upkeep of this building is tremendous with our current level of visitation. When you add several thousand school kids each year, the traffic through the building, the noise level within the building, compromises the structure and takes away from the experience of viewing great art. I can see creating*

educational programs that go out to the schools, but not bringing huge school groups here; and certainly not serving as some sort of after-school day care. No. I cannot see that.

A university administrator: *The important thing is to add lively contemporary exhibits that will attract both university students and community adults and provide new insight and dialogue about current events. We can bring attention to the museum and spur dialogue by having an occasional controversial exhibit, such as Islamic art, and exhibits that appeal to Hispanics and African-Americans. This approach would entail bringing in traveling exhibitions from major museums and loaning out portions of the Venable collection in exchange.*

Head of the art history department: *The key thing is that the museum will not have the artistic resources or the financial resources to serve the community at large. We have a wonderful opportunity to integrate the museum with the academic faculty and make it a teaching institution. It can be a major resource for both undergraduate and graduate students in art education and in art history. Using the collections inside and the structure itself as a classroom, we can also work with engineering students, architecture students, and students in the liberal arts. This is a unique opportunity that will distinguish our art history department's mission from others in the country.*

A faculty member of the art history department: *The best use of the museum's relationship with the University is to concentrate on training PhD level students in art history and to support scholarly research. I strongly urge the museum to focus on graduate education, which would increase the stature of the University nationally. Graduate students would be involved in the design of exhibits that would fit their research. Trying to make the museum popular on campus or in the community will waste our limited resources. Our PhD students will be sought after by art history departments throughout the country, adding also to the prestige of the Venable Museum of Art.*

Head of the university's new department of public history: *It is imperative, upon selection of the new museum director, that the Board relinquish some of its power in the rethinking of the current collection and the selection and design of future exhibits to trained museum professionals—not art history experts. The professional expertise of the director and the staff; their knowledge of best practices in the field; their cognizance of trends and innovations in the museum field, will ultimately determine the success or failure of this museum.*

You have been invited to interview for the position of museum director and must now consider how you would answer questions that might arise during the interview process and how you would move the museum forward if you took the job.

CASE FOR ANALYSIS | Covington Corrugated Parts & Services[87]

Larisa Harrison grimaced as she tossed her company's latest quarterly earnings onto the desk. When sales at Virginia-based Covington Corrugated Parts & Services surged past the $10 million mark some time back, Larisa was certain the company was well positioned for steady growth. Today Covington, which provides precision machine parts and service to the domestic corrugated box and paperboard industry, still enjoys a dominant market share, but sales and profits are showing clear signs of stagnation.

More than two decades ago, Larisa's grandfather loaned her the money to start the business and then handed over the barn on what had been the family's Shenandoah Valley farm to serve as her first factory. He had been a progressive thinker compared to many of his contemporaries who scoffed at the idea of a woman running a machine parts plant, and he saw no reason why a smart, ambitious 27-year-old woman couldn't run anything she wanted to. His old-fashioned friends no longer scoffed when Larisa became one of the major employers in the local area. Today, Covington operates from a 50,000 square-foot factory located near I-81 just a few miles from that old family barn. The business allowed Larisa to realize what had once seemed an almost impossible goal: She was making a good living without having to leave her close-knit extended family and rural roots. She also felt a sense of satisfaction at employing about 150 people, many of them neighbors. They were among the most hard-working, loyal workers you'd find anywhere. However, many of her original employees were now nearing retirement. Replacing those skilled workers was going to be difficult, she realized from experience. The area's brightest and best young people were much more likely to move away in search of employment than their parents had been. Those who remained behind just didn't seem to have the work ethic Larisa had come to expect in her employees.

Other problems were looming as well. Covington's market share, once at a formidable 70 percent, was slipping fast, brought about not only by the emergence of new direct competitors but also by changes in the industry. The box and paperboard industry had never been particularly recession resistant, with demand fluctuating with manufacturing output. The rocky economy had hurt the whole industry, including Covington's largest customers. Added to that, alternative shipping products, such as flexible plastic films and reusable plastic containers, were becoming more prevalent. It remained to be seen how much of a dent they'd make in the demand for boxes and paperboard. Even more worrying, consolidation in the industry had wiped out hundreds of the smaller U.S. plants that Covington once served, with many of the survivors either opening overseas facilities or entering into joint ventures abroad. The surviving manufacturers were investing in higher quality machines from Germany that broke down less frequently, thus requiring fewer of Covington's parts.

Covington was clearly at a crossroads, and its managers were arguing about which direction the company should take. If Covington wanted to grow, business as usual wasn't going to work. But no one could seem to agree on the best way to achieve growth. The marketing manager was pushing for moving into new products and services, perhaps even serving other industries, while the director of finance believed the plant needed to become more efficient, even lay off employees, and offer customers the lowest cost. Larisa cringed as she heard that statement because her focus was always on what was best for her employees. The finance director added that efficiency and profitability should be the key criteria by which Covington measured its performance, whereas the marketing manager vehemently argued that the company would be effective only if it focused on new customers and customer satisfaction in the changing industry environment, which would mean taking some financial risks. "I know 'corrugated' is in our name," he said, "but we've already moved beyond that to servicing other types of paperboard-making equipment. Why not become the all-around provider, serving any manufacturer that makes containers and packing materials, whether it's paper, plastic, or whatever?" It was truly an ambitious idea, but he was so fired up about it that he had investigated possible acquisitions and partnership opportunities. The finance director was livid. "If anyone is looking into mergers and acquisitions, it should be me, not the marketing manager," she had shouted at the most recent managers' meeting. Meanwhile, the vice president of manufacturing presented a plan for expanding market share by exporting parts globally, which set both the marketing manager and the finance director off. "Why haven't we even heard about this before now?" the marketing manager asked. "I'm not saying I disagree with it, but communication in this place is atrocious. I never even got a copy of the last finance report." The director of finance quickly shot back with a charge that the marketing manager didn't seem to care about profit and loss anyway so why should he need a copy of the report.

As Larisa considered the chaos into which the most recent meeting had degenerated, she thought back to her days in graduate school and realized that organization design was part of the problem. Covington had succeeded for two decades with a loose, even haphazard structure, because everyone seemed focused on building the business. People simply did what needed to be done. However, the company had never been under threat before. "Perhaps we just aren't as well organized as we need to be to handle the challenges Covington is facing," she thought. As she watched the last shift workers walk to their cars, Larisa pulled out a report that a consultant friend had developed for her a few months ago. The report emphasized:

- Covington rated very high on employee morale.
- Covington was rated low on innovation and change.
- The Covington culture emphasized production efficiency.

- The Covington culture was not intensely focused on developing new customers.
- Each department did its job well, but collaboration across departments was rated low to medium.
- Price competition would probably intensify as the customer base grew smaller.
- The industry would continue to change toward fewer paperboard machines and toward higher quality imported machines.

Larisa scribbled a few notes on a pad:
How should we decide what strategy to pursue?
Who should have authority and responsibility for what?
How do we improve communications?
What criteria should we use to measure performance and ensure accountability?

Larisa knew that as soon as she or her team could determine some answers, she would sleep at least a little better.

NOTES

1. Evelyn M. Rusli, "Instagram Pictures Itself Making Money," *The Wall Street Journal Online*, September 8, 2013, http://online.wsj.com/news/articles/SB100014241278873245773045790592300069305894 (accessed February 17, 2014).

2. Christopher Weaver and Louise Radnofsky, "Federal Health Site Stymied by Lack of Direction," *The Wall Street Journal Online*, October 28, 2013, http://online.wsj.com/news/articles/SB100014240527023046825045791580435377193338 (accessed February 18, 2014).

3. Amitai Etzioni, *Modern Organizations* (Englewood Cliffs, NJ: Prentice Hall, 1964), 6.

4. John P. Kotter, "What Effective General Managers Really Do," *Harvard Business Review*, November–December 1982, 156–167; Henry Mintzberg, *The Nature of Managerial Work* (New York: Harper & Row, 1973); and Henry Mintzberg, *Managing* (San Francisco: Berrett-Kohler Publishers, 2009).

5. Charles C. Snow and Lawrence G. Hrebiniak, "Strategy, Distinctive Competence, and Organizational Performance," *Administrative Science Quarterly* 25 (1980), 317–335; and Robert J. Allio, "Strategic Thinking: The Ten Big Ideas," *Strategy & Leadership* 34, no. 4 (2006), 4–13.

6. Based on A. G. Lafley and Roger Martin, "Instituting a Company-Wide Strategic Conversation at Procter & Gamble," *Strategy & Leadership* 41, no. 4 (2013), 4–9.

7. Miguel Bustillo, "Corporate News—Boss Talk: Wal-Mart's U.S. Chief Aims for Turnaround," *The Asian Wall Street Journal*, March 22, 2011, 22; and Miguel Bustillo, "Wal-Mart Tries to Recapture Mr. Sam's Winning Formula," *The Wall Street Journal Online*, February 22, 2011, http://online.wsj.com/article/SB1000142405274870380390457615275311178930.html (accessed July 17, 2012).

8. Gary Hamel and C. K. Prahalad, "Strategic Intent," *Harvard Business Review* July–August 2005, 148–161.

9. Ibid.

10. Barbara Bartkus, Myron Glassman, and R. Bruce McAfee, "Mission Statements: Are They Smoke and Mirrors?" *Business Horizons*, November–December 2000, 23–28; and Mark Suchman, "Managing Legitimacy: Strategic and Institutional Approaches," *Academy of Management Review* 20, no. 3 (1995), 571–610.

11. CVS Health, "Our New Name," http://www.cvshealth.com/research-insights/health-topics/our-new-name (accessed December 12, 2014).

12. Bill George, "The Company's Mission Is the Message," *Strategy + Business*, Issue 33 (Winter 2003), 13–14; and Jim Collins and Jerry Porras, *Built to Last: Successful Habits of Visionary Companies* (New York: Harper Business, 1994).

13. Hamel and Prahalad, "Strategic Intent."

14. Arthur A. Thompson, Jr. and A. J. Srickland III, *Strategic Management: Concepts and Cases*, 6th ed. (Homewood, IL: Irwin, 1992); and Briance Mascarenhas, Alok Baveja, and Mamnoon Jamil, "Dynamics of Core Competencies in Leading Multinational Companies," *California Management Review* 40, no. 4 (Summer 1998), 117–132.

15. Issie Lapowsky, "Logistics; No Time to Spare; Tackling Last-Minute Jobs," *Inc.*, July–August 2011, 106, 108.

16. Brad Stone, "What's in the Box? Instant Gratification," *Bloomberg Businessweek*, November 29–December 5, 2010, 39–40; Stephanie Clifford, "Same-Day Delivery Test at Wal-Mart," *The New York Times*, October 10, 2012, B1; and S. Levy, "CEO of the Internet: Jeff Bezos Owns the Web in More Ways than You Think," *Wired*, December 2011, www.wired.com/magazine/2011/11/ff_bezos/ (accessed July 24, 2012).

17. Charles Perrow, "The Analysis of Goals in Complex Organizations," *American Sociological Review* 26 (1961), 854–866.

18. Johannes U. Stoelwinde and Martin P. Charns, "The Task Field Model of Organization Analysis and Design," *Human Relations* 34 (1981), 743–762; and Anthony Raia, *Managing by Objectives* (Glenview, IL: Scott Foresman, 1974).

19. Henrich Greve, "UPS's Christmas Failure Delivers a Powerful Lesson About Alliances," *Strategy + Business Blog*, January 16, 2014, http://www.strategy-business.com/blog/UPSs-Christmas-Failure-Delivers-a-Powerful-Lesson-about-Alliances?gko=e33d3 (accessed February 19, 2014).

20. Paul Beckett, Vibhuti Agarwal, and Julie Jargon, "Starbucks Brews Plan to Enter India," *The Wall Street Journal Online*, January 14, 2011, http://online.wsj.com/article/SB100014240527487035834045760795933558838756.html (accessed July 16, 2011).

21. James Dao, "Wal-Mart Plans to Hire Any Veteran Who Wants a Job," *The New York Times*, January 14, 2013, http://www.nytimes.com/2013/01/15/us/wal-mart-to-announce-extensive-plan-to-hire-veterans.html?_r=0 (accessed February 19, 2014).

22. Christina Passariello, "To L'Oreal, Brazil's Women Need Fresh Style of Shopping," *The Wall Street Journal*, January 21, 2011, B1.

23. Reed Abelson, "Managing Outcomes Helps a Children's Hospital Climb in Renown," *The New York Times*, September 15, 2007, C1.

24. Robert L. Porter and Gary P. Latham, "The Effect of Employee Learning Goals and Goal Commitment on Departmental Performance," *Journal of Leadership & Organizational Studies* 20, no. 1 (2013), 62–68.

25. William Alden and Sydney Ember, "Wall St. Shock: Take a Day Off, Even a Sunday," *The New York Times*, January 11, 2014, A1.

26. Brooks Barnes, "Animation Meets Economic Reality," *The New York Times*, April 4, 2011, B1.

27. A. G. Lafley and Ram Charan, *The Game Changer: How You Can Drive Revenue and Profit Growth with Innovation* (New York: Crown Business, 2008); Larry Huston and Nabil Sakkab, "Connect and Develop; Inside Procter & Gamble's New Model for Innovation," *Harvard Business Review*, March 2006, 58–66; G. Gil Cloyd, "P&G's Secret: Innovating Innovation," *Industry Week*, December 2004, 26–34; and "P&G Sets Two New Goals for Open Innovation Partnerships," Press Release (October 28, 2010), Procter & Gamble website, http://www.pginvestor.com/phoenix.zhtml?c=104574&p=irol-newsArticle&ID=1488508 (accessed July 15, 2011).

28. Amy Chozick, Nathaniel Popper, Edward Wong, and David Carr, "At Bloomberg, Signs of Change in News Mission," *The New York Times*, November 25, 2013, A1.

29. This discussion is based on Anne-Claire Pache and Filipe Santos, "Inside the Hybrid Organization: Selective Coupling as a Response to Competing Institutional Logics," *Academy of Management Journal* 56, no. 4 (2013), 972–1011.

30. Stephen Friedman and James K. Sebenius, "Organization Transformation: The Quiet Role of Coalitional Leadership," *Ivey Business Journal*, January–February 2009, www.iveybusinessjournal.com/topics/leadership/organizational-transformation-the-quiet-role-of-coalitional-leadership (accessed January 27, 2012); and Gerald R. Ferris et al., "Political Skill in Organizations," *Journal of Management*, June 2007, 290–320.

31. See studies reported in Gary P. Latham and Edwin A. Locke, "Enhancing the Benefits and Overcoming the Pitfalls of Goal Setting," *Organizational Dynamics* 35, no. 4 (2006), 332–340.

32. Porter and Latham, "The Effect of Employee Learning Goals and Goal Commitment on Departmental Performance."

33. Adam Bryant, "Tell Me the Problem and 3 Ways to Solve It" (an interview with Jennifer Dulski, Corner Office column), *The New York Times*, December 1, 2013, BU2.

34. James D. Thompson, *Organizations in Action* (New York: McGraw Hill, 1967), 83–98.

35. Michael E. Porter, "What Is Strategy?" *Harvard Business Review*, November–December 1996, 61–78.

36. This discussion is based on Michael E. Porter, *Competitive Strategy: Techniques for Analyzing Industries and Competitors* (New York: Free Press, 1980).

37. Scott Sloan, "Lexington's Trader Joe's Opens Friday," *Kentucky.com*, June 28, 2012, http://www.kentucky.com/2012/06/28/2241801/lexingtons-trader-joes-opens-friday.html (accessed July 17, 2012); Mark Mallinger, "The Trader Joe's Experience: The Impact of Corporate Culture on Business Strategy," *Graziadio Business Review*, Graziadio School of Business and Management, Pepperdine University, 10, no. 2 (2007), http://www.gbr.pepperdine.edu/2010/08/the-trader-joes-experienc/ (accessed July 17, 2012); Shan Li, "Can Trader Joe's Stay 'Homey' as It Grows?"; and Beth Kowitt, "Inside Trader Joe's," *Fortune* (September 6, 2010), 86ff.

38. Alan Ruddock, "Keeping Up with O'Leary," *Management Today*, September 2003, 48–55; and Jane Engle, "Flying High for Pocket Change; Regional Carriers Offer Inexpensive Travel Alternative," *South Florida Sun Sentinel*, February 13, 2005, 5.

39. Michael E. Porter, "Strategy and the Internet," *Harvard Business Review*, March 2001, 63–78; and John Magretta, "Why Business Models Matter," *Harvard Business Review*, May 2002, 86.

40. Jack Nicas, "Allegiant Air: The Tardy, Gas-Guzzling, Most Profitable Airline in America," *The Wall Street Journal*, June 4, 2013, http://online.wsj.com/article/SB10001424127887324423904578525310460541592.html (accessed September 16, 2013).

41. Richard Teitelbaum, "The Wal-Mart of Wall Street," *Fortune*, October 13, 1997, 128–130.

42. Raymond E. Miles and Charles C. Snow, *Organizational Strategy, Structure, and Process* (New York: McGraw-Hill, 1978).

43. Nicholas Casey, "New Nike Sneaker Targets Jocks, Greens, Wall Street," *The Wall Street Journal*, February 15, 2008, B1.

44. Norihiko Shirouzu, "Chinese Begin Volvo Overhaul," *The Wall Street Journal*, June 7, 2011, B1.

45. Geraldine Fabrikant, "The Paramount Team Puts Profit Over Splash," *The New York Times*, June 30, 2002, Section 3, 1, 15.

46. Greg Bensinger, "Amazon Revenue, Spending Grow Apace," *The Wall Street Journal*, April 26, 2013, B4; and Mylene Mangalindan, "Slow Slog for Amazon's Digital Media—Earnings Today May Provide Data on What Works," *The Wall Street Journal*, April 23, 2008, B1.

47. Susan Berfield, "The End: Barnes & Noble in Silicon Valley," *Bloomberg Businessweek*, July 25, 2013, http://www.businessweek.com/articles/2013-07-25/the-end-barnes-and-noble-in-silicon-valley (accessed February 20, 2014).

48. "On the Staying Power of Defenders, Analyzers, and Prospectors: Academic Commentary by Donald C. Hambrick," *Academy of Management Executive* 17, no. 4 (2003), 115–118.

49. Etzioni, *Modern Organizations*, 8; and Gary D. Sandefur, "Efficiency in Social Service Organizations," *Administration and Society* 14 (1983), 449–468.

50. Richard M. Steers, *Organizational Effectiveness: A Behavioral View* (Santa Monica, CA: Goodyear, 1977), 51.

51. Michael Hammer, "The 7 Deadly Sins of Performance Measurement (and How to Avoid Them)," *MIT Sloan Management Review* 48, no. 3 (Spring 2007), 19–28.

52. Karl E. Weick and Richard L. Daft, "The Effectiveness of Interpretation Systems," in Kim S. Cameron and David A. Whetten, eds., *Organizational Effectiveness: A Comparison of Multiple Models* (New York: Academic Press, 1982).

53. This discussion is based on Robert D. Herman and David O. Renz, "Advancing Nonprofit Organizational Effectiveness Research and Theory," *Nonprofit Management and Leadership* 18, no. 4 (Summer 2008), 399–415; Eric J. Walton and Sarah Dawson, "Managers' Perceptions of Criteria of Organizational Effectiveness," *Journal of Management Studies* 38, no. 2 (March 2001), 173–199; and K. S. Cameron and D. A. Whetton, "Organizational Effectiveness: One Model or Several?" in *Organizational Effectiveness: A Comparison of Multiple Models*, K. S. Cameron and D. A. Whetton, eds., (New York: Academic Press, 1983), 1–24.

54. Story told in Herman and Renz, "Advancing Nonprofit Organizational Effectiveness Research and Theory."

55. Graham Kenny, "From the Stakeholder Viewpoint: Designing Measurable Objectives," *Journal of Business Strategy* 33, no. 6 (2012), 40–46.

56. Most of these indicators are from Cristina B. Gibson, Mary E. Zellmer-Bruhn, and Donald P. Schwab, "Team Effectiveness in Multinational Organizations: Evaluation Across Contexts," *Group & Organizational Management* 28, no. 4 (December 2003), 444–474.

57. Herman and Renz, "Advancing Nonprofit Organizational Effectiveness Research and Theory"; Y. Baruch and N. Ramalho, "Communalities and Distinctions in the Measurement of Organizational Performance and Effectiveness Across For-Profit and Nonprofit Sectors," *Nonprofit and Voluntary Sector Quarterly* 35, no. 1 (2006), 39–65; A. M. Parhizgari and G. Ronald Gilbert, "Measures of Organizational Effectiveness: Private and Public Sector Performance," *Omega; The International Journal of Management Science* 32 (2004), 221–229; David L. Blenkhorn and Brian Gaber, "The Use of 'Warm Fuzzies' to Assess Organizational

Effectiveness," *Journal of General Management,* 21, no. 2 (Winter 1995), 40–51; and Scott Leibs, "Measuring Up," *CFO* (June 2007), 63–66.

58. Reported in David H. Freedman, "What's Next: The Dashboard Dilemma," *Inc.,* November 1, 2006, http://www.inc.com/magazine/20061101/column-freedman.html (accessed July 14, 2011).

59. Kim S. Cameron, "A Study of Organizational Effectiveness and Its Predictors," *Management Science* 32 (1986), 87–112; and Joseph R. Matthews, "Assessing Organizational Effectiveness: The Role of Performance Measures," *The Library Quarterly* 81, no. 1 (2011), 83–110.

60. James L. Price, "The Study of Organizational Effectiveness," *Sociological Quarterly* 13 (1972), 3–15; and Steven Strasser, J. D. Eveland, Gaylord Cummins, O. Lynn Deniston, and John H. Romani, "Conceptualizing the Goal and Systems Models of Organizational Effectiveness—Implications for Comparative Evaluation Research," *Journal of Management Studies* 18 (1981), 321–340.

61. Richard H. Hall and John P. Clark, "An Ineffective Effectiveness Study and Some Suggestions for Future Research," *Sociological Quarterly* 21 (1980), 119–134; Price, "The Study of Organizational Effectiveness"; and Perrow, "The Analysis of Goals in Complex Organizations."

62. Gautam Naik, "Poverty: The New Search for Solutions; Baby Steps: Cincinnati Applies a Corporate Model to Saving Infants," (Third in a Series), *The Wall Street Journal,* June 20, 2006, A1.

63. David J. Collis and Cynthia A. Montgomery, "Competing on Resources," *Harvard Business Review,* July–August 2008, 140–150.

64. The discussion of the resource-based approach is based in part on Michael V. Russo and Paul A. Fouts, "A Resource-Based Perspective on Corporate Environmental Performance and Profitability," *Academy of Management Journal* 40, no. 3 (June 1997), 534–559; and Jay B. Barney, J. L. "Larry" Stempert, Loren T. Gustafson, and Yolanda Sarason, "Organizational Identity within the Strategic Management Conversation: Contributions and Assumptions," in David A. Whetten and Paul C. Godfrey, eds., *Identity in Organizations: Building Theory through Conversations* (Thousand Oaks, CA: Sage Publications, 1998), 83–98.

65. These are based on David J. Collis and Cynthia A. Montgomery, "Competing on Resources," *Harvard Business Review,* July–August 2008, 140–150; J. Barton Cunningham, "A Systems-Resource Approach for Evaluating Organizational Effectiveness," *Human Relations* 31 (1978), 631–656; and Ephraim Yuchtman and Stanley E. Seashore, "A System Resource Approach to Organizational Effectiveness," *Administrative Science Quarterly* 12 (1967), 377–395.

66. Roger Noble, "How Shriners Hospitals for Children Found the Formula for Performance Excellence," *Global Business and Organizational Excellence,* July–August 2009, 7–15.

67. Based on Collis and Montgomery, "Competing on Resources."

68. Richard I. Priem, "Is the Resource-Based 'View' a Useful Perspective for Strategic Management Research?" *Academy of Management Review* 26, no. 1 (2001), 22–40.

69. Chris Argyris, *Integrating the Individual and the Organization* (New York: Wiley, 1964); Warren G. Bennis, *Changing Organizations* (New York: McGraw-Hill, 1966); Rensis Likert, *The Human Organization* (New York: McGraw-Hill, 1967); and Richard Beckhard, *Organization Development Strategies and Models* (Reading, MA: Addison-Wesley, 1969).

70. Cheri Ostroff and Neal Schmitt, "Configurations of Organizational Effectiveness and Efficiency," *Academy of Management Journal* 36 (1993), 1345–1361.

71. J. Barton Cunningham, "Approaches to the Evaluation of Organizational Effectiveness," *Academy of Management Review* 2 (1977), 463–474; and Beckhard, *Organization Development.*

72. Craig Torres and Anthony Feld, "Campbell's Quest for Productivity," *Businessweek,* November 24, 2010, 15–16.

73. Jeanne Michalski, "BNSF's Leadership Engine," *Organizational Dynamics* 42 (2013), 35–45.

74. Anne S. Tusi, "A Multiple Constituency Model of Effectiveness: An Empirical Examination at the Human Resource Subunit Level," *Administrative Science Quarterly* 35 (1990), 458–483; Charles Fombrun and Mark Shanley, "What's In a Name? Reputation Building and Corporate Strategy," *Academy of Management Journal* 33 (1990), 233–258; and Terry Connolly, Edward J. Conlon, and Stuart Jay Deutsch, "Organizational Effectiveness: A Multiple Constituency Approach," *Academy of Management Review* 5 (1980), 211–217.

75. Frank Friedlander and Hal Pickle, "Components of Effectiveness in Small Organizations," *Administrative Science Quarterly* 13 (1968), 289–304.

76. Jessica E. Vascellaro, "Facebook Taps Consumer Card—Social Networking Site Wants to Know More than Just Who Your Friends Are," *The Wall Street Journal,* April 22, 2010, B2.

77. Tusi, "A Multiple Constituency Model of Effectiveness."

78. Fombrun and Shanley, "What's In a Name?"

79. Kim S. Cameron, "The Effectiveness of Ineffectiveness," in Barry M. Staw and L. L. Cummings, eds., *Research in Organizational Behavior* (Greenwich, CT: JAI Press, 1984), 235–286; and Rosabeth Moss Kanter and Derick Brinkerhoff, "Organizational Performance: Recent Developments in Measurement," *Annual Review of Sociology* 7 (1981), 321–349.

80. Eric J. Walton and Sarah Dawson, "Managers' Perceptions of Criteria of Organizational Effectiveness," *Journal of Management Studies* 38, no. 2 (2001), 173–199.

81. Beth Dickey, "NASA's Next Step," *Government Executive,* April 15, 2004, http://www.govexec.com/features/ 0404 -15/0404-15s1.htm 34 (accessed July 19, 2011).

82. Neil King Jr. and Russell Gold, "BP Crew Focused on Costs: Congress," *The Wall Street Journal Online,* June 15, 2010, http://online.wsj.com/article/SB10001424052748704324304 575306800201158346.html (accessed July 19, 2011).

83. Robert E. Quinn and John Rohrbaugh, "A Spatial Model of Effectiveness Criteria: Towards a Competing Values Approach to Organizational Analysis," *Management Science* 29, no. 3 (1983), 363–377; and Walton and Dawson, "Managers' Perceptions of Criteria of Organizational Effectiveness."

84. Regina M. O'Neill and Robert E. Quinn, "Editor's Note: Applications of the Competing Values Framework," *Human Resource Management* 32 (Spring 1993), 1–7.

85. Robert E. Quinn and Kim Cameron, "Organizational Life Cycles and Shifting Criteria of Effectiveness: Some Preliminary Evidence," *Management Science* 29 (1983), 33–51.

86. Dongwook Chung, "A Management 180," *T + D,* July 2013, 56–59.

87. Based on Ron Stodghill, "Boxed Out," *FSB,* April 2005, 69–72; "SIC 2653 Corrugated and Solid Fiber Boxes," *Reference for Business, Encyclopedia of Business,* 2nd ed., http://www.referenceforbusiness.com/industries/Paper-Allied /Corrugated-Solid-Fiber-Boxes.html (accessed November 11, 2011); "Paper and Allied Products," *U.S. Trade and Industry Outlook 2000,* 10–12 to 10–15; "Smurfit-Stone Container: Market Summary," *Business Week Online,* May 4, 2006; and Bernard A. Deitzer and Karl A. Shilliff, "Incident 15," *Contemporary Management Incidents* (Columbus, OH: Grid, Inc., 1977), 43–46.

3 | Fundamentals of Organization Structure

Learning Objectives

After reading this chapter you should be able to:

1. Define the three key components of organization structure.
2. Explain the vertical and horizontal information-sharing concepts of structure.
3. Understand the role of task forces and teams in organization structure.
4. Identify departmental grouping options, such as functional, divisional, and matrix.
5. Understand the strengths and weaknesses of various structural forms.
6. Explain new horizontal and virtual network structural forms.
7. Describe the symptoms of structural deficiency within an organization.

Before reading this chapter, please check whether you agree or disagree with each of the following statements:

1 A popular form of organizing is to have employees work on what they want in whatever department they choose so that motivation and enthusiasm stay high.

I AGREE _____   I DISAGREE _____

2 Committees and task forces whose members are from different departments are often worthless for getting things done.

I AGREE _____   I DISAGREE _____

3 Top managers are smart to maintain organizational control over the activities of key work units rather than contracting out some work unit tasks to other firms.

I AGREE _____   I DISAGREE _____

Carlos Ghosn brought Nissan back from the brink of bankruptcy in the late 1990s, but his skills at restructuring were put to the test once again when Japan's Number 2 automaker began showing surprisingly weak profit and declining market share in 2013. Top executives pinpointed the cause. It wasn't in the design studio or on the factory floor, they say, or even in the planning office. The problem was the organization structure, with one chief operating officer overseeing a rapidly expanding number of opportunities and investments around the globe. In the new structure, three executive vice presidents will oversee planning and execution. They will work closely together from the beginning, which will enable them to spot problems quickly, balance resources, and coordinate investments among regions. The primary goal of the new structure is to improve coordination so that problems can be solved quickly. The goals are achievable, Ghosn says, with the right management structure in place so that people are collaborating. "We need a management team that delivers," he said.[1]

Organization structure is one factor that helps companies execute their strategies and achieve their goals. Lack of coordination and collaboration is a tremendous problem for many organizations today, as it was at Nissan. The World Bank, for example, recently conducted a survey of employees that revealed a "terrible" environment for collaboration at the huge economic development institution that works in more than 100 countries.[2] Many companies use structural innovations such as teams and matrix designs to achieve the coordination and flexibility they need. Teams, for example, are part of the strategy used by the Federal Bureau of Investigation (FBI) to combat terrorism. Like other organizations, the FBI must find ways to accomplish more with limited resources. One innovation was the creation of Flying Squads, which are teams of volunteer agents and support staff from various offices who are ready to spring into action when minimally staffed FBI offices around the world request assistance.[3] Jeff Bezos of Amazon organizes around the concept of the "two-pizza team." The company, he said, should be organized into autonomous groups of fewer than 10 people—small enough that, when working late, the team could be fed with two pizzas.[4]

Because of the complexity of today's environment, many organizations are more complex and amorphous than they used to be. Wyeth Pharmaceuticals formed a joint venture with Accenture called the Alliance for Clinical Data Excellence designed to "bring together the best of both Wyeth and Accenture" for managing Wyeth's entire clinical testing operation—from protocol design to patient recruitment to site monitoring.[5] Accenture doesn't have a formal headquarters, no official branches, no permanent offices. The company's chief technologist is located in Germany, its head of human resources is in Chicago, the chief financial officer is in Silicon Valley, and most of its consultants are constantly on the move.[6] Wyeth and Accenture reflect the structural trend among organizations toward outsourcing, alliances, and virtual networking.

Still other firms continue to be successful with traditional functional structures that are coordinated and controlled through the vertical hierarchy. Organizations use a wide variety of structural alternatives to help them achieve their purpose and goals, and nearly every firm needs to undergo reorganization at some point to help meet new challenges. Structural changes are needed to reflect new strategies or respond to changes in other contingency factors introduced in Chapters 1 and 2: environment, technology, size and life cycle, and culture.

Purpose of This Chapter

This chapter introduces basic concepts of organization structure and shows how to design structure as it appears on the organization chart. First, we define structure and provide an overview of structural design. Next, an information-sharing perspective explains how to design vertical and horizontal linkages to provide needed information flow and coordination. The chapter then presents basic design options, followed by strategies for grouping organizational activities into functional, divisional, matrix, horizontal, virtual network, or hybrid structures. The final section examines how the application of basic structures depends on the organization's situation (various contingencies) and outlines the symptoms of structural misalignment.

Organization Structure

The following three key components define **organization structure**:

1. Organization structure designates formal reporting relationships, including the number of levels in the hierarchy and the span of control of managers and supervisors.
2. Organization structure identifies the grouping together of individuals into departments and of departments into the total organization.
3. Organization structure includes the design of systems to ensure effective communication, coordination, and integration of efforts across departments.[7]

These three elements of structure pertain to both vertical and horizontal aspects of organizing. For example, the first two elements are the structural *framework*, which is the vertical hierarchy.[8] The third element pertains to the pattern of *interactions* among organizational employees. An ideal structure encourages employees to provide horizontal information and coordination where and when it is needed.

Organization structure is reflected in the organization chart. It isn't possible to see the internal structure of an organization the way we might see its manufacturing tools, offices, website, or products. Although we might see employees going about their duties, performing different tasks, and working in different locations, the only way to actually see the structure underlying all this activity is through the organization chart. The organization chart is the visual representation of a whole set of underlying activities and processes in an organization. Exhibit 3.1 shows a simple organization chart for a traditional organization. An organization chart can

EXHIBIT 3.1
A Sample Organization Chart

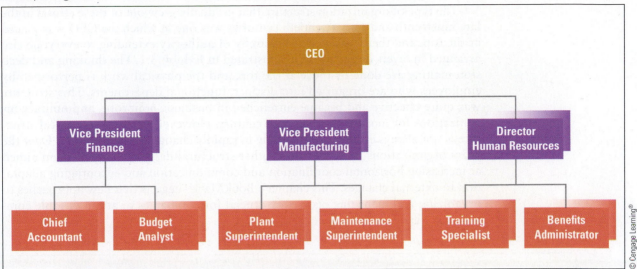

© Cengage Learning®

be quite useful in understanding how a company works. It shows the various parts of an organization, how they are interrelated, and how each position and department fits into the whole.

The concept of an organization chart, showing what positions exist, how they are grouped, and who reports to whom, has been around for centuries.[9] For example, diagrams outlining church hierarchy can be found in medieval churches in Spain. However, the use of the organization chart for business stems largely from the Industrial Revolution. As we discussed in Chapter 1, as work grew more complex and was

performed by greater numbers of workers, there was a pressing need to develop ways of managing and controlling organizations. The growth of the railroads provides an example. After the collision of two passenger trains in Massachusetts in 1841, the public demanded better control of the operation. As a result, the board of directors of the Western Railroad took steps to outline "definite responsibilities for each phase of the company's business, drawing solid lines of authority and command for the railroad's administration, maintenance, and operation."[10]

Exhibit 3.2 shows an interesting example of an early organization chart created by Daniel McCallum for the Erie Railroad in 1855. Faced with financial strain and slumping productivity, McCallum created charts to explain the railroad's operations to investors and to show the division of responsibilities for superintendents along hundreds of miles

EXHIBIT 3.2
Organization Chart for the Erie Railroad, 1855

Source: Erie Railroad Organization Chart of 1855. Library of Congress, Haer, N.Y.

of rail lines. McCallum divided the railroad into geographic divisions of manageable size, with each division headed by a superintendent.[11]

The type of organization structure that gradually grew out of these efforts in the late nineteenth and early twentieth centuries was one in which the CEO was placed at the top, and there was a clear hierarchy of authority extending to everyone else arranged in layers down below, as illustrated in Exhibit 3.1. The thinking and decision making are done by those at the top, and the physical work is performed by employees who are organized into distinct, functional departments. This structure was quite effective and became entrenched in business, nonprofit, and military organizations for most of the twentieth century. However, this type of vertical structure is not always effective, particularly in rapidly changing environments. Over the years organizations have developed other structural designs, many of them aimed at increasing horizontal coordination and communication and encouraging adaptation to external changes. This chapter's BookMark suggests that new approaches to organizing and managing people are crucial for companies to attain durable competitive advantages in the twenty-first century.

ASSESS YOUR ANSWER

1 A popular form of organizing is to have employees work on what they want in whatever department they choose so that motivation and enthusiasm stay high.

ANSWER: *Disagree.* A small number of firms have tried this approach with some success, but a typical organization needs to structure its work activities, positions, and departments in a way that ensures work is accomplished and coordinated to meet organizational goals. Many managers try to give some consideration to employee choices as a way to keep enthusiasm high.

Information-Sharing Perspective on Structure

The organization should be designed to provide both vertical and horizontal information flow as necessary to accomplish the organization's overall goals. If the structure doesn't fit the information requirements of the organization, people either will have too little information or will spend time processing information that is not vital to their tasks, thus reducing effectiveness.[12] However, there is an inherent tension between vertical and horizontal mechanisms in an organization. Whereas vertical linkages are designed primarily for control, horizontal linkages are designed for coordination and collaboration, which usually means reducing control.

Centralized Versus Decentralized

One question is the level at which decisions are made in the organization, because that determines where information is needed. Centralization and decentralization pertain to the hierarchical level at which decisions are made. **Centralization** means that decision authority is located near the top of the organization. With **decentralization**, decision authority is pushed downward to lower organization levels.

Organizations can choose whether to orient toward a traditional organization designed for efficiency, which emphasizes vertical communication and control (a mechanistic design, as described in Chapter 1), or toward a contemporary

BOOKMARK 3.0   HAVE YOU READ THIS BOOK?

The Future of Management
By Gary Hamel with Bill Breen

Management breakthroughs such as the principles of scientific management, divisionalized organization structure, and using brand managers for horizontal coordination have created more sustained competitive advantage than any hot new product or service innovation, says Gary Hamel in *The Future of Management*, written with Bill Breen. Wait a minute—haven't those ideas been around since—well, *forever*? Exactly the point, says Hamel. In fact, he points out that many of today's managers are running twenty-first-century organizations using ideas, practices, and structural mechanisms invented a century or more ago. At that time, the principles of vertical hierarchy, specialization, bureaucratic control, and strong centralization were radical new approaches developed to solve the problem of inefficiency. They are too static, regimented, and binding today when the pace of change continues to accelerate. Today's organizations, Hamel argues, have to become "as strategically adaptable as they are operationally efficient."

SOME STRUCTURAL INNOVATORS
Hamel suggests that the practice of management must undergo a transformation akin to that which occurred with the Industrial Revolution and the advent of scientific management. Here, from *The Future of Management*, are a few examples that offer glimpses of what is possible when managers build structure around principles of community, creativity, and information sharing rather than strict hierarchy:

- *Whole Foods Market.* Teams are the basic organizational unit at Whole Foods, and they have a degree of autonomy nearly unprecedented in the retail industry. Each store is made up of eight or so self-directed teams that oversee departments such as fresh produce, prepared foods, dairy, or checkout. Teams are responsible for all key operating decisions, including pricing, ordering, hiring, and in-store promotions.
- *W. L. Gore.* W. L. Gore's innovation was to organize work so that good things happen whether managers are "in control" or not. Gore, best known for Gore-Tex fabric, lets employees decide what they want to do. There are no management layers, few titles, and no organization charts. As at Whole Foods, the core operating units are small teams, but at Gore people can choose which teams to work on and say no to requests from anyone. Gore also builds in strong accountability—people are reviewed by at least 20 of their peers every year.
- *Visa.* Everybody's heard of Visa, but few people know anything about the organization behind the brand. Visa is the world's first almost-entirely virtual company. In the early 1970s, a group of banks formed a consortium that today has grown into a global network of 21,000 financial institutions and more than 1.3 billion cardholders. The organization is largely self-organizing, continually evolving as conditions change.

HOW TO BE A MANAGEMENT INNOVATOR
Most companies have a system for product innovation, but Hamel notes that few have a well-honed process for management innovation. *The Future of Management* provides detailed steps managers can take to increase the chances of a breakthrough in management thinking. Hamel considers the rise of modern management and organization design the most important innovation of the twentieth century. It is time now, though, for twenty-first-century ideas.

The Future of Management, by Gary Hamel with Bill Breen, is published by Harvard Business School Press.

---

flexible learning organization, which emphasizes horizontal communication and coordination (an organic design). Exhibit 3.3 compares organizations designed for efficiency with those designed for learning and adaptation. An emphasis on efficiency and control is associated with specialized tasks, a hierarchy of authority, rules and regulations, formal reporting systems, few teams or task forces, and centralized decision making. Emphasis on learning and adaptation is associated with shared tasks; a relaxed hierarchy; few rules; face-to-face communication; many teams and task forces; and informal, decentralized decision making.

Organizations may have to experiment to find the correct degree of centralization or decentralization to meet their needs. For example, a study by William Ouchi found that three large school districts that shifted to a more flexible, decentralized

EXHIBIT 3.3
The Relationship of
Organization Design
to Efficiency Versus
Learning Outcomes

structure, giving school principals more autonomy, responsibility, and control over resources, performed better and more efficiently than large districts that were highly centralized.[13] Government leaders in Great Britain hope the same thing will happen when they decentralize the country's National Health Service. The system is undergoing the most radical restructuring since it was founded in 1948, with a key part of the plan to shift control of the multibillion dollar annual healthcare budget to doctors at the local level. Leaders believe decentralization will cut costs, simplify and streamline procedures, and reduce inefficiency by "putting power in the hands of patients and clinicians."[14]

Even Japanese companies such as Toyota, which have a strong tradition of centralization, are seeing the power of decentralization for promoting a sense of ownership.

 **IN PRACTICE**

Toyota

"We didn't have to go back to Japan for approval on everything," said Randy Stephens, the chief engineer at the Toyota Technical Center near Ann Arbor, Michigan, where the new version of the Avalon was designed and engineered. "We might go back to review the status of the project, but there is a feeling of ownership of this car here."

The new version of the Avalon, designed and engineered in Michigan and built in Kentucky, is being promoted as the company's most American vehicle ever. It is the first prototype not developed in Japan, and it is testing how well Toyota can decentralize decision making to the company's subsidiaries. Following four years of crisis related to safety issues and recalls, Toyota managers have been gradually rebuilding a stronger company, which includes delegating responsibilities more globally.

The company was strongly criticized for its need to coordinate every decision regarding the safety issues and recalls from headquarters. Executives have since overhauled the quality control process and decentralized more decision making to regional managers in charge of safety in North America, Europe, and Asia.[15]

Although many decisions will still rest with executives at headquarters, Toyota has realized that some decisions need to be made close to the action. Regional managers believe the problems Toyota went through have given top executives freedom to take risks they might not have taken otherwise.[16]

However, not every organization should decentralize all decisions. Within many companies, there is often a "tug of war between centralization and decentralization" as top executives want to centralize some operations to eliminate duplication, while business managers want to maintain decentralized control.[17] Managers are always searching for the best combination of vertical control and horizontal collaboration, centralization and decentralization, for their own situations.[18]

Vertical Information Sharing

Organization design should facilitate the communication among employees and departments that is necessary to accomplish the organization's overall task. Managers create *information linkages* to facilitate communication and coordination among organizational elements. **Vertical linkages** are used to coordinate activities between the top and bottom of an organization and are designed primarily for control of the organization. Employees at lower levels should carry out activities consistent with top-level goals, and top executives must be informed of activities and accomplishments at the lower levels. Organizations may use any of a variety of structural devices to achieve vertical linkage, including hierarchical referral, rules and plans, and formal management information systems.[19]

Hierarchical Referral. The first vertical device is the hierarchy, or chain of command, which is illustrated by the vertical lines in Exhibit 3.1. If a problem arises that employees don't know how to solve, it can be referred up to the next level in the hierarchy. When the problem is solved, the answer is passed back down to lower levels. The lines of the organization chart act as communication channels.

Rules and Plans. The next linkage device is the use of rules and plans. To the extent that problems and decisions are repetitive, a rule or procedure can be established so employees know how to respond without communicating directly with their manager. Rules and procedures provide a standard information source enabling employees to be coordinated without actually communicating about every task. At PepsiCo's Gemesa cookie business in Mexico, for example, managers carefully brief production workers on goals, processes, and procedures so that employees themselves do most of the work of keeping the production process running smoothly, enabling the plants to operate with fewer managers.[20] Plans also provide standing information for employees. The most widely used plan is the budget. With carefully designed and communicated budget plans, employees at lower levels can be left on their own to perform activities within their resource allotment.

Vertical Information Systems. A **vertical information system** is another strategy for increasing vertical information capacity. Vertical information systems include the periodic reports, written information, and computer-based communications distributed to managers. Information systems make communication up and down the hierarchy more efficient.

In today's world of corporate financial scandals and ethical concerns, many top managers are considering strengthening their organization's linkages for vertical information and control. The other major issue in organizing is to provide adequate horizontal linkages for coordination and collaboration.

Horizontal Information Sharing and Collaboration

Horizontal communication overcomes barriers between departments and provides opportunities for coordination and collaboration among employees to achieve unity of effort and organizational objectives. **Collaboration** means a joint effort between people from two or more departments to produce outcomes that meet a common goal or shared purpose and that are typically greater than what any of the individuals or departments could achieve working alone.[21] To understand the value of collaboration, consider the 2011 U.S. mission to raid Osama bin Laden's compound in Pakistan. The raid could not have succeeded without close collaboration between the Central Intelligence Agency (CIA) and the U.S. military. There has traditionally been little interaction between the nation's intelligence officers and its military officers, but the war on terrorism has changed that mindset. During planning for the bin Laden mission, military officers spent every day for months working closely with the CIA team in a remote, secure facility on the CIA campus. "This is the kind of thing that, in the past, people who watched movies thought was possible, but no one in the government thought was possible," one official later said of the collaborative mission.[22]

Horizontal linkage refers to communication and coordination horizontally across organizational departments. Its importance is articulated by comments made by Lee Iacocca when he took over Chrysler Corporation in the 1980s. The following quote might be three decades old, but it succinctly captures a problem that still occurs in organizations all over the world:

> What I found at Chrysler were thirty-five vice presidents, each with his own turf. ... I couldn't believe, for example, that the guy running engineering departments wasn't in constant touch with his counterpart in manufacturing. But that's how it was. Everybody worked independently. I took one look at that system and I almost threw up. That's when I knew I was in really deep trouble. ... Nobody at Chrysler seemed to understand that interaction among the different functions in a company is absolutely critical. People in engineering and manufacturing almost have to be sleeping together. These guys weren't even flirting![23]

During his tenure at Chrysler, Iacocca pushed horizontal coordination to a high level. All the people working on a specific vehicle project—designers, engineers, and manufacturers, as well as representatives from marketing, finance, purchasing, and even outside suppliers—worked together on a single floor so they could easily communicate. Horizontal linkage mechanisms often are not drawn on the organization chart, but nevertheless are a vital part of organization structure. Small organizations usually have a high level of interaction among all employees, but in a large organization such as Chrysler, Microsoft, or Toyota, providing mechanisms to ensure horizontal information sharing is critical to effective collaboration, knowledge sharing, and decision making.[24] For example, poor coordination and lack of information sharing has been blamed for delaying Toyota's decisions and response time to quality and safety issues related to sticky gas petals, faulty brakes, and other problems.[25] The following devices are structural alternatives that can improve horizontal coordination and information flow.[26] Each device enables people to exchange information.

Information Systems. A significant method of providing horizontal linkage in today's organizations is the use of cross-functional information systems. Computerized information systems enable managers or frontline workers throughout the organization to routinely exchange information about problems, opportunities, activities, or decisions. For example, at Veterans Administration (VA) hospitals around the country, a sophisticated system called Vista enables people all across the organization to access complete patient information and provide better care. By enabling close coordination and collaboration, technology helped transform the VA into one of the highest-quality, most cost-effective medical providers in the United States.[27]

Some organizations also encourage employees to use the company's information systems to build relationships all across the organization, aiming to support and enhance ongoing horizontal coordination across projects and geographical boundaries. CARE International, one of the world's largest private international relief organizations, enhanced its personnel database to make it easy for people to find others with congruent interests, concerns, or needs. Each person in the database has listed past and current responsibilities, experience, language abilities, knowledge of foreign countries, emergency experiences, skills and competencies, and outside interests. The database makes it easy for people working across borders to seek each other out, share ideas and information, and build enduring horizontal connections.[28]

Liaison Roles. A higher level of horizontal linkage is direct contact between managers or employees affected by a problem. One way to promote direct contact is to create a special **liaison role**. A liaison person is located in one department but has the responsibility for communicating and achieving coordination and collaboration with another department. Liaison roles often exist between engineering and manufacturing departments because engineering has to develop and test products to fit the limitations of manufacturing facilities. An engineer's office might be located in the manufacturing area so the engineer is readily available for discussions with manufacturing supervisors about engineering problems with the manufactured products. A research and development person might sit in on sales meetings to coordinate new product development with what sales people think customers are wanting.

Task Forces. Liaison roles usually link only two departments. When linkage involves several departments, a more complex device such as a task force is required. A **task force** is a temporary committee composed of representatives from each organizational unit affected by a problem.[29] Each member represents the interest of a department or division and can carry information from the meeting back to that department.

Task forces are an effective horizontal linkage device for temporary issues. They solve problems by direct horizontal collaboration and reduce the information load on the vertical hierarchy. Typically, they are disbanded after their tasks are accomplished. Organizations have used task forces for everything from organizing the annual company picnic to solving expensive and complex manufacturing problems. One example comes from Georgetown Preparatory School in North Bethesda, Maryland, which used a task force made up of teachers, administrators, coaches, support staff, and outside consultants to develop a flu preparedness plan. When the H1N1 flu threat hit several years ago, Georgetown was much better equipped than most educational institutions to deal with the crisis because they had a plan in place.[30]

Full-time Integrator. A stronger horizontal linkage device is to create a full-time position or department solely for the purpose of coordination. A full-time **integrator** frequently has a title, such as product manager, project manager, program manager, or brand manager. Unlike the liaison person described earlier, the integrator does not report to one of the functional departments being coordinated. He or she is located outside the departments and has the responsibility for coordinating several departments. The brand manager for Planters Peanuts, for example, coordinates the sales, distribution, and advertising for that product.

The integrator can also be responsible for an innovation or change project, such as coordinating the design, financing, and marketing of a new product. An organization chart that illustrates the location of project managers for new product development is shown in Exhibit 3.4. The project managers are drawn to the side to

EXHIBIT 3.4
Project Manager Location in the Structure

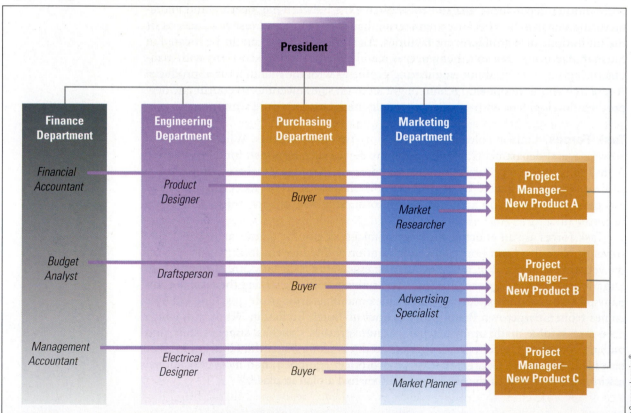

© Cengage Learning®

indicate their separation from other departments. The arrows indicate project members assigned to the new product development. New Product A, for example, has a financial accountant assigned to keep track of costs and budgets. The engineering member provides design advice, and purchasing and manufacturing members represent their areas. The project manager is responsible for the entire project. He or she sees that the new product is completed on time, is introduced to the market, and achieves other project goals. The horizontal lines in Exhibit 3.4 indicate that project managers do not have formal authority over team members with respect to giving pay raises, hiring, or firing. Formal authority rests with the managers of the functional departments, who have direct authority over subordinates within their departments.

Integrators need excellent people skills. Integrators in most companies have a lot of responsibility but little authority. The integrator has to use expertise and persuasion to achieve coordination. He or she spans the boundary between departments and must be able to get people together, maintain their trust, confront problems, and resolve conflicts and disputes in the interest of the organization.[31]

Teams. Project teams tend to be the strongest horizontal linkage mechanism. **Teams** are permanent task forces and are often used in conjunction with a full-time integrator. When activities among departments require strong coordination and collaboration over a long period of time, a cross-functional team is often the solution. *Special project teams* may be used when organizations have a large-scale project, a major innovation, or a new product line. JetBlue Airways put together a special project team made up of crew schedulers, systems operators, dispatchers, reservations agents, and other employees to revise how the airline handles and recovers from "irregular operations," such as severe weather. How effectively airlines manage and recover from these events dramatically affects performance and customer satisfaction, but effectiveness requires close coordination. At the first team meeting, leaders presented a simulated emergency and asked the team to map out how they would respond. As team members went through the process, they began to spot problems. The goal of the team is to work out solutions to help JetBlue improve both regular on-time performance and its recovery time from major events.[32]

Many of today's companies use virtual cross-functional teams. A **virtual team** is one that is made up of organizationally or geographically dispersed members who are linked primarily through advanced information and communications technologies. Members frequently use the Internet and collaboration software to work together rather than meet face to face.[33] IBM's virtual teams, for instance, collaborate primarily via internal websites using wiki technology.[34] At Nokia, virtual team members working in several different countries across time zones and cultures have a virtual work space that members can access 24 hours a day. In addition, Nokia provides an online resource where virtual workers are encouraged to post photos and share personal information.[35]

An illustration of how teams provide strong horizontal coordination is shown in Exhibit 3.5. Wizard Software Company develops and markets software for various web, desktop, and mobile applications, from games and social media products to financial services. Wizard uses teams to coordinate each product line across the research, programming, and marketing departments, as illustrated by the dashed lines and shaded areas in the exhibit. Members from each team meet at the beginning of each day as needed to resolve problems concerning customer needs, backlogs,

EXHIBIT 3.5
Teams Used for Horizontal Coordination at Wizard Software Company

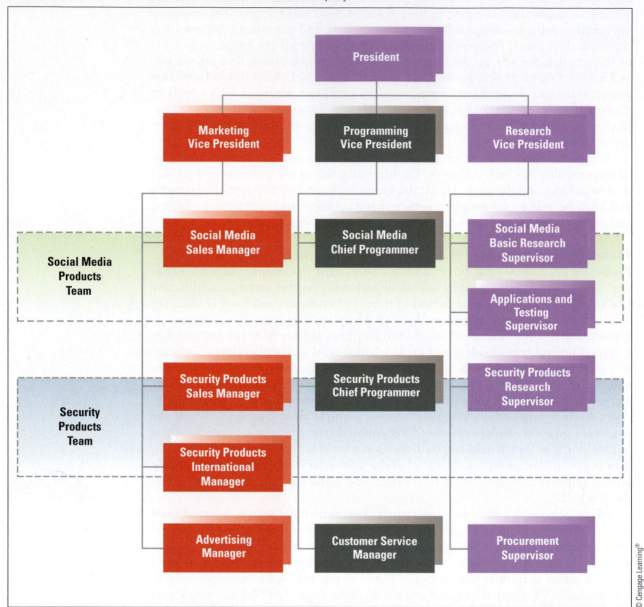

© Cengage Learning®

programming changes, scheduling conflicts, and any other problem with the product line. Are you cut out for horizontal teamwork? Complete the questionnaire in the "How Do You Fit the Design?" box to assess your feelings about working on a team.

Exhibit 3.6 summarizes the mechanisms for achieving horizontal linkages. These devices represent alternatives that managers can select to increase horizontal coordination and collaboration in any organization. The higher-level devices provide more horizontal information capacity, although the cost to the organization in terms of time and human resources is greater. If horizontal communication is insufficient, departments will find themselves out of synchronization and will not contribute to

HOW DO YOU FIT THE DESIGN?

THE PLEASURE/PAIN OF WORKING ON A TEAM

Your approach to your job or schoolwork may indicate whether you thrive on a team. Answer the following questions about your work preferences. Please answer whether each item is Mostly True or Mostly False for you.

	Mostly True	Mostly False
1. I prefer to work on a team rather than do individual tasks.	——	——
2. Given a choice, I try to work by myself rather than face the hassles of group work.	——	——
3. I enjoy the personal interaction when working with others.	——	——
4. I prefer to do my own work and let others do theirs.	——	——
5. I get more satisfaction from a group victory than an individual victory.	——	——
6. Teamwork is not worthwhile when people do not do their share.	——	——
7. I feel good when I work with others, even when we disagree.	——	——
8. I prefer to rely on myself rather than others to do a job or assignment.	——	——

Scoring: Give yourself one point for each odd-numbered item you marked as Mostly True and one point for each even-numbered item you marked Mostly False. Your score indicates your preference for teamwork versus individual work. If you scored 2 or fewer points, you definitely prefer individual work. A score of 7 or above suggests that you prefer working in teams. A score of 3–6 indicates comfort working alone and in a team.

Interpretation: Teamwork can be either frustrating or motivating depending on your preference. On a team you will lose some autonomy and have to rely on others who may be less committed than you. On a team you have to work through other people and you lose some control over work procedures and outcomes. On the other hand, teams can accomplish tasks far beyond what an individual can do, and working with others can be a major source of satisfaction. If you definitely prefer individual work, then you would likely fit better in a functional structure within a vertical hierarchy or in the role of individual contributor. If you prefer teamwork, then you are suited to work in the role of a horizontal linkage, such as on a task force or as an integrator, and would do well in a horizontal or matrix organization structure.

Source: Based on Jason D. Shaw, Michelle K. Duffy, and Eric M. Stark, "Interdependence and Preference for Group Work: Main and Congruence Effects on the Satisfaction and Performance of Group Members," *Journal of Management* 26, no. 2 (2000), 259–279.

the overall goals of the organization. When the amount of horizontal coordination needed is high, managers should select higher-level mechanisms.

Relational Coordination

The highest level of horizontal coordination illustrated in Exhibit 3.6 is relational coordination. **Relational coordination** refers to "frequent, timely, problem-solving communication carried out through relationships of shared goals, shared knowledge, and mutual respect."[36] Relational coordination isn't a device or mechanism like the other elements listed in Exhibit 3.6, but rather is part of the very fabric and culture of the organization. In an organization with a high level of relational

EXHIBIT 3.6
Ladder of Mechanisms
for Horizontal Linkage
and Coordination

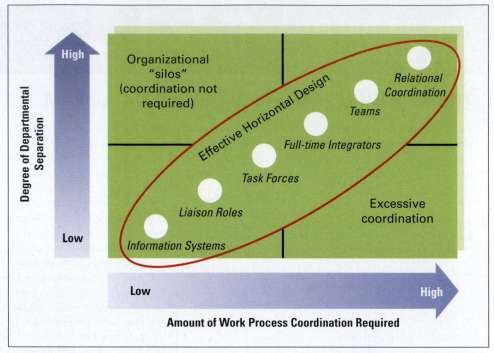

Sources: Based on Exhibit 1 in Nicolay Worren, "Hitting the Sweet Spot Between Separation and Integration in Organization Design," *People & Strategy* 34, no. 1 (2011), 24–30; and Richard L. Daft, *Organization Theory and Design*, 11th ed. (Cincinnati, OH: Cengage/Southwestern), 106.

coordination, people share information freely across departmental boundaries, and people interact on a continuous basis to share knowledge and solve problems. Coordination is carried out through a web of ongoing positive relationships rather than because of formal coordination roles or mechanisms.[37] Employees coordinate and collaborate directly with each other across units.

Building relational coordination into the fabric of the organization requires the active role of managers. Managers invest in training people in the skills needed to interact with one another and resolve cross-functional conflicts, build trust and credibility by showing they care about employees, and intentionally foster relationships based on shared goals rather than emphasizing goals of the separate departments. People are given freedom from strict work rules so they have the flexibility to interact and contribute wherever they are needed, and rewards are based on team efforts and accomplishments. Frontline supervisors have small spans of control so they can develop close working relationships with subordinates and coach and mentor employees. Managers also create specific cross-functional roles that promote coordination across boundaries. Southwest Airlines provides a good illustration.

IN PRACTICE

Southwest Airlines

Airlines face many challenges, but one that they face hundreds of times on a daily basis is getting airplanes loaded and off the ground safely and on time. Flight departure is a highly complex process. It involves numerous employees from various departments—such as ticket agents, pilots, flight attendants, baggage handlers, gate agents, mechanics, ramp agents, and fuel attendants—performing multiple tasks within a limited time period, under uncertain and ever-changing conditions. If all these groups aren't tightly coordinated, a successful on-time departure is difficult to achieve.

Southwest Airlines has the shortest turnaround time in the business, partly because managers promote relational coordination to achieve superior on-time performance and a high level of customer satisfaction. In any airline, there can be serious disagreements among employees about who is to blame when a flight is delayed, so Southwest managers created what they call *team delay*. Rather than searching for who is to blame when something goes wrong, the team delay is used to point out problems in coordination between various groups. Emphasis on the team focuses everyone on the shared goals of on-time departure, accurate baggage handling, and customer satisfaction. Because delay becomes a team problem, people are motivated to work closely together and coordinate their activities rather than looking out for themselves and trying to avoid or shift blame. Supervisors work closely with employees, but their role is less "being the boss," more facilitating learning and helping people do their jobs. Southwest uses a small supervisory span of control—about one supervisor for every eight or nine frontline employees—so that supervisors have the time to coach and assist employees, who are viewed as internal customers.[38]

By using practices that facilitate relational coordination, Southwest managers ensure that all the departments involved in flight departure are tightly coordinated. When relational coordination is high, people share information and coordinate their activities without having to have bosses or formal mechanisms telling them to do so.

U.S. Lieutenant General David M. Rodriguez, the first commander of the International Security Assistance Force Joint Command and deputy commander of U.S. forces in Afghanistan, fostered relational coordination among U.S. and Afghan military leaders as well as low-ranking commanders, civilian leaders, and others. His operations center had the feel of a newsroom, in which people eagerly talked to one another and shared their knowledge. Guidelines from high-ranking officers got bottom-up refinement from captains and sergeants. Rodriguez understood that people have to "work together and figure out how to maximize the effectiveness of the team." He worked hard to build relationships based on mutual trust, respect, and shared goals and commitments. "We ask them to hold us accountable and we attempt to hold them accountable in a type of shared responsibility," Rodriguez said in an interview.[39] Whether in the military or in business, trust grows and knowledge and collaboration result when leaders build solid relationships.

BRIEFCASE

As an organization manager, keep these guidelines in mind:

Recognize that the strongest horizontal linkage mechanisms are more costly in terms of time and human resources but are necessary when the organization needs a high degree of horizontal coordination to achieve its goals. When very high levels of coordination and knowledge sharing are needed, build relational coordination into the culture of the organization.

Organization Design Alternatives

The overall design of organization structure indicates three things: required work activities, reporting relationships, and departmental groupings.

Required Work Activities

Departments are created to perform tasks considered strategically important to the company. In a typical manufacturing company, for example, work activities fall into a range of functions that help the organization accomplish its goals, such as a human resource department to recruit and train employees, a purchasing department to obtain supplies and raw materials, a production department to build products, and a sales department to sell products. As organizations grow larger and more complex, managers find that more functions need to be performed. Organizations typically define new positions, departments, or divisions as a way to accomplish new tasks deemed valuable by the organization. For example, British oil giant BP added a new safety division in the wake of the Deepwater Horizon oil spill.

Reporting Relationships

Once required work activities and departments are defined, the next question is how these activities and departments should fit together in the organizational hierarchy. Reporting relationships, often called the *chain of command*, are represented by vertical lines on an organization chart. The chain of command should be an unbroken line of authority that links all persons in an organization and shows who reports to whom. In a large organization such as General Electric, BP, L'Oreal, or Microsoft, 100 or more charts might be needed to identify reporting relationships among thousands of employees. The definition of departments and the drawing of reporting relationships define how employees are to be grouped into departments.

Departmental Grouping Options

Options for departmental grouping, including functional grouping, divisional grouping, multifocused grouping, horizontal grouping, and virtual network grouping, are illustrated in Exhibit 3.7. **Departmental grouping** affects employees because they share a common supervisor and common resources, are jointly responsible for performance, and tend to identify and collaborate with one another.[40]

Functional grouping places together employees who perform similar functions or work processes or who bring similar knowledge and skills to bear. For example, all marketing people work together under the same supervisor, as do all manufacturing employees, all human resources people, and all engineers. For an Internet company, all the people associated with maintaining the website might be grouped together in one department. In a scientific research firm, all chemists may be grouped in a department different from biologists because they represent different disciplines.

Divisional grouping means people are organized according to what the organization produces. All the people required to produce toothpaste—including personnel in marketing, manufacturing, and sales—are grouped together under one executive. In huge corporations, such as Time Warner Corporation, some product or service lines may represent independent businesses, such as Warner Brothers Entertainment (movies and videos), Time Inc. (publisher of magazines such as *Sports Illustrated*, *Time*, and *People*), and Turner Broadcasting (cable television networks).

Multifocused grouping means an organization embraces two or more structural grouping alternatives simultaneously. These structural forms are often called *matrix* or *hybrid*. They will be discussed in more detail later in this chapter. An organization may need to group by function and product division simultaneously or might need to combine characteristics of several structural options.

Horizontal grouping means employees are organized around core work processes, the end-to-end work, information, and material flows that provide value directly to customers. All the people who work on a core process are brought together in a group rather than being separated into functional departments. At field offices of the U.S. Occupational Safety and Health Administration, for example, teams of workers representing various functions respond to complaints from American

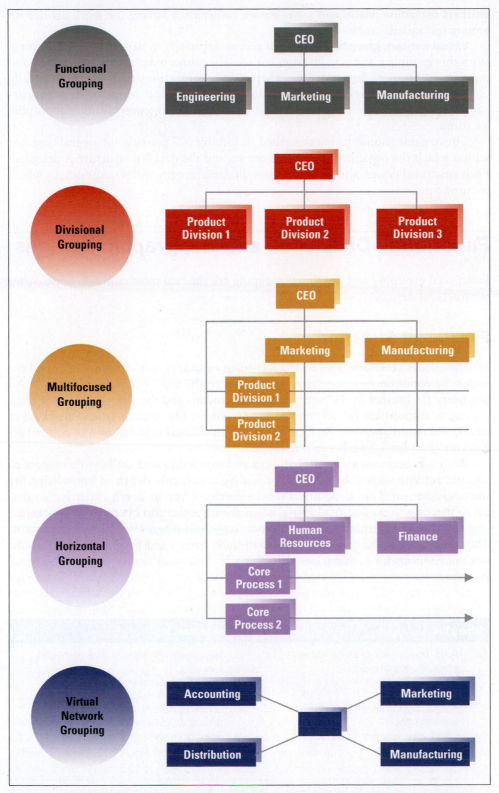

EXHIBIT 3.7
Structural Design Options
for Grouping Employees
into Departments

Source: Adapted from David Nadler and Michael Tushman, *Strategic Organization Design* (Glenview, IL: Scott Foresman, 1988), 68.

workers regarding health and safety issues, rather than having the work divided up among specialized employees.[41]

Virtual network grouping is the most recent approach to departmental grouping. With this grouping, the organization is a loosely connected cluster of separate components. In essence, departments are separate organizations that are electronically connected for the sharing of information and completion of tasks. Departments can be spread all over the world rather than located together in one geographic location.

The organizational forms described in Exhibit 3.7 provide the overall options within which the organization chart is drawn and the detailed structure is designed. Each structural design alternative has significant strengths and weaknesses, to which we now turn.

Functional, Divisional, and Geographic Designs

Functional grouping and divisional grouping are the two most common approaches to structural design.

Functional Structure

In a **functional structure**, also called a U-form (unitary), activities are grouped together by common function from the bottom to the top of the organization.[42] All engineers are located in the engineering department, and the vice president of engineering is responsible for all engineering activities. The same is true in marketing, R&D, and manufacturing. An example of the functional organization structure was shown in Exhibit 3.1 earlier in this chapter.

With a functional structure, all human knowledge and skills with respect to specific activities are consolidated, providing a valuable depth of knowledge for the organization. This structure is most effective when in-depth expertise is critical to meeting organizational goals, when the organization needs to be controlled and coordinated through the vertical hierarchy, and when efficiency is important. The structure can be quite effective if there is little need for horizontal coordination. Exhibit 3.8 summarizes the strengths and weaknesses of the functional structure.

EXHIBIT 3.8
Strengths and Weaknesses of Functional Organization Structure

Strengths	Weaknesses
1. Allows economies of scale within functional departments	1. Slow response time to environmental changes
2. Enables in-depth knowledge and skill development	2. May cause decisions to pile on top; hierarchy overload
3. Enables organization to accomplish functional goals	3. Leads to poor horizontal coordination among departments
4. Is best with only one or a few products	4. Results in less innovation
	5. Involves restricted view of organizational goals

Source: Based on Robert Duncan, "What Is the Right Organization Structure?" *Organizational Dynamics* (Winter 1979), 59–80.

One strength of the functional structure is that it promotes economy of scale within functions. Economy of scale results when all employees are located in the same place and can share facilities. Producing all products in a single plant, for example, enables the plant to acquire the latest machinery. Constructing only one facility instead of separate facilities for each product line reduces duplication and waste. The functional structure also promotes in-depth skill development of employees. Employees are exposed to a range of functional activities within their own department.[43] One interesting example comes from India, where Dr. Devi Shetty runs a hospital that performs open heart surgery for about 10 percent of the cost charged by hospitals in the United States, without reduced quality, by applying standardized operating procedures and principles of mass production.

IN PRACTICE

Narayana Hrudayalaya Hospital

You might not want to think about going on the assembly line when you go in for heart surgery, but Dr. Devi Shetty, who was Mother Teresa's cardiac surgeon in the early 1990s, offers cutting-edge medical care at a fraction of the cost charged in the United States by applying the principles of Henry Ford's mass production. By driving huge volumes, Dr. Shetty drives down costs.

"What health care needs is process innovation, not product innovation," Dr. Shetty says. When services can be broken down into explicit steps, employees can follow set rules and procedures while they do the same function over and over, in line with a trend toward *lean services* that looks at how to design service work to improve both quality and efficiency. "In healthcare, you can't do one thing and reduce the price," Dr. Shetty says. "We have to do 1,000 small things."

When services can be standardized, a tight, centralized functional structure can be effective. Because doctors perform so many heart surgeries, they get better and better at what they do. The hospital reports a 1.4 percent mortality rate within 30 days of one of the most common procedures, compared with an average of 1.9 percent in the United States.[44]

The functional structure works just fine for Narayana Hrudayalaya Hospital. The organization has chosen to stay medium-sized and focus on a few procedures.

The main weakness of the functional structure is a slow response to environmental changes that require coordination across departments. The vertical hierarchy becomes overloaded. Decisions pile up, and top managers do not respond fast enough. Other disadvantages of the functional structure are that innovation is slow because of poor coordination, and each employee has a restricted view of overall goals.

Functional Structure with Horizontal Linkages

Some organizations perform very effectively with a functional structure, and organizing by functions is still the prevalent approach to organization design.[45] However, in today's fast-moving world, very few companies can be successful with a strictly functional structure. For example, Watershed Asset Management is organized by functions such as legal, accounting, and investment, but to ensure coordination and collaboration, founder Meridee A. Moore has everyone sit in one big open room. "There's not much that is distilled or screened," she says. "When we're working on something, there's a lot of back and forth."[46] For a small organization, this informal coordination works fine, but as organizations grow larger, they typically need stronger mechanisms for horizontal linkage.

Managers improve horizontal coordination by using information systems, liaison roles, full-time integrators or project managers (illustrated in Exhibit 3.4), task forces, or teams (illustrated in Exhibit 3.5), and by creating the conditions that encourage relational coordination. One interesting use of horizontal linkages occurred at Karolinska Hospital in Stockholm, Sweden, which had 47 functional departments. Even after top executives cut that down to 11, coordination was still inadequate. The top executive team set about reorganizing workflow at the hospital around patient care. Instead of bouncing a patient from department to department, Karolinska now envisions the illness to recovery period as a process with "pit stops" in admissions, X-ray, surgery, and so forth. The most interesting aspect of the approach is the new position of nurse coordinator. Nurse coordinators serve as full-time integrators, troubleshooting transitions within or between departments. The improved horizontal coordination dramatically improved productivity and patient care at Karolinska.[47] The hospital is effectively using horizontal linkages to overcome some of the disadvantages of the functional structure.

Divisional Structure

With a **divisional structure**, also called an M-form (multidivisional) or a decentralized form, separate divisions can be organized with responsibility for individual products, services, product groups, major projects or programs, divisions, businesses, or profit centers.[48] This structure is sometimes also called a product structure or strategic business unit structure. The distinctive feature of a divisional structure is that grouping is based on *organizational outputs*. For example, LEGO Group shifted from a functional structure to a divisional structure with three product divisions: DUPLO, with its big bricks for the youngest children; LEGO construction toys; and a third category for other forms of LEGO quality play materials such as buildable jewelry. Each division contained the functional departments necessary for that toy line.[49] United Technologies Corporation (UTC), which is among the 50 largest U.S. industrial firms, has numerous divisions, including Carrier (air conditioners and heating), Otis (elevators and escalators), Pratt & Whitney (aircraft engines), and Sikorsky (helicopters).[50] The Chinese online-commerce company Taobao is divided into three divisions that provide three different types of services: linking individual buyers and sellers; a marketplace for retailers to sell to consumers; and a service for people to search across Chinese shopping websites.[51]

Organizations tend to shift from functional to divisional structures as they become more complex.[52] The difference between a divisional structure and a functional structure is illustrated in Exhibit 3.9. The functional structure can be redesigned into separate product groups, and each group contains the functional departments of R&D, manufacturing, accounting, and marketing. Coordination is maximized across functional departments within each product group. The divisional structure promotes flexibility and change because each unit is smaller and can adapt to the needs of its environment. Moreover, the divisional structure *decentralizes* decision making because the lines of authority converge at a lower level in the hierarchy. The functional structure, by contrast, is *centralized* because it forces decisions all the way to the top before a problem affecting several functions can be resolved.

EXHIBIT 3.9

Reorganization from Functional Structure to Divisional Structure at Info-Tech

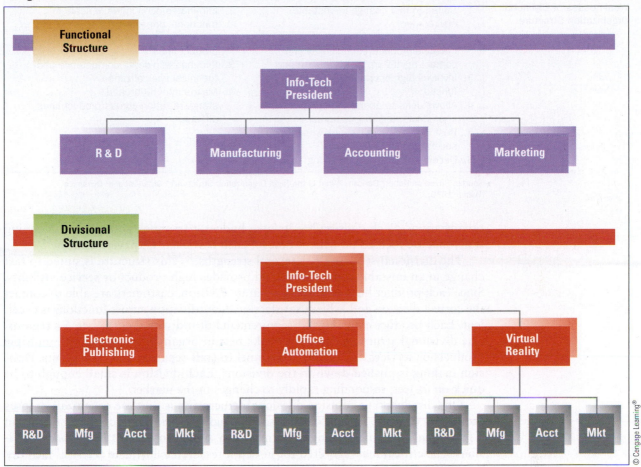

Strengths and weaknesses of the divisional structure are summarized in Exhibit 3.10. The divisional organization structure is excellent for achieving coordination across functional departments. It works well when organizations can no longer be adequately controlled through the traditional vertical hierarchy and when goals are oriented toward adaptation and change. Giant, complex organizations such as General Electric, Time Warner, and Johnson & Johnson are subdivided into a series of smaller, self-contained organizations for better control and coordination. In these large, complex companies, the units are sometimes called divisions, businesses, or strategic business units. Johnson & Johnson is organized into three major divisions: Consumer Products, Medical Devices and Diagnostics, and Pharmaceuticals, yet within those three major divisions are 250 separate operating units in 57 countries.[53] Some U.S. government organizations also use a divisional structure to better serve the public. One example is the Internal Revenue Service, which wanted to be more customer oriented. The agency shifted its focus to informing, educating, and serving the public through four separate divisions serving distinct taxpayer groups—individual taxpayers, small businesses, large businesses, and tax-exempt

EXHIBIT 3.10
Strengths and
Weaknesses of Divisional
Organization Structure

Strengths	Weaknesses
1. Suited to fast change in unstable environment 2. Leads to customer satisfaction because product responsibility and contact points are clear 3. Involves high coordination across functions 4. Allows units to adapt to differences in products, regions, customers 5. Best in large organizations with several products 6. Decentralizes decision making	1. Eliminates economies of scale in functional departments 2. Leads to poor coordination across product lines 3. Eliminates in-depth competence and technical specialization 4. Makes integration and standardization across product lines difficult

Source: Based on Robert Duncan, "What Is the Right Organization Structure?" *Organizational Dynamics* (Winter 1979).

organizations. Each division has its own budget, personnel, policies, and planning staffs that are focused on what is best for each particular taxpayer segment.[54]

The divisional structure has several strengths.[55] This structure is suited to fast change in an unstable environment and provides high product or service visibility. Since each product line has its own separate division, customers are able to contact the correct division and achieve satisfaction. Coordination across functions is excellent. Each product can adapt to requirements of individual customers or regions. The divisional structure typically works best in organizations that have multiple products or services and enough personnel to staff separate functional units. Decision making is pushed down to the divisions. Each division is small enough to be quick on its feet, responding rapidly to changes in the market.

One disadvantage of using divisional structuring is that the organization loses economies of scale. Instead of 50 research engineers sharing a common facility in a functional structure, 10 engineers may be assigned to each of five product divisions. The critical mass required for in-depth research is lost, and physical facilities have to be duplicated for each product line. Another problem is that product lines become separate from each other, and coordination across product lines can be difficult. As a Johnson & Johnson executive once said, "We have to keep reminding ourselves that we work for the same corporation."[56]

Some companies that have a large number of divisions have had real problems with cross-unit coordination. Sony lost the digital music player business to Apple partly because of poor coordination. With the introduction of the iPod, Apple quickly captured 60 percent of the U.S. market versus 10 percent for Sony. The digital music business depends on seamless coordination. Sony's Walkman didn't even recognize some of the music sets that could be made with the company's SonicStage software and thus didn't mesh well with the division selling music downloads.[57] Unless effective horizontal mechanisms are in place, a divisional structure can hurt overall performance. One division may produce products or programs that are incompatible with products sold by another division, as at Sony. Customers can become frustrated when a sales representative from one division is unaware of developments in other divisions. Task forces and other horizontal linkage devices are needed to coordinate across divisions. A lack of technical specialization is also a problem in a divisional structure. Employees identify with the product line rather than with a functional specialty. R&D personnel, for example, tend to do applied research to benefit the product line rather than basic research to benefit the entire organization.

Poor coordination and collaboration among divisions are blamed for Microsoft's late entry into the profitable smartphone and tablet markets. Top managers are trying to change that with a massive, but tricky, reorganization.

IN PRACTICE
Microsoft

Microsoft is having a hard time keeping pace with Apple and Google. While those companies were bringing hot new products to market, Microsoft "became a high-tech equivalent of a Detroit car-maker, bringing flashier models of the same old thing off the assembly line." One big reason is that the company's divisions have long been at war with one another. Potential innovative technologies for tablets and smartphones were killed, delayed, or derailed by in-fighting and power plays. Steven A. Ballmer, the former longtime CEO of Microsoft, said, "To execute, we've got to move from multiple Microsofts to one Microsoft."

Top executives are implementing a major reorganization that dissolves the existing eight product divisions in favor of four units based on broad themes that will, it is hoped, encourage greater collaboration and teamwork. The goal, said Ballmer, is to organize things so as "to drive a cross-company team for success." Whereas each division once had its own finance and marketing departments, those functions have been centralized to force groups to work more closely together to create complete products where all the hardware, software, and services work together. Each major initiative will have a high-level corporate champion who will be a direct report to the CEO, to ensure the proper flow of information and to keep everyone pulling in the same direction.

In a telephone interview, Qi Lu, the head of Bing and Microsoft's other Internet initiatives, said the old structure was similar to baseball, in that it gave individual players opportunities to perform. A better model for the new Microsoft, he says, is football: "You have to huddle before every play."[58]

It remains to be seen if Microsoft's long-feuding divisions can huddle and put the good of the whole above their individual goals. The company's problems became so worrisome that in early October 2013, three of the top 20 shareholders began lobbying the board to pressure Bill Gates to step down as chairman of the company he co-founded 38 years ago.[59] Microsoft will likely use a variety of structural mechanisms to encourage greater collaboration across the organization's four broad units and try to put the spark back in the company.

The problem of coordination and collaboration is also amplified in the international arena because organizational units are differentiated not only by goals and work activities, but also by geographical distance, time differences, cultural values, and perhaps language. How can managers ensure that needed coordination and collaboration will take place in their company, both domestically and globally? Coordination is the outcome of information and cooperation. Managers can design systems and structures, as described earlier, to promote horizontal coordination and collaboration.

Geographic Structure

Another basis for structural grouping is the organization's users or customers. The most common structure in this category is geography. Each region of the country may have distinct tastes and needs. Each geographic unit includes all functions required to produce and market products or services in that region. Large nonprofit organizations such as the Girl Scouts of the USA, Habitat for Humanity, Make-A-Wish Foundation, and the United Way of America frequently use a type of geographic structure, with a central headquarters and semiautonomous local units. The national organization provides brand recognition, coordinates fund-raising services, and handles some shared administrative functions, while day-to-day control and decision making is decentralized to local or regional units.[60] World Bank, mentioned in the chapter opening, uses a complex type of geographic divisional structure, organized country by country and region by region. Because of poor coordination and collaboration across regions, Jim Yong Kim, who took over as president in 2012, has planned a sweeping reorganization, overlaying the structure with 14 "global practices," including agriculture, energy, and education, that cut across the bank's different projects, funds, and geographies. The goal is to encourage greater coordination and collaboration.[61]

For multinational corporations, self-contained units are created for different countries and parts of the world. Exhibit 3.11 shows an example of a geographic structure for a cosmetics company. This structure focuses managers and employees on specific geographic regions and sales targets. Walmart Stores are organized by geographic regions, such as Walmart Japan, Walmart India, Walmart Brazil, Walmart China, and Walmart Asia. Until recently, U.S. operations were organized largely by function, but managers restructured U.S. operations into three geographic divisions, West, South, and North, making the U.S. organization more like how Walmart operates internationally. Using a geographic structure helps the company expand into new markets and use resources more efficiently.[62]

The strengths and weaknesses of a geographic divisional structure are similar to the divisional organization characteristics listed in Exhibit 3.10. The organization can adapt to the specific needs of its own region, and employees identify with regional goals rather than with national goals. Horizontal coordination within a region is emphasized rather than linkages across regions or to the national office. For example, Jim Yong Kim, president of World Bank, said, "When we asked technical people how much time they spent supporting other regions, the answer was less than 1 percent."

EXHIBIT 3.11
Geographic Structure for Cosmetics Company

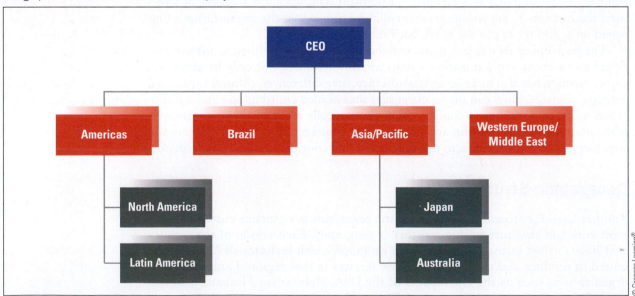

© Cengage Learning®

Matrix Structure

Sometimes, an organization's structure needs to be multifocused in that both product and function or product and geography are emphasized at the same time. One way to achieve this is through the **matrix structure**.[63] The matrix can be used when both technical expertise and product innovation and change are important for meeting organizational goals. The matrix structure often is the answer when organizations find that the functional, divisional, and geographic structures combined with horizontal linkage mechanisms will not work.

The matrix is a strong form of horizontal linkage. The unique characteristic of the matrix organization is that both product divisions and functional structures (horizontal and vertical) are implemented simultaneously, as shown in Exhibit 3.12. The product managers and functional managers have equal authority within the organization, and employees report to both of them. The matrix structure is similar to the use of full-time integrators or product managers described earlier in this

EXHIBIT 3.12

Dual-Authority Structure in a Matrix Organization

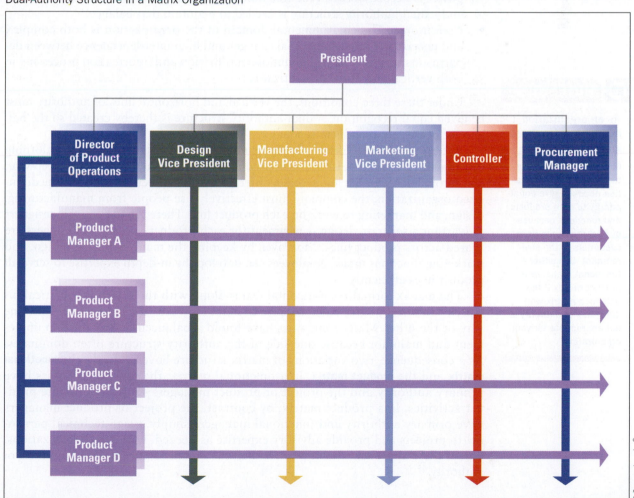

© Cengage Learning®

chapter (Exhibit 3.4), except that in the matrix structure the product managers (horizontal) are given formal authority equal to that of the functional managers (vertical).

Conditions for the Matrix

A dual hierarchy may seem an unusual way to design an organization, but the matrix is the correct structure when the following conditions are present:[64]

- *Condition 1.* Pressure exists to share scarce resources across product lines. The organization is typically medium-sized and has a moderate number of product lines. It feels pressure for the shared and flexible use of people and equipment across those products. For example, the organization is not large enough to assign engineers full-time to each product line, so engineers are assigned part-time to several products or projects.
- *Condition 2.* Environmental pressure exists for two or more critical outputs, such as for in-depth technical knowledge (functional structure) and frequent new products (divisional structure). This dual pressure means a balance of power is needed between the functional and product sides of the organization, and a dual-authority structure is needed to maintain that balance.
- *Condition 3.* The environmental domain of the organization is both complex and uncertain. Frequent external changes and high interdependence between departments require a large amount of coordination and information processing in both vertical and horizontal directions.

Under these three conditions, the vertical and horizontal lines of authority must be given equal recognition. A dual-authority structure is thereby created so the balance of power between them is equal.

Referring again to Exhibit 3.12, assume the matrix structure is for a clothing manufacturer. Product A is footwear, product B is outerwear, product C is sleepwear, and so on. Each product line serves a different market and customers. As a medium-sized organization, the company must effectively use people from manufacturing, design, and marketing to work on each product line. There are not enough designers to warrant a separate design department for each product line, so the designers are shared across product lines. Moreover, by keeping the manufacturing, design, and marketing functions intact, employees can develop the in-depth expertise to serve all product lines efficiently.

The matrix formalizes horizontal teams along with the traditional vertical hierarchy and tries to give equal balance to both. However, the matrix may shift one way or the other. Many companies have found a balanced matrix hard to implement and maintain because one side of the authority structure often dominates. As a consequence, two variations of matrix structure have evolved—the **functional matrix** and the **product matrix**. In a functional matrix, the functional bosses have primary authority and the project or product managers simply coordinate product activities. In a product matrix, by contrast, the project or product managers have primary authority and functional managers simply assign technical personnel to projects and provide advisory expertise as needed. For many organizations, one of these approaches works better than the balanced matrix with dual lines of authority.[65]

As an organization manager, keep these guidelines in mind:

Consider a matrix structure when the organization needs to give equal priority to both products and functions because of dual pressures from customers in the environment. Use either a functional matrix or a product matrix if the balanced matrix with dual lines of authority is not appropriate for your organization.

All kinds of organizations have experimented with the matrix, including hospitals, consulting firms, banks, insurance companies, government agencies, and many types of industrial firms.[66] This structure has been used successfully by global organizations such as Ford Motor, Procter & Gamble (P&G), Unilever, and Dow Chemical, which fine-tuned the matrix to suit their own particular goals and culture.

Strengths and Weaknesses

The matrix structure is best when environmental change is high and when goals reflect a dual requirement, such as for both product and functional goals. The dual-authority structure facilitates communication and coordination to cope with rapid environmental change and enables an equal balance between product and functional bosses. The matrix facilitates discussion and adaptation to unexpected problems. It tends to work best in organizations of moderate size with a few product lines. The matrix is not needed for only a single product line, and too many product lines make it difficult to coordinate both directions at once. Exhibit 3.13 summarizes the strengths and weaknesses of the matrix structure based on what we know of organizations that use it.[67]

One strength of the matrix is that it enables an organization to meet dual demands from customers in the environment. Resources (people, equipment) can be flexibly allocated across different products, and the organization can adapt to changing external requirements.[68] This structure also provides an opportunity for employees to acquire either functional or general management skills, depending on their interests.

One disadvantage of the matrix is that some employees experience dual authority, reporting to two bosses and sometimes juggling conflicting demands. This can be frustrating and confusing, especially if roles and responsibilities are not clearly defined by top managers.[69] Employees working in a matrix need excellent interpersonal and conflict-resolution skills, which may require special training in human relations. The matrix also forces managers to spend a great deal of time in meetings.[70]

EXHIBIT 3.13
Strengths and Weaknesses of Matrix Organization Structure

Strengths	Weaknesses
1. Achieves coordination necessary to meet dual demands from customers	1. Causes participants to experience dual authority, which can be frustrating and confusing
2. Flexible sharing of human resources across products	2. Means participants need good interpersonal skills and extensive training
3. Suited to complex decisions and frequent changes in unstable environment	3. Is time consuming; involves frequent meetings and conflict-resolution sessions
4. Provides opportunity for both functional and product skill development	4. Will not work unless participants understand it and adopt collegial rather than vertical-type relationships
5. Best in medium-sized organizations with multiple products	5. Requires great effort to maintain power balance

Source: Based on Robert Duncan, "What Is the Right Organization Structure? Decision Tree Analysis Provides the Answer," *Organizational Dynamics* (Winter 1979), 429.

Many people working in matrix structures say they spend two days a week in meetings and only 50 percent of the content is relevant to them or their jobs.[71] If managers do not adapt to the information and power sharing required by the matrix, the system will not work. Managers must collaborate with one another rather than rely on vertical authority in decision making. The successful implementation of one matrix structure occurred at a steel company in Great Britain.

IN PRACTICE

Englander Steel

As far back as anyone could remember, the steel industry in England was stable and certain. Then in the 1980s and 1990s, excess European steel capacity, an economic downturn, the emergence of the mini mill electric arc furnace, and competition from steelmakers in Germany and Japan forever changed the steel industry. By the turn of the century, traditional steel mills in the United States, such as Bethlehem Steel and LTV Corporation, were facing bankruptcy. Mittal Steel in Asia and Europe's leading steelmaker, Arcelor, started acquiring steel companies to become world steel titans (the two merged in 2006 to become ArcelorMittal). The survival hope of small traditional steel manufacturers was to sell specialized products. A small company could market specialty products aggressively and quickly adapt to customer needs. Complex process settings and operating conditions had to be rapidly changed for each customer's order—a difficult feat for the titans.

Englander Steel employed 2,900 people, made 400,000 tons of steel a year (about 1 percent of Arcelor's output), and was 180 years old. For 160 of those years, a functional structure worked fine. As the environment became more turbulent and competitive, however, Englander Steel managers realized they were not keeping up. Fifty percent of Englander's orders were behind schedule. Profits were eroded by labor, material, and energy cost increases. Market share declined.

In consultation with outside experts, the president of Englander Steel saw that the company had to walk a tightrope. It had to specialize in a few high-value-added products tailored for separate markets, while maintaining economies of scale and sophisticated technology within functional departments. The dual pressure led to an unusual solution for a steel company: a matrix structure.

Englander Steel had four product lines: open-die forgings, ring-mill products, wheels and axles, and sheet steel. A business manager was given responsibility for and authority over each line, which included preparing a business plan and developing targets for production costs, product inventory, shipping dates, and gross profit. The managers were given authority to meet those targets and to make their lines profitable. Functional vice presidents were responsible for technical decisions. Functional managers were expected to stay abreast of the latest techniques in their areas and to keep personnel trained in new technologies that could apply to product lines. With 20,000 recipes for specialty steels and several hundred new recipes ordered each month, functional personnel had to stay current. Two functional departments—field sales and industrial relations—were not included in the matrix because they worked independently. The final design was a hybrid matrix structure with both matrix and functional relationships, as illustrated in Exhibit 3.14.

Implementation of the matrix was slow. Middle managers were confused. Meetings to coordinate orders across functional departments seemed to be held every day. After about a year of training by external consultants, Englander Steel was on track. Ninety percent of the orders were now delivered on time and market share recovered. Both productivity and profitability increased steadily. The managers thrived on matrix involvement. Meetings to coordinate product and functional decisions provided a growth experience. Middle managers began including younger managers in the matrix discussions as training for future management responsibility.[72]

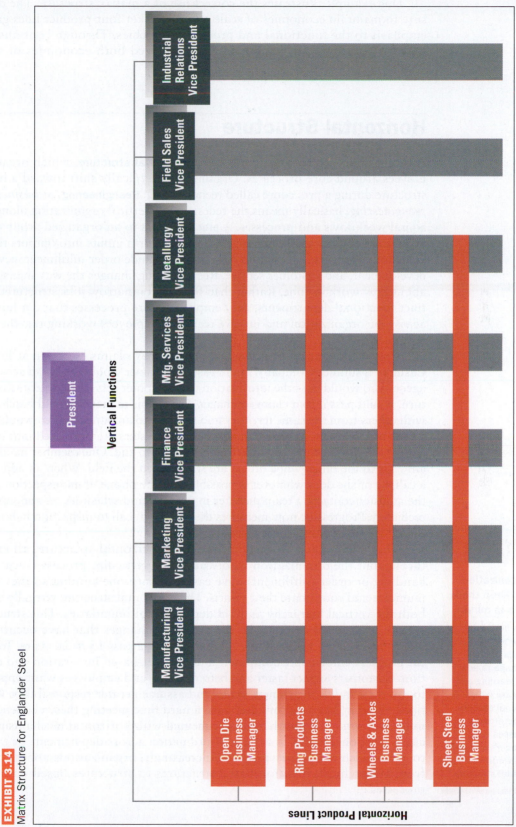

EXHIBIT 3.14
Matrix Structure for Englander Steel

© Cengage Learning®

This example illustrates the correct use of a matrix structure. The dual pressure to maintain economies of scale and to market four product lines gave equal emphasis to the functional and product hierarchies. Through continuous meetings for coordination, Englander Steel achieved both economies of scale and flexibility.

Horizontal Structure

A recent approach to organizing is the **horizontal structure**, which organizes employees around core processes. Organizations typically shift toward a horizontal structure during a procedure called reengineering. **Reengineering**, or *business process reengineering*, basically means the redesign of a vertical organization along its horizontal workflows and processes. A **process** refers to an organized group of related tasks and activities that work together to transform inputs into outputs that create value for customers.[73] Examples of processes include order fulfillment, new product development, and customer service. Reengineering changes the way managers think about how work is done. Rather than focusing on narrow jobs structured into distinct functional departments, they emphasize core processes that cut horizontally across the organization and involve teams of employees working together to serve customers.

A good illustration of process is provided by claims handling at Progressive Casualty Insurance Company. In the past, a customer would report an accident to an agent, who would pass the information to a customer service representative, who, in turn, would pass it to a claims manager. The claims manager would batch the claim with others from the same territory and assign it to an adjuster, who would schedule a time to inspect the vehicle damage. Today, adjusters are organized into teams that handle the entire claims process from beginning to end. One member handles claimant calls to the office while others are stationed in the field. When an adjuster takes a call, he or she does whatever is possible over the phone. If an inspection is needed, the adjuster contacts a team member in the field and schedules an appointment immediately. Progressive now measures the time from call to inspection in hours rather than the 7 to 10 days it once took.[74]

When a company is reengineered to a horizontal structure, all employees throughout the organization who work on a particular process (such as claims handling or order fulfillment) have easy access to one another so they can communicate and coordinate their efforts. The horizontal structure virtually eliminates both the vertical hierarchy and old departmental boundaries. This structural approach is largely a response to the profound changes that have occurred in the workplace and the business environment over the past 15 to 20 years. Technological progress emphasizes computer- and Internet-based integration and coordination. Customers expect faster and better service, and employees want opportunities to use their minds, learn new skills, and assume greater responsibility. Organizations mired in a vertical mindset have a hard time meeting these challenges. Thus, numerous organizations have experimented with horizontal mechanisms such as cross-functional teams to achieve coordination across departments or task forces to accomplish temporary projects. Increasingly, organizations are shifting away from hierarchical, function-based structures to structures based on horizontal processes.

BRIEFCASE

As an organization manager, keep these guidelines in mind:

Consider a horizontal structure when customer needs and demands change rapidly and when learning and innovation are critical to organizational success. Carefully determine core processes and train managers and employees to work within the horizontal structure.

Characteristics

An illustration of a company reengineered into a horizontal structure appears in Exhibit 3.15. Such an organization has the following characteristics:[75]

- Structure is created around cross-functional core processes rather than tasks, functions, or geography. Thus, boundaries between departments are obliterated. Ford Motor Company's Customer Service Division, for example, has core process groups for business development, parts supply and logistics, vehicle service and programs, and technical support.
- Self-directed teams, not individuals, are the basis of organizational design and performance. Schwa, a restaurant in Chicago that serves elaborate multicourse meals, is run by a team. Members rotate jobs so that everyone is sometimes a chef; sometimes a dishwasher; sometimes a waiter; or sometimes the person who answers the phone, takes reservations, or greets customers at the door.[76]
- Process owners have responsibility for each core process in its entirety. For Ford's parts supply and logistics process, for example, a number of teams may work on jobs such as parts analysis, purchasing, material flow, and distribution, but a process owner is responsible for coordinating the entire process.
- People on the team are given the skills, tools, motivation, and authority to make decisions central to the team's performance. Team members are cross-trained to perform one another's jobs, and the combined skills are sufficient to complete a major organizational task.

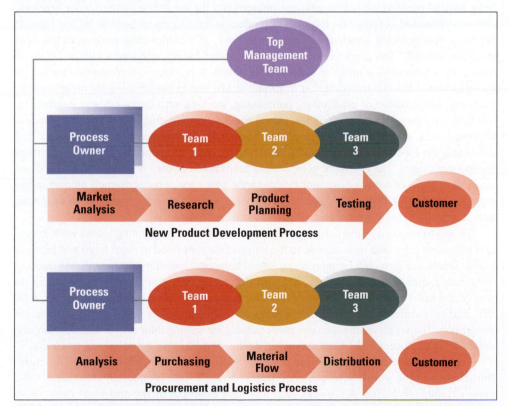

EXHIBIT 3.15
A Horizontal Structure

Sources: Based on Frank Ostroff, *The Horizontal Organization* (New York: Oxford University Press, 1999); John A. Byrne, "The Horizontal Corporation," *BusinessWeek*, December 20, 1993, 76–81; and Thomas A. Stewart, "The Search for the Organization of Tomorrow," *Fortune*, May 18, 1992, 92–98.

- Teams have the freedom to think creatively and respond flexibly to new challenges that arise.
- Customers drive the horizontal corporation. Effectiveness is measured by end-of-process performance objectives (based on the goal of bringing value to the customer), as well as customer satisfaction, employee satisfaction, and financial contribution.
- The culture is one of openness, trust, and collaboration, focused on continuous improvement. The culture values employee empowerment, responsibility, and well-being.

General Electric's Salisbury, North Carolina, plant shifted to a horizontal structure to improve flexibility and customer service.

 **IN PRACTICE**

GE Salisbury

General Electric's plant in Salisbury, North Carolina, which manufactures electrical lighting panel boards for industrial and commercial purposes, used to be organized functionally and vertically. Because no two GE customers have identical needs, each panel board has to be configured and built to order, which frequently created bottlenecks in the standard production process. In the mid-1980s, faced with high product-line costs, inconsistent customer service, and a declining market share, managers began exploring new ways of organizing that would emphasize teamwork, responsibility, continuous improvement, empowerment, and commitment to the customer.

By the early 1990s, GE Salisbury had made the transition to a horizontal structure that links sets of multiskilled teams who are responsible for the entire build-to-order process. The new structure is based on the goal of producing lighting panel boards "of the highest possible quality, in the shortest possible cycle time, at a competitive price, with the best possible service." The process consists of four linked teams, each made up of 10 to 15 members representing a range of skills and functions. A production-control team serves as process owner (as illustrated earlier in Exhibit 3.15) and is responsible for order receipt, planning, coordination of production, purchasing, working with suppliers and customers, tracking inventory, and keeping all the teams focused on meeting objectives. The fabrication team cuts, builds, welds, and paints the various parts that make up the steel box that will house the electrical components panel, which is assembled and tested by the electrical components team. The electrical components team also handles shipping. A maintenance team takes care of heavy equipment maintenance that cannot be performed as part of the regular production process. Managers have become *associate advisors* who serve as guides and coaches and bring their expertise to the teams as needed.

The key to success of the horizontal structure is that all the operating teams work in concert with each other and have access to the information they need to meet team and process goals. Teams are given information about sales, backlogs, inventory, staffing needs, productivity, costs, quality, and other data, and each team regularly shares information about its part of the build-to-order process with the other teams. Joint production meetings, job rotation, and cross-training of employees are some of the mechanisms that help ensure smooth integration. The linked teams assume responsibility for setting their own production targets, determining production schedules, assigning duties, and identifying and solving problems.

Productivity and performance have dramatically improved with the horizontal structure. Bottlenecks in the workflow, which once wreaked havoc with production schedules, have been virtually eliminated. A six-week lead time has been cut to two-and-a-half days. More subtle but just as important are the increases in employee and customer satisfaction that GE Salisbury has realized since implementing its new structure.[77]

Strengths and Weaknesses

As with all structures, the horizontal structure has both strengths and weaknesses, as listed in Exhibit 3.16.

The most significant strength of the horizontal structure is enhanced coordination, which can dramatically increase the company's flexibility and response to changes in customer needs. The structure directs everyone's attention toward the customer, leading to greater customer satisfaction as well as improvements in productivity, speed, and efficiency. In addition, because there are no boundaries between functional departments, employees take a broader view of organizational goals rather than being focused on the goals of a single department. The horizontal structure promotes an emphasis on teamwork and cooperation so that team members share a commitment to meeting common objectives. Finally, the horizontal structure can improve the quality of life for employees by giving them opportunities to share responsibility, make decisions, and contribute significantly to the organization. Employees are typically enthusiastic about their involvement in bigger projects rather than narrow departmental tasks. At Lockheed Martin's Missiles and Fire Control division's Pike County Operations in Troy, Alabama, all employees work in self-directed teams that set performance goals and make decisions related to assembling and testing advanced missile systems. Teams at Pike County Operations have contributed to 100 percent on-time delivery with zero customer rejects for the division.[78]

A weakness of the horizontal structure is that it can harm rather than help organizational performance unless managers carefully determine which core processes are critical for bringing value to customers. Simply defining the processes around which to organize can be difficult. In addition, shifting to a horizontal structure is complicated and time consuming because it requires significant changes in culture, job design, management philosophy, and information and reward systems. Traditional managers may balk when they have to give up power and authority to serve instead as coaches and facilitators of teams. Employees have to be trained to work effectively in a team environment. Finally, because of the cross-functional nature of

Strengths	Weaknesses
1. Promotes flexibility and rapid response to changes in customer needs	1. Determining core processes is difficult and time consuming
2. Directs the attention of everyone toward the production and delivery of value to the customer	2. Requires changes in culture, job design, management philosophy, and information and reward systems
3. Each employee has a broader view of organizational goals	3. Traditional managers may balk when they have to give up power and authority
4. Promotes a focus on teamwork and collaboration	4. Requires significant training of employees to work effectively in a horizontal team environment
5. Improves quality of life for employees by offering them the opportunity to share responsibility, make decisions, and be accountable for outcomes	5. Can limit in-depth skill development

EXHIBIT 3.16
Strengths and Weaknesses of Horizontal Structure

Sources: Based on Frank Ostroff, *The Horizontal Organization: What the Organization of the Future Looks Like and How It Delivers Value to Customers* (New York: Oxford University Press, 1999); and Richard L. Daft, *Organization Theory and Design*, 6th ed. (Cincinnati, OH: South-Western, 1998), 253.

work, a horizontal structure can limit in-depth knowledge and skill development unless measures are taken to give employees opportunities to maintain and build technical expertise.

Virtual Networks and Outsourcing

Recent developments in organization design extend the concept of horizontal coordination and collaboration beyond the boundaries of the traditional organization. The most widespread design trend in recent years has been the outsourcing of various parts of the organization to outside partners.[79] **Outsourcing** means to contract out certain tasks or functions, such as manufacturing, human resources, or credit processing, to other companies.

All sorts of organizations are jumping on the outsourcing bandwagon. The Ohio State University is outsourcing its parking system. The City of Maywood, California, decided to outsource everything from street maintenance to policing and public safety. The budget for the police department used to be nearly $8 million. Now the city pays about half that to the Los Angeles County Sheriff's Department, and residents say service has improved.[80] The U.S. military is also increasingly using private military company contractors to handle just about everything except the core activity of fighting battles and securing defensive positions. Kellogg Brown & Root, a subsidiary of the Halliburton Corporation, for instance, builds and maintains military bases and provides catering and cleaning services. In the business world, Hitachi once made all its own televisions with Hitachi-made components, but the company now outsources manufacturing and gets key components from outside suppliers. Wachovia Corporation transferred administration of its human resources programs to Hewitt Associates, and British food retailer J. Sainsbury's lets Accenture handle its entire information technology department. About 20 percent of drug manufacturer Eli Lilly & Company's chemistry work is done in China by start-up labs such as Chem-Explorer, and companies such as India's Wipro, France's S.R. Teleperformance, and the U.S.-based Convergys manage call center and technical support operations for big computer and cell phone companies around the world.[81] The pharmaceuticals company Pfizer is using an innovative approach that lets some employees pass off certain parts of their jobs to an outsourcing firm in India with a click of a button. Rather than shifting entire functions to contractors, this "personal outsourcing" approach allows people to shift only certain tedious and time-consuming tasks to be handled by the outsourcing partner while they focus on higher-value work.[82]

Once, a company's units of operation "were either within the organization and 'densely connected' or they were outside the organization and not connected at all," as one observer phrased it.[83] Today, the lines are so blurred that it can be difficult to tell what is part of the organization and what is not. IBM handles back-office operations for many large companies, but it also outsources some of its own activities to other firms, which in turn may farm out some of their functions to still other organizations.[84]

A few organizations carry outsourcing to the extreme to create a virtual network structure. With a **virtual network structure**, sometimes called a *modular structure*, the firm subcontracts most of its major functions or processes to separate companies and coordinates their activities from a small headquarters organization.[85]

BRIEFCASE

As an organization manager, keep these guidelines in mind:

Use a virtual network structure for extreme flexibility and rapid response to changing market conditions. Focus on key activities that give the organization its competitive advantage and outsource other activities to carefully selected partners.

How the Structure Works

The virtual network organization may be viewed as a central hub surrounded by a network of outside specialists. For example, Philip Rosedale runs LoveMachine from his home and coffee shops around San Francisco. LoveMachine makes software that lets employees send Twitter-like messages to say "Thank you," or "Great job!" When the message is sent, everyone in the company gets a copy, which builds morale, and the basic software is free to companies that want to use it. LoveMachine has no full-time development staff, but instead works with a network of freelancers who bid on jobs such as creating new features and fixing glitches. Rosedale also contracts out payroll and other administrative tasks.[86]

With a network structure, rather than being housed under one roof or located within one organization, services such as accounting, design, manufacturing, marketing, and distribution are outsourced to separate companies or individuals that are connected electronically to a central office. Organizational partners located in different parts of the world may use networked computers or the Internet to exchange data and information so rapidly and smoothly that a loosely connected network of suppliers, manufacturers, and distributors can look and act like one seamless company. The virtual network form incorporates a free-market style to replace the traditional vertical hierarchy. Subcontractors may flow into and out of the system as needed to meet changing needs. The Georgia town of Sandy Springs is run almost entirely by subcontractors.

IN PRACTICE

Sandy Springs, Georgia

The Atlanta suburb of Sandy Springs has 94,000 residents but just seven city employees, including the city manager, John F. McDonough. The entire city is run from a generic, one-story industrial park, where the seven employees paid by the city work alongside those paid by outside contractors, and no one knows the difference.

If you go to get a business license, for example, you'll talk to someone who works for Severn Trent, a multinational company based in Coventry, England. To get a building permit, you'll talk with an employee of the Collaborative of Boston, Massachusetts. If you've got a problem with your trash collection, you'll need to have a word with someone who works for URS Corporation, based in San Francisco, California. Of course, as far as you know, all of these people work for the city of Sandy Springs. Even the city's courts and administrative work are handled by outside contractors. The city does have its own police force and fire department, but the 911 call center is operated by an outside contractor, IXP, with headquarters in Cranbury, New Jersey.

Sandy Springs isn't the most outsourced city in the United States. That distinction still belongs to Maywood, California, which has only one employee and runs everything else through contracts. One city council member in Maywood says the approach has driven up the cost of running the town. "Let's say a tree falls on a car," the council member said. "Previously, we had an employee who would deal with it. Now you have to make an appointment and they'll come when they can. They're not our people to control anymore." The city manager of Sandy Springs says they have sidestepped such issues. The key, he explains, is in the fine art of drafting the right contracts.[87]

When a business chooses to use a network structure, the hub maintains control over processes in which it has world-class or difficult-to-imitate capabilities and then transfers other work activities—along with the control over them—to other organizations. These partner organizations organize and accomplish their work using their own ideas, assets, and tools.[88] The idea is that a firm can concentrate

on what it does best and contract out everything else to companies with distinctive competence in those specific areas, enabling the organization to do more with less.[89] The "heart-healthy" food company Smart Balance, for example, was able to innovate and expand rapidly by using a virtual network approach. Smart Balance has only about 67 employees, but 400 people are working for the company through various contractors and subcontractors. Each morning, full-time employees and virtual workers exchange a flurry of e-mail messages and phone calls to update each other on what took place the day before and what needs to happen today. Executives spend much of their time managing relationships.[90]

With a network structure such as that used by the city of Sandy Springs or at Smart Balance, it is difficult to answer the question "Where is the organization?" in traditional terms. The different organizational parts are drawn together contractually and coordinated electronically, creating a new form of organization. Much like building blocks, parts of the network can be added or taken away to meet changing needs.[91] Exhibit 3.17 illustrates a simplified network structure for a business such as Smart Balance, showing some of the functions that can be outsourced to other companies.

Strengths and Weaknesses

Exhibit 3.18 summarizes the strengths and weaknesses of the virtual network structure.[92] One of the major strengths is that the organization, no matter how small, can be truly global, drawing on resources worldwide to achieve the best quality and price and then selling products or services worldwide just as easily through subcontractors. The network structure also enables a new or small company to develop products or services and get them to market rapidly without huge investments in factories, equipment, warehouses, or distribution facilities. The ability to arrange and rearrange resources to meet changing needs and best serve customers gives the network structure extreme flexibility and rapid response. New technologies can be developed quickly by tapping into a worldwide network of experts. The organization can continually redefine itself to meet changing product or market opportunities. A final strength is

Strengths	Weaknesses
1. Enables even small organizations to obtain talent and resources worldwide	1. Managers do not have hands-on control over many activities and employees
2. Gives a company immediate scale and reach without huge investments in factories, equipment, or distribution facilities	2. Requires a great deal of time to manage relationships and potential conflicts with contract partners
3. Enables the organization to be highly flexible and responsive to changing needs	3. There is a risk of organizational failure if a partner fails to deliver or goes out of business
4. Reduces administrative overhead costs	4. Employee loyalty and corporate culture might be weak because employees feel they can be replaced by contract services

EXHIBIT 3.18
Strengths and
Weaknesses of Virtual
Network Structure

Sources: Based on R.E. Miles and C.C. Snow, "The New Network Firm: A Spherical Structure Built on a Human Investment Philosophy," *Organizational Dynamics* (Spring 1995), 5–18; Gregory G. Dess, Abdul M. A. Rasheed, Kevin J. McLaughlin, and Richard L. Priem, "The New Corporate Architecture," *Academy of Management Executive* 9, no. 3 (1995), 7–20; N. Anand and R.L. Daft, "What Is the Right Organization Design?" *Organizational Dynamics* 36, no. 4 (2007), 329–344; and H.W. Chesbrough and D.J. Teece, "Organizing for Innovation: When Is Virtual Virtuous?" *Harvard Business Review*, August 2002, 127–134.

reduced administrative overhead. Large teams of staff specialists and administrators are not needed. Managerial and technical talent can be focused on key activities that provide competitive advantage while other activities are outsourced.

The virtual network structure also has a number of weaknesses. The primary weakness is a lack of control. The network structure takes decentralization to the extreme. Managers do not have all operations under their jurisdiction and must rely on contracts, coordination, and negotiation to hold things together. This also means increased time spent managing relationships with partners and resolving conflicts. K'Nex Brands LP, a family-owned toy company near Philadelphia, brought most of the production of its plastic building toys back to its factory in the United States from subcontractors in China, for instance, to maintain greater control over quality and materials. The safety of toys made in overseas factories is a growing concern for parents, and as wages and transportation costs rise in China, K'Nex managers saw a competitive advantage in bringing production back in-house.[93]

3 Top managers are smart to maintain organizational control over the activities of key work units rather than contracting out some work unit tasks to other firms.

ANSWER: *Disagree.* Virtual networks and outsourcing forms of organization design have become popular because they offer increased flexibility and more rapid response in a fast-changing environment. Outsourced departments can be added or dropped as conditions change. Keeping control over all activities in-house might be more comfortable for some managers, but it discourages flexibility.

ASSESS YOUR ANSWER

A problem of equal importance is the risk of failure if one organizational partner fails to deliver, has a plant burn down, or goes out of business. Managers in the headquarters organization have to act quickly to spot problems and find new arrangements. Finally, from a human resource perspective, employee loyalty can be weak in a network organization because of concerns over job security. Employees may feel that they can be replaced by contract services. In addition, it is more difficult to develop a cohesive corporate culture. Turnover may be higher because emotional commitment between the organization and employees is low. With changing products, markets, and partners, the organization may need to reshuffle employees at any time to get the correct mix of skills and capabilities.

Hybrid Structure

As a practical matter, many structures in the real world do not exist in the pure forms we have outlined in this chapter. Most large organizations, in particular, often use a **hybrid structure** that combines characteristics of various approaches tailored to specific strategic needs. Most companies combine characteristics of functional, divisional, geographic, horizontal, or network structures to take advantage of the strengths of various structures and avoid some of the weaknesses. Hybrid structures tend to be used in rapidly changing environments because they offer the organization greater flexibility.

One type of hybrid that is often used is to combine characteristics of the functional and divisional structures. When a corporation grows large and has several products or markets, it typically is organized into self-contained divisions of some type. Functions that are important to each product or market are decentralized to the self-contained units. However, some functions that are relatively stable and require economies of scale and in-depth specialization are also centralized at headquarters. For example, Starbucks has a number of geographic divisions, but functions such as marketing, legal, and supply chain operations are centralized.[94] Sun Petroleum Products Corporation (SPPC) reorganized to a hybrid structure to be more responsive to changing markets. The hybrid organization structure adopted by SPPC is illustrated in part 1 of Exhibit 3.19. Three major product divisions—fuels, lubricants, and chemicals—were created, each serving a different market and requiring a different strategy and management style. Each product-line vice president is now in charge of all functions for that product, such as marketing, planning, supply and distribution, and manufacturing. However, activities such as human resources, legal, technology, and finance were centralized as functional departments at headquarters in order to achieve economies of scale. Each of these departments provides services for the entire organization.[95]

A second hybrid approach that is increasingly used today is to combine characteristics of functional, divisional, and horizontal structures. Ford Motor Company's Customer Service Division, a global operation made up of 12,000 employees serving nearly 15,000 dealers, provides an example of this type of hybrid. Beginning in 1995, when Ford launched its "Ford 2000" initiative aimed at becoming the world's leading automotive firm in the twenty-first century, top executives grew increasingly concerned about complaints regarding customer service. They decided that the horizontal model offered the best chance to gain a faster, more efficient, integrated approach to customer service. Part 2 of Exhibit 3.19 illustrates a portion of the Customer Service Division's hybrid structure. Several horizontally aligned groups, made up of multiskilled teams, focus on core processes such as parts supply and logistics (acquiring parts and getting them to dealers quickly and efficiently), vehicle service and programs (collecting and disseminating information about repair problems), and technical support (ensuring that every service department receives updated technical information). Each group has a process owner who is responsible for seeing that the teams meet overall objectives. Ford's Customer Service Division

BRIEFCASE

EXHIBIT 3.19
Two Hybrid Structures

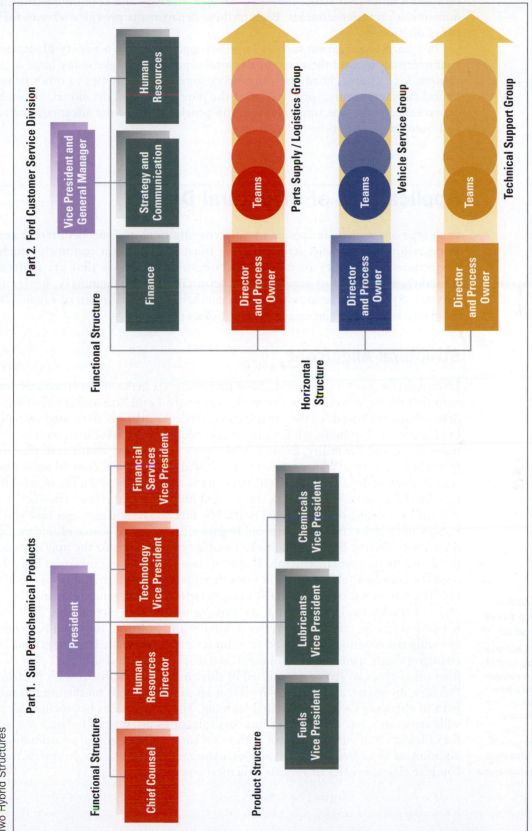

Part 1. Sun Petrochemical Products

Functional Structure

President

Chief Counsel — Human Resources Director — Technology Vice President — Financial Services Vice President

Product Structure

Fuels Vice President — Lubricants Vice President — Chemicals Vice President

Part 2. Ford Customer Service Division

Functional Structure

Vice President and General Manager

Finance — Strategy and Communication — Human Resources

Horizontal Structure

Director and Process Owner — Teams — Parts Supply / Logistics Group

Director and Process Owner — Teams — Vehicle Service Group

Director and Process Owner — Teams — Technical Support Group

Sources: Based on Linda S. Ackerman, "Transition Management: An In-Depth Look at Managing Complex Change," *Organizational Dynamics* (Summer 1982), 46–66; and Frank Ostroff, *The Horizontal Organization* (New York: Oxford University Press, 1999), Figure 2.1, 34.

retained a functional structure for its finance, strategy and communications, and human resources departments. Each of these departments provides services for the entire division.[96]

In a huge organization such as Ford, managers may use a variety of structural characteristics to meet the needs of the total organization. Like many large organizations, for example, Ford also outsources some of its activities to other firms. A hybrid structure is often preferred over the pure functional, divisional, horizontal, or virtual network structure because it can provide some of the advantages of each and overcome some of the disadvantages.

Applications of Structural Design

Each type of structure is applied in different situations and meets different needs. In describing the various structures, we touched briefly on conditions such as environmental stability or change and organizational size that are related to structure. Each form of structure—functional, divisional, matrix, horizontal, network, hybrid—represents a tool that can help managers make an organization more effective, depending on the demands of its situation.

Structural Alignment

Ultimately, the most important decision that managers make about structural design is to find the right balance between vertical control and horizontal coordination, depending on the needs of the organization. Vertical control is associated with goals of efficiency and stability, while horizontal coordination is associated with learning, innovation, and flexibility. Exhibit 3.20 shows a simplified continuum that illustrates how structural approaches are associated with vertical control versus horizontal coordination. The functional structure is appropriate when the organization needs to be coordinated through the vertical hierarchy and when efficiency is important for meeting organizational goals. The functional structure uses task specialization and a strict chain of command to gain efficient use of scarce resources, but it does not enable the organization to be flexible or innovative. At the opposite end of the scale, the horizontal structure is appropriate when the organization has a high need for coordination among functions to achieve innovation and promote learning. The horizontal structure enables organizations to differentiate themselves and respond quickly to changes, but at the expense of efficient resource use. The virtual network structure offers even greater flexibility and potential for rapid response by allowing the organization to add or subtract pieces as needed to adapt and meet changing needs from the environment and marketplace. Exhibit 3.20 also shows how other types of structure defined in this chapter—functional with horizontal linkages, divisional, and matrix—represent intermediate steps on the organization's path to efficiency or innovation and learning. The exhibit does not include all possible structures, but it illustrates how organizations attempt to balance the needs for efficiency and vertical control with innovation and horizontal coordination. In addition, as described in the chapter, many organizations use a hybrid structure to combine characteristics of various structural types.

BRIEFCASE

As an organization manager, keep these guidelines in mind:

Find the correct balance between vertical control and horizontal coordination to meet the needs of the organization. Consider a structural reorganization when symptoms of structural deficiency are observed.

EXHIBIT 3.20
Relationship of Structure to Organization's Need for Efficiency Versus Learning

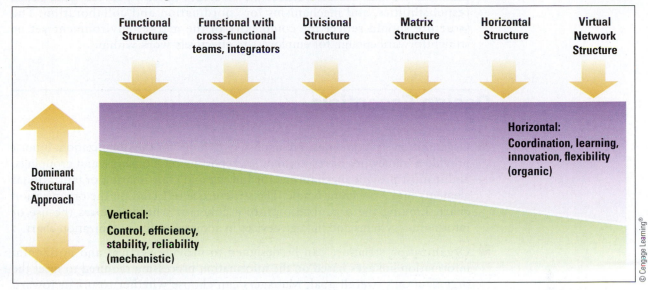

Symptoms of Structural Deficiency

Top executives periodically evaluate organization structure to determine whether it is appropriate to changing needs. Managers try to achieve the best fit between internal reporting relationships and the needs of the external environment. As a general rule, when organization structure is out of alignment with organization needs, one or more of the following **symptoms of structural deficiency** appear.[97]

- *There is an absence of collaboration among units.* Organization structure should encourage collaboration when and where it is needed to meet organizational goals. It should enable resolution of conflicting departmental needs and goals into a single set of goals for the entire organization. When departments act at cross-purposes or are under pressure to achieve departmental goals at the expense of organizational goals, the structure is often at fault. Horizontal linkage mechanisms are not adequate.

- *Decision making is delayed or lacking in quality.* Decision makers may be overloaded because the hierarchy funnels too many problems and decisions to them. Delegation to lower levels may be insufficient. Another cause of poor-quality decisions is that information may not reach the correct people. Information linkages in either the vertical or horizontal direction may be inadequate to ensure decision quality.

- *The organization does not respond innovatively to a changing environment.* One reason for lack of innovation is that departments are not coordinated horizontally. The identification of customer needs by the marketing department and the identification of technological developments in the research department must be coordinated. Organization structure also has to specify departmental responsibilities that include environmental scanning and innovation.

- *Employee performance declines and goals are not being met.* Employee performance may decline because the structure doesn't provide clear goals, responsibilities, and mechanisms for coordination and collaboration. The structure should reflect the complexity of the market environment yet be straightforward enough for employees to effectively work within.

Design Essentials

■ Organization structure must accomplish two things for the organization. It must provide a framework of responsibilities, reporting relationships, and groupings, and it must provide mechanisms for linking and coordinating organizational elements into a coherent whole. The structure is reflected on the organization chart. Linking the organization into a coherent whole requires the use of information systems and linkage devices in addition to the organization chart.

■ Organization structure can be designed to provide vertical and horizontal information linkages based on the information processing required to meet the organization's overall goal. Managers can choose whether to orient toward a traditional organization designed for efficiency, which emphasizes vertical linkages such as hierarchy, rules and plans, and formal information systems (a mechanistic design), or toward a contemporary organization designed for learning and adaptation, which emphasizes horizontal communication and coordination (an organic design). Vertical linkages are not sufficient for most organizations today. Organizations provide horizontal linkages through cross-functional information systems, liaison roles, temporary task forces, full-time integrators, and teams, and by creating the conditions to enable relational coordination.

■ Alternatives for grouping employees and departments into overall structural design include functional grouping, divisional grouping, multifocused grouping, horizontal grouping, and virtual network grouping. The choice among functional, divisional, and horizontal structures determines where coordination and integration will be greatest. With functional and divisional structures, managers also use horizontal linkage mechanisms to complement the vertical dimension and achieve integration of departments and levels into an organizational whole. With a horizontal structure, activities are organized horizontally around core work processes.

■ A virtual network structure extends the concept of horizontal coordination and collaboration beyond the boundaries of the organization. Core activities are performed by a central hub while other functions and activities are outsourced to contract partners.

■ The matrix structure attempts to achieve an equal balance between the vertical and horizontal dimensions of structure. Most organizations do not exist in these pure forms, using instead hybrid structures that incorporate characteristics of two or more types of structure.

■ Ultimately, managers attempt to find the correct balance between vertical control and horizontal coordination. Signs of structural misalignment include lack of collaboration, delayed decision making, lack of innovation, and poor employee performance.

■ Finally, an organization chart is only so many lines and boxes on a piece of paper. The purpose of the organization chart is to encourage and direct employees into activities and communications that enable the organization to achieve its goals. The organization chart provides the structure, but employees provide the behavior. The chart is a guideline to encourage people to work together, but management must implement the structure and carry it out.

⟫ KEY CONCEPTS

centralization	horizontal structure	relational coordination
collaboration	hybrid structure	symptoms of structural deficiency
decentralization	integrator	task force
departmental grouping	liaison role	teams
divisional grouping	matrix structure	vertical information system
divisional structure	multifocused grouping	vertical linkages
functional grouping	organization structure	virtual network grouping
functional matrix	outsourcing	virtual network structure
functional structure	process	virtual team
horizontal grouping	product matrix	
horizontal linkage	reengineering	

⟫ DISCUSSION QUESTIONS

1. What is the definition of *organization structure?* Does organization structure appear on the organization chart? Explain.
2. When is a functional structure preferable to a divisional structure?
3. Large corporations tend to use hybrid structures. Why?
4. What are the primary differences in structure between a traditional, mechanistic organization designed for efficiency and a more contemporary, organic organization designed for learning?
5. What is the difference between a task force and a team? Between liaison role and integrating role? Which of these provides the greatest amount of horizontal coordination?
6. As a manager, how would you create an organization with a high degree of relational coordination?
7. What conditions usually have to be present before an organization should adopt a matrix structure?
8. The manager of a consumer products firm said, "We use the brand manager position to train future executives." Why do you think the brand manager position is considered a good training ground? Discuss.
9. Why do companies using a horizontal structure have cultures that emphasize openness, employee empowerment, and responsibility? What do you think a manager's job would be like in a horizontally organized company?
10. Describe the virtual network structure. What are the advantages and disadvantages of using this structure compared to performing all activities in-house within an organization?

⟫ CHAPTER 3 WORKBOOK   You and Organization Structure[98]

To better understand the importance of organization structure in your life, do the following assignment.

Select one of the following situations to organize:

- A copy and print shop
- A travel agency
- A sports rental (such as Jet Skis or snowmobiles) in a resort area
- A bakery

Background

Organization is a way of gaining some power against random forces in the environment. The environment provides the organization with inputs, which include raw materials, human resources, and financial resources. There is a service or product to produce that involves technology. The output goes to clients, a group that must be nurtured. The complexities of the environment and the technology determine the complexity of the organization.

Planning Your Organization

1. Write down the mission or purpose of the organization in a few sentences.
2. What are the specific tasks to be completed to accomplish the mission?
3. Based on the specifics in question 2, develop an organization chart. Each position in the chart will perform a specific task or is responsible for a certain outcome.
4. You are into your third year of operation, and your business has been very successful. You want to add a second location a few miles away. What issues will you face running the business at two locations? Draw an organization chart that includes the two business locations.
5. Twenty years later you have 75 business locations in five states. What are the issues and problems that have to be dealt with through organizational structure? Draw an organization chart for this organization, indicating such factors as who is responsible for customer satisfaction, how you will know if customer needs are met, and how information will flow within the organization.

CASE FOR ANALYSIS | C & C Grocery Stores, Inc.[99]

The first C & C Grocery store was started in 1947 by Doug Cummins and his brother Bob. Both were veterans who wanted to run their own business, so they used their savings to start the small grocery store in Charlotte, North Carolina. The store was immediately successful. The location was good, and Doug Cummins had a winning personality. Store employees adopted Doug's informal style and "serve the customer" attitude. C & C's increasing circle of customers enjoyed an abundance of good meats and produce.

By 1997, C & C had over 200 stores. A standard physical layout was used for new stores. Company headquarters moved from Charlotte to Atlanta in 1985. The organization chart for C & C is shown in Exhibit 3.21. The central offices in Atlanta handled personnel, merchandising, financial, purchasing, real estate, and legal affairs for the entire chain. For management of individual stores, the organization was divided by regions. The southern, southeastern, and southwestern regions each had about 70 stores. Each region was divided into five districts of 10 to 15 stores each. A district director was responsible for supervision and coordination of activities for the 10 to 15 district stores.

Each district was divided into four lines of authority based on functional specialty. Three of these lines reached into the stores. The produce department manager within each store reported directly to the produce specialist for the division, and the same was true for the meat department manager, who reported directly to the district meat specialist. The meat and produce managers were responsible for all activities associated with the acquisition and sale of perishable products. The store manager's responsibility included the grocery line, front-end departments, and store operations. The store manager was responsible for appearance of personnel, cleanliness, adequate checkout service, and price accuracy. A grocery manager reported to the store manager, maintained inventories, and restocked shelves for grocery items. The district merchandising office was responsible for promotional campaigns, advertising circulars, district advertising, and attracting customers into the stores. The grocery merchandisers were expected to coordinate their activities with each store in the district.

Business for the C & C chain has dropped off in all regions in recent years—partly because of a declining economy, but mostly because of increased competition from large discount retailers such as Walmart, Target, and Costco. When these large discounters entered the grocery business, they brought a level of competition unlike any C & C had seen before. C & C had managed to hold its own against larger supermarket chains, but now even the big chains were threatened by Walmart, which became number 1 in grocery sales in 2001. C & C managers knew they couldn't compete on price, but they were considering ways they could use advanced information technology to improve service and customer satisfaction and distinguish the store from the large discounters.

However, the most pressing problem was how to improve business with the resources and stores they now had. A consulting team from a major university was hired to investigate store structure and operations. The consultants visited several stores in each region, talking to about 50 managers and employees. The consultants wrote a report that pinpointed four problem areas to be addressed by store executives.

1. *The chain was slow to adapt to change.* Store layout and structure were the same as had been designed 15 years ago. Each store did things the same way, even though some stores were in low-income areas and other stores in suburban areas. A new computerized supply chain management system for ordering and stocking had been developed, but after two years it was only partially implemented in the stores. Other proposed information technology (IT) initiatives were still "on the back burner," not yet even in the development stage.

EXHIBIT 3.21

Organization Structure for C & C Grocery Stores, Inc.

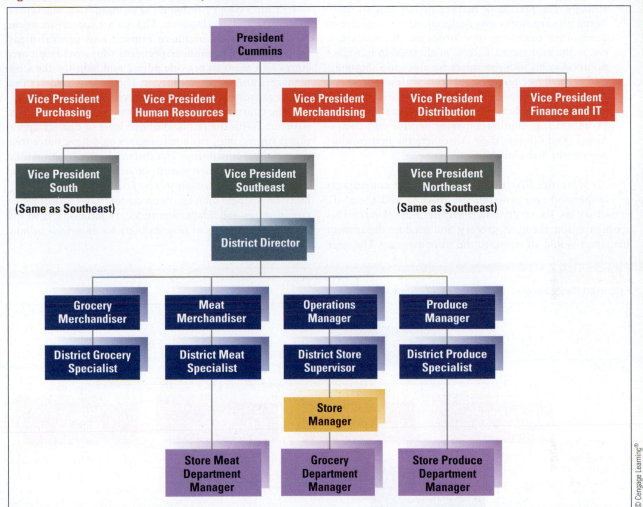

2. *Roles of the district store supervisor and the store manager were causing dissatisfaction.* Store managers wanted more decentralization and freedom to tailor store inventory, and to carry specialty products, to fit their specific market clientele as a way to boost sales. The store managers also wanted to learn general management skills for potential promotion into district or regional management positions. However, their jobs restricted them to narrow operational activities with little authority and they learned little about merchandising, meat, and produce. Moreover, district store supervisors used store visits to inspect for cleanliness and adherence to operating standards rather than to train the store manager and help coordinate operations with perishable departments. Close supervision on the operational

details had become the focus of operations management rather than development, training, and coordination.

3. *Cooperation within stores was low and morale was poor. The informal, friendly atmosphere originally created by Doug Cummins was gone.* One example of this problem occurred when the grocery merchandiser and store manager in a Louisiana store decided to promote Coke and Diet Coke as a loss leader. Thousands of cartons of Coke were brought in for the sale, but the stockroom was not prepared and did not have room. The store manager wanted to use floor area in the meat and produce sections to display Coke cartons, but those managers refused. The produce department manager said that Diet Coke did not help his sales and it was okay with him if there was no promotion at all.

4. *Long-term growth and development of the store chain would probably require reevaluation of long-term strategy.* The percent of market share going to traditional grocery stores was declining nationwide due to competition from large superstores and discount retailers. In the near future, C & C might need to introduce nonfood items into the stores for one-stop shopping, add specialty or gourmet sections within stores, and investigate how new technology could help distinguish the company, such as through targeted marketing and promotion, providing superior service and convenience, and offering their customers the best product assortment and availability.

To solve the first three problems, the consultants recommended reorganizing the district and the store structure as illustrated in Exhibit 3.22. Under this reorganization, the meat, grocery, and produce department managers would all report to the store manager. The store manager would have complete store control and would be responsible for coordination of all store activities. The district supervisor's role would be changed from supervision to training and development. The district supervisor would head a team that included himself and several meat, produce, and merchandise specialists who would visit area stores as a team to provide advice and help for the store managers and other employees. The team would act in a liaison capacity between district specialists and the stores.

The consultants were enthusiastic about the proposed structure. With the removal of one level of district operational supervision, store managers would have more freedom and responsibility. The district liaison team would establish a cooperative team approach to management that could be adopted within stores. Focusing store responsibility on a single manager would encourage coordination within stores and adaptation to local conditions. It would also provide a focus of responsibility for storewide administrative changes.

EXHIBIT 3.22

Proposed Reorganization of C & C Grocery Stores, Inc.

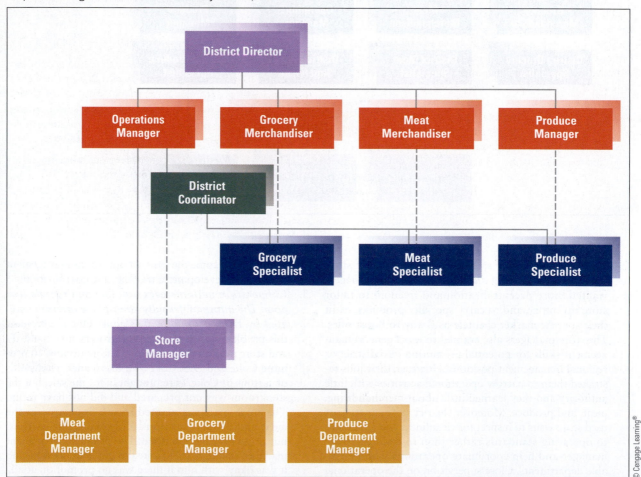

© Cengage Learning®

The consultants also believed that the proposed structure could be expanded to accommodate nongrocery lines and gourmet units if these were included in C & C's future plans. Within each store, a new department manager could be added for pharmacy, gourmet/specialty items, or other major departments. The district team could be expanded to include specialists in these lines, as well as an information technology coordinator to act as liaison for stores in the district.

CASE FOR ANALYSIS | Aquarius Advertising Agency[100]

The Aquarius Advertising Agency is a medium-sized firm that offered two basic services to its clients: customized plans for the content of an advertising campaign (e.g., slogans and layouts) and complete plans for media (e.g., radio, TV, newspapers, billboards, and Internet). Additional services included aid in marketing and distribution of products and marketing research to test advertising effectiveness.

Its activities were organized in a traditional manner. The organization chart is shown in Exhibit 3.23. Each department included similar functions.

Each client account was coordinated by an account executive who acted as a liaison between the client and the various specialists on the professional staff of the operations and marketing divisions. The number of direct communications and contacts between clients and Aquarius specialists, clients and account executives, and Aquarius specialists and account executives is indicated in Exhibit 3.24. These sociometric data were gathered by a consultant who conducted a study of the patterns of formal and informal communication. Each intersecting cell of Aquarius personnel and the clients contains an index of the direct contacts between them.

Although an account executive was designated to be the liaison between the client and specialists within the agency, communications frequently occurred directly between clients and specialists and bypassed the account executive. These direct contacts involved a wide range of interactions, such as meetings, telephone calls, and e-mail messages. A large number of direct communications occurred between agency specialists and their counterparts in the client organization. For example, an art specialist working as one member of a team on a particular client account would often be contacted directly by the client's in-house art specialist, and agency research personnel had direct communication with research personnel of the client firm. Also, some of the unstructured contacts often led to more formal meetings with clients in which agency personnel made presentations, interpreted and defended agency policy, and committed the agency to certain courses of action.

Both hierarchical and professional systems operated within the departments of the operations and marketing divisions. Each department was organized hierarchically with a director, an assistant director, and several levels of authority. Professional communications were widespread and mainly concerned with sharing knowledge and techniques, technical evaluation of work, and development of professional interests. Control in each department was exercised mainly through control of promotions and supervision of work done by subordinates. Many account executives, however, felt the need for more influence, and one commented:

Creativity and art. That's all I hear around here. It is hard as hell to effectively manage six or seven hotshots who claim they have to do their own thing. Each of them tries to sell his or her idea to the client, and most of the time I don't know what has happened until a week later. If I were a despot, I would make all of them check with me first to get approval. Things would sure change around here.

The need for reorganization was made more acute by changes in the environment. Within a short period of time, there was a rapid turnover in the major accounts handled by the agency. It was typical for advertising agencies to gain or lose clients quickly, often with no advance warning as consumer behavior and lifestyle changes emerged and product innovations occurred.

An agency reorganization was one solution proposed by top management to increase flexibility in this unpredictable environment. The reorganization would be aimed at reducing the agency's response time to environmental changes and at increasing cooperation and communication among specialists from different departments. The top managers are not sure what type of reorganization is appropriate. They would like your help analyzing their context and current structure and welcome your advice on proposing a new structure.

EXHIBIT 3.23

Aquarius Advertising Agency Organization Chart

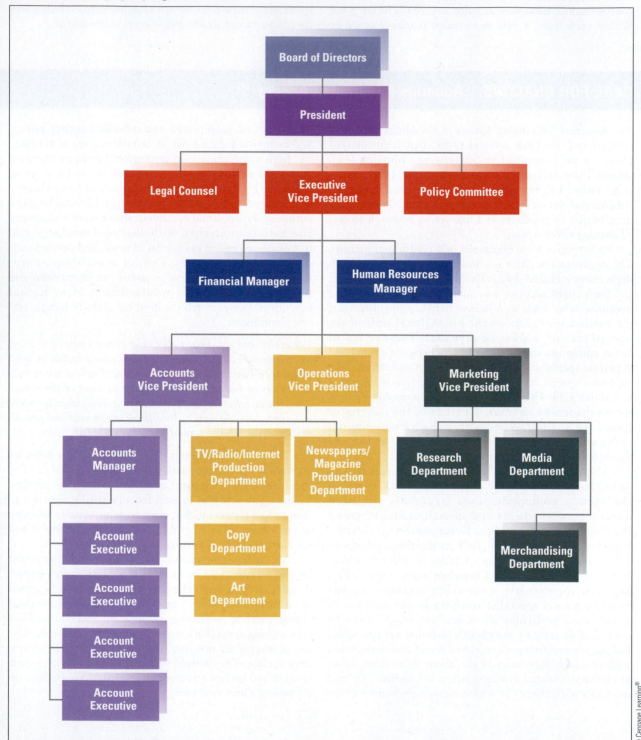

EXHIBIT 3.24

Sociometric Index of Aquarius Personnel and Clients
F = Frequent—daily
O = Occasional—once or twice per project
N = None

	Clients	Account Manager	Account Executives	TV/Radio Specialists	Newspaper/Magazine Specialists	Copy Specialists	Art Specialists	Merchandising Specialists	Media Specialists	Research Specialists
Clients	X	F	F	N	N	O	O	O	O	O
Account Manager		X	F	N	N	N	N	N	N	N
Account Executives			X	F	F	F	F	F	F	F
TV/Radio Specialists				X	N	O	O	N	N	O
Newspaper/Magazine Specialists					X	O	O	N	O	O
Copy Specialists						X	N	O	O	O
Art Specialists							X	O	O	O
Merchandising Specialists								X	F	F
Media Specialists									X	F
Research Specialists										X

© Cengage Learning®

NOTES

1. Phred Dvorak and Yoshio Takahashi, "Nissan Pins Revival on Leadership Trio," *The Wall Street Journal Online*, November 21, 2013, http://online.wsj.com/news/articles/SB100014240 52702304607104579211641207439728 (accessed February 24, 2014).

2. Annie Lowrey, "World Bank, Rooted in Bureaucracy, Proposes a Sweeping Reorganization," *The New York Times*, October 7, 2013, B2.

3. Dan Carrison, "Borrowing Expertise from the FBI," *Industrial Management*, May–June 2009, 23–26.

4. Reported in Brad Stone, *The Everything Store: Jeff Bezos and the Age of Amazon* (New York: Little, Brown, 2013), 168–169.

5. Pete Engardio with Michael Arndt and Dean Foust, "The Future of Outsourcing," *BusinessWeek*, January 30, 2006, 50–58; "Working with Wyeth to Establish a High— Performance Drug Discovery Capability," Accenture website,

http://www.accenture.com/SiteCollectionDocuments
/PDF/wyeth (accessed July 18, 2011); and Ira Spector,
"Industry Partnerships: Changing the Way R&D Is
Conducted," *Applied Clinical Trials Online*, March 1, 2006,
http://appliedclinicaltrialsonline.findpharma.com
/appliedclinicaltrials/article/articleDetail.jsp?id=310807
(accessed July 18, 2011).

6. Carol Hymowitz, "Have Advice, Will Travel; Lacking
   Permanent Offices, Accenture's Executives Run 'Virtual'
   Company on the Fly," *The Wall Street Journal*, June 5, 2006, B1.

7. John Child, *Organization* (New York: Harper & Row, 1984).

8. Stuart Ranson, Bob Hinings, and Royston Greenwood, "The
   Structuring of Organizational Structures," *Administrative
   Science Quarterly* 25 (1980), 1–17; and Hugh Willmott,
   "The Structuring of Organizational Structures: A Note,"
   Administrative Science Quarterly 26 (1981), 470–474.

9. This section is based on Frank Ostroff, *The Horizontal Organization: What the Organization of the Future Looks Like
   and How It Delivers Value to Customers* (New York: Oxford
   University Press, 1999).

10. Stephen Salsbury, *The State, the Investor, and the Railroad:
    The Boston & Albany, 1825–1867* (Cambridge: Harvard
    University Press, 1967), 186–187.

11. "The Cases of Daniel McCallum and Gustavus Swift,"
    Willamette University, http://www.willamette.edu/~fthompso
    /MgmtCon/McCallum.htm (accessed July 29, 2011);
    "The Rise of the Professional Manager in America,"
    ManagementGuru.com, http://www.mgmtguru.com/mgt301
    /301_Lecture1Page7.htm (accessed July 29, 2011); and Alfred
    D. Chandler, *Strategy and Structure: Chapters in the History
    of the American Industrial Enterprise* (Cambridge, MA:
    Massachusetts Institute of Technology Press, 1962).

12. David Nadler and Michael Tushman, *Strategic Organization
    Design* (Glenview, IL: Scott Foresman, 1988).

13. William C. Ouchi, "Power to the Principals: Decentralization
    in Three Large School Districts," *Organization Science* 17,
    no. 2 (March–April 2006), 298–307.

14. Sarah Lyall, "Britain Plans to Decentralize Health Care,"
    The New York Times, July 24, 2010, www.nytimes
    .com/2010/07/25/world/europe/25britain.
    html?pagewanted=all (accessed August 14, 2012).

15. Hiroko Tabuchi and Bill Vlasic, "Battered by Expensive Crises,
    Toyota Declares a Rebirth," *The New York Times*, January 3,
    2013, B1.

16. Ibid.

17. Andrew Campbell, Sven Kunisch, and Günter Müller-Stewens,
    "To Centralize or Not to Centralize?" *McKinsey Quarterly*,
    June 2011, www.mckinseyquarterly.com/To_centralize_or
    _not_to_centralize_2815 (accessed August 14, 2012).

18. Ibid.; and "Country Managers: From Baron to Hotelier," *The
    Economist*, May 11, 2002, 55–56.

19. Based on Jay R. Galbraith, *Designing Complex Organizations*
    (Reading, MA: Addison-Wesley, 1973), and *Organization
    Design* (Reading, MA: Addison-Wesley, 1977), 81–127.

20. George Anders, "Overseeing More Employees—With Fewer
    Managers," *The Wall Street Journal*, March 24, 2008, B6.

21. Thomas Kayser, "Six Ingredients for Collaborative Partner-
    ships," *Leader to Leader*, Summer 2011, 48–54.

22. Siobhan Gorman and Julian E. Barnes, "Spy, Military Ties
    Aided bin Laden Raid," *The Wall Street Journal*, May 23,
    2011, http://online.wsj.com/article/SB1000142405274870408
    3904576334160172068344.html (accessed May 23, 2011).

23. Lee Iacocca with William Novak, *Iacocca: An Autobiography*
    (New York: Phantom Books, 1984), 152–153.

24. Ronald J. Recardo and Kleigh Heather, "Ten Best Practices
    for Restructuring the Organization," *Global Business and
    Organizational Excellence*, January–February 2013, 23–37;
    Kirsten Foss and Waymond Rodgers, "Enhancing Information
    Usefulness by Line Managers' Involvement in Cross-Unit
    Activities," *Organization Studies* 32, no. 5 (2011), 683–703;
    M. Casson, *Information and Organization* (Oxford: Oxford
    University Press, 1997); Justin J. P. Jansen, Michiel P.
    Tempelaar, Frans A. J. van den Bosch, and Henk W. Volberda,
    "Structural Differentiation and Ambidexterity: The Mediating
    Role of Integration Mechanisms," *Organization Science* 20,
    no. 4 (July–August 2009), 797–811; and Galbraith, *Designing
    Complex Organizations*.

25. "Panel Says Toyota Failed to Listen to Outsiders," *USA Today*,
    May 23, 2011, http://content.usatoday.com/communities
    /driveon/post/2011/05/toyota-panel-calls-for-single-us-chief
    -paying-heed-to-criticism/1#.VDU5Q7N0x1s (accessed
    October 7, 2014).

26. These are based in part on Galbraith, *Designing Complex
    Organizations*; and Recardo and Heather, "Ten Best Practices
    for Restructuring the Organization."

27. David Stires, "How the VA Healed Itself," *Fortune*, May 15,
    2006, 130–136.

28. Jay Galbraith, Diane Downey, and Amy Kates, "How Net-
    works Undergird the Lateral Capability of an Organization—
    Where the Work Gets Done," *Journal of Organizational
    Excellence* (Spring 2002), 67–78.

29. Walter Kiechel III, "The Art of the Corporate Task Force,"
    Fortune, January 28, 1991, 104–105; and William J. Altier,
    "Task Forces: An Effective Management Tool," *Management
    Review*, February 1987, 52–57.

30. Margaret Frazier, "Flu Prep," *The Wall Street Journal*, March
    25–26, 2006, A8.

31. Paul R. Lawrence and Jay W. Lorsch, "New Managerial
    Job: The Integrator," *Harvard Business Review*, November–
    December 1967, 142–151.

32. Dan Heath and Chip Heath, "Blowing the Baton Pass," *Fast
    Company*, July–August 2010, 46–48.

33. Anthony M. Townsend, Samuel M. DeMarie, and Anthony R.
    Hendrickson, "Virtual Teams: Technology and the Workplace
    of the Future," *Academy of Management Executive* 12, no. 3
    (August 1998), 17–29.

34. Erin White, "How a Company Made Everyone a Team
    Player," *The Wall Street Journal*, August 13, 2007, B1.

35. Pete Engardio, "A Guide for Multinationals: One of the
    Greatest Challenges for a Multinational Is Learning How to
    Build a Productive Global Team," *BusinessWeek*, August 20,
    2007, 48–51; and Lynda Gratton, "Working Together . . .
    When Apart," *The Wall Street Journal*, June 18, 2007.

36. Jody Hoffer Gittell, *The Southwest Airlines Way: Using the
    Power of Relationships to Achieve High Performance*
    (New York: McGraw-Hill, 2003).

37. This discussion is based on Jody Hoffer Gittell,
    "Coordinating Mechanisms in Care Provider Groups:
    Relational Coordination as a Mediator and Input
    Uncertainty as a Moderator of Performance Effects,"
    Management Science 48, no. 11 (November 2002), 1408–
    1426; J. H. Gittell, "The Power of Relationships," *Sloan
    Management Review* (Winter 2004), 16–17; and J. H. Gittell,
    The Southwest Airlines Way.

38. Based on the story in Jody Hoffer Gittell, "Paradox of Coordination and Control," *California Management Review* 42, no. 3 (Spring 2000), 101–117.

39. "Transcript of Stripes Interview with Lt. Gen. David M. Rodriguez," *Stars and Stripes*, December 31, 2009, http://www.stripes.com/news/transcript-of-stripes-interview-with-lt-gen-david-m-rodriguez-1.97669# (accessed July 21, 2011); and Robert D. Kaplan, "Man Versus Afghanistan," *The Atlantic*, April 2010, 60–71. Note: Rodriguez was scheduled to leave Afghanistan in late July 2011.

40. Henry Mintzberg, *The Structuring of Organizations* (Englewood Cliffs, NJ: Prentice-Hall, 1979).

41. Frank Ostroff, "Stovepipe Stomper," *Government Executive*, April 1999, 70.

42. Raymond E. Miles, Charles C. Snow, Øystein D. Fjeldstad, Grant Miles, and Christopher Lettl, "Designing Organizations to Meet 21st-Century Opportunities and Challenges," *Organizational Dynamics* 39, no. 2 (2010), 93–103.

43. Based on Robert Duncan, "What Is the Right Organization Structure?" *Organizational Dynamics*, Winter 1979, 59–80; and W. Alan Randolph and Gregory G. Dess, "The Congruence Perspective of Organization Design: A Conceptual Model and Multivariate Research Approach," *Academy of Management Review* 9 (1984), 114–127.

44. Geeta Anand, "The Henry Ford of Heart Surgery," *The Wall Street Journal*, November 25, 2009, A16.

45. Survey reported in Timothy Galpin, Rod Hilpirt, and Bruce Evans, "The Connected Enterprise: Beyond Division of Labor," *Journal of Business Strategy* 28, no. 2 (2007), 38–47.

46. Adam Bryant, "An Office? She'll Pass on That," (an interview with Meridee A. Moore, Corner Office column), *The Wall Street Journal*, March 7, 2010, BU2.

47. Rahul Jacob, "The Struggle to Create an Organization for the 21st Century," *Fortune*, April 3, 1995, 90–99.

48. R. E. Miles et al., "Designing Organizations to Meet 21st-Century Opportunities and Challenges."

49. David C. Robertson with Bill Breen, *Brick by Brick: How LEGO Rewrote the Rules of Innovation and Conquered the Global Toy Industry* (New York: Crown Business, 2013), 32.

50. N. Anand and Richard L. Daft, "What Is the Right Organization Design?" *Organizational Dynamics* 36, no. 4 (2007), 329–344.

51. Loretta Chao, "Alibaba Breaks Up E-Commerce Unit," *The Wall Street Journal*, June 17, 2011, B2.

52. Yue Maggie Zhou, "Designing for Complexity: Using Divisions and Hierarchy to Manage Complex Tasks," *Organization Science* 24, no. 2 (March–April 2013), 339–355.

53. Geoff Colvin and Jessica Shambora, "J&J: Secrets of Success," *Fortune*, May 4, 2009, 117–121.

54. Eliza Newlin Carney, "Calm in the Storm," *Government Executive*, October 2003, 57–63; and Brian Friel, "Hierarchies and Networks," *Government Executive*, April 2002, 31–39.

55. Based on Duncan, "What Is the Right Organization Structure?"

56. Joseph Weber, "A Big Company That Works," *BusinessWeek*, May 4, 1992, 124.

57. Phred Dvorak and Merissa Marr, "Stung by iPod, Sony Addresses a Digital Lag," *The Wall Street Journal*, December 30, 2004, B1.

58. Nick Wingfield, "Microsoft Overhauls, the Apple Way," http://www.nytimes.com/2013/07/12/technology/microsoft-revamps-structure-and-management.html?pagewanted=all (accessed October 7, 2014); Brian R. Fitzgerald, "Microsoft Memo: The Highlights," *The Wall Street Journal*, July 13, 2013, http://blogs.wsj.com/digits/2013/07/11/microsoft-memo-the-highlights/ (accessed February 25, 2014); and quote from Kurt Eichenwald, "Microsoft's Lost Decade," *Vanity Fair*, August 2012, 108–135.

59. Susanna Kim, "Major Microsoft Investors Want Bill Gates Out as Chairman," *ABC News*, October 2, 2013, http://abcnews.go.com/Business/microsoft-shareholders-call-bill-gates-step-chairman/story?id=20443636 (accessed October 2, 2013).

60. Maisie O'Flanagan and Lynn K. Taliento, "Nonprofits: Ensuring That Bigger Is Better," *McKinsey Quarterly*, no. 2 (2004), 112ff.

61. Lowrey, "World Bank, Rooted in Bureaucracy, Proposes a Sweeping Reorganization."

62. Mae Anderson, "Wal-Mart Reorganizes U.S. Operations to Help Spur Growth," *USA Today*, January 28, 2010, http://www.usatoday.com/money/industries/retail/2010-01-28-walmart-reorganization_N.htm (accessed July 21, 2011); and "Organizational Chart of Wal-Mart Stores," The Official Board.com, http://www.theofficialboard.com/org-chart/wal-mart-stores (accessed July 21, 2011).

63. Jay R. Galbraith, "The Multi-Dimensional and Reconfigurable Organization," *Organizational Dynamics* 39, no. 2 (2010), 115–125; Thomas Sy and Laura Sue D'Annunzio, "Challenges and Strategies of Matrix Organizations: Top-Level and Mid-Level Managers' Perspectives," *Human Resource Planning* 28, no. 1 (2005), 39–48; and Stanley M. Davis and Paul R. Lawrence, *Matrix* (Reading, MA: Addison-Wesley, 1977), 11–24. For a current perspective on matrix management, see Kevan Hall, *Making the Matrix Work: How Matrix Managers Engage People and Cut Through Complexity* (London: Nicholas Brealey Publishing, 2013).

64. Davis and Lawrence, *Matrix*.

65. Steven H. Appelbaum, David Nadeau, and Michael Cyr, "Performance Evaluation in a Matrix Organization: A Case Study (Part One)," *Industrial and Commercial Training* 40, no. 5 (2008), 236–241; Erik W. Larson and David H. Gobeli, "Matrix Management: Contradictions and Insight," *California Management Review* 29 (Summer 1987), 126–138; and Sy and D'Annunzio, "Challenges and Strategies of Matrix Organizations."

66. Davis and Lawrence, *Matrix*, 155–180.

67. Robert C. Ford and W. Alan Randolph, "Cross-Functional Structures: A Review and Integration of Matrix Organizations and Project Management," *Journal of Management* 18 (June 1992), 267–294; and Duncan, "What Is the Right Organization Structure?"

68. Lawton R. Burns, "Matrix Management in Hospitals: Testing Theories of Matrix Structure and Development," *Administrative Science Quarterly* 34 (1989), 349–368; and Sy and D'Annunzio, "Challenges and Strategies of Matrix Organizations."

69. Carol Hymowitz, "Managers Suddenly Have to Answer to a Crowd of Bosses" (In the Lead column), *The Wall Street Journal*, August 12, 2003, B1; and Michael Goold and Andrew Campbell, "Making Matrix Structures Work: Creating Clarity on Unit Roles and Responsibilities," *European Management Journal* 21, no. 3 (June 2003), 351–363.

70. Christopher A. Bartlett and Sumantra Ghoshal, "Matrix Management: Not a Structure, a Frame of Mind," *Harvard Business Review*, July–August 1990, 138–145.

71. Kevan Hall, "Revisiting Matrix Management," *People & Strategy* 36, no. 1 (2013), 4–5.

72. This case was inspired by John E. Fogerty, "Integrative Management at Standard Steel" (unpublished manuscript, Latrobe, Pennsylvania, 1980); Stanley Reed with Adam Aston, "Steel: The Mergers Aren't Over Yet," *Business Week*, February 21, 2005, 6; Michael Arndt, "Melting Away Steel's Costs," *Business Week*, November 8, 2004, 48; and "Steeling for a Fight," *The Economist*, June 4, 1994, 63.

73. Michael Hammer, "Process Management and the Future of Six Sigma," *Sloan Management Review*, Winter 2002, 26–32; and Michael Hammer and Steve Stanton, "How Process Enterprises *Really* Work," *Harvard Business Review* 77 (November–December 1999), 108–118.

74. Hammer, "Process Management and the Future of Six Sigma."

75. Based on Ostroff, *The Horizontal Organization*; and Anand and Daft, "What Is the Right Organization Design?"

76. Julia Moskin, "Your Waiter Tonight . . . Will Be the Chef," *The New York Times*, March 12, 2008, F1.

77. Frank Ostroff, *The Horizontal Organization*, 102–114.

78. Jill Jusko, "Engaged Teams Keep Lockheed Martin Delivering on Time, Every Time," *Industry Week*, January 2013, 26.

79. See Anand and Daft, "What Is the Right Organization Design?"; Pete Engardio, "The Future of Outsourcing," *Business Week*, January 30, 2006, 50–58; Jane C. Linder, "Transformational Outsourcing," *MIT Sloan Management Review*, Winter 2004, 52–58; and Denis Chamberland, "Is It Core or Strategic? Outsourcing as a Strategic Management Tool," *Ivey Business Journal*, July–August 2003, 1–5.

80. Bob Sechler, "Colleges Shedding Non-Core Operations," *The Wall Street Journal*, April 2, 2012, A6; and David Streitfeld, "A City Outsources Everything. California's Sky Doesn't Fall," *The New York Times*, July 20, 2010, A1.

81. Anand and Daft, "What Is the Right Organization Design?"; Yuzo Yamaguchi and Daisuke Wakabayashi, "Hitachi to Outsource TV Manufacture," *The Wall Street Journal Online*, July 10, 2009, http://online.wsj.com/article /SB124714255400717925.html (accessed July 17, 2009); Engardio, "The Future of Outsourcing"; Chamberland, "Is It Core or Strategic?"; and Keith H. Hammonds, "Smart, Determined, Ambitious, Cheap: The New Face of Global Competition," *Fast Company*, February 2003, 91–97.

82. Jena McGregor, "The Chore Goes Offshore," *Business Week*, March 23 & 30, 2009, 50–51.

83. David Nadler, quoted in "Partners in Wealth: The Ins and Outs of Collaboration," *The Economist*, January 21–27, 2006, 16–17.

84. Ranjay Gulati, "Silo Busting: How to Execute on the Promise of Customer Focus," *Harvard Business Review*, May 2007, 98–108.

85. The discussion of virtual networks is based on Anand and Daft, "What Is the Right Organization Design?"; Melissa A. Schilling and H. Kevin Steensma, "The Use of Modular Organizational Forms: An Industry-Level Analysis," *Academy of Management Journal* 44, no. 6 (2001), 1149–1168; Raymond E. Miles and Charles C. Snow, "The New Network Firm: A Spherical Structure Built on a Human Investment Philosophy," *Organizational Dynamics*, Spring 1995, 5–18; and R. E. Miles, C. C. Snow, J. A. Matthews, G. Miles,

and H. J. Coleman Jr., "Organizing in the Knowledge Age: Anticipating the Cellular Form," *Academy of Management Executive* 11, no. 4 (1997), 7–24.

86. Darren Dahl, "Want a Job? Let the Bidding Begin; a Radical Take on the Virtual Company," *Inc.*, March 2011, 93–96.

87. David Segal, "A Georgia Town Takes the People's Business Private," *The New York Times*, June 24, 2012, BU1.

88. Paul Engle, "You *Can* Outsource Strategic Processes," *Industrial Management*, January–February 2002, 13–18.

89. Don Tapscott, "Rethinking Strategy in a Networked World," *Strategy + Business* 24 (Third Quarter, 2001), 34–41.

90. Joann S. Lublin, "Smart Balance Keeps Tight Focus on Creativity" (Theory & Practice column), *The Wall Street Journal*, June 8, 2009; and Rebecca Reisner, "A Smart Balance of Staff and Contractors," *Business Week Online*, June 16, 2009, http://www.businessweek.com/managing/content /jun2009/ca20090616_217232.htm (accessed April 30, 2010).

91. Gregory G. Dess, Abdul M. A. Rasheed, Kevin J. McLaughlin, and Richard L. Priem, "The New Corporate Architecture," *Academy of Management Executive* 9, no. 3 (1995), 7–20.

92. This discussion of strengths and weaknesses is based on Miles and Snow, "The New Network Firm"; Dess et al., "The New Corporate Architecture"; Anand and Daft, "What Is the Right Organization Design?"; Henry W. Chesbrough and David J. Teece, "Organizing for Innovation: When Is Virtual Virtuous?" *Harvard Business Review*, August 2002, 127–134; Cecily A. Raiborn, Janet B. Butler, and Marc F. Massoud, "Outsourcing Support Functions: Identifying and Managing the Good, the Bad, and the Ugly," *Business Horizons* 52 (2009), 347–356; and M. Lynne Markus, Brook Manville, and Carole E. Agres, "What Makes a Virtual Organization Work?" *Sloan Management Review*, Fall 2000, 13–26.

93. James R. Hagerty, "A Toy Maker Comes Home to the U.S.A.," *The Wall Street Journal*, March 11, 2013, B1.

94. "Organization Chart for Starbucks," The Official Board. com, http://www.theofficialboard.com/org-chart/starbucks (accessed July 21, 2011).

95. Linda S. Ackerman, "Transition Management: An In-depth Look at Managing Complex Change," *Organizational Dynamics*, Summer 1982, 46–66.

96. Based on Ostroff, *The Horizontal Organization*, 29–44.

97. Based on Child, *Organization*, Ch. 1; and Jonathan D. Day, Emily Lawson, and Keith Leslie, "When Reorganization Works," *The McKinsey Quarterly*, 2003 Special Edition: The Value in Organization, 21–29.

98. Adapted by Dorothy Marcic from "Organizing," in Donald D. White and H. William Vroman, *Action in Organizations*, 2nd ed. (Boston: Allyn & Bacon, 1982), 154; and Cheryl Harvey and Kim Morouney, "Organization Structure and Design: The Club Ed Exercise," *Journal of Management Education* (June 1985), 425–429.

99. Prepared by Richard L. Daft, from Richard L. Daft and Richard Steers, *Organizations: A Micro/Macro Approach* (Glenview, IL: Scott Foresman, 1986). Reprinted with permission.

100. Adapted from John F. Veiga and John N. Yanouzas, "Aquarius Advertising Agency," *The Dynamics of Organization Theory* (St. Paul, MN: West, 1984), 212–217, with permission.

Open System Design Elements

3

PART

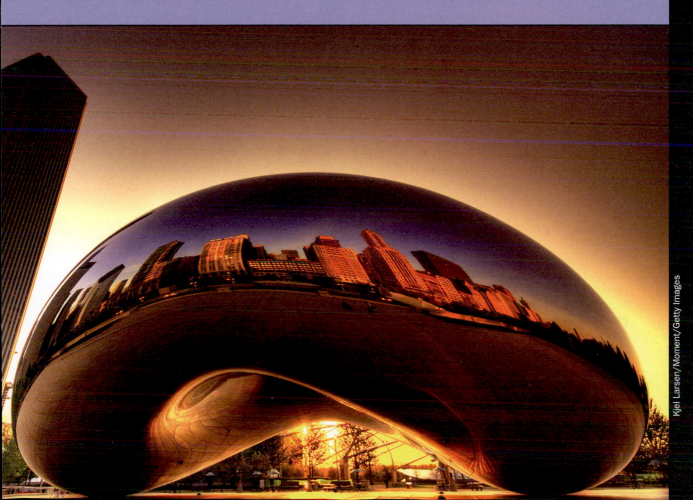

Kjel Larsen/Moment/Getty Images

4 The External Environment

Learning Objectives

After reading this chapter you should be able to:

1. Define the task environment and its key sectors.
2. Define the general environment and its key sectors.
3. Explain environmental complexity and environmental dynamism.
4. Describe the environmental uncertainty model.
5. Explain how organizations adapt to complexity and dynamism in a changing environment.
6. Understand how the environment affects organizational differentiation and integration.
7. Describe how the environment affects organic versus mechanistic management processes.
8. Specify how organizations depend on financial resources.
9. Recognize how organizations influence key environment sectors.

Before reading this chapter, please check whether you agree or disagree with each of the following statements:

1 The best way for an organization to cope with a complex environment is to develop a complex structure (rather than keep it simple and uncomplicated).

   I AGREE _____   I DISAGREE _____

2 In a volatile, fast-changing environment, serious planning activities are a waste of time and resources.

   I AGREE _____   I DISAGREE _____

3 Managers of business organizations should not get involved in political activities.

   I AGREE _____   I DISAGREE _____

Gregg Steinhafel, who joined Target as a buyer in 1979 and took over as the CEO in 2008, earned a reputation for stocking the stores with trendy merchandise at low prices. Target's bulls-eye logo became one of the best-known trademarks in retail. It seemed that Target could do no wrong, but in the past few years, things have been rough for Steinhafel and Target. The biggest problem was a disastrous security failure during the 2013 holiday shopping season, when malicious software quietly gathered account information from 40 million credit and debit cards as the data moved unencrypted through Target's cash register systems. News of the data breach seriously hurt Target, reducing traffic at stores and making it more difficult for executives to deal with other issues. Executives were already struggling with a costlier-than-expected expansion into Canada and taking over online operations from Amazon, which ran Target's back-end operations until 2011. When Target first took over the website, it was unreliable, crashing at times when demand was high for hot-selling products. All of these issues led to the layoff of 475 people and the elimination of 700 open positions at headquarters, the largest round of corporate layoffs since 2009. Morale is in the pits. "Target's staff needs to be utterly focused on reinvigorating the business and the data breach diverted their attention at a critical time," said Amy Koo, an analyst with consultancy Kantar Retail.[1]

Changes in the environment can create both threats and opportunities for organizations. The data breach was a serious external threat to Target, and managers will likely be dealing with the fallout for years. All organizations face tremendous uncertainty in dealing with events in the external environment and often have to adapt quickly to new competition, economic turmoil, changes in consumer interests, or innovative technologies. Cybercrime, such as the data breach at Target, is a growing threat from the environment to every organization.

Purpose of This Chapter

The purpose of this chapter is to develop a framework for assessing environments and how organizations can respond to them. First we identify the organizational domain and the sectors that influence the organization. Then we explore two major environmental forces on the organization—the need for information and the need for financial resources. Organizations respond to these forces through structural design; planning systems; and attempts to adapt to and influence various people, events, and organizations in the external environment.

The Organization's Environment

In a broad sense the environment is infinite and includes everything outside the organization. However, the analysis presented here considers only those aspects of the environment to which the organization is sensitive and must respond to survive. Thus, **organizational environment** is defined as everything that exists outside the boundary of the organization and has the potential to affect all or part of the organization.

The environment of an organization can be understood by analyzing its domain within external sectors. An organization's **domain** is the chosen environmental field of action. It is the territory an organization stakes out for itself with respect to products, services, and markets served. Domain defines the organization's niche and defines those external sectors with which the organization will interact to accomplish its goals.

The environment comprises several **sectors** or subdivisions that contain similar elements. Eleven sectors can be analyzed for each organization: industry, raw materials, human resources, financial resources, market, technology, economic conditions, government, natural, sociocultural, and international. The sectors and a hypothetical organizational domain are illustrated in Exhibit 4.1. For most companies, the sectors in Exhibit 4.1 can be further categorized as either the task environment or the general environment.

Task Environment

The **task environment** includes sectors with which the organization interacts directly and that have a direct impact on the organization's ability to achieve its goals. The task environment typically includes the industry, raw materials, and market sectors, and perhaps the human resources and international sectors.

The following examples illustrate how each of these sectors can affect organizations:

- In the *industry sector*, the retail industry in South Korea has always been dominated by big department stores, but as smartphone use has surged in the country over the past few years, companies saw new ways to reach consumers. South Korea has a low number of women in the workforce, so there is a ready audience of affluent television and Internet shoppers. Online and home shopping competitors are growing in popularity, and posters on subway station walls allow people to make purchases simply by snapping a picture of a barcode.[2]
- In the *raw materials sector*, Tyson Foods is spending hundreds of millions of dollars to build 90 chicken farms in China to guarantee a supply of high-quality birds, which the company then processes and sells to fast food companies, wholesalers, and other meatpackers that use the meat in sausage and other products. In the United States, Tyson pays independent farmers to raise chickens, but it has little control over product quality and safety in China so it decided to run its own farms, hoping safe products will build its brand in a country where the company is not well known.[3]

BRIEFCASE

As an organization manager, keep these guidelines in mind:

Organize elements in the external environment into 11 sectors for analysis: industry, raw materials, human resources, financial resources, market, technology, economic conditions, government, natural, sociocultural, and international. Focus on sectors that may experience significant change at any time.

EXHIBIT 4.1

An Organization's Environment

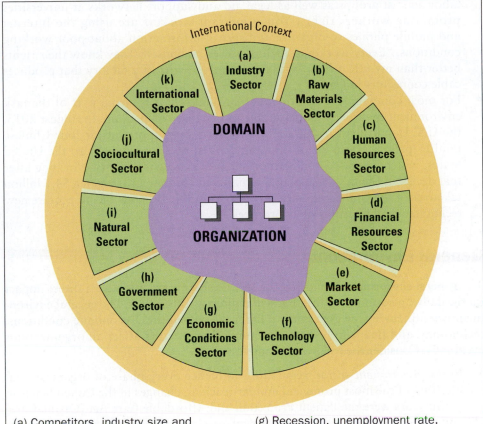

(a) Competitors, industry size and competitiveness, related industries

(b) Suppliers, manufacturers, real estate, services

(c) Labor market, employment agencies, universities, training schools, employees in other companies, unionization

(d) Stock markets, banks, savings and loans, private investors

(e) Customers, clients, potential users of products and services

(f) Techniques of production, science, computers, information technology, e-commerce

(g) Recession, unemployment rate, inflation rate, rate of investment, economics, growth

(h) City, state, federal laws and regulations, taxes, services, court system, political processes

(i) Green movement, sustainability, natural resource management

(i) Age, values, beliefs, education, religion, work ethic, consumer movements

(j) Competition from and acquisition by foreign firms, entry into overseas markets, foreign customs, regulations, exchange rate

© Cengage Learning®

- In the *market sector*, smart companies are keeping tabs on social media (tweets, Facebook) to see what customers and potential customers care about, gain rapid insight into trends, and learn what words to use in marketing. For example, companies such as Mars, the maker of M&Ms, and Kraft, which makes different varieties of macaroni and cheese, are tweaking their products, particularly the use of certain food dyes, to address customer concerns.[4]

- The *human resources sector* is of significant concern to every business. In China, a new labor movement is challenging business leaders with emerging labor activist groups as well as legal aid and support networks at universities promoting workers rights. Young migrant workers are using the Internet and mobile phones to organize and spread information about poor working conditions. "Every worker is a labor lawyer by himself. They know their rights better than my HR officer," said the German owner of a factory that produces cable connectors in China.[5]

- For most companies today, the *international sector* is also a part of the task environment because of globalization and intense competition. In August 2013, the U.S. Department of Agriculture (USDA) gave approval for four Chinese poultry processors to begin shipping cooked poultry products to the United States, which increased competition for U.S. processing plants. Not long after that decision, China's Shuanghui International Holding Ltd. began a $4.7 billion takeover of the U.S.-based pork processor Smithfield Foods Inc. to acquire new technology and improve safety practices.[6]

General Environment

The **general environment** includes those sectors that might not have a direct impact on the daily operations of a firm but will indirectly influence it. The general environment often includes the government, natural, sociocultural, economic conditions, technology, and financial resources sectors. These sectors affect all organizations eventually. Consider the following examples:

- In the *government sector*, regulations influence every phase of organizational life. Two of the most prominent and far-reaching changes in the United States in recent years were the Patient Protection and Affordable Care Act (ObamaCare) and the Dodd–Frank Act (financial regulatory reform).[7] Small companies in particular are struggling with the time and expense required to meet provisions of new healthcare and financial reform laws.

- The *natural sector* of the external environment, including all elements that occur naturally on earth, is of growing importance as consumers, organizations, and managers become increasingly sensitive to diminishing natural resources and the environmental impact of a company's products and business practices. Many companies have adopted a philosophy of *sustainability*, which refers to economic development that meets the needs of the current generation while preserving the environment for the needs of future generations as well. Caesars Entertainment, one of the world's largest gaming companies, created a scorecard to keep track of how well the company was doing at reducing energy consumption, recycling waste, reducing water consumption, and meeting other "green" goals. Managers found that the more information guests had about Caesars' sustainability practices, the better they felt about the company and the more likely they were to enjoy their stay at the casino and to book future visits.[8]

- One significant element in the *sociocultural sector* is pressure from advocacy groups to improve working conditions for employees hired by contractors for large companies such as Walmart, Apple, and Amazon. Walmart recently suspended one of its seafood suppliers in the South after immigrant workers said they had been forced to work more than 80 hours a week, threatened with beatings, and told their families in Mexico would be hurt if they complained to government agencies. The National Guestworker Alliance released a list of 644 federal citations at 12 Walmart food suppliers. "We work with more than 60,000 suppliers in the United States and we have rigorous standards in place that our suppliers are required to follow," said Lorenzo Lopez, a Walmart spokesman, adding that Walmart is conducting its own investigation and will terminate its relationship with any suppliers that violate its ethical standards.[9]

- General *economic conditions* often affect the way a company must do business. The global recession that began in 2008 affected companies in all industries. Briggs Inc., a small New York City company that plans customized events for corporations wanting to woo top clients or reward staff or client loyalty, had to make some changes when it began losing customers. Even huge, elite corporations were hesitant to spend extravagantly in the weakening economy, so Briggs began looking for ways to save clients' money, such as moving events to smaller venues, scaling down décor, and adding extras that didn't add to the cost. Companies can hold stylish and unique events in boutique hotels instead of Fifth Avenue locations, for instance. The strategy was a financial burden for Briggs, but it helped the company hold onto clients for the long term.[10]

- The *technology sector* is an area in which massive changes have occurred in recent years. Technology for mobile Internet is a rapidly growing area. Although technology has created some jobs, analysts say it is eliminating many more than it is creating. In countries from the United States to Canada to Japan, studies have found substantial drops in white-collar jobs linked to adoption of new technology. Today, software is picking out worrisome spots on medical scans, spotting profits in stock trades in milliseconds, sifting through documents for evidence in court cases, and recording power usage beamed from digital utility meters at millions of homes. A consultant estimates that 2 million jobs in human resources, finance, information technology, and procurement have disappeared in the United States and Europe since 2008 and been replaced by technology. When business conditions improve, many managers realize they don't have to rehire.[11]

- All businesses have to be concerned with *financial resources*, and this sector is often the first and foremost in the minds of entrepreneurs. Many small-business owners turned to online person-to-person (P-to-P) lending networks for small loans as banks tightened their lending standards. Jeff Walsh, for example, borrowed around $22,000 through Prosper.com for his coin laundry business. Alex Kalempa needed $15,000 to expand his business of developing racing shift systems for motorcycles, but banks offered him credit lines of only $500 to $1,000. Kalempa went to LendingClub.com, where he got the $15,000 loan at an interest rate several points lower than the banks were offering.[12]

International Environment

The international sector can directly affect many organizations, and it has become extremely important in the last few years. The auto industry, for example, has experienced profound shifts as China recently emerged as the world's largest auto market. In response, car makers are moving international headquarters into China and designing features that appeal to the Chinese market, including bigger, limousine-like back seats, advanced entertainment systems, and light-colored interiors. These trends, inspired by the Chinese market, are reflected in models sold around the world.[13]

In addition, international events can influence all the domestic sectors of the environment. For example, adverse weather and a workers' strike in Western Africa, which supplies about two-thirds of the world's cocoa beans, sharply increased raw material costs for Choco-Logo, a small maker of gourmet chocolates in Buffalo, New York.[14] Farmers, fertilizer companies, food manufacturers, and grocers in the United States faced new competitive issues because of an unexpected grain shortage and rising costs related to international changes. Strong economic growth in developing countries enabled millions of people to afford richer diets, including grain-fed meat, which directly contributed to the grain shortage in the United States.[15] Countries and organizations around the world are connected as never before, and economic, political, and sociocultural changes in one part of the world eventually affect other areas.

Every organization faces uncertainty domestically as well as globally. Consider the fate of the Richard Ginori porcelain tableware factory in Italy.

IN PRACTICE

Richard Ginori

Founded in 1735, the Richard Ginori factory has produced singular, handcrafted, elegantly decorated porcelain tableware that graced the tables of Italy's wealthy, was customized for luxury liners and lavish hotels, and has been used at the Vatican. But after years of struggling, the factory declared bankruptcy in January 2013.

Changes and uncertainty in the environment have been too much for Ginori to handle. Formal dining has been gradually dying out, and along with it the market for handmade porcelain, which is slow and expensive to produce. To try to compete, Ginori began producing more everyday products, including tableware as a promotional giveaway for a supermarket. That only weakened the brand, some say, and put it in direct competition with cheaper ceramics. Italians now buy about 60 percent of their tableware from China. The lobbying association that represents 273 Italian ceramics manufacturers has accused the Chinese of dumping products in the Italian market below the cost of manufacturing.

Court-appointed liquidators have been searching for a buyer for what's left of Ginori. The city of Sesto Fiorentino and the 300 employees of the factory who fret by the front gates can do little to determine what happens with all the uncertainty in the environment. "Foreign capital is welcome," said Mayor Gianni Gianassi, "but the heads and the hands of the factory must remain Tuscan."[16]

All organizations have to adapt to both subtle and massive shifts in the environment. In the following sections, we discuss in greater detail how companies can cope with and respond to environmental complexity and dynamism.

The Changing Environment

How does the environment influence an organization? The patterns and events occurring in the environment can be described along three primary dimensions: dynamism (whether events in the environment are stable or unstable), complexity (whether the environment is simple or complex), and abundance (amount of financial resources available to support the organization's growth).[17] These dimensions are illustrated in Exhibit 4.2. As the environment becomes more complex, events become less stable, and financial resources become less available, the level of uncertainty increases. These dimensions boil down to two essential ways the environment influences organizations: (1) the need for information about

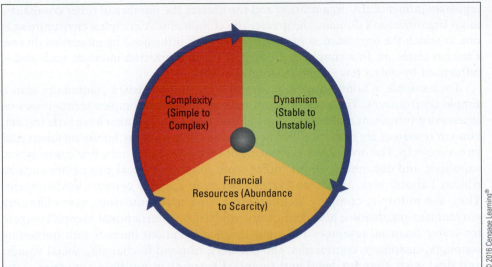

© 2016 Cengage Learning®

EXHIBIT 4.2
Factors Causing
Uncertainty for the
Organization

changes in the environment and (2) the need for resources from the environment. The environmental conditions of complexity and dynamism create a greater need to gather information and to respond to changes based on that information. The organization also is concerned with scarce financial resources and with the need to ensure availability of resources, which will be discussed later in this chapter.

Environmental uncertainty pertains primarily to those sectors illustrated in Exhibit 4.1 that an organization deals with on a regular, day-to-day basis. Although sectors of the general environment—such as economic conditions, social trends, or technological changes—can create uncertainty for organizations, determining an organization's environmental uncertainty generally means focusing on sectors of the *task environment,* such as how many elements (e.g., people, other organizations, events) the organization deals with regularly and how rapidly these various elements change. To assess uncertainty, each sector of the organization's task environment can be analyzed along dimensions such as stability or instability and degree of complexity.[18] The total amount of uncertainty felt by an organization is the uncertainty accumulated across relevant task environment sectors.

Organizations must cope with and manage uncertainty to be effective. **Uncertainty** means that decision makers do not have sufficient information about environmental factors, and they have a difficult time predicting external changes. Uncertainty increases the risk of failure for organizational decisions and makes it difficult to compute costs and probabilities associated with decision alternatives.[19] The remainder of this section will focus on the information perspective, which is concerned with uncertainty created by the extent to which the environment is complex and the extent to which events are dynamic. Later in the chapter, we discuss how organizations influence the environment to acquire needed financial resources.

Complexity

Environmental **complexity** refers to heterogeneity, or the number and dissimilarity of external elements (e.g., competitors, suppliers, industry changes, government regulations) that affect an organization's operations. The more external elements regularly influence the organization and the greater the number of other companies in an organization's domain, the greater the complexity. A complex environment is one in which the organization interacts with and is influenced by numerous diverse external elements. In a simple environment, the organization interacts with and is influenced by only a few similar external elements.

For example, a family-owned hardware store in a suburban community is in a simple environment. The store does not have to deal with complex technologies or extensive government regulations, and cultural and social changes have little impact. Human resources are not a problem because the store is run by family members and part-time help. The only external elements of real importance are a few competitors, suppliers, and customers. On the other hand, pharmaceutical companies such as Abbott Laboratories, Merck, and Pfizer operate in a highly complex environment. They use multiple, complex technologies; cope with numerous ever-changing government regulations; are significantly affected by international events; compete for scarce financial resources and highly trained scientists; interact with numerous suppliers, customers, contractors, and partners; respond to changing social values; and deal with complex legal and financial systems in multiple countries. This large number of external elements in a drug company's domain creates a complex environment. Abbott recently announced plans to split into two separate companies to better cope with the complexity of the environment. Other companies, such as Merck and Schering Plough, merged to better cope with uncertainty.[20]

Dynamism

Dynamism refers to whether the environment in which the organization operates is stable or unstable. An environmental domain is stable if it remains essentially the same over a period of months or years. Under unstable conditions, environmental elements shift rapidly. Consider what is happening in the environment for digital camera makers.

IN PRACTICE

Fujifilm Holding Corporation

Uh-oh! Managers at Fuji got high marks for seeing the trend toward digital cameras and responding faster than Kodak, but even they failed to prepare for the dynamism in the environment for compact digital cameras.

Adding Wi-Fi technology for Internet connectivity is common in many consumer electronics, but for the most part digital cameras remain stand-alone devices. It's an oversight that is hurting not only Fuji but also Panasonic, Olympus, Canon, and other camera makers. The number of photos being taken is soaring, but most people are using their smartphones so they can easily share the photos on Facebook, Instagram, and other social media. Shipments of compact digital cameras plummeted 42 percent in the first five months of 2013. "It's the classic case of an industry that is unable to adapt," said Christopher Chute, a digital imaging analyst at research firm IDC.

Fujifilm said it planned to cut production of point-and-shoot models by 50 percent, but even that might not be enough. "Everyone in this industry recognizes the market is changing," said Hiroshi Tanaka, corporate vice president at Fujifilm. "The question is what we can do about it."

Shigenobu Nagamori, CEO of Nidec Corporation, a supplier of components used in a variety of consumer electronic products, offers a warning to manufacturers hoping for the compact digital camera's rebound: "I told them to assume that the inexpensive cameras are dead, just like the PCs," he said.[21]

As this example shows, instability often occurs when consumer interests shift, new technologies are introduced, or competitors react with aggressive moves and countermoves regarding advertising and new products or services. Sometimes specific, unpredictable events—such as the data breach at Target described in the chapter opening example, reports of lead-tainted paint in Mattel toys made in China, the Pakistani government's attempt to block access to certain videos on YouTube, or the discovery of heart problems related to pain drugs such as Vioxx and Celebrex—create unstable conditions for organizations. Today, freewheeling bloggers, Twitterers, and YouTubers are a tremendous source of instability for scores of companies. For example, when United Airlines refused to compensate a musician for breaking his $3,500 guitar, he wrote a song and posted a derogatory music video about his lengthy negotiations with the company on YouTube. Word spread quickly across the Internet, and United just as quickly responded with a settlement offer.[22] Similarly, Domino's Pizza managers had to act quickly after two pranksters posted a video showing employees fouling a pizza on the way to delivery. Domino's responded with a video of its own. The company president apologized and thanked the online community for bringing the issue to his attention. He promised that the wrongdoers would be prosecuted and outlined steps Domino's was taking to ensure the episode would never happen again. By engaging in an online conversation about the crisis, Domino's demonstrated concern for its customers and squelched further rumors and fears.[23]

Environmental domains are increasingly unstable for most organizations.[24] This chapter's BookMark on page 150 examines the volatile nature of today's business world and gives some tips for managing in a fast-shifting environment. Although environments are more unstable for most organizations today, an example of a traditionally stable environment is a public utility.[25] In the rural Midwest, demand and supply factors for a public utility are stable. A gradual increase in demand may occur, which is easily predicted over time. Toy companies, by contrast, have an unstable environment. Hot new toys are difficult to predict, a problem compounded by the fact that children are losing interest in toys at a younger age, their interest captured by video and computer games, electronics, and the Internet. Adding to the instability for toymakers is the shrinking retail market, with big toy retailers going out of business trying to compete with discounters such as Walmart. Toymakers are trying to attract more customers in developing markets such as China, Poland, Brazil, and India to make up for the declining U.S. market, but hitting the target in those countries has proven to be a challenge. Companies such as Fisher-Price, owned by Mattel, can find their biggest products languishing on shelves as shoppers turn to less expensive locally made toys in countries where brand consciousness doesn't come into play. As one toy analyst said, "Chinese kids have been growing for 5,000 years without the benefits of Fisher-Price."[26]

Framework

The simple–complex and stable–unstable dimensions are combined into a framework for assessing environmental uncertainty in Exhibit 4.3. In the *simple, stable* environment, uncertainty is low. There are only a few external elements in a limited number of environmental sectors (e.g., suppliers, customers) to contend with, and they tend to remain stable. The *complex, stable* environment represents somewhat greater uncertainty. A large number of elements (e.g., suppliers, customers, government regulations, industry changes, unions, economic conditions) have to be scanned, analyzed, and acted upon for the organization to perform well. External elements do not change rapidly or unexpectedly in this environment.

Confronting Reality: Doing What Matters to Get Things Right

By Lawrence A. Bossidy and Ram Charan

The business world is changing at an increasingly rapid pace. That is the reality that spurred Larry Bossidy, retired chairman and CEO of Honeywell International, and Ram Charan, a noted author, speaker, and business consultant, to write *Confronting Reality: Doing What Matters to Get Things Right*. Too many managers, they believe, are tempted to hide their heads in the sand of financial issues rather than face the confusion and complexity of the organization's environment.

LESSONS FOR FACING REALITY

For many companies, today's environment is characterized by global hypercompetition, declining prices, and the growing power of consumers. Bossidy and Charan offer some lessons to leaders for navigating in a fast-changing world.

- *Understand the environment as it is now and is likely to be in the future, rather than as it was in the past.* Relying on the past and conventional wisdom can lead to disaster. Kmart, for example, stuck to its old formula as Walmart gobbled its customers and carved out a new business model. Few could have predicted in 1990, for example, that Walmart would now be America's biggest seller of groceries.
- *Seek out and welcome diverse and unorthodox ideas.* Managers need to be proactive and open-minded toward conversing with employees, suppliers, customers, colleagues, and anyone else they come in contact with. What are people thinking about? What changes and opportunities do they see? What worries them about the future?
- *Avoid the common causes of manager failure to confront reality: filtered information, selective hearing,* wishful thinking, fear, emotional overinvestment in a failing course of action, and unrealistic expectations. For example, when sales and profits fell off a cliff at data-storage giant EMC, managers displayed a bias toward hearing good news and believed the company was only experiencing a blip in the growth curve. When Joe Tucci was named CEO, however, he was determined to find out if the slump was temporary. By talking directly with top leaders at his customers' organizations, Tucci was able to face the reality that EMC's existing business model based on high-cost technology was dead. Tucci implemented a new business model to fit that reality.
- *Ruthlessly assess your organization.* Understanding the internal environment is just as important. Managers need to evaluate whether their company has the talent, commitment, and attitude needed to drive the important changes. At EMC, Tucci realized his sales force needed an attitude shift to sell software, services, and business solutions rather than just expensive hardware. The arrogant, hard-driving sales tactics of the past had to be replaced with a softer, more customer-oriented approach.

STAYING ALIVE

Staying alive in today's business environment requires that managers stay alert. Managers should always be looking at their competitors, broad industry trends, technological changes, shifting government policies, changing market forces, and economic developments. At the same time, they work hard to stay in touch with what their customers really think and really want. By doing so, leaders can confront reality and be poised for change.

Confronting Reality: Doing What Matters to Get Things Right, by Lawrence A. Bossidy and Ram Charan, is published by Crown Business Publishing.

Even greater uncertainty is felt in the *simple, unstable* environment.[27] Rapid change creates uncertainty for managers. Even though the organization has few external elements, those elements are hard to predict (such as shifting social trends or changing customer interests), and they react unexpectedly to organizational initiatives. The greatest uncertainty for an organization occurs in the *complex, unstable* environment. A large number of elements in numerous environmental sectors impinge upon the organization, and they shift frequently or react strongly to organizational initiatives. When several sectors change simultaneously, the environment becomes turbulent.[28]

EXHIBIT 4.3

Framework for Assessing Environmental Uncertainty

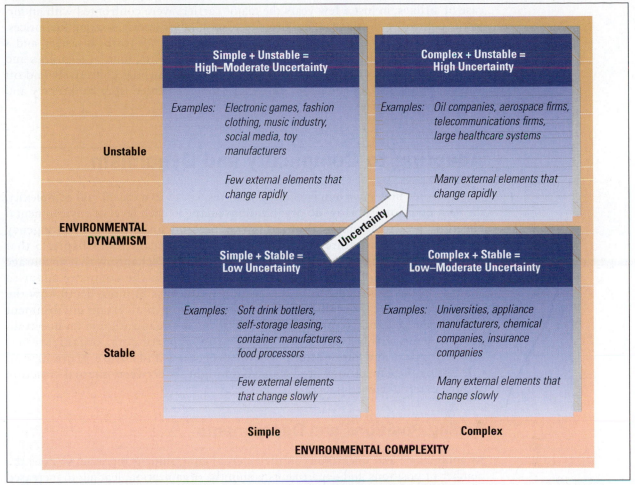

Sources: Based on Robert Duncan, "Characteristics of Organizational Environments and Perceived Environments Uncertainty," *Administrative Science Quarterly* 17 (September 1972), 313–327; Robert B. Duncan, "Multiple Decision-Making Structures in Adapting to Environmental Uncertainty: The Impact on Organizational Effectiveness," *Human Relations* 26, no. 3 (1973), 273–291; and Robert B. Duncan, "Modifications in Decision Structure in Adapting to the Environment: Some Implications for Organizational Learning," *Decision Sciences* 5, no. 4 (October 1974), 705–725.

A soft drink distributor functions in a simple, stable environment. Demand changes only gradually. The distributor has an established delivery route, and supplies of soft drinks arrive on schedule. State universities, appliance manufacturers, and insurance companies are in somewhat stable, complex environments. A large number of external elements are present, but although they change, changes are gradual and predictable.

Toy manufacturers are in simple, unstable environments. Organizations that design, make, and sell toys, as well as those that make electronic games or are involved in the clothing or music industry, face shifting supply and demand. Fashion apparel company Zara launches around 11,000 new products annually to try to meet changing customer tastes, for example.[29] Although there may be few elements to contend with—e.g., suppliers, customers, competitors—they are difficult to predict and change abruptly and unexpectedly.

The telecommunications industry, the oil industry, and airlines face complex, unstable environments. Many external sectors are changing simultaneously. In the case of airlines, in just a few years the major carriers were confronted with an air-traffic controller shortage, aging fleets of planes, labor unrest, soaring fuel prices, the entry of new low-cost competitors, a series of major air-traffic disasters, and a drastic decline in customer demand. Within just a few years, four large airlines and many smaller ones went through bankruptcy, and the airlines collectively laid off 170,000 employees. In late 2013, American Airlines emerged from bankruptcy and merged with US Airways.[30]

Adapting to Complexity and Dynamism

Once you see how environments differ with respect to dynamism and complexity, the next question is, "How do organizations adapt to each level of environmental uncertainty?" Environmental uncertainty represents an important contingency for organization structure and internal behaviors. Recall from Chapter 3 that organizations facing uncertainty often use structural mechanisms that encourage horizontal communication and collaboration to help the company adapt to changes in the environment. In this section we discuss in more detail how the environment affects organizations. An organization in a certain environment will be managed and controlled differently from an organization in an uncertain environment with respect to positions and departments, organizational differentiation and integration, control processes, and future planning and forecasting. Organizations need to have the right fit between internal structure and the external environment.

Adding Positions and Departments

As complexity and uncertainty in the external environment increase, so does the number of positions and departments within the organization, leading to increased internal complexity. This relationship is part of being an open system. Each sector in the external environment requires an employee or department to deal with it. The human resource department deals with unemployed people who want to work for the company. The marketing department finds customers. Procurement employees obtain raw materials from hundreds of suppliers. The finance group deals with bankers. The legal department works with the courts and government agencies. E-business departments handle electronic commerce, and information technology departments deal with the increasing complexity of computerized information and knowledge management systems. For example, President Barack Obama added a chief technology officer position and a chief information officer position to the U.S. government. Many organizations added chief compliance officer or chief governance officer positions to deal with the complexities associated with the 2002 Sarbanes–Oxley Act, often referred to as SOX. SOX required several types of corporate governance reforms, including better internal monitoring to reduce the risk of fraud, certification of financial results by top executives, improved measures for internal auditing, and enhancing public financial disclosure. Adding new positions and departments is a common way for organizations to adapt to growing environmental uncertainty. After the disastrous explosion and oil spill in the Gulf of Mexico, BP embarked on a major restructuring of its exploration, development, and production operations (referred to as *upstream*) to try to make sure a similar event never happens again. To improve risk management, CEO Robert W. Dudley appointed a dedicated chief executive for the entire upstream operations worldwide.[31]

Building Relationships

The traditional approach to coping with environmental uncertainty was to establish buffer departments. The purpose of **buffering roles** is to absorb uncertainty from the environment.[32] The technical core performs the primary production activity of an organization. Buffer departments surround the technical core and exchange materials, resources, and money between the environment and the organization. They help the technical core function efficiently. The purchasing department buffers the technical core by stockpiling supplies and raw materials. The human resource department buffers the technical core by handling the uncertainty associated with finding, hiring, and training production employees.

A more recent approach many organizations use is to drop the buffers and expose the technical core to the uncertain environment. These organizations no longer create buffers because they believe being well connected to customers and suppliers is more important than internal efficiency. Highly uncertain environments require rapid transfer of information and knowledge so the organization can adapt quickly. Teams, as described in Chapter 3, often work directly with customers and other parties outside the organization.[33] At Total Attorneys, a Chicago-based company that provides software and services to small law firms, cross-functional teams work with customers who test and provide feedback on products as they are developed.[34] Opening up the organization to the environment by building closer relationships with external parties makes it more fluid and adaptable.

Boundary-spanning roles link and coordinate an organization with key elements in the external environment. Boundary spanning is primarily concerned with the exchange of information to detect and bring into the organization information about changes in the environment and to send information into the environment that presents the organization in a favorable light.[35]

Organizations have to keep in touch with what is going on in the environment so that managers can respond to market changes and other developments. A study of high-tech firms found that 97 percent of competitive failures resulted from lack of attention to market changes or the failure to act on vital information.[36] To detect and bring important information into the organization, boundary personnel scan the environment. For example, a market research department scans and monitors trends in consumer tastes. Boundary spanners in engineering and research and development departments scan new technological developments, innovations, and raw materials. Boundary spanners prevent the organization from stagnating by keeping top managers informed about environmental changes. The greater the uncertainty in the environment, the greater the importance of boundary spanners.[37]

One approach to boundary spanning is **business intelligence**, which refers to the high-tech analysis of large amounts of internal and external data to spot patterns and relationships that might be significant. For example, Verizon uses business intelligence to actively monitor customer interactions so that it can catch problems and fix them almost immediately.[38] Tools to automate the process are a hot area of software, with companies spending billions on business intelligence software in recent years.[39]

Business intelligence is related to another important area of boundary spanning, known as *competitive intelligence* (CI). CI gives top executives a systematic way to collect and analyze public information about rivals and use it to make better decisions.[40] Using techniques that range from Internet surfing to digging through trash cans, intelligence professionals dig up information on competitors' new products, manufacturing costs, or training methods and share it with top leaders. Intelligence teams are the newest wave of CI activities. An **intelligence team** is a cross-functional group of managers and employees, usually led by a CI professional, who work together to gain a deep understanding of a specific business issue, with the aim of presenting insights, possibilities, and recommendations to top leaders.[41] Intelligence teams can provide insights that enable managers to make more informed decisions about goals, as well as devise contingency plans and scenarios related to major competitive issues.

The boundary task of sending information into the environment to represent the organization is used to influence other people's perception of the organization. In the marketing department, advertising and sales people represent the organization to customers. Purchasers may call on suppliers and describe purchasing needs. The legal department informs lobbyists and elected officials about the organization's needs or views on political matters. Many companies set up special web pages and blogs to present the organization in a favorable light.

ASSESS YOUR ANSWER

1 The best way for an organization to cope with a complex environment is to develop a complex structure (rather than keep it simple and uncomplicated).

ANSWER: *Agree.* As an organization's environment becomes more complex, the organization has to add jobs, departments, and boundary-spanning roles to cope with all the elements in the environment. When environmental sectors are complex, there is no way for an organization to stay simple and uncomplicated and continue to be effective.

Differentiation and Integration

Another response to environmental uncertainty is the amount of differentiation and integration among departments. Organizational **differentiation** refers to "the differences in cognitive and emotional orientations among managers in different functional departments, and the difference in formal structure among these departments."[42] When the external environment is complex and rapidly changing, organizational departments become highly specialized to handle the uncertainty in that part of the external environment each department works with. Success in each environmental sector (human resources, technology, government, and so forth) requires special expertise and behavior. Employees in an R&D department thus have unique attitudes, values, goals, and education that distinguish them from employees in manufacturing or sales departments.

A study by Paul Lawrence and Jay Lorsch examined three organizational departments—manufacturing, research, and sales—in 10 corporations.[43] This study

EXHIBIT 4.4

Organizational Departments Differentiate to Meet Needs of Subenvironments

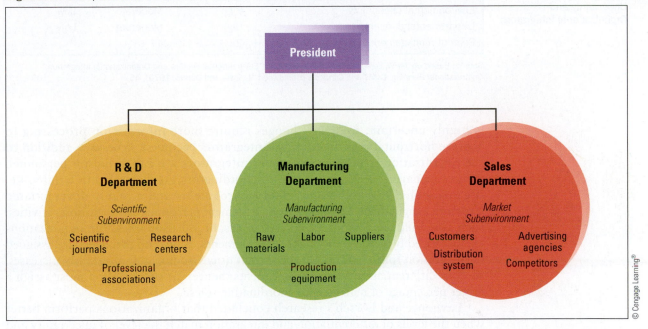

EXHIBIT 4.5

Differences in Goals and Orientations Among Organizational Departments

Characteristic	R&D Department	Manufacturing Department	Sales Department
Goals	New developments, quality	Efficient production	Customer satisfaction
Time horizon	Long	Short	Short
Interpersonal orientation	Mostly task	Task	Social
Formality of structure	Low	High	High

Source: Based on Paul R. Lawrence and Jay W. Lorsch, *Organization and Environment* (Homewood, IL: Irwin, 1969), 23–29.

found that each department evolved toward a different orientation and structure to deal with specialized parts of the external environment. Exhibit 4.4 illustrates the market, scientific, and manufacturing subenvironments identified by Lawrence and Lorsch. As shown in the exhibit, each department interacted with different external groups. The differences that evolved among departments within the organizations are shown in Exhibit 4.5. To work effectively with the scientific subenvironment, R&D had a goal of quality work, a long time horizon (up to five years), an informal structure, and task-oriented employees. Sales was at the opposite extreme. It had a goal of customer satisfaction, was oriented toward the short term (two weeks or so), had a very formal structure, and was socially oriented.

One outcome of high differentiation is that coordination and collaboration among departments become difficult. More time and resources must be devoted to achieving coordination when attitudes, goals, and work orientation differ so widely. **Integration** is the quality of collaboration among departments.[44] Formal integrators are often required to coordinate departments. When the environment

EXHIBIT 4.6
Environmental
Uncertainty and
Organizational Integrators

Industry	Plastics	Foods	Container
Environmental uncertainty	High	Moderate	Low
Departmental differentiation	High	Moderate	Low
Percent management in integrating roles	22	17	0

Source: Based on Jay W. Lorsch and Paul R. Lawrence, "Environmental Factors and Organizational Integration," *Organizational Planning: Cases and Concepts* (Homewood, IL: Irwin and Dorsey, 1972), 45.

is highly uncertain, frequent changes require more information processing to achieve horizontal coordination, so integrators become a necessary addition to the organization structure. Sometimes integrators are called liaison personnel, project managers, brand managers, or coordinators. As illustrated in Exhibit 4.6, organizations with highly uncertain environments and a highly differentiated structure assign about 22 percent of management personnel to integration activities, such as serving on committees, on task forces, or in liaison roles.[45] In organizations characterized by very simple, stable environments, almost no managers are assigned to integration roles. Exhibit 4.6 shows that as environmental uncertainty increases, so does differentiation among departments; hence, the organization must assign a larger percentage of managers to coordinating roles.

Lawrence and Lorsch's research concluded that organizations perform better when the levels of differentiation and integration match the level of uncertainty and complexity in the environment. Organizations that performed well in uncertain environments had high levels of both differentiation and integration, while those performing well in less uncertain environments had lower levels of differentiation and integration. A recent study of 266 modern manufacturing firms in nine countries confirmed that high levels of integration are associated with better performance in complex environments.[46]

Organic Versus Mechanistic Management Processes

Recall our discussion of organic and mechanistic designs from Chapter 1. The degree of uncertainty in the external environment is one primary contingency that shapes whether an organization will function best with an organic or a mechanistic design. Tom Burns and G. M. Stalker observed 20 industrial firms in England and discovered that internal management processes were related to the external environment.[47] When the external environment was stable, the internal organization was characterized by standard rules, procedures, a clear hierarchy of authority, formalization, and centralization. Burns and Stalker called this a **mechanistic** organization system, as described in Chapter 1 and illustrated in Exhibit 1.7.

In rapidly changing environments, the internal organization was much looser, free-flowing, and adaptive, with a loose hierarchy and decentralized decision making. Burns and Stalker used the term **organic** to characterize this type of organization. Complete the questionnaire in the "How Do You Fit the Design?" box for some insight into whether you are more suited to working in an organic organization or a mechanistic one.

As environmental uncertainty increases, organizations tend to become more organic, which means decentralizing authority and responsibility to lower levels, encouraging employees to take care of problems by working directly with one

BRIEFCASE

As an organization manager, keep these guidelines in mind:

Match internal organization structure to the external environment. If the external environment is complex, make the organization structure complex. Associate a stable environment with a mechanistic structure and an unstable environment with an organic structure. If the external environment is both complex and changing rapidly, make the organization highly differentiated and organic, and use mechanisms to achieve coordination across departments.

another, encouraging teamwork, and taking an informal approach to assigning tasks and responsibility. Thus, the organization is more fluid and is able to adapt continually to changes in the external environment.[48] Guiltless Gourmet, which sells low-fat tortilla chips and other high-quality snack foods, provides an example. When large companies like Frito Lay entered the low-fat snack-food market, Guiltless Gourmet shifted to a flexible network structure to remain competitive. The company redesigned itself to become basically a full-time marketing organization, while production and other activities were outsourced. An 18,000-square-foot plant in Austin was closed, and the workforce was cut from 125 to about 10 core people who handle marketing and sales promotions. The flexible structure allowed Guiltless Gourmet to adapt quickly to changing market conditions.[49]

HOW DO YOU FIT THE DESIGN?

MIND AND ENVIRONMENT

Does your mind best fit an organization in a certain or an uncertain environment? Think back to how you thought or behaved as a student, as an employee, or in a formal or informal leader position. Please answer whether each of the following items was Mostly True or Mostly False for you.

	Mostly True	Mostly False
1. I always offered comments on my interpretation of data or issues.	___	___
2. I welcomed unusual viewpoints of others even if we were working under pressure.	___	___
3. I made it a point to attend industry trade shows and company (school) events.	___	___
4. I explicitly encouraged others to express opposing ideas and arguments.	___	___
5. I asked "dumb" questions.	___	___
6. I enjoyed hearing about new ideas even when working toward a deadline.	___	___
7. I expressed a controversial opinion to bosses and peers.	___	___
8. I suggested ways of improving my and others' ways of doing things.	___	___

Scoring: Give yourself one point for each item you marked as Mostly True. If you scored less than 5, your mindfulness level may be suited to an organization in a stable rather than unstable environment. A score of 5 or above suggests a higher level of mindfulness and a better fit for an organization in an uncertain environment.

Interpretation: In an organization in a highly uncertain environment everything seems to be changing. In that case, an important quality for a professional employee or manager is "mindfulness," which includes the qualities of being open-minded and an independent thinker. In a stable environment, an organization will be more "mechanistic," and a manager without mindfulness may perform okay because much work can be done in the traditional way. In an uncertain environment, everyone needs to facilitate new thinking, new ideas, and new ways of working. A high score on this exercise suggests higher mindfulness and a better fit with an "organic" organization in an uncertain environment.

Sources: These questions are based on ideas from R. L. Daft and R. M. Lengel, *Fusion Leadership*, Chapter 4 (San Francisco, CA: Berrett Koehler, 2000); B. Bass and B. Avolio, *Multifactor Leadership Questionnaire*, 2nd ed. (Menlo Park, CA: Mind Garden, Inc); and Karl E. Weick and Kathleen M. Sutcliffe, *Managing the Unexpected: Assuring High Performance in an Age of Complexity* (San Francisco, CA: Jossey-Bass, 2001).

Planning, Forecasting, and Responsiveness

The whole point of increasing internal integration and shifting to a more organic design is to enhance the organization's ability to quickly respond to sudden changes in an uncertain environment. It might seem that in an environment where everything is changing all the time, planning is useless. However, in uncertain environments, planning and environmental forecasting actually become *more* important as a way to keep the organization geared for a coordinated, speedy response. When the environment is stable, the organization can concentrate on current operational problems and day-to-day efficiency. Long-range planning and forecasting are not needed because environmental demands in the future will be much the same as they are today.

With increasing environmental uncertainty, planning and forecasting become necessary.[50] Indeed, surveys of multinational corporations have found that as environments become more turbulent, managers increase their planning activities, particularly in terms of planning exercises that encourage learning, continual adaptation, and innovation.[51] For example, following the September 11, 2001, terrorist attacks in the United States, there was a surge in the use of scenario and contingency planning as a way to manage uncertainty. Although their popularity waned for several years, these approaches made a comeback due to increasing environmental turbulence and the recent global financial crisis. Japanese consumer electronics makers such as Sony, Panasonic, and Sharp, for example, have been struggling with falling sales in almost every product category and have had to plan for a different future. Sony's plan was to make a push into the medical field with an investment into the endoscope maker Olympus.[52]

With scenario planning, managers mentally rehearse different scenarios based on anticipating various changes that could affect the organization. Scenarios are like stories that offer alternative, vivid pictures of what the future will look like and how managers will respond. Royal Dutch/Shell Oil has long used scenario building and has been a leader in speedy response to massive changes that other organizations failed to perceive until it was too late.[53] Planning can soften the adverse impact of external shifts. Organizations that have unstable environments often establish a separate planning department. In an unpredictable environment, planners scan environmental elements and analyze potential moves and countermoves by other organizations.

ASSESS YOUR ANSWER

2 In a volatile, fast-changing environment, serious planning activities are a waste of time and resources.

ANSWER: *Disagree.* General Colin Powell once said, "No battle plan survives contact with the enemy."[54] Yet no wise general would go into battle without one. Serious planning becomes more important in a turbulent environment, even though a plan will not last long. Planning and environmental forecasting help managers anticipate and be prepared to respond to changes. Lack of planning makes more sense in a stable, easily predictable environment.

Planning, however, cannot substitute for other actions, such as effective boundary spanning and adequate internal integration and coordination. The organizations that are most successful in uncertain environments are those that keep everyone in close touch with the environment so they can spot threats and opportunities, enabling the organization to respond immediately.

Framework for Adapting to Complexity and Dynamism

Exhibit 4.7 summarizes the ways in which environmental uncertainty influences organizational characteristics. The complexity and dynamism dimensions are combined and illustrate four levels of uncertainty. The low uncertainty environment is simple and stable. Organizations in this environment can have few departments and a mechanistic design. In a low–moderate uncertainty environment, more departments are needed, along with more integrating roles to coordinate the departments. Some planning may occur. Environments that are high–moderate uncertainty are simple but unstable. Organization design is organic and decentralized. Planning is emphasized,

EXHIBIT 4.7
Contingency Framework for Environmental Uncertainty and Organizational Responses

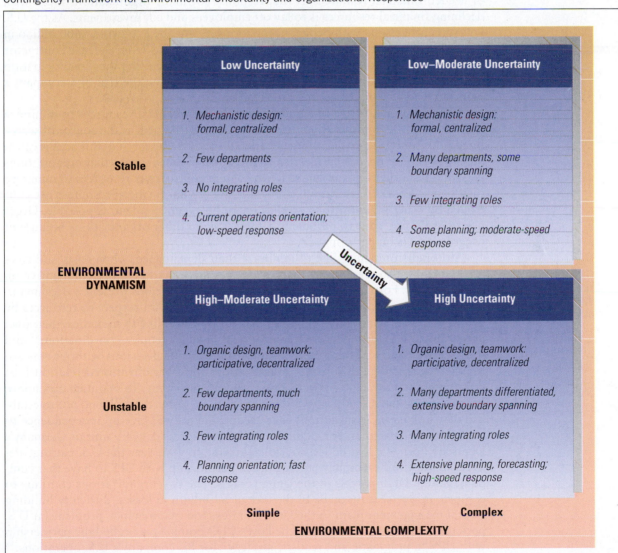

and managers are quick to make internal changes as needed. The high uncertainty environment is both complex and unstable and is the most difficult environment from a management perspective. Organizations are large and have many departments, but they are also organic. A large number of management personnel are assigned to co-ordination and integration, and the organization uses boundary spanning, planning, and forecasting to enable a high-speed response to environmental changes.

Dependence on Financial Resources

Thus far, this chapter has described several ways in which organizations adapt to the lack of information and to the uncertainty caused by environmental dynamism and complexity. We turn now to the third characteristic of the organization–environment relationship that affects organizations, which is the abundance or scarcity of needed financial resources. A first response for many organizations faced with declining financial resources is to lay off employees and cut investments. As the U.S. government wrestled with budget negotiations in late 2012 to avoid $600 billion in cuts to government spending, for example, organizations from defense contractor Lockheed Martin to health insurer Aetna were already cutting jobs in anticipation of reduced financial resources.[55] Downsizing, or reducing the size of a company's workforce, will be discussed in more detail in Chapter 9.

Companies also strive to acquire control over financial resources to minimize their dependence on other organizations.[56] The environment is the source of scarce financial resources essential to organizational survival. Research in this area is called the *resource-dependence perspective*. **Resource dependence** means that organizations depend on the environment but strive to acquire control over resources to minimize their dependence. Organizations are vulnerable if vital financial resources are controlled by other organizations, so they try to be as independent as possible. Organizations do not want to become too vulnerable to other organizations because of negative effects on performance.

Although companies like to minimize their dependence, when costs and risks are high they also team up to share scarce resources and be more competitive on a global basis. Formal relationships with other organizations present a dilemma to managers. Organizations seek to reduce vulnerability with respect to resources by developing links with other organizations, but they also like to maximize their own autonomy and independence. Organizational linkages require coordination,[57] and they reduce the freedom of each organization to make decisions without concern for the needs and goals of other organizations. Interorganizational relationships thus represent a trade-off between resources and autonomy. To maintain autonomy, organizations that already have abundant financial resources will tend not to establish new linkages. Organizations that need resources will give up independence to acquire those resources. For example, DHL, the express delivery unit of Germany's Deutsche Post AG, lost billions of dollars trying to take over the U.S. package delivery market and eventually entered into a partnership with UPS to have that company handle DHL parcels in the United States. The two organizations continue to compete in overseas markets. In the face of $3 billion in losses, difficulty building a local management team in the United States, and maintenance problems at U.S. package handling facilities, Deutsche Post's CEO Frank Appel called the partnership with UPS "a pragmatic and realistic strategy" for his company's U.S. operations.[58] Resource dependence will be discussed in more detail in Chapter 5.

Influencing Financial Resources

In response to the need for resources, organizations try to maintain a balance between depending on other organizations and preserving their own independence. Organizations maintain this balance through attempts to modify, manipulate, or control elements of the external environment (such as other organizations, government regulators) to meet their needs.[59] To survive, the focal organization often tries to reach out and change or control its environment. Two strategies can be adopted to influence resources in the external environment: establish favorable relationships with other organizations and shape the organization's environment.[60] Techniques to accomplish each of these strategies are summarized in Exhibit 4.8. As a general rule, when organizations sense that valued resources are scarce, they will use the strategies in Exhibit 4.8 rather than go it alone. Notice how dissimilar these strategies are from the responses to environmental dynamism and complexity described in Exhibit 4.7. The dissimilarity reflects the difference between responding to the need for resources and responding to the need for information.

Establishing Formal Relationships

Building formal relationships includes techniques such as acquiring ownership, establishing joint ventures and partnerships, developing connections with important people in the environment, recruiting key people, and using advertising and public relations.

Acquire an Ownership Stake. Companies use various forms of ownership to reduce uncertainty in an area important to the acquiring company. For example, a firm might buy a part of or a controlling interest in another company, giving it access to technology, products, or other resources it doesn't currently have.

A greater degree of ownership and control is obtained through acquisition or merger. An *acquisition* involves the purchase of one organization by another so that the buyer assumes control, such as when Google bought YouTube, eBay bought PayPal, and Walmart purchased Britain's ASDA Group. A *merger* is the unification of two or more organizations into a single unit.[61] Sirius Satellite Radio and XM Satellite Radio Holdings merged to become Sirius XM Radio. The merger enabled the companies to combine resources and share risks to be more competitive against digital music providers and other emerging types of music distribution. In the past few years, there has been a huge wave of acquisition and merger activity in the tele-communications and advertising industries, reflecting how these companies cope with the tremendous uncertainty they face. For example, Omnicom and Publicis opted to try to merge to create the largest advertising company in the world in order to compete in a new environment of fewer resources.

Establishing Formal Relationships	Influencing Key Sectors
1. Acquire an ownership stake	1. Change where you do business (your domain)
2. Form joint ventures and partnerships	2. Use political activity, regulation
3. Lock in key players	3. Join in trade associations
4. Recruit executives	4. Avoid illegitimate activities
5. Use advertising and public relations	

EXHIBIT 4.8
Organizing Strategies for Controlling the External Environment

© Cengage Learning®

IN PRACTICE

Omnicom and Publicis

Once upon a time, advertising was controlled by small, independent shops led by creative people. They grew, then merged, then grew some more. Today, advertising and marketing is big business. Well, make that "Big Data" business. The attempted merger of Omnicom and Publicis is not so much a response to competition from other advertising agencies, but to bolster against the likes of IBM, Google, Salesforce, and Oracle. "Fighting that fight is a potentially losing battle," said Darren Herman, chief digital media officer at the Media Kitchen, an agency owned by MDC Partners.

When the merger of Omnicom and Publicis was announced in Paris, Maurice Lévy, CEO of Publicis, said the "billions of people" online are providing data that offer the opportunity to use advertising technologies to crunch data and target specific messages to very narrow audiences. Ad agencies have long worked hand-in-hand with Google, Facebook, and Twitter, but now those companies and others, including IBM, Oracle, Microsoft, and numerous data analytics start-ups, also work directly with companies to develop targeted ad campaigns, cutting out the advertising agency. Some companies, including Nike, Progressive, and Procter & Gamble, use fast-paced, algorithmic bidding systems to target individual consumers. Advertising agencies are under pressure like never before. The attempted merger is a sign that the marketing business is becoming more personalized and more competitive. "All of a sudden the new set of companies playing in this space is not only large and profitable, but they are competing with companies that are very large and profitable," said an analyst of the mergers in advertising.[62]

Form Joint Ventures and Partnerships. When there is a high level of complementarity between the business lines, geographical positions, or skills of two companies, the firms often go the route of a strategic alliance rather than ownership through merger or acquisition.[63] Such alliances are formed through contracts and joint ventures.

Contracts and joint ventures reduce uncertainty through a legal and binding relationship with another firm. Contracts come in the form of *license agreements* that involve the purchase of the right to use an asset (such as a new technology) for a specific time and *supplier arrangements* that contract for the sale of one firm's output to another. Contracts can provide long-term security by tying customers and suppliers to specific amounts and prices. For example, the Italian fashion house Versace forged a deal to license its primary asset—its name—for a line of designer eyeglasses.[64]

Joint ventures result in the creation of a new organization that is formally independent of the parents, although the parents will have some control.[65] Madrid-based tech start-up FON formed a joint venture with British phone carrier BT to install FON wi-fi technology in the modems of nearly 2 million BT customers. Office Depot and Reliance Retail Limited, a division of India's largest private-sector employer, entered into a joint venture to provide office products and services to business customers in India. Food and agricultural corporation Cargill Inc. has numerous joint ventures around the world, such as the one with Spanish cooperative Hojiblanca to source, trade, and supply customers worldwide with private label and bulk olive oils. As evidenced by these short examples, many joint ventures are undertaken to share risks when companies are doing business in other countries or on a global scale.

Lock in Key Players. Cooptation occurs when leaders from important sectors in the environment are made part of an organization. It takes place, for example, when influential customers or suppliers are appointed to the board of directors, such as when the senior executive of a bank sits on the board of a manufacturing company. As a board member, the banker may become psychologically coopted into the interests of the manufacturing firm.

An **interlocking directorate** is a formal linkage that occurs when a member of the board of directors of one company sits on the board of directors of another company. The individual is a communications link between companies and can influence policies and decisions. When one individual is the link between two companies, this is typically referred to as a **direct interlock**. An **indirect interlock** occurs when a director of company A and a director of company B are both directors of company C. They have access to one another but do not have direct influence over their respective companies.[66] Research shows that, as a firm's financial fortunes decline, direct interlocks with financial institutions increase. Financial uncertainty facing an industry also has been associated with greater indirect interlocks between competing companies.[67] However, during the economic turmoil of recent years, some companies, including Apple and Google, have run up against a long-standing U.S. federal law that bars direct interlocks between competing companies. Arthur Levinson, chairman of Roche Holding AG's Genentech, for example, resigned from the Google board after the Federal Trade Commission began investigating his participation on both the Google and Apple boards. Similarly, Eric Schmidt, executive chairman and former CEO of Google, resigned from the Apple board for the same reason, as the two companies compete in a growing number of businesses.[68]

Important business or community leaders also can be appointed to other organizational committees or task forces. By serving on committees or advisory panels, these influential people learn about the needs of the company and are more likely to consider the company's interests in their decision making. Today, many companies face uncertainty from environmental pressure groups, so organizations are trying to bring in leaders from this sector, such as when DuPont appointed environmentalists to its biotechnology advisory panel.[69]

Recruit Executives. Transferring or exchanging executives also offers a method of establishing favorable linkages with external organizations. For example, the high-frequency trading firm Getco LLC hired a former associate director in the Securities and Exchange Commission's Division of Trading and Markets to be part of its regulatory and compliance team.[70] The aerospace industry often hires retired generals and executives from the Department of Defense. These generals have personal friends in the department, so the aerospace companies obtain better information about technical specifications, prices, and dates for new weapons systems. They can learn the needs of the defense department and are able to present their case for defense contracts in a more effective way. Companies without personal contacts find it nearly impossible to get a defense contract. Having channels of influence and communication between organizations reduces financial uncertainty and dependence for an organization.

Get Your Side of the Story Out. A traditional way of establishing favorable relationships is through advertising. Organizations spend large amounts of money to influence the tastes and opinions of consumers. Advertising is especially important in highly competitive industries and in industries that experience variable demand. For example, since the U.S. Food and Drug Administration loosened regulations to permit advertising of prescription drugs in the United States, the major pharmaceutical companies have spent nearly $5 billion annually on advertisements such as a cute cartoon bee pushing Nasonex spray for allergies or heart attack survivors promoting the benefits of cholesterol-fighting Crestor.[71]

Public relations is similar to advertising, except that stories often are free and aimed at public opinion. Public relations people cast an organization in a favorable light in speeches, on websites, in press reports, and on television. Public relations attempts to shape the company's image in the minds of customers, suppliers, government officials, and the broader public. Google is a master at shaping its image through donations, fellowship programs, and at conferences that establish a network of ties to advocacy organizations, public intellectuals, and academic institutions that often take Google's side in public debates and national policy issues. By encouraging and sometimes supporting groups that hold viewpoints similar to its own, Google has an ongoing widespread PR campaign that one reporter referred to as "subtle acts of persuasion."[72] Blogging, tweeting, and social networking have become important components of public relations activities for many companies today.[73]

Influencing Key Sectors

In addition to establishing favorable linkages, organizations often try to change the environment. There are four techniques for influencing or changing a firm's environment.

Change Where You Do Business. Early in this chapter, we talked about the organization's *domain* and the 10 sectors of the environment. An organization's domain is not fixed. Managers make decisions about which business to be in; the markets to enter; and the suppliers, banks, employees, and location to use; and this domain can be changed if necessary to keep the organization competitive.[74] An organization can seek new environmental relationships and drop old ones. Walmart, which has long focused on its big box retail stores, is finally trying to get into e-commerce "for real," while Amazon is trying to build a physical presence across the nation.

IN PRACTICE

Amazon and Walmart

Who would have thought Walmart would one day be playing catch-up to Amazon? That seems to be happening, as the country's largest brick-and-mortar retailer struggles to build an online presence to compete with the conqueror of the online shopping world, Amazon, which is beginning to build warehouses and pickup locations across the country that will invade Walmart's turf.

Amazon has decided it wants to control *all* shopping, not just online shopping. Thus, to remain competitive, Walmart is trying to learn the rules of the technology business from the ground up at its dot-com division, Walmart Global E-Commerce, where it has started @WalmartLabs. Managers at the two giants are now shifting their domains so that Walmart is becoming more technology oriented and Amazon is competing more in physical space. Both companies believe the future is a combination of stores and online.

Walmart Global E-Commerce, which is located in Silicon Valley, has acquired a number of start-ups that build tools to crunch data, create mobile apps, or speed up websites, and the purchases included the founders and engineers. The company offers "hack days," when engineers can work on anything they want. It has also hired 150 people from companies such as Yahoo and eBay. Walmart is hoping to turn its 4,100 stores in the United States and many of its 6,200 overseas stores into e-commerce assets. Many items ordered online can be shipped from stores. It is also allowing customers to pick up online orders from stores and is trying same-day delivery in test markets.[75]

Walmart managers know they need to alter the domain to be more competitive against Amazon as shopping habits continue to shift more toward online. Managers have many reasons for altering an organization's domain. They may try to find a domain where there is little competition, no government regulation, abundant suppliers, affluent customers, and barriers to keep competitors out. Acquisition and divestment are two techniques for altering the domain. For example, Google acquired YouTube to expand its domain beyond search, and Facebook recently paid $16 billion for WhatsApp, a text-messaging application with 450 million users. An example of divestment was when Google sold the Motorola Mobility smartphone unit to Lenovo for $2.9 billion in February 2014 to get out of the business of manufacturing phones.[76]

Get Political. Political activity includes techniques to influence government legislation and regulation. Political strategy can be used to erect regulatory barriers against new competitors or to squash unfavorable legislation. Corporations also try to influence the appointment to agencies of people who are sympathetic to their needs.

Health insurance companies heavily lobbied federal and state officials to try to ward off strict regulation of insurance premiums and company profits under ObamaCare. Large retailers such as Walmart and Target are lobbying to change laws so that Amazon.com will be required to collect sales taxes. And Facebook has a Washington office with a staff of eight people lobbying legislators primarily regarding tighter privacy restrictions on online companies.[77]

Many CEOs believe they should participate directly in lobbying. CEOs have easier access than lobbyists and can be especially effective when they do the politicking. Political activity is so important that "informal lobbyist" is an unwritten part of almost any CEO's job description.[78] Top executives at Amerilink Telecom Corporation did some serious politicking as they tried to open the U.S. market to telecommunications equipment manufactured by China's Huawei Technologies Company.

IN PRACTICE

Huawei Technologies

Huawei Technologies tried for years to break into the U.S. market, but security concerns have thwarted its ambitions. Alleged ties to the Chinese government and military have had U.S. officials worried that allowing equipment from the company could disrupt or intercept critical U.S. communications.

Huawei is the world's largest telecommunications company and a leader in the "plumbing" of mobile phone networks. Sales in 2012 were more than $35.4 billion. The company says more than a third of the world's population is hooked up to networks that use Huawei gear—and that's what has U.S. officials worried. For one of its recent efforts in the United States, a bid for a multibillion-dollar network upgrade at Sprint Nextel, Huawei partnered with the U.S. consulting firm Amerilink, a company founded by William Owens, former vice chairman of the Joint Chiefs of Staff under President Bill Clinton. Owens and other top executives immediately launched an extensive lobbying campaign, meeting with numerous officials from Congress and the Obama administration. In addition, the company recruited several former government officials to aid in lobbying, including former Congressional leader Richard Gebhardt, Gordon England, who served as deputy secretary of defense and homeland security under President George W. Bush, and former World Bank president James Wolfensohn.

Despite the heavy lobbying efforts, Huawei's joint bid with Amerilink was rejected by Sprint after government officials allegedly expressed serious concerns to Sprint managers about security risks. In addition, the United States has launched a quiet lobbying effort of its own to persuade other countries to reject Huawei's equipment. South Korea recently agreed that Huawei equipment will not be used or connected to U.S. military bases in that country and that sensitive U.S.–South Korea communications will be routed over separate networks.[79]

Despite the failure of the lobbying efforts so far, this example shows how companies use political activity to try to influence government opinion and legislation that affects the organization's success.

3 **Managers of business organizations should not get involved in political activities.**

ANSWER: *Disagree.* Smart business managers get involved in lobbying and other political activities to try to make sure the consequences of new laws and regulations are mostly positive for their own firms. Companies pay huge fees to associations and lobbyists to make sure government actions work out in their favor.

Unite with Others. Much of the work to influence the external environment is accomplished jointly with other organizations that have similar interests. For example, most large pharmaceutical companies belong to Pharmaceutical Research and Manufacturers of America. Manufacturing companies are part of the National Association of Manufacturers, and retailers join the Retail Industry Leaders Association. The American Petroleum Institute is the leading trade group for oil and gas companies. By pooling resources, these organizations can pay people to carry out activities such as lobbying legislators, influencing new regulations, developing public relations campaigns, and making campaign contributions. Primerica is using the resources and influence of the American Council of Life Insurers to push for changes in state licensing exams, which the company believes put minorities at a disadvantage. Primerica, unlike most large insurance companies, focuses on selling basic term life insurance and depends almost exclusively on middle-income consumers rather than selling pricier policies. Company managers say the way the test questions are phrased limits their ability to expand their corps of minority agents that could better serve minority communities.[80]

Don't Fall into Illegitimate Activities. Illegitimate activities represent the final technique companies sometimes use to control their environmental domain, but this technique typically backfires. Conditions such as low profits, pressure from senior managers, or scarce environmental resources may lead managers to adopt behaviors not considered legitimate.[81] One study found that companies in industries with low demand, shortages, and strikes were more likely to be convicted for illegal activities, suggesting that illegal acts are an attempt to cope with resource scarcity. Some nonprofit organizations have been found to use illegitimate or illegal actions to bolster their visibility and reputation as they compete with other organizations for scarce grants and donations, for example.[82]

Bribery is one of the most frequent types of illegitimate activity, particularly in companies operating globally. Energy companies face tremendous uncertainty, for example, and need foreign governments to approve giant investments and authorize risky projects. Under pressure to win contracts in Nigeria, Albert "Jack" Stanley, a former executive at KBR (then a division of Halliburton Company), admits he orchestrated a total of about $182 million in bribes to get Nigerian officials to approve the construction of a liquefied natural gas plant in that country. Stanley faces up to seven years in prison and a hefty fine after pleading guilty.[83] Other types of illegitimate activities include payoffs to foreign governments, illegal political contributions, promotional gifts, and price-fixing. For nearly a decade, executives from Procter & Gamble (P&G), Colgate-Palmolive, Unilever, and Henkel AG secretly met in restaurants around Paris to allegedly fix the price of laundry detergent in France. The managers used fake names and discussed elaborate and complex pricing mechanisms in meetings that sometimes lasted as long as four hours. The scheme went on for years until members had a disagreement over price increases and promotions and one member handed over a 282-page report to French antitrust authorities. The companies involved were eventually fined a total of €361 ($484 million).[84]

Organization–Environment Integrative Framework

The relationships illustrated in Exhibit 4.9 summarize the two major themes about organization–environment relationships discussed in this chapter. One theme is that the amount of complexity and dynamism in an organization's domain influences

EXHIBIT 4.9

Relationship Between Environmental Characteristics and Organizational Actions

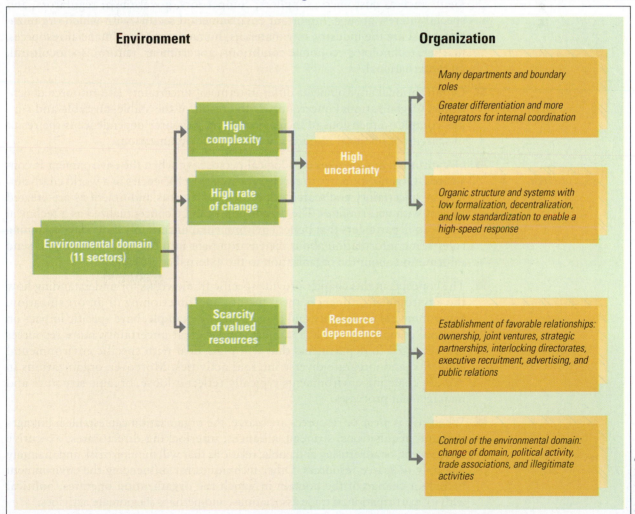

the need for information and hence the uncertainty felt within an organization. Greater information uncertainty is resolved through greater structural flexibility (an organic design) and the assignment of additional departments and boundary roles. When uncertainty is low, management structures can be more mechanistic, and the number of departments and boundary roles can be fewer. The second theme pertains to the scarcity of financial resources. The more dependent an organization is on other organizations for those resources, the more important it is to either establish favorable linkages with those organizations or control entry into the domain. If dependence on external resources is low, the organization can maintain autonomy and does not need to establish linkages or control the external domain.

Design Essentials

- Dynamism and complexity in the external environment have major implications for organization design and management action. Organizations are open social systems. Most are involved with hundreds of elements in the external environment, such as customers, suppliers, competitors, government regulators, and special interest groups. Important environmental sectors with which organizations deal are the industry, raw materials, human resources, financial resources, market, technology, economic conditions, government, natural, sociocultural, and international.

- Organizational environments differ in terms of uncertainty and resource dependence. Organizational uncertainty is the result of the stable–unstable and simple–complex dimensions of the environment. Resource dependence is the result of scarcity of financial resources needed by the organization.

- Organization design takes on a logical perspective when the environment is considered. Organizations try to survive and achieve efficiencies in a world characterized by uncertainty and scarcity. Specific departments and functions are created to deal with uncertainties. The organization can be conceptualized as a technical core and departments that buffer environmental uncertainty. Boundary-spanning roles bring information about the environment into the organization and send information about the organization to the external environment.

- The concepts in this chapter provide specific frameworks for understanding how the environment influences the structure and functioning of an organization. Environmental complexity and dynamism, for example, have specific impact on internal complexity and adaptability. Under great uncertainty, more resources are allocated to departments that will plan, deal with specific environmental elements, and integrate diverse internal activities. Moreover, organizations in rapidly changing environments typically reflect a loose, organic structure and management processes.

- When risk is great or resources are scarce, the organization can establish linkages through acquisitions, strategic alliances, interlocking directorates, executive recruitment, or advertising and public relations that will minimize risk and maintain a supply of scarce resources. Other techniques for influencing the environment include a change of the domain in which the organization operates, political activity, participation in trade associations, and perhaps illegitimate activities.

■ Two important themes in this chapter are that organizations can learn and adapt to the environment and that organizations can change and control the environment. These strategies are especially true for large organizations that command many resources. Such organizations can adapt when necessary but can also neutralize or change problematic areas in the environment.

⟫ KEY CONCEPTS

boundary-spanning roles	domain	mechanistic
buffering roles	dynamism	organic
business intelligence	general environment	organizational environment
complexity	indirect interlock	resource dependence
cooptation	integration	sectors
differentiation	intelligence team	task environment
direct interlock	interlocking directorate	uncertainty

⟫ DISCUSSION QUESTIONS

1. Define *organizational environment*. Would the task environment of a new Internet-based company be the same as that of a large government agency? Discuss.
2. What are some forces that influence environmental uncertainty? Which typically has the greatest impact on uncertainty—environmental complexity or environmental dynamism? Why?
3. Name some factors causing environmental complexity for an organization of your choice. How might this environmental complexity lead to organizational complexity? Explain.
4. Discuss the importance of the international sector for today's organizations, compared to domestic sectors. What are some ways in which the international sector affects organizations in your city or community?
5. Describe differentiation and integration. In what type of environmental uncertainty will differentiation and integration be greatest? Least?
6. How do you think planning in today's organizations compares to planning 25 years ago? Do you think planning becomes more important or less important in a world where everything is changing fast and crises are a regular part of organizational life? Why?
7. What is an organic organization? A mechanistic organization? How does the environment influence organic and mechanistic designs?
8. Why do organizations become involved in interorganizational relationships? Do these relationships affect an organization's dependency? Performance?
9. Assume you have been asked to calculate the ratio of staff employees to production employees in two organizations—one in a simple, stable environment and one in a complex, shifting environment. How would you expect these ratios to differ? Why?
10. Is changing the organization's domain a feasible strategy for coping with a threatening environment? Explain. Can you think of an organization in the recent news that has changed its domain?

⟫ CHAPTER 4 WORKSHOP Organizations You Rely On[85]

Below, list four organizations you somehow rely on in your daily life for some resource. Examples might be a restaurant, a clothing store, a university, your family, the post office, your wireless provider, an airline, a pizzeria that delivers, and your place of work. In the first column, list those four organizations. Then, in column 2, choose another organization you could use in case the one in column 1 was not available. In column 3, evaluate your level of dependence on the organizations listed in column 1 as Strong, Medium, or Weak. Finally, in column 4, rate the certainty of that organization being able to meet your needs as High (certainty), Medium, or Low.

Organization	Backup Organization	Level of Dependence	Level of Certainty
1.			
2.			
3.			
4.			

Questions

1. Do you have adequate backup organizations for those of high resource dependence? How might you create even more backups?
2. What would you do if an organization you rated high for dependence and high for certainty suddenly became high dependence and low certainty? How would your behavior relate to the concept of resource dependence?
3. Have you ever used any behaviors similar to those in Exhibit 4.8 to manage your relationships with the organizations listed in column 1?

CASE FOR ANALYSIS | CPI Corporation: What Happened?[86]

They are the most treasured possessions; they line mantels and living room walls; they are the first items frantically sought by family members following fires or natural disasters. They are family photographs.

Considering the popularity and demand for beloved photographs, it seems logical that the market leader in the portrait studio industry, with a 60-year history of success and the convenience of store locations within retail giants Walmart, Sears, and BabiesRUs, would have the confidence of a secure and bright future. That was the apparent situation for CPI Corporation, the store-within-a-store portrait studios. With over 1,500 locations, the studios offered consumers the convenience of inexpensive family portrait packages, combined with one-stop shopping for family and household needs.

Then abruptly, in April 2013, CPI announced closure of all of the company's U.S. locations. That announcement and immediate slamming of the doors caught everyone, including employees and customers, by surprise. As families scrambled to locate and retrieve their photographs, employees absorbed the blow of a sudden loss of salary and benefits, including health insurance.

But in recent years, there had been voices of concern and questions about direction at CPI. At a board meeting in St. Louis in 2006, then-CEO Paul Rasmussen expressed concerns with the need for improvement of the customer in-store experience and his own awareness of the lengthy wait times for photo sessions, followed by additional lengthy wait times (up to six weeks) for delivery of the photos from a central printing location.

The abruptness of the closures may have been the only real surprise to many competitors who continue to thrive and who expressed amazement that the industry leader failed to blaze the way with cutting-edge technology.

"There's no reason why CPI didn't invent Instagram (photo sharing)," said Mitch Goldstone, CEO of ScanMy-Photos.com. "CPI had the greatest opportunity. They had a huge customer base nation-wide that they let disappear overnight."

Aware of its corporate strengths, CPI increasingly failed to read and respond to the changing environment in which it conducted business. A glance through its recent history reveals potential problem areas for the company. Rasmussen's 2006 urging to board members to shorten in-store wait times and to modernize backdrops and traditional posing styles was ignored in favor of finding ways to attract additional customers. Consumer expectations were changing toward the immediate gratification enabled by the iPhone age with digital photography and instant access/sharing capabilities for their photographs. CPI, however, remained committed to centralization of printing and avoided the cost of updating stores with digital technology.

Meanwhile, competitors discovered innovative ways to build technology into their services and products. Companies such as Picture Perfect offered one-hour digital printing. ScanMyPhotos.com provided the convenience of online photo services. And Lifetouch, whose store-within-a-store photo studios are located in JCPenney and Target stores, expanded their market into providing school pictures.

As technological trends and consumer behaviors and attitudes changed, CPI continued holding on to its own success model. In April 2013, with loan obligations of $98.5 million, CPI closed all U.S. locations. By June, competitor Lifetouch Portrait Studios, Inc. had entered a "stalking horse" agreement to purchase all CPI assets and awaited competing offers.

Photography and digital technology continue to evolve at an unimaginable pace, and consumers feel empowered in their abilities to now go beyond taking, sharing, and printing photographs to explore the design and manipulation and animation of photographs. As business competitors within the industry weigh their future, how will they pay attention and adjust their business strategies in order to remain viable and avoid the CPI fate?

CASE FOR ANALYSIS | The Paradoxical Twins: Acme and Omega Electronics[87]

Part I

In 1986, Technological Products of Erie, Pennsylvania, was bought out by a Cleveland manufacturer. The Cleveland firm had no interest in the electronics division of Technological Products and subsequently sold to different investors two plants that manufactured computer chips and printed circuit boards. Integrated circuits, or chips, were the first step into microminiaturization in the electronics industry, and both plants had developed some expertise in the technology, along with their superior capabilities in manufacturing printed circuit boards. One of the plants, located in nearby Waterford, was renamed Acme Electronics; the other plant, within the city limits of Erie, was renamed Omega Electronics, Inc.

Acme retained its original management and upgraded its general manager to president. Omega hired a new president who had been a director of a large electronic research laboratory and upgraded several of the existing personnel within the plant. Acme and Omega often competed for the same contracts. As subcontractors, both firms benefited from the electronics boom and both looked forward to future growth and expansion. The world was going digital, and both companies began producing digital microprocessors along with the production of circuit boards. Acme had annual sales of $100 million and employed 550 people. Omega had annual sales of $80 million and employed 480 people. Acme regularly achieved greater net profits, much to the chagrin of Omega's management.

Inside Acme

The president of Acme, John Tyler, was confident that, had the demand not been so great, Acme's competitor would not have survived. "In fact," he said, "we have been able to beat Omega regularly for the most profitable contracts, thereby increasing our profit." Tyler credited his firm's greater effectiveness to his managers' abilities to run a "tight ship." He explained that he had retained the basic structure developed by Technological Products because it was most efficient for high-volume manufacturing. Acme had detailed organization charts and job descriptions. Tyler believed everyone should have clear responsibilities and narrowly defined jobs, which would lead to efficient performance and high company profits. People were generally satisfied with their work at Acme; however, some of the managers voiced the desire to have a little more latitude in their jobs.

Inside Omega

Omega's president, Jim Rawls, did not believe in organization charts. He felt his organization had departments similar to Acme's, but he thought Omega's plant was small enough that things such as organization charts just put artificial barriers between specialists who should be working together. Written memos were not allowed since, as Rawls expressed it, "the plant is small enough that if people want to communicate, they can just drop by and talk things over."

The head of the mechanical engineering department said, "Jim spends too much of his time and mine making sure everyone understands what we're doing and listening to suggestions." Rawls was concerned with employee satisfaction and wanted everyone to feel part of the organization. The top management team reflected Rawls's attitudes. They also believed that employees should be familiar with activities throughout the organization so that cooperation between departments would be increased. A newer member of the industrial engineering department said, "When I first got here, I wasn't sure what I was supposed to do. One day I worked with some mechanical engineers and the next day I helped the shipping department design some packing cartons. The first months on the job were hectic, but at least I got a real feel for what makes Omega tick."

Part II

In the 1990s, mixed analog and digital devices began threatening the demand for the complex circuit boards manufactured by Acme and Omega. This *system-on-a-chip* technology combined analog functions, such as sound, graphics, and power management, together with digital circuitry, such as logic and memory, making it highly useful for new products such as cellular phones and wireless computers. Both Acme and Omega realized the threat to their futures and began aggressively to seek new customers.

In July 1992, a major photocopier manufacturer was looking for a subcontractor to assemble the digital memory units of its new experimental copier. The projected contract for the job was estimated to be $7 million to $9 million in annual sales.

Both Acme and Omega were geographically close to this manufacturer, and both submitted highly competitive bids for the production of 100 prototypes. Acme's bid was slightly lower than Omega's; however, both firms were asked to produce 100 units. The photocopier manufacturer told both firms that speed was critical because its president had boasted to other manufacturers that the firm would have a finished copier available by Christmas. This boast, much to the designer's dismay, required pressure on all subcontractors to begin prototype production before the final design of the copier was complete. This meant Acme and Omega would have at most two weeks to produce the prototypes or would delay the final copier production.

Part III

Inside Acme

As soon as John Tyler was given the blueprints (Monday, July 13, 1992), he sent a memo to the purchasing department asking to move forward on the purchase of all necessary materials. At the same time, he sent the blueprints to the drafting department and asked that it prepare manufacturing prints. The industrial engineering department was told to begin methods design work for use by the production department supervisors. Tyler also sent a memo to all department heads and executives indicating the critical time constraints of this job and how he expected that all employees would perform as efficiently as they had in the past.

The departments had little contact with one another for several days, and each seemed to work at its own speed. Each department also encountered problems. Purchasing could not acquire all the parts on time. Industrial engineering had difficulty arranging an efficient assembly sequence. Mechanical engineering did not take the deadline seriously and parceled its work to vendors so the engineers could work on other jobs scheduled previously. Tyler made it a point to stay in touch with the photocopier manufacturer to let it know things were progressing and to learn of any new developments. He traditionally worked to keep important clients happy. Tyler telephoned someone at the photocopier company at least twice a week and got to know the head designer quite well.

On July 17, Tyler learned that mechanical engineering was far behind in its development work, and he "hit the roof." To make matters worse, purchasing had not obtained all the parts, so the industrial engineers decided to assemble the product without one part, which would be inserted at the last minute. On Thursday, July 23, the final units were being assembled, although the process was delayed several times. On Friday, July 24, the last units were finished while Tyler paced around the plant. Late that afternoon, Tyler received a phone call from the head designer of the photocopier manufacturer, who told Tyler that he had received a call on Wednesday from Jim Rawls of Omega. He explained that Rawls's workers had found an error in the design of the connector cable and taken corrective action on their prototypes. He told Tyler that he had checked out the design error and that Omega was right. Tyler, a bit overwhelmed by this information, told the designer that he had all the memory units ready for shipment and that, as soon as they received the missing component on Monday or Tuesday, they would be able to deliver the final units. The designer explained that the design error would be rectified in a new blueprint he was sending over by messenger and that he would hold Acme to the Tuesday delivery date.

When the blueprint arrived, Tyler called in the production supervisor to assess the damage. The alterations in the design would call for total disassembly and the unsoldering of several connections. Tyler told the supervisor to put extra people on the alterations first thing Monday morning and to try to finish the job by Tuesday. Late Tuesday afternoon, the alterations were finished and the missing components were delivered. Wednesday morning, the production supervisor discovered that the units would have to be torn apart again to install the missing component. When John Tyler was told this, he again "hit the roof." He called industrial engineering and asked if it could help out. The production supervisor and the methods engineer couldn't agree on how to install the component. John Tyler settled the argument by ordering that all units be taken apart again and the missing component installed. He told shipping to prepare cartons for delivery on Friday afternoon.

On Friday, July 31, 50 prototypes were shipped from Acme without final inspection. John Tyler was concerned about his firm's reputation, so he waived the final inspection after he personally tested one unit and found it operational. On Tuesday, August 4, Acme shipped the last 50 units.

Inside Omega

On Friday, July 10, Jim Rawls called a meeting that included department heads to tell them about the potential contract they were to receive. He told them that as soon as he received the blueprints, work could begin. On Monday, July 13, the prints arrived and again the department heads met to discuss the project. At the end of the meeting, drafting had agreed to prepare manufacturing prints, while industrial engineering and production would begin methods design.

Two problems arose within Omega that were similar to those at Acme. Certain ordered parts could not be delivered on time, and the assembly sequence was difficult to engineer. The departments proposed ideas to help one another, however, and department heads and key employees had daily meetings to discuss progress. The head of electrical engineering knew of a Japanese source for the components that could not be purchased from normal suppliers. Most problems were solved by Saturday, July 18.

On Monday, July 20, a methods engineer and the production supervisor formulated the assembly plans, and production was set to begin on Tuesday morning. On Monday afternoon, people from mechanical engineering, electrical engineering, production, and industrial engineering got together to produce a prototype just to ensure that there would be no snags in production. While they were building the unit, they discovered an error in the connector cable design. All the engineers agreed, after checking and rechecking the blueprints, that the cable was erroneously designed. People from mechanical engineering and electrical engineering spent Monday night redesigning the cable, and on Tuesday morning, the drafting department finalized the changes in the manufacturing prints. On Tuesday morning, Rawls was a bit apprehensive about the design changes and decided to get formal approval. Rawls received word on Wednesday from the head designer at the photocopier firm that they could proceed with the design changes as discussed on the phone. On Friday, July 24, the final units were inspected by quality control and were then shipped.

Part IV

Ten of Acme's final memory units were defective, whereas all of Omega's units passed the photocopier firm's tests. The photocopier firm was disappointed with Acme's delivery delay and incurred further delays in repairing the defective Acme units. However, rather than give the entire contract to one firm, the final contract was split between Acme and Omega with two directives added: maintain zero defects and reduce final cost. In 1993, through extensive cost-cutting efforts, Acme reduced its unit cost by 20 percent and was ultimately awarded the total contract.

» NOTES

1. Paul Ziobro and Joann S. Lublin, "Target's Data Breach Adds to CEO's Sack of Woe," *The Wall Street Journal Online*, January 23, 2014, http://online.wsj.com/news/articles/SB10 0014240527023048565045793391940501258 (accessed January 23, 2014).

2. Evan Ramstad, "A New Look for South Korean Retail," *The Wall Street Journal*, April 16, 2013, B8.

3. David Kesmodel, "Inside China's Supersanitary Chicken Farms; Looking to Capitalize on Food-Safety Concerns, Tyson Shifts from Using Independent Breeders," *The Wall Street Journal Online*, December 9, 2013, http://online.wsj

.com/news/articles/SB10001424052702303559504579197662165181956 (accessed March 3, 2014).

4. Stephanie Strom, "Social Media as a Megaphone to Push Food Makers to Change," *The New York Times*, December 31, 2013, B1.

5. Dexter Roberts, "A New Labor Movement Is Born in China," *BusinessWeek*, June 14–June 20, 2010, 7–8.

6. Stephanie Strom, "Chinese Chicken Processors Are Cleared to Ship to U.S.," *The New York Times*, August 31, 2013, B3; and Kesmodel, "Inside China's Supersanitary Chicken Farms."

7. "What's in Health Care Bill? Take a Dose," *CBS News .com*, March 19, 2010, http://www.cbsnews.com /-stories/2010/03/19/politics/main6314410.shtml (accessed June 1, 2010); "Another View: Full Speed Ahead on Banking Reforms," *San Gabriel Valley Tribune*, February 25, 2010; and "Government and Regulatory Reform," National Federation of Independent Business, http://www .nfib.com/issues-elections/government-and-regulatory -reform?gclid=CIf_5oWLpKoCFcjAKgodhh2GYA& (accessed July 28, 2011).

8. Bruce Posner and David Kiron, "How Caesars Entertainment Is Betting on Sustainability," *MIT Sloan Management Review*, Summer 2013, 63–73.

9. Steven Greenhouse, "Wal-Mart Suspends Supplier of Seafood," *The New York Times*, June 30, 2012, B1.

10. Simona Covel, "Briggs Retains Clients by Helping Them Cut Costs," *The Wall Street Journal Online*, May 2, 2008, http://online.wsj.com/article/SB120943805522951855 .html (accessed May 2, 2008).

11. "AP IMPACT: Middle-Class Jobs Cut In Recession Feared Gone for Good, Lost to Technology," *The Washington Post*, January 23, 2013.

12. Jane J. Kim, "Where Either a Borrower or a Lender Can Be," *The Wall Street Journal*, March 12, 2008, D1, D3.

13. Norihiko Shirouzu, "Chinese Inspire Car Makers' Designs," *The Wall Street Journal*, October 28, 2009.

14. Alex Salkever, "Anatomy of a Business Decision; Case Study: A Chocolate Maker Is Buffeted by Global Forces Beyond His Control," *Inc.*, April 2008, 59–63.

15. Scott Kilman, "Consumers Feel Impact of Rising Grain Costs," *The Wall Street Journal*, August 8, 2008, A1, A11.

16. Elisabetta Povoledo, " 'Ferrari of Porcelain' Struggles to Find Buyer, Reflecting Hard Times in Italy," *The New York Times*, February 9, 2013, B1.

17. For an extended discussion of environmental change and uncertainty, see Randall D. Harris, "Organizational Task Environments: An Evaluation of Convergent and Discriminant Validity," *Journal of Management Studies* 41, no. 5 (July 2004), 857–882; Allen C. Bluedorn, "Pilgrim's Progress: Trends and Convergence in Research on Organizational Size and Environment," *Journal of Management* 19 (1993), 163–191; Howard E. Aldrich, *Organizations and Environments* (Englewood Cliffs, NJ: Prentice Hall, 1979); and Fred E. Emery and Eric L. Trist, "The Casual Texture of Organizational Environments," *Human Relations* 18 (1965), 21–32.

18. Gregory G. Dess and Donald W. Beard, "Dimensions of Organizational Task Environments," *Administrative Science Quarterly* 29 (1984), 52–73; Ray Jurkovich, "A Core Typology of Organizational Environments," *Administrative Science Quarterly* 19 (1974), 380–394; and Robert B. Duncan, "Characteristics of Organizational Environments and Perceived Environmental Uncertainty," *Administrative Science Quarterly* 17 (1972), 313–327.

19. Christine S. Koberg and Gerardo R. Ungson, "The Effects of Environmental Uncertainty and Dependence on Organizational Structure and Performance: A Comparative Study," *Journal of Management* 13 (1987), 725–737; and

Frances J. Milliken, "Three Types of Perceived Uncertainty About the Environment: State, Effect, and Response Uncertainty," *Academy of Management Review* 12 (1987), 133–143.

20. Jonathan D. Rockoff, "Abbott to Split Into Two Companies," *The Wall Street Journal Online*, October 20, 2011, http://online.wsj.com/news/articles/SB10001424052 970204485304576640740820288766 (accessed October 20, 2011).

21. Daisuke Wakabayashi, "The Point-and-Shoot Camera Faces Its Existential Moment," *The Wall Street Journal*, July 30, 2013, http://online.wsj.com/article/SB10001424 127887324251504578580263719432252.html (accessed August 26, 2013).

22. Reported in Pekka Aula, "Social Media, Reputation Risk and Ambient Publicity Management," *Strategy & Leadership* 38, no. 6 (2010), 43–49.

23. Jay Stuller, "The Need for Speed," *The Conference Board Review*, Fall 2009, 34–41; and Richard S. Levick, "Domino's Discovers Social Media," *BusinessWeek*, April 21, 2009, http://www.businessweek.com /stories/2009-04-21/dominos-discovers-social -mediabusinessweek-business-news-stock-market-and -financial-advice (accessed October 8, 2014).

24. See Ian P. McCarthy, Thomas B. Lawrence, Brian Wixted, and Brian R. Gordon, "A Multidimensional Conceptualization of Environmental Velocity," *Academy of Management Review* 35, no. 4 (2010), 604–626, for an overview of the numerous factors that are creating environmental instability for organizations.

25. J. A. Litterer, *The Analysis of Organizations*, 2nd ed. (New York: Wiley, 1973), 335.

26. Constance L. Hays, "More Gloom on the Island of Lost Toy Makers," *The New York Times*, February 23, 2005, C1; and Nicholas Casey, "Fisher-Price Game Plan: Pursue Toy Sales in Developing Markets," *The Wall Street Journal*, May 29, 2008, B1, B2.

27. Rosalie L. Tung, "Dimensions of Organizational Environments: An Exploratory Study of Their Impact on Organizational Structure," *Academy of Management Journal* 22 (1979), 672–693.

28. Joseph E. McCann and John Selsky, "Hyper-Turbulence and the Emergence of Type 5 Environments," *Academy of Management Review* 9 (1984), 460–470.

29. McCarthy et al., "A Multidimensional Conceptualization of Environmental Velocity."

30. Terry Maxon, "Judge OKs American Airlines-US Airways Merger, American's Exit from Bankruptcy," *DallasNews .com*, November 27, 2013, http://aviationblog.dallasnews .com/2013/11/judge-oks-american-airlines-us-airways -merger-americans-exit-from-bankruptcy.html/ (accessed March 4, 2014); and Susan Carey and Melanie Trottman, "Airlines Face New Reckoning as Fuel Costs Take Big Bite," *The Wall Street Journal*, March 20, 2008, A1, A15.

31. Julia Werdigier, "BP Appoints New Chief of Production," *The New York Times*, November 24, 2012, B3.

32. James D. Thompson, *Organizations in Action* (New York: McGraw-Hill, 1967), 20–21.

33. Jennifer A. Marrone, "Team Boundary Spanning: A Multilevel Review of Past Research and Proposals for the Future," *Journal of Management* 36, no. 4 (July 2010), 911–940.

34. Darren Dahl, "Strategy: Managing Fast, Flexible, and Full of Team Spirit," *Inc.*, May 2009, 95–97.

35. David B. Jemison, "The Importance of Boundary Spanning Roles in Strategic Decision-Making," *Journal of Management Studies* 21 (1984), 131–152; and Mohamed Ibrahim Ahmad At-Twaijri and John R. Montanari, "The Impact of Context and Choice on the Boundary-Spanning Process: An Empirical Extension," *Human Relations* 40 (1987), 783–798.

36. Reported in Michelle Cook, "The Intelligentsia," *Business 2.0*, July 1999, 135–136.

37. Robert C. Schwab, Gerardo R. Ungson, and Warren B. Brown, "Redefining the Boundary-Spanning Environment Relationship," *Journal of Management* 11 (1985), 75–86.

38. Patricia Buhler, "Business Intelligence: An Opportunity for a Competitive Advantage," *Supervision*, March 2013, 8–11; and Tom Duffy, "Spying the Holy Grail," *Microsoft Executive Circle*, Winter 2004, 38–39.

39. Reported in Julie Schlosser, "Looking for Intelligence in Ice Cream," *Fortune*, March 17, 2003, 114–120.

40. Ken Western, "Ethical Spying," *Business Ethics*, September/October 1995, 22–23; Stan Crock, Geoffrey Smith, Joseph Weber, Richard A. Melcher, and Linda Himelstein, "They Snoop to Conquer," *BusinessWeek*, October 28, 1996, 172–176; and Kenneth A. Sawka, "Demystifying Business Intelligence," *Management Review* 85, no. 10 (October 1996), 47–51.

41. Liam Fahey and Jan Herring, "Intelligence Teams," *Strategy & Leadership* 35, no. 1 (2007), 13–20.

42. Jay W. Lorsch, "Introduction to the Structural Design of Organizations," in Gene W. Dalton, Paul R. Lawrence, and Jay W. Lorsch, eds., *Organizational Structure and Design* (Homewood, IL: Irwin and Dorsey, 1970), 5.

43. Paul R. Lawrence and Jay W. Lorsch, *Organization and Environment* (Homewood, IL: Irwin, 1969).

44. Lorsch, "Introduction to the Structural Design of Organizations," 7.

45. Jay W. Lorsch and Paul R. Lawrence, "Environmental Factors and Organizational Integration," in J. W. Lorsch and Paul R. Lawrence, eds., *Organizational Planning: Cases and Concepts* (Homewood, IL: Irwin and Dorsey, 1972), 45.

46. Virpi Turkulainen and Mikko Ketokivi, "The Contingent Value of Organizational Integration," *Journal of Organization Design* 2, no. 2 (2013), 31–43.

47. Tom Burns and G. M. Stalker, *The Management of Innovation* (London: Tavistock, 1961).

48. John A. Courtright, Gail T. Fairhurst, and L. Edna Rogers, "Interaction Patterns in Organic and Mechanistic Systems," *Academy of Management Journal* 32 (1989), 773–802.

49. Dennis K. Berman, "Crunch Time," *BusinessWeek Frontier*, April 24, 2000, F28–F38.

50. Thomas C. Powell, "Organizational Alignment as Competitive Advantage," *Strategic Management Journal* 13 (1992), 119–134; Mansour Javidan, "The Impact of Environmental Uncertainty on Long-Range Planning Practices of the U.S. Savings and Loan Industry," *Strategic Management Journal* 5 (1984), 381–392; Tung, "Dimensions of Organizational Environments"; and Thompson, *Organizations in Action*.

51. Peter Brews and Devavrat Purohit, "Strategic Planning in Unstable Environments," *Long Range Planning* 40 (2007), 64–83; and Darrell Rigby and Barbara Bilodeau, "A Growing Focus on Preparedness," *Harvard Business Review*, July–August 2007, 21–22.

52. Hiroko Tabuchi, "Japan's Electronics Behemoths Speak of Dire Times Ahead," *The New York Times*, November 2, 2012, B6.

53. Ian Wylie, "There Is No Alternative To . . .," *Fast Company*, July 2002, 106–110.

54. General Colin Powell, quoted in Oren Harari, "Good/Bad News About Strategy," *Management Review* 84, no. 7, July 1995, 29–31.

55. Kate Linebaugh and Siobhan Hughes, "Companies Warn About Cutbacks," *The Wall Street Journal*, November 14, 2012, A6.

56. Jeffrey Pfeffer and Gerald Salancik, *The External Control of Organizations: A Resource Dependent Perspective* (New York: Harper & Row, 1978); David Ulrich and Jay B. Barney, "Perspectives in Organizations: Resource Dependence, Efficiency, and Population," *Academy of Management Review* 9 (1984), 471–481; and Amy J. Hillman, Michael C. Withers, and Brian J. Collins, "Resource Dependence Theory: A Review," *Journal of Management* 35, no. 6 (2009), 1404–1427.

57. Andrew H. Van de Ven and Gordon Walker, "The Dynamics of Interorganizational Coordination," *Administrative Science Quarterly* (1984), 598–621; and Huseyin Leblebici and Gerald R. Salancik, "Stability in Interorganizational Exchanges: Rulemaking Processes of the Chicago Board of Trade," *Administrative Science Quarterly* 27 (1982), 227–242.

58. Mike Esterl and Corey Dade, "DHL Sends an SOS to UPS in $1 Billion Parcel Deal," *The Wall Street Journal*, May 29, 2008, B1.

59. Judith A. Babcock, *Organizational Responses to Resource Scarcity and Munificence: Adaptation and Modification in Colleges Within a University* (Ph.D. diss., Pennsylvania State University, 1981).

60. Peter Smith Ring and Andrew H. Van de Ven, "Developmental Processes of Corporative Interorganizational Relationships," *Academy of Management Review* 19 (1994), 90–118; Jeffrey Pfeffer, "Beyond Management and the Worker: The Institutional Function of Management," *Academy of Management Review* 1 (April 1976), 36–46; and John P. Kotter, "Managing External Dependence," *Academy of Management Review* 4 (1979), 87–92.

61. Bryan Borys and David B. Jemison, "Hybrid Arrangements as Strategic Alliances: Theoretical Issues in Organizational Combinations," *Academy of Management Review* 14 (1989), 234–249.

62. Tanzina Vega, "Two Ad Giants Chasing Google in Merger Deal," *The New York Times*, July 29, 2013, A1.

63. Julie Cohen Mason, "Strategic Alliances: Partnering for Success," *Management Review* 82, no. 5 (May 1993), 10–15.

64. Teri Agins and Alessandra Galloni, "After Gianni; Facing a Squeeze, Versace Struggles to Trim the Fat," *The Wall Street Journal*, September 30, 2003, A1, A10.

65. Borys and Jemison, "Hybrid Arrangements as Strategic Alliances."

66. Donald Palmer, "Broken Ties: Interlocking Directorates and Intercorporate Coordination," *Administrative Science Quarterly* 28 (1983), 40–55; F. David Shoorman, Max H. Bazerman, and Robert S. Atkin, "Interlocking Directorates: A Strategy for Reducing Environmental Uncertainty," *Academy of Management Review* 6 (1981), 243–251; and Ronald S. Burt, *Toward a Structural Theory of Action* (New York: Academic Press, 1982).

67. James R. Lang and Daniel E. Lockhart, "Increased Environmental Uncertainty and Changes in Board Linkage Patterns," *Academy of Management Journal* 33 (1990), 106–128; and Mark S. Mizruchi and Linda Brewster Stearns, "A Longitudinal Study of the Formation of Interlocking Directorates," *Administrative Science Quarterly* 33 (1988), 194–210.

68. Miguel Bustillo and Joann S. Lublin, "Board Ties Begin to Trip Up Companies," *The Wall Street Journal*, April 8, 2010, B1.

69. Claudia H. Deutsch, "Companies and Critics Try Collaboration," *The New York Times*, May 17, 2006, G1.

70. Tom McGinty, "SEC 'Revolving Door' Under Review; Staffers Who Join Companies They Once Regulated Draw Lawmakers' Ire," *The Wall Street Journal*, June 16, 2010, C1.

71. Keith J. Winstein and Suzanne Vranica, "Drug Ads' Impact Questioned," *The Wall Street Journal*, September 3, 2008, B7.

72. Rob Levine, "Google's Spreading Tentacles of Influence," *Bloomberg Businessweek*, October 31–November 6, 2011, 43–44.

73. Aula, "Social Media, Reputation Risk and Ambient Publicity Management."

74. Kotter, "Managing External Dependence."

75. Claire Cain Miller and Stephanie Clifford, "To Catch Up, Walmart Moves to Amazon Turf," *The New York Times*, October 20, 2013, A1.

76. Matt Rosoff, "Google's 15 Biggest Acquisitions and What Happened to Them," *Business Insider*, March 14, 2011, http://www.businessinsider.com/googles-15 -biggest-acquisitions-and-what-happened-to-them-2011-3 (accessed July 28, 2011); and Kathy Bergen and Ameet Sachdev, "Lenovo Takes On a Fixer-Upper with Motorola Acquisition," *Seattle Times*, February 9, 2014, http:// seattletimes.com/html/businesstechnology/2022861882 _motorolalenovoxml.html (accessed March 6, 2014).

77. Robert Pear, "Health Insurance Companies Try to Shape Rules," *The New York Times*, May 15, 2010, http://www .nytimes.com/2010/05/16/health/policy/16health

.html (accessed May 15, 2010); Miguel Bustillo and Stu Woo, "Retailers Push Amazon on Taxes; Wal-Mart, Target and Others Look to Close Loophole for Online Sellers," *The Wall Street Journal*, March 17, 2011, B1; and Sara Forden, "Facebook Seeks Friends in Washington amid Privacy Talk," *BusinessWeek*, December 2, 2010, http:// www.businessweek.com/news/2010-12-02/facebook-seeks -friends-in-washington-amid-privacy-talk.html (accessed July 28, 2011).

78. David B. Yoffie, "How an Industry Builds Political Advantage," *Harvard Business Review* (May–June 1988), 82–89; and Jeffrey H. Birnbaum, "Chief Executives Head to Washington to Ply the Lobbyist's Trade," *The Wall Street Journal*, March 19, 1990, A1, A16.

79. Adam Entous, "U.S.-South Korea Communications Won't Use Huawei Gear," *The Wall Street Journal Online*, February 13, 2014, http://online.wsj.com/news/articles/SB100014240 52702303704304579381742601220138 (accessed March 6, 2014); Emily Rauhala, "Huawei: The Chinese Company That Scares Washington," *Time*, April 4, 2013, http://world .time.com/2013/04/04/huawei-the-chinese-company-that -scares-washington/ (accessed March 6, 2014); Spencer E. Ante and Shayndi Raice, "Dignitaries Come on Board to Ease Huawei into U.S.," *The Wall Street Journal Online*, September 21, 2010, http://online.wsj.com/article/SB100014 24052748704416904575501892440266992.html (accessed September 23, 2010); P. Goldstein, "Former Defense Official Joins Amerilink in Huawei Lobbying Bid," *FierceWireless. com*, October 22, 2010, http://www. fiercewireless.com/ story/former-defense-official-joins-amerilink-huawei- lobbing-bid/2010-10-22 (accessed July 26, 2011); Joann S. Lublin and Shayndi Raice, "U.S. Security Fears Kill Huawei, ZTE Bids," *The Asian Wall Street Journal*, November 8, 2010, 17; and Shayndi Raice, "Huawei and U.S. Partner Scale Back Business Tie-Up," *The Wall Street Journal*, February 10, 2011, B5.

80. Leslie Scism, "Insurer Pushes to Weaken License Test," *The Wall Street Journal*, April 25, 2011, A1.

81. Anthony J. Daboub, Abdul M. A. Rasheed, Richard L. Priem, and David A. Gray, "Top Management Team Characteristics and Corporate Illegal Activity," *Academy of Management Review* 20, no. 1 (1995), 138–170.

82. Barry M. Staw and Eugene Szwajkowski, "The Scarcity- Munificence Component of Organizational Environments and the Commission of Illegal Acts," *Administrative Science Quarterly* 20 (1975), 345–354; and Kimberly D. Elsbach and Robert I. Sutton, "Acquiring Organizational Legitimacy Through Illegitimate Actions: A Marriage of Institutional and Impression Management Theories," *Academy of Management Journal* 35 (1992), 699–738.

83. Russell Gold, "Halliburton Ex-Official Pleads Guilty in Bribe Case," *The Wall Street Journal*, September 4, 2005, A1, A15.

84. Max Colchester and Christina Passariello, "Dirty Secrets in Soap Prices," *The Wall Street Journal*, December 9, 2011, http://online.wsj.com/news/articles/SB100014240529702034 13304577086251676539124 (accessed December 19, 2011).

85. Adapted by Dorothy Marcic from "Organizational Dependencies," in Ricky W. Griffin and Thomas C. Head, *Practicing Management*, 2nd ed. (Dallas: Houghton Mifflin), 2–3.

86. Based on Tom Gara and Karen Talley, "Portrait of a Studio Missing the Boat," *The Wall Street Journal Online*, April 9, 2013, http://online.wsj.com/news/articles/SB10001424 127887323820304578411103993150918 (accessed April 15, 2014); Kavita Kumar, "The Fall of CPI," *St. Louis Post-Dispatch*, April 14, 2013, http://www.stltoday.com/business /local/the-fall-of-cpi/article_28fa0d94-0575-5e06-8ad0 -4de245e07eeb.html (accessed April 15, 2014); and Jim Suhr, "CPI Corp., Sears' and Walmart Portrait Photographer, Abruptly Shuts Down," *The Huffington Post*, http://www .huffingtonpost.com/2013/04/07/cpi-corp-shut-down_n _3033911.html (accessed April 15, 2014).

87. Adapted from John F. Veiga, "The Paradoxical Twins: Acme and Omega Electronics," in John F. Veiga and John N. Yanouzas, *The Dynamics of Organizational Theory* (St. Paul, MN: West, 1984), 132–138.

Interorganizational Relationships

Learning Objectives

After reading this chapter you should be able to:

1. Define an organizational ecosystem and the changing role of competition.
2. Explain the changing role of management in interorganizational relationships.
3. Discuss types of resource-dependence relationships and the power implications.
4. Describe the role of collaborative networks.
5. Explain the interorganizational shift from adversaries to partners.
6. Understand the population-ecology perspective and its key concepts.
7. Specify the key aspects of institutionalism.

Before reading this chapter, please check whether you agree or disagree with each of the following statements:

1 Organizations should strive to be as independent and self-sufficient as possible so that their managers aren't put in the position of "dancing to someone else's tune."

    I AGREE _____   I DISAGREE _____

2 The success or failure of a start-up is largely determined by the smarts and management ability of the entrepreneur.

    I AGREE _____   I DISAGREE _____

3 Managers should quickly copy or borrow techniques being used by other successful companies to make their own organization more effective and to keep pace with changing times.

    I AGREE _____   I DISAGREE _____

MANAGING BY DESIGN QUESTIONS

Several garment factory fires in Bangladesh in 2012 and the collapse of another apparel plant in 2013 that killed more than 1,100 workers put the spotlight on poor working conditions in that country. The incidents set off public outrage, requiring the retailers such as Walmart, Target, and H&M that use Bangladesh contractors to respond. It's a serious problem, and even though Walmart publicly blacklisted about 250 Bangladesh suppliers found to have safety problems and other retailers took similar steps, it wasn't enough to salve the public's anger. Now, major U.S. retailers including Gap, Walmart, Target, Macy's, Costco, and VF Corporation have banded together in a group called the Alliance for Bangladesh Worker Safety. The group's primary goals are to improve working conditions and prevent such disasters. It has come up with common fire and building safety standards and formed a board that includes four company representatives, former U.S. ambassador to Bangladesh Jim Moriarty, and fire safety consultant Randy Tucker. The group will provide $100 million in low-cost loans. The alliance falls short of the commitment made by an alliance of mostly European companies, including H&M, that has agreed to directly pay for the costs of repair and renovation of some 5,000 Bangladesh garment factories. Yet it is definitely a step in the right direction. Former U.S. Representative Ellen O'Kane Tauscher, who will serve as chairman of the board, says her job is to ensure accountability. "We expect scrutiny, but it is also important to give us time to put the plans into action."[1]

When dealing with a massive, complex problem, like the organizational catastrophes in Bangladesh, even the most sophisticated and capable organization will soon reach the limit of its effectiveness. Today's organizations face numerous complex problems because of the complexity and uncertainty of the environment, as discussed in the previous chapter. Thus, a widespread organizational trend is to reduce boundaries and increase collaboration between companies, sometimes even between competitors. For example, Poste Italiane S.p.A., which serves as Italy's postal service as well as a bank, credit card firm, and mobile phone company, created one of the most sophisticated cyber security operations in the world. CEO Massimo Sarmi realized that to achieve true security for customers against cybercrime, he needed to collaborate with other organizations. He began reaching out around the globe. Poste Italiane has signed a memorandum of understanding with the U.S. Secret Service, for example, and joined the electronic crime task force in New York City. The company has partnered with companies such as software firm Microsoft, energy company Enel, and Visa/MasterCard, and academic organizations such as George Mason University and the University of London, to open a global Cyber Security Program of Excellence. The center is promoting international cooperation regarding cyber security and studying ways to make the Internet more dynamically secure through active defense. "[T]he problem is global," Sarmi says. "It's not national or local."[2]

In many industries, the business environment is so complicated that no single company can develop all the expertise and resources needed to stay competitive. Why? Globalization and rapid advances in technology, communications, and transportation have created amazing new opportunities, but they have also raised the cost of doing business and made it increasingly difficult for any company to take advantage of those opportunities on its own. In this new economy, webs of organizations are emerging. Collaboration and partnership is the new way of doing business. Organizations think of themselves as teams that create value jointly rather than as autonomous companies that are in competition with all others.

Purpose of This Chapter

This chapter explores the most recent trend in organizing, which is the increasingly dense web of relationships among organizations. Companies have always been dependent on other organizations for supplies, materials, and information. The question involves the way these relationships are managed. At one time it was a matter of a large, powerful company tightening the screws on small suppliers. Today a company can choose to develop positive, trusting relationships. The notion of horizontal relationships described in Chapter 3 and the understanding of environmental uncertainty in Chapter 4 are leading to the next stage of organizational evolution, which is a web of horizontal relationships *across* organizations. Organizations can choose to build relationships in many ways, such as appointing preferred suppliers, establishing agreements, business partnering, joint ventures, or even mergers and acquisitions.

Interorganizational research has yielded perspectives such as resource dependence, collaborative networks, population ecology, and institutionalism. The sum total of these ideas can be daunting because it means managers no longer can rest in the safety of managing a single organization. They have to figure out how to manage a whole set of interorganizational relationships, which is a great deal more challenging and complex.

Organizational Ecosystems

Interorganizational relationships are the relatively enduring resource transactions, flows, and linkages that occur among two or more organizations.[3] Traditionally, these transactions and relationships have been seen as a necessary evil to obtain what an organization needs. The presumption has been that the world is composed of distinct businesses that thrive on autonomy and compete for supremacy. A company may be forced into interorganizational relationships depending on its needs and the instability and complexity of the environment.

A new view described by James Moore argues that organizations are now evolving into business ecosystems. An **organizational ecosystem** is a system formed by the interaction of a community of organizations and their environment. An ecosystem cuts across traditional industry lines.[4] A similar concept is the *megacommunity approach*, in which businesses, governments, and nonprofit organizations join together across sectors and industries to tackle huge, compelling problems of mutual interest, such as energy development, world hunger, or cybercrime.[5]

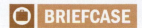

BRIEFCASE

As an organization manager, keep these guidelines in mind:

Look for and develop relationships with other organizations. Don't limit your thinking to a single industry or business type. Build an ecosystem of which your organization is a part.

Is Competition Dead?

No company can go it alone under a constant onslaught of international competitors, changing technology, and new regulations. Organizations around the world are embedded in complex networks of confusing relationships—collaborating in some markets, competing fiercely in others. The number of corporate alliances has been increasing at a rate of 25 percent annually, and many of those have been between competitors.[6] Hyundai, Chrysler, and Mitsubishi jointly run the Global Engine Manufacturing Alliance to build four-cylinder engines. Volvo is now owned by Zhejiang Geely Holding Group of China, but it maintains an alliance with previous owner Ford Motor Company to supply engines and certain other components.[7]

Traditional competition, which assumes a distinct company competing for survival and supremacy with other standalone businesses, no longer exists because each organization both supports and depends on the others for success, and perhaps for survival. However, most managers recognize that the competitive stakes are higher than ever in a world where market share can crumble overnight, and no industry is immune from almost instant obsolescence.[8] In today's world, a new form of competition is in fact intensifying.[9]

For one thing, companies now need to co-evolve with others in the ecosystem so that everyone gets stronger. Consider the wolf and the caribou. Wolves cull weaker caribou, which strengthens the herd. A strong herd means that wolves must become stronger themselves. With co-evolution, the whole system becomes stronger. In the same way, companies co-evolve through discussion with each other, shared visions, alliances, and managing complex relationships.

Exhibit 5.1 illustrates the complexity of an ecosystem by showing the myriad overlapping relationships among high-tech companies. Since the time this chart was created, many of these companies have merged, been acquired, or gone out of business. Ecosystems constantly change and evolve, with some relationships growing stronger while others weaken or are terminated. The changing pattern of relationships and interactions in an ecosystem contributes to the health and vitality of the system as an integrated whole.[10]

In an organizational ecosystem, conflict and cooperation exist at the same time. For example, consider what is happening with Apple and Samsung.

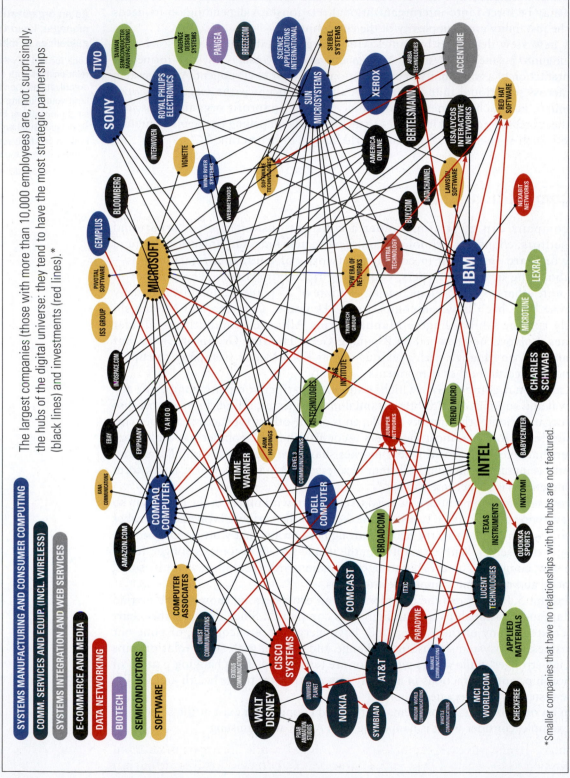

The largest companies (those with more than 10,000 employees) are, not surprisingly, the hubs of the digital universe: they tend to have the most strategic partnerships (black lines) and investments (red lines).*

EXHIBIT 5.1
An Organizational Ecosystem

SYSTEMS MANUFACTURING AND CONSUMER COMPUTING
COMM. SERVICES AND EQUIP. (INCL. WIRELESS)
SYSTEMS INTEGRATION AND WEB SERVICES
E-COMMERCE AND MEDIA
DATA NETWORKING
BIOTECH
SEMICONDUCTORS
SOFTWARE

*Smaller companies that have no relationships with the hubs are not featured.

© Cengage Learning®

Samsung is Apple's most ferocious rival in the smartphone wars. The company is also Apple's biggest supplier of the sophisticated processors and memory chips used for many of Apple's iPhones, iPods, and iPads, and it also produces screens for some products.

☑ IN PRACTICE

Apple and Samsung

A decade ago, when Apple first began collaborating with Samsung, the two companies didn't really compete, but that changed when Samsung got into producing smartphones that today eclipse the iPhone in terms of units shipped. Apple managers have tried to find alternate suppliers for some of the parts it uses from Samsung, but it isn't easy. The two firms have worked together for more than half a decade to build custom chips. Apple executives realized Samsung had ambitions to compete with their company, but they needed the technology that only Samsung could deliver in large quantities. Samsung, meanwhile, needed the business. Apple remains Samsung's biggest customer. An attempt by Apple to begin using Sharp for screens on the third-generation iPad faltered when Sharp missed the launch deadline. Soon after, Samsung bought a 3 percent stake in Sharp and agreed to buy more LCD screens from them. The move made Samsung Sharp's key client, potentially preventing Apple from gaining more bargaining power.

For now, Apple and Samsung need each other. If Apple pulled all of its business, Samsung would lose a huge portion of its sales and earnings. Apple will likely continue searching for a way to "divorce" Samsung, but for now the two companies are locked in a relationship that is usually, although perhaps not always, mutually beneficial. Even as they collaborate, the two companies have spent the better part of two years suing and countersuing over the look, feel, and features of their phones.[11]

Some companies believe cooperation is essential to success. Google, for example, has a whole team dedicated to giving away technology to the competition. Microsoft also tends to support and cooperate with a wide range of companies that help sell software and services. It has invested $2 billion to a leveraged buy-out of Dell Computer. Microsoft, executives say, "is committed to the long-term success of the entire PC ecosystem."[12]

Other companies, such as Apple, are less willing to cooperate, although they do so when it clearly benefits them. "Open systems don't always win," warned the recently deceased Steve Jobs, Apple's co-founder and former CEO, who always kept tight control and close watch over his company's products.[13] In general, cooperation has become the rule in many industries and especially in high-tech firms. The business press is full of articles that talk about *frenemies*, reflecting the trend toward companies being both friends and enemies, collaborators and competitors. Many companies that long prided themselves on independence have shifted to an ecosystem approach. Mutual dependencies and partnerships have become a fact of life. Is competition dead? Companies today may use their strength to achieve victory over competitors, but ultimately cooperation carries the day.

The Changing Role of Management

Within business ecosystems managers learn to move beyond traditional responsibilities of corporate strategy and designing hierarchical structures and control systems. Managers have to look beyond the boundaries of their own company and build relationships with a network of partners. If a top manager looks down to enforce order and uniformity, the company is missing opportunities for new and evolving external relationships.[14] In this new world, managers think about horizontal processes rather than vertical structures. Important initiatives are not just top down; they cut across the boundaries separating organizational units. Moreover, horizontal relationships now include linkages with suppliers and customers, who become part of the team. Business leaders can learn to lead economic co-evolution. Managers learn to see and appreciate the rich environment of opportunities that grow from cooperative relationships with other contributors to the ecosystem. Rather than trying to force suppliers into low prices or customers into high prices, managers strive to strengthen the larger system evolving around them, finding ways to understand this big picture and how to contribute. For example, managers at luxury retailer Neiman Marcus are cooperating with managers at cheap-chic retailer Target and with fashion designers in an experiment that pushes the boundaries of retail and potentially expands the customer base for all. For the holiday shopping season, a limited edition collection of 50 designer items from fashion houses including Diane Von Furstenberg, Tory Burch, Derek Lam, Rodarte, and 20 other designers will be offered at an average price of $60 at both retail chains. Neiman had contacts with the designers, while Target had an extensive supply chain to produce items in bulk. Executives from the two retailers met in person to brainstorm how the experiment might work, then began negotiating with designers.[15]

This is a broader leadership role than ever before. Managers in charge of coordinating with other companies must learn new executive skills. For example, Federal investigations have found that the inability of managers to collaborate and communicate effectively across organizational boundaries played a significant role in the BP-Transocean Deepwater Horizon oil spill, as we described in Chapter 1. One question raised by investigators concerned an argument between a BP manager and a Transocean manager that occurred on the rig the day of the explosion. BP and Federal agency managers also had trouble collaborating effectively in clean-up efforts.[16]

A study of executive roles by the Hay Group distinguished between *operations roles* and *collaborative roles*. Most traditional managers are skilled in handling operations roles, which have traditional vertical authority and are accountable for business results primarily through direct control over people and resources. Collaborative roles, on the other hand, don't have direct authority over horizontal colleagues or partners, but are nonetheless accountable for specific business results. Managers in collaborative roles have to be highly flexible and proactive. They achieve results through personal communication and assertively seeking out needed information and resources.[17]

The old way of managing relied almost exclusively on operations roles, defending the organization's boundaries and maintaining direct control over resources. Today, though, collaborative roles are becoming more important for success. When partnerships fail, it is usually because of an inability of the partners to develop trusting, collaborative relationships rather than due to the lack of a solid business plan or strategy. In successful alliances, people work together almost as if they were members of the same organization.[18] Consider the U.S. war against terrorism. As we discussed in the opening section of this chapter, interorganizational collaboration is essential for tackling large, complex problems. To fight terrorism, the U.S. government not only collaborates with governments of other countries but also with numerous private security companies. At the Pentagon's National Military Command Center, employees of private contracting firms work side-by-side with military personnel monitoring potential crises worldwide and providing information to top leaders. "We could not perform our mission without them," said Ronald Sanders, former chief of human capital at the Office of the Director of National Intelligence. "They serve as our reserves, providing flexibility and expertise we can't acquire. Once they are on board, we treat them as if they're part of the total force."[19]

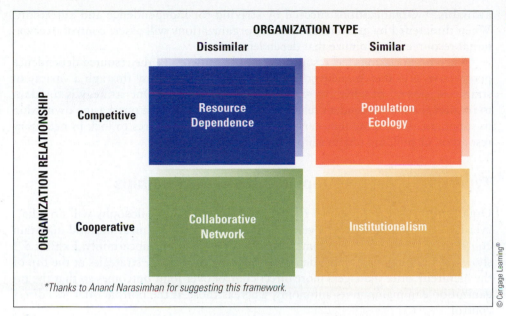

EXHIBIT 5.2
A Framework of
Interorganizational
Relationships*

*Thanks to Anand Narasimhan for suggesting this framework.

Interorganizational Framework

Appreciating the larger organizational ecosystem is one of the most exciting areas of organization theory. The models and perspectives for understanding interorganizational relationships ultimately help managers change their role from top-down management to horizontal coordination across organizations. Exhibit 5.2 shows a framework for analyzing the different views of interorganizational relationships. Relationships among organizations can be characterized by whether the organizations are dissimilar or similar and whether relationships are competitive or cooperative. By understanding these perspectives, managers can assess their environment and adopt strategies to suit their needs. The first perspective is called resource-dependence theory, which was described briefly in Chapter 4. It describes rational ways organizations deal with each other to reduce their dependence on the environment. The second perspective is about collaborative networks, wherein organizations allow themselves to become dependent on other organizations to increase value and productivity for all. The third perspective is population ecology, which examines how new organizations fill niches left open by established organizations and how a rich variety of new organizational forms benefits society. The final approach is called institutionalism, which explains why and how organizations legitimate themselves in the larger environment and design structures by borrowing ideas from each other. These four approaches to the study of interorganizational relationships are described in the remainder of this chapter.

Resource Dependence

Resource dependence represents the traditional view of relationships among organizations. As described in Chapter 4, **resource-dependence theory** argues that organizations try to minimize their dependence on other organizations for the supply of important resources and try to influence the environment to make resources available.[20] Organizations succeed by striving for independence and autonomy. When threatened by greater dependence, organizations will assert control over external resources to minimize that dependence.

When organizations feel resource or supply constraints, the resource-dependence perspective says they maneuver to maintain their autonomy through a variety of strategies, several of which were described in Chapter 4. One strategy is to adapt to or alter the interdependent relationships. This could mean purchasing ownership in suppliers, developing long-term contracts or joint ventures to lock in necessary resources, or building relationships in other ways.

Types of Resource-Dependence Relationships

Organizations operating under the resource-dependence philosophy will do whatever is needed to avoid excessive dependence on other organizations and maintain control of resources and outcomes, thereby reducing their uncertainty. Exhibit 5.3 shows a hierarchy of resource-dependence relationships. The strategies at the top of the hierarchy offer managers more direct control over joint outcomes so that the organization can maintain its autonomy, whereas those at the bottom offer less direct control.

Acquisition/Merger. This type of relationship offers the greatest amount of control over joint outcomes because the acquiring firm absorbs all of the resources, assets, and liabilities of the target organization. For example, Mattel recently acquired Canada's Mega Brands Inc. to expand its line of toys and compete with LEGO in the market for plastic construction blocks. Mattel will own the company and control what happens with it.[21]

Joint Venture. A joint venture offers less control than full ownership. As Peter Drucker once said, "Businesses once grew by one of two ways: grass roots up, or by acquisition. . . . Today they grow through alliances—all kinds of dangerous alliances. Joint ventures and partnering which, by the way, very few people understand."[22] A **joint venture** is a new and distinct organizational entity set up by two or more organizations to jointly develop an innovative product or shared technology. The successful video streaming site HULU, for example, is a joint venture that was set up by News Corporation (which owns Fox), Disney (which owns ABC), and Comcast

Types of Resource-Dependence Relationships

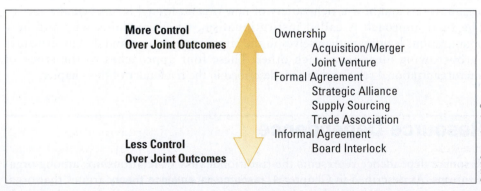

(which owns NBC). Although the three compete with one another on the television airwaves, they knew they could be more competitive together than separately with video streaming.[23] Whirlpool has a joint venture with Hisense-Kelon Holdings Co. to make refrigerators and washers in China.[24]

Strategic Alliance. A **strategic alliance** is less formal and binding than a joint venture. It is a collaborative agreement between two or more organizations that contribute resources to a common endeavor while maintaining their individuality. One example is a strategic partnership between NBCUniversal News Group and NowThis News, a start-up that creates short news segments tailored for social media sites such as Instagram and Snapchat and stored on mobile apps for viewers to watch throughout the day. NowThis News creates 10-, 15-, and 30-second news segments focusing on the top serious stories of the day. The partnership with NBC is expected to facilitate the evolution to linking to longer videos for those who want more information.[25]

Supply Sourcing. Many organizations establish contracts with key suppliers to acquire resources to supplement in-house resources and capabilities. Rather than going it alone, companies such as Apple, Walmart, Dell, and Tesco develop deep, mutually beneficial relationships to make sure they have the supplies and resources they need. As one example, SCA (Svenska Cellulosa Aktiebolaget) uses fiber from recycled paper to make napkins, toilet paper, and paper towels for restaurants, offices, schools, and other institutions. When the supply of recycled paper went down in recent years due to reduced paper waste along with competition for the fiber from Chinese paper companies, SCA developed partnerships with numerous recycling centers, providing them with financial backing to upgrade equipment in exchange for the centers selling recovered fiber exclusively to SCA.[26] At the same time, companies don't want to become too dependent on one supplier. Apple, which for years has used a single company, Foxconn, to assemble iPhones and iPads, recently began using a second company, Pegatron Corp., as the primary assembler for the iPad Mini tablets and a low-cost iPhone. The goal is to reduce risk and overdependence on one company in the supply chain.[27]

 BRIEFCASE

Trade Association. A **trade association** is a federation that allows organizations, often in the same industry, to meet, share information, and monitor one another's activities. A trade association can also use collective resources to lobby for government policies to protect the industry. Membership in the Smoke Free Alternatives Trade Association (SFATA) is growing as opposition to the electronic cigarette industry grows and "vaping" increases in popularity.[28] SFATA has lobbied to keep the federal government from regulating electronic cigarettes the same way tobacco is regulated, believing that "self-regulation is pivotal to the success of the industry."[29]

Board Interlock. A board interlock occurs when a director serves on the boards of multiple companies, creating connections among the companies. The candy company Hershey, for example, has for decades had a board with at least a dozen interlocks with other companies at any one time.[30] This practice also occurs frequently in Silicon Valley, where venture capitalist Marc Andreessen is a director of several firms, including eBay, Hewlett-Packard, and Facebook.[31]

Power Implications

In resource-dependence relationships, large independent companies have power over smaller suppliers or partners. When a large company such as Amazon has power over small publishing companies, for instance, it can ask the companies for shipping deals or lower prices and the publishing companies have no choice but to go along. One former Amazon executive in charge of vendor relations in Europe admits that after Amazon grew large and powerful he took "an almost sadistic delight" in pressuring book publishers to give the online company better financial terms.[32] As Facebook has grown more powerful, it is using its muscle to put restrictions and limits on independent developers that create applications for the social networking site.

IN PRACTICE

Facebook

Antoine Morcos instantly lost nearly half a million registered users for his photo-sharing application Vintage Camera when Facebook unexpectedly cut ties with the third-party app and blocked access to it from Facebook. "I was really shocked," Morcos said. He received an e-mail from Facebook saying they had received too many complaints about Vintage Camera. Morcos believes the real issue is that the app competes with Facebook-owned Instagram.

Vintage Camera isn't alone. Facebook has recently blocked a growing number of third-party apps, including messaging app Voxer, Yandex NV's Wonder social discovery app, and Twitter's Vine video app. Developers say Facebook is using its power to block applications that compete with Facebook-owned services. Message Me, a messaging service, found itself restricted from accessing users' friends lists after the founders snubbed Facebook's takeover advances. As Facebook continues to grow, it is struggling to balance developers, advertisers, and its own new products. Independent developers feel that they are getting squeezed out unless they are willing to play by Facebook's ever-changing rules.[33]

Resource dependence can work in the opposite direction too. Auto companies such as Toyota and General Motors are working to develop a new type of electric motor that doesn't require the use of neodymium, a rare earth mineral that is almost entirely mined and refined in China. Chinese suppliers have power over the auto companies as they strive to create more hybrid and electric vehicles, and the price of the mineral has soared.[34] Power relationships in various industries are always shifting.

Collaborative Networks

The **collaborative-network perspective** is an emerging alternative to resource-dependence theory. Companies join together to become more competitive and to share scarce resources. Large aerospace firms partner with one another and with smaller companies and suppliers to design next-generation jets. Large pharmaceutical companies join with small biotechnology firms to share resources and knowledge and spur innovation. Consulting firms, investment companies, and accounting firms may join in an alliance to meet customer demands for expanded services.[35] Five leading medical groups spanning several states and millions of patients joined in a consortium to share electronic data, including patient health records. Geisinger Health System, Kaiser Permanente, Mayo Clinic, Intermountain Healthcare, and Group Health Cooperative believe using and sharing digitized patient records can help healthcare providers make smarter decisions and provide better care, such as referring a patient to a specialist in another system.[36] Corporate alliances require managers who are good at building personal networks across boundaries. How effective are you at networking? Complete the questionnaire in the "How Do You Fit the Design?" box to find out.

HOW DO YOU FIT THE DESIGN?

PERSONAL NETWORKING

Are you a natural at reaching out to others for personal networking? Having multiple sources of information is a building block for partnering with people in other organizations. To learn something about your networking, answer the following questions. Please answer whether each item is Mostly True or Mostly False for you in school or at work.

	Mostly True	Mostly False
1. I learn early on about changes going on in the organization and how they might affect me or my job.	___	___
2. I network as much to help other people solve problems as to help myself.	___	___
3. I join professional groups and associations to expand my contacts and knowledge.	___	___
4. I know and talk with peers in other organizations.	___	___
5. I act as a bridge from my work group to other work groups.	___	___
6. I frequently use lunches to meet and network with new people.	___	___
7. I regularly participate in charitable causes.	___	___
8. I maintain a list of friends and colleagues to whom I send holiday cards.	___	___
9. I maintain contact with people from previous organizations and school groups.	___	___
10. I actively give information to subordinates, peers, and my boss.	___	___

Scoring: Give yourself one point for each item marked as Mostly True. A score of 7 or higher suggests very active networking. If you scored 3 or less, reaching out to others may not be natural for you and will require extra effort.

Interpretation: In a world of adversarial relationships between organizations, networking across organizational boundaries was not important. In a world of interorganizational partnerships, however, many good things flow from active networking, which will build a web of organizational relationships to get things done. If you are going to manage relationships with other organizations, networking is an essential part of your job. Networking builds social, work, and career relationships that facilitate mutual benefit. People with large, active networks tend to enjoy and contribute to partnerships and have broader impact on interorganizational relationships.

Why Collaboration?

Why all this interest in interorganizational collaboration? Some companies have moved away from the idea of remaining independent to allow themselves to develop mutually dependent relationships with other organizations and accomplish things none of the organizations could do alone. There has been a tremendous surge in the formation of strategic alliances, for example, over the past three decades, with both large established firms and small entrepreneurial firms taking advantage of the benefits of collaboration.[37] Some key reasons for collaboration include sharing risks when entering new markets, mounting expensive new programs and reducing costs, and enhancing the organization's profile in selected industries or technologies. Cooperation and collaboration is a prerequisite for greater innovation, adaptation, problem solving, and performance.[38] Partnerships are also a major avenue for entering global markets, with both large and small firms developing partnerships overseas and in North America. Joint ventures with organizations in other countries, for example, make up a substantial portion of U.S. firms' foreign investment and entry strategies.[39]

North American companies traditionally have worked alone, competing with each other and believing in the tradition of individualism and self-reliance, but they have learned from their international experience just how effective interorganizational relationships can be. Both Japan and Korea have long traditions of corporate clans or industrial groups that collaborate and assist each other. North Americans typically have considered interdependence a bad thing, believing it would reduce competition. However, the experience of collaboration in other countries has shown that competition among companies can be fierce in some areas even as they collaborate in others. It is as if the brothers and sisters of a single family went into separate businesses and want to outdo one another, but they will help each other out when push comes to shove.

ASSESS YOUR ANSWER

1 Organizations should strive to be as independent and self-sufficient as possible so that their managers aren't put in the position of "dancing to someone else's tune."

ANSWER: *Disagree.* Trying to be separate and independent is the old way of thinking. This view says organizations should minimize their dependence on other firms so that they don't become vulnerable. Today, though, successful companies see collaboration as a better approach to maintaining a balance of power and getting things done.

Interorganizational linkages provide a kind of safety net that encourages long-term investment, information sharing, and risk taking. Organizations can achieve higher levels of innovation and performance as they learn to shift from an adversarial to a partnership mindset.[40] Consider the following examples:

- General Motors and Ford Motor Company compete fiercely to sell cars and trucks, but they have joined together to develop new transmissions with 9 speeds for front-wheel-drive vehicles and 10 speeds for rear-drive cars and trucks. The new transmissions are part of the companies' efforts to meet upcoming standards for fuel efficiency and carbon dioxide emissions in the United States and Europe. By cooperating on design, engineering, and testing, the companies will save hundreds of millions of dollars. The two automakers have already collaborated on a 6-speed automatic transmission. "We've already proven that Ford and GM transmission engineers work extremely well together," said Ford's vice president of powertrain engineering.[41]

- Microsoft and Oracle recently struck a deal to allow pieces of Oracle's business software to work with Microsoft's software and online services. The deal between the often feuding technology giants comes as both companies are fighting competition from web-based alternatives to some of their key products. Moreover, the companies have common customers that want help getting products to work together. Steven Ballmer, former CEO of Microsoft, said the two firms have long had a "behind the scenes collaboration," but that was no longer enough during a time when customers want all their cloud services to work together easily. Oracle CEO Larry Ellison hinted that his company will be partnering with other firms as well.[42]

- Roche Holding AG and AstraZeneca PLC developed a partnership to share data on early-stage drug design to increase the odds of developing safe and effective drugs. The data will also be shared with a third company, MedChemica Ltd., which specializes in scrutinizing chemical compounds to pinpoint chemical structures that might create safety problems. The companies say they hope other pharmaceutical companies will join the data-sharing partnership, leading to the creation of safer, more effective drugs.[43] Pharmaceutical companies have until recently been protective of their research data, but there is a noted trend toward collaboration, such as the recently formed Accelerating Medicines Partnership.

IN PRACTICE

Accelerating Medicines Partnership

Companies have spent billions of dollars racing to beat one another to find breakthrough drugs for diseases like Alzheimer's. Now, 10 big pharmaceutical companies have formed a five-year collaborative agreement with the National Institutes of Health (NIH) to share scientists, tissue and blood samples, and research data. By collaborating, the scientists hope to interpret Alzheimer's, Type 2 diabetes, lupus, and rheumatoid arthritis in a way none of the companies have been able to do on their own and identify targets for new drugs.

Called the Accelerating Medicines Partnership, the group includes companies that compete vigorously, such as Bristol-Myers Squibb, Johnson & Johnson, GlaxoSmithKline, Eli Lilly, Sanofi, and Merck. The pact prevents any company from using a discovery until the project makes data on the discovery public. "The moment the project results are out," said David Wholley of the NIH, "all-out competition resumes to develop the winning drug."

Getting the pact pulled together wasn't easy. At times, some of the participants "weren't even talking with one another." Jan Lundbert, who leads Eli Lilly & Company's research laboratories, said figuring out how to collaborate despite being rivals had a "bonding role: Do we respect each other as scientists and as human beings?"[44]

From Adversaries to Partners

Fresh flowers are blooming on the battle-scarred landscape where once-bitter rivalries once took place. In North America, collaboration among organizations initially occurred in nonprofit social service and mental health organizations, where public interest was involved. Community organizations collaborated to achieve greater effectiveness and better use of scarce resources.[45] With the push from international competitors and international examples, hard-nosed American business managers soon began shifting to a new partnership paradigm on which to base their relationships.

Exhibit 5.4 provides a summary of this change in mindset. Rather than organizations maintaining independence, the new model is based on interdependence and trust. Performance measures for the partnership are loosely defined, and problems are resolved through discussion and dialogue. Managing strategic relationships with other firms has become a critical management skill, as discussed in this chapter's BookMark. In the new orientation, people try to add value to both sides and believe in high commitment rather than suspicion and competition. Companies work toward equitable profits for both sides rather than just for their own benefit. The new model is characterized by lots of shared information, including electronic linkages and face-to-face discussions to provide feedback and solve problems. Sometimes people from other companies are on site to enable very close coordination. Partners develop equitable solutions to conflicts rather than relying on legal contracts and lawsuits. Contracts may be loosely specified, and it is not unusual for business partners to help each other outside whatever is specified in the contract.[46]

BRIEFCASE

As an organization manager, keep these guidelines in mind:

Seek collaborative partnerships that enable mutual dependence and enhance value and gain for both sides. Get deeply involved in your partner's business, and vice versa, to benefit both.

EXHIBIT 5.4

Changing Characteristics of Interorganizational Relationships

Traditional Orientation: Adversarial	New Orientation: Partnership
Low dependence	**High dependence**
Suspicion, competition, arm's length	Trust, addition of value to both sides, high commitment
Detailed performance measures, closely monitored	Loose performance measures; problems discussed
Price, efficacy, own profits	Equity, fair dealing, both profit
Limited information and feedback	Electronic linkages to share key information, problem feedback, and discussion
Legal resolution of conflict	Mechanisms for close coordination; people on site
Minimal involvement and up-front investment, separate resources	Involvement in partner's product design and production, shared resources
Short-term contracts	Long-term contracts
Contract limiting the relationship	Business assistance beyond the contract

Sources: Based on Mick Marchington and Steven Vincent, "Analysing the Influence of Institutional, Organizational, and Interpersonal Forces in Shaping Inter-Organizational Relations," *Journal of Management Studies* 41, no. 6 (September 2004), 1029–1056; Jeffrey H. Dyer, "How Chrysler Created an American Keiretsu," *Harvard Business Review*, July–August 1996, 42–56; Myron Magnet, "The New Golden Rule of Business," *Fortune*, February 21, 1994, 60–64; and Peter Grittner, "Four Elements of Successful Sourcing Strategies," *Management Review*, October 1995, 41–45.

BOOKMARK 5.0 HAVE YOU READ THIS BOOK?

Managing Strategic Relationships: The Key to Business Success
By Leonard Greenhalgh

What determines organizational success in the twenty-first century? According to Leonard Greenhalgh, author of *Managing Strategic Relationships: The Key to Business Success,* it's how successfully managers support, foster, and protect collaborative relationships both inside and outside the firm. In separate chapters, the book offers strategies for managing relationships between people and groups within the company and with other organizations. Effectively managing relationships generates a sense of commonwealth and consensus, which ultimately results in competitive advantage.

MANAGING RELATIONSHIPS IN A NEW ERA
Greenhalgh says managers need a new way of thinking to fit the realities of the new era. He offers the following guidelines:

- *Recognize that detailed legal contracts can undermine trust and goodwill.* Greenhalgh stresses the need to build relationships that are based on honesty, trust, understanding, and common goals instead of on narrowly defined legal contracts that concentrate on what one business can give to the other.
- *Treat partners like members of your own organization.* Members of partner organizations need to be active participants in the learning experience by becoming involved in training, team meetings, and other activities. Giving a partner organization's employees a chance to make genuine contributions promotes deeper bonds and a sense of unity.
- *Top managers must be champions for the alliance.* Managers from both organizations have to act in ways that signal to everyone inside and outside the organization a new emphasis on partnership and collaboration. Using ceremony and symbols can help instill a commitment to partnership in the company culture.

A PARTNERSHIP PARADIGM
To succeed in today's environment, old-paradigm management practices based on power, hierarchy, and adversarial relationships must be traded for new-era commonwealth practices that emphasize collaboration and communal forms of organization. The companies that will thrive, Greenhalgh believes, "are those that really have their act together—those that can successfully integrate strategy, processes, business arrangements, resources, systems, and empowered workforces." That can be accomplished, he argues, only by effectively creating, shaping, and sustaining strategic collaborative relationships.

Managing Strategic Relationships: The Key to Business Success, by Leonard Greenhalgh, is published by The Free Press.

In this new view of partnerships, dependence on another company is seen to reduce rather than increase risks. Greater value can be achieved by both parties. By being entwined in a system of interorganizational relationships, everyone does better because they help one another. This is a far cry from the belief that organizations do best by being autonomous. The partnership mindset can be seen in a number of industries. For example, aircraft manufacturers EADS, Embraer, and Boeing have teamed up to develop aviation biofuel.[47] Top medical centers, such as the Mayo Clinic, the MD Anderson Cancer Center, and Community Health Systems, have formed partnerships with networks of clinics or smaller nonprofit hospitals to expand their services and leverage their brands.[48] Auto companies have formed numerous partnerships to share development costs for new electric and hybrid vehicles. Canada's Bombardier and its suppliers were linked together almost like one organization to build the Continental business jet.[49]

By breaking down boundaries and becoming involved in partnerships with an attitude of fair dealing and adding value to both sides, today's companies are changing the concept of what makes an organization.

Population Ecology

This section introduces a different perspective on relationships among organizations. The **population-ecology perspective** differs from the other perspectives because it focuses on organizational diversity and adaptation within a population of organizations.[50] A **population** is a set of organizations engaged in similar activities with similar patterns of resource utilization and outcomes. Organizations within a population compete for similar resources or similar customers, such as financial institutions in the Seattle area or car dealerships in Houston, Texas.

Within a population, the question asked by ecology researchers is about the large number and variation of organizations in society. Why are new organizational forms that create such diversity constantly appearing? The answer is that individual organizational adaptation is severely limited compared to the changes demanded by the environment. Innovation and change in a population of organizations take place through the birth of new types of organizations more so than by the reform and change of existing organizations. Indeed, organizational forms are considered relatively stable, and the good of a whole society is served by the development of new forms of organization through entrepreneurial initiatives. New organizations meet the new needs of society more than established organizations that are slow to change.[51]

What does this theory mean in practical terms? It means that large, established organizations often become dinosaurs. Consider that among the companies that appeared on the first *Fortune* 500 list in 1955, only 71 stayed on the list for 50 years. Some were bought out or merged with other companies. Others simply declined and disappeared. Large, established firms often have tremendous difficulty adapting to a rapidly changing environment. Hence, new organizational forms that fit the current environment emerge, fill a new niche, and over time take away business from established companies.[52] According to the population-ecology view, when looking at an organizational population as a whole, the changing environment determines which organizations survive or fail. The assumption is that individual organizations suffer from structural inertia and find it difficult to adapt to environmental changes. Thus, when rapid change occurs, old organizations are likely to decline or fail, and new organizations emerge that are better suited to the needs of the environment.

What Hinders Adaptation?

Why do established organizations have such a hard time adapting? Michael Hannan and John Freeman, originators of the population-ecology model of organization, argue that there are many limitations on the ability of organizations to change. The limitations come from heavy investment in plants, equipment, and specialized personnel; limited information; the established viewpoints of decision makers; the organization's own successful history that justifies current procedures; and the difficulty of changing corporate culture. True transformation is a rare and unlikely event in the face of all these barriers.[53] Consider the story of Barnes & Noble.

IN PRACTICE

Barnes & Noble Versus Amazon

When Jeff Bezos gave a talk to a class at the Harvard Business School in 1997, one student bluntly told him, "You seem like a really nice guy . . . but you really need to sell to Barnes & Noble and get out now." Bezos told the class the student might be right but said "I think you might be underestimating the degree to which established brick-and-mortar business, or any company that might be used to doing things a certain way, will find it hard to be nimble or focus attention on a new channel. I guess we'll see."[54]

Bezos had a natural understanding of how hard it is for established organizations to adapt. He knew Barnes & Noble's managers would have trouble seriously competing online because they wouldn't want to risk losing money on an unproven new venture. They would be reluctant to pull talented and resourceful employees away from the bookstore business and put them to work on an effort that would, at least for a time, take money away from the profitable stores. Barnes & Noble also wasn't equipped to package and ship one or two books to individual customers; it was geared to shipping boxes and boxes of books to a set number of locations. Making the switch would be difficult and full of errors. For Amazon, on the other hand, shipping one book at a time was just everyday business.[55]

Back in 1997, few people thought Amazon was a threat to Barnes & Noble. The story of how this new company defeated a giant illustrates that it is extremely difficult for large established companies to shift to a new way of doing things. Another example comes from Kodak, which actually invented some of the earliest digital photographic technology but couldn't accept that customers would give up on the company's traditional film. Kodak had been successful for so long and was so large and entrenched in its way of doing business that it couldn't change substantively even when managers wanted to.[56]

The population-ecology model is developed from theories of natural selection in biology, and the terms *evolution* and *selection* are used to refer to the underlying behavioral processes. Theories of biological evolution try to explain why certain life forms appear and survive whereas others perish. Some theories suggest the forms that survive are typically best fitted to the immediate environment. The environment of the 1940s and 1950s was suitable to Woolworth, but new organizational forms like Walmart and other superstores became dominant in the 1980s. Now, the environment is shifting again, indicating that the "big box" era is coming to a close. With more people shopping online, smaller stores once again have an advantage in bricks-and-mortar retail. Walmart is planning to open dozens of small-scale Walmart Express stores in urban areas. Best Buy is also opting for smaller storefronts called Best Buy Mobile and searching for ways to fill unused floor space in its large outlets.[57] No company is immune to the processes of social change. In recent years, technology has brought tremendous environmental change, leading to the decline of many outdated organizations and a proliferation of new companies such as Pinterest, Facebook, and Twitter.

BRIEFCASE

As an organization manager, keep these guidelines in mind:

Adapt your organization to new variations being selected and retained in the external environment. If you are starting a new organization, find a niche that contains a strong environmental need for your product or service, and be prepared for a competitive struggle over scarce resources.

Organizational Form and Niche

The population-ecology model is concerned with organizational forms. **Organizational form** is an organization's specific technology, structure, products, goals, and personnel, which can be selected or rejected by the environment. Each new organization tries to find a **niche** (i.e., a domain of unique environmental resources and needs) sufficient to support it. The niche is usually small in the early stages of an organization but may increase in size over time if the organization is successful. If the organization doesn't find an appropriate niche, it will decline and may perish.

From the viewpoint of a single firm, luck, chance, and randomness play important parts in survival. New products and ideas are continually being proposed by both entrepreneurs and large organizations. Whether these ideas and organizational forms survive or fail is often a matter of chance—whether external circumstances happen to support them. A woman starting a small electrical contracting business in a rapidly growing area such as Austin, Texas, or Raleigh, North Carolina (the two fastest growing cities in 2014), would have an excellent chance of success. If the same woman were to start the same business in a declining community elsewhere in the United States, her chance of success would be far less. Success or failure of a single firm thus is predicted by the characteristics of the environment as much as by the skills or strategies used by the organization's managers.

2 **The success or failure of a start-up is largely determined by the smarts and management ability of the entrepreneur.**

> **ANSWER:** *Disagree.* Luck is often as important as smarts because larger forces in the environment, typically unseen by managers, allow some firms to succeed and others to fail. If a start-up happens to be in the right place at the right time, chances for success are much higher, regardless of management ability.

ASSESS YOUR ANSWER

Process of Ecological Change

The population-ecology model assumes that new organizations are always appearing in the population. Thus, organizational populations are continually undergoing change. The process of change in the population occurs in three stages: variation, selection, and retention, as summarized in Exhibit 5.5.

- *Variation.* **Variation** means the appearance of new, diverse forms in a population of organizations. These new organizational forms are initiated by entrepreneurs, established with venture capital by large corporations, or set up by governments seeking to provide new services. Some forms may be conceived to cope with a perceived need in the external environment. In recent years, a large number of new firms have been initiated to develop applications for smartphones and social networking sites, to develop computer software, to provide consulting and other services to large corporations, and to develop products and technologies for Internet commerce. Other new organizations produce a traditional product or service, but do it using new technology, new business models, or new management techniques that make the new companies far more able to survive. Organizational variations are analogous to mutations in biology, and they add to the scope and complexity of organizational forms in the environment.

EXHIBIT 5.5

Elements in the
Population Ecology
Model of Organizations

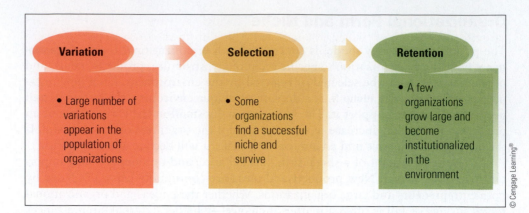

- *Selection.* **Selection** refers to whether a new organizational form is suited to the environment and can survive. Only a few variations are "selected in" by the environment and survive over the long term. Some variations will suit the external environment better than others. Some prove beneficial and thus are able to find a niche and acquire the resources from the environment necessary to survive. Other variations fail to meet the needs of the environment and perish. When there is insufficient demand for a firm's product or service and when insufficient resources are available to the organization, that organization will be "selected out."

- *Retention.* **Retention** is the preservation and institutionalization of selected organizational forms. Certain technologies, products, and services are highly valued by the environment. The retained organizational form may become a dominant part of the environment. Many forms of organization have been institutionalized, such as government, schools, churches, and automobile manufacturers. McDonald's, which owns 43 percent of the fast-food market and provides the first job for many teenagers, has become institutionalized in American life.

Institutionalized organizations like McDonald's seem to be relatively permanent features in the population of organizations, but they are not permanent in the long run. The environment is always shifting, and if the dominant organizational forms don't adapt to external change, they will gradually diminish and be replaced by other organizations.

From the population-ecology perspective, the environment is the important determinant of organizational success or failure. The organization must meet an environmental need or else it will be selected out. The principles of variation, selection, and retention lead to the establishment of new organizational forms in a population of organizations.

Strategies for Survival

Another principle that underlies the population-ecology model is the **struggle for existence**, or competition. Organizations and populations of organizations are engaged in a competitive struggle over resources, and each organizational form is fighting to survive. The struggle is most intense among new organizations, and both the birth and survival frequencies of new organizations are related to factors in the larger environment. Historically, for example, factors such as size of urban area, percentage of immigrants, political turbulence, industry growth rate, and environmental variability have influenced the launching and survival of newspapers, telecommunication firms, railroads, government agencies, labor unions, and even voluntary organizations.[58]

In the population-ecology perspective, **generalist** and **specialist** strategies distinguish organizational forms in the struggle for survival. Organizations with a wide niche or domain—that is, those that offer a broad range of products or services or that serve a broad market—are generalists. Organizations that provide a narrower range of goods or services or that serve a narrower market are specialists.

In the natural environment, a specialist form of flora and fauna would evolve in protective isolation in a place like Hawaii, where the nearest body of land is 2,000 miles away. The flora and fauna are heavily protected. In contrast, a place like Costa Rica, which experienced wave after wave of external influences, developed a generalist set of flora and fauna that has better resilience and flexibility for adapting to a broad range of environments. In the business world, Amazon.com started with a specialist strategy, selling books over the Internet, but evolved to a generalist strategy with the addition of music, DVDs, electronics, and a wide range of other goods; creation of the Kindle digital reader; and more recently the addition of a streaming video service offering thousands of movies and TV shows. A company such as Olmec Corporation, which sells African-American and Hispanic dolls, would be considered a specialist, whereas Mattel is a generalist, marketing a broad range of toys for boys and girls of all ages.[59] Apple uses a specialist strategy with its iPhone, offering only one smartphone model, whereas Samsung uses a generalist strategy creating multiple versions of myriad phone products.[60]

Specialists are generally more competitive than generalists in the narrow area in which their domains overlap. However, the breadth of the generalist's domain serves to protect it somewhat from environmental changes. Though demand may decrease for some of the generalist's products or services, it usually increases for others at the same time. In addition, because of the diversity of products, services, and customers, generalists are able to reallocate resources internally to adapt to a changing environment, whereas specialists are not. However, because specialists are often smaller companies, they can sometimes move faster and be more flexible in adapting to changes.[61] Managerial impact on company success often comes from selecting a strategy that steers a company into an open niche.

Institutionalism

The institutional perspective provides yet another view of interorganizational relationships.[62] The **institutional perspective** describes how organizations survive and succeed through congruence between an organization and the expectations from its environment. The **institutional environment** is composed of norms and values from stakeholders (e.g., customers, investors, associations, boards, other organizations, government, and the community). Thus, the institutional view believes that organizations adopt structures and processes to please outsiders, and these activities come to take on rule-like status in organizations. The institutional environment reflects what the greater society views as correct ways of organizing and behaving.[63]

Legitimacy is defined as the general perception that an organization's actions are desirable, proper, and appropriate within the environment's system of norms, values, and beliefs.[64] Institutional theory thus is concerned with the set of intangible norms and values that shape behavior, as opposed to the tangible elements of technology and structure. Organizations and industries must fit within the cognitive and emotional expectations of their audience. For example, people will not deposit money in a bank unless it sends signals of compliance with norms of wise financial management. Consider also your local government and whether it could raise property taxes for increased school funding if community residents did not approve of the school district's policies and activities.

Most organizations are concerned with legitimacy, as reflected in the annual *Fortune* magazine survey that ranks corporations based on their reputations and the annual Global RepTrak 100 conducted by the Reputation Institute. Success and a good reputation go hand in hand. The fact that there is a payoff for having a good reputation is verified by a study of organizations in the airline industry. Having a good reputation was significantly related to higher levels of performance based on measures such as return on assets and net profit margin.[65]

Many corporations actively shape and manage their reputations to increase their competitive advantage. In the wake of the mortgage meltdown and the failure of giants Bear Stearns and Lehman Brothers, for example, many companies in the finance industry began searching for new ways to bolster legitimacy. Citigroup, Merrill Lynch, and Wachovia all ousted their chief executives over mortgage-related issues, partly as a way to signal a commitment to better business practices. The board of oil giant BP asked Tony Hayward to resign as CEO due to his mishandling of the Deepwater Horizon oil spill crisis and brought in a new CEO they believed could take the steps needed to restore the company's reputation.[66]

The notion of legitimacy answers an important question for institutional theorists: Why is there so much homogeneity in the forms and practices of established organizations? For example, visit banks, high schools, hospitals, government departments, or business firms in a similar industry, in any part of the country, and they will look strikingly similar. When an organizational field is just getting started, such as in Internet-related businesses, diversity is the norm. New organizations fill emerging niches. Once an industry becomes established, however, there is an invisible push toward similarity. *Isomorphism* is the term used to describe this move toward similarity.

The Institutional View and Organization Design

The institutional view also sees organizations as having two essential dimensions—technical and institutional. The technical dimension is the day-to-day work, technology, and operating requirements. The institutional structure is that part of the organization most visible to the outside public. Moreover, the technical dimension is governed by norms of rationality and efficiency, but the institutional dimension is governed by expectations from people and organizations in the external environment. As a result of pressure to conduct business in a proper and correct way, the formal structures of many organizations reflect the expectations and values of the environment rather than the demand of work activities. This means that an organization may incorporate positions or activities (e.g., e-commerce division, chief compliance officer, social media director) perceived as important by the larger society to increase its legitimacy and survival prospects, even though these elements may decrease efficiency. For example, many small companies set up websites, even though the benefits gained from the site are sometimes outweighed by the costs of maintaining it. Having a website is perceived as essential by the larger society today. The formal structure and design of an organization may not be rational with respect to workflow and products or services, but it will ensure survival in the larger environment.

Organizations adapt to the environment by signaling their congruence with the demands and expectations stemming from cultural norms, standards set by professional bodies, funding agencies, and customers. Structure is something of a facade disconnected from technical work through which the organization obtains approval, legitimacy, and continuing support. The adoption of structures thus might not be linked to actual production needs and might occur regardless of whether specific internal problems are solved. Formal structure is separated from technical action in this view.[67]

BRIEFCASE

As an organization manager, keep these guidelines in mind:

Pursue legitimacy with your organization's major stakeholders in the external environment. Adopt strategies, structures, and management techniques that meet the expectations of significant parties, thereby ensuring their cooperation and access to resources.

Institutional Similarity

Many aspects of structure and behavior may be targeted toward environmental acceptance rather than toward internal technical efficiency. Interorganizational relationships thus are characterized by forces that cause organizations in a similar population to look like one another. **Institutional similarity**, called *institutional isomorphism* in the academic literature, is the emergence of a common structure and approach among organizations in the same field. Isomorphism is the process that causes one unit in a population to resemble other units that face the same set of environmental conditions.[68]

Exactly how does increasing similarity occur? How are these forces realized? Exhibit 5.6 provides a summary of three mechanisms for institutional adaptation. These three core mechanisms are *mimetic forces*, which result from responses to uncertainty; *coercive forces*, which stem from political influence; and *normative forces*, which result from common training and professionalism.[69]

Mimetic Forces. Most organizations, especially business organizations, face great uncertainty. It is not clear to senior executives exactly what products, services, technologies, or management practices will achieve desired goals, and sometimes the goals themselves are not clear. In the face of this uncertainty, **mimetic forces**, the pressures to copy or model other organizations, occur. Executives observe an innovation in a firm generally regarded as successful, so the practice is quickly

EXHIBIT 5.6
Three Mechanisms for Institutional Adaptation

	Mimetic	Coercive	Normative
Reason to become similar:	Uncertainty	Dependence	Duty, obligation
Events:	Innovation visibility	Political law, rules, sanctions	Professionalism—certification, accreditation
Social basis:	Culturally supported	Legal	Moral
Example:	Reengineering, benchmarking	Pollution controls, school regulations	Accounting standards, consultant training

Source: Adapted from W. Richard Scott, *Institutions and Organizations* (Thousand Oaks, CA: Sage, 1995).

copied. McDonald's revived stagnant sales by adding healthier menu items and new types of beverages, so other fast-food chains began doing the same. "You need to learn from your competition," said David Novak, CEO of Yum Brands, the parent company of KFC, Taco Bell, and Pizza Hut. SanDisk, Microsoft, Samsung, and other companies came out with their own digital music players to try to capture some of the success Apple enjoyed with its iPod.[70] Many large companies enter specific foreign markets when managers see their firm's biggest rivals doing so, even if entering the market is highly risky. Managers don't want to take a chance on losing out.[71]

Many times, this modeling of other organizations is done without any clear proof that performance will be improved. Mimetic processes explain why fads and fashions occur in the business world. Once a new idea starts, many organizations grab onto it, only to learn that the application is difficult and may cause more problems than it solves. This was the case with the recent merger wave that swept many industries. The past few decades have seen the largest merger and acquisition wave in history, but evidence shows that many of these mergers did not produce the expected financial gains and other benefits. The sheer momentum of the trend was so powerful that many companies chose to merge not because of potential increases in efficiency or profitability but simply because it seemed like the right thing to do.[72]

Techniques such as outsourcing, teams, Six Sigma quality programs, brainstorming, and the balanced scorecard have all been adopted without clear evidence that they will improve efficiency or effectiveness. The one certain benefit is that management's feelings of uncertainty will be reduced, and the company's image will be enhanced because the firm is seen as using the latest management techniques. A study of 100 organizations confirmed that those companies associated with using popular management techniques were more admired and rated higher in quality of management, even though these organizations often did not reflect higher economic performance.[73] Perhaps the clearest example of official copying is the technique of benchmarking that occurs as part of the total quality movement. *Benchmarking* means identifying who is best at something in an industry and then duplicating the technique for creating excellence, perhaps even improving it in the process. Many organizations, however, simply copy what a competitor is doing without understanding why it is successful or how it might mesh—or clash—with their own organization's way of doing business.[74]

The mimetic process occurs because managers face high uncertainty, they are aware of innovations occurring in the environment, and the innovations are culturally supported, thereby giving legitimacy to adopters. This is a strong mechanism by which a group of banks, or high schools, or manufacturing firms begin to look and act like one another.

ASSESS YOUR ANSWER

3 Managers should quickly copy or borrow techniques being used by other successful companies to make their own organization more effective and to keep pace with changing times.

ANSWER: *Agree.* Managers frequently copy techniques used by other, successful organizations as a way to appear legitimate and up to date. Copying other firms is one reason organizations may begin to look and act similar in their structures, processes, and management systems.

Coercive Forces. All organizations are subject to pressure, both formal and informal, from government, regulatory agencies, and other important organizations in the environment, especially those on which a company is dependent. **Coercive forces** are the external pressures exerted on an organization to adopt structures, techniques, or behaviors similar to other organizations. For example, large corporations have recently been putting pressure on service providers, such as accounting or law firms, to step up their diversity efforts. Managers in these corporations have felt pressure to increase diversity within their own organizations and they want the firms with which they do business to reflect a commitment to hiring and promoting more women and minorities as well.[75]

Some pressures may have the force of law, such as government mandates to adopt new pollution control equipment or new safety standards. New regulations and government oversight boards have been set up for the mortgage and finance industries following the Wall Street meltdown. As one example, the Credit Card Accountability, Responsibility, and Disclosure (CARD) Act requires credit card companies to add specific warnings regarding late payments and the total amount of interest customers will pay if they make only the minimum payment.

Coercive pressures may also occur between organizations where there is a power difference, as described in the resource-dependence section earlier in this chapter. Large retailers and manufacturers often insist that certain policies, procedures, and techniques be used by their suppliers. As part of its new sustainability push, for instance, Walmart is requiring its 100,000 or so suppliers to calculate the "full environmental costs" of making their products (such as water use, carbon dioxide emissions, and waste) and provide this information for the company to distill into a rating system that shoppers will see alongside the price of the item.[76]

As with other changes, those brought about because of coercive forces may not make the organization more effective, but it will look more effective and will be accepted as legitimate in the environment. Organizational changes that result from coercive forces occur when an organization is dependent on another, when there are political factors such as rules, laws, and sanctions involved, or when some other contractual or legal basis defines the relationship. Organizations operating under those constraints will adopt changes and relate to one another in a way that increases homogeneity and limits diversity.

BRIEFCASE

As an organization manager, keep this guideline in mind:

Enhance legitimacy by borrowing good ideas from other firms, complying with laws and regulations, and following procedures considered best for your company.

Normative Forces. The third reason organizations change according to the institutional view is normative forces. **Normative forces** are pressures to achieve standards of professionalism and to adopt techniques that are considered by the professional community to be up to date and effective. Changes may be in any area, such as information technology, accounting requirements, marketing techniques, or collaborative relationships with other organizations.

Professionals share a body of formal education based on university degrees and professional networks through which ideas are exchanged by consultants and professional leaders. Universities, consulting firms, trade associations, and professional training institutions develop norms among professional managers. People are exposed to similar training and standards and adopt shared values, which are implemented in organizations with which they work. Business schools teach finance, marketing, and human resource majors that certain techniques are better than others, so using those techniques becomes a standard in the field. In one study, for example, a radio station changed from a functional to a multidivisional structure because a consultant recommended it as a "higher standard" of doing business. There was no proof that this structure was better, but the radio station wanted legitimacy and to be perceived as fully professional and up to date in its management techniques.

Companies accept normative pressures to become like one another through a sense of obligation or duty to high standards of performance based on professional norms shared by managers and specialists in their respective organizations. These norms are conveyed through professional education and certification and have almost a moral or ethical requirement based on the highest standards accepted by the profession at that time. In some cases, though, normative forces that maintain legitimacy break down, as they did recently in the mortgage and finance industries, and coercive forces are needed to shift organizations back toward acceptable standards.

An organization may use any or all of the mechanisms of mimetic, coercive, or normative forces to change itself for greater legitimacy in the institutional environment. Firms tend to use these mechanisms when they are acting under conditions of dependence, uncertainty, ambiguous goals, and reliance on professional credentials. The outcome of these processes is that organizations become far more homogeneous than would be expected from the natural diversity among managers and environments.

Design Essentials

- This chapter has been about the important evolution in interorganizational relationships. At one time organizations considered themselves autonomous and separate, trying to outdo other companies. Today more organizations see themselves as part of an ecosystem. The organization may span several industries and will be anchored in a dense web of relationships with other companies. In this ecosystem, collaboration is as important as competition. Indeed, organizations may compete and collaborate at the same time, depending on the location and issue. In business ecosystems, the role of management is changing to include the development of horizontal relationships with other organizations.

- Four perspectives have been developed to explain relationships among organizations. The resource-dependence perspective is the most traditional, arguing that organizations try to avoid excessive dependence on other organizations. In this view, organizations devote considerable effort to controlling the environment to ensure ample resources while maintaining independence. Types of resource-dependence relationships include acquisitions or mergers, joint ventures, strategic alliances, supply sourcing, trade associations, and board interlocks.

- The collaborative-network perspective is an emerging alternative to resource dependence. Organizations welcome collaboration and interdependence with other organizations to enhance value for both. Many executives are changing mindsets away from autonomy toward collaboration, often with former corporate enemies. The new partnership mindset emphasizes trust, fair dealing, and achieving profits for all parties in a relationship.

- The population-ecology perspective explains why organizational diversity continuously increases with the appearance of new organizations filling niches left open by established companies. This perspective asserts that large companies usually cannot adapt to meet a changing environment; hence, new companies emerge with the appropriate form and skills to serve new needs. Through the process of variation, selection, and retention, some organizations will survive and grow while others perish. Companies may adopt a generalist or specialist strategy to survive in the population of organizations.

■ The institutional perspective argues that interorganizational relationships are shaped as much by a company's need for legitimacy as by the need to provide products and services. The need for legitimacy means that the organization will adopt structures and activities that are perceived as valid, proper, and up to date by external stakeholders. In this way, established organizations copy techniques from one another and begin to look very similar. The emergence of common structures and approaches in the same field is called institutional similarity or institutional isomorphism. Three core mechanisms explain increasing organizational homogeneity: mimetic forces, which result from responses to uncertainty; coercive forces, which stem from power differences and political influences; and normative forces, which result from common training and professionalism.

■ Each of the four perspectives is valid. They represent different lenses through which the world of interorganizational relationships can be viewed: organizations experience a competitive struggle for autonomy; they can thrive through collaborative relationships with others; the slowness to adapt provides openings for new organizations to flourish; and organizations seek legitimacy as well as profits from the external environment. The important thing is for managers to be aware of interorganizational relationships and to consciously manage them.

KEY CONCEPTS

coercive forces	legitimacy	resource-dependence theory
collaborative-network perspective	mimetic forces	retention
generalist	niche	selection
institutional environment	normative forces	specialist
institutional perspective	organizational ecosystem	strategic alliance
institutional similarity	organizational form	struggle for existence
interorganizational relationships	population	trade association
joint venture	population-ecology perspective	variation

DISCUSSION QUESTIONS

1. The concept of business ecosystems implies that organizations are more interdependent than ever before. From personal experience, do you agree? Explain.

2. How do you feel about the prospect of becoming a manager and having to manage a set of relationships with other companies rather than just managing your own company? Discuss.

3. Assume you are the manager of a small firm that is dependent on a large manufacturing customer that uses the resource-dependence perspective. Put yourself in the position of the small firm, and describe what actions you would take to survive and succeed. What actions would you take from the perspective of the large firm?

4. Many managers today were trained under assumptions of adversarial relationships with other companies. Do you think operating as adversaries is easier or more difficult than operating as partners with other companies? Discuss.

5. Discuss how the adversarial versus partnership orientations work among students in class. Is there a sense of competition for grades? Is it possible to develop true partnerships in which your work depends on others?

6. The population-ecology perspective argues that it is healthy for society to have new organizations emerging and old organizations dying as the environment changes. Do you agree? Why would European countries pass laws to sustain traditional organizations and inhibit the emergence of new ones?

7. Discuss how the process of variation, selection, and retention might explain innovations that take place within an organization.

8. Do you believe that legitimacy really motivates a large, powerful organization such as Walmart? Is acceptance by other people a motivation for individuals as well? Explain.

9. How does the desire for legitimacy result in organizations becoming more similar over time?

10. How do mimetic forces differ from normative forces? Give an example of each.

CHAPTER 5 WORKSHOP   The Shamatosi[77]

Instructions

1. Divide into groups of three. Half the groups, on one side of the room, are "1s" and the other half are "2s."

2. The 1s are Pharmacology; the 2s are Radiology. Read *only* your own role, not the other one.

3. Any students not in a negotiating group can be assigned to observe a specific negotiation meeting.

4. Both groups want to purchase Shamatosi plants owned by DBR.

5. Each group has 10 minutes to prepare a negotiation strategy for meeting with the other side.

6. One Pharmacology group meets with one Radiology group so that all groups meet with one counterpart.

7. You have 15 minutes to try and negotiate a possible agreement to purchase Shamatosi plants from DBR.

8. You should decide whether you can form an agreement to move ahead jointly or whether you will go into competition with each other. An agreement would consider the price offered for the plants, how the cost is shared, to where plants will be delivered (which company), and how plants are best utilized.

9. Groups report to the whole class on results of negotiation. Observers can comment on their observations, such as level of trust and/or disclosure and ease/difficulties of reaching an agreement between companies.

10. Instructor leads a discussion on interorganizational agreements, decision-making, and joint ventures.

Role of Team from Pharmacology, Inc.:

Dr. Bernice Hobbs, a biological researcher for Pharmacology, Inc., a major pharmaceutical company, has monitored with mounting concern the reports from Brazil's Amazon rainforest. Everything from world weather patterns to providing an estimated one in four ingredients in medicine is tied to securing the world's rainforests. But over the past decade, scientists and pharmaceutical companies, along with environmental groups and others, have observed with alarm the destruction of the rainforests, and with it the destruction of entire species of plant, animal, and insect life.

As Hobbs monitors the situation, she is particularly concerned about conditions with regard to a particular plant found in limited quantities near the Rio Negro. Rainforest trees have shallow roots because the major nutrients for growth are located near the surface level. Biologists discovered a rare tiny plant growth called Shamatosi embedded among the trees near the Rio Negro. For a number of years, researchers have explored potential medical uses for these tiny plants.

Dr. Hobbs has been working with the leaves of the tiny Shamatosi plant and has discovered the plant's potential as a cancer-suppressing drug after breast cancer surgery. For a number of years the leading drug in this category has been Tamoxifen, a synthetic drug described as "remarkable" and credited with saving more lives than any other oncological drug by the lead investigator for a major breast cancer research group. However, research has also shown that Tamoxifen raises the risk of cancer in the lining of the uterus and can lead to blood clots in the lungs. There is also a growing level of concern as Tamoxifen resistance has developed. The medicine developed by Hobbs may avoid these problems and bring a new treatment into the list of options for doctors and their patients. But more research is needed. Hobbs needs to have access to as many leaves as possible from the Shamatosi plant.

DBR, the Brazilian timber company, has possession of several thousand Shamatosi plants from this year's season that have been replanted in portable crates. Your company, Pharmacology, Inc., has authorized $1.5 million for your team to bid to obtain the plants. You cannot go over this budget. Your team will meet with a team from Radiology, Inc., which also wants to purchase the Shamatosi plants from DBR, about a possible agreement for purchasing and using the plants for research.

Role of Team from Radiology, Inc.:

Dr. Alberto Dominguez, a biochemist for Radiology, Inc. who has expertise in treating radiation exposure, monitors with mounting concern the reports from Brazil's Amazon rainforest. Everything from world weather patterns to providing an estimated one in four ingredients in medicine is tied to securing the world's rainforests. But over the past decade, scientists and pharmaceutical companies, along with environmental groups and others, have observed with alarm the destruction of the rainforests, and with it the destruction of entire species of plant, animal, and insect life.

As Dominguez monitors the situation, he is particularly concerned about conditions concerning a particular plant found in limited quantities near the Rio Negro. Rainforest trees have shallow roots because the major nutrients for growth are located near the surface level. Biologists discovered a rare tiny plant growth called Shamatosi embedded among the trees near the Rio Negro. For a number of years, researchers have explored potential medical uses for these tiny plants.

Dr. Dominquez has been working with the roots of the Shamatosi plant in response to incidents involving radiation exposure. The worldwide expansion of nuclear facilities, the lessons from the 1986 Chernobyl disaster, and the resulting cases of thyroid cancer among thousands of children and adolescents, led to intensive research by Dominguez and his colleagues to provide the swiftest response with the most powerful medicine. For years, Potassium iodide (KI) was issued in kits provided by organizations such as the Centers for Disease Control. However, KI was found deficient in protecting many body parts, such as the liver and intestines. Dominguez discovered the tiny Shamatosi plant, and his research indicated the potential for medicines from the root of this plant to provide additional protection, even for incidents of large-scale or prolonged exposure. The March 2011 Tohoku earthquake and tsunami, and the resultant radiation exposure caused by the meltdown at the Fukushima Daiichi nuclear power plant, intensified concerns among scientists to find and develop a new medicine. Dominguez needs as many plants as possible.

DBR, the Brazilian timber company, has possession of several thousand Shamatosi plants from this year's season that have been replanted in portable crates. Your company, Radiology, Inc., has authorized your team to bid $1.5 million to obtain the plants. You cannot go over this budget. Your team will meet with a team from Pharmacology, Inc., which also wants to purchase the Shamatosi plants from DBR, about a possible agreement for purchasing and using the plants for research.

CASE FOR ANALYSIS | Why is Cooperation So Hard?

Armando Bronaldo immigrated to the United States six years ago after working as design leader for an Italian company specializing in home sound systems. Armed with a vision and 15 years of experience, he founded his own company, Technologia, as the supplier of sound translation components including the base radiator, dome tweeter (for high frequency), composite cone (for midrange sound), the binding post (for sound translator delivery), and ohms impedance (for conducting sound through the speakers). As it builds its reputation for quality and supply chain service and delivery, Technologia relies heavily on continuing a solid relationship with AUD, a manufacturer of home sound systems, under the management of CEO Audie Richards. AUD was the company's first contractual partner, currently accounting for 50 percent of the small supplier's business. The initial agreement with AUD has grown and the current business relationship brings a steady stream of orders that has enabled Bronaldo, even in a tough economy, to add workers over the last three years. Bronaldo loves the reliability of selling to AUD, but he sometimes questions whether the business relationship is overbalanced in favor of the powerful manufacturer.

"I think in the beginning Audie played his hand well, knowing that we were a start-up and trying to secure a solid customer base. In my eagerness to get the contract and in trying to please the head of a big company, I found myself saying 'Yes' and carrying out his wishes and demands," Bronaldo admits. "Because we were a young company and because he is, by far, our biggest customer, I think he got into the habit of assuming the focus would remain on *his* needs and *his* profits throughout the business relationship. But now, with our feet under us as a company, I think it is time to look again at the relationship between the two companies."

Richards is satisfied with the present arrangement he has with Technologia and sees himself as both partner and mentor, as he recently explained to a colleague. "Bronaldo came to this country and started his company and I was willing to give him a chance, set up our logistics, and make it possible for him to grow his company. I think it's worked out very well for AUD. And now he talks about wanting to change the way we do things. I'm suspicious about what he has in mind. But he needs us more than we need him. Look, I've got a good supplier; he gets lots of business from us; I see no reason to change it."

Although the relationship and dialogue at the top management level is strained, mid-level managers at both companies *do* talk and are eager to explore and implement a new vendor managed inventory (VMI) system that builds a partnership of strong interdependence and equity. Instead of sending purchase orders, VMI involves sharing daily electronic information about AUD's sales, so inventory is replaced automatically by Technologia. Mid-level managers Larry Stansell (AUD) and Victoria Santos (Technologia) regularly correspond and meet to find potential areas for close cooperation, information sharing, and problem feedback.

"I know that Richards is suspicious, but it really is time for these two guys to take a new look at this business relationship and how they can address issues that could be beneficial to both," Santos says. "The playing field has changed. Technologia is stronger."

"But the relationship has not changed and I don't think it will until Bronaldo finds a way to reduce his dependence on AUD. In the meantime, flexibility, information sharing, and reconsidering a range of cost-efficient options is important," Stansell admits, "But we have to start with the discussion of whether AUD calls all the shots between our two organizations."

"Yes, and that discussion must include logistical issues," Santos says.

"Delivery, the disagreements about the pallets . . ."

"Richards set up all of that initially—what would work best for delivery to AUD," Santos says. "But Bronaldo insists that PM rather than AM pick-ups would be better and that a change in pallet companies, from Bradley Packaging to Eastmont Packaging, would cut costs per trip by reducing mileage. Plus Eastmont has a new custom-made pallet that provides greater load stabilization necessary for high-tech components. The savings for Technologia would be shared with AUD."

"But Bradley has a long-time business relationship of its own with AUD," Stansell points out.

"So, what we're saying here is that it is not *just* a discussion about these two organizations, but a consideration of the whole supply chain. The cost of lost flexibility, the lack of shared information. It's costing both of them. And the sudden spikes in production requests by AUD, in response to its retail customers, create unnecessary problems in production planning at Technologia and unnecessary stress for the management and workers at both companies."

"VMI could be a powerful tool that empowers and brings value to both sides," Stansell says. "Through this system, Technologia will be able to create orders for us based on direct access to our orders and demand information—both short and long-range needs. . . ."

"And then, we can work together, determining the most cost-efficient way to manage and deliver the inventory," Santos continues. "We'll look at the entire supply chain to see where changes and even minor tweaks can be made to bring down costs and make the partnership strong, but there would have to be equal give and take."

"Flexibility on both sides is necessary to make this work," Stansell points out. "This is not a competition. Nobody has to be *right*."

"But getting top management on board to make this work is our real challenge," Santos says. "And we have to start looking ahead. VMI could be a stepping-stone to Jointly Managed Inventory (JMI), an even deeper collaboration, allowing the increased tactical planning and the real integration of Technologia and AUD's point of sale systems. That will offer optimal cost sharing and real time sales data, allowing us to stay ahead of the curve in production planning as well as logistics to meet AUD's needs in real time."

"So, what's our next step?" Stansell asks. "How can we make this happen?"

CASE FOR ANALYSIS | Oxford Plastics Company[78]

Oxford Plastics manufactures high-quality plastics and resins for use in a variety of products, from lawn ornaments and patio furniture to automobiles. The Oxford plant located near Beatty, a town of about 45,000 in a southeastern state, employs about 3,000 workers. It plays an important role in the local economy and, indeed, that of the entire state, which offers few well-paying factory jobs.

In early 2004, Sam Henderson, plant manager of the Beatty facility, notified Governor Tom Winchell that Oxford

was ready to announce plans for a major addition to the factory—a state-of-the-art color lab and paint shop that would enable better and faster matching of colors to customer requirements. The new shop would keep Oxford competitive in the fast-paced global market for plastics, as well as bring the Beatty plant into full compliance with updated U.S. Environmental Protection Agency (EPA) regulations.

Plans for the new facility were largely complete. The biggest remaining task was identifying the specific location. The new color lab and paint shop would cover approximately 25 acres, requiring Oxford to purchase some additional land adjacent to its 75-acre factory campus. Henderson was somewhat concerned with top management's preferred site because it fell outside the current industrial zoning boundary, and, moreover, would necessitate destruction of several 400- to 500-year-old beech trees. The owner of the property, a nonprofit agency, was ready to sell, whereas property located on the other side of the campus might be more difficult to obtain in a timely manner. Oxford was on a tight schedule to get the project completed. If the new facility wasn't up and running in a timely manner, there was a chance the EPA could force Oxford to stop using its old process—in effect, shutting down the factory.

The governor was thrilled with Oxford's decision to build the new shop in Beatty and he urged Henderson to immediately begin working closely with local and state officials to circumvent any potential problems. It was essential, he stressed, that the project not be bogged down or thwarted by conflict among different interest groups, as it was too important to the economic development of the region. Governor Winchell assigned Beth Friedlander, director of the Governor's Office of Economic Development, to work closely with Henderson on the project. However, Winchell was not willing to offer his commitment to help push through the rezoning, as he had been an enthusiastic public supporter of environmental causes.

Following his conversation with Governor Winchell, Henderson sat down to identify the various people and organizations that would have an interest in the new color lab project and that would need to collaborate in order for it to proceed in a smooth and timely manner. They are as follows:

Oxford Plastics

- Mark Thomas, vice president of North American Operations. Thomas would be flying in from Oxford's Michigan headquarters to oversee land purchase and negotiations regarding the expansion.
- Sam Henderson, Beatty plant manager, who has spent his entire career at the Beatty facility, beginning on the factory floor fresh out of high school.
- Wayne Talbert, local union president. The union is strongly in favor of the new shop being located in Beatty because of the potential for more and higher-wage jobs.

State Government

- Governor Tom Winchell, who can exert pressure on local officials to support the project.
- Beth Friedlander, director of the Governor's Office of Economic Development.
- Manu Gottlieb, director of the State Department of Environmental Quality.

City Government

- Mayor Barbara Ott, a political newcomer who has been in office for less than a year and who campaigned on environmental issues.
- Major J. Washington, the Chamber of Commerce chair of local economic development.

Public

- May Pinelas, chairman of Historic Beatty who argues vociferously that the future of the region lies in historic and natural preservation and tourism.
- Tommy Tompkins, president of the Save Our Future Foundation, a coalition of private individuals and representatives from the local university who have long been involved in public environmental issues and have successfully thwarted at least one previous expansion project.

Henderson is feeling torn about how to proceed. He thinks to himself, "To move forward, how will I build a coalition among these diverse organizations and groups?" He understands the need for Oxford to move quickly, but he wants Oxford to have a good relationship with the people and organizations that will surely oppose destruction of more of Beatty's natural beauty. Henderson has always liked finding a win-win compromise, but there are so many groups with an interest in this project that he's not sure where to start. Maybe he should begin by working closely with Beth Friedlander from the governor's office—there's no doubt this is an extremely important project for the state's economic development. On the other hand, it's the local people who are going to be most affected and most involved in the final decisions. Oxford's vice president has suggested a press conference to announce the new shop at the end of the week, but Henderson is worried about putting the news out cold. Perhaps he should call a meeting of interested parties now and let everyone get their feelings out into the open? He knows it could get emotional, but he wonders if things won't get much uglier later on if he doesn't.

▶ NOTES

1. Based on Shelly Banjo and Suzanne Kapner, "Retailers to Implement Bangladesh Factory Plan," *The Wall Street Journal*, August 20, 2013, B3.

2. Fernando Napolitano, "The Megacommunity Approach to Tackling the World's Toughest Problems," *Strategy + Business*, August 24, 2010, http://www.strategy-business.com /article/10305?gko=73c6d (accessed August 1, 2011).

3. Christine Oliver, "Determinants of Interorganizational Relationships: Integration and Future Directions," *Academy of Management Review* 15 (1990), 241–265.

4. James Moore, *The Death of Competition: Leadership and Strategy in the Age of Business Ecosystems* (New York: HarperCollins, 1996).

5. Mark Gerencser, Reginald Van Lee, Fernando Napolitano, and Christopher Kelly, *Megacommunities: How Leaders of Government, Business, and Non-Profits Can Tackle Today's Global Challenges Together* (New York: Palgrave Macmillan, 2008).

6. Jonathan Hughes and Jeff Weiss, "Simple Rules for Making Alliances Work," *Harvard Business Review*, November 2007, 122–131; Howard Muson, "Friend? Foe? Both? The Confusing World of Corporate Alliances," *Across the Board*, March–April 2002, 19–25; and Devi R. Gnyawali and Ravindranath Madhavan, "Cooperative Networks and Competitive Dynamics: A Structural Embeddedness Perspective," *Academy of Management Review* 26, no. 3 (2001), 431–445.

7. Katie Merx, "Automakers Interconnected Around World," *Edmonton Journal*, April 6, 2007, H14; and Keith Bradsher, "Ford Agrees to Sell Volvo to a Fast-Rising Chinese Company," *The New York Times Online*, March 28, 2010, http://www.nytimes.com/2010/03/29/business/global/29auto .html (accessed August 1, 2011).

8. Thomas Petzinger, Jr., *The New Pioneers: The Men and Women Who Are Transforming the Workplace and Marketplace* (New York: Simon & Schuster, 1999), 53–54.

9. James Moore, "The Death of Competition," *Fortune*, April 15, 1996, 142–144.

10. Brian Goodwin, *How the Leopard Changed Its Spots: The Evolution of Complexity* (New York: Touchstone, 1994), 181, quoted in Petzinger, *The New Pioneers*, 53.

11. Jessica E. Lessin, Lorraine Luk, and Na Juro Osawa, "Apple Finds It Difficult to Divorce Samsung," *The Wall Street Journal*, June 29, 2013, A1.

12. Shira Ovide and Anupreeta Das, "Microsoft Takes a Side in PC War," *The Wall Street Journal*, February 6, 2013, B1.

13. Greg Ferenstein, "In a Cutthroat World, Some Web Giants Thrive by Cooperating," *The Washington Post*, February 19, 2011, http://www.washingtonpost.com/business/in-a -cutthroat-world-some-web-giants-thrive-by -cooperating/2011/02/19/ABmYSYQ_story.html (accessed February 19, 2011); and Jessica E. Vascellaro and Yukari Iwatani Kane, "Apple, Google Rivalry Heats Up," *The Wall Street Journal*, December 11, 2009, B1.

14. Sumantra Ghoshal and Christopher A. Bartlett, "Changing the Role of Top Management: Beyond Structure and Process," *Harvard Business Review*, January–February 1995, 86–96.

15. Ann Zimmerman and Dana Mattioli, "Retail's New Odd Couple," *The Wall Street Journal*, July 11, 2012, B1.

16. Ian Urbina, "In Gulf, It Was Unclear Who Was in Charge of Oil Rig," *The New York Times*, June 5, 2010, http://www .nytimes.com/2010/06/06/us/06rig.html (accessed August 5, 2011).

17. "Toward a More Perfect Match: Building Successful Leaders by Effectively Aligning People and Roles," Hay Group Working Paper (2004); and "Making Sure the Suit Fits," *Hay Group Research Brief* (2004). Available from Hay Group, The McClelland Center, 116 Huntington Avenue, Boston, MA 02116, or at http://www.haygroup.com.

18. Hughes and Weiss, "Simple Rules for Making Alliances Work."

19. Dana Priest and William M. Arkin, "Top Secret America, A *Washington Post* Investigation; Part II: National Security Inc.," July 20, 2010, http://projects.washingtonpost.com /top-secret-america/articles/national-security-inc/1/ (accessed November 28, 2011).

20. J. Pfeffer and G. R. Salancik, *The External Control of Organizations: A Resource Dependence Perspective* (New York: Harper & Row, 1978); and Amy J. Hillman, Michael C. Withers, and Brian J. Collins, "Resource Dependence Theory: A Review," *Journal of Management* 35, no. 6 (2009), 1404–1427.

21. Paul Ziobro, "Mattel Puts a Target on Lego," *The Wall Street Journal*, February 28, 2014, http://online.wsj.com/news /articles/SB100014240527023038013045794106715979 45030 (accessed March 10, 2014).

22. Peter Drucker, quoted in Rajesh Kumar and Anoop Nathwani, "Business Alliances: Why Managerial Thinking and Biases Determine Success," *Journal of Business Strategy* 33, no 5 (2012), 44–50.

23. Patrick Hull, "Joint Ventures Provide Opportunities for Entrepreneurs," *Forbes*, July 21, 2013, http://www.forbes .com/sites/patrickhull/2013/06/21/joint-ventures-provide -opportunities-for-entrepreneurs/ (accessed March 10, 2014).

24. James R. Hagerty, "Whirlpool Expands in China," *The Wall Street Journal*, March 19, 2012, http://online.wsj.com/news /articles/SB10001424052702303812904577291793985890430 (accessed March 12, 2014).

25. Leslie Kaufman, "NBC's News Unit Teams with Video Clip Start-Up," *The New York Times*, January 13, 2014, B3.

26. Ellen Byron, "Theory & Practice: Tight Supplies, Tight Partners," *The Wall Street Journal*, January 10, 2011, B5.

27. Eva Dou, "Apple Shifts from Foxconn to Pegatron," *The Wall Street Journal*, May 30, 2013, B5.

28. Ashleigh Barry and Marcey Goulder, "As 'Vaping Bars' Thrive, Jury Remains Out on E-Cigarettes," *The Columbus Dispatch*, March 9, 2014, http://www .dispatch.com/content/stories/business/2014/03/09 /as-vaping-bars-thrive-jury-remains-out-on-e-cigarettes .html?utm_source=rss&utm_medium=rss&utm _campaign=as-vaping-bars-thrive-jury-remains-out-on-e -cigarettes (accessed March 11, 2014)

29. "About SFATA," Smoke Free Alternatives Trade Association Website, http://www.sfata.org/about-sfata/ (accessed March 11, 2014).

30. Brian L. Connelly and Erik J. Van Slyke, "The Power and Peril of Board Interlocks," *Business Horizons* 55 (2012), 403–408.

31. Greg Bensinger and David Benoit, "Ichan Targets Silicon Valley Directors' Club," *The Wall Street Journal Online*, February 24, 2014, http://online.wsj.com/news/articles/SB10001424052702304610404579402831365897274 (accessed March 10, 2014).

32. Brad Stone, *The Everything Store: Jeff Bezos and the Age of Amazon* (New York: Little Brown and Company, 2013), 245.

33. Evelyn M. Rusli, "Facebook Takes Aim at Apps Makers," *The Wall Street Journal*, March 18, 2013, B1.

34. Mike Ramsey, "Toyota Tries to Break Reliance on China," *The Wall Street Journal*, January 14, 2011, B1.

35. Mitchell P. Koza and Arie Y. Lewin, "The Co-Evolution of Network Alliances: A Longitudinal Analysis of an International Professional Service Network," Center for Research on New Organizational Forms, Working Paper 98–09–02; and Kathy Rebello with Richard Brandt, Peter Coy, and Mark Lewyn, "Your Digital Future," *BusinessWeek*, September 7, 1992, 56–64.

36. Steve Lohr, "Big Medical Groups Begin Patient Data-Sharing Project," *The New York Times*, April 6, 2011, http://bits.blogs.nytimes.com/2011/04/06/big-medical-groups-begin-patient-data-sharing-project/ (accessed April 6, 2011).

37. Eugene Geh, "Understanding Strategic Alliances from the Effectual Entrepreneurial Firm's Perspective—An Organization Theory Perspective," *SAM Advanced Management Journal* (Autumn 2011), 27–36.

38. Saul Berman and Peter Korsten, "Embracing Connectedness: Insights from the IBM 2012 CEO Study," *Strategy & Leadership* 41, no. 2 (2013), 46–57; Christine Oliver, "Determinants of Interorganizational Relationships: Integration and Future Directions," *Academy of Management Review*, 15 (1990), 241–265; and Ken G. Smith, Stephen J. Carroll, and Susan Ashford, "Intra- and Interorganizational Cooperation: Toward a Research Agenda," *Academy of Management Journal* 38 (1995), 7–23.

39. Paul W. Beamish and Nathaniel C. Lupton, "Managing Joint Ventures," *Academy of Management Perspectives*, May 2009, 75–94.

40. Timothy M. Stearns, Alan N. Hoffman, and Jan B. Heide, "Performance of Commercial Television Stations as an Outcome of Interorganizational Linkages and Environmental Conditions," *Academy of Management Journal* 30 (1987), 71–90; David A. Whetten and Thomas K. Kueng, "The Instrumental Value of Interorganizational Relations: Antecedents and Consequences of Linkage Formation," *Academy of Management Journal* 22 (1979), 325–344; G. Ahuja, "Collaboration Networks, Structural Holes, and Innovation: A Longitudinal Study," *Administrative Science Quarterly* 45 (2000), 425–455; and Corey C. Phelps, "A Longitudinal Study of the Influence of Alliance Network Structure and Composition on Firm Exploratory Innovation," *Academy of Management Journal* 53, no. 4 (2010), 890–913.

41. Lindsay Brooke, "Ford-G.M. Teamwork on Transmissions," *The New York Times*, April 21, 2013, AU4.

42. Shira Ovide and Don Clark, "Oracle, Microsoft Strike Deal to Make Core Software Work Easily Together," *The Wall Street Journal*, June 25, 2013, B4.

43. Jeanne Whalen, "Roche, AstraZeneca Agree to Share Drug Research Data," *The Wall Street Journal*, June 26, 2013, B3.

44. Monica Langley and Jonathan D. Rockoff, "Drug Companies Join NIH in Study of Alzheimer's, Diabetes, Rheumatoid Arthritis, Lupus," *The Wall Street Journal*, February 3, 2014, http://online.wsj.com/news/articles/SB10001424052702303519404579353442155924498 (accessed March 12, 2014).

45. Keith G. Provan and H. Brinton Milward, "A Preliminary Theory of Interorganizational Network Effectiveness: A Comparative Study of Four Community Mental Health Systems," *Administrative Science Quarterly* 40 (1995), 1–33.

46. Peter Smith Ring and Andrew H. Van de Ven, "Developmental Processes of Corporate Interorganizational Relationships," *Academy of Management Review* 19 (1994), 90–118; Jeffrey H. Dyer, "How Chrysler Created an American *Keiretsu*," *Harvard Business Review*, July–August 1996, 42–56; Peter Grittner, "Four Elements of Successful Sourcing Strategies" *Management Review*, October 1995, 41–45; Myron Magnet, "The New Golden Rule of Business," *Fortune*, February 21, 1994, 60–64; and Mick Marchington and Steven Vincent, "Analysing the Influence of Institutional, Organizational and Interpersonal Forces in Shaping Inter-Organizational Relationships," *Journal of Management Studies* 41, no. 6 (September 2004), 1029–1056.

47. Travis Hessman, "Collaborating with the Competition," *Industry Week*, June 2013, 52, 54.

48. Anna Wilde Mathews, "Cleveland Clinic, Hospital Operator Forge Alliance," *The Wall Street Journal*, March 21, 2013, B8.

49. Philip Siekman, "The Snap-Together Business Jet," *Fortune*, January 21, 2002, 104[A]–104[H].

50. This section draws from Joel A. C. Baum, "Organizational Ecology," in Stewart R. Clegg, Cynthia Hardy, and Walter R. Nord, eds., *Handbook of Organization Studies* (Thousand Oaks, CA: Sage, 1996); Jitendra V. Singh, *Organizational Evolution: New Directions* (Newbury Park, CA: Sage, 1990); Howard Aldrich, Bill McKelvey, and Dave Ulrich, "Design Strategy from the Population Perspective," *Journal of Management* 10 (1984), 67–86; Howard E. Aldrich, *Organizations and Environments* (Englewood Cliffs, NJ: Prentice Hall, 1979); Michael Hannan and John Freeman, "The Population Ecology of Organizations," *American Journal of Sociology* 82 (1977), 929–964; Dave Ulrich, "The Population Perspective: Review, Critique, and Relevance," *Human Relations* 40 (1987), 137–152; Jitendra V. Singh and Charles J. Lumsden, "Theory and Research in Organizational Ecology," *Annual Review of Sociology* 16 (1990), 161–195; Howard E. Aldrich, "Understanding, Not Integration: Vital Signs from Three Perspectives on Organizations," in Michael Reed and Michael D. Hughes, eds., *Rethinking Organizations: New Directions in Organizational Theory and Analysis* (London: Sage, 1992); Jitendra V. Singh, David J. Tucker, and Robert J. House, "Organizational Legitimacy and the Liability of Newness," *Administrative Science*

Quarterly 31 (1986), 171–193; and Douglas R. Wholey and Jack W. Brittain, "Organizational Ecology: Findings and Implications," *Academy of Management Review* 11 (1986), 513–533.

51. Derek S. Pugh and David J. Hickson, *Writers on Organizations* (Thousand Oaks, CA: Sage, 1996); and Lex Donaldson, *American Anti-Management Theories of Organization* (New York: Cambridge University Press, 1995).

52. Jim Collins, "The Secret of Enduring Greatness," *Fortune*, May 5, 2008, 72–76; Julie Schlosser and Ellen Florian, "In the Beginning; Fifty Years of Amazing Facts," *Fortune*, April 5, 2004, 152–159; and "The Fortune 500; 500 Largest U. S. Corporations," *Fortune*, May 23, 2011, F1–F26.

53. Hannan and Freeman, "The Population Ecology of Organizations."

54. Quoted in Brad Stone, *The Everything Store*, p. 65.

55. Brad Stone, *The Everything Store*; Julie Bosman, "The Bookstore's Last Stand," *The New York Times*, January 29, 2012, BU1; and Jeffrey A. Trachtenberg and Martin Peers, "Barnes & Noble Seeks Next Chapter," *The Wall Street Journal Online*, January 6, 2012, http://online.wsj.com/news/articles/SB10001424052970203513604577142481239801336 (accessed January 6, 2012).

56. Damon Darlin, "Always Pushing Beyond the Envelope," *The New York Times*, August 8, 2010, BU5.

57. Miguel Bustillo, "As Big Boxes Shrink, They Also Rethink," *The Wall Street Journal*, March 3, 2011, B1.

58. David J. Tucker, Jitendra V. Singh, and Agnes G. Meinhard, "Organizational Form, Population Dynamics, and Institutional Change: The Founding Patterns of Voluntary Organizations," *Academy of Management Journal* 33 (1990), 151–178; Glenn R. Carroll and Michael T. Hannan, "Density Delay in the Evolution of Organizational Populations: A Model and Five Empirical Tests," *Administrative Science Quarterly* 34 (1989), 411–430; Jacques Delacroix and Glenn R. Carroll, "Organizational Foundings: An Ecological Study of the Newspaper Industries of Argentina and Ireland," *Administrative Science Quarterly* 28 (1983), 274–291; Johannes M. Pennings, "Organizational Birth Frequencies: An Empirical Investigation," *Administrative Science Quarterly* 27 (1982), 120–144; David Marple, "Technological Innovation and Organizational Survival: A Population Ecology Study of Nineteenth-Century American Railroads," *Sociological Quarterly* 23 (1982), 107–116; and Thomas G. Rundall and John O. McClain, "Environmental Selection and Physician Supply," *American Journal of Sociology* 87 (1982), 1090–1112.

59. "Amazon.com Inc.; Amazon Announces Digital Video License Agreement with NBCUniversal Domestic TV Distribution," *Computers, Networks & Communication*, August 11, 2011, 93; and Maria Mallory with Stephanie Anderson Forest, "Waking Up to a Major Market," *BusinessWeek*, March 23, 1992, 70–73.

60. Jessica E. Vascellaro and Evan Ramstad, "The Two-Horse Smartphone Race," *The Wall Street Journal*, April 24, 2012, B1.

61. Arthur G. Bedeian and Raymond F. Zammuto, *Organizations: Theory and Design* (Orlando, FL: Dryden Press, 1991); and Richard L. Hall, *Organizations: Structure, Process and Outcomes* (Englewood Cliffs, NJ: Prentice Hall, 1991).

62. M. Tina Dacin, Jerry Goodstein, and W. Richard Scott, "Institutional Theory and Institutional Change: Introduction to the Special Research Forum," *Academy of Management Journal* 45, no. 1 (2002), 45–47. Thanks to Tina Dacin for her material and suggestions for this section of the chapter.

63. J. Meyer and B. Rowan, "Institutionalized Organizations: Formal Structure as Myth and Ceremony," *American Journal of Sociology* 83 (1990), 340–363; and Royston Greenwood and Danny Miller, "Tackling Design Anew: Getting Back to the Heart of Organizational Theory," *Academy of Management Perspectives*, November 2010, 78–88.

64. Mark C. Suchman, "Managing Legitimacy: Strategic and Institutional Approaches," *Academy of Management Review* 20 (1995), 571–610.

65. Richard J. Martinez and Patricia M. Norman, "Whither Reputation? The Effects of Different Stakeholders," *Business Horizons* 47, no. 5 (September–October 2004), 25–32.

66. Guy Chazan and Monica Langley, "Dudley Faces Daunting To-Do List," *The Wall Street Journal Europe*, July 27, 2010, 17.

67. Pamela S. Tolbert and Lynne G. Zucker, "The Institutionalization of Institutional Theory," in Stewart R. Clegg, Cynthia Hardy, and Walter R. Nord, eds., *Handbook of Organization Studies* (Thousand Oaks, CA: Sage, 1996).

68. Pugh and Hickson, *Writers on Organizations*; and Paul J. DiMaggio and Walter W. Powell, "The Iron Cage Revisited: Institutional Isomorphism and Collective Rationality in Organizational Fields," *American Sociological Review* 48 (1983), 147–160.

69. This section is based largely on DiMaggio and Powell, "The Iron Cage Revisited"; Pugh and Hickson, *Writers on Organizations*; and W. Richard Scott, *Institutions and Organizations* (Thousand Oaks, CA: Sage, 1995).

70. Janet Adamy, "Yum Uses McDonald's as Guide in Bid to Heat Up Sales," *The Wall Street Journal*, December 13, 2007, A21; and Nick Wingfield and Robert A. Guth, "IPod, TheyPod: Rivals Imitate Apple's Success," *The Wall Street Journal*, September 18, 2006, B1.

71. Kai-Yu Hsieh and Freek Vermeulen, "Me Too or Not Me? The Influence of the Structure of Competition on Mimetic Market Entry," *Academy of Management Annual Meeting Proceedings* (2008), 1–6.

72. Ellen R. Auster and Mark L. Sirower, "The Dynamics of Merger and Acquisition Waves," *The Journal of Applied Behavioral Science* 38, no. 2 (June 2002), 216–244; and Monica Yang and Mary Anne Hyland, "Who Do Firms Imitate? A Multilevel Approach to Examining Sources of Imitation in Choice of Mergers and Acquisitions," *Journal of Management* 32, no. 3 (June 2006), 381–399.

73. Barry M. Staw and Lisa D. Epstein, "What Bandwagons Bring: Effects of Popular Management Techniques on Corporate Performance, Reputation, and CEO Pay," *Administrative Science Quarterly* 45, no. 3 (September 2000), 523–560.

74. Jeffrey Pfeffer and Robert I. Sutton, "The Trouble with Benchmarking," *Across the Board* 43, no. 4 (July–August 2006), 7–9.

75. Karen Donovan, "Pushed by Clients, Law Firms Step Up Diversity Efforts," *The New York Times*, July 21, 2006, C6.

76. Miguel Bustillo, "Wal-Mart to Assign New 'Green' Ratings," *The Wall Street Journal*, July 16, 2009, B1.

77. Based on Donald D. Bowen, Roy J. Lewicki, Francine S. Hall, and Douglas T. Hall, "The Ugli Orange Case," *Experiences in Management and Organizational Behavior*, 4th ed. (Chicago, IL: Wiley, 1997), 134–136; "Amazon Rainforest," BluePlanetBiomes.org, http://www.blueplanetbiomes.org /amazon.htm (accessed August 24, 2011); and "Rainforest Plants," BluePlanetBiomes.org, http://www.blueplanetbiomes .org/rnfrst_plant_page.htm (accessed August 24, 2011).

78. Based in part on "Mammoth Motors' New Paint Shop," a role play originally prepared by Arnold Howitt, executive director of the A. Alfred Taubman Center for State and Local Government at the Kennedy School of Government, Harvard University, and subsequently edited by Gerald Cormick, a principal in the CSE Group and senior lecturer for the Graduate School of Public Affairs at the University of Washington.

6 | Designing Organizations for the International Environment

Learning Objectives

After reading this chapter you should be able to:

1. Discuss organizational motivations for entering the global arena.
2. Explain the stages of international development.
3. Recognize the three major challenges global design faces.
4. Understand globalization versus multidomestic strategies.
5. Describe structural design options for international operations.
6. Identify mechanisms for global coordination, knowledge transfer, and resolving the tension between global uniformity and local responsiveness.
7. Understand the transnational model of organizing.

Entering the Global Arena

Motivations for Global Expansion · Stages of International Development · Global Expansion Through International Alliances and Acquisitions

The Challenges of Global Design

Increased Complexity and Differentiation · Increased Need for Coordination · More Difficult Transfer of Knowledge and Innovation

Designing Structure to Fit Global Strategy

Strategies for Global Versus Local Opportunities · International Division · Global Product Division Structure · Global Geographic Division Structure · Global Matrix Structure

Additional Global Coordination Mechanisms

Global Teams · Headquarters Planning · Expanded Coordination Roles · Benefits of Coordination

The Transnational Model of Organization

Design Essentials

Before reading this chapter, please check whether you agree or disagree with each of the following statements:

1 The only way an organization can reasonably expect to be successful in different countries is to customize its products and services to suit the local interests, preferences, and values in each country.

I AGREE _____   I DISAGREE _____

2 It is an especially difficult challenge to work on a global team to coordinate one's own activities and share new ideas and insights with colleagues in different divisions around the world.

I AGREE _____   I DISAGREE _____

3 The most advanced multinational corporations have developed systems for maintaining tight headquarters control over subsidiaries in dozens of countries.

I AGREE _____   I DISAGREE _____

British grocery retailer Tesco isn't accustomed to failure, but after spending five years and a billion pounds (about $1.61 billion), Tesco managers began preparing to sell or close the company's 199 Fresh & Easy markets and get out of the United States for good. "It's likely . . . that our presence in America will come to an end," Tesco CEO Philip Clarke said when he made the announcement. Fresh & Easy was a novel format for Americans—stores that were larger than convenience stores but smaller than supermarkets and that focused on selling fresh foods. As it turned out, Americans found the format neither fresh nor easy. Managers imported British favorites instead of adapting to American tastes, and each store carried the same selection of prepackaged meals and other products, no matter its location. There was no deli section where food could be made to order. Prepackaged sandwiches are commonplace to the British, but to American shoppers they seemed like something from a vending machine. The timing didn't help either. Fresh & Easy opened in the United States just before the subprime mortgage crisis and subsequent recession devastated many of the areas in California, Arizona, and Nevada where it located its earliest stores. The chain never turned a profit.[1]

That's the reality of international business. When an organization decides to do business in another country, managers face a whole new set of challenges and roadblocks. They sometimes find that transferring their domestic success internationally requires a totally different approach. Tesco, a highly successful grocery retailer in the United Kingdom, has also had problems in other countries, particularly Poland, the Czech Republic, Slovakia, and China, although it has been successful in some global markets. In general, food retailers that succeed in overseas markets do so by buying local companies that already have strong businesses with local managers in place, such as when Walmart bought British supermarket chain Asda in 1999. In the fall of 2013, Yucaipa Companies of Los Angeles agreed to buy 150 Fresh & Easy stores, mostly in California.[2]

Other companies have also struggled in the international arena. Deere & Company, the world's largest maker of farm equipment, is trying hard to penetrate Russia's farm equipment market, but the Russian government passed a law excluding farm machinery built outside the country from financing, so farmers had no way to buy from Deere. The company has now opened a plant near Moscow but still faces tremendous risks and uncertainties in Russia. Giant retailer Walmart entered South Korea with high hopes in 1996, but 10 years later it sold all its South Korean stores to a local retailer and withdrew from that country. Similarly, the company abandoned the German market after spending eight years trying to break into the competitive discount retailing environment in that country.[3] It is not the only successful organization to have pulled out of one or another foreign market battered and bruised, its managers scratching their heads over what went wrong.

Succeeding on a global scale isn't easy. Managers have to make tough decisions about strategic approach, how best to get involved in international markets, and how to design the organization to reap the benefits of international expansion. Despite the challenges, managers in most organizations think the potential rewards outweigh the risks. U.S.-based firms set up foreign operations to provide goods and services needed by consumers in other countries, as well as to obtain lower costs or technical know-how for producing products and services to sell domestically. In return, companies from Japan, Germany, China, the United Kingdom, and other countries compete with U.S. organizations on their own turf as well as abroad. Understanding and addressing the challenges of international business is more important today than ever before.

Purpose of This Chapter

This chapter explores how managers design an organization for the international environment. We begin by looking at some of the primary motivations for organizations to expand internationally, the typical stages of international development, and the use of alliances and acquisitions as ways to expand internationally. Then, the chapter discusses some of the specific design challenges global organizations face, examines global strategic approaches, considers the application of various structural designs for global advantage, and looks at coordination mechanisms used in global organizations. Finally, the chapter takes a look at the *transnational model*, a type of global organization that achieves high levels of the varied capabilities needed to succeed in a complex and volatile international environment.

Entering the Global Arena

Only a few decades ago, many companies could afford to ignore the international environment. Not today. The world is rapidly developing into a unified global field, and every company and manager needs to think globally. Brazil, Russia, India, and China (often referred to as BRIC) as well as other emerging economies are growing rapidly as providers of both products and services to the United States, Canada, Europe, and other developed nations. At the same time, these regions are becoming major markets for the products and services of North American firms.[4] China, with the fastest-growing middle class in history, is the largest or second-largest market for a variety of products and services, including mobile phones, automobiles, consumer electronics, luxury goods, and Internet use.[5]

Alay Mulally, CEO of U.S.-based Ford Motor Company, spends about a third of his time on matters related to China. Mulally is planning to build five additional plants in that country and double the number of dealerships.[6] China also has 1.22 billion mobile phone subscribers, and leading smartphone manufacturers Apple and South Korea's Samsung have new competition from Chinese mobile phone maker Xiaomi, as well as China's Lenovo and Acer, which recently entered the smartphone market.[7] Over the next few decades, the BRIC countries will have tremendous spending power as around a billion people become part of a new middle class.[8] For today's companies, the whole world is a source of business threats and opportunities. The BookMark discusses some of the factors contributing to our increasingly interconnected world and how this interconnection affects organizations.

Motivations for Global Expansion

Economic, technological, and competitive forces have combined to push many companies from a domestic to a global focus. Extraordinary advances in communications, technology, and transportation have created a new, highly competitive landscape.[9]

BOOKMARK 6.0   HAVE YOU READ THIS BOOK?

The World Is Flat: A Brief History of the Twenty-First Century
By Thomas L. Friedman

The global competitive playing field is being leveled. How fast is globalization happening? Three-time Pulitzer-Prize winning *New York Times* columnist Thomas L. Friedman started working on the second edition of his best-selling book, *The World Is Flat*, before the first edition was barely off the press. However, Friedman asserts that the forces causing this accelerated phase of globalization actually began to unfold in the final years of the twentieth century.

WHAT MAKES THE WORLD GO FLAT?
Friedman outlines 10 forces that flattened the world, which he calls flatteners. Many of these forces are directly or indirectly related to advanced technology, including the following:

- *Work flow software*. A dizzying array of software programs enable computers to easily communicate with one another. That's what makes it possible for a company like animation studio Wild Brain to make films with a team of production employees spread all over the world or for Boeing airplane factories to automatically resupply global customers with parts. It means companies can create global virtual offices as well as outsource pieces of their operations to whoever can do the job best and most efficiently, no matter in which country they are located.
- *Supply chaining*. Work flow software also enhances supply chaining, the horizontal collaboration among suppliers, retailers, and customers that became a

phenomenon in the 1990s. In turn, the more supply chains grow and proliferate, the flatter the world becomes. Supply chaining forces the adoption of common standards and technologies among companies so that every link can interact seamlessly.

- *The steroids*. Friedman refers to a variety of new technologies as steroids "because they are amplifying and turbocharging all the other flatteners." Perhaps the most significant element is the wireless revolution, which enables you to "take everything that has been digitized, made virtual and personal, and do it from anywhere." As Alan Cohen, senior vice president at Airespace, says, "Your desk goes with you everywhere you are now. And the more people have the ability to push and pull information from anywhere to anywhere faster, the more barriers to competition and communication disappear."

HOW TO BENEFIT FROM A FLATTER WORLD
A flatter, interconnected world means employees and organizations can collaborate and compete more successfully than ever, whatever their size and wherever they are located. But the benefits of a flatter world are not automatic. Friedman offers strategies for how companies can align themselves with the new reality of globalization. He warns U.S. companies (and employees) that they should embrace the idea that there will no longer be such a thing as an American firm or an American job. In a flat world, the best companies are the best global collaborators.

The World Is Flat, by Thomas L. Friedman, is published by Farrar, Straus & Giroux.

The importance of the global environment for today's organizations is reflected in the shifting global economy. As one indication, *Fortune* magazine's list of the Global 500, the world's 500 largest companies by revenue, indicates that economic clout is being diffused across a broad global scale. Exhibit 6.1 lists the number of companies on the Global 500 for a variety of countries in 2006, 2008, and 2013. Note the general decline in North America and Western Europe and the increase in countries such as China, Brazil, Taiwan, and Russia. China, in particular, is coming on strong. China's GDP surpassed Japan's in the second half of 2010, making that country the second-largest economy in the world (after the United States).[10] Consider that in 1993, China had only three companies on the *Fortune* Global 500 list and now has 89. Japan, on the other hand, has declined in importance, dropping from 149 companies in 1993 down to 64 by 2008 and 62 by 2013.[11]

As power continues to shift, organizations are viewing participation in global business as a necessity. Indeed, in some industries a company can be successful only by succeeding on a global scale. In general, three primary factors motivate companies to expand internationally: economies of scale, economies of scope, and

	Number of Companies on the Global 500 List		
	2006	2008	2013
United States	170	153	132
Japan	70	64	62
China	20	29	89
France	38	39	31
Germany	35	37	29
Britain	38	34	26
Switzerland	12	14	14
South Korea	12	15	2
Netherlands	14	13	11
Canada	14	14	9
Italy	10	10	8
Spain	9	11	8
India	6	7	8
Taiwan	3	6	6
Australia	8	8	8
Brazil	4	5	8
Russia	5	5	7
Mexico	5	5	3
Sweden	6	6	3
Singapore	1	1	2

Source: Based on data from "Global 500," *Fortune* magazine's annual ranking of the world's largest corporations for 2006, 2008, and 2013, http://money.cnn.com/magazines/fortune/global500/ (accessed December 7, 2011, and March 14, 2014).

low-cost production factors.[12] Recall from Chapter 2 that companies are always striving for greater efficiency and effectiveness, and expanding globally is one way to achieve these goals.

Economies of Scale. Building a global presence expands an organization's scale of operations, enabling it to realize **economies of scale**. The trend toward large organizations was initially sparked by the Industrial Revolution, which created pressure in many industries for larger factories that could seize the benefits of economies of scale offered by new technologies and production methods. Through large-volume production, these industrial giants were able to achieve the lowest possible cost per unit of production. However, for many companies, domestic markets no longer provide the high level of sales needed to maintain enough volume to achieve scale economies. For farm equipment manufacturers such as Deere & Company, for example, growth comes primarily from overseas, where more land is coming under cultivation and more farmers are mechanizing. Most farm equipment in North America is relatively new, according to a recent report on the farm machinery market. "While there could be some growth left [in North America], we're nearer to the peak than the trough," said the report. Deere is looking to the BRIC countries to lift sales outside the United States so the company can achieve scale economies.[13]

The Hollywood movie industry has also recently expanded its international outlook as sales of movie tickets and DVDs have declined in the United States and increased in other countries. The studios are using more international stars and retooling scripts to appeal to an international audience. One film industry veteran said, "No studio head is going to make a big expensive movie . . . unless it has worldwide appeal. You can't pay back that production cost on the domestic model alone."[14] International ticket sales now account for up to 80 percent of a movie's total gross. Paramount Pictures has tried hard to make "Star Trek Into Darkness," the latest in the franchise, successful overseas. Cast members and producers traveled around the globe to do advanced marketing. Paramount went out of its way to cast foreign actors, and the writers tried to craft a story that would keep loyal fans interested but not turn off people in other countries who knew nothing about the other movies.[15] Domestic markets have become saturated for many U.S. companies, and the only potential for growth lies overseas. Starbucks has targeted Asia for rapid international growth, planning to open thousands of stores in China, India, and Vietnam.[16] Asia has been a successful source of growth for Starbucks, but Vietnam, unlike elsewhere in Asia, has its own deep-rooted coffee culture and the company is having to adapt how it brews and serves coffee to succeed.[17] Economies of scale also enable companies to obtain volume discounts from suppliers, lowering the organization's cost of production.

Economies of Scope. A second factor is the enhanced potential for exploiting **economies of scope**. *Scope* refers to the number and variety of products and services a company offers as well as the number and variety of regions, countries, and markets it serves. Hollywood's DreamWorks SKG sold a 50 percent stake to India's Reliance Big Entertainment because the company has a presence in every entertainment platform. It can sell DreamWorks movies through its theaters, its satellite networks, its movie rental service, its radio stations, and its mobile phones.[18]

BRIEFCASE

As an organization manager, keep this guideline in mind:

Consider building an international presence to realize economies of scale, exploit economies of scope, or obtain scarce or low-cost production factors such as labor and raw materials.

Companies that have a presence in multiple countries gain marketing power and synergy compared to the same-size firm that has a presence in fewer countries. For example, an advertising agency with a presence in several global markets gains a competitive edge serving large companies that span the globe. Or consider the case of McDonald's, which has to obtain nearly identical ketchup and sauce packets for its restaurants around the world. A supplier that has a presence in every country McDonald's serves has an advantage because it provides cost, consistency, and convenience benefits to McDonald's, which does not have to deal with a number of local suppliers in each country. Economies of scope can also increase a company's market power as compared to competitors, because the company develops broad knowledge of the cultural, social, economic, and other factors that affect its customers in varied locations and can provide specialized products and services to meet those needs. Amway had to change everything about the company to survive and prosper in China, and the expanded scope has helped the company thrive in other areas as well.

IN PRACTICE

Amway

Amway started in 1959 with a direct sales model of independent entrepreneurs selling straight to consumers. By the late 1980s, more than half of Amway's revenues were coming from outside the United States, so when the company began selling in the People's Republic of China in 1995, it already had experience in that part of the world. Within a few years, China was a $200 million business and growing fast. Then, China pulled the plug, outlawing direct selling because of unethical actions of some non-Amway sellers.

Amway could be put out of business. Or, argued Eva Cheng, who ran Amway China at the time, it could cooperate with the Chinese government to find a solution. Over the next several years, regulatory changes in China required that Amway ask hard questions and repeatedly revise its business model. In fact, the company changed its business model five times in order to do business in China. For one thing, the company established physical stores, selling products to people who came in off the street, something it had never done before. Rather than importing products from the United States, it began manufacturing them in China. Managers changed their entire distributor compensation system in China. They also began doing brand advertising since they could no longer rely on the word-of-mouth marketing that drove direct sales. Amway took the long-term view, and today, China is the company's largest market.

The changes Amway made in China were a huge leap in scope at the time, but it has since successfully used some of them in other markets. In addition, being forced to revise the business model made managers realize the importance of regularly questioning the business model and adapting to succeed in different global markets.[19]

Low-Cost Production Factors. The third major force motivating global expansion relates to **factors of production**. One of the earliest, and still one of the most powerful, motivations for U.S. companies to invest abroad is the opportunity to obtain raw materials, labor, and other resources at the lowest possible cost. Organizations have long turned overseas to secure raw materials that were scarce or unavailable in their home country. In the early twentieth century, for example, tire companies went abroad to develop rubber plantations to supply tires for America's growing automobile industry. Today, U.S. paper manufacturers such as Weyerhaeuser and

International Paper Co., forced by environmental concerns to look overseas for new timberlands, are managing millions of acres of tree farms in New Zealand and other areas.[20]

Many companies also turn to other countries as a source of cheap labor. Apple's iPhones and iPads are made overseas by contract manufacturers such as Foxconn Technologies and Pegatron Corporation. Despite criticism of their labor practices, it is unlikely any of those jobs will come back to the United States. When he talked with President Barack Obama at a dinner in California in February 2011, Steve Jobs told Obama the scale, speed, and flexibility of the factories and the skills and diligence of the workers overseas were almost as important as the low costs.[21]

Textile manufacturing in the United States is now practically nonexistent as companies have lowered costs by shifting most production to Asia, Mexico, Latin America, and the Caribbean. Manufacturing of non-upholstered furniture has rapidly followed the same pattern, with companies closing plants in the United States and importing high-quality wooden furniture from China, where as many as 30 workers can be hired for the cost of one cabinetmaker in the United States.[22] Mexico is taking center stage in the production of cars. One in 10 cars sold in the United States in 2011 was made in Mexico.[23] But the trend isn't limited to manufacturing. A growing number of service firms in India write software; perform consulting work; and handle technical support, accounting, and data processing for some of the biggest corporations in the United States. One index lists more than 900 business services companies in India that employ around 575,000 people.[24]

Stages of International Development

No company can become a global giant overnight. Managers have to consciously adopt a strategy for global development and growth. Organizations enter foreign markets in a variety of ways and follow diverse paths. However, the shift from domestic to global typically occurs through stages of development, as illustrated in Exhibit 6.2.[25] In stage one, the **domestic stage**, the company is domestically oriented,

	I. Domestic	II. International	III. Multinational	IV. Global
Strategic orientation	Domestically oriented	Export-oriented, multidomestic	Multinational	Global
Stage of development	Initial foreign involvement	Competitive positioning	Explosion	Global
Structure	Domestic structure plus export department	Domestic structure plus international division	Worldwide geographic product structure	Matrix, transnational structure
Market potential	Moderate, mostly domestic	Large, multidomestic	Very large, multinational	Whole world

EXHIBIT 6.2
Four Stages of International Evolution

Sources: Based on Nancy J. Adler, *International Dimensions of Organizational Behavior*, 4th ed. (Cincinnati, OH: South-Western, 2002), 8–9; and Theodore T. Herbert, "Strategy and Multinational Organization Structure: An Interorganizational Relationships Perspective," *Academy of Management Review* 9 (1984), 259–271.

but managers are aware of the global environment and may want to consider initial foreign involvement to expand production volume and realize economies of scale. Market potential is limited and is primarily in the home country. The structure of the company is domestic, typically functional or divisional, and initial foreign sales is handled through an export department. The details of freight forwarding, customs problems, and foreign exchange are handled by outsiders. Candy company Hershey is an example of a company in this stage. The company is domestically oriented, and managers are just beginning to consider expanding foreign markets, particularly China. To better cater to Chinese tastes, Hershey plans to open the Shanghai-based Asia Innovation Center.[26]

In stage two, the **international stage**, the company takes exports seriously and begins to think multidomestically. **Multidomestic** means competitive issues in each country are independent of other countries; the company deals with each country individually. The concern is with international competitive positioning compared with other firms in the industry. At this point, an international division has replaced the export department, and specialists are hired to handle sales, service, and warehousing abroad. Multiple countries are identified as a potential market. Purafil, with headquarters in Doraville, Georgia, manufactures air filters that remove pollution and cleanse the air in 60 different countries.[27] The company first began exporting in the early 1990s and now earns 60 percent of its revenues from overseas. A service example is AlertDriving, a firm that provides online training courses to companies with vehicle fleets. The company must tailor its products and marketing to the expectations, driving habits, and geographical nuances in the 20 or so countries where it exports.[28]

In stage three, the **multinational stage**, the company has extensive experience in a number of international markets and has established marketing, manufacturing, or research and development (R&D) facilities in several foreign countries. The organization obtains a large percentage of revenues from sales outside the home country. Explosive growth occurs as international operations take off, and the company has business units scattered around the world along with suppliers, manufacturers, and distributors. Companies in the multinational stage include Siemens of Germany, Sony of Japan, and Coca-Cola of the United States. Aditya Birla Group is an example of a multinational based in India. The company began in 1850 as the Birla family's trading company. Starting in the 1970s in Southeast Asia, the Birla Group has expanded around the world, operating in 33 countries and producing and selling such products as fiber, chemicals, cement, metals, yarns and textiles, apparel, fertilizer, and carbon black. In 2010, around 60 percent of the company's revenues came from outside India.[29]

The fourth and ultimate stage is the **global stage**, which means the company transcends any single country. The business is not merely a collection of domestic industries; rather, subsidiaries are interlinked to the point where competitive position in one country significantly influences activities in other countries.[30] Truly **global companies** no longer think of themselves as having a single home country and, indeed, have been called *stateless corporations*.[31] This represents a new and dramatic evolution from the multinational company of the 1960s and 1970s. At this stage, ownership, control, and top management tend to be dispersed among several nationalities.[32] Nestlé SA provides a good example. The company gets most of its sales from outside the "home" country of Switzerland, and its 280,000 employees are spread all over the world. CEO Paul Bulcke is Belgian, Chairman Peter Brabeck-Letmathe was born in Austria, and more than half of the company's

HOW DO YOU FIT THE DESIGN?

WHAT IS YOUR CULTURAL INTELLIGENCE?

Instructions: To what extent does each of the following statements characterize your behavior? Please honestly answer each item below as Mostly True or Mostly False for you.

	Mostly True	Mostly False
1. I think about how I'm going to relate to people from a different culture before I meet them.	___	___
2. I understand the major religions and how they impact other cultures.	___	___
3. I know about the geography, history, and cultural leaders of several countries.	___	___
4. I regularly discuss world events with family and friends.	___	___
5. I seek out opportunities to interact with people from different cultures.	___	___
6. I can adapt to living in a different culture with relative ease.	___	___
7. I am confident that I can befriend locals in a culture that is unfamiliar to me.	___	___
8. I find work on a multicultural team very satisfying.	___	___
9. I regularly associate with people from cultural backgrounds different from me.	___	___
10. I alter my facial expressions and gestures as needed to facilitate a cross-culture interaction.	___	___
11. I am quick to change the way I behave when a cross-culture encounter seems to require it.	___	___
12. I take pleasure in talking with someone whose English is limited.	___	___

Scoring and Interpretation: The scores for these questions pertain to some aspect of *cultural intelligence*, which is a manager's capability to function well in situations characterized by cultural diversity. Give yourself 1 point for each Mostly True item as indicated below:

Cognitive CQ, items 1–4. Score = ____.
Emotional CQ, items 5–8. Score = ____.
Behavioral CQ, items 9–12. Score = ____.

Cognitive CQ pertains to the head, emotional CQ pertains to the heart, and behavioral CQ pertains to the body. If you have sufficient international experience and CQ to have scored 3–4 on all three parts, then consider yourself at a high level of CQ. If you scored 1–2 on all three parts, it is time to learn more about other national cultures. Hone your observational skills, take courses, look for international travel opportunities, and learn to pick up on clues about how people from a different country respond to various situations. Compare your scores to other students. If you are not fascinated by diverse people and cultures, how might you develop greater empathy for people who are different from you?

Sources: Based on P. Christopher Earley and Elaine Mosakowski, "Cultural Intelligence," *Harvard Business Review*, October 2004, 139–146; Soon Ang, Lynn Van Dyne, Christine Koh, K. Yee Ng, Klaus J. Templer, Cheryl Tay, and N. Anand Chandrasekar, "Cultural Intelligence: Its Measurement and Effects on Cultural Judgment and Decision Making, Cultural Adaptation, and Task Performance," *Management and Organization Review* 3 (2007), 335–371; and David C. Thomas and Kerr Inkson, *Cultural Intelligence: People Skills for Global Business* (San Francisco: Berrett-Koehler, 2004).

managers are non-Swiss. Nestlé has hundreds of brands and has production facilities or other operations in almost every country in the world.[33] How effective would you be managing in a global corporation and interacting with people from many different cultures? Complete the questionnaire in the "How Do You Fit the Design?" box to assess your level of cultural intelligence.

Global companies operate in truly global fashion, and the entire world is their marketplace. Global companies such as Nestlé, Royal Dutch/Shell, Unilever, and Matsushita Electric may operate in more than a hundred countries. The structural problem of holding together this huge complex of subsidiaries scattered thousands of miles apart is immense. Organization structure for global companies can be extremely complex and often evolves into an international matrix or transnational model, which will be discussed later in this chapter.

Global Expansion Through International Alliances and Acquisitions

As an organization manager, keep this guideline in mind:

Develop international strategic alliances, such as licensing and joint ventures, as fast and inexpensive ways to become involved in international sales and operations.

One of the most popular ways companies get involved in international operations is through international alliances. Companies in rapidly changing industries such as media and entertainment, pharmaceuticals, biotechnology, and software might have hundreds of these relationships.[34]

Typical alliances include licensing, joint ventures, and acquisitions.[35] Recall our discussion of these techniques from the previous chapter as types of resource-dependence relationships. They are also used for expanding internationally. For example, when entering new markets, particularly in developing areas of the world, retailers such as Saks Fifth Avenue and Barneys New York limit their risks by licensing their names to foreign partners. Saks has licensed stores in Riyadh and Dubai, Saudi Arabia, and in Mexico, for instance, and Barneys has a licensed store in Japan. Both firms, as well as other U.S.-based department stores, are currently making a strong international push in light of weak sales and stiff competition in the United States.[36] As described in the previous chapter, a **joint venture** is a separate entity created with two or more active firms as sponsors. This is a popular approach to sharing development and production costs and penetrating new markets.[37] Joint ventures may be with either customers or competitors. Competing firms Sprint, Deutsche Telecom, and Telecom France cooperate with each other and with several smaller firms in a joint venture that serves the telecommunication needs of global corporations in 65 countries.[38] Navistar International Corporation, based in Warrenville, Illinois, formed a joint venture with rival Mahindra & Mahindra Ltd., a fast-growing equipment maker in India, to build trucks and buses for export.[39] Walmart thought it got a foothold in India's fast-growing but difficult retail market through a joint venture with Bharti Enterprises to establish Bharti Walmart Private Limited.[40] Unfortunately, the problems engulfing India's economy, charges of corruption, and government regulations that created obstacles caused the two firms to end their partnership in late 2013, with Walmart buying out its part of the venture.[41]

Companies often seek joint ventures to achieve production cost savings through economies of scale, to share complementary technological strengths, to distribute new products and services through another country's distribution channels, or to take advantage of a partner's knowledge of local markets. However, when they can persuade senior managers of foreign companies to stay on, many companies prefer acquisitions because they offer greater control than joint ventures. Walmart, for instance, established a joint venture with Seiyu Ltd., a national grocery chain in Japan, and then acquired the chain in full several years ago after it gained more experience in the Japanese market.[42] Acquisitions have been China's preferred way of expanding internationally.

Perhaps China's biggest international acquisition success story is Lenovo, which acquired the personal computer business, including ThinkPad laptops, from IBM in 2005. The company struggled for a few years, but Lenovo kept several key managers of the IBM unit and split headquarters between Beijing and Morrisville, North Carolina, where the IBM unit had been located. These moves helped put the company on solid footing. Since Lenovo took over, ThinkPad sales have doubled and profit margins have remained above 5 percent.

Chinese companies have also acquired a number of other foreign firms, including Volvo, AMC movie theaters, Ferretti Italian luxury yachts, and Smithfield Foods, which has long supplied U.S. grocery stores with Smithfield hams, Eckrich sausages, Armour meatballs, and Farmland bacon. The $4.7 billion purchase of Smithfield by Shuanghui International Holdings Ltd. was the largest Chinese acquisition to date, but Chinese companies probably will not stop there. Although China didn't start investing in developed markets in earnest until the 2000s, the rate at which Chinese investment is increasing and the diversity of industries and geographical areas are astounding. These acquisitions will likely reshape the global business landscape.[43]

IN PRACTICE

China's International Expansion

Home-grown Chinese brands have struggled internationally, but Chinese companies have learned that they can succeed by buying strong brands overseas and keeping them healthy. In many cases, the Chinese companies keep local managers and let them run the companies. When China's property conglomerate Dalian Wanda Group Corporation bought AMC Entertainment Holdings Inc., for example, it sent a financial team to the United States, but it let U.S. management decide how to use their strategic budget.[44]

The Challenges of Global Design

Managers taking their companies international face a tremendous challenge in how to capitalize on the incredible opportunities that global expansion presents. Exhibit 6.3 illustrates the three primary challenges global organizational design faces: greater complexity and differentiation, an increased need for integration, and more difficulty transferring knowledge and innovation. Organizations have to accept an extremely high level of environmental complexity in the international domain and address the many differences that occur among countries. For instance, each country has its own history, culture, laws, and regulatory system. People eat different foods, observe different religions, have different attitudes, and subscribe to different social customs.[45] This environmental complexity and country variations require greater organizational differentiation, as described in Chapter 4.

At the same time, organizations must find ways to effectively achieve coordination and collaboration among far-flung units and facilitate the development and transfer of organizational knowledge and innovation for global learning.[46] Although many small companies are involved in international business, most international companies grow very large, creating a huge coordination problem. Exhibit 6.4 provides some understanding of the size and impact of international firms by comparing the revenues of several large multinational companies with the gross domestic product (GDP) of selected countries.

EXHIBIT 6.3
Challenges of Global
Design

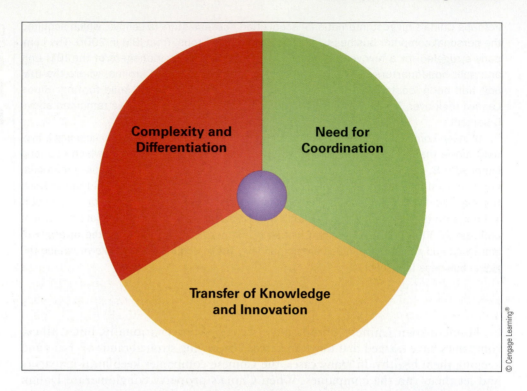

EXHIBIT 6.4
Comparison of Leading
Multinationals and
Selected Countries, 2010
(in U.S. dollars)

Company	Revenue*	Country	Annual GDP†
Walmart	421.89 billion	Norway	414.46 billion
ExxonMobil	354.67 billion	Thailand	318.85 billion
Chevron	196.34 billion	Czech Republic	192.15 billion
Fannie Mae	153.83 billion	Peru	152.83 billion
General Electric	151.63 billion	New Zealand	140.43 billion
Berkshire Hathaway	136.19 billion	Hungary	128.96 billion
General Motors	135.59 billion	Bangladesh	104.92 billion
Bank of America	134.19 billion	Vietnam	103.57 billion

*This size comparison is assuming revenues were valued at the equivalent of GDP.
†Gross domestic product.

Source: Based on Vincent Trivett, "25 US Mega Corporations: Where They Rank If They Were Countries" (with data from *Fortune/CNNMoney* and IMF), June 27, 2011, *BusinessInsider.com*, http://www.businessinsider.com/25-corporations-bigger-tan-countries-2011-6?op=1 (accessed April 30, 2014).

Increased Complexity and Differentiation

When organizations enter the international arena, they encounter a greater level of internal and external complexity than anything experienced on the domestic front. Companies have to create a structure to operate in numerous countries that differ in economic development, language, political systems and government regulations, cultural norms and values, and infrastructure such as transportation and communication facilities. For example, we mentioned computer maker Lenovo earlier as a Chinese company, but Lenovo is incorporated in Hong Kong, it has nine operational hubs, and its top managers and corporate functions are spread around the world. The CEO is in Singapore; the chairman in Raleigh, North Carolina; and the chief financial officer in Hong Kong. Worldwide marketing is coordinated in India.[47]

All the complexity in the international environment is mirrored in a greater internal organizational complexity. Recall from Chapter 4 that as environments become more complex and uncertain, organizations grow more highly differentiated, with many specialized positions and departments to cope with specific sectors in the environment. Top management might need to set up specialized departments to deal with the diverse government, legal, and accounting regulations in various countries, for example. In India, Internet companies such as Google, Yahoo, and Facebook are expected to help enforce certain standards and take down content considered incendiary, but the rules can be difficult to interpret. India is a democracy and in principle supports freedom of speech on the Internet as well as in print. Yet with the country's volatile mix of religions and ethnic politics, the Indian government reserves the right to impose "reasonable restrictions" on free speech to maintain public order. Most companies want to follow local laws and sentiments, but they also want to exercise discretion regarding what they believe should be allowable, so they often use teams of lawyers and other experts to monitor complaints and decide how to respond.[48]

In addition to departments to deal with diverse laws and regulations, companies operating internationally need more boundary-spanning departments to sense and respond to the external environment. Some companies disperse operations such as engineering, design, manufacturing, marketing, and sales around the world. In particular, many organizations have set up global product development systems to achieve greater access to international expertise and design products that are better suited to global markets. A Deloitte Research study found that 48 percent of North American and Western European manufacturers surveyed had set up engineering operations in other countries.[49] International organizations also might implement a variety of strategies, a broader array of activities, and a much larger number of products and services on an international level.

Increased Need for Coordination

As organizations become more differentiated, with multiple products, divisions, departments, and positions scattered across numerous countries, managers face a tremendous coordination challenge. *Coordination* refers to the quality of collaboration across organizational units. The question is how to achieve the integration and collaboration that is necessary for a global organization to reap the benefits of economies of scale, economies of scope, and labor and production cost efficiencies that international expansion offers. Recall from Chapter 4 that even in a domestic firm, high differentiation among departments requires that more time and resources be devoted to achieving coordination because employees' attitudes, goals, and work orientations differ widely. Imagine what it must be like for an international organization, whose operating units are divided not only by goals and work attitudes but by geographic distance, time differences, cultural values, and perhaps even language as well. Companies must find ways to share information, ideas, new products, and technologies across the organization. All organizations working globally face the challenge of getting all the pieces working together in the right way at the right time and in the right place.

More Difficult Transfer of Knowledge and Innovation

The third piece of the international challenge is for organizations to learn from their international experiences by sharing knowledge and innovations across the enterprise. The diversity of the international environment offers extraordinary opportunities for learning, development of diverse capabilities, and startling innovations in products and services. Essilor International SA, the world's largest manufacturer of ophthalmic corrective lenses, for example, engineers its lenses in Germany, makes blanks from high-transparency polymers in the United States, and adds microthin coatings in Japan.[50]

Some experts believe a great percentage of radical innovations will come from companies in emerging markets such as China and India in the coming years.[51] The old approach to innovation was for innovations in products and services to come primarily from developed countries and gravitate to less developed areas of the world, but a new approach referred to as *trickle-up innovation* or *reverse innovation* has companies paying attention more than ever to the need for mechanisms that encourage sharing across the international enterprise. Consider products for the healthcare profession. GE Healthcare had a solid presence in China, but its high-end ultrasound machines and other products didn't meet the needs of healthcare practitioners working in poorly funded, low-tech hospitals or clinics in rural villages. Price, portability, and ease of use were the important criteria. GE Healthcare formed a semiautonomous "local growth team" in China that, drawing on local talent and combining product development, sourcing, manufacturing, and marketing in one business unit, created a portable ultrasound machine that sold for less than 15 percent of the cost of the company's high-end ultrasound machines. GE now sells the product around the world, and it grew to a $278 million global product line within six years.[52] GE's CEO Jeffrey Immelt says, "If we don't come up with innovations in poor countries and take them global, new competitors from the developing world—like Mindray, Suzlon, and Goldwind—will."[53] Exhibit 6.5 lists some additional examples of trickle-up innovation.

Organizational units in each location acquire the skills and knowledge to meet environmental challenges that arise in that particular locale. As the trend toward trickle-up innovation shows, much of that knowledge, which may be related to product improvements, operational efficiencies, technological advancements, or myriad other competencies, is relevant across multiple countries, so organizations need systems that promote the transfer of knowledge and innovation across the global enterprise. A classic example comes from Procter & Gamble (P&G). Liquid Tide was one of P&G's most successful U.S. product launches in the 1980s, but the product came about from the sharing of innovations developed in diverse parts of the firm. Liquid Tide incorporated a technology for helping to suspend dirt in wash water from P&G headquarters in the United States, the formula for its cleaning agents from P&G technicians in Japan, and special ingredients for fighting mineral salts present in hard water from company scientists in Brussels.[54]

Company	Innovation and Application
Groupe Danone	Built tiny plants in Bangladesh that produce one-hundredth of the yogurt a typical Danone factory produces and then discovered that they can operate almost as efficiently as the firm's large factories, spurring Danone to adapt the concept to other markets
Nestlé	Took the Maggi brand dried noodles created as a low-cost meal for rural Pakistan and India and repositioned it as a budget-friendly health food in Australia and New Zealand
General Electric	Created an inexpensive portable electrocardiogram machine for sale in India, where medical practitioners face power fluctuations, lack of funding and space for big machines, high levels of dust, and difficulty replacing parts in expensive equipment, and now sells it in the United States as well as other countries around the world
Hewlett-Packard	Has a team in India looking for ways to migrate web-interface applications created for mobile phones in Asia and Africa to developed markets in the United States and Europe
John Deere	John Deere India developed a high-quality low-cost tractor for farmers in India that is now increasingly in demand in the United States among farmers reeling from the recession and that will play a big role in Deere's expansion in Russia

EXHIBIT 6.5
Examples of Trickle-Up Innovation

Sources: These examples are from Michael Fitzgerald, "As the World Turns," *Fast Company*, March 2009, 33–34; Reena Jana, "Inspirations from Emerging Economies," *BusinessWeek*, March 23 & 30, 2009, 38–41; Jeffrey R. Immelt, Vijay Govindarajan, and Chris Trimble, "How GE Is Disrupting Itself," *Harvard Business Review*, October 2009, 3–11; and Navi Radjou, "Polycentric Innovation: A New Mandate for Multinationals," *The Wall Street Journal Online*, November 9, 2009, http://online.wsj.com/article/SB125774328035737917.html (accessed November 13, 2009).

Getting employees to transfer ideas and knowledge across national boundaries can be exceedingly challenging. When Luxembourg-based steelmaker ArcelorMittal wanted its Burns Harbor, Indiana, mill to begin using hypermodern equipment and techniques similar to a mill in Gent, Belgium, to boost productivity and profitability, employees weren't overjoyed. They had long been accustomed to using paper and pencil to calculate the right mix of iron ore, coking coal, and limestone for every batch of steel; they resisted attending classes to learn to follow a computer's instructions. In a process called "twinning," two mills of similar size, age, and product mix are benchmarked against each other, with the weaker company told to copy the practices of the stronger one. So ArcelorMittal flew more than 100 U.S. engineers and managers to Gent, Belgium, and told them to "do as the Belgians do." Today, the Burns Harbor mill has record output, with productivity approaching the level of the Belgian mill. Workers say twinning has helped avoid catastrophe and that their jobs are different, but better.[55] Many organizations tap only a fraction of the potential that is available from the cross-border transfer of knowledge and innovation. People scattered at different locations around the world sometimes have trouble building trusting relationships. Other reasons include:[56]

- Language barriers, cultural dissimilarities, and geographic distances can prevent managers from spotting the knowledge and opportunities that exist across disparate country units.
- Sometimes managers don't appreciate the value of organizational integration and want to protect the interests of their own division rather than cooperate with other divisions.

- Divisions sometimes view knowledge and innovation as power and want to hold onto it as a way to gain an influential position within the global firm.
- The "not-invented-here" syndrome makes some managers reluctant to tap into the know-how and expertise of other units.
- Much of an organization's knowledge is in the minds of employees and cannot easily be written down and shared with other units.

Organizations have to encourage both the development and the sharing of knowledge, implement systems for tapping into knowledge wherever it exists, and share innovations to meet global challenges. Managers strive to find the right strategy and structure for their particular situations.

Designing Structure to Fit Global Strategy

As we discussed in Chapter 3, an organization's structure must fit its situation by providing sufficient information processing for coordination and control while focusing employees on specific functions, products, or geographic regions. Organization design for international firms follows a similar logic, with special interest in global versus local strategic opportunities.

Strategies for Global Versus Local Opportunities

When organizations venture into the international domain, managers attempt to formulate a coherent global strategy that will provide synergy among worldwide operations for the purpose of achieving common organizational goals. One dilemma they face is choosing whether to emphasize global **standardization** versus local responsiveness. Managers must decide whether they want each global affiliate to act autonomously or whether activities should be standardized across countries. These decisions are reflected in the choice between a *globalization* versus a *multidomestic* global strategy.

The **globalization strategy** means that product design, manufacturing, and marketing strategy are standardized throughout the world, which is less costly than creating different products for different markets.[57] For example, Black & Decker became much more competitive internationally when it standardized its line of power hand tools. Some products, such as Coca-Cola, are naturals for globalization because only advertising and marketing need to be tailored for different regions. In general, services are less suitable for globalization because different customs and habits often require a different approach to providing service. Meliá Hotels International, the largest hotel chain in Spain and one of the top 20 hotel companies worldwide, for example, partners with local companies in joint ventures and other partnerships to acquire the know-how to operate in 35 different countries, including China, Bulgaria, the United States, Indonesia, Greece, Croatia, Brazil, Egypt, and the United Kingdom.[58] A lack of local knowledge was part of Walmart's trouble in the South Korean market. The retailer continued to use Western-style displays and marketing strategies, whereas successful South Korean retailers build bright, eye-catching displays and hire clerks to promote their goods using megaphones and hand-clapping. Walmart similarly flubbed in Indonesia, where it closed its stores after only a year. Customers didn't like the brightly lit, highly organized stores, and because no haggling was permitted, they perceived the goods as being overpriced.[59]

Other companies have also begun shifting away from a strict globalization strategy. Economic and social changes, including a backlash against huge global corporations, have prompted consumers to be less interested in global brands and more in favor of products that have a local feel.[60] However, a globalization strategy can save a company money because it helps reap economy-of-scale efficiencies by standardizing product design and manufacturing, using common suppliers, introducing products around the world faster, coordinating prices, and eliminating overlapping facilities.[61] Gillette Company, which makes grooming products such as the Mach3 shaving system for men and the Venus razor for women, has large production facilities that use common suppliers and processes to manufacture products whose technical specifications are standardized around the world.[62]

---

1 **The only way an organization can reasonably expect to be successful in different countries is to customize its products and services to suit the local interests, preferences, and values in each country.**

> **ANSWER:** *Disagree.* It is the case that people around the world often want products and services that are tailored to their local needs and interests, and many organizations are quite successful by responding to local market demands. However, other international organizations attain competitive advantages by using the same product design and marketing strategies in many countries throughout the world.

ASSESS YOUR ANSWER

A **multidomestic strategy** means that competition in each country is handled independently of competition in other countries. Thus, a multidomestic strategy would encourage product design, assembly, and marketing tailored to the specific needs of each country. Some companies have found that their products do not thrive in a single global market. For instance, people in different countries have very different expectations for personal-care products such as deodorant or toothpaste. Many people in parts of Mexico use laundry detergent for washing dishes. Even American fast food chains, once considered ultimate examples of standardization for a world market, have felt the need to be more responsive to local and national differences. The menus at McDonald's restaurants vary widely around the world, for example, although procurement and distributions systems are standardized and centralized.[63] When KFC (Yum Brands) entered Asia in 1973, it tried to use a globalization strategy, but the 11 restaurants it opened closed within two years. Managers tried again with a multidomestic strategy and achieved remarkable success, particularly in China, where the chain gained a 40 percent market share, compared to 16 percent for McDonald's.[64]

Different global organization designs are better suited to the need for either global standardization or local responsiveness. Research on more than 100 international firms based in Spain provided support for the connection between international structure and strategic focus.[65] The model in Exhibit 6.6 illustrates how organization design and international strategy fit the needs of the environment.[66]

EXHIBIT 6.6
Model to Fit Organization
Structure to International
Advantages

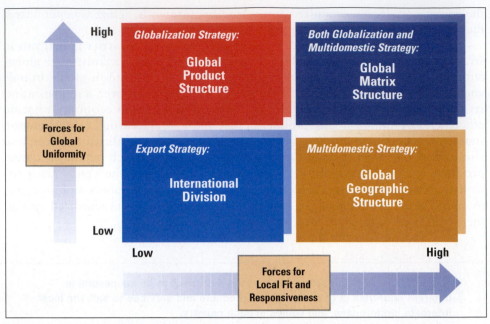

Sources: Based on Christopher A. Bartlett and Sumantra Ghoshal, *Text, Cases, and Readings in Cross-Border Management*, 3rd ed. (New York: Irwin McGraw-Hill, 2000), 395; Roderick E. White and Thomas A. Poynter, "Organizing for Worldwide Advantage," *Business Quarterly*, Summer 1989, 84–89; Gunnar Hedlund, "The Hypermodern MNC—A Heterarchy?" *Human Resource Management* 25, no. 1 (Spring 1986), 9–36; and J. M. Stopford and L. T. Wells, Jr., *Managing the Multinational Enterprise* (New York: Basic Books, 1972).

Companies can be characterized by whether their product and service lines have potential for globalization, which means advantages through worldwide standardization. Companies that sell similar products or services across many countries have a globalization strategy. On the other hand, some companies have products and services appropriate for a multidomestic strategy, which means local-country advantages through differentiation and customization to meet local needs.

As indicated in Exhibit 6.6, when forces for both global standardization and local responsiveness in many countries are low, simply using an international division with the domestic structure is an appropriate way to handle international business. For some industries, however, technological, social, or economic forces may create a situation in which selling standardized products worldwide provides a basis for competitive advantage because it enables the company to keep costs lower than if it had to provide products tailored to each market. In these cases, a global product structure is appropriate. This structure provides product managers with authority to handle their product lines on a global basis and enables the company to take advantage of a unified global marketplace. In other cases, companies can gain competitive advantages through local responsiveness—by responding to unique needs in the various countries in which they do business. For these companies, a worldwide geographic structure is appropriate. Each country or region will have subsidiaries that modify products and services to fit that locale. A good illustration is the advertising firm of Ogilvy & Mather, which divides its operations into four primary geographic regions because advertising approaches need to be modified to fit the tastes, preferences, cultural values, and government regulations in different parts of the world.[67] Children are frequently used to advertise products in the United States, but this approach in France is against the law. The competitive claims of rival products regularly seen on U.S. television would violate government regulations in Germany.[68]

In many instances, companies need to respond to both global and local opportunities simultaneously, in which case the global matrix structure can be used. Part of the product line may need to be standardized globally and other parts tailored to the needs of local countries. In reality, there has been an escalating tension for most companies between the need for global uniformity and the need for local fit and responsiveness. Here's what Panasonic has done to address the tension.

IN PRACTICE
Panasonic

Panasonic established its first manufacturing joint venture in China in 1987 and soon had more than 40 China-based manufacturing operations. By the early 2000s, China was Panasonic's manufacturing hub for home appliances, but the goal was to achieve efficiency and low costs in making products for export. Most product development was done in Japan, and little effort was made to understand the Chinese market for appliances.

Then, Panasonic managers noticed that the Chinese company Haier was quickly outpacing it, growing 20 to 30 percent annually while Panasonic's growth in China stayed flat. They realized they needed to adjust their strategy to keep from falling behind not just in China but in all their markets. Over time, Panasonic learned to treat the goal of meeting local consumers' needs as equally important as the goal of achieving competitive advantage through uniformity with global integrated operations. The company created the Shanghai-based China Lifestyle Research Center, which was Panasonic's first real effort to develop a deep understanding of consumer lifestyles in any market outside of Japan. From the beginning the director of the center embraced the tension between global uniformity and local adaptation. One adaptation for the Chinese market was slimmer refrigerators to fit in the smaller 55-centimeter-wide spaces typical of kitchens there. Sales zoomed.

Over time, as knowledge flowed from China to the rest of the company and from the various business units to China, Panasonic began initiatives to better understand consumers in other diverse markets all over the world. Today, the company continues its "tension-embracing philosophy" of being both efficient on a worldwide scale and local in its focus on consumer needs.[69]

Thus, even companies that don't use a matrix structure as shown in Exhibit 6.6 often use various mechanisms to address the tension between the need for global uniformity and the need for local responsiveness. Now let's discuss each of the structures in Exhibit 6.6 in more detail.

International Division

As companies begin to explore international opportunities, they typically start with an export department that grows into an **international division**. The international division has a status equal to the other major departments or divisions within the company and is illustrated in Exhibit 6.7. Whereas the domestic divisions are typically organized along functional or product lines, the international division is organized according to geographic interests, as illustrated in Exhibit 6.7. The international division has its own hierarchy to handle business (licensing,

EXHIBIT 6.7
Domestic Hybrid
Structure with
International Division

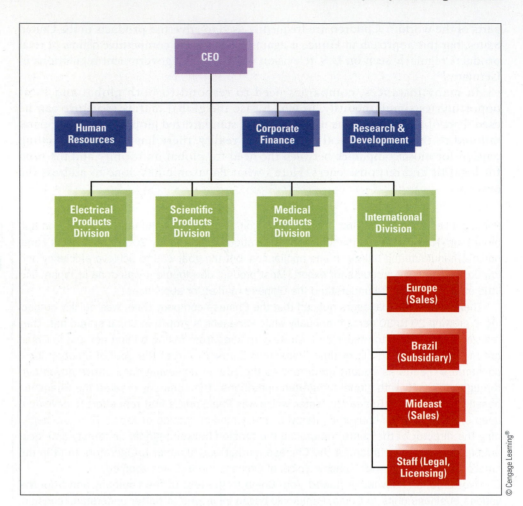

joint ventures) in various countries, selling the products and services created by the domestic divisions, opening subsidiary plants, and in general moving the organization into more sophisticated international operations.

Although functional structures are often used domestically, they are less frequently used to manage a worldwide business.[70] Lines of functional hierarchy running around the world would extend too long, so some form of product or geographic structure is used to subdivide the organization into smaller units. Firms typically start with an international department and, depending on their strategy, later use product or geographic division structures or a matrix. One study found that 48 percent of organizations identified as global leaders use divisional structures, while 28 percent reported using matrix structures.[71]

Global Product Division Structure

In a **global product structure**, the product divisions take responsibility for global operations in their specific product area. This is one of the most commonly used structures through which managers attempt to achieve global goals because it provides a fairly straightforward way to effectively manage a variety of businesses and products around the world. Managers in each product division can focus on organizing for international operations as they see fit and directing employees' energy toward their own division's unique set of global problems or opportunities.[72] In addition, the structure provides top managers at headquarters with a broad perspective on competition, enabling the entire corporation to respond more rapidly to a changing global environment.[73] Service companies can also use a divisional structure. For example, Italian bank UniCredit, with headquarters in Milan and more than 9,600 branches in 22 countries, has three product divisions: Family and SME (household and small and mid-sized business banking), Corporate and Investment Banking, and Private Banking and Asset Management. The company also has one geographic-based division to focus on operations and growth in Central and Eastern European countries.[74]

With a global product structure, each division's manager is responsible for planning, organizing, and controlling all functions for the production and distribution of its products or services for any market around the world. As we saw in Exhibit 6.6, the global product structure works best when the company has opportunities for worldwide production and sale of standard products for all markets, thus providing economies of scale and standardization of production, marketing, and advertising.

Eaton Corporation has used a form of worldwide product structure, as illustrated in Exhibit 6.8. In this structure, the automotive components group, industrial group, and so on are responsible for the manufacture and sale of products worldwide. The vice president of the international division is responsible for coordinators in each region, including a coordinator for Japan, Australia, South America, and northern Europe. The coordinators find ways to share facilities and improve production and delivery across all product lines sold in their regions. These coordinators fulfill the same function as integrators described in Chapter 3.

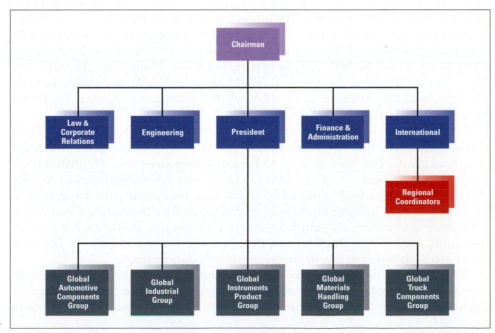

EXHIBIT 6.8
Partial Global Product Structure Used by Eaton Corporation

Source: Based on *New Directions in Multinational Corporate Organization* (New York: Business International Corp., 1981).

The product structure is great for standardizing production and sales around the globe, but it also has problems. Often the product divisions do not work well together, competing instead of cooperating in some countries; and some countries may be ignored by product managers. The solution adopted by Eaton Corporation of using country coordinators who have a clearly defined role is a superb way to overcome these problems. Haier uses a radical type of product structure that breaks the company into 2,000 semiautonomous teams of 10 to 30 employees, each with its own P&L, and each focused on coordinating a specific product or project across several countries.[75]

Global Geographic Division Structure

As an organization manager, keep these guidelines in mind:

Choose a global product structure when the organization can gain competitive advantages through a globalization strategy (global uniformity). Choose a global geographic structure when the company has advantages with a multidomestic strategy (local fit and responsiveness). Use an international division when the company is primarily domestic and has only a few international operations.

A regionally based organization is well suited to companies that want to emphasize adaptation to regional or local market needs through a multidomestic strategy, as illustrated earlier in Exhibit 6.6. The **global geographic structure** divides the world into geographic regions, with each geographic division reporting to the CEO. Each division has full control of functional activities within its geographic area. For example, Nestlé, with headquarters in Switzerland, puts great emphasis on the autonomy of regional managers who know the local culture. The largest branded food company in the world, Nestlé rejects the idea of a single global market and has used a partial geographic structure to focus on the local needs and competition in each country. Local managers have the authority to tinker with a product's flavoring, packaging, portion size, or other elements as they see fit. Many of the company's 8,000 brands are registered in only one country.[76]

Companies that use this type of structure have typically been those with mature product lines and stable technologies. They can find low-cost manufacturing within countries as well as meet different needs across countries for marketing and sales. However, several business and organizational trends have led to a broadening of the kinds of companies that use the global geographic structure.[77] The growth of service organizations has outpaced manufacturing for several years, and services by their nature must occur on a local level. Starbucks Coffee Company uses a three-region organization structure: China and Asia Pacific, which consists of the Japan, Korea, Hong Kong, Thailand, Malaysia, Singapore, Indonesia, Philippines, Australia, and New Zealand markets; the Americas, which includes the United States, Canada, Mexico, and Latin America; and EMEA, which encompasses, Europe, the United Kingdom, Russia, the Middle East, and Africa.[78]

In addition, to meet new competitive threats, many manufacturing firms are emphasizing the ability to customize their products to meet specific needs, which requires a greater emphasis on local and regional responsiveness. All organizations are compelled by current environmental and competitive challenges to develop closer relationships with customers, which may lead companies to shift from product-based to geographic-based structures. India's Bupharm, a young and growing pharmaceuticals company, created geographic divisions for its sales operation, such as Asia Pacific, Latin America, and Europe, to help the company better serve customers in the 40 countries where it does business.[79]

The problems encountered by senior management using a global geographic structure result from the autonomy of each regional division. For example, it is difficult to do planning on a global scale—such as new-product R&D—because

each division acts to meet only the needs of its region. New domestic technologies and products can be difficult to transfer to international markets because each division thinks it will develop what it needs. Likewise, it is difficult to rapidly introduce products developed offshore into domestic markets, and there is often duplication of line and staff managers across regions. Because regional divisions act to meet specific needs in their own areas, tracking and maintaining control of costs can be a real problem. The following example illustrates how executives at Colgate-Palmolive overcame some of the problems associated with the geographic structure.

For several years, Colgate-Palmolive Company, which manufactures and markets personal-care, household, and specialty products, used a global geographic structure of the form illustrated in Exhibit 6.9. Colgate has a long, rich history of international involvement and has relied on regional divisions in North America, Europe, Latin America, the Far East, and the South Pacific to stay on the competitive edge. Well over half of the company's total sales are generated outside of the United States.

☑ IN PRACTICE

Colgate-Palmolive Company

The regional approach supports Colgate's cultural values, which emphasize individual autonomy, an entrepreneurial spirit, and the ability to act locally. Each regional president reports directly to the chief operating officer, and each division has its own staff functions such as human resources (HR), finance, manufacturing, and marketing. Colgate handled the problem of coordination across geographic divisions by creating an *international business development group* that is responsible for long-term company planning and worldwide product coordination and communication. It used several product team leaders, many of whom had been former country managers with extensive experience and knowledge. The product leaders are essentially coordinators and advisors to the geographic divisions; they have no power to direct, but they have the ability and the organizational support needed to exert substantial influence. The addition of this business development group quickly reaped positive results in terms of more rapid introduction of new products across all countries and better, lower-cost marketing.

The success of the international business development group prompted Colgate's top management to add two additional coordinating positions—a *vice president of corporate development* to focus on acquisitions and a *worldwide sales and marketing group* that coordinates sales and marketing initiatives across all geographic locations. With these worldwide positions added to the structure, Colgate maintains its focus on each region and achieves global coordination for overall planning, faster product introductions, and enhanced sales and marketing efficiency.[80]

Global Matrix Structure

We've discussed how Eaton used a global product division structure and found ways to coordinate across worldwide divisions. Colgate-Palmolive used a global geographic division structure and found ways to coordinate across geographic regions. Each of these companies emphasized a single dimension. Recall from Chapter 3 that a matrix structure provides a way to achieve vertical and horizontal

EXHIBIT 6.9
Global Geographic Structure of Colgate-Palmolive Company

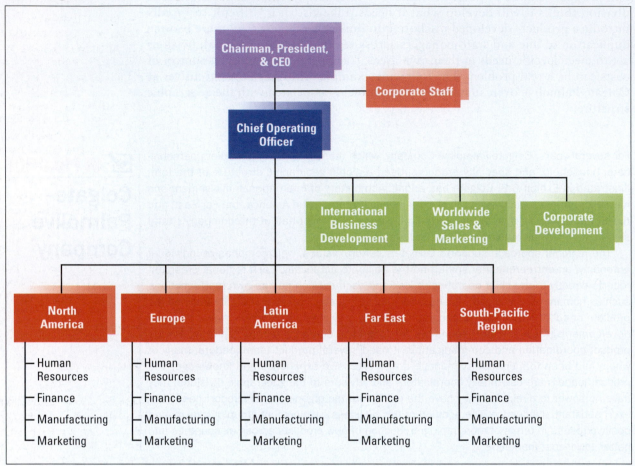

Source: Based on Robert J. Kramer, *Organizing for Global Competitiveness: The Geographic Design* (New York: The Conference Board, 1993), 30.

coordination simultaneously along two dimensions. A **global matrix structure** is similar to the matrix described in Chapter 3, except that for multinational corporations the geographic distances for communication are greater and coordination is more complex.

The matrix works best when pressure for decision making balances the interests of both product standardization and geographic localization and when coordination to share resources is important. The matrix can support a mixed globalization and multidomestic strategy, as illustrated in Exhibit 6.6; that is, it can enable a global firm to achieve aspects of both global uniformity and local diversification and responsiveness.[81] For many years, ABB (Asea Brown Boveri), a global leader in power and automation technologies, with headquarters in Zurich, used a global matrix structure that worked extremely well to coordinate a 150,000-employee company operating in approximately 100 countries.

ABB has given new meaning to the notion of "being local worldwide." ABB has used a complex global matrix structure similar to Exhibit 6.10 to achieve worldwide economies of scale combined with local flexibility and responsiveness.

At the top are the chief executive officer and an executive committee of 10 top managers, who hold frequent meetings around the world. Along one side of the matrix are product division managers for Power Products, Power Systems, Discrete Automation and Motion, Low Voltage Products, and Process Automation. Each division manager is responsible for handling business on a global scale, allocating export markets, establishing cost and quality standards, and creating mixed-nationality teams to solve problems. Each division is subdivided into smaller units over which the division manager also has responsibility.

Along the other side of the matrix is a regional structure; ABB has eight regional managers for Northern Europe; Central Europe; Mediterranean; North America; South America; India, Middle East, and Africa; North Asia; and South Asia. Under the regional managers are country managers who run local companies that cross business areas and are responsible for local balance sheets, income statements, and career ladders.

The matrix structure converges at the level of the local companies. The presidents of local companies report to two bosses—the product division leader, who coordinates on a global scale, and the regional president, who runs the company of which the local organization is a subsidiary.

ABB's philosophy is to decentralize things to the lowest levels. Global managers are generous, patient, and multilingual. They must work with teams made up of different nationalities and be culturally sensitive. They craft strategy and evaluate performance for people and subsidiaries around the world. Regional managers, by contrast, are line managers responsible for several country subsidiaries. They must cooperate with product division managers to achieve worldwide efficiencies and the introduction of new products. Finally, the presidents of local companies have both a global boss—the product division manager—and a regional boss, and they learn to coordinate the needs of both.[82]

✔ IN PRACTICE
ABB Group

EXHIBIT 6.10
Global Matrix Structure

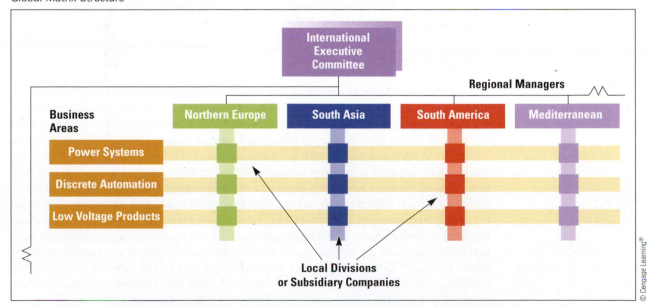

© Cengage Learning®

ABB is a large, successful company that achieved the benefits of both product and geographic organizations through this matrix structure. However, over the past several years, as ABB has faced increasingly complex competitive issues, leaders have transformed the company toward a complex structure called the *transnational model*, which will be discussed later in this chapter.

In the real world, as with the domestic hybrid structure, many international firms such as ABB, Colgate, UniCredit, Nestlé, or Eaton Corporation apply a *global hybrid* or *mixed structure*, in which two or more different structures or elements of different structures are used. Hybrid structures are typical in highly volatile environments. UniCredit, for example, combines elements of functional, geographic, and product divisions to respond to dynamic market conditions in the multiple countries where it operates.[83]

There is no *ideal* structure, and organizations that operate on a global scale frequently have to make adjustments to their structures to overcome the challenges of doing business in a global environment. In the following sections, we will look at some additional coordination mechanisms used to address the challenges of operating on a global scale.

Additional Global Coordination Mechanisms

There are many instances of well-known companies that have trouble transferring successful ideas, products, and services from their home country to the international domain. As we discussed earlier in the chapter, greater complexity and differentiation, an increased need for coordination, and more difficult transfer of knowledge and innovation present challenges for global organization design. In addition, managers have to address the tension between the desire to achieve worldwide efficiency and uniformity and the desire to achieve local fit and responsiveness in each market they serve. Managers meet these global challenges in a variety of ways. Some of the most common are the use of global teams, stronger headquarters planning and control, and specific coordination roles.

Global Teams

One of the most valuable mechanisms for global coordination and the transfer of knowledge and innovation has been the use of global teams. In addition to these uses of teams, today's organizations are using teams specifically to address the tension between global uniformity and local responsiveness.[84] **Global teams**, also called *transnational teams*, are cross-border work groups made up of multiskilled, multinational members whose activities span multiple countries.[85] Typically, teams are of two types: intercultural teams, whose members come from different countries and meet face to face, and virtual global teams, whose members remain in separate locations around the world and conduct their work electronically.[86] Heineken formed the European Production Task Force, a 13-member team made up of multinational members, to meet regularly and come up with ideas for optimizing the company's production facilities across Europe.[87] German steelmaker ThyssenKrupp uses global virtual teams, applying sophisticated computer networks and software to link and coordinate team members working across three continents to run a virtually integrated steel operation.[88]

However, building effective global teams is not easy. Cultural and language differences can create misunderstandings, and resentments and mistrust can quickly derail the team's efforts. Consider what happened in one virtual team made up of members from India, Israel, Canada, the United States, Singapore, Spain, Brussels, Great Britain, and Australia:

> Early on . . . team members were reluctant to seek advice from teammates who were still strangers, fearing that a request for help might be interpreted as a sign of incompetence. Moreover, when teammates did ask for help, assistance was not always forthcoming. One team member confessed to carefully calculating how much information she was willing to share. Going the extra mile on behalf of a virtual teammate, in her view, came at a high price of time and energy, with no guarantee of reciprocation.[89]

As this quote shows, it is easy for an "us against them" mentality to develop, which is just the opposite of what organizations want from global teams.[90] No wonder when the executive council of *CIO* magazine asked global chief information officers to rank their greatest challenges, managing virtual global teams ranked as the most pressing issue.[91] L'Oréal, the French global cosmetics giant, is one of the most effective companies at building teams that improve coordination, transfer knowledge and innovation, help resolve the tension between uniformity and local responsiveness, and thwart the "us against them" mentality.

IN PRACTICE
L'Oréal

The global–local tension is often greatest when product development requires subtle, complex knowledge that can't be easily codified and written down. This so-called tacit knowledge resides in people's minds and is usually revealed only in action and interaction, which means it is subject to misinterpretation when it crosses borders. The cosmetics firm L'Oréal exemplifies this tension as well as any other company, because personal-care needs are unique to each culture. Yet the company has managed to be both very global and very local. It has offices in 130 countries, and in 2012 more than half of the company's sales came from new markets outside the United States and Europe, mostly in developing countries.

The upper management team has always been strongly rooted in L'Oréal's home culture, so how does the firm bridge its products to other cultures? Product development is the firm's competitive advantage, so L'Oréal recruits and builds product development teams that report to managers who have mixed cultural backgrounds. A team of three or four people will usually have at least two who are multicultural, such as a Lebanese-Spanish-American manager working with a French-Irish-Cambodian or an Indian-American-French project manager. Product development teams share their ideas with each other and with top management as work progresses over the period of about a year. "Their background is a kind of master class in holding more than one idea at a time," said one director. "They think as if they were French, American, or Chinese, and all of these together at once."

How does that flexible perspective lead to knowledge transfer and innovation? A French-Irish-Cambodian manager working on skin care noticed that many tinted face creams in Asia had a lifting effect. At the time, most face creams in Europe were either tinted, and considered makeup, or lifting, and considered skin care. The manager drew on his knowledge of Asian beauty trends and suggested a tinted cream for the French market that was a huge success.

As the firm grows around the world, some of these multicultural managers are beginning to find their way into senior management in the company, a sign that the approach is working. L'Oréal is beginning to place multicultural managers at the center of interactions among brands, regions, and functions and is increasingly encouraging the flow of knowledge from subsidiaries back to the home country as well as the old way from the home country to far-flung subsidiaries.[92]

2 It is an especially difficult challenge to work on a global team to coordinate one's own activities and share new ideas and insights with colleagues in different divisions around the world.

> **ANSWER:** *Agree.* The problems of different languages, locations, cultural values, and business practices make membership on an international team especially difficult. Global teams can be effective only if members have the patience and skills to surmount the barriers and openly share information and ideas. Global teams perform better when they are made up of people who are culturally astute and genuinely want to coordinate and communicate with their counterparts in other countries.

Headquarters Planning

A second approach to achieving stronger global coordination is for headquarters to take an active role in planning, scheduling, and control to keep the widely distributed pieces of the global organization working together and moving in the same direction. In one survey, 70 percent of global companies reported that the most important function of corporate headquarters was to "provide enterprise leadership."[93] For example, Panasonic's Global Consumer Marketing organization, described in the earlier In Practice, is directed from the top of the organization. Top leaders make decisions about resource allocation to further the goals of embracing the global–local tension. If top leaders don't make decisions that both further the cultivation of a global mindset and promote greater understanding of local markets in various countries, instead acting as mere observers, the goals aren't likely to be met.[94]

Without strong leadership, highly autonomous divisions can begin to act like independent companies rather than coordinated parts of a global whole. To counteract this, top management may delegate responsibility and decision-making authority in some areas, such as adapting products or services to meet local needs, while maintaining strong control through centralized systems in other areas to provide the coordination and integration needed.[95] Plans, schedules, and formal rules and procedures can help ensure greater communication among divisions and with headquarters as well as foster cooperation and synergy among far-flung units to achieve the organization's goals in a cost-efficient way. Top managers can provide clear strategic direction, guide far-flung operations, and resolve competing demands from various units.

Expanded Coordination Roles

Organizations may also implement structural solutions to achieve stronger coordination and collaboration.[96] Creating specific organizational roles or positions for coordination is a way to integrate all the pieces of the enterprise to achieve a strong competitive position. In successful international firms, the role of top *functional managers*, for example, is expanded to include responsibility for coordinating across countries, identifying and linking the organization's expertise and resources worldwide. In an international organization, the manufacturing manager has to be aware of and coordinate with manufacturing operations of the company in various parts of the world so that the company achieves manufacturing efficiency and shares technology and ideas across units. A new manufacturing technology developed to improve efficiency in a company's Brazilian operations may be valuable for European and North American plants as well. Manufacturing managers are responsible for being aware of new developments wherever they occur and for using their knowledge to improve the organization. Similarly, marketing managers, HR managers, and other functional managers at an international company are involved not only in activities for their particular location but in coordinating with their sister units in other countries as well.

Whereas functional managers coordinate across countries, *country managers* coordinate across functions. A country manager for an international firm has to co-ordinate all the various functional activities located within the country to meet the problems, opportunities, needs, and trends in the local market, enabling the organization to achieve multinational flexibility and rapid response. The country manager in Venezuela for a global consumer products firm such as Colgate-Palmolive would coordinate everything that goes on in that country, from manufacturing to HR to marketing, to ensure that activities meet the language, cultural, government, and legal requirements of Venezuela. The country manager in Ireland or Canada would do the same for those countries. Country managers also help with the transfer of ideas, trends, products, and technologies that arise in one country and might have significance on a broader scale. Some organizations also use *business integrators* to provide coordination on a regional basis that might include several countries. These managers reach out to various parts of the organization to resolve problems and coordinate activities across groups, divisions, or countries.

Another coordination role is that of formal *network coordinator* to coordinate information and activities related to key customer accounts. These coordinators would enable a manufacturing organization, for example, to provide knowledge and integrated solutions across multiple businesses, divisions, and countries for a large retail customer such as Tesco, Walmart, or Carrefour. Top managers in successful global firms also encourage and support informal networks and relationships to keep information flowing in all directions. Much of an organization's information exchange occurs not through formal systems or structures but through informal channels and relationships. By supporting these informal networks, giving people across boundaries opportunities to get together and develop relationships, and then ways to keep in close touch, executives enhance organizational coordination.[97]

BRIEFCASE

As an organization manager, keep these guidelines in mind:

Use mechanisms such as global teams, head-quarters planning, and specific coordination roles to provide needed coordination and integration among far-flung international units. Emphasize information and knowledge sharing to help the organization learn and improve on a global scale.

Benefits of Coordination

International companies have a hard time staying competitive without strong inter-unit coordination and collaboration. Those firms that stimulate and support collaboration are typically better able to leverage dispersed resources and capabilities to reap operational and economic benefits.[98] Benefits that result from inter-unit collaboration include the following:

- *Cost savings.* Collaboration can produce real, measurable results in the way of cost savings from the sharing of best practices across global divisions. For example, at BP, a business unit head in the United States improved inventory turns and cut the working capital needed to run U.S. service stations by learning the best practices from BP operations in the United Kingdom and the Netherlands.
- *Better decision making.* By sharing information and advice across divisions, managers can make better business decisions that support their own unit as well as the organization as a whole.

- *Greater revenues.* By sharing expertise and products among various divisions, organizations can reap increased revenues. BP again provides an example. More than 75 people from various units around the world flew to China to assist the team developing an acetic acid plant there. As a result, BP finished the project and began realizing revenues sooner than project planners had expected.

- *Increased innovation.* The sharing of ideas and technological innovations across units stimulates creativity and the development of new products and services. McDonald's is taking an approach called "freedom within a framework" that allows regional and national managers to develop practices and products suited to the local area. The company then makes sure international managers have plenty of both formal and informal ways to communicate and share ideas. The Big Tasty, a whopping 5.5-oz. beef patty slathered in barbeque sauce and topped with three slices of cheese, was created in a test kitchen in Germany and launched in Sweden, but as word spread, the sandwich was adopted by restaurants in places like Brazil, Italy, and Portugal, where it became a huge hit.[99]

The Transnational Model of Organization

Because traditional approaches have been inadequate to meet the demands of a rapidly changing, complex global environment, many large international companies are moving toward a *transnational model* of organization, which is highly differentiated to address the increased complexity of the global environment yet offers very high levels of coordination, learning, and transfer of organizational knowledge and innovations. The **transnational model** represents the most advanced kind of international organization. It reflects the ultimate in both organizational complexity, with many diverse units, and organizational coordination, with mechanisms for integrating the varied parts. The transnational model is useful for large, multinational companies with subsidiaries in many countries that try to exploit both global and local advantages as well as technological advancements, rapid innovation, and global learning and knowledge sharing. Rather than building capabilities primarily in one area, such as global efficiency, local responsiveness, or global learning, the transnational model seeks to achieve all three simultaneously. Dealing with multiple, interrelated, complex issues requires a complex form of organization and structure.

The transnational model represents the most current thinking about the kind of structure needed by highly complex global organizations such as Philips NV, illustrated in Exhibit 6.11. Incorporated in the Netherlands, Philips has hundreds of operating units all over the world and is typical of global companies such as Unilever, Matsushita, or Procter & Gamble.[100] Large professional service firms such as KPMG and PricewaterhouseCoopers (PwC) also use the transnational structure. PwC, for example, has more than 160,000 people in 757 offices in 151 countries. The company provides a highly diversified range of knowledge-based services that have to be customized to specific clients in specific locales, so local offices need discretion and autonomy. At the same time, PwC needs consistent operating standards and control systems worldwide.[101]

The units of a transnational organization network, as illustrated in Exhibit 6.11, are far-flung. Achieving coordination, a sense of participation and involvement by subsidiaries, and a sharing of information, knowledge, new technology, and customers is a tremendous challenge. For example, a global corporation like Philips,

EXHIBIT 6.11
International Organizational Units and Interlinkages Within Philips NV

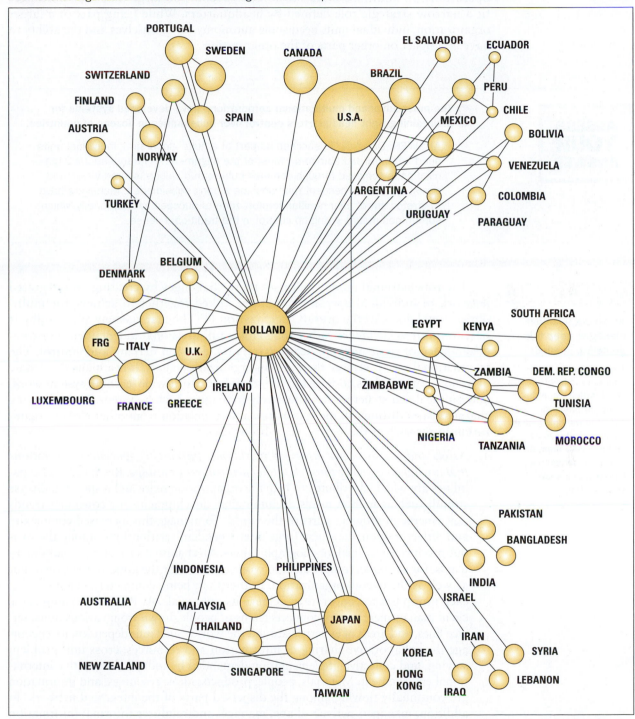

Source: Republished with permission of Academy of Management (NY), from Sumantra Ghoshal and Christopher Bartlett, "The Multinational Corporation as an Interorganizational Network," *The Academy of Management Review*, 15 (1990), 603–625; permission conveyed through Copyright Clearance Center, Inc.

Unilever, or PwC is so large that size alone is a huge problem in coordinating global operations. In addition, some subsidiaries become so large that they no longer fit a narrow strategic role defined by headquarters. While being part of a larger organization, individual units need some autonomy for themselves and the ability to have an impact on other parts of the organization.

BRIEFCASE

As an organization manager, keep this guideline in mind:

Strive toward a transnational model of organization when the company has to respond to multiple global forces simultaneously and needs to promote worldwide integration, learning, and knowledge sharing.

The transnational model addresses these challenges by creating an integrated network of individual operations that are linked together to achieve the multidimensional goals of the overall organization.[102] The management philosophy is based on *interdependence* rather than either full divisional independence or total dependence of these units on headquarters for decision making and control. The transnational model is more than just an organization chart. It is a managerial state of mind, a set of values, a shared desire to make a worldwide learning system work, and an idealized structure for effectively managing such a system. The following characteristics distinguish the transnational organization from other global organization forms such as the matrix, described earlier.

1. *Assets and resources are dispersed worldwide into highly specialized operations that are linked together through interdependent relationships.* Resources and capabilities are widely distributed to help the organization sense and respond to diverse stimuli such as market needs, technological developments, or consumer trends that emerge in different parts of the world. To manage this increased complexity and differentiation, managers forge interdependent relationships among the various product, functional, or geographic units. Mechanisms such as cross-subsidiary teams, for example, compel units to work together for the good of their own unit as well as the overall organization. Rather than being completely self-sufficient, each group has to cooperate to achieve its own goals. At PwC, for example, the client management system connects teams of people drawn from various units, service lines, and areas of expertise around the world. Such interdependencies encourage the collaborative sharing of information and resources, cross-unit problem solving, and collective implementation demanded by today's competitive international environment. Materials, people, products, ideas, resources, and information are continually flowing among the dispersed parts of the integrated network. In addition, managers actively shape, manage, and reinforce informal information networks that cross functions, products, divisions, and countries.

2. *Structures are flexible and ever-changing.* The transnational operates on a principle of *flexible centralization*. It may centralize some functions in one country, some in another, yet decentralize still other functions among its many geographically

dispersed operations. An R&D center may be centralized in Holland and a purchasing center may be located in Sweden, while financial accounting responsibilities are decentralized to operations in many countries. A unit in Hong Kong may be responsible for coordinating activities across Asia, while activities for all other countries are coordinated by a large division headquarters in London. The transnational model requires that managers be flexible in determining structural needs based on the benefits to be gained. Some functions, products, and geographic regions by their nature may need more central control and coordination than others. In addition, coordination and control mechanisms will change over time to meet new needs or competitive threats. Some companies have begun setting up multiple headquarters in different countries as the organization gets too large and too complex to manage from one place and to get closer to important markets. Irdeto Holdings BV, for example, has headquarters in both Hoofddorp, the Netherlands, and Beijing, and the CEO moved to China with his family. IBM created a growth-markets headquarters in Shanghai that is responsible for Asia (non-Japan), Latin America, Russia, Eastern Europe, the Middle East, and Africa. Japan's Nissan located global headquarters for its luxury Infiniti brand in Hong Kong.[103]

3. *Subsidiary managers initiate strategy and innovations that become strategy for the corporation as a whole.* In traditional structures, managers have a strategic role only for their division. In a transnational structure, various centers and subsidiaries can shape the company from the bottom up by developing creative responses and initiating programs in response to local needs, then dispersing those innovations worldwide. Transnational companies recognize each of the worldwide units as a source of capabilities and knowledge that can be used to benefit the entire organization. In addition, environmental demands and opportunities vary from country to country, and exposing the whole organization to this broader range of environmental stimuli triggers greater learning and innovation.

4. *Unification and coordination are achieved primarily through corporate culture, shared vision and values, and management style, rather than through formal structures and systems.* A study by Hay Group found that one of the defining characteristics of companies that succeed on a global scale is that they successfully coordinate worldwide units and subsidiaries around a common strategic vision and values rather than relying on formal coordination systems alone.[104] Achieving unity and coordination in an organization in which employees come from a variety of different national backgrounds, are separated by time and geographic distance, and have different cultural norms is more easily accomplished through shared understanding than through formal systems. Top leaders build a context of shared vision, values, and perspectives among managers who in turn cascade these elements through all parts of the organization. Selection and training of managers emphasizes flexibility and open-mindedness. In addition, people are often rotated through different jobs, divisions, and countries to gain broad experience and become socialized into the corporate culture. Achieving coordination in a transnational organization is a much more complex process than simple centralization or decentralization of decision making. It requires shaping and adapting beliefs, culture, and values so that everyone participates in information sharing and learning.

Taken together, these characteristics facilitate strong coordination, organizational learning, and knowledge sharing on a broad global scale. The transnational model is truly a complex and messy way to conceptualize organization structure, but it is becoming increasingly relevant for large, global firms that treat the whole world as their playing field and do not have a single country base. The autonomy of organizational parts gives strength to smaller units and allows the firm to be flexible in responding to rapid change and competitive opportunities on a local level, while the emphasis on interdependency enables global efficiencies and organizational learning. Each part of the transnational company is aware of and closely integrated with the organization as a whole so that local actions complement and enhance other company parts.

Design Essentials

- ■ This chapter examined how managers design organizations for a complex international environment. Almost every company today is affected by significant global forces, and many are developing overseas operations to take advantage of global markets. Three primary motivations for global expansion are to realize economies of scale, exploit economies of scope, and achieve scarce or low-cost factors of production such as labor, raw materials, or land. One popular way to become involved in international operations is through strategic alliances with international firms. Alliances include licensing, joint ventures, and acquisitions.

- ■ Organizations typically evolve through four stages, beginning with a domestic orientation, shifting to an international orientation, then changing to a multinational orientation, and finally moving to a global orientation that sees the whole world as a potential market. Organizations typically use an export department, then use an international department, and eventually develop into a worldwide geographic or product structure.

- ■ Succeeding on a global scale is not easy. Three primary challenges facing global organizational design are addressing environmental complexity through greater organizational complexity and differentiation, achieving integration and coordination among the highly differentiated units, and implementing mechanisms for the transfer of knowledge and innovations.

- ■ Organizations try to match their design to fit their strategic goals. Geographic structures are most effective for organizations that can benefit from a multidomestic strategy, meaning that products and services will do best if tailored to local needs and cultures. A product structure supports a globalization strategy, which means that products and services can be standardized and sold worldwide. Huge global firms might use a matrix structure to respond to both local and global forces simultaneously. Many firms use hybrid structures by combining elements of two or more different structures to meet the dynamic conditions of the global environment.

- ■ Additional coordination mechanisms to address the problem of integration and knowledge transfer are through global teams, stronger headquarters planning and control, and specific coordination roles. Teams can also be a good way to help resolve the tension between the desire for global uniformity and the desire for local responsiveness.

- ■ Companies operating globally need broad coordination methods, and some are moving toward the transnational model of organization. The transnational model is based on a philosophy of interdependence. It is highly differentiated yet offers very high levels of coordination, learning, and transfer of knowledge across far-flung divisions. The transnational model represents the ultimate global design in terms of both organizational complexity and organizational integration. Each part of the transnational organization is aware of and closely integrated with the organization as a whole so that local actions complement and enhance other company parts.

≫ KEY CONCEPTS

domestic stage	global product structure	multidomestic
economies of scale	global stage	multidomestic strategy
economies of scope	global teams	multinational stage
factors of production	globalization strategy	standardization
global companies	international division	transnational model
global geographic structure	international stage	
global matrix structure	joint venture	

≫ DISCUSSION QUESTIONS

1. Name some companies that you think could succeed today with a globalization strategy and explain why you selected those companies. How does the globalization strategy differ from a multidomestic strategy?

2. Why do you think the tension between a desire for global uniformity and local responsiveness is greater today than in the past?

3. Many American companies enter China through joint ventures with local firms, but China is succeeding in the United States primarily with a strategy of buying companies outright. What are some factors that might account for this difference?

4. Do you think it makes sense for a transnational organization to have more than one headquarters? What might be some advantages associated with two headquarters, each responsible for different things? Can you think of any drawbacks?

5. What are some of the primary reasons a company decides to expand internationally? Identify a company in the news that has recently built a new overseas facility. Which of the three motivations for global expansion described in the chapter do you think best explains the company's decision? Discuss.

6. When would an organization consider using a matrix structure? How does the global matrix differ from the domestic matrix structure described in Chapter 3?

7. Name some of the elements that contribute to greater complexity for international organizations. How do organizations address this complexity? Do you think these elements apply to a company such as Spotify that wants to expand its music streaming service internationally? Discuss.

8. Traditional values in Mexico support high power distance and a low tolerance for uncertainty. What would you predict about a company that opens a division in Mexico and tries to implement global teams characterized by shared power and authority and the lack of formal guidelines, rules, and structure?

9. Do you believe it is possible for a global company to simultaneously achieve the goals of global efficiency and integration, national responsiveness and flexibility, and the worldwide transfer of knowledge and innovation? Discuss.

10. Compare the description of the transnational model in this chapter to the elements of organic versus mechanistic organization designs described in Chapter 1. Do you think the transnational model seems workable for a huge global firm? Discuss.

≫ CHAPTER 6 WORKSHOP   Made in the U.S.A.?

In March 2011, ABC World News ran a special series called "Made in America." In the opening program, correspondents David Muir and Sharyn Alfonsi removed all foreign made products from a family's Dallas, Texas, home and found that there was virtually nothing left when they finished. How many items in your home were made in America? For this exercise, pick three different consumer products from your home (e.g., a shirt, a toy or game, a phone, a shoe, a sheet or pillowcase, a coffeemaker). Try to find the following information for each product, as shown in the table. To find this information, use websites, articles on the company from various business newspapers and magazines, and the labels on the items or user manuals. You could also try calling the company and talking with someone there.

Product	What country do materials come from?	Where is it manufactured or assembled?	Which country does the marketing and advertising?	In what different countries is the product sold?
1.				
2.				
3.				

What can you conclude about international products and organizations based on your analysis?

CASE FOR ANALYSIS | TopDog Software[105]

At the age of 39, after working for nearly 15 years at a leading software company on the West Coast, Ari Weiner and his soon-to-be-wife, Mary Carpenter, had cashed in their stock options, withdrawn all their savings, maxed out their credit cards, and started their own business, naming it TopDog Software after their beloved Alaskan malamute. The two had developed a new software package for root cause analysis (RCA) applications that they were certain was far superior to anything on the market at that time. TopDog's software was particularly effective for use in design engineering organizations because it provided a highly efficient way to eliminate problems in new digital manufacturing processes, including product development, software engineering, hardware design, manufacturing, and installation. The software, which could be used as a standalone product or easily integrated with other software packages, dramatically expedited problem identification and corrective actions in the work of design engineering firms. The use of TopDog's RCA software would find an average of 30 to 50 root cause problems and provide 20 to 30 corrective actions that lowered defect rates by 50 percent, saving tens and sometimes hundreds of thousands of dollars with each application.

The timing proved to be right on target. RCA was just getting hot, and TopDog was poised to take advantage of the trend as a niche player in a growing market. Weiner and Carpenter brought in two former colleagues as partners and were soon able to catch the attention of a venture capitalist firm to gain additional funding. Within a couple of years, TopDog had 28 employees and sales had reached nearly $4 million.

Now, though, the partners are facing the company's first major problem. TopDog's head of sales, Samantha Jenkins, has learned of a new company based in Norway that is beta testing a new RCA package that promises to outpace TopDog's—and the Norway-based company,

FastData, has been talking up its global aspirations in the press. "If we stay focused on the United States and they start out as a global player, they'll kill us within months!" Sam moaned. "We've got to come up with an international strategy to deal with this kind of competition."

In a series of group meetings, off-site retreats, and one-on-one conversations, Weiner and Carpenter have gathered opinions and ideas from their partners, employees, advisors, and friends. Now they have to make a decision—should TopDog go global? And if so, what approach would be most effective? There's a growing market for RCA software overseas, and new companies such as FastData will soon be cutting into TopDog's U.S. market share as well. Samantha Jenkins isn't alone in her belief that TopDog has no choice but to enter new international markets or get eaten alive. Others, however, are concerned that TopDog isn't ready for that step. The company's resources are already stretched to the limit, and some advisors have warned that rapid global expansion could spell disaster. TopDog isn't even well established in the United States, they argue, and expanding internationally could strain the company's capabilities and resources. Others have pointed out that none of the managers has any international experience, and the company would have to hire someone with significant global exposure to even think about entering new markets.

Although Mary tends to agree that TopDog for the time being should stay focused on building its business in the United States, Ari has come to believe that global expansion of some type is a necessity. But if TopDog does eventually decide on global expansion, he wonders how on earth they should proceed in a huge, complex world environment. Sam, the sales manager, is arguing that the company should set up its own small foreign offices from scratch and staff them primarily with local people. Building a U.K. office and an Asian office, she asserts, would give TopDog an ideal base for penetrating markets around the world. However, it would be quite expensive, not to mention the complexities of dealing with language and cultural differences, legal and government regulations, and other matters. Another option would be to establish alliances or joint ventures with small European and Asian companies that could benefit from adding RCA applications to their suite of products. The companies could share expenses in setting up foreign production facilities and a global sales and distribution network. This would be a much less costly operation and would give TopDog the benefit of the expertise of the foreign partners. However, it might also require lengthy negotiations and would certainly mean giving up some control to the partner companies.

One of TopDog's partners is urging still a third, even lower-cost approach, that of licensing TopDog's software to foreign distributors as a route to international expansion. By giving foreign software companies rights to produce, market, and distribute its RCA software, TopDog could build brand identity and customer awareness while keeping a tight rein on expenses. Ari likes the low-cost approach, but he wonders if licensing would give TopDog enough participation and control to successfully develop its international presence. As another day winds down, Weiner and Carpenter are no closer to a decision about global expansion than they were when the sun came up.

CASE FOR ANALYSIS | Rhodes Industries

David Javier was reviewing the consulting firm's proposed changes in organization structure for Rhodes Industries (RI). As Javier read the report, he wondered whether the changes recommended by the consultants would do more harm than good for RI. Javier had been president of RI for 18 months, and he was keenly aware of the organizational and coordination problems that needed to be corrected in order for RI to improve profits and growth in its international businesses.

Company Background

Rhodes Industries was started in the 1950s in Southern Ontario, Canada, by Robert Rhodes, an engineer who was an entrepreneur at heart. He started the business by first making pipe and then glass for industrial uses. As soon as the initial business was established, however, he quickly branched into new areas such as industrial sealants, coatings, and cleaners, and even into manufacturing mufflers and parts for the trucking industry. Much of this expansion occurred by acquiring small firms in Canada and the United States during the 1960s. RI had a conglomerate-type structure with rather diverse subsidiaries scattered around North America, all reporting directly to the Ontario headquarters. Each subsidiary was a complete local business and was allowed to operate independently so long as it contributed profits to RI.

During the 1970s and 1980s, the president at the time, Clifford Michaels, brought a strong international focus to RI. His strategy was to acquire small companies worldwide with the belief that they could be formed into a cohesive unit that would bring RI synergies and profits through low cost of manufacturing and by serving businesses in international markets. Some of RI's businesses were acquired simply because they were available at a good price, and RI found itself in new lines of business such as consumer products (paper and envelopes) and electrical equipment (switchboards, light bulbs, and security systems), in addition to its previous lines of business. Most of these products had local brand names or were manufactured for major international companies such as General Electric or Corning Glass.

During the 1990s, a new president of RI, Sean Rhodes, the grandson of the founder, took over the business and adopted the strategy of focusing RI on three lines of business—Industrial Products, Consumer Products, and Electronics. He led the acquisition of more international businesses that fit these three categories and divested a few businesses that didn't fit. Each of the three divisions had manufacturing plants as well as marketing and distribution systems in North America, Asia, and Europe. The Industrial Products division included pipe, glass, industrial sealants and coatings, cleaning equipment, and truck parts. The Electronics division included specialty light bulbs, switchboards, computer chips, and resistors and capacitors for original equipment manufacturers. Consumer Products included dishes and glassware, paper and envelopes, and pencils and pens.

Structure

In 2004 David Javier replaced Sean Rhodes as president. He was very concerned about whether a new organization structure was needed for RI. The current structure was based on three major geographic areas—North America, Asia, and Europe—as illustrated in Exhibit 6.12. The various autonomous units within those regions reported to the office of the regional vice president. When several units existed in a single country, one of the subsidiary presidents was also responsible for coordinating the various

EXHIBIT 6.12
Rhodes Industries Organization Chart

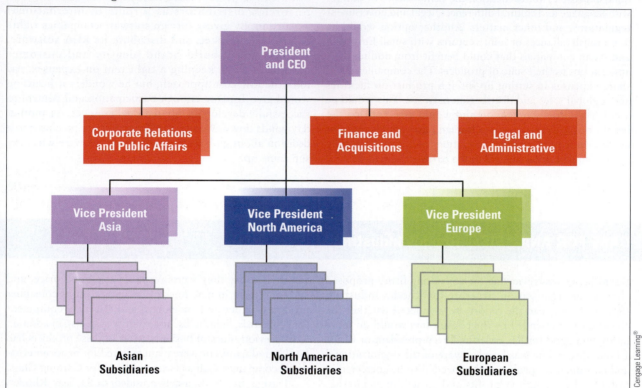

© Cengage Learning®

businesses in that country, but most coordination was done through the regional vice president. Businesses were largely independent, which provided flexibility and motivation for the subsidiary managers.

The headquarters functional departments in Ontario were rather small. The three central departments—Corporate Relations and Public Affairs, Finance and Acquisitions, and Legal and Administrative—served the corporate business worldwide. Other functions such as HR management, new product development, marketing, and manufacturing all existed within individual subsidiaries and there was little coordination of these functions across geographic regions. Each business devised its own way to develop, manufacture, and market its products in its own country and region.

Organizational Problems

The problems Javier faced at RI, which were confirmed in the report on his desk, fell into three areas. First, each subsidiary acted as an independent business, using its own reporting systems and acting to maximize its own profits. This autonomy made it increasingly difficult to consolidate financial reports worldwide and to gain the efficiencies of uniform information and reporting systems.

Second, major strategic decisions were made to benefit individual businesses or for a country's or region's local interests. Local projects and profits received more time and resources than did projects that benefited RI worldwide. For example, an electronics manufacturer in Singapore refused to increase production of chips and capacitors for sale in the United Kingdom because it would hurt the bottom line of the Singapore operation. However, the economies of scale in Singapore would more than offset shipping costs to the United Kingdom and would enable RI to close expensive manufacturing facilities in Europe, increasing RI's efficiency and profits.

Third, there had been no transfer of technology, new product ideas, or other innovations within RI. For example, a cost-saving technology for manufacturing light bulbs in Canada had been ignored in Asia and Europe. A technical innovation that provided homeowners with cell phone access to home security systems developed in Europe had been ignored in North America. The report on Javier's desk stressed that RI was failing to disperse important innovations throughout the organization. These ignored innovations could provide significant improvements in both manufacturing and marketing worldwide. The report said, "No one at RI understands all the products and locations in a way that allows RI to capitalize on manufacturing improvements and new product opportunities." The report also said that better worldwide coordination would reduce RI's costs by 7 percent each year and increase market potential by 10 percent. These numbers were too big to ignore.

Recommended Structure

The report from the consultant recommended that RI try one of two options for improving its structure. The first alternative was to create a new international department at headquarters with the responsibility to coordinate technology transfer and product manufacturing and marketing worldwide (Exhibit 6.13). This department would have a product director for each major product line—Industrial, Consumer, and Electronics—who would have authority to coordinate activities and innovations worldwide. Each product director would have a team that would travel to each region and carry information on innovations and improvements to subsidiaries in other parts of the world.

The second recommendation was to reorganize into a worldwide product structure, as shown in Exhibit 6.14. All subsidiaries worldwide associated with a product line would report to the product line business manager. The business manager and staff would be responsible for developing business strategies and for coordinating all manufacturing efficiencies and product developments worldwide for its product line.

This worldwide product structure would be a huge change for RI. Many questions came to Javier's mind. Would the subsidiaries still be competitive and adaptive in local markets if forced to coordinate with other subsidiaries around the world? Would business managers be able to change the habits of subsidiary managers toward more global behavior? Would it be a better idea to appoint product director coordinators as a first step or jump to the business manager product structure right away? Javier had a hunch that the move to worldwide product coordination made sense, but he wanted to think through all the potential problems and how RI would implement the changes.

EXHIBIT 6.13
Proposed Product Director Structure

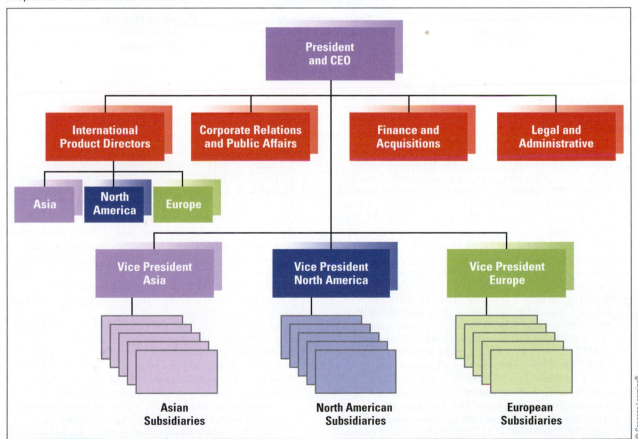

© Cengage Learning®

EXHIBIT 6.14
Proposed Worldwide Business Manager Structure

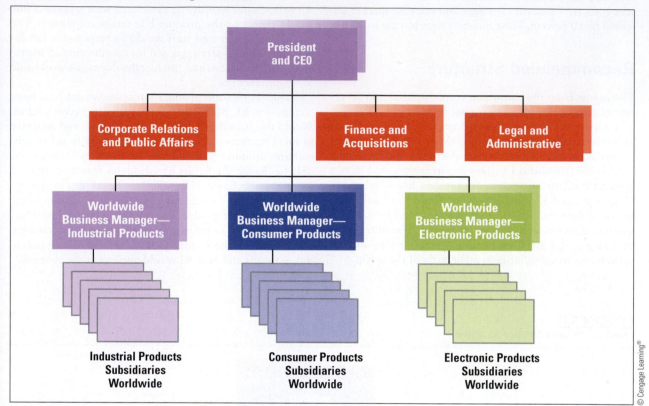

 NOTES

1. Paul Sonne and Peter Evans, "The $1.6 Billion Grocery Flop: Tesco Poised to Quit U.S.," *The Wall Street Journal*, December 5, 2012, http://online.wsj.com/news/articles/SB10001424127887324640104578160514192695162 (accessed December 6, 2012); and Shan Li, "Tesco May Sell All Fresh & Easy Stores," *Los Angeles Times*, December 6, 2012, http://articles.latimes.com/2012/dec/06/business/la-fi-tesco-fresh-easy-20121206 (accessed December 6, 2012).

2. Stuart Pfeifer, "Ron Burkle's Yucaipa Buying Fresh & Easy Stores from Tesco," *Los Angeles Times*, September 10, 2013, http://articles.latimes.com/2013/sep/10/business/la-fi-burkle-fresh-easy-20130911 (accessed March 14, 2014).

3. Bob Tita, "Deere Enhances Focus on Russia," *The Wall Street Journal*, March 24, 2011, http://online.wsj.com/article/SB1000142405274870460470457622068400380807 2.html (accessed August 9, 2011);Choe Sang-Hun, "Wal-Mart Selling Stores and Leaving South Korea," *The New York Times*, May 23, 2006, C5; and Miguel Bustillo, Robb Stewart, and Paul Sonne, "Wal-Mart Bids $4.6 Billion for South Africa's Massmart," *The Wall Street Journal*, September 28, 2010), http://online.wsj.com/article/SB10001424052748704654004575517300108186976.html (accessed September 28, 2010).

4. Michael A. Hitt and Xiaoming He, "Firm Strategies in a Changing Global Competitive Landscape," *Business Horizons* 51 (2008), 363–369.

5. George Stalk and David Michael, "What the West Doesn't Get About China," *Harvard Business Review*, June 2011, 25–27; and Zoe McKay, "Consumer Spending in China: To Buy or Not To Buy," *Forbes.com*, June 15, 2012, www.forbes.com/sites/insead/2012/06/15/consumer-spending-in-china-to-buy-or-not-to-buy/ (accessed June 29, 2012); and Adam Davidson, "Come On, China, Buy Our Stuff!" *The New York Times*, January 25, 2012, www.nytimes.com/2012/01/29/magazine/come-on-china-buy-our-stuff.html?pagewanted=all (accessed June 29, 2012).

6. Mike Ramsey, "Ford's CEO Revs up Auto Maker's China Role," *The Wall Street Journal*, April 16, 2013, B7.

7. Ian DeMartino, "Xiaomi Soars Past Apple and Samsung, Best Selling Smartphone in China in December," *GizChina.com*, http://www.gizchina.com/2014/02/08/xiaomi-soars-past-apple-samsung-best-selling-smartphone-china-december/ (accessed March 14, 2014); and Bruce Einhorn, "Lenovo Takes on Apple and Samsung in Smartphone Market," *Bloomberg BusinessWeek*, January 30, 2014, http://www.businessweek.com/articles/2014-01-30

/lenovo-takes-on-apple-and-samsung-in-smartphone-market (accessed March 14, 2014).

8. Qamar Rizvi, "Going International: A Practical, Comprehensive Template for Establishing a Footprint in Foreign Markets," *Ivey Business Journal*, May–June 2010, http://www.iveybusinessjournal.com/topics/global-business/going–international-a-practical-comprehensive-template -for-establishing-a-footprint-in-foreign-markets (accessed August 9, 2011).

9. Michael A. Hitt and Xiaoming He, "Firm Strategies in a Changing Global Competitive Landscape," *Business Horizons* 51 (2008), 363–369.

10. D. Barboza, "China Passes Japan as Second-Largest Economy," *The New York Times*, August 14, 2010, http://www.nytimes.com/2010/08/16/business/global/16yuan.html (accessed August 12, 2011).

11. Jenny Mero, "Power Shift," *Fortune*, July 21, 2008, 161; and "The Fortune Global 500," *Fortune*, http://money.cnn.com /magazines/fortune/global500/2013/ (accessed March 14, 2014).

12. This discussion is based heavily on Christopher A. Bartlett and Sumantra Ghoshal, *Transnational Management: Text, Cases, and Readings in Cross-Border Management*, 3rd ed. (Boston: Irwin McGraw-Hill, 2000), 94–96; and Anil K. Gupta and Vijay Govindarajan, "Converting Global Presence into Global Competitive Advantage," *Academy of Management Executive* 15, no. 2 (2001), 45–56.

13. Shruti Date Singh with Ganesh Nagarajan, "Small Is Beautiful," *Bloomberg Businessweek* (September 26–October 2, 2011), 33–34.

14. Lauren A.E. Schuker, "Plot Change: Foreign Forces Transform Hollywood Films," *The Wall Street Journal*, July 31, 2010, A1.

15. Brooks Barnes, "Paramount Hopes New 'Star Trek' Is a Global Crowd-Pleaser," *The New York Times*, May 3, 2013, B1.

16. Mariko Sanchanta, "Starbucks Plans Major China Expansion," *The Wall Street Journal*, April 13, 2010, http://online.wsj.com /article/SB1000142405270230460420457518149089123167 2.html (accessed April 16, 2010); and Paul Beckett, Vibhuti Agarwal, and Julie Jargon, "Starbucks Brews Plan to Enter India," *The Wall Street Journal*, January 14, 2011, http://online .wsj.com/article/SB100014240527487035834045760795935 58838756.html (accessed July 16, 2011).

17. James Hookway, "Starbucks Brings Its Culture to Vietnam," *The Wall Street Journal*, May 18, 2013, B3.

18. Eric Bellman, "Indian Firm Takes a Hollywood Cue, Using DreamWorks to Expand Empire," *The Wall Street Journal*, September 22, 2009, B1.

19. Doug DeVos, "How I Did It . . . Amway's President on Reinventing the Business to Succeed in China," *Harvard Business Review*, April 2013, 41–44.

20. Jim Carlton, "Branching Out; New Zealanders Now Shear Trees Instead of Sheep," *The Wall Street Journal*, May 29, 2003, A1, A10.

21. Charles Duhigg and Keith Bradsher, "How U.S. Lost Out on iPhone Work," *The New York Times*, January 22, 2012, A1; and David Barboza and Charles Duhigg, "China Plant Again Faces Labor Issue on iPhones," *The New York Times*, September 11, 2012, B1.

22. Dan Morse, "Cabinet Decisions; in North Carolina, Furniture Makers Try to Stay Alive," *The Wall Street Journal*, February 20, 2004, A1.

23. Nicholas Casey, "In Mexico, Auto Plants Hit the Gas," *The Wall Street Journal*, November 20, 2012, A1.

24. Keith H. Hammonds, "Smart, Determined, Ambitious, Cheap: The New Face of Global Competition," *Fast Company*, February 2003, 91–97; and W. Michael Cox and Richard Alm, "China and India: Two Paths to Economic Power," *Economic Letter*, Federal Reserve Bank of Dallas (August 2008), http://dallasfed.org/assets/documents/research /eclett/2008/el0808.pdf (accessed October 14, 2014).

25. Based on Nancy J. Adler, *International Dimensions of Organizational Behavior*, 4th ed. (Cincinnati, OH: South-Western, 2002); Theodore T. Herbert, "Strategy and Multinational Organizational Structure: An Interorganizational Relationships Perspective," *Academy of Management Review* 9 (1984), 259–271; and Laura K. Rickey, "International Expansion—U.S. Corporations: Strategy, Stages of Development, and Structure" (unpublished manuscript, Vanderbilt University, 1991).

26. Colum Murphy and Laurie Burkitt, "Hershey Launches New Brand in China," *The Wall Street Journal*, May 21, 2013, B1.

27. Julia Boorstin, "Exporting Cleaner Air," segment of "Small and Global," *Fortune Small Business*, June 2004, 36–48; and Purafil website, http://www.purafil.com/company/facts.aspx (accessed August 8, 2011).

28. Emily Maltby, "Expanding Abroad? Avoid Cultural Gaffes," *The Wall Street Journal*, January 19, 2010.

29. Vikas Sehgal, Ganesh Panneer, and Ann Graham, "A Family-Owned Business Goes Global," *Strategy + Business* (September 13, 2010), http://www.strategy-business.com /article/00045?gko=aba49 (accessed August 9, 2011).

30. Michael E. Porter, "Changing Patterns of International Competition," *California Management Review* 28 (Winter 1986), 9–40.

31. William J. Holstein, "The Stateless Corporation," *BusinessWeek*, May 14, 1990, 98–115.

32. Nancy J. Adler, *International Dimensions of Organizational Behavior*, 4th ed. (Cincinnati, OH: South-Western, 2002), 8–9; and William Holstein, Stanley Reed, Jonathan Kapstein, Todd Vogel, and Joseph Weber, "The Stateless Corporation," *BusinessWeek*, May 14, 1990, 98–105.

33. Deborah Ball, "Boss Talk: Nestlé Focuses on Long Term," *The Wall Street Journal*, November 2, 2009; Transnationale website, http://www.transnationale.org/companies/nestle .php (accessed March 17, 2010); Company-Analytics website, http://www.company-analytics.org/company/nestle.php (accessed March 17, 2010); and Nestle website, http://www .nestle.com (accessed March 17, 2010).

34. Debra Sparks, "Partners," *BusinessWeek*, Special Report: Corporate Finance, October 25, 1999, 106–112.

35. David Lei and John W. Slocum, Jr., "Global Strategic Alliances: Payoffs and Pitfalls," *Organizational Dynamics*, 19, no. 3 (Winter 1991), 17–29.

36. Vanessa O'Connell, "Department Stores: Tough Sell Abroad," *The Wall Street Journal*, May 22, 2008, B1.

37. Paul W. Beamish and Nathaniel C. Lupton, "Managing Joint Ventures," *Academy of Management Perspectives*, 23, no. 2 (May 2009), 75–94; Stratford Sherman, "Are Strategic Alliances Working?" *Fortune*, September 21, 1992, 77–78; and David Lei, "Strategies for Global Competition," *Long-Range Planning* 22 (1989), 102–109.

38. Cyrus F. Freidheim, Jr., *The Trillion-Dollar Enterprise: How the Alliance Revolution Will Transform Global Business* (New York: Perseus Books, 1998).

39. Pete Engardio, "Emerging Giants," *BusinessWeek*, July 31, 2006, 40–49.

40. Eric Bellman and Kris Hudson, "Wal-Mart to Enter India in Venture," *The Wall Street Journal*, November 28, 2006, A3.

41. Neha Thirani Bagri, "Wal-Mart Drops Ambitious Expansion Plan for India," *The Wall Street Journal*, October 20, 2013, B3.

42. Shelly Banjo, "Japan Ready for Wal-Mart," *The Wall Street Journal*, September 28, 2012, B6.

43. Laurie Burkitt, "USA Inc., a Division of China Corp.," *The Wall Street Journal*, May 31, 2013, B1; and Joel Backaler, "What the Shuanghui-Smithfield Acquisition Means for Chinese Overseas Investment," *Forbes*, November 5, 2013, http://www.forbes.com/sites/joelbackaler/2013/11/05/what -the-shuanghui-smithfield-acquisition-means-for-chinese -overseas-investment/ (accessed March 18, 2014).

44. Burkitt, "USA Inc., A Division of China Corp."

45. C.K. Prahalad and Hrishi Bhattacharyya, "Twenty Hubs and No HQ," *Strategy + Business* (February 26, 2008), http://www.strategy-business.com/article/08102?gko=8c379 (accessed July 25, 2009).

46. The discussion of these challenges is based on Bartlett and Ghoshal, *Transnational Management*.

47. Phred Dvorak, "Why Multiple Headquarters Multiply," *The Wall Street Journal*, November 19, 2007, B1.

48. Amol Sharma and Jessica E. Vascellaro, "Google and India Test the Limits of Liberty," *The Wall Street Journal*, January 4, 2010, A16.

49. Peter Koudal and Gary C. Coleman, "Coordinating Operations to Enhance Innovation in the Global Corporation," *Strategy & Leadership* 33, no. 4 (2005), 20–32; and Steven D. Eppinger and Anil R. Chitkara, "The New Practice of Global Product Development," *MIT Sloan Management Review* 47, no. 4 (Summer 2006), 22–30.

50. Yves Doz and Keeley Wilson, "Leading Ideas: Overcoming the Global Innovation Trade-Off," *Strategy + Business* 69 (Winter 2012), http://www.strategy-business.com/article/00145?pg=all (accessed March 18, 2014).

51. David W. Norton and B. Joseph Pine II, "Unique Experiences: Disruptive Innovations Offer Customers More 'Time Well Spent,'" *Strategy & Leadership* 37, no. 6 (2009), 4; and "The Power to Disrupt," *The Economist*, April 17, 2010, 16.

52. Jeffrey R. Immelt, Vijay Govindarajan, and Chris Trimble, "How GE Is Disrupting Itself," *Harvard Business Review*, October 2009, 3–11; C.K. Prahalad and Hrishi Bhattacharyya, "How to Be a Truly Global Company," *Strategy + Business* 64 (Autumn 2011), http://www.strategy -business.com/article/11308?pg=all (accessed March 19, 2014); Daniel McGinn, "Cheap, Cheap, Cheap," *Newsweek.com*, January 21, 2010, http://www.newsweek.com/2010/01/20 /cheap-cheap-cheap.html (accessed September 3, 2010); and Reena Jana, "Inspiration from Emerging Economies," *BusinessWeek*, March 23 & 30, 2009, 38–41.

53. Jeffrey Immelt, quoted in Vijay Govindarajan and Chris Trimble, "Reverse Innovation: Is It in Your Strategic Plan?" *Leadership Excellence*, May 2012, 7.

54. P. Ingrassia, "Industry Is Shopping Abroad for Good Ideas to Apply to Products," *The Wall Street Journal*, April 29, 1985, A1.

55. John W. Miller, "Indiana Steel Mill Revived with Lessons from Abroad," *The Wall Street Journal*, May 21, 2012, A1.

56. Based on Gupta and Govindarajan, "Converting Global Presence into Global Competitive Advantage"; Yves Doz and Keeley Wilson, "Leading Ideas: Overcoming the Global Innovation Trade-Off," *Strategy + Business* 69 (Winter 2012), http://www.strategy-business.com/article/00145?pg=all (accessed March 18, 2014); Giancarlo Ghislanzoni, Risto Penttinen, and David Turnbull, "The Multilocal Challenge: Managing Cross-Border Functions," *The McKinsey Quarterly*, March 2008, http://www.mckinseyquarterly .com/The_multilocal_challenge_Managing_cross-border _functions_2116 (accessed August 11, 2011); and Bert Spector, Henry W. Lane, and Dennis Shaughnessy, "Developing Innovation Transfer Capacity in a Cross-National Firm," *The Journal of Applied Behavioral Science* 45, no. 2 (June 2009), 261–279.

57. Kenichi Ohmae, "Managing in a Borderless World," *Harvard Business Review*, May–June 1989, 152–161.

58. Paloma Almodóvar Martínez and José Emilio Navas López, "Making Foreign Market Entry Decisions," *Global Business and Organizational Excellence*, January–February 2009, 52–59.

59. Choe Sang-Hun, "Wal-Mart Selling Stores and Leaving South Korea"; and Constance L. Hays, "From Bentonville to Beijing and Beyond," *The New York Times*, December 6, 2004, C6.

60. Conrad de Aenlle, "Famous Brands Can Bring Benefit, or a Backlash," *The New York Times*, October 19, 2003, Section 3, 7.

61. Cesare R. Mainardi, Martin Salva, and Muir Sanderson, "Label of Origin: Made on Earth," *Strategy + Business* 15 (Second Quarter 1999), 42–53; and Joann S. Lublin, "Place vs. Product: It's Tough to Choose a Management Model," *The Wall Street Journal*, June 27, 2001, A1, A4.

62. Mainardi, Salva, and Sanderson, "Label of Origin."

63. Prahalad and Bhattacharyya, "How to Be a Truly Global Company."

64. William Mellor, "Local Menu, Managers Are KFC's Secret in China," *The Washington Post*, February 12, 2011, http://www.washingtonpost.com/wp-dyn/content /article/2011/02/12/AR2011021202412.html (accessed February 13, 2011); and Julie Jargon and Laurie Burkitt, "KFC's Crisis in China Tests Ingenuity of Man Who Built Brand," *The Wall Street Journal*, January 12, 2014, http:// online.wsj.com/news/articles/SB1000142405270230375440 4579312681624114274 (accessed March 19, 2014).

65. José Pla-Barber, "From Stopford and Wells's Model to Bartlett and Ghoshal's Typology: New Empirical Evidence," *Management International Review* 42, no. 2 (2002), 141–156.

66. Sumantra Ghoshal and Nitin Nohria, "Horses for Courses: Organizational Forms for Multinational Corporations," *Sloan Management Review* 34, no. 2 (Winter 1993), 23–35; and Roderick E. White and Thomas A. Poynter, "Organizing for Worldwide Advantage," *Business Quarterly*, Summer 1989, 84–89.

67. Robert J. Kramer, *Organizing for Global Competitiveness: The Country Subsidiary Design* (New York: The Conference Board, 1997), 12.

68. Laura B. Pincus and James A. Belohlav, "Legal Issues in Multinational Business: To Play the Game, You Have to Know the Rules," *Academy of Management Executive* 10, no. 3, 1996, 52–61.

69. Toshiro Wakayama, Junjiro Shintaku, and Tomofumi Amano, "What Panasonic Learned in China," *Harvard Business Review*, December 2012, 109–113.

70. John D. Daniels, Robert A. Pitts, and Marietta J. Tretter, "Strategy and Structure of U.S. Multinationals: An Exploratory Study," *Academy of Management Journal* 27 (1984), 292–307.

71. Hay Group Study, reported in Mark A. Royal and Melvyn J. Stark, "Why Some Companies Excel at Conducting Business Globally," *Journal of Organizational Excellence*, Autumn 2006, 3–10.

72. Robert J. Kramer, *Organizing for Global Competitiveness: The Product Design* (New York: The Conference Board, 1994).

73. Robert J. Kramer, *Organizing for Global Competitiveness: The Business Unit Design* (New York: The Conference Board, 1995), 18–19.

74. Tina C. Ambos, Bodo B. Schlegelmilch, Björn Ambos, and Barbara Brenner, "Evolution of Organisational Structure and Capabilities in Internationalising Banks," *Long Range Planning* 42 (2009), 633–653; "Divisions," UniCredit website, http://www.unicreditgroup.eu/en/Business/Strategic_Business_Areas.htm (accessed August 10, 2011); and "Organizational Model," UniCredit website, http://www.unicreditgroup.eu/en/Business/Organizational_structure.htm (accessed August 10, 2011).

75. John Jullens, "How Emerging Giants Can Take on the World," *Harvard Business Review*, December 2013, 121–125.

76. Carol Matlack, "Nestlé Is Starting to Slim Down at Last; But Can the World's No. 1 Food Colossus Fatten Up Its Profits As It Slashes Costs?" *BusinessWeek*, October 27, 2003, 56.

77. Robert J. Kramer, *Organizing for Global Competitiveness: The Geographic Design* (New York: The Conference Board, 1993).

78. Starbucks Corporation 2012 Annual Report, http://www.google.com/url?sa=t&rct=j&q=starbucks%20company%20structure%202012&source=web&cd=7&ved=0CDUQFjAG&url=http%3A%2F%2Fphx.corporate-ir.net%2FExternal.File%3Fitem%3DUGFyZW50SUQ9NDkxNTE3fENoaWxkSUQ9NTI4OTE2fFR5cGU9MQ%3D%3D%26t%3D1&ei=zvYpU9GmLeWwygH3nYGACg&usg=AFQjCNE7nmyBSaYAZPruBGBP-Gn6u797Lw (accessed March 19, 2013).

79. Rakesh Sharma and Jyotsna Bhatnagar, "Talent Management—Competency Development: Key to Global Leadership," *Industrial and Commercial Training* 41, no. 3 (2009), 118–132.

80. Kramer, *Organizing for Global Competitiveness: The Geographic Design*, 29–31.

81. Jane XJ. Qiu and Lex Donaldson, "Stopford and Wells Were Right! MNC Matrix Structures *Do* Fit a 'High-High' Strategy," *Management International Review* 52 (2012), 671–689.

82. "Group Structure," ABB website, http://new.abb.com/about/abb-in-brief/group-structure (accessed March 10, 2014); William Taylor, "The Logic of Global Business: An Interview with ABB's Percy Barnevik," *Harvard Business Review*, March–April 1991, 91–105; Carla Rappaport, "A Tough Swede Invades the U.S.," *Fortune*, January 29, 1992, 76–79; Raymond E. Miles and Charles C. Snow, "The New Network Firm: A Spherical Structure Built on a Human Investment Philosophy," *Organizational Dynamics* 23, no. 4 (Spring 1995), 5–18; and Manfred F.R. Kets de Vries, "Making a Giant Dance," *Across the Board*, October 1994, 27–32.

83. Ambos et al., "Evolution of Organisational Structure and Capabilities in Internationalising Banks"; and "Organizational Structure Map," UniCredit website, http://www.-nicreditgroup.eu/ucg-static/downloads/-Organizational_structure_map.pdf (accessed August 10, 2011).

84. Hae-Jung Hong and Yves Doz, "L'Oréal Masters Multiculturalism," *Harvard Business Review*, June 2013, 114–199; and Prahalad and Bhattacharyya, "How to Be a Truly Global Company."

85. Vijay Govindarajan and Anil K. Gupta, "Building an Effective Global Business Team," *MIT Sloan Management Review* 42, no. 4 (Summer 2001), 63–71.

86. Charlene Marmer Solomon, "Building Teams Across Borders," *Global Workforce*, November 1998), 12–17.

87. Charles C. Snow, Scott A. Snell, Sue Canney Davison, and Donald C. Hambrick, "Use Transnational Teams to Globalize Your Company," *Organizational Dynamics* 24, no. 4 (Spring 1996), 50–67.

88. Robert Guy Matthews, "Business Technology: Thyssen's High-Tech Relay—Steelmaker Uses Computer Networks to Coordinate Operations on Three Continents," *The Wall Street Journal*, December 14, 2010, B9.

89. Benson Rosen, Stacie Furst, and Richard Blackburn, "Overcoming Barriers to Knowledge Sharing in Virtual Teams," *Organizational Dynamics* 36, no. 3 (2007), 259–273.

90. Gupta and Govindarajan, "Converting Global Presence into Global Competitive Advantage"; and Nadine Heintz, "In Spanish, It's *Un Equipo*; in English, It's a Team; Either Way, It's Tough to Build," *Inc.*, April 2008, 41–42.

91. Richard Pastore, "Global Team Management: It's a Small World After All," *CIO*, January 23, 2008, http://www.cio.com/article/174750/Global_Team_Management_It_s_a_Small_World_After_All (accessed May 20, 2008).

92. Hong and Doz, "L'Oréal Masters Multiculturalism."

93. Robert J. Kramer, *Organizing for Global Competitiveness: The Corporate Headquarters Design* (New York: The Conference Board, 1999).

94. Wakayama, Shintaku, and Amano, "What Panasonic Learned in China."

95. Ghislanzoni et al., "The Multilocal Challenge."

96. Based on Christopher A. Bartlett and Sumantra Ghoshal, *Managing Across Borders: The Transnational Solution*, 2nd ed. (Boston: Harvard Business School Press, 1998), Chapter 11, 231–249.

97. See Jay Galbraith, "Building Organizations Around the Global Customer," *Ivey Business Journal*, September–October 2001, 17–24, for a discussion of both formal and informal lateral networks in multinational companies.

98. This section and the BP examples are based on Morten T. Hansen and Nitin Nohria, "How to Build Collaborative Advantage," *MIT Sloan Management Review* 46, no. 1 (Fall 2004), 22ff.

99. Peter Gumbel, "Big Mac's Local Flavor," *Fortune*, May 5, 2008, 114–121.

100. Sumantra Ghoshal and Christopher Bartlett, "The Multinational Corporation as an Interorganizational Network," *Academy of Management Review* 15 (1990), 603–625.

101. Royston Greenwood, Samantha Fairclough, Tim Morris, and Mehdi Boussebaa, "The Organizational Design of Transnational Professional Service Firms," *Organizational Dynamics* 39, no. 2 (2010), 173–183.

102. The description of the transnational organization is based on Bartlett and Ghoshal, *Transnational Management* and *Managing Across Borders*.

103. Bettina Wassener, "Living in Asia Appeals to More Company Leaders," *The New York Times*, June 21, 2012, B3; Nirmalya Kumar and Phanish Puranam, "Have You Restructured for Global Success?" *Harvard Business Review*, October 2011, 123–128; and Dvorak, "Why Multiple Headquarters Multiply."

104. Royal and Stark, "Why Some Companies Excel at Conducting Business Globally."

105. Based on Timo O.A. Lehtinen, Mika V. Mäntylä, and Jari Vanhanen, "Development and Evaluation of a Lightweight Root Cause Analysis Method (ARCA Method): Field Studies at Four Software Companies," *Information and Software Technology* 53 (2011), 1045–1061; and Walter Kuemmerle, "Go Global—Or No?" *Harvard Business Review*, June 2001, 37–49.

Internal Design Elements

4

PART

Kjel Larsen/Moment/Getty Images

Manufacturing and Service Technologies

Learning Objectives

After reading this chapter you should be able to:

1. Identify and define an organization's core technology.
2. Explain the impact of core technology on organization design.
3. Describe Woodward's model of technical complexity, structure, and performance.
4. Understand lean manufacturing, kaizen, and the smart factory.
5. Describe the nature of service technology and its impact on organization design.
6. Recognize departmental technology and its relationship to department design.
7. Identify three types of interdependence and the respective structural priority.
8. Understand the sociotechnical systems concept.

Before reading this chapter, please check whether you agree or disagree with each of the following statements:

MANAGING BY DESIGN QUESTIONS

1 Lean manufacturing is a super-efficient form of manufacturing that produces products of top quality.

I AGREE _____   I DISAGREE _____

2 The best way for a company to provide good service is to have abundant and clear rules and procedures and make sure everyone follows them to the letter.

I AGREE _____   I DISAGREE _____

3 The design characteristics and management processes that are effective for a television station's sales department probably would not work so well for the news department.

I AGREE _____   I DISAGREE _____

An auto parts factory sends engineers around the world to learn about new production methods. A team of airline employees studies the pit stop techniques used by NASCAR racing crews. A small clothing manufacturer in New York invests in a computerized German-made knitting machine. What do all these organizations have in common? They are looking for ways to provide goods and services more efficiently and effectively.

For many manufacturers in the United States, it's a do-or-die situation. Manufacturing has been on the decline in the United States and other developed countries for years. The American manufacturing sector lost 5.8 million jobs between 1990 and 2012, according to data from the Bureau of Labor Statistics.[1] However, some manufacturing companies are applying new technology to gain a new competitive edge. Manufacturing is returning to the United States, but with a twist. It is machines, not people, who are doing most of the work these days. Parkdale Mills in South Carolina, the country's largest buyer of raw cotton, reopened in 2010 and produces about 2.5 million pounds of yarn a week with 140 workers. In 1980, that production level would have needed more than 2,000 employees. "With all the challenges we've had with cheap imports, we knew in order to survive, we'd have to take technology as far as we could," said Anderson Warlick, Parkdale's CEO. Other manufacturers are also looking at the United States as a better place to do business. A survey found that one-third of companies with manufacturing overseas were considering bringing at least some of their production back to the United States.[2] It is all because of changing technology. In IBM's 2012 CEO Study, technology topped the list of external forces that executives expect to significantly influence their organizations over the next few years.[3]

Service companies also need to keep pace with changing technology and continually strive for better approaches. Many service firms are fighting for their lives as global competition intensifies, and the cost of ineffective or outdated technology and procedures can be organizational decline and failure. This chapter explores both service and manufacturing technologies. **Technology** refers to the work processes, techniques, machines, and actions used to transform organizational inputs (materials, information, ideas) into outputs (products and services).[4] Technology is an organization's production process and includes work procedures as well as machinery.

One important theme in this chapter is how core technology influences organization design. Understanding core technology provides insight into how an organization can be designed for efficient performance.[5] An organization's **core technology** is the work process that is directly related to the organization's mission, such as teaching in a high school, medical services in a health clinic, or manufacturing at American Axle & Manufacturing (AAM). At AAM, the core technology begins with raw materials (e.g., steel, aluminum, and composite metals). Employees take action on the raw material to make a change in it (e.g., they cut and forge metals and assemble parts), thus transforming the raw material into the output of the organization (e.g., axles, drive shafts, crankshafts, and transmission parts). For a service organization like UPS, the core technology includes the production equipment (e.g., sorting machines, package handling equipment, trucks, and airplanes) and procedures for delivering packages and overnight mail. In addition, as at companies like UPS and AAM, computers and information technology have revolutionized work processes in both manufacturing and service organizations. The specific impact of new information technology on organizations will be described in Chapter 8.

Exhibit 7.1 features an example of core technology for a manufacturing plant. Note how the core technology consists of raw material inputs, a transformation work process (e.g., milling, inspection, assembly) that changes and adds value to the raw material and produces the ultimate product or service output that is sold to consumers in the environment. In today's large, complex organizations, core work processes vary widely and sometimes can be hard to pinpoint. A core technology can

EXHIBIT 7.1
Core Transformation Process for a Manufacturing Company

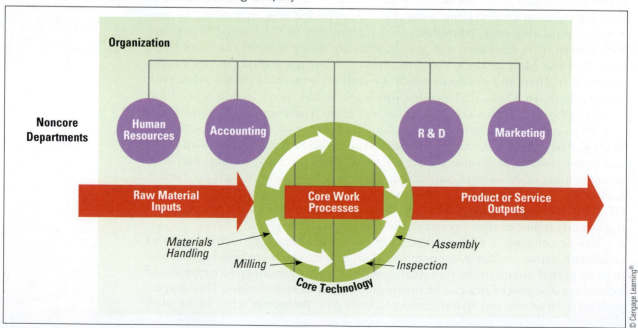

© Cengage Learning®

be partly understood by examining the raw materials flowing into the organization,[6] the variability of work activities,[7] the degree to which the production process is mechanized,[8] the extent to which one task depends on another in the workflow,[9] or the number of new product or service outputs.[10]

Organizations are also made up of many departments, each of which may use a different work process (technology) to provide a good or service within the organization. A **noncore technology** is a department work process that is important to the organization but is not directly related to its primary mission. In Exhibit 7.1, noncore work processes are illustrated by the departments of human resources (HR), accounting, research and development (R&D), and marketing. Thus, R&D transforms ideas into new products, and marketing transforms inventory into sales, each using a somewhat different work process. The output of the HR department is people to work in the organization, and accounting produces accurate statements about the organization's financial condition.

Purpose of This Chapter

In this chapter, we discuss both core and noncore work processes and their relationship to organization design. The nature of the organization's work processes must be considered in designing the organization for maximum efficiency and effectiveness. The optimum organization design is based on a variety of elements. Exhibit 7.2 illustrates that forces affecting organization design come from both outside and inside the organization. External strategic needs, such as environmental conditions, strategic direction, and organizational goals, create top-down pressure for designing the organization in such a way as to fit the environment and accomplish goals. These pressures on design have been discussed in previous chapters. However, decisions about design should also take into consideration pressures from the bottom

EXHIBIT 7.2
Pressures Affecting Organization Design

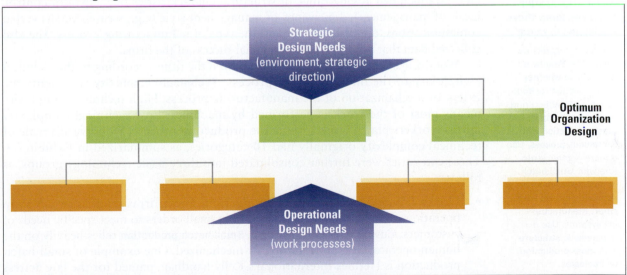

Source: Based on David A. Nadler and Michael L. Tushman, with Mark B. Nadler, *Competing by Design: The Power of Organizational Architecture* (New York: Oxford University Press, 1997), 54.

up—from the work processes that are performed to produce the organization's products or services. The operational work processes will influence the structural design associated with both the core technology and noncore departments. Thus, the subject with which this chapter is concerned is, "How should the organization be designed to accommodate and facilitate its operational work processes?"

The remainder of the chapter will unfold as follows. First, we examine how the technology for the organization as a whole influences organization structure and design. This discussion includes both manufacturing and service technologies. Second, we examine differences in departmental technologies and how the technologies influence the design and management of organizational subunits. Third, we explore how interdependence—flow of materials and information—among departments affects organization design.

Core Organization Manufacturing Technology

Manufacturing technologies include traditional manufacturing processes and contemporary applications, such as the smart factory and lean manufacturing.

Manufacturing Firms

The first and most influential study of manufacturing technology was conducted by Joan Woodward, a British industrial sociologist. Her research began as a field study of management principles in south Essex. The prevailing management wisdom at the time (1950s) was contained in what were known as universal principles of management. These principles were "one best way" prescriptions that effective organizations were expected to adopt. Woodward surveyed 100 manufacturing firms firsthand to learn how they were organized.[11] She and her research team visited each firm, interviewed managers, examined company records, and observed the manufacturing operations. Her data included a wide range of structural characteristics (e.g., span of control, levels of management), dimensions of management style (e.g., written versus verbal communications, use of rewards), and the type of manufacturing process. She also collected data that reflected the commercial success of the firms.

Woodward developed a scale and organized the firms according to the technical complexity of the manufacturing process. **Technical complexity** represents the extent of mechanization of the manufacturing process. High technical complexity means most of the work is performed by machines. Low technical complexity means workers play a larger role in the production process. Woodward's scale of technical complexity originally had 10 categories, as summarized in Exhibit 7.3. These categories were further consolidated into three basic technology groups, as follows:

- *Group I: Small-batch and unit production.* These firms tend to be job shop operations that manufacture and assemble small orders to meet specific needs of customers. Custom work is the norm. **Small-batch production** relies heavily on the human operator; it is thus not highly mechanized. One example of small-batch production is Hermes International's Kelly handbag, named for the late actress Grace Kelly. Craftsmen stitch the majority of each $7,000 bag by hand and sign

BRIEFCASE

As an organization manager, keep these guidelines in mind:

Use the categories developed by Woodward to diagnose whether the production technology in a manufacturing firm is small batch, mass production, or continuous process. Use a more organic structure with small-batch or continuous-process technologies and with smart manufacturing systems. Use a mechanistic structure with mass-production technologies.

EXHIBIT 7.3

Woodward's Classification of 100 British Firms According to Their Systems of Production

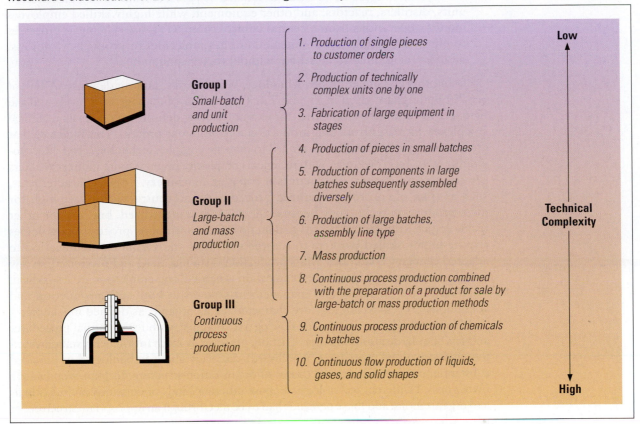

Source: Adapted from Joan Woodward, *Management and Technology* (London: Her Majesty's Stationery Office, 1958). Used with permission of Her Britannic Majesty's Stationery Office.

it when they finish.[12] A traditional distribution center at Amazon might also be considered a small-batch service operation. Workers pick products off shelves and assemble orders one at a time for customers.

- *Group II: Large-batch and mass production.* **Large-batch production** is a manufacturing process characterized by long production runs of standardized parts. Output often goes into inventory from which orders are filled because customers do not have special needs. Examples include traditional assembly lines, such as for automobiles.

- *Group III: Continuous-process production.* In **continuous-process production**, the entire process is mechanized. There is no starting and stopping. This represents mechanization and standardization one step beyond those in an assembly line. Automated machines control the continuous process, and outcomes are highly predictable. Amazon's new fully automated distribution centers could be considered continuous-process production. Amazon recently bought Kiva Systems, which provides robots that bring all the items needed for a customer's order to a worker. Other robots then take the filled boxes to the shipping door[13]. Other examples would include chemical plants, oil refineries, liquor producers, pharmaceuticals, and nuclear power plants. Royal Dutch Shell's new "Pearl GTL" (gas-to-liquid) plant in Qatar provides an illustration. At the new processing facility, natural gas flows through a maze of pipes, storage tanks, gasification units, distillers, reactors, and other equipment, while highly skilled employees monitor operations from a central control room. GTL uses chemical processes to physically change the composition of gas molecules to produce a colorless, odorless fuel similar to diesel but without diesel's pollutants.[14]

Using this classification of technology, Woodward's data made sense. A few of her key findings are given in Exhibit 7.4. The number of management levels and the manager-to-total personnel ratio, for example, show definite increases as technical complexity increases from unit production to continuous process. This indicates that greater management intensity is needed to manage complex technology. The direct-to-indirect labor ratio decreases with technical complexity because more indirect workers are required to support and maintain complex machinery. Other characteristics, such as span of control, formalized procedures, and centralization, are high for mass-production technology because the work is standardized, but low for other technologies. Unit (small-batch) production and continuous-process technologies require highly skilled workers to run the machines and verbal communication to adapt to changing conditions. Mass production is standardized and routinized, so few exceptions occur, little verbal communication is needed, and employees are less skilled.

Overall, the structure and management systems in both unit production and continuous-process technology are characterized as organic, as defined in Chapter 1 and Chapter 4. They are more free-flowing and adaptive, with fewer formal procedures and less standardization. Mass production, however, is mechanistic, with standardized jobs and formalized procedures. Woodward's discovery about technology thus provided substantial new insight into the causes of organization structure. In Joan Woodward's own words, "Different technologies impose different kinds of demands on individuals and organizations, and those demands had to be met through an appropriate structure."[15]

EXHIBIT 7.4

Relationship Between Technical Complexity and Structural Characteristics

Structural Characteristic	Technology		
	Unit Production	Mass Production	Continuous Process
Number of management levels	3	4	6
Supervisor span of control	23	48	15
Direct/indirect labor ratio	9:1	4:1	1:1
Manager/total personnel ratio	Low	Medium	High
Workers' skill level	High	Low	High
Formalized procedures	Low	High	Low
Centralization	Low	High	Low
Amount of verbal communication	High	Low	High
Amount of written communication	Low	High	Low
Overall structure	Organic	Mechanistic	Organic

Source: Based on *Management and Technology* by Joan Woodward (London: Her Majesty's Stationery Office, 1958).

Strategy, Technology, and Performance

Another portion of Woodward's study examined the success of the firms along dimensions such as profitability, market share, stock price, and reputation. As indicated in Chapter 2, the measurement of effectiveness is not simple or precise, but Woodward was able to rank firms on a scale of commercial success according to whether they displayed above-average, average, or below-average performance on strategic objectives.

Woodward compared the structure-technology relationship against commercial success and discovered that successful firms tended to be those that had complementary structures and technologies. Many of the organizational characteristics of the successful firms were near the average of their technology category, as shown in Exhibit 7.4. Below-average firms tended to depart from the structural characteristics for their technology type. Another conclusion was that structural characteristics could be interpreted as clustering into organic and mechanistic management systems, as defined in Chapters 1 and 4. Successful small-batch and continuous-process organizations had organic designs, and successful mass-production organizations had mechanistic designs. Subsequent research has replicated her findings.[16]

What this illustrates for today's companies is that strategy, structure, and technology need to be aligned, especially when competitive conditions change.[17] For example, consider changes in the mattress business that required Sealy to adopt a more organic design. With the increasing popularity of mattresses from Sleep Number and Tempur-Pedic, combined with the slowdown in the housing market, Sealy managers saw sales of the company's high-end Stearns & Foster line decline significantly. Sealy revamped how it designs mattresses, using cross-functional teams and joining with design firm IDEO to design a prettier bed that differentiated Stearns & Foster and tapped into people's belief that they were truly getting a premium product.[18] The company also adopted lean manufacturing (discussed later in this chapter) to be more competitive in the new environment.

Failing to adopt appropriate new technologies to support strategy, or adopting a new technology and failing to realign strategy to match it, can lead to poor performance. Today's increased global competition means more volatile markets, shorter product life cycles, and more sophisticated and knowledgeable consumers; and flexibility to meet these new demands has become a strategic imperative.[19] Manufacturing companies can adopt new technologies to support the strategy of flexibility. However, organization design and management processes must also be realigned, as a highly mechanistic design hampers flexibility and prevents the company from reaping the benefits of the new technology.[20]

BRIEFCASE

As an organization manager, keep this guideline in mind:

When adopting a new technology, realign strategy, structure, and management processes to achieve top performance.

Contemporary Applications

The factory of today is far different from the industrial firms Woodward studied in the 1950s. In particular, computers and information technology have revolutionized all types of manufacturing—small batch, large batch, and continuous process. At the Marion, North Carolina, plant of Rockwell Automation's Power Systems Division, for example, highly trained employees can quickly handle a build-on-demand unit of one, thanks to computers, wireless technology, and radio-frequency identification (RFID) systems. In one instance, the Marion plant built, packaged, and delivered a replacement bearing for installation in an industrial air-conditioning unit in Texas only 15 hours after the customer called for help.[21]

Trends

As illustrated by the earlier example of the Parkdale textile factory, technology has transformed today's factories. For the most part, they no longer are hot, dusty, crowded shops full of overworked employees but rather streamlined, modern installations where the air quality, temperature, and humidity are tightly controlled for the sake of sophisticated machinery. Technology has also transformed the service industry. Yet there are both good and bad aspects of the increasing complexity of technology.

Extreme Complexity. Boeing called the production of its 787 Dreamliner a "reinvention of manufacturing." New technology enabled the plane to be made from composites, a first for the industry. It is 20 percent more fuel efficient and has 20 percent fewer emissions. But the launch of the plane was delayed by years, and when it did come out, it was plagued by one after another quality problem, including fuel leaks, a cracked cockpit window, wiring problems, and overheating batteries.[22]

Boeing isn't the only company to suffer from pushing the boundaries of complex new technology. As another example, think about the problems in the cruise industry.

IN PRACTICE
Carnival Cruise Lines

In the fall of 2013, a string of incidents at Carnival Cruise Lines had some customers vowing never to cruise with Carnival again. In the worst episode, an engine room fire left the Carnival Triumph stranded without power in the Gulf of Mexico with 4,200 people on board. As the four-day cruise doubled in length, food and water were scarce, passengers sweltered with no air-conditioning, and the media reported overflowing toilets and described the scene as "hellish." Carnival managers are reevaluating the strategy of building ever larger ships that are almost too complex to handle when an emergency arises.

The dangers of that strategy became most visible when the Costa Concordia ran aground and capsized off the coast of Italy, killing 32 people. The accident revealed fatal flaws in Carnival's safety and emergency procedures. Captain Francesco Schettino made many errors and is said to have contributed to the crisis by failing to respond for 45 minutes after the crew told him that the ship was flooding and its motors were dead. However, part of the danger also came from the huge size of the ship and the lack of industry oversight. Today's largest cruise ships are nearly five times the size they were in 1985.[23]

The recent string of accidents in the cruise industry has prompted safety experts and regulators to push for more accountability, saying the strategy of building supersize ships is fraught with risk. "Given the size of today's ships, any problem immediately becomes a very big problem," said Michael Bruno, dean of the engineering school at the Stevens Institute of Technology.[24] This chapter's BookMark provides a historical look at the dangers of failing to understand and effectively manage highly complex technological advances.

BOOKMARK 7.0 HAVE YOU READ THIS BOOK?

Inviting Disaster: Lessons from the Edge of Technology
By James R. Chiles

Dateline: Paris, France, July 25, 2000. Less than two minutes after Air France Concorde Flight 4590 departs from Charles DeGaulle Airport, something goes horribly wrong. Trailing fire and billowing black smoke, the huge plane rolls left and crashes into a hotel, killing all 109 people aboard and four more on the ground. It's just one of the technological disasters James R. Chiles describes in his book, *Inviting Disaster: Lessons from the Edge of Technology*.

One of Chiles's main points is that advancing technology makes possible the creation of machines that strain the human ability to understand and safely operate them. For example, managers' overconfidence that they understood blowout preventer technology contributed to the 2010 BP-Transocean oil rig disaster at Deepwater Horizon, and the inability to safely manage complex nuclear technology led to dangerous radiation leaks at Japan's Fukushima Daiichi nuclear power plant following a 2011 earthquake and tsunami. Chiles asserts that the margins of safety are growing thinner as the energies we harness become more powerful and the time between invention and use grows shorter. He believes that today, "for every twenty books on the pursuit of success, we need a book on how things fly into tiny pieces despite enormous effort and the very highest ideals." All complex systems, he reminds us, are destined to fail at some point.

HOW THINGS FLY INTO PIECES: EXAMPLES OF SYSTEM FRACTURES

Chiles uses historical calamities such as the sinking of the *Titanic* and modern disasters such as the explosion of the space shuttle *Challenger* to illustrate the dangers of *system fracture*, a chain of events that involves human error in response to malfunctions in complex machinery. Disaster begins when one weak point links up with others.

- *Sultana* (American steamboat on the Mississippi River near Memphis, Tennessee), April 25, 1865. The boat, designed to carry a maximum of 460 people, was carrying more than 2,000 Union ex-prisoners north—as well as 200 additional crew and passengers—when three of the four boilers exploded, killing 1,800 people. One of the boilers had been temporarily patched to cover a crack, but the patch was too thin. Operators failed to compensate by resetting the safety valve.

- *Piper Alpha* (offshore drilling rig in the North Sea), July 6, 1988. The offshore platform processed large volumes of natural gas from other rigs via pipe. A daytime work crew, which didn't complete the repair of a gas-condensate pump, relayed a verbal message to the next shift, but workers turned the pump on anyway. When the temporary seal on the pump failed, a fire trapped crewmen with no escape route, killing 167 crew and rescue workers.

- *Union Carbide (India) Ltd.* (release of highly toxic chemicals into a community), Bhopal, Madhya Pradesh, India, December 3, 1984. Three competing theories exist for how water got into a storage tank, creating a violent reaction that sent highly toxic methyl isocyanate for herbicides into the environment, causing an estimated 7,000 deaths: (1) poor safety maintenance, (2) sabotage, or (3) worker error.

WHAT CAUSES SYSTEM FRACTURES?

There is a veritable catalog of causes that lead to such disasters, from design errors, insufficient operator training, and poor planning to greed and mismanagement. Chiles wrote his book as a reminder that technology takes us into risky locales, whether it be outer space, up a 2,000-foot tower, or into a chemical processing plant. Chiles also cites examples of potential disasters that were averted by quick thinking and appropriate response. To help prevent system fractures, managers can create organizations in which people throughout the company are expert at picking out the subtle signals of real problems—and where they are empowered to report them and take prompt action.

Inviting Disaster: Lessons from the Edge of Technology, by James R. Chiles, is published by HarperBusiness.

What About People? At a Philips factory in China, hundreds of workers assemble electric shavers by hand. At a sister plant in the Netherlands, 128 robotic arms do the same work, guided by video cameras. The arms work so fast they are enclosed in cages to keep them from injuring the few humans supervising them. The factory in the Netherlands has about a tenth as many workers as the one in China. UPS and FedEx still employ tens of thousands of people to load and unload trucks, but robotic automation is in the near future.[25] A new breed of dexterous robots are replacing workers in both manufacturing and service operations.

The technological and the human systems of an organization are intertwined. So what happens to the people when robots or other machines take over doing the work? Like it or not, it is the wave of the future, and probably the only way manufacturers in developed countries can compete with low-wage countries. Technological advances typically destroy some jobs but create others, but as we described in Chapter 4 and earlier in this chapter, recent technological advances are destroying more jobs than they are creating. Even white-collar jobs in finance, human resources, and other functions are being replaced by sophisticated information technology (IT). IT will be discussed in more detail in the next chapter.

Advanced technology is making companies more efficient and more productive, but there are some things robots can't do. Harley-Davidson, for example, found that humans are much more flexible, as we described in a Chapter 1 In Practice example, so the company still uses people to build motorcycles that have 1,200 different configurations. Human beings can adjust on the fly, whereas robots cannot. At Harley, and at other companies, robots do the simple and repetitive tasks and people handle the more complex and dynamic ones. Speaking of robots, "it's not a one-for-one replacement," says Rodney Brooks, a former MIT robotics professor. "People are so much better at certain things."[26]

The Smart Factory

Two significant contemporary applications of advanced technology for mass production are the smart factory and lean manufacturing. Most of today's factories use a variety of new manufacturing technologies, including robots, numerically controlled machine tools, RFID, wireless technology, and computerized software for product design, engineering analysis, and remote control of machinery. A study found, for example, that manufacturers in the United States use more than six times the amount of information-processing equipment (computers, etc.) as they used 20 years ago.[27] This increase reflects the growing uncertainty and tough challenges manufacturing organizations face, including globalization of operations, increased competition, greater product complexity, and the need to coordinate with a larger number of business partners.[28] The ultimate automated factories are referred to as **smart factories**.[29] Also called *digital factories*, *computer-integrated manufacturing*, *flexible manufacturing systems*, *advanced manufacturing technology*, or *agile manufacturing*, smart factories link manufacturing components that previously stood alone. Thus, robots, machines, product design, and engineering analysis are coordinated by a single computer system in an interconnected web of information and production.[30]

The smart factory typically includes several subcomponents:

- *Computer-aided design (CAD).* Computers are used to assist in the drafting, design, and engineering of new parts. Designers guide their computers to draw specified configurations on the screen, including dimensions and component details. Hundreds of design alternatives can be explored, as can scaled-up or scaled-down versions of the original.[31]
- *Computer-aided manufacturing (CAM).* Computer-controlled machines in materials handling, fabrication, production, and assembly greatly increase the speed at which items can be manufactured. CAM also permits a production line to shift rapidly from producing one product to any variety of other products by changing software codes in the computer. CAM enables the production line to quickly honor customer requests for changes in product design and product mix.[32]

- *Robots*. Automakers have been using large robots on the assembly line for years, but a new generation of smaller, simpler robots enables small and medium size manufacturers to benefit from them also. These new robots can communicate and collaborate with human employees and help with every phase of the manufacturing process, from delivering parts to assembling products to warehousing to packing and shipping.[33] Aided by new imaging and human interface software and advances in object detection and sensor technology, these robots can be used by manufacturers of all sizes because they can run "cage-free." They can sense and react to their "co-workers," have built-in safety mechanisms, and are capable of making commonsense decisions while performing repetitive tasks.[34]
- *3-D Printing*. Also known as *additive manufacturing*, 3-D printing builds objects one successive layer of material at a time. The technology lets engineers model an object, whether it is a Barbie doll or a Ford truck axle, on a computer and print it out with plastic, metal, or composite materials rather than cutting or drilling the object from molds. This results in less wasted materials and allows manufacturers to get products to customers more quickly. [35]

In a smart factory, a new product can be designed on the computer and a prototype can be produced untouched by human hands. The ideal factory can switch quickly from one product to another, working fast and with precision, without paperwork or record keeping to bog down the system.[36] In addition, new software can coordinate information from multiple departments and organizations involved in a design, and virtual designs can even include an entirely new factory.

The Siemens Electronic Works facility in Amberg, Germany, is a good example of a smart factory. Its integrated smart machines coordinate the production and distribution of the company's Simatic control devices, which involves a custom, build-to-order process involving more than 1.6 billion components from 250 suppliers to make 950 different products in 50,000 annual product variations. And they do it all with a 99 percent reliability rate and record only about 15 defects per million.[37] Automakers also provide good examples of the benefits of the smart factory. Honda has achieved an amazing degree of flexibility at its plant in East Liberty, Ohio. Considered the most flexible auto manufacturer in North America, the Honda plant can switch from making Civic compacts to making the longer, taller CRV crossover in as little as five minutes. All that's needed to switch assembly from one type of vehicle to another is to put different "hands" on the robots to handle different parts. The ability to quickly adjust inventory levels of different types of vehicles has been a key strategic advantage for Honda in an era of volatile gasoline prices and shifting vehicle popularity.[38]

Lean Manufacturing

The smart factory reaches its ultimate level to improve quality, customer service, and cost cutting when all parts are used interdependently and combined with flexible management processes in a system referred to as lean manufacturing. **Lean manufacturing** uses highly trained employees at every stage of the production process, who take a painstaking approach to squeeze out all waste to improve value to the customer. Lean manufacturing is typically combined with Six Sigma. *Six Sigma* is a highly ambitious quality standard that specifies a goal of no more than 3.4 defects per million parts.[39] However, Six Sigma has deviated from its precise definition to become a generic term for a quality-control approach that emphasizes a disciplined and relentless pursuit of higher quality and lower costs. In a survey by *Industry Week* and the Manufacturing Performance Institute asking 745 manufacturers which improvement programs they used, lean manufacturing was by far the most common answer, with more than 40 percent reporting the use of lean manufacturing techniques.[40]

Lean Six Sigma uses a team-driven holistic approach to eliminating waste and improving quality.[41] It incorporates technological elements, such as CAD/CAM, but the heart of lean Six Sigma is not machines or software, but people. Lean manufacturing requires changes in organizational systems, such as decision-making processes and management processes, as well as an organizational culture that supports active employee participation, a quality perspective, and focus on the customer. Employees are trained to attack waste and strive for continuous improvement in all areas.[42]

Kaizen. One lesson of lean manufacturing is that there is always room for improvement. Continuous improvement, or *kaizen*, is the implementation of a large number of small, incremental improvements in all areas of the organization on an ongoing basis. All employees learn that they are expected to contribute by initiating changes in their own job activities. The basic philosophy is that improving things a little bit at a time, all the time, has the highest probability of success. Innovations can start simple, and employees can build on their success in this unending process. A commitment to *kaizen* has allowed La-Z-Boy in Dayton, Tennessee, to thrive even during the recent recession.

 **IN PRACTICE**

La-Z-Boy

"If we were doing business the same way we did in 2005," said La-Z-Boy's Continuous Improvement Manager David Robinson, "somebody else would be here because we would already be closed. We are $50 million a year better now than we were."

The facility's managers and engineers were trained in Six Sigma, and cross-functional teams have completed 24 *kaizen* events focused on safety, quality, and productivity. A significant process improvement at the Dayton facility is the Flawless Launch Program, which assigns a production engineer to make sure quality and manufacturability are designed into all new products. That way, Robinson points out, the company knows the tooling and equipment that will be needed to produce the product repeatedly, at low cost, and relatively error-free. As an example, he points to the plant's first attempt to manufacture an electric lift chair. It had about a 40 percent failure rate in the field. After reintroducing it with the flawless launch process, Robinson reports, "We now have a fraction of 1 percent failure in the field."[43]

La-Z-Boy managers embarked on their lean manufacturing quest some years ago, as did many North American companies that started studying the practices of lean manufacturing pioneer Toyota and other Japanese companies. For example, a small improvement at Toyota's new Miyagi factory is to position vehicles side-by-side on the assembly line rather than tip-to-tail, which cuts installation costs and increases productivity because workers don't have to walk as far between cars.[44]

ASSESS YOUR ANSWER

1 **Lean manufacturing is a super-efficient form of manufacturing that produces products of top quality.**

ANSWER: *Agree.* Lean manufacturing techniques have been implemented in hundreds of organizations all over the world and have led to dramatic improvements in quality, productivity, and efficiency. Lean manufacturing continues to be an important tool for manufacturing firms, and smart managers in service firms are also learning to benefit from lean thinking.

Mass Customization. Lean manufacturing and the smart factory have paved the way for **mass customization**, which refers to using mass-production technology to quickly and cost-effectively assemble goods that are uniquely designed to fit the demands of individual customers. The goal is to provide customers with exactly what they want when they want it.[45] Mass customization has been applied to products as diverse as farm machinery, water heaters, clothing, computers, and industrial detergents.[46] A customer can order a Sony laptop with one of several hard drive capacities, processing chip speeds, and software packages, or a BMW automobile with the exact combination of features and components desired. About 60 percent of the cars BMW sells in Europe are built to order.[47] Oshkosh Truck Company thrived during an industry-wide slump in sales by offering customized fire, cement, garbage, and military trucks. Firefighters often travel to the plant to watch their new vehicle take shape, sometimes bringing paint chips to customize the color of their fleet.[48]

The awesome advantage of the smart factory is that products of different sizes, types, and customer requirements freely intermingle on the assembly line, enabling large factories to deliver a wide range of custom-made products at low mass-production costs.[49] Computerized machines can make instantaneous changes—such as putting a larger screw in a different location—without slowing the production line. A manufacturer can turn out an infinite variety of products in unlimited batch sizes, as illustrated in Exhibit 7.5.

EXHIBIT 7.5

Relationship of Smart Manufacturing Technology to Traditional Technologies

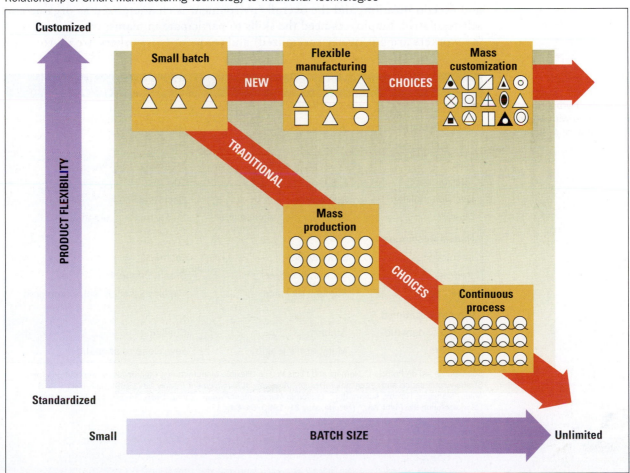

Source: Based on Jack Meredith, "The Strategic Advantages of New Manufacturing Technologies for Small Firms," *Strategic Management Journal* 8 (1987), 249–258; Paul Adler, "Managing Flexible Automation," *California Management Review* (Spring 1988), 34–56; and Otis Port, "Custom-made Direct from the Plant," *BusinessWeek/21st Century Capitalism*, November 18, 1994, 158–159.

In traditional manufacturing systems studied by Woodward, choices were limited to the diagonal. Small batch allowed for high product flexibility and custom orders, but because of the "craftsmanship" involved in custom-making products, batch size was necessarily small. Mass production could have large-batch size, but offered limited product flexibility. Continuous process could produce a single standard product in unlimited quantities. The smart factory allows plants to break free of this diagonal and to increase both batch size and product flexibility at the same time. When taken to its ultimate level, the smart factory allows for mass customization, with each specific product tailored to customer specification. This high-level use of smart systems has been referred to as *computer-aided craftsmanship*.[50]

Performance and Structural Implications

Studies suggest that in smart factories, machine utilization is more efficient, labor productivity increases, scrap rates decrease, and product variety and customer satisfaction increase.[51] Many U.S. manufacturing companies are reinventing the factory using digital systems and lean manufacturing techniques to increase productivity.

Research into the relationship between the smart factory and organizational characteristics has discovered the organizational patterns summarized in Exhibit 7.6. Compared with traditional mass-production technologies, the smart factory has a narrow span of control, few hierarchical levels, adaptive tasks, low specialization, and decentralization, and the overall environment is characterized as organic and self-regulative. Employees need the skills to participate in teams; training is broad (so workers are not overly specialized) and frequent (so workers are up to date).

EXHIBIT 7.6

Comparison of Organizational Characteristics Associated with Mass Production and Smart Factories

Characteristic	Mass Production	Smart Factory
Structure		
Span of control	Wide	Narrow
Hierarchical levels	Many	Few
Tasks	Routine, repetitive	Adaptive, craftlike
Specialization	High	Low
Decision making	Centralized	Decentralized
Overall	Bureaucratic, mechanistic	Self-regulating, organic
Human Resources		
Interactions	Standalone	Teamwork
Training	Narrow, one time	Broad, frequent
Expertise	Manual, technical	Cognitive, social; solve problems
Interorganizational		
Customer demand	Stable	Changing
Suppliers	Many, arm's length	Few, close relationships

Sources: Based on Patricia L. Nemetz and Louis W. Fry, "Flexible Manufacturing Organizations: Implications for Strategy Formulation and Organization Design," *Academy of Management Review* 13 (1988), 627–638; Paul S. Adler, "Managing Flexible Automation," *California Management Review*, Spring 1988, 34–56; and Jeremy Main, "Manufacturing the Right Way," *Fortune*, May 21, 1990, 54–64.

Expertise tends to be cognitive so workers can process abstract ideas and solve problems. Interorganizational relationships in smart factories are characterized by changing demand from customers—which is easily handled with the new technology—and close relationships with a few suppliers that provide top-quality raw materials.[52]

Technology alone cannot give organizations the benefits of flexibility, quality, increased productivity, and greater customer satisfaction. Research suggests that organizational structures and management processes also must be redesigned to take advantage of the new technology.[53] When top managers make a commitment to implement new structures and processes that empower workers and support a learning and knowledge-creating environment, the smart factory can help companies be more competitive.[54]

Core Organization Service Technology

Another big change occurring in the technology of organizations is the growing service sector. More than half of all businesses in the United States are service organizations, and according to one estimate nearly 90 percent of the U.S. workforce is employed in services, such as restaurants, hospitals, hotels and resorts, airlines, retail, financial services, and information services.[55]

Service Firms

Service technologies are different from manufacturing technologies and, in turn, require a different organization design.

Definition. Whereas manufacturing organizations achieve their primary purpose through the production of products, service organizations accomplish their primary purpose through the production and provision of services, such as education, healthcare, transportation, banking, and hospitality. Studies of service organizations have focused on the unique dimensions of service technologies. The characteristics of service technology are compared to those of manufacturing technology in Exhibit 7.7.

The most obvious difference is that service technology produces an *intangible output*, such as social networking provided by Facebook, rather than a tangible product, such as a refrigerator produced by General Electric. A service is abstract and often consists of knowledge and ideas rather than a physical product. Thus, whereas manufacturers' products can be inventoried for later sale, services are characterized by *simultaneous production and consumption*. A client meets with a doctor or attorney, for example, and students and teachers come together in the classroom or over the Internet. A service is an intangible product that does not exist until it is requested by the customer. It cannot be stored, inventoried, or viewed as a finished good. If a service is not consumed immediately upon production, it disappears.[56] This typically means that service firms are *labor* and *knowledge intensive*, with many employees needed to meet the needs of customers, whereas manufacturing firms tend to be *capital intensive*, relying on mass production, continuous process, and smart manufacturing technologies.[57]

EXHIBIT 7.7
Differences Between Manufacturing and Service Technologies

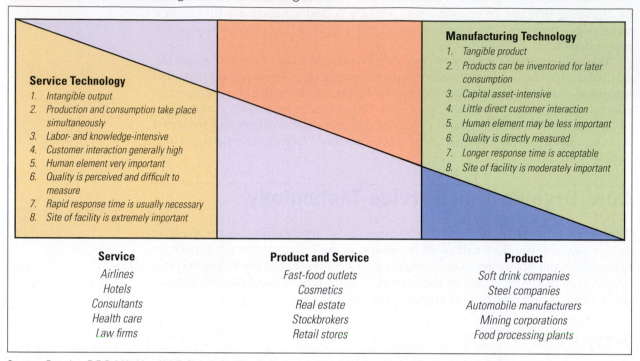

Service Technology	**Manufacturing Technology**
1. Intangible output	1. Tangible product
2. Production and consumption take place simultaneously	2. Products can be inventoried for later consumption
3. Labor- and knowledge-intensive	3. Capital asset-intensive
4. Customer interaction generally high	4. Little direct customer interaction
5. Human element very important	5. Human element may be less important
6. Quality is perceived and difficult to measure	6. Quality is directly measured
7. Rapid response time is usually necessary	7. Longer response time is acceptable
8. Site of facility is extremely important	8. Site of facility is moderately important

Service	**Product and Service**	**Product**
Airlines	Fast-food outlets	Soft drink companies
Hotels	Cosmetics	Steel companies
Consultants	Real estate	Automobile manufacturers
Health care	Stockbrokers	Mining corporations
Law firms	Retail stores	Food processing plants

Sources: Based on F. F. Reichheld and W. E. Sasser, Jr., "Zero Defections: Quality Comes to Services," *Harvard Business Review* 68 (September–October 1990), 105–111; and David E. Bowen, Caren Siehl, and Benjamin Schneider, "A Framework for Analyzing Customer Service Orientations in Manufacturing," *Academy of Management Review* 14 (1989), 75–95.

As an organization manager, keep these guidelines in mind:

Use the concept of service technology to evaluate the production process in nonmanufacturing firms. Services are intangible and must be located close to the customer. Hence, service organizations may have an organization design with fewer boundary roles, greater geographical dispersion, decentralization, highly skilled employees in the technical core, and generally less control than in manufacturing organizations.

Direct interaction between customer and employee is generally very high with services, while there is little direct interaction between customers and employees in the technical core of a manufacturing firm. This direct interaction means that the *human element* (employees) becomes extremely important in service firms. Whereas most people never meet the workers who manufactured their cars, they interact directly with the salesperson who sells them a new truck or the Avis associate who rents them a car while on vacation. The treatment received from the salesperson— or from a doctor, lawyer, or hairstylist—affects the perception of the service received and the customer's level of satisfaction. The *quality of a service is perceived* and cannot be directly measured and compared in the same way that the quality of a tangible product can. Another characteristic that affects customer satisfaction and perception of quality service is *rapid response time*. A service must be provided when the customer wants and needs it. When you take a friend to dinner, you want to be seated and served in a timely manner; you would not be very satisfied if the hostess or manager told you to come back tomorrow when there would be more tables or servers available to accommodate you.

The final defining characteristic of service technology is that *site selection is often much more important* here than with manufacturing. Because services are intangible, they have to be located where the customer wants to be served. Services are dispersed and located geographically close to customers. For example, fast-food franchises usually disperse their facilities into local stores. Most towns of even moderate size today have two or more McDonald's restaurants rather than one large one, for example, in order to provide service where customers want and need it.

In reality, it is difficult to find organizations that reflect 100 percent service or 100 percent manufacturing characteristics. Some service firms take on characteristics of manufacturers, and vice versa. Many manufacturing firms are placing a greater emphasis on customer service to differentiate themselves and be more competitive. In addition, manufacturing organizations have departments such as purchasing, human resources, and marketing that are based on service technology. On the other hand, organizations such as gas stations, stockbrokers, retail stores, and restaurants belong to the service sector, but the provision of a product is a significant part of the transaction. The vast majority of organizations involve some combination of products and services. The important point is that all organizations can be classified along a continuum that includes both manufacturing and service characteristics, as illustrated in Exhibit 7.7. This chapter's "How Do You Fit the Design?" questionnaire will give you some insight into whether you are better suited to be a manager in a service organization or a manufacturing firm.

The Trend Toward Lean Services. Service firms have always tended toward providing *customized output*—that is, providing exactly the service each customer wants and needs. When you visit a hairstylist, you don't automatically get the same cut the stylist gave the three previous clients. The stylist cuts your hair the way you request it. Pandora.com, whose mission is "to play only music you love," provides its 250 million or so registered users with a custom radio channel that broadcasts a set of music that fits their preferences.[58]

Customer expectations of what constitutes good service are rising. Zappos.com provides free shipping on both orders and returns. Amazon.com not only aims to have the lowest price and the fastest delivery, it also helps outside retailers bring their customer service up to par and covers for their service shortcomings if they don't. Insurance and financial services giant USAA cross-trained its agents and call center representatives so that customers can get answers to their questions about any product or service rather than being switched around from one agent to another.[59] At Montefiore Medical Center in the Bronx, New York, rather than having specialized medical, surgical, cardiothoracic, and neurosurgical intensive care units (ICUs), Dr. Vladimir Kvetan combined them into a central critical-care department to increase efficiency and improve patient care. Kvetan, director of critical-care medicine, is continually thinking of ways to provide better care more efficiently, which means Montefiore rarely encounters the critical-care bottlenecks that many other large hospitals experience.[60]

The expectation for better service is pushing service firms in industries from food service to package delivery to take a lesson from manufacturing.[61] Japan Post, under pressure to cut a $191 million loss on operations, hired Toyota's Toshihiro Takahashi to help apply the principles of the lean Toyota Production System to the collection, sorting, and delivery of mail. In all, Takahashi's team came up with 370 improvements and reduced the post office's person-hours by 20 percent. The waste reduction is expected to cut costs by around $350 million a year.[62] Numerous other service firms, in the United States as well as in other countries, have also applied lean principles in recent years. Starbucks Corporation hired a vice president of lean thinking who has been traveling the world with a *lean team* to work with employees to find ways to cut waste and improve customer service. Panera Bread Company is looking for ways to improve sales and profits because long lines at the sandwich chain's outlets have caused some customers to walk out and inaccurate orders have caused others not to return.[63] Another good example comes from Seattle Children's Hospital, which applied lessons from manufacturing to increase efficiency and improve patient care.

HOW DO YOU FIT THE DESIGN?

MANUFACTURING VERSUS SERVICE

The questions that follow ask you to describe your behavior. For each question, check the answer that best describes you.

1. I am usually running late for class or other appointments:
   a. Yes
   b. No

2. When taking a test I prefer:
   a. Subjective questions (discussion or essay)
   b. Objective questions (multiple choice)

3. When making decisions, I typically:
   a. Go with my gut—what feels right
   b. Carefully weigh each option

4. When solving a problem, I would more likely:
   a. Take a walk, mull things over, and then discuss
   b. Write down alternatives, prioritize them, and then pick the best

5. I consider time spent daydreaming as:
   a. A viable tool for planning my future
   b. A waste of time

6. To remember directions, I typically:
   a. Visualize the information
   b. Make notes

7. My work style is mostly:
   a. Juggle several things at once
   b. Concentrate on one task at a time until complete

8. My desk, work area, and laundry area are typically:
   a. Cluttered
   b. Neat and organized

Scoring: Count the number of checked "a" items and "b" items. Each "a" represents right-brain processing, and each "b" represents left-brain processing. If you scored 6 or higher on either, you have a distinct processing style. If you checked fewer than 6 for either, you probably have a balanced style.

Interpretation: People have two thinking processes—one visual and intuitive in the right half of the brain, and the other verbal and analytical in the left half of the brain. The thinking process you prefer predisposes you to certain types of knowledge and information—technical reports, analytical information, and quantitative data (left brain) versus talking to people, thematic impressions, and personal intuition (right brain)—as effective input to your thinking and decision making. Manufacturing organizations typically use left-brain processing to handle data based on physical, measurable technology. Service organizations typically use right-brain processing to interpret less tangible situations and serve people in a direct way. Left-brain processing has been summarized as based on logic; right-brain processing has been summarized as based on love.

Source: Adapted from Carolyn Hopper, *Practicing Management Skills* (Houghton Mifflin, 2003); and Jacquelyn Wonder and Priscilla Donovan, "Mind Openers," *Self* (March 1984).

IN PRACTICE

Seattle Children's Hospital

Ten years ago, Seattle Children's Hospital set a goal to become the top hospital of its type in the country. But with healthcare costs rising nationwide, administrators needed to find ways not only to improve patient care but also cut costs. They did it by applying lean techniques through a program called "Continuous Performance Improvement" (CPI). The main goals of CPI are to reduce waste and increase value for customers (patients).

CPI examines every aspect of patients' experience, from the time they arrive in the parking lot until they are discharged. Managers involved all hospital staff in studying the flow of medicines, patients, and information in the same way plant managers study the flow of materials in a manufacturing plant, and asked them to find ways to improve processes. Patients often had to wait for a non-emergency MRI for nearly a month. Now, that wait time has been cut to one or two days thanks to more efficient scheduling. Standardizing the instrument cart for specific types of surgeries cut inventory costs and reduced instrument preparation errors. An operating room team saw that a tonsillectomy procedure required filling out 21 separate forms and worked to cut that number down to 11. Overhauling the procedure for sterilizing surgical instruments increased the number of surgeries the hospital could perform. Overall, the CPI program helped cut costs per patient by 3.7 percent, for a savings of $23 million. The hospital has also been able to serve thousands more patients without expanding or adding beds.

A key aspect of the CPI program was shifting corporate culture by training doctors, nurses, administrators, and others in new methods and ways of thinking. Using CPI, teams can make changes any time they think they can improve a process or cut waste (defined as anything that doesn't add value for the patient). Even small changes that increase efficiency and improve patient care are celebrated by hospital administrators. "Their support fosters the idea that everyone can make positive changes in their departments," said one physician.[64]

With the costs of medical care soaring, other healthcare organizations are also taking a continuous improvement approach to cutting costs without sacrificing quality of care. "In healthcare, you can't do one big thing and reduce the price," says Dr. Devi Shetty, who runs a hospital in India that performs open-heart surgery for about 10 percent of the cost charged by hospitals in the United States (described in a Chapter 3 In Practice). "We have to do 1,000 small things."[65]

Designing the Service Organization

The feature of service technologies with a distinct influence on organizational structure and control systems is the need for technical core employees to be close to the customer.[66] The differences between service and product organizations necessitated by customer contact are summarized in Exhibit 7.8.

The impact of customer contact on organization design is reflected in the use of boundary roles and structural disaggregation.[67] Boundary roles are used extensively in manufacturing firms to handle customers and to reduce disruptions for the technical core. They are used less in service firms because a service is intangible and cannot be passed along by boundary spanners, so service customers must interact directly with technical employees, such as doctors or brokers.

A service firm deals in information and intangible outputs and does not need to be large. Its greatest economies are achieved through disaggregation into small units that can be located close to customers. Stockbrokers, doctors' clinics,

	Service	Product
Structural Characteristic		
1. Separate boundary roles	Few	Many
2. Geographical dispersion	Much	Little
3. Decision making	Decentralized	Centralized
4. Formalization	Lower	Higher
Human Resources		
1. Employee skill level	Higher	Lower
2. Skill emphasis	Interpersonal	Technical

EXHIBIT 7.8
Configuration and Structural Characteristics of Service Organizations Versus Product Organizations

© Cengage Learning®

consulting firms, and banks disperse their facilities into regional and local offices. Manufacturing firms, on the other hand, tend to aggregate operations in a single area that has raw materials and an available workforce. A large manufacturing firm can take advantage of economies derived from expensive machinery and long production runs.

Service technology also influences internal organization characteristics used to direct and control the organization. For one thing, the skills of technical core employees typically need to be higher. These employees need enough knowledge and awareness to handle customer problems rather than just enough to perform mechanical tasks. Employees need social and interpersonal skills as well as technical skills.[68] Because of higher skills and structural dispersion, decision making often tends to be decentralized in service firms, and formalization tends to be low. Although some service organizations, such as many fast-food chains, have set rules and procedures for customer service, employees in service organizations typically have more freedom and discretion on the job. Managers at Home Depot have learned that how employees are managed has a great deal to do with the success of a service organization.

IN PRACTICE

Home Depot Inc.

Home Depot grew to be the world's largest home improvement retailer largely on the strength of its employees. Many people hired to work in the stores were former plumbers, carpenters, or other skilled tradesmen who understood the products and took pride in helping do-it-yourself customers find the right tools and supplies and know how to use them.

To cut costs, however, the company began hiring more part-time employees and instituted a salary cap that made jobs less appealing to experienced workers. As a further way to reduce costs, managers began measuring every aspect of the stores' productivity, such as how long it took to unload shipments of goods or how many extended warranties each employee sold per week. Customers began complaining that they could never find anyone to assist them—and even when they did, many employees didn't have the knowledge and experience to be of much help. Some customers took their business elsewhere, even if it meant going to small shops where they would pay higher prices but get better service.

Home Depot managers have been working hard to get things back on track. The stores are hiring more full-timers again, instituting new training programs, and looking for other ways to make sure service employees are knowledgeable and helpful.[69]

Managers at Home Depot can use an understanding of the nature of service technology to help them align strategy, structure, and management processes and make the retailer more effective. Service technologies require structures and systems that are quite different from those for a traditional manufacturing technology. For example, the concept of separating complex tasks into a series of small jobs and exploiting economies of scale is a cornerstone of traditional manufacturing, but researchers have found that applying it to service organizations often does not work so well.[70] Some service firms have redesigned jobs to separate low- and high-customer-contact activities, with more rules and standardization in the low-contact jobs. High-touch service jobs, like those on the Home Depot sales floor, need more freedom and less control to satisfy customers.

2 The best way for a company to provide good service is to have abundant and clear rules and procedures and make sure everyone follows them to the letter.

ANSWER: *Disagree.* Service employees need good interpersonal skills and a degree of autonomy to be able to satisfy each customer's specific needs. Although many service organizations have some standard procedures for serving customers, service firms are typically low on both centralization and formalization. Abundant rules can take away both personal autonomy and the personal touch.

Now let's turn to another perspective on technology, that of production activities within specific organizational departments. Departments often have characteristics similar to those of service technology, providing services to other departments within the organization.

Noncore Departmental Technology

This section shifts to the department level of analysis for departments not within the technical core. For example, refer back to Exhibit 7.1 on page 260, which illustrates human resources, accounting, research and development, and marketing departments that are outside of the technical core. Each of these (and other noncore) departments in an organization has its own production process that consists of a distinct technology. A company such as Tenneco, a maker of auto parts, might have departments for engineering, research and development, human resources, marketing, quality control, finance, and dozens of other functions. This section analyzes the nature of departmental technology and its relationship with departmental design.

The framework that has had the greatest impact on the understanding of departmental technologies was developed by Charles Perrow.[71] Perrow's model has been useful for a broad range of technologies, which made it ideal for research into departmental activities.

Variety

Perrow specified two dimensions of departmental activities that were relevant to organization structure and processes. The first is the number of exceptions in the work. This refers to task **variety**, which is the frequency of unexpected and novel events that occur in the conversion process. Task variety concerns whether work activities are performed the same way every time or differ from time to time as employees transform the organization's inputs into outputs.[72] When individuals encounter a large number of unexpected situations, with frequent problems, variety is considered high. When there are few problems, and when day-to-day job requirements are repetitive, technology contains little variety. Variety in departments can range from repeating a single act, such as on a traditional assembly line, to working on a series of unrelated problems, such as in a hospital emergency room.

Analyzability

The second dimension of technology concerns the **analyzability** of work activities. When the conversion process is analyzable, the work can be reduced to mechanical steps and participants can follow an objective, computational procedure to solve problems. Problem solution may involve the use of standard procedures, such as instructions and manuals, or technical knowledge, such as that in a textbook or handbook. On the other hand, some work is not analyzable. When problems arise, it is difficult to identify the correct solution. There is no store of techniques or procedures to tell a person exactly what to do. The cause of or solution to a problem is not clear, so employees rely on accumulated experience, intuition, and judgment. The final solution to a problem is often the result of wisdom and experience and not the result of standard procedures. For example, Philippos Poulos, a tone regulator at Steinway & Sons, has an unanalyzable technology. Tone regulators carefully check each piano's hammers to ensure that they produce the proper "Steinway sound."[73] These quality-control tasks require years of experience and practice. Standard procedures will not tell a person how to do such tasks.

Framework

The two dimensions of departmental technology and examples of departmental activities that would fit on Perrow's framework are shown in Exhibit 7.9. The dimensions of variety and analyzability form the basis for four major categories of technology: routine, craft, engineering, and nonroutine.

Categories of Departmental Technology. **Routine technologies** are characterized by little task variety and the use of objective, computational procedures. The tasks are formalized and standardized. Examples include an automobile assembly line and a bank teller department.

Craft technologies are characterized by a fairly stable stream of activities, but the conversion process is not analyzable or well understood. Tasks require extensive training and experience because employees respond to intangible factors on the basis of wisdom, intuition, and experience. Although advances in machine technologies seem to have reduced the number of craft technologies in organizations, craft technologies are still important. For example, steel furnace engineers continue to mix steel based on intuition and experience, pattern makers at fashion houses such as Louis Vuitton, Zara, or H&M convert rough designers' sketches into saleable garments, and teams of writers for television series such as *Glee* or *The Mentalist* convert ideas into story lines.

Engineering technologies tend to be complex because there is substantial variety in the tasks performed. However, the various activities are usually handled on the basis of established formulas, procedures, and techniques. Employees normally refer to a well-developed body of knowledge to handle problems. Engineering and accounting tasks usually fall in this category.

Nonroutine technologies have high task variety, and the conversion process is not analyzable or well understood. In nonroutine technology, a great deal of effort is devoted to analyzing problems and activities. Several equally acceptable options typically can be found. Experience and technical knowledge are used to solve problems and perform the work. Basic research, strategic planning, and other work that involves new projects and unexpected problems are nonroutine. The biotechnology industry also represents a nonroutine technology. Breakthroughs in understanding metabolism and physiology at a cellular level depend on highly trained employees who use their experience and intuition, as well as scientific knowledge.[74]

EXHIBIT 7.9

Framework for Department Technologies

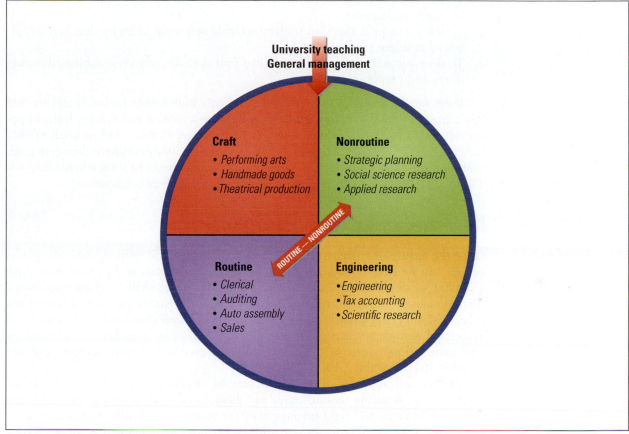

Sources: Based on R. L. Daft and N. Macintosh, "A New Approach to the Design and Use of Management Information," *California Management Review* 20 (August 1978), 82–92; R. L. Daft and N. Macintosh, "The Technology of User Departments and Information Design," *Information and Management* I (April 1978), 122–131; and R. L. Daft and N. Macintosh, "A Tentative Exploration into the Amount and Equivocality of Information Processing in Organizational Work Units," *Administrative Science Quarterly* 26 (June 1981), 207–224.

Routine Versus Nonroutine. Variety and analyzability can be combined into a single dimension of technology. This dimension is called *routine versus nonroutine technology*. The analyzability and variety dimensions are often correlated in departments, meaning that technologies high in variety tend to be low in analyzability, and technologies low in variety tend to be analyzable. Departments can be evaluated along a single dimension of routine versus nonroutine, as illustrated in Exhibit 7.9, that combines both analyzability and variety, which is a useful shorthand measure for analyzing departmental technology.

The following questions show how departmental technology can be analyzed for determining its placement on Perrow's technology framework in Exhibit 7.9.[75] Employees normally circle a number from 1 to 7 in response to each question.

Variety:

1. To what extent would you say your work is routine?
2. Does almost everyone in this unit do about the same job in the same way most of the time?
3. Are unit members performing repetitive activities in doing their jobs?

Analyzability:

1. To what extent is there a clearly known way to do the major types of work you normally encounter?
2. To what extent is there an understandable sequence of steps that can be followed in doing your work?
3. To do your work, to what extent can you actually rely on established procedures and practices?

If answers to the preceding questions indicate high scores for analyzability and low scores for variety, the department would have a routine technology. If the opposite occurs, the technology would be nonroutine. Low variety and low analyzability indicate a craft technology, and high variety and high analyzability indicate an engineering technology. As a practical matter, most departments fit somewhere along the diagonal and can be most easily characterized as routine or nonroutine.

Department Design

Once the nature of a department's technology has been identified, the appropriate design can be determined. Department technology tends to be associated with a cluster of departmental characteristics, such as the skill level of employees, formalization, and methods of communication. Definite patterns exist in the relationship between work unit technology and design characteristics, which are associated with departmental performance.[76] Key relationships between technology and other dimensions of departments are described in this section and are summarized in Exhibit 7.10.

The overall design of departments may be characterized as either organic or mechanistic. Routine technologies are associated with a mechanistic design, with formal rules and rigid management processes. Nonroutine technologies are associated with an organic design, and department management is more flexible and free-flowing. The specific design characteristics of formalization, centralization, employee skill level, span of control, and communication and coordination vary, depending on work unit technology. For example, consider the organization of departments that provide food to hospital patients.

IN PRACTICE

Memorial Sloan-Kettering Cancer Center

For many years, hospital food service units reflected a routine technology. Workers followed a standard menu, prepared meals according to standard recipes, and followed standard rules and procedures. In recent years, some hospitals have shifted to a nonroutine approach.

Pnina Peled, head chef at Memorial Sloan-Kettering Cancer Center, recently made her first lemon-flavored pizza. Peled is always thinking of new ways to get patients to eat. A teenage patient wanted pizza but could only taste lemon, so Peled created a pizza with a lemon Alfredo sauce. At Memorial Sloan-Kettering, patients "now order what they want to eat, when they are ready to eat," says Veronica McLymont, director of food and nutrition services. That means less food waste, but it also means kitchen staff has to be better trained, more experienced, and more flexible, and people need more discretion in their behavior to provide personalized food service. Hospitals such as Memorial Sloan-Kettering, Rex Healthcare in Raleigh, North Carolina, MD Anderson Cancer Center in Houston, and Brigham and Women's Hospital in Boston are retraining kitchen staff, giving them more flexibility in line with a nonroutine service technology.[77]

EXHIBIT 7.10
Relationship of Department Technology to Structural and Management Characteristics

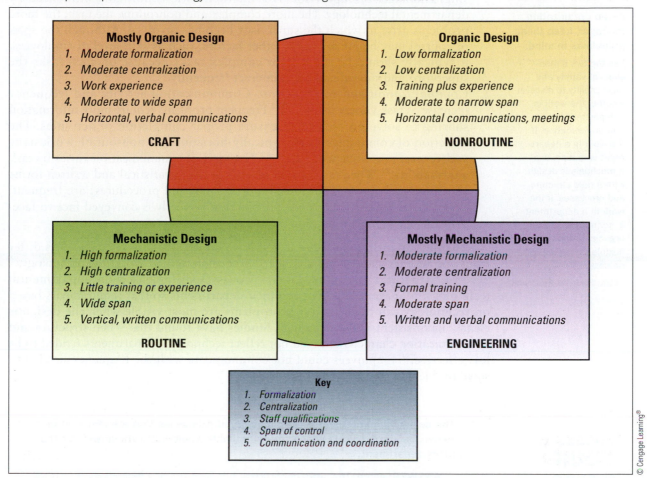

1. *Formalization.* Routine technology is characterized by standardization and division of labor into small tasks that are governed by formal rules and procedures. For non-routine tasks, the structure is less formal and less standardized. When variety is high, as in a research department, fewer activities are covered by formal procedures.[78]

2. *Decentralization.* In routine technologies, most decision making about task activities is centralized to management.[79] In engineering technologies, employees with technical training tend to acquire moderate decision authority because technical knowledge is important to task accomplishment. Production employees who have years of experience obtain decision authority in craft technologies because they know how to respond to problems. Decentralization to employees is greatest in nonroutine settings, where many decisions are made by employees.

3. *Employee skill level.* Work staff in routine technologies typically require little education or experience, which is congruent with repetitious work activities. In work units with greater variety, staff members are more skilled and often have formal training in technical schools or universities. Training for craft activities, which are less analyzable, is more likely to be through job experience. Nonroutine activities require both formal education and job experience.[80]

4. *Span of control.* Span of control is the number of employees who report to a single manager or supervisor. This characteristic is normally influenced by departmental technology. The more complex and nonroutine the task, the more problems arise in which the supervisor becomes involved. Although the span of control may be influenced by other factors, such as skill level of employees, it typically should be smaller for complex tasks because on such tasks the supervisor and subordinate must interact frequently.[81]

5. *Communication and coordination.* Communication activity and frequency increase as task variety increases.[82] Frequent problems require more information sharing to solve problems and ensure proper completion of activities. The direction of communication is typically horizontal in nonroutine work units and vertical in routine work units.[83] The form of communication varies by task analyzability.[84] When tasks are highly analyzable, statistical and written forms of communication (e.g., memos, reports, rules, and procedures) are frequent. When tasks are less analyzable, information typically is conveyed face to face, over the telephone, or in group meetings.

Two important points are reflected in Exhibit 7.10. First, departments differ from one another and can be categorized according to their workflow technology.[85] Second, structural and management processes differ based on departmental technology. Managers should design their departments so that requirements based on technology can be met. Design problems are most visible when the design is clearly inconsistent with technology. Studies have found that when structure and communication characteristics did not reflect technology, departments tended to be less effective.[86] Employees could not communicate with the frequency needed to solve problems.

ASSESS YOUR ANSWER

3 The design characteristics and management processes that are effective for a television station's sales department probably would not work so well for the news department.

ANSWER: *Agree.* The news department has a nonroutine technology compared to the sales department. No one knows what newsworthy events are going to happen during the day, when or where they will happen, or how they will need to be covered. Sales tasks, particularly telephone sales to repeat customers involving standard rates for advertising, can be performed using standard procedures, but gathering and reporting news events can't be standardized. A sales department would be characterized as routine because there is little variety and tasks are well understood.

Workflow Interdependence Among Departments

The final characteristic of technology that influences organization design is called interdependence. **Interdependence** means the extent to which departments depend on each other for information, resources, or materials to accomplish their tasks. Low interdependence means that departments can do their work independently of each other and have little need for interaction, consultation, or exchange of materials. High interdependence means departments must constantly exchange resources.

Types

James Thompson defined three types of interdependence that influence organization structure.[87] These interdependencies are illustrated in Exhibit 7.11 and are discussed in the following sections.

Pooled. **Pooled interdependence** is the lowest form of interdependence among departments. In this form, work does not flow between units. Each department is part of the organization and contributes to the common good of the organization, but works independently. Subway restaurants or Bank of America branches are examples of pooled interdependence. An outlet in Chicago need not interact with an outlet in Urbana. Pooled interdependence may be associated with the relationships within a *divisional structure*, defined in Chapter 3. Divisions or branches share financial resources from a common pool, and the success of each division contributes to the success of the overall organization.

Thompson proposed that pooled interdependence would exist in firms with what he called a mediating technology. A **mediating technology** provides products or services that mediate or link clients from the external environment and, in so doing, allows each department to work independently. Banks, brokerage firms, and real estate offices all mediate between buyers and sellers, but the offices work independently within the organization.

EXHIBIT 7.11

Thompson's Classification of Interdependence and Management Implications

Form of Interdependence	Demands on Horizontal Communication, Decision Making	Type of Coordination Required	Priority for Locating Units Close Together
Pooled (bank) ... Clients	Low communication	Standardization, rules, procedures Divisional structure	Low
Sequential (assembly line) ... Client	Medium communication	Plans, schedules, feedback Task forces	Medium
Reciprocal (hospital) ... Client	High communication	Mutual adjustment, relational coordination, teamwork Horizontal structure	High

© Cengage Learning®

The management implications associated with pooled interdependence are quite simple. Thompson argued that managers should use rules and procedures to standardize activities across departments. Each department should use the same procedures and financial statements so the outcomes of all departments can be measured and pooled. Very little day-to-day coordination is required among units.

Sequential. When interdependence is of serial form, with parts produced in one department becoming inputs to another department, it is called **sequential interdependence**. The first department must perform correctly for the second department to perform correctly. This is a higher level of interdependence than pooled interdependence because departments exchange resources and depend on others to perform well. Sequential interdependence creates a greater need for horizontal mechanisms such as integrators or task forces.

Sequential interdependence occurs in what Thompson called **long-linked technology**, which "refers to the combination in one organization of successive stages of production; each stage of production uses as its inputs the production of the preceding stage and produces inputs for the following stage."[88] An example of sequential interdependence comes from the shipbuilding industry. Until recently, ship designers made patterns and molds out of paper and plywood, which were passed on to assembly. The cutting department depended on accurate measurements from the designers, and the assembly department depended on accurate parts from the cutting department. This sequential interdependence meant that mistakes in measurements or pattern mix-ups often caused errors in the cutting and assembly process, leading to delays and increased costs. Naval architect Filippo Cali created a complex software program that computerizes the process of making patterns and molds, thus eliminating many of the problems between design and assembly.[89] Another example of sequential interdependence would be an automobile assembly line, which must have all the parts it needs to keep production rolling, such as engines, steering mechanisms, and tires.

The management requirements for sequential interdependence are more demanding than those for pooled interdependence. Coordination among the linked plants or departments is required. Since the interdependence implies a one-way flow of materials, extensive planning and scheduling are generally needed. Department B needs to know what to expect from Department A so both can perform effectively. Some day-to-day communication among plants or departments is also needed to handle unexpected problems and exceptions that arise.

Reciprocal. The highest level of interdependence is **reciprocal interdependence**. This exists when the output of operation A is the input to operation B, and the output of operation B is the input back again to operation A. The outputs of departments influence those departments in reciprocal fashion.

Reciprocal interdependence tends to occur in organizations with what Thompson called **intensive technologies**, which provide a variety of products or services in combination to a client. A firm developing new products provides an example of reciprocal interdependence. Intense coordination is needed between design, engineering, manufacturing, and marketing to combine all their resources to suit the customer's product need. For example, Callaway Golf introduces seven to eight new products every year to keep its edge as one of the industry's most innovative manufacturers.

Maintaining that pace requires tight coordination between design teams, engineers, marketing staff, and even lawyers. Teams have to communicate and quickly and securely share information created with CAD and CAM software with manufacturing partners in China, Japan, Korea, Mexico, and Taiwan. With the use of collaborative software, everyone involved in the process is able to access files 24 hours a day to keep track of the project. On a typical business day, 200 different users will access documents and collaborate with others.[90] Hospitals are also excellent examples of reciprocal interdependence because they provide coordinated services to patients.

Reciprocal interdependence requires that departments work together intimately and frequently. A study of top management teams confirms that the effective performance of teams characterized by high interdependence depends on good communication and close coordination.[91] With reciprocal interdependence, the structure must allow for frequent horizontal communication and adjustment, perhaps using cross-functional teams or a horizontal structure. Extensive planning is required, but plans will not anticipate or solve all problems. Daily interaction and mutual adjustment among departments are required. People from several departments might need to be involved in face-to-face coordination, teamwork, and decision making. For these reasons, managers in organizations characterized by reciprocal interdependence often organize work in such a way to encourage and support *relational coordination*, as described in Chapter 3, so that people share information and coordinate across departments as a normal part of their everyday work lives. Coordination and information sharing is built into the fabric of the organization.[92] Southwest Airlines provides a good example.

IN PRACTICE

Southwest Airlines

For all airlines, flight departure is a highly complex process that involves numerous employees from various departments, performing multiple tasks under uncertain and ever-changing conditions. Exhibit 7.12 illustrates the highly interdependent nature of the flight departure process, which involves ticket agents, pilots, flight attendants, baggage handlers, gate agents, operations agents, mechanics, cabin cleaners, ramp agents, cargo handlers, fuel attendants, and caterers. Tight coordination among these groups is essential for a successful on-time departure.

As described in Chapter 3, Southwest Airlines has the shortest turnaround time in the industry. How do they do it? Southwest promotes relational coordination among all these interdependent groups, some of which are illustrated in Exhibit 7.12, to achieve superior on-time performance and a high level of customer satisfaction. Southwest managers created what they call *team delay*, which helps people pinpoint problems in coordination between various groups rather than searching for who is to blame when something goes wrong. The emphasis on the team focuses everyone on shared goals of safety, on-time departure, accurate baggage handling, and customer satisfaction. People are motivated to work together and coordinate their activities rather than look out for themselves and try to avoid or shift blame. Supervisors work closely with employees to facilitate learning and help people accomplish their jobs.

Southwest puts a lot of emphasis on hiring people with a collaborative attitude. Rather than focusing on technical skills, Southwest focuses on hiring people who are oriented toward teamwork. Training and development activities and organizational stories reinforce teamwork and mutual respect. One story is told that a pilot came for an interview at Southwest and treated an administrative assistant with disrespect. He didn't get the job. "We all succeed together—and all fail together," is the philosophy at Southwest, as one field manager put it.[93]

EXHIBIT 7.12
Interdependence of
Departments Involved
in the Flight Departure
Process

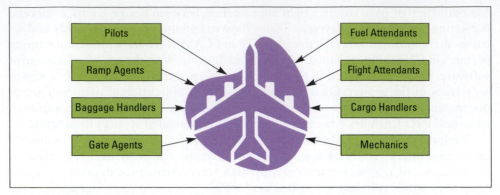

Source: Based on Jody Hoffer Gittell, "Organizing Work to Support Relational Coordination," *International Journal of Human Resource Management* 11, no. 3 (June 2000), 517–539.

By using practices that support teamwork, shared goals, mutual respect, and shared responsibility and accountability, Southwest facilitates relational coordination so that interdependent departments are tightly coordinated. Reciprocal interdependence is the most complex interdependence for organizations to handle and the most challenging for managers in designing the organization.

Structural Priority

As indicated in Exhibit 7.11, because decision making, communication, and coordination problems are greatest for reciprocal interdependence, reciprocal interdependence should receive first priority in organization structure. Activities that are reciprocally interdependent should be grouped close together in the organization so that managers have easy access to one another for mutual adjustment. These units should report to the same person on the organization chart and should be physically close so the time and effort for coordination can be minimized. A horizontal structure, with linked sets of teams working on core processes, can provide the close coordination needed to support reciprocal interdependence. Poor coordination will result in poor performance for the organization. If reciprocally interdependent units are not located close together, the organization should design mechanisms for coordination, such as daily meetings between departments or an intranet to facilitate communication. The next priority is given to sequential interdependencies, and finally to pooled interdependencies. This strategy of organizing keeps the communication channels short where coordination is most critical to organizational success.

Structural Implications

Most organizations experience various levels of interdependence, and structure can be designed to fit these needs, as illustrated in Exhibit 7.13.[94] In a manufacturing firm, new product development entails reciprocal interdependence among the design, engineering, purchasing, manufacturing, and sales departments. Perhaps a horizontal structure or cross-functional teams could be used to handle the back-and-forth flow of information and resources. Once a product is designed, its actual

EXHIBIT 7.13
Primary Means to
Achieve Coordination for
Different Levels of Task
Interdependence in a
Manufacturing Firm

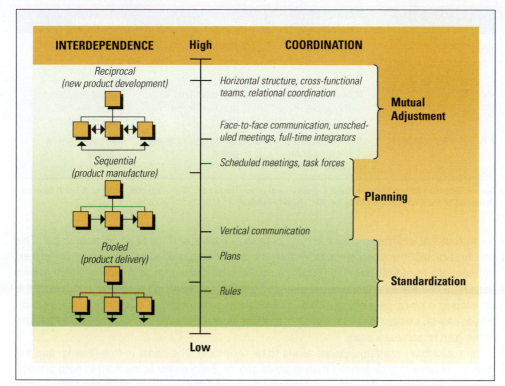

Source: Adapted from Andrew H. Van de Ven, Andre Delbecq, and Richard Koenig, "Determinants of Communication Modes within Organizations," *American Sociological Review* 41 (1976), 330.

manufacture would be sequential interdependence, with a flow of goods from one department to another, such as among purchasing, inventory, production control, manufacturing, and assembly. The actual ordering and delivery of products is pooled interdependence, with warehouses working independently. Customers could place an order with the nearest facility, which would not require coordination among warehouses, except in unusual cases such as a stock outage.

The three levels of interdependence are illustrated by a study of athletic teams that examined interdependency among players and how it influences other aspects of baseball, football, and basketball teams.

☑ IN PRACTICE

Athletic Teams

A major difference among baseball, football, and basketball is the interdependence among players. Baseball is low in interdependence, football is medium, and basketball represents the highest player interdependence. The relationships among interdependence and other characteristics of team play are illustrated in Exhibit 7.14.

Pete Rose said, "Baseball is a team game, but nine men who reach their individual goals make a nice team." In baseball, interdependence among team players is low and can be defined as pooled. Each member acts independently, taking a turn at bat and playing his or her own position. When interaction does occur, it is between only two or three players, as in a double play. Players are physically dispersed, and the rules of the game are the primary means of coordinating players. Players practice and develop their skills individually, such as by taking batting practice and undergoing physical conditioning. Management's job is to select good players. If each player is successful as an individual, the team should win.

EXHIBIT 7.14

Relationships Among
Interdependence and
Other Characteristics of
Team Play

	Baseball	Football	Basketball
Interdependence	Pooled	Sequential	Reciprocal
Physical dispersion of players	High	Medium	Low
Coordination	Rules that govern the sport	Game plan and position roles	Mutual adjustment and shared responsibility
Key management job	Select players and develop their skills	Prepare and execute game	Influence flow of game

Source: Based on William Pasmore, Carol E. Francis, and Jeffrey Haldeman, "Sociotechnical Systems: A North American Reflection on the Empirical Studies of the 70s," *Human Relations* 35 (1982), 1179–1204.

In football, interdependence among players is higher and tends to be sequential. The line first blocks the opponents to enable the backs to run or pass. Plays are performed sequentially from first down to fourth down. Physical dispersion is medium, which allows players to operate as a coordinated unit. The primary mechanism for coordinating players is developing a game plan along with rules that govern the behavior of team members. Each player has an assignment that fits with other assignments, and management designs the game plan to achieve victory.

In basketball, interdependence tends to be reciprocal. The game is free-flowing, and the division of labor is less precise than in other sports. Each player is involved in both offense and defense, handles the ball, and attempts to score. The ball flows back and forth among players. Team members interact in a dynamic flow to achieve victory. Management skills involve the ability to influence this dynamic process, either by substituting players or by working the ball into certain areas. Players must learn to adapt to the flow of the game and to one another as events unfold.

Interdependence among players is a primary factor explaining the difference among the three sports. Baseball is organized around an autonomous individual, football around groups that are sequentially interdependent, and basketball around the free flow of reciprocal players.[95]

Sociotechnical Systems

So far, this chapter has described models for analyzing how manufacturing, service, and department technologies influence structure and management processes. The relationship between a new technology and the organization seems to follow a pattern, beginning with immediate effects on the content of jobs followed (after a longer period) by impact on the design of the organization. The ultimate impact of technology on employees can be partially understood through the concept of sociotechnical systems.

The **sociotechnical systems approach** recognizes the interaction of technical and human needs in effective job design, combining the needs of people with the organization's need for technical efficiency. The *socio* portion of the approach refers to the people and groups that work in organizations and how work is organized and coordinated. The *technical* portion refers to the materials, tools, machines, and processes used to transform organizational inputs into outputs.

EXHIBIT 7.15
Sociotechnical Systems Model

The Social System

- *Individual and team behaviors*
- *Organizational/team culture*
- *Management practices*
- *Leadership style*
- *Degree of communication openness*
- *Individual needs and desires*

Design for Joint Optimization

Work roles, tasks, workflow

Goals and values

Skills and abilities

The Technical System

- *Type of production technology (small batch, mass production, digital, service, etc.)*
- *Level of interdependence (pooled, sequential, reciprocal)*
- *Physical work setting*
- *Complexity of production process (variety and analyzability)*
- *Nature of raw materials*
- *Time pressure*

Sources: Based on T. Cummings, "Self-Regulating Work Groups: A Socio-Technical Synthesis," *Academy of Management Review* 3 (1978), 625–634; Don Hellriegel, John W. Slocum, and Richard W. Woodman, *Organizational Behavior*, 8th ed. (Cincinnati, OH: South-Western, 1998), 492; and Gregory B. Northcraft and Margaret A. Neale, *Organizational Behavior: A Management Challenge*, 2nd ed. (Fort Worth, TX: The Dryden Press, 1994), 551.

Exhibit 7.15 illustrates the three primary components of the sociotechnical systems model.[96] The *social system* includes all human elements—such as individual and team behaviors, organizational culture, management practices, and degree of communication openness—that can influence the performance of work. The *technical system* refers to the type of production technology, the level of interdependence, the complexity of tasks, and so forth. The goal of the sociotechnical systems approach is to design the organization for **joint optimization**, which means that an organization functions best when the social and technical systems are designed to fit the needs of one another. Indeed, according to sociotechnical theory, merging people and technology effectively will create a harmonious relationship because people understand the advantages of the new technology and embrace it rather than fight against it.[97] Designing the organization to meet human needs while ignoring the technical systems, or changing technology to improve efficiency while ignoring human needs, may inadvertently cause performance problems. For example, no matter how much technology advances, says evolutionary psychologist Robin Dunbar, human beings are limited in the number of "meaningful social connections" they can sustain. Based on anthropological and historical studies, that number is 150. That is why when a branch of W. L. Gore & Associates exceeds 150 employees, it breaks in two and creates a new office. When a group begins to lose its sense of meaningful connection, managers know, people don't communicate and collaborate in a way that creates the bonds of a superior organization.[98] The sociotechnical systems approach attempts to find a balance between what people want and need and the technical requirements of the organization's production system.[99]

One example comes from a museum that installed a closed-circuit television system. Rather than having several guards patrolling the museum and grounds, the television could easily be monitored by a single guard. Although the technology saved money because only one guard was needed per shift, it led to unexpected performance problems. Guards had previously enjoyed the social interaction provided by patrolling; monitoring a closed-circuit television led to alienation and boredom. When a Federal agency did an 18-month test of the system, only 5 percent of several thousand experimental covert intrusions were detected by the guard.[100] The system was inadequate because human needs were not taken into account.

Sociotechnical principles evolved from the work of the Tavistock Institute, a research organization in England, during the 1950s and 1960s.[101] Examples of organizational change using sociotechnical systems principles have occurred in numerous organizations, including General Motors, Volvo, the Tennessee Valley Authority (TVA), and Procter & Gamble.[102] Although there have been failures, in many of these applications the joint optimization of changes in technology and structure to meet the needs of people as well as efficiency improved performance, safety, quality, absenteeism, and turnover. In some cases, work design was not the most efficient based on technical and scientific principles, but employee involvement and commitment more than made up for the difference. Thus, once again research shows that new technologies need not have a negative impact on people because the technology often requires higher-level mental and social skills and can be organized to encourage the involvement and commitment of employees, thereby benefiting both the employee and the organization.

The sociotechnical systems principle that states that people should be viewed as resources and provided with appropriate skills, meaningful work, and suitable rewards becomes even more important in today's world of growing technological complexity.[103] One study of paper manufacturers found that organizations that put too much faith in machines and technology and pay little attention to the appropriate management of people do not achieve advances in productivity and flexibility. Today's most successful companies strive to find the right mix of machines, robots, and people and the most effective way to coordinate them.[104]

Design Essentials

■ Several important ideas in the technology literature stand out. The first is Woodward's research into manufacturing technology. Woodward went into organizations and collected practical data on technology characteristics, organization structure, and management systems. She found clear relationships between technology and structure in high-performing organizations. Her findings are so clear that managers can analyze their own organizations along the same dimensions of technology and structure. In addition, technology and structure can be co-aligned with organizational strategy to meet changing needs and provide new competitive advantages.

■ The second important idea is that service technologies differ in a systematic way from manufacturing technologies. Service technologies are characterized by intangible outcomes and direct client involvement in the production process. Service firms do not have the fixed, machine-based technologies that appear in manufacturing organizations; hence, organization design often differs as well.

■ A third significant idea is Perrow's framework applied to department technologies. Understanding the variety and analyzability of a technology tells one about the management style, structure, and process that should characterize that department. Routine technologies are characterized by a mechanistic design and nonroutine technologies by an organic design. Applying the wrong management system to a department will result in dissatisfaction and reduced efficiency.

■ The fourth important idea is interdependence among departments. The extent to which departments depend on each other for materials, information, or other resources determines the amount of coordination required between them. As interdependence increases, demands on the organization for coordination increase. Organization design must allow for the correct amount of communication and coordination to handle interdependence across departments.

■ The fifth idea is that smart factories and lean manufacturing are being adopted by organizations and having impact on organization design. For the most part, the impact is positive, with shifts toward more organic designs both on the shop floor and in the management hierarchy. These technologies replace routine jobs, give employees more autonomy, produce more challenging jobs, encourage teamwork, and let the organization be more flexible and responsive. The new technologies are enriching jobs to the point where organizations are happier places to work.

■ Several principles of sociotechnical systems theory, which attempts to design the technical and human aspects of an organization to fit one another, are increasingly important as advances in technology alter the nature of jobs and social interaction in today's companies.

KEY CONCEPTS

analyzability	lean manufacturing	sequential interdependence
continuous-process production	long-linked technology	service technology
core technology	mass customization	small-batch production
craft technologies	mediating technology	smart factories
engineering technologies	noncore technology	sociotechnical systems approach
intensive technologies	nonroutine technologies	technical complexity
interdependence	pooled interdependence	technology
joint optimization	reciprocal interdependence	variety
large-batch production	routine technologies	

DISCUSSION QUESTIONS

1. Where would your university or college department be located on Perrow's technology framework? Would a department devoted exclusively to teaching be in a different quadrant from a department devoted exclusively to research?

2. Explain Thompson's levels of interdependence. What is the level of interdependence among departments (finance, marketing) in a business school? What kinds of coordination mechanisms might be used to handle that interdependence?

3. What relationships did Woodward discover between supervisor span of control and technological complexity?

4. How do smart factories and lean manufacturing differ from other manufacturing technologies? Why are these new approaches needed in today's environment?

5. What is a service technology? Are different types of service technologies likely to be associated with different organization designs? Explain.

6. Lean concepts such as continuous improvement and waste reduction have long been used by manufacturing companies. Discuss how service firms can apply the same concepts. Why do you think many service companies are adopting these ideas?

7. Why might administrators at a hospital such as Seattle Children's Hospital, described on page 276, want to foster relational coordination?

8. A top executive claimed that top-level management is a craft technology because the work contains intangibles, such as handling personnel, interpreting the environment, and coping with unusual situations that have to be learned through experience. If this is true, is it

appropriate to teach management in a business school? Does teaching management from a textbook assume that the manager's job is analyzable, and hence that formal training rather than experience is most important?

9. To what extent does the development of new technologies simplify and routinize the jobs of employees?

Can you give an example? Can new technology also lead to jobs with greater variety and complexity? Discuss.

10. Describe the sociotechnical systems model. Why might some managers oppose a sociotechnical systems approach?

▶▶ CHAPTER 7 WORKSHOP   Bistro Technology[105]

You will be analyzing the work technology used in three different restaurants—McDonald's, Subway, and a typical family restaurant. Your instructor will tell you whether to do this assignment as individuals or in a group.

You must visit all three restaurants and infer how the work is done, according to the following criteria. You are not allowed to interview any employees, but instead you will be an observer. Take lots of notes when you are there.

	McDonald's	Subway	Family Restaurant
Organization goals: Speed, service, atmosphere, and so on.			
Type of technology using Woodward's model.			
Organization structure: Mechanistic or organic?			
Team versus individual: Do people work together or alone?			
Interdependence: How do employees depend on each other?			
Tasks: Routine versus nonroutine—how varied are tasks?			

Questions

1. Is the technology used the best one for each restaurant, considering its goals and environment?
2. From the preceding data, determine if the structure and other characteristics fit the technology.
3. If you were part of a consulting team assigned to improve the operations of each organization, what recommendations would you make?

CASE FOR ANALYSIS | AV Corporate: Software Tool Project[106]

Kenneth Tirona has been working for the second largest information security company in the world for the past three years. He started out as a Quality Assurance Specialist and is now a project manager in the Product

Research and Development Department who is familiar with the internal processes of the Anti Virus Operations Department. The company's organizational setup is shown in Exhibit 7.16.

EXHIBIT 7.16
Partial Organization Chart for AV Corporate

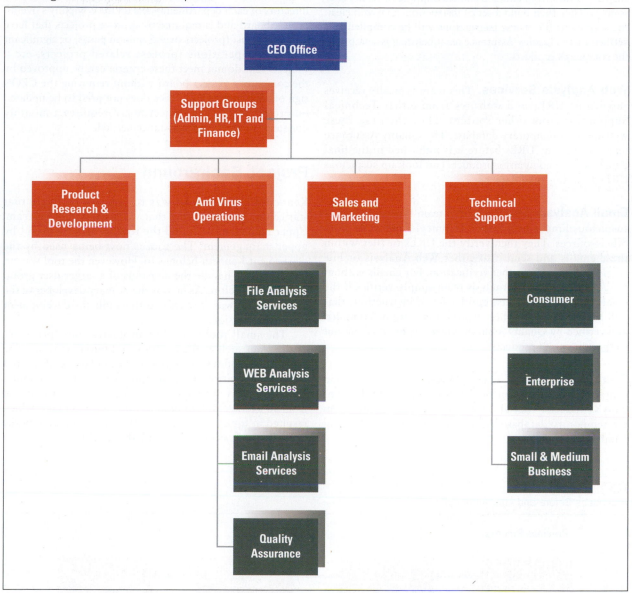

Organization Background

Marketing

The Marketing Department is involved not just in typical sales and marketing but also in Product Development where they assist the Product Research and Development Department in conducting market studies for potential products and finally in Beta testing upcoming products.

Product Research and Development

The Product Research and Development Department is in charge of driving the entire project from start to finish. The department typically interfaces with Marketing at the start of the project to understand the requirements needed by customers and then develop these new products.

Technical Support

Technical Support is the customer facing side of the business and deals with issues and requests after a product is launched. They routinely escalate other issues to the Anti Virus Operations Department if required. These issues typically lead to new "instructions" that are sent out to products used by customers.

Anti-Virus Operations

This department typically supplies the "instructions" that are updated regularly for the company's products. These instructions are based on File, Web, and Email analysis conducted by engineers. They also provide support as needed by Technical Support.

File Analysis Services. This team typically receives suspicious files from either Technical Support or from other sources. They then build a set of instructions that will clean the suspicious file. These instructions will be compiled and verified by the Quality Assurance team before it is sent out to the company's products.

Web Analysis Services. This team typically receives suspicious URLs and websites from either Technical Support or from other sources. They then tag these websites in a temporary database. The Quality Assurance team verifies the URLs before it is published in the final database. The company's products can look up suspicious URLs from this final database.

Email Analysis Services. This team typically receives suspicious Emails from either Technical Support or from other sources. They then verify the URLs or files within these emails and send it to either Web Analysis or File Analysis teams for further verification. For emails without files/URLs, the Email Analysis team simply verifies if the email is spam. They then build a set of instructions that will block the spam. These instructions will be compiled and verified by Quality Assurance team before it is sent out to the company's products.

Quality Assurance. Quality Assurance is the team in charge of verifying instructions before it is sent to the company's products. They also verify suspicious websites from the temporary database before it is published in the final database.

Office of the Chief Executive Officer (CEO)

Top management – which includes the CEO and the directors of each department – sits on the company's overall project board and is required to approve projects that have significant cost (projects over 5 million pesos) or significant impact to operations (process related projects, etc.). Projects that do not meet these criteria can be approved by the company's project board without requiring the CEO's sign off. While the CEO office does not need to be updated on project status, the project board requires a monthly update of progress and assistance needed.

Project Background

Kenneth's latest project was to improve software that started out as a small tool that was used within his team. Upper management found the tool to be very useful by upper management. The tool is now being used by the department Kenneth belongs to. However, the tool was no longer able to handle the demands of a larger user group compared to before. As he was the primary developer of the small tool, he was very excited to handle the development of the next version.

The small tool typically automates some processes of the team such as file analysis and initial analysis. The tool also provides sonic input for Secondary Analysis and Report Generation which helps speed up those manual processes. This automation helped cut down processing from an average of 245 minutes to just 60 minutes, which resulted in four times as much analyses being done in the time allocated, as illustrated in Exhibit 7.17.

EXHIBIT 7.17
Processes Before and After Automation

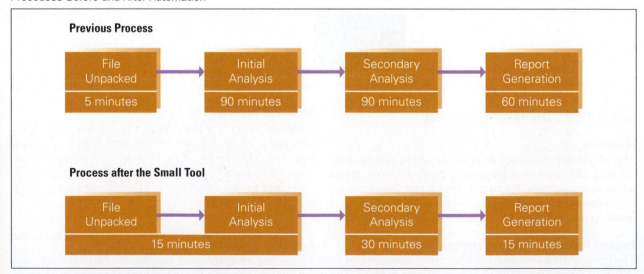

EXHIBIT 7.18
Routing of Customer Support Cases

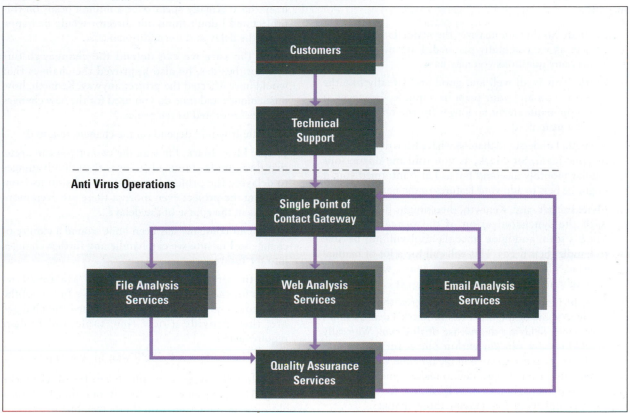

Kenneth started by interviewing managers from the different teams under the Anti Virus Department to gather their inputs. After completing the feature requirements for the new version, Kenneth pitched the project idea to management and approval was given. He was allocated a budget of 1.5 million pesos for the six month project and kept management updated at the end of each month.

The managers from the different teams routinely met to discuss ongoing issues and improvements in the organization. As this project affected all of them, it was one of the regular items discussed in weekly management meetings. The managers are independent of each other and are free to implement changes for their own team. However, changes that impact processes across teams must be clearly communicated to all affected teams and approved by a 60 percent majority of the management through voting. This ensures that everyone is made aware of changes to be done that affect multiple teams.

In AV Corporate, customers typically submit support cases to the Technical Support Team which resolves product-related cases and further forwards Anti Virus related cases to the Anti Virus Operations Department (see

Exhibit 7.18). These cases are received by a Single Point of Contact Gateway–a team composed of four people–that routes the case depending on the analysis requested. Cases related to files are routed to the File Analysis Services team, and such cases include files that wreak havoc on customers' computers. Cases related to websites, such as customers requesting analysis on whether a certain website is fraudulent, phishing, and so on, are routed to the Web Analysis Services team. Finally, the Email Analysis Services team receives email-related cases and typically analyzes if emails are spam.

These three teams typically perform similar tasks using tools shared throughout Anti Virus Operations; however, they also have their specialized tools within their respective teams and have varying processes. Before the three teams provide a final solution for services requested from them, a Quality Assurance Services team checks the solution provided before it is delivered to customers.

As the project was approaching completion, Kenneth optimistically presented the prototype to management. The management panel was composed of Mark Rago, manager for File Analysis Services, Joseph Rosario, manager for

Web Analysis Services and Elvie Talavera, manager for Email Analysis Services. The following is a transcript of the meeting:

Kenneth: So that summarizes the major features of the project as we originally planned. I am now ready to answer any questions you may have.

Mark: This is all well and good and I really like the progress you and your team have made. However, it seems the requirement no longer fits the new processes that my team needs.

Kenneth: I understand that there have been developments in your team, Sir Mark, as you told me during our regular monthly meetings but as I also informed you, it might be best to add your features to the next project.

Elvie: In that case, Kenneth, there might be a problem with the synchronization of the process between Mark's team and mine since the tool will not be able to handle their needs. This will call for a lot of manual interfaces between Mark and my team, which means we might also prefer waiting for the next . . .

Joseph: Hold on, Elvie. While I agree that we have changed some of the processes in Mark's team, I don't agree with delaying the release of this tool. We really need this new version within our team and would really like to see it released in the timeline we discussed. In fact, my team also wanted to make some changes to the requirements but we actually waited for this project to be completed before making those changes.

Mark: I find that really unfair, Joseph, since all of us have been touching base with Kenneth throughout the project. I'm sure Kenneth was very accommodating in handling the changes within all our teams but if we can manage a delayed release date then perhaps your team can proceed with those changes you have been pushing back and allow for ample time for Kenneth to incorporate them into the tool.

Joseph: I think we should stick to the current project and adjust to the new technology instead of delaying it. We have already spent over a million pesos on this project and I don't think our director would be happy about the delay and the additional cost.

Elvie: I'm sure we can defend the changes to our director. Besides, he also approved the changes that would have affected the project anyway. Kenneth, how much money and time do you need for the new changes to be incorporated to the project?

Kenneth: It would depend on the changes required.

Joseph: Elvie, Mark, I'm sure the two of you can argue that there are far more advantages than disadvantages to delaying the project but what would stop us from delaying the project even more if there are even more changes in the course of the delay?

Mark: Our company has been built around a culture of change so I'm sure we can handle any further changes into the future.

Kenneth: Sir Joseph, Sir Mark and Ma'am Elvie, thanks for the inputs so far. What if we first pool the new requirements, see how complicated the changes are, then provide a new time table and budget requirements?

Mark: Thanks Kenneth. We'll wait for your updates.

This left Kenneth very much confused after the meeting. This project was definitely one that he hoped would change his career for the better but it had the potential of being a perpetual project, especially since minor changes in any of the three teams' processes could affect the project at different times throughout its duration.

Kenneth took some time to go over his notes to review the detailed processes for each team that evolved during the course of the project and take note of the processes that shared resources (items shaded in blue are shared resources).

Core Process	Web Analysis	File Analysis	Email Analysis
Download and Unpack	File Downloading	*None*	File Downloading
	File Unpacking	File Unpacking	File Unpacking
Automated Analysis	File Analysis	File Analysis	File Analysis
	URL Analysis	*None*	URL Analysis
	Text Analysis	*None*	Text Analysis
	URL Correlation	*None*	URL Correlation
Manual Analysis	Behavior Analysis	Behavior Analysis	Behavior Analysis

Download and Unpack– For Web and Email Analysis Services, the file is first downloaded then unpacked.

Automated Analysis– All Analysis Services require File Analysis if files are downloaded, however, only Web and Email Analysis Services require URL Analysis, Text Analysis and URL Correlation. All these services are typically handled by an automated system.

Manual Analysis– A behavior analysis is provided once all automated analysis is complete. This service requires an engineer to manually create behavior descriptions of the threat.

Author's Note

Manuel C. Manuel III is an Assistant Professor at and College Secretary of the College of Business Administration, University of the Philippines, Diliman.

This case study was developed in collaboration with Peter Michael Tongco, a recent MBA graduate (Class of 2011) at the University of the Philippines. The case is not designed to illustrate effective or ineffective handling of managerial situations. Certain names have been disguised.

❯❯ NOTES

1. Reported in Stephanie Clifford, "Textile Plants Humming, but Not with Workers," *The New York Times*, September 20, 2013, A22.
2. Clifford, "Textile Plants Humming, but Not with Workers."
3. Saul Berman and Peter Korsten, "Embracing Connectedness: Insights from the IBM 2012 CEO Study," *Strategy & Leadership* 41, no. 2 (2013), 46–57.
4. Charles Perrow, "A Framework for the Comparative Analysis of Organizations," *American Sociological Review* 32 (1967), 194–208; and R. J. Schonberger, *World Class-Manufacturing: The Next Decade* (New York: The Free Press, 1996).
5. Wanda J. Orlikowski, "The Duality of Technology: Rethinking the Concept of Technology in Organizations," *Organization Science* 3 (1992), 398–427.
6. Linda Argote, "Input Uncertainty and Organizational Coordination in Hospital Emergency Units," *Administrative Science Quarterly* 27 (1982), 420–434; Charles Perrow, *Organizational Analysis: A Sociological Approach* (Belmont, CA: Wadsworth, 1970); and William Rushing, "Hardness of Material as Related to the Division of Labor in Manufacturing Industries," *Administrative Science Quarterly* 13 (1968), 229–245.
7. Lawrence B. Mohr, "Organizational Technology and Organization Structure," *Administrative Science Quarterly* 16 (1971), 444–459; and David Hickson, Derek Pugh, and Diana Pheysey, "Operations Technology and Organization Structure: An Empirical Reappraisal," *Administrative Science Quarterly* 14 (1969), 378–397.
8. Joan Woodward, *Industrial Organization: Theory and Practice* (London: Oxford University Press, 1965); and Joan Woodward, *Management and Technology* (London: Her Majesty's Stationery Office, 1958).
9. Hickson, Pugh, and Pheysey, "Operations Technology and Organization Structure"; and James D. Thompson, *Organizations in Action* (New York: McGraw-Hill, 1967).
10. Edward Harvey, "Technology and the Structure of Organizations," *American Sociological Review* 33 (1968), 241–259.
11. Based on Woodward, *Industrial Organization* and *Management and Technology*.
12. Christina Passariello, "Brand-New Bag: Louis Vuitton Tried Modern Methods on Factory Lines—For Craftsmen, Multitasking Replaces Specialization," *The Wall Street Journal*, October 9, 2006, A1.
13. John Letzing, "Amazon Adds That Robotic Touch," *The Wall Street Journal*, March 20, 2012, B1.
14. Guy Chazan, "Clean-Fuels Refinery Rises in Desert," *The Wall Street Journal*, April 16, 2010, B8; and "Renewed Optimism for the Future of GTL, CTL, and BTL," *Oil and Gas News*, July 11, 2011.
15. Woodward, *Industrial Organization*, vi.
16. William L. Zwerman, *New Perspectives on Organizational Theory* (Westport, CT: Greenwood, 1970); and Harvey, "Technology and the Structure of Organizations."
17. Dean M. Schroeder, Steven W. Congden, and C. Gopinath, "Linking Competitive Strategy and Manufacturing Process Technology," *Journal of Management Studies* 32, no. 2 (March 1995), 163–189.
18. Daniel Roberts, "Going to the Mattresses," *Fortune*, September 24, 2012, 28–29; and Jake Stiles, "Lean Initiatives Help Sealy Prepare for Market Rebound," *IndustryWeek*, May 6, 2009, http://www.industryweek.com/articles/lean_initiatives_help_sealy_-prepare_for_market_rebound_19073.aspx?ShowAll=1 (accessed August 17, 2011).
19. Fernando F. Suarez, Michael A. Cusumano, and Charles H. Fine, "An Empirical Study of Flexibility in Manufacturing," *Sloan Management Review*, Fall 1995, 25–32.
20. Raymond F. Zammuto and Edward J. O'Connor, "Gaining Advanced Manufacturing Technologies' Benefits: The Roles of Organization Design and Culture," *Academy of Management Review* 17, no. 4 (1992), 701–728; and Schroeder, Congden, and Gopinath, "Linking Competitive Strategy and Manufacturing Process Technology."
21. John S. McClenahen, "Bearing Necessities," *Industry Week*, October 2004, 63–65.
22. James Surowiecki, "Requiem for a Dreamliner?" *The New Yorker*, February 4, 2013, 2; Nancy Trejos, "Boeing Faces More Dreamliner Problems," *USA Today*, September 26, 2013, http://www.usatoday.com/story/todayinthesky/2013/09/26/norwegian-air-polish-lot-boeing-dreamliner/2878019/

(accessed November 13, 2013); and "Boeing 787 Dreamliner: A Timeline of Problems," *The Telegraph*, July 28, 2013, http://www.telegraph.co.uk/travel/travelnews/10207415/ (accessed November 13, 2013).

23. Dov Gardin, "Carnival Cruise Lines: What They Should Have Done," *Risk Management Monitor*, February 22, 2013, http://www.riskmanagementmonitor.com/carnival-cruise-lines-what-they-should-have-done/ (accessed October 25, 2013); Lateef Mungin and Mark Morgenstein, "Carnival Cruise Line in More Troubled Waters," *CNN*, March 16, 2013, http://www.cnn.com/2013/03/15/travel/carnival-problems (accessed October 25, 2013); and Jad Mouawad, "Too Big to Sail?" *The New York Times*, October 28, 2013, B1.

24. Quoted in Mouawad, "Too Big to Sail?"

25. John Markoff, "Skilled Work, Without the Worker," *The New York Times*, August 19, 2012, A1.

26. Quoted in Sam Grobart, "What Machines Can't Do," *Bloomberg BusinessWeek*, December 17–December 30, 2012, 4–5.

27. Heritage Foundation statistic, based on data from the U.S. Department of Labor, Bureau of Labor Statistics, "Multifactor Productivity, 1987–2007," and reported in James Sherk, "Technology Explains Drop in Manufacturing Jobs," *Backgrounder*, October 12, 2010, 1–8.

28. John Teresko, "Winning with Digital Manufacturing," *Industry Week*, July 2008, 45–47.

29. Travis Hessman, "The Dawn of the Smart Factory," *Industry Week*, February 2013, 14–19.

30. Hessman, "The Dawn of the Smart Factory"; Jim Brown, "Leveraging the Digital Factory," *Industrial Management*, July–August 2009, 26–30; Teresko, "Winning with Digital Manufacturing"; Jack R. Meredith, "The Strategic Advantages of the Factory of the Future," *California Management Review* 29 (Spring 1987), 27–41; and Althea Jones and Terry Webb, "Introducing Computer Integrated Manufacturing," *Journal of General Management* 12 (Summer 1987), 60–74.

31. Paul S. Adler, "Managing Flexible Automation," *California Management Review* (Spring 1988), 34–56.

32. Bela Gold, "Computerization in Domestic and International Manufacturing," *California Management Review* (Winter 1989), 129–143.

33. Travis Hessman, "The New Age of Robotics," *Industry Week*, August 2013, 22–25.

34. Brown, "Leveraging the Digital Factory."

35. Clint Boulton, "Barbies, Auto Parts Hot Off the Press," *The Wall Street Journal*, June 6, 2013, B1.

36. Graham Dudley and John Hassard, "Design Issues in the Development of Computer Integrated Manufacturing (CIM)," *Journal of General Management* 16 (1990), 43–53.

37. Hessman, "The Dawn of the Smart Factory."

38. Kate Linebaugh, "Honda's Flexible Plants Provide Edge; Company Can Rejigger Vehicle Output to Match Consumer Demand Faster Than Its Rivals," *The Wall Street Journal*, September 23, 2008, B1.

39. Tracy Mayor, "Six Sigma Comes to IT: Targeting Perfection," *CIO*, December 1, 2003, 62–70; Hal Plotkin, "Six Sigma: What It Is and How to Use It," *Harvard Management*

Update, June 1999, 3–4; Tom Rancour and Mike McCracken, "Applying Six Sigma Methods for Breakthrough Safety Performance," *Professional Safety* 45, no. 10 (October 2000), 29–32; G. Hasek, "Merger Marries Quality Efforts," *Industry Week*, August 21, 2000, 89–92; and Lee Clifford, "Why You Can Safely Ignore Six Sigma," *Fortune*, January 22, 2001, 140.

40. 2006 Census of Manufacturers, reported in "Lean Choices," sidebar in Jonathan Katz, "Back to School," *Industry Week*, May 2007, 14.

41. Chris Liebtag, "Making Change with Lean Six Sigma Generates Many Happy Returns for CPA Firm Rea & Associates," *Global Business and Organizational Excellence*, May/June 2013,16–27.

42. Jeffrey K. Liker and James M. Morgan, "The Toyota Way in Services: The Case of Lean Product Development," *Academy of Management Perspectives*, May 2006, 5–20; and Brian Heymans, "Leading the Lean Enterprise," *Industrial Management*, September–October 2002, 28–33.

43. Steve Minter, "La-Z-Boy Never Rests on Continuous Improvement," *Industry Week*, January 2013, 25.

44. Chester Dawson, "For Toyota, Patriotism and Profits May Not Mix," *The Wall Street Journal*, November 29, 2011, http://online.wsj.com/news/articles/SB100014240529702037 33504577025523618197732 (accessed March 27, 2014).

45. B. Joseph Pine II, *Mass Customization: The New Frontier in Business Competition* (Boston: Harvard Business School Press, 1999); and Fabrizio Salvador, Pablo Martin De Holan, and Frank Piller, "Cracking the Code of Mass Customization," *Sloan Management Review*, Spring, 2009, 71–78.

46. Barry Berman, "Should Your Firm Adopt a Mass Customization Strategy?" *Business Horizons*, July–August 2002, 51–60.

47. Erick Schonfeld, "The Customized, Digitized, Have-It-Your-Way Economy," *Fortune*, September 28, 1998, 115–124.

48. Mark Tatge, "Red Bodies, Black Ink," *Forbes*, September 18, 2000, 114–115.

49. Zammuto and O'Connor, "Gaining Advanced Manufacturing Technologies' Benefits."

50. Joel D. Goldhar and David Lei, "Variety Is Free: Manufacturing in the Twenty-First Century," *Academy of Management Executive* 9, no. 4 (1995), 73–86.

51. Meredith, "The Strategic Advantages of the Factory of the Future."

52. Patricia L. Nemetz and Louis W. Fry, "Flexible Manufacturing Organizations: Implementations for Strategy Formulation and Organization Design," *Academy of Management Review* 13 (1988), 627–638; Paul S. Adler, "Managing Flexible Automation," *California Management Review* (Spring 1988), 34–56; Jeremy Main, "Manufacturing the Right Way," *Fortune*, May 21, 1990, 54–64; and Frank M. Hull and Paul D. Collins, "High-Technology Batch Production Systems: Woodward's Missing Type," *Academy of Management Journal* 30 (1987), 786–797.

53. Goldhar and Lei, "Variety Is Free: Manufacturing in the Twenty-First Century"; P. Robert Duimering, Frank Safayeni, and Lyn Purdy, "Integrated Manufacturing: Redesign the Organization before Implementing Flexible Technology,"

Sloan Management Review (Summer 1993), 47–56; and Zammuto and O'Connor, "Gaining Advanced Manufacturing Technologies' Benefits."

54. Goldhar and Lei, "Variety Is Free: Manufacturing in the Twenty-First Century."

55. Estimate reported in "Services Firms Expand at Slowest Pace in 17 Months," *MoneyNews.com*, August 3, 2011, http://www.moneynews.com/Economy/ism-economy-Service-Sector/2011/08/03/id/405915 (accessed August 15, 2011).

56. Byron J. Finch and Richard L. Luebbe, *Operations Management: Competing in a Changing Environment* (Fort Worth, TX: The Dryden Press, 1995), 51.

57. This discussion is based on David E. Bowen, Caren Siehl, and Benjamin Schneider, "A Framework for Analyzing Customer Service Orientations in Manufacturing," *Academy of Management Review* 14 (1989), 79–95; Peter K. Mills and Newton Margulies, "Toward a Core Typology of Service Organizations," *Academy of Management Review 5* (1980), 255–265; and Peter K. Mills and Dennis J. Moberg, "Perspectives on the Technology of Service Operations," *Academy of Management Review 7* (1982), 467–478.

58. "Pandora Announces Listener Milestone," Pandora Press Release (July 12, 2011), http://blog.pandora.com/archives/press/2011/07/pandora_announc_1.html (accessed August 17, 2011).

59. Jena McGregor, "When Service Means Survival," *BusinessWeek*, March 2, 2009, 26–30; and Heather Green, "How Amazon Aims to Keep You Clicking," *BusinessWeek*, March 2, 2009, 37–40.

60. Melinda Beck, "Critical (Re)thinking: How ICUs Are Getting a Much-Needed Makeover," *The Wall Street Journal*, March 28, 2011, http://online.wsj.com/article/ SB10001424052748704132204576190632996146752 .html (accessed October 5, 2012).

61. Liker and Morgan, "The Toyota Way in Services."

62. Paul Migliorato, "Toyota Retools Japan," *Business 2.0*, August 2004, 39–41.

63. Julie Jargon, "Latest Starbucks Buzzword: 'Lean' Japanese Techniques," *The Wall Street Journal*, August 4, 2009; and Julie Jargon, "Panera Says It Can't Handle Crush," *The Wall Street Journal*, October 23, 2013, http://online.wsj.com/news/articles/SB100014240527023036153045791534509096617 02 (accessed March 28, 2014).

64. Julie Weed, "Factory Efficiency Comes to the Hospital," *The New York Times*, July 9, 2010.

65. Geeta Anand, "The Henry Ford of Heart Surgery," *The Wall Street Journal*, November 25, 2009, A16.

66. Richard B. Chase and David A. Tansik, "The Customer Contact Model for Organization Design," *Management Science* 29 (1983), 1037–1050.

67. Ibid.

68. David E. Bowen and Edward E. Lawler III, "The Empowerment of Service Workers: What, Why, How, and When," *Sloan Management Review* (Spring 1992), 31–39; Gregory B. Northcraft and Richard B. Chase, "Managing Service Demand at the Point of Delivery," *Academy of Management Review* 10 (1985), 66–75; and Roger W. Schmenner, "How Can Service Businesses Survive and Prosper?" *Sloan Management Review* 27 (Spring 1986), 21–32.

69. Ann Zimmerman, "Home Depot Tries to Make Nice to Customers," *The Wall Street Journal*, February 20, 2007, D1.

70. Richard Metters and Vincente Vargas, "Organizing Work in Service Firms," *Business Horizons*, July–August 2000, 23–32.

71. Perrow, "A Framework for the Comparative Analysis of Organizations" and *Organizational Analysis*.

72. Brian T. Pentland, "Sequential Variety in Work Processes," *Organization Science* 14, no. 5 (September–October 2003), 528–540.

73. Jim Morrison, "Grand Tour. Making Music: The Craft of the Steinway Piano," *Spirit*, February 1997, 42–49, 100.

74. Stuart F. Brown, "Biotech Gets Productive," *Fortune*, special section, "Industrial Management and Technology," January 20, 2003, 170[A]–170[H].

75. Michael Withey, Richard L. Daft, and William C. Cooper, "Measures of Perrow's Work Unit Technology: An Empirical Assessment and a New Scale," *Academy of Management Journal* 25 (1983), 45–63.

76. Christopher Gresov, "Exploring Fit and Misfit with Multiple Contingencies," *Administrative Science Quarterly* 34 (1989), 431–453; and Dale L. Goodhue and Ronald L. Thompson, "Task-Technology Fit and Individual Performance," *MIS Quarterly*, June 1995, 213–236.

77. Dawn Fallik, "New Hospital Cuisine: Dishes Made to Order," *The Wall Street Journal*, February 21, 2012, http://online.wsj .com/news/articles/SB10001424052970204642604577213390021632180 (accessed February 24, 2012).

78. Gresov, "Exploring Fit and Misfit with Multiple Contingencies"; Charles A. Glisson, "Dependence of Technological Routinization on Structural Variables in Human Service Organizations," *Administrative Science Quarterly* 23 (1978), 383–395; and Jerald Hage and Michael Aiken, "Routine Technology, Social Structure and Organizational Goals," *Administrative Science Quarterly* 14 (1969), 368–379.

79. Gresov, "Exploring Fit and Misfit with Multiple Contingencies"; A. J. Grimes and S. M. Kline, "The Technological Imperative: The Relative Impact of Task Unit, Modal Technology, and Hierarchy on Structure," *Academy of Management Journal* 16 (1973), 583–597; Lawrence G. Hrebiniak, "Job Technologies, Supervision and Work Group Structure," *Administrative Science Quarterly* 19 (1974), 395–410; and Jeffrey Pfeffer, *Organizational Design* (Arlington Heights, IL: AHM, 1978), Chapter 1.

80. Patrick E. Connor, *Organizations: Theory and Design* (Chicago: Science Research Associates, 1980); and Richard L. Daft and Norman B. Macintosh, "A Tentative Exploration into Amount and Equivocality of Information Processing in Organizational Work Units," *Administrative Science Quarterly* 26 (1981), 207–224.

81. Paul D. Collins and Frank Hull, "Technology and Span of Control: Woodward Revisited," *Journal of Management Studies* 23 (1986), 143–164; Gerald D. Bell, "The Influence of Technological Components of Work upon Management Control," *Academy of Management Journal* 8 (1965), 127–132; and Peter M. Blau and Richard A. Schoenherr, *The Structure of Organizations* (New York: Basic Books, 1971).

82. W. Alan Randolph, "Matching Technology and the Design of Organization Units," *California Management Review* 22–23 (1980–81), 39–48; Daft and Macintosh, "A Tentative Exploration into Amount and Equivocality of Information Processing"; and Michael L. Tushman, "Work Characteristics and Subunit Communication Structure: A Contingency Analysis," *Administrative Science Quarterly* 24 (1979), 82–98.

83. Andrew H. Van de Ven and Diane L. Ferry, *Measuring and Assessing Organizations* (New York: Wiley, 1980); and Randolph, "Matching Technology and the Design of Organization Units."

84. Richard L. Daft and Robert H. Lengel, "Information Richness: A New Approach to Managerial Behavior and Organization Design," in Barry Staw and Larry L. Cummings, eds., *Research in Organizational Behavior*, 6 (Greenwich, CT: JAI Press, 1984), 191–233; Richard L. Daft and Norman B. Macintosh, "A New Approach into Design and Use of Management Information," *California Management Review* 21 (1978), 82–92; Daft and Macintosh, "A Tentative Exploration into Amount and Equivocality of Information Processing"; W. Alan Randolph, "Organizational Technology and the Media and Purpose Dimensions of Organizational Communication," *Journal of Business Research* 6 (1978), 237–259; Linda Argote, "Input Uncertainty and Organizational Coordination in Hospital Emergency Units," *Administrative Science Quarterly* 27 (1982), 420–434; and Andrew H. Van de Ven and Andre Delbecq, "A Task Contingent Model of Work Unit Structure," *Administrative Science Quarterly* 19 (1974), 183–197.

85. Peggy Leatt and Rodney Schneck, "Criteria for Grouping Nursing Subunits in Hospitals," *Academy of Management Journal* 27 (1984), 150–165; and Robert T. Keller, "Technology-Information Processing," *Academy of Management Journal* 37, no. 1 (1994), 167–179.

86. Gresov, "Exploring Fit and Misfit with Multiple Contingencies;" Michael L. Tushman, "Technological Communication in R&D Laboratories: The Impact of Project Work Characteristics," *Academy of Management Journal* 21 (1978), 624–645; and Robert T. Keller, "Technology-Information Processing Fit and the Performance of R&D Project Groups: A Test of Contingency Theory," *Academy of Management Journal* 37, no. 1 (1994), 167–179.

87. James Thompson, *Organizations in Action* (New York: McGraw-Hill, 1967).

88. Ibid., 40.

89. Gene Bylinsky, "Shipmaking Gets Modern," *Fortune*, special section, "Industrial Management and Technology," January 20, 2003, 170[K]–170[L].

90. Brad Kenney, "Callaway Improves Long Game with Collaborative Tech," *Industry Week*, June 2008, 72.

91. Murray R. Barrick, Bret H. Bradley, Amy L. Kristof-Brown, and Amy E. Colbert, "The Moderating Role of Top Management Team Interdependence: Implications for Real Teams and Working Groups," *Academy of Management Journal* 50, no. 3 (2007), 544–557.

92. Jody Hoffer Gittell, "Organizing Work to Support Relational Coordination," *The International Journal of Human Resource Management* 11, no. 3 (June 2000), 517–539.

93. Jody Hoffer Gittell, "Paradox of Coordination and Control," *California Management Review* 42, no. 3 (Spring 2000), 101–117.

94. This discussion is based on Christopher Gresov, "Effects of Dependence and Tasks on Unit Design and Efficiency," *Organization Studies* 11 (1990), 503–529; Andrew H. Van de Ven, Andre Delbecq, and Richard Koenig, "Determinants of Coordination Modes within Organizations," *American Sociological Review* 41 (1976), 322–338; Argote, "Input Uncertainty and Organizational Coordination in Hospital Emergency Units"; Jack K. Ito and Richard B. Peterson, "Effects of Task Difficulty and Interdependence on Information Processing Systems," *Academy of Management Journal* 29 (1986), 139–149; and Joseph L. C. Cheng, "Interdependence and Coordination in Organizations: A Role-System Analysis," *Academy of Management Journal* 26 (1983), 156–162.

95. Robert W. Keidel, "Team Sports Models as a Generic Organizational Framework," *Human Relations* 40 (1987), 591–612; Robert W. Keidel, "Baseball, Football, and Basketball: Models for Business," *Organizational Dynamics* (Winter 1984), 5–18; and Nancy Katz, "Sports Teams as a Model for Workplace Teams: Lessons and Liabilities," *Academy of Management Executive* 15, no. 3 (2001), 56–67.

96. Based on Don Hellriegel, John W. Slocum, Jr., and Richard W. Woodman, *Organizational Behavior*, 8th ed. (Cincinnati, OH: SouthWestern, 1998), 491–495; and Gregory B. Northcraft and Margaret A. Neale, *Organizational Behavior: A Management Challenge*, 2nd ed. (Fort Worth, TX: The Dryden Press, 1994), 550–553.

97. William H. Bishop, "The Elements of Leadership in a Global Environment," *Global Business and Organizational Excellence* 32, no. 5 (July–August 2013), 78–85.

98. Drake Bennett, "The Dunbar Number," *Bloomberg BusinessWeek*, January 10, 2013, 52–56.

99. F. Emery, "Characteristics of Sociotechnical Systems," Tavistock Institute of Human Relations, document 527 (1959); William Pasmore, Carol Francis, and Jeffrey Haldeman, "Sociotechnical Systems: A North American Reflection on Empirical Studies of the 70s," *Human Relations* 35 (1982), 1179–1204; and William M. Fox, "Sociotechnical System Principles and Guidelines: Past and Present," *Journal of Applied Behavioral Science* 31, no. 1 (March 1995), 91–105.

100. W. S. Cascio, *Managing Human Resources* (New York: McGraw-Hill, 1986), 19.

101. Eric Trist and Hugh Murray, eds., *The Social Engagement of Social Science: A Tavistock Anthology*, vol. II (Philadelphia: University of Pennsylvania Press, 1993); and William A. Pasmore, "Social Science Transformed: The Socio-Technical Perspective," *Human Relations* 48, no. 1 (1995), 1–21.

102. R. E. Walton, "From Control to Commitment in the Workplace," *Harvard Business Review* 63, no. 2 (1985),

76–84; E. E. Lawler, III, *High Involvement Management* (San Francisco: Jossey-Bass, 1986), 84; and Hellriegel, Slocum, and Woodman, *Organizational Behavior*, 491.

103. William A. Pasmore, "Social Science Transformed: The Socio-Technical Perspective," *Human Relations* 48, no. 1 (1995), 1–21.

104. David M. Upton, "What Really Makes Factories Flexible?" *Harvard Business Review*, July–August 1995, 74–84.

105. Adapted loosely by Dorothy Marcic from "Hamburger Technology," in Douglas T. Hall et al., *Experiences in Management and Organizational Behavior*, 2nd ed. (New York: Wiley, 1982), 244–247, as well as "Behavior, Technology, and Work Design" in A. B. Shani and James B. Lau, *Behavior in Organizations* (Chicago: Irwin, 1996), M16–23 to M16–26.

106. Manuel C. Manuel III, "AV Corporate: Software Tool Project," *Journal of the International Academy for Case Studies* 19, no. 1 (2013). Used with permission.

8 | Technology for Control, Social Business, and Big Data

Learning Objectives

After reading this chapter you should be able to:

1. Explain how information technology applications have evolved.
2. Discuss how a decentralized philosophy of control differs from a hierarchical philosophy of control.
3. Explain the feedback control model.
4. Describe the balanced scorecard's value for organizational control.
5. Specify IT mechanisms for facilitating employee coordination and efficiency.
6. Explain how IT can be used for social network analysis (SNA) and the value of SNA for managers.
7. Describe social business and how it is being used to improve relationships within the organization and with customers and other stakeholders.
8. Define how big data analytics is distinct from previous data analysis activities within organizations, and specify various approaches to organizing big data scientists within the organization.

Information Technology Evolution

The Philosophy and Focus of Control Systems
   The Changing Philosophy of Control · Feedback Control Model · Organization Level: The Balanced Scorecard · Department Level: Behavior Versus Outcome Control

Facilitating Employee Coordination and Efficiency
   Knowledge Management · Social Network Analysis

Adding Strategic Value
   Social Business · Structural Design for Social Business · Big Data · Big Data and Organization Structure

Impact on Organization Design

Design Essentials

Before reading this chapter, please check whether you agree or disagree with each of the following statements:

1 For a manager, it should not matter much exactly how or when people get their work done, just as long as they produce good results.

I AGREE _____   I DISAGREE _____

2 Savvy organizations should encourage managers to use Twitter.

I AGREE _____   I DISAGREE _____

3 Big data analytics gives good results for making decisions by using carefully selected samples of data.

I AGREE _____   I DISAGREE _____

A few weeks before the H1N1 flu virus made headlines, engineers from Google published a surprising paper in the scientific journal *Nature*. It explained how Google could predict the spread of the winter flu in the United States down to specific regions and even states. Google gets more than 3 billion search queries every day and saves them all. Engineers took the 50 million most common search terms and compared the list with Centers for Disease Control data on the spread of seasonal flu between 2003 and 2008, looking for correlations between the frequency of certain search queries and the spread of flu. They processed 450 million different mathematical models to test the terms, comparing their predictions against actual flu cases. The Google team struck gold: the software found a combination of 45 search terms that had a strong correlation between their predictions and the official figures. The *Nature* paper was largely overlooked outside the world of computer scientists, but it created a splash among health officials. When a new virus emerges and spreads quickly, the only hope health officials have is to slow the spread of the disease, but to do that they need to know where it already is. Although the CDC receives information from doctors, public health clinics, and hospitals, the data are always a couple of weeks out of date. With a rapidly spreading disease, two weeks is an eternity. Google's method, built on the power of "big data," could tell where the flu had spread in near real time, not a week or two after the fact.[1]

Big data is one of the most recent advances in the field of information technology (IT), and it is reshaping companies and entire businesses. Amazon.com collects tons of data on customers, including what books they buy, what else they look at, how they navigate through the website, and how much they are influenced by promotions and reviews. The company uses algorithms that predict and suggest what books a customer might be interested in reading next. Moreover, the predictions get better every time a customer responds to or ignores a recommendation.[2] Many organizations have also been transformed by other forms of IT. Effectively using IT in knowledge-based firms such as consulting firm KPMG, Amerex Brokers, a brokerage firm specializing in energy resources, and Business Wire, which provides business and corporate information, has long been fundamental. Today, IT has become a crucial factor helping companies in all industries maintain a competitive edge in the face of growing global competition and rising customer demands for speed, convenience, quality, and value. The primary benefits of IT for organizations include its potential for improving decision making as well as for enhancing control, efficiency, and coordination of the organization internally and with external partners and customers. Some organization theorists believe IT is gradually replacing the traditional hierarchy in coordinating and controlling organizational activities.[3]

Purpose of This Chapter

Information is the lifeblood of organizations. Managers spend at least 80 percent of their time actively exchanging information. They need this information to hold the organization together. The vertical and horizontal information linkages described in Chapter 3 are designed to provide managers with relevant information for decision making, coordination, evaluation, and control. It isn't just facilities, equipment, or even products and services that define organization success, but rather the information managers possess and how they use it. Highly successful organizations today are typically those that apply information technology (IT) most effectively.

The ways in which managers collect and use information has changed dramatically over the years. This chapter examines the evolution of IT. The chapter begins by looking at IT systems applied to organizational operations and then examines how IT is used for control and coordination of the organization, including a discussion of knowledge management. The next sections consider how IT can add strategic value through the use of social business and big data applications. These recent IT innovations are a natural outgrowth of earlier applications such as business intelligence and knowledge management and have led to a quantum leap in strengthening internal and external relationships, organizational understanding, and strategic success. The final section of the chapter presents an overview of how IT affects organization design.

Information Technology Evolution

Exhibit 8.1 illustrates the evolution of IT. First-line management is typically concerned with well-defined problems about operational issues and past events. Top management, by contrast, deals mostly with uncertain, ambiguous issues, such as strategy and planning. As computer-based IT systems have grown increasingly sophisticated, applications have grown to support effective management coordination, control, and decision making about complex and uncertain problems.

Initially, IT systems in organizations were applied to operations. These initial applications were based on the notion of machine-room efficiency—that is, current operations could be performed more efficiently with the use of computer technology. The goal was to reduce labor costs by having computers take over some tasks. These systems became known as **transaction processing systems** (TPSs), which automate the organization's routine, day-to-day business transactions. A TPS collects data from transactions such as sales, purchases from suppliers, and inventory changes, and stores them in a database. For example, at Enterprise Rent-A-Car, a computerized system keeps track of the 1.4 million transactions the company logs every hour. The system can provide front-line employees with up-to-the-minute information on car availability and other data, enabling them to provide exceptional customer service.[4] Midland Memorial Hospital in Texas recently adopted IT for

EXHIBIT 8.1

Evolution of Organizational Applications of IT

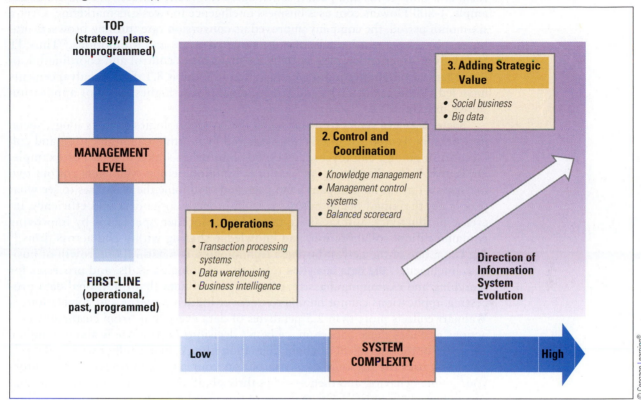

electronic medical records. The system helped Midland catch up on a $16.7 million coding and billing backlog for 4,500 patient records in only four weeks, a process that likely would have taken six months or more without the system.[5]

In recent years, the use of data warehousing and business intelligence software has expanded the usefulness of these accumulated data. **Data warehousing** is the use of huge databases that combine all of a company's data and allow users to access the data directly, create reports, and obtain responses to what-if questions. Software for business intelligence, also called *analytic software*, helps users make sense of all these data. **Business intelligence** refers to the high-tech analysis of a company's data in order to make better strategic decisions.[6] Sometimes referred to as *data mining*, business intelligence means searching out and analyzing data from multiple sources across the enterprise, and increasingly from outside sources as well, to identify patterns and relationships that might be significant. Retailers are some of the biggest users of business intelligence software. Managers at companies such as Wet Seal, a specialty clothing store selling mainly to teenage girls, and Elie Tahari, a maker of designer clothes, need to spot changing trends fast, so they are continually mining sales data. Wet Seal created a web feature called Outfitter that allows users to put together their own outfits online; mining the 300,000 user-generated outfits gave managers an early lead on the trend toward wearing dressy tops with casual pants and jeans.[7]

By collecting the right data and using business intelligence software to analyze them and spot trends and patterns, managers can make smarter decisions. For example, 1-800-Flowers.com uses business intelligence to tweak its marketing. Over a six-month period, the company improved its conversion rate (turning browsers into buyers) by 20 percent because of more targeted pages and promotions.[8] Thus, IT has evolved to more complex systems for managerial control and coordination of the organization, the second stage illustrated in Exhibit 8.1. Further advancements have led to the use of IT to add strategic value, the highest level of application shown in Exhibit 8.1.

Social business refers to using social media technologies such as blogs, social networks, or Twitter for interacting with and facilitating communication and collaboration among employees, customers, and other stakeholders. For example, Dr. Pepper built a Facebook fan base of 8.5 million people. Managers put out two messages a day on the company's fan page and then mine the responses to see what people are thinking.[9] Social business can improve an organization's efficiency, increase productivity, and facilitate faster and smoother operations by improving communication, collaboration, and knowledge sharing within and across firms.[10] Big Data, one of the newest business technologies, is a natural outgrowth of business intelligence. **Big data analytics** refers to technologies, skills, and processes for searching and examining massive, complex sets of data that traditional data processing applications cannot handle to uncover hidden patterns and correlations.[11] Walmart collects more than 2.5 petabytes of data every hour from customer transactions and uses those data to make better decisions (a petabyte is about a million gigabytes or the equivalent of about 20 million filing cabinets full of written data).[12] Facebook uses the personal data you put on your page and tracks and monitors your online behavior, and then searches through all those data to identify and suggest potential "friends."[13] The majority of this chapter focuses on these two higher-level stages in the evolution of IT.

The Philosophy and Focus of Control Systems

Managers consider both control of the overall organization and control of departments, teams, and individuals. Some control strategies apply to the top levels of an organization, where the concern is for the entire organization or major divisions. Control is also an issue at the lower, operational level, where department managers and supervisors focus on the performance of teams and individual employees.

The Changing Philosophy of Control

Managers' approach to control is changing in many organizations. In connection with the shift to employee participation and empowerment, many companies are adopting a *decentralized* rather than a *hierarchical* control process. Hierarchical control and decentralized control represent different philosophies of corporate culture. Most organizations display some aspects of both hierarchical and decentralized control, but managers generally emphasize one or the other, depending on the organizational culture and their own beliefs about control.

Hierarchical control involves monitoring and influencing employee behavior through extensive use of rules, policies, hierarchy of authority, written documentation, reward systems, and other formal mechanisms.[14] In contrast, decentralized control relies on cultural values, traditions, shared beliefs, and trust to foster compliance with organizational goals. Managers operate on the assumption that employees are trustworthy and willing to perform effectively without extensive rules and close supervision.

Exhibit 8.2 contrasts the use of hierarchical and decentralized methods of control. Hierarchical methods define explicit rules, policies, and procedures for employee behavior. Control relies on centralized authority, the formal hierarchy, and close personal supervision. Responsibility for quality control rests with quality control inspectors and supervisors rather than with employees. Job descriptions generally are specific and task related, and managers define minimal standards for acceptable employee performance. In exchange for meeting the standards, individual employees are given extrinsic rewards such as wages, benefits, and possibly promotions up the hierarchy. Employees rarely participate in the control process, with any participation being formalized through mechanisms such as grievance procedures. With hierarchical control, the organizational culture is somewhat rigid, and managers do not consider culture a useful means of controlling employees and the organization. Technology often is used to control the flow and pace of work or to monitor employees, such as by measuring the number of minutes employees spend on phone calls or how many keystrokes they make at the computer.

EXHIBIT 8.2

Hierarchical and Decentralized Methods of Control

	Hierarchical Control	Decentralized Control
Basic assumptions	People are incapable of self-discipline and cannot be trusted. They need to be monitored and controlled closely.	People work best when they are fully committed to the organization.
Actions	Uses detailed rules and procedures and formal control systems.	Features limited use of rules; relies on shared values, group and self-control, selection, and socialization.
	Uses top-down authority, formal hierarchy, position power, supervision, quality control inspectors.	Relies on flexible authority, flat structure, and expert power; everyone monitors quality.
	Relies on task-related job descriptions.	Relies on results-based job descriptions; emphasizes goals to be achieved.
	Emphasizes extrinsic rewards (pay, benefits, status).	Emphasizes extrinsic and intrinsic rewards (meaningful work, opportunities for growth).
	Features rigid organizational culture and distrust of cultural norms as means of control.	Features adaptive culture; culture recognized as means for uniting individual, team, and organizational goals for overall control.
Consequences	Employees follow instructions and do *just* what they are told.	Employees take initiative and seek responsibility.
	Employees feel a sense of indifference toward work.	Employees are actively engaged and committed to their work.
	Employee absenteeism and turnover is high.	Employee turnover is low.

Sources: Based on Naresh Khatri et al., "Medical Errors and Quality of Care: From Control to Commitment," *California Management Review* 48, no. 3 (Spring, 2006), 118; Richard E. Walton, "From Control to Commitment in the Workplace," *Harvard Business Review*, March–April 1985, 76–84; and Don Hellriegel, Susan E. Jackson, and John W. Slocum, Jr., *Management*, 8th ed. (Cincinnati, OH: South-Western, 1999), 663.

The hierarchical approach to control is strongly evident in many Japanese companies. Japanese culture reflects an obsession with rules that can excel at turning chaos to order. For example, after the devastating 2011 earthquake and tsunami, the Japanese efficiently organized evacuation centers for families who lost homes during the disaster. Self-governing committees managed these temporary shelters and laid out in painstaking detail the daily responsibilities of the residents. People were assigned specific tasks, including sorting the garbage, washing the bathrooms, and cleaning fresh-water tanks. This hierarchical method of managing the temporary evacuation centers helped survivors find routine and responsibility, which could play a big role in reducing the long-term psychological and physical toll of this natural disaster.[15]

Decentralized control is based on values and assumptions that are almost opposite to those of hierarchical control. Rules and procedures are used only when necessary. Managers rely instead on shared goals and values to control employee behavior. The organization places great emphasis on the selection and socialization of employees to ensure that workers have the appropriate values needed to influence behavior toward meeting company goals. No organization can control employees 100 percent of the time, and self-discipline and self-control are what keep people performing their jobs up to standard. Empowerment of employees, effective socialization, and training all can contribute to internal standards that provide self-control. Nick Sarillo, who owns two Nick's Pizza & Pub shops in Illinois, says his management style is "trust and track," which means giving people the tools and information they need, telling them the result they need to achieve, and then letting them get there in their own way. At the same time, Sarillo keeps track of results so the company stays on solid ground.[16]

With decentralized control, power is more dispersed and is based on knowledge and experience as much as formal position. The organizational structure is flat and horizontal, with flexible authority and teams of workers solving problems and making improvements. Everyone is involved in quality control on an ongoing basis. Job descriptions generally are results-based, with an emphasis more on the outcomes to be achieved than on the specific tasks to be performed. Managers use not only extrinsic rewards such as pay, but the intrinsic rewards of meaningful work and the opportunity to learn and grow. Technology is used to empower employees by giving them the information they need to make effective decisions, work together, and solve problems. People are rewarded for team and organizational success as well as their individual performance, and the emphasis is on equity among employees. Employees participate in a wide range of areas, including setting goals, determining standards of performance, governing quality, and designing control systems.

With decentralized control, the culture is adaptive, and managers recognize the importance of organizational culture for uniting individual, team, and organizational goals for greater overall control. Ideally, with decentralized control, employees will pool their areas of expertise to arrive at procedures that are better than managers could come up with working alone. Campbell Soup is using decentralized control by enlisting its workers to help squeeze efficiency out of its plants. At the plant in Maxton, North Carolina, factory workers huddle every morning with managers to find ways to save the company money. These employees are part of a decentralized culture where both managers and employees share the company's goals and collaborate on ways to improve efficiency. The daily worker–manager huddles are about "getting everybody involved," says "Big John" Filmore, a 28-year plant veteran. "Instead of being told what to do, we get to tell people about our problems," he said.[17]

Feedback Control Model

All effective control systems involve the use of feedback to determine whether organizational performance meets established standards to help the organization attain its goals. Managers set up systems for organizational control that consist of the four key steps in the **feedback control model** illustrated in Exhibit 8.3.

The cycle of control includes setting strategic goals for departments or the organization as a whole, establishing metrics and standards of performance, comparing metrics of actual performance to standards, and correcting or changing activities as needed. An example from Jefferson Pilot Financial, a full-service life insurance and annuities company, illustrates the feedback control model. Executives established goals for one department to reduce the time between receiving an application and issuing a policy by 60 percent and to reduce the number of reissued policies due to errors by 40 percent. When performance was measured, the unit had met its goal of reducing reissues by 40 percent and had surpassed the application-to-policy goal, reducing turnaround time by 70 percent.[18] Feedback control helps managers make needed adjustments in work activities, standards of performance, or goals to help the organization be successful. Complete the questionnaire in the "How Do You Fit the Design?" box to see how effective you are at setting goals.

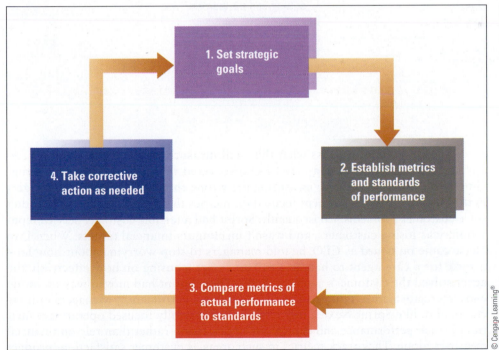

EXHIBIT 8.3
A Simplified Feedback Control Model

1. Set strategic goals

2. Establish metrics and standards of performance

3. Compare metrics of actual performance to standards

4. Take corrective action as needed

© Cengage Learning®

HOW DO YOU FIT THE DESIGN?

IS GOAL-SETTING YOUR STYLE?

How do your work habits fit with making plans and setting goals? Answer the following questions as they apply to your work or study behavior. Please answer whether each item is Mostly True or Mostly False for you.

	Mostly True	Mostly False
1. I set clear, specific goals in more than one area of my work and life.	_____	_____
2. I have a definite outcome in life I want to achieve.	_____	_____
3. I prefer general to specific goals.	_____	_____
4. I work better without specific deadlines.	_____	_____
5. I set aside time each day or week to plan my work.	_____	_____
6. I am clear about the measures that indicate when I have achieved a goal.	_____	_____
7. I work better when I set more challenging goals for myself.	_____	_____
8. I help other people clarify and define their goals.	_____	_____
9. Trying for specific goals makes life more fun than being without goals.	_____	_____

Scoring: Give yourself one point for each item you marked as Mostly True, except items 3 and 4. For items 3 and 4 give yourself one point for each one you marked Mostly False. If you scored 4 or less, goal-setting behavior may not be natural for you. A score of 6 or above suggests a positive level of goal-setting behavior and better preparation for a managerial role in an organization.

Interpretation: An important part of organization life is setting goals, measuring results, and reviewing progress for people and departments. Most organizations have goal-setting and review systems. The preceding questions indicate the extent to which you have already adopted the disciplined use of goals in your life and work. Research indicates that setting clear, specific, and challenging goals in key areas will produce better performance. Not everyone thrives under a disciplined goal-setting system, but as an organization manager, setting goals, assessing results, and holding people accountable will enhance your impact. Goal-setting can be learned.

BRIEFCASE

As an organization manager, keep these guidelines in mind:

Devise control systems that consist of the four essential steps of the feedback control model: set goals, establish standards of performance, measure actual performance, and correct or change activities as needed.

Managers carefully assess what they will measure and how they define it. At Sprint Nextel Corporation, a new CEO discovered that the company was struggling because managers were measuring the wrong things. For example, managers in the customer care department focused on metrics that controlled costs but didn't solve customer problems. Consequently, Sprint had a terrible customer service reputation, was losing customers, and wasn't meeting its financial targets. When Dan Hesse came on board as CEO, he told managers to stop worrying about how long it took for a care agent to handle a call and start focusing on how effectively the agent solved the customer's problem. Before long, Sprint had moved way up in the consumer satisfaction ratings and was adding new customers.[19] Managers at most companies, like Sprint Nextel, use a number of carefully focused operational metrics to track performance and control the organization rather than rely on financial measures alone. They track metrics in such areas as customer satisfaction, product quality, employee commitment and turnover, operational performance, innovation, and corporate social responsibility, for example, as well as financial results.

Organization Level: The Balanced Scorecard

A recent control system innovation is to integrate internal financial measurements and statistical reports with a concern for markets and customers, as well as employees. The **balanced scorecard** (BSC) is a comprehensive management control system that balances traditional financial measures with operational measures relating to a company's critical success factors.[20] A BSC contains four major perspectives, as illustrated in Exhibit 8.4: financial performance, customer service, internal business processes, and the organization's capacity for learning and growth.[21]

Within these four areas, managers identify key performance indicators (KPIs) the organization will track. The *financial perspective* reflects a concern that the organization's activities contribute to improving short- and long-term financial

EXHIBIT 8.4

Major Perspectives of the Balanced Scorecard

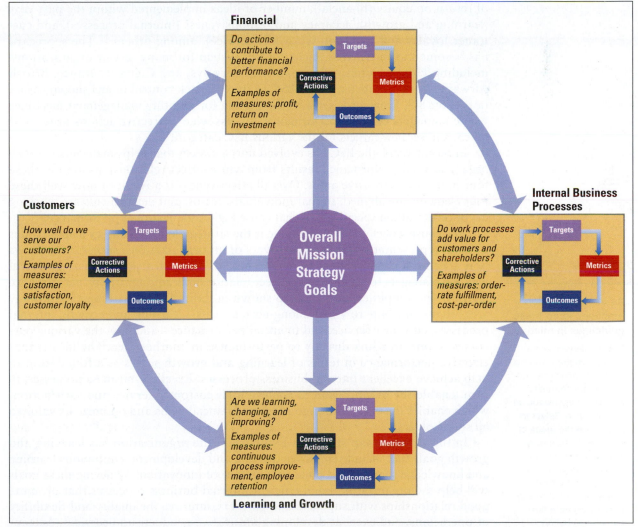

Sources: Based on Robert S. Kaplan and David P. Norton, "Using the Balanced Scorecard as a Strategic Management System," *Harvard Business Review*, January–February 1996, 75–85; Chee W. Chow, Kamal M. Haddad, and James E. Williamson, "Applying the Balanced Scorecard to Small Companies," *Management Accounting* 79, no. 2 (August 1997), 21–27; and Cathy Lazere, "All Together Now," *CFO*, February 1998, 28–36.

performance. It includes traditional measures such as net income and return on investment. *Customer service indicators* measure such things as how customers view the organization as well as customer retention and satisfaction. *Business process indicators* focus on production and operating statistics, such as order fulfillment or cost per order. The final component looks at the organization's *potential for learning and growth*, focusing on how well resources and human capital are being managed for the company's future. Measurements include such things as employee retention, business process improvements, and the introduction of new products. The components of the scorecard are designed in an integrative manner so that they reinforce one another and link short-term actions with long-term strategic goals, as illustrated in Exhibit 8.4. Managers can use the scorecard to set goals, allocate resources, plan budgets, and determine rewards.

Although these elements sound like they apply most clearly to product-based firms, the scorecard can also be applied to both for-profit and nonprofit service organizations. A large technology service provider, for example, identified KPIs of return on equity (financial), number of ideas implemented within the past year (learning and growth), accuracy and responsiveness (internal processes), and customer loyalty and retention (customer service), among others.[22] The scorecard has become the core management control system for many service organizations, including Hilton Hotels, Allstate, British Airways, and Cigna Insurance. British Airways clearly ties its use of the BSC to the feedback control model shown earlier in Exhibit 8.3. Scorecards serve as the agenda for monthly management meetings, where managers evaluate performance, discuss what corrective actions need to be taken, and set new targets for the various BSC categories.[23]

In recent years, the BSC has evolved into a system that helps managers see how organizational performance results from cause–effect relationships among these four mutually supportive areas. Overall effectiveness is a result of how well these four elements are aligned, so that individuals, teams, and departments are working in concert to attain specific goals that cause high organizational performance.[24]

The cause–effect control technique is the strategy map. A **strategy map** provides a visual representation of the key drivers of an organization's success and shows how specific outcomes in each area are linked.[25] The strategy map is a powerful way for managers to see the cause–effect relationships among various performance metrics. The simplified strategy map shown in Exhibit 8.5 illustrates the four key areas that contribute to a firm's long-term success—learning and growth, internal processes, customer service, and financial performance—and how the various outcomes in one area link directly to performance in another area. The idea is that effective performance in terms of learning and growth serves as a foundation to help achieve excellent internal business processes. Excellent business processes, in turn, enable the organization to achieve high customer service and satisfaction, which enables the organization to reach its financial goals and optimize its value to all stakeholders.

In the strategy map shown in Exhibit 8.5, the organization has learning and growth goals that include employee training and development, continuous learning and knowledge sharing, and building a culture of innovation. Achieving these goals will help the organization build efficient internal business processes that promote good relationships with suppliers and partners, improve the quality and flexibility of operations, and excel at developing innovative products and services. Accomplishing internal process goals, in turn, enables the organization to maintain strong

BRIEFCASE

As an organization manager, keep these guidelines in mind:

Use a balanced scorecard to integrate various control dimensions and get a more complete picture of organizational performance. Select indicators in the areas of financial performance, customer service, internal processes, and learning and growth, and consider a strategy map to visualize how outcomes are linked.

EXHIBIT 8.5
A Strategy Map for Performance Management

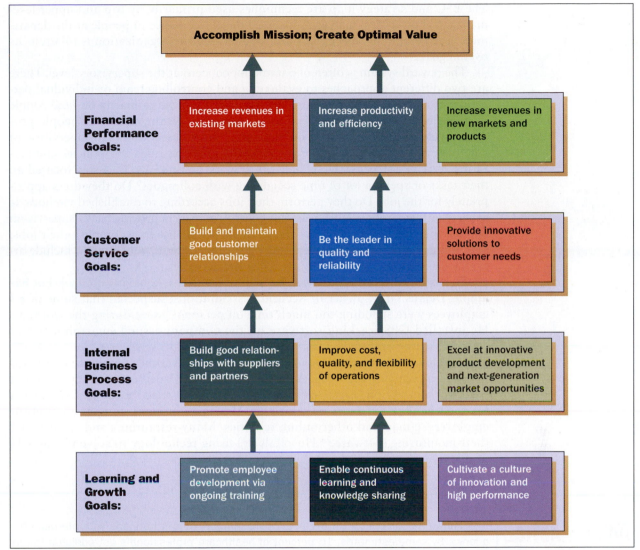

Sources: Based on Robert S. Kaplan and David P. Norton, "Mastering the Management System," *Harvard Business Review*, January 2008, 63–77; and R. S. Kaplan and D. P. Norton, "Having Trouble with Your Strategy? Then Map It," *Harvard Business Review*, September–October 2000, 167–176.

relationships with customers, be a leader in quality and reliability, and provide innovative solutions to emerging customer needs. At the top of the strategy map, the accomplishment of these lower-level goals helps the organization increase revenues in existing markets, reduce costs through better productivity and efficiency, and grow by selling new products and services in new market segments.

In a real-life organization, the strategy map would typically be more complex and would state concrete, specific goals; desired outcomes; and metrics relevant to the particular business. However, the generic map shown in Exhibit 8.5 gives an idea of how managers can use strategy maps to set goals, track metrics, assess performance, and make changes as needed.

Department Level: Behavior Versus Outcome Control

The BSC and strategy map are techniques used primarily by top and upper-level managers. Lower-level managers focus on the performance of people at the department level, who must meet goals and standards if the organization is to attain its overall goals.

The reward system is often of paramount concern at the supervisory level. There are two different approaches to evaluating and controlling team or individual performance and allocating rewards. One approach focuses primarily on *how* people do their jobs, whereas the other focuses primarily on the *outcomes* people produce.[26] **Behavior control** is based on managers' direct observation and supervision of employee actions to see whether the individual follows rules and policies and performs tasks as instructed. Do people get to work on time? Do they stay focused on their tasks or spend a lot of time socializing with colleagues? Do they dress appropriately for the job? Do they perform their jobs according to established methods or supervisor instructions? With behavior control, managers provide heavy supervision and monitoring, pay attention to the methods people use to accomplish their jobs, and evaluate and reward people based on specific criteria, which might include areas such as appearance, punctuality, skills, and activities.

IT has increased the potential for managers to use behavior control. For example, Dennis Gray, owner of Accurid Pest Solutions, suspected that some of his employees were spending too much time on personal issues during the workday. He installed GPS tracking software on the company-issued smartphones and found that one employee was visiting the same address several times a week. The employee admitted he was meeting a woman. Another employee confessed that he was blowing off work. A survey found that 37 percent of companies that send workers out on service calls now track the real-time location of employees via their handheld devices or vehicles.[27] Managers in many companies monitor employees' e-mail and other online activities. Many restaurants and retailers use theft-monitoring software.[28] Hospitals are using technology to solve the age-old problem of missing drugs.

IN PRACTICE

University of Tennessee Medical Center

It is known as "diversion" in the healthcare industry, and it happens with alarming frequency. By some estimates, 15 percent of healthcare professionals get addicted to prescription drugs at some point in their careers by siphoning off drugs for their own use. Controlled substances may also be stolen by patients and visitors.

Drug inventory losses cost hospitals millions of dollars each year and represent a threat to both patient and community safety. Kim New, a compliance specialist at University of Tennessee Medical Center, regularly scans medical surveillance reports to look for patterns of suspicious activity. Automated dispensing machines improve the security of controlled substances by documenting the dispensing of doses and the disposal of unused medicines. Drugs are available in a single-use vial, and if a patient is given a smaller dose, nurses and other staff are required to dispose of the rest following a strict protocol that requires a witness. By scanning the automated reports, New discovered that one nurse was waiting until the end of her shift to dispose of multiple partially used vials. As it turns out, she was collecting leftover medication and injecting herself in the parking lot after work. New says the automated reports have enabled the hospital to catch about one staffer a month diverting drugs.[29]

Monitoring the status of controlled substances in healthcare organizations is essential, but for many organizations, such close monitoring is counterproductive. A second approach to control is to pay less attention to what people *do* than to what they *accomplish*. **Outcome control** is based on monitoring and rewarding results, and managers might pay little attention to how those results are obtained. With outcome control, managers don't supervise employees in the traditional sense. People have a great deal of autonomy in terms of how they do their jobs—and sometimes in terms of where and when they do their jobs—as long as they produce desired outcomes. Rather than monitoring how many hours an employee works, for example, managers focus on how much work the employee accomplishes.

The Results-Only Work Environment (ROWE) program at Best Buy provides an illustration of outcome control carried to the extreme. When Best Buy managers noticed an alarming increase in turnover of headquarters employees, they began looking for ways to reverse the trend. They realized that the Best Buy culture that emphasized long hours, mandatory procedures, and managers "acting like hall monitors" was no longer working. A new system allowed people to work when and where they wanted as long as they got the job done. The experiment started in one department where morale had reached a dismal low. It worked so well that it eventually spread throughout headquarters. The results? From 2005 to 2007, the turnover rate in departments using ROWE decreased nearly 90 percent, while productivity shot up 41 percent. Although the ROWE system was discontinued as Best Buy went into decline in recent years, it worked extremely well as a means of outcome control. Senior Vice President John Thompson, who was at first skeptical, became a strong believer when he saw the results. "I was always looking to see if people were here. I should have been looking at what they were getting done," Thompson said.[30]

With outcome control such as the ROWE system, IT is used not to monitor and control individual employee behavior but rather to assess performance outcomes. For example, at Best Buy, the manager of the online orders department could use IT to measure how many orders per hour his team processed, even if one team member was working down the hall, one working from home, one taking the afternoon off, and another working from her vacation cabin 400 miles away.[31] Good performance metrics are key to making an outcome control system work effectively.

However, outcome control is not necessarily the best for all situations. In some cases, behavior control is more appropriate and effective, but in general, managers in successful organizations are moving away from closely monitoring and controlling behavior toward allowing employees more discretion and autonomy in how they do their jobs. The BookMark describes a simple tool that managers can use to give employees more autonomy yet maintain control over critical work activities. In most organizations, managers use both behavior and outcome control.

1 **For a manager, it should not matter much exactly how or when people get their work done, just as long as they produce good results.**

> **ANSWER:** *Agree.* Focusing on results, or outcomes, can be a highly effective approach to department level control in many organizations. Employees resent being micromanaged and don't like being treated like children. Most managers find it necessary to set some reasonable boundaries for correct behavior, but greater control emphasis is placed on outcome control to achieve highest performance.

ASSESS YOUR ANSWER

BOOKMARK 6.0 HAVE YOU READ THIS BOOK?

The Checklist Manifesto: How to Get Things Right

By Atul Gawande

Buildings crumble because design modifications don't take critical engineering specifications into account. Factory fires, oil rig explosions, and mine accidents occur because important safety measures are overlooked. And every year in the United States alone nearly 100,000 people die from hospital-acquired infections because simple sterilization steps are missed. "The volume and complexity of what we know has exceeded our individual ability to deliver its benefits correctly, safely, or reliably," says Atul Gawande, a physician and author of *The Checklist Manifesto: How to Get Things Right*.

A SIMPLE WAY TO CONTROL COMPLEX WORK

Gawande's book describes how using a checklist can reduce and eliminate many errors in complex jobs by making priorities clear, helping people remember specific critical steps that can easily be forgotten in the midst of complexity, and preventing communication breakdowns. Using examples from surgery, foreign intelligence, construction, aviation, rock concerts, software design, and other areas, Gawande shows how the right checklist improves outcomes by catching the "mental flaws inherent in all of us—flaws of memory and attention and thoroughness." Here's how to effectively use a checklist:

- *Keep it simple*. A checklist shouldn't try to detail every step involved in a process such as conducting surgery, setting up for a rock concert, or designing a new piece of software. Rather, it should be simple and precise, spelling out "only the most critical and important steps" that are prone to errors. A good checklist makes priorities clear to everyone using it.

- *Remember that complexity obscures the obvious*. A checklist should make sure people don't make stupid mistakes because they are overwhelmed by a complex situation. A critical care specialist created a five-step checklist designed to reduce IV line infections of patients in the intensive care unit: wash your hands with soap; sterilize the patient's skin; put sterile drapes over the entire patient; wear a mask, gown, and gloves; put a sterile dressing over the insertion site. The rate of infections dropped from 11 percent to 0 within a year.

- *Make it a communication tool*. A checklist forces communication where it is needed. For instance, in construction, even a minor change in the support structure can affect a range of other planned steps, such as plumbing and electrical. Checklists can be used to make sure people in charge of different aspects of a project are consulted about any decision that potentially affects their part of the project. "Just ticking boxes is not the ultimate goal here," Gawande writes. "Embracing a culture of teamwork and discipline is."

CHECKLISTS HELP DECENTRALIZE POWER

Good checklists enable managers to "push the power of decision making out to the periphery and away from the center," Gawande says. Checklists mean managers can focus less on strict forms of behavior control. "They supply a set of checks to ensure the stupid but critical stuff is not overlooked, and they supply another set of checks to ensure people talk and coordinate and accept responsibility while nonetheless being left the power to manage the nuances and unpredictabilities the best they know how."

The Checklist Manifesto: How to Get Things Right, by Atul Gawande, is published by Metropolitan Books.

Facilitating Employee Coordination and Efficiency

IT is also used for improving coordination and knowledge sharing among employees, enhancing efficiency, and improving collaboration within the organization.

Knowledge Management

One common form of corporate information sharing is an **intranet**, a private, companywide information system that uses the communications protocols and standards of the Internet but is accessible only to people within the company. To view files and information, users simply navigate the site with a standard web browser, clicking on links. Intranets can improve internal communications and unlock hidden information. They enable employees to keep in touch with what's going on around the organization, quickly and easily find information they need, share ideas, and work on projects collaboratively.

A primary use of intranets is for knowledge management. **Knowledge management** refers to the efforts to systematically find, organize, and make available a company's intellectual capital and to foster a culture of continuous learning and knowledge sharing.[32] The company's **intellectual capital** is the sum of its knowledge, experience, understanding, relationships, processes, innovations, and discoveries.

Companies need ways to transfer both codified knowledge and tacit knowledge across the organization.[33] **Codified knowledge** is formal, systematic knowledge that can be articulated, written down, and passed on to others in documents, rules, or general instructions. Tacit knowledge, on the other hand, is often difficult to put into words. **Tacit knowledge** might include how to interpret the look on a negotiator's face or the learned experience of working with a client over a long period of time. It is based on personal experience, rules of thumb, intuition, and judgment. It includes professional know-how and expertise, individual insight and experience, and creative solutions that are difficult to communicate and pass on to others. As much as 80 percent of an organization's valuable knowledge may be tacit knowledge that is not easily captured and transferred.[34] Some companies use **expert-locator systems** that identify and catalog experts in a searchable database so people can quickly identify who has knowledge they can use.[35]

Two approaches to knowledge management are outlined in Exhibit 8.6.[36] The first approach deals primarily with the collection and sharing of codified knowledge, largely through the use of sophisticated IT systems. Codified knowledge may include intellectual properties such as patents and licenses; work processes such as policies and procedures; specific information on customers, markets, suppliers, or competitors; competitive intelligence reports; and benchmark data. The second approach focuses on leveraging individual expertise and know-how—tacit

EXHIBIT 8.6
Two Approaches to Knowledge Management

Codified Provide high-quality, reliable, and fast information systems for access of explicit, reusable knowledge		**Tacit** Channel individual expertise to provide creative advice on strategic problems
People-to-documents approach *Develop an electronic document system that codifies, stores, disseminates, and allows reuse of knowledge*	**Knowledge Management Strategy**	**Person-to-person approach** *Develop networks for linking people so that tacit knowledge can be shared*
Invest heavily in information technology, with a goal of connecting people with reusable, codified knowledge	**Information Technology Approach**	*Invest moderately in information technology, with a goal of facilitating conversations and the personal exchange of tacit knowledge*

Source: Based on Morten T. Hansen, Nitin Nohria, and Thomas Tierney, "What's Your Strategy for Managing Knowledge?" *Harvard Business Review*, March–April 1999, 106–116.

BRIEFCASE

As an organization manager, keep these guidelines in mind:

Establish systems to facilitate both codified and tacit knowledge sharing among employees to help the organization learn and improve. Use social network analysis to learn about informal relationships and patterns of influence.

knowledge—by connecting people face to face or through interactive social media. Tacit knowledge includes professional know-how, individual insights and creativity, and personal experience and intuition. With this approach, managers concentrate on developing personal networks that link people together for the sharing of tacit knowledge. The organization uses IT systems primarily for facilitating conversation and person-to-person sharing of experience, insight, and ideas.

Consider the example of Converteam, a company with headquarters in the United Kingdom that maintains power generation and propulsion systems for hundreds of ships and oil exploration platforms around the world. Employees working in China, India, Brazil, the United States, and Norway need a way to share knowledge and expertise among themselves and with headquarters. An IT system includes contact details for engineers working in various countries along with an expertise inventory. Engineers can contact one another directly regarding new products, challenges, and so forth, rather than having to go through headquarters.[37]

Encouraging and facilitating the sharing of tacit knowledge isn't easy. Despite the fact that companies have spent billions on software and other technology for knowledge management, there is some indication that knowledge sharing has fallen short of managers' goals. For instance, 60 percent of employees surveyed by a Harris poll said work was often duplicated in their organizations because people were unaware of one another's work. Fifty-four percent said their companies missed opportunities to innovate because of poor collaboration and information sharing, and 51 percent said managers regularly made poor decisions because employee knowledge isn't effectively tapped.[38] For example, through conversation and ongoing interaction, salespeople often come to know what top executives in a client's organization want in a product or service. With this tacit knowledge, the salespeople could help develop better solutions for the client, refine their firm's marketing message, and increase their company's revenue. Yet most organizations lack the internal information-sharing networks to tap into this tacit knowledge. Salespeople naturally concentrate on forming networks with customers and potential customers, not with people inside the company.[39] Managers should understand and manage internal information networks so that tacit knowledge can be shared more easily.

Social Network Analysis

A valuable technique enabled by IT is called **social network analysis** (SNA), which can help managers learn about informal relationships and network structures within an organization. With SNA they can know who has influence and who doesn't, who people turn to for answers, who has the knowledge and technical capability to be innovative, and who has leadership potential. SNA was developed by scientists as a social theory to diagram relationships among people that differ from the formal hierarchy. Social networks include people who turn to one another for help, advice, information, and support, whether or not they are in the same work group. It is within these networks that much of an organization's work gets done.[40] "There is a secret structure at every organization that spells success or failure. You can't see it in the org chart or in the flow of money on the spreadsheet. But within this [informal] structure, the assistant in the third cubicle from the elevator may be more crucial than the suit in the fancy corner office," says corporate anthropologist Karen Stephenson.[41]

People play different roles in social networks. Three roles, or patterns of relationships, seen over and over in organizations are the hub, the broker, and the peripheral player. *Hubs* are people who are at the center of an information network. These are people who are sought out for their knowledge and information. Hubs tend to have more influence than other employees. They may have technical expertise and organizational memory, as well as a set of relationships that helps them get information that other people need. Hubs are the "go to" people in an organization. If they don't know the answer, they know where to find it. A long-time salesperson might be a hub because he or she has developed connections with other salespeople as well as with clients, managers, and people in other departments, and has years of knowledge about how the organization works. *Peripheral players* have the fewest number of connections and operate on the boundaries of a network. They are marginal players, but they can still be important because they may have niche expertise or valuable outside contacts. These might not be needed on a daily basis but could be useful during a crisis or for specialized projects. Of particular importance are the *brokers*, the people who have a knack for connecting people across boundaries and subgroups.[42] Brokers link specialized pools of knowledge and integrate the larger network within the organization. For example, a well-known investment bank won the business of a major account from a rival bank thanks to David Hawkins, a manager who played a broker role. The client had been with the rival bank for years. However, Hawkins had connections to different product and service groups within his bank that the executive at the rival bank didn't have within his firm. Hawkins served as a link across his bank's groups and introduced the client to them, which enabled his bank to create a more targeted and customized financial solution that met the client's unique needs.[43]

Exhibit 8.7 illustrates the three roles in a hypothetical organization, showing how the broker connects different parts of the larger network. Understanding these informal networks offers a competitive advantage to a company. By knowing who is

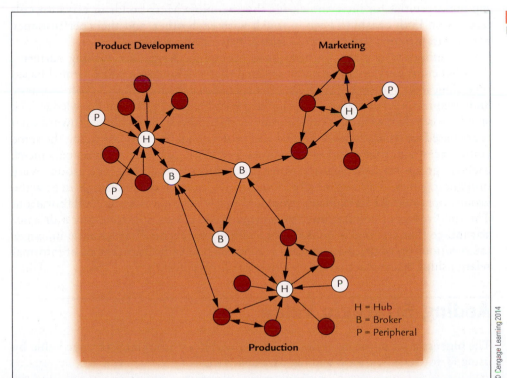

© Cengage Learning 2014

EXHIBIT 8.7
Roles in a Social Network

facilitating high performance in others, who is collaborating, and who has personal connections, managers have a tool through which to help the company improve, innovate, expand, and grow.[44] IBM has been using SNA for years. SNA experts work with companies to find their hidden networks by asking employees simple questions like the following:

> "To whom do you go for a quick decision?"
> "Whom do you hang out with socially?"
> "To whom do you turn for advice?"
> "Whom do you go to with a good idea?"
> "To whom do you go for career advice?"[45]

SNA can be administered in the form of an electronic employee survey or by tracking e-mail messages among employees. Here are some examples of information that a sophisticated network tracking system might provide:

- Who is working with whom in the company's social network?
- Who are the informal leaders, and who has leadership potential?
- How does knowledge and information flow through an organization?
- Who is being overutilized, and who is being underutilized?
- Who are the experts in a company before they retire so their knowledge can be stored or transferred?[46]

Social network analysis can uncover hidden workplace relationships. It offers clear delineation of relationships through data, facts, and statistics instead of relying on rumor and innuendo. These data can be used to change the organization. For example, after reviewing the results of the SNA, the packaged food giant Mars found that the people in the snack food division in New Jersey weren't talking enough with peers in the Los Angeles food division, creating duplication of work and missing opportunities for tacit knowledge sharing. Now Mars builds in ways for colleagues on both coasts to keep in touch with each other, and their performance reviews are based in part on their informal networking activities.[47]

Sometimes a stronger intervention is needed to change networking patterns. A global consulting organization discovered that two subgroups had formed based on technical and nontechnical skills. Clients needed a combination of "soft" strategy and organizational design smarts combined with "harder" technical knowledge. The split between the two groups came about because individuals gravitated toward each other based on common work-related and professional interests, attending the same conferences, and time spent working together. With guidance from management, each subgroup learned what the other group offered to clients. The groups were brought together to discuss the situation, which ultimately led to changes in how the groups operated. These changes promoted knowledge sharing and collaboration. The final result of collaborative groups gave the consulting company a distinct advantage that resulted in more sales and happier clients.[48] Systematic manager interventions based on SNA can help a company build a healthy pattern of informal relationships that replace ad hoc dysfunctional relationships.[49]

Adding Strategic Value

The highest level in the evolution of IT in Exhibit 8.1 is adding strategic value by using IT for social business and big data analytics.

Social Business

As described earlier, *social business* refers to using social media technologies for interacting with and facilitating communication and collaboration among employees, customers, and other stakeholders. **Social media** include company online community pages and forums, blogs and wikis for virtual collaboration, social media sites such as Facebook or LinkedIn, video channels such as YouTube, and microblogging platforms such as Twitter and China's Sina Weibo.

Social media can provide for more effective sharing of tacit knowledge.[50] For example, the simplicity and informality of Twitter make it a fast and easy way for people to communicate. People can send a question and quickly get responses from all over the organization or from outsiders. Because of the popularity of Facebook and Twitter in people's personal lives, most employees are comfortable with the idea of "following" and communicating with their colleagues online. Using social networks for a business enables people to easily connect with one another across organizational and geographical boundaries based on professional relationships, shared interests, problems, or other criteria. A Symantec salesman in Dubai created a group on the company's network that exchanges sales tips from employees around the world.[51] People can use the social network to search for tags that will identify others with knowledge and resources that can help them solve a problem or do their jobs better. Moreover, the nature of social networking builds trust so that people are more likely to cooperate and share information.[52]

In addition, social media technology is being used by companies to build trusting relationships with customers.[53] An early leader in this realm was Morgan Stanley Wealth Management. As director of digital strategy, Lauren Boyman worked closely with the company's sales manager and investment advisors to use Twitter and other social media for communicating with clients.[54]

2 **Savvy organizations should encourage managers to use Twitter.**

ANSWER: *Agree.* Twitter and other microblogging platforms are an increasingly popular way for managers to communicate, both with employees and with customers. Blogging and microblogging have become almost as common for some managers as using e-mail. Employees expect managers to use Twitter at least occasionally.

ASSESS **YOUR** ANSWER

Just as importantly, social media can build stronger, more authentic relationships between managers and employees.

Mark Reuss left General Motors (GM) in Australia to run GM's operations in North America just after GM had filed for bankruptcy and was implementing plans to eliminate more than 2,000 U.S. dealerships. He knew every move he made would affect how well the company weathered the tough period and how successful it was on the other side of the bankruptcy.

Reuss chose to communicate with the dealer network through a "get to know you" messaging part of Facebook rather than through e-mails or other corporate communications. The strategy helped build trust and credibility because Reuss made himself accessible and was willing to engage others authentically. "No matter what happened," Reuss said, "they knew that I was listening and that they had . . . someone to talk to in the company and they could do it instantly. And if you look at how we got through that period and the dealers that we have and the trust that I have built . . . it's because of that conversation on Facebook."[55]

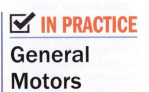
☑ **IN PRACTICE**
General Motors

Other managers are also finding social media a great way to quickly build trust and credibility. Shortly after arriving as the new CEO of MassMutual, Roger Crandall attended the company's biggest sales conference and was asked by an employee with a Flip cam if she could record him at the conference and post the video on the company intranet's community page. "A Week in the Life" was available for the whole company to watch in real time and "was a great way to create a personal connection," Crandall said.[56] Some managers have begun incorporating video streams into their blogs because they allow them to engage with people in real time on a highly personal level.[57]

Many organizations, from small entrepreneurial firms and nonprofit agencies to huge corporations, are using social media for business purposes. Danish shipping and energy company Maersk Group had a 100-year history of keeping a low public profile, but the company is now a social business leader. Maersk is on Facebook, Twitter, YouTube, Tumblr, Google+, Sina Weibo, LinkedIn, and more. As the public began expecting more transparency from companies, Maersk found itself hosting conversations and asking customers and others to engage with the company. Social media is also used at Maersk for internal collaboration. One unit, Damco, established the Damco People's Network to help salespeople in Copenhagen, for example, connect with their counterparts in other countries, such as China, where there were potential leads. Another unit is using Chatter to connect sales teams around the globe and create a knowledge database. When you get people who don't already know one another connected to a global network, says corporate brand manager Anna Granholm-Brun, "magic starts to happen."[58]

Structural Design for Social Business

Maersk isn't the only company using social media to communicate with customers. Many organizations, including Ford Motor Company, Harrah's Entertainment, McDonald's, Petco, and AT&T, have hired *social media directors* who are in charge of a blend of activities such as marketing and promotions, customer service, and support.[59] Like most new activities or techniques within organizations, social business typically starts slowly and gains momentum. Unlike some other activities, social business often starts *bottom-up*, that is, with lower-level employees and managers who see value in using social media, and then spreads throughout the rest of the organization. Facebook was founded in 2004 and Twitter in 2006, but most organizations began actively using social media for business only within the last few years.

Because of its value in connecting with customers, social business first spread to marketing and public relations or corporate communications departments. Social networks, Twitter, and blogs are particularly popular customer-facing technologies. In 2013, 77 percent of *Fortune* 500 companies reported having active Twitter accounts and 70 percent were on Facebook. Interestingly, only 34 percent reported having corporate blogs.[60]

Social media directors and social business teams typically report to either the marketing or corporate communications department, but social business teams are increasingly reporting to top management in order to serve departments across the enterprise. Of companies surveyed in 2013, three-quarters said they had a dedicated social media team to serve the entire company; however, only 14 percent have a separate social media department. Organizations use a variety of models to facilitate and support social media programs.[61] One of the most popular approaches is to use a social media command center.[62]

BRIEFCASE

As an organization manager, keep these guidelines in mind:

Use social media to improve communication and collaboration among employees, customers, and other stakeholders. Consider a social media director and team to lead the social business initiative and develop a social media command center.

AP Images/Carla K. Johnson

EXHIBIT 8.8
A Social Media Command
Center

Source: AP Photos

A **social media command center** is a dedicated office where a company can monitor what is being said about the company on social media platforms. Exhibit 8.8 shows a social media command center. For some companies, this is a state-of-the-art room manned by a full social business team. For others, it is a couple of desks in a room. From the command center, staff can get instant feedback about what customers are talking about, which trends are emerging, the most recent customer complaints about the company or others in the industry, and how competitors are doing. The Coca-Cola Company, for example, recently pulled an advertising campaign for Diet Coke using the theme "You're on" after the ads were mocked on social media. Some bloggers said they evoked a cocaine habit and the history of Diet Coke's sibling, Coke, which once included small amounts of the drug as an ingredient.[63] Command center findings can be shared across the organization. Cisco set up a two-screen kiosk in front of its CEO and CMO's offices to give those top leaders an ongoing look at what was being said about the company in real time. Dell uses its command center to uncover information to help staff better understand customers. Gatorade was one of the pioneers with its Mission Control Center, which provides valuable social intelligence concerning how products are resonating with customers, detailed sentiment about marketing campaigns, and so forth.[64] Wells Fargo Bank built its Social Media Command Center to be an early alert system for customer service and risk management issues. Managers are aware that even one small misstep in social channels could have serious consequences so one goal of the bank's social business program is to balance the potential for employee engagement with mitigating the risk such engagement can create.[65]

Big Data

One of the hottest terms in IT is big data. **Big data** refers to any massive data set that exceeds the boundaries and conventional processing capabilities of IT. Big data requires a nontraditional approach; it requires that managers throw out the old way of thinking and take a totally new approach. Exhibit 8.9 illustrates how big data are different from regular data.

EXHIBIT 8.9
Big Data Is Really Big

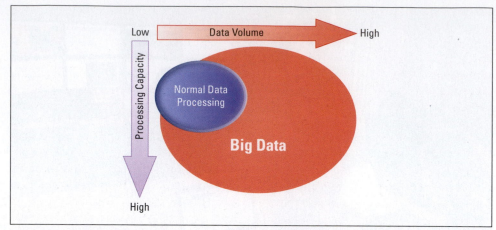

Source: Based on Steve Duplessie, "Big Data: A Better Definition," Enterprise Strategy Group blog, January 6, 2012, http://www.esg-global.com/blogs/big-data-a-better-definition/ (accessed December 20, 2014).

Big data includes data sets with sizes beyond the ability of traditional software tools to manage and process the data within an acceptable time frame. As described earlier, *big data analytics* refers to the process of examining these large data sets to uncover hidden patterns, correlations, and other useful information and make better decisions. Because the data sets are so massive, big data analytics often cannot be done with existing advanced analytics tools; thus a new class of big data technology has emerged.

Exhibit 8.10 illustrates five elements of big data, each of which is discussed in the following sections.

EXHIBIT 8.10
Elements of Big Data Function

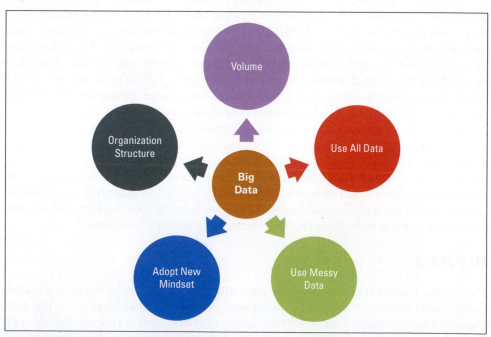

Source: Based on Figure 1.1 Cracking the Big Data Nut, in David Loshin, *Big Data Analytics: From Strategic Planning to Enterprise Integration with Tools, Techniques, NoSQL, and Graph* (Morton Kaufmann, 2009), 3.

Volume. Big data are *really* big. They are so big they are hard to comprehend. What is a zettabyte or a yottabyte, anyway? Quintillions of bytes of data are created every day, and as IBM figures it, about 90 percent of the data that exist in the world today were created within the last two years.[66] Data can be collected easily and often without awareness on the part of individuals being recorded. Many automobiles are recording data all the time. Our physical locations have become data. If you start up Google maps on your smartphone, it immediately knows where you are. Even our interactions with each other have become data, say Viktor Mayer-Schönberger and Kenneth Cukier, the authors of a book on big data, who refer to this new phenomenon as the "datafication of everything."[67]

If all the data available today were printed in books, they say the books would cover the entire surface of the United States 52 layers thick. Placed on CD-ROMs and stacked up, they would stretch to the moon in five separate piles.[68] We are drowning in data, but making them mean something is the challenge. For example, Dell realized there were over seven septillion possible configurations of Dell products on its website. To create a new system of "optimized configuration," the analytics team looked for the most common configurations people were choosing, narrowing the seven septillion down to a couple million, even identifying a few models that could be stocked into preconfigured inventory, saving both Dell and customers time and money.[69] "Storing data, recording data is cheap today," says Radhika Subramanian, CEO of analytics solutions provider Emcien. "Now data is everywhere. Everyone has data. It's like dirt."[70]

Use All Data. Using big data, people and companies can do things that weren't possible with smaller amounts. Rather than using just a sample of their data, companies now have the power to capture and store all the data from their operations, which can lead to interesting correlations. For example, one company found that people who buy small felt pads for the bottom of chair legs to protect their wooden floors are typically good credit risks. An analysis of used cars found that orange cars are half as likely as others to have defects.[71] So what? Managers with a big data mindset embrace these correlations, even if they don't see an immediate underlying cause or purpose. Some correlations prove highly valuable. In *Predictive Analytics*, Eric Siegel talks about how companies use big data to quantify how likely it is that a particular customer will default on a loan, upgrade to a higher level of cable service, or look for another job, for example. Citizens Bank was able to cut losses from check fraud by 20 percent thanks to better data analysis. FedEx can reportedly identify with 65 to 90 percent accuracy which customers are likely to move to a competitor, enabling the company to offer incentives to stay.[72]

Use Messy Data. As the size of data sets increases, so do inaccuracies. Think about a small grocery store, which may count the money in the cash register each night down to the last penny. The same couldn't be done for a country's gross domestic product. A devotion to rigid exactness is given up in a big data world; managers are content with a general direction. Big data are often messy, vary in quality, and come from different sources. Because there is less error than from using sampling, though, managers can live with these inaccuracies. Amazon ran a test to see whether personal book recommendations from editorial staff or from data-based computer analyses generated more book sales. The computer analysis won hands-down. Websites collect massive amounts of messy data on customers. By using all the data and looking at correlations, companies such as Amazon, Netflix, eHarmony, LinkedIn, and Facebook can recommend books, products, friends, dates, and groups without even knowing why people might be interested in them.[73]

Adopt a New Mindset. The big data approach requires a new mindset. It requires surrendering to the data. "I was very sad about the editorial team getting beaten," said Greg Linden at Amazon. "But the data doesn't lie, and the cost was very high."[74] One of the earliest encounters many people had with the big data mindset was the 2011 movie "Moneyball." Brad Pitt portrays Billy Beane, the legendary general manager for the Oakland Athletics baseball team, who in 2002 built one of Major League Baseball's winningest teams with one of its smallest budgets. Rather than rely on the intuition of scouts, who would sometimes reject a player because he "didn't look like a major leaguer," Beane relied heavily on data and statistical analysis. If the analysis said an overweight college catcher that nobody else wanted should be a number-one draft pick, Beane went for it. The movie focuses on clashes between the analytics expert and the chief scout and manager, who had a hard time letting go of the idea of making decisions based on intuition and years of experience. Since that time, most other sports teams have adopted big data statistical techniques to some degree for making decisions. "There's still a place for [guys with stopwatches or playing hunches], but technology has changed the game forever," said Steve Greenberg, former deputy commissioner of Major League Baseball.[75]

Such clashes are playing out in companies across the world as managers with a big data mindset run up against those who believe decisions should be made based on historical information and manager experience. That might be why many big data supporters start new companies, such as Google's Larry Page and Sergey Brin, Amazon's Jeff Bezos, eBay's Pierre Omidyar, and FlightCaster.com's Bradford Cross. Cross and some friends analyzed every flight over the previous 10 years, matched against historic and current weather data, to predict if a flight in the United States was likely to be delayed. FlightCaster lost its first-mover advantage when a larger firm, FlyOnTime.us, began doing the same thing, and Cross sold his firm to Next Jump, a company that manages corporate discount programs using big data techniques.[76]

ASSESS YOUR ANSWER

3 Big data analytics gets the best results with carefully selected samples of data.

ANSWER: *Disagree.* Big data analytics uses all data, not just samples as in traditional data analysis. By using all the data, the findings are considered more accurate for the entire population. This is a major departure from traditional data collection based on small samples.

Big Data and Organization Structure

One crucial question concerns how to organize big data activity within the enterprise. Should the function be centralized or decentralized? Should data specialists be located in a central pool or attached to business units or functions? To which existing unit or function should they report? As with many other activities within organizations, there is no "one best way." Exhibit 8.11 illustrates four structural options for setting up a big data operation. Various structural forms may work best depending on the size and type of organization.

Outsourcing. The first option is to outsource analytics activities. This is a popular choice because many companies don't have the knowledge and experience to put together an analytics team. In addition, finding big data scientists and analysts is not always easy. Because big data analysis is such a hot topic, there is a shortage of skilled analysts looking for jobs. Numerous business process organizations (BPOs) handle call center operations, computer programming, legal research, accounting, and other

EXHIBIT 8.11
Alternative Structures for Organizing Big Data Analytics

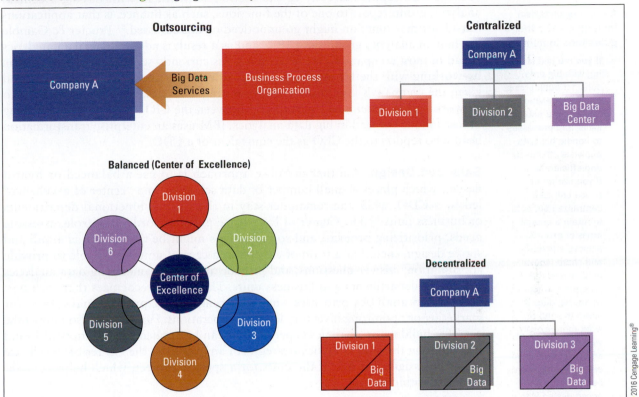

© 2016 Cengage Learning®

services for organization, and business analytics is the latest on the menu of services these firms offer. BPOs in India, for example, have highly skilled analytics teams.

One benefit of outsourcing is that it increases flexibility by making fixed costs variable. Setting up an in-house division can be expensive. For companies that don't have in-house capabilities, outsourcing provides a way to quickly obtain the resources to execute analytics projects and gain important insights at a lower cost. In markets where finding workers with analytics skills is difficult, outsourcing might be the only way to get a foothold in analytics and achieve an advantage over competitors. The outsourcing firm can often provide resources and training for the company's own employees.[77]

Another form of outsourcing is to use **data intermediaries**, firms that collect data from multiple organizations and analyze the combined data for them.[78] For example, Visa and MasterCard do analysis on the billions of transactions from cardholders in 210 countries to predict consumer and business trends and sell the data to others. A division called MasterCard Advisors discovered that when people fill up their gas tanks at around 4:00 P.M., they are likely to spend between $35 and $50 at a grocery store or restaurant within the next hour.[79]

Centralized. For companies that want to set up an in-house unit for analytics, the big question is whether to centralize or decentralize. The first in-house model in Exhibit 8.11 centralizes analytics by locating all big data experts in a single department.[80] The advantages are that this achieves a critical mass of analysts and is the easiest way to ensure that the unit can obtain the necessary data and develop the necessary expertise to efficiently test and use various statistical, data-mining, and predictive models. Managers have to decide whether the unit will report to one of the departments, such as finance or marketing, or to a chief data officer (CDO), who reports directly to the CEO. The problem with having a central analytics group report to one of the functions, such as finance, is that applications outside of that function might go unnoticed or unaddressed.[81] Procter & Gamble has had an analytics group since 1992 and as a result is adopting big data analytics ahead of most companies. At P&G, the CIO is currently serving the CDO function by working with the business units to introduce new analytical approaches, and given the company's long history incorporating analytics, this approach seems to be working fine. Intel uses a partnership between the CIO and the chief marketing officer to take the lead in big data analytics. IBM uses an enterprise transformation head who reports to the CEO as the equivalent of a CDO.[82]

Balanced Design. Another in-house approach is to use a balanced or hybrid design, which places a small number of data scientists in a "center of excellence" led by a CDO, while the remainder stay in the various functional departments or business units.[83] The Center of Excellence plays a coordination role, assessing needs, prioritizing projects, and so forth. This might be thought of as a hub and spoke design, such that a team of experts in a central unit is available to provide coordination, answer questions, and provide assistance concerning data analytics to various departments and business units. This design recognizes that each unit has its own analytics priorities, such as strengthening promotional efforts for marketing or optimizing inventory levels for operations. However, it also honors the need for building up analytics expertise that can be applied organization-wide and coordinating the data analytics strategy. An analyst from the Center of Excellence might be assigned to one of the units for a specific project, which helps to build expertise within the unit.[84]

Decentralized. This approach totally decentralizes data analytics, so that data scientists are spread throughout the organization, with a small group of analysts in each department or business unit. This fully decentralized approach is the easiest way for analysts to collaborate with the respective departments or business units and tailor their models to each unit's needs, but it makes it difficult to share innovative solutions across unit boundaries and achieve critical mass on organization-wide problems and opportunities. In addition, with a small group, there is the question of whether each group will have the expertise needed to obtain the necessary data and deploy the appropriate analytical models.[85] Caesars Entertainment went from decentralized to centralized analytics to increase efficiency and effectiveness of the big data analytics function.

 **IN PRACTICE**

Caesars Entertainment

Caesars Entertainment, with more than 70,000 employees and casino resorts on four continents, is devoted to the use of big data analytics. CEO Gary Loveman, a classically trained economist, has woven analytics into the culture of the organization.

At one time, each Caesars property had its own analytics team of three or four people, but Loveman and chief analytics officer Ruben Sigala believed greater centralization was needed to reap the benefits of data analytics. Over the past several years, Caesars has undergone a reorganization to centralize analytics in order to build a deeper understanding of the total enterprise. Data analytics is used not only to understand customers and create a richer customer experience at each property but also to improve operations—everything from food and beverage analytics to human resources analytics. Centralizing analytics has given all the operations a uniform view of their business and a common language across the organization. Centralization of the analytics function has enabled the team to develop and provide world-class analytical support to each of the businesses and to facilitate innovation across different areas of the organization and through partnerships outside the organization.[86]

Impact on Organization Design

Managers and organization theorists have been studying the relationship between technology and organization design and functioning for more than half a century. As we mentioned in Chapter 7, in IBM's 2012 CEO Study, technology topped the list of external forces that executives expect to significantly influence their organizations over the next few years.[87] In recent years, the advances in IT have had the greatest impact in most organizations.[88] Some specific implications of these advances for organization design are smaller organizations, decentralized structures, improved internal and external coordination, and new network organization structures.

1. *Smaller organizations*. Some Internet-based businesses exist almost entirely in cyberspace; there is no formal organization in terms of a building with offices, desks, and so forth. One or a few people may maintain the site from their homes or a rented work space. Even for traditional businesses, new IT enables the organization to do more work with fewer people. Customers can buy insurance, clothing, tools and equipment, and practically anything else over the Internet without ever speaking to an agent or salesperson. In addition, new IT systems automatically handle many administrative duties within organizations, reducing the need for clerical staff. The Michigan Department of Transportation (MDOT) used to need an army of workers to verify contractors' work. Large projects often required as many as 20 inspectors on-site every day to keep track of thousands of work items. Today, MDOT rarely sends more than one field technician to a site. The employee enters data into a laptop computer using road construction management software tied to computers at headquarters. The system can automatically generate payment estimates and handle other administrative processes that used to take hours of labor.[89] Thanks to IT, today's companies can also outsource many functions and thus use fewer in-house resources.

2. *Decentralized organization structures*. Although management philosophy and corporate culture have a substantial impact on whether IT is used to decentralize information and authority or to reinforce a centralized authority structure,[90] most organizations today use technology to further decentralization. With IT, information that may have previously been available only to top managers at headquarters can be quickly and easily shared throughout the organization, even across great geographical distances. In the IBM study mentioned earlier, CEOs see technology as an enabler of openness, collaboration, and less rigid hierarchies.[91] Managers in varied business divisions or offices can now have the information they need to make important decisions quickly rather than waiting for decisions from headquarters. Social business technologies that enable people to meet, coordinate, and collaborate online facilitate communication and decision making among distributed, autonomous groups of workers, such as in virtual teams.

BRIEFCASE

As an organization manager, keep this guideline in mind:

With greater use of IT, consider smaller organizational units, decentralized structures, improved internal coordination, and the possibility of outsourcing or a network structure.

3. *Improved horizontal coordination and collaboration.* Perhaps one of the greatest outcomes of IT is its potential to improve coordination, communication, and collaboration across the firm. IT applications can connect people even when their offices, factories, or stores are scattered around the world, and many traditional tools companies use look outdated to young employees. A banking executive from Argentina participating in IBM's 2012 study said, "We are the e-mail generation; they are the social network generation." IBM makes extensive use of virtual teams, whose members use a wide variety of social business tools to easily communicate and collaborate. One team made up of members in the United States, Germany, and the United Kingdom used collaboration software as a virtual meeting room to solve a client's tough technical problem within the space of just a few days.[92] Siemens uses a global intranet that connects 450,000 employees around the world to share knowledge and collaborate on projects.[93] MITRE Corporation, an organization that provides consulting and research and development services, primarily to U.S. government clients such as the Department of Defense and the Federal Aviation Administration, uses social networking to overcome traditional barriers such as tenure, location, and functional affiliation that had previously limited information sharing and collaboration at the firm.[94]

4. *Enhanced network structures.* The high level of cross-organization collaboration needed in a virtual network organization structure, described in Chapter 3, would not be possible without the use of advanced IT. In the business world, these are also sometimes called *modular structures* or *virtual organizations*. Outsourcing has become a major trend, thanks to computer technology that can tie companies together into a seamless information flow. For example, Hong Kong's Li & Fung is one of the biggest providers of clothing for retailers such as Abercrombie & Fitch, Guess, Ann Taylor, and Disney, but the company doesn't own any factories, machines, or fabrics. Li & Fung specializes in managing information, relying on an electronically connected web of 7,500 partners in 37 countries to provide raw materials and assemble the clothes. IT enables Li & Fung to stay in touch with worldwide partners and move items quickly from factories to retailers. It also lets retailers track orders as they move through production and make last-minute changes and additions.[95] With a network structure, most activities are outsourced so that different companies perform the various functions needed by the organization. The speed and ease of electronic communication makes the network structure a viable option for companies that want to keep costs low but expand activities or market presence.

Design Essentials

■ Today's most successful organizations are generally those that most effectively apply information technology. IT systems have evolved to a variety of applications to meet organizations' information needs. Operations applications are applied to well-defined tasks at lower organization levels and help improve efficiency. These include transaction processing systems, data warehousing, and business intelligence.

■ Advanced IT systems are also used for better control and coordination of the organization. Many organizations are shifting from a *hierarchical* to a *decentralized* control process that relies on shared values rather than strict rules and close supervision for control. With decentralized control, everyone needs access to good information.

■ At the organization level of control, an innovation called the *balanced scorecard* provides managers with a balanced view of the organization by integrating traditional financial measurements and statistical reports with a concern for markets, customers, and employees. Managers also use strategy maps to see the cause-effect relationships among these critical success factors. At the department level, managers use behavior control or outcome control. Behavior control involves close monitoring of employee activities, whereas outcome control measures and rewards results. Most managers use a combination of behavior and outcome control, with a greater emphasis on outcome control because it leads to better performance and higher motivation.

■ Two primary ways to increase coordination are with knowledge management and social network analysis. Managers use intranets and other IT systems to promote the sharing of both codified and tacit knowledge. Social network analysis helps managers identify the hubs of informal information exchanges within the organization and the informal leaders who serve to connect people and groups across organizational boundaries.

■ Social business, which refers to using social media technologies for interacting with and facilitating communication and collaboration among employees, customers, and other stakeholders, is a rapidly growing area of activity. Many companies have social media directors and social media teams that typically report to the marketing or corporate communications department. These teams keep tabs on the company's online reputation by tracking what is being said about the organization on social networking sites, blogs, and other online media, often via a social media command center, and they can share this information across the organization.

■ Big data is one of the most recent advances in the field of information technology. Big data analytics, a direct outgrowth of earlier business intelligence applications, uses new technologies to examine these large data sets to uncover hidden patterns, correlations, and other useful information and make better decisions. Elements of big data are its massive volume, the potential to use all the data rather than just samples, the use of "messy" data, and the need for a new mindset. Some companies outsource big data activities to business process organizations or use data intermediaries, because it is tough to build big data capabilities in-house. As more people gain the skills, however, more organizations are building their own big data analytics departments. Companies can choose to centralize big data activities, decentralize big data to departments or divisions, or use a Center of Excellence.

■ These advances in IT are having a significant impact on organization design, and some experts suggest that IT may eventually replace traditional hierarchy as a primary means of coordination and control. Technology has enabled creation of the network organization structure, in which a company subcontracts most of its major functions to separate companies. Other specific implications of advanced IT for organization design include smaller organizations, decentralized organization structures, and improved internal and external coordination.

KEY CONCEPTS

balanced scorecard	decentralized control	social business
behavior control	expert-locator system	social network analysis
big data	feedback control model	social media
big data analytics	hierarchical control	social media command center
business intelligence	intellectual capital	strategy map
codified knowledge	intranet	tacit knowledge
data intermediaries	knowledge management	transaction processing systems
data warehousing	outcome control	

DISCUSSION QUESTIONS

1. Do you think technology for social business will eventually enable top managers to do their jobs with little face-to-face communication? Discuss.

2. What types of information technology do you as a student use on a regular basis? How might your life be different if this technology were not available to you?

3. How might a hospital administrator trying to implement cross-functional teams use social network analysis to improve communication and collaboration among nurses, doctors, technicians, and other staff?

4. Discuss some ways a large insurance company such as Allstate, Progressive, or State Farm might use social media tools such as microblogs or social networking. Do you think these tools are more applicable to a service company than to a manufacturing organization? Discuss.

5. Describe how the four balanced scorecard components discussed in the chapter might be used for feedback control within organizations. Which of these components is more similar to outcome control? Behavior control?

6. Describe your use of codified knowledge when you research and write a term paper. Do you also use tacit knowledge regarding this activity? Discuss.

7. Why is knowledge management particularly important to a company that wants to learn and change continuously rather than operate at a stable state?

8. Caesars Entertainment centralized its big data analytics function to be more efficient. Can you think of some competitive issues that might lead a company to go from a centralized big data function to a function that decentralizes to various units?

9. How might social media be used to develop more trusting relationships between management and employees? Between a company and its customers?

10. Why do you think the application of advanced IT typically leads to greater decentralization in an organization? Might it also be used for greater centralization in some organizations? Explain.

CHAPTER 8 WORKSHOP   Balanced Scorecard Exercise

Read the measures and objectives listed below for a business firm and a healthcare organization. Make a check for each objective/measure in the correct balanced scorecard column. If you think an objective/measure fits into two balanced scorecard categories, write the numbers 1 and 2 for your first versus second preference.

	Financial	Customers	Business Processes	Learning & Growth
Business Firm				
Return on capital employed (ROCE)	_____	_____	_____	_____
Build employee recreation venue by December 2016	_____	_____	_____	_____
Develop new products within a time period of eight months	_____	_____	_____	_____
Provide team leader training program by July 2015	_____	_____	_____	_____
Achieve 98 percent customer satisfaction by December 2017	_____	_____	_____	_____
Number of monthly customer complaints	_____	_____	_____	_____
Reduce cost per unit sold by 10 percent	_____	_____	_____	_____
Increase customer retention by 15 percent	_____	_____	_____	_____

	Financial	Customers	Business Processes	Learning & Growth
Improve employee satisfaction scores by 20 percent				
Lead market in speed of delivery by 2016				
Lowest industry cost by 2017				
Improve profits by 12 percent over the next year				
Budget forecast accuracy				
Introduce three new products by December 2016				
Percent training completed				
Number of leaders ready for promotion				
Completed succession plan				
Percentage of part-time employees				
Sales growth to increase 1 percent monthly				
Number of employee grievances				
Employee engagement scores				
Number of employee terminations				
Policy implementation time lag				
Vendor on-time delivery rate				
Total annual revenues				
Utility consumption costs				
Workers' compensation claims				
EBITDA				
Healthcare Organization				
Fundraising targets				
Patient satisfaction				
Appointments accommodated on time				
Percentage of patients restored to full functioning				
Number of patients wanting service				
Percentage of clinical support staff				
Nurse satisfaction				
Length of physician employment				
Patient satisfaction with scheduling				
Wait time satisfaction				
Patient perception of quality				
Cost of patient care				
Profitability				
Staff compliance with privacy regulations				
Bed utilization rate				
Falls per 100 patients				
Percentage of nurse master's degrees				
Speed of patient admissions and discharge				
Education for family member care giving				
Quality of pain control				
Percentage of medicines filled accurately				
Nurse turnover rate				
Nurse shortage rate				
Completion rate of prescribed services				
Total labor costs				
Operating margins				
Amount of charity care				
Unpaid cost of public programs				
Smoking cessation program effectiveness				
Medicare reimbursement audit results				
Education completion rate				

CASE FOR ANALYSIS | Century Medical[96]

Sam Nolan clicked the mouse for one more round of solitaire on the computer in his den. He'd been at it for more than an hour, and his wife had long ago given up trying to persuade him to join her for a movie or a rare Saturday night on the town. The mind-numbing game seemed to be all that calmed Sam enough to stop thinking about work and how his job seemed to get worse every day.

Nolan was chief information officer at Century Medical, a large medical products company based in Connecticut. He had joined the company four years ago, and since that time Century had made great progress integrating technology into its systems and processes. Nolan had already led projects to design and build two highly successful systems for Century. One was a benefits-administration system for the company's HR department. The other was a complex web-based purchasing system that streamlined the process of purchasing supplies and capital goods. Although the system had been up and running for only a few months, modest projections were that it would save Century nearly $2 million annually.

Previously, Century's purchasing managers were bogged down with shuffling paper. The purchasing process would begin when an employee filled out a materials request form. Then the form would travel through various offices for approval and signatures before eventually being converted into a purchase order. The new web-based system allowed employees to fill out electronic request forms that were automatically e-mailed to everyone whose approval was needed. The time for processing request forms was cut from weeks to days or even hours. When authorization was complete, the system would automatically launch a purchase order to the appropriate supplier. In addition, because the new system had dramatically cut the time purchasing managers spent shuffling paper, they now had more time to work collaboratively with key stakeholders to identify and select the best suppliers and negotiate better deals.

Nolan thought wearily of all the hours he had put in developing trust with people throughout the company and showing them how technology could not only save time and money but also support team-based work and give people more control over their own jobs. He smiled briefly as he recalled one long-term HR employee, 61-year-old Ethel Moore. She had been terrified when Nolan first began showing her the company's intranet, but she was now one of his biggest supporters. In fact, it had been Ethel who had first approached him with an idea about a web-based job-posting system. The two had pulled together a team and developed an idea for linking Century managers, internal recruiters, and job applicants using artificial intelligence software on top of an integrated web-based system. Nolan's dream was to eventually integrate the job-posting system into a social media command center

that would communicate jobs and marketing information externally via Twitter, blogs, and other media. When Nolan had presented the idea to his boss, Executive Vice President Sandra Ivey, she had enthusiastically endorsed it, and within a few weeks the team had authorization to proceed with the web-based job-posting project.

But everything began to change when Ivey resigned her position six months later to take a plum job in New York. Ivey's successor, Tom Carr, seemed to have little interest in the project. During their first meeting, Carr had openly referred to the project as a waste of time and money. He immediately disapproved several new features suggested by the company's internal recruiters, even though the project team argued that the features could double internal hiring and save millions in training costs. "Just stick to the original plan and get it done. All this stuff needs to be handled on a personal basis anyway," Carr countered. "You can't learn more from a computer than you can talking to real people—and as for internal recruiting, it shouldn't be so hard to talk to people if they're already working right here in the company." Carr seemed to have no understanding of how and why technology was being used. He became irritated when Ethel Moore referred to the system as "web-based." He boasted that he had never visited Century's intranet site and suggested that "social media is a child's plaything" that has no place in a hospital. Even Ethel's enthusiasm couldn't get through to him. She tried to show him some of the HR resources available on the intranet and explain how it had benefited the department and the company, but he waved her away. "Technology is for those people in the IT department. My job is people, and yours should be too." Ethel was crushed, and Nolan realized it would be like beating his head against a brick wall to try to persuade Carr to the team's point of view. Near the end of the meeting, Carr even jokingly suggested that the project team should just buy a couple of filing cabinets and save everyone some time and money.

Just when the team thought things couldn't get any worse, Carr dropped the other bomb. They would no longer be allowed to gather data and feedback from users of the new system. Nolan feared that without the input of potential users, the system wouldn't meet their needs, or even that users would boycott the system because they hadn't been allowed to participate. No doubt that would put a great big "I told you so" smile right on Carr's face.

Nolan sighed and leaned back in his chair. The project had begun to feel like a joke. The vibrant and innovative HR department his team had imagined and a social media initiative now seemed like nothing more than a pipe dream. But despite his frustration, a new thought entered Nolan's mind: "Is Carr just stubborn and narrow-minded or does he have a point that HR is a people business that doesn't need a high-tech job-posting system?"

CASE FOR ANALYSIS | Is Anybody Listening?

Bart Gaines glanced at the caller ID panel and reluctantly answered the phone.

"Bart, you and Craig and I need to discuss what we plan to do about T-latch."

Again? Bart thought, but he answered back, "Sure, LeRon. You set up something. I'm in."

T-latch was an innovative specialty rear-seat door latch and a highly touted safety feature for a major auto maker's new line of family vehicles. For an industry plagued by several years of mechanical recalls, disastrous investigative media reports, and high-profile lawsuits, top management and marketing enthusiastically embraced the emphasis on family safety. In a tough economy, a new mid-priced, high-mileage family vehicle appealed to consumers, and a series of touching ads reassured potential buyers of the auto company's renewed focus on "safety for those you love."

However, amid the advertising media blitz, the first nervous rumblings about T-latch safety began, strangely from the data analytics people, who saw a correlation between cold weather and T-latch repair. A team of three engineers from manufacturing, Bart Gaines, LeRon Cathy, and Craig Langley, examined additional data, and the correlations suggested that extreme temperatures could sometimes cause cracks, resulting in rear doors popping open during even minor mishaps, putting rear-seat passengers (particularly children) at a small risk of injury or death. In these initial stages of their concern, the three agreed that any discussion of the issue would take place via phone rather than through e-mails until they knew the extent of the problem.

"As more of these vehicles hit the highway, it is a matter of time until the press and public will be screaming for investigations and filing lawsuits," LeRon mentioned during one conference call. "A huge chunk of responsibility falls into our laps, guys."

"But we need to look at several issues here," Craig pointed out. "We can't just hand top management a bombshell like this when sales are skyrocketing and when our own evidence is minimal and based on data correlations. This will not be well-received and we can't just give them a 'what if' scenario. I mean, our guys are saying this can happen, but do we need more tests or what?"

"Let's do this," Bart suggested. "Let's take some time and carefully word a memo to some of the guys in middle management saying that we've detected a potential problem that shows up in extreme conditions and suggesting they determine the next step before contacting top management."

"That sounds good," Craig said. "But let's limit the chatter about this in the memo and not sound like we're panicking over this. We just want them to see what should be done here and we will do what they suggest."

The trio carefully crafted a memo voicing their concerns and sent it up the chain of command to middle managers at corporate headquarters. Within a short time, they received a curt, "We'll check it out." A subsequent report that the team saw no problems with T-latch surprised the three engineers. "Did you check it in extreme temperatures?" the trio countered.

"Everything is fine," was the reply. "Listen, this is the best family vehicle produced in years. Top management is thrilled with sales, the public loves it, and we've seen no evidence of a major safety problem."

When the engineers teleconferenced days later, Bart told his friends that he felt like the NASA engineers who repeatedly complained about the O-rings before the tragic *Challenger* explosion in 1986. "That was also a problem with temperature and remember, no one listened to them either," he warned. Then Bart added, "Why don't the people above us pay attention to this problem based on data from our own systems? Are they distracted by big sales or don't they believe the data on this kind of problem?"

Of the three, Craig was least convinced of the danger or the need to keep pursuing the issue. "You know, maybe we are over-reacting. Sure, there's some danger that has shown up, but is it any more than the danger that's present any time you get behind the wheel of a vehicle?"

"Tell me, Craig," LeRon said. "Knowing what we know, would you put your kids in the back seat of this vehicle?"

"That's not fair, LeRon. I believe in our company and all I'm saying is that we sent them our concerns and that managers higher up the chain have looked into this and they are satisfied. Let's just give this some time."

"Maybe he's right," Bart said. "It may work itself out or middle management may send something to design. They'll certainly issue a recall for buyers to take the vehicle into the dealership for adjustments if there is a major problem."

The fact that *someone* at corporate knew of their concerns, and that top management would probably be unresponsive to bad news about the vehicle with sales running high, convinced the trio to back off and let middle and senior managers handle the issue.

Over the winter months two tragic accidents (one in Minnesota and the other in Colorado) resulted in the deaths of three children, and while investigations by the National Highway Traffic Safety Administration (NHTSA) were still under way, no mention had been made connecting the tragedies to problems with T-latch. Nevertheless, Bart placed a call to LeRon.

"What do you think, LeRon?"

"I'm one step ahead, Bart. I've already placed a call to my management, and they said it's too early to jump the gun on this thing. But they are willing to release a few summarized versions of memos to the very top brass. They will be the kind of bullet-point summaries that management likes. This will make them aware of potential problems without going too negative on their major new line."

"That will mean more delays."

"Production is running high and the company is grabbing every possible award. The guys believe we don't have sufficient evidence of a major problem and that it is still too early to force the company to make

announcements or changes in the vehicle. Listen, they're not trying to put anyone at risk. The main focus here is on family safety. But there's no definitive information on this even from NHTSA. The information will be issued as needed. I'm thinking that maybe I agree on this and I'm sure Craig would agree also."

"Ok." Bart hung up the phone, picked up a T-latch sample from his desk, and examined it. *Well, we'll just wait and see what happens*, he thought and placed it in a desk drawer.

NOTES

1. Based on Viktor Mayer-Schönberger and Kenneth Cukier, *Big Data: A Revolution That Will Transform How We Live, Work, and Think* (Boston: Houghton Mifflin Harcourt, 2013), 1–2.
2. Andrew McAfee and Erik Brynjolfsson, "Big Data: The Management Revolution," *Harvard Business Review*, October 2012, 61–68.
3. Raymond F. Zammuto, Terri L. Griffith, Ann Majchrzak, Deborah J. Dougherty, and Samer Faraj, "Information Technology and the Changing Fabric of Organization," *Organization Science* 18, no. 5 (September–October 2007), 749–762.
4. Erik Berkman, "How to Stay Ahead of the Curve," *CIO*, February 1, 2002, 72–80; and Heather Harreld, "Pick-Up Artists," *CIO*, November 1, 2000, 148–154.
5. Laura Landro, "An Affordable Fix for Modernizing Medical Records," *The Wall Street Journal*, April 30, 2009, A11.
6. "Business Intelligence," special advertising section, *Business 2.0*, February 2003, S1–S4; Alice Dragoon, "Business Intelligence Gets Smart," *CIO*, September 15, 2003, 84–91; and Steve Lohr, "A Data Explosion Remakes Retailing," *The New York Times*, January 3, 2010, BU3.
7. Lohr, "A Data Explosion Remakes Retailing."
8. Ibid.
9. Geoffrey A. Fowler, "Leadership: Information Technology (A Special Report)—Are You Talking to Me?" *The Wall Street Journal*, April 25, 2011, R5.
10. Jacques Bughin, Michael Chui, and James Manyika, "Capturing Business Value with Social Technologies," *McKinsey Quarterly*, November 2012, http://www.mckinsey.com/insights/high_tech_telecoms_internet/capturing_business_value_with_social_technologies (accessed September 27, 2013); and Roland Deiser and Sylvain Newton, "Six Social-Media Skills Every Leader Needs," *McKinsey Quarterly*, Issue 1, February 2013, http://www.mckinsey.com/insights/high_tech_telecoms_internet/six_social-media_skills_every_leader_needs (accessed August 21, 2013).
11. Darrell K. Rigby, *Management Tools 2013: An Executive's Guide* (Boston, MA: Bain & Company, 2013), http://www.bain.com/Images/MANAGEMENT_TOOLS_2013_An_Executives_guide.pdf (accessed August 27, 2013); Margaret Rouse, "Big Data Analytics," *TechTarget.com*, January 10, 2012, http://searchbusinessanalytics.techtarget.com/definition/big-data-analytics (accessed August 27, 2013); and David Kiron, Renee Boucher Ferguson, and Pamela Kirk Prentice, "From Value to Vision: Reimagining the Possible with Data Analytics," *MIT Sloan Management Review Special Report*, March 5, 2013, http://sloanreview.mit.edu/reports/analytics-innovation/ (accessed August 27, 2013).
12. McAfee and Brynjolfsson, "Big Data: The Management Revolution."
13. Examples reported in Steve Lohr, "Sure, Big Data Is Great. But So Is Intuition," *The New York Times*, December 29, 2012; Thomas H. Davenport and Jeanne G. Harris, *Competing on Analytics: The New Science of Winning* (Boston, MA: Harvard Business School Press, 2007); and McAfee and Brynjolfsson, "Big Data: The Management Revolution."
14. William G. Ouchi, "Markets, Bureaucracies, and Clans," *Administrative Science Quarterly* 25 (1980), 129–141; and B. R. Baligia and Alfred M. Jaeger, "Multinational Corporations: Control Systems and Delegation Issues," *Journal of International Business Studies* (Fall 1984), 25–40.
15. Daisuke Wakabayashi and Toko Sekiguchi, "Disaster in Japan: Evacuees Set Rules to Create Sense of Normalcy," *The Wall Street Journal*, http://online.wsj.com/article/SB10001424052748703784004576220382991112672.html (accessed October 3, 2012).
16. Ian Mount, "A Pizzeria Owner Learns the Value of Watching the Books," *The New York Times*, October 25, 2012, B8.
17. Craig Torres and Anthony Feld, "Campbell's Quest for Productivity," *Bloomberg BusinessWeek*, November 29–December 5, 2010, 15–16.
18. Cynthia Karen Swank, "The Lean Service Machine," *Harvard Business Review*, October 2003, 123–129.
19. Shayndi Raice, "Sprint Tackles Subscriber Losses; Carrier Stems Defections as Customer-Service Gains Take Root," *The Wall Street Journal Online*, December 17, 2010, http://online.wsj.com/article/SB10001424052748704073804576023572789952028.html (accessed December 17, 2010).
20. Robert Kaplan and David Norton, "The Balanced Scorecard: Measures That Drive Performance," *Harvard Business Review*, January–February 1992, 71–79; "On Balance," a CFO Interview with Robert Kaplan and David Norton, *CFO*, February 2001, 73–78; Chee W. Chow, Kamal M. Haddad, and James E. Williamson, "Applying the Balanced Scorecard

to Small Companies," *Management Accounting* 79, no. 2 (August 1997), 21–27; and Meena Chavan, "The Balanced Scorecard: A New Challenge," *Journal of Management Development* 28, no. 5 (2009), 393–406.

21. Based on Kaplan and Norton, "The Balanced Scorecard"; Chow, Haddad, and Williamson, "Applying the Balanced Scorecard"; and C. A. Latshaw and Y. Choi, "The Balanced Scorecard and the Accountant as a Valued Strategic Partner," *Review of Business* 23, no. 1 (2002), 27–29.

22. Rajesh Tyagi and Praveen Gupta, "Gauging Performance in the Service Industry," *Journal of Business Strategy* 34, no. 3 (2013), 4–15.

23. Nils–Göran Olve, Carl-Johan Petri, Jan Roy, and Sofie Roy, "Twelve Years Later: Understanding and Realizing the Value of Balanced Scorecards," *Ivey Business Journal*, May–June 2004, 1–7.

24. Geary A. Rummler and Kimberly Morrill, "The Results Chain," *TD*, February 2005, 27–35; Chavan, "The Balanced Scorecard: A New Challenge"; and John C. Crotts, Duncan R. Dickson, and Robert C. Ford, "Aligning Organizational Processes with Mission: The Case of Service Excellence," *Academy of Management Executive* 19, no. 3 (August 2005), 54–68.

25. This discussion is based on Robert S. Kaplan and David P. Norton, "Mastering the Management System," *Harvard Business Review*, January 2008, 63–77; and Robert S. Kaplan and David P. Norton, "Having Trouble with Your Strategy? Then Map It," *Harvard Business Review*, September–October 2000, 167–176.

26. This discussion of behavior versus outcome control is based in part on Erin Anderson and Vincent Onyemah, "How Right Should the Customer Be?" *Harvard Business Review*, July–August 2006, 59–67; and Bruno S. Frey, Fabian Homberg, and Margit Osterloh, "Organizational Control Systems and Pay-for-Performance in the Public Service," *Organization Studies* 34, no. 7 (2013), 949–972.

27. Spencer E. Ante and Lauren Weber, "Memo to Workers: The Boss Is Watching; Tracking Technology Shakes Up the Workplace," *The Wall Street Journal*, October 22, 2013, http://online.wsj.com/news/articles/SB10001424052702303672404579151440488919138 (accessed April 22, 2014).

28. Pui-Wing Tam, Erin White, Nick Wingfield, and Kris Maher, "Snooping E-Mail by Software Is Now a Workplace Norm," *The Wall Street Journal*, March 9, 2005, B1; and Ante and Weber, "Memo to Workers."

29. Laura Landro, "Hospitals Address a Drug Problem: Software and Robots Help Secure and Monitor Medications," *The Wall Street Journal*, February 23, 2014, http://online.wsj.com/news/articles/SB10001424052702304104504579377283066012564 (accessed April 22, 2014).

30. Bill Ward, "Power to the People: Thanks to a Revolutionary Program Called ROWE, Best Buy Employees Can Lead Lives—Professional and Personal—On Their Own Terms," *Star Tribune*, June 1, 2008, E1; Michelle Conlin, "Smashing the Clock," *BusinessWeek*, December 11, 2006, 60ff; and Jyoti Thottam, "Reworking Work," *Time*, July 25, 2005, 50–55.

31. Conlin, "Smashing the Clock."

32. Based on Andrew Mayo, "Memory Bankers," *People Management*, January 22, 1998, 34–38; William Miller,

"Building the Ultimate Resource," *Management Review*, January 1999, 42–45; and Todd Datz, "How to Speak Geek," *CIO Enterprise*, Section 2, April 15, 1999, 46–52.

33. This discussion is based in part on Gustavo Guzman and Luiz F. Trivelato, "Transferring Codified Knowledge: Socio-Technical Versus Top-Down Approaches," *The Learning Organization* 15, no. 3 (2008), 251–276; Ikujiro Nonaka and Hirotaka Takeuchi, *The Knowledge-Creating Company: How Japanese Companies Create the Dynamics of Innovation* (New York: Oxford University Press, 1995), 8–9; Robert M. Grant, "Toward a Knowledge-Based Theory of the Firm," *Strategic Management Journal* 17 (Winter 1996), 109–122; and Martin Schulz, "The Uncertain Relevance of Newness: Organizational Learning and Knowledge Flows," *Academy of Management Journal* 44, no. 4 (2001), 661–681.

34. The description of tacit knowledge is based on Matt Palmquist, "(Tacit) Knowledge Is Power," *Strategy + Business*, April 9, 2014, http://www.strategy-business.com/blog/Tacit-Knowledge-Is-Power (accessed April 22, 2014); and C. Jackson Grayson, Jr., and Carla S. O'Dell, "Mining Your Hidden Resources," *Across the Board*, April 1998, 23–28.

35. Dorit Nevo, Izak Benbasat, and Yair Wand, "Knowledge Management; Who Knows What?" *The Wall Street Journal*, October 26, 2009.

36. Based on Morten T. Hansen, Nitin Nohria, and Thomas Tierney, "What's Your Strategy for Managing Knowledge?" *Harvard Business Review*, March–April 1999, 106–116.

37. Mark Easterby-Smith and Irina Mikhailava, "Knowledge Management: In Perspective," *People Management*, June 2011, 34–37.

38. David Gilmore, "How to Fix Knowledge Management," *Harvard Business Review*, October 2003, 16–17.

39. Palmquist, "(Tacit) Knowledge Is Power."

40. Phyllis Korkki, "The Leaders Who Aren't Always Followed," *The New York Times*, April 13, 2014, BU3.

41. Karen Stephenson, quoted in Ethan Watters, "The Organization Woman," *Business 2.0*, April 2006, 106–110.

42. Korkki, "The Leaders Who Aren't Always Followed."

43. This example is from Rob Cross and Robert J. Thomas, "How Top Talent Uses Networks and Where Rising Stars Get Trapped," *Organizational Dynamics* 37, no. 2 (2008), 165–180.

44. Jennifer Reingold and Jia Lynn Yang, "The Hidden Workplace: There's the Organization Chart—and Then There's the Way Things Really Work," *Fortune*, July 23, 2007, 98–106.

45. Ethan Watters, "The Organization Woman."

46. Susannah Patton, "Who Knows Whom and Who Knows What?" *CIO Magazine*, June 15, 2005, 51–56.

47. Ibid.

48. Rob Cross, Stephen P. Borgatti, and Andrew Parker, "Making Invisible Work Visible: Using Social Network Analysis to Support Strategic Collaboration," *California Management Review* 44, no. 2 (Winter 2002), 25–46.

49. Lowell L. Bryan, Eric Matson, and Leigh M. Weiss, "Harnessing the Power of Informal Employee Networks," *McKinsey Quarterly*, November 2007, http://www.mckinsey.com/insights/organization/harnessing_the_power_of_informal_employee_networks (accessed April 23, 2014).

50. This discussion is based on Verne G. Kopytoff, "Companies Stay in the Loop by Using In-House Social Networks," *The New York Times*, June 27, 2011, B3; Daniel Burrus, "Social Networks in the Workplace: The Risk and Opportunity of Business 2.0," *Strategy & Leadership* 38, no. 4 (2010), 50–53; Evelyn Nussenbaum, "Tech to Boost Teamwork," *Fortune Small Business*, February 2008, 51–54; Nevo et al., "Knowledge Management"; and "Building the Web 2.0 Enterprise: McKinsey Global Survey Results," *The McKinsey Quarterly*, July 2008, http://www.mckinseyquarterly.com /Building_the_Web_20_Enterprise_McKinsey_Global _-Survey_2174 (accessed October 18, 2011).

51. Kopytoff, "Companies Stay in the Loop."

52. Nevo et al., "Knowledge Management."

53. Roland Deiser and Sylvain Newton, "Six Social-Media Skills Every Leader Needs," *McKinsey Quarterly*, Issue 1, February 2013, http://www.mckinsey.com/insights/high_tech_telecoms _internet/six_social-media_skills_every_leader_needs (accessed August 21, 2013).

54. David Kiron, Douglas Palmer, and Robert Berkman, "The Executive's Role in Social Business," *MIT Sloan Management Review*, Summer 2013, 83–89.

55. Ibid.

56. Ibid.

57. Deiser and Newton, "Six Social-Media Skills Every Leader Needs."

58. Anna Granholm-Brun, interviewed by Robert Berkman, "Turning a 'No Comment' Company into a Social Media Leader," *MIT Sloan Management Review*, August 2013, 1–4.

59. Felix Gillette, "Twitter, Twitter, Little Stars," *Bloomberg Businessweek*, July 19–July 25, 2010, 64–67.

60. Nora Ganim Barnes, Ava M. Lescault, and Stephanie Wright, "2013 *Fortune* 500 Are Bullish on Social Media: Big Companies Get Excited About Google+, Instagram, Foursquare and Pinterest," University of Massachusetts, Dartmouth Center for Marketing Research, http://www.umassd.edu/media /umassdartmouth/cmr/studiesandresearch/2013_Fortune_500 .pdf (accessed May 5, 2014).

61. This discussion is based on Brian Solis and Charlene Li, "The State of Social Business 2013: The Maturing of Social Media into Social Business," Altimeter Group, http://www .altimetergroup.com/research/reports/the_state_of_social _business_2013 (accessed May 5, 2014).

62. The discussion of command centers is based on Amanda Nelson, "Everything You Need to Know About Social Media Command Centers," *Salesforce.com*, May 30, 2013 http:// blogs.salesforce.com/company/2013/05/social-media -command-centers.html (accessed May 5, 2014); Joel Windels, "Social Media Command Centers Are Coming of Age," *Brandwatch.com*, February 12, 2014, http://www .brandwatch.com/2014/02/social-media-command-centers -come-of-age/ (accessed May 5, 2014).

63. Stuart Elliott, "Mocked on Internet, Diet Coke Alters Ads," *The New York Times*, May 7, 2014, B6.

64. Nelson, "Everything You Need to Know About Social Media Command Centers."

65. Susan Etlinger, Andrew Jones, and Charlene Li, *Shiny Object or Digital Intelligence Hub? Evolution of the Enterprise Social Media Command Center*, Altimeter, March 18, 2014,

http://www.slideshare.net/Altimeter/report-evolution-of -the-enterprise-social-media-command-center-susan-etlinger (accessed May 5, 2014).

66. Travis Hessman, "Putting Big Data to Work," *Industry Week*, April 2013, 14–18.

67. Alden M. Hayashi, "Thriving in a Big Data World," *MIT Sloan Management Review*, Winter 2014, 35–39; and Mayer-Schönberger and Cukier, *Big Data*.

68. Mayer-Schönberger and Cukier, *Big Data*.

69. Hessman, "Putting Big Data to Work."

70. Quoted in Hessman, "Putting Big Data to Work."

71. Reported in Hayashi, "Thriving in a Big Data World"; and Mayer-Schönberger and Cukier, *Big Data*.

72. Reported in Hayashi, "Thriving in a Big Data World."

73. Mayer-Schönberger and Cukier, *Big Data*, 51–52.

74. Quoted in Mayer-Schönberger and Cukier, *Big Data*, 52.

75. Matthew Futterman, "Friday Journal—Baseball After Moneyball," *The Wall Street Journal*, September 23, 2011, D1.

76. Mayer-Schönberger and Cukier, *Big Data*, 129–130.

77. This discussion is based on David Fogarty and Peter C. Bell, "Should You Outsource Analytics?" *MIT Sloan Management Review*, Winter 2014, 41–45.

78. Mayer-Schönberger and Cukier, *Big Data*, 134–135.

79. Mayer-Schönberger and Cukier, *Big Data*, 127.

80. This discussion is based on Robert L. Grossman and Kevin P. Siegel, "Organization Models for Big Data and Analytics," *Journal of Organization Design* 3, no. 1 (2014), 20–25; and Jay R. Galbraith, "Organization Design Challenges Resulting from Big Data," *Journal of Organization Design* 3, no. 1 (2014), 2–13.

81. Thomas H. Davenport, "Five Ways to Organize Your Data Scientists," *The Wall Street Journal*, August 22, 2013, http:// blogs.wsj.com/cio/2013/08/22/five-ways-to-organize-your -data-scientists/ (accessed April 25, 2014).

82. Galbraith, "Organization Design Challenges Resulting from Big Data."

83. Davenport, "Five Ways to Organize Your Data Scientists"; and Grossman and Siegel, "Organization Models for Big Data and Analytics."

84. Based on Brad Brown, David Court, and Paul Wilmott, "Mobilizing Your C-Suite for Big-Data Analytics," *McKinsey Quarterly*, November 2013, 14–21.

85. Davenport, "Five Ways to Organize Your Data Scientists"; and Grossman and Siegel, "Organization Models for Big Data and Analytics."

86. Ruben Sigala, interviewed by Renee Boucher Ferguson, "A Process of Continuous Innovation: Centralizing Analytics at Caesars," *MIT Sloan Management Review*, Fall 2013, 1–6.

87. Saul Berman and Peter Korsten, "Embracing Connectedness: Insights from the IBM 2012 CEO Study," *Strategy & Leadership* 41, no. 2 (2013), 46–57.

88. Zammuto et al., "Information Technology and the Changing Fabric of Organization."

89. Stephanie Overby, "Paving over Paperwork," *CIO*, February 1, 2002, 82–86.

90. Siobhan O'Mahony and Stephen R. Barley, "Do Digital Telecommunications Affect Work and Organization? The State of Our Knowledge," *Research in Organizational Behavior* 21 (1999), 125–161.

91. Berman and Korsten, "Embracing Connectedness."

92. "Big and No Longer Blue," *The Economist*, January 21–27, 2006, http://www.economist.com/node/5380442 (accessed October 18, 2011).

93. "Mandate 2003: Be Agile and Efficient," *Microsoft Executive Circle*, Spring 2003, 46–48.

94. Salvatore Parise, Bala Iyer, Donna Cuomo, and Bill Donaldson, "MITRE Corporation: Using Social Technologies to Get Connected," *Ivey Business Journal*, January–February 2011, http://www.iveybusinessjournal.com/topics/strategy /mitre-corporation-using-social-technologies-to-get-connected (accessed August 25, 2011).

95. Joanne Lee-Young and Megan Barnett, "Furiously Fast Fashions," *The Industry Standard*, June 11, 2001, 72–79.

96. Based on Carol Hildebrand, "New Boss Blues," *CIO Enterprise*, Section 2, November 15, 1998, 53–58; and Megan Santosus, "Advanced Micro Devices' Web-Based Purchasing System," *CIO*, Section 1, May 15, 1998, 84.

Organization Size, Life Cycle, and Decline

Learning Objectives

After reading this chapter you should be able to:

1. Explain the advantages and disadvantages of large organization size.
2. Define organizational life cycle and explain the four stages.
3. Define the characteristics of bureaucracy.
4. Explain how bureaucracy is used for control.
5. Discuss approaches to reducing bureaucracy in large organizations.
6. Contrast market and clan control with bureaucratic control.
7. Describe the model of decline stages and methods of downsizing.

"Southwest is in a better position today than it has ever been in its history," says the airline's CEO Gary Kelly. But look closely, and Southwest is beginning to show signs of growing old. Even Kelly, when pressed, admits that not only the airline industry, but Southwest's position in that industry, has changed. Its growth has stalled. The low fares that were long the core selling point with customers aren't so low anymore. The three larger U.S. airlines—American Airlines Group, United Continental Holdings, and Delta Air Lines—offer programs and services that capture business travelers. Ultra-discounters undercut Southwest's fares. Southwest also has out-of-date phone and computer systems that have caused problems when things go wrong, such as the snowstorms that cancelled thousands of flights in the winter of 2014. Workers had to manually reschedule each passenger. At Midway Airport in Chicago on January 2, 2014, Southwest lost 7,500 bags. Many employees long for the days of co-founder and former CEO and executive chairman Herb Kelleher, who was known for his outlandish costumes, love of Wild Turkey bourbon, and riding Harley-Davidson motorcycles. "Ever since Herb . . . left, this has been more of a corporation and less of a family," said union representative Randy Barnes.[1]

As organizations like Southwest grow large and complex, they need more complex systems and procedures for guiding and controlling the organization. Moreover, the addition of more complex systems and procedures can cause problems of inefficiency, rigidity, and slow response time, meaning that the company has a hard time innovating or adapting quickly to changes in the environment or to customer needs. In a recent video posted online, the current Southwest CEO Gary Kelly asked his predecessor, "How do you respond to employees concerned about change?" Herb Kelleher responded: "What I tell them is . . . 'What we're talking about here is your future. If we don't change, you won't have one'."[2]

Southwest Airlines has enjoyed a long period of "youth," staying in the innovative, adaptable start-up mindset longer than most organizations, but every organization—from locally owned restaurants and auto body shops to large international firms, nonprofit organizations, and law-enforcement agencies—eventually wrestles with questions about organizational size, bureaucracy, and control. During the twentieth century, large organizations became widespread, and bureaucracy has become a major topic of study in organization theory and design.[3] Most large organizations have bureaucratic characteristics, which can be very effective. These organizations provide us with abundant goods and services and accomplish astonishing feats—explorations of Mars, overnight delivery of packages to any location in the world, the scheduling and coordination of thousands of airline flights a day—that are testimony to their effectiveness. On the other hand, bureaucracy is also accused of many sins, including inefficiency, rigidity, and demeaning routinized work that alienates both employees and the customers an organization tries to serve.

Purpose of This Chapter

In this chapter, we explore the question of large versus small organizations and how size relates to structure and control. Organization size is a major contingency that influences organization design and functioning, just as do the contingencies—technology, environment, goals—discussed in previous chapters. In the first section, we look at the advantages of large versus small size. Then, we explore what is called an organization's life cycle and the structural characteristics at each stage. Next, we examine the historical need for bureaucracy as a means to control large organizations and compare bureaucratic control to various other control strategies. Finally, the chapter looks at the causes of organizational decline and discusses some methods for dealing with downsizing. By the end of this chapter, you should be able to recognize when bureaucratic control can make an organization effective and when other types of control are more appropriate.

Organization Size: Is Bigger Better?

The question of big versus small begins with the notion of growth and the reasons so many organizations feel the need to grow large.

Pressures for Growth

Do you ever dream of starting a small company? Many people do, and entrepreneurial start-ups are the lifeblood of the U.S. economy. Yet the hope of practically every entrepreneur is to have his or her company grow fast and grow large, maybe even to eventually make the *Fortune* 500 list.[4] Sometimes this goal is more urgent than to make the best products or show the greatest profits. However, there are some thriving companies where managers have resisted the pressure for endless growth to focus instead on different goals, as discussed in this chapter's BookMark.

Recent economic woes and layoffs at many large firms have spurred budding entrepreneurs to take a chance on starting their own company or going it alone in a sole proprietorship. However, industry consolidation, global expansion, and diversification have made firms considerably larger over the past few decades. In 1960, the combined revenues of the top 50 U.S. firms amounted to $103 billion, nearly $2.1 billion per company. In 2010, that amount had increased to $5.1 trillion, or $102 billion per company.[5] In addition, despite the proliferation of new, small organizations, giants such as Toyota, General Electric, Samsung, and Walmart have continued to grow.

Small Giants: Companies That Choose to Be Great Instead of Big

By Bo Burlingham

The conventional business mindset is to equate growth with success, but Bo Burlingham, an editor-at-large at *Inc.* magazine, reminds us that there is a different class of great companies that focus not on getting bigger, but on getting better. He calls them *Small Giants*. In his book of the same name, Burlingham looks at 14 small companies that are admired in their industries and recognized for their accomplishments—and in which managers have made a conscious decision not to significantly expand, go public, or become part of a larger firm.

WHAT GIVES SMALL GIANTS THEIR *MOJO*?

The companies Burlingham profiles come from a wide range of industries and vary a great deal in terms of the number of employees, corporate structure, management approach, and stage of the life cycle. What makes them similar? Burlingham describes seven shared characteristics that give these companies an almost magical quality. Here are three of them:

- *The founders and leaders made a mindful choice to build the kind of business they wanted to "live in" rather than accommodate a business shaped by outside forces.* Danny Meyer, owner of the Union Square Café, says he "earned more money by choosing the right things to say no to than by choosing things to say yes to." Fritz Maytag of Anchor Brewery, content to limit his distribution to northern California, even

helped rival brewers develop their skills to accommodate growing demand for his kind of beer.
- *Each of the small giants is intimately connected with the community in which it does business.* CitiStorage, the premier independent records-storage company in the United States, built its warehouse in a depressed inner-city neighborhood to save money. But it quickly bonded with the community by hiring local residents, opening the facility for community events, and making generous donations to the local school.
- *Their leaders have a passion for the business.* Whether it's making music, creating special effects, designing and manufacturing constant torque hinges, brewing beer, or planning commercial construction projects, the leaders of these companies show a true passion for the subject matter as well as a deep emotional commitment to the business and its employees, customers, and suppliers.

DO YOU WANT TO BUILD A SMALL GIANT?

One beneficial outcome of Burlingham's book has been to prove to new or aspiring entrepreneurs that better doesn't have to mean bigger. For some, this strategy eases the urge to seize every opportunity to expand. But Burlingham warns that resisting the pressures for growth takes strength of character. This fun-to-read book provides great insight into some entrepreneurs and managers who summoned the fortitude to make the choices that were right for them.

Small Giants: Companies That Choose to Be Great Instead of Big, by Bo Burlingham, is published by Portfolio, a division of the Penguin Group.

Companies in all industries, from retail, to aerospace, to media, strive for growth to acquire the size and resources needed to compete on a global scale, to invest in new technology, and to control distribution channels and guarantee access to markets.[6] There are a number of other pressures for organizations to grow. Many executives have found that firms must grow to stay economically healthy. To stop growing is to stagnate. To be stable means that customers may not have their demands fully met or that competitors will increase market share at the expense of your company. Rovio Entertainment struck gold with the launch of Angry Birds and grew dramatically in 2012. Yet top executives know continued growth depends on whether Rovio can pivot from "a hot Nordic game developer into a global entertainment powerhouse." If Rovio doesn't come out with new games that succeed with customers, it cannot continue to grow.[7] At Walmart, managers have vowed to continue an emphasis on growth even if it means a decreasing return on investment (ROI). They are ingrained with the idea that to stop growing is to stagnate and die. Walmart's chief financial officer Tom Schoewe said that even if the ROI could "come down a bit and we could grow faster, that would be just fine by me."[8]

Large size enables companies to take risks that could ruin smaller firms, and scale is crucial to economic health in some industries. There is currently a wave of mergers in the U.S. healthcare industry, for example, as hospitals, medical groups, and insurers strive to control healthcare costs and meet challenges brought about by the Affordable Care Act.[9] For marketing-intensive companies such as Coca-Cola and Procter & Gamble, greater size provides power in the marketplace and thus increased revenues.[10] Through a series of mergers and acquisitions, the Belgium brewing company Interbrew (now Anheuser-Busch InBev) became the world's largest brewer and distributor of beer, giving the company tremendous power in the industry. In addition, growing organizations are vibrant, exciting places to work, enabling these companies to attract and keep quality employees. When the number of employees is expanding, the company can offer many challenges and opportunities for advancement.

Dilemmas of Large Size

Organizations feel compelled to grow, but how much and how large? What size organization is better poised to compete in a fast-changing global environment? The arguments are summarized in Exhibit 9.1.

EXHIBIT 9.1
Differences Between Large and Small Organizations

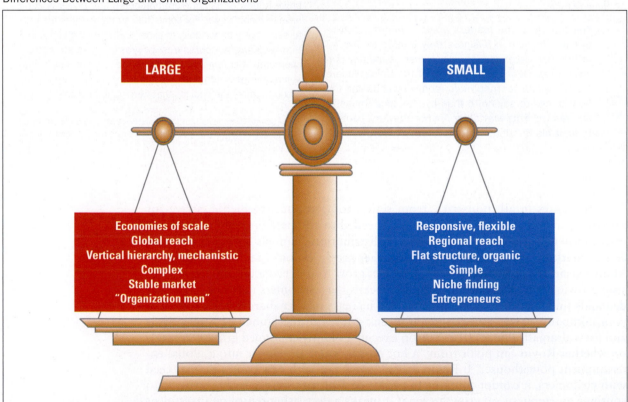

LARGE	SMALL
Economies of scale	Responsive, flexible
Global reach	Regional reach
Vertical hierarchy, mechanistic	Flat structure, organic
Complex	Simple
Stable market	Niche finding
"Organization men"	Entrepreneurs

Source: Based on John A. Byrne, "Is Your Company Too Big?" *Businessweek*, March 27, 1989, 84–94.

Large. Huge resources and economies of scale and scope are needed for many organizations to compete globally. Only large organizations can build the massive Keystone Pipeline, an oil pipeline system running from Western Canada down through the United States. Only a large corporation like General Electric can afford to build ultra-efficient $2 million wind turbines that contain 8,000 different parts.[11] Only a large Johnson & Johnson can invest hundreds of millions of dollars in new products such as bifocal contact lenses and a patch that delivers contraceptives through the skin. In addition, large firms were able to weather the economic woes of recent years much more easily than small firms, many of which are still struggling or out of business.[12] A recent study that looked at 99 developing countries found that large firms had significantly higher productivity than small firms. The connection between size and productivity is also especially strong in the United States because of economies of scale and scope.[13] Large firms can provide greater social support to the communities they serve. After the 2011 earthquake, tsunami, and nuclear disaster in Japan, the insurance company Aflac, which derives most of its revenue from that country, gave customers a six-month grace period to pay their insurance premiums. In addition, Aflac donated millions of dollars to relief efforts.[14] Large organizations also are able to get back to business more quickly following a disaster, giving employees and communities a sense of security during an uncertain time.

Large companies are standardized, often mechanistically run, and complex. The complexity offers hundreds of functional specialties within the organization to perform multifaceted tasks and to produce varied and complicated products. Moreover, large organizations, once established, can be a presence that stabilizes a market for years. Managers can join the company and expect a career reminiscent of the "organization men" of the 1950s and 1960s. The organization can provide longevity, raises, and promotions.

Small. The competing argument says small is beautiful because the crucial requirements for success in a global economy are responsiveness and flexibility in fast-changing markets. Small scale can provide significant advantages in terms of quick reaction to changing customer needs or shifting environmental and market conditions.[15] In addition, small organizations often enjoy greater employee commitment because it is easier for people to feel like part of a community. Employees typically work on a variety of tasks rather than narrow, specialized jobs. For many people, working in a small company is more exciting and fulfilling than working in a huge organization. Where would you be happier as a manager? Complete the questionnaire in this chapter's "How Do You Fit the Design?" box on page 348 for some insight.

Many large companies have grown even larger through merger or acquisition in recent years, yet research indicates that few mergers live up to their expected performance levels. Studies by consulting firms such as McKinsey & Company, Hay Group, and others suggest that performance declines in almost 20 percent of acquired companies after acquisition. By some estimates, 90 percent of mergers and acquisitions never live up to expectations. Many researchers and analysts agree that, frequently, bigness just doesn't add up to better performance.[16] Consider Pulte Group, the nation's second largest home-builder, which acquired Centex Corporation in 2009. The challenges of integrating the two companies, combined with a weakening housing market, wreaked havoc on Pulte's profitability. Between the time of the acquisition and mid-2011, Pulte had just one profitable quarter and had lost millions of dollars.[17]

BRIEFCASE

As an organization manager, keep these guidelines in mind: Decide whether your organization should act like a large or small company. To the extent that economies of scale, global reach, and complexity are important, introduce greater bureaucratization as the organization increases in size. As it becomes necessary, add rules and regulations, written documentation, job specialization, technical competence in hiring and promotion, and decentralization.

HOW DO YOU FIT THE DESIGN?

WHAT SIZE ORGANIZATION FOR YOU?

How do your work preferences fit organization size? Answer the following questions as they reflect your likes and dislikes. Please answer whether each item is Mostly True or Mostly False for you.

	Mostly True	Mostly False
1. I value stability and predictability in the organization I work for.	_____	_____
2. Rules are meant to be broken.	_____	_____
3. Years of service should be an important determinant of pay and promotion.	_____	_____
4. I generally prefer to work on lots of different things rather than specialize in a few things.	_____	_____
5. Before accepting a job, I would want to make sure the company had good benefits.	_____	_____
6. I would rather work on a team where managerial responsibility is shared than work in a department with a single manager.	_____	_____
7. I would like to work for a large, well-known company.	_____	_____
8. I would rather earn $90,000 a year as a VP in a small company than earn $100,000 a year as a middle manager in a big company.	_____	_____

Scoring: Give yourself one point for each odd-numbered item you marked Mostly True and one point for each even-numbered item you marked Mostly False.

Interpretation: Working in a large organization is a very different experience from working in a small organization. The large organization is well-established, provides good benefits, is stable, and has rules, well-defined jobs, and a clear management hierarchy of authority. A small organization may be struggling to survive, but it offers excitement, multitasking, risk, and the sharing of responsibility. If you scored 6 or more, a large organization may be for you. If you scored 3 or less, you may be happier in a smaller, less-structured organization.

Source: From Don Hellriegel, Susan E. Jackson, and John W. Slocum. *Managing: A Competency-Based Approach*, 11th ed. (Mason, OH: South-Western, a part of Cengage Learning, Inc., 2008). Reproduced by permission. http://www.cengage.com/permissions.

Despite the increasing size of many companies, the economic vitality of the United States as well as most of the rest of the developed world is tied to small and midsized businesses. According to the Small Business Administration, small businesses represent about half the private sector economy and 99 percent of all businesses in the United States. The 27.9 million small firms in the United States account for more than half of all U.S. sales and 55 percent of all jobs.[18] In addition, small firms accounted for 64 percent of net new jobs created between 1993 and 2011, and about 67 percent since the latest recession (from mid-2009 to 2011).[19] A large percentage of exporters are small businesses. The growth of the Internet and other information technologies has made it easier for small companies to compete with larger firms. The growing service sector also contributes to a decrease in average organization size, as many service companies remain small to better serve customers.

Small organizations have a flat structure and an organic, free-flowing management style that encourages entrepreneurship and innovation. Today's leading biotechnology drugs, for example, were all discovered by small firms such as Gilead Sciences, which developed anti-retroviral drugs to treat HIV, rather than by huge pharmaceutical companies such as Pfizer.[20] Moreover, the personal involvement of employees in small firms encourages motivation and commitment because employees personally identify with each other and with the company's mission. Based on studies of primitive societies, religious sects, military organizations, and some businesses, anthropologist Robin Dunbar proposed that 150 is the optimum size for any group trying to achieve a goal, as we described in Chapter 7. Dunbar says that beyond that size, the group's effectiveness wanes because too many rules, procedures, and red tape slow things down and sap group morale, enthusiasm, and commitment.[21]

Big-Company/Small-Company Hybrid. The paradox is that the advantages of small companies sometimes enable them to succeed and, hence, grow large. Small companies can become victims of their own success as they grow, shifting to a mechanistic design emphasizing vertical hierarchy and spawning "organization men" rather than entrepreneurs. Giant companies are "built for optimization, not innovation."[22] Big companies become committed to their existing products and technologies and have a hard time supporting innovation for the future.

The solution is what Jack Welch, retired chairman and CEO of General Electric, called the "big-company/small-company hybrid" that combines a large corporation's resources and reach with a small company's simplicity and flexibility. These companies incorporate structures and processes that enable them to be both adaptable and efficient at the same time. That is, they use an *ambidextrous approach*, incorporating structures and processes that are appropriate for both small-company creativeness and large-company systems for exploiting innovations. For example, a loose, flexible structure and greater employee freedom are excellent for the creation and initiation of ideas; however, these same conditions often make it difficult to implement a change because employees are less likely to comply. With an ambidextrous approach, managers encourage flexibility and freedom to innovate and propose new ideas within some departments, but they use a more rigid, centralized, and standardized approach for implementing innovations across the organization.[23] For example, Mike Lawrie, CEO of the London-based software company Misys, created a separate unit for Misys Open Source Solutions, a venture aimed at creating a potentially disruptive technology in the healthcare industry. Lawrie wanted creative people to have the time and resources they needed to work on new software that holds the promise of seamless data exchange among hospitals, physicians, insurers, and others involved in the healthcare system. Implementation of new ideas, where routine and precision is important, occurs within the regular organization.[24] The divisional structure, described in Chapter 3, is another way some large organizations attain a big-company/small-company hybrid. By reorganizing into groups of small companies, huge corporations such as Johnson & Johnson capture the mindset and advantages of smallness. Johnson & Johnson is actually a group of 250 separate companies operating in 57 countries.[25] Michael Dell is trying to bring the luster back to his organization by giving divisions the autonomy to act like start-ups.

BRIEFCASE

As an organization manager, keep this guideline in mind:

If responsiveness, flexibility, simplicity, and niche finding are important, subdivide the organization into simple, autonomous divisions that have freedom and a small-company approach.

IN PRACTICE

Dell Inc.

Dell was once the top PC maker in the world. Now it ranks third, behind Hewlett-Packard and Lenovo. It also faces stiff competition from IBM, HP, and Oracle in the market for corporate computing. As it transitions from a PC company to a "solutions company," founder Michael Dell is trying to return Dell to its entrepreneurial roots.

Dell is moving into new areas such as cybersecurity and data center design and management, and letting those new units operate more autonomously. Forrest Norrod, who runs the unit designing data centers, says he has permission to ignore some of the corporate office's "help." Michael Dell says he wants the units to act more creatively and less bureaucratically so he is taking a hands-off approach. Norrod's division is housed at Dell's Parmer South campus, eight miles from headquarters. When employees couldn't find rulers to measure server racks, they used dollar bills. One employee built a special chassis in his garage. Duct tape has been used to attach a power supply. It might not seem like the way to run a computing giant, but Norrod and Michael Dell agree that it is the way to run a fast, flexible, entrepreneurial start-up. That might be the best chance Dell has to get ahead of its larger tech rivals.[26]

Other companies are also finding ways to be both big and small. Retail giant Lowe's, for example, uses the advantage of size in areas such as advertising, purchasing, and raising capital, but it also gives each individual store manager the autonomy needed to serve customers as if it were a small, hometown shop. To avoid the problem of isolated top managers, mutual fund manager Vanguard requires everyone—even the CEO—to spend some time each month manning the phones and talking directly to customers.[27] Small companies that are growing can use these ideas to help their organizations retain the flexibility and customer focus that fueled their growth.

Organizational Life Cycle

A useful way to think about organizational growth and change is the concept of an organizational **life cycle**,[28] which suggests that organizations are born, grow older, and eventually die. Organization structure, leadership style, and administrative systems follow a fairly predictable pattern through stages in the life cycle. Stages are sequential and follow a natural progression.

Stages of Life-Cycle Development

Research on organizational life cycle suggests that four major stages characterize organizational development.[29] Exhibit 9.2 illustrates these four stages and the problems associated with transition to each stage.

Definitions. Growth is not easy. Each time an organization enters a new stage in the life cycle, it enters a whole new ball game with a new set of rules for how the organization functions internally and how it relates to the external environment.[30]

1. *Entrepreneurial stage.* When an organization is born, the emphasis is on creating a product or service and surviving in the marketplace. The founders are entrepreneurs, and they devote their full energies to the technical activities of production and marketing. The organization is informal and non-bureaucratic. The hours of work are long. Control is based on the owners' personal supervision. Growth is from a creative new product or service. For example, Andrew

Mason turned a failed social action website into the daily deals phenomenon Groupon in 1998. Dennis Crowley and Naveen Selvadurai created the first version of Foursquare—a mobile networking service that lets users share their locations with friends, bookmark information about venues they want to visit, and share tips and experiences—at Crowley's kitchen table in New York City's East Village. They launched the service in 2009 in Austin, Texas, and by January 2014 it had 45 million users worldwide. Crowley acts as CEO and continues to personally provide oversight of the company, which has grown to about 140 employees.[31]

The founding of Foursquare is reminiscent of Apple (originally Apple Computer), which was in the **entrepreneurial stage** when it was created by Steve Jobs and Stephen Wozniak in Wozniak's parents' garage in 1976.

Crisis: Need for leadership. As the organization starts to grow, the larger number of employees causes problems. The creative and technically oriented owners are confronted with management issues, but they may prefer to focus their energies on making and selling the product or inventing new products and services. At this time of crisis, entrepreneurs must either adjust the structure of the organization to accommodate continued growth or else bring in strong managers who can do so. For example, when a valued female engineer at GitHub quit because of a culture of bullying and disrespect toward women, CEO Chris Wanstrath realized GitHub had no system to handle this kind of issue. He promptly hired a senior human resources executive. Groupon experienced phenomenal growth, but founder Andrew Mason didn't seem interested in managing a large company and he was forced out in early 2013. "I view Mason as a visionary idea generator," said one analyst. "Few would argue with how impressive the Groupon organization was as it grew. However, at some point, it became the overgrown toddler of the Internet . . . not quite ready to make adult decisions."[32]

2. *Collectivity stage.* If the leadership crisis is resolved, strong leadership is obtained and the organization begins to develop clear goals and direction. Departments are established along with a hierarchy of authority, job assignments, and a beginning division of labor. In the **collectivity stage**, employees identify with the mission of the organization and spend long hours helping the organization succeed. Members feel part of a collective. Communication and control are mostly informal, although a few formal systems begin to appear. Apple was in the collectivity stage during its rapid growth years from 1978 to 1981. Jobs remained as CEO and visionary leader, although A. C. Markkula had been brought in as CEO to handle most of the management responsibilities. Employees threw themselves into the business as the major product line was established and more than 2,000 dealers signed on.

Crisis: Need for delegation. If the new management has been successful, lower-level employees gradually find themselves restricted by the strong top-down leadership. Lower-level managers begin to acquire confidence in their own functional areas and want more discretion. An autonomy crisis occurs when top managers, who were successful because of their strong leadership and vision, do not want to give up responsibility. Top managers want to make sure that all parts of the organization are coordinated and pulling together. The organization needs to find mechanisms to control and coordinate departments without direct supervision from the top. For example, when Diamond Wipes International reached a point where costly mistakes were being made because of poor communication among departments, Taiwanese entrepreneur Eve Yen hired a general manager and charged him with coordinating the work of all departments.[33]

BRIEFCASE

As an organization manager, keep these guidelines in mind: Grow when possible. With growth, you can provide opportunities for employee advancement and greater profitability and effectiveness. Apply new management systems and structural configurations at each stage of an organization's development. Interpret the needs of the growing organization and respond with the management and internal systems that will carry the organization through to the next stage of development.

EXHIBIT 9.2
Organizational Life Cycle

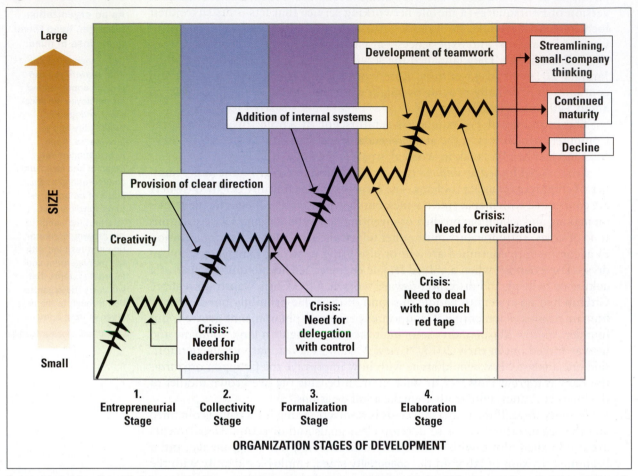

Large

SIZE

Small

Creativity

Provision of clear direction

Addition of internal systems

Development of teamwork

Streamlining, small-company thinking

Continued maturity

Decline

Crisis: Need for leadership

Crisis: Need for delegation with control

Crisis: Need to deal with too much red tape

Crisis: Need for revitalization

1. **Entrepreneurial Stage**

2. **Collectivity Stage**

3. **Formalization Stage**

4. **Elaboration Stage**

ORGANIZATION STAGES OF DEVELOPMENT

Source: Adapted from Robert E. Quinn and Kim Cameron, "Organizational Life Cycles and Shifting Criteria of Effectiveness: Some Preliminary Evidence," *Management Science* 29 (1983), 33–51; and Larry E. Greiner, "Evolution and Revolution as Organizations Grow," *Harvard Business Review* 50 (July–August 1972), 37–46.

ASSESS YOUR ANSWER

1 **It is wise for the entrepreneur who starts a new company to maintain hands-on management control as the company grows.**

ANSWER: *Disagree.* Entrepreneurs typically enjoy using their creativity to make and sell a new product or service. Many stay hands-on too long because they have a hard time shifting to the role of managing other people and setting up procedures and systems the company needs as it grows. In most cases, successful entrepreneurs bring in skilled managers to run the business and take the organization to the next level.

3. *Formalization stage.* The **formalization stage** involves the installation and use of rules, procedures, and control systems. In the formalization stage, communication is less frequent and more formal, and more likely to follow the hierarchy of authority. Engineers, human resource specialists, and other staff may be added. Top management becomes concerned with issues such as strategy and planning and leaves the operations of the firm to middle management. Product

groups or other decentralized units may be formed to improve coordination. Incentive systems based on profits may be implemented to ensure that managers work toward what is best for the overall company. Facebook is currently in the early formalization stage. The board is working with founder and CEO Mark Zuckerberg and COO Sheryl Sandberg to develop rules and procedures to guide the company and ensure oversight. Zuckerberg's power has been almost absolute, but Facebook has reached the stage where formal rules and controls are necessary.[34] When effective, the new coordination and control systems enable the organization to continue growing by establishing linkage mechanisms between top management and field units. Internet companies such as eBay and Amazon. com are currently in the late formalization stage of the life cycle, with managers devising new systems to manage the growing complexity of operations.

Crisis: Too much red tape. At this point in the organization's development, the proliferation of systems and programs may begin to strangle middle-level executives. The organization seems bureaucratized. Middle management may resent the intrusion of staff. Innovation may be restricted. The organization seems too large and complex to be managed through formal programs. Google is currently at this crisis point, with co-founder Larry Page returning to try to cut the bureaucracy and bring back an entrepreneurial spirit.

4. *Elaboration stage.* The solution to the red tape crisis is a new sense of collaboration and teamwork. Throughout the organization, managers develop skills for confronting problems and working together. Bureaucracy may have reached its limit. Social control and self-discipline reduce the need for additional formal controls. Managers learn to work within the bureaucracy without adding to it. Formal systems may be simplified and replaced by manager teams and task forces. To achieve collaboration, teams are often formed across functions or divisions of the company. The organization may also be split into multiple divisions to maintain a small-company philosophy. Apple is currently in the **elaboration stage** of the life cycle, as are such large companies as Toyota, General Electric, Caterpillar, and Southwest Airlines, described in the chapter opening example.

Crisis: Need for revitalization. After the organization reaches maturity, it may enter periods of temporary decline.[35] A need for renewal may occur every 10 to 20 years. The organization shifts out of alignment with the environment or perhaps becomes slow moving and over-bureaucratized, so it must go through a stage of streamlining and innovation. Top managers are often replaced during this period. At Apple, the top spot changed hands a number of times as the company struggled to revitalize over the years between 1985 and 1997. CEOs John Sculley, Michael Spindler, and Gilbert Amelio were each ousted by the board as Apple's problems deepened. Steve Jobs returned in mid-1997 to run the company he had founded nearly 25 years earlier. Jobs quickly reorganized the company, weeded out inefficiencies, and refocused Apple on innovative products for the consumer market. Jobs moved the company into a whole new direction with the iPod music system and the iPhone. Sales and profits zoomed and Apple entered a long period of success.[36] In the years since he had left Apple, Jobs had gained management skills and experience, but he was also smart enough to bring in other skilled managers. For instance, Timothy D. Cook, hired by Jobs in 1998, has been referred to as "the story behind the story" and has long handled day-to-day operations while Jobs provided visionary leadership. Cook took over as CEO in mid-2011 following Jobs's resignation and subsequent death.[37] Apple is still successful, but it will continue to face the problems all mature organizations deal with. All mature organizations must go through periods of revitalization or they will decline, as shown in the last stage of Exhibit 9.2.

Summary. Eighty-four percent of businesses that make it past the first year still fail within five years because they can't make the transition from the entrepreneurial stage.[38] The transitions become even more difficult as organizations progress through future stages of the life cycle. Organizations that do not successfully resolve the problems associated with these transitions are restricted in their growth and may even fail. From within an organization, the life-cycle crises are very real. Larry Page is trying to resolve the crisis of too much bureaucracy at Google.

Google

For technology companies, life cycles are getting shorter. To stay competitive, companies like Facebook, Netflix, and Google have to successfully progress through stages of the cycle faster. It might seem hard to believe that Google was launched in 1998, and even harder to believe that it has reached the stage of becoming overly bureaucratic. The company is just over 15 years old, but in tech years that is practically ancient.

Larry Page, one of the co-founders of perhaps the best-known search site on the Internet, is on a mission to pull Google through its midlife crisis and get it to act like a hot young start-up again. He has reshaped the top leadership team, handpicking people to run areas and requiring them to spend part of each day sitting in an open bullpen of desks on the fourth floor of Building 1900 in the Googleplex. It's an idea he got from former New York City Mayor Michael Bloomberg as a way to get everybody together for a fixed number of hours and speed up decision making. Page also cut many products and reorganized the company into seven divisions to focus on the most promising ones, tying year-end bonuses to the overall success of efforts. Whereas in the past, a decision required that Page, co-founder Sergey Brin, and executive chairman Eric Schmidt all weigh in, Page is now willing to make a decision quickly, even if it isn't perfect. He is forcing managers to settle disputes in person like in smaller, entrepreneurial companies, rather than via e-mail.[39]

Organizational Characteristics During the Life Cycle

As organizations evolve through the four stages of the life cycle, changes take place in structure, control systems, innovation, and goals. The organizational characteristics associated with each stage are summarized in Exhibit 9.3.

Entrepreneurial. Initially, the organization is small, non-bureaucratic, and a one-person show. The top manager provides the structure and control system. Organizational energy is devoted to survival and the production of a single product or service.

Collectivity. This is the organization's youth. Growth is rapid, and employees are excited and committed to the organization's mission. The structure is still mostly informal, although some procedures are emerging. Strong charismatic leaders provide direction and goals for the organization. Continued growth is a major goal.

Formalization. At this point, the organization is entering midlife. Bureaucratic characteristics emerge. The organization adds staff support groups, formalizes procedures, and establishes a clear hierarchy and division of labor. At the formalization stage, organizations may also develop complementary products to offer a complete product line. Innovation may be achieved by establishing a separate research and development (R&D) department. Major goals are internal stability and market expansion. Top management delegates, but it also implements formal control systems.

Organization Characteristics During Four Stages of Life Cycle

Characteristic	1. Entrepreneurial Nonbureaucratic	2. Collectivity Prebureaucratic	3. Formalization Bureaucratic	4. Elaboration Very Bureaucratic
Structure	Informal, one-person show	Mostly informal, some procedures	Formal procedures, division of labor, new specialties added	Teamwork within bureaucracy, small-company thinking
Products or services	Single product or service	Major product or service, with variations	Line of products or services	Multiple product or service lines
Reward and control systems	Personal, paternalistic	Personal, contribution to success	Impersonal, formalized systems	Extensive, tailored to product and department
Innovation	By owner-manager	By employees and managers	By separate innovation group	By institutionalized R&D department
Goal	Survival	Growth	Internal stability, market expansion	Reputation, complete organization
Top management style	Individualistic, entrepreneurial	Charismatic, direction-giving	Delegation with control	Team approach, attack bureaucracy

Source: Adapted from Larry E. Greiner, "Evolution and Revolution as Organizations Grow," *Harvard Business Review* 50 (July–August 1972), 37–46; G. L. Lippitt and W. H. Schmidt, "Crises in a Developing Organization," *Harvard Business Review* 45 (November–December 1967), 102–112; B. R. Scott, "The Industrial State: Old Myths and New Realities," *Harvard Business Review* 51 (March–April 1973), 133–148; and Robert E. Quinn and Kim Cameron, "Organizational Life Cycles and Shifting Criteria of Effectiveness," *Management Science* 29 (1983), 33–51.

Elaboration. The mature organization is large and bureaucratic, with extensive control systems, rules, and procedures. Organization managers attempt to develop a team orientation within the bureaucracy to prevent further bureaucratization. Top managers are concerned with establishing a complete organization. Organizational stature and reputation are important. Innovation is institutionalized through an R&D department. Management may attack the bureaucracy and streamline it.

Summary. Growing organizations move through stages of a life cycle, and each stage is associated with specific characteristics of structure, control systems, goals, and innovation. The life-cycle phenomenon is a powerful concept used for understanding problems facing organizations and how managers can respond in a positive way to move an organization to the next stage.

Organizational Size, Bureaucracy, and Control

As organizations progress through the life cycle, they usually take on bureaucratic characteristics as they grow larger and more complex. The systematic study of bureaucracy was launched by Max Weber, a sociologist who studied government organizations in Europe and developed a framework of administrative characteristics that would make large organizations rational and efficient.[40] Weber wanted to understand how organizations could be designed to play a positive role in the larger society.

What Is Bureaucracy?

Although Weber perceived **bureaucracy** as a threat to basic personal liberties, he also recognized it as the most efficient possible system of organizing. He predicted the triumph of bureaucracy because of its ability to ensure more efficient functioning of organizations in both business and government settings. Weber identified a set of organizational characteristics, shown in Exhibit 9.4, that could be found in successful bureaucratic organizations.

Rules and standard procedures enabled organizational activities to be performed in a predictable, routine manner. Specialized duties meant that each employee had a clear task to perform. Hierarchy of authority provided a sensible mechanism for supervision and control. Technical competence was the basis by which people were hired rather than friendship, family ties, and favoritism. The separation of the position from the position holder meant that individuals did not own or have an inherent right to the job, which promoted efficiency. Written records provided an organizational memory and continuity over time.

Although bureaucratic characteristics carried to an extreme are widely criticized today, the rational control introduced by Weber was a significant idea and a new form of organization. Bureaucracy provided many advantages over organization forms based on favoritism, social status, family connections, or graft. For example, an investigation of Kabul Bank uncovered massive fraud that led to the collapse of Afghanistan's largest financial institution. Bank officers and their friends and relatives got rich off $861 million in fraudulent loans. In some

EXHIBIT 9.4

Weber's Dimensions of Bureaucracy

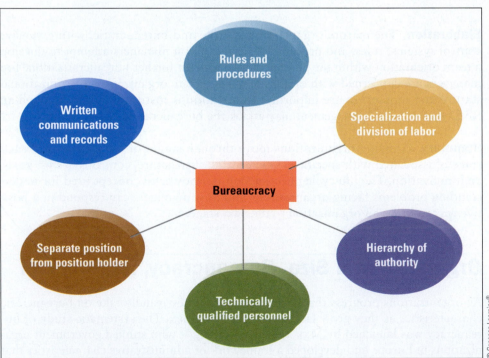

© Cengage Learning®

cases, loans were taken out to repay previous loans. Company documents and financial statements were fabricated, and in some cases money was smuggled out of the country on airline food trays.[41] In China, the tradition of giving government posts to relatives is still widespread, but China's emerging class of educated people doesn't like seeing the best jobs going to children and other relatives of officials.[42] The United States, as well, sees its share of corruption, as evidenced by the case of Illinois Governor Rod Blagojevich, who was accused of a wide-ranging corruption that included trying to sell the Senate seat vacated by President Barack Obama.[43] By comparison with these examples, the logical and rational form of organization described by Weber allows work to be conducted fairly, efficiently, and according to established rules.

A study of empirical organization research over four decades confirms the validity and persistence of Weber's model of bureaucracy, showing positive relationships among elements such as specialization, formalization, and standardization, as shown in Exhibit 9.4.[44] Bureaucratic characteristics can have a positive effect for many large organizations, such as United Parcel Service (UPS), one of today's most efficient large corporations.

IN PRACTICE

United Parcel Service (UPS)

UPS, sometimes called *Big Brown* for the color of delivery trucks and employee uniforms, is the largest package-distribution company in the world, delivering over 15 million packages a day, and a global leader in supply chain, logistics, and information services. The company operates in more than 200 countries and territories around the world.

How did UPS become so successful? Many efficiencies were realized through adoption of the bureaucratic model of organization. UPS operates according to a mountain of rules and regulations. It teaches drivers an astounding 340 precise steps to correctly deliver a package. For example, it tells them how to load their trucks, how to unbuckle their seat belts (with the left hand), how to step off the truck, how to walk (briskly, but no running), and how to carry their keys. Strict dress codes are enforced—clean uniforms (called *browns*) every day, black or brown polished shoes with nonslip soles, no shirt unbuttoned below the first button, no hair below the shirt collar, no beards, no tattoos visible during deliveries, and so on. Before each shift, drivers conduct a "Z-scan," a Z-shaped inspection of the sides and front of their vehicles. There are safety rules for drivers, loaders, clerks, and managers. Employees are asked to clean off their desks at the end of each day so they can start fresh the next morning. Managers are given copies of policy books with the expectation that they will use them regularly, and memos on various policies and rules circulate by the hundreds every day.

Despite the strict rules and numerous policies, employees are satisfied and UPS has a high employee retention rate. Employees are treated well and paid well, and the company has maintained a sense of equality and fairness. Everyone is on a first-name basis. The policy book states, "A leader does not have to remind others of his authority by use of a title. Knowledge, performance, and capacity should be adequate evidence of position and leadership." Technical qualification, not favoritism, is the criterion for hiring and promotion. Top executives started at the bottom—former CEO James Kelly began his career as a temporary holiday-rush driver, for example. The emphasis on equality, fairness, and a promote-from-within mentality inspires loyalty and commitment throughout the ranks.[45]

UPS illustrates how bureaucratic characteristics increase with large size. UPS is so productive and dependable that it dominates the small package delivery market. As it expands and transitions into a global, knowledge-based logistics business, UPS managers may need to find effective ways to reduce the bureaucracy. New technology and new services place more demands on workers, who may need more flexibility and autonomy to perform well. Now, let's look at some specific ways size affects organization structure and control.

Size and Structural Control

In the field of organization theory, organization size has been described as an important contingency that influences structural design and methods of control. Should an organization become more bureaucratic as it grows larger? In what size organizations are bureaucratic characteristics most appropriate? More than 100 studies have attempted to answer these questions.[46] Most of these studies indicate that large organizations are different from small organizations along several dimensions of bureaucratic structure, including formalization, centralization, and personnel ratios.

Formalization and Centralization. **Formalization**, as described in Chapter 1, refers to rules, procedures, and written documentation, such as policy manuals and job descriptions, that prescribe the rights and duties of employees.[47] The evidence supports the conclusion that large organizations are more formalized, as at UPS. The reason is that large organizations rely on rules, procedures, and paperwork to achieve standardization and control across their large numbers of employees and departments, whereas top managers can use personal observation to control a small organization.[48] For example, a locally owned coffee shop in a small town doesn't need the detailed manuals, policies, and procedures that Starbucks uses to standardize and control its operations around the world.

Centralization refers to the level of hierarchy with authority to make decisions. In centralized organizations, decisions tend to be made at the top. In decentralized organizations, similar decisions would be made at a lower level.

Decentralization represents a paradox because, in the perfect bureaucracy, all decisions would be made by the top administrator, who would have perfect control. However, as an organization grows larger and has more people and departments, decisions cannot be passed to the top because senior managers would be overloaded. Thus, the research on organization size indicates that larger organizations permit greater decentralization.[49] In small start-up organizations, on the other hand, the founder or top executive can effectively be involved in every decision, large and small.

Personnel Ratios. Another characteristic of bureaucracy relates to **personnel ratios** for administrative, clerical, and professional support staff. The most frequently studied ratio is the administrative ratio.[50] Two patterns have emerged. The first is that the ratio of top administration to total employees is typically smaller in large organizations,[51] indicating that organizations experience administrative economies as they grow larger. However, recent studies of large colleges and universities have found that the number of administrators at some has grown eight to ten times as much over the past decade as the number of faculty. According to the U.S. Department of Education, the number of employees hired by institutions of higher education to manage and administer people, programs, and regulations grew 50 percent faster than the number of instructors between 2001 and 2011.[52] Because of differences in how institutions classify employees, however, some of these people might actually be clerical and professional support staff rather than administrative staff. The second pattern concerns clerical and professional support staff ratios.[53] These groups tend to *increase* in proportion to organization size. The clerical ratio increases because of the greater communication and reporting requirements needed as organizations grow larger. The professional staff ratio increases because of the greater need for specialized skills in larger, complex organizations.

Exhibit 9.5 illustrates administrative and support ratios for small and large organizations. As organizations increase in size, the administrative ratio declines and the ratios for other support groups increase.[54] The net effect for direct workers is that they decline as a percentage of total employees. In summary, whereas top administrators do not make up a disproportionate number of employees in large organizations, the idea that proportionately greater overhead is required in large organizations is supported. With the declining U.S. economy, many companies have been struggling to cut overhead costs. Keeping costs for administrative, clerical, and professional support staff low represents an ongoing challenge for large organizations.

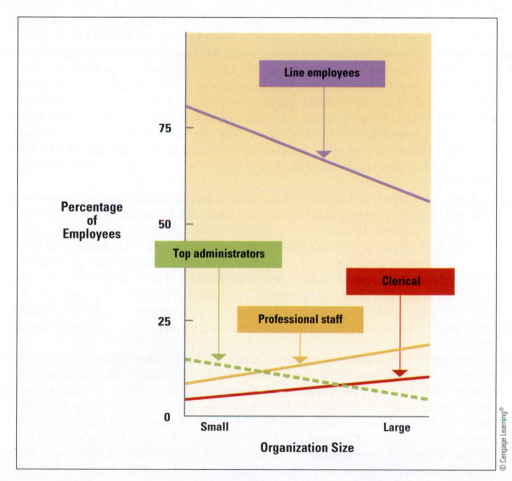

EXHIBIT 9.5
Percentage of Personnel Allocated to Administrative and Support Activities

© Cengage Learning®

Bureaucracy in a Changing World

Evidence found in buildings occupied by terrorist cells suggests that rather than being a "fly-by-night, fragmented terror organization, al-Qaida is attempting to behave like a multinational corporation." The groups closely document their expenses, from a $0.60 snack cake to $330 spent for 3,300 rounds of ammunition. The strict bureaucracy, says one expert, has helped al-Qaida not only to endure but to spread. "They have so few ways to keep control. . . . They have to run it like a business."[55] Even al-Qaida benefits from the use of bureaucratic principles for bringing order.

Weber's prediction of the triumph of bureaucracy proved accurate. Bureaucratic characteristics have many advantages and have worked extremely well for many of the needs of the industrial age.[56] By establishing a hierarchy of authority and specific rules and procedures, bureaucracy provides an effective way to bring order to large groups of people and minimize abuses of power. Bureaucracy provides for systematic and rational ways to organize and manage tasks too complex to be understood and handled by a few individuals, thus greatly improving the efficiency and effectiveness of large organizations. Impersonal relationships based on roles rather than people also reduced the favoritism and nepotism characteristic of many preindustrial organizations.

However, the machinelike bureaucratic system of the industrial age doesn't always work so well as organizations face new challenges and need to respond quickly. The Vatican's bureaucracy, for example, has been blamed for the inability of the Catholic Church to respond to and better serve its members. Pope Francis is only the latest of popes who have tried for decades—and so far failed—to change the Vatican. "Instead of transforming the structure," said a former superior general of a Roman Catholic religious order, "the structure transforms you." Communication among the various departments moves at a snail's pace. Some Vatican officials now use Twitter, but responses are slow in coming. One official said, "Here, the Roman mechanisms are designed to prevent people with a good idea from carrying it forward."[57]

Businesses have the same problem. Some current and former employees of Microsoft say the company has become slow and muscle-bound by heavy bureaucracy in recent years. Almost every significant action requires a lawyer's signature, they say, and getting approval for even routine matters can take weeks. One employee left the company because he was tired of being inundated with paperwork. "The smallest issue would balloon into a nightmare of a thousand e-mails," he says.[58] Managers are trying to find ways to cut the bureaucracy so people can do their jobs more effectively and help Microsoft stay competitive. Like Microsoft, many organizations are fighting against increasing formalization and professional staff ratios.

The problems caused by over-bureaucratization are evident in the inefficiencies of some large U.S. government organizations. In response to President Barack Obama's demand that his cabinet secretaries find $100 million in budget cuts, for example, the U.S. Office of Thrift Supervision (a division of the Treasury Department) identified unused phone lines that were costing $320,000 annually.[59] One recent study found an average of 18 Federal management layers between the top and bottom of most agencies, such as between the secretary of agriculture and the forest ranger or the secretary of the interior and the oil rig inspector.[60] Some agencies have so many clerical staff members and confusing job titles that no one is really sure who does what. Richard Cavanagh, once an aide to President Jimmy Carter, reports his favorite Federal title as the "administrative assistant to the assistant administrator for administration of the General Services Administration."[61] Some critics have blamed government bureaucracy for intelligence, communication, and accountability failures related to the 2001 terrorist attacks, the Columbia space shuttle disaster, the abuses at Abu Ghraib prison, and slow responses to the 2010 Gulf oil spill and the 2012 Hurricane Sandy disasters. "Every time you add a layer of bureaucracy, you delay the movement of information up the chain of command. . . . And you dilute the information because at each step some details are taken out," says Richard A. Posner, a Federal appeals court judge who has written a book on intelligence reform.[62] Many business organizations, too, need to reduce formalization and bureaucracy. Narrowly defined job descriptions and excessive rules, for example, tend to limit the creativity, flexibility, and rapid response needed in today's knowledge-based organizations.

Organizing Temporary Systems

How can organizations overcome the problems of bureaucracy in rapidly changing environments? Some are implementing innovative structural solutions. One structural concept is to use temporary systems or structures to respond to an emergency or crisis situation. This approach is often used by organizations such as police and fire departments or other emergency management agencies to maintain the efficiency and control benefits of bureaucracy yet prevent the problem of slow response.[63] The approach is being adapted by other types of organizations to help them respond quickly to new opportunities, unforeseen competitive threats, or organizational crises.

The basic idea is that the organization can glide smoothly between a highly formalized, hierarchical structure that is effective during times of stability and a more flexible, loosely structured one needed to respond well to unexpected and demanding environmental conditions. The hierarchical side with its rules, procedures, and chain of command helps maintain control and ensure adherence to rules that have been developed and tested over many years to cope with well-understood problems and situations. During times of high uncertainty, however, the most effective structure is one that loosens the lines of command and enables people to work across departmental and hierarchical lines to anticipate, avoid, and solve unique problems within the context of a clearly understood mission and guidelines. The approach can be seen in action at the Salvation Army, which has been called "the most effective organization in the world."

The Salvation Army provides day-to-day assistance to the homeless and economically disadvantaged. In addition, the organization rushes in whenever there is a major disaster—whether it be a tornado, flood, hurricane, airplane crash, or terrorist attack—to network with other agencies to provide disaster relief. The Army's management realizes that emergencies demand high flexibility. At the same time, the organization must have a high level of control and accountability to ensure its continued existence and meet its day-to-day responsibilities. As a former national commander puts it, "We have to have it both ways. We can't choose to be flexible and reckless or to be accountable and responsive. . . . We have to be several different kinds of organization at the same time."

IN PRACTICE

Salvation Army

In the early emergency moments of a crisis, the Salvation Army deploys a temporary organization that has its own command structure. People need to have a clear sense of who's in charge to prevent the rapid response demands from degenerating into chaos. For example, when the Army responds to a disaster such as the 2014 mudslide in Snohomish County, Washington, manuals clearly specify in advance who is responsible for talking to the media, who is in charge of supply inventories, who liaises with other agencies, and so forth. This model for the temporary organization keeps the Salvation Army responsive and consistent. However, in the later recovery and rebuilding phases of a crisis, supervisors frequently give people general guidelines and allow them to improvise the best solutions. There isn't time for supervisors to review and sign off on every decision that needs to be made to get families and communities reestablished.

Thus, the Salvation Army actually has people simultaneously working in all different types of structures, from traditional vertical command structures, to horizontal teams, to a sort of network form that relies on collaboration with other agencies. Operating in such a fluid way enables the organization to accomplish amazing results. In one year, the Army assisted more than 2.3 million people caught in disasters in the United States, in addition to many more served by regular day-to-day programs. It has been recognized as a leader in putting money to maximal use, meaning donors are willing to give because they trust the organization to be responsible and accountable at the same time it is flexible and innovative in meeting human needs.[64]

Other Approaches to Busting Bureaucracy

Organizations are taking a number of other, less dramatic steps to reduce bureaucracy, often *driven by top leaders*. Many are cutting layers of the hierarchy, keeping headquarters staff small, and giving lower-level employees greater freedom to make decisions rather than burdening them with excessive rules and regulations. The commitment of top leadership is essential when an organization needs to reduce bureaucracy and become more flexible and responsive.[65] Consider the following examples:

As an organization manager, keep these guidelines in mind:

Consider using a temporary systems approach to maintain the efficiency and control benefits of bureaucracy but prevent the problem of slow response to rapid environmental change. Enable the organization to glide smoothly from a formalized system during times of stability to a more flexible, loosely structured one when facing threats, crises, or unexpected environmental changes.

- As described earlier, Larry Page recently returned as CEO of Google to try to cut through the bureaucracy that has built up as Google became a big corporation. One mechanism Page is using to speed decision making and restore the sense of a start-up is a daily "bullpen" session. Every afternoon, Page and other top executives work together in a public area of Google's headquarters so employees can directly approach them about issues or concerns. "The more people say that you can't have a big company act like a small company, the more determined [Larry Page] is to figure out how to do just that," said Steven Levy, the author of a book about Google.[66]

- Executives at a multinational consumer goods manufacturer created small teams based in each geographic region to focus on customer needs and competitive conditions in each area. They also streamlined procedures for how teams and divisions communicate and work with headquarters. This cut in half the number of rounds of consultations related to an issue, leading to faster decision making and less frustration and wasted time for employees and customers.[67] The point is to reduce red tape that inhibits the flexibility and autonomy of divisions and teams.

- At the London-based pharmaceuticals company GlaxoSmithKline PLC, top executives gave frontline scientists, not managers or a research committee, the authority to set priorities and allocate resources for drugs in development. The shift in who decides which drug research projects to fund has brought an entrepreneurial spirit to the giant firm similar to that of a small biotechnology company.[68]

Another attack on bureaucracy is from the increasing professionalism of employees. *Professionalism* is defined as the length of formal training and experience of employees. More employees need college degrees, MBAs, and other professional degrees to work as attorneys, researchers, engineers, or doctors at Google, Zurich Financial Services, or GlaxoSmithKline. Some Internet-based companies are staffed entirely by well-educated knowledge workers. Studies of professionals show that formalization is not needed because professional training regularizes a high standard of behavior for employees, which acts as a substitute for bureaucracy.[69] Companies enhance this trend when they provide ongoing training for *all* employees, from the front office to the shop floor, in a push for continuous individual and organizational learning. Increased training substitutes for bureaucratic rules and procedures that can constrain the creativity of employees in solving problems and also enhances individual and organizational capability.

A form of organization called the *professional partnership* has emerged that is made up completely of professionals.[70] These organizations include accounting firms, medical practices, law firms, and consulting firms. The general finding concerning professional partnerships is that branches have substantial autonomy and decentralized authority to make necessary decisions. They work with a consensus orientation rather than the top-down direction typical of traditional business and government organizations. Thus, the trend of increasing professionalism combined with rapidly changing environments is leading to less bureaucracy in corporate North America.

Bureaucracy Versus Other Forms of Control

Even though many organizations are trying to reduce bureaucracy and streamline rules and procedures that constrain employees, every organization needs systems for guiding and controlling the organization. Employees may have more freedom in today's companies, but control is still a major responsibility of management.

Managers at the top and middle levels of an organization can choose among three overall control strategies. These strategies come from a framework for organizational control proposed by William Ouchi of the University of California at Los Angeles. Ouchi suggested three control strategies that organizations could adopt—bureaucratic, market, and clan.[71] Each form of control uses different types of information. However, all three types may appear simultaneously in an organization. The requirements for each control strategy are given in Exhibit 9.6.

Bureaucratic Control

Bureaucratic control is the use of rules, policies, hierarchy of authority, written documentation, standardization, and other bureaucratic mechanisms to standardize behavior and assess performance. Bureaucratic control uses the bureaucratic

Type	Requirements
Bureaucratic	Rules, standards, hierarchy, legitimate authority
Market	Prices, competition, exchange relationship
Clan	Tradition, shared values and beliefs, trust

EXHIBIT 9.6
Three Organizational Control Strategies

Source: Based on William G. Ouchi, "A Conceptual Framework for the Design of Organizational Control Mechanisms," *Management Science* 25 (1979), 833–848.

characteristics defined by Weber and illustrated in the UPS case. The primary purpose of bureaucratic rules and procedures is to standardize and control employee behavior.

Recall that as organizations progress through the life cycle and grow larger, they become more formalized and standardized. Within a large organization, thousands of work behaviors and information exchanges take place both vertically and horizontally. Rules and policies evolve through a process of trial and error to regulate these behaviors. Some degree of bureaucratic control is used in virtually every organization. Rules, regulations, and directives contain information about a range of behaviors. For example, note the variety of behaviors managers seek to control through the rules at an exclusive yacht club, listed in Exhibit 9.7.

To make bureaucratic control work, managers must have the authority to maintain control over the organization. Weber argued that legitimate, rational authority granted to managers was preferred over other types of control (e.g., favoritism or payoffs) as the basis for organizational decisions and activities. Within the larger society, however, Weber identified three types of authority that could explain the creation and control of a large organization.[72]

Rational–legal authority is based on employees' belief in the legality of rules and the right of those elevated to positions of authority to issue commands. Rational–legal authority is the basis for both creation and control of most government organizations and is the most common base of control in organizations worldwide. **Traditional authority** is the belief in traditions and in the legitimacy of the status of people exercising authority through those traditions. Traditional authority is the basis for control for monarchies, churches, and some organizations in Latin America and the Persian Gulf. **Charismatic authority** is based on devotion to the exemplary character or to the heroism of an individual person and the order defined by him or her. Revolutionary military organizations are often based on the leader's charisma, as are North American organizations led by charismatic individuals such as Steve Jobs, the recently deceased CEO of Apple, or media entrepreneur Oprah Winfrey, who runs a successful magazine and a television network among other enterprises.

More than one type of authority—such as long tradition and the leader's special charisma—may exist in organizations, but rational–legal authority is the most widely used form to govern internal work activities and decision making,

EXHIBIT 9.7
Examples of Rules at a Yacht Club

Northeast Harbor Yacht Club Rules for Employees

- Employees shall maintain a clean and well-dressed appearance at work.
- The summer uniform is green shorts, black or brown belt, white shirt tucked in, and boat shoes. Frayed clothing is not allowed at the club.
- Employees should arrive at work at or before the agreed-upon shift time.
- Employees shall not smoke or consume alcohol on club property at any time.
- Employees are required to be polite and helpful to members at all times.
- Employees should remain a respectful distance from members and should not accept social invitations from members.
- Employees should not be on club property when they are not working.
- Employees are not permitted to use the club phones to make or receive personal calls.
- Instructors must provide their own manuals and radio.
- Maintenance employees must provide and use their own tools.

particularly in large organizations. Bureaucratic control can be highly effective and rules and standardization are important when safety is at stake. "The existence of rules and regulations, and the bureaucrats who enforce them . . . puts a check on the kinds of initiatives that can lead to catastrophe."[73] Newell Rubbermaid, for example, carefully follows standard procedures for building and testing car seats and strollers for infants. Also consider environmental safety in drilling the Marcellus Shale, a vast underground rock formation rich in natural gas.

☑ IN PRACTICE

East Resources Inc. and Royal Dutch Shell PLC

East Resources Inc. was among the first companies to drill into the Marcellus Shale, starting in 2008, and regulators cited the company for spills or other environmental infractions repeatedly. Then, Royal Dutch Shell bought East Resources and brought its bureaucratic control to the operation.

The first thing Shell did was shut down the rigs and retrain all the workers. Since taking over in 2010, Shell has averaged less than one violation for every four wells. The same pattern can be seen across the Marcellus Shale. As larger companies with standardized procedures buy out smaller firms, environmental and safety records are improving. The larger firms have developed more rigorous approaches because they know that even one mistake can affect their ability to do business in all areas. Most of these companies have learned from the BP disaster that it is better to be safe than sorry. Smaller firms typically use riskier procedures. Inspection records show that large companies such as Shell, Exxon, and Chevron averaged 38 violations for every 100 Marcellus wells they drilled. Midsized companies averaged 69 citations per 100 wells; and the smallest firms averaged 139 citations per 100 wells.

A senior policy advisor at the Environmental Defense Fund said "there is reason to think . . . that as more of the business is handled by large companies, we will see an improvement in environmental performance."[74]

Of course, some companies have also found that too many rules can get in the way of serving customers. Employees at Starbucks, which grew rapidly from six stores in 1987 into a huge corporation with thousands of stores around the world, are being strangled by meticulous rules and policies that no longer work. Consistency is important for any company, and rules and procedures that facilitated predictable outcomes enabled Starbucks to grow and succeed. However, applying rules inflexibly and blindly soon started to cause problems. One software entrepreneur and *Inc.* magazine contributor tells a story about an order taker in a Starbucks store who got into a prolonged shouting match with a customer who wanted to pick up her sandwich at the front counter. "They're not allowed to give it to you up here!" the employee kept shouting at the shocked and frustrated customer.[75]

Market Control

Market control occurs when price competition is used to evaluate the output and productivity of an organization or its major departments and divisions. The idea of market control originated in economics.[76] A dollar price is an efficient form of control because managers can compare prices and profits to evaluate the efficiency of the corporation. Top managers nearly always use the price mechanism to evaluate performance in their corporations. Corporate sales and costs are summarized in a profit-and-loss statement that can be compared against performance in previous years or with that of other corporations.

⬡ BRIEFCASE

As an organization manager, keep these guidelines in mind:

Implement one of the three basic choices—bureaucratic, clan, market—as the primary means of organizational control. Use bureaucratic control when organizations are large, have a stable environment, and use routine technology. Use clan control in small, uncertain departments. Use market control when outputs can be priced and when competitive bidding is available.

The use of market control requires that outputs be sufficiently explicit for a price to be assigned and that competition exist. Without competition, the price does not accurately reflect internal efficiency. Even some government and nonprofit organizations are effectively using market control. For example, the U.S. Federal Aviation Administration took bids to operate its payroll computers. The Department of Agriculture beat out IBM and two other private companies to win the bid.[77] The city of Indianapolis requires all its departments to bid against private companies. When the transportation department was underbid by a private company on a contract to fill potholes, the city's union workers made a counterproposal that involved eliminating most of the department's middle managers and reengineering union jobs to save money. Eighteen supervisors were laid off, costs were cut by 25 percent, and the department won the bid.[78]

Market control was once used primarily at the level of the entire organization, but it is increasingly used in product divisions or individual departments. Profit centers are self-contained product divisions, such as those described in Chapter 3. Each division contains resource inputs needed to produce a product. Each division can be evaluated on the basis of profit or loss compared with other divisions. ABB, a global electrical contractor and manufacturer of electrical equipment, includes three different types of profit centers, all operating according to their own bottom line and all interacting through buying and selling with one another and with outside customers.[79] The network organization, also described in Chapter 3, illustrates market control as well. Different companies compete on price to provide the functions and services required by the hub organization. The organization typically contracts with the company that offers the best price and value.

Clan Control

Clan control is the use of social characteristics, such as shared values, commitment, traditions, and beliefs, to control behavior. Organizations that use clan control have strong cultures that emphasize shared values and trust among employees.[80] Clan control is important when ambiguity and uncertainty are high. High uncertainty means the organization cannot put a price on its services, and things change so fast that rules and regulations are not able to specify every correct behavior. Under clan control, people may be hired because they are committed to the organization's purpose, such as in a religious organization or an organization focused on a social mission. New employees are typically subjected to a long period of socialization to gain acceptance by colleagues. There is strong pressure to conform to group norms, which govern a wide range of employee behaviors. Managers act primarily as mentors, role models, and agents for transmitting values.[81]

ASSESS YOUR ANSWER

2 A manager should emphasize shared values, trust, and commitment to the organization's mission as the primary means of controlling employee behavior.

ANSWER: *Agree or disagree.* Clan control, which relies on culture, trust, commitment, and shared values and traditions, can be highly effective and is particularly useful in departments or organizations experiencing high uncertainty or environmental turbulence. However, other forms of control, such as bureaucratic or market control, are also effective and appropriate under the right circumstances.

Traditional control mechanisms based on strict rules and close supervision are inadequate for controlling behavior in conditions of high uncertainty and rapid change.[82] In addition, the use of computer networks and the Internet, which often leads to a democratic spread of information throughout the organization, is influencing companies to depend less on bureaucratic control and more on shared values that guide individual actions for the corporate good.[83]

A similar concept is *self-control*. Whereas clan control is a function of being socialized into a group, self-control stems from individual values, goals, and standards. Managers attempt to induce a change such that individual employees' own internal values and work preferences are brought in line with the organization's values and goals.[84] With self-control, employees generally set their own goals and monitor their own performance, yet companies relying on self-control need strong leaders who can clarify boundaries within which people exercise their own knowledge and discretion.

Clan control or self-control may also be used in some departments, such as strategic planning, where uncertainty is high and performance is difficult to measure. Managers of departments that rely on these informal control mechanisms must not assume that the absence of written, bureaucratic control means no control is present. Clan control is invisible yet very powerful. One study found that the actions of employees were controlled even more powerfully and completely with clan control than with a bureaucratic hierarchy.[85] When clan control works, bureaucratic control is not needed, as managers at the following "bossless" companies have learned.

IN PRACTICE
Menlo Innovations, FAVI

Richard Sheridan, James Goebel, Robert Simms, and Thomas Meloche founded Menlo Innovations to create custom software for organizations, but one of their primary goals was to create a unique culture that embraces the values of equality, teamwork, trust, learning, and fun. Menlo infuses happiness into the often lonely grueling work of software development by making it communal. At many software companies developers work alone and are driven to meet rigorous performance goals, but at Menlo, everyone works in a large, open room with no barriers of any kind to limit communication and information sharing. Employees work in pairs, sharing a single computer and passing the mouse back and forth as they brainstorm ideas and troubleshoot problems. Menlo's bossless hiring process is called "Extreme Interviewing," and it bears a striking resemblance to speed-dating. Applicants, sometimes as many as five for each open position, are brought into the office for a series of rapid-fire interviews with a range of current employees. The emphasis is on "kindergarten skills": curiosity, interest in learning, the ability to "play well with others," generosity. Technical proficiency is less important than a candidate's "ability to make [his or her] partner look good." Menlo became one of *Inc.* 500's fastest growing privately held firms in the United States.

One company that shifted from a traditional bureaucratic control approach to bosslessness is FAVI. When CEO Jean-François Zobrist took over FAVI, a 600-person French company that designs and manufactures automotive components, he eliminated the traditional hierarchy. There is no personnel department, no middle management, no time clocks, no employee handbooks. "I told them 'tomorrow when you come to work, you do not work for me or for a boss. You work for your customer. I don't pay you. They do.'" FAVI hasn't been late with a customer order in 10 years.[86]

Clan control works just fine for Menlo Innovations and FAVI, as it does for many other organizations experimenting with bossless designs. The key is establishing strong clan-type values that guide employee behavior. As we discussed in the previous chapter, managers' approach to control is changing in many organizations.

In connection with the shift to more collaborative forms of working and the trend toward bossless organization design, many companies are adopting a *decentralized* approach more in line with clan control rather than a *hierarchical* process associated with bureaucratic control.

Organizational Decline and Downsizing

Earlier in the chapter, we discussed the organizational life cycle, which suggests that organizations are born, grow older, and eventually die. Size can become a burden for many organizations. For example, Hostess Brands, perhaps best known for the cream-filled pastry Twinkies, ceased operation in 2012, after being in business under one name or another for about 82 years. Some of the brands were purchased by other firms and will live on, but the company itself ceased to exist, brought down by excessive debt, mounting labor costs and union strife, and mismanagement.[87] General Motors collapsed under its own weight and had to go through bankruptcy and a forced restructuring. Not only was the company laboring under a financial burden of huge pension and healthcare obligations, but its cumbersome bureaucracy had made it hard for GM to connect with the needs of consumers. Regional managers said their ideas and suggestions for product changes or advertising approaches never reached decision makers or fell on deaf ears.[88] Nearly every organization goes through periods of temporary decline. In addition, a reality in today's environment is that for some companies, continual growth and expansion may not be possible.

All around, we see evidence that some organizations have stopped growing, and many are declining. Huge financial services firms, such as Lehman Brothers and Bear Stearns, disintegrated partly as a result of unfettered growth and ineffective control. With the declining economy, many big corporations have made significant job cuts in recent years. Local governments have been forced to close schools, lay off police officers, and shut down fire stations as tax revenues have declined. Colleges and universities have instituted hiring freezes, halted construction projects, and scaled back on maintenance tasks such as power washing of windows and sidewalks.[89]

In this section, we examine the causes and stages of organizational decline and then discuss how leaders can effectively manage the downsizing that is a reality in today's companies.

Definition and Causes

The term **organizational decline** is used to define a condition in which a substantial, absolute decrease in an organization's resource base occurs over time.[90] Organizational decline is often associated with environmental decline in the sense that an organizational domain experiences either a reduction in size (such as shrinkage in customer demand or erosion of a city's tax base) or a reduction in shape (such as a shift in customer demand). In general, the following three factors are considered responsible for causing organizational decline.

1. *Organizational atrophy.* Atrophy occurs when organizations grow older and become inefficient and overly bureaucratized. The organization's ability to adapt to its environment deteriorates. Often, atrophy follows a long period of success because an organization takes success for granted, becomes attached to practices and structures that worked in the past, and fails to adapt to changes in the

environment.[91] A prime example is BlackBerry, which pioneered the smartphone revolution but failed to prepare for competition and changes in the market. Some warning signals for organizational atrophy include excess administrative and support staff, cumbersome administrative procedures, lack of effective communication and coordination, and outdated organizational structure.[92]

2. *Vulnerability.* Vulnerability reflects an organization's strategic inability to prosper in its environment. This often happens to small organizations that are not yet fully established. They are vulnerable to shifts in consumer tastes or in the economic health of the larger community. Some organizations are vulnerable because they are unable to define the correct strategy to fit the environment. Vulnerable organizations typically need to redefine their environmental domain to enter new industries or markets.

3. *Environmental decline or competition.* Environmental decline refers to reduced energy and resources available to support an organization. When the environment has less capacity to support organizations, the organization has to either scale down operations or shift to another domain.[93] Managers at the American Red Cross, for example, are struggling with raising enough funds to cover expenses. Donations have been declining for several years, and recent major disasters such as Typhoon Haiyan in the Philippines, earthquakes in Japan, China, Pakistan, and elsewhere, a massive mudslide in Washington, and Hurricane Sandy in the northeastern United States, have strained the organization's resources. Steep drops in the stock market, widespread job losses, rising prices, and general pessimism about the U.S. economy have created a tough fund-raising environment for all nonprofits.[94] New competition and fast-shifting industries can also be a problem. Well-established companies such as Hewlett-Packard, Dell, and Cisco were unprepared for the faster-than-expected move by both businesses and consumers from PCs to mobile phones and tablets. The companies that are winning in the new environment are those like Apple and Amazon, not the old-guard firms like HP, Dell, and Cisco.[95]

All three of these factors were involved in the decline of Eastman Kodak, once an American icon of the photograph industry.

☑ IN PRACTICE
Eastman Kodak

Founded in 1880, Eastman Kodak became one of America's most well-known companies, helping to create the industry for camera film and then dominating it for decades. At its peak, Kodak employed 145,000 people worldwide. But a combination of factors led Kodak down a long and winding path to bankruptcy. The company filed for Chapter 11 in January 2012 and is a shadow of its former self.

The primary causes of decline were competition and industry changes, but atrophy and vulnerability were also involved. Kodak actually invented one of the first digital cameras and spent hundreds of millions of dollars developing digital technology, but managers couldn't move forward when it came time to go to market for fear of cannibalizing their lucrative film business. Fujifilm had been competing aggressively with Kodak in the market for traditional film for several years, undercutting prices and adopting a low-cost strategy, and Fuji was quick to jump on the digital bandwagon.

Kodak began trying to fight back, but managers couldn't find the right strategy to compete in an increasingly digital world. In 2003, the company ceased investing in its traditional film business, alienating some long-time customers. It was too late getting into digital to compete with Fuji and other major digital players. A decision to bet on inkjet printers didn't go anywhere. Since 2004, Kodak has reported only one full year of profits. Kodak will continue operating while it goes through bankruptcy, and managers hope they can turn things around.[96]

When managers are hit with all three causes of decline, such as at Kodak, it is exceedingly difficult to survive. In some cases, the only option is to shut things down in an orderly fashion. In the next section, we examine the stages of organizational decline and some common mistakes managers make that can lead to dissolution.

A Model of Decline Stages

Based on an extensive review of organizational decline research, a model of decline stages has been proposed and is summarized in Exhibit 9.8. This model suggests that decline, if not managed properly, can move through five stages resulting in organizational dissolution.[97]

1. *Blinded stage.* The first stage of decline is the internal and external change that threatens long-term survival and may require the organization to tighten up. The organization may have excess personnel, cumbersome procedures, or lack of harmony with customers. Leaders often miss the signals of decline at this point, and the solution is to develop effective scanning and control systems that indicate when something is wrong. With timely information, alert executives can bring the organization back to top performance.

2. *Inaction stage.* The second stage of decline is called *inaction* in which denial occurs despite signs of deteriorating performance. Leaders may try to persuade employees and other stakeholders that all is well. In some cases, managers use "creative

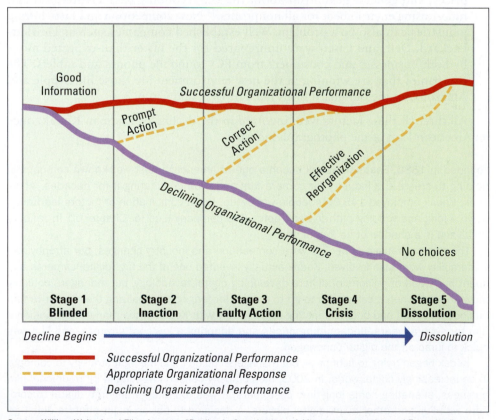

Source: William Weitzel and Ellen Jonsson, "Decline in Organizations: A Literature Integration and Extension," *Administrative Science Quarterly* 34 (March 1989), 99–109. Reprinted by permission of SAGE Publications.

BRIEFCASE

As an organization manager, keep these guidelines in mind:

Understand the causes and stages of decline. Be vigilant to detect signs of decline in the organization and take action as quickly as possible to reverse course. Quick action in the early stages prevents the organization from deteriorating to a stage-4 crisis, when a turnaround becomes much more difficult.

EXHIBIT 9.8
Stages of Decline and the Widening Performance Gap

accounting" to make things look fine during this period. The solution is for leaders to acknowledge decline and take prompt action to realign the organization with the environment. Leadership actions may include adopting new problem-solving approaches, increasing decision-making participation, and encouraging employee and customer expression of dissatisfaction to learn what is wrong.

3. *Faulty action stage.* In the third stage, the organization is facing serious problems, and indicators of poor performance cannot be ignored. Failure to adjust to the declining spiral at this point can lead to organizational failure. Leaders are forced by severe circumstances to consider major changes. Actions may involve retrenchment, including downsizing personnel. Leaders should reduce employee uncertainty by clarifying values and providing information. A major mistake at this stage decreases the organization's chance for a turnaround.

4. *Crisis stage.* In the fourth stage, the organization still has not been able to deal with decline effectively and is facing a panic. The organization may experience chaos, efforts to go back to basics, sharp changes, and anger. It is best for managers to prevent a stage-4 crisis; at this stage, the only solution is major reorganization. The social fabric of the organization is eroding, and dramatic actions are necessary, such as replacing top administrators and instituting revolutionary changes in structure, strategy, and culture. Workforce downsizing may be severe.

5. *Dissolution stage.* This stage of decline is irreversible. The organization is suffering loss of markets and reputation, the loss of its best personnel, and capital depletion. The only available strategy is to close down the organization in an orderly fashion and reduce the separation trauma of employees.

Properly managing organizational decline is necessary if an organization is to avoid dissolution. Managers have a responsibility to detect the signs of decline, acknowledge them, implement necessary action, and reverse course. Some of the most difficult decisions pertain to **downsizing**, which refers to intentionally reducing the size of a company's workforce.

Downsizing Implementation

The economic downturn has made downsizing a common practice in U.S. corporations. In addition, downsizing has been an integral part of organizational life for the past couple of decades as companies make changes to cope with global competition and a rapidly shifting environment.[98] Reengineering projects, mergers and acquisitions, the implementation of advanced technology, and the trend toward outsourcing have all led to job reductions.[99]

Some researchers have found that massive downsizing has often not achieved the intended benefits, and in some cases has significantly harmed the organization.[100] Honeywell CEO David Cote agrees that widespread layoffs hurt companies in the long run. During the recent recession, Honeywell took a different approach, thinking not just of a response to the recession but looking at what was best for efficiency and the profitability of Honeywell over the long term and would not hurt the company's ability to succeed in the recovery. They decided massive layoffs were not the answer.[101] There are times, though, when downsizing is a necessary part of managing organizational decline. A number of techniques can help smooth the downsizing process and ease tensions for employees who leave and for those who remain.[102]

 BRIEFCASE

As an organization manager, keep these guidelines in mind:

When layoffs are necessary, handle them with care. Treat departing employees humanely, communicate with employees and provide as much information as possible, provide assistance to displaced workers, and remember the emotional needs of remaining employees.

1. *Establish criteria for future work needs.* Downsizing should be used as a way to make the organization stronger and more competitive when conditions change, not just as a way to cut workers. Managers need to identify what types of jobs and tasks will need to be performed in the future. Then, they can identify the knowledge, skills, abilities, and work experience that will be needed in the future and base job cuts on these criteria. Without this understanding, managers risk downsizing the very people who have the skills and abilities the organization needs to rebound.[103]

2. *Search for alternatives.* Managers can use creative approaches to cut costs and limit the number of people they have to let go during a decline. Honeywell used furloughs and benefit cuts to limit layoffs during the recent recession. With furloughs, employees take unpaid leaves, but remained employed. Connecticut's state government, Tri-Star Industries, and numerous other organizations are using work-sharing programs, where employees work fewer hours. Other organizations are cutting pay, offering unpaid or partially paid sabbaticals, having mandatory shutdown days, and applying other techniques to avoid across-the-board job cuts.[104]

3. *Communicate more, not less.* Some managers seem to think the less that's said about a pending layoff, the better. Not so. Rumors can be much more damaging than open communication. At 3Com Corporation (now part of Hewlett-Packard), managers drew up a three-stage plan as they prepared for layoffs. First, they warned employees several months ahead that layoffs were inevitable. Soon thereafter, they held on-site presentations at all locations to explain to employees why the layoffs were needed and to provide as much information as they could about what employees should expect.[105] Managers should remember that it is impossible to "overcommunicate" during turbulent times. Remaining employees need to know what is expected of them, whether future layoffs are a possibility, and what the organization is doing to help co-workers who have lost their jobs.

4. *Provide assistance to displaced workers.* The organization has a responsibility to help displaced workers cope with the loss of their jobs and get reestablished in the job market. The organization can provide training, severance packages, extended benefits, and outplacement assistance. At eBay, managers provided each laid-off employee five months of severance pay, four months of health benefits, and several months of outplacement services. "How you treat the leavers has a strong impact on how the stayers feel about the company," said eBay's senior HR executive.[106] Counseling services for both employees and their families can ease the trauma associated with a job loss. A growing number of companies are giving laid-off workers continued access to employee assistance programs to help them cope with stress, depression, and other problems.[107]

5. *Help the survivors thrive.* There has been much research on the "layoff survivor syndrome."[108] Many people experience guilt, anger, confusion, and sadness after the loss of colleagues, and managers should acknowledge these feelings. Survivors also might be concerned about losing their own jobs, lose confidence in company management, and grow depressed and cynical. People sometimes have difficulty adapting to the changes in job duties, responsibilities, and reporting relationships after a downsizing. It is extremely important that managers don't hide behind closed doors, no matter how depressed they might be feeling themselves. They need to get out and interact with employees, doing everything they can to reduce the uncertainty, stress, and confusion people are feeling. "One of the worst actions management can take during this time is to not acknowledge the situation and the impact it is having on employees," advises management consultant Simma Lieberman.[109]

3 After a necessary downsizing, managers should not spend much time helping laid-off workers but focus instead on making sure the remaining employees are taken care of to do what is needed to revive the company.

> **ANSWER:** *Disagree.* One way to take care of remaining employees after a downsizing is to take care of the people who were laid off. Helping laid-off employees sends a signal to remaining workers that the organization cares about the departed co-workers and friends, which helps get the company going again. Managing downsizing means providing assistance to both departing and remaining employees.

Even the best-managed organizations may sometimes need to lay off employees in a turbulent environment or to revitalize the organization and reverse decline. Leaders can attain positive results if they handle downsizing in a way that lets departing employees leave with dignity and enables remaining organization members to be motivated, productive, and committed to a better future.

Design Essentials

- Organizations experience many pressures to grow, and large size is crucial to economic health in some industries. Size enables economies of scale, provides a wide variety of opportunities for employees, and allows companies to invest in expensive and risky projects. However, large organizations have a hard time adapting to rapid changes in the environment. Large organizations are typically standardized, mechanistically run, and complex. Small organizations typically have a flatter structure and an organic, free-flowing management. They can respond more quickly to environmental changes and are more suited to encouraging innovation and entrepreneurship. Managers in large or growing firms try to find mechanisms to make their organizations more flexible and responsive.

- Organizations evolve through distinct life-cycle stages as they grow and mature. Organization structure, internal systems, and management issues are different for each stage of development. Growth creates crises and revolutions along the way toward large size. A major task of managers is to guide the organization through the entrepreneurial, collectivity, formalization, and elaboration stages of development.

- As organizations progress through the life cycle and grow larger and more complex, they generally take on bureaucratic characteristics, such as rules, division of labor, written records, hierarchy of authority, and impersonal procedures. Bureaucracy is a logical form of organizing that lets firms use resources efficiently. In many large corporate and government organizations, however, bureaucracy has come under attack with attempts to decentralize authority, flatten organization structure, reduce rules and written procedures, and create a small-company mindset. These companies are willing to trade economies of scale for responsive, adaptive organizations. Many companies are subdividing to gain small-company advantages. Another approach to overcoming the problems of bureaucracy is to use temporary systems, enabling the organization to glide smoothly between a highly formalized, hierarchical style that is effective during times of stability and a more flexible, loosely structured one needed to respond to unexpected or volatile environmental conditions.

■ All organizations, large and small, need systems for control. Managers can choose among three overall control strategies: bureaucratic, market, and clan. Bureaucratic control relies on standard rules and the rational–legal authority of managers. Market control is used where product or service outputs can be priced and competition exists. Clan control and self-control are associated with uncertain and rapidly changing organization processes. They rely on commitment, tradition, and shared values for control. Managers may use a combination of control approaches to meet the organization's needs. In general, today's companies are shifting from a hierarchical to a decentralized approach to control.

■ Many organizations have stopped growing, and some are declining. Organizations go through stages of decline, and it is the responsibility of managers to detect the signs of decline, implement necessary action, and reverse course. One of the most difficult decisions pertains to downsizing the workforce. To smooth the downsizing process, managers can establish criteria for the types of jobs and skills that will be needed in a recovery, search for creative alternatives to massive layoffs, communicate with employees and provide as much information as possible, provide assistance to displaced workers, and remember to address the emotional needs of those who remain with the organization.

》 KEY CONCEPTS

bureaucracy	downsizing	market control
bureaucratic control	elaboration stage	organizational decline
centralization	entrepreneurial stage	personnel ratios
charismatic authority	formalization	rational–legal authority
clan control	formalization stage	traditional authority
collectivity stage	life cycle	

》 DISCUSSION QUESTIONS

1. Why do large organizations tend to have larger ratios of clerical and administrative support staff? Why are they typically more formalized than small organizations?

2. Apply the concept of life cycle to an organization with which you are familiar, such as a local business. What stage is the organization in now? How did the organization handle or pass through its life-cycle crises?

3. Why do you think organizations feel pressure to grow? How do you think the companies described in the chapter's BookMark, *Small Giants*, resist that pressure?

4. Describe the three bases of authority identified by Weber. Is it possible for each of these types of authority to function at the same time within an organization? Discuss.

5. Look through several recent issues of a business magazine such as *Fortune, Businessweek*, or *Fast Company* and find examples of two companies that are using approaches to busting bureaucracy. Discuss the techniques these companies are applying.

6. In writing about types of control, William Ouchi said, "The Market is like the trout and the Clan like the salmon, each a beautiful highly specialized species which requires uncommon conditions for its survival. In comparison, the bureaucratic method of control is the catfish—clumsy, ugly, but able to live in the widest range of environments and ultimately, the dominant species." Discuss what Ouchi meant with that analogy.

7. Government organizations often seem more bureaucratic than for-profit organizations. Could this partly be the result of the type of control used in government organizations? Explain.

8. How does the Salvation Army manage to be "several different kinds of organization at the same time"? Does the Salvation Army's approach seem workable for a large media company like Time Warner or Disney that wants to reduce bureaucracy?

9. Numerous large financial institutions, including Lehman Brothers and Merrill Lynch, experienced significant decline or dissolution in recent years. Which of the three causes of organizational decline described in the chapter seems to apply most clearly to these firms?

10. Do you think a "no growth" philosophy of management should be taught in business schools? Discuss.

⊗ CHAPTER 9 WORKSHOP Classroom Control

Think back to one of your most favorite and least favorite courses in school. How did the instructor control you and other students in those courses? Write down your answers for the comparisons below.

How were rules, standards, or legitimate authority used to influence student behavior?

Favorite class:

Least favorite class:

How were competition and measured outcomes used to influence student behavior?

Favorite class:

Least favorite class:

How were shared values, norms, expectations, and self-control used to influence student behavior?

Favorite class:

Least favorite class:

Questions

1. How did the differences in *type* of control influence how much you liked each course?

2. How did the *amount* of control asserted over students influence how much you liked each course?

3. How did size of each class influence the type and amount of control used by the instructor?

4. Discuss your answers with other students to learn how your perceptions of control are similar or different.

CASE FOR ANALYSIS │ Yahoo: *"Get to Work!"*

High-tech within the corporate world was developed, in part, on the notion of mobile strategy and convenience—the ability to communicate, work remotely and accomplish the same results; cutting the corporate and personal carbon footprint by reducing commute times; and reducing wasted time through workplace flexibility.

Flex time was touted as a solution and an attractive perk for job seekers, particularly in the tech industries. Workers were actually *doing* and modeling what they insisted was possible for future workers. Then, it changed. Suddenly, the brakes were applied.

"Get to work" was what your mom said; what your coach said; what your teacher said. Suddenly, for Yahoo employees, it was what your boss said in a surprise memo from new CEO Marissa Mayer. *Entrepreneur* called it Mayer's "dumbest move," and it ignited a national debate over the concept of workplace bureaucracy versus flexibility.

Created by Stanford grad students Jerry Yang and David Filo, and launched as Yahoo in 1994, the company grabbed the spotlight, riding the dot-com bubble to both an all-time high and an all-time low in tech stock pricing,

rejecting an acquisition bid from Microsoft, and suffering through its largest layoff of employees (2,000) in 2012. In a five-year period, 2009–2014, Yahoo had six CEOs bringing constantly changing visions and executives to the company.

In May 2013 the last, Marissa Mayer, came over from Google and immediately set off a fire-storm with the memo informing employees to get to work and announcing that Yahoo's work-at-home policy had been overturned. Empty parking lots, offices, and cubicles would henceforth be teeming with employees.

Seen by Mayer and a significant number of employees as a boost for low morale, the move was criticized by others within the company and across industries as a slap in the face at the notion of flexibility and remote workforce productivity.

The general target for the new corporate ruling appeared to be the 200 or so employees who had routinely abused the work-from-home privilege by doing things like starting their own businesses while no one was watching. But if remote productivity and collaboration won't work within the tech industry, others pointed out, what is the message for other industries? Was this a high profile example of a tech company shooting itself in the foot?

Supporters of the change defended the move as a need for control in this particular company based on the constant directional changes at Yahoo, the low morale of employees, and the lack of face-time and collaboration needed to keep up with the innovations of rivals. *The New York Times* quoted one former Yahoo official as saying, "In the tech world it was such a bummer to say you worked for Yahoo." The situation had gotten that bad.

Mayer's turnaround strategy required employee *skin in the game*—getting employees into the office. The company responded to critics with one blanket statement about the change: "This isn't a broad industry view about working from home. This is about what is right for Yahoo, right now."

The previous situation was viewed by Mayer as cultural self-strangulation. With no one in the building, and a revolving CEO door, projects slowed or were completely abandoned. Meanwhile, Facebook and other rivals were surging ahead, rolling out innovations, grabbing advertisers, and cornering the social media market while Yahoo hesitated.

Mayer jumped in, revamping the recently acquired Flickr, which had seemingly abandoned a potential leadership role in photo-sharing to rival Instagram. With new hires and a total redesign and update of Flickr, the move was heralded by *Entrepreneur* as Mayer's smartest. In addition, the new CEO quickly replaced employee BlackBerrys with Android and iPhones, with corporate picking up the tab for monthly usage. With bodies now working on-site, and in an effort to create an atmosphere of meeting and collaboration, Mayer offered free food in the cafeteria and insisted on day-long Friday question/answer/planning meetings between senior executives and all employees.

Yahoo must make up time and get up to speed within the industry quickly. Rivals are not waiting and some new ones doubtlessly lurk in the shadows. While some criticize what they see as Mayer's infantilizing of employees and clamping down on others as she adds an on-site nursery for her own child, others have developed a wait and see attitude—not only within the walls of Yahoo, but nationwide, as companies weigh the future of remote workforce cultures.

CASE FOR ANALYSIS | Sunflower Incorporated[110]

Sunflower Incorporated is a large distribution company with more than 5,000 employees and gross sales of more than $700 million (2008). The company purchases salty snack foods and liquor and distributes them to independent retail stores throughout the United States and Canada. Salty snack foods include corn chips, potato chips, cheese curls, tortilla chips, pretzels, and peanuts. The United States and Canada are divided into 22 regions, each with its own central warehouse, salespeople, finance department, and purchasing department. The company distributes national and local brands and packages some items under private labels. Competition in this industry is intense. The demand for liquor has been declining, and snack food competitors like Procter & Gamble and Frito-Lay have developed new products and low-carb options to gain market share from smaller companies like Sunflower. The head office encourages each region to be autonomous because of local tastes and practices. In the northeastern United States, for example, people consume a greater percentage of Canadian whiskey and American bourbon, whereas in the West they consume more light liquors, such as vodka, gin, and rum. Snack foods in the Southwest are often seasoned to reflect Mexican tastes, and customers in the Northeast buy a greater percentage of pretzels.

Early in 2003, Sunflower began using a financial reporting system that compared sales, costs, and profits across company regions. Each region was a profit center, and top management was surprised to learn that profits varied widely. By 2006, the differences were so great that management decided some standardization was necessary. Managers believed highly profitable regions were sometimes using lower-quality items, even seconds, to boost profit margins. This practice could hurt Sunflower's image. Most regions were facing cutthroat price competition to hold market share. Triggered by price cuts by Eagle Snacks, national distributors such as Frito-Lay, Borden, Nabisco, Procter & Gamble (Pringles), and Kraft Foods (Planters Peanuts) were pushing to hold or increase market share by cutting prices and launching new products. Independent snack food distributors had a tougher and tougher time competing, and many were going out of business.

As these problems accumulated, Joe Steelman, president of Sunflower, decided to create a new position to monitor pricing and purchasing practices. Loretta Williams was hired from the finance department of a competing organization. Her new title was director of pricing and purchasing, and she reported to the vice president of finance, Peter Langly. Langly gave Williams great latitude in organizing her job and encouraged her to establish whatever rules and procedures were necessary. She was also encouraged to gather information from each region. Each region was notified of her appointment by an official memo sent to the 22 regional directors. A copy of the memo was posted on each warehouse bulletin board. The announcement was also made in the company newspaper.

After three weeks on the job, Williams decided two problems needed her attention. Over the long term, Sunflower should make better use of information technology. Williams believed information technology could provide more information to headquarters for decision making. Top managers in the divisions were connected to headquarters by an intranet, but lower-level employees and salespeople were not connected. Only a few senior managers in about half the divisions used the system regularly.

In the short term, Williams decided fragmented pricing and purchasing decisions were a problem and these decisions should be standardized across regions. This strategy should be undertaken immediately. As a first step, she wanted the financial executive in each region to notify her of any change in local prices of more than 3 percent. She also decided that all new contracts for local purchases of more than $5,000 should be cleared through her office. (Approximately 60 percent of items distributed in the regions were purchased in large quantities and supplied from the home office. The other 40 percent were purchased and distributed within the region.) Williams believed the only way to standardize operations was for each region to notify the home office in advance of any change in prices or purchases. She discussed the proposed policy with Langly. He agreed, so they submitted a formal proposal to the president and board of directors, who approved the plan. The changes represented a complicated shift in policy procedures, and Sunflower was moving into peak holiday season, so Williams wanted to implement the new procedures right away. She decided to send an e-mail message followed by a fax to the financial and purchasing executives in each region notifying them of the new procedures. The change would be inserted in all policy and procedure manuals throughout Sunflower within four months.

Williams showed a draft of the message to Langly and invited his comments. Langly said the message was a good idea but wondered if it was sufficient. The regions handled hundreds of items and were accustomed to decentralized decision making. Langly suggested that Williams ought to visit the regions and discuss purchasing and pricing policies with the executives. Williams refused, saying that such trips would be expensive and time consuming. She had so many things to do at headquarters and said that the trips were impossible to schedule. Langly also suggested waiting to implement the procedures until after the annual company meeting in three months, when Williams could meet the regional directors personally. Williams said this would take too long because the procedures would then not take effect until after the peak sales season. She believed the procedures were needed now. The messages went out the next day.

During the next few days, e-mail replies came in from seven regions. The managers said they were in agreement and were happy to cooperate.

Eight weeks later, Williams had not received notices from any regions about local price or purchase changes. Other executives who had visited regional warehouses indicated to her that the regions were busy as usual. Regional executives seemed to be following usual procedures for that time of year. She telephoned one of the regional managers and discovered that he did not know who she was and had never heard of her position. Besides, he said, "we have enough to worry about reaching profit goals without additional procedures from headquarters." Williams was chagrined that her position and her suggested changes in procedure had no impact. She wondered whether field managers were disobedient or whether she should have used another communication strategy.

▶▶ NOTES

1. Jack Nicas and Susan Carey, "Southwest Airlines, Once a Brassy Upstart, Is Showing Its Age," *The Wall Street Journal Online*, April 1, 2014, http://online.wsj.com/news/articles/SB10001424052702303949704579459643375588678 (accessed April 14, 2014).

2. Ibid.

3. James Q. Wilson, *Bureaucracy* (New York: Basic Books, 1989); and Charles Perrow, *Complex Organizations: A Critical Essay* (Glenview, IL: Scott, Foresman, 1979), 4.

4. Tom Peters, "Rethinking Scale," *California Management Review* (Fall 1992), 7–29.

5. Statistics reported in Claudio Feser, "Long Live Bureaucracy!" *Leader to Leader* (Summer 2012), 57–62.

6. Donald V. Potter, "Scale Matters," *Across the Board*, July–August 2000, 36–39.

7. Juhana Rossi, "Angry Birds Maker at Pivot Point," *The Wall Street Journal Online*, April 3, 2013, http://online.wsj.com/news/articles/SB10001424127887323646604578400201763339218 (accessed April 3, 2013).

8. Kris Hudson, "Wal-Mart Sticks with Fast Pace of Expansion Despite Toll on Sales," *The Wall Street Journal*, April 13, 2006, A1.

9. Christopher Weaver, "Managed Care Enters the Exam Room as Insurers Buy Doctors Groups," *The Washington Post*, July 1, 2011, http://www.washingtonpost.com/insurers-quietly-gaining-control-of-doctors-covered-by-companies-plans/2011/06/29/AG5DNftH_story.html (accessed September 6, 2011).

10. James B. Treece, "Sometimes, You Still Gotta Have Size," *Businessweek*, October 22, 1993, 200–201.

11. Nelson D. Schwartz, "Is G.E. Too Big for Its Own Good?" *The New York Times*, July 22, 2007, Section 3, 1.

12. Scott Thurm, "For Big Companies, Life Is Good," *The Wall Street Journal*, April 9, 2012, B1.

13. James Surowiecki, "Big Is Beautiful," *The New Yorker*, October 31, 2011, 38.

14. Ken Belson, "After the Disasters in Japan, a Stoic Response from Aflac," *The New York Times*, April 16, 2011, B4.

15. Frits K. Pil and Matthias Holweg, "Exploring Scale: The Advantages of Thinking Small," *MIT Sloan Management Review*, Winter 2003, 33–39; and David Sadtler, "The Problem with Size," *Management Today*, November 2007, 52–55.

16. See Keith H. Hammonds, "Size Is Not a Strategy," *Fast Company*, September 2002, 78–86; David Henry, "Mergers: Why Most Big Deals Don't Pay Off," *Businessweek*, October 14, 2002, 60–70; and Tom Brown, "How Big Is Too Big?" *Across the Board*, July–August 1999, 15–20, for a discussion.

17. Chip Jarnagan and John W. Slocum, Jr., "Creating Corporate Cultures Through Mythopoetic Leadership," *Organizational Dynamics* 36, no. 3 (2007), 288–302; and Robbie Whelan and Dawn Wotapka, "Corporate News: Home Builder Pulte to Lay Off Executives," *The Wall Street Journal*, May 13, 2011, B2.

18. Winslow Sargeant, "Small Business Economy 2012," SBA Office of Advocacy, http://www.sba.gov/sites/default/files/files/Small_Business_Economy_2012(2).pdf (accessed September 6, 2013); and "Small Business Trends," Small Business Administration, http://www.sba.gov/content/small-business-trends (accessed September 6, 2013).

19. Bureau of Labor Statistics data, reported by U.S. Small Business Administration Office of Advocacy, September 2012, http://www.sba.gov/sites/default/files/FAQ_Sept_2012.pdf (accessed September 6, 2013).

20. "The Hot 100," *Fortune*, September 5, 2005, 75–80.

21. Reported in Sadtler, "The Problem with Size."

22. Gary Hamel, quoted in Hammonds, "Size Is Not a Strategy."

23. For more information on the ambidextrous approach, see Charles A. O'Reilly III and Michael L. Tushman, "Organizational Ambidexterity in Action: How Managers Explore and Exploit," *California Management Review* 53, no. 4 (Summer 2011), 5–22; and S. Raisch et al., "Organizational Ambidexterity: Balancing Exploitation and Exploration for Sustained Performance," *Organization Science* 20, no. 4 (July–August 2009), 685–695.

24. Michael L. Tushman, Wendy K. Smith, and Andy Binns, "The Ambidextrous CEO," *Harvard Business Review*, June 2011, 74–80.

25. "Our Company," Johnson & Johnson website, http://www.jnj.com/connect/about-jnj/ (accessed August 31, 2011).

26. Anne VanderMey, "Dell Gets in Touch with Its Inner Entrepreneur," *Fortune*, December 12, 2011, 58.

27. Reported in Jerry Useem, "The Big…Get Bigger," *Fortune*, April 30, 2007, 81–84.

28. John R. Kimberly, Robert H. Miles, and associates, *The Organizational Life Cycle* (San Francisco: Jossey-Bass, 1980); Ichak Adices, "Organizational Passages—Diagnosing and Treating Lifecycle Problems of Organizations," *Organizational Dynamics*, Summer 1979, 3–25; Danny Miller and Peter H. Friesen, "A Longitudinal Study of the Corporate Life Cycle," *Management Science* 30 (October 1984), 1161–1183; and Neil C. Churchill and Virginia L. Lewis, "The Five Stages of Small Business Growth," *Harvard Business Review* 61 (May–June 1983), 30–50.

29. Larry E. Greiner, "Evolution and Revolution as Organizations Grow," *Harvard Business Review* 50 (July–August 1972), 37–46; and Robert E. Quinn and Kim Cameron, "Organizational Life Cycles and Shifting Criteria of Effectiveness: Some Preliminary Evidence," *Management Science* 29 (1983), 33–51.

30. George Land and Beth Jarman, "Moving Beyond Breakpoint," in Michael Ray and Alan Rinzler, eds., *The New Paradigm* (New York: Jeremy P. Tarcher/Perigee Books, 1993), 250–266; and Michael L. Tushman, William H. Newman, and Elaine Romanelli, "Convergence and Upheaval: Managing the Unsteady Pace of Organizational Evolution," *California Management Review* 29 (1987), 1–16.

31. Sam Gustin, "The Next Tech Titan? 10 Hottest Technology Start-Ups of 2010," DailyFinance.com, August 12, 2010, http://www.dailyfinance.com/2010/08/12/the-next-tech-tian-10-hottest-technology-start-ups-of-2010/ (accessed September 1, 2011); and "About Foursquare," https://foursquare.com/about (accessed April 16, 2014).

32. Claire Cain Miller, "Yes, Silicon Valley, Sometimes You Need More Bureaucracy," *The New York Times*, May 1, 2014, B3; and David Streitfeld, "Groupon Dismisses Chief After a Dismal Quarter," *The New York Times*, February 28, 2013, http://www.nytimes.com/2013/03/01/technology/groupon-dismisses-its-chief-andrew-mason.html?_r=0 (accessed April 17, 2014).

33. Eve Yen, "Delegate Smart," *Fortune Small Business*, April 2009, 33–34.

34. Jeffrey Sonnenfeld, "Analysis: Facebook Board Must Learn to Deal with Genius CEO," *The Washington Post*, May 19, 2012, http://www.washingtonpost.com/analysis-facebook-board-must-learn-to-deal-with-genius-ceo/2012/05/18/gIQADEFtYU_story.html (accessed April 17, 2014); and Shayndi Raice, "Is Facebook Ready for the Big Time?" *The Wall Street Journal Online*, January 14, 2012, http://online.wsj.com/news/articles/SB10001424405297020454240457715 7113178985408 (accessed January 20, 2012).

35. David A. Whetten, "Sources, Responses, and Effects of Organizational Decline," in Kimberly, Miles, and Associates, *The Organizational Life Cycle*, 342–374.

36. Peter Burrows, "Opening Remarks: The Essence of Apple," *Bloomberg Businessweek*, January 24–January 30, 2011, 6–8; Brent Schlender, "How Big Can Apple Get?" *Fortune* (February 21, 2005), 67–76; and Josh Quittner with Rebecca Winters, "Apple's New Core—Exclusive: How Steve Jobs Made a Sleek Machine That Could Be the Home-Digital Hub of the Future," *Time*, January 14, 2002, 46.

37. Nick Wingfield, "Apple's No. 2 Has Low Profile, High Impact," *The Wall Street Journal*, October 16, 2006, B1, B9; and Garrett Sloane, "Apple Gets Cored; End of an Era as Legend Steve Jobs Resigns," *The New York Post*, August 25, 2011, 27.

38. Land and Jarman, "Moving Beyond Breakpoint."

39. Brad Stone, "The Education of Larry Page," *Bloomberg Businessweek*, April 9–April 15, 2012, 12–14; and Claire Cain Miller, "Google's Chief Works to Trim a Bloated Ship," *The New York Times*, November 10, 2011, A1.

40. Max Weber, *The Theory of Social and Economic Organizations*, translated by A. M. Henderson and T. Parsons (New York: Free Press, 1947).

41. Rahim Faiez, "Review: Kabul Bank Sent Millions of Dollars Abroad," Associated Press story in *HeartlandConnection.com*, November 28, 2012, http://www.heartlandconnection.com/news/story.aspx?id=830523#.U0_n5ZhOV1s (accessed November 28, 2012).

42. Barry Kramer, "Chinese Officials Still Give Preference to Kin, Despite Peking Policies," *The Wall Street Journal*, October 29, 1985, 1, 21.

43. John Chase, "Delay Requested for Indictment; 3 More Months Sought in Case Against Governor," *The Chicago Tribune*, January 1, 2009, 4.

44. Eric J. Walton, "The Persistence of Bureaucracy: A Meta-Analysis of Weber's Model of Bureaucratic Control," *Organization Studies* 26, no. 4 (2005), 569–600.

45. Nadira A. Hira, "The Making of a UPS Driver," *Fortune*, November 12, 2007, 118–129; Devin Leonard, "UPS's Holiday Shipping Master: They Call Him Mr. Peak," *Bloomberg Businessweek*, December 19, 2013, http://www.businessweek.com/articles/2013-12-18/upss-holiday-shipping-master-scott-abell-they-call-him-mr-dot-peak#p4 (accessed April 17, 2014); "Logistics: Squeezing More Green Out of Brown," *Bloomberg Businessweek*, September 20–September 26, 2010, 43; David J. Lynch, "Thanks to Its CEO, UPS Doesn't Just Deliver," *USA Today*, July 24, 2006, http://www.usatoday.com/money/companies/management/2006-07-23-ups_x.htm?tab1=t2 (accessed July 24, 2006); Kelly Barron, "Logistics in Brown," *Forbes*, January 10, 2000, 78–83; Scott Kirsner, "Venture Vèritè: United Parcel Service," *Wired*, September 1999, 83–96; Kathy Goode, Betty Hahn, and Cindy Seibert, *United Parcel Service: The Brown Giant* (unpublished manuscript, Texas A&M University, 1981); and "About UPS," UPS corporate website, http://www.ups.com/content/ corp/about/index.html?WT.svl=SubNav (accessed October 27, 2008).

46. See Allen C. Bluedorn, "Pilgrim's Progress: Trends and Convergence in Research on Organizational Size and Environment," *Journal of Management Studies* 19 (Summer 1993), 163–191; John R. Kimberly, "Organizational Size and the Structuralist Perspective: A Review, Critique, and Proposal," *Administrative Science Quarterly* (1976), 571–597; and Richard L. Daft and Selwyn W. Becker, "Managerial, Institutional, and Technical Influences on Administration: A Longitudinal Analysis," *Social Forces* 59 (1980), 392–413.

47. James P. Walsh and Robert D. Dewar, "Formalization and the Organizational Life Cycle," *Journal of Management Studies* 24 (May 1987), 215–231.

48. Nancy M. Carter and Thomas L. Keon, "Specialization as a Multidimensional Construct," *Journal of Management Studies* 26 (1989), 11–28; Cheng-Kuang Hsu, Robert M. March, and Hiroshi Mannari, "An Examination of the Determinants of Organizational Structure," *American Journal of Sociology* 88 (1983), 975–996; Guy Geeraerts, "The Effect of Ownership on the Organization Structure in Small Firms," *Administrative Science Quarterly* 29 (1984), 232–237; Bernard Reimann, "On the Dimensions of Bureaucratic Structure: An Empirical Reappraisal," *Administrative Science Quarterly* 18 (1973), 462–476; Richard H. Hall, "The Concept of Bureaucracy: An Empirical Assessment," *American Journal of Sociology* 69 (1963), 32–40; and William A. Rushing, "Organizational Rules and Surveillance: A Proposition in Comparative Organizational Analysis," *Administrative Science Quarterly* 10 (1966), 423–443.

49. Jerald Hage and Michael Aiken, "Relationship of Centralization to Other Structural Properties," *Administrative Science Quarterly* 12 (1967), 72–91.

50. Peter Brimelow, "How Do You Cure Injelitance?" *Forbes*, August 7, 1989, 42–44; Jeffrey D. Ford and John W. Slocum, Jr., "Size, Technology, Environment and the Structure of Organizations," *Academy of Management Review* 2 (1977), 561–575; and John D. Kasarda, "The Structural Implications of Social System Size: A Three-Level Analysis," *American Sociological Review* 39 (1974), 19–28.

51. Graham Astley, "Organizational Size and Bureaucratic Structure," *Organization Studies* 6 (1985), 201–228; Spyros K. Lioukas and Demitris A. Xerokostas, "Size and Administrative Intensity in Organizational Divisions," *Management Science* 28 (1982), 854–868; Peter M. Blau, "Interdependence and Hierarchy in Organizations," *Social Science Research* 1 (1972), 1–24; Peter M. Blau and R. A. Schoenherr, *The Structure of Organizations* (New York: Basic Books, 1971); A. Hawley, W. Boland, and M. Boland, "Population Size and Administration in Institutions of Higher Education," *American Sociological Review* 30 (1965), 252–255; Richard L. Daft, "System Influence on Organization Decision-Making: The Case of Resource Allocation," *Academy of Management Journal* 21 (1978), 6–22; and B. P. Indik, "The Relationship Between Organization Size and the Supervisory Ratio," *Administrative Science Quarterly* 9 (1964), 301–312.

52. John Hechinger, "The Troubling Dean-to-Professor Ratio," *Bloomberg Businessweek*, November 26–December 2, 2012, 40–42; and Douglas Belkin and Scott Thurm, "Deans List: Hiring Spree Fattens College Bureaucracy—And Tuition," *The Wall Street Journal*, December 29, 2012, A1.

53. T. F. James, "The Administrative Component in Complex Organizations," *Sociological Quarterly* 13 (1972), 533–539; Daft, "System Influence on Organization Decision-Making: The Case of Resource Allocation"; E. A. Holdaway and E. A. Blowers, "Administrative Ratios and Organization Size: A Longitudinal Examination," *American Sociological Review* 36 (1971), 278–286; and John Child, "Parkinson's Progress: Accounting for the Number of Specialists in Organizations," *Administrative Science Quarterly* 18 (1973), 328–348.

54. Richard L. Daft and Selwyn Becker, "School District Size and the Development of Personnel Resources," *Alberta Journal of Educational Research* 24 (1978), 173–187.

55. Rukmini Callimachi, "0.60 for Cake: Al-Qaida Records Every Expense," Associated Press, December 20, 2013, http://bigstory.ap.org/article/060-cake-al-qaida-records-every-expense (accessed April 17, 2014).

56. Based on Gifford and Elizabeth Pinchot, *The End of Bureaucracy and the Rise of the Intelligent Organization* (San Francisco: Berrett-Koehler Publishers, 1993), 21–29.

57. Rachel Donadio and Jim Yardley, "Vatican's Bureaucracy Tests Even the Infallible," *The New York Times*, March 19, 2013, A1.

58. Victoria Murphy, "Microsoft's Midlife Crisis," *Forbes*, October 3, 2005, 88.

59. Jonathan Weisman, "In a Savings Shocker, the Government Discovers that Paper Has Two Sides," *The Wall Street Journal,* July 29, 2009, A1.

60. Study by Paul C. Light, reported in Paul C. Light, "The Easy Way Washington Could Save $1 Trillion; How an Independent Agency Could Squeeze $1 Trillion in Savings from the Bureaucracy," *The Wall Street Journal*, July 7, 2011, http://online.wsj.com/article/SB1000142405270230476060457642826241993539.html (accessed September 6, 2011).

61. Jack Rosenthal, "Entitled: A Chief for Every Occasion, and Even a Chief Chief," *New York Times Magazine*, August 26, 2001, 16.

62. Scott Shane, "The Beast That Feeds on Boxes: Bureaucracy," *The New York Times,* April 10, 2005, Section 4, 3.

63. Gregory A. Bigley and Karlene H. Roberts, "The Incident Command System: High-Reliability Organizing for Complex and Volatile Task Environments," *Academy of Management Journal* 44, no. 6 (2001), 1281–1299.

64. Robert A. Watson and Ben Brown, *The Most Effective Organization in the U.S.: Leadership Secrets of the Salvation Army* (New York: Crown Business, 2001), 159–181.

65. Julian Birkinshaw and Suzanne Heywood, "Putting Organizational Complexity in Its Place," *McKinsey Quarterly*, Issue 3 (2010), 122–127.

66. Amir Efrati, "At Google, Page Aims to Clear Red Tape," *The Wall Street Journal*, March 26, 2011, B1; and Jessica Guynn, "New CEO Stirs Up Google Ranks; Larry Page Promotes Seven Execs to Run the Company's Most Important Divisions," *Los Angeles Times*, April 9, 2011, B1.

67. Birkinshaw and Heywood, "Putting Organizational Complexity in Its Place."

68. Jeanne Whalen, "Bureaucracy Buster? Glaxo Lets Scientists Choose Its New Drugs," *The Wall Street Journal*, March 27, 2006, B1.

69. Philip M. Padsakoff, Larry J. Williams, and William D. Todor, "Effects of Organizational Formalization on Alienation among Professionals and Nonprofessionals," *Academy of Management Journal* 29 (1986), 820–831.

70. Royston Greenwood, C. R. Hinings, and John Brown, "'P2-Form' Strategic Management: Corporate Practices in Professional Partnerships," *Academy of Management Journal* 33 (1990), 725–755; and Royston Greenwood and C. R. Hinings, "Understanding Strategic Change: The Contribution of Archetypes," *Academy of Management Journal* 36 (1993), 1052–1081.

71. William G. Ouchi, "Markets, Bureaucracies, and Clans," *Administrative Science Quarterly* 25 (1980), 129–141; idem, "A Conceptual Framework for the Design of Organizational Control Mechanisms," *Management Science* 25 (1979), 833–848; and Jay B. Barney, "An Interview with William Ouchi," *Academy of Management Executive* 18, no. 4 (November 2004), 108–116.

72. Weber, *The Theory of Social and Economic Organizations*, 328–340.

73. Raymond Fisman and Tim Sullivan, "The Unsung Beauty of Bureaucracy," *The Wall Street Journal*, March 15, 2013, http://online.wsj.com/news/articles/SB10001424127887324077704578360243017096714 (accessed April 17, 2014).

74. Daniel Gilbert and Russell Gold, "As Big Drillers Move In, Safety Goes Up," *The Wall Street Journal*, April 2, 2013, A1.

75. Joel Spolsky, "Good System, Bad System; Starbucks' Meticulous Policy Manual Shows Employees How to Optimize Profits. Too Bad It Undercuts Basic Customer Service," *Inc.* (August 2008), 67.

76. Oliver A. Williamson, *Markets and Hierarchies: Analyses and Antitrust Implications* (New York: Free Press, 1975).

77. David Wessel and John Harwood, "Capitalism Is Giddy with Triumph: Is It Possible to Overdo It?" *The Wall Street Journal,* May 14, 1998, A1, A10.

78. Anita Micossi, "Creating Internal Markets," *Enterprise*, April 1994, 43–44.

79. Raymond E. Miles, Henry J. Coleman, Jr., and W. E. Douglas Creed, "Keys to Success in Corporate Redesign," *California Management Review* 37, no. 3 (Spring 1995), 128–145.

80. Ouchi, "Markets, Bureaucracies, and Clans."

81. Jeffrey Kerr and John W. Slocum, Jr., "Managing Corporate Culture Through Reward Systems," *Academy of Management Executive* 19, no. 4 (2005), 130–138.

82. Richard Leifer and Peter K. Mills, "An Information Processing Approach for Deciding upon Control Strategies and Reducing Control Loss in Emerging Organizations," *Journal of Management* 22, no. 1 (1996), 113–137.

83. Stratford Sherman, "The New Computer Revolution," *Fortune*, June 14, 1993, 56–80.

84. Leifer and Mills, "An Information Processing Approach for Deciding upon Control Strategies"; and Laurie J. Kirsch, "The Management of Complex Tasks in Organizations: Controlling the Systems Development Process," *Organization Science* 7, no. 1 (January–February 1996), 1–21.

85. James R. Barker, "Tightening the Iron Cage: Concertive Control in Self-Managing Teams," *Administrative Science Quarterly* 38 (1993), 408–437.

86. "Core Value: Teamwork," segment in Leigh Buchanan, "2011 Top Small Company Workplaces: Core Values," *Inc.* (June 2011): 60–74; Matthew Shaer, "The Boss Stops Here," *New York Magazine*, June 24–July 1, 2013, 26-34; and Leigh Buchanan, "Taking Teamwork to the Extreme" in the Culture segment of "The Audacious 25: Meet the Scrappiest, Smartest, Most Disruptive Companies of the Year," *Inc.*, May 2013, 54–76 (Menlo profile is on page 76); and Matthew E. May, "Mastering the Art of Bosslessness," *Fast Company*, September 26, 2012, http://www.fastcompany.com/3001574/mastering-art-bosslessness (accessed August 20, 2013).

87. Steven Greenhouse and Michael J. De La Merced, "Court Allows Liquidation of Hostess," *The New York Times*, November 21, 2012, http://dealbook.nytimes .com/2012/11/21/judge-approves-hostess-brands-plan -to-close-down/?_php=true&_type=blogs&_r=0 (accessed November 22, 2012).

88. Lee Hawkins Jr., "Lost in Transmission—Behind GM's Slide: Bosses Misjudged New Urban Tastes; Local Dealers, Managers Tried Alerting Staid Bureaucracy," *The Wall Street Journal*, March 8, 2006, A1.

89. Deepak K. Datta, James P. Guthrie, Dynah Basuil, and Alankrita Pandey, "Causes and Effects of Employee Downsizing: A Review and Synthesis," *Journal of Management* 36, no. 1 (January 2010), 281–348; Jack Healy, "Big Companies Around Globe Lay Off Tens of Thousands," *The New York Times*, January 27, 2009; Kevin Sack, "A City's Wrenching Budget Choices," *The New York Times*, July 4, 2011; Tamar Lewin, For Colleges, Small Cutbacks Are Adding Up to Big Savings," *The New York Times*, June 19, 2009, A19.

90. Kim S. Cameron, Myung Kim, and David A. Whetten, "Organizational Effects of Decline and Turbulence," *Administrative Science Quarterly* 32 (1987), 222–240.

91. Danny Miller, "What Happens after Success: The Perils of Excellence," *Journal of Management Studies* 31, no. 3 (May 1994), 325–358.

92. Leonard Greenhalgh, "Organizational Decline," in Samuel B. Bacharach, ed., *Research in the Sociology of Organizations* 2 (Greenwich, CT: JAI Press, 1983), 231–276; and Peter Lorange and Robert T. Nelson, "How to Recognize—and Avoid—Organizational Decline," *Sloan Management Review* (Spring 1987), 41–48.

93. Kim S. Cameron and Raymond Zammuto, "Matching Managerial Strategies to Conditions of Decline," *Human Resources Management* 22 (1983), 359–375; and Leonard Greenhalgh, Anne T. Lawrence, and Robert I. Sutton, "Determinants of Workforce Reduction Strategies in Organizations," *Academy of Management Review* 13 (1988), 241–254.

94. Stephanie Strom, "Short on Fund-Raising, Red Cross Will Cut Jobs," *The New York Times*, January 16, 2008, A15.

95. Quentin Hardy, "As Computing Changes, Hewlett-Packard Struggles to Follow," *The New York Times*, May 24, 2012, B1.

96. Dana Mattioli, Joann S. Lublin, and Ellen Byron, "Kodak Struggles to Find Its Moment," *The Wall Street Journal* August 11, 2011; Michael J. De La Merced, "Eastman Kodak Files for Bankruptcy," *The New York Times*, January 19, 2012, http://dealbook.nytimes.com/2012/01/19/eastman -kodak-files-for-bankruptcy/?_php=true&_type=blogs&_r=0 (accessed January 19, 2012); and Mike Spector, Dana Mattioli, and Katy Stech, "Kodak Files for Bankruptcy Protection," *The Wall Street Journal*, January 19, 2012, http:// online.wsj.com/news/articles/SB3000142405297020455904 577169920031456052 (accessed January 19, 2012).

97. William Weitzel and Ellen Jonsson, "Reversing the Downward Spiral: Lessons from W. T. Grant and Sears Roebuck," *Academy of Management Executive* 5 (1991), 7–21; and William Weitzel and Ellen Jonsson, "Decline in Organizations: A Literature Integration and Extension," *Administrative Science Quarterly* 34 (1989), 91–109.

98. Datta et al., "Causes and Effects of Employee Downsizing"; and William McKinley, Carol M. Sanchez, and Allen G. Schick, "Organizational Downsizing: Constraining, Cloning, Learning," *Academy of Management Executive* 9, no. 3 (1995), 32–42.

99. Datta et al., "Causes and Effects of Employee Downsizing"; Gregory B. Northcraft and Margaret A. Neale, *Organizational Behavior: A Management Challenge*, 2nd ed. (Fort Worth, TX: The Dryden Press, 1994), 626; and A. Catherine Higgs, "Executive Commentary" on McKinley, Sanchez, and Schick, "Organizational Downsizing: Constraining, Cloning, Learning," *Academy of Management Executive* 9, no. 3 (1995), 43–44.

100. Wayne Cascio, "Use and Management of Downsizing as a Corporate Strategy," Society for Human Resource Management Foundation (2009), http://www.shrm .org/about/foundation/ products/Documents/609%20 Exec%20Briefing-%20 Downsizing%20FINAL.pdf (accessed September 8, 2011); Wayne Cascio, "Strategies for Responsible Restructuring," *Academy of Management Executive* 16, no. 3 (2002), 80–91; James R. Morris, Wayne F. Cascio, and Clifford E. Young, "Downsizing after All These Years: Questions and Answers about Who Did It, How Many Did It, and Who Benefited from It," *Organizational Dynamics* (Winter 1999), 78–86; Brett C. Luthans and Steven M. Sommer, "The Impact of Downsizing on Workplace Attitudes," *Group and Organization Management* 2, no. 1 (1999), 46–70; and Pat Galagan, "The Biggest Losers: The Perils of Extreme Downsizing," *T+D*, November 2010, 27–29.

101. David Cote, "Honeywell's CEO on How He Avoided Layoffs," *Harvard Business Review*, July 2013, 43–46.

102. These techniques are based on Cascio, "Use and Management of Downsizing as a Corporate Strategy"; Mitchell Lee Marks and Kenneth P. De Meuse, "Resizing the Organization: Maximizing the Gain While Minimizing the Pain of Layoffs, Divestitures, and Closings," *Organizational Dynamics* 34, no. 2 (2005), 19–35; Bob Nelson, "The Care of the Un-Downsized," *Training and Development*, April 1997, 40–43; Joel Brockner, "Managing the Effects of Layoffs on Survivors," *California Management Review* (Winter 1992), 9–28; Kim S. Cameron, "Strategies for Successful Organizational Downsizing," *Human Resource Management* 33, no. 2 (Summer 1994), 189–211; and Stephen Doerflein and James Atsaides, "Corporate Psychology: Making Downsizing Work," *Electrical World*, September–October 1999, 41–43.

103. Michael A. Campion, Laura Guerrero, and Richard Posthuma, "Reasonable Human Resource Practices for Making Employee Downsizing Decisions," *Organizational Dynamics* 40 (2011), 174–180.

104. Cote, "Honeywell's CEO on How He Avoided Layoffs"; Steven Greenhouse, "To Avoid Layoffs, Some Companies Turn to Work-Sharing," http://www.nytimes .com/2009/06/16/business/economy/16workshare .html?pagewanted=all (accessed September 8, 2011); Kathleen Madigan, "More Firms Cut Pay to Save Jobs," *The Wall Street Journal*, June 9, 2009, A4; and Cascio, "Use and Management of Downsizing as a Corporate Strategy."

105. Matt Murray, "Stress Mounts as More Firms Announce Large Layoffs, But Don't Say Who or When" (Your Career Matters column), *The Wall Street Journal*, March 13, 2001, B1, B12.

106. Ebay example reported in Cascio, "Use and Management of Downsizing as a Corporate Strategy."

107. Joann S. Lublin, "Theory & Practice: Employers See Value in Helping Those Laid Off; Some Firms Continue Access to Programs That Assist Workers," *The Wall Street Journal*, September 24, 2007, B3.

108. Marks and De Meuse, "Resizing the Organization"; Jeanenne LaMarch, "How Companies Reduce the Downside of Downsizing," *Global Business and Organizational Excellence* 29, no. 1 (November–December 2009), 7–16; and Cascio, "Use and Management of Downsizing as a Corporate Strategy."

109. Matt Villano, "Career Couch: Dealing with Low Morale After Others Are Laid Off," *The New York Times*, July 29, 2007, BU17.

110. This case was inspired by "Frito-Lay May Find Itself in a Competition Crunch," *Businessweek*, July 19, 1982, 186; Jim Bohman, "Mike-Sells Works to Remain on Snack Map," *Dayton Daily News*, February 27, 2005, D1; "Dashman Company" in Paul R. Lawrence and John A. Seiler, *Organizational Behavior and Administration: Cases, Concepts, and Research Findings* (Homewood, IL: Irwin and Dorsey, 1965), 16–17; and Laurie M. Grossman, "Price Wars Bring Flavor to Once Quiet Snack Market," *The Wall Street Journal*, May 23, 1991, B1, B3.

Managing Dynamic Processes

5

PART

Kjel Larsen/Moment/Getty Images

10 Organizational Culture and Ethical Values

Learning Objectives

After reading this chapter you should be able to:

1. Know the nature of organizational culture and its manifestations.
2. Describe the four types of organizational culture.
3. Explain the relationship between culture and performance.
4. Identify some sources of ethical values and principles.
5. Define corporate social responsibility.
6. Explain how managers shape organizational culture and ethical values.

Before reading this chapter, please check whether you agree or disagree with each of the following statements:

1 Top managers typically should focus their energy more on strategy and structure than on corporate culture.

I AGREE _____   I DISAGREE _____

2 Being ethical and socially responsible is not just the right thing for a corporation to do; it is a critical issue for business success.

I AGREE _____   I DISAGREE _____

3 The single best way to make sure an organization stays on solid ethical ground is to have a strong code of ethics and make sure all employees are familiar with its guidelines.

I AGREE _____   I DISAGREE _____

When people think of working at a technology start-up, some of the terms that come to mind are *long hours, collaboration, creativity, cohesiveness, challenge, camaraderie,* and *fun.* Terms you don't often hear in connection with entrepreneurial start-ups are *internal competitiveness, adversity, confrontation,* and *threat.* Well, unless you talk to Amazon escapees, as some former employees and managers call themselves. Some former employees refer to Amazon's internal environment as a "gladiator culture" where a fierce competitiveness among employees seems embedded in everything. Some people say they wouldn't think of returning to work there. Others, however, love the pace and challenge of such a confrontational culture and find they can't work effectively anywhere else. Professional networking site LinkedIn has plenty of executives who left Amazon and then returned because they missed the challenge. "Inside the company," writes Brad Stone in his story of the e-commerce giant, "this is referred to as a boomerang."[1]

Amazon is a highly successful company, and it has employees and managers who enjoy their jobs and generally like the way things are done at the company. It also has managers and employees who think the cultural values and ways of doing things are detrimental to employee happiness and long-term company success. Every organization, like Amazon, has particular values that characterize how people should behave and how the organization carries out everyday business. One of the most important jobs organizational leaders do is instill and support the kind of values needed for the company to thrive.

Strong cultures can have a profound impact on a company, which can be either positive or negative for the organization. At J. M. Smucker & Company, the first manufacturer ever to earn the top spot on *Fortune* magazine's list of "The 100 Best Companies to Work For," strong values of cooperation, caring for employees and customers, and an "all for one, one for all" attitude enable the company to consistently meet productivity, quality, and customer-service goals in the challenging environment of the food industry.[2] Negative cultural norms, however, can damage a company just as powerfully as positive ones can strengthen it. An independent review of Barclay's, ordered in the wake of an interest rate–rigging scandal, for example, found problems with the culture. As managers pushed to change Barclay's from a retail bank to a global financial giant over the past two decades, they created a culture that "tended to favor transactions over relationships, the short term over sustainability, and financial over other business purposes," the report said. The desire to increase profits became all consuming. New CEO Antony P. Jenkins has announced a plan to improve Barclay's culture, including reining in aggressive risk-taking behavior. In an internal memo, he told staff members who were unwilling to help Barclay's rebuild its reputation that they should leave the organization.[3]

A related concept concerning the influence of norms and values on how people work together and how they treat one another and customers is called *social capital*. **Social capital** refers to the quality of interactions among people and whether they share a common perspective. In organizations with a high degree of social capital, relationships are based on trust, mutual understandings, and shared norms and values that enable people to cooperate and coordinate their activities to achieve goals.[4] An organization can have either a high or a low level of social capital. One way to think of social capital is as *goodwill*. When relationships both within the organization and with customers, suppliers, and partners are based on honesty, trust, and respect, a spirit of goodwill exists and people willingly cooperate to achieve mutual benefits. A high level of social capital enables frictionless social interactions and exchanges that help facilitate smooth organizational functioning. Relationships based on cutthroat competition, self-interest, and subterfuge can be devastating to a company. Social capital relates to both corporate culture and ethics, which is the subject matter of this chapter.

Purpose of This Chapter

This chapter explores ideas about corporate culture and associated ethical values and how these are influenced by managers. The first section describes the nature of corporate culture, its origins and purpose, and how to identify and interpret culture by looking at the organization's rites and ceremonies, stories and sayings, symbols, organization structures, power relationships, and control systems. We then examine how culture reinforces the strategy and structural design the organization needs to be effective in its environment and discuss the important role of culture in organizational learning and high performance. Next, the chapter turns to ethical values and corporate social responsibility. We consider how managers implement the structures and systems that influence ethical and socially responsible behavior. The chapter also discusses how managers shape culture and ethical values in a direction suitable for strategy and performance outcomes. The chapter closes with a brief overview of the complex cultural and ethical issues that managers face in an international environment.

Organizational Culture

The popularity of the corporate culture topic raises a number of questions. Can we identify cultures? Can culture be aligned with strategy? How can cultures be managed or changed? The best place to start is by defining culture and explaining how it is reflected in organizations.

What Is Culture?

Culture is the set of values, norms, guiding beliefs, and understandings that is shared by members of an organization and taught to new members as the correct way to think, feel, and behave.[5] It is the unwritten, feeling part of the organization. Culture represents the informal organization, whereas topics discussed in previous chapters,

EXHIBIT 10.1
Levels of Corporate
Culture

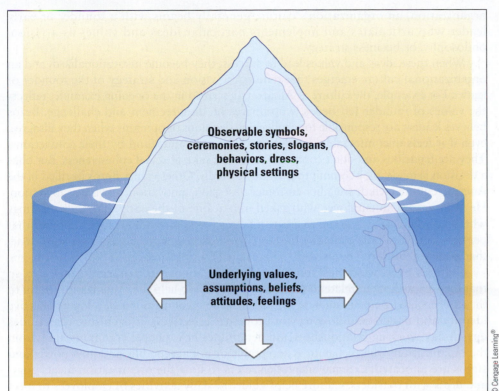

© Cengage Learning®

such as structure, size, and strategy, represent the formal organization. Every organization has two sides at work: formal structures and systems and the informal values, norms, and assumptions of the corporate culture.[6] Everyone participates in culture, but culture generally goes unnoticed. It is only when managers try to implement new strategies, structures, or systems that go against basic cultural norms and values that they come face to face with the power of culture.

Organizational culture exists at two levels, as illustrated in Exhibit 10.1. On the surface are visible artifacts and observable behaviors—the ways people dress and act; office layouts; the type of control systems and power structures used by the company; and the symbols, stories, and ceremonies organization members share. The visible elements of culture, however, reflect deeper values in the minds of organization members. These underlying values, assumptions, beliefs, and thought processes operate unconsciously to define the culture.[7] For example, at tomato processor Morning Star, described in Chapter 1 of this text, administrative offices are located near the factory floor so managers and employees can interact as equals. At Germany's TeamBank, top managers made the informal *Du* the mandatory form of address rather than the formal *Sie* commonly used in German workplaces. These are observable symbols. The underlying values are openness, collaboration, egalitarianism, and teamwork.[8] The attributes of culture display themselves in many ways but typically evolve into a patterned set of activities carried out through social interactions.[9] Those patterns can be used to interpret culture.

Emergence and Purpose of Culture

Culture provides people with a sense of organizational identity and generates in them a commitment to beliefs and values that are larger than themselves.[10] Though ideas that become part of the culture can come from anywhere within the organization, an organization's culture generally begins with a founder or early leader who articulates and implements particular ideas and values as a vision, philosophy, or business strategy.

When these ideas and values lead to success, they become institutionalized, and an organizational culture emerges that reflects the vision and strategy of the founder or leader. For example, the culture at Amazon, described in the opening example, reflects the values of founder Jeff Bezos, who thrives on disagreement and challenge. Bezos believes leaders are responsible for challenging decisions or opinions when they disagree, even if it feels uncomfortable. Leaders have courage and stand by their convictions. They are tenacious and don't compromise for the sake of social cohesiveness. But once a decision is made, they commit to it wholeheartedly. Other values Bezos instilled in the Amazon culture include frugality, customer obsession, innovation, and a bias for action. He bluntly told an employee who asked him at one of the early all-hands meetings when the company was going to create a better work–life balance for employees that perhaps this wasn't the company for her. "The reason we are here is to get stuff done, that is the top priority," Bezos said. "That is the DNA of Amazon."[11]

Cultures serve two critical functions in organizations: (1) to integrate members so that they know how to relate to one another and (2) to help the organization adapt to the external environment. **Internal integration** means that members develop a collective identity and understand how to work together effectively. It is culture that guides day-to-day working relationships and determines how people communicate within the organization, what behavior is acceptable or not acceptable, and how power and status are allocated. **External adaptation** refers to how the organization meets goals and deals with outsiders. Culture helps guide the daily activities of employees to meet certain goals. It can help the organization respond rapidly to customer needs or the moves of a competitor. For example, consider how the culture at Billtrust, a small New Jersey–based automated and electronic billing services firm, fosters internal integration and helps the company adapt to the external environment.

IN PRACTICE
Billtrust

Over a two-year period, Billtrust grew from 45 to 145 employees, and increasing business meant more new people would be coming on board. That was good news, but founder Flint Lane wanted to be sure the culture that promoted fun, open communication, teamwork, and interdepartmental interaction remained strong.

Billtrust has an open-door policy to encourage people to take ownership of their jobs and talk to managers about whatever is on their minds. As the company grew, managers decided to add a monthly town-hall-style meeting for all employees. It begins at 11:37 A.M., an offbeat time, chosen so that people can demonstrate their commitment to the company by making timeliness a priority. At these meetings, Lane and other managers encourage people to ask candid questions, and they respond openly and honestly. The company also hosts a number of companywide events, including an annual team table tennis tournament, two yearly bowling tournaments, and regular summer cookouts where departments take turns supplying a "grill master" whose skills are evaluated by colleagues.

These events serve to bond the growing workforce into a united whole and reinforce the cultural values. As one new employee put it, "Everyone else offered me a job, but Billtrust offered me something I could become a part of."[12]

The organization's culture also guides employee decision making in the absence of written rules or policies.[13] Thus, both functions of culture are related to building the organization's social capital by forging either positive or negative relationships both within the organization and with outsiders.

Interpreting Culture

To identify and interpret culture requires that people make inferences based on observable artifacts. Artifacts can be studied but are hard to decipher accurately. An award ceremony in one company might have a different meaning than it does in another company. To understand what is really going on in an organization requires detective work and probably some experience as an insider. Exhibit 10.2 shows some aspects of the organization that can be observed to help decode the organizational culture.[14] These include rites and ceremonies, stories and sayings, symbols, organization structures, power relationships, and control systems.[15]

Rites and Ceremonies. Cultural values can typically be identified in **rites and ceremonies**, the elaborate, planned activities that make up a special event and are often conducted for the benefit of an audience. Managers hold rites and ceremonies to provide dramatic examples of what a company values. These are special occasions that reinforce specific values, create a bond among people for sharing an important understanding, and anoint and celebrate heroes and heroines who symbolize important beliefs and activities.[16]

One type of rite that appears in organizations is a *rite of passage*, which facilitates the transition of employees into new social roles. Organizations as diverse as religious orders, sororities and fraternities, businesses, and the military use rites to initiate new members and communicate important values. Another type often used is a *rite of integration*, which creates common bonds and good feelings among employees and increases commitment to the organization. Consider the following examples:

- A rite of passage at Gentle Giant, a Somerville, Massachusetts, moving company that has won nine Best of Boston awards from *Boston* magazine, is the "stadium run." CEO Larry O'Toole decided to have new hires run the tiers of Harvard University stadium as a way to emphasize that people at the company work hard, challenge themselves, and go the distance rather than letting up if things get tough. After the run, O'Toole provides a hearty breakfast and gives an orientation speech. "You're not a Gentle Giant until you've done the run," said employee Kyle Green.[17]

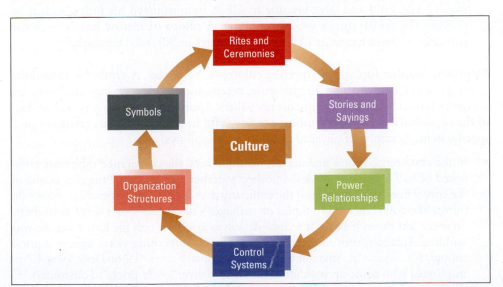

EXHIBIT 10.2
Observable Aspects of Organizational Culture

Sources: Based on Gerry Johnson, "Managing Strategic Change—Strategy, Culture, and Action," *Long Range Planning* 25, no. 1 (1992), 28–36, and Gerry Johnson, "Rethinking Incrementalism," *Strategic Management Journal* 9, no. 1 (1988), 75–91.

- Pope Francis, leading an organization that has been rife with scandal, has used rites to capture attention and reenergize jaded and hurting Catholics around the world. For example, to symbolize the values of humility and inclusivity, he modified a traditional ritual by washing the feet of prisoners at a youth detention center on Holy Thursday instead of washing the feet of priests, as his predecessors had done. The ritual also reportedly included two females and two Muslims for the first time. This might be considered a rite of integration.[18]

Stories and Sayings. **Stories** are narratives based on true events that are frequently shared among employees and told to new employees to inform them about an organization. Many stories are about company **heroes** who serve as models or ideals for upholding cultural norms and values. Some stories are considered **legends** because the events are historic and may have been embellished with fictional details.[19] Stories keep alive the primary values of the organization and provide a shared understanding among all employees. **Sayings** are mottoes or mantras that encapsulate key cultural values, such as Walmart's "always low prices." Examples of how stories and sayings shape culture are as follows:

- At Brinker Capital, managers wanted a culture where people are held accountable, but CEO Noreen Beaman knew that sometimes people make mistakes. She made a big one early in her career. The point is to solve the problem and not make the same mistake again. One of the company's sayings is "Find it, fix it, prevent it." Lush Cosmetics uses the motto, "We reserve the right to make mistakes." Another firm uses the tag line, "Set Targets, Keep Score, Win" to emphasize values of competitiveness, risk-taking, and taking ownership for results.[20]
- Sometimes a saying grows out of a story, such as LEGO's "Only the best is good enough." As the story goes, back when the company was still making wooden toys, founder Ole Kirk's son Godtfred boasted that he had saved money by using just two coats of varnish rather than the usual three coats on a shipment of toy ducks going out that day. Ole was offended by the deception and made Godtfred go back to the train station, retrieve the shipment, and spend the night correcting his error. Godtfred, who worked for the company from the time he was 12 years old and later became its CEO, immortalized his father's ideal by carving the motto into a wooden plague. A photo of it now hangs over the entrance to the cafeteria at LEGO headquarters in Billund, Denmark.[21]

Symbols. Another tool for interpreting culture is the **symbol**. A symbol is something that represents another thing. In one sense, ceremonies, stories, sayings, and rites are all symbols because they symbolize deeper values. Another symbol is a physical artifact of the organization. Physical symbols are powerful because they focus attention on a specific item. Examples of physical symbols are as follows:

- In the conference rooms at Amazon headquarters, the conference tables are composed of half a dozen door-desks pushed together side by side. Frugality is one of the core values at Amazon, and the company doesn't believe in spending money on things like conference room tables or manager's desks that don't serve customers. Founder Jeff Bezos believes if a door-desk was good enough for him when he was building Amazon from scratch in his garage 20 something years ago, it is good enough for anyone at Amazon today. The company gives "Door-Desk awards" to employees who come up with ideas that help deliver lower prices to customers.[22]
- When employees at Foot Levelers, a maker of chiropractic products, see the "Rudy in Progress" sign taped to the conference room door, they know there's

a group of new employees watching a DVD of *Rudy*, the 1993 inspirational football drama about the ungifted but determined Notre Dame football player Rudy Ruettiger, who finally took the field in the last minutes of a game against Georgia Tech and sacked the quarterback. The film is a symbol of the high value the company puts on determination, passion, commitment, and tenacity. Whenever an employee approaches a manager with a tough problem, the manager will ask "Did you Rudy that?" meaning did you do all that you possibly can to try to solve the problem.[23]

Organization Structures. How the organization is designed is also a reflection of its culture. Does it have a rigid *mechanistic* structure or a flexible *organic* structure, as described in Chapters 1 and 4? Is there a tall or a flat hierarchy, as discussed in Chapter 3? The way in which people and departments are arranged into a whole, and the degree of flexibility and autonomy people have, tells a lot about which cultural values are emphasized in the organization. Here are a couple of examples:

- Nordstrom's structure reflects the emphasis the department store chain puts on empowering and supporting lower-level employees. Nordstrom is known for its extraordinary customer service. Its organization chart, shown in Exhibit 10.3, symbolizes that managers are to support the employees who give the service rather than exercise tight control over them.[24]
- To get a struggling Chrysler back on its feet quickly after bankruptcy reorganization, CEO Sergio Marchionne cut several layers of management to flatten the structure and get top executives closer to the business of making and selling vehicles. Marchionne also chose a fourth-floor office in the

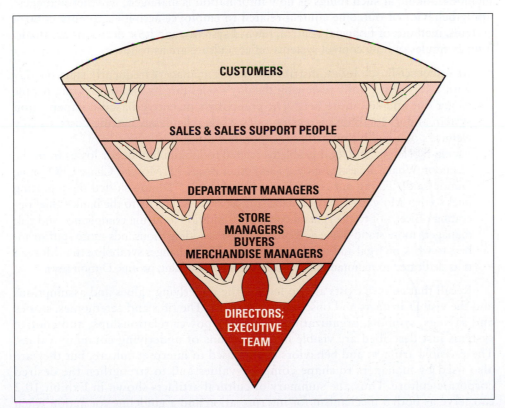

EXHIBIT 10.3
Organization Chart for Nordstrom Inc.

CUSTOMERS

SALES & SALES SUPPORT PEOPLE

DEPARTMENT MANAGERS

STORE MANAGERS
BUYERS
MERCHANDISE MANAGERS

DIRECTORS;
EXECUTIVE
TEAM

Source: Used with permission of Nordstrom, Inc.

technical center, rather than occupy the top-floor executive suite, to symbolize the importance of top executives being close to the engineers and supervisors making day-to-day decisions.[25]

Power Relationships. Looking at power relationships means deciphering who influences or manipulates or has the ability to do so. Which people and departments are the key power holders in the organization? In some companies, finance people are quite powerful, whereas in others engineers and designers have the most power. Another aspect is considering whether power relationships are formal or informal, such as whether people have power based primarily on their position in the hierarchy or based on other factors, such as their expertise or admirable character. Consider the following examples:

- An investment firm in Atlanta, Georgia, has an "inner sanctum" with special offices, restrooms, and a dining room for senior executives. The entry door has an electronic lock that only members can access. Mid-level managers hold the title of "director" and eat in a separate dining room. First-level supervisors and other employees share a general cafeteria. Dining facilities and titles signal who has more power in the vertical hierarchy of the organization.
- At W. L. Gore, few people have titles, and no one has a boss. Rather than people having power based on their position, leaders emerge based on who has a good idea and can recruit people to work on it.[26]

Control Systems. The final element shown in Exhibit 10.2 relates to control systems or the inner workings of how the organization controls people and operations. This includes looking at such things as how information is managed, whether managers apply behavior or outcome control related to employee activities, quality control systems, methods of financial control, reward systems, and how decisions are made. Two examples of how control systems reflect culture are as follows:

- At Anheuser-Busch InBev, distribution center managers frequently start the day with a sort of pep rally reviewing the day's sales targets and motivating people to get out and sell more beer. The company's incentive-based compensation system and its focus on increasing sales while relentlessly cutting costs are key elements of a highly competitive corporate culture.[27]
- Facing regulatory and legal problems related to multibillion dollar losses from the "London Whale" investment fiasco and other issues, J.P. Morgan Chase CEO Jamie Dimon said, "Fixing our control issues is job no. 1." Dimon shifted the reporting lines so that Morgan's top compliance officer reports directly to the bank's chief operating officer, not to the general counsel. In addition to giving compliance and risk managers more stand-alone authority, Dimon is adding thousands more staff members to work on legal and regulatory matters. These changes symbolize that Morgan is as dedicated to maintaining control as it is to recording profits, Dimon says.[28]

Recall that culture exists at two levels—the underlying values and assumptions and the visible artifacts and observable behaviors. The rites and ceremonies, stories and sayings, symbols, organization structures, power relationships, and control systems just described are visible manifestations of underlying company values. These visible artifacts and behaviors can be used to interpret culture, but they are also used by managers to shape company values and to strengthen the desired corporate culture. Thus, the summary of cultural artifacts shown in Exhibit 10.2 can serve as both a mechanism for interpretation and a guideline for action when managers need to change or strengthen cultural values.[29]

Organization Design and Culture

Managers want a corporate culture that reinforces the strategy and structural design that the organization needs to be effective within its environment. For example, if the external environment requires flexibility and responsiveness, such as the environment for Internet-based companies like Twitter, Pandora, Pinterest, or Hulu, the culture should encourage adaptability. The correct relationship among cultural values, organizational strategy and structure, and the environment can enhance organizational performance.[30]

Cultures can be assessed along many dimensions, such as the extent of collaboration versus isolation among people and departments, the importance of control and where control is concentrated, or whether the organization's time orientation is short range or long range.[31] Here we focus on two specific dimensions: (1) the extent to which the competitive environment requires flexibility or stability and (2) the extent to which the organization's strategic focus and strength are internal or external. Four categories of culture associated with these differences, as illustrated in Exhibit 10.4, are adaptability, mission, clan, and bureaucratic.[32] These four categories relate to the fit among cultural values, strategy, structure, and the environment. Each can be successful, depending on the needs of the external environment and the organization's strategic focus.

EXHIBIT 10.4
Four Types of Organizational Culture

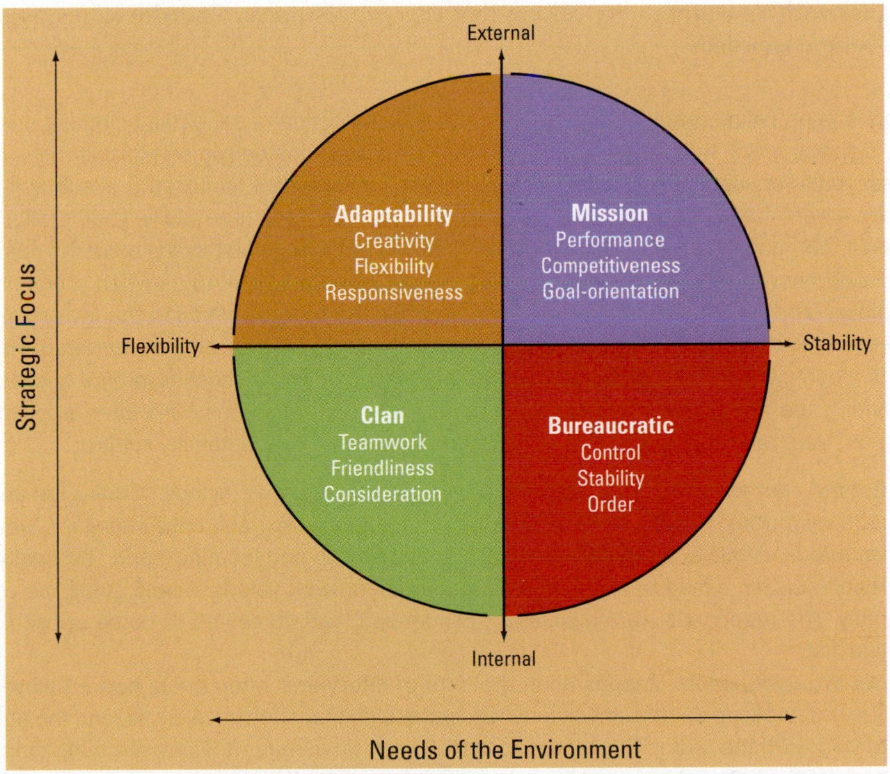

Sources: Based on Daniel R. Denison and Aneil K. Mishra, "Toward a Theory of Organizational Culture and Effectiveness," *Organization Science* 6, no. 2 (March–April 1995), 204–223; R. E. Quinn, *Beyond Rational Management: Mastering the Paradoxes and Competing Demands of High Performance* (San Francisco: Jossey-Bass, 1988); and Mohamed Hafar, Wafi Al-Karaghouli, and Ahmad Ghoneim, "An Empirical Investigation of the Influence of Organizational Culture on Individual Readiness for Change in Syrian Manufacturing Organizations," *Journal of Organizational Change Management* 27, no. 1 (2014), 5–22.

1 **Top managers typically should focus their energy more on strategy and structure than on corporate culture.**

> **ANSWER:** *Disagree.* Smart top managers know that for the organization to be successful, the right culture has to support and reinforce the strategy and structure to be effective in its environment. Someone once said, "Culture eats strategy for lunch." Managers can invest all the time and resources they have in defining a killer strategy, but implementing it will be impossible if the cultural values are out of line.

The Adaptability Culture

The **adaptability culture** is characterized by strategic focus on the external environment through flexibility and change to meet customer needs. The culture encourages entrepreneurial values, norms, and beliefs that support the capacity of the organization to detect, interpret, and translate signals from the environment into new behavior responses. This type of company, however, doesn't just react quickly to environmental changes—it actively creates change. Innovation, creativity, and risk taking are valued and rewarded.

Most Internet-based companies use the adaptability type of culture, as do many companies in the marketing, electronics, and cosmetics industries, because they must move quickly to satisfy customers. Zappos.com became a hugely successful Internet retailer with an adaptability culture that encourages open-mindedness, teamwork, and a little weirdness.

IN PRACTICE

Zappos

Zappos is an online retailer best known for its wide selection of shoes and clothing and its free shipping policy. But for CEO Tony Hsieh, the real purpose of the company is *cultivating happiness*, both for customers and employees. Hsieh's management theory goes like this: if you create a work culture that fosters well-being, good practices and (eventually) good profits will naturally flow out of the operation. So far, his theory is producing outstanding business results.

Hsieh knows firsthand how important a strong, adaptable culture is when it comes to employee and customer happiness. Before Zappos, he had experienced the joyless grind of working in a job that had no meaning, where technical skill was all that mattered. Hsieh wrote a book, *Delivering Happiness*, to document his journey from "chasing profits to chasing passion," the life lessons he has learned, and how those lessons have been applied at Zappos. Here are some key points from Hsieh for building an adaptability culture:

- *Get the right values.* Zappos has a set of 10 core values that include "Create fun and a little weirdness"; "Deliver WOW through service"; "Embrace and drive change"; "Be adventurous, creative, and open-minded"; "Pursue growth and learning"; and "Be humble." Hsieh sent an e-mail to all employees asking them what values should guide the company. The responses were discussed, condensed, and combined to come up with the final list.
- *Get the right people.* Zappos does two sets of interviews when hiring new employees. The first focuses on relevant experience, professional and technical skills, and the ability to work with the team. The second focuses purely on culture fit. There are questions for each of the core values, such as "How weird are you?" People are carefully selected to fit the Zappos culture, even if that means rejecting people with stronger technical skills.
- *Make culture a top priority.* All employees attend a four-week training session and commit the core values to memory. At the end of training, they're offered a $2,000 bonus to resign if they believe they aren't a good fit with the culture (the amount varies each year). Every year, Zappos puts out a *Culture Book*, in which employees share their own stories about what the Zappos culture means to them.[33]

The Zappos values may seem slightly wacky, but by encouraging fun, flexibility, and creativity, they also keep people adaptable and poised for change, which is perfect for companies in rapidly changing industries.

The Mission Culture

An organization concerned with serving specific customers in the external environment, but without the need for rapid change, is suited to the mission culture. The **mission culture** is characterized by emphasis on a clear vision of the organization's purpose and on the achievement of goals, such as sales growth, profitability, or market share, to help achieve the purpose. Individual employees may be responsible for a specified level of performance, and the organization promises specified rewards in return. Managers shape behavior by envisioning and communicating a desired future state for the organization. Because the environment is stable, they can translate the vision into measurable goals and evaluate employee performance for meeting them. In some cases, mission cultures reflect a high level of competitiveness and a profit-making orientation. Amazon reflects aspects of a mission culture with its emphasis on competitiveness, assertiveness, and achieving growing sales and market share.

Anheuser-Busch InBev, mentioned earlier in the chapter, also reflects a mission culture. Professionalism, ambition, and aggressiveness are key values. Managers keep employees focused on achieving high sales and profit levels, and those who meet the demanding goals are handsomely rewarded. Bonuses and promotions are based on performance, not seniority, and top executives are unapologetic about giving special treatment to high achievers.[34]

The Clan Culture

The **clan culture** has a primary focus on the involvement and participation of the organization's members and on rapidly changing expectations from the external environment. This culture is similar to the clan form of control described in Chapter 9. More than any other, this culture focuses on meeting the needs of employees as the route to high performance. Involvement and participation create a sense of responsibility and ownership and, hence, greater commitment to the organization.

In a clan culture, an important value is taking care of employees and making sure they have whatever they need to help them be satisfied as well as productive. The approach to culture taken by William Rogers, CEO of UKRD, which owns a number of commercial radio stations in the United Kingdom, reflects a clan culture. "If your people are the key to great performance, then facilitating their enjoyment, engagement, and commitment are fundamental to ultimate success . . .," Rogers says. "Our values are intended to change people's lives for the better." When UKRD leaders visit one of the 17 stations around the country for a meeting, they build in plenty of time to talk to people and say goodbyes around the station. Every year, all of the company's teams take a day out to talk together about the values, behaviors, and working environment they want. UKRD has a "cast-iron commitment" to a *people first* culture, and any manager who doesn't live up to that is asked to leave.[35]

The Bureaucratic Culture

The **bureaucratic culture** has an internal focus and a consistency orientation for a stable environment. This type of culture supports a methodical approach to doing business. Symbols, heroes, and ceremonies reinforce the values of cooperation,

 BRIEFCASE

As an organization manager, keep these guidelines in mind:

Make sure corporate culture is consistent with strategy and the environment. Shape culture to fit the needs of both. Four types of culture are adaptability culture, mission culture, clan culture, and bureaucratic culture.

tradition, and following established policies and practices as ways to achieve goals. Personal involvement is somewhat lower here, but that is outweighed by a high level of consistency, conformity, and collaboration among members. This organization succeeds by being highly integrated and efficient.

Today, most managers are shifting away from bureaucratic cultures because of a need for greater flexibility. However, SAS Institute and Pacific Edge Software (now part of Serena Software) have successfully used some elements of a bureaucratic culture to keep projects on time and on budget and to ensure saner lives for employees. Emphasis on order and discipline means the formal workweek at SAS is 35 hours, for instance. Although sometimes being careful means being slow, Pacific Edge and SAS have managed to keep pace with the demands of the external environment.[36]

Some people like the order and predictability of a bureaucratic culture, whereas other people would feel stifled and constrained by too much discipline and would be happier working in some other type of culture. Complete the questionnaire in the "How Do You Fit the Design?" box to get an idea of which type of culture—adaptability, mission, clan, or bureaucratic—you would be most comfortable and successful working in.

Culture Strength and Organizational Subcultures

Culture strength refers to the degree of agreement among members of an organization about the importance of specific values. If widespread consensus exists about the importance of those values, the culture is cohesive and strong; if little agreement exists, the culture is weak.[37] A strong culture reflects clear values and social norms—that is, people know what is expected. There is generally little differentiation among people within the culture and a low tolerance for deviation from the norm. Resistance to change is strong because people like the culture and want to keep things as they are.[38]

A strong culture is typically associated with the frequent use of ceremonies, symbols, and stories and sayings that express key values, as described earlier, and managers align structures and processes to support the cultural values. These elements increase employee commitment to the values and strategy of a company. However, culture is not always uniform throughout the organization, particularly in large companies. Even in organizations that have strong cultures, there may be several sets of subcultures. **Subcultures** develop to reflect the common problems, goals, and experiences that members of a team, department, or other unit share. An office, branch, or unit of a company that is physically separated from the company's main operations may also take on a distinctive subculture.

For example, although the dominant culture of an organization may be a mission culture, various departments may also reflect characteristics of adaptability, clan, or bureaucratic cultures. The manufacturing department of a large organization may thrive in an environment that emphasizes order, efficiency, and obedience to rules, whereas the research and development (R&D) department may be characterized by employee empowerment, flexibility, and customer focus. This is similar to the concept of differentiation described in Chapter 4, where employees in manufacturing, sales, and research departments studied by Paul Lawrence and Jay Lorsch[39] developed different values with respect to time horizon, interpersonal relationships, and formality in order to perform the job of each particular department most effectively. Consider how the credit division of Pitney Bowes, a huge corporation that manufactures postage meters, copiers, and other office equipment, developed a distinctive subculture to encourage innovation and risk-taking.

HOW DO YOU FIT THE DESIGN?

CORPORATE CULTURE PREFERENCE

The fit between a manager or employee and corporate culture can determine both personal success and satisfaction. To understand your culture preference, rank the following items from 1 to 8 based on the strength of your preference (1 = highest preference; 8 = lowest preference).

1. The organization is very personal, much like an extended family. ___

2. The organization is dynamic and changing, where people take risks. ___

3. The organization is achievement oriented, with the focus on competition and getting jobs done. ___

4. The organization is stable and structured, with clarity and established procedures. ___

5. Management style is characterized by teamwork and participation. ___

6. Management style is characterized by innovation and risk-taking. ___

7. Management style is characterized by high-performance demands and achievement. ___

8. Management style is characterized by security and predictability. ___

Scoring: To compute your preference for each type of culture, add together the scores for each set of two questions as follows:

Clan culture—total for questions 1, 5:___

Adaptability culture—total for questions 2, 6:___

Mission culture—total for questions 3, 7:___

Bureaucratic culture—total for questions 4, 8:___

Interpretation: Each of the preceding questions pertains to one of the four types of culture in Exhibit 10.4. A lower score means a stronger preference for that specific culture. You will likely be more comfortable and more effective as a manager in a corporate culture that is compatible with your personal preferences. A higher score means the culture would not fit your expectations, and you would have to change your style to be effective. Review the text discussion of the four culture types. Do your cultural preference scores seem correct to you? Can you think of companies that would fit your culture preference?

Source: Adapted from Kim S. Cameron and Robert E. Quinn, *Diagnosing and Changing Organizational Culture* (Reading, MA: Addison-Wesley, 1999).

Pitney Bowes, a maker of postage meters and other office equipment, has long thrived in an environment of order and predictability. Its headquarters reflects a typical corporate environment and an orderly culture with its blank walls and bland carpeting. But step onto the third floor of the Pitney Bowes building in Shelton, Connecticut, and you might think you're at a different company. The domain of Pitney Bowes Credit Corporation (PBCC) looks more like an indoor theme park, featuring cobblestone-patterned carpets, faux gas lamps, and an ornate town square-style clock. It also has a French-style café, a 1950s-style diner, and the "Cranial Kitchen," where employees sit in cozy booths to surf the Internet or watch training videos. The friendly hallways encourage impromptu conversations, where people can exchange information and share ideas they wouldn't otherwise share.

PBCC traditionally helped customers finance their business with the parent company. However, Matthew Kisner, PBCC's president and CEO, worked with other managers to redefine the division as a *creator* of services rather than just a provider of services. Rather than just financing sales and leasing of existing products, PBCC now creates new services for customers to buy. For example, Purchase Power is a revolving line of credit that helps

IN PRACTICE
Pitney Bowes Credit Corporation

companies finance their postage costs. It was profitable within nine months and quickly signed up more than 400,000 customers. When PBCC redefined its job, it began redefining its subculture to match by emphasizing values of teamwork, risk taking, and creativity. "We wanted a fun space that would embody our culture," Kisner says. "No straight lines, no linear thinking. Because we're a financial services company, our biggest advantage is the quality of our ideas." So far, PBCC's new approach is working. In one year, the division, whose 600 employees make up less than 2 percent of Pitney Bowes' total workforce, generated 36 percent of the company's net profits.[40]

Subcultures typically include the basic values of the dominant organizational culture plus additional values unique to members of the subculture. However, subcultural differences can sometimes lead to conflicts between departments, especially in organizations that do not have strong overall corporate cultures. When subcultural values become too strong and outweigh the corporate cultural values, conflicts may emerge and hurt organizational performance. Conflict will be discussed in detail in Chapter 13.

BRIEFCASE

As an organization manager, keep this guideline in mind:

Consciously manage culture to shift values toward high performance and goal accomplishment.

Constructive Culture, Learning, and Performance

Culture can play an important role in creating an organizational climate that enables learning and innovative response to challenges, competitive threats, or new opportunities. A strong culture that encourages responsiveness and change enhances organizational performance by energizing and motivating employees, unifying people around shared goals and a higher mission, and shaping and guiding behavior so that everyone's actions are aligned with strategic priorities. Thus, creating and influencing a *constructive culture* is one of a manager's most important jobs. The right culture can drive high performance.[41] Aaron Levie, who co-founded Box, a Los Altos, California-based company that provides online file storage for businesses, when he was 20 years old, offers a good example of creating a constructive culture.

☑ **IN PRACTICE**

Box

Aaron Levie, the CEO of Box, says his primary goals are "to innovate and to disrupt." "Also, I want to avoid being disrupted." Those goals are reflected in the company's culture, which emphasizes speed, flexibility, and pushing the boundaries. Levie is constantly reminding people that they can do things 10 times bigger, 10 times better, and 10 times faster," a core value he calls "10X." Other core values are "Get s— done" and "Take risks. Fail fast."

Taking risks is essential for the company to remain competitive, but failing fast means people can correct mistakes quickly. For a company of 600 people competing with companies that have tens of thousands, speed is crucial. The culture is focused on how much people can get done in as little time as possible. Goals are set very high, and the culture values solving any problem that comes along as a team. No one at Box has a private office, including Levie. The open office plan lets people interact and collaborate continually. The 44 rooms that could be offices serve as conference rooms instead, where people brainstorm and hash out ideas. The glass walls are meant to be written on. People are encouraged to "throw their ideas on the wall."

The fast pace and aggressive goals can mean high pressure, but Box also encourages fun. "We have one of the world's best jugglers and one of the country's best baton twirlers," Levie says. "Circus skills are a pretty important quality around here."[42]

A number of studies have found a positive relationship between culture and performance.[43] In *Corporate Culture and Performance*, Kotter and Heskett provided evidence that companies that intentionally managed cultural values outperformed similar companies that did not. Some companies have developed systematic ways to measure and manage the impact of culture on organizational performance.[44] Even the U.S. federal government is recognizing the link between culture and effectiveness. The U.S. Office of Personnel Management created its Organizational Assessment Survey as a way for federal agencies to measure culture factors and shift values toward high performance.[45]

Strong cultures that don't encourage constructive adaptation and responsiveness, however, can hurt the organization. A danger for many successful organizations is that the culture becomes set and the company fails to adapt as the environment changes. When organizations are successful, the values, ideas, and practices that helped attain success become institutionalized. As the environment changes, these values may become detrimental to future performance. Many organizations become victims of their own success, clinging to outmoded and even destructive values and behaviors. When the actions of top managers are unethical, for instance, the entire culture can become contaminated. Consider what happened at News Corporation, a corporate giant with a lucrative string of media properties all over the world. Rupert Murdoch, chairman and CEO, has been accused in the media of frequently applying unethical, sometimes seedy tactics in his business dealings. "Bury your mistakes," Murdoch was fond of saying.[46] After journalists working for News Corporation newspapers allegedly hacked private voice-mail messages and offered bribes to police in the pursuit of hot scoops, scandal rocked the organization. As reported in *The New York Times*, journalists went so far as to hack the voice mail of a murdered 13-year-old girl, Milly Dowler, while she was still listed as missing.[47] Mark Lewis, the lawyer for the family of the murdered girl, pointed out: "This is not just about one individual, but about the culture of an organization."[48] This unethical culture might have been successful at one time in helping the organization scoop the competition, but in today's environment, it has seriously damaged the corporation's reputation.

Thus, the impact of a strong culture is not always positive. Typically, healthy cultures not only provide for smooth internal integration but also encourage adaptation to the external environment. Non-constructive cultures encourage rigidity and stability. As illustrated in Exhibit 10.5, constructive corporate cultures have different values and behavior patterns than non-constructive cultures.[49] In constructive cultures, managers are concerned with customers and employees, as well as with the internal processes and procedures that bring about useful change. Behavior is flexible, and managers initiate change when needed, even if it involves risk. In non-constructive cultures, managers are more concerned about themselves or their own special projects, and their values discourage risk-taking and change. Thus, strong, healthy cultures help organizations adapt to the external environment, whereas strong, unhealthy cultures can encourage organizations to march resolutely in the wrong direction.

BRIEFCASE

As an organization manager, keep these guidelines in mind:

To support a learning orientation, emphasize cultural values of openness and collaboration, equality and trust, continuous improvement, and risk-taking. Build a strong internal culture that encourages adaptation to changing environmental conditions.

EXHIBIT 10.5
Constructive Versus Non-
Constructive Cultures

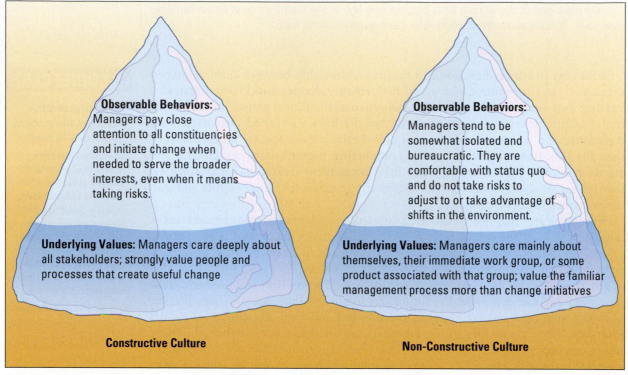

Observable Behaviors:
Managers pay close
attention to all constituencies
and initiate change when
needed to serve the broader
interests, even when it means
taking risks.

Underlying Values: Managers care deeply about
all stakeholders; strongly value people and
processes that create useful change

Constructive Culture

Observable Behaviors:
Managers tend to be
somewhat isolated and
bureaucratic. They are
comfortable with status quo
and do not take risks to
adjust to or take advantage of
shifts in the environment.

Underlying Values: Managers care mainly about
themselves, their immediate work group, or some
product associated with that group; value the familiar
management process more than change initiatives

Non-Constructive Culture

Source: Based on John P. Kotter and James L. Heskett, *Corporate Culture and Performance* (New York: The Free Press, 1992), 51.

Ethical Values and Social Responsibility

Of the values that make up an organization's culture, ethical values are now considered among the most important and have gained renewed emphasis in today's era of financial scandals and moral lapses. A survey by the Ethics Resource Center indicates that 41 percent of the 6,400 U.S. employees surveyed say they have observed wrongdoing at work. That sounds high, but it is actually down from 45 percent in 2011 and 55 percent in 2007. The bad news, though, is that 60 percent of the ethical violations were by someone with managerial authority. In addition, the percentage of employees who say they were retaliated against for reporting ethical wrongdoing remains about the same as in the earlier surveys.[50] And the problem isn't limited to U.S. corporations. Business leaders in countries such as Germany and Japan have also been reeling in recent years from one headline-grabbing scandal after another.[51] Top corporate managers are under scrutiny from the public as never before, and even small companies are finding a need to put more emphasis on ethics to restore trust among their customers and the community.

Sources of Individual Ethical Principles

Ethics refers to the code of moral principles and values that governs the behaviors of a person or group with respect to what is right or wrong. Ethical values set standards as to what is good or bad in conduct and decision making.[52] Ethics are personal and unique to each individual, although in any given group, organization, or society, there are many areas of consensus about what constitutes ethical behavior.[53] Each person is a creation of his or her time and place in history. National culture, religious heritage, historical background, and so forth lead to the development of societal morality, or society's view of what is right and wrong. Societal morality is often reflected in norms of behavior and values about what makes sense for an orderly society. Some principles are codified into laws and regulations, such as laws against drunk driving, robbery, or murder.

These laws, as well as unwritten societal norms and values, shape the local environment within which each individual acts, such as a person's community, family, and place of work. Individuals absorb the beliefs and values of their family, community, culture, society, religious community, and geographic environment, typically discarding some and incorporating others into their own personal ethical standards. Each person's ethical stance is thus a blending of his or her historical, cultural, societal, and family backgrounds and influences.

It is important to look at individual ethics because ethical behavior always involves an individual action, whether it is a decision to act or the failure to take action against wrongdoing by others. In organizations, an individual's ethical stance may be affected by peers, subordinates, and supervisors, as well as by the organizational culture. Organizational culture often has a profound influence on individual choices and can support and encourage ethical actions or promote unethical and socially irresponsible behavior.

Managerial Ethics

Many of the recent scandals in the news have dealt with people and corporations that broke the law. A coalition of children's advocacy, health, and public interest groups has filed complaints with the Federal Trade Commission, for instance, alleging that online marketing by McDonald's HappyMeal.com, Nick.com, the Nickelodeon site, General Mills' RessesPuffs.com, SubwayKids.com, and Turner's CartoonNetwork. com violates a federal law protecting children's privacy. Since it is illegal to collect e-mail addresses and send marketing materials directly to children, critics say, these and other companies use tactics such as getting website users to play games and share them with friends, so the site can then target those friends with marketing messages.[54] Many companies have been accused of paying bribes in foreign countries, which is a violation of U.S. law.[55] But it is important to remember that ethical decisions go far beyond behaviors governed by law.[56] The **rule of law** arises from a set of codified principles and regulations that describe how people are required to act, that are generally accepted in society, and that are enforceable in the courts.[57]

For example, federal prosecutors recently uncovered a test cheating ring in which people paid others to take teacher certification exams for them using false identification. Several people have been indicted on conspiracy charges of wire, mail, and Social Security fraud, and some have already gone to prison for their participation in a scheme that spanned 15 years across three Southern states.[58] This is a clear incident of breaking the law, but the U.S. military is investigating allegations of cheating among navy and air force instructors at the military's nuclear-reactor training center in Charleston, South Carolina, and nuclear missile crews in Montana that are not as clear-cut. Navy officials have decertified about 30 senior enlisted sailors and the air force has suspended 92 junior officers while they are being investigated for the cheating allegations. No laws were broken, but Admiral Jonathan Greenert of the U.S. Navy said, "This is contrary to our core values. The foundation of our conduct throughout the Navy is integrity."[59]

EXHIBIT 10.6

Relationship Between the
Rule of Law and Ethical
Standards

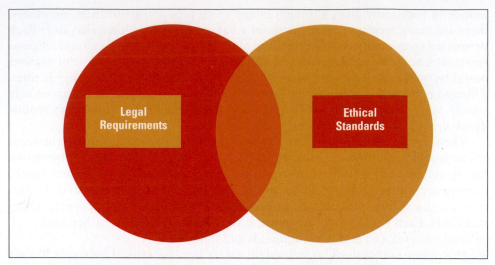

Legal
Requirements

Ethical
Standards

Source: LaRue Tone Hosmer, *The Ethics of Management*, 2nd ed. (Homewood, IL: Irwin, 1991).

The relationship between ethical standards and legal requirements is illustrated in Exhibit 10.6. Ethical standards for the most part apply to behavior not covered by the law, and the rule of law applies to behaviors not necessarily covered by ethical standards. Current laws often reflect combined moral judgments, but not all moral judgments are codified into law. The morality of aiding a drowning person, for example, is not specified by law, and driving on the right-hand side of the road has no moral basis; but in acts such as robbery or murder, rules and moral standards overlap. Many people believe that if you are not breaking the law, then you are behaving in an ethical manner, but this is not always true. Many behaviors have not been codified, and managers must be sensitive to emerging norms and values about those issues.

Managerial ethics are principles that guide the decisions and behaviors of managers with regard to whether they are right or wrong. The following examples illustrate the need for managerial ethics:[60]

- Top executives are considering promoting a rising sales manager who consistently brings in $70 million a year and has cracked open new markets in places like Brazil and Russia that are important for international growth. However, female employees have been complaining for years that the manager is verbally abusive to them, tells offensive jokes, and throws temper tantrums if female employees don't do exactly as he says.
- The manager of a beauty supply store is told that she and her salespeople can receive large bonuses for selling a specified number of boxes of a new product, a permanent-wave solution that costs nearly twice as much as what most of her salon customers typically use. She orders her salespeople to store the old product in the back and tell customers there's been a delay in delivery.
- A North American manufacturer operating abroad was asked to make cash payments (a bribe) to government officials and was told by local business partners that it was consistent with local customs, despite being illegal in North America.

As these examples illustrate, being ethical is about making decisions. Managers make choices every day about whether to be honest or deceitful with customers and suppliers, treat employees with respect or disdain, and be a good or a harmful corporate citizen. Some issues are exceedingly difficult to resolve and often represent ethical dilemmas. An **ethical dilemma** arises in a situation concerning right and wrong in which values are in conflict.[61] Right or wrong cannot be clearly identified in such situations. For a salesperson at the beauty supply store, for example, the value conflict is between being honest with customers and adhering to the boss's expectations. The manufacturing manager may feel torn between respecting and following local customs in a foreign country or adhering to U.S. laws concerning bribes. Sometimes, each alternative choice or behavior seems undesirable. Ethical dilemmas are not easy to resolve, but top executives can aid the process by establishing organizational values that give people guidelines for making the best decision from a moral standpoint.

Corporate Social Responsibility

The notion of **corporate social responsibility (CSR)** is an extension of the idea of managerial ethics and refers to management's obligation to make choices and take action so that the organization contributes to the welfare and interest of all organizational stakeholders, such as employees, customers, shareholders, the community, and the broader society.[62] For example, MAS Holdings, a family-owned apparel manufacturer in Sri Lanka, has made a commitment to contribute to economic development while also improving the lives of employees, their families, and the community. In an era when clothing manufacturers are in the news every week for another ethical, labor relations, or safety violation, MAS Holdings is making the news for its owners' belief that businesses have the power to make a positive difference in the lives of employees and the community. MAS, the largest supplier for Victoria's Secret, provides transportation to and from work, free meals, and medical care to all 45,000 employees in 28 plants. More than 90 percent of its workers are women, so MAS builds factories in rural areas with easy access so women can work close to their homes and families.[63]

CSR was once seen as the purview of small, offbeat companies like Patagonia or The Body Shop, but it has moved firmly into the mainstream of organizational thinking and behavior. IBM's Corporate Service Corps sends teams of volunteer employees on month-long assignments to work with projects such as reforming Kenya's postal system or designing an online education program in India. Campbell Soup gave a local food bank in Camden, New Jersey, access to its production lines to turn wilting food donations into jars of salsa that raised $100,000.[64] Whirlpool donates a refrigerator and range to every home built by Habitat for Humanity in North America. PepsiCo made a commitment to voluntarily remove high-calorie sweetened drinks from schools in more than 200 countries. Giant corporations from Walmart to General Electric have announced ambitious environmental responsibility goals. More than 1,000 companies around the world have published reports proclaiming their concern for employees, the environment, and their local communities.[65] In addition, many companies, including GE, Nestlé, IBM, PepsiCo, and Johnson & Johnson, are pursuing strategies and business opportunities that embrace a conscious capitalism model. **Conscious capitalism**, which has also been referred to as a *shared value* approach, refers to organizational policies and practices that both enhance the economic success of a company and advance the economic and social conditions of the communities in which the company operates.[66] Hindustan Unilever, for example, uses a direct-to-home distribution system for its hygiene products in parts of India, whereby women from low-income households in villages of less than 2,000 people are given micro loans and training to start their own small businesses. The system benefits communities by giving women

BRIEFCASE

As an organization manager, keep these guidelines in mind:

Take control of ethical values in the organization and make a commitment to corporate social responsibility. Recognize that ethics is not the same as following the law, and help people learn how to make ethical decisions.

skills and opportunities that sometimes double their household income, as well as by reducing the spread of disease by bringing hygiene products into isolated areas. It also benefits the company by extending its market and building its brand in hard-to-reach areas. The project now accounts for 5 percent of Hindustan Unilever's revenue in India.[67] The BookMark further describes the philosophy of conscious capitalism.

ASSESS YOUR ANSWER

2 Being ethical and socially responsible is not just the right thing for a corporation to do; it is a critical issue for business success.

> **ANSWER:** *Agree.* Following years of scandal, employees and the public are demanding a more ethical and socially responsible approach to business. Businesses as well as nonprofits and governmental organizations are looking for ways to restore trust. A new generation of job seekers takes a company's social responsibility into account when considering job offers, so companies that want to hire the best are paying attention.

BOOKMARK 10.0   HAVE YOU READ THIS BOOK?

Conscious Capitalism: Liberating the Heroic Spirit of Business
By John Mackey and Raj Sisodia

In *Conscious Capitalism*, John Mackey, founder and co-CEO of Whole Foods, and marketing professor Raj Sisodia start with the premise that business is "fundamentally good and ethical" because it enables people to live more vibrant and fulfilling lives. In just 200 years, they say, we have gone from 85 percent of the world's population living in extreme poverty to just 16 percent. But they challenge business leaders to open their eyes, minds, and hearts and understand the perspectives of their stakeholders so that "the truth, beauty, goodness, and heroism of free-enterprise capitalism" can be realized.

FOUR TENETS OF CONSCIOUS CAPITALISM
To practice conscious capitalism, business managers have to embrace the right beliefs. Here are the four tenets of conscious capitalism:

- *Have a higher purpose.* No business can practice conscious capitalism without a higher purpose. It is purpose that enables managers to transcend a narrow-minded focus on profit, infuse the organization with energy and relevance, and create engagement among employees and other stakeholders.
- *Recognize each stakeholder group as important and interdependent.* The authors refer to this as *stakeholder integration*. Conscious businesses strive to satisfy the needs of all stakeholders,

including investors who seek profits. Trade-offs are not necessary, the authors say: "Together we can create our future reality, so we should do so consciously, collaboratively, and responsibly."
- *Conscious businesses need conscious leaders.* Leaders of conscious capitalism businesses embrace "decentralization, empowerment, innovation, and collaboration." Leaders are motivated by service to the higher purpose and the goal of aligning the interests of all stakeholders. The authors offer practical advice on how to evolve into a more conscious leader.
- *Embrace conscious business values.* The conscious capitalism culture embodies trust, accountability, fairness, love, transparency, integrity, caring, loyalty, personal growth, and egalitarianism.

IT *DOES* PAY TO DO GOOD
Money is one measure of value, but it is by no means the only measure. Mackey and Sisodia believe the primary business model will eventually be one of conscious capitalism rather than profit. They say hard data show that, in the long run, conscious businesses outperform traditionally run organizations by a wide margin. Companies that embrace a conscious capitalism philosophy include Google, the Container Store, Costco, Pedigree, Medtronic, Trader Joe's, Panera Bread, and Harley-Davidson.

Conscious Capitalism: Liberating the Heroic Spirit of Business, by John Mackey and Raj Sisodia, is published by Harvard Business Review Press.

Does It Pay to Be Good?

The relationship of ethics and CSR to an organization's financial performance concerns both managers and organization scholars and has generated a lively debate.[68] Hundreds of studies have been undertaken to determine whether heightened ethical and social responsiveness increases or decreases a company's financial performance.[69] Studies have provided varying results, but they have generally found a positive relationship between ethical and socially responsible behavior and a firm's financial performance. For example, a recent study of the top 100 global corporations that have made a commitment to **sustainability**, which means to weave environmental and social efforts to preserve natural resources into all their decisions, had significantly higher sales growth, return on assets, profits, and cash flow from operations in at least some areas of the business.[70] Another review of the financial performance of large U.S. corporations considered "best corporate citizens" found that they enjoy both superior reputations and superior financial performance.[71] Although results from these studies are not proof, they do provide an indication that using resources for ethics and social responsibility does not hurt companies.[72]

Companies are also making an effort to measure the nonfinancial factors that create value. Researchers find, for example, that people prefer to work for companies that demonstrate a high level of ethics and social responsibility; thus, these organizations can attract and retain high-quality employees.[73] Sarah Antonette says she joined PNC Financial Services rather than two other companies that offered her a job because of PNC's strong employee volunteer program.[74] One vice president at Timberland says she has turned down lucrative offers from other companies because she prefers to work at a company that puts ethics and social responsibility ahead of just making a profit.[75] And a survey of 13- to 25-year-olds found that 79 percent say they want to work for a company that cares about how it affects or contributes to society.[76] Customers pay attention too. A study by Walker Research indicates that, price and quality being equal, two-thirds of customers say they would switch brands to do business with a company that is ethical and socially responsible.[77]

As discussed earlier in the chapter, long-term organizational success relies largely on social capital, which means companies need to build a reputation for honesty, fairness, and doing the right thing. Companies that put ethics on the back burner in favor of fast growth and short-term profits ultimately suffer. To gain and keep the trust of employees, customers, investors, and the general public, organizations must put ethics and social responsibility first.

> **BRIEFCASE**
>
> **As an organization manager, keep these guidelines in mind:**
>
> Act as a leader for the internal culture and ethical values that are important to the organization. Treat people fairly, hold yourself and others to high ethical standards, and communicate a vision for putting ethics before short-term interests. Remember that actions speak louder than words.

How Managers Shape Culture and Ethics

In the early days after founding Wendy's, Dave Thomas was known for going into his restaurants and throwing out full trays of food that weren't properly prepared.[78] During Michael Bloomberg's first term as mayor of New York City, he commuted to work the same way millions of other New Yorkers do, by foot and by subway. By sharing the struggle and hardship of fellow citizens—the uncomfortable temperatures, the crushing crowds, the delays when trains were late—Bloomberg signaled that his talk about goals for changing the city's traffic congestion and cutting carbon emissions was more than just talk.[79] The behavior of top managers is watched, and it makes a difference in how people throughout the organization behave.

In a study of ethics policy and practice in successful, ethical companies, no point emerged more clearly than the role of top management in providing commitment, leadership, and examples for ethical behavior.[80] The CEO and other top managers must be committed to specific ethical values and provide constant leadership in tending and renewing the values. Values can be communicated in a number of ways—speeches, company publications, policy statements, and, especially, personal actions. People follow and model what they see managers doing. If managers lie and bend the rules, so will employees. Top leaders are responsible for creating and sustaining a culture that emphasizes the importance of ethical behavior for every employee. When Vic Sarni was CEO of PPG Industries, he often called himself the chief ethics officer. Sarni didn't believe in using special staff departments to investigate ethical complaints; instead, he personally headed the firm's ethics committee. This sent a powerful symbolic message that ethics was important in the organization.[81] However, managers throughout the organizations also need to espouse and model ethical values. Employees are often influenced most by the managers and supervisors they work with closely rather than by distant top leaders. Formal ethics programs are worthless if managers do not live up to high standards of ethical conduct.[82]

The following sections examine how managers signal and implement values through leadership as well as through the formal systems of the organization.

Values-Based Leadership

Employees learn what values are important in the organization by watching managers. Managers have to discover their own personal values and the values they want to guide the team or organization and actively communicate the values to others through both words and actions.[83] Understanding one's own values clarifies what is important, which is essential for effective management, because people have different priorities, and values may change over time. Exhibit 10.7 shows some interesting changes in how managers from different generations prioritized values in one study. The exhibit lists values that were ranked differently by each group, showing only those rankings that were statistically significant.

The underlying value system of an organization cannot be managed in the traditional way. Issuing an authoritative directive, for example, has little or no impact on an organization's value system. Organizational values are developed and

EXHIBIT 10.7
Some Differences in Manager Rankings of Ethical Values by Generation

Value	Ranking by Baby Boom Managers	Ranking by Gen X Managers	Ranking by Gen Y Managers
Ambition	5	12	6
Broadminded	15	10	7
Courageous	9	6	13
Equality	15	13	10
Independent	6	15	2

Source: Based on Table 3, Generation Differences in Managers' Terminal and Instrumental Value Rankings, in Edward F. Murphy, Jr., Jane Whitney Gibson, and Regina A. Greenwood, "Analyzing Generational Values Among Managers and Non-Managers for Sustainable Organizational Effectiveness," *SAM Advanced Management Journal* (Winter 2010), 33–55.

strengthened primarily through **values-based leadership,** a relationship between a leader and followers that is based on shared, strongly internalized values that are advocated and acted upon by the leader.[84] Craig Jelinek, the new CEO of Costco, has vowed to continue the strong values-based leadership of co-founder and former CEO Jim Sinegal.

IN PRACTICE

Costco

In 2009, as the recession deepened and many employers were slashing jobs and cutting salaries, Costco CEO Jim Sinegal was handing out raises. Costco is the second-largest retailer in the United States, behind Walmart, and while Walmart leaders are seeing growing troubles, Costco leaders seem to be seeing nothing but growing sales and profits.

Minimum wage in the United States is still a paltry $7.25 per hour, but Costco's starting hourly wage is around $12.00. Because people stay around so long, the average hourly wage paid to Costco workers is $20.89, and the company offers good healthcare benefits even to part-time employees. New CEO Craig Jelinek recently wrote a public letter urging Congress to up the minimum wage. The letter sparked an interest in Costco's culture and business philosophy. Wall Street has repeatedly been critical of Costco leaders, asking them to reduce wages and health benefits. Instead, leaders have increased them every three years since the company began. In 2009, according to CFO Richard Galanti, "the first thing out of Jim [Sinegal's] mouth was, 'This economy is bad. We should be figuring out how to give them more, not less.' " Galanti admits Costco could make more money if the average wage was two or three dollars lower. "But we're not going to do it."

Jelinek, who took over as CEO in 2012, has vowed to continue Sinegal's values-based legacy. For instance, Jelinek is paid well, but the CEO earns only about 28 times more than the average employee, whereas CEOs in many companies earn a whopping 380 times more than the average employee. Costco doesn't hire business school graduates as managers. It cultivates employees who work the floor and sponsors them through graduate school. Turnover is around 5 percent, extremely low for the retail industry. "If you treat consumers with respect and treat employees with respect, good things are going to happen to you," Jelinek says.[85]

Leaders at Costco believe values of taking a long-term view and treating people humanely are just good business.

General Norman Schwarzkopf once said, "Leadership is a combination of strategy and character. If you must be without one, be without the strategy."[86] Good leaders know their every act and statement has an impact on culture and values. Employees learn about values, beliefs, and goals from watching managers, just as students learn which topics are important for an exam, what professors like, and how to get a good grade from watching professors. Actions speak louder than words, so values-based leaders "walk their talk."[87] "Just saying you're ethical isn't very useful," says Charles O. Holliday Jr., former chairman and CEO of DuPont. "You have to earn trust by what you do every day."[88]

Exhibit 10.8 outlines some of the characteristics that define values-based leaders.[89] Values-based leaders treat others with care, are helpful and supportive of others, and put effort into maintaining positive interpersonal relationships. They treat everyone fairly and with respect. Values-based leaders accept others' mistakes and failures and are never condescending. They hold themselves to high ethical standards and continuously strive to be honest, humble, and trustworthy and to be consistently ethical in both their public and private lives. However, they are open about and accept responsibility for their own ethical failings.

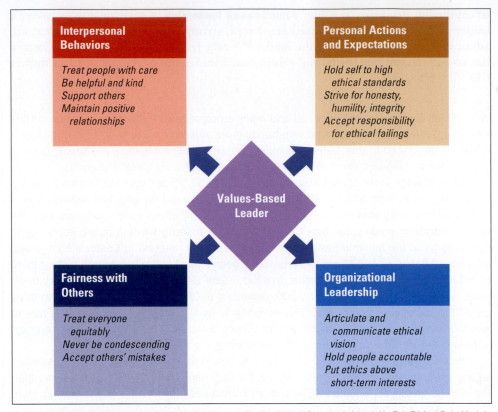

Source: Based on Gary Weaver, Linda Klebe Treviño, and Bradley Agle, "'Somebody I Look Up To': Ethical Role Models in Organizations," *Organizational Dynamics* 34, no. 4 (2005), 313–330.

Values-based leaders also clearly articulate and communicate an uncompromising vision for high ethical standards in the organization, and they institutionalize the vision by holding themselves and others accountable and by putting ethics above short-term personal or company interests. They continuously strengthen ethical values through everyday behaviors, rituals, ceremonies, and symbols, as well as through organizational systems and policies.

Formal Structure and Systems

Another set of tools managers can use to shape cultural and ethical values is the formal structure and systems of the organization. These systems can be especially effective for influencing managerial ethics.

Structure. Most experts agree that a formal ethics program is necessary to ensure an ethical culture, especially for large organizations.[90] This not only allocates organization time and energy to the problem but symbolizes to everyone the importance of ethics. Top executives can assign responsibility for ethical values to a specific position. One example is an **ethics committee**, which is a cross-functional group of executives who oversee company ethics. The committee provides rulings on questionable ethical issues and assumes responsibility for disciplining wrongdoers. By appointing top-level executives to serve on the committee, the organization signals the importance of ethics.

Today, many organizations are setting up ethics departments that manage and coordinate all corporate ethics activities. These departments are headed by a chief ethics or **compliance officer**, a high-level company executive who oversees all aspects

of ethics, including establishing and broadly communicating ethical standards, setting up ethics training programs, supervising the investigation of ethical problems, and advising managers on the ethical aspects of corporate decisions. For this to be an effective position, the compliance officer should have direct access to the company's board and not be subject to being fired by the CEO.[91]

Ethics offices sometimes also work as counseling centers to help employees resolve tricky ethical dilemmas. The focus is as much on helping employees make the right decisions as on disciplining wrongdoers. Most ethics offices have confidential **ethics hotlines** that employees can use to seek guidance as well as report questionable behavior. One organization calls its hotline a "Guide Line" to emphasize its use as a tool for making ethical decisions as well as reporting lapses.[92] According to Gary Edwards, president of the Ethics Resource Center, between 65 and 85 percent of calls to hotlines in the organizations he advises are calls for counsel on ethical issues.[93]

Disclosure Mechanisms. A confidential hotline is also an important mechanism for employees to voice concerns about ethical practices. Holding organizations accountable depends to some degree on individuals who are willing to speak up if they suspect illegal, dangerous, or unethical activities. **Whistle-blowing** involves employee disclosure of illegal, immoral, or illegitimate practices on the part of the organization.[94] As ethical problems in the corporate world increase, many companies are looking for ways to protect whistle-blowers. In addition, calls are increasing for stronger legal protection for those who report illegal or unethical business activities.[95] When there are no protective measures, whistle-blowers suffer, and the company may continue its unethical or illegal practices. A new whistle-blower bounty program, created as part of the Dodd-Frank finance regulatory overhaul law, is designed to reward whistle-blowers and prevent what happened to Matthew Lee, a former senior vice president in Lehman Brothers' accounting division. Lee lost his job just weeks after he raised concerns about how the firm was hiding risks by temporarily "parking" $50 billion in risky loan assets off its balance sheet. Lawrence McDonald, a former Lehman trader who has written a book about the giant firm's collapse, says Lehman routinely sacked or sidelined whistle-blowers, which allowed the company to continue its risky and unethical behavior.[96] Unlike Lee, a whistle-blower who helped stop a multimillion-dollar fraud at another company was given $50,000 in August 2012, a percentage of the amount collected in the case.[97]

Many governments, including the United States and Japan, have passed laws aimed at protecting whistle-blowers, but that isn't enough. Enlightened managers strive to create an organizational climate and culture in which people feel free to point out problems and managers take swift action to address concerns about unethical or illegal activities. Organizations can view whistle-blowing as a benefit to the company, helping prevent the kind of disasters that have hit companies such as Enron, Bear Stearns, Countrywide, News Corporation, and Lehman Brothers.

Code of Ethics. At a minimum, every company needs a code of ethics that is easy to understand, includes examples, and explains expected behaviors and sanctions.[98] A **code of ethics** is a formal statement of the company's values concerning ethics and social responsibility; it clarifies to employees what the company stands for and its expectations for employee conduct. The code of ethics at Lockheed Martin, for example, states that the organization "aims to set the standard for ethical conduct" through adhering to the values of honesty, integrity, respect, trust, responsibility, and citizenship. The code specifies the types of behaviors expected to honor these values and encourages employees to use available company resources to help make ethical choices and decisions.[99] Codes of ethics may cover a broad range of issues, including statements of the company's guiding values; guidelines related to issues such as workplace safety, the security of proprietary information, or employee privacy; and commitments to environmental responsibility, product safety, and other matters of concern to stakeholders. Swiss bank UBS AG, for example, developed a strong code of ethics addressing issues such as financial crime, competition, and confidentiality, including outlining sanctions against employees who violate the code. The code explicitly bans staff from helping clients cheat on their taxes, in response to a damaging investigation into the use of hidden offshore accounts. The Internal Revenue Service gave the largest-ever whistle-blower award—$104 million—to a former UBS banker who helped expose the fraud.[100] In an important step, the new code prohibits retaliation by managers against employees who report misconduct.[101]

Some companies use broader values statements within which ethics is a part. These statements define ethical values as well as corporate culture and contain language about company responsibility, quality of products, and treatment of employees. A formal statement of values can serve as a fundamental organizational document that defines what the organization stands for and clarifies the expected ethical behaviors and choices.[102]

Although written codes of ethics and value statements are important, it is essential that top managers support and reinforce the codes through their actions, including rewards for compliance and discipline for violations. Otherwise, a code of ethics is nothing more than a piece of paper. Indeed, one study found that companies with a written code of ethics are just as likely as those without a code to be found guilty of illegal activities.[103]

ASSESS YOUR ANSWER

3 The single best way to make sure an organization stays on solid ethical ground is to have a strong code of ethics and make sure all employees are familiar with its guidelines.

ANSWER: *Disagree.* Having a strong code of ethics can be an important part of creating an ethical organization, but managers' actions are more powerful in determining whether people live up to high ethical standards. If managers and top leaders are dishonest, unprincipled, or ruthless and create a culture that supports or ignores these behaviors in others, employees will put little stock in the formal ethics code.

Corporate Culture and Ethics in a Global Environment

Organizations operating on a global basis often face particularly tough ethical challenges because of the various cultural and market factors they deal with. The greater complexity of the environment and organizational domain creates a greater potential for ethical problems or misunderstandings.[104]

The global supply chain is a source of ongoing challenges for managers, for example. The global supply chain is so broad and diffuse that managers often have a hard time even knowing what firms they are doing business with, much less what is going on in all those different contractors and subcontractors. Amazon has distribution centers in Germany and because of high costs in that country, it often works with third parties to hire and manage thousands of temporary immigrant workers from Poland, Spain, Romania, and other European countries, allowing

Amazon to adjust to seasonal needs. The company became embroiled in an ethical quagmire after German public television aired a documentary in which workers said security guards from HESS (short for Hensel European Security Services) intimidate them, search them for pilfered food, and spot-check their cramped living quarters unannounced. The program showed some guards wearing clothing from Thor Steinar, a German fashion label popular with the country's neo-Nazi community. Amazon immediately stopped doing business with HESS, whose executives denied the allegations and said, "We explicitly distance ourselves from any form of political radicalism." Germany's Labor Ministry is also investigating.[105]

Many companies retract their orders and stop doing business with companies that are found to use unsafe or unethical practices. A more recent approach some are taking is to work closely with overseas factories to improve their conditions, which managers say benefits both sides of the equation.[106]

Another concern when doing business globally is that employees from different countries may have varied attitudes and beliefs that make it difficult to establish a sense of community and cohesiveness based on the corporate culture. In fact, research has indicated that national culture has a greater impact on employees than does corporate culture, and differences in national culture also create tremendous variance in ethical attitudes.[107] Managers often struggle to translate the ideas for developing strong, ethical corporate cultures to a complex global environment. Accenture, a management consulting, technology services, and outsourcing company with 140,000 employees in 48 countries, worked with liaisons in each region, called "Geographic Ethics Leads," to make sure the ethics code was written in appropriate language and addressed to the needs of employees in the different regions. These liaisons received input from employees at focus group sessions held in each country. Thus, although there are core ethical values in common, the company's code of ethics is customized for each country where Accenture has offices.[108]

Design Essentials

- This chapter covered a range of material on corporate culture, the importance of cultural and ethical values, and techniques managers can use to influence these values. Cultural and ethical values help determine the organization's social capital, and the right values can contribute to organizational success.

- Culture is the set of key values, beliefs, and norms shared by members of an organization. Organizational cultures serve two critically important functions— to integrate members so that they know how to relate to one another and to help the organization adapt to the external environment. Culture can be interpreted by looking at the organization's rites and ceremonies, stories and sayings, symbols, structures, control systems, and power relationships. Managers can also use these elements to influence culture.

- Organizational culture should reinforce the strategy and structure that the organization needs to be successful in its environment. Four types of culture that may exist in organizations are adaptability culture, mission culture, clan culture, and bureaucratic culture. When widespread consensus exists about the importance of specific values, the organizational culture is strong and cohesive. However, even in organizations with strong cultures, several sets of subcultures may emerge, particularly in large organizations.

■ Strong cultures can be either constructive or non-constructive. Constructive cultures have different values and different behavior patterns than non-constructive cultures. Strong but unhealthy cultures can be detrimental to a company's chances for success. On the other hand, strong constructive cultures can play an important role in creating high performance and innovative responses to challenges, competitive threats, or new opportunities.

■ An important aspect of organizational values is managerial ethics, which is the set of values governing behavior with respect to what is right or wrong. Corporate social responsibility (CSR) is an extension of managerial ethics and refers to management responsibility to make choices that contribute to the welfare of society as well as the organization. Many companies are embracing the concept of conscious capitalism, which means adopting policies and practices that enhance the competitiveness of a company while simultaneously advancing the economic and social conditions of the communities in which it operates.

■ The chapter also discussed how managers shape culture and ethics. One important idea is values-based leadership, which means leaders define a vision of proper values, communicate it throughout the organization, and institutionalize it through everyday behavior, rituals, ceremonies, and symbols. Formal systems are also important for shaping ethical values. Formal systems include an ethics committee, an ethics department, disclosure mechanisms for whistle-blowing, ethics training programs, and a code of ethics or values statement that specifies desired ethical values and behaviors.

■ As business increasingly crosses geographical and cultural boundaries, leaders face difficult challenges in establishing strong cultural and ethical values with which all employees can identify and agree. The global supply chain is an area of growing ethical concerns.

KEY CONCEPTS

adaptability culture	ethics	rule of law
bureaucratic culture	ethics committee	sayings
clan culture	ethics hotlines	social capital
code of ethics	external adaptation	stories
compliance officer	heroes	subcultures
conscious capitalism	internal integration	sustainability
corporate social responsibility (CSR)	legends	symbol
culture	managerial ethics	values-based leadership
culture strength	mission culture	whistle-blowing
ethical dilemma	rites and ceremonies	

DISCUSSION QUESTIONS

1. How much do you think it is possible for an outsider to discern about the underlying cultural values of an organization by analyzing symbols, ceremonies, dress, or other observable aspects of culture, compared to an insider with several years of work experience? Specify a percentage (e.g., 10 percent, 70 percent) and discuss your reasoning.

2. Many of the companies on *Fortune* magazine's list of most admired companies are also on its list of most profitable ones. Some people say this proves that high social capital translates into profits. Other people suggest that high profitability is the primary reason the companies have a good culture and are admired in the first place. Discuss your thinking about these two differing interpretations.

3. Can a strong bureaucratic culture also be a constructive culture, as defined in the text and in Exhibit 10.5? Discuss.
4. Why is values-based leadership so important to the influence of culture? Does a symbolic act communicate more about company values than an explicit statement? Discuss.
5. Can you recall a situation in which either you or someone you know was confronted by an ethical dilemma, such as being encouraged to inflate an expense account or trade answers on a test? Do you think the decision was affected more by individual moral values or by the accepted values within the team or company? Explain.
6. In a survey of 20,000 people in 16 European countries plus Russia, Turkey, and the United States, 55 percent of respondents said cheating in business is more common than it was 10 years ago. Do you believe this is truly the case, or have new forms of media simply made cheating more visible? Discuss.
7. What importance would you attribute to leadership statements and actions for influencing ethical values and decision making in an organization?
8. Why has globalization contributed to more complex ethical issues? Do you think it's possible for a company operating in many different countries to have a cohesive corporate culture? To have uniform ethical values?
9. Explain the concept of conscious capitalism. Do you think managers in companies that take a shared value approach are more likely to behave in ethical and socially responsible ways? Discuss.
10. Codes of ethics have been criticized for transferring responsibility for ethical behavior from the organization to the individual employee. Do you agree? Do you think a code of ethics is valuable for an organization?

CHAPTER 10 WORKSHOP The Power of Ethics[109]

This exercise will help you to better understand the concept of ethics and what it means to you.
A. Spend about five minutes individually answering the four questions below.
B. Divide into groups of four to six members.
C. Have each group try to achieve consensus with answers to each of the four questions. For question 3, choose one scenario to highlight. You will have 20 to 40 minutes for this exercise, depending on the instructor.
D. Have groups share their answers with the whole class, after which the instructor will lead a discussion on ethics and its power in business.

Questions

1. In your own words, define the concept of ethics in one or two sentences.
2. If you were a manager, how would you motivate your employees to follow ethical behavior? Use no more than two sentences.
3. Describe a situation in which you were faced with an ethical dilemma. What was your decision and behavior? How did you decide to do that? Can you relate your decision to any concept in the chapter?
4. What do you think is a powerful ethical message for people who report to you? Where did you get it from? How might it influence your own behavior in the future?

CASE FOR ANALYSIS | Implementing Change at National Industrial Products[110]

Curtis Simpson sat staring out the window of his office. What would he say to Tom Lawrence when they met this afternoon? Tom had clearly met the challenge Simpson set for him when he hired him as president of National Industrial Products (National) a little more than a year ago, but the company seemed to be coming apart at the seams. As chairman and CEO of Simpson Industries, which had bought National several years ago, Simpson was faced with the task of understanding the problem and clearly communicating his ideas and beliefs to Lawrence.

National Industrial Products is a medium-sized producer of mechanical seals, pumps, and other flow-control products. When Simpson Industries acquired the company, it was under the leadership of Jim Carpenter, who had been CEO for almost three decades and was very well liked by employees. Carpenter had always treated his employees like family. He knew most of them by name, often visited them in their homes if they were ill, and spent part of each day just chatting with workers on the factory floor. National sponsored an annual holiday party for its workers as well as company picnics and other social events several times a year, and Carpenter was always in attendance. He considered these activities to be just as important as his visits with customers or negotiations with suppliers. Carpenter believed it was important to treat people right so they would have a sense of loyalty to the company. If business was slow, he would find something else for workers to do, even if it was just sweeping the parking lot, rather than lay people off. He figured the company couldn't afford to lose skilled workers who were so difficult to replace. "If you treat people right," he said, "they'll do a good job for you without your having to push them."

Carpenter had never set performance objectives and standards for the various departments, and he trusted his managers to run their departments as they saw fit. He offered training programs in communications and HR for managers and team leaders several times each year. Carpenter's approach had seemed to work quite well for much of National's history. Employees were very loyal to Carpenter and the company, and there were many instances in which workers had gone above and beyond the call of duty. For example, when two National pumps that supplied water to a U.S. Navy ship failed on a Saturday night just before the ship's scheduled departure, two employees worked throughout the night to make new seals and deliver them for installation before the ship left port. Most managers and employees had been with the company for many years, and National boasted the lowest turnover rate in the industry.

However, as the industry began to change in recent years, National's competitiveness began to decline. Four of National's major rivals had recently merged into two large companies that were better able to meet customer needs, which was one factor that led to National being acquired by Simpson Industries. Following the acquisition, National's sales and profits had continued to decline, while costs kept going up. In addition, Simpson Industries' top executives were concerned about low productivity at National. Although they had been happy to have Carpenter stay on through the transition, within a year they had gently pressured him into early retirement. Some of the top managers believed Carpenter tolerated poor performance and low productivity in order to maintain a friendly atmosphere. "In today's world, you just can't do that," one had said. "We've got to bring in someone who can implement change and turn this company around in a hurry, or National's going to go bankrupt." That's when Tom Lawrence was brought on board, with a mandate to cut costs and improve productivity and profits.

Lawrence had a growing reputation as a young, dynamic manager who could get things done fast. He quickly began making changes at National. First, he cut costs by discontinuing the company-sponsored social activities, and he even refused to allow the impromptu birthday celebrations that had once been a regular part of life at National. He cut the training programs in communications and HR, arguing that they were a waste of time and money. "We're not here to make people feel good," he told his managers. "If people don't want to work, get rid of them and find someone else who does." He often referred to workers who complained about the changes at National as "crybabies."

Lawrence established strict performance standards for his vice presidents and department managers and ordered them to do the same for their employees. He held weekly meetings with each manager to review department performance and discuss problems. All employees were now subject to regular performance reviews. Any worker who had substandard performance was to be given one warning and then fired if performance did not improve within two weeks. And, whereas managers and sales representatives had once been paid on a straight salary basis, with seniority being the sole criterion for advancement, Lawrence implemented a revised system that rewarded them for meeting productivity, sales, and profit goals. For those who met the standards, rewards were generous, including large bonuses and perks such as company cars and first-class air travel to industry meetings. Those who fell behind were often chided in front of their colleagues to set an example, and if they didn't shape up soon, Lawrence didn't hesitate to fire them.

By the end of Lawrence's first year as president of National, production costs had been reduced by nearly 20 percent, while output was up 10 percent and sales increased by nearly 10 percent as well. However, three experienced and well-respected National managers had left the company for jobs with competitors, and turnover among production workers had increased alarmingly. In the tight labor market, replacements were not easily found. Most disturbing to Simpson were the results of a survey he had commissioned by an outside consultant. The survey indicated that morale at National was in the pits. Workers viewed their supervisors with antagonism and a touch of fear. They expressed the belief that managers were obsessed with profits and quotas and cared nothing about workers' needs and feelings. They also noted that the collegial, friendly atmosphere that had made National a great place to work had been replaced by an environment of aggressive internal competition and distrust.

Simpson was pleased that Lawrence has brought National's profits and productivity up to the standards Simpson Industries expects. However, he was concerned that the low morale and high turnover would seriously damage the company in the long run. Was Lawrence correct that many of the employees at National are just being "crybabies"? Were they so accustomed to being coddled by Carpenter that they weren't willing to make the changes necessary to keep the company competitive? Finally, Simpson wondered if a spirit of competition can exist in an atmosphere of collegiality and cooperativeness such as that fostered by Carpenter.

CASE FOR ANALYSIS | The Boys Versus Corporate

NASCAR fans expect their drivers to be smart, crafty, and calculating and, if need be, playing just this side of the rule book—in the garage and on the track. Loyal fans "know" their drivers and can easily picture themselves drinking a beer or spending an afternoon tinkering under the hood with a favorite driver. In the wild, fast-paced world of NASCAR, drivers can joke and pal around with competitors one day and trade word-for-word or, if necessary, fist-for-fist with a rival the next day. They defiantly wear monikers like "Fireball" and "The Intimidator."

And why not? The roots of the sport trace back to Prohibition when moonshine runners in souped-up cars raced across the hills of Appalachia outsmarting and outrunning the "Feds" and "Revenuers," taking risks with life and the law to make deliveries. As reputations grew, the desire for head-to-head competition to establish bragging rights resulted in informal races.

As the popularity of these races increased, one driver, Big Bill France, gathered drivers and set up a meeting in Daytona in December 1947 to establish and standardize rules for the many tracks scattered across the region. At that meeting, a new governing organization, the National Association for Stock Car Auto Racing (NASCAR) was born. Two months later, drivers met in the first NASCAR sanctioned race.

Across decades, NASCAR has remained a "family business" with third-generation Brian France named as CEO in 2014. Still headquartered in Daytona, with offices scattered around the country, NASCAR has expanded into Mexico and Canada. "The Boys" became "Big Business" and the nation's second largest spectator sport with television coverage in over 150 countries and team sponsorships attracting Fortune 500 companies.

By contrast, the majority of the racing teams remained based in the hills around Charlotte, North Carolina, setting up an organizational tug-of-war. Drivers and the fan base remain faithful to traditional stock car racing and to the traditional tracks, devoted to the notion of "let the boys drive," including rule-breaking to gain an advantage.

The outlaw image is cherished by NASCAR's fan base, as one sports columnist warned: "If the outlaw blood ever is completely drained, then NASCAR will be as colorless as the white flag that signals one lap to go. And its popularity could be just as fleeting."

From the beginnings to recent history, it would appear there are few worries about the loss of that "outlaw image" and controversies are epic. In 1983, Richard Petty's Charlotte victory was allowed to "stand" despite over-the-limit engine cylinders. To the delight of fans, popular driver Junior Johnson continued the wild ways of his youth running moonshine for his dad, sneaking in illegal car modifications when he could, if it meant tearing down and

rebuilding a car. He often got into trouble with NASCAR, but stock car traditionalists were thrilled.

Two of the sport's biggest scandals occurred in 2001 and 2013. In a NASCAR move overshadowed by the death of Dale Earnhardt Sr. at the 2001 Daytona 500, eighteen teams were fined/penalized for rules violations. At Richmond in 2013 leading up to the Daytona 500, another six teams were penalized and fined. In that rules violation dragnet, Michael Waltrip made NASCAR history with the largest-ever fine ($300,000), a penalty of 100 championship points, and a penalty of 100 team points for the use of what fans and the media have come to call "rocket fuel." Year after year, drivers and crews get angry, apologize, and then shrug off the controversies as they continue to search for the "winning edge."

At the other end of the tug-of-war lies corporate NASCAR, the media, and sponsors concerned about image and any hint of impropriety—a modern version of those chasing the moonshine runners. *Their* focus is on safety, rules, fines, and penalties. The NASCAR rule book is in a constant state of growth and revision. Along with pre-race inspections, the winning vehicle is stripped down and examined for any evidence of tampering or cheating. There are currently six penalty levels for rule violations for drivers, crews, and vehicles ranging from P-1 (minor infractions) to P-6 (suspension).

Even the crucial area of driver safety enters into this cultural tug-of-war. Drivers claim that NASCAR is more concerned with the crackdown on rules violations than on driver safety. NASCAR's focus ranges from assigning and revoking car numbers at will, and the strict enforcement of a no-communications ban between crews/drivers and their rivals, to points penalties for drivers who refuse to talk to the media. Teams point out the frequency with which serious issues such as safety regulations seem to *follow* high-profile wrecks and deaths.

Fire retardant suits were required following the fiery death of Glen "Fireball" Roberts. The throttle "kill-switch" came on the heels of Adam Petty's death. Rules governing G-forces on drivers during crashes came after a series of deaths in 2000–2001. And the relocation of the driver's seat near the center of the vehicle, along with the requirement for installation of HANS (Head & Neck Support Device) came after the death of Dale Earnhardt.

Meanwhile, sport officials and sponsors appear to freak out over minute vehicle modifications that can give a driver an edge. Those modifications are not unethical, say stock car traditionalists; they are part of the culture—rivals and team crews discovering that undetectable edge that brings victory.

No one was prepared for NASCAR's latest move. In 2014, new CEO Brian France and NASCAR suddenly threw a monkey-wrench into tradition in a move that is both exciting for spectators and dangerous for drivers.

In a sudden shift, NASCAR set new rules for qualifying, replacing the one-car-at-a-time-against-the-clock qualifying with a new all-cars-on-the-track-at-once qualifying round.

The change will ignite the fan base with increased action and is both challenging and dangerous for drivers who must suddenly use both speed and strategy in the race for pole position, creating, in effect, "a race-before-the-race."

While some drivers are thrilled by the change, others are concerned with safety issues as drivers jockey to the front, scrambling for position, or hold back, preferring not to start too close to the front of the race. There are also concerns about the effects on asphalt with the transfer of energy from car to surface during an additional day of 43 cars with 750 horsepower racing at speeds of 150 mph.

As the sport enters a new era under the leadership of a new CEO, observers might ask how the NASCAR organization, teams, and sponsors might work through issues of ethics and values to create a unified culture.

❯❯ NOTES

1. Brad Stone, *The Everything Store: Jeff Bezos and the Age of Amazon* (New York: Little, Brown and Company 2013), 327–328.
2. Julia Boorstin, "Secret Recipe: J. M. Smucker," *Fortune*, January 12, 2004, 58–59.
3. Mark Scott, "Report Faults 'at All Costs' Attitude at Barclay's That Encouraged Risk," *The New York Times*, April 4, 2013, B2.
4. Mark C. Bolino, William H. Turnley, and James M. Bloodgood, "Citizenship Behavior and the Creation of Social Capital in Organizations," *Academy of Management Review* 27, no. 4 (2002), 505–522; and Don Cohen and Laurence Prusak, *In Good Company: How Social Capital Makes Organizations Work* (Boston: Harvard Business School Press, 2001), 3–4.
5. W. Jack Duncan, "Organizational Culture: 'Getting a Fix' on an Elusive Concept," *Academy of Management Executive* 3 (1989), 229–236; Linda Smircich, "Concepts of Culture and Organizational Analysis," *Administrative Science Quarterly* 28 (1983), 339–358; and Andrew D. Brown and Ken Starkey, "The Effect of Organizational Culture on Communication and Information," *Journal of Management Studies* 31, no. 6 (November 1994), 807–828.
6. See Jon Katzenbach and Zia Khan, "Leading Outside the Lines," *Strategy + Business*, April 26, 2010, http://www.strategy-business.com/article/10204?gko=788c9 (accessed September 9, 2010) for the idea of the formal versus the informal organization.
7. Edgar H. Schein, "Organizational Culture," *American Psychologist* 45, February 1990, 109–119.
8. Doug Kirkpatrick, "Self-Management's Success at Morning Star," *T+D*, October 2012, 25–27; and Christoph H. Loch, Fabian J. Sting, Arnd Huchzermeier, and Christiane Decker, "Finding the Profit in Fairness," *Harvard Business Review*, September 2012, 111–115.
9. Harrison M. Trice and Janice M. Beyer, "Studying Organizational Cultures Through Rites and Ceremonials," *Academy of Management Review* 9 (1984), 653–669; Janice M. Beyer and Harrison M. Trice, "How an Organization's Rites Reveal Its Culture," *Organizational Dynamics* 15 (Spring 1987), 5–24; Steven P. Feldman, "Management in Context: An Essay on the Relevance of Culture to the Understanding of Organizational Change," *Journal of Management Studies* 23 (1986), 589–607; and Mary Jo Hatch, "The Dynamics of Organizational Culture," *Academy of Management Review* 18 (1993), 657–693.
10. This discussion is based on Edgar H. Schein, *Organizational Culture and Leadership*, 2nd ed. (Homewood, IL: Richard D. Irwin, 1992); and John P. Kotter and James L. Heskett, *Corporate Culture and Performance* (New York: Free Press, 1992).
11. Stone, *The Everything Store*, 328 and 88–90.
12. Jim Kanir, "Culture Champions," *T+D*, January 2013, 80.
13. Larry Mallak, "Understanding and Changing Your Organization's Culture," *Industrial Management* (March–April 2001), 18–24.
14. Based on Gerry Johnson, "Managing Strategic Change—Strategy, Culture, and Action," *Long Range Planning* 25, no. 1 (1992), 28–36.
15. For an expanded list of various elements that can be used to assess or interpret corporate culture, see "10 Key Cultural Elements," sidebar in Micah R. Kee, "Corporate Culture Makes a Fiscal Difference," *Industrial Management* (November–December 2003), 16–20.
16. Gazi Islam and Michael J. Zyphur, "Rituals in Organizations: A Review and Expansion of Current Theory," *Group & Organization Management* 34, no. 1 (2009), 114–139; Trice and Beyer, "Studying Organizational Cultures through Rites and Ceremonials"; and Terrence E. Deal and Allan A. Kennedy, "Culture: A New Look through Old Lenses," *Journal of Applied Behavioral Science* 19 (1983), 498–505.
17. Leigh Buchanan, "Managing: Welcome Aboard. Now, Run!" *Inc.*, March 2010, 95–96.
18. Susan Cramm, "Leadership Gone Viral," *Strategy + Business*, January 17, 2014, http://www.strategy-business.com/blog/Leadership-Gone-Viral (accessed May 6, 2014); and Claudio Lavanga, "Pope Washes Feet of Young Detainees in Holy Thursday Ritual," NBCNews.com, March 28, 2013, http://worldnews.nbcnews.com/_news/2013/03/28/17502522-pope-washes-feet-of-young-detainees-in-holy-thursday-ritual?lite (accessed May 6, 2014).
19. Trice and Beyer, "Studying Organizational Cultures through Rites and Ceremonials."
20. Adam Bryant, "Noreen Beaman of Brinker Capital, on Accountability" (Corner Office column), *The New York Times*, January 25, 2014, http://www.nytimes.com/2014/01/26/business/noreen-beaman-of-brinker-capital-on-accountability.html?_r=0 (accessed May 6, 2014); Lucas Conley, "Rinse and Repeat," *Fast Company*, July 2005, 76–77; and Robert Bruce Shaw and Mark Ronald, "Changing Culture—Patience Is Not a Virtue," *Leader to Leader*, Fall 2012, 50–55.
21. David C. Robertson with Bill Breen, *Brick by Brick: How LEGO Rewrote the Rules of Innovation and Conquered the Global Toy Industry* (New York: Crown Business, 2013), 17.
22. Quoted in Stone, *The Everything Store*, 300 and 174.
23. Buchanan, "Managing: Welcome Aboard. Now, Run!"
24. "FYI: Organization Chart of the Month," *Inc.*, April 1991, 14.

25. Neal E. Boudette, "Fiat CEO Sets New Tone at Chrysler," *The Wall Street Journal Online*, June 19, 2009, http://online .wsj.com/article/SB124537403628329989.html?utm _source=feedburner&utm_medium=feed&utm_campaign =Feed%3A+wsj%2Fxml%2Frss%2F3_7011+%28WSJ.com %3A+What%27s+News+US%29#mod=rss_whats_news_us (accessed September 12, 2011).

26. Gary Hamel with Bill Breen, *The Future of Management* (Boston: Harvard Business School Press, 2007).

27. Matt Moffett, "At InBev, a Gung-Ho Culture Rules; American Icon Anheuser, A Potential Target, Faces Prospect of Big Changes," *The Wall Street Journal*, May 28, 2008, B1; and Matt Moffett, "InBev's Chief Built Competitive Culture," *The Wall Street Journal*, June 13, 2008, B6.

28. Monica Langley and Dan Fitzpatrick, "Embattled J.P. Morgan Bulks Up Overnight," *The Wall Street Journal*, September 12, 2013, http://online.wsj.com/news/articles/SB1000142412788 7324755104579071304170686532 (accessed May 7, 2014).

29. Johnson, "Managing Strategic Change—Strategy, Culture, and Action."

30. Jennifer A. Chatman and Sandra Eunyoung Cha, "Leading by Leveraging Culture," *California Management Review* 45, no. 4 (Summer 2003), 20–34; and Abby Ghobadian and Nicholas O'Regan, "The Link between Culture, Strategy, and Performance in Manufacturing SMEs," *Journal of General Management* 28, no. 1 (Autumn 2002), 16–34.

31. James R. Detert, Roger G. Schroeder, and John J. Mauriel, "A Framework for Linking Culture and Improvement Initiatives in Organizations," *Academy of Management Review* 25, no. 4 (2000), 850–863.

32. Based on Daniel R. Denison, *Corporate Culture and Organizational Effectiveness* (New York: Wiley, 1990), 11–15; Daniel R. Denison and Aneil K. Mishra, "Toward a Theory of Organizational Culture and Effectiveness," *Organization Science* 6, no. 2 (March–April 1995), 204–223; R. Hooijberg and F. Petrock, "On Cultural Change: Using the Competing Values Framework to Help Leaders Execute a Transformational Strategy," *Human Resource Management* 32 (1993), 29–50; and R. E. Quinn, *Beyond Rational Management: Mastering the Paradoxes and Competing Demands of High Performance* (San Francisco: Jossey-Bass, 1988).

33. Carlin Flora, "Paid to Smile," *Psychology Today*, September–October 2009, 59; and Tony Hsieh, *Delivering Happiness: A Path to Profits, Passion, and Purpose* (New York: Business Plus, 2010).

34. Moffett, "InBev's Chief Built Competitive Culture."

35. William Rogers, "Sound Advice," *People Management*, August 2012, 40–43.

36. Gerald D. Klein, "Creating Cultures That Lead to Success: Lincoln Electric, Southwest Airlines, and SAS Institute," *Organizational Dynamics* 41 (2012), 32–43; and Rekha Balu, "Pacific Edge Projects Itself," *Fast Company*, October 2000, 371–381.

37. Bernard Arogyaswamy and Charles M. Byles, "Organizational Culture: Internal and External Fits," *Journal of Management* 13 (1987), 647–659.

38. Based on Table 1, Tightness-Looseness of Cultures, in Michael Harvey et al., "Corralling the 'Horses' to Staff the Global Organization of 21st Century," *Organizational Dynamics* 39, no. 3 (2010), 258–268.

39. Paul R. Lawrence and Jay W. Lorsch, *Organization and Environment* (Homewood, IL: Irwin, 1969).

40. Scott Kirsner, "Designed for Innovation," *Fast Company*, November 1998, 54, 56.

41. Chatman and Cha, "Leading by Leveraging Culture"; and Jeff Rosenthal and Mary Ann Masarech, "High-Performance Cultures: How Values Can Drive Business Results," *Journal of Organizational Excellence*, Spring 2003, 3–18.

42. Aaron Levie, as told to Memon Yaqub, "I'm Obsessed with Speed," *Inc.*, November 2012, 100–103.

43. Ghobadian and O'Regan, "The Link between Culture, Strategy and Performance"; G. G. Gordon and N. DiTomaso, "Predicting Corporate Performance from Organizational Culture," *Journal of Management Studies* 29, no. 6 (1992), 783–798; and G. A. Marcoulides and R. H. Heck, "Organizational Culture and Performance: Proposing and Testing a Model," *Organization Science* 4 (1993), 209–225.

44. John P. Kotter and James L. Heskett, *Corporate Culture and Performance* (New York: The Free Press, 1992); and Kee, "Corporate Culture Makes a Fiscal Difference."

45. Tressie Wright Muldrow, Timothy Buckley, and Brigitte W. Schay, "Creating High-Performance Organizations in the Public Sector," *Human Resource Management* 41, no. 3 (Fall 2002), 341–354.

46. David Carr, "Troubles That Money Can't Dispel," *The New York Times Online*, July 18, 2011, B1.

47. John F. Burns and Jeremy W. Peters, "Two Top Deputies Resign as Crisis Isolates Murdoch," *The New York Times Online*, July 16, 2011, www.hongkong-mart.com/forum /viewtopic.php?f=2&t=367 (accessed June 13, 2012).

48. Carr, "Troubles That Money Can't Dispel."

49. Kotter and Heskett, *Corporate Culture and Performance*.

50. Jena McGregor, "Ethical Misconduct, by the Numbers," *The Washington Post*, February 4, 2014, http://www .washingtonpost.com/blogs/on-leadership/wp/2014/02/04 /ethical-misconduct-by-the-numbers/ (accessed May 8, 2014).

51. Mike Esterl, "Executive Decision: In Germany, Scandals Tarnish Business Elite," *The Wall Street Journal*, March 4, 2008, A1; and Martin Fackler, "The Salaryman Accuses," *The New York Times*, June 7, 2008, C1.

52. Gordon F. Shea, *Practical Ethics* (New York: American Management Association, 1988); Linda K. Treviño, "Ethical Decision Making in Organizations: A Person–Situation Interactionist Model," *Academy of Management Review* 11 (1986), 601–617; and Linda Klebe Treviño and Katherine A. Nelson, *Managing Business Ethics: Straight Talk about How to Do It Right*, 2nd ed. (New York: John Wiley & Sons Inc., 1999).

53. This discussion of the sources of individual ethics is based on Susan H. Taft and Judith White, "Ethics Education: Using Inductive Reasoning to Develop Individual, Group, Organizational, and Global Perspectives," *Journal of Management Education* 31, no. 5 (October 2007), 614–646.

54. Natasha Singer, "Web Sites Accused of Collecting Data on Children," *The New York Times*, August 22, 2012, B1.

55. Samuel Rubenfeld, "Survey Finds 25% of People Paid Bribes in Last Year," *The Wall Street Journal*, July 9, 2013, http:// blogs.wsj.com/riskandcompliance/2013/07/09/survey-finds -one-fourth-of-people-paid-bribes-in-last-year/ (accessed May 9, 2014); and James B. Stewart, "Bribery, But Nobody Was Charged," *The New York Times*, June 25, 2011, B1.

56. Dawn-Marie Driscoll, "Don't Confuse Legal and Ethical Standards," *Business Ethics*, July–August 1996, 44.

57. LaRue Tone Hosmer, *The Ethics of Management*, 2nd ed. (Homewood, IL: Irwin, 1991).

58. Motoko Rich, "2 More Educators in the South Are Charged in Test Cheating," *The New York Times*, June 21, 2013, http://www.nytimes.com/2013/06/22/us/2-more-educators-in-the-south-are-charged-in-test-cheating.html?_r=0 (accessed June 29, 2013).

59. Julian E. Barnes, "Navy Probes Allegation of Instructors' Cheating," *The Wall Street Journal*, February 4, 2014, http://online.wsj.com/news/articles/SB10001424052702304851104579363402001370472 (accessed May 9, 2014).

60. Some of these incidents are from Hosmer, *The Ethics of Management*.

61. Linda K. Treviño and Katherine A. Nelson, *Managing Business Ethics: Straight Talk About How to Do It Right* (New York: John Wiley & Sons, Inc., 1995), 4.

62. N. Craig Smith, "Corporate Social Responsibility: Whether or How?" *California Management Review* 45, no. 4 (Summer 2003), 52–76; and Eugene W. Szwajkowski, "The Myths and Realities of Research on Organizational Misconduct," in James E. Post, ed., *Research in Corporate Social Performance and Policy*, vol. 9 (Greenwich, CT: JAI Press, 1986), 103–122.

63. D. Bright, K. Cameron, and A. Caza, "The Amplifying and Buffering Effects of Virtuousness in Downsized Organizations," *Journal of Business Ethics* 64 (2006), 249–269; as described in Mario Fernando and Shamika Almeida, "The Organizational Virtuousness of Strategic Corporate Social Responsibility: A Case Study of the Sri Lankan Family-Owned Enterprise MAS Holdings," *European Management Journal* 30 (2012), 564–576.

64. "Volunteerism as a Core Competency," *Bloomberg BusinessWeek*, November 12–November 18, 2012, 53–54.

65. "Habitat for Humanity," Whirlpool Corporation website, http://www.whirlpoolcorp.com/responsibility/building_communities/habitat_for_humanity.aspx (accessed September 13, 2011); Bruce Horovitz, "Pepsi Is Dropping Out of Schools Worldwide by 2012," *USA Today*, March 16, 2011, http://www.usatoday.com/money/industries/food/2010-03-16-pepsicutsschoolsoda_N.htm (accessed September 13, 2011); Kate O'Sullivan, "Virtue Rewarded," *CFO*, October 2006, 46–52.

66. Definition is based on John Mackey and Raj Sisodia, *Conscious Capitalism: Liberating the Heroic Spirit of Business* (Boston: Harvard Business Review Press, 2013); and Michael E. Porter and Mark R. Kramer, "Creating Shared Value: How to Reinvent Capitalism—and Unleash a Wave of Innovation and Growth," *Harvard Business Review*, January–February 2011, 62–77.

67. Porter and Kramer, "Creating Shared Value."

68. Homer H. Johnson, "Does It Pay to Be Good? Social Responsibility and Financial Performance," *Business Horizons*, November–December 2003, 34–40; Jennifer J. Griffin and John F. Mahon, "The Corporate Social Performance and Corporate Financial Performance Debate: Twenty-Five Years of Incomparable Research," *Business and Society* 36, no. 1 (March 1997), 5–31; Beckey Bright, "How More Companies Are Embracing Social Responsibility as Good Business," *The Wall Street Journal*, March 10, 2008, R3; Bernadette M. Ruf et al., "An Empirical Investigation of the Relationship Between Change in Corporate Social Performance and Financial Performance: A Stakeholder Theory Perspective," *Journal of Business Ethics* 32, no. 2 (July 2001), 143ff; and Philip L. Cochran and Robert A. Wood, "Corporate Social Responsibility and Financial Performance," *Academy of Management Journal* 27 (1984), 42–56.

69. Heli Wang, Jaepil Choi, and Jiatao Li, "Too Little or Too Much? Untangling the Relationship Between Corporate Philanthropy and Firm Financial Performance," *Organization Science* 19, no. 1 (January–February 2008), 143–159; Philip L. Cochran, "The Evolution of Corporate Social Responsibility," *Business Horizons* 50 (2007), 449–454; Paul C. Godfrey, "The Relationship Between Corporate Philanthropy and Shareholder Wealth: A Risk Management Perspective," *Academy of Management Review* 30, no. 4 (2005), 777–798; Oliver Falck and Stephan Heblich, "Corporate Social Responsibility: Doing Well by Doing Good," *Business Horizons* 50 (2007), 247–254; J. A. Pearce II and J. P. Doh, "The High Impact of Collaborative Social Initiatives," *MIT Sloan Management Review*, Spring 2005, 31–39; Curtis C. Verschoor and Elizabeth A. Murphy, "The Financial Performance of Large U.S. Firms and Those with Global Prominence: How Do the Best Corporate Citizens Rate?" *Business and Society Review* 107, no. 3 (Fall 2002), 371–381; Johnson, "Does It Pay to Be Good?"; and Dale Kurschner, "5 Ways Ethical Business Creates Fatter Profits," *Business Ethics*, March–April 1996, 20–23.

70. Rashid Ameer and Radiah Othman, "Sustainability Practices and Corporate Financial Performance: A Study Based on the Top Global Corporations," *Journal of Business Ethics* 108, no. 1 (June 2012), 61–79.

71. Verschoor and Murphy, "The Financial Performance of Large U.S. Firms."

72. Richard McGill Murphy, "Why Doing Good Is Good For Business," *Fortune*, February 8, 2010, 90–95; Jean B. McGuire, Alison Sundgren, and Thomas Schneeweis, "Corporate Social Responsibility and Firm Financial Performance," *Academy of Management Journal* 31 (1988), 854–872; Falck and Heblich, "Corporate Social Responsibility: Doing Well by Doing Good"; and Geoffrey B. Sprinkle and Laureen A. Maines, "The Benefits and Costs of Corporate Social Responsibility," *Business Horizons* 53 (2010), 445–453.

73. Daniel W. Greening and Daniel B. Turban, "Corporate Social Performance as a Competitive Advantage in Attracting a Quality Workforce," *Business and Society* 39, no. 3 (September 2000), 254; and Kate O'Sullivan, "Virtue Rewarded," *CFO*, October 2006, 47–52.

74. Sarah E. Needleman, "The Latest Office Perk: Getting Paid to Volunteer," *The Wall Street Journal*, April 29, 2008, D1.

75. Christopher Marquis, "Doing Well and Doing Good," *The New York Times*, July 13, 2003, Section 3, 2; and Joseph Pereira, "Career Journal: Doing Good and Doing Well at Timberland," *The Wall Street Journal*, September 9, 2003, B1.

76. Reported in Needleman, "The Latest Office Perk."

77. "The Socially Correct Corporate Business," in Leslie Holstrom and Simon Brady, "The Changing Face of Global Business," a special advertising section, *Fortune*, July 24, 2000, S1–S38.

78. Example told in Shaw and Ronald, "Changing Culture—Patience Is Not a Virtue."

79. Alan Deutschman, *Walk the Walk; The #1 Rule for Leaders* (New York: Portfolio/Penguin, 2010), 93–94.

80. *Corporate Ethics: A Prime Business Asset* (New York: The Business Round Table, February 1988).

81. Treviño and Nelson, *Managing Business Ethics*, 201.
82. Gary R. Weaver, Linda Klebe Treviño, and Bradley Agle, "'Somebody I Look Up To': Ethical Role Models in Organizations," *Organizational Dynamics* 34, no. 4 (2005), 313–330; Andrew W. Singer, "The Ultimate Ethics Test," *Across the Board*, March 1992, 19–22; Ronald B. Morgan, "Self and Co-Worker Perceptions of Ethics and Their Relationships to Leadership and Salary," *Academy of Management Journal* 36, no. 1 (February 1993), 200–214; and Joseph L. Badaracco Jr. and Allen P. Webb, "Business Ethics: A View from the Trenches," *California Management Review* 37, no. 2 (Winter 1995), 8–28.
83. Alan Lewis, "Values Compass: Align Around True North Values," *Leadership Excellence*, February 2012, 13; Krista Jaakson, "Management by Values: Are Some Values Better than Others?" *Journal of Management Development* 29, no. 9 (2010), 795–806; and Kathy Whitmire, "Leading Through Shared Values," *Leader to Leader*, Summer 2005, 48–54.
84. This definition is based on Robert J. House, Andre Delbecq, and Toon W. Taris, "Value Based Leadership: An Integrated Theory and an Empirical Test" (working paper).
85. Brad Stone, "Costco CEO Craig Jelinek Leads the Cheapest, Happiest Company in the World," *Bloomberg BusinessWeek*, June 6, 2013, http://www.businessweek.com/articles/2013-06-06/costco-ceo-craig-jelinek-leads-the-cheapest-happiest-company-in-the-world (accessed June 7, 2013); "Costco's Profit Soars to $537 Million Just Days After CEO Endorses Minimum Wage Increase," *The Huffington Post*, March 13, 2013, http://www.huffingtonpost.com/2013/03/12/costco-profit_n_2859250.html (accessed June 7, 2013); Bud Meyers, "Hail to the Chief (Executive Officer) Craig Jelinek of Costco!," *The Daily Kos*, March 8, 2013, http://www.dailykos.com/story/2013/03/08/1192632/-Hail-to-the-Chief-Executive-Officer-Craig-Jelinek-of-Costco (accessed June 8, 2013); and Satinder Dhiman and Joan Marques, "The Role and Need of Offering Workshops and Courses on Workplace Spirituality," *Journal of Management Development* 30, no. 9 (2011), 816–835.
86. As quoted in Arkadi Kuhlmann, "Culture-Driven Leadership," *Ivey Business Journal*, March–April 2010, http://www.iveybusinessjournal.com/topics/leadership/culture-driven-leadership (accessed September 13, 2011).
87. Thomas J. Peters and Robert H. Waterman Jr., *In Search of Excellence* (New York: Harper & Row, 1982); and Kuhlmann, "Culture-Driven Leadership."
88. Carol Hymowitz, "CEOs Must Work Hard to Maintain Faith in the Corner Office" (In the Lead column), *The Wall Street Journal*, July 9, 2002, B1.
89. Based on Weaver et al., "Somebody I Look Up To."
90. Mark S. Schwartz, "Developing and Sustaining an Ethical Corporate Culture: The Core Elements," *Business Horizons* 56 (2013), 39–50.
91. Ibid.; and Gregory J. Millman and Ben DiPietro, "More Compliance Chiefs Get Direct Line to Boss," *The Wall Street Journal*, January 15, 2014, http://online.wsj.com/news/articles/SB10001424052702303330204579250723925965180 (accessed May 9, 2014).
92. Treviño and Nelson, *Managing Business Ethics*, 212.
93. Beverly Geber, "The Right and Wrong of Ethics Offices," *Training*, October 1995, 102–118.
94. Janet P. Near and Marcia P. Miceli, "Effective Whistle-Blowing," *Academy of Management Review* 20, no. 3 (1995), 679–708.
95. Jene G. James, "Whistle-Blowing: Its Moral Justification," in Peter Madsen and Jay M. Shafritz, eds., *Essentials of Business Ethics* (New York: Meridian Books, 1990), 160–190; and Janet P. Near, Terry Morehead Dworkin, and Marcia P. Miceli, "Explaining the Whistle-Blowing Process: Suggestions from Power Theory and Justice Theory," *Organization Science* 4 (1993), 393–411.
96. Christine Seib and Alexandra Frean, "Lehman Whistleblower Lost Job Month After Speaking Out," *The Times*, March 17, 2010.
97. Christian Berthelsen, "Whistleblower to Get Big Payment in Bank of New York–Virginia Deal," *The Wall Street Journal*, November 9, 2012, C1.
98. Schwartz, "Developing and Sustaining an Ethical Corporate Culture."
99. "Setting the Standard," Lockheed Martin's website, http://www.lockheedmartin.com/exeth/html/code/code.html (accessed August 7, 2001).
100. Schwartz, "Developing and Sustaining an Ethical Corporate Culture."
101. Katharina Bart, "UBS Lays Out Employee Ethics Code," *The Wall Street Journal*, January 12, 2010, http://online.wsj.com/article/SB10001424052748704586504574653901865050062.html?KEYWORDS=%22Ubs+lays+out+employee+ethics+code%22 (accessed January 15, 2010).
102. Carl Anderson, "Values-Based Management," *Academy of Management Executive* 11, no. 4 (1997), 25–46.
103. Ronald E. Berenbeim, *Corporate Ethics Practices* (New York: The Conference Board, 1992).
104. Jerry G. Kreuze, Zahida Luqmani, and Mushtaq Luqmani, "Shades of Gray," *Internal Auditor*, April 2001, 48.
105. Vanessa Fuhrmans, "Amazon Acts on German Controversy; Online Retailer Cuts Ties with Security Firm After a Television Documentary on Working Conditions," *The Wall Street Journal*, February 19, 2013, B3.
106. Jens Hansegard, Tripti Lahiri, and Chritina Passariello, "Retailers' Dilemma: To Ax or Help Fix Bad Factories," *The Wall Street Journal*, May 28, 2011, http://online.wsj.com/article/SB10001424127887323336104578501143973731324.html (accessed September 5, 2013).
107. S. C. Schneider, "National vs. Corporate Culture: Implications for Human Resource Management," *Human Resource Management*, Summer 1988, 239; and Terence Jackson, "Cultural Values and Management Ethics: A 10-Nation Study," *Human Relations* 54, no. 10 (2001), 1267–1302.
108. K. Matthew Gilley, Christopher J. Robertson, and Tim C. Mazur, "The Bottom-Line Benefits of Ethics Code Commitment," *Business Horizons* 53 (2010), 31–37.
109. Adapted by Dorothy Marcic from Allayne Barrilleaux Pizzolatto's "Ethical Management: An Exercise in Understanding Its Power," *Journal of Management Education* 17, no. 1 (February 1993), 107–109.
110. Based on Gary Yukl, "Consolidated Products," in *Leadership in Organizations*, 4th ed. (Englewood Cliffs, NJ: Prentice-Hall, 1998), 66–67; John M. Champion and John H. James, "Implementing Strategic Change," in *Critical Incidents in Management: Decision and Policy Issues*, 6th ed. (Homewood, IL: Irwin, 1989), 138–140; and William C. Symonds, "Where Paternalism Equals Good Business," *BusinessWeek*, July 20, 1998, 16E4, 16E6.

11 | Innovation and Change

Learning Objectives

After reading this chapter you should be able to:

1. Describe the types of strategic change.
2. Explain the necessary elements for successful organizational change.
3. Understand techniques for encouraging technology change.
4. Discuss the horizontal coordination model for new products.
5. Demonstrate how innovation speed provides competitive advantage.
6. Describe the dual-core approach to organizational change.
7. Explain the techniques for bringing about culture change in organizations.
8. Use techniques for overcoming resistance to change.

Before reading this chapter, please check whether you agree or disagree with each of the following statements:

1 The most important aspect for creating an innovative company is requiring people to come up with new ideas.

I AGREE _____   I DISAGREE _____

2 Asking customers what they want is the best way to create new products that will be successful in the marketplace.

I AGREE _____   I DISAGREE _____

3 Changing a company's culture is probably one of the hardest jobs a manager can undertake.

I AGREE _____   I DISAGREE _____

Online retailer Zappos is building a smaller headquarters to encourage employee collisions. It's not an attempt to spark fights or increase trips to the emergency room. Managers are hoping to spur more collaboration and information transfer by having people bump into each other and start spontaneous conversations. Researchers studying patterns of interaction among research scientists at the University of Michigan found that when the scientists shared the same buildings and overlapped in their daily walking patterns, they were much more likely to collaborate. In fact, collaborations increased by up to 20 percent for every 100 feet of "zonal overlap." Zappos managers decided to build a smaller headquarters, allotting about 100 square feet per worker instead of 150 square feet. Break rooms will be "really small, so people literally collide," said Patrick Olson, senior manager of campus development for Zappos.[1]

Zappos isn't alone in its efforts to try to engineer serendipity into the workplace. Years ago, Steve Jobs designed the headquarters for Pixar with centrally located bathrooms so people would run into each other.[2] AT&T, Plantronics, Twitter, Capgemini, and many other companies have sent teams to co-working spaces, where they work alongside people from other companies.[3] Many people think the way to encourage chance encounters and spur innovation is to make companies more like cities. Zappos is opening its lobby as a free co-working space so people can mingle with employees from other companies and visitors, like in a hotel lobby. "Those ground floor connection points, we see that as magic," Olson says.[4]

Companies and managers are searching for any innovation edge they can find. Every company faces a challenge in keeping up with changes in the external environment. New discoveries, new inventions, and new approaches quickly replace standard ways of doing things. Tremendous leaps in technology have revolutionized the way we live. Many of us now text and tweet and "friend" people online more often than we interact with them face to face. The pace of change is revealed in the fact that the parents of today's college-age students grew up without iPads, social networking, global positioning systems, streaming video, and even the Internet. As teenagers, they couldn't have imagined communicating instantly with people around the world, carrying all their favorite music with them wherever they went, or downloading an entire book onto a device as small as a notepad. High-tech industries seem to change every nanosecond, so companies such as Apple, Google, Cisco, Facebook, Intel, and Twitter are continually innovating to keep up. But companies in all industries face greater pressures for innovation today. Bob Jordon, executive vice president and chief commercial officer for Southwest Airlines, spoke for managers all over the world when he said, "We have to innovate to survive."[5]

Purpose of This Chapter

This chapter explores how organizations change and how managers direct the innovation and change process. First we look at how difficult innovation can be and discuss the challenge of disruptive innovation. The next section describes the four types of change—technology, product, structure, people—occurring in organizations, and how to manage change successfully. The chapter then describes the organization structure and management approach for facilitating each type of change. Management techniques for influencing both the creation and implementation of change are also covered. The final section of the chapter looks at implementation techniques managers can use to successfully implement change and innovation.

The Strategic Role of Change

If there is one theme or lesson that emerges from previous chapters, it is that organizations must run fast to keep up with changes taking place all around them. Large organizations must find ways to act like small, flexible organizations. Manufacturing firms need to reach out for new smart manufacturing technology and service firms for new information technology (IT). Today's organizations must keep themselves open to continuous innovation, not only to prosper but merely to survive in a world of disruptive change and increasingly stiff competition.

Innovate or Fail

Powerful environmental forces drive the need for major organizational change.[6] Technological advances, changing markets, increasing government regulation, e-business and mobile commerce, shifting social attitudes, global economic turbulence, social media and the information revolution, and the growing power of Arab countries and the BRIC nations (Brazil, Russia, India, and China) have brought about an uncertain globalized economy that affects every business, from the largest to the smallest, creating more threats as well as more opportunities.

Organizations can respond to environmental shifts with three types of change and innovation.[7] *Episodic change* is what many long-time managers are accustomed to. This type of change occurs occasionally, with periods of relative stability, and managers can respond with technical, product, or structural innovations as needed. Most organizations today, however, experience *continuous change* because of a rapidly shifting environment. This type of change occurs frequently, with fewer and shorter periods of stability. Managers embrace change as an ongoing organizational process, using research and development (R&D) to build a flow of new product and service innovations to meet shifting needs. In many industries today, the environment has become so turbulent that managers encounter *disruptive change and innovation.*

EXHIBIT 11.1
Stages of Disruptive Innovation

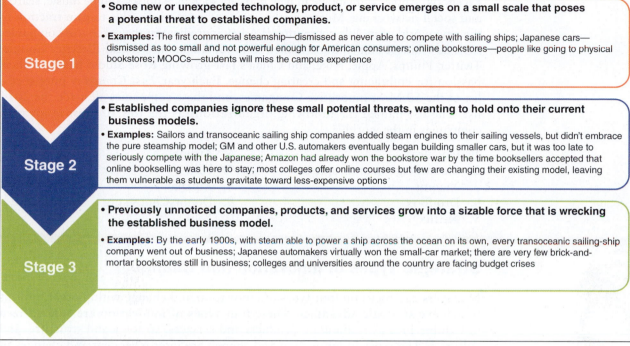

Source: Based on Clayton M. Christensen and Michael B. Horn, "Innovation Imperative: Change Everything," *The New York Times*, November 1, 2013, http://www.nytimes.com/2013/11/03/education/edlife/online-education-as-an-agent-of-transformation.html?_r=0 (accessed May 15, 2014); and Melissa A. Korn, "Coursera Defends MOOCs as Road to Learning," *The Wall Street Journal*, May 15, 2013, B5.

As shown in Exhibit 11.1, **disruptive innovation** refers to innovations in products or services that typically start small and end up completely replacing an existing product or service technology for producers and consumers. Companies that initiate a disruptive innovation typically win big; companies affected by a disruptive innovation may be put out of business. Established companies typically ignore the initial small innovation because they want to hang onto their established business models. Most students probably aren't old enough to remember how American car companies poked fun at the first automobiles from Japan, but GM and Ford managers stopped laughing when cars from Toyota and Subaru began stealing market share. Another disruptive innovation, the DVD, all but wiped out the videotape industry, and now streaming video is threatening the same fate for DVDs. Digital cameras appear to be virtually eliminating the photographic film industry and the smartphone is threatening the compact digital camera. People prefer to use their smartphones for snapshots because they can easily share the photos on social networks. Sales of point-and-shoot cameras continue to fall.[8] MOOCs, which stands for *massive, open, online classes*, could become a disruptive innovation to the traditional and expensive classroom-based form of delivering courses for a college education. Coursera, a Mountain View, California, company, has 3.5 million registered users for its 370 mostly free online college courses.[9] Yet traditional colleges are making the same mistake that the U.S. auto manufacturers made. Many of them are offering online courses, but they aren't significantly changing their existing business model to save students time and money.[10] Many disruptive innovations come from small entrepreneurial firms like Coursera.

Innovation, and particularly coping with disruptive innovation, is not easy. Microsoft, once considered a technology leader, has had trouble competing with Facebook, Apple, and Google in new markets such as e-books, online music, search, and social networking. Moreover, the company hasn't been able to gain traction in the new world of mobile computing.[11] A key ingredient in the success of companies such as Chinese smartphone maker Xiaomi, Amazon, General Electric, Google, Twitter, Philips, Apple, Nike, and China's fast-growing Rose Studio has been their passion for embracing and creating change. Each year, *Fast Company* publishes a list of the 50 Most Innovative Companies, and these companies all made the 2014 list. The list named the following organizations as the top 10 most innovative companies in the world:[12]

1. Google
2. Bloomberg Philanthropies
3. Xiaomi
4. DropBox
5. Netflix
6. Airbnb
7. Nike
8. ZipDial
9. DonorsChoose.org
10. Yelp

Strategic Types of Innovation and Change

Managers can focus on four types of innovation and change within organizations to achieve strategic advantage. These four types of innovation are summarized in Exhibit 11.2 as technology, products and services, strategy and structure, and culture.[13] The types of innovation and change are interdependent and changes in one area often require changes in other areas as well. A new product may require changes in the production technology, or a change in structure may require new employee skills. For example, when Shenandoah Life Insurance Company acquired new computer technology to process claims, the technology was not fully used until clerks were restructured into teams of five to seven members that were compatible with the technology. The structural change was an outgrowth of the technology change. Organizations are interdependent systems, and changing one part often has implications for other parts of the organization.

EXHIBIT 11.2
The Four Types of
Innovation and Change

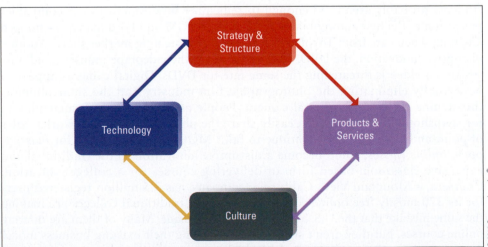

© 2016 Cengage Learning®

Technology innovations are changes in an organization's production process, including its knowledge and skill base, that enable distinctive competence. These changes are designed to make production more efficient or to produce greater volume. Innovations in technology involve the techniques for making products or services. They include work methods, equipment, and workflow. For example, Hammond's Candies saves hundreds of thousands of dollars a year by implementing technology changes suggested by employees. One example was tweaking a machine gear that reduced the number of employees needed on an assembly line from five to four. Another idea was a new way to package candy canes that would protect them from getting broken while en route to stores.[14]

Product and service innovations pertain to the product or service outputs of an organization. New products include small adaptations of existing products or entirely new product lines. New products and services are normally designed to increase the market share or to develop new markets, customers, or clients. Elkay Manufacturing introduced an adaptation of an existing product with its EZH2O water fountain.

✅ IN PRACTICE

Elkay Manufacturing

You probably remember it from school. There might be one outside your classroom right now: the water fountain. It hasn't changed much for decades. Then, a few years ago, managers at Elkay Manufacturing started noticing what they call "the airport dance": people doing a shuffle as they tried to tilt their bottles at the right angle to fill them at the water fountain without splashing water all over themselves.

Elkay began redesigning the water fountain to create a "bottle filling station" instead. About half of the water people consume these days comes from taps, including drinking fountains. Elkay managers wanted a fountain where people could fill their bottles without ever even touching the fountain, to avoid the concern many people have about germs. Moreover, they thought filling a 16-ounce bottle should take less than 10 seconds. Early in the project, one engineer said that wasn't possible. Another engineer, who joined Elkay from an auto parts company, found a way to speed up the flow. The result was a machine that fills a 16-ounce bottle in about 5 seconds if the water is at room temperature or a few seconds longer if it goes through refrigeration pipes. The traditional water fountain needed at least 20 seconds.

The addition of a digital counter on Elkay's first EZH20 model ended up helping "make this thing go viral," said one manager who had originally thought the digital counter was a dumb idea. College students liked tracking how many plastic bottles were being kept out of landfills. Some held intra-campus competitions to see who could reuse the most bottles. Incoming freshmen at Muhlenberg College in Allentown, Pennsylvania, which has installed 49 of the new EZH20 stations, receive a free stainless steel water bottle. The college says sales of bottled water have fallen 90 percent. Students say that's at least 1.4 million plastic bottles that have been kept out of landfills.[15]

Other companies have also introduced new types of water fountains designed to fill water bottles. Elkay says its new fountains have been installed in hundreds of colleges and universities and at least 15 airports including Chicago's O'Hare and New York's LaGuardia.

Strategy and structure innovations pertain to the administrative domain in an organization. The administrative domain involves the supervision and management of the organization. These innovations include changes in organization structure, strategic management, policies, reward systems, labor relations, coordination devices,

management information and control systems, and accounting and budgeting systems. Strategy, structure, and system changes are usually top-down—that is, mandated by top management—whereas product and technology changes often come from the bottom up. At StockPot, a division within the Campbell Soup Company that makes fresh refrigerated soup for the food service industry, former general manager Ed Carolan and his management team changed the strategy to focus more on large grocery retailers. To make the strategy successful, they identified a new set of key performance metrics to track how effectively the company was meeting goals of competitive costs, high quality, and great service. The changes were highly effective for improving the division's financial performance.[16] An example of a top-down structure change comes from ICU Medical Inc., where Dr. George Lopez, founder and CEO, made the decision to implement self-directed teams, even though some managers and employees at first hated the idea. This change also proved to be successful in the long run.[17]

Culture innovations refer to changes in the values, attitudes, expectations, beliefs, abilities, and behavior of employees. Culture innovations pertain to changes in how employees think; these are changes in mindset rather than technology, structure, or products. Washington, D.C. Metropolitan Police chief Cathy Lanier is changing the culture of the department to focus on preventing crime as much as fighting crime. "We went from beating people up, wrestling them, handcuffing them, to 'How do we prevent these things from happening?'" said Al Durham, assistant police chief in Washington, D.C. "Even as a patrol cop, if you work hard, if you focus, you can make major changes in people's lives every single day," Lanier says.[18]

Culture change can be particularly difficult because people don't change their attitudes and beliefs easily. Culture was discussed in detail in the previous chapter, and we will talk more about how to change culture later in this chapter.

Elements for Successful Change

Regardless of the type or scope of change, there are identifiable stages of innovation, which generally occur as a sequence of events, though innovation stages may overlap.[19] In the research literature on innovation, **organizational change** is considered the adoption of a new idea or behavior by an organization.[20] **Organizational innovation**, in contrast, is the adoption of an idea or behavior that is new to the organization's industry, market, or general environment.[21] The first organization to introduce a new product is considered the innovator, and organizations that copy it are considered to adopt changes. For purposes of managing change, however, the terms *innovation* and *change* will be used interchangeably because the **change process** within organizations tends to be identical whether a change is early or late with respect to other organizations in the environment. Innovations typically are assimilated into an organization through a series of steps or elements. Organization members first become aware of a possible innovation, evaluate its appropriateness, and then evaluate and choose the idea.[22] The required elements of successful change are summarized in Exhibit 11.3. For a change to be successfully implemented, managers must make sure each element occurs in the organization. If one of the elements is missing, the change process will fail.

EXHIBIT 11.3
Sequence of Elements for Successful Change

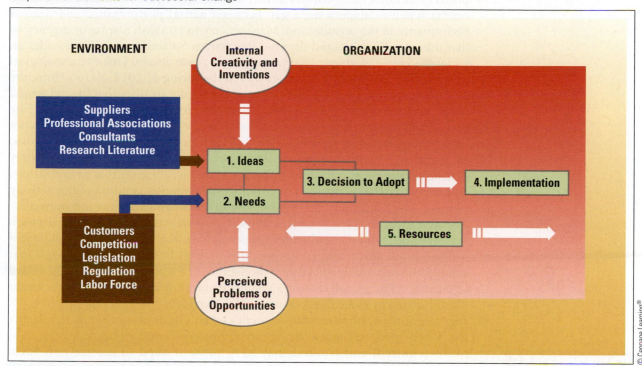

© Cengage Learning®

1. *Ideas.* Change is an outward expression of ideas. No company can remain competitive without new ideas.[23] An idea is a new way of doing things. It may be a new product or service, a new management concept, or a new procedure for working together in the organization. Ideas can come from within or from outside the organization. Internal creativity is a dramatic aspect of organizational change. **Creativity** is the generation of novel ideas that may meet perceived needs or respond to opportunities. For example, an employee at Boardroom Inc., a publisher of books and newsletters, came up with the idea of cutting the dimensions of the company's books by a quarter inch. Managers learned that the smaller size would reduce shipping rates, and implementation of the idea led to annual savings of more than $500,000.[24] Some techniques for spurring internal creativity are to increase the diversity within the organization, make sure employees have plenty of opportunities to interact with people different from themselves, give people time and freedom for experimentation, and support risk-taking and learning.[25] Eli Lilly, the Indianapolis-based pharmaceutical company, holds "failure parties" to commemorate brilliant, efficient scientific work that nevertheless resulted in failure. The company's scientists are encouraged to take risks and look for alternative uses for failed drugs. Lilly's osteoporosis drug Evista was a failed contraceptive. Strattera, which treats attention deficit/hyperactivity disorder, had been unsuccessful as an antidepressant. The blockbuster impotence drug Viagra was originally developed to treat severe heart pain.[26]

2. *Need.* Ideas are generally not seriously considered unless there is a perceived problem or crisis that provides a need for change. A perceived need for change occurs when managers see a gap between actual performance and desired performance in the organization. Managers try to establish a sense of urgency so that others will understand the need for change. Sometimes a crisis provides an undoubted sense of urgency. Sony, for example, once defined Japan's technological expertise but is now fighting for its life. In the spring of 2012, Kazuo Hirai, the new CEO, stood before the company and outlined a strategy that he said would return the company to profitability. "The time for Sony to change is now," he said. "I believe Sony can change." Unfortunately, so far, his call for change has not been heeded and Sony continues to flounder.[27] In many cases, there is no crisis, so managers have to recognize a need and communicate it to others.[28] A study of innovativeness in industrial firms, for example, suggests that organizations that encourage close attention to customers and market conditions and actively support entrepreneurial activity produce more ideas and are more innovative.[29]

3. *Decision to adopt.* The decision to adopt occurs when managers or other decision makers choose to go ahead with a proposed idea. Key managers and employees need to be in agreement to support the change. For a major organizational change, the decision might require the signing of a legal document by the board of directors. For a small change, a middle manager or lower-level manager might be authorized to make the decision to adopt an idea.

4. *Implementation.* Implementation occurs when organization members actually use a new idea, technique, or behavior. Materials and equipment may have to be acquired, and workers may have to be trained to use the new idea. Implementation is a very important step because without it, previous steps are to no avail. Implementation of change is often the most difficult part of the change process. Until people use the new idea, no change has actually taken place.

5. *Resources.* Human energy and activity are required to bring about change. Change does not happen on its own; it requires time and resources, for both creating and implementing a new idea. Employees have to provide energy to see both the need and the idea to meet that need. Someone must develop a proposal and provide the time and effort to implement it. Most innovations go beyond ordinary budget allocations and require special funding. Some companies use task forces, as described in Chapter 3, to focus resources on a change. Others set up seed funds or venture funds that employees with promising ideas can tap into. At Eli Lilly, a "blue sky fund" pays researchers for working on projects that don't appear to make immediate commercial sense.[30]

As an organization manager, keep these guidelines in mind:

Make sure every change undertaken has a definite need, idea, adoption decision, implementation strategy, and resources. Avoid failure by not proceeding until each element is accounted for.

One point about Exhibit 11.3 is especially important. Needs and ideas are listed simultaneously at the beginning of the change sequence. Either may occur first. Many organizations adopted the computer, for example, because it seemed a promising idea for improving efficiency. The search for a vaccine against the HIV virus, on the other hand, was stimulated by a severe need. Whether the need or the idea occurs first, for the change to be accomplished, each of the steps in Exhibit 11.3 must be completed.

Technology Change

In today's business world, any company that isn't continually developing, acquiring, or adapting new technology will likely be out of business in a few years. Managers can create the conditions to encourage technology innovations. However, organizations face a contradiction when it comes to technology change because the conditions that promote new ideas are not generally the best for implementing those ideas for routine production. An innovative organization is characterized by flexibility and empowered employees and the absence of rigid work rules.[31] As discussed earlier in this book, an organic, free-flowing organization is typically associated with change and is considered the best organization form for adapting to a chaotic environment. Complete the questionnaire in this chapter's "How Do You Fit the Design?" to see if you have characteristics associated with innovativeness.

The flexibility of an organic organization is attributed to people's freedom to be creative and introduce new ideas. Organic organizations encourage a bottom-up innovation process. Ideas bubble up from middle- and lower-level employees because they have the freedom to propose ideas and to experiment. A mechanistic structure, in contrast, stifles innovation with its emphasis on rules and regulations, but it is often the best structure for efficiently producing routine products. The challenge for managers is to create both organic and mechanistic conditions within the organization to achieve both innovation and efficiency. To attain both aspects of technological change, many organizations use an ambidextrous approach.

HOW DO YOU FIT THE DESIGN?

ARE YOU INNOVATIVE?

Think about your current life. Indicate whether each of the following items is Mostly True or Mostly False for you.

	Mostly True	Mostly False
1. I am always seeking new ways to do things.	_____	_____
2. I consider myself creative and original in my thinking and behavior.	_____	_____
3. I rarely trust new gadgets until I see whether they work for people around me.	_____	_____
4. In a group or at work I am often skeptical of new ideas.	_____	_____
5. I typically buy new foods, gear, and other innovations before other people do.	_____	_____
6. I like to spend time trying out new things.	_____	_____
7. My behavior influences others to try new things.	_____	_____
8. Among my co-workers, I will be among the first to try out a new idea or method.	_____	_____

Scoring: To compute your score on the Personal Innovativeness scale, add the number of Mostly True answers to items 1, 2, 5, 6, 7, and 8 and the Mostly False answers to items 3 and 4.

Interpretation: *Personal Innovativeness* reflects the awareness of a need to innovate and a readiness to try new things. Innovativeness is also thought of as the degree to which a person adopts innovations earlier than other people in the peer group. Innovativeness is considered a positive quality for people in creative companies, creative departments, venture teams, or corporate entrepreneurship. A score of 6–8 indicates that you are very innovative and likely are one of the first people to adopt changes. A score of 4–5 would suggest that you are average or slightly above average in innovativeness compared to others. A score of 0–3 means that you may prefer the tried and true and hence are not excited about new ideas or innovations. As a manager, a high score suggests you will emphasize innovation and change.

Source: Based on H. Thomas Hurt, Katherine Joseph, and Chester D. Cook, "Scales for the Measurement of Innovativeness," *Human Communication Research* 4, no. 1 (1977), 58–65; and John E. Ettlie and Robert D. O'Keefe, "Innovative Attitudes, Values, and Intentions in Organizations," *Journal of Management Studies* 19, no. 2 (1982), 163–182.

The Ambidextrous Approach

Recent thinking has refined the idea of organic versus mechanistic structures with respect to innovation creation versus innovation utilization. Organic characteristics such as decentralization and employee freedom are excellent for initiating ideas, but these same conditions often make it hard to implement a change because employees are less likely to comply. Employees can ignore the innovation because of decentralization and a generally loose structure.

How does an organization solve this dilemma? One remedy is for the organization to use an **ambidextrous approach** —to incorporate structures and management processes that are appropriate to both the creation and the implementation of innovation.[32] Ambidexterity has become a hot topic in the field of organizational studies over the last several years.[33] Another way to think of the ambidextrous approach is to look at the organization design elements that are important for *exploring* new ideas versus the design elements that are most suitable for *exploiting* current capabilities.[34] Exploration means encouraging creativity and developing new ideas, whereas exploitation means implementing those ideas to produce routine products. The organization can be designed to behave in an organic way for exploring new ideas and in a mechanistic way to exploit and use the ideas. Exhibit 11.4 illustrates how one department is structured organically to explore and develop new ideas and another department is structured mechanistically for routine implementation of innovations. Research indicates that organizations that use an ambidextrous approach by designing for both exploration and exploitation perform better and are significantly more successful in launching innovative new products or services.[35]

For example, a study of long-established Japanese companies such as Honda and Canon that have succeeded in breakthrough innovations found that these companies use an ambidextrous approach.[36] To develop ideas related to a new technology, the companies assign teams of young staff members who are not entrenched in the "old way of doing things" to work on the project. The teams are headed by an esteemed elder and are charged with doing whatever is needed to develop new ideas and products, even if it means breaking rules that are important in the larger organization for implementing the new ideas.

A recent study by Booz & Company emphasizes the two parts of the innovation process by looking at what they call *idea generation* and *idea conversion*, which roughly correspond to exploration and exploitation. Idea generation refers to coming

EXHIBIT 11.4
Division of Labor in the Ambidextrous Organization

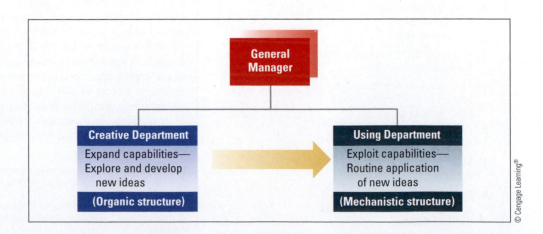

© Cengage Learning®

up with new ideas for products or services; idea conversion means the efforts to convert those ideas to product development processes. Interestingly, 46 percent of companies in the Booz study see themselves as doing both stages poorly, and only 25 percent see themselves as doing both stages well.[37]

The Bottom-Up Approach

Innovative companies recognize that many useful ideas come from the people who are daily doing the work, serving the customers, fighting off the competition, and figuring out how best to get their jobs done. Thus, companies that want to support innovation implement a variety of mechanisms, systems, and processes that encourage a bottom-up flow of ideas and make sure they get heard and acted upon by top executives.[38] Google lets employees try hundreds of small experiments at any given time. The company intentionally puts out imperfect or unfinished products to test the response and get ideas for how to perfect them.[39] Many successful innovations start with small experiments rather than with grand ideas. Mike Hall, CEO of Borrego Solar Systems, holds internal "innovation challenge" contests on the company intranet to get his shy, introverted engineers to speak up with their ideas for improving the business. Employees vote on their favorites and the winner takes home a cash prize. One idea that was quickly implemented was using software that enables sales and engineering teams to collaborate.[40]

Other companies use an approach sometimes referred to as "innovation communities." At Intuit, managers sponsor Design for Delight (D4D) forums, typically attended by more than 1,000 employees. Two employees who had been at Intuit for only a few months came up with the idea of an online social network for the D4D initiative. In the first year, the network generated 32 ideas that made it to market.[41] Japanese pharmaceutical firm Eisai Company has held more than 400 innovation community forums since 2005 to focus on specific healthcare related issues. One idea that is now on the market in Japan is technology for dispensing medications in a jelly-like substance that Alzheimer's patients can easily swallow.[42] Taco Bell headquarters staff gathered for an all-day idea session to consider new product concepts that eventually led to the Doritos Locos Taco, which triggered a 13 percent jump in sales for the company and required the chain to hire 15,000 additional staff members.

Taco Bell's Doritos Locos Taco (DLT) began with a trip to Home Depot. Staff members had to buy paint-spray guns to blast Doritos flavoring onto taco shells. But after prototype development, consumer taste tests were disappointing. "It was a total buzzkill," said Steve Gomez, Taco Bell's food innovation expert.

Teams from Taco Bell and Frito-Lay spent months trying to get the right formula and technology so that the shells wouldn't break but would still snap and crunch. More than two years of working day and night, and 40 recipes later, the DLT team was ready for a testing in a handful of restaurants. The pressure was intense. One of the early reviews said, "It's everything I expected and more." When the DLT went nationwide, it was a smash hit, with millions of tacos sold in the first week alone. After Nacho Cheese and Cool Ranch, a spicy Doritos Flamas-flavored taco is next up. "It's not just a product; it's now a platform," said Taco Bell's CEO Greg Creed.[43]

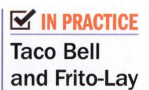

IN PRACTICE

Taco Bell and Frito-Lay

Taco Bell is also mulling over other possibilities for new products, and is considering crowdsourcing the next iteration of the DLT. Frito-Lay has brought out Taco Bell flavored Doritos. Many of today's successful innovators bring in people from outside the organization, as Taco Bell did with Frito-Lay and is considering doing with crowdsourcing.

Just as important as creating ideas is turning them into action. "There's nothing worse for morale than when employees feel like their ideas go nowhere," says Larry Bennett, a professor of entrepreneurship. At Borrego Solar Systems, the CEO assigns each idea he wants to implement to an executive sponsor, and employees can track the progress of implementation on the intranet.[44]

Techniques for Encouraging Technology Change

Some specific techniques used by companies to maintain an ambidextrous approach and encourage a bottom-up flow of ideas are switching structures, separate creative departments, venture teams, corporate entrepreneurship, and collaborative teams.

Switching Structures. **Switching structures** means an organization creates an organic structure when such a structure is needed for the initiation of new ideas.[45] Some of the ways organizations have switched structures to achieve the ambidextrous approach are as follows:

- Mike Lawrie, CEO of the London-based software company Misys, created a separate unit for Misys Open Source Solutions, a venture aimed at creating a potentially disruptive innovation in the healthcare industry. Lawrie wanted creative people to have the time and resources they needed to work on new software that holds the promise of seamless data exchange among hospitals, physicians, insurers, and others involved in the healthcare system. After creation in the new venture, implementation of the new ideas, where routine and precision are important, occurs within the more mechanistic, regular organization.[46]
- Managers at Gardetto's, a snack-food business acquired by General Mills in 1999, would send small teams of workers to Eureka Ranch for two and a half days of "fun and freedom." Part of each day would be for play, such as Nerf gun battles; then the teams would participate in brainstorming exercises with the idea of generating as many new ideas as possible by the end of the day. After two and a half days, the group returned to the regular organizational structure to put the best of the ideas into action.[47]
- The NUMMI plant, a Toyota–GM joint venture in Fremont, California, that operated from 1984 to 2010, created a separate, organically organized, cross-functional subunit, called the Pilot Team, to design production processes for new car and truck models. When the model moved into production, workers returned to their regular jobs on the shop floor.[48]

Each of these organizations found creative ways to be ambidextrous, establishing organic conditions for developing new ideas in the midst of more mechanistic conditions for implementing and using those ideas.

Creative Departments. In many large organizations the initiation of innovation is assigned to separate **creative departments**.[49] Staff departments such as research and development, engineering, design, and systems analysis create changes for adoption in other departments. Departments that initiate change are organically structured to facilitate the generation of new ideas and techniques. Departments that use those innovations tend to have a mechanistic structure more suitable for efficient production.

One example of a creative department is the research lab at Oksuka Pharmaceutical Company. To get the kind of creative spirit that is willing to try new things and look for the unexpected, Oksuka's president Tatsuo Higuchi says its research labs "put a high value on weird people."[50] However, in the department that manufactures drugs, where routine and precision is important, a pharmaceutical company would prefer to have less-unusual people who are comfortable following rules and standard procedures.

Another type of creative department is the **idea incubator**, an increasingly popular way to facilitate the development of new ideas within the organization. An idea incubator provides a safe harbor where ideas from employees throughout the organization can be developed without interference from company bureaucracy or politics.[51] Companies as diverse as Boeing, Adobe Systems, Yahoo!, Ziff-Davis, and UPS are using incubators to support the development of creative ideas.

Venture Teams. **Venture teams** are a technique used to give free rein to creativity within organizations. Venture teams are often given a separate location and facilities so they are not constrained by organizational procedures. A venture team is like a small company within a large company. Numerous organizations have used the venture team concept to free creative people from the bureaucracy of a large corporation.[52] In late 2003, Amazon began setting up satellite locations in geographic regions with pools of technical talent to work on specific, isolated projects. They called these offices *remote development centers*. The idea was to harness the energy and flexibility of a start-up and minimize the need for communication with the larger company. The first development center tackled the problem of indexing and searching Amazon's growing product catalog.[53]

One type of venture team is called a *skunkworks*.[54] A **skunkworks** is a separate, small, informal, highly autonomous, and often secretive group that focuses on breakthrough ideas for the business. The original skunkworks was created by Lockheed Martin more than 50 years ago and is still in operation. The essence of a skunkworks is that highly talented people are given the time and freedom to let creativity reign. The Google X lab is a top-secret lab in an undisclosed location where engineers are working on shoot-for-the-moon ideas like driverless cars, space elevators that can collect information from or haul things into space, and robots that can attend a conference for you while you stay at the office. This skunkworks was so secretive that until *The New York Times* wrote about it, even many of Google's employees didn't know it existed.[55]

A variation of the venture team concept is the **new-venture fund**, which provides financial resources for employees to develop new ideas, products, or businesses. Royal Dutch Shell puts 10 percent of its R&D budget into the GameChanger program, which provides seed money for innovation projects that are highly ambitious, radical, or long term and would get lost in the larger product development system.[56]

Corporate Entrepreneurship. Corporate entrepreneurship attempts to develop an internal entrepreneurial spirit, philosophy, and structure that will produce a higher-than-average number of innovations. Corporate entrepreneurship may involve the use of creative departments and new-venture teams, but it also attempts to release the creative energy of all employees in the organization. The most successful companies over the long term are ones in which innovation is an everyday way of thinking, an ongoing process rather than a one-time event. This chapter's BookMark describes some lessons from Pixar for how to keep people's creative juices flowing. ING Direct (now Capital One 360) built entrepreneurship into the corporate culture. The company's list of guiding principles includes the guideline, "We will never be finished." Managers want people to always be inventing what's next.[57]

BOOKMARK 11.0   HAVE YOU READ THIS BOOK?

Creativity Inc.: Overcoming the Unseen Forces That Stand in the Way of True Inspiration
By Ed Catmull

Pixar Animation Studios has put out some amazingly successful films. It is also an amazingly successful business. Moreover, Pixar's leaders have been credited with reinvigorating Disney Animation Studios, which was on its last legs when Pixar was bought by Disney in 2006. The management philosophy at Pixar, and now at Disney Animation Studios, is a radical one: Let the creative people have creative control, and financial success will follow. Ed Catmull, president and one of the co-founders of Pixar, wrote *Creativity Inc.* not only to explain how Pixar produced 14 box office hits in a row, but how any company can reboot employees' creative juices.

THE SOURCES OF PIXAR'S MAGIC
The book gives numerous tips for how to manage and motivate a creative workforce, based on what Catmull has learned from his experiences at Pixar.

- *Embrace New Experiences.* When Catmull was first recruited by George Lucas to work special effects images into live-action footage, the film editors at Lucasfilm resisted working with a computer. Only when John Lasseter was hired and brought his enthusiastic emphasis on storytelling to the organization did people begin to have a shift in mindset. To prevent the risk-averse repackaging of what worked well before, for example, teams do field research before every film. For *Ratatouille*, the film about a Parisian rat who wants to be a chef, a team went to Paris to eat, visit kitchens, talk to chefs, and even slosh through the Paris sewer system.
- *Encourage Everyone to Speak with Candor.* "A hallmark of a creative culture is that people feel free to share ideas, opinions, and criticisms," Catmull writes. Pixar's primary mechanism for ensuring candor is the Braintrust, a group of creative people who meet every few months and are expected to say whatever they think.

No one has any authority, and the director isn't obligated to follow any suggestions, but the results of putting smart, creative people together and encouraging them to speak candidly can be phenomenal. "Candor could not be more crucial to our creative process. Why? Because early on, all of our movies suck," Catmull writes. Pixar dares to attempt movies about talking toys, rats preparing food, and other off-the-wall themes, but it almost never gets them right on the first pass.

- *Give Everyone a Voice.* Pixar is focused on protecting creative people and giving them the autonomy they need to create. However, Catmull learned after *Toy Story* came out that the production managers had been very unhappy working on the film and were reluctant to sign up for the next one. This could seriously hurt the company. Catmull discovered that the production people felt that they were treated like second-class citizens by the artists. Surprised because no one had taken advantage of the "open door policy" to complain during filming, he called everyone together and said that anyone should feel free to talk to anyone else at any time, without fear of embarrassment or reprimand. "People talking directly to one another, then letting the manager find out later, was more efficient than trying to make sure that everything happened in the 'right' order and through the 'proper' channels," Catmull writes.

WHAT IS THE ROLE OF THE LEADER?
Leaders can miss a lot, Catmull says. It is partly because they are so busy, but also because everyone has blind spots that become more pronounced as they move higher in power and prestige. Leaders can't totally avoid this, he says, but they can be aware of it and remember that there is so much that they don't know. "The better approach," he says, "is to accept that we can't understand every facet of a complex environment and to focus, instead, on techniques to deal with combining different viewpoints."

Creativity Inc., by Ed Catmull, is published by Random House.

An important outcome of corporate entrepreneurship is to facilitate **idea champions**. These go by a variety of names, including *advocate, intrapreneur*, or *change agent*. Idea champions provide the time and energy to make things happen. They fight to overcome natural resistance to change and to convince others of the merit of a new idea.[58] Some companies are using the results of their social network analysis, as describe in Chapter 8, to pinpoint people who might have influence over colleagues and can help implement a new idea. HealthFitness Corporation, which provides corporate health services, for example, had invested $30 million in a new technology platform. Client expectations were high, but some employees weren't on board with the new idea. Managers identified 30 or so people with high influence and gave them extra insight into the project. With these people supporting the project and building positive buzz, the project was implemented much more smoothly.[59]

The importance of the idea champion is illustrated by a fascinating fact discovered by Texas Instruments: When TI reviewed 50 successful and unsuccessful technical projects, it discovered that every failure was characterized by the absence of a volunteer champion. There was no one who passionately believed in the idea, who pushed the idea through every obstacle to make it work. TI took this finding so seriously that now its number-one criterion for approving new technical projects is the presence of a zealous champion.[60] Similarly, at SRI International, a contract research and development firm, managers use the saying "no champion, no product, no exception."[61] Research confirms that successful new ideas are generally those that are backed by someone who believes in the idea wholeheartedly and is determined to convince others of its value. Numerous studies support the importance of idea champions as a factor in the success of new products.[62]

Companies encourage idea champions by providing freedom and slack time to creative people. Companies such as IBM, Texas Instruments, General Electric, and 3M allow employees to develop new technologies without company approval. Sometimes referred to as *bootlegging*, the unauthorized research often pays big dividends. The talking educational toy Speak & Spell was developed "under the table" at TI beginning in the 1970s. The product was a hit, but more importantly, it contained TI's first digital-signal processing-chip, which grew into an enormous, highly profitable business when cell phones and other portable devices came along years later.[63]

> **1** The most important aspect for creating an innovative company is requiring people to come up with new ideas.
>
> **ANSWER:** *Disagree.* New ideas are essential for innovation, but managers can't simply issue directives ordering people to come up with new ideas. Managers create the conditions that are conducive to both the creation of new ideas and their implementation. Organizing to sustain innovation is as important as organizing to spur creativity.

New Products and Services

Although the concepts just discussed are important to product and service as well as technology changes, other factors also need to be considered. In many ways, new products and services are a special case of innovation because they are used by customers outside the organization. Since new products are designed for sale in the environment, uncertainty about the suitability and success of an innovation is very high.

New Product Success Rate

Research has explored the enormous uncertainty associated with the development and sale of new products.[64] To understand what this uncertainty can mean to organizations, consider that Microsoft spent two years and hundreds of millions of dollars creating a new line of smartphones, called Kin One and Kin Two, and then pulled them from the market after less than two months because no one was buying. Even Google has struggled with new product development. The launch of Nexus Q, a black ball meant to stream video and music, was delayed and customers who had already ordered it received it free because it was deemed to be too expensive for the benefits. CNN named it one of the top 10 "tech fails" of 2012.[65] And remember Zune, Microsoft's music player designed to compete with the iPod? If you don't, that's fine; neither does anyone else.[66]

Products from companies in other industries can suffer the same fate. Coca-Cola invested $50 million in an advertising campaign for C2, a new cola that had half the calories and carbs but (supposedly) all the taste of regular Coke and was aimed at a market of 20- to 40-year-old men. The benefits weren't distinctive enough and the product flopped. P&G introduced a new product called "Scentstories" that looked like a CD player and emitted an air freshener every 30 minutes. Consumers were confused by the product and the marketing messages, thinking the product involved both music and scent.[67] McDonald's Arch Deluxe hamburger, designed to appeal to "adult tastes," flopped despite millions invested in research and development and a $100 million advertising campaign.[68] Developing and producing products that fail is a part of business in all industries. Toy companies introduce thousands of new products a year, and many of them fail. U.S. food companies put approximately 5,000 new products in supermarkets each year, but the failure rate of new food products is 70 to 80 percent.[69] Organizations take the risk because product innovation is one of the most important ways companies adapt to changes in markets, technologies, and competition.[70]

Although measuring the success of new products is tricky, a survey by the Product Development and Management Association (PDMA) sheds some light on the commercialization success rates of new products across a variety of industries.[71] PDMA compiled survey results from over 400 PDMA members. The findings about success rates are shown in Exhibit 11.5. On the average, only 28 percent of all projects undertaken in the R&D laboratories passed the testing stage, which

EXHIBIT 11.5
New Product Success Rates

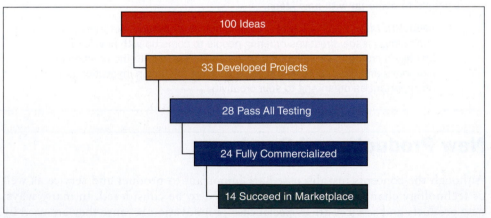

Source: Based on M. Adams and the Product Development and Management Association, "Comparative Performance Assessment Study 2004," available for purchase at http://www.pdma.org (search on CPAS). Results reported in Jeff Cope, "Lessons Learned—Commercialization Success Rates: A Brief Review," *RTI Tech Ventures* newsletter 4, no. 4 (December 2007).

means all technical problems were solved and the projects moved on to production. Less than one-fourth of all product ideas (24 percent) were fully marketed and commercialized, and only 14 percent achieved economic success.[72]

Reasons for New Product Success

The next question to be considered is: Why are some products more successful than others? Recent research at the Massachusetts Institute of Technology (MIT) suggests that keeping research and manufacturing close together helps companies be more innovative and more successful with their innovations. General Electric custom-built a large manufacturing facility in upstate New York to be near its research campus, where a new secret battery technology was being invented. The idea was to knit together design, prototyping, manufacturing, testing, and production for uses of the new battery technology.[73] Other studies indicate that innovation success is related to collaboration between technical and marketing departments. Successful new products and services seem to be technologically sound and also carefully tailored to customer needs.[74] A study called Project SAPPHO examined 17 pairs of new product innovations, with one success and one failure in each pair, and concluded the following:

1. Successful innovating companies had a much better understanding of customer needs and paid much more attention to marketing.
2. Successful innovating companies made more effective use of outside technology and outside advice, even though they did more work in-house.
3. Top management support in the successful innovating companies was from people who were more senior and had greater authority.

Thus there is a distinct pattern of tailoring innovations to customer needs, making effective use of technology, and having influential top managers support the project. These ideas taken together indicate that the effective design for new product innovation is associated with horizontal coordination across departments.

Horizontal Coordination Model

The organization design for achieving new product innovation involves three components—departmental specialization, boundary spanning, and horizontal coordination. These components are similar to the horizontal coordination mechanisms discussed in Chapter 3, such as teams, task forces, and project managers, and the differentiation and integration ideas discussed in Chapter 4. Exhibit 11.6 illustrates these components in the **horizontal coordination model**.

Specialization. The key departments in new product development are R&D, marketing, and production. The specialization component means that the personnel in all three of these departments are highly competent at their own tasks. The three departments are differentiated from each other and have skills, goals, and attitudes appropriate for their specialized functions.

Boundary Spanning. This component means each department involved with new products has excellent linkage with relevant sectors in the external environment. R&D personnel are linked to professional associations and to colleagues in other R&D departments. They are aware of recent scientific developments. Marketing personnel are closely linked to customer needs. They listen to what customers have to say, and they analyze competitor products and

EXHIBIT 11.6
Horizontal Coordination Model for New Product Innovations

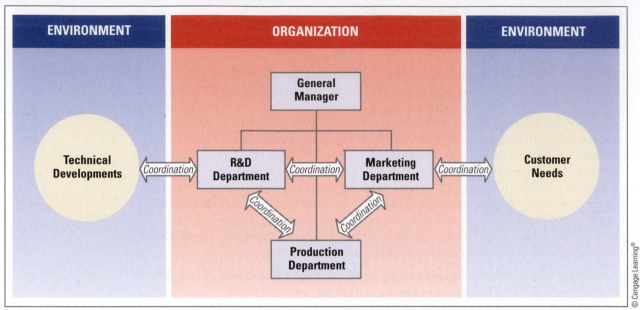

© Cengage Learning®

suggestions by distributors. One study compared companies with good product development track records to those with poor track records and found that the best performers keep in close touch with customers throughout the product development process and carefully research what customers want and need.[75] Kimberly-Clark had amazing success with Huggies Pull-Ups because marketing researchers worked closely with customers in their own homes and recognized the emotional appeal of pull-on diapers for toddlers. By the time competitors caught on, Kimberly-Clark was selling $400 million worth of Huggies annually.[76] Procter & Gamble's product development teams conduct "transaction learning experiments," whereby they produce and sell small quantities of a new product online, at mall kiosks, and at amusement parks to gauge customer interest, thus letting consumers "vote with their wallets" on the desirability of a new product.[77]

Horizontal Coordination. This component means that technical, marketing, and production people share ideas and information. Research people inform marketing of new technical developments to learn whether the developments are applicable to customers. Marketing people provide customer complaints and information to R&D to use in the design of new products. People from both R&D and marketing coordinate with production because new products have to fit within production capabilities so costs are not exorbitant. The decision to launch a new product is ultimately a joint decision among all three departments. At Avocent, an information technology management company, managers redesigned the product development process so that programmers, testers, and customers work on the same team and follow a project from start to finish. After a spate of quality and safety issues and the recall of millions of vehicles, Toyota revamped its process for developing new cars to increase communication across departments. GM is likely to do the same, as safety issues continue to emerge. What began in February 2014 as a recall of around 800,000 vehicles related to faulty ignition switches had grown to more than 2 million by May and will probably expand further. CEO Mary Barra announced the creation of a safety team, which will likely be charged with increasing communication and collaboration across departments to prevent safety and quality lapses.[78] Horizontal coordination, using mechanisms such as cross-functional teams, increases both the amount and the variety of information for new product development, enabling the design of products that meet customer needs and circumventing manufacturing, quality, and marketing problems.[79] Corning used a horizontal linkage model to create a new product for the mobile phone industry.

✓ IN PRACTICE
Corning, Inc.

If you have ever had a cell phone with a plastic screen, you probably know that the plastic can scratch and even break easily. A small team in Corning's specialty materials division spotted an opportunity. They began looking for a way that mobile phone screens could be made out of a super-strong but flexible glass that the company had originally attempted (unsuccessfully) to sell for automobile windshields in the 1960s. Just producing an experimental batch to gauge customer interest would cost as much as $300,000, but managers took the risk because the project had a strong idea champion.

Once the test run was completed and potential customers expressed excitement, managers had to move quickly. Corning took the project from concept to commercial success in an amazingly short period of time. One reason is that the company had both the right culture and the right systems. Corning divisions and departments know that top managers expect, support, and reward collaboration on promising new product launches. Innovation at Corning is managed not by lone inventors or small teams in silos, but rather by multidisciplinary groups all across the organization. Thus, employees from R&D, manufacturing, and sales quickly agreed to serve on the team developing the new glass product.

By 2013, Corning's cell phone glass, called Gorilla Glass, was used on more than 1 billion smartphones and tablets and was a $1 billion–a-year business, landing Corning at Number 36 on *Fast Company*'s list of most innovative companies. Gorilla Glass 2, released in 2012, is up to 20 percent thinner, so companies can make slimmer devices. Version 3 promises to be 40 percent more scratch resistant. As more displays incorporate touch screens, the company keeps innovating.[80]

By using a horizontal linkage model for new product development, Corning has been highly effective in taking products from idea to success in the marketplace. Famous innovation failures—such as New Coke, Microsoft's Zune music player, and the U.S. Mint's Susan B. Anthony dollar, perhaps the most unpopular coin in American history—usually violate the horizontal linkage model. Employees fail to connect with customer needs and market forces or internal departments fail to adequately share needs and coordinate with one another. Research has confirmed a connection between effective boundary spanning that keeps the organization in touch with market forces, smooth coordination among departments, and successful product development.[81]

Open Innovation and Crowdsourcing

Many successful companies include customers, strategic partners, suppliers, and other outsiders directly in the product and service development process. One of the hottest trends is *open innovation*.[82]

⊙ BRIEFCASE

As an organization manager, keep these guidelines in mind:

Encourage marketing, research, and production departments to develop linkages to each other and to their environments when new products or services are needed. Consider bringing customers, suppliers, and others from outside the boundaries of the organization into the product development process.

In the past, most businesses generated their own ideas in-house and then developed, manufactured, marketed, and distributed them, which represents a closed innovation approach. Today, though, forward-looking companies are trying a different method. **Open innovation** means extending the search for and commercialization of new products beyond the boundaries of the organization and even beyond the boundaries of the industry.[83] For example, game maker Rovio extended the commercialization of the Angry Birds brand into books, movies, and toys by letting outsiders license the popular gaming app.[84] Collaboration with other firms and with customers and other outsiders provides many benefits, including faster time to market, lower product development costs, improved quality, and better adaptation of products to customer needs. It can also stimulate stronger internal coordination across departments. Because open innovation requires the involvement of people from different areas of the company, it forces managers to set up stronger internal coordination and knowledge-sharing mechanisms.[85]

Booz & Company research shows that firms with robust open innovation capabilities are seven times more effective in terms of generating returns on their overall research and development investment than firms with weak capabilities.[86] Consumer products giant Procter & Gamble is probably the best-known proponent of open innovation. Some of the company's best-selling products, including the Swiffer SweeperVac, Olay Regenerist, and Mr. Clean Magic Eraser, were developed in whole or in part by someone outside the company. P&G gets more than 50 percent of its innovation from outside company walls.[87] Even Apple, which has always been famously "closed" in many ways, found a way to tap into the power of open innovation. Former CEO Steve Jobs maintained close control over the company's product design and development, and the company is tight-lipped about the principles that guided its decade-long journey from virtual irrelevance as a maker of computers to the world's largest technology company, with leading products in the hardware, software, music, video, communication, and e-publishing industries. Managers knew that success in some of these industries requires a more open approach. For example, although the company sets guidelines and technological constraints, it allows anyone to create and market mobile applications for the iPhone in exchange for a small share of the revenue generated by the apps.[88]

The Internet has made it possible for companies such as Eli Lilly, Procter & Gamble, IBM, and General Electric to tap into ideas from around the world and let hundreds of thousands of people contribute to the innovation process. The approach to open innovation that solicits ideas, services, or information from online volunteers rather than from traditional employees is referred to as **crowdsourcing** (a combination of "crowd" and "outsourcing").[89] The most straightforward way to enlist the help of a crowd is with a contest.[90] Elastec/American Marine, based in Carmi, Illinois, won a $1 million prize for a new oil recovery system that can recover oil from the ocean's surface at a rate of 4,600 gallons a minute, more than 4 times the industry standard.[91] Rob McEwen, the chairman and CEO of Canadian mining group Goldcorp, created the Goldcorp Challenge, putting Red Lake's previously closely guarded topographic data online and offering $575,000 in prize money to anyone who could identify rich drill sites. More than 1,400 technical experts in 50 countries offered alternatives to the problem, and two teams working together in Australia pinpointed locations that have made Red Lake one of the world's richest gold mines.[92] There has been a huge surge of interest in Internet-based innovation contests over the past few years, giving companies a chance to integrate external with internal input into the front end of new product development.[93]

2 Asking customers what they want is the best way to create new products that will be successful in the marketplace.

> **ANSWER:** *Agree or disagree.* It depends on the organization. Bringing customers into the product development process has been highly beneficial for many companies. However, many products developed based on what customers say they want do not succeed. In addition, some highly innovative companies, like Apple, believe relying too much on customer input limits the pie-in-the-sky thinking needed to create truly breakthrough products.

Achieving Competitive Advantage: The Need for Speed

In a survey conducted by IBM and *Industry Week* magazine, 40 percent of respondents identified collaborating with customers and suppliers as having the most significant impact on product development time-to-market.[94] The rapid development of new products and services can be a strategic weapon in an ever-shifting global marketplace.[95]

In general, faster new product development is associated with lower development costs and greater success because firms can gain favorable market position, more readily adapt to changing environments, and quickly address shifting consumer demands.[96] Clothing retailer Zara gets new styles into stores twice a week, for example. The company produces about 450 million items a year. High-tech equipment enables the chain's factories to adjust to sudden production changes. Callaway Golf introduces seven to eight new products every year to keep its edge as one of the industry's most innovative manufacturers.[97] Speed is a cornerstone of Fiat Chrysler CEO Sergio Marchionne's strategy for reviving Chrysler. Cost cutting by previous managers had led to a dearth of new products, and Marchionne knows the company must catch up fast to stay competitive. Marchionne recently announced an ambitious goal to increase sales at Fiat Chrysler from 4.4 million in 2013 to 7 million vehicles. The company will introduce 8 new models by 2018 and is also revamping older models to keep them fresh and stylish. Urgency and quick decision making are the new watchwords at Chrysler.[98] Dodge showed up at Number 11 on *Fast Company's* list of the Most Innovative Companies for 2014 "for being part of the conversation, no matter what." Dodge's late-2013 spokesman, Ron Burgundy from *Anchorman 2*, boosted Durango sales 59 percent in October of that year, but threw the company a curveball when he went on a late-night talk show (in character) and said, "What's so amazing about it is, it's a terrible car. Just horrible craftsmanship." Dodge loved it. Apparently so did everyone else. Sales kept climbing.[99]

Strategy and Structure Change

The preceding discussion focused on new production processes and products, which are based in the technology of an organization. The expertise for such innovation lies within the technical core and professional staff groups, such as research and engineering. This section turns to an examination of strategy and structure changes.

All organizations need to make changes in their strategies, structures, management processes, and administrative procedures from time to time. In the past, when the environment was relatively stable, most organizations focused on small, incremental changes to solve immediate problems or take advantage of new opportunities. However, over the past couple of decades, companies throughout the world have faced the need to make radical changes in strategy, structure, and management processes to adapt to new competitive demands.[100]

Many organizations are cutting out layers of management and decentralizing decision making. LEGO's Ninjago: Masters of Spinjitzu toy series illustrates how the company decentralized innovation and decision making. Back in 2004, LEGO was a hierarchical organization, "with the big dogs at the peak of the pyramid" making all the decisions. But this was a do or die survival period for the company, and some top leaders felt a new structural approach was needed. They flipped the top-down approach by defining the outcomes they wanted and giving teams almost complete freedom to set their own targets and make decisions about innovation. When Ninjago: Masters of Spinjitzu launched in January of 2011, it set new financial records for LEGO, proving the success of the decentralized model.[101] LEGO's most recent decentralization success was *The Lego Movie*, a computer-animated adventure comedy released in early 2014 that garnered nearly universally favorable reviews and stayed at the top of the box office in North America for three weekends in a row.

There is a strong shift within organizations toward more horizontal structures, with teams of front-line workers empowered to make decisions and solve problems on their own. Some companies are breaking totally away from traditional organization forms and shifting toward virtual network strategies and structures. Numerous companies are reorganizing and shifting their strategies to incorporate e-business. These types of changes are the responsibility of the organization's top managers, and the overall process of change is typically different from the process for innovation in technology or new products.

The Dual-Core Approach

The **dual-core approach** to organizational change compares management and technical innovation. **Management innovation** refers to the adoption and implementation of a management practice, process, structure, strategy, or technique that is new to the organization and is intended to further organizational goals.[102] This type of change pertains to the design and structure of the organization itself, including restructuring, downsizing, teams, control systems, information systems, and departmental grouping. The implementation of a balanced scorecard, as described in Chapter 8, for example, would be a management innovation, as would the establishment of a joint venture for global expansion, as described in Chapter 6, or the shift to a virtual network organization structure, described in Chapter 3. One recent management innovation that some companies are adopting is *jugaad* (pronounced joo-gaardh). Jugaad basically refers to a management mindset used widely by Indian companies such as Tata Group and Infosys Technologies that strives to meet customers' immediate needs quickly and inexpensively. With research and development budgets strained in a difficult economy, it's an approach U.S. managers are picking up on.[103]

Research into management change suggests two things. First, management changes occur less frequently than do technical changes. Second, management changes occur in response to different environmental sectors and follow a different internal process than do technology-based changes.[104] The dual-core approach to organizational change identifies the unique processes associated with management change.[105] Organizations—schools, hospitals, city governments, welfare agencies, government bureaucracies, and many business firms—can be conceptualized as having two cores: a *technical core* and a *management core*. Each core has its own employees, tasks, and environmental domain. Innovation can originate in either core.

The management core is above the technical core in the hierarchy. The responsibility of the management core includes the structure, control, and coordination of the organization itself and concerns the environmental sectors of government, financial resources, economic conditions, human resources, and competitors. The technical core is concerned with the transformation of raw materials into organizational products and services and involves the environmental sectors of customers and technology.[106]

The point of the dual-core approach is that many organizations—especially nonprofit and government organizations—must adopt frequent management changes and need to be structured differently from organizations that rely on frequent technical and product changes for competitive advantage.

Organization Design for Implementing Management Change

The findings from research comparing management and technical change suggest that a mechanistic organization structure is appropriate for frequent management changes, including changes in goals, strategy, structure, control systems, and human resources.[107] Organizations that successfully adopt many management changes often have a larger administrative ratio, are larger in size, and are centralized and formalized compared with organizations that adopt many technical changes.[108] The reason is the top-down implementation of changes in response to changes in the government, financial, or legal sectors of the environment. If an organization has an organic structure, lower-level employees have more freedom and autonomy and, hence, may resist top-down initiatives.

The innovation approaches associated with management versus technical change are summarized in Exhibit 11.7. Technical change, such as changes in production techniques and innovative technology for new products, is facilitated by an organic structure, which allows ideas to bubble upward from lower- and middle-level employees. Organizations that must adopt frequent management changes, in contrast, tend to use a top-down process and a mechanistic structure. For example, changes such as implementation of Six Sigma methods, application of the balanced scorecard, decentralization of decision making, or downsizing and restructuring are facilitated by a top-down approach.

Research into civil service reform found that the implementation of management innovation was extremely difficult in organizations that had an organic technical core. The professional employees in a decentralized agency could resist civil service changes. By contrast, organizations that were considered more bureaucratic and mechanistic in the sense of high formalization and centralization adopted management changes readily.[109]

What about business organizations that are normally technologically innovative in bottom-up fashion but suddenly face a crisis and need to reorganize? Or a technically innovative, high-tech firm that must reorganize frequently to

BRIEFCASE

As an organization manager, keep these guidelines in mind:

Facilitate changes in strategy and structure by adopting a top-down approach. Use a mechanistic structure when the organization needs to adopt frequent management changes in a top-down fashion.

EXHIBIT 11.7
Dual-Core Approach to
Organization Change

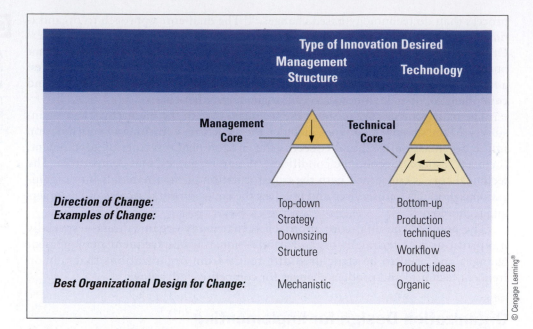

accommodate changes in production technology or the environment? Technically innovative firms may suddenly have to restructure, reduce the number of employees, alter pay systems, disband teams, or form a new division.[110] The answer is to use a top-down change process. The authority for strategy and structure change lies with top management, who should initiate and implement the new strategy and structure to meet environmental circumstances. Employee input may be sought, but top managers have the responsibility to direct the change. For example, top managers at GlaxoSmithKline, the large pharmaceutical company with headquarters in the United Kingdom, implemented top-down change to improve drug discovery.

 **IN PRACTICE**
GlaxoSmith-Kline

Large pharmaceutical companies such as Pfizer, AstraZeneca, and GlaxoSmithKline have grown even larger over the past decade or so through mergers and acquisitions. Yet, while the increasing size brought power in sales and marketing, the growing bureaucracy hampered research and development efforts. The amount of money big companies invested in R&D of new drugs has tripled over the past 15 years, but the number of new drugs has declined, with most new pharmaceuticals being invented by small biotechnology start-ups.

Andrew Witty, CEO of GlaxoSmithKline, decided to try an experimental approach that would get his R&D scientists thinking and acting more like those start-ups. He broke the R&D unit into small groups of 20 to 60 people, called Discovery Performance Units (DPUs). Each group has scientists from all disciplines working together and focusing their combined expertise on finding new drugs for specific types of diseases, such as cancer or auto-immune diseases. Previously, chemist David Wilson says he could go days on end without ever seeing a biologist. Now, he says, the mix of disciplines has led to quick decisions and productive brainstorming.

Witty gave the DPUs three-year budgets with specific goals and set up a review board to track progress and decide whether to continue funding them. The units were told that if they don't produce, they could be disbanded and employees terminated. "If we fail, there must be consequences that may go all the way to termination," said Moncef Slaoui, Glaxo's head of R&D.[111]

Most researchers at Glaxo welcomed the creation of the DPUs. Witty says morale in the research unit was "terrible" when he arrived. Implementing the new R&D approach has spurred an entrepreneurial drive and given people a chance to focus their energies on the most promising areas of research. If the units don't perform as needed to help the company discover cutting-edge drugs, Witty and other top managers may have to implement more difficult top-down changes by terminating employees and outsourcing more R&D work.

Even the shift to a bossless system is directed from the top, as illustrated in the following example.

IN PRACTICE
Zappos

As described in the chapter opening example, Zappos leaders aren't afraid to take risks and try new approaches. In late 2013, CEO Tony Hseih asked his employees to embark on another radical change. He called everyone together and announced that Zappos would be restructured into a "holocracy." There would be no job titles and no managers; all work would be done in circles instead of layers. Zappos employees were expected to alter every aspect of how they worked, virtually overnight.

So far, Zappos is the biggest company to adopt this management system that is gaining popularity in the business world. By the end of 2014, all 1500 Zappos employees will be organized into 400 circles. The idea behind a holocracy is that by redistributing authority so that all employees become leaders in their own roles, organizations can solve problems and achieve goals more quickly. It will be an organization made up of entrepreneurial leaders who fulfill their own roles but also share a common purpose and are accountable to the larger organization.[112]

It's still too early to see how this top-down change at Zappos is succeeding. Zappos is an unusual company and employees are likely to embrace the new structure. However, in general, top-down changes related to restructuring and downsizing can be painful for employees, so top managers should move quickly and authoritatively to make them as humane as possible.[113] A study of successful corporate transformations, which frequently involve painful changes, found that managers followed a fast, focused approach. When top managers spread difficult changes such as downsizing over a long time period, employee morale suffers and the change is much less likely to lead to positive outcomes.[114]

Top managers should also remember that top-down change means initiation of the idea occurs at upper levels and is implemented downward. It does not mean that lower-level employees are not educated about the change or allowed to participate in it.

Culture Change

Organizations are made up of people and their relationships with one another. Changes in strategy, structure, technologies, and products do not happen on their own, and changes in any of these areas involve changes in people as well. Employees must learn how to use new technologies, or market new products, or work effectively in interdisciplinary teams, as at GlaxoSmithKline. Sometimes achieving a new way of thinking requires a focused change in the underlying corporate cultural values and norms. Changing corporate culture fundamentally shifts how work is done in an organization and can lead to renewed commitment and empowerment of employees, as well as a stronger bond between the company and its customers.[115]

However, changing culture can be particularly difficult because it challenges people's core values and established ways of thinking and doing things. Mergers and acquisitions often illustrate how tough culture change can be. Consider an example from Japan. Officers of Mizuho Financial Group, which was formed from the merger of Dai-Ichi, Fuji Bank, and Industrial Bank of Japan in 2002, say cultural differences between the units created the biggest hurdle to integrating operations. Mizuho's structure, culture, and management systems have been under scrutiny since the bank suffered a prolonged computer system breakdown following the March 11, 2011, earthquake that hit Japan. Bank officials have vowed to create a unified corporate culture and speed the integration to prevent similar problems and improve Mizuho's financial performance, which is lagging that of other large Japanese banks.[116] Although cultural issues can sometimes make or break the success of a merger, many managers fail to consider culture as part of their merger and acquisition plans, says Chuck Moritt, a senior partner in Mercer's M&A consulting business.[117]

Forces for Culture Change

In addition to mergers, a number of other recent trends have contributed to a need for cultural makeovers at many companies. For example, reengineering and the shift to horizontal forms of organizing, which we discussed in Chapter 3, require greater focus on employee empowerment, collaboration, information sharing, and meeting customer needs, which means managers and employees need a new mindset. Mutual trust, risk-taking, and tolerance for mistakes become key cultural values in the horizontal organization.

Another force for culture change is the diversity of today's workforce. Diversity is a fact of life for today's organizations, and many are implementing new recruiting, mentoring, and promotion methods, diversity training programs, tough policies regarding sexual harassment and racial discrimination, and new benefits programs that respond to a more diverse workforce. Companies such as Pfizer, BAE, Dow Chemical, and Google are training employees and managers to recognize "unconscious bias," which refers to a hidden preference for certain groups or types of people that can influence decisions in hiring, performance appraisal, promotions, and so forth. After Dow sent hundreds of managers to unconscious bias training, the number of women in higher level positions increased. Executives believe the training played a role in realizing those diversity gains.[118] However, the underlying culture of an organization also has to change or all other efforts to support diversity will fail.

Finally, a growing emphasis on learning and adaptation in organizations calls for new cultural values. Recall from Chapter 1 that flexible, organic organizations that support learning and adaptation typically have more horizontal structures with empowered teams working directly with customers. There are few rules and procedures for performing tasks, and knowledge and control of tasks are located with employees rather than supervisors. Information is broadly shared, and employees, customers, suppliers, and partners all play a role in determining the organization's strategic direction. When managers want to shift to a more organic organization design, they have to instill new values, new attitudes, and new ways of thinking and working together.

Changing a company's culture is probably one of the hardest jobs a manager can undertake.

ANSWER: *Agree.* Changing people and culture is typically much more difficult than changing any other aspect of the organization. Managers often underestimate the difficulty of changing culture and fail to appreciate that it takes a determined, consciously planned effort over a long period of time.

Organization Development Culture Change Interventions

Managers use a variety of approaches and techniques for changing corporate culture, some of which we discussed in Chapter 10. One method of quickly bringing about culture change is known as **organization development** (OD), which focuses on the human and social aspects of the organization as a way to improve the organization's ability to adapt and solve problems. OD emphasizes the values of human development, fairness, openness, freedom from coercion, and individual autonomy that allows workers to perform the job as they see fit, within reasonable organizational constraints.[119] In the 1970s, OD evolved as a separate field that applied the behavioral sciences in a process of planned organization-wide change, with the goal of increasing organizational effectiveness. Today, the concept has been enlarged to examine how people and groups can change to an adaptive culture in a complex and turbulent environment. Organization development is not a step-by-step procedure to solve a specific problem but a process of fundamental change in the human and social systems of the organization, including organizational culture.[120]

OD uses knowledge and techniques from the behavioral sciences to create a learning environment through increased trust, open confrontation of problems, employee empowerment and participation, knowledge and information sharing, the design of meaningful work, cooperation and collaboration between groups, and the full use of human potential.

OD interventions involve training of specific groups or of everyone in the organization. For OD interventions to be successful, senior management in the organization must see the need for OD and provide enthusiastic support for the change. Techniques used by many organizations for improving people skills through OD include the following.

Large Group Intervention. Most early OD activities involved small groups and focused on incremental change. However, in recent years there has been growing interest in the application of OD techniques to large group settings, which are more attuned to bringing about radical or transformational change in organizations operating in complex environments.[121] The **large group intervention** approach, sometimes referred to as "whole system in the room,"[122] brings together participants from all parts of the organization—often including key stakeholders from outside the organization as well—in an off-site setting to discuss problems or opportunities and plan for change. A large group intervention might involve 50 to 500 people and last for several days. For example, the global furniture retailer IKEA used the large-group intervention approach to completely re-conceptualize how the company operates. During 18 hours of meetings held over several days, 52 stakeholders

 BRIEFCASE

As an organization manager, keep this guideline in mind:

Work with organization development consultants for large-scale changes in the attitudes, values, or skills of employees, and when trying to change the overall culture toward a more adaptable one.

created a new system for product design, manufacturing, and distribution, which involved cutting layers of hierarchy and decentralizing the organization.[123] All of the departments that had information, resources, or an interest in the design outcome worked together to create and implement the new system.

Using an off-site setting limits interference and distractions, enabling participants to focus on new ways of doing things. General Electric's "Work Out" program, an ongoing process of solving problems, learning, and improving, begins with large-scale off-site meetings that get people talking across functional, hierarchical, and organizational boundaries. Hourly and salaried workers come together from many different parts of the organization and join with customers and suppliers to discuss and solve specific problems.[124] The process forces a rapid analysis of ideas, the creation of solutions, and the development of a plan for implementation. Over time, Work Out creates a culture where ideas are rapidly translated into action and positive business results.[125]

Team Building. Team building promotes the idea that people who work together can work as a team. A work team can be brought together to discuss conflicts, goals, the decision-making process, communication, creativity, and leadership. The team can then plan to overcome problems and improve results. Team-building activities are also used in many companies to train task forces, committees, and new product development groups. These activities enhance communication and collaboration and strengthen the cohesiveness of organizational groups and teams.

Interdepartmental Activities. Representatives from different departments are brought together in a neutral location to expose problems or conflicts, diagnose the causes, and plan improvements in communication and coordination. This type of intervention has been applied to union–management conflict, headquarters–field office conflict, interdepartmental conflict, and mergers.[126] One archival records-storage company found interdepartmental meetings to be a key means of building a culture based on team spirit and customer focus. People from different departments met for hour-long sessions every two weeks and shared their problems, told stories about their successes, and talked about things they had observed in the company. The meetings helped people understand the problems faced by other departments and see how everyone depended on each other to do their jobs successfully.[127]

UnitedHealth Group, the nation's largest health insurer and one of the most powerful companies in the healthcare industry, has used OD interventions to build a more humane and collaborative environment at the giant company.

IN PRACTICE
UnitedHealth Group

"We were too self-centered and needlessly aggressive," said Stephen Helmsley, CEO of UnitedHealth Group. Helmsley says the atmosphere within the company was toxic when he took over, with a lot of IQ, but not much EQ. To encourage more civil, emotionally intelligent, and collaborative behavior, Helmsley sent 8,000 managers to three-day sensitivity training programs to become more aware of their own biases and impact and be more sensitive to other people. "I'm not proud that we needed to change, but we did," he says.

Interestingly, Helmsley, a former accountant with a reputation as a numbers man, was not recruited for his people skills, but that is what he has brought to the company. Today, people at UnitedHealth are respectful of their role in one of the most sensitive areas of human endeavor. One of the guidelines people live by is "Assume positive intent." A major team building experience at UnitedHealth is the annual broomball tournament held at headquarters in Minnesota. Inaugurated in 2010, the tournament is now a prized tradition held every winter, with 90 teams representing every area of the company participating. This and other OD activities have contributed to a drop in turnover, from 20 percent in 2008 to 8 percent in 2012.[128]

Stephen Helmsley hopes OD can help him in his efforts to dispel "the image of a greedy colossus driven by numbers." Leading a healthcare revolution is a tough, never-ending challenge, especially "trying to find the right balance between the analytical and the emotional," he says.[129]

Strategies for Implementing Change

Managers and employees can think of inventive ways to improve the organization's technology, creative ideas for new products and services, fresh approaches to strategies and structures, or ideas for fostering adaptive cultural values, but until the ideas are put into action, they are worthless to the organization. Implementation is the most crucial part of the change process, but it is also the most difficult. Change is frequently disruptive and uncomfortable for managers as well as employees. Change is complex, dynamic, and messy, and implementation requires strong and persistent leadership. In this final section, we briefly discuss the role of leadership for change, some reasons for resistance to change, and techniques that managers can use to overcome resistance and successfully implement change.

Leadership for Change

One survey found that among companies that are successful innovators, 80 percent have top leaders who are innovation champions; that is, they frequently reinforce the value and importance of innovation. These leaders think about innovation, demonstrate its importance through their actions, and follow through to make sure people are investing time and resources in innovation issues.[130]

The leadership style of the top executive sets the tone for how effective an organization is at continuous adaptation and innovation. One style of leadership, referred to as *transformational leadership*, is particularly suited for bringing about change. Top leaders who use a transformational leadership style enhance organizational innovation both directly, by creating a compelling vision, and indirectly, by creating an environment that supports exploration, experimentation, risk-taking, and sharing of ideas.[131]

Successful change can happen only when managers and employees are willing to devote the time and energy needed to reach new goals. In addition, people need the coping skills to endure possible stress and hardship. Understanding and appreciating the *curve of change* enables managers to guide people successfully through the difficulties of change. The change curve, illustrated in Exhibit 11.8, is the psychological process people go through during a significant change.

For example, a manager sees a need for a change in work procedures in her department and initiates the change with high expectations for a smooth implementation and a positive outcome. As time progresses, people have difficulty altering their attitudes and behaviors. Employees may question why they need to do things a new way, the supervisor may begin to feel overwhelmed and frustrated, and everyone can potentially reach a point of despair that change is really possible. Performance may decline dramatically as people wrestle with the new procedures and resist the shift to a new way of working. Good change leaders drive through this period of despair rather than allowing it to sabotage the change effort. With effective change leadership, the changes can take hold and lead toward better performance.

EXHIBIT 11.8
The Change Curve

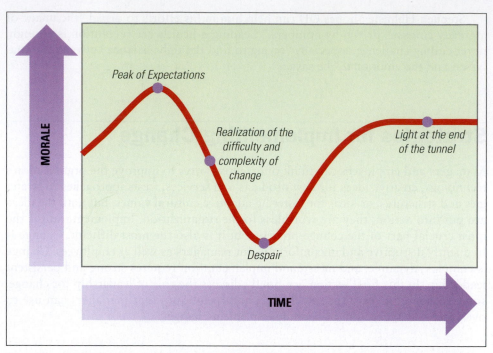

Source: Based on "Gartner Hype Cycle: Interpreting Technology Hype," Gartner Research, http://www.gartner.com /technology/research/methodologies/hype-cycle.jsp (accessed May 20, 2011); "The Change Equation and Curve," *21st Century Leader*, http://www.21stcenturyleader.co.uk/change_equation (accessed May 20, 2011); David M. Schneider and Charles Goldwasser, "Be a Model Leader of Change," *Management Review*, March 1998, 41–45; and Daryl R. Conner, *Managing at the Speed of Change* (New York: Villard Books, 1992).

Managers at Procter & Gamble prepare themselves for a "60-day immune response" from users of a new work process. They expect that it takes 60 days to overcome resistance, work out the bugs in the new process, and reach the light at the end of the tunnel, when everyone begins to see positive results of the change.[132] Having a clearly communicated vision that embodies flexibility and openness to new ideas, methods, and styles sets the stage for a change-oriented organization and helps employees cope with the chaos and tension associated with change.

Techniques for Implementation

Top leaders articulate the vision and set the tone, but managers and employees throughout the organization are involved in the process of change. A number of techniques can be used to successfully implement change.[133]

1. *Establish a sense of urgency for change.* Once managers identify a true need for change, they thaw resistance by creating a sense of urgency in others that the change is really needed. Organizational crises can help unfreeze employees and make them willing to invest the time and energy needed to adopt new techniques or procedures. When there is no obvious crisis, managers have to find creative ways to make others aware of the need for change.

2. *Establish a coalition to guide the change.* Effective change managers build a coalition of people throughout the organization who have enough power and influence to steer the change process. For implementation to be successful, there must be a shared commitment to the need and possibilities for change.

Top management support is crucial for any major change project, and lack of top management support is one of the most frequent causes of implementation failure.[134] In addition, the coalition should involve lower-level supervisors and middle managers from across the organization. For smaller changes, the support of influential managers in the affected departments is important.

3. *Create a vision and strategy for change.* Leaders who have taken their companies through major successful transformations often have one thing in common: They focus on formulating and articulating a compelling vision and strategy that will guide the change process. Even for a small change, a vision of how the future can be better and strategies to get there are important motivations for change.

4. *Find an idea that fits the need.* Finding the right idea often involves search procedures—talking with other managers, assigning a task force to investigate the problem, sending out a request to suppliers, or asking creative people within the organization to develop a solution. This is a good opportunity to encourage employee participation because employees need the freedom to think about and explore new options.[135]

5. *Create change teams.* This chapter has emphasized the need for resources and energy to make change happen. Separate creative departments, new-venture groups, and ad hoc teams or task forces are ways to focus energy on both creation and implementation. A separate department has the freedom to create a new technology that fits a genuine need. A task force can be created to see that implementation is completed. The task force can be responsible for communication, involvement of users, training, and other activities needed for change.

6. *Foster idea champions.* One of the most effective weapons in the battle for change is the idea champion. The most effective champion is a volunteer champion who is deeply committed to a new idea. The idea champion sees that all technical activities are correct and complete. An additional champion, such as a manager sponsor, may also be needed to persuade people about implementation.

BRIEFCASE

As an organization manager, keep these guidelines in mind:

Understand the curve of change so you can prevent yourself and others from falling prey to frustration and despair when implementing a major change. To achieve successful implementation, use techniques such as obtaining top management support, implementing the change in a series of steps, and assigning change teams or idea champions.

Techniques for Overcoming Resistance

Many good ideas are never used because managers failed to anticipate or prepare for resistance to change by consumers, employees, or other managers. No matter how impressive the performance characteristics of an innovation, its implementation will conflict with some interests and jeopardize some alliances in the organization. To increase the chance of successful implementation, managers acknowledge the conflict, threats, and potential losses perceived by employees. Several strategies can be used by managers to overcome resistance:

1. *Top management support.* The visible support of top management makes people aware of the importance of the change. For instance, one of the primary correlates of the success of new business ventures is the strong support of top managers, which gives the project legitimacy.[136] Top management support is especially important when a change involves multiple departments or when resources are being reallocated among departments. Without top management support, changes can get bogged down in squabbling among departments or contradictory orders from lower-level managers.

2. *Participation and involvement.* Early and extensive participation in a change should be part of implementation. Participation gives those involved a sense of control over the change activity. They understand it better, and they become

committed to its successful implementation.[137] At Domino's Pizza, some franchise owners resisted the switch to a new point-of-sale (POS) system that headquarters managers mandated as part of a drive to improve accuracy, boost efficiency, and increase profits. The franchisees hadn't been involved in the process of designing and configuring the new system, and many of them wanted to stay with the system they were accustomed to. "It was hard for a lot of us to embrace," said Tony Osani, who owns 16 Domino's restaurants in the Huntsville, Alabama, area.[138] The team-building and large group intervention activities described earlier can be effective ways to involve employees in a change process.

3. *Alignment with needs and goals of users.* The best strategy for overcoming resistance is to make sure change meets a real need. Employees in R&D often come up with great ideas that solve nonexistent problems. This happens because initiators fail to consult with the intended users. Resistance can be frustrating for managers, but moderate resistance to change is good for an organization. Resistance provides a barrier to frivolous changes and to change for the sake of change. The process of overcoming resistance to change normally requires that the change be good for its users. When David Zugheri wanted to switch to a primarily paperless system at First Houston Mortgage, he emphasized to employees that storing customer records electronically meant they could now work from home when they needed to care for a sick child, or take a vacation and still keep track of critical accounts. "I could literally see their attitudes change through their body language," Zugheri says.[139]

4. *Communication and training.* Communication means informing users about the need for change and the consequences of a proposed change, preventing rumors, misunderstanding, and resentment. In one study of change efforts, the most commonly cited reason for failure was that employees learned of the change from outsiders. Top managers concentrated on communicating with the public and shareholders but failed to communicate with the people who would be most intimately involved with and most affected by the change—their own employees.[140] Open communication often gives managers an opportunity to explain what steps will be taken to ensure that the change will have no adverse consequences for employees. Training is also needed to help people understand and cope with their role in the change process.

5. *An environment that affords psychological safety.* Psychological safety means that people feel a sense of confidence that they will not be embarrassed or rejected by others in the organization. People need to feel secure and capable of making the changes that are asked of them.[141] Change requires that employees be willing to take risks and do things differently, but many people are fearful of trying something new if they think they might be embarrassed by mistakes or failure. Managers support psychological safety by creating a climate of trust and mutual respect in the organization. "Not being afraid someone is laughing at you helps you take genuine risks," says Andy Law, one of the founders of St. Luke's, an advertising agency based in London.[142]

Learning to manage change effectively, including understanding the change curve and knowing ways to overcome resistance, is crucial, particularly when top-down changes are needed. The failure to recognize and overcome resistance is one of the primary reasons managers fail to implement new strategies that can keep their companies competitive.[143] Smart managers approach the change process mindfully and consistently, planning for implementation and preparing for resistance.

🔘 **BRIEFCASE**

As an organization manager, keep this guideline in mind:

Overcome resistance to change by actively communicating with workers and encouraging their participation in the change process.

Design Essentials

■ Organizations face a dilemma. Managers prefer to organize day-to-day activities in a predictable, routine manner. However, change—not stability—is the natural order of things in today's global environment. Thus, organizations need to build in change as well as stability, to facilitate innovation as well as efficiency. Today's environment creates demands for three types of change—episodic change, continuous change, and disruptive change.

■ Four categories of innovation—technology, products and services, strategy and structure, and culture—may give an organization a competitive edge, and managers can make certain each of the necessary ingredients for change is present.

■ For technology innovation, which is of concern to most organizations, an organic structure that encourages employee autonomy works best because it encourages a flow of ideas throughout the organization. Other approaches are to establish a separate department charged with creating new technical ideas, establish venture teams or idea incubators, apply a variety of mechanisms, systems, and processes that encourage a bottom-up flow of ideas and make sure they get heard and acted upon by top executives, and encourage idea champions. New products and services generally require cooperation among several departments, so horizontal linkage is an essential part of the innovation process. The latest trend is open innovation, which brings customers, suppliers, and other outsiders directly into the search for and development of new products. Crowdsourcing is a growing part of the open innovation trend.

■ For changes in strategy and structure, a top-down approach is typically best. These innovations are in the domain of top managers who take responsibility for restructuring, for downsizing, and for changes in policies, goals, and control systems.

■ Culture changes are also generally the responsibility of top management. Some recent trends that may create a need for broad-scale culture change in the organization are reengineering, the shift to horizontal forms of organizing, and greater organizational diversity. All of these changes require significant shifts in employee and manager attitudes and ways of working together. One method for bringing about this level of culture change is organization development (OD). OD focuses on the human and social aspects of the organization and uses behavioral science knowledge to bring about changes in attitudes and relationships.

■ Finally, the implementation of change can be difficult. Strong leadership is needed to guide employees through the turbulence and uncertainty and build organization-wide commitment to change. Understanding the curve of change can help leaders push through the despair and frustration often associated with major change.

■ Managers can increase the likelihood of success by thoughtfully planning how to deal with resistance. Implementation techniques are to establish a sense of urgency that change is needed; create a powerful coalition to guide the change; formulate a vision and strategy to achieve the change; and foster change teams and idea champions. To overcome resistance, managers can gain the support of top management, include users in the change process, align the change with the needs and goals of users, and provide psychological safety.

KEY CONCEPTS

ambidextrous approach	idea champions	product and service innovations
change process	idea incubator	skunkworks
creative departments	large group intervention	strategy and structure innovations
creativity	management innovation	switching structures
crowdsourcing	new-venture fund	team building
culture innovations	open innovation	technology innovations
disruptive innovation	organization development	venture teams
dual-core approach	organizational change	
horizontal coordination model	organizational innovation	

DISCUSSION QUESTIONS

1. Why do you think crowdsourcing has become popular in recent years? What might be some disadvantages of taking a crowdsourcing approach? When might a company be better off taking a more limited approach to open innovation?

2. Describe the dual-core approach. How does the process of management innovation normally differ from technology change? Discuss.

3. What does it mean to say managers should organize for both exploration and exploitation?

4. Do you think factory employees would typically be more resistant to changes in production methods, changes in structure, or changes in culture? Why? What steps could managers take to overcome this resistance?

5. "Change requires more coordination than does the performance of normal organizational tasks. Any time you change something, you discover its connections to other parts of the organization, which have to be changed as well." Discuss whether you agree or disagree with this quote, and why.

6. A noted organization theorist said, "Pressure for change originates in the environment; pressure for stability originates within the organization." Do you agree? Discuss.

7. Of the five elements in Exhibit 11.3 required for successful change, which element do you think managers are most likely to overlook? Discuss.

8. How do the underlying values of organization development compare to the values underlying other types of change? Why do the values underlying OD make it particularly useful in shifting to a constructive culture as described in Chapter 10 (Exhibit 10.5)?

9. The manager of R&D for a drug company said that only 5 percent of the company's new products ever achieve market success. She also said the industry average is 10 percent and wondered how her organization might increase its success rate. If you were acting as a consultant, what advice would you give her about designing organization structure to improve market success?

10. Examine the change curve illustrated in Exhibit 11.8 and the five techniques for overcoming resistance to change discussed at the end of the chapter. Describe at which point along the change curve managers could use each of the five techniques to successfully implement a major change.

CHAPTER 11 WORKSHOP   Innovation Climate[144]

In order to examine differences in the level of innovation encouragement in organizations, you will be asked to rate two organizations. The first should be an organization in which you have worked, or the university. The second should be someone else's workplace—that of a family member, a friend, or an acquaintance. You will have to interview that person to answer the following questions. You should put your own answers in column A, your interviewee's answers in column B, and what you think would be the ideal in column C.

Innovation Measures

Item of Measure	A Your Organization	B Other Organization	C Your Ideal
Score items 1–5 on this scale: 1 = *don't agree at all* to 5 = *agree completely*			
1. Creativity is encouraged here.[†]			
2. People are allowed to solve the same problems in different ways.[†]			
3. I get to pursue creative ideas.[‡]			
4. The organization publicly recognizes and also rewards those who are innovative.[‡]			
5. Our organization is flexible and always open to change.[†]			
Score items 6–10 on the opposite scale: 1 = *agree completely* to 5 = *don't agree at all*			
6. The primary job of people here is to follow orders that come from the top.[†]			
7. The best way to get along here is to think and act like others.[†]			
8. This place seems to be more concerned with the status quo than with change.[†]			
9. People are rewarded more if they don't rock the boat.[‡]			
10. New ideas are great, but we don't have enough people or money to carry them out.[‡]			

[†] These items indicate the organization's innovation climate.
[‡] These items show resource support.

Questions

1. What comparisons in terms of innovation climates can you make between these two organizations?
2. How might productivity differ between a climate that supports innovation and a climate that does not?
3. Where would you rather work? Why?

CASE FOR ANALYSIS | Shoe Corporation of Illinois[145]

Shoe Corporation of Illinois (SCI) produces a line of women's shoes that sell in the lower-price market for $27.99 to $29.99 per pair. Profits averaged 30 cents to 50 cents per pair 10 years ago, but according to the president and the controller, labor and materials costs have risen so much in the intervening period that profits today average only 25 cents to 30 cents per pair.

Production at both the company's plants totals 12,500 pairs per day. The two factories are located within a radius of 60 miles of Chicago: one at Centerville, which produces 4,500 pairs per day, and the other at Meadowvale, which produces 8,000 pairs per day. Company headquarters is located in a building adjacent to the Centerville plant.

It is difficult to give an accurate picture of the number of items in the company's product line. Shoes change in style perhaps more rapidly than any other style product, including garments. This is chiefly because it is possible to change production processes quickly and because, historically, each company, in attempting to get ahead of competitors, gradually made style changes more frequently. At present, including both major and minor style changes, SCI offers 100 to 120 different products to customers each year.

A partial organizational chart, showing the departments involved in this case, appears in Exhibit 11.9.

Competitive Structure of the Industry

Very large general shoe houses, such as International and Brown, carry a line of women's shoes and are able to undercut prices charged by SCI, principally because of the policy in the big companies of producing large numbers of "stable" shoes, such as the plain pump and the loafer. They do not attempt to change styles as rapidly as their smaller competitors. Thus, without constant changes in production processes and sales presentations, they are able to keep costs substantially lower.

Charles F. Allison, the president of SCI, feels that the only way for a small independent company to be competitive is to change styles frequently, taking advantage of the flexibility of a small organization to create designs that appeal to customers. Thus, demand can be created and a price set high enough to make a profit. Allison, incidentally, appears to have an artistic talent in styling and a record of successful judgments in approving high-volume styles over the years.

Regarding how SCI differs from its large competitors, Allison has said:

You see, Brown and International Shoe Company both produce hundreds of thousands of the same pair of shoes. They store them in inventory at their factories. Their cus-

tomers, the large wholesalers and retailers, simply know their line and send in orders. They do not have to change styles nearly as often as we do. Sometimes I wish we could do that, too. It makes for a much more stable and orderly system. There is also less friction between people inside the company. The salespeople always know what they're selling; the production people know what is expected of them. The plant personnel are not shook up so often by someone coming in one morning and tampering with their machine lines or their schedules. The styling people are not shook up so often by the plant saying, "We can't do your new style the way you want it."

To help SCI be more competitive against larger firms, Allison recently created an e-commerce department. Although his main interest was in marketing over the Internet, he also hoped new technology would help reduce some of the internal friction by giving people an easier way to communicate. He invested in a sophisticated new computer system and hired consultants to set up a company intranet and provide a few days' training to upper and middle managers. Katherine Olsen came on board as director of e-commerce, charged primarily with coordinating Internet marketing and sales. When she took the job, she had visions of one day offering consumers the option of customized shoe designs. However, Olsen was somewhat surprised to learn that most employees still refused to use the intranet even for internal communication and coordination. The process for deciding on new styles, for example, had not changed since the 1980s.

Major Style Changes

The decision about whether to put a certain style into production requires information from a number of different people. Here is what typically happens in the company. It may be helpful to follow the organization chart (see Exhibit 11.9) tracing the procedure.

M. T. Lawson, the styling manager, and his designer, John Flynn, originate most of the ideas about shape, size of heel, use of flat sole or heels, and findings (the term used for ornaments attached to, but not part of, the shoes—bows, straps, and so forth). They get their ideas principally from reading style and trade magazines or by copying top-flight designers. Lawson corresponds with publications and friends in large stores in New York, Rome, and Paris to obtain pictures and samples of up-to-the-minute style innovations. Although he uses e-mail occasionally, Lawson prefers telephone contact and receiving drawings or samples by overnight mail. Then, he and Flynn discuss various ideas and come up with design options.

EXHIBIT 11.9
Partial Organization Chart of Shoe Corporation of Illinois

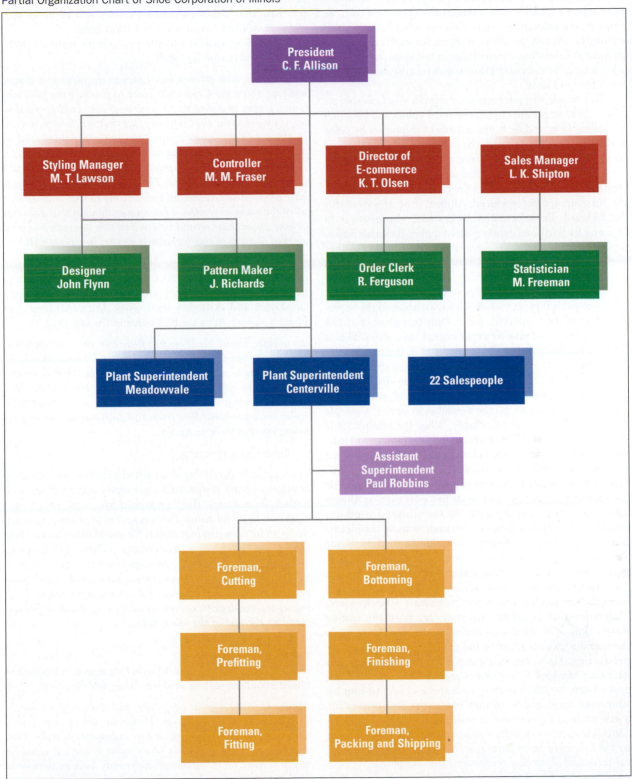

When Lawson decides on a design, he takes a sketch to Allison, who either approves or disapproves it. If Allison approves, he (Allison) then passes the sketch on to L. K. Shipton, the sales manager, to find out what lasts (widths) should be chosen. Shipton, in turn, forwards the design to Martin Freeman, a statistician in the sales department, who maintains summary information on customer demand for colors and lasts.

To compile this information, Freeman visits salespeople twice a year to get their opinions on the colors and lasts that are selling best, and he keeps records of shipments by color and by last. For these needs, he simply totals data that are sent to him by the shipping foreman in each of the two plants.

When Freeman has decided on the lasts and colors, he sends Allison a form that lists the colors and lasts in which the shoe should be produced. Allison, if he approves this list, forwards the information to Lawson, who passes it on to Jenna Richards, an expert pattern maker. Richards makes a paper pattern and then constructs a prototype in leather and paper. She sends this to Lawson, who in turn approves or disapproves it. He forwards any approved prototype to Allison. Allison, if he, too, approves, notifies Lawson, who takes the prototype to Paul Robbins, assistant to the superintendent of the Centerville plant. Only this plant produces small quantities of new or experimental shoe styles. This is referred to as a "pilot run" by executives at the plant.

Robbins then literally carries the prototype through the six production departments of the plant—from cutting to finishing—discussing it with each foreman, who in turn works with employees on the machines in having a sample lot of several thousand pairs made. When the finished lot is delivered by the finishing foreman to the shipping foreman (because of the importance of styling, Allison has directed that each foreman personally deliver styling goods in process to the foreman of the next department), the latter holds the inventory in storage and sends one pair each to Allison and Lawson. If they approve of the finished product, Allison instructs the shipping foreman to mail samples to each of the company's twenty-two salespeople throughout the country. Olsen also receives samples, photos, and drawings to post on the web page and gauge customer interest.

Salespeople have instructions to take the samples immediately (within one week) to at least 10 customers. Orders for already established shoes are normally sent to Ralph Ferguson, a clerk in Shipton's office, who records them and forwards them to the plant superintendents for production. However, salespeople have found by experience that Martin Freeman has a greater interest in the success of new "trials," so they rush these orders to him by overnight mail, and he in turn places the first orders for a new style in the interoffice mail to the plant superintendents. He then sends off a duplicate of the order, mailed in by the salespeople, to Ferguson for entering in his statistical record of all orders received by the company.

Three weeks after the salespeople receive samples, Allison requires Ralph Ferguson to give him a tabulation of orders. At that time, he decides whether the salespeople

and the web page should push the item and the superintendents should produce large quantities, or whether he will tell them that although existing orders will be produced, the item will be discontinued in a short time.

According to Allison, the procedures outlined here have worked reasonably well.

The average time from when Lawson decides on a design until we notify the Centerville plant to produce the pilot run is two weeks to a month. Of course, if we could speed that up, it would make the company just that much more secure in staying in the game against the big companies, and in taking sales away from our competitors. There seems to be endless bickering among people around here involved in the styling phase of the business. That's to be expected when you have to move fast—there isn't much time to stop and observe all of the social amenities. I have never thought that a formal organization chart would be good in this company—we've worked out a customary system here that functions well.

M. T. Lawson, manager of styling, said that within his department all work seems to get out in minimum time; he also stated that both Flynn and Richards are good employees and skilled in their work. He mentioned that Flynn had been in to see him twice in the last year

to inquire about his [Flynn's] future in the company. He is 33 years old and has three children. I know that he is eager to make money, and I assured him that over the years we can raise him right along from the $60,000 we are now paying. Actually, he has learned a lot about shoe styles since we hired him from the design department of a fabric company six years ago.

John Flynn revealed:

I was actually becoming dissatisfied with this job. All shoe companies copy styles—it's a generally accepted practice within the industry. But I've picked up a real feel for designs, and several times I've suggested that the company make all its own original styles. We could make SCI a style leader and also increase our volume. When I ask Lawson about this, he says it takes too much time for the designer to create originals—that we have all we can handle to do research in trade magazines and maintain contracts feeding us the results of experts. Beside, he says our styles are standing the test of the marketplace.

Projects X and Y

Flynn also said that he and Martin Freeman had frequently talked about the styling problem. They felt that:

Allison is really a great president, and the company surely would be lost without him. However, we've seen times when he lost a lot of money on bad judgments in styles. Not many times—perhaps six or seven times in the last eighteen months. Also, he is, of course, extremely busy as president of the corporation. He must look after everything from financing from the banks to bargaining with the union. The result is that he is sometimes unavailable to do his styling approvals for several days, or even two weeks. In a business like this, that kind of delay can cost money. It also makes him slightly edgy. It tends, at times when he has many other things to do, to make him look quickly at the styles we submit, or the prototypes Richards makes, or even the finished shoes that are sent for approval by the shipping foreman. Sometimes I worry that he makes two kinds of errors. He simply rubber-stamps what we've done, which makes sending these things to him a waste of time. At other times he makes snap judgments of his own, overruling those of us who have spent so much time and expertise on the shoe. We do think he has good judgment, but he himself has said at times that he wishes he had more time to concentrate on styling and approval of prototypes and final products.

Flynn further explained (and this was corroborated by Freeman) that the two had worked out two plans, which they referred to as "project X" and "project Y." In the first, Flynn created an original design that was not copied from existing styles. Freeman then gave special attention to color and last research for the shoe and recommended a color line that didn't exactly fit past records on consumer purchases—but one he and Flynn thought would have "great consumer appeal." This design and color recommendation was accepted by Lawson and Allison; the shoe went into production and was one of the three top sellers during the calendar year. The latter two men did not know that the shoe was styled in a different way from the usual procedure.

The result of a second, similar project (Y) was put into production the next year, but this time sales were discontinued after three weeks.

Problem between Lawson and Robbins

Frequently, perhaps 10 to 12 times a year, disagreement arises between Mel Lawson, manager of styling, and Paul Robbins, assistant to the superintendent of the Centerville plant. Robbins said:

The styling people don't understand what it means to produce a shoe in the quantities that we do, and to make the changes in production that we have to. They dream up a style quickly, out of thin air. They do not realize that we have a lot of machines that have to be adjusted and that some things they dream up take much longer on certain machines than others, thus creating a bottleneck in the production line. If they put a bow or strap in one position rather than another, it may mean we have to keep people idle on later machines while there is a pileup on the sewing machines on which this complicated little operation is performed. This costs the plant money. Furthermore, there are times when they get the prototype here late, and either the foremen and I work overtime or the trial run won't get through in time to have new production runs on new styles, to take the plant capacity liberated by our stopping production on old styles. Lawson doesn't know much about production and sales and the whole company. I think all he does is to bring shoes down here to the plant, sort of like a messenger boy. Why should he be so hard to

get along with? He isn't getting paid any more than I am, and my position in the plant is just as important as his.

Lawson, in turn, said that he has a difficult time getting along with Robbins:

There are many times when Robbins is just unreasonable. I take prototypes to him five or six times a month, and other minor style changes to him six or eight times. I tell him every time that we have problems in getting these ready, but he knows only about the plant, and telling him doesn't seem to do any good. When we first joined the company, we got along all right, but he has gotten harder and harder to get along with.

Other Problems

Ralph Ferguson, the clerk in the sales department who receives orders from salespeople and forwards totals for production schedules to the two plant superintendents, has complained that the salespeople and Freeman are bypassing him in their practice of sending experimental shoe orders to Freeman. He insisted that his job description (one of only two written descriptions in the company) gives him responsibility for receiving all orders throughout the company and for maintaining historical statistics on shipments.

Both the salespeople and Freeman, on the other hand, said that before they started the new practice (that is, when Ferguson still received the experimental shoe orders), there were at least 8 or 10 instances a year when these were delayed from 1 to 3 days on Ferguson's desk. They reported that Ferguson just wasn't interested in new styles, so the salespeople "just started sending them to Freeman." Ferguson acknowledged that there were times of short delay, but said that there were good reasons for them:

They [the salespeople and Freeman] are so interested in new designs, colors, and lasts that they can't understand the importance of a systematic handling of the whole order procedure, including both old and new shoe styles. There must be accuracy. Sure, I give some priority to experimental orders, but sometimes when rush orders for existing company products are piling up, and when there's a lot of planning I have to do to allocate production between Centerville and Meadowvale, I decide which comes first—processing of these, or processing the experimental shoe orders. Shipton is my boss, not the salespeople or Freeman. I'm going to insist that these orders come to me.

The Push for New Technology

Katherine Olsen believes many of these problems could be solved through better use of technology. She has approached Charles Allison several times about the need to make greater use of the expensive and sophisticated computer information systems he had installed. Although Allison always agrees with her, he has so far done nothing to help solve the problem. Olsen thinks the new technology could dramatically improve coordination at SCI.

Everyone needs to be working from the same data at the same time. As soon as Lawson and Flynn come up with a new design, it should be posted on the intranet so all of us can be informed. And everyone needs access to sales and order information, production schedules, and shipping deadlines. If everyone—from Allison down to the people in the production plants—was kept up to date throughout the entire process, we wouldn't have all this confusion and bickering. But no one around here wants to give up any control—they all have their own little operations and don't want to share information with anyone else. For example, I *sometimes don't even know there's a new style in the works until I get finished samples and photos. No one seems to recognize that one of the biggest advantages of the Internet is to help stay ahead of changing styles. I know that Flynn has a good feel for design, and we're not taking advantage of his abilities. But I also have information and ideas that could help this company keep pace with changes and really stand out from the crowd. I don't know how long we expect to remain competitive using this cumbersome, slow-moving process and putting out shoes that are already behind the times.*

CASE FOR ANALYSIS | Southern Discomfort[146]

Jim Malesckowski remembered the call of two weeks ago as if he had just put down the telephone receiver: "I just read your analysis and I want you to get down to Mexico right away," Jack Ripon, his boss and chief executive officer, had blurted in his ear. "You know we can't make the plant in Oconomo work anymore—the costs are just too high. So go down there, check out what our operational costs would be if we move, and report back to me in a week."

As president of the Wisconsin Specialty Products Division of Lamprey Inc., Jim knew quite well the challenge of dealing with high-cost labor in a third-generation, unionized, U.S. manufacturing plant. And although he had done the analysis that led to his boss's knee-jerk response, the call still stunned him. There were 520 people who made a living at Lamprey's Oconomo facility, and if it closed, most of them wouldn't have a chance of finding another job in the town of 9,900 people.

Instead of the $16-per-hour average wage paid at the Oconomo plant, the wages paid to the Mexican workers—who lived in a town without sanitation and with an unbelievably toxic effluent from industrial pollution—would amount to about $1.60 an hour on average. That would be a savings of nearly $15 million a year for Lamprey, to be offset in part by increased costs for training, transportation, and other matters.

After two days of talking with Mexican government representatives and managers of other companies in the town, Jim had enough information to develop a set of comparative figures of production and shipping costs. On the way home, he started to outline the report, knowing full well that unless some miracle occurred, he would be ushering in a blizzard of pink slips for people he had come to appreciate.

The plant in Oconomo had been in operation since 1921, making special apparel for people suffering from injuries and other medical conditions. Jim had often talked with employees who would recount stories about their fathers or grandfathers working in the same Lamprey company plant—the last of the original manufacturing operations in town.

But friendship aside, competitors had already edged past Lamprey in terms of price and were dangerously close to overtaking it in product quality. Although both Jim and the plant manager had tried to convince the union to accept lower wages, union leaders resisted. In fact, on one occasion when Jim and the plant manager tried to discuss a cell manufacturing approach, which would cross-train employees to perform up to three different jobs, local union leaders could barely restrain their anger. Jim thought he sensed an underlying fear, meaning the union reps were aware of at least some of the problems, but he had been unable to get them to acknowledge this and move on to open discussion.

A week passed and Jim had just submitted his report to his boss. Although he didn't specifically bring up the point, it was apparent that Lamprey could put its investment dollars in a bank and receive a better return than what its Oconomo operation was currently producing.

The next day, he would discuss the report with the CEO. Jim didn't want to be responsible for the plant's dismantling, an act he personally believed would be wrong as long as there was a chance its costs can be lowered. "But Ripon's right," he said to himself. "The costs are too high, the union's unwilling to cooperate, and the company needs to make a better return on its investment if it's to continue at all. It sounds right but feels wrong. What should I do?"

⊗ NOTES

1. Rachel Emma Silverman, "The Science of Serendipity in the Workplace," *The Wall Street Journal*, May 1, 2013, B1.
2. Ibid.
3. Greg Lindsay, "Looking Beyond the Cube," *Fast Company*, March 2013, 34–38.
4. Silverman, "The Science of Serendipity in the Workplace."
5. Quoted in Anne Fisher, "America's Most Admired Companies," *Fortune*, March 17, 2008, 65–67.
6. Based on John P. Kotter, *The New Rules: How to Succeed in Today's Post-Corporate World* (New York: The Free Press, 1995); Steve Lohr, "How Crisis Shapes the Corporate Model," *The New York Times*, March 29, 2009, BU4; David K. Carr, Kelvin J. Hard, and William J. Trahant, *Managing the Change Process: A Field Book for Change Agents, Consultants, Team Leaders, and Reengineering Managers* (New York: McGraw-Hill, 1996); and Joseph

McCann, "Organizational Effectiveness: Changing Concepts for Changing Environments," *Human Resource Planning* 27, no. 1 (2004), 42–50.

7. This discussion of three types of change is based in part on Joseph McCann, "Organizational Effectiveness: Changing Concepts for Changing Environments."

8. Daisuke Wakabayashi, "The Point-and-Shoot Camera Faces Its Existential Moment," *The Wall Street Journal*, July 30, 2013, http://online.wsj.com/article/SB10001424127887324251504578580263719432252.html (accessed August 26, 2013).

9. Melissa A. Korn, "Coursera Defends MOOCs as Road to Learning," *The Wall Street Journal*, May 15, 2013, B5.

10. Clayton M. Christensen and Michael B. Horn, "Innovation Imperative: Change Everything," *The New York Times*, November 1, 2013, http://www.nytimes.com/2013/11/03/education/edlife/online-education-as-an-agent-of-transformation.html?_r=0 (accessed May 15, 2014).

11. Kurt Eichenwald, "Microsoft's Lost Decade," *Vanity Fair*, August 2012, 108–135; and Don Clark, "Microsoft, Intel Brave a Mobile World," *The Wall Street Journal*, April 15, 2013, B2.

12. "The World's 50 Most Innovative Companies," *Fast Company*, March 2014, 74–148.

13. Joseph E. McCann, "Design Principles for an Innovating Company," *Academy of Management Executive* 5, no. 2 (May 1991), 76–93.

14. Teri Evans, "Entrepreneurs Seek to Elicit Workers' Ideas—Contests with Cash Prizes and Other Rewards Stimulate Innovation in Hard Times," *The Wall Street Journal*, December 22, 2009, B7.

15. James R. Hagerty, "With Bottle-Fillers in Mind, the Water Fountain Evolves," *The Wall Street Journal*, March 24, 2013, B1.

16. Jon Katzenbach and Zia Khan, "Leading Outside the Lines," *Strategy + Business*, April 26, 2010, http://www.strategy-business.com/article/10204?gko=788c9 (accessed September 9, 2010).

17. Erin White, "How a Company Made Everyone a Team Player," *The Wall Street Journal*, August 13, 2007, B1, B7.

18. Judy Oppenheimer, "A Top Cop Who Gets It," *More*, June 2009, 86–91, 144.

19. Richard A. Wolfe, "Organizational Innovation: Review, Critique and Suggested Research Directions," *Journal of Management Studies* 31, no. 3 (May 1994), 405–431.

20. John L. Pierce and Andre L. Delbecq, "Organization Structure, Individual Attitudes and Innovation," *Academy of Management Review* 2 (1977), 27–37; and Michael Aiken and Jerald Hage, "The Organic Organization and Innovation," *Sociology* 5 (1971), 63–82.

21. Richard L. Daft, "Bureaucratic versus Non-bureaucratic Structure in the Process of Innovation and Change," in Samuel B. Bacharach, ed., *Perspectives in Organizational Sociology: Theory and Research* (Greenwich, CT: JAI Press, 1982), 129–166.

22. Alan D. Meyer and James B. Goes, "Organizational Assimilation of Innovations: A Multilevel Contextual Analysis," *Academy of Management Journal* 31 (1988), 897–923.

23. Richard W. Woodman, John E. Sawyer, and Ricky W. Griffin, "Toward a Theory of Organizational Creativity," *Academy of Management Review* 18 (1993), 293–321.

24. John Grossman, "Strategies: Thinking Small," *Inc.*, August 2004, 34–36.

25. Robert I. Sutton, "Weird Ideas That Spark Innovation," *MIT Sloan Management Review* (Winter 2002), 83–87; Robert Barker, "The Art of Brainstorming," *BusinessWeek*, August 26, 2002, 168–169; Gary A. Steiner, ed., *The Creative Organization* (Chicago: University of Chicago Press, 1965), 16–18; and James Brian Quinn, "Managing Innovation: Controlled Chaos," *Harvard Business Review*, May–June 1985, 73–84.

26. Thomas M. Burton, "Flop Factor: By Learning from Failures, Lilly Keeps Drug Pipeline Full," *The Wall Street Journal*, April 21, 2004, A1, A12.

27. Hiroko Tabuchi, "How the Parade Passed Sony By," *The New York Times*, April 15, 2012, BU1.

28. John P. Kotter, *Leading Change* (Boston: Harvard Business School Press, 1996), 20–25; and John P. Kotter, "Leading Change," *Harvard Business Review*, March–April 1995, 59–67.

29. G. Tomas M. Hult, Robert F. Hurley, and Gary A. Knight, "Innovativeness: Its Antecedents and Impact on Business Performance," *Industrial Marketing Management* 33 (2004), 429–438.

30. Burton, "Flop Factor."

31. D. Bruce Merrifield, "Intrapreneurial Corporate Renewal," *Journal of Business Venturing* 8 (September 1993), 383–389; Linsu Kim, "Organizational Innovation and Structure," *Journal of Business Research* 8 (1980), 225–245; and Tom Burns and G. M. Stalker, *The Management of Innovation* (London: Tavistock Publications, 1961).

32. Robert B. Duncan, "The Ambidextrous Organization: Designing Dual Structures for Innovation," in Ralph H. Killman, Louis R. Pondy, and Dennis Slevin, eds., *The Management of Organization* 1 (New York: North-Holland, 1976), 167–188; M. L. Tushman and C. A. O'Reilly III, "Building an Ambidextrous Organization: Forming Your Own 'Skunk Works,'" *Health Forum Journal* 42, no. 2 (March–April 1999), 20–23; and J. C. Spender and Eric H. Kessler, "Managing the Uncertainties of Innovation: Extending Thompson (1967)," *Human Relations* 48, no. 1 (1995), 35–56.

33. Julian Birkinshaw and Kamini Gupta, "Clarifying the Distinctive Contribution of Ambidexterity to the Field of Organization Studies," *The Academy of Management Perspectives* 27, no. 4 (2013), 287–298; Constantine Andriopoulos and Marianne W. Lewis, "Managing Innovation Paradoxes: Ambidexterity Lessons from Leading Product Design Companies," *Long Range Planning* 43 (2010), 104–122; Charles A. O'Reilly III and Michael L. Tushman, "The Ambidextrous Organization," *Harvard Business Review*, April 2004, 74–81; Sebastian Raisch and Julian Birkinshaw, "Organizational Ambidexterity: Antecedents, Outcomes, and Moderators," *Journal of Management* 34, no 3 (June 2008), 375–409.

34. J. G. March, "Exploration and Exploitation in Organizational Learning," *Organization Science* 2 (1991), 71–87; and R. Duane Ireland and Justin W. Webb, "Crossing the Great Divide of Strategic Entrepreneurship: Transitioning Between Exploration and Exploitation," *Business Horizons* 52 (2009), 469–479. For a review of the research on exploration and exploitation, see A. K. Gupta, K. G. Smith, and C. E. Shalley, "The Interplay Between Exploration and Exploitation," *Academy of Management Journal* 49, no. 4 (2006), 693–706.

35. M. H. Lubatkin, Z. Simsek, Y. Ling, and J. F. Veiga, "Ambidexterity and Performance in Small- to Medium-Sized Firms: The Pivotal Role of Top Management Team

Behavioral Integration," *Journal of Management* 32, no. 5 (October 2006), 646–672; and O'Reilly and Tushman, "The Ambidextrous Organization."

36. Tushman and O'Reilly, "Building an Ambidextrous Organization."

37. Barry Jaruzelski, John Loehr, and Richard Holman, "Making Ideas Work," *Strategy + Business* (Winter 2012), 2–14.

38. J. C. Spender and Bruce Strong, "Who Has Innovative Ideas? Employees." *The Wall Street Journal,* August 23, 2010, R5; and Rachel Emma Silverman, "How to Be Like Apple," *The Wall Street Journal,* August 29, 2011, http://online.wsj.com/article/SB1000142405311190400930457653284266785 4706.html (accessed September 16, 2011).

39. Erik Brynjolfsson and Michael Schrage, "The New, Faster Face of Innovation; Thanks to Technology, Change Has Never Been So Easy or So Cheap," *The Wall Street Journal,* August 17, 2009; and Vindu Goel, "Why Google Pulls the Plug," *The New York Times,* February 15, 2009.

40. Darren Dahl, "Technology: Pipe Up, People! Rounding Up Staff Ideas," *Inc.,* February 2010, 80–81.

41. Roger L. Martin, "The Innovation Catalysts," *Harvard Business Review,* June 2011, 82–87.

42. Spender and Strong, "Who Has Innovative Ideas?"

43. Austin Carr, "The Hard Sell at Taco Bell," *Fast Company,* July–August 2013, 36–38.

44. Dahl, "Technology: Pipe Up, People!"

45. Edward F. McDonough III and Richard Leifer, "Using Simultaneous Structures to Cope with Uncertainty," *Academy of Management Journal* 26 (1983), 727–735.

46. Michael L. Tushman, Wendy K. Smith, and Andy Binns, "The Ambidextrous CEO," *Harvard Business Review,* June 2011, 74–80.

47. Todd Datz, "Romper Ranch," *CIO Enterprise* Section 2 (May 15, 1999), 39–52.

48. Paul S. Adler, Barbara Goldoftas, and David I. Levine, "Ergonomics, Employee Involvement, and the Toyota Production System: A Case Study of NUMMI's 1993 Model Introduction," *Industrial and Labor Relations Review* 50, no. 3 (April 1997), 416–437.

49. Judith R. Blau and William McKinley, "Ideas, Complexity, and Innovation," *Administrative Science Quarterly* 24 (1979), 200–219.

50. Peter Landers, "Back to Basics; With Dry Pipelines, Big Drug Makers Stock Up in Japan," *The Wall Street Journal,* November 24, 2003, A1, A7.

51. Sherri Eng, "Hatching Schemes," *The Industry Standard,* November 27–December 4, 2000, 174–175.

52. Donald F. Kuratko, Jeffrey G. Covin, and Robert P. Garrett, "Corporate Venturing: Insights from Actual Performance," *Business Horizons* 52 (2009), 459–467.

53. Brad Stone, *The Everything Store: Jeff Bezos and the Age of Amazon* (New York: Little Brown), 199.

54. Christopher Hoenig, "Skunk Works Secrets," *CIO,* July 1, 2000, 74–76.

55. Claire Cain Miller and Nick Bilton, "Google's Lab of Wildest Dreams," *The New York Times,* November 13, 2011, www.nytimes.com/2011/11/14/technology/ at-google-x-a-top -secret-lab-dreaming-up-the-future .html?pagewanted=all (accessed November 14, 2011).

56. James I. Cash, Jr., Michael J. Earl, and Robert Morison, "Teaming Up to Crack Innovation and Enterprise Integration," *Harvard Business Review,* November 2008, 90–100.

57. Arkadi Kuhlmann, "Reinventing Innovation," *Ivey Business Journal,* May–June 2010, 6.

58. Jane M. Howell and Christopher A. Higgins, "Champions of Technology Innovation," *Administrative Science Quarterly* 35 (1990), 317–341; and Jane M. Howell and Christopher A. Higgins, "Champions of Change: Identifying, Understanding, and Supporting Champions of Technology Innovations," *Organizational Dynamics* (Summer 1990), 40–55.

59. Rachel Feintzeig, "Office 'Influencers' Are In High Demand," *The Wall Street Journal,* February 12, 2014, http://online.wsj.com/news/articles/SB10001424052702303874504579375313680290816 (accessed May 20, 2014).

60. Thomas J. Peters and Robert H. Waterman, Jr., *In Search of Excellence* (New York: Harper & Row, 1982).

61. Curtis R. Carlson and William W. Wilmot, *Innovation: The Five Disciplines for Creating What Customers Want* (New York: Crown Business, 2006).

62. Robert I. Sutton, "The Weird Rules of Creativity," *Harvard Business Review,* September 2001, 94–103; and Julian Birkinshaw and Michael Mol, "How Management Innovation Happens," *MIT Sloan Management Review* (Summer 2006), 81–88. See Lionel Roure, "Product Champion Characteristics in France and Germany," *Human Relations* 54, no. 5 (2001), 663–682, for a review of the literature related to product champions.

63. Peter Lewis, "Texas Instruments' Lunatic Fringe," *Fortune,* September 4, 2006, 120–128.

64. Joan Schneider and Julie Hall, "Why Most Product Launches Fail," *Harvard Business Review*, April 2011, 21–23; G. A. Stevens and J. Burley, "3,000 Raw Ideas = 1 Commercial Success!" *Research Technology Management* 40, no. 3 (May–June 1997), 16–27; R. P. Morgan, C. Kruytbosch, and N. Kannankutty, "Patenting and Invention Activity of U.S. Scientists and Engineers in the Academic Sector: Comparisons with Industry," *Journal of Technology Transfer* 26 (2001), 173–183; Edwin Mansfield, J. Rapaport, J. Schnee, S. Wagner, and M. Hamburger, *Research and Innovation in Modern Corporations* (New York: Norton, 1971); Christopher Power with Kathleen Kerwin, Ronald Grover, Keith Alexander, and Robert D. Hof, "Flops," *BusinessWeek,* August 16, 1993, 76–82; and Modesto A. Maidique and Billie Jo Zirger, "A Study of Success and Failure in Product Innovation: The Case of the U.S. Electronics Industry," *IEEE Transactions in Engineering Management* 31 (November 1984), 192–203.

65. Claire Cain Miller, "Back to the Drawing Board for Nexus Q," *The New York Times,* August 9, 2012, B1; and Doug Gross, "The Top 10 Tech Fails of 2012," CNN Tech Website, December 28, 2012, http://www.cnn.com/2012/12/28/tech /web/tech-fails-2012/index.html?hpt=hp_bn5 (accessed May 20, 2014).

66. Holman W. Jenkins, Jr., "The Microsoft Solution," *The Wall Street Journal Europe,* July 29, 2010, 13.

67. Schneider and Hall, "Why Most Product Launches Fail."

68. Andrew Bordeaux, "10 Famous Product Failures and the Advertisements That Did Not Sell Them," *Growthink.com,* December 17, 2007, http://www.growthink.com/content/10 -famous-product-failures-and-advertisements-did-not-sell -them (accessed September 16, 2011); and Jane McGrath, "Five Failed McDonald's Menu Items," HowStuffWorks.com, http://money.howstuffworks.com/5-failed-mcdonalds-menu -items3.htm (accessed September 16, 2011).

69. Linton, Matysiak & Wilkes Inc. study results reported in "Market Study Results Released: New Product Introduction Success, Failure Rates Analyzed," *Frozen Food Digest,* July 1, 1997.

70. Deborah Dougherty and Cynthia Hardy, "Sustained Product Innovation in Large, Mature Organizations: Overcoming Innovation-to-Organization Problems," *Academy of Management Journal* 39, no. 5 (1996), 1120–1153.

71. M. Adams and the Product Development and Management Association, "Comparative Performance Assessment Study 2004," available for purchase at http://www.pdma .org. Results reported in Jeff Cope, "Lessons Learned—Commercialization Success Rates: A Brief Review," *RTI Tech Ventures* newsletter 4, no. 4 (December 2007).

72. Ibid.

73. Annie Lowrey, "Ideas on an Assembly Line," *The New York Times*, December 14, 2012, B1.

74. Shona L. Brown and Kathleen M. Eisenhardt, "Product Development: Past Research, Present Findings, and Future Directions," *Academy of Management Review* 20, no. 2 (1995), 343–378; F. Axel Johne and Patricia A. Snelson, "Success Factors in Product Innovation: A Selective Review of the Literature," *Journal of Product Innovation Management* 5 (1988), 114–128; Antonio Bailetti and Paul F. Litva, "Integrating Customer Requirements into Product Designs," *Journal of Product Innovation Management* 12 (1995), 3–15; Jay W. Lorsch and Paul R. Lawrence, "Organizing for Product Innovation," *Harvard Business Review*, January–February 1965, 109–122; and Science Policy Research Unit, University of Sussex, *Success and Failure in Industrial Innovation* (London: Centre for the Study of Industrial Innovation, 1972).

75. Study reported in Mike Gordon, Chris Musso, Eric Rebentisch, and Nisheeth Gupta, "Business Insight (A Special Report): Innovation—The Path to Developing Successful New Products," *The Wall Street Journal*, November 30, 2009, R5.

76. Dorothy Leonard and Jeffrey F. Rayport, "Spark Innovation through Empathic Design," *Harvard Business Review*, November–December 1997, 102–113.

77. Bruce Brown and Scott D. Anthony, "How P&G Tripled Its Innovation Success Rate," *Harvard Business Review*, June 2011, 64–72.

78. Janet Rae-Dupree, "Even the Giants Can Learn to Think Small," *The New York Times*, August 3, 2008, BU4; Mike Ramsey and Norihiko Shirouzu, "Toyota Is Changing How It Develops Cars," *The Wall Street Journal*, July 5, 2010, http://www.in.com/news/business/fullstory-toyota-is -changing-how-it-develops-cars-14559691-in-1.html (accessed September 16, 2011); and Tim Higgins, "GM Adds Team to Focus on Safety During Car Development," *Bloomberg*, April 16, 2014, http://www.bloomberg.com /news/2014-04-15/barra-adds-team-to-focus-on-safety-of-gm -vehicles-in-development.html (accessed May 24, 2014).

79. Brown and Eisenhardt, "Product Development"; and Dan Dimancescu and Kemp Dwenger, "Smoothing the Product Development Path," *Management Review*, January 1996, 36–41.

80. William J. Holstein, "Five Gates to Innovation," *Strategy + Business*, March 1, 2010, www.strategy-business.com/ article/00021?gko=0bd39 (accessed September 16, 2011); and "Corning: For Becoming the 800-Pound Gorilla of the Touch Screen Business," segment of "The World's 50 Most Innovative Companies," *Fast Company*, March 2013, 86–156.

81. Kenneth B. Kahn, "Market Orientation, Interdepartmental Integration, and Product Development Performance," *The Journal of Product Innovation Management* 18 (2001),

314–323; and Ali E. Akgün, Gary S. Lynn, and John C. Byrne, "Taking the Guesswork Out of New Product Development: How Successful High-Tech Companies Get That Way," *Journal of Business Strategy* 25, no. 4 (2004), 41–46.

82. The discussion of open innovation is based on Henry Chesbrough, *Open Innovation* (Boston, MA: Harvard Business School Press, 2003); Henry Chesbrough, "The Era of Open Innovation," *MIT Sloan Management Review* (Spring 2003), 35–41; Julian Birkinshaw and Susan A. Hill, "Corporate Venturing Units: Vehicles for Strategic Success in the New Europe," *Organizational Dynamics* 34, no. 3 (2005), 247–257; Amy Muller and Liisa Välikangas, "Extending the Boundary of Corporate Innovation," *Strategy & Leadership* 30, no. 3 (2002), 4–9; and Navi Radjou, "Networked Innovation Drives Profits," *Industrial Management*, January–February 2005, 14–21.

83. Chesbrough, *Open Innovation*.

84. Amy Muller, Nate Hutchins, and Miguel Cardoso Pinto, "Applying Open Innovation Where Your Company Needs It Most," *Strategy & Leadership* 40, no. 2 (2012), 35–42.

85. Martin W. Wallin and Georg Von Krogh, "Organizing for Open Innovation: Focus on the Integration of Knowledge," *Organizational Dynamics* 39, no. 2 (2010), 145–154; Bettina von Stamm, "Collaboration with Other Firms and Customers: Innovation's Secret Weapon," *Strategy & Leadership* 32, no. 3 (2004), 16–20; and Bas Hillebrand and Wim G. Biemans, "Links between Internal and External Cooperation in Product Development: An Exploratory Study," *The Journal of Product Innovation Management* 21 (2004), 110–122.

86. Barry Jaruzelski and Richard Holman, "Casting a Wide Net: Building the Capabilities for Open Innovation," *Ivey Business Journal* March–April 2011, http://www .iveybusinessjournal.com/topics/innovation/casting-a-wide -net—building-the-capabilities-for-open-innovation (accessed September 19, 2011).

87. A. G. Lafley and Ram Charan, *The Game Changer: How You Can Drive Revenue and Profit Growth with Innovation* (New York: Crown Business, 2008); Larry Huston and Nabil Sakkab, "Connect and Develop: Inside Procter & Gamble's New Model for Innovation," *Harvard Business Review*, March 2006, 58–66; and G. Gil Cloyd, "P&G's Secret: Innovating Innovation," *Industry Week*, December 2004, 26–34.

88. Farhad Manjoo, "Apple Nation," *Fortune*, July–August 2010, 68–112; and Jorge Rufat-Latre, Amy Muller, and Dave Jones, "Delivering on the Promise of Open Innovation," *Strategy & Leadership* 38, no. 6 (2010), 23–28.

89. David Lerman and Liz Smith, "Wanted: Big Ideas from Small Fry," *Bloomberg BusinessWeek*, August 30–September 5, 2010, 49–51; Steve Lohr, "The Crowd Is Wise (When It's Focused)," *The New York Times*, July 19, 2009, BU4; and S. Lohr, "The Corporate Lab As Ringmaster," *The New York Times*, August 16, 2009, BU3.

90. Kevin J. Boudreau and Karim R. Lakhani, "Using the Crowd as an Innovation Partner," *Harvard Business Review*, April 2013, 61–67; Andy Meek "May the Best Business Win; Innovation Contests Can Spur New Products—and Boost Worker Morale," *Inc.*, February 2012, 86–87.

91. Meek "May the Best Business Win."

92. Olivier Leclerc and Mihnea Moldoveanu, "Five Routes to More Innovative Problem Solving," *McKinsey Quarterly*, April 2013, http://www.mckinsey.com/insights/strategy/five _routes_to_more_innovative_problem_solving (accessed May 14, 2013).

93. Sabrina Adamczyk, Angelika C. Bullinger, and Kathrin M. Möslein, "Innovation Contests: A Review, Classification and Outlook," *Creativity and Innovation Management* 21, no. 4 (2012), 335–355.

94. Reported in Jill Jusko, "A Team Effort," *Industry Week,* January 2007, 42, 45.

95. John A. Pearce II, "Speed Merchants," *Organizational Dynamics* 30, no. 3 (2002), 191–205; Kathleen M. Eisenhardt and Behnam N. Tabrizi, "Accelerating Adaptive Processes: Product Innovation in the Global Computer Industry," *Administrative Science Quarterly* 40 (1995), 84–110; Dougherty and Hardy, "Sustained Product Innovation in Large, Mature Organizations"; and Karne Bronikowski, "Speeding New Products to Market," *Journal of Business Strategy,* September–October 1990, 34–37.

96. Pinar Cankurtaran, Fred Langerak, and Abbie Griffin, "Consequences of New Product Development Speed: A Meta-Analysis," *Journal of Product Innovation Management* 30, no. 3 (2013), 465–486.

97. Susan Berfield and Manuel Baigorri, "Zara's Fast Fashion Edge," *Bloomberg BusinessWeek,* November 13, 2013, http://www.businessweek.com/articles/2013-11-14/2014-outlook-zaras-fashion-supply-chain-edge (accessed May 20, 2014); Brad Kenney, "Callaway Improves Long Game with Collaborative Tech," *Industry Week*, June 2008, 72.

98. Paul A. Eisenstein, "Not Your Dad's Chrysler: Fiat Merger Brings Exotic Cars, Style," *NBC News,* May 12, 2014, http://www.nbcnews.com/business/autos/not-your-dads-chrysler-fiat-merger-brings-exotic-cars-style-n103006 (accessed May 20, 2014); Bernie Woodall, "Fiat Chrysler Will Be OK If It Misses Lofty Targets: Marchionne," *Reuters,* May 13, 2014, http://www.reuters.com/article/2014/05/13/us-fiat-chrysler-markets-idUSBREA4C0XI20140513 (accessed May 20, 2014); and Alex Taylor III, "Chrysler's Speed Merchant," *Fortune,* September 6, 2010, 77–82.

99. "The World's 50 Most Innovative Companies," *Fast Company,* March 2014, 74–148 (Dodge is on page 86).

100. Raymond E. Miles, Henry J. Coleman, Jr., and W. E. Douglas Creed, "Keys to Success in Corporate Redesign," *California Management Review* 37, no. 3 (Spring 1995), 128–145.

101. David C. Robertson with Bill Breen, *Brick by Brick: How LEGO Rewrote the Rules of Innovation and Conquered the Global Toy Industry* (New York: Crown Business, 2013), 265–266.

102. Julian Birkinshaw, Gary Hamel, and Michael J. Mol, "Management Innovation," *Academy of Management Review* 33, no. 4 (2008), 825–845.

103. Reena Jana, "From India, The Latest Management Fad," *BusinessWeek,* December 14, 2009, 57; Navi Radjou, "Jugaad: The Art of Converting Adversity Into Opportunity," *Forbes* (March 23, 2014), http://www.forbes.com/sites/ashoka/2014/03/23/jugaad-the-art-of-converting-adversity-into-opportunity/ (accessed May 24, 2014); and Rebecca Bundhun, "Home and Away: Indians Successful All Around the World, *The National,* May 24, 2014, http://www.thenational.ae/business/industry-insights/economics/home-and-away-indians-successful-all-around-the-world (accessed May 24, 2014).

104. Fariborz Damanpour and William M. Evan, "Organizational Innovation and Performance: The Problem of 'Organizational Lag,'" *Administrative Science Quarterly* 29 (1984), 392–409; David J. Teece, "The Diffusion of an Administrative Innovation,"

Management Science 26 (1980), 464–470; John R. Kimberly and Michael J. Evaniski, "Organizational Innovation: The Influence of Individual, Organizational and Contextual Factors on Hospital Adoption of Technological and Administrative Innovation," *Academy of Management Journal* 24 (1981), 689–713; Michael K. Moch and Edward V. Morse, "Size, Centralization, and Organizational Adoption of Innovations," *American Sociological Review* 42 (1977), 716–725; and Mary L. Fennell, "Synergy, Influence, and Information in the Adoption of Administrative Innovation," *Academy of Management Journal* 27 (1984), 113–129.

105. Richard L. Daft, "A Dual-Core Model of Organizational Innovation," *Academy of Management Journal* 21 (1978), 193–210.

106. Daft, "Bureaucratic versus Nonbureaucratic Structure"; and Robert W. Zmud, "Diffusion of Modern Software Practices: Influence of Centralization and Formalization," *Management Science* 28 (1982), 1421–1431.

107. Daft, "A Dual-Core Model of Organizational Innovation"; and Zmud, "Diffusion of Modern Software Practices."

108. Fariborz Damanpour, "The Adoption of Technological, Administrative, and Ancillary Innovations: Impact of Organizational Factors," *Journal of Management* 13 (1987), 675–688.

109. Gregory H. Gaertner, Karen N. Gaertner, and David M. Akinnusi, "Environment, Strategy, and the Implementation of Administrative Change: The Case of Civil Service Reform," *Academy of Management Journal* 27 (1984), 525–543.

110. Claudia Bird Schoonhoven and Mariann Jelinek, "Dynamic Tension in Innovative, High Technology Firms: Managing Rapid Technology Change through Organization Structure," in Mary Ann Von Glinow and Susan Albers Mohrman, eds., *Managing Complexity in High Technology Organizations* (New York: Oxford University Press, 1990), 90–118.

111. Jeanne Whalen, "Glaxo Tries Biotech Model to Spur Drug Innovations," *The Wall Street Journal,* July 1, 2010, A1.

112. Sally Helgesen, "An Extreme Take on Restructuring: No Job Titles, No Managers, No Politics," *Strategy + Business,* February 11, 2014, http://www.strategy-business.com/blog/An-Extreme-Take-on-Restructuring-No-Job-Titles?gko=9b214 (accessed May 21, 2014); and Camille Sweeney and Josh Gosfield, "No Managers Required: How Zappos Ditched the Old Corporate Structure for Something New," *Fast Company,* January 6, 2014, http://www.fastcompany.com/3024358/bottom-line/no-managers-required-how-zappos-ditched-the-old-corporate-structure-for-somethin (accessed June 16, 2014).

113. David Ulm and James K. Hickel, "What Happens after Restructuring?" *Journal of Business Strategy,* July–August 1990, 37–41; and John L. Sprague, "Restructuring and Corporate Renewal: A Manager's Guide," *Management Review,* March 1989, 34–36.

114. Stan Pace, "Rip the Band-Aid Off Quickly," *Strategy & Leadership* 30, no. 1 (2002), 4–9.

115. Benson L. Porter and Warrington S. Parker, Jr., "Culture Change," *Human Resource Management* 31 (Spring–Summer 1992), 45–67.

116. Atsuko Fukase, "New CEO, New Mizuho Culture," *The Asian Wall Street Journal,* June 23, 2011, 22.

117. Reported in "Mergers Don't Consider Cultures," *ISHN,* September 2011, 14.

118. Joann S. Lublin, "Bringing Hidden Biases Into the Light," *The Wall Street Journal Online*, January 9, 2014, http://online.wsj.com/news/articles/SB10001424052702303754404579308562690896896 (accessed May 30, 2014).

119. W. Warner Burke, "The New Agenda for Organization Development," in Wendell L. French, Cecil H. Bell, Jr., and Robert A. Zawacki, *Organization Development and Transformation: Managing Effective Change* (Burr Ridge, IL: Irwin McGraw-Hill, 2000), 523–535.

120. W. Warner Burke, *Organization Development: A Process of Learning and Changing*, 2nd ed. (Reading, MA: Addison-Wesley, 1994); and Wendell L. French and Cecil H. Bell, Jr., "A History of Organization Development," in French, Bell, and Zawacki, *Organization Development and Transformation*, 20–42.

121. French and Bell, "A History of Organization Development."

122. The information on large group intervention is based on Kathleen D. Dannemiller and Robert W. Jacobs, "Changing the Way Organizations Change: A Revolution of Common Sense," *The Journal of Applied Behavioral Science* 28, no. 4 (December 1992), 480–498; Barbara B. Bunker and Billie T. Alban, "Conclusion: What Makes Large Group Interventions Effective?" *The Journal of Applied Behavioral Science* 28, no. 4 (December 1992), 570–591; and Marvin R. Weisbord, "Inventing the Future: Search Strategies for Whole System Improvements," in French, Bell, and Zawacki, *Organization Development and Transformation*, 242–250.

123. Marvin Weisbord and Sandra Janoff, "Faster, Shorter, Cheaper May Be Simple; It's Never Easy," *The Journal of Applied Behavioral Science* 41, no. 1 (March 2005), 70–82.

124. J. Quinn, "What a Workout!" *Performance*, November 1994, 58–63; and Bunker and Alban, "Conclusion: What Makes Large Group Interventions Effective?"

125. Dave Ulrich, Steve Kerr, and Ron Ashkenas, with Debbie Burke and Patrice Murphy, *The GE Work Out: How to Implement GE's Revolutionary Method for Busting Bureaucracy and Attacking Organizational Problems—Fast!* (New York: McGraw-Hill, 2002).

126. Paul F. Buller, "For Successful Strategic Change: Blend OD Practices with Strategic Management," *Organizational Dynamics* (Winter 1988), 42–55.

127. Norm Brodsky, "Everybody Sells," (Street Smarts column), *Inc.*, June 2004, 53–54.

128. Shawn Tully, "Can UnitedHealth Really Fix the System?" *Fortune*, May 29, 2013, 187–194.

129. Ibid.

130. Pierre Loewe and Jennifer Dominiquini, "Overcome the Barriers to Effective Innovation," *Strategy & Leadership* 34, no. 1 (2006), 24–31.

131. Bernard M. Bass, "Theory of Transformational Leadership Redux," *Leadership Quarterly* 6, no. 4 (1995), 463–478; and Dong I. Jung, Chee Chow, and Anne Wu, "The Role of Transformational Leadership in Enhancing Organizational Innovation: Hypotheses and Some Preliminary Findings," *The Leadership Quarterly* 14 (2003), 525–544.

132. Todd Datz, "No Small Change," *CIO*, February 15, 2004, 66–72.

133. These techniques are based on John P. Kotter's eight-stage model of planned organizational change, Kotter, *Leading Change*, 20–25.

134. Everett M. Rogers and Floyd Shoemaker, *Communication of Innovations: A Cross Cultural Approach*, 2nd ed. (New York: Free Press, 1971); and Stratford P. Sherman, "Eight Big Masters of Innovation," *Fortune*, October 15, 1984, 66–84.

135. Richard L. Daft and Selwyn W. Becker, *Innovation in Organizations* (New York: Elsevier, 1978); and John P. Kotter and Leonard A. Schlesinger, "Choosing Strategies for Change," *Harvard Business Review* 57 (1979), 106–114.

136. Donald F. Kuratko, Jeffrey G. Covin, and Robert P. Garrett, "Corporate Venturing: Insights from Actual Performance," *Business Horizons* 52 (2009), 459–467.

137. Philip H. Mirvis, Amy L. Sales, and Edward J. Hackett, "The Implementation and Adoption of New Technology in Organizations: The Impact on Work, People, and Culture," *Human Resource Management* 30 (Spring 1991), 113–139; Arthur E. Wallach, "System Changes Begin in the Training Department," *Personnel Journal* 58 (1979), 846–848, 872; and Paul R. Lawrence, "How to Deal with Resistance to Change," *Harvard Business Review* 47 (January–February 1969), 4–12, 166–176.

138. Julie Jargon, "Business Technology: Domino's IT Staff Delivers Slick Site, Ordering System," *The Wall Street Journal*, November 24, 2009, B5.

139. Darren Dahl, "Trust Me: You're Gonna Love This; Getting Employees to Embrace New Technology," *Inc.*, November 2008, 41.

140. Peter Richardson and D. Keith Denton, "Communicating Change," *Human Resource Management* 35, no. 2 (Summer 1996), 203–216.

141. Edgar H. Schein and Warren Bennis, *Personal and Organizational Change via Group Methods* (New York: Wiley, 1965); and Amy Edmondson, "Psychological Safety and Learning Behavior in Work Teams," *Administrative Science Quarterly* 44 (1999), 350–383.

142. Diane L. Coutu, "Creating the Most Frightening Company on Earth; An Interview with Andy Law of St. Luke's," *Harvard Business Review*, September–October 2000, 143–150.

143. Lawrence G. Hrebiniak, "Obstacles to Effective Strategy Implementation," *Organizational Dynamics* 35, no. 1 (2006), 12–31.

144. Adapted by Dorothy Marcic from Susanne G. Scott and Reginald A. Bruce, "Determinants of Innovative Behavior: A Path Model of Individual Innovation in the Workplace," *Academy of Management Journal* 37, no. 3 (1994), 580–607.

145. Written by Charles E. Summer. Copyright 1978.

146. Doug Wallace, "What Would You Do?" *Business Ethics*, March/April 1996, 52–53. Reprinted with permission from *Business Ethics*, PO Box 8439, Minneapolis, MN 55408; phone: 612-879-0695.

12 | Decision-Making Processes

Learning Objectives

After reading this chapter you should be able to:

1. Define organizational decision making.
2. Explain programmed versus nonprogrammed decisions.
3. Discuss the rational and bounded rationality approaches to decision making.
4. Describe the management science approach to decision making.
5. Understand the Carnegie and incremental decision models.
6. Explain the garbage can model of decision making.
7. Discuss the contingency decision-making framework.
8. Explain the role of high-velocity environments, mistakes, and cognitive biases in decision making.

Before reading this chapter, please check whether you agree or disagree with each of the following statements:

1 Managers should use the most objective, rational process possible when making a decision.

   I AGREE _____   I DISAGREE _____

2 When a manager knows the best solution to a serious organizational problem and has the necessary authority, it is best to simply make the decision and implement it rather than involve other managers in the decision process.

   I AGREE _____   I DISAGREE _____

3 Making a poor decision can help a manager and organization learn and get stronger.

   I AGREE _____   I DISAGREE _____

What is one activity every manager—no matter what level of the hierarchy, what industry, or what size or type of organization—engages in every day? Decision making. Managers are often referred to as *decision makers*, and every organization grows, prospers, or fails as a result of the choices managers make. However, many decisions can be risky and uncertain, without any guarantee of success. Ron Johnson, who was the brain behind Apple's retail stores and formerly a successful executive at Target, thought he had the winning formula to bring department store chain J.C. Penney back from the brink. Johnson decided to remake Penney into a more upscale, youth-oriented retailer, but the decision failed. Johnson was ousted after only 16 months, and Penney lost $1 billion during his one full year as CEO.[1] Or consider the damage done to the reputation of General Motors (GM) when investigations into quality and safety problems revealed that managers had delayed decisions that might have saved lives. Top executives at GM have admitted some managers knew about faulty ignition switches for more than a decade before crashes and deaths linked to the problem caused them to issue a recall of 2.6 million vehicles. By May 2014, the faulty switch had been linked to 47 crashes and 13 deaths, but investigators believe there are likely many more that were caused by the problem.[2] In hindsight, the decision to issue a recall seems like a no-brainer, but the situation wasn't so clear-cut at the time. Decision making is done amid constantly changing factors, unclear information, and conflicting points of view, and even the best managers in the most successful companies sometimes make big blunders.

Yet managers also make many successful decisions every day. Apple has topped *Fortune* magazine's list of the world's most admired companies for seven straight years (2008–2014), but the company was all but dead in the mid-1990s. If the board had not decided to bring back co-founder Steve Jobs as CEO (he had been fired from his own company years earlier), Apple might not even exist today. In 1996, Apple lost $816 million on sales of $9.8 billion. Yet, thanks to decisions made by Jobs (who led the company from 1997 until he died in 2011) and other top managers, Apple is soaring today. Since 2010, Apple has been the largest U.S. corporation in terms of market valuation. The decision to bring Jobs back has been called one of the greatest business decisions of all time.[3] There are also examples from industries very different from the one Apple operates in. Decisions made by the leadership team of Delta Airlines CEO Richard Anderson helped Delta (Number 48 on *Fortune*'s 2014 list of most admired companies) earn $2.7 billion in profit in 2013, an all-time record for the airline industry. Examples of Anderson's unorthodox thinking include the decision to reward frequent-flyers based on the price of their ticket, not the number of miles flown. That means business travelers, who usually pay higher prices, get rewarded, and more corporate business is going Delta's way. Another decision was to forgo purchasing next-generation jets in favor of buying and refurbishing older aircraft.[4]

Purpose of This Chapter

At any time, an organization may be identifying problems and implementing alternatives for hundreds of decisions. Managers and organizations somehow muddle through these processes.[5] The purpose here is to analyze these processes to learn what decision making is actually like in organizational settings. Decision-making processes can be thought of as the brain and nervous system of an organization. Decision making is the end use of the information and control systems described in Chapter 8.

First, the chapter defines decision making and the different types of decisions managers make. The next section describes an ideal model of decision making and then examines how individual managers actually make decisions. The chapter also explores several models of organizational decision making, each of which is appropriate in a different organizational situation. The next section combines the models into a single framework that describes when and how the various approaches should be used. Finally, the chapter discusses special issues related to decision making, such as high-velocity environments, decision mistakes and learning, and ways to overcome cognitive biases that hinder effective decision making.

Types of Decisions

Organizational decision making is formally defined as the process of identifying and solving problems. The process has two major stages. In the **problem identification** stage, information about environmental and organizational conditions is monitored to determine if performance is satisfactory and to diagnose the cause of shortcomings. The **problem solution** stage is when alternative courses of action are considered and one alternative is selected and implemented.

Organizational decisions vary in complexity and can be categorized as programmed or nonprogrammed.[6] **Programmed decisions** are repetitive and well defined, and procedures exist for resolving the problem. They are well structured because criteria of performance are normally clear, good information is available about current performance, alternatives are easily specified, and there is relative certainty that the chosen alternative will be successful. Examples of programmed decisions include decision rules, such as when to replace an office copy machine, when to reimburse managers for travel expenses, or whether an applicant has sufficient qualifications for an assembly-line job. Many companies adopt rules based on experience with programmed decisions. For example, a rule for hotel managers assigning staff for banquets is to allow one server per 30 guests for a sit-down function and one server per 40 guests for a buffet.[7]

Nonprogrammed decisions are novel and poorly defined, and no procedure exists for solving the problem. They are used when an organization has not seen a problem before and may not know how to respond. Clear-cut decision criteria do not exist. Alternatives are fuzzy. There is uncertainty about whether a proposed solution will solve the problem. Typically, few alternatives can be developed for a nonprogrammed decision, so a single solution is custom-tailored to the problem.

Managers at fast-food chain McDonald's face various decisions, some programmed and some nonprogrammed.

IN PRACTICE

McDonald's

McDonald's opens hundreds of new restaurants a year. When managers face the decision about opening a new restaurant in the United States, they either know or can easily find all the information they need to make a good prediction of how well a restaurant will do in a particular location. They can analyze local demographics, traffic patterns, prices and availability of real estate, and where competitors are in the area. Combining these data with restaurant revenue and cost models, managers can make a reasonably good choice for a new location. This represents a *programmed decision*.

Another decision McDonald's managers encounter regularly is not so easy. The company frequently introduces new menu items, but many of them don't do so well. When managers want to introduce a new sandwich, they have a lot of data about demographics and so forth. But they can't predict whether a large number of people will like the new offering. Consider the Arch Deluxe hamburger, mentioned in Chapter 11, which flopped despite millions invested in research and development and a $100 million advertising campaign.[8] Introducing a new sandwich would be considered a *nonprogrammed decision*.

One of the toughest decisions McDonald's managers face is to open a restaurant for the first time in an emerging market. They can analyze all the factors as if for a store in the United States, but managers have much less information and less understanding of the local market. Its products are new to the region; the store will be facing unfamiliar competitors; it has less experience with suppliers; and hiring and training practices have to be built from the ground up. This is a truly nonprogrammed decision and could even turn into a "wicked" decision if some managers disagree over where and how to enter the new market.[9]

Many nonprogrammed decisions, such as the decision to enter a new market for McDonald's, involve strategic planning where uncertainty is great and decisions are complex. Particularly complex nonprogrammed decisions are often referred to as wicked decisions because simply defining the problem can turn into a major task. Wicked problems are associated with manager conflicts over decision objectives as well as over viable alternatives, rapidly changing circumstances, and unclear linkages among decision elements. Managers dealing with a wicked decision may hit on a solution that merely proves they failed to correctly define the problem to begin with.[10] Organizational scholar Russell Ackoff once said, "Managers don't solve simple, isolated problems. They manage messes." *Messes*, Ackoff explained, involve highly interconnected problems and constantly changing, interdependent circumstances.[11] In other words, a mess is a wicked problem. Under conditions of such extreme uncertainty, even a good choice can produce a bad outcome.[12] An example of a wicked decision is what to do about Edward Snowden, the former contract worker at the National Security Agency who leaked information about U.S. security programs to the press and is now living under asylum in Russia. Some say that if he comes back to the United States, he should be offered a plea bargain or clemency. Others say he should go to prison. Even after Snowden's NBC television interview with Brian Williams, in which Snowden explained his decision to go

EXHIBIT 12.1
Decision Making in
Today's Environment

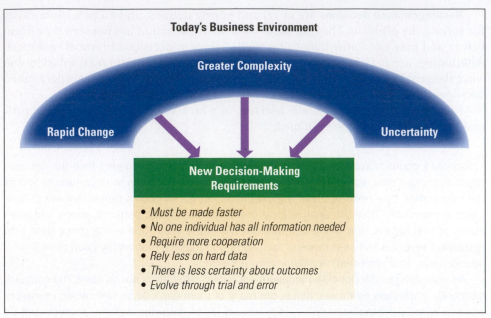

Source: Based on John P. Kotter, *Leading Change* (Boston, MA: Harvard Business School Press, 1996), 56.

public and emphasized that he did it for the benefit of his country, lawmakers and the general public were still divided on whether Snowden acted as a traitor or a patriot.[13] Other examples of wicked decisions include how to reverse J.C. Penney's decline and restore the company's reputation and how to solve the crisis in Detroit, the largest city in the United States ever to file for bankruptcy.

Managers and organizations are dealing with a higher percentage of nonprogrammed and wicked decisions because of the complex and rapidly changing environment. As outlined in Exhibit 12.1, the rapid pace, complexity, and uncertainty of today's environment creates new demands on decision makers. For one thing, decisions have to be made faster than when the environment was more stable. No individual manager has the information needed to make all major decisions, which means good decision making depends on cooperation and information sharing. Decisions rely less on hard data, and there is less certainty about the outcomes. Many decisions evolve through trial and error. For example, Walmart managers eliminated 9 percent of merchandise in an effort to simplify and smarten up cluttered stores and increase sales of higher-value items, but the decision hurt sales. Walmart lost market share for the first time in a decade. Managers recently announced a campaign called "It's Back" to showcase the return of about 8,500 items to store shelves and adopted a new motto—"Low prices. Every day. On everything."[14]

Individual Decision Making

Individual decision making by managers can be described in two ways. First is the **rational approach**, which suggests an ideal method for how managers should try to make decisions. Second is the **bounded rationality perspective**, which describes how decisions actually have to be made under severe time and resource constraints. The rational approach is an ideal that managers may work toward but rarely reach.

Rational Approach

The rational approach to individual decision making stresses the need for systematic analysis of a problem followed by choice and implementation in a logical, step-by-step sequence. When eighteenth-century politician and diplomat Benjamin Franklin was faced with a difficult problem, for example, he would divide a sheet of paper into two columns labeled "Pro" and "Con" and write down various reasons for or against a particular decision. Over several days Franklin would narrow down the list based on a system of weighting the value of each *pro* or *con* until he reached a determination of the best decision. Franklin believed that by using this rational approach, he was "less liable to make a rash step."[15] For managers, too, the rational approach was developed to guide individual decision making because many managers were observed to be unsystematic and arbitrary in their approach to organizational decisions.

Although the rational model is an ideal not fully achievable in a manager's real world of uncertainty, complexity, and rapid change highlighted in Exhibit 12.1, the model does help managers think about decisions more clearly and rationally. Managers should use systematic procedures to make decisions whenever possible. When managers have a deep understanding of the rational decision-making process, it can help them make better decisions even when there is a lack of clear information. The authors of a popular book on decision making use the example of the U.S. Marines, who have a reputation for handling complex problems quickly and decisively. The Marines are trained to quickly go through a series of mental routines that help them analyze the situation and take action.[16]

According to the rational approach, decision making can be broken down into eight steps, as illustrated in Exhibit 12.2 and demonstrated by department store manager Linda Koslow in the following discussion.[17] Koslow was general manager of the Marshall Field's Oakbrook, Illinois, store before the chain was purchased by Macy's.[18]

1. *Monitor the decision environment.* In the first step, a manager monitors internal and external information that will indicate deviations from planned or acceptable behavior. He or she talks to colleagues and reviews financial statements, performance evaluations, industry indices, competitors' activities, and so forth. For example, during the pressure-packed five-week Christmas season, Linda Koslow checks out competitors around the mall, eyeing whether they are marking down merchandise. She also scans printouts of her store's previous day's sales to learn what is or is not moving.
2. *Define the decision problem.* The manager responds to deviations by identifying essential details of the problem: where, when, who was involved, who was affected, and how current activities are influenced. For Koslow, this means defining whether store profits are low because overall sales are less than expected or because certain lines of merchandise are not moving as expected.
3. *Specify decision objectives.* The manager determines what performance outcomes should be achieved by a decision.
4. *Diagnose the problem.* In this step, the manager digs below the surface to analyze the cause of the problem. He or she might gather additional data to facilitate this diagnosis. Understanding the cause enables appropriate treatment. For Koslow at Marshall Field's, the cause of slow sales might be competitors' marking down of merchandise or Marshall Field's failure to display hot-selling items in a visible location.

EXHIBIT 12.2
Steps in the Rational
Approach to Decision
Making

© Cengage Learning®

5. *Develop alternative solutions.* Before a manager can move ahead with a decisive action plan, he or she must have a clear understanding of the various options available to achieve desired objectives. The manager may seek ideas and suggestions from other people. Koslow's alternatives for increasing profits could include buying fresh merchandise, running a sale, or reducing the number of employees.

6. *Evaluate alternatives.* This step may involve the use of statistical techniques or personal experience to gauge the probability of success. The manager assesses the merits of each alternative, as well as the probability that it will achieve the desired objectives.

7. *Choose the best alternative.* This step is when the manager uses his or her analysis of the problem, objectives, and alternatives to select a single alternative that has the best chance for success. At Marshall Field's, Koslow may choose to reduce the number of staff as a way to meet the profit goals rather than increase advertising or markdowns.

8. *Implement the chosen alternative.* Finally, the manager uses managerial, administrative, and persuasive abilities and gives directions to ensure that the decision is carried out, sometimes called execution of the decision. This might

be considered the core of the decision process because any decision that isn't successfully implemented is a failed decision, no matter how good the chosen alternative might be.[19] Managers have to mobilize the people and resources to put the decision into action. Execution may be the hardest step of decision making. The monitoring activity (step 1) begins again as soon as the solution is implemented. For many managers, the decision cycle is a continuous process, with new decisions made daily based on monitoring the environment for problems and opportunities.

The first four steps in this sequence are the problem identification stage, and the next four steps are the problem solution stage of decision making, as indicated in Exhibit 12.2. A manager normally goes through all eight steps in making a decision, although each step may not be a distinct element. Managers may know from experience exactly what to do in a situation, so one or more steps will be minimized. The following example illustrates how the rational approach is used to make a decision about a personnel problem.

1. *Monitor the decision environment.* It is Monday morning, and Joe DeFoe, Saskatchewan Consulting's accounts receivable supervisor, is absent again.

2. *Define the decision problem.* This is the fourth consecutive Monday DeFoe has been absent. Company policy forbids unexcused absenteeism, and DeFoe has been warned about his excessive absenteeism on the last two occasions. A final warning is in order but can be delayed, if warranted.

3. *Specify decision objectives.* DeFoe should attend work regularly and establish the invoice collection levels of which he is capable. The time period for solving the problem is two weeks.

4. *Diagnose the problem.* Discreet discussions with DeFoe's co-workers and information gleaned from DeFoe indicate that DeFoe has a drinking problem. He apparently uses Mondays to dry out from weekend benders. Discussion with other company sources confirms that DeFoe is a problem drinker.

5. *Develop alternative solutions.* (1) Fire DeFoe. (2) Issue a final warning without comment. (3) Issue a warning and accuse DeFoe of being an alcoholic to let him know you are aware of his problem. (4) Talk with DeFoe to see if he will discuss his drinking. If he admits he has a drinking problem, delay the final warning and suggest that he enroll in the company's new employee assistance program for help with personal problems, including alcoholism. (5) Talk with DeFoe to see if he will discuss his drinking. If he does not admit he has a drinking problem, let him know that the next absence will cost him his job.

6. *Evaluate alternatives.* The cost of training a replacement is the same for each alternative. Alternative 1 ignores cost and other criteria. Alternatives 2 and 3 do not adhere to company policy, which advocates counseling where appropriate. Alternative 4 is designed for the benefit of both DeFoe and the company. It might save a good employee if DeFoe is willing to seek assistance. Alternative 5 is primarily for the benefit of the company. A final warning might provide some incentive for DeFoe to admit he has a drinking problem. If so, dismissal might be avoided, but further absences will no longer be tolerated.

7. *Choose the best alternative.* DeFoe does not admit that he has a drinking problem. Choose alternative 5.

8. *Implement the chosen alternative.* Write up the case and issue the final warning.[20]

✓ IN PRACTICE

Saskatchewan Consulting

In the preceding example, issuing the final warning to Joe DeFoe was a programmed decision. The standard of expected behavior was clearly defined, information on the frequency and cause of DeFoe's absence was readily available, and acceptable alternatives and procedures were described. The rational procedure works best in such cases, when the decision maker has sufficient time for an orderly, thoughtful process. Moreover, Saskatchewan Consulting had mechanisms in place to successfully implement the decision once it was made. Some managers even apply a rational approach to encouraging and managing creative thinking about problems and solutions. The Lilly Foundation works with the World Health Organization's Stop TB Partnership to come up with ideas that will help people with tuberculosis get the drugs they need more easily and consistently. When they have idea sessions, they start with defining the problem and breaking it down before they start looking for alternative solutions.[21]

When decisions are nonprogrammed, ill-defined, and piling on top of one another, the individual manager should still try to use the steps in the rational approach, but he or she often will have to take shortcuts by relying on intuition and experience. Deviations from the rational approach are explained by the bounded rationality perspective.

Bounded Rationality Perspective

The point of the rational approach is that managers should try to use systematic procedures to arrive at good decisions. When managers are dealing with well-understood issues, they generally use rational procedures to make decisions.[22] Yet research into managerial decision making shows that managers often are unable to follow an ideal procedure. Many decisions must be made very quickly. Time pressure, a large number of internal and external factors affecting a decision, and the ill-defined nature of many problems make systematic analysis virtually impossible. Managers have only so much time and mental capacity and, hence, cannot evaluate every goal, problem, and alternative. The attempt to be rational is bounded (limited) by the enormous complexity of many problems. There is a limit to how rational managers can be. Jeff Bezos of Amazon talks about the *narrative fallacy*, a term coined by Nassim Nicholas Taleb in his book *The Black Swan*. The narrative fallacy says that because of the human brain's limited ability to consider all factors, people are biologically inclined to convert complex realities into more easily understandable narratives. Bezos required that all senior executives read *The Black Swan* so that they could avoid this tendency toward oversimplification when it wasn't justified.[23]

Bounded rationality should not always be used, but it is useful for certain decisions. *Bounded rationality* is the term coined by organizational scholar Herbert Simon. Simon believed that a perfect solution might exist for a problem, but because of the bounded mind people are not able to conduct the necessary cognitive steps to reach it.[24] To understand the bounded rationality approach, think about how most new managers select a job upon graduation from college. Even this seemingly simple decision can quickly become so complex that a bounded rationality approach is used. Graduating students typically search for a job until they have two or three acceptable job offers, at which point their search activity rapidly diminishes. Hundreds of firms may be available for interviews, and two or three job offers are far short of the maximum number that would be possible if students made the decision based on perfect rationality.

Constraints and Tradeoffs. Not only are large organizational decisions too complex to fully comprehend, but several constraints impinge on the decision maker, as illustrated in Exhibit 12.3. For many decisions, the organizational circumstances are ambiguous, requiring social support, a shared perspective on what happens, and acceptance and agreement. Other organizational constraints on decision making outlined in Exhibit 12.3 include corporate culture and ethical values, as discussed in Chapter 10, and the organization's structure and design. For example, the corporate culture of BP acted as a constraint on decisions managers made that contributed to the disastrous Deepwater Horizon explosion and oil spill in the Gulf of Mexico. Taking risky shortcuts was deeply ingrained into the culture of the company. BP was drilling one of the deepest oil wells in history, for example, but managers decided to use only one strand of steel casing instead of the recommended two or more. Rather than using the recommended 21 centralizers, which ensure that the well doesn't veer off-course as it drills deeper, BP managers decided to use only six. They also skipped a crucial test to verify the sturdiness of the cement holding the well at the bottom of the sea, deciding instead to depend solely on the blowout preventer as a safeguard. Most oil companies typically build in additional safeguards so problems can be fixed before the blowout preventer is needed, but BP's aggressive, risk-taking culture constrained managers from taking the more cautious and time-consuming approach.[25]

Constraints also exist at the personal level. Personal constraints—such as decision style, work pressure, desire for prestige, or simple feelings of insecurity—may constrain either the search for alternatives or the acceptability of an alternative. All of these factors constrain a perfectly rational approach that should

EXHIBIT 12.3

Constraints and Tradeoffs During Nonprogrammed Decision Making

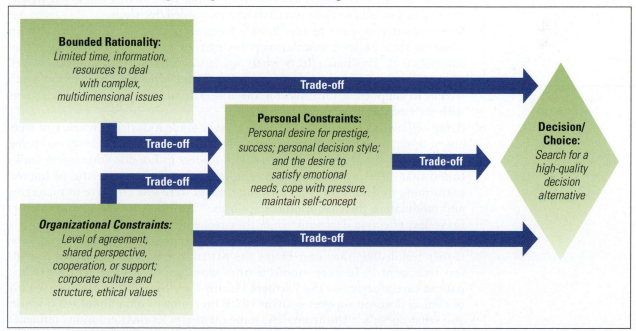

Source: Adapted from Irving L. Janis, *Crucial Decisions* (New York: Free Press, 1989); and A. L. George, *Presidential Decision Making in Foreign Policy: The Effective Use of Information and Advice* (Boulder, CO: Westview Press, 1980).

lead to an obviously ideal choice.[26] Some managers, for example, make many of their decisions within a mindset of trying to please upper managers, people who are perceived to have power within the organization, or others they respect and want to emulate.[27] Other managers are constrained by an unadaptive decision style. Michael Dell reportedly has a cautious decision style that has constrained his acceptance of alternatives for fixing the problems his computer company has been facing. Dell was highly successful for many years, but while other companies such as IBM and Apple moved into entirely new businesses, Dell got stuck in the business of making personal computers and providing niche services. Dell failed to appreciate the shifts in the industry away from computer hardware and to search for alternatives for moving his company into new areas. In addition, insiders say he repeatedly blocked former CEO Kevin Rollins's efforts to expand beyond PCs, starting in 2002. His aversion to risk and uncertainty acted as a personal constraint on decision making.[28]

In addition, many managers have biases that cloud their judgment and act as constraints when making decisions. Check out the Manager's Workshop on page 503 at the end of the chapter to see if you let biases affect your decisions. Some of the most common individual biases are listed next. Later in the chapter we will talk about other biases that influence organizational-level decisions. Awareness of the following four biases can help you make better decisions as an individual.[29]

1. *Being influenced by initial impressions.* When considering decisions, the mind often gives disproportionate weight to the first information it receives. These initial impressions, statistics, or estimates act as an anchor to our subsequent thoughts and judgments. Anchors can be as simple as a random comment by a colleague or a statistic read in a newspaper. Past events and trends also act as anchors. For example, in business, managers frequently look at the previous year's sales when estimating sales for the coming year. Giving too much weight to the past can lead to poor forecasts and misguided decisions.

2. *Seeing what you want to see.* People frequently look for information that supports their existing instinct or point of view and avoid information that contradicts it. This bias affects where managers look for information, as well as how they interpret the information they find. People tend to give too much weight to supporting information and too little to information that conflicts with their established viewpoints.

3. *Being influenced by emotions.* If you've ever made a decision when you were angry, upset, or even very happy, you might already know the danger of being influenced by emotions. A recent study of traders in London investment banks found that effective regulation of emotions was a characteristic of higher-performing traders. Lower-performing traders were less effective in managing and modulating their emotional responses.[30] Another finding is that doctors make less effective decisions when they feel emotions of like or dislike for a patient. If they like a patient, they are less likely to prescribe a painful procedure. If they feel dislike, they may blame the patient for the condition and provide less treatment.[31] To keep emotion from clouding their judgment regarding patient care, doctors in the Partners Health Care System incorporate the use of clinical decision support systems based on reams of data about what works and what doesn't.[32] Unfortunately, some managers let their emotions influence their decisions on a regular basis. Managers make better decision when—to the extent possible—they take emotions out of the decision-making process.

4. *Being overconfident.* Most people overestimate their ability to predict uncertain outcomes. A manager at a fast-food chain was sure that low employee turnover was a key driver of customer satisfaction and store profitability, so he decided to invest in programs to keep employees happy. However, when managers analyzed store data, they found that some locations with high turnover were highly profitable, while some with low turnover were struggling.[33] Overconfidence can be particularly dangerous when making risky decisions.

The Role of Intuition. The bounded rationality perspective is often associated with intuitive decision processes. In **intuitive decision making**, experience and judgment rather than sequential logic or explicit reasoning are used to make decisions.[34] Most researchers have found that effective managers use a combination of rational analysis and intuition in making complex decisions under time pressure.[35] Go to the "How Do You Fit the Design?" box for some insight into your use of rationality versus intuition in making decisions.

Intuition is not arbitrary or irrational because it is based on years of practice and hands-on experience, often stored in the subconscious. When managers use their intuition based on long experience with organizational issues, they more rapidly

HOW DO YOU FIT THE DESIGN?

MAKING IMPORTANT DECISIONS

How do you make important decisions? To find out, think about a time when you made an important career decision or made a major purchase or investment. To what extent does each of the following words describe how you reached the final decision? Please check five words that best describe how you made your final choice.

1. Logic _____

2. Inner knowing _____

3. Data _____

4. Felt sense _____

5. Facts _____

6. Instincts _____

7. Concepts _____

8. Hunch _____

9. Reason _____

10. Feelings _____

Scoring: Give yourself one point for each odd-numbered item you checked, and subtract one point for each even-numbered item you checked. The highest possible score is +5 and the lowest possible score is –5.

Interpretation: The odd-numbered items pertain to a linear decision style and the even-numbered items pertain to a nonlinear decision approach. Linear means using logical *rationality* to make decisions, which would be similar to the decision process in Exhibit 12.2. Nonlinear means using primarily *intuition* to make decisions, as described in the text. If you scored from +3 to –5, then intuition and a satisficing model is your dominant approach to major decisions. If you scored from +3 to +5, then the rational model of decision making as described in the text is your dominant approach. The rational approach is taught in business schools, but many managers use intuition based on experience, especially at senior management levels when there is little tangible data to evaluate.

Source: Adapted from Charles M. Vance, Kevin S. Groves, Yongsun Paik, and Herb Kindler, "Understanding and Measuring Linear–Nonlinear Thinking Style for Enhanced Management Education and Professional Practice," *Academy of Management Learning & Education* 6, no. 2 (2007), 167–185.

perceive and understand problems, and they develop a gut feeling or hunch about which alternative will solve a problem, speeding the decision-making process.[36] The value of intuition for effective decision making is supported by a growing body of research from psychology, organizational science, and other disciplines.[37]

When someone has a depth of experience and knowledge in a particular area, the right decision often comes quickly and effortlessly because the individual recognizes patterns based on information that has been largely forgotten by the conscious mind. This ability could be seen among soldiers in Iraq who were responsible for stopping many roadside bomb attacks by recognizing patterns. High-tech gear designed to detect improvised explosive devices, or IEDs, was merely a supplement rather than a replacement to the ability of the human brain to sense danger and act on it. Soldiers with experience in Iraq unconsciously knew when something didn't look or feel right. It might be a rock that wasn't there yesterday, a piece of concrete that looked too symmetrical, odd patterns of behavior, or just a different feeling of tension in the air.[38] Similarly, in the business world, managers continuously perceive and process information that they may not consciously be aware of, and their base of knowledge and experience helps them make decisions that may be characterized by uncertainty and ambiguity.

Managers use previous experience and judgment to incorporate intangible elements at both the problem identification and problem solution stages.[39] A study of manager problem finding showed that 30 of 33 problems were ambiguous and ill-defined.[40] Bits and scraps of unrelated information from informal sources resulted in a pattern in the manager's mind. The manager could not prove a problem existed but knew intuitively that a certain area needed attention. A too-simple view of a complex problem is often associated with decision failure,[41] so managers learn to listen to their intuition rather than accepting that things are going okay.

Intuitive processes are also used in the problem solution stage. Executives frequently make decisions without explicit reference to the impact on profits or to other measurable outcomes.[42] As we saw in Exhibit 12.3, many intangible factors—such as a person's concern about the support of other executives, fear of failure, and social attitudes—influence selection of the best alternative. These factors cannot be quantified in a systematic way, so intuition guides the choice of a solution. Managers may make a decision based on what they sense to be right rather than on what they can document with hard data.

ASSESS YOUR ANSWER

1 **Managers should use the most objective, rational process possible when making a decision.**

ANSWER: *Disagree.* Striving for perfect rationality in decision making is ideal but not realistic. Many complex decisions do not lend themselves to a step-by-step analytical process. There are also numerous constraints on decision makers. When making nonprogrammed decisions, managers may try to follow the steps in the rational decision-making process, but they also have to rely on experience and intuition.

This chapter's BookMark discusses how managers can give their intuition a better chance of leading to successful decisions. Remember that the bounded rationality perspective and the use of intuition apply mostly to nonprogrammed decisions. The novel, unclear, complex aspects of nonprogrammed decisions mean hard data and logical procedures are not available. Studies of executive decision making find that managers simply cannot use the rational approach for nonprogrammed strategic decisions, such as whether to market a controversial new prescription drug, whether to invest in a complex new project, or whether a city has a need for and can reasonably adopt an enterprise resource planning system.[43] For decisions such as these, managers have limited time and resources, and some factors simply cannot be measured and analyzed. Trying to quantify such information could cause mistakes because it may oversimplify decision criteria. Intuition can balance and supplement rational analysis to help managers make better decisions. A new trend in decision making is referred to as **quasirationality**, which basically means combining intuitive and analytical thought.[44] There are many situations in which neither analysis nor intuition is sufficient for making a good decision, so managers use a combination of processes.

BOOKMARK HAVE YOU READ THIS BOOK?

Blink: The Power of Thinking without Thinking
By Malcolm Gladwell

Snap decisions can be just as good as—and sometimes better than—decisions that are made cautiously and deliberately. Yet they can also be seriously flawed or even dangerously wrong. That's the premise of Malcolm Gladwell's *Blink: The Power of Thinking Without Thinking*. Gladwell explores how our *adaptive unconscious* arrives at complex, important decisions in an instant—and how we can train it to make those decisions good ones.

SHARPENING YOUR INTUITION
Even when we think our decision making is the result of careful analysis and rational consideration, Gladwell says, most of it actually happens subconsciously in a split second. This process, which he refers to as *rapid cognition*, provides room for both amazing insight and grave error. Here are some tips for improving rapid cognition:

- *Remember that more is not better.* Gladwell argues that giving people too much data and information hampers their ability to make good decisions. He cites a study showing that emergency room doctors who are best at diagnosing heart attacks gather less information from their patients than other doctors do. Rather than overloading on information, search out the most meaningful parts.
- *Practice thin-slicing.* The process Gladwell refers to as *thin-slicing* is what harnesses the power of the adaptive unconscious and enables us to make smart decisions with minimal time and information. Thin-slicing

means focusing on a thin slice of pertinent data or information and allowing your intuition to do the work for you. Gladwell cites the example of a Pentagon war game, in which an enemy team of commodities traders defeated a U.S. Army that had "an unprecedented amount of information and intelligence" and "did a thoroughly rational and rigorous analysis that covered every conceivable contingency." The commodities traders were used to making thousands of instant decisions an hour based on limited information. Managers can practice spontaneous decision making until it becomes second nature.

- *Know your limits.* Not every decision should be based on intuition. When you have a depth of knowledge and experience in an area, you can put more trust in your gut feelings. Gladwell also cautions to beware of biases that interfere with good decision making. *Blink* suggests that we can teach ourselves to sort through first impressions and figure out which are important and which are based on subconscious biases such as stereotypes or emotional baggage.

PUT IT TO WORK
Blink is filled with lively and interesting anecdotes, such as how experienced firefighters can "slow down a moment" and create an environment where spontaneous decision making can take place. Gladwell asserts that a better understanding of the process of split-second decision making can help people make better decisions in all areas of their lives, as well as help them anticipate and avoid miscalculations.

Blink: The Power of Thinking Without Thinking, by Malcolm Gladwell, is published by Little Brown.

Organizational Decision Making

Organizations are composed of managers who make decisions using both rational and intuitive processes, but organization-level decisions are not usually made by a single manager. Many organizational decisions involve several managers. Problem identification and problem solution involve many departments, multiple viewpoints, and even other organizations, which are beyond the scope of an individual manager.

The processes by which decisions are made in organizations are influenced by a number of factors, particularly the organization's own internal structures and the degree of stability or instability of the external environment.[45] Research into organization-level decision making has identified four primary types of organizational decision-making processes: the management science approach, the Carnegie model, the incremental decision model, and the garbage can model.

Management Science Approach

The **management science approach** to organizational decision making is the analog to the rational approach by individual managers. Management science came into being during World War II.[46] At that time, mathematical and statistical techniques were applied to urgent, large-scale military problems that were beyond the ability of individual decision makers.

Mathematicians, physicists, and operations researchers used systems analysis to develop artillery trajectories, antisubmarine strategies, and bombing strategies such as salvoing (discharging multiple shells simultaneously). Consider the problem of a battleship trying to sink an enemy ship several miles away. The calculation for aiming the battleship's guns should consider distance, wind speed, shell size, speed and direction of both ships, pitch and roll of the firing ship, and curvature of the earth. Methods for performing such calculations using trial and error and intuition are not accurate, take far too long, and may never achieve success.

This is where management science came in. Analysts were able to identify the relevant variables involved in aiming a ship's guns and could model them with the use of mathematical equations. Distance, speed, pitch, roll, shell size, and so on could be calculated and entered into the equations. The answer was immediate, and the guns could begin firing. Factors such as pitch and roll were soon measured mechanically and fed directly into the targeting mechanism. Today, the human element is completely removed from the targeting process. Radar picks up the target, and the entire sequence is computed automatically.

Management science yielded astonishing success for many military problems. This approach to decision making diffused into corporations and business schools, where techniques were studied and elaborated. Operations research departments use mathematical models to quantify relevant variables and develop a quantitative representation of alternative solutions and the probability of each one solving the problem. These departments also use such devices as linear programming, Bayesian statistics, PERT charts, and computer simulations.

Management science is an excellent device for organizational decision making when problems are analyzable and when the variables can be identified and measured. Mathematical models can contain a thousand or more variables, each one relevant in some way to the ultimate outcome. Management science techniques have been used to correctly solve problems as diverse as finding the right spot for

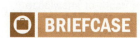

BRIEFCASE

As an organization manager, keep this guideline in mind:

Use a rational decision approach—computation and management science—when a problem situation is well understood and can be broken down into variables that can be measured and analyzed.

a church camp, test-marketing the first of a new family of products, drilling for oil, and radically altering the distribution of telecommunications services.[47] Other problems amenable to management science techniques are the scheduling of ambulance technicians, turnpike toll collectors, and airline crew members.[48]

Management science, especially with increasingly sophisticated computer technology and software, can accurately and quickly solve problems that have too many explicit variables for adequate human processing. For example, Alaska Airlines has been using management science techniques to make flight decisions since 1980, when Mount St. Helens erupted near the airline's home base and crippled the company for days. A team of aviation and weather experts developed computer models to predict the trajectory of volcanic ash and often enable flights to work around it.[49] The location of Malaysia Airlines Flight 370, the plane that disappeared over the Indian Ocean in early March 2014, remains a mystery, but officials are using management science to pinpoint the best areas to search. A team of international experts is using radar data, and also including factors such as the position of an Inmarsat PLC satellite when the plane exchanged digital handshakes with it, incorporating arcane calculations to reflect changes in temperature of the satellite as well as the communications equipment on board the plane. The analysis included changes in temperature of the satellite on each occasion that the plane made contact with it and also evaluated data from hundreds of other flights in the same region. Without management science techniques, such analysis would be prohibitively time consuming or even impossible.[50]

Management science is covering a broader range of problems than ever before, thanks partly to the emergence of big data techniques, as described in Chapter 8. Consider baseball and the story told in the 2011 movie *Moneyball*.[51] As described in Chapter 8, Brad Pitt portrays Billy Beane, the legendary general manager for the Oakland A's, who in 2002 built one of Major League Baseball's winningest teams with one of its smallest budgets. Rather than rely on the intuition of scouts, who would sometimes reject a player because he "didn't look like a major leaguer," Beane relied heavily on data and statistical analysis. Since that time, most other teams have adopted management science techniques for analyzing various types of data to make decisions.[52]

Managers in other types of organizations are also applying technology to make more decisions. At Walt Disney World in Orlando, Florida, managers use sophisticated computerized systems to analyze data and make decisions that minimize wait times for visitors, maximize ride capacity, optimize staffing efficiency, and increase souvenir-selling opportunities.[53] Even doctors' offices are turning to management science to manage their practices more efficiently, such as by predicting demand for appointments based on the number of patients in their practice, the average no-show rate, and other factors.[54]

One problem with the management science approach is that quantitative data are not rich and do not convey tacit knowledge, as described in Chapter 8. Informal cues that indicate the existence of problems have to be sensed on a more personal basis by managers.[55] The most sophisticated mathematical analyses are of no value if the important factors cannot be quantified and included in the model. Such things as competitor reactions, consumer tastes, and product warmth are qualitative dimensions. In these situations, the role of management science is to supplement manager decision making. Quantitative results can be given to managers for discussion and interpretation along with their informal opinions, judgment, and intuition, in line with a quasirationality approach. The final decision can include both qualitative factors and quantitative calculations.

Carnegie Model

The **Carnegie model** of organizational decision making is based on the work of Richard Cyert, James March, and Herbert Simon, who were all associated with Carnegie Mellon University.[56] Their research helped formulate the bounded rationality approach to individual decision making, as well as provide new insights about organizational decisions.

Until their work, research in economics assumed that business firms made decisions as a single entity, as if all relevant information were funneled to the top decision maker for a choice. Research by the Carnegie group indicated that organization-level decisions involved many managers and that a final choice was based on a coalition among those managers. A **coalition** is an alliance among several managers who agree about organizational goals and problem priorities.[57] It could include managers from line departments, staff specialists, and even external groups, such as powerful customers, bankers, or union representatives.

Management coalitions are needed during decision making for two reasons. First, organizational goals are often ambiguous, and operative goals of departments are often inconsistent. When goals are ambiguous and inconsistent, managers disagree about problem priorities. They must bargain about problems and build a coalition around the question of which problems to address. For example, Randy Komisar, a partner with Kleiner Perkins Caufield & Byers, advises using a technique called "the balance sheet" when a company is facing decisions about which new opportunities to invest in or which problems to solve. Managers from across departments sit around a table, and each person lists on paper the good and bad points about a specific opportunity. This is similar to the "Pro" and "Con" list Benjamin Franklin used for making rational decisions as an individual. In this case, though, managers then share their thoughts and ideas with others and typically find shared interests. The process "mitigates a lot of the friction that typically arises when people marshal the facts that support their case while ignoring those that don't," Komisar says.[58]

The second reason for coalitions is that individual managers intend to be rational but function with human cognitive limitations and other constraints, as described earlier. Managers do not have the time, resources, or mental capacity to identify all dimensions and to process all information relevant to a decision. These limitations lead to coalition-building behavior. Managers talk to each other and exchange points of view to gather information and reduce ambiguity. People who have relevant information or a stake in a decision outcome are consulted. Building a coalition will lead to a decision that is supported by interested parties. Managers at *The New York Times* reached a decision to begin a paid subscription plan for the newspaper's website through a process of coalition building.

 **IN PRACTICE**

The New York Times

The decision to ask readers to begin paying for online access to *The New York Times* wasn't made lightly. In fact, executives and senior editors spent most of 2009 debating the question, analyzing various options, and reaching agreement to implement the new subscription plan.

Arthur Sulzberger, Jr., chairman of the company, and several other top executives embraced the idea of a pay model. However, other senior managers and editors vehemently opposed the plan. These managers and editors had spent years working to build *NYTimes.com* into the most visited newspaper site in the world. They argued that a subscription model would jeopardize the paper's online reach and was out of step with the digital age.

Some advertising managers were worried that it would also jeopardize digital advertising revenues, which were just starting to recover from the recession. Others argued that the paper needed a subscription source of revenue or more layoffs would be needed.

Debate and discussion continued, both formally and informally. Eventually, a coalition came together around the idea of a tiered subscription service that allows website visitors to read 20 articles a month at no charge before being asked to select one of three subscription models at various price levels. Articles that people access through social networks such as Facebook and Twitter or search engines such as Google won't count toward the monthly limit. The fact that content can still easily be "shared, tweeted, blogged" assuaged some of the concerns from digital managers and helped get them on board to support the decision. As Martin A. Nisenholtz, senior vice president for digital operations, put it, "On the one hand, I think there is [still] some anxiety around it. On the other hand, I think the model we have chosen mitigates 90 percent of it."[59]

The decision to charge for access has not hurt *The Times*.[60] By successfully building a coalition to support the decision within the organization, managers improved the chances of success.

The process of coalition building has several implications for organizational decision behavior. First, decisions are made to *satisfice* rather than to optimize problem solutions. **Satisficing** means organizations accept a satisfactory rather than a maximum level of performance, enabling them to achieve several goals simultaneously. In decision making, the coalition will accept a solution that is perceived as satisfactory to all coalition members, as at *The New York Times*.

Second, managers are concerned with immediate problems and short-run solutions. They engage in what Cyert and March called *problemistic search*.[61] **Problemistic search** means managers look around the immediate environment for a solution to quickly resolve a problem. Although managers at *The Times* studied various options that were being used by other companies, they didn't consider every possible approach that could be taken to an online subscription model. Managers don't expect a perfect solution when the situation is ill-defined and conflict-laden. This contrasts with the management science approach, which assumes that analysis can uncover every reasonable alternative. The Carnegie model says that search behavior is just sufficient to produce a satisfactory solution and that managers typically adopt the first satisfactory solution that emerges.

Third, discussion and bargaining are especially important in the problem identification stage of decision making. Unless coalition members perceive a problem, action will not be taken. However, a coalition of key managers is also important for smooth implementation of a decision. When top managers perceive a problem or want to make a major decision, they need to reach agreement with other managers to support the decision.[62]

The decision process described in the Carnegie model is summarized in Exhibit 12.4. The Carnegie model points out that building agreement through a managerial coalition is a major part of organizational decision making. This is especially true at upper management levels. Discussion and bargaining are time consuming, so search procedures are usually simple and the selected alternative satisfices rather than optimizes problem solution. When problems are programmed—are clear and have been seen before—the organization will rely on previous procedures and routines. Rules and procedures prevent the need for renewed coalition formation and political bargaining. Nonprogrammed decisions, however, require bargaining and conflict resolution.

EXHIBIT 12.4
Choice Processes in the Carnegie Model

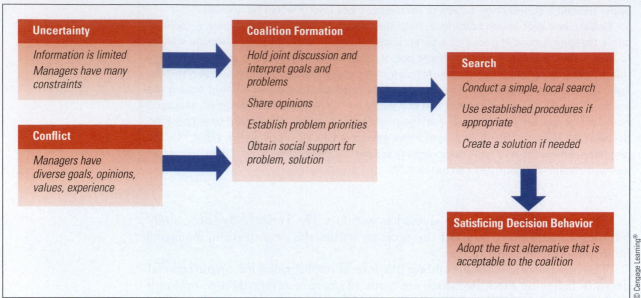

2 When a manager knows the best solution to a serious organizational problem and has the necessary authority, it is best to simply make the decision and implement it rather than involve other managers in the decision process.

ANSWER: *Disagree.* Few organizational decisions are made by a single manager. Organizational decision making is a social process that combines multiple perspectives. Managers have to talk to one another about problem priorities and exchange opinions and viewpoints to reach agreement. When managers don't build coalitions, important problems may go unsolved and good decisions may fail because other managers don't buy into the decisions and effectively implement them.

Incremental Decision Model

Henry Mintzberg and his associates at McGill University in Montreal approached organizational decision making from a different perspective. They identified 25 decisions made in organizations and traced the events associated with these decisions from beginning to end.[63] Their research identified each step in the decision sequence. This theory of decision making, called the **incremental decision model**, places less emphasis on the political and social factors described in the Carnegie model but tells more about the structured sequence of activities undertaken from the discovery of a problem to its solution.[64]

Sample decisions in Mintzberg's research included choosing which jet aircraft to acquire for a regional airline, developing a new supper club, designing a new container terminal in a harbor, identifying a new market for a deodorant, installing a controversial new medical treatment in a hospital, and firing a star radio announcer.[65]

The scope and importance of these decisions are revealed in the length of time taken to complete them. Most of these decisions took more than a year, and one-third of them took more than two years. Most of these decisions were nonprogrammed and required custom-designed solutions.

One discovery from this research is that major organizational choices are usually a series of small choices that combine to produce the major decision. Thus, many organizational decisions are a series of nibbles rather than a big bite. Consider the multiple decisions Alan Mulally made to save Ford from the brink of bankruptcy.

IN PRACTICE
Ford Motor Company

"The American auto industry should pass the hat and build a statue to Alan," said the chief executive of AutoNation Inc., a large dealership chain that operates 40 Ford franchises. He was referring to Alan Mulally, who came to Ford in 2006 with no experience in the auto industry. As Mulally prepared to retire in 2014, he was recognized as one of the best CEOs in the industry.

The decisions Mulally made to revive Ford reflect an incremental decision model. When he first arrived as CEO, Ford was losing billions of dollars and burning through cash. Mulally mortgaged most of the company's assets to borrow $23.5 billion to keep the company solvent. Another early decision was to change how the management team operated, breaking down regional rivalries and demanding accountability. Mulally set up a monthly meeting where each manager reported on his areas of responsibility and coded them to show what was on target and what wasn't. The first time a manager confessed that a new vehicle project was "red" (not on target), Mulally clapped to show that reporting problems was better than hiding them.

Soon, Mulally decided to implement a "One Ford" strategy that included cutting back the number of vehicles produced, designing new models to be sold around the world rather than for each market in order to achieve economies of scale, focusing on the Ford brand, and making vehicles more attractive by adding new technology, safety features, and better gas mileage. When the financial crisis hit in late 2008 and Ford was again experiencing huge losses, Mulally appeared before Congress with the CEOs of GM and Chrysler to ask for a bailout. But Mulally had a change of mind and decided that the company needed to do anything it could to avoid taking government help.

The decision to turn down a government bailout bolstered the company's reputation, and with improving sales and cost-cutting measures Mulally implemented, Ford surprised everyone by making money in 2009.[66]

These multiple decisions had a positive impact at Ford. In 2014, Ford was making more money than ever and its market value has increased by $8 billion since Mulally arrived.

Managers also use the incremental decision process to make single big decisions. Organizations move through several decision points and may hit barriers along the way. Mintzberg called these barriers *decision interrupts*. An interrupt may mean an organization has to cycle back through a previous decision and try something new. Decision loops or cycles are one way the organization learns which alternatives will work. The ultimate solution may be very different from what was initially anticipated.

The pattern of decision stages discovered by Mintzberg and his associates is shown in Exhibit 12.5. Each box indicates a possible step in the decision sequence. The steps take place in three major decision phases: identification, development, and selection.

BRIEFCASE

As an organization manager, keep these guidelines in mind:

Take risks and move the company ahead by increments when a problem is defined but solutions are uncertain. Try solutions step by step to learn whether they work.

EXHIBIT 12.5
The Incremental Decision Model

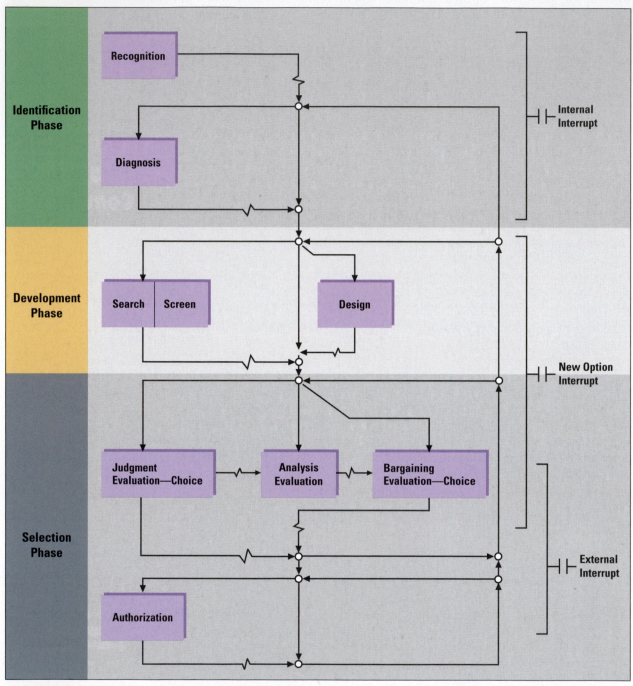

Source: Based on Henry Mintzberg, Duru Raisinghani, and André Théorêt, "Structure of Unstructured Decision Processes," *Administrative Science Quarterly* vol. 21(June 1976), 246–275. SAGE Publications.

Identification Phase. The identification phase begins with *recognition*. Recognition means one or more managers become aware of a problem and the need to make a decision. Recognition is usually stimulated by a problem or an opportunity. A problem exists when elements in the external environment change or when internal performance is perceived to be below standard. In the case of firing a radio announcer, comments about the announcer came from listeners, other announcers, and advertisers. Managers interpreted these cues until a pattern emerged that indicated a problem had to be dealt with.

The second step is *diagnosis*, in which more information is gathered if needed to define the problem situation. Diagnosis may be systematic or informal, depending upon the severity of the problem. Severe problems do not allow time for extensive diagnosis; the response must be immediate. Mild problems are usually diagnosed in a more systematic manner.

Development Phase. In the development phase, a solution is shaped to solve the problem defined in the identification phase. The development of a solution takes one of two directions. First, *search* procedures may be used to seek out alternatives within the organization's repertoire of solutions. In the case of firing a star announcer, for example, managers asked what the radio station had done the last time an announcer had to be let go. To conduct the search, organization participants may look into their own memories, talk to other managers, or examine the formal procedures of the organization.

The second direction of development is to *design* a custom solution. This happens when the problem is novel so that previous experience has no value. Mintzberg found that in these cases, key decision makers have only a vague idea of the ideal solution. Gradually, through a trial-and-error process, a custom-designed alternative will emerge. Development of the solution is a groping, incremental procedure, building a solution brick by brick.

Selection Phase. The selection phase is when the solution is chosen. This phase is not always a matter of making a clear choice among alternatives. In the case of custom-made solutions, selection is more an evaluation of the single alternative that seems feasible.

Evaluation and choice may be accomplished in three ways. The *judgment* form of selection is used when a final choice falls upon a single decision maker, and the choice involves judgment based upon experience. In *analysis*, alternatives are evaluated on a more systematic basis, such as with management science techniques. Mintzberg found that most decisions did not involve systematic analysis and evaluation of alternatives. *Bargaining* occurs when selection involves a group of decision makers. Each decision maker may have a different stake in the outcome, so conflict emerges. Discussion and bargaining occur until a coalition is formed, as in the Carnegie model described earlier.

When a decision is formally accepted by the organization, *authorization* takes place. The decision may be passed up the hierarchy to the responsible hierarchical level. Authorization is often routine because the expertise and knowledge rest with the lower-level decision makers who identified the problem and developed the solution. A few decisions may be rejected because of implications not anticipated by lower-level managers.

Dynamic Factors. Note that the right hand side of the chart in Exhibit 12.5 shows lines running back toward the beginning of the decision process. These lines represent loops or cycles that take place in the decision process. Organizational decisions do not follow an orderly progression from recognition through authorization. Minor problems arise that force a loop back to an earlier stage. These are decision interrupts. If a custom-designed solution is perceived as unsatisfactory, the organization may have to go back to the very beginning and reconsider whether the problem is truly worth solving. Feedback loops can be caused by problems of timing, politics, disagreement among managers, inability to identify a feasible solution, turnover of managers, or the sudden appearance of a new alternative. For example, when a small Canadian airline made the decision to acquire jet aircraft, the board authorized the decision, but shortly after, a new chief executive was brought in who canceled the contract, recycling the decision back to the identification phase. He accepted the diagnosis of the problem but insisted upon a new search for alternatives. Then a foreign airline went out of business and two used aircraft became available at a bargain price. This presented an unexpected option, and the chief executive used his own judgment to authorize the purchase of the aircraft.[67]

Because most decisions take place over an extended period of time, circumstances change. Decision making is a dynamic process that may require a number of cycles before a problem is solved.

Organizational Decisions and Change

At the beginning of this chapter, we discussed how the rapidly changing business environment is creating greater uncertainty for decision makers. Many organizations are marked by a tremendous amount of uncertainty at both the problem identification and problem solution stages. Two approaches to decision making have evolved to help managers cope with this uncertainty and complexity. One approach is to combine the Carnegie and incremental models just described. The second is a unique approach called the garbage can model.

Combining the Incremental and Carnegie Models

The Carnegie description of coalition building is especially relevant for the problem identification stage. When issues are ambiguous, or if managers disagree about problem severity, discussion, negotiation, and coalition building are needed. The incremental model tends to emphasize the steps used to reach a solution. After managers agree on a problem, the step-by-step process is a way of trying various solutions to see what will work. When problem solution is unclear, a trial-and-error solution may be designed.

The application of the Carnegie and incremental models to the stages in the decision process is illustrated in Exhibit 12.6. The two models do not disagree with one another. They describe different approaches for how organizations make decisions when either problem identification or problem solution is uncertain. When both parts of the decision process are simultaneously highly uncertain, the organization is in an extremely difficult position. Decision processes in that situation may be a combination of the Carnegie and incremental models, and this combination may evolve into a situation described in the garbage can model.

Garbage Can Model

The **garbage can model** is one of the most recent and interesting descriptions of organizational decision processes. It is not directly comparable to the earlier models, because the garbage can model deals with the pattern or flow of multiple decisions

BRIEFCASE

As an organization manager, keep these guidelines in mind:

Apply both the Carnegie model and the incremental decision model in a situation with high uncertainty about both problems and solutions. Decision making may also employ garbage can procedures. Move the organization toward better performance by proposing new ideas, spending time working in important areas, and persisting with potential solutions.

EXHIBIT 12.6
Decision Process When Problem Identification and Problem Solution Are Uncertain

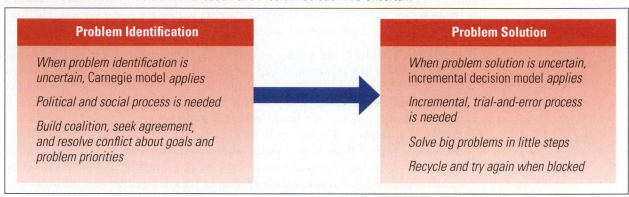

within organizations, whereas the incremental and Carnegie models focus on how a single decision is made. The garbage can model helps you think of the whole organization and the frequent decisions being made by managers throughout. At any time, managers throughout an organization are considering various decisions and actions, such as hiring new employees, developing a new product, or investing in a joint venture. Often, individual managers evaluate alternatives and then top level executives combine their opinions and suggestions to reach a final decision.[68] Sometimes, however, the decision-making process is much messier.

Organized Anarchy. The garbage can model was developed to explain the pattern of decision making in organizations that experience extremely high uncertainty. Michael Cohen, James March, and Johan Olsen, the originators of the model, called the highly uncertain conditions an **organized anarchy**, which is an extremely organic organization.[69] Organized anarchies do not rely on the normal vertical hierarchy of authority and bureaucratic decision rules. They result from three characteristics:

1. *Problematic preferences.* Goals, problems, alternatives, and solutions are ill-defined. Ambiguity characterizes each step of a decision process.
2. *Unclear, poorly understood technology.* Cause-and-effect relationships within the organization are difficult to identify. An explicit database that applies to decisions is not available.
3. *Turnover.* Organizational positions experience turnover of participants. In addition, employees are busy and have only limited time to allocate to any one problem or decision. Participation in any given decision will be fluid and limited.

An organized anarchy is characterized by rapid change and a collegial, nonbureaucratic environment. No organization fits this extremely organic circumstance all the time, although today's Internet-based companies, as well as organizations in rapidly changing industries, may experience it much of the time. Many organizations will occasionally find themselves in positions of making decisions under unclear, problematic circumstances. The garbage can model is useful for understanding the pattern of these decisions.

Streams of Events. The unique characteristic of the garbage can model is that the decision process is not seen as a sequence of steps that begins with a problem and ends with a solution. Indeed, problem identification and problem solution may not be connected to each other. An idea may be proposed as a solution when no problem is specified. A problem may exist and never generate a solution. Decisions are the outcome of independent streams of events within the organization. The four streams relevant to organizational decision making are as follows:

1. *Problems.* Problems are points of dissatisfaction with current activities and performance. They represent a gap between desired performance and current activities. Problems are perceived to require attention. However, they are distinct from solutions and choices. A problem may lead to a proposed solution or it may not. Problems may not be solved when solutions are adopted.

2. *Potential solutions.* A solution is an idea somebody proposes for adoption. Such ideas form a flow of alternative solutions through the organization. Ideas may be brought into the organization by new personnel or may be invented by existing personnel. Participants may simply be attracted to certain ideas and push them as logical choices regardless of problems. Attraction to an idea may cause an employee to look for a problem to which the idea can be attached and, hence, justified. The point is that solutions exist independent of problems.

3. *Participants.* Organization participants are employees who come and go throughout the organization. People are hired, reassigned, and fired. Participants vary widely in their ideas, perception of problems, experience, values, and training. The problems and solutions recognized by one manager will differ from those recognized by another manager.

4. *Choice opportunities.* Choice opportunities are occasions when an organization usually makes a decision. They occur when contracts are signed, people are hired, or a new product is authorized. They also occur when the right mix of participants, solutions, and problems exists. Thus, a manager who happened to learn of a good idea may suddenly become aware of a problem to which it applies and, hence, can provide the organization with a choice opportunity. Match-ups of problems and solutions often result in decisions.

With the concept of four streams, the overall pattern of organizational decision making takes on a random quality. Problems, solutions, participants, and choices all flow through the organization. In one sense, the organization is a large garbage can in which these streams are being stirred, as illustrated in Exhibit 12.7. When a problem, solution, and participant happen to connect at one point, a decision may be made and the problem may be solved; but if the solution does not fit the problem, the problem may not be solved.

Thus, when viewing the organization as a whole and considering its high level of uncertainty, one sees problems arise that are not solved and solutions tried that do not work. Organizational decisions are disorderly and not the result of a logical, step-by-step sequence. Events may be so ill-defined and complex that decisions, problems, and solutions act as independent events. When they connect, some problems are solved, but many are not.[70]

Consequences. There are four specific consequences of the garbage can decision process for organizational decision making:

1. *Solutions may be proposed even when problems do not exist.* An employee might be sold on an idea and might try to sell it to the rest of the organization. An example was the adoption of computers by many organizations during the 1970s. The computer was an exciting solution and was pushed by both computer

EXHIBIT 12.7
Illustration of
Independent Streams of
Events in the Garbage
Can Model of Decision
Making

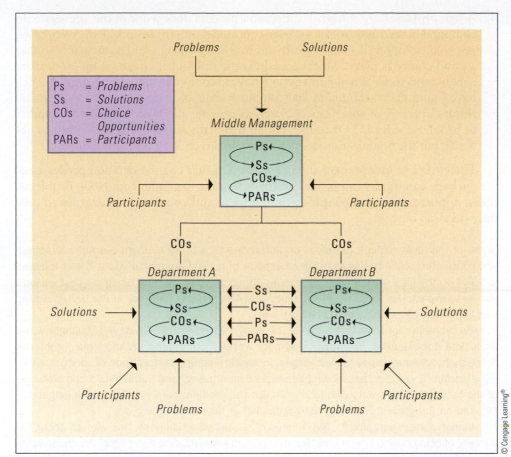

© Cengage Learning®

manufacturers and systems analysts within organizations. The computer did not solve any problems in those initial applications. Indeed, some computers caused more problems than they solved.

2. *Choices are made without solving problems.* A choice—for example, creating a new department or revising work procedures—may be made with the intention of solving a problem; but, under conditions of high uncertainty, the choice may be incorrect. Moreover, many choices just seem to happen. People decide to quit, the organization's budget is cut, or a new policy bulletin is issued. These choices may be oriented toward problems but do not necessarily solve them.

3. *Problems may persist without being solved.* Organization participants get used to certain problems and give up trying to solve them; or participants may not know how to solve certain problems because the technology is unclear. A university in Canada was placed on probation by the American Association of University Professors because a professor had been denied tenure without due process. The probation was a nagging annoyance that the administrators wanted to remove. Fifteen years later, the nontenured professor died. The probation continues because the university did not acquiesce to the demands of the heirs to reevaluate the case. The university would like to solve the problem, but administrators are not sure how, and they do not have the resources to allocate to it. The probation problem persists without a solution.

4. *A few problems are solved.* The decision process does work in the aggregate. In computer simulations of the garbage can model, important problems were often resolved. Solutions do connect with appropriate problems and participants so that a good choice is made. More recently, some researchers have set up laboratory experiments to see if real humans do what the computer simulations predict. They have found that real humans and computer simulations produce almost identical results in terms of some aspects, such as number of choices made and number of problems solved.[71] Of course, not all problems are resolved when choices are made, but the organization does move in the direction of problem reduction.

The effects of independent streams and the rather chaotic decision processes of the garbage can model can be seen in the following example from Nike. Problems, ideas, opportunities, and people seem to appear and combine haphazardly to produce decision outcomes.

IN PRACTICE

Nike

Some of the most difficult decisions organizations face today concern overseas suppliers and contractors. Nike has been in the crosshairs of activist groups for years. It was founded in 1964 on the idea of producing high-quality shoes at lower costs by using low-cost workers in overseas factories (choice). At the time, only 4 percent of footwear in the United States was imported. Today, that figure is 98 percent.

The problems for Nike first arose in the early 1990s, when activist Jeff Ballinger wrote an article documenting low wages and poor working conditions in Indonesia (problem). Since then, Nike has made many changes, including writing a factory code of conduct, creating a nonprofit group to establish independent monitoring, and publishing a complete list of the factories it contracts with (choices). But the problem persists. Today, challenges are focused on Bangladesh, and the internal conflict at Nike is still going on.

Hannah Jones (participant), Nike's head of sustainable business, has warned about the dangers of doing business with Bangladesh suppliers for years. She argues that the cheap costs offered by manufacturers there are not worth risking human lives or Nike's reputation (solution). Another faction within the company, led by COO Eric Sprunk (participants), argues that Nike has the power and ability to put controls in place that will guarantee worker safety (solution) so that Nike can match its rivals' cost advantages (problem) by producing in Bangladesh.

The twin goals of maintaining low costs and maintaining safe and humane working conditions (choices) have divided the company. One set of executives has continually urged that Nike publicly acknowledge labor problems (solution), while another camp says such problems are common in the apparel industry and there's no need for Nike to make itself more of a target (solution). Finally, CEO Phil Knight vowed in a speech to root out child labor and be more transparent about the company's supply chain (choice). Nike worked with its main soccer-ball manufacturing partner, Saga Sports, to end the practice of having some production done at private homes (choice), a practice linked to child labor. However, when the owner of the factory died, it was taken over by family members who reintroduced the practice (problem). What should be done? Some executives said $100 million worth of soccer balls should be pulled (solution). It would take 18 months to resume production levels. Eventually, the company pulled the soccer balls (choice), sending a strong message to the supplier base.

The issue of Bangladesh is similarly split. Some manufacturing managers argue for going more aggressively into the country because of its low labor costs (solution). Others say it's not worth the cost in terms of human suffering and potential damage to Nike's reputation (solution). Eventually, members of the corporate responsibility and production units (participants) took a joint trip to Bangladesh to see what was going on in factories there (choice). At one factory, they found fire and safety hazards that led Nike to make the decision to cut ties with that particular company (choice). Nike decided to continue doing business with four other factories that didn't have similar safety problems.[72]

The story of Nike's challenges with suppliers illustrates the garbage can model of decision making and the seemingly random flow of people, problems, potential solutions, and choice opportunities through an organization. Problems are not solved in a simple, logical, step-by-step sequence. Some problems have been solved at Nike, or at least reduced, but many persist despite the proposed solutions and decision choices that were made. Some events occurred by chance, such as the factory owner who died and passed the factory on to family members who reinstituted child labor. Managers are trying various solutions to solve supplier problems, and some will be solved. Others may persist for years. New choices will be made and other choice opportunities embraced or rejected as people with various ideas come and go and outside forces continue to change.

Contingency Decision-Making Framework

This chapter has covered several approaches to organizational decision making, including management science, the Carnegie model, the incremental decision model, and the garbage can model. It has also discussed rational and intuitive decision processes used by individual managers and looked at individual cognitive biases and other constraints that impinge on decision making. Each decision approach is a relatively accurate description of the actual decision process, yet all differ from each other. Management science, for example, reflects a different set of decision assumptions and procedures than does the garbage can model.

One reason for having different approaches is that they appear in different organizational situations. The use of an approach is contingent on the organization setting. Two characteristics of organizations that determine the use of decision approaches are (1) problem consensus and (2) technical knowledge about the means to solve those problems.[73] Analyzing organizations along these two dimensions suggests which approach is most appropriate for making decisions.

Problem Consensus

Problem consensus refers to the agreement among managers about the nature of a problem or opportunity and about which goals and outcomes to pursue. This variable ranges from complete agreement to complete disagreement. When managers agree, there is little uncertainty—the problems and goals of the organization are clear and so are standards of performance. When managers disagree, organization direction and performance expectations are in dispute, creating a situation of high uncertainty. One example of problem uncertainty occurred at Rockford Health System. Human resource managers wanted to implement a new self-service benefits system, which would allow employees to manage their own benefits and free up HR employees for more strategic activities. Finance managers, on the other hand, argued that the cost of the software licenses was too high and would hurt the company's bottom line. Managers in other departments also disagreed with the new system because they feared adoption of an expensive new HR system meant they might not get their departmental projects approved.[74]

Problem consensus tends to be low when organizations are differentiated, as described in Chapter 4. Recall that uncertain environments cause organizational departments to differentiate from one another in goals and attitudes to specialize in specific environmental sectors. This differentiation leads to disagreement and conflict, as with the manufacturing and corporate responsibility units at Nike, so managers must make a special effort to build coalitions during decision making. For example, NASA was severely criticized for failing to identify problems with the *Columbia* space shuttle that might have prevented the February 2003 disaster. A part of the reason was high differentiation and conflicting opinions between safety managers and scheduling managers, in which pressure to launch on time overrode safety concerns. In addition, after the launch, engineers three times requested—and were denied—better photos to assess the damage from a piece of foam debris that struck the shuttle's left wing just seconds after launch. Investigations later indicated that the damage caused by the debris may have been the primary physical cause of the explosion. Mechanisms for hearing dissenting opinions and building coalitions can improve decision making at NASA and other organizations dealing with complex problems.[75]

Problem consensus is especially important for the problem identification stage of decision making. When problems are clear and agreed on, they provide clear standards and expectations for performance. When problems are not agreed on, problem identification is uncertain and management attention must be focused on gaining agreement about goals and priorities.

Technical Knowledge about Solutions

Technical knowledge refers to understanding and agreement about how to solve problems and reach organizational goals. This variable can range from complete agreement and certainty to complete disagreement and uncertainty about cause–effect relationships leading to problem solution. One example of low technical knowledge occurred at Dr. Pepper/Seven-Up Inc. Managers agreed on the problem to be solved—they wanted to increase market share from 6 to 7 percent. However, the means for achieving this increase in market share were not known or agreed on. A few managers wanted to use discount pricing in supermarkets. Other managers believed they should increase the number of soda fountain outlets in restaurants and fast-food chains. A few other managers insisted that the best approach was to increase advertising. Managers did not know what would cause an increase in market share. Eventually, the advertising judgment prevailed, but it did not work very well. The failure of the decision reflected managers' low technical knowledge about how to solve the problem.

When means are well understood, the appropriate alternatives can be identified and calculated with some degree of certainty. When means are poorly understood, potential solutions are ill-defined and uncertain. Intuition, judgment, and trial and error become the basis for decisions.

Contingency Framework

Exhibit 12.8 describes the **contingency decision-making framework**, which brings together the two dimensions of problem consensus and technical knowledge about solutions. Each cell represents an organizational situation that is appropriate for the decision-making approaches described in this chapter.

Cell 1. In cell 1 of Exhibit 12.8, rational decision procedures are used because problems are agreed on and cause–effect relationships are well understood, so there is little uncertainty. Decisions can be made in a computational manner. Alternatives can be

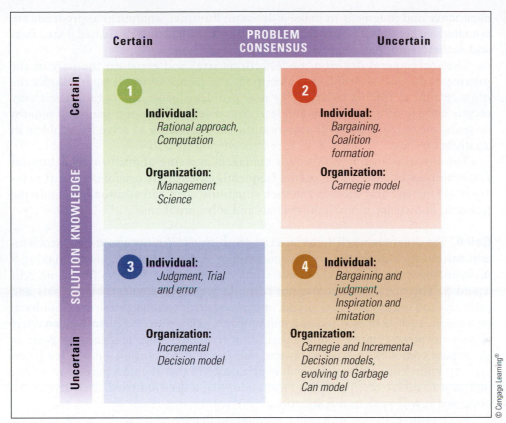

EXHIBIT 12.8

Contingency Framework for Using Decision Models

identified and the best solution adopted through analysis and calculations. The rational models described earlier in this chapter, both for individuals and for the organization, are appropriate when problems and the means for solving them are well defined.

Cell 2. In cell 2, there is high uncertainty about problems and priorities, so bargaining and compromise are used to reach consensus. Tackling one problem might mean the organization must postpone action on other issues. The priorities given to respective problems are decided through discussion, debate, and coalition building.

Managers in this situation should use broad participation to achieve consensus in the decision process. Opinions should be surfaced and discussed until compromise is reached. The organization will not otherwise move forward as an integrated unit. The Carnegie model applies when there is dissension about organizational problems. When groups within the organization disagree or when the organization is in conflict with constituencies (government regulators, suppliers, unions), bargaining and negotiation are required. The bargaining strategy is especially relevant to the problem identification stage of the decision process. Once bargaining and negotiation are completed, the organization will have support for one direction.

Cell 3. In a cell 3 situation, problems and standards of performance are certain, but alternative technical solutions are vague and uncertain. Techniques to solve a problem are ill-defined and poorly understood. When an individual manager faces this situation, intuition will be the decision guideline. The manager will rely on past experience and judgment to make a decision. Rational, analytical approaches are not effective because the alternatives cannot be identified and calculated. Hard facts and accurate information are not available.

The incremental decision model reflects trial and error on the part of the organization. Once a problem is identified, a sequence of small steps enables the organization to learn a solution. As new problems arise, the organization may recycle back to an earlier point and start over. Eventually, over a period of months or years, the organization will acquire sufficient experience to solve the problem in a satisfactory way.

The situation in cell 3, of senior managers agreeing about problems but not knowing how to solve them, occurs frequently in business organizations. If managers use incremental decisions in such situations, they will eventually acquire the technical knowledge to accomplish goals and solve problems.

Cell 4. The situation in cell 4, characterized by high uncertainty about both problems and solutions, is difficult for decision making. An individual manager making a decision under this high level of uncertainty can employ techniques from both cells 2 and 3. The manager can attempt to build a coalition to establish goals and priorities and use judgment, intuition, or trial and error to solve problems. Additional techniques, such as inspiration and imitation, also may be required. **Inspiration** refers to an innovative, creative solution that is not reached by logical means. Inspiration sometimes comes like a flash of insight, but—similar to intuition—it is often based on deep knowledge and understanding of a problem that the unconscious mind has had time to mull over.[76] **Imitation** means adopting a decision tried elsewhere in the hope that it will work in this situation.

For example, in one university, accounting department faculty were unhappy with their current circumstances but could not decide on the direction the department should take. Some faculty members wanted a greater research orientation, whereas others wanted greater orientation toward business firms and accounting applications. The disagreement about goals was compounded because neither group was sure about the best technique for achieving its goals. The ultimate solution was inspirational on the part of the dean. An accounting research center was established with funding from major accounting firms. The funding was used to finance research activities for faculty interested in basic research and to provide contact with business firms for other faculty. The solution provided a common goal and unified people within the department to work toward that goal.

When an entire organization is characterized by high uncertainty regarding both problems and solutions, elements of the garbage can model will appear. Managers may first try techniques from both cells 2 and 3, but logical decision sequences starting with problem identification and ending with problem solution will not occur. Potential solutions will precede problems as often as problems precede solutions. In this situation, managers should encourage widespread discussion of problems and idea proposals to facilitate the opportunity to make choices. Eventually, through trial and error, the organization will solve some problems.

Research has found that decisions made following the prescriptions of the contingency decision-making framework tend to be more successful. However, the study noted that nearly 6 of 10 strategic management decisions failed to follow the framework, leading to a situation in which misleading or missing information decreased the chance of an effective decision choice.[77] Managers can use the contingency framework in Exhibit 12.8 to improve the likelihood of successful organizational decisions.

Special Decision Circumstances

In a highly competitive world beset by global competition and rapid change, decision making seldom fits the traditional rational, analytical model. Today's managers have to make high-stakes decisions more often and more quickly than ever before in an environment that is increasingly less predictable. Interviews with CEOs in high-tech industries, for example, found that they strive to use some type of rational process, but the uncertainty and change in the industry often make that approach unsuccessful. The way these managers actually reach decisions is through a complex interaction with other managers, subordinates, environmental factors, and organizational events.[78] Issues of particular concern for today's decision makers are coping with high-velocity environments, learning from decision mistakes, and understanding and overcoming cognitive biases in decision making.

High-Velocity Environments

In some industries, the rate of competitive and technological change is so extreme that market data are either unavailable or obsolete, strategic windows open and shut quickly, perhaps within a few months, and the cost of poor decisions may be company failure. Research has examined how successful companies make decisions in these **high-velocity environments**, especially to understand whether organizations abandon rational approaches or have time for incremental implementation.[79]

A comparison of successful with unsuccessful decisions in high-velocity environments found the following patterns:

- Successful decision makers tracked information in real time to develop a deep and intuitive grasp of the business. Two to three intense meetings per week with all key players were usual. Decision makers closely tracked operating statistics to constantly feel the pulse of what was happening. Unsuccessful firms were more concerned with future planning and forward-looking information, with only a loose grip on immediate happenings.
- During a major decision, successful companies began immediately to build multiple alternatives. Implementation of alternatives sometimes ran in parallel before managers settled on a final choice. Companies that made decisions slowly developed just one alternative, moving to another only after the first one failed.
- Fast, successful decision makers sought advice from everyone and depended heavily on one or two savvy, trusted colleagues as counselors. Slow companies were unable to build trust and agreement among the best people.
- Fast companies involved everyone in the decision and tried for consensus; but if consensus did not emerge, the top manager made the choice and moved ahead. Waiting for everyone to be on board created more delays than was warranted. Slow companies delayed decisions to achieve a uniform consensus.
- Fast, successful choices were well integrated with other decisions and the overall strategic direction of the company. Less successful choices considered the decision in isolation from other decisions; the decision was made in the abstract.[80]

When speed matters, a slow decision can be as ineffective as the wrong decision. Managers can learn to make decisions quickly. To improve the chances of a good decision under high-velocity conditions, some organizations stimulate constructive

 BRIEFCASE

As an organization manager, keep this guideline in mind:

Track real-time information, build multiple alternatives simultaneously, and try to involve everyone—but move ahead anyway when making decisions in a high-velocity environment.

conflict through a technique called **point–counterpoint**, which divides decision makers into two groups and assigns them different, often competing responsibilities.[81] The groups develop and exchange proposals and debate options until they arrive at a common set of understandings and recommendations. Groups can often make better decisions because multiple and diverse opinions are considered. In the face of complexity and uncertainty, the more people who have a say in the decision making, the better.

In group decision making, a consensus may not always be reached, but the exercise gives everyone a chance to consider options and state their opinions, and it gives top managers a broader understanding. Typically, those involved support the final choice. However, if a very speedy decision is required, top managers are willing to make the decision and move forward.

Decision Mistakes and Learning

Organizational decisions result in many errors, especially when made in conditions of great uncertainty. Managers simply cannot determine or predict which alternative will solve a problem. In these cases, managers must make the decision—and take the risk—often in the spirit of trial and error. If an alternative fails, they can learn from it and try another alternative that better fits the situation. Each failure provides new information and insight. The point for managers is to move ahead with the decision process despite the potential for mistakes. "Chaotic action is preferable to orderly inaction."[82]

In some organizations, managers are encouraged to instill a climate of experimentation to facilitate creative decision making. If one idea fails, another idea should be tried. Failure often lays the groundwork for success, such as when technicians at 3M developed Post-it Notes based on a failed product—a not-very-sticky glue. Managers in the most innovative companies believe that if all their new products succeed, they're doing something wrong, not taking the necessary risks to develop new markets. In other words, they recognize that when failure teaches the company something new, it lays the groundwork for success.

Only by making mistakes can managers and organizations go through the process of **decision learning** and acquire sufficient experience and knowledge to perform more effectively in the future. Some companies even give awards for failures that lead to learning. Grey Advertising awards an annual "Heroic Failure" trophy, to reward the "glorious defeats that can make success itself look timid."[83] At Intuit, one winner of the failure award was the team that developed an aggressive marketing campaign to target young tax filers. Through a website called RockYourRefund.com, Intuit offered discounts to Best Buy and other companies and the ability to deposit tax refunds directly into prepaid Visa cards issued by hip-hop star and entrepreneur Russell Simmons. The campaign was a bust, with Intuit doing "very few returns" through the site. A postmortem of the project gave the team lessons they applied to future projects, such as the fact that young people shun websites that feel too much like advertising. "It's only a failure if we fail to get the learning," said former Intuit chairman Scott Cook.[84]

Based on what has been said about decision making in this chapter, one can expect companies to be ultimately successful in their decision making by adopting a learning approach toward solutions. They will make mistakes along the way, but they will resolve uncertainty through the trial-and-error process.

Making a poor decision can help a manager and organization learn and get stronger.

> **ANSWER:** *Agree.* Managers don't want people to intentionally make poor decisions, of course, but smart managers encourage people to take risks and experiment, which can lead to failed decisions. Learning from the failures is the key to growing and improving. In addition, although managers strive to make good decisions, they understand that decisions sometimes must be made quickly based on limited information and that trial and error is an important way the organization learns and grows stronger.

Cognitive Biases

While encouraging risk-taking and accepting mistakes can lead to learning, one error managers strive to avoid is allowing cognitive biases to influence their decision making. **Cognitive biases** are severe errors in judgment that all humans are prone to and that typically lead to bad choices.[85] Three common biases are escalating commitment, loss aversion, and groupthink.

Escalating Commitment. One well-known cognitive bias is referred to as **escalating commitment**. Research suggests that organizations often continue to invest time and money in a solution despite strong evidence that it is not working. Several explanations are given for why managers escalate commitment to a failing decision.[86] Many times managers simply keep hoping they can recoup their losses. For example, after the Fukushima Daiichi nuclear power plant was damaged by a 2011 earthquake in Japan, managers at Tokyo Electric Power Company delayed using seawater to cool the damaged nuclear reactors because they wanted to protect their investment and knew that using seawater could render the reactors permanently inoperable. The company reversed its decision and began using seawater only when Japan's prime minister ordered it to do so after an explosion at the facility.[87]

In addition, managers block or distort negative information when they are personally responsible for a bad decision. Another explanation is that consistency and persistence are valued in contemporary society. Consistent managers are considered better leaders than those who switch around from one course of action to another, so managers have a hard time pulling the plug despite evidence that a decision was wrong.

Prospect Theory. Most people are naturally loss averse, so the fear of failure is more powerful than the opportunity for success when making a decision.[88] The pain one feels from losing a 10-dollar bill is typically much more powerful than the happiness one gets from finding a 20-dollar one. **Prospect theory**, developed by psychologists Daniel Kahneman and Amos Tversky, suggests that the threat of a loss has a greater impact on a decision than the possibility of an equivalent gain.[89] Therefore, most managers have a tendency to analyze problems in terms of what they fear losing rather than what they might gain. When faced with a specific decision, they overweight the value of potential losses and underweight the value of potential gains. In addition, research indicates that the regret associated with a decision that results in a loss is stronger than the regret of a missed opportunity. Thus, managers might avoid potentially wonderful opportunities that also have potentially negative outcomes. This tendency can create a pattern of overly-cautious decisions that leads to chronic underperformance in the organization.[90] Prospect theory also helps explain the phenomenon of escalating commitment, discussed in the previous section. Managers don't want to lose or be associated with a failing project, so they keep throwing good money after bad.

Groupthink. Many decisions in organizations are made by groups, and the desire to go along with the group can bias decisions. Subtle pressures for conformity exist in almost any group, and particularly when people like one another, they tend to avoid anything that might create disharmony. **Groupthink** refers to the tendency of people in groups to suppress contrary opinions.[91] When people slip into groupthink, the desire for harmony outweighs concerns over decision quality. Group members emphasize maintaining unity rather than realistically challenging problems and alternatives. People censor their personal opinions and are reluctant to criticize the opinions of others.

Overcoming Cognitive Biases

How can managers avoid the problems of groupthink, escalating commitment, and being influenced by loss aversion? Several ideas have been proposed that help managers be more realistic and objective when making decisions. Two of the most effective are to use evidence-based management and to encourage dissent and diversity.

Evidence-Based Management. **Evidence-based management** means a commitment to make more informed and intelligent decisions based on the best available facts and evidence.[92] It means being aware of one's biases, seeking and examining evidence with rigor. Managers practice evidence-based decision making by being careful and thoughtful rather than carelessly relying on assumptions, past experience, rules of thumb, or intuition. For example, Dawn Zier was hired as CEO of Nutrisystem to turn things around, but when she would ask people questions, she says "they would answer a little too quickly, without even having time to think about it." When Zier dug deeper, she usually found that "the facts weren't always the facts being presented." She embarked on a culture change initiative to build a culture where people focus on hard evidence rather than "fantasy or wishing that something happened." The company's motto is now, "Just the Facts," where the word *Facts* stands not only for evidence but also for the values of focus, accountability, customer-centric, team, and success.[93]

A global survey by McKinsey & Company found that when managers incorporate thoughtful analysis into decision making, they get better results. Studying the responses of more than 2,000 executives regarding how their companies made a specific decision, McKinsey concluded that techniques such as detailed analysis, risk assessment, financial models, and considering comparable situations typically contribute to better financial and operational outcomes.[94] However, a recent review of the decisions of 39 senior general managers found that they used only limited sources of evidence in making most of their decisions. Managers can enhance the effectiveness of decisions by using more sources of evidence.[95] Evidence-based management can be particularly useful for overcoming fear of loss and the problem of escalating commitment. To practice evidence-based management, managers use data and facts to the extent possible to inform their decisions. Many manager problems are uncertain, and hard facts and data aren't available, but by always seeking evidence, managers can avoid relying on faulty assumptions. Decision makers can also do a postmortem of decisions to evaluate what worked, what didn't, and how to do things better. The best decision makers have a healthy appreciation for what they don't know. They are always questioning and encouraging others to question their knowledge and assumptions. They foster a culture of inquiry, observation, and experimentation.

Encourage Dissent and Diversity. Dissent and diversity can be particularly useful in complex circumstances because they open the decision process to a wide variety of ideas and opinions rather than being constrained by personal biases or groupthink.[96] One way to encourage dissent is to ensure that the group is diverse in terms of age and gender, functional area of expertise, hierarchical level, and experience with the business. Some groups assign a **devil's advocate**, who has the role of challenging the assumptions and assertions made by the group.[97] The devil's advocate may force the group to rethink its approach to the problem and avoid reaching premature decisions. Consider the situation of soldiers involved in volatile military operations in Iraq and Afghanistan, where faulty decisions could be deadly. At Fort Leavenworth's University of Foreign Military and Cultural Studies, the U.S. Army trained a group of soldiers to act as devil's advocates. Members of the "Red Team," as graduates were called, were deployed to various brigades to question prevailing assumptions and make sure decisions were considered from alternate points of view. "This is having someone inside that says, 'Wait a minute, not so fast,' " says Greg Fontenot, the program director. The goal, he says, was to avoid "getting sucked into that groupthink."[98]

Another approach, referred to as *ritual dissent*, puts parallel teams to work on the same problem in a large group meeting. Each team appoints a spokesperson who presents the team's finding and ideas to another team, which is required to listen quietly. Then, the spokesperson turns to face away from the team, which rips into the presentation no-holds-barred while the spokesperson is required to listen quietly. Each team's spokesperson does this with every other team in turn, so that by the end of the session all ideas have been well-dissected and discussed.[99] The point–counterpoint method described earlier is also effective for encouraging dissent. Whatever techniques they use, good managers find ways to get a diversity of ideas and opinions on the table when making complex decisions.

Design Essentials

- Most organizational decisions are not made in a logical, rational manner. Most decisions do not begin with the careful analysis of a problem, followed by systematic analysis of alternatives, and finally implementation of a solution. On the contrary, decision processes are characterized by conflict, coalition building, trial and error, speed, and mistakes. Managers operate under many constraints that limit rationality; hence, they use satisficing and intuition as well as rational analysis in their decision making. Individual cognitive biases are one significant constraint that managers should be aware of.

■ Another important idea is that individuals make decisions, but most organizational decisions are not made by a single individual. Organizational decision-making approaches include the management science approach, the Carnegie model, the incremental decision model, and the garbage can model.

■ Only in rare circumstances do managers analyze problems and find solutions by themselves. Many problems are not clear, so widespread discussion and coalition building take place. Once goals and priorities are set, alternatives to achieve those goals can be tried. When a manager does make an individual decision, it is often a small part of a larger decision process. Organizations solve big problems through a series of small steps. A single manager may initiate one step but should be aware of the larger decision process to which it belongs.

■ The greatest amount of conflict and coalition building occurs when problems are not agreed on. Priorities must be established to indicate which goals are important and which problems should be solved first. If a manager attacks a problem other people do not agree with, the manager will lose support for the solution to be implemented. Thus, time and activity should be spent building a coalition in the problem identification stage of decision making. Then the organization can move toward solutions. Under conditions of low technical knowledge, the solution unfolds as a series of incremental trials that will gradually lead to an overall solution.

■ The most novel description of decision making is the garbage can model. This model describes how decision processes can seem almost random in highly organic organizations. Decisions, problems, ideas, and people flow through organizations and mix together in various combinations. Through this process, the organization gradually learns. Some problems may never be solved, but many are, and the organization will move toward maintaining and improving its level of performance.

■ Many organizations operating in high-velocity environments must make decisions with speed, which means staying in immediate touch with operations and the environment. Moreover, in an uncertain world, organizations will make mistakes, and mistakes made through trial and error should be appreciated. Encouraging trial-and-error increments facilitates organizational learning.

■ On the other hand, allowing cognitive biases to cloud decision making can have serious negative consequences for an organization. Managers can avoid the biases of escalating commitment, loss aversion, and groupthink by using evidence-based management and by encouraging diversity and dissent in the decision-making process.

❯❯ KEY CONCEPTS

bounded rationality perspective	groupthink	problem consensus
Carnegie model	high-velocity environments	problem identification
coalition	imitation	problem solution
cognitive biases	incremental decision model	problemistic search
contingency decision-making framework	inspiration	programmed decisions
decision learning	intuitive decision making	prospect theory
devil's advocate	management science approach	quasirationality
escalating commitment	nonprogrammed decisions	rational approach
evidence-based management	organizational decision making	satisficing
garbage can model	organized anarchy	technical knowledge
	point–counterpoint	

▶▶ DISCUSSION QUESTIONS

1. When you are faced with choosing between several valid options, how do you typically make your decision? How do you think managers typically choose between several options? What are the similarities between your decision process and what you think managers do?

2. A professional economist once told his class, "An individual decision maker should process all relevant information and select the economically rational alternative." Do you agree? Why or why not?

3. If managers frequently use experience and intuition to make complex, nonprogrammed decisions, how do they apply evidence-based management, which seems to suggest that managers should rely on facts and data?

4. The Carnegie model emphasizes the need for a political coalition in the decision-making process. When and why are coalitions necessary?

5. What are the three major phases in Mintzberg's incremental decision model? Why might an organization recycle through one or more phases of the model?

6. An organization theorist once told her class, "Organizations never make big decisions. They make small decisions that eventually add up to a big decision." Explain the logic behind this statement.

7. How would you make a decision to select a building site for a new waste-treatment plant in the Philippines? Where would you start with this complex decision, and what steps would you take? Explain which decision model in the chapter best describes your approach.

8. Why would managers in high-velocity environments worry more about the present than the future? Would an individual manager working in this type of environment be more likely to succeed with a rational approach or an intuitive approach? Discuss.

9. Can you think of a decision you have made in your personal, school, or work life that reflects a stronger desire to avoid a loss than to make a gain? How about a time when you stayed with an idea or project for too long, perhaps even escalating your commitment, to avoid a failure? Discuss.

10. Why are decision mistakes usually accepted in organizations but penalized in college courses and exams that are designed to train managers?

▶▶ CHAPTER 12 WORKSHOP   Do Biases Influence Your Decision Making?[100]

All of us have biases, but most of us have a hard time seeing our own. What biases influence your decisions and solutions to problems? Answer the following questions to get an idea of the difficulties and mistakes that likely await you as a manager.

1. A piece of paper is folded in half, in half again, and so on. After 100 folds, how thick will it be? Take your best guess: _____. I am 90 percent sure that the correct answer lies between _____ and _____.

2. Which of the following figures is most different from the others?

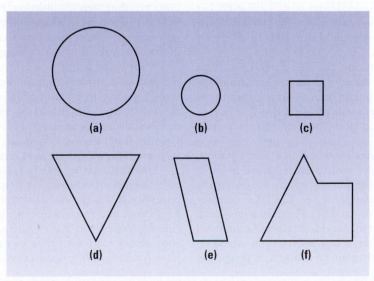

From the Shoptalk on page 289 of Management / 11e

3. As owner and CEO of your company, you decided to invest $100 million to build pilotless drones that cannot be detected by enemy radar. When the project is 90 percent complete, a competing firm begins marketing a completed drone that cannot be detected by radar. In addition, their drone is much faster, smaller, cheaper, and more sophisticated than the drone that your company is developing. The question is: Should you invest the last 10 percent of the research funds to finish your drone? Check one of the following answers.

_____ No; there is no reason to continue spending money on the project.

_____ Yes; after investing $90 million, we might as well finish the project.

4. Give a quick (five-second) estimate of the following product without actually calculating it:

$8 \times 7 \times 6 \times 5 \times 4 \times 3 \times 2 \times 1 =$ _____.

5. Robert is envious, stubborn, critical, impulsive, industrious, and intelligent. In general, how emotional do you think Robert is? (Circle one number.)

Not emotional　　1 2 3 4 5 6 7 8 9　　Extremely
at all　　　　　　　　　　　　　　　　emotional

6. Which would you choose between the two alternatives below?

_____ Alternative A: A 50 percent chance of gaining $1,000

_____ Alternative B: A sure gain of $500

Which would you choose between the two alternatives below?

_____ Alternative C: A 50 percent chance of losing $1,000

_____ Alternative D: A sure loss of $500

After you have specified an answer to each problem, you will find the answers and a description of the potential related bias on page 506.

CASE FOR ANALYSIS | Cracking the Whip[101]

Harmon Davidson stared dejectedly at the departing figure of his management survey team leader. Their meeting had not gone well. Davidson had relayed to Al Pitcher complaints about his handling of the survey. Pitcher had responded with adamant denial and unveiled scorn.

Davidson, director of headquarters management, was prepared to discount some of the criticism as resentment of outsiders meddling with "the way we've always done business," exacerbated by the turbulence of continual reorganization. But Davidson could hardly ignore the sheer volume of complaints or his high regard for some of their sources. "Was I missing danger signals about Pitcher from the start?" Davidson asked himself. "Or was I just giving a guy I didn't know a fair chance with an inherently controversial assignment?"

With his division decimated in the latest round of downsizing at the Department of Technical Services (DTS) earlier that year, Davidson had been asked to return to the headquarters management office after a five-year hiatus. The director, Walton Drummond, had abruptly taken early retirement.

One of the first things Davidson had learned about his new job was that he would be responsible for a comprehensive six-month survey of the headquarters management structure and processes. The DTS secretary had promised the survey to the White House as a prelude to the agency's next phase of management reform. Drummond had already picked the five-person survey team consisting of two experienced management analysts, a promising younger staff member, an intern, and Pitcher, the team leader. Pitcher was fresh from the Treasury Department, where he had participated in a similar survey. But having gone off after retirement for an extended mountain-climbing expedition in Asia, Drummond was unavailable to explain his survey plans or any understandings he had reached with Pitcher.

Davidson had been impressed with Pitcher's energy and motivation. He worked long hours, wrote voluminously if awkwardly, and was brimming with the latest organizational theory. Pitcher had other characteristics, however, that were disquieting. He seemed uninterested in DTS's history and culture and was paternalistic toward top managers, assuming they were unsophisticated and unconcerned about modern management.

A series of presurvey informational briefings for headquarters office heads conducted by Davidson and Pitcher seemed to go swimmingly. Pitcher deferred to his chief on matters of philosophy and confined his remarks to schedule and procedures. He closed his segment on a friendly note, saying, "If we do find opportunities for improvement, we'll try to have recommendations for you."

But the survey was barely a week old when the director of management received his first call from an outraged customer. It was the assistant secretary for public affairs, Erin Dove, and she was not speaking in her usual upbeat tones. "Your folks have managed to upset my whole supervisory staff with their comments about how we'll have to change our organization and methods," she said.

"I thought you were going through a fact-finding study. This guy Pitcher sounds like he wants to remake DTS headquarters overnight. Who does he think he is?"

When Davidson asked him about the encounter with public affairs, Pitcher expressed puzzlement that a few summary observations shared with supervisors in the interest of "prompt informal feedback" had been interpreted as such disturbing conclusions. "I told them we'll tell them how to fix it," he reassured his supervisor.

"Listen, Al," Davidson remonstrated gently. "These are very accomplished managers who aren't used to being told they have to fix anything. This agency's been on a roll for years, and the need for reinvention isn't resonating all that well yet. We've got to collect and analyze the information and assemble a convincing case for change, or we'll be spinning our wheels. Let's hold off on the feedback until you and I have reviewed it together."

But two weeks later, Technology Development Director Phil Canseco, an old and treasured colleague, was on Davidson's doorstep looking as unhappy as Erin Dove had sounded on the phone. "Harmon, buddy, I think you have to rein in this survey team a bit," he said. "Several managers who were scheduled for survey interviews were working on a 24-hour turnaround to give a revised project budget to the Appropriations subcommittee that day. My deputy says Pitcher was put out about postponing interviews and grumbled about whether we understood the new priorities. Is he living in the real world?"

Canseco's comments prompted Davidson to call a few of his respected peers who had dealt with the survey team. With varying degrees of reluctance, they all criticized the team leader and, in some cases, team members, as abrasive and uninterested in the rationales offered for existing structure and processes.

And so Davidson marshaled all of his tact for a review with the survey team leader. But Pitcher was in no mood for either introspection or reconsideration. He took the view that he had been brought in to spearhead a White House-inspired management improvement initiative in a glamour agency that had never had to think much about efficiency. He reminded Davidson that even he had conceded that managers were due some hard lessons on this score. Pitcher didn't see any way to meet his deadline except by adhering to a rigorous schedule, since he was working with managers disinclined to cooperate with an outsider pushing an unpopular exercise. He felt Davidson's role was to hold the line against unwarranted criticisms from prima donnas trying to discredit the survey.

Many questions arose in Davidson's mind about the survey plan and his division's capacity to carry it out. Had they taken on too much with too little? Had the right people been picked for the survey team? Had managers and executives, and even the team, been properly prepared for the survey?

But the most immediate question was whether Al Pitcher could help him with these problems.

CASE FOR ANALYSIS | Medici Mediterranean Restaurant

Gui-do. Gui-do.

As Alissa Mason drove up the mountain through the rain, she turned up the volume on the radio to clear her mind. However, even the steady rhythm of the truck's windshield wipers steered her mind back to *the problem*—Gui-do, Gui-do. Ten years earlier, Alissa's dream of opening a Mediterranean-style restaurant came true with the launching of *Medici*. Even now, Alissa smiled, recalling how the once-annoying habit of mispronunciation (*Medi-ki*) by ranchers and townspeople had become yet another endearing quality of owning a business in a small town.

In 2000, a graduation gift from her rancher dad provided Alissa the opportunity to travel throughout the Mediterranean region, culminating in a stint at a cooking school in Tuscany. Upon return to her hometown, and armed with a dream, her MBA, and a box load of ideas for tantalizing meals, Alissa was certain she had the recipe for success. She was right.

The opening of the new restaurant in her hometown was a triumph and its popularity and reputation for delicious food spread rapidly, attracting state and regional press coverage. In addition to a strong local customer base, Medici's location on the route from the interstate to several popular mountain resorts offered opportunities to become a favorite stopover for tourists, skiers, and hikers. Within a few years, the amazing success of the business and the constant barrage of suggestions for a second location closer to the resorts encouraged Alissa to consider expansion. The problem would be how she would manage locations almost an hour apart while maintaining the level of quality and service customers expected.

Guido Bertolli appeared to be the answer to her prayers. A handsome, charming Italian, Guido was a talented chef from a large family of talented chefs. The youngest of four brothers, Guido realized he would not inherit the family restaurant and decided to immigrate to America to build a reputation as a chef away from his dominating father and brothers.

Guido's experience and amazing talents as a chef, his natural ease in managing staff, and the charm and joy he displayed in his interaction with customers soon convinced Alissa that she had found the perfect person to direct the new restaurant. Looking back, she realized her own enthusiasm for expansion and a starry-eyed impression of the Italian, shared by an adoring public, led to mistakes in her business judgment.

Following a fabulous opening, the new restaurant soared to financial success, far out-pacing its small-town sister location. But by the end of the second year, problems loomed. Alissa's travels to the resort location became more frequent, cutting into the time needed at the original restaurant. Crowds filled the resort location. ("We love Guido." "You're so lucky to have found him.") Patrons waited patiently in lines. However, delivery problems led to frequent changes in popular menu items. Recurring delinquency in the payment of bills and invoices, as well as Guido's increasingly lax attitude regarding his presence on site, led to confrontations. Realizing his value to the organization, Alissa always accepted Guido's promises to do better. Each time, the problems returned, and staff frustration at both locations increased.

Recently, rumors reached Alissa that Guido was exploring the possibility of opening his own rival Mediterranean restaurant. Alissa was not sure she wanted to keep Guido, but she did not want her popular chef to move and take devoted customers with him. The bottom line—the clientele wanted Guido. Alissa was certain he would be able to obtain financial backing for his venture based upon his talents and popularity. She realized she must do something before Guido moved further into the process.

As she drove, Alissa was aware of the increasing stress. The situation with Guido was taking over every aspect of her life. The time for serious discussion loomed. For days she had weighed her options.

Status Quo

Alissa liked Guido and would like to avoid another confrontation. Her own management style was nonconfrontational and she wondered if sitting down with Guido to discuss a more manageable plan for handling office management details at his location would be a good solution until she could be certain of his future plans. The thought of hiring someone to assist Guido with the business details occurred to her, but that meant the addition of another full-time employee—a step she was not sure she could take at this time.

Discipline or Fire Guido

With a repeat of the same problems that had been addressed on previous occasions, Alissa felt that disciplinary steps were futile. However, firing Guido set up the very situation—her talented chef as a rival—that she wanted to avoid. Still, with his shaky business skills, there was no guarantee he would be able to create a strong business plan, secure financial backing, and sustain a rival restaurant, despite his popularity and talents as a chef. It would not be the first time a great chef failed as an owner.

Focus on Medici II

Alissa wondered if it would be better to move the entire operation to the resort. The original restaurant had her heart, but the resort location had the talented chef and the bulk of the clientele. If she closed the first location and maintained only the resort location, she would take over the business side, relieve Guido of the responsibility for which he was obviously ill-suited, and maintain more control over his work habits.

Offer Guido a Partnership

Rewarding Guido with a partnership might be a way to keep him and impose a stronger sense of loyalty as well as pride in building a greater sense of urgency for his reputation and success as a businessman. However, if she offered Guido a minority stake, she would give up a portion of control and increase his role in the direction and day-to-day operations of the business.

Decision Time

As Alissa pulled into the parking lot, the rain ended and Guido stepped out of the doorway and waved. With no clear answer, she walked with Guido to his office.

▶▶ ANSWERS TO QUESTIONS IN "WORKSHOP"

1. The answer is unbelievably huge: roughly 800,000, 000,000,000,000 times the distance between the Earth and the Sun. Your mind was likely anchored in the thinness of a sheet of paper, thereby leading you to dramatically underestimate the effect of doubling the thickness 100 times. Initial mental anchoring to a low or high point leads to frequent incorrect solutions. How certain did you feel about your answer? This is an example of *overconfidence*, a major cause of manager mistakes.

2. Every figure is different in some way. Figure (a) has the greatest area, (b) has the least area, (c) is the only square, (d) is the only three-sided figure, (e) is the most narrow and lopsided, and (f) is the least symmetrical and five-sided. Did you stop after finding one correct answer? *Failure to go beyond initial impressions and dig below the surface* often prevents managers from understanding what the real problem is or identifying the correct or best solution.

3. If you checked "yes," you felt the desire to continue investing in a previous decision even when it was failing, which is called *escalating commitment*. This is a mistake that many managers make because they are *emotionally attached* to the previous decision, even one as hopeless as this inadequate drone.

4. The median estimate from students is 2,250. When the numbers are given in reverse order starting with 1×2, and so on, the median estimate is 512. The correct answer is 40,320. The *order in which information is presented* makes a difference to a person's solution, and acting quickly produces an answer that is far from correct.

5. When judging people, early information has more impact than later information, called the *primacy effect*. Reversing the word sequence so that *intelligent* and *industrious* come first creates a more favorable impression. Respondents rate Robert more or less emotional depending on the order of the descriptive words. Were you guilty of rating Robert as more emotional because of being *influenced by initial impressions*?

6. Although the options are numerically equivalent, most people choose alternatives B and C. People hate losing more than they enjoy winning, and hence about 80 percent choose a sure small gain (B), and 70 percent will take more risk in the hope of avoiding a loss (C). *Taking emotions out of the process* typically leads to better decisions.

❯❯ NOTES

1. Jennifer Reingold, "How to Fail in Business While Really, Really Trying," *Fortune*, April 7, 2014, 80–90.

2. "GM Faulty Ignition Crashes Now 47," *CNN*, May 25, 2014, http://money.cnn.com/2014/05/24/autos/gm-faulty-ignition-crashes/ (accessed May 27, 2014); and Jeff Bennett, "GM Now Says It Detected Ignition Switch Problem Back in 2001," March 12, 2014, http://online.wsj.com/news/articles/SB10001424052702303403604579585891316612268?mod=Business_newsreel_1 (accessed May 27, 2014).

3. Adam Lashinsky, "Apple Brings Back Steve Jobs," *Fortune*, October 8, 2012, 178–184 (adapted from *The Greatest Business Decisions of All Time* by Verne Harnish and the editors of *Fortune*); Betsy Morris, "What Makes Apple Golden?" *Fortune*, March 17, 2008, 68–74; E. S. Browning, Steven Russolillo, and Jessica Vascellaro, "Apple Now Biggest-Ever U.S. Company," *The Wall Street Journal Europe*, August 22, 2012, 24; and "World's Most Admired Companies," *Fortune*, http://money.cnn.com/magazines/fortune/most-admired/2014/snapshots/670.html (accessed May 28, 2014).

4. Shawn Tully, "Delta Takes Off," *Fortune*, March 17, 2014, 114–120.

5. Charles Lindblom, "The Science of 'Muddling Through,' " *Public Administration Review* 29 (1954), 79–88.

6. Herbert A. Simon, *The New Science of Management Decision* (Englewood Cliffs, NJ: Prentice-Hall, 1960), 1–8.

7. Paul J. H. Schoemaker and J. Edward Russo, "A Pyramid of Decision Approaches," *California Management Review*, Fall 1993, 9–31.

8. Andrew Bordeaux, "10 Famous Product Failures and the Advertisements That Did Not Sell Them," *Growthink.com*, December 17, 2007, http://www.growthink.com/content/10-famous-product-failures-and-advertisements-did-not-sell-them (accessed September 16, 2011); and Jane McGrath, "Five Failed McDonald's Menu Items," HowStuffWorks.com, http://money.howstuffworks.com/5-failed-mcdonalds-menu-items3.htm (accessed September 16, 2011).

9. Hugh Courtney, Dan Lovallo, and Carmini Clarke, "Deciding How to Decide," *Harvard Business Review*, November 2013, 62–70.

10. Michael Pacanowsky, "Team Tools for Wicked Problems," *Organizational Dynamics* 23, no. 3 (Winter 1995), 36–51.

11. Russell L. Ackoff, quoted in Ian I. Mitroff, Can M. Alpaslan, and Richard O. Mason, "The Messy Business of Management," *MIT Sloan Management Review*, Fall 2012, 96.

12. The idea of a good choice potentially producing a bad outcome under uncertain conditions is attributed to Robert Rubin, reported in David Leonhardt, "This Fed Chief May Yet Get a Honeymoon," *The New York Times*, August 23, 2006, C1.

13. David Firestone, "What Should Happen to Edward Snowden?" *The New York Times*, January 2, 2014, http://takingnote.blogs.nytimes.com/2014/01/02/what-should-happen-to-edward-snowden/ (accessed May 28, 2014).

14. Ylan Q. Mui, "Wal-Mart to Reinstate Dropped Products, Emphasize Price," *The Washington Post*, April 11, 2011, http://www.washingtonpost.com/business/economy/wal-mart-to-reinstate-products-emphasize-price/2011/04/11/AFrwLWMD_story.html (accessed September 26, 2011).

15. As described in a letter Franklin wrote in 1772, quoted in J. Edward Russo and Paul J. H. Shoemaker, *Decision Traps: Ten Barriers to Brilliant Decision-Making and How to Overcome Them* (New York: Fireside/Simon & Schuster, 1989).

16. Karen Dillon, "The Perfect Decision" (an interview with John S. Hammond and Ralph L. Keeney), *Inc.*, October 1998, 74–78; and John S. Hammond and Ralph L. Keeney, *Smart Choices: A Practical Guide to Making Better Decisions* (Boston: Harvard Business School Press, 1998).

17. Earnest R. Archer, "How to Make a Business Decision: An Analysis of Theory and Practice," *Management Review* 69 (February 1980), 54–61; Boris Blai, "Eight Steps to Successful Problem Solving," *Supervisory Management*, January 1986, 7–9; and Thomas S. Bateman, "Leading with Competence: Problem-Solving by Leaders and Followers," *Leader to Leader*, Summer 2010, 38–44.

18. Francine Schwadel, "Christmas Sales' Lack of Momentum Tests Store Manager's Mettle," *The Wall Street Journal*, December 16, 1987, 1.

19. Noel M. Tichy and Warren G. Bennis, "Making Judgment Calls: The Ultimate Act of Leadership," *Harvard Business Review*, October 2007, 94–102.

20. Adapted from Archer, "How to Make a Business Decision," 59–61.

21. Joseph V. Sinfield, Tim Gustafson, and Brian Hindo, "The Discipline of Creativity," *MIT Sloan Management Review*, Winter 2014, 24–26.

22. James W. Dean, Jr., and Mark P. Sharfman, "Procedural Rationality in the Strategic Decision-Making Process," *Journal of Management Studies* 30 (1993), 587–610.

23. Brad Stone, *The Everything Store: Jeff Bezos and the Age of Amazon* (New York: Little Brown, 2013), 12–13.

24. Jörn S. Basel and Rolf Brühl, "Rationality and Dual Process Models of Reasoning in Managerial Cognition and Decision Making," *European Management Journal* 31 (2013), 745–754.

25. Joe Nocera, "BP Ignored the Omens of Disaster," *The New York Times*, June 19, 2010, B1.

26. Irving L. Janis, *Crucial Decisions: Leadership in Policymaking and Crisis Management* (New York: The Free Press, 1989); and Paul C. Nutt, "Flexible Decision Styles and the Choices of Top Executives," *Journal of Management Studies* 30 (1993), 695–721.

27. Art Kleiner, "Core Group Therapy," *Strategy + Business*, Issue 27 (Second Quarter, 2002), 26–31.

28. Katie Benner, "Michael Dell's Dilemma," *Fortune*, June 13, 2011, 41–44.

29. This section is based on John S. Hammond, Ralph L. Keeney, and Howard Raiffa, *Smart Choices: A Practical Guide to Making Better Decisions* (Boston: Harvard Business School Press, 1999); Max H. Bazerman and Dolly Chugh, "Decisions Without Blinders," *Harvard Business Review*, January 2006, 88–97; J. S. Hammond, R. L. Keeney, and H. Raiffa, "The Hidden Traps in Decision Making," *Harvard Business Review*, September–October 1998, 47–58; Oren Harari, "The Thomas Lawson Syndrome," *Management Review*, February 1994, 58–61; Dan Ariely, "Q&A: Why Good CIOs Make Bad Decisions," *CIO*, May 1, 2003, 83–87; Leigh Buchanan, "How to Take Risks in a Time of Anxiety," *Inc.*, May 2003, 76–81; and Max H. Bazerman, *Judgment in Managerial Decision Making*, 5th ed. (New York: John Wiley & Sons, 2002).

30. Mark Fenton-O'Creevy et al., "Thinking, Feeling, and Deciding: The Influence of Emotions on the Decision Making and Performance of Traders," *Journal of Organizational Behavior* 32 (2011), 1044–1061.

31. Example from Jerome Groopman, *How Doctors Think* (New York: Houghton Mifflin, 2007).

32. Example from Thomas H. Davenport and Brook Manville, "From the Judgment of Leadership to the Leadership of Judgment: The Fallacy of Heroic Decision Making," *Leader to Leader*, Fall 2012, 26–31.

33. David Larcker and Brian Tayan study, reported in Michael J. Mauboussin, "The True Measures of Success," *Harvard Business Review*, October 2012, 46–56.

34. Herbert A. Simon, "Making Management Decisions: The Role of Intuition and Emotion," *Academy of Management Executive* 1 (February 1987), 57–64; and Daniel J. Eisenberg, "How Senior Managers Think," *Harvard Business Review* 62, November–December 1984, 80–90.

35. Jaana Woiceshyn, "Lessons from 'Good Minds': How CEOs Use Intuition, Analysis, and Guiding Principles to Make Strategic Decisions," *Long Range Planning* 42 (2009), 298–319; and Ann Hensman and Eugene Sadler-Smith, "Intuitive Decision Making in Banking and Finance," *European Management Journal* 29 (2011), 51–66.

36. Eduardo Salas, Michael A. Rosen, and Deborah DiazGranados, "Expertise-Based Decision Making in Organizations," *Journal of Management* 36, no. 4 (July 2010), 941–973; Kurt Matzler, Franz Bailom, and Todd A. Mooradian, "Intuitive Decision Making," *MIT Sloan Management Review* 49, no. 1 (Fall 2007), 13–15; Stefan Wally and J. Robert Baum, "Personal and Structural Determinants of the Pace of Strategic Decision Making," *Academy of Management Journal* 37, no. 4 (1994), 932–956; and Orlando Behling and Norman L. Eckel, "Making Sense Out of Intuition," *Academy of Management Executive* 5, no. 1 (1991), 46–54.

37. For a recent overview of the research on expertise-based intuition, see Salas et al., "Expertise-Based Decision Making in Organizations." Also see Eric Dane and Michael G. Pratt, "Exploring Intuition and Its Role in Managerial Decision Making," *Academy of Management Review* 32, no. 1 (2007), 33–54; Gary Klein, *Intuition at Work: Why Developing Your Gut Instincts Will Make You Better at What You Do* (New York: Doubleday, 2002); Milorad M. Novicevic, Thomas J. Hench, and Daniel A. Wren, "'Playing By Ear . . . In an Incessant Din of Reasons': Chester Barnard and the History of Intuition in Management Thought," *Management Decision* 40, no. 10 (2002), 992–1002; Alden M. Hayashi, "When to Trust Your Gut," *Harvard Business Review*, February 2001, 59–65; Brian R. Reinwald, "Tactical Intuition," *Military Review* 80, no. 5 (September–October 2000), 78–88; Thomas A. Stewart, "How to Think with Your Gut," *Business 2.0*, November 2002, http://www.business2.com/articles (accessed November 7, 2002); Henry Mintzberg and Frances Westley, "Decision Making: It's Not What You Think," *MIT Sloan Management Review*, Spring 2001, 89–93; and Carlin Flora, "Gut Almighty," *Psychology Today*, May–June 2007, 68–75.

38. Benedict Carey, "Hunches Prove to Be Valuable Assets in Battle," *The New York Times*, July 28, 2009, A1.

39. Thomas F. Issack, "Intuition: An Ignored Dimension of Management," *Academy of Management Review* 3 (1978), 917–922.

40. Marjorie A. Lyles, "Defining Strategic Problems: Subjective Criteria of Executives," *Organizational Studies* 8 (1987), 263–280; and Marjorie A. Lyles and Ian I. Mitroff, "Organizational Problem Formulation: An Empirical Study," *Administrative Science Quarterly* 25 (1980), 102–119.

41. Marjorie A. Lyles and Howard Thomas, "Strategic Problem Formulation: Biases and Assumptions Embedded in Alternative Decision-Making Models," *Journal of Management Studies* 25 (1988), 131–145.

42. Ross Stagner, "Corporate Decision-Making: An Empirical Study," *Journal of Applied Psychology* 53 (1969), 1–13.

43. W. A. Agor, "The Logic of Intuition: How Top Executives Make Important Decisions," *Organizational Dynamics* 14, no. 3 (1986), 5–18; and Paul C. Nutt, "Types of Organizational Decision Processes," *Administrative Science Quarterly* 29 (1984), 414–450.

44. Mandeep K. Dhami and Mary E. Thomson, "On the Relevance of Cognitive Continuum Theory and Quasirationality for Understanding Management Judgment and Decision Making," *European Management Journal* 30 (2012), 316–326.

45. Nandini Rajagopalan, Abdul M. A. Rasheed, and Deepak K. Datta, "Strategic Decision Processes: Critical Review and Future Directions," *Journal of Management* 19 (1993), 349–384; Paul J. H. Schoemaker, "Strategic Decisions in Organizations: Rational and Behavioral Views," *Journal of Management Studies* 30 (1993), 107–129; Charles J. McMillan, "Qualitative Models of Organizational Decision Making," *Journal of Management Studies* 5 (1980), 22–39; and Paul C. Nutt, "Models for Decision Making in Organizations and Some Contextual Variables Which Stimulate Optimal Use," *Academy of Management Review* 1 (1976), 84–98.

46. Hugh J. Miser, "Operations Analysis in the Army Air Forces in World War II: Some Reminiscences," *Interfaces* 23 (September–October 1993), 47–49; and Harold J. Leavitt, William R. Dill, and Henry B. Eyring, *The Organizational World* (New York: Harcourt Brace Jovanovich, 1973), chap. 6.

47. Stephen J. Huxley, "Finding the Right Spot for a Church Camp in Spain," *Interfaces* 12 (October 1982), 108–114; and James E. Hodder and Henry E. Riggs, "Pitfalls in Evaluating Risky Projects," *Harvard Business Review*, January–February 1985, 128–135.

48. Edward Baker and Michael Fisher, "Computational Results for Very Large Air Crew Scheduling Problems," *Omega* 9 (1981), 613–618; and Jean Aubin, "Scheduling Ambulances," *Interfaces* 22 (March–April, 1992), 1–10.

49. Scott McCartney, "The Middle Seat: How One Airline Skirts the Ash Cloud," *The Wall Street Journal*, April 22, 2010, D1.

50. Daniel Stacey, Andy Pasztor, and Jon Ostrower, "New Data, Analysis, and Luck Help Narrow Flight 370 Search Zone," *The Wall Street Journal*, April 16, 2014, http://online.wsj.com/news/articles/SB10001424052702303887804579504142188688308 (accessed May 29, 2014).

51. The movie is based on the bestselling book by Michael Lewis, *Moneyball: The Art of Winning an Unfair Game* (New York: W. W. Norton & Company, 2003).

52. Matthew Futterman, "Friday Journal—Baseball After Moneyball," *The Wall Street Journal*, September 23, 2011, D1.

53. Stephen Baker, "Math Will Rock Your World," *BusinessWeek*, January 23, 2006, 54–60; Julie Schlosser, "Markdown Lowdown," *Fortune*, January 12, 2004, 40; and Brooks Barnes, "Disney Technology Tackles a Theme Park Headache: Lines," *The New York Times*, December 28, 2010, B1.

54. Baker, "Math Will Rock Your World"; and Laura Landro, "The Informed Patient: Cutting Waits at the Doctor's Office—New Programs Reorganize Practices to Be More Efficient," *The Wall Street Journal*, April 19, 2006, D1.

55. Richard L. Daft and John C. Wiginton, "Language and Organization," *Academy of Management Review* (1979), 179–191.

56. Based on Richard M. Cyert and James G. March, *A Behavioral Theory of the Firm* (Englewood Cliffs, NJ: Prentice-Hall, 1963); and James G. March and Herbert A. Simon, *Organizations* (New York: Wiley, 1958).

57. William B. Stevenson, Joan L. Pearce, and Lyman W. Porter, "The Concept of 'Coalition' in Organization Theory and Research," *Academy of Management Review* 10 (1985), 256–268.

58. Anne Mulcahy, Randy Komisar, and Martin Sorrell, "How We Do It: Three Executives Reflect on Strategic Decision Making," *McKinsey Quarterly*, March, 2010, 46–57.

59. Jeremy W. Peters, "The Times's Online Pay Model Was Years in the Making," *The New York Times*, March 20, 2011, http://www.nytimes.com/2011/03/21/business/media/21times.html?pagewanted=all (accessed September 27, 2011); and J. W. Peters, "New York Times is Set to Begin Charging for Web Access; Chairman Concedes Plan is Risky but Says It's an 'Investment in Our Future,'" *International Herald Tribune*, March 18, 2011, 15.

60. Jeremy W. Peters, "Optimism for Digital Plan; but Times Co. Posts Loss," *The New York Times*, July 22, 2011, B3.

61. Cyert and March, *A Behavioral Theory of the Firm*, 120–222.

62. Lawrence G. Hrebiniak, "Top-Management Agreement and Organizational Performance," *Human Relations* 35 (1982), 1139–1158; and Richard P. Nielsen, "Toward a Method for Building Consensus During Strategic Planning," *Sloan Management Review*, Summer 1981, 29–40.

63. Based on Henry Mintzberg, Duru Raisinghani, and André Théorêt, "The Structure of 'Unstructured' Decision Processes," *Administrative Science Quarterly* 21 (1976), 246–275.

64. Lawrence T. Pinfield, "A Field Evaluation of Perspectives on Organizational Decision Making," *Administrative Science Quarterly* 31 (1986), 365–388.

65. Mintzberg et al., "The Structure of 'Unstructured' Decision Processes."

66. Neal E. Boudette, Christina Rogers, and Joann S. Lublin, "Mulally's Legacy: Setting Ford on a Stronger Course," *The Wall Street Journal*, April 21, 2014, http://online.wsj.com/news/articles/SB10001424052702304049904579515852823291232 (accessed May 29, 2014).

67. Mintzberg et al., "The Structure of 'Unstructured' Decision Processes," 270.

68. Michael Christensen and Thorbjörn Knudsen, "How Decisions Can Be Organized—and Why It Matters," *Journal of Organization Design* 2, no. 3 (2013), 41–50.

69. Michael D. Cohen, James G. March, and Johan P. Olsen, "A Garbage Can Model of Organizational Choice," *Administrative Science Quarterly* 17, March 1972, 1–25; Michael D. Cohen and James G. March, *Leadership and Ambiguity: The American College President* (New York: McGraw-Hill, 1974); and Alessandro Lomi and J. Richard Harrison, eds. *Research in the Sociology of Organizations, vol. 36: The Garbage Can Model of Organizational Choice: Looking Forward at Forty* (Bingley, UK: Emerald Books, 2012).

70. Michael Masuch and Perry LaPotin, "Beyond Garbage Cans: An AI Model of Organizational Choice," *Administrative Science Quarterly* 34 (1989), 38–67.

71. See John F. Padgett, "Book Review Essay: Recycling Garbage Can Theory," *Administrative Science Quarterly* 58, no. 3 (2013), 472–482, for an overview of garbage can theory and various empirical studies and computer simulations. This is a review of Lomi and Harrison, eds. *Research in the Sociology of Organizations, vol. 36: The Garbage Can Model.*

72. Shelly Banjo, "Inside Nike's Struggle to Balance Cost and Worker Safety in Bangladesh," *The Wall Street Journal*, April 21, 2014, http://online.wsj.com/news/articles/SB 10001424052702303873604579493502231397942 (accessed May 30, 2014); Max Nisen, "How Nike Solved Its Sweatshop Problem," *Business Insider*, May 9, 2013, http://www.businessinsider.com/how-nike-solved-its-sweatshop-problem-2013-5 (accessed May 30, 2014); and Miguel Bustillo, "Nike Tries to Avoid Bangladesh, Risky Cities," *The Wall Street Journal Online*, November 29, 2012, http://online.wsj.com/news/articles/SB100014241278873240208045781499591783958054 (accessed May 30, 2014).

73. Adapted from James D. Thompson, *Organizations in Action* (New York: McGraw-Hill, 1967), chap. 10; McMillan, "Qualitative Models of Organizational Decision Making," 25; and Clayton M. Christensen, Matt Marx, and Howard H. Stevenson, "The Tools of Cooperation and Change," *Harvard Business Review*, October 2006, 73–80.

74. Ben Worthen, "Cost Cutting Versus Innovation: Reconcilable Difference," *CIO*, October 1, 2004, 89–94.

75. Beth Dickey, "NASA's Next Step," *Government Executive*, April 15, 2004, 34–42; and Jena McGregor, "Gospels of Failure," *Fast Company*, February 2005, 61–67.

76. Mintzberg and Westley, "Decision Making: It's Not What You Think."

77. Paul C. Nutt, "Selecting Decision Rules for Crucial Choices: An Investigation of the Thompson Framework," *The Journal of Applied Behavioral Science* 38, no. 1 (March 2002), 99–131; and Paul C. Nutt, "Making Strategic Choices," *Journal of Management Studies* 39, no. 1 (January 2002), 67–95.

78. George T. Doran and Jack Gunn, "Decision Making in High-Tech Firms: Perspectives of Three Executives," *Business Horizons*, November–December 2002, 7–16.

79. L. J. Bourgeois III and Kathleen M. Eisenhardt, "Strategic Decision Processes in High Velocity Environments: Four Cases in the Microcomputer Industry," *Management Science* 34 (1988), 816–835.

80. Kathleen M. Eisenhardt, "Speed and Strategic Choice: How Managers Accelerate Decision Making," *California Management Review*, Spring 1990, 39–54.

81. David A. Garvin and Michael A. Roberto, "What You Don't Know About Making Decisions," *Harvard Business Review*, September 2001, 108–116.

82. Karl Weick, *The Social Psychology of Organizing*, 2nd ed. (Reading, MA: Addison-Wesley, 1979), 243.

83. Sue Shellenbarger, "Better Ideas Through Failure," *The Wall Street Journal*, September 27, 2011, D1; and "Culture of Creativity," Grey Advertising Website, http://grey.com/us/culture (accessed May 19, 2014).

84. Jena McGregor, "How Failure Breeds Success," *BusinessWeek*, July 10, 2006, 42–52.

85. For discussions of various cognitive biases, see Daniel Kahneman, Dan Lovallo, and Olivier Sibony, "Before You Make That Big Decision . . .," *Harvard Business Review*, June 2011, 50–60; John S. Hammond, Ralph L. Keeney, and Howard Raiffa, *Smart Choices: A Practical Guide to Making Better Decisions* (Boston: Harvard Business School Press, 1999); Max H. Bazerman and Dolly Chugh, "Decisions Without Blinders," *Harvard Business Review*, January 2006, 88–97; J. S. Hammond, R. L. Keeney, and H. Raiffa, "The Hidden Traps in Decision Making," *Harvard Business Review*, September–October 1998, 47–58; Oren Harari, "The Thomas Lawson Syndrome," *Management Review*, February 1994, 58–61; and Max H. Bazerman, *Judgment in Managerial Decision Making*, 5th ed. (New York: John Wiley & Sons, 2002).

86. Helga Drummond, "Too Little Too Late: A Case Study of Escalation in Decision Making," *Organization Studies* 15, no. 4 (1994), 591–607; Joel Brockner, "The Escalation of Commitment to a Failing Course of Action: Toward Theoretical Progress," *Academy of Management Review* 17 (1992), 39–61; Barry M. Staw and Jerry Ross, "Knowing When to Pull the Plug," *Harvard Business Review* 65, March–April 1987, 68–74; and Barry M. Staw, "The Escalation of Commitment to a Course of Action," *Academy of Management Review* 6 (1981), 577–587.

87. Norihiko Shirouzu, Phred Dvorak, Yuka Hayashi, and Andrew Morse, "Bid to 'Protect Assets' Slowed Reactor Fight," *The Wall Street Journal*, March 19, 2011, A1.

88. Alastair Dryburgh, "Everything You Know About Business Is Right; Is Failure More Powerful Than Success?" *Management Today*, February 1, 2013, 16.

89. Daniel Kahneman and Amos Tversky, "Prospect Theory: An Analysis of Decision Under Risk," *Econometrica* 47 (1979), 263–292.

90. Kahneman et al., "Before You Make That Big Decision . . . ."

91. Irving L. Janis, *Groupthink: Psychological Studies of Policy Decisions and Fiascoes*, 2nd ed. (Boston: Houghton Mifflin, 1982).

92. This section is based on Jeffrey Pfeffer and Robert I. Sutton, "Evidence-Based Management," *Harvard Business Review*, January 2006, 62–74; Rosemary Stewart, *Evidence-Based Management: A Practical Guide for Health Professionals* (Oxford: Radcliffe Publishing, 2002); and Joshua Klayman, Richard P. Larrick, and Chip Heath, "Organizational Repairs," *Across the Board*, February 2000, 26–31.

93. Adam Bryant, "When Your Company Is Adrift, Raise Your Sails" (interview with Dawn Zier), *The New York Times*, January 31, 2014, B2.

94. "How Companies Make Good Decisions: McKinsey Global Survey Results," *The McKinsey Quarterly*, January 2009, http://www.mckinseyquarterly.com/How_companies_make_good_decisions_McKinsey_Global_Survey_Results_2282 (accessed February 3, 2009).

95. Jan Francis-Smythe, Laurie Robinson, and Catharine Ross, "The Role of Evidence in General Managers' Decision-Making," *Journal of General Management* 38, no. 4 (Summer 2013), 3–21.

96. Michael A. Roberto, "Making Difficult Decisions in Turbulent Times," *Ivey Business Journal*, May–June 2003, 1–7; Kathleen M. Eisenhardt, "Strategy as Strategic Decision Making," *Sloan Management Review*, Spring 1999, 65–72; and Garvin and Roberto, "What You Don't Know About Making Decisions."

97. David M. Schweiger and William R. Sandberg, "The Utilization of Individual Capabilities in Group Approaches to Strategic Decision Making," *Strategic Management Journal* 10 (1989), 31–43; and "The Devil's Advocate," *Small Business Report*, December 1987, 38–41.

98. Anna Mulrine, "To Battle Groupthink, the Army Trains a Skeptics Corps," *U.S. News & World Report*, May 26–June 2, 2008, 30–32.

99. "Tools for Managing in a Complex Context," sidebar in David J. Snowden and Mary E. Boone, "A Leader's Framework for Decision Making," *Harvard Business Review*, November 2007, 69–76.

100. Questions 1 and 3–6 are from research studies reviewed in Scott Plous, *The Psychology of Judgment and Decision Making* (Philadelphia: Temple University Press, 1993); question 2 is based on an item in the *Creativity in Action Newsletter*, as reported in Arthur B. VanGundy, *Idea Power: Techniques & Resources to Unleash the Creativity in Your Organization* (New York: AMACOM, 1992).

101. This case was prepared by David Hornestay and appeared in *Government Executive*, 30, no. 8 (August 1998), 45–46, as part of a series of case studies examining workplace dilemmas confronting Federal managers. Reprinted by permission of *Government Executive*.

13 | Conflict, Power, and Politics

Learning Objectives

After reading this chapter you should be able to:

1. Describe the sources of intergroup conflict in organizations.
2. Explain the rational versus political models of conflict.
3. Describe power versus authority and their sources in organizations.
4. Explain the concept of empowerment.
5. Understand the sources of horizontal power in organizations.
6. Define politics and understand when political activity is necessary.
7. Identify tactics for increasing and for using power.

Interdepartmental Conflict in Organizations
Sources of Conflict · Rational Versus Political Model · Tactics for Enhancing Collaboration

Power and Organizations
Individual Versus Organizational Power · Power Versus Authority · Vertical Sources of Power · The Power of Empowerment · Horizontal Sources of Power

Political Processes in Organizations
Definition · When to Use Political Activity

Using Soft Power and Politics
Tactics for Increasing Power · Political Tactics for Using Power

Design Essentials

In the summer of 2013, executives from Omnicom Group Inc. and Publicis Groupe SA announced with much fanfare in Paris that the two companies were merging to create the largest advertising agency in the world. As the summer of 2014 approached, however, the deal had not been completed and clashes over position and power were largely to blame. For one thing, the two sides couldn't agree on which company would legally be the acquirer, which held up the filing of necessary paperwork. Beyond that, each company wanted its senior executives to fill top positions in the new company. The deal was talked up as a "merger of equals," and John Wren of Omnicom and Maurice Lévy of Publicis agreed to serve as co-CEOs for the first 30 months. But both men have strong personalities, which clashed from the start. Communicating about the details of the merger grew increasingly complicated. Martin Sorrell, CEO of one of the major rivals of the companies, said, "You have one talking Chinese and the other talking Japanese" to illustrate the conflicting messages the Omnicom and Publicis leaders were sending out about the status of the proposed merger. The battle for control went on for nearly a year before Wren and Lévy issued a joint statement in May 2014 saying that the deal was off. "It seems incredulous that this merger fell apart because of disagreements over roles and responsibilities," said Brian Wieser, an analyst at Pivotal Research Group.[1]

It wasn't just roles and responsibilities, of course. What was really at stake was control of the company, and each side wanted to have the most power. It isn't the first organizational project to be derailed because of power clashes between leaders. Managers at Research in Motion (now called BlackBerry Enterprise Mobility) argued for years about whether the company should retain its corporate and professional focus that once made the BlackBerry smartphone preferred by corporations, government agencies, and the military or begin catering to the needs and interests of ordinary consumers with machines that could easily play games and access movies and music.[2] The power struggle made it hard for the company to reinvent itself for a new era, and BlackBerry is no longer in the running for being the top smartphone.

Conflict such as that at BlackBerry and over the Omnicom Publicis merger is a natural outcome of the close interaction of people who may have diverse opinions and values, pursue different objectives, and have differential access to information and resources within the organization. Individuals and groups use power and political activity to handle their differences and manage the inevitable conflicts that arise.[3] Too much conflict can be harmful to an organization. However, conflict can also be a positive force because it challenges the status quo, encourages new ideas and approaches, and leads to needed change.[4] Some degree of conflict occurs in all human relationships—between friends, romantic partners, and teammates, as well as between parents and children, teachers and students, and bosses and employees. Conflict is not necessarily a negative force; it results from the normal interaction of varying human interests. Within organizations, individuals and groups frequently have different interests and goals they wish to achieve through the organization. Managers can effectively use power and politics to manage conflict, get the most out of employees, enhance job satisfaction and team identification, achieve important goals, and realize high organizational performance.

Purpose of This Chapter

In this chapter we discuss the nature of conflict and the use of power and political tactics to manage and reduce conflict among individuals and groups. The notions of conflict, power, and politics have appeared in previous chapters. In Chapter 3 we talked about horizontal linkages such as task forces and teams that encourage collaboration among functional departments. Chapter 4 introduced the concept of differentiation, which means that different departments pursue different goals and may have different attitudes and values. Chapter 5 touched on conflict and power relationships among organizations. Chapter 10 discussed the emergence of subcultures, and in Chapter 12 coalition building was proposed as one way to resolve disagreements among managers and departments.

The first sections of this chapter explore the nature of intergroup conflict, characteristics of organizations that contribute to conflict, the use of a political versus a rational model of organization to manage conflicting interests, and some tactics for reducing conflict and enhancing collaboration. Subsequent sections examine individual and organizational power, the vertical and horizontal sources of power for managers and other employees, and how power is used to attain organizational goals. We also look at the trend toward empowerment, sharing power with lower-level employees. The latter part of the chapter turns to politics, which is the application of power and influence to achieve desired outcomes. We discuss ways managers increase their power and various political tactics for using power to influence others and accomplish desired goals.

Interdepartmental Conflict in Organizations

Conflict among departments and groups in organizations, called *intergroup conflict*, requires three ingredients: group identification, observable group differences, and frustration. First, employees have to perceive themselves as part of an identifiable group or department.[5] Second, there has to be an observable group difference of some form. Groups may be located on different floors of the building, members may have different social or educational backgrounds, or members may work in different departments. The ability to identify oneself as a part of one group and to observe differences in comparison with other groups is necessary for conflict.[6]

The third ingredient is frustration. Frustration means that if one group achieves its goal, the other will not; it will be blocked. Frustration need not be severe and only needs to be anticipated to set off intergroup conflict. Intergroup conflict will appear when one group tries to advance its position in relation to other groups. **Intergroup conflict** can be defined as the behavior that occurs among organizational groups when participants identify with one group and perceive that other groups may block their group's goal achievement or expectations.[7] Conflict means that groups clash directly, that they are in fundamental opposition. Conflict is similar to competition but more severe. **Competition** is rivalry among groups in the pursuit of a common prize, whereas conflict presumes direct interference with goal achievement.

Intergroup conflict within organizations can occur horizontally across departments or vertically between different levels of the organization.[8] The production department of a manufacturing company may have a dispute with quality control because new quality procedures reduce production efficiency. R&D managers often conflict with finance managers because the finance managers' pressure to control costs reduces the amount of funding for new R&D projects. Teammates may argue about the best way to accomplish tasks and achieve goals.

Vertical conflict may occur when employees clash with bosses about new work methods, reward systems, or job assignments. Another typical area of conflict is between groups such as unions and management or franchise owners and headquarters. For example, franchise owners for McDonald's, Taco Bell, Burger King, and KFC have clashed with headquarters because of the increase of company-owned stores in neighborhoods that compete directly with franchisees.[9]

Conflict can also occur between different divisions or business units within an organization, such as between the trading and investment banking division and the retail banking division at Morgan Stanley. Traders and investment banking employees have typically looked down on the retail business, seeing themselves as the "elite" of Wall Street. Today, though, banks are under pressure from shareholders to increase profits by finding ways for retail and investment banking to cooperate. Morgan Stanley has recently made a number of changes intended to increase collaboration and communication between the two divisions. However, as one analyst said, "Morgan Stanley has a horrible history of getting these two groups to work together."[10] In global organizations, conflicts between regional managers and business division managers, among different divisions, or between divisions and headquarters are common because of the complexities of international business, as described in Chapter 6. Similar problems occur between distinct organizations. As we briefly discussed in Chapter 5, with so many companies involved in interorganizational collaboration, conflicts and shifting power relationships are inevitable.

Sources of Conflict

Some specific organizational characteristics can generate conflict. These **sources of intergroup conflict** are goal incompatibility, differentiation, task interdependence, and limited resources. These characteristics of organizational relationships are determined by the organizational structure and the contingency factors of environment, size, technology, and strategy and goals, which have been discussed in previous chapters. These characteristics, in turn, help shape the extent to which a rational model of behavior versus a political model of behavior is used to accomplish objectives.

Goal Incompatibility. The goals of each department reflect the specific objectives members are trying to achieve. The achievement of one department's goals often interferes with another department's goals, leading to conflict. University police, for example, have a goal of providing a safe and secure campus. They can achieve their goal by locking all buildings on evenings and weekends and not distributing keys. Without easy access to buildings, however, progress toward the science department's research goals will proceed slowly. On the other hand, if scientists come and go at all hours and security is ignored, police goals for security will not be met. Goal incompatibility throws the departments into conflict with each other.

1 **A certain amount of conflict is good for an organization.**

> **ANSWER:** *Agree.* Conflict is inevitable in all human relationships, including those in organizations, and is often a good thing. Some conflict can be healthy because it contributes to diverse thinking and leads to change. If there is no conflict whatsoever, there is likely no growth and development either.

In business organizations, the IT department is frequently in conflict with managers of business departments because of goal incompatibility. Business managers often want new devices or new systems and don't understand why the CIO turns down the requests. The CIO, however, is responsible for making sure any changes don't jeopardize the safety and security of the company's overall IT systems and processes.[11] The potential for conflict is perhaps greater between marketing and manufacturing than between other departments because the goals of these two departments are frequently at odds. Exhibit 13.1 shows examples of goal conflict between typical marketing and manufacturing departments. Marketing strives to increase the breadth of the product line to meet customer tastes for variety. A broad

EXHIBIT 13.1
Marketing–Manufacturing Areas of Potential Goal Conflict

	MARKETING Versus MANUFACTURING	
Goal Conflict	**Operative Goal Is Customer Satisfaction**	**Operative Goal Is Production Efficiency**
Conflict Area	**Typical Comment**	**Typical Comment**
1. Breadth of product line	"Our customers demand variety."	"The product line is too broad—all we get are short, uneconomical runs."
2. New product introduction	"New products are our lifeblood."	"Unnecessary design changes are prohibitively expensive."
3. Product scheduling	"We need faster response. Our customer lead times are too long."	"We need realistic commitments that don't change like wind direction."
4. Physical distribution	"Why don't we ever have the right merchandise in inventory?"	"We can't afford to keep huge inventories."
5. Quality	"Why can't we have reasonable quality at lower cost?"	"Why must we always offer options that are too expensive and offer little customer utility?"

Sources: Based on Benson S. Shapiro, "Can Marketing and Manufacturing Coexist?" *Harvard Business Review* 55, September–October 1977, 104–114; and Victoria L. Crittenden, Lorraine R. Gardiner, and Antonie Stam, "Reducing Conflict Between Marketing and Manufacturing," *Industrial Marketing Management* 22 (1993), 299–309.

product line means short production runs, so manufacturing has to bear higher costs.[12] Typical areas of goal conflict are quality, cost control, and new products or services. Goal incompatibility is probably the greatest cause of intergroup conflict in organizations.[13]

Differentiation. *Differentiation* was defined in Chapter 4 as "the differences in cognitive and emotional orientations among managers in different functional departments." Functional specialization requires people with specific education, skills, attitudes, and time horizons. For example, people may join a sales department because they have ability and aptitude consistent with sales work. After becoming members of the sales department, they are influenced by departmental norms and values.

Departments or divisions within an organization often differ in values, attitudes, and standards of behavior, and these subcultural differences lead to conflicts.[14] Consider an encounter between a sales manager and a research and development (R&D) scientist about a new product:

> *The sales manager may be outgoing and concerned with maintaining a warm, friendly relationship with the scientist. He may be put off because the scientist seems withdrawn and disinclined to talk about anything other than the problems in which he is interested. He may also be annoyed that the scientist seems to have such freedom in choosing what he will work on. Furthermore, the scientist is probably often late for appointments, which, from the salesman's point of view, is no way to run a business. Our scientist, for his part, may feel uncomfortable because the salesman seems to be pressing for immediate answers to technical questions that will take a long time to investigate. All the discomforts are concrete manifestations of the relatively wide differences between these two men in respect to their working and thinking styles.*[15]

Task Interdependence. Task interdependence refers to the dependence of one unit on another for materials, resources, or information. As described in Chapter 7, *pooled interdependence* means there is little interaction; *sequential interdependence* means the output of one department goes to the next department; and *reciprocal interdependence* means that departments mutually exchange materials and information.[16]

Generally, as interdependence increases, the potential for conflict increases.[17] In the case of pooled interdependence, units have little need to interact. Conflict is at a minimum. Sequential and reciprocal interdependence require employees to spend time coordinating and sharing information. Employees must communicate frequently, and differences in goals or attitudes will surface. Conflict is especially likely to occur when agreement is not reached about the coordination of services to each other. Greater interdependence means departments often exert pressure for a fast response because departmental work has to wait on other departments.[18]

Limited Resources. Another major source of conflict involves competition between groups for what members perceive as limited resources.[19] Organizations have limited money, physical facilities, staff resources, and human resources to share among departments. In their desire to achieve goals, groups want to increase their resources. This throws them into conflict. Managers may develop strategies, such as inflating budget requirements or working behind the scenes, to obtain a desired level of resources.

BRIEFCASE

As an organization manager, keep these guidelines in mind:

Recognize that some interdepartmental conflict is natural and can benefit the organization. Associate the organizational design characteristics of goal incompatibility, differentiation, task interdependence, and resource scarcity with greater conflict among groups. Expect to devote more time and energy to resolving conflict in these situations.

Resources also symbolize power and influence within an organization. The ability to obtain resources enhances prestige. Departments typically believe they have a legitimate claim on additional resources. However, exercising that claim results in conflict. Conflict over limited resources also occurs frequently among government, nonprofit, and membership organizations. Consider the nation's labor unions, which are fighting each other these days for members and dues as much or more than they are fighting corporate management. Branches of the U.S. military are in conflict as they battle to keep their share of a shrinking defense budget.

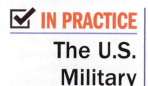

IN PRACTICE

The U.S. Military

Former U.S. defense secretary Chuck Hagel recommended cutting the U.S. Army to its smallest size since before World War II. This and other recommended force reductions triggered the most intense conflict among branches of the U.S. military in two decades.

The formula for military spending has roughly been 30 percent for the Air Force, between 30 and 35 percent for the Navy and Marine Corps, and about 25 percent for the Army. When the Pentagon revises its assignment of missions to the various services, their share of military spending can go either up or down. Officials with the Marines are proposing to focus on quick-response forces worldwide, which they believe will best match the kind of military operations the United States will need in coming years. The trouble is that the Army is also building small teams of soldiers who can move quickly to different parts of the world. This means retooling procedures, such as stationing Army helicopters aboard Navy warships to support the small teams of ground troops. That puts the Army in direct conflict with the Marines, which currently base helicopters on Navy ships. The army chief of staff said his service needs to be able to deploy quickly in the opening days of a military conflict. "The Marines know that. They're not built for that," he said. The Marine commandant fired back: "Just the same way America doesn't need a second land army, America doesn't need a second Marine Corps."[20]

Rational Versus Political Model

The sources of intergroup conflict are listed in Exhibit 13.2. The degree of goal incompatibility, differentiation, interdependence, and competition for limited resources determines whether a rational or political model of behavior is used within the organization to accomplish goals.

When goals are in alignment, there is little differentiation, departments are characterized by pooled interdependence, and resources seem abundant, managers can use a **rational model** of organization, as outlined in Exhibit 13.2. As with the rational approach to decision making described in Chapter 12, the rational model of organization is an ideal that is not fully achievable in the real world, though managers strive to use rational processes whenever possible. In the rational organization, behavior is not random or accidental. Goals are clear and choices are made in a logical way. When a decision is needed, the goal is defined, alternatives are identified, and the choice with the highest probability of success is selected. The rational model is also characterized by centralized power and control, extensive information systems, and an efficiency orientation.[21]

The opposite view of organizational processes is the **political model**, also described in Exhibit 13.2. When differences are great, organization groups have separate interests, goals, and values. Disagreement and conflict are normal, so power and influence are needed to reach decisions. Groups will engage in the push

EXHIBIT 13.2
Sources of Conflict and Use of Rational Versus Political Model

Sources of Potential Intergroup Conflict	When Conflict Is Low, Rational Model Describes Organization		When Conflict Is High, Political Model Describes Organization
• Goal incompatibility	Consistent across participants	Goals	Inconsistent, pluralistic within the organization
• Differentiation	Centralized	Power and control	Decentralized, shifting coalitions and interest groups
• Task interdependence	Orderly, logical, rational	Decision process	Disorderly, result of bargaining and interplay among interests
• Limited resources	Norm of efficiency	Rules and norms	Free play of market forces; conflict is legitimate and expected
	Extensive, systematic, accurate	Information	Ambiguous; information used and withheld strategically

© Cengage Learning®

and pull of debate to decide goals and reach decisions. Information is ambiguous and incomplete. The political model describes the way organizations operate much of the time. Although managers strive to use a rational approach, the political model prevails because each department has different interests it wants met and different goals it wants to achieve. Purely rational procedures do not work for many circumstances.

Typically, both rational and political processes are used in organizations. Neither the rational model nor the political model characterizes things fully, but each will be used some of the time. Managers may strive to adopt rational procedures but will find that politics is needed to accomplish objectives. When managers fail to effectively apply the political model, conflict can escalate and prevent the organization from achieving important outcomes.

Consider what happened at Premio Foods, where CEO Marc Cinque and Charlean Gmunder, the vice president of operations, tried to use a rational model but discovered that a political model was needed. Gmunder suggested implementing a new computerized system that would overhaul the company's outdated method of forecasting and ordering and require changes in every department. She presented facts and statistics to Cinque showing that the system would increase annual cash flow by $500,000 and save up to $150,000 a year by cutting wasted material. But even though "the numbers made it clear," Cinque hesitated primarily because many of his senior managers expressed strong objections. After Cinque finally decided to go with the system, the conflict intensified. Gmunder couldn't get the information she needed from some managers, and some would show up late to meetings or skip them altogether. Gmunder had failed to build a coalition to support the new system. To salvage the project, Cinque formed a team that included senior managers from various departments to discuss their concerns and involve them in determining how the new system should work.[22]

BRIEFCASE

As an organization manager, keep these guidelines in mind:

Use a political model of organization when differences among groups are great, goals are ill-defined, or there is competition for limited resources. Use the rational model when alternatives are clear, goals are defined, and managers can estimate the outcomes accurately. In these circumstances, coalition building, cooptation, or other political tactics are not needed and will not lead to better decisions.

EXHIBIT 13.3
Top 10 Problems from
Too Much Conflict

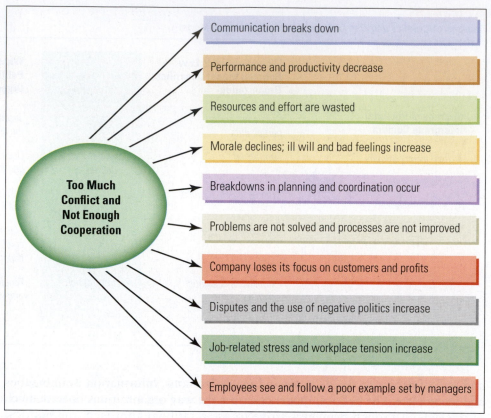

Source: Based on survey results reported in Clinton O. Longenecker and Mitchell Neubert, "Barriers and Gateways to Management Cooperation and Teamwork," *Business Horizons*, November–December 2000, 37–44.

Most organizations have at least moderate conflict among departments or other organizational groups. When conflict becomes too strong and managers do not work together, it creates many problems for organizations. Exhibit 13.3 lists the top 10 problems caused by a lack of cooperation that were identified by one survey of managers.[23]

Tactics for Enhancing Collaboration

Good managers strive to minimize conflict and prevent it from hurting organizational performance and goal attainment. Effective conflict management can have a direct, positive effect on team and organization performance.[24] Thus, managers consciously apply a variety of techniques to overcome conflict by stimulating cooperation and collaboration among departments to support the attainment of organizational goals. **Tactics for enhancing collaboration** include the following:

1. *Create integration devices.* As described in Chapter 3, teams, task forces, and project managers who span the boundaries between departments can be used as integration devices. Bringing together representatives from conflicting departments in joint problem-solving teams is an effective way to enhance collaboration because representatives learn to understand each other's point of view.[25] Sometimes a full-time integrator is assigned to achieve cooperation and collaboration by meeting with members of the respective departments

and exchanging information. The integrator has to understand each group's problems and must be able to move both groups toward a solution that is mutually acceptable.[26]

Teams and task forces reduce conflict and enhance cooperation because they integrate people from different departments. Integration devices can also be used to enhance cooperation between labor and management. **Labor-management teams**, which are designed to increase worker participation and provide a cooperative model for solving union-management problems, are increasingly being used at companies such as Goodyear, Ford Motor Company, and Alcoa. At the International Specialty Products Corporation plant in Calvert City, Kentucky, a union-management partnership enabled the company to improve quality, reduce costs, and enhance profitability. The plant leadership team is made up of two managers and two union members, and each of the plant's seven operating areas is jointly led by a management representative and a union representative.[27] Although unions continue to battle over traditional issues such as wages, these integration devices are creating a level of cooperation that many managers would not have believed possible just a few years ago. Bob King, president of the United Auto Workers, said the UAW learned the hard way that cooperation was important for helping keep the auto makers profitable. The "old 'Us vs. Them' mentality" is a relic of the past, King says.[28]

2. *Use confrontation and negotiation.* **Confrontation** occurs when parties in conflict directly engage one another and try to work out their differences. **Negotiation** is the bargaining process that often occurs during confrontation and that enables the parties to systematically reach a solution. These techniques bring appointed representatives from the departments together to work out a serious dispute. Confrontation and negotiation involve some risk. There is no guarantee that discussions will focus on a conflict or that emotions will not get out of hand. However, if members are able to resolve the conflict on the basis of face-to-face discussions, they will find new respect for each other, and future collaboration becomes easier. The beginnings of relatively permanent attitude change are possible through direct negotiation.

Confrontation and negotiation are successful when managers engage in a *win-win strategy.* Win-win means both sides adopt a positive attitude and strive to resolve the conflict in a way that will benefit each other.[29] If the negotiations deteriorate into a strictly win-lose strategy (each group wants to defeat the other), the confrontation will be ineffective. The differences between win-win and win-lose strategies of negotiation are shown in Exhibit 13.4. With a win-win strategy—which includes defining the problem as mutual, communicating openly, and avoiding threats—understanding can be changed while the dispute is resolved.

One type of negotiation, used to resolve a disagreement between workers and management, is referred to as **collective bargaining**. The bargaining process is usually accomplished through a union and results in an agreement that specifies each party's responsibilities for the next two to three years.

3. *Schedule intergroup consultation.* When conflict is intense and enduring, and department members are suspicious and uncooperative, top managers may intervene as third parties to help resolve the conflict or bring in third-party consultants from outside the organization.[30] This process, sometimes called *workplace mediation,* is a strong intervention to reduce conflict because it involves bringing the disputing parties together and allowing each side to present its version of the situation. The technique has been developed by such psychologists as Robert Blake, Jane Mouton, and Richard Walton.[31]

EXHIBIT 13.4
Negotiating Strategies

Win-Lose Strategy	Win-Win Strategy
1. Define the problem as a win-lose situation.	1. Define the conflict as a mutual problem.
2. Pursue own group's outcomes.	2. Pursue joint outcomes.
3. Force the other group into submission.	3. Find creative agreements that satisfy both groups.
4. Be deceitful, inaccurate, and misleading in communicating the group's needs, goals, and proposals.	4. Be open, honest, and accurate in communicating the group's needs, goals, and proposals.
5. Use threats (to force submission).	5. Avoid threats (to reduce the other's defensiveness).
6. Communicate strong commitment (rigidity) regarding one's position.	6. Communicate flexibility of position.

Source: Adapted from David W. Johnson and Frank P. Johnson, *Joining Together: Group Theory and Group Skills* (Englewood Cliffs, NJ: Prentice-Hall, 1975), 182–183.

Department members attend a workshop, which may last for several days, away from day-to-day work problems. This approach is similar to the organization development (OD) approach described in Chapter 11. The conflicting groups are separated, and each group is invited to discuss and make a list of its perceptions of itself and the other group. Group representatives publicly share these perceptions, and together the groups discuss the results. Intergroup consultation can be quite demanding for everyone involved, but if handled correctly, these sessions can help department employees understand each other much better and lead to improved attitudes and better working relationships for years to come.

4. *Practice member rotation.* Rotation means that individuals from one department can be asked to work in another department on a temporary or permanent basis. The advantage is that individuals become submerged in the values, attitudes, problems, and goals of the other department. In addition, individuals can explain the problems and goals of their original departments to their new colleagues. This enables a frank, accurate exchange of views and information. Rotation works slowly to reduce conflict but is very effective for changing the underlying attitudes and perceptions that promote conflict.[32] Some years ago, Ben Horowitz, co-founder of venture capital firm Andreessen Horowitz, used what he calls the *Freaky Friday* Management Technique to solve a difficult conflict between the Sales Engineering and Customer Support departments.

 **IN PRACTICE**

The *Freaky Friday* Management Technique

When the Customer Support and Sales Engineering teams went to war with one another, Ben Horowitz didn't know what to do. Both teams were made up of first-rate people and were led by excellent managers. The sales engineers complained that customer support refused to fix problems, did not respond with urgency, and generally failed to provide the kind of service that led to customer satisfaction. On the other hand, customer support said the sales engineers didn't listen to suggested fixes for problems and made the support team's job harder by assigning every problem top priority. The teams just could not get along. But for the company to function, they had to work together smoothly and constantly.

Horowitz happened to watch the movie *Freaky Friday* during this time period and came up with an idea. In the movie, a mother and daughter become completely frustrated with one another's lack of understanding and appreciation and wish that they could switch places. Because this is a movie, they miraculously do just that! Throughout the rest of the movie, "by being inside each other's bodies, both characters develop an understanding of the challenges the other faces," Horowitz writes. He wonders if the same thing could work with his sales engineering and customer support managers. The next day, he tells the managers they will be switching places. Like the characters in *Freaky Friday*, they will keep their own minds but get new bodies.

The reaction he got was equivalent to Jamie Lee Curtis and Lindsay Lohan screaming in horror in the film. But after a week of experiencing the other's challenges, the managers discovered the core issues that were leading to conflict between the two departments. Moreover, they quickly implemented some simple solutions that resolved disputes and got people working together harmoniously. "From that day to the day we sold the company," Horowitz says, those two teams "worked better together than any other major groups in the company—all thanks to *Freaky Friday*, perhaps the most insightful management training film ever made."[33]

5. *Create shared mission and superordinate goals.* Another strategy is for top management to create a shared mission and establish superordinate goals that require cooperation among departments.[34] As discussed in Chapter 10, organizations with strong, constructive cultures, where employees share a larger vision for their company, are more likely to have a united, cooperative workforce. Studies have shown that when employees from different departments see that their goals are linked, they will openly share resources and information.[35] To be effective, superordinate goals must be substantial, and employees must be granted the time and incentives to work cooperatively in pursuit of the superordinate goals rather than departmental subgoals.

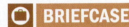

BRIEFCASE

As an organization manager, keep these guidelines in mind:

If conflict becomes too strong, use tactics for enhancing collaboration, including integration devices, confrontation, intergroup consultation, member rotation, and superordinate goals. Select the technique that fits the organization and the conflict.

Power and Organizations

Power is an intangible force in organizations. It cannot be seen, but its effect can be felt. *Power* is often defined as the potential ability of one person (or department) to influence other people (or departments) to carry out orders[36] or to do something they would not otherwise have done.[37] Other definitions stress that power is the ability to achieve goals or outcomes that power holders desire.[38] The achievement of desired outcomes is the basis of the definition used here: **power** is the ability of one person or department in an organization to influence other people to bring about desired outcomes. It is the potential to influence others within the organization with the goal of attaining desired outcomes for power holders. Powerful managers, for instance, are often able to get bigger budgets for their departments, more favorable production schedules, and more control over the organization's agenda.[39]

Power exists only in a relationship between two or more people, and it can be exercised in either vertical or horizontal directions. The source of power often derives from an exchange relationship in which one person, department, or organization provides scarce or valued resources to other people, departments, or organizations. When one is dependent on another, a power relationship emerges in which the side with the resources has greater power.[40] Power holders can achieve compliance with their requests.

As an illustration of dependence increasing one's power, consider AMC's hit show "Mad Men," which is in its final season. The show's creator, Matthew Weiner, had tremendous power in the relationship with AMC and could virtually dictate the terms of his contract. Until recently, AMC had little original programming and was dependent on "Mad Men" for the advertising revenues and prestige it brought to the cable network. In his last round of negotiations, Weiner walked away with a three-year deal worth $30 million, one of the biggest of its kind in cable television, and the network also dropped some of its demands regarding cast budget cuts and advertising slots. Weiner was considered the heart and soul of "Mad Men," so AMC was dependent upon him to keep the hit show going.[41] The final season was split into two seasons, one of the few decisions Weiner didn't dictate. "This was an edict that was given to me that proved to be successful for AMC. I have fought many battles with them in the past, and I understood where they were coming from (with this idea) and I didn't have any say in it," Weiner said.[42]

Individual Versus Organizational Power

In popular literature, power is often described as a personal characteristic, and a frequent topic is how one person can influence or dominate another person.[43] You probably recall from an earlier management or organizational behavior course that managers have five sources of personal power.[44] *Legitimate power* is the authority granted by the organization to the formal management position a manager holds. *Reward power* stems from the ability to bestow rewards—a promotion, raise, or pat on the back—to other people. The authority to punish or recommend punishment is called *coercive power. Expert power* derives from a person's greater skill or knowledge about the tasks being performed. The last, *referent power*, is derived from personal characteristics: people admire the manager and want to be like or identify with the manager out of respect and admiration. Each of these sources may be used by individuals within organizations.

Power in organizations, however, is often the result of structural characteristics.[45] Organizations are large, complex systems that may contain hundreds, even thousands, of people. These systems have a formal hierarchy in which some tasks are more important regardless of who performs them. In addition, some positions have access to more information and greater resources, or their contribution to the organization is more critical. Executive assistants to CEOs, for example, have tremendous power because they have direct access to the top executive, have information other people don't have, and can determine who gets to talk to the boss and who doesn't. John Mannuck, CEO of Techmer PM LLC, says he depends on his assistant Nicole Brannick to tell him who he needs to speak with urgently and who can wait. Anikka Fragodt, who was Mark Zuckerberg's assistant for seven years, starting with him when the company had only about 100 employees, was one of only four people who knew about Zuckerberg's secret wedding to Priscilla Chan in advance of the event.[46]

Power Versus Authority

Anyone in an organization can exercise power to achieve desired outcomes. For example, when the Discovery Channel wanted to extend its brand beyond cable television, Tom Hicks began pushing for a focus on the Internet. Even though Discovery's CEO favored exploring interactive television instead, Hicks organized a grassroots campaign that eventually persuaded the CEO to focus on Internet publishing, indicating that Hicks had power within the organization. Eventually, Hicks was put in charge of running Discovery Channel Online.[47]

The concept of formal authority is related to power but is narrower in scope. **Authority** is also a force for achieving desired outcomes, but only as prescribed by the formal hierarchy and reporting relationships. Three properties identify authority:

1. *Authority is vested in organizational positions.* People have authority because of the positions they hold, not because of personal characteristics or resources.
2. *Authority is accepted by subordinates.* Subordinates comply because they believe position holders have a legitimate right to exercise authority.[48] In most North American organizations, employees accept that supervisors can legitimately tell them what time to arrive at work, the tasks to perform while they're there, and what time they can go home.
3. *Authority flows down the vertical hierarchy.*[49] Authority exists along the formal chain of command, and positions at the top of the hierarchy are vested with more formal authority than are positions at the bottom.

Formal authority is exercised downward along the hierarchy. Organizational power, on the other hand, can be exercised upward, downward, and horizontally in organizations. In addition, managers can have formal authority but little real power. When Kevin Sharer looks back on his three years as executive vice president of marketing at telecommunications company MCI, he can now see why those years were so frustrating. Sharer, who later served as CEO and chairman of Amgen Inc., had great ideas for changing things, but he failed to build credibility with his new colleagues, and his ideas and suggestions went unheeded despite his impressive job title.[50] In the following sections we examine how employees throughout the organization can tap into both vertical and horizontal sources of power.

Vertical Sources of Power

All employees along the vertical hierarchy have access to some sources of power. Although a large amount of power is typically allocated to top managers by the organization structure, people throughout the organization often obtain power disproportionate to their formal positions and can exert influence in an upward direction, as Tom Hicks did at the Discovery Channel. There are four major sources of vertical power: formal position, resources, control of information, and network centrality.[51]

Formal Position. Certain rights, responsibilities, and prerogatives accrue to top positions. People throughout the organization accept the legitimate right of top managers to set goals, make decisions, and direct activities. This is *legitimate power*, as defined earlier. Senior managers often use symbols and language to perpetuate their legitimate power. For example, the new administrator at a large hospital in the San Francisco area symbolized his legitimate position power by issuing a newsletter with his photo on the cover and airing a 24-hour-a-day video to personally welcome patients.[52]

The amount of power provided to middle managers and lower-level participants can be built into the organization's structural design. The allocation of power to middle managers and staff is important because power enables people to be productive. When job tasks are nonroutine and when employees participate in self-directed teams and problem-solving task forces, this encourages them to be flexible and creative and to use their own discretion. Allowing people to make their own decisions increases their power.

BRIEFCASE

As an organization manager, keep this guideline in mind:

Understand and use the vertical sources of power in organizations, including formal position, resources, control of information, and network centrality.

Power is also increased when a position encourages contact with high-level people. Access to powerful people and the development of a relationship with them provide a strong base of influence.[53] For example, D'Andra Galarza, executive assistant for a president at NBCUniversal, says people treat her with kid gloves and are always trying to wheedle information out of her. "People know I know everything," she says. "If I was working for a VP, it wouldn't be that way."[54]

The logic of designing positions for more power assumes that an organization does not have a limited amount of power to be allocated among high-level and low-level employees. The total amount of power in an organization can be increased by designing tasks and interactions along the hierarchy so everyone can exert more influence. If the distribution of power is skewed too heavily toward the top, research suggests that the organization will be less effective.[55]

Resources. Organizations allocate huge amounts of resources. Buildings are constructed, salaries are paid, and equipment and supplies are purchased. Each year, new resources are allocated in the form of budgets. These resources are allocated downward from top managers. Top managers often own stock, which gives them property rights over resource allocation. In many of today's organizations, however, employees throughout the organization also share in ownership, which increases their power.

In most cases, top managers control the resources and, hence, can determine their distribution. Resources can be used as rewards and punishments, which are additional sources of power. Resource allocation creates a dependency relationship. Lower-level participants depend on top managers for the financial and physical resources needed to perform their tasks. Top management can exchange resources in the form of salaries and bonuses, personnel, promotions, and physical facilities for compliance with the outcomes they desire.

Control of Information. The control of information can be a significant source of power. Managers recognize that information is a primary business resource and that by controlling what information is collected, how it is interpreted, and how it is shared, they can influence how decisions are made.[56] In many of today's companies, information is openly and broadly shared, which increases the power of people throughout the organization.

However, top managers generally have access to more information than do other employees. This information can be released as needed to shape the decisions of other people. In one healthcare organization, Clark Ltd., the senior information technology manager controlled information given to the board of directors and thereby influenced the board's decision to eliminate the existing computer systems of the business units and move all the software onto one new IT platform. She knew this was the only way to bring costs into line, but it would cause short-term problems for the business unit managers who were likely to resist.[57] The board of directors had formal authority to decide whether to adopt the plan for unifying IT systems and from which company the new system would be purchased. The management services group was asked to recommend which of six companies should receive the order. Kate Kenny was in charge of the management services group, and Kenny disagreed with other managers about which system to purchase. As shown in Exhibit 13.5, other managers had to go through Kenny to have their viewpoints heard by the board. Kenny shaped the board's thinking toward selecting the system she preferred by controlling information given to them.

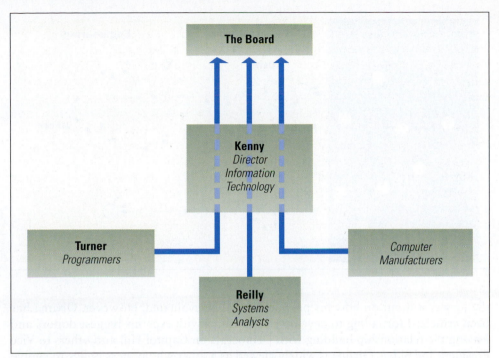

EXHIBIT 13.5
Information Flow for
IT System Decision at
Clark Ltd.

Source: Andrew M. Pettigrew, *The Politics of Organizational Decision-Making* (London: Tavistock, 1973), 235. Reprinted by permission of the author.

Middle managers and lower-level employees may also have access to information that can increase their power. An assistant to a senior executive can often control information that other people want and will thus be able to influence those people. Top executives depend on people throughout the organization for information about problems or opportunities. Middle managers or lower-level employees may manipulate the information they provide to top managers in order to influence decision outcomes.

Network Centrality. Network centrality means being centrally located in the organization and having access to information and people that are critical to the company's success. Managers as well as lower-level employees are more effective and more influential when they put themselves at the center of a communication network, building connections with people throughout the company. For example, in Exhibit 13.6, Radha has a well-developed communication network, sharing information and assistance with many people across the marketing, manufacturing, and engineering departments. Contrast Radha's contacts with those of Jasmine or Kirill. Who do you think is likely to have greater access to resources and more influence in the organization?

Think about the importance of networks of relationships in the political arena. Abraham Lincoln is considered by historians to be one of the greatest U.S. presidents partly because he built relationships and listened carefully to a broad range of people both inside and outside of his immediate circle when the nation was so bitterly divided over the Civil War. He included people who didn't agree with him and were critical of his goals and plans.[58] As for President Barack Obama,

EXHIBIT 13.6
An Illustration of Network Centrality

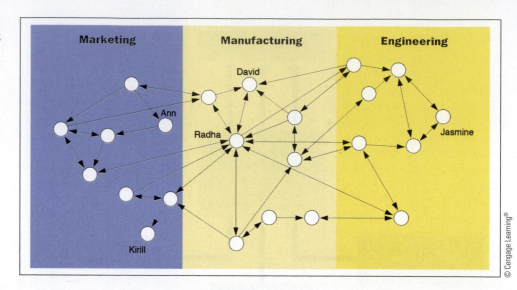

the jury is still out on how his presidency will be evaluated. However, Obama has been criticized for failing to develop relationships with even his biggest donors and leaving the relationship building with Democrats on Capitol Hill and others to Vice President Joe Biden. Obama is widely viewed as a loner who prefers policy to people and consults primarily with a close circle of advisers.[59]

People at all levels of the hierarchy can use the idea of network centrality to accomplish goals and be more successful. People can increase their network centrality by becoming knowledgeable and expert about certain activities or by taking on difficult tasks and acquiring specialized knowledge that makes them indispensable to managers above them. People who show initiative, work beyond what is expected, take on undesirable but important projects, and show interest in learning about the company and industry often find themselves with influence. Physical location also helps because some locations are in the center of things. Central location lets a person be visible to key people and become part of important interaction networks.

ASSESS YOUR ANSWER

2 A factory worker on the assembly line is in a low power position and should accept that he or she will have little influence over what happens.

ANSWER: *Disagree.* Although an assembly line worker typically has little formal power and authority, all employees have access to some sources of power. It is up to the individual to network or gather information to expand his or her power in the organization. In addition, when employees band together, they can have a tremendous amount of power. Managers can't accomplish goals unless employees cooperate and do the work they're supposed to do.

People. Top leaders often increase their power by surrounding themselves with a group of loyal executives.[60] Loyal managers keep the leader informed and in touch with events and report possible disobedience or troublemaking in the organization. Top executives can use their central positions to build alliances and exercise substantial power when they have a management team that is fully in support of their decisions and actions.

Many top executives strive to build a cadre of loyal and supportive managers to help them achieve their goals for the organization. Smart managers also actively work to build bridges and win over potential opponents. Gary Loveman, who left a position as associate professor at Harvard Business School to be the chief operating officer of casino company Harrah's, provides a good example. Some Harrah's executives, including the CFO, resented Loveman's appointment and could have derailed his plans for the company. Because he knew the CFO's information, knowledge, and support would be critical for accomplishing his plans, Loveman made building a positive relationship with the CFO a priority. He stopped by his office frequently to talk, kept him informed about what he was doing and why, and took care to involve him in important meetings and decisions. Building positive relationships enabled Loveman to accomplish goals that eventually led to him being named CEO of Harrah's.[61]

This idea works for lower-level employees and managers too. Lower-level people have greater power when they have positive relationships and connections with higher-ups. By being loyal and supportive of their bosses, employees sometimes gain favorable status and exert greater influence.

BRIEFCASE

As an organization manager, keep these guidelines in mind:

Do not leave lower organization levels powerless. If vertical power is too heavy in favor of top management, empower lower levels by giving people the tools they need to perform better: information, knowledge and skills, and the power to make substantive decisions.

The Power of Empowerment

In forward-thinking organizations, top managers want lower-level employees to have greater power so they can do their jobs more effectively. These managers intentionally push power down the hierarchy and share it with employees to enable them to achieve goals. **Empowerment** is power sharing, the delegation of power or authority to subordinates in an organization.[62] Increasing employee power improves morale, heightens motivation for task accomplishment, and prevents petty interpersonal rivalries. "When people feel powerless, they behave in petty ways," says management expert Rosabeth Moss-Kanter. "They become rule-minded and are overcontrolling because they are trying to grab hold of some little piece of the world that they do control . . . ."[63] Empowered employees can improve their own effectiveness, choosing how to do a task and using their creativity.[64]

Empowering employees involves giving them three elements that enable them to act more freely to accomplish their jobs: information, knowledge, and power.[65]

1. *Employees receive information about company performance.* In companies where employees are fully empowered, all employees have access to all financial and operational information.
2. *Employees have knowledge and skills to contribute to company goals.* Companies use training programs and other development tools to help people acquire the knowledge and skills they need to contribute to organizational performance.
3. *Employees have the power to make substantive decisions.* Empowered employees have the authority to directly influence work procedures and organizational performance, such as through quality circles or self-directed work teams.

Many of today's organizations are implementing empowerment programs, but they are empowering employees to varying degrees. At some companies, empowerment means encouraging employees' ideas while managers retain final authority for decisions; at others, it means giving people almost complete freedom and power to make decisions and exercise initiative and imagination.[66] The continuum of empowerment can run from a situation in which front-line employees have almost no discretion, such as on a traditional assembly line, to full empowerment, where employees even participate in formulating organizational strategy. There are several examples of organizations that push empowerment to the maximum. One of the most interesting is tomato processor Morning Star, which we first described in Chapter 1.

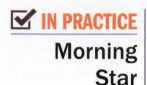

IN PRACTICE
Morning Star

Morning Star is the world's largest tomato processor, with three factories where 400 or so employees produce tomato paste, diced tomatoes, and other products for companies such as Heinz and Campbell Soup Company, bringing in over $700 million a year in revenues.

Chris Rufer founded Morning Star more than 40 years ago with the idea of pushing empowerment to the maximum by letting people manage themselves. At Morning Star, nobody gives orders, and nobody takes them. Here are the principles on which the company operates:

- No one has a boss
- Accountability is to the customer and the team rather than to a manager
- There are no titles or promotions
- Anyone can spend the company's money
- Compensation is decided by peers

Rufer believes if people can manage the complexities of their own lives without a boss, there is no reason they can't manage themselves in the workplace. However, as the company grew from the original 24 colleagues to around 400 (employment swells to 2,400 during tomato season), some people had trouble working in an environment with no bosses and no hierarchy. Rufer created the Morning Star Self-Management Institute to provide training for people in the principles and systems of self-management. Today, every colleague writes a personal mission statement and is responsible for accomplishing it, including obtaining whatever tools and resources are needed. That means anyone can order supplies and equipment, and colleagues are responsible for initiating the hiring process when they need more help.

Every year, each individual negotiates a Colleague Letter of Understanding (CLOU) with the people most affected by his or her work. Every CLOU has clearly defined metrics that enable people to track their progress in achieving goals and meeting the needs of colleagues. "Around here," one associate said, "nobody's your boss and everybody's your boss."[67]

Horizontal Sources of Power

Horizontal power pertains to relationships across departments, divisions, or other units. All vice presidents are usually at the same level on the organization chart. Does this mean each department has the same amount of power? No. Horizontal power is not defined by the formal hierarchy or the organization chart. Each department makes a unique contribution to organizational success. Some departments will have greater say and will achieve their desired outcomes, whereas others will not. Researcher and scholar Charles Perrow surveyed managers in several industrial firms.[68] He bluntly asked, "Which department has the most power?" among four major departments: production, sales and marketing, R&D, and finance and accounting.

In most firms, sales had the greatest power. In a few firms, production was also quite powerful. On average, the sales and production-type departments were more powerful than Research & Development and HR, although substantial variation existed. Differences in the amount of horizontal power clearly occurred in those firms. Exhibit 13.7 illustrates the difference in power among several departments in a technology firm. In another recent study of 55 top-level decisions in 14 organizations in the United Kingdom, researchers found that production, finance, and marketing had the greatest influence on strategic decisions compared

Ratings of Power Among Departments in a Technology Firm

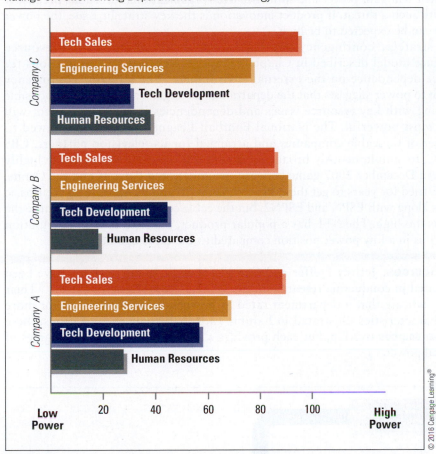

to R&D, HR, and purchasing.[69] Power shifts among departments depending on circumstances. Today, finance departments have gained power in many companies because of the urgent need to control costs in a tough economy. Ethics and compliance offices may have greater power because they help reduce uncertainty for top leaders regarding ethical scandals and financial malfeasance. In the Federal government, watchdog and regulatory agencies for Wall Street have increased power because of the 2008 financial meltdown. Under the leadership of former chairman Sheila Bair, for example, the Federal Deposit Insurance Corporation (FDIC) gained broad new powers to police large financial institutions, including installing examiners at financial firms to monitor their managers' activities.[70]

Horizontal power is difficult to measure because power differences are not defined on the organization chart. However, some initial explanations for power differences, such as those shown in Exhibit 13.7, have been found. The theoretical concept that explains relative power is called strategic contingencies.[71]

Strategic Contingencies. **Strategic contingencies** are events and activities both inside and outside an organization that are essential for attaining organizational goals. Departments involved with strategic contingencies for the organization tend to have greater power. Departmental activities are important when they provide strategic value by solving problems or crises for the organization. For example, if an organization faces an intense threat from lawsuits and regulations, the legal department will gain power and influence over organizational decisions because it copes with such a threat. If product innovation is the key strategic issue, the power of R&D can be expected to be high.

The strategic contingency approach to power is similar to the resource dependence model described in Chapters 4 and 5. Recall that organizations try to reduce dependence on the external environment. The strategic contingency approach to power suggests that the departments or organizations most responsible for dealing with key resource issues and dependencies in the environment will become most powerful. The National Football League, for instance, bowed to the power of the cable companies and arranged for its television partners, CBS and NBC, to simultaneously broadcast along with the NFL Network the highly anticipated December 2007 game between the undefeated Patriots and the Giants. The NFL tried for years to get the cable companies to add its network to their basic packages along with ESPN and ESPN2, but the cable companies refused because the price was too high. The NFL has a popular product, but with limited distribution options, it is in a low power position compared to the cable operators.[72]

Power Sources. Jeffrey Pfeffer and Gerald Salancik, among others, have been instrumental in conducting research on the strategic contingencies theory.[73] Their findings indicate that a department rated as powerful may possess one or more of the characteristics illustrated in Exhibit 13.8.[74] In some organizations, these five **power sources** overlap, but each provides a useful way to evaluate sources of horizontal power.

EXHIBIT 13.8
Strategic Contingencies that Influence Horizontal Power among Departments

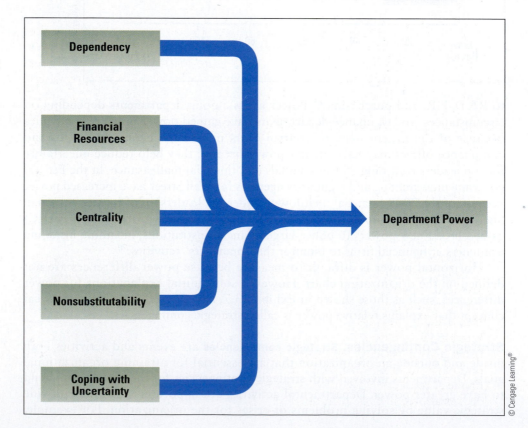

1. *Dependency*. Interdepartmental **dependency** is a key element underlying relative power. Power is derived from having something someone else wants. The power of theatrical stagehands provides an excellent example of how dependency increases power.

> ☑ **IN PRACTICE**
>
> ## International Alliance of Theatrical Stage Employees
>
> The power of labor unions in the United States has weakened significantly in recent years, but not for the International Alliance of Theatrical Stage Employees, which has retained its clout and even grown stronger. For example, the 2,600 active members of Local 1 are the talent behind some of the most opulent performance sets in New York City, from Carnegie Hall to the Metropolitan Opera, to Lincoln Center, to the New York City Ballet. Stagehands for some performances earn more money than principal cast members.
>
> The primary reason is that they have specialized, hard-to-replace skills. Good stagehands are not easy to find. They create the razzle-dazzle behind the Rockettes "Radio City Christmas Spectacular," raise the 45-foot Christmas tree for "George Balanchine's The Nutcraker," and are responsible for making the lavish ballroom set spin for the Metropolitan Opera's "Die Fledermaus." Bringing these dazzling stage effects to life requires talent, experience, and hard work. Unlike many tasks, the jobs of these highly skilled trades people cannot be easily outsourced. "Their jobs are extremely complex, extremely high-tech and possibly extremely dangerous," said Martha S. LoMonaco, a theater professor at Fairfield University.
>
> If the stagehands walk out, the performance cannot go on. They set up and break down complicated sets, handle the lighting and sound equipment, and manage special effects. Even the threat of a strike can be enough for Local 1 to win favorable contract terms. There have been only a few strikes in the union's 127-year history. Like the theater owners and managers, the stagehands also understand that they only work when they have a show.[75]

The same features of dependency and power can be seen in other organizations. The power of department A over department B is greater when department B depends on department A.[76] Materials, information, and resources may flow between departments in one direction, such as in the case of sequential task interdependence (see Chapter 7). In such cases, the department receiving resources is in a lower power position than the department providing them. The number and strength of dependencies are also important. When seven or eight departments must come for help to the engineering department, for example, engineering is in a strong power position. In contrast, a department that depends on many other departments is in a low power position. Likewise, a department in an otherwise low power position might gain power through dependencies. If a factory cannot produce without the expertise of maintenance workers to keep the machines working, the maintenance department is in a strong power position because it has control over a strategic contingency.

2. *Financial resources*. Control over resources is an important source of power in organizations. Money can be converted into other kinds of resources that are needed by other departments. Money generates dependency; departments that provide financial resources have something other departments want. Departments that generate income for an organization have greater power. Exhibit 13.7 showed tech sales as the most powerful unit in most technology firms. This is because salespeople find customers and bring in money, thereby removing an important problem for the organization. An ability to provide financial resources also explains why certain departments are powerful in other organizations, such as universities.

Budget allocation in a state university is not a straightforward process determined by such things as the number of undergraduate students, the number of graduate students, and the number of faculty in each department. In most universities, important resources come from research grants and the quality of students and faculty. Departments that generate large research grants are more powerful, for instance, because research grants contain a sizable overhead payment to university administration. This overhead money pays for a large share of the university's personnel and facilities. The size of a department's graduate student body and the national prestige of the department also add to power. Graduate students and national prestige are nonfinancial resources that add to the reputation and effectiveness of the university. How do university departments use their power? Generally, they use it to obtain even more resources from the rest of the university. Very powerful departments receive university resources, such as graduate student fellowships, internal research support, and summer faculty salaries, far in excess of their needs based on the number of students and faculty.[77]

As shown by this example, power accrues to departments that bring in or provide resources that are highly valued by an organization. Power enables those departments to obtain more of the scarce resources allocated within the organization. "Power derived from acquiring resources is used to obtain more resources, which in turn can be employed to produce more power—the rich get richer."[78]

3. *Centrality*. **Centrality** reflects a department's role in the primary activity of an organization.[79] One measure of centrality is the extent to which the work of the department affects the final output of the organization. For example, the production department is more central and usually has more power than staff groups (assuming no other critical contingencies). Centrality is associated with power because it reflects the contribution made to the organization. The corporate finance department of an investment bank generally has more power than the stock research department. When the finance department has the limited task of recording money and expenditures, it tends to be low in power because it is not responsible for obtaining critical resources or for producing the products of the organization. Today, however, finance departments have greater power in many organizations because of the greater need for controlling costs.

4. *Nonsubstitutability*. Power is also determined by **nonsubstitutability**, which means that a department's function cannot be performed by other readily available resources, such as the stagehands described earlier. If an organization has no alternative sources of skill and information, a department's power will be greater. This can be one reason top managers use outside consultants. Consultants might be used as substitutes for staff people to reduce the power of staff groups.

The impact of substitutability on power was studied for programmers in computer departments.[80] When computers were first introduced, programming was a rare and specialized occupation. Programmers controlled the use of organizational computers because they alone possessed the knowledge to program them. Over a period of about 10 years, computer programming became a more common activity. People could be substituted easily, and the power of programming departments dropped. Substitutability affects the power of organizations as well. Major record labels once had tremendous power over artists in the music industry because they had almost total control over which artists got their music recorded and in front of consumers. Today, though, new and established bands can release albums directly on the Internet without going through a label. In addition, Walmart, the largest music retailer in the United States, has entered the music making and marketing business, buying albums directly from artists like the Eagles and Journey. Intense marketing helped the Eagles' "Long Road Out of Eden" sell 711,000 copies through Walmart in its first week, without a traditional record company ever being involved.[81]

5. *Coping with Uncertainty.* Elements in the environment can change swiftly and can be unpredictable and complex. In the face of uncertainty, little information is available to managers on appropriate courses of action. Departments that reduce this uncertainty for the organization will increase their power.[82] When market research personnel accurately predict changes in demand for new products, they gain power and prestige because they have reduced a critical uncertainty. But forecasting is only one technique. Sometimes uncertainty can be reduced by taking quick and appropriate action after an unpredictable event occurs.

Departments can cope with critical uncertainties by (1) obtaining prior information, (2) prevention, and (3) absorption.[83] *Obtaining prior information* means a department can reduce an organization's uncertainty by forecasting an event. Departments increase their power through *prevention* by predicting and forestalling negative events. *Absorption* occurs when a department takes action after an event to reduce its negative consequences. With the increasing legal and regulatory challenges organizations face, in-house legal departments have grown in power. "Sometimes the [general counsel] will be paid more than the president of a business unit," says Cynthia Dow, an executive search consultant for Russell Reynolds Associates Inc.[84] Consider the following case from the healthcare industry.

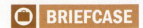

IN PRACTICE

Carilion Health System

Because hospitals and other healthcare providers have to deal with so many complex legal and regulatory matters, the legal department is usually in a high power position. That is certainly the case at Carilion Health System, based in Roanoke, Virginia. Some years ago, the legal department successfully fought off a U.S. Department of Justice antitrust lawsuit and played a crucial role in negotiating a merger between Carilion and Roanoke's only other hospital.

Since then, the legal department has been kept busy not only with regulatory issues but also with trying to get payment from patients who say they can't pay their high medical bills. Because Roanoke is now a "one-market town" in terms of healthcare, critics say Carilion is getting away with charging excessive fees, thereby hurting patients, businesses, insurers, and the entire community. The Roanoke City District Court devotes one morning a week to cases filed by Carilion, which during one recent fiscal year sued nearly 10,000 patients, garnished the wages of more than 5,000 people, and placed liens on nearly 4,000 homes.

The negative press resulting from this, along with a backlash from independent doctors who say Carilion is intentionally stifling competition, means the public relations department has a chance to increase its power as well. The department is actively involved in efforts to bolster Carilion's image as a good corporate citizen, emphasizing that it only sues patients it believes have the ability to pay and pointing out the millions of dollars Carilion dispenses to charity care each year.[85]

At Carilion, the legal department absorbed a critical uncertainty by fighting off the antitrust lawsuit and helping Carilion grow in size and power. It continues to take action after uncertainties appear (such as patients who don't pay).

Horizontal power relationships in organizations change as strategic contingencies change. Whereas the legal department will likely continue in a high power position at Carilion, the need of the hospital to improve its reputation and fend off growing criticism could lead to an increase in the power of the public relations department. The public relations department can gain power by being involved in activities targeted toward both prevention and absorption. Departments that help organizations cope with new strategic issues will increase their power.

Political Processes in Organizations

Politics, like power, is intangible and difficult to measure. It is hidden from view and is hard to observe in a systematic way. Two surveys uncovered the following reactions of managers toward political behavior.[86]

1. Most managers have a negative view toward politics and believe that politics will more often hurt than help an organization in achieving its goals.
2. Managers believe that political behavior is common in practically all organizations.
3. Most managers think that political behavior occurs more often at upper rather than lower levels in organizations.
4. Managers believe political behavior arises in certain decision domains, such as structural change, but is absent from other decisions, such as handling employee grievances.

Based on these surveys, politics seems more likely to occur at the top levels of an organization and around certain issues and decisions. Moreover, managers do not approve of political behavior. The remainder of this chapter explores more fully what political behavior is, when it should be used, the type of issues and decisions most likely to be associated with politics, and some political tactics that may be effective.

Definition

Power has been described as the available force or potential for achieving desired outcomes. *Politics* is the use of power to influence decisions in order to achieve those outcomes. The exercise of power to influence others has led to two ways to define politics: as self-serving behavior or as a natural organizational decision process. The first definition emphasizes that politics is self-serving and involves activities that are not sanctioned by the organization.[87]

In this view, politics involves deception and dishonesty for purposes of individual self-interest and leads to conflict and disharmony within the work environment. This dark view of politics is widely held by laypeople, and political activity certainly can be used in this way. Studies have shown that workers who perceive this kind of political activity within their companies often have related feelings of anxiety and job dissatisfaction. Research also supports the belief that an inappropriate use of politics is related to low employee morale, inferior organizational performance, and poor decision making.[88] This view of politics explains why managers in the aforementioned surveys did not approve of political behavior.

Although politics can be used in a negative, self-serving way, the appropriate use of political behavior can serve organizational goals.[89] The second view sees politics as a natural organizational process for resolving differences among organizational interest groups.[90] Politics is the process of bargaining and negotiation that is used to overcome conflicts and differences of opinion. In this view, politics is similar to the coalition-building decision processes described in Chapter 12.

The organization theory perspective views politics as described in the second definition. Politics is simply the activity through which power is exercised in the resolution of conflicts and uncertainty. Politics is neutral and is not necessarily harmful to the organization. The formal definition of organizational politics is as follows: **organizational politics** involves activities to acquire, develop, and use power and other resources to influence others and obtain the preferred outcome when there is uncertainty or disagreement about choices.[91]

Political behavior can be either a positive or a negative force. Politics is the use of power to get things accomplished—good things as well as bad. Uncertainty and conflict are natural and inevitable, and politics is the mechanism for reaching agreement. Politics includes informal discussions that enable people to arrive at consensus and make decisions that otherwise might be stalemated or unsolvable.

3 When managers use politics, it usually leads to conflict and disharmony and will likely disrupt the smooth functioning of the organization.

> **ANSWER:** *Disagree.* Politics is a natural organizational process for resolving differences and getting things done. Although politics can be used for negative and self-serving purposes, political activity is also the primary way managers are brought together to accomplish good things. Being political is part of the job of a manager, but managers should take care to use politics to serve the interests of the organization rather than themselves.

ASSESS **YOUR** ANSWER

When to Use Political Activity

Politics is a mechanism for arriving at consensus when uncertainty is high and there is disagreement over goals or problem priorities. Recall the rational versus political models described in Exhibit 13.2. The political model is associated with conflict over goals, shifting coalitions and interest groups, ambiguous information, and uncertainty. Thus, political activity tends to be most visible when managers confront nonprogrammed decisions, as described in Chapter 12, and is related to the Carnegie model of decision making. Because managers at the top of an organization generally deal with more nonprogrammed decisions than do managers at lower levels, more political activity will appear at higher levels. Moreover, some issues are associated with inherent disagreement. Resources, for example, are critical for the survival and effectiveness of departments, so resource allocation often becomes a political issue. Rational methods of allocation do not satisfy participants. Three **domains of political activity** (areas in which politics plays a role) in most organizations are structural change, management succession, and resource allocation.

Structural reorganizations strike at the heart of power and authority relationships. Reorganizations such as those discussed in Chapter 3 change responsibilities and tasks, which also affects the underlying power base from strategic contingencies. For these reasons, a major reorganization can lead to an explosion of political activity.[92] Managers may actively bargain and negotiate to maintain the responsibilities and power bases they have. Mergers and acquisitions also frequently create tremendous political activity.

Organizational changes such as hiring new executives, promotions, and transfers have great political significance, particularly at top organizational levels where uncertainty is high and networks of trust, cooperation, and communication among executives are important.[93] Hiring decisions can generate uncertainty, discussion, and disagreement. Managers can use hiring and promotion to strengthen network alliances and coalitions by putting their own people in prominent positions.

The third area of political activity is resource allocation. Resource-allocation decisions encompass all resources required for organizational performance, including salaries, operating budgets, employees, office facilities, equipment, and use of the company airplane. Resources are so vital that disagreement about priorities exists, and political processes help resolve the dilemmas.

Using Soft Power and Politics

One theme in this chapter has been that power in organizations is not primarily a phenomenon of the individual. It is related to the resources departments command, the role departments play in an organization, and the environmental contingencies with which departments cope. Position and responsibility, more than personality and style, may determine a manager's ability to influence outcomes in the organization.

However, power is used through individual political behavior. To fully understand the use of power within organizations, it is important to look at both structural components and individual behavior.[94] Although power often comes from larger organizational forms and processes, the political use of power involves individual-level activities and skills. To learn about your political skills, complete the questionnaire in the "How Do You Fit the Design?" box. Managers with political skill are more effective at influencing others and thus getting what they want, for the organization and for their own careers.[95] These managers have honed their abilities to observe and understand patterns of interaction and influence in the organization. They are skilled at developing relationships with a broad network of people and can adapt their behavior and approach to diverse people and situations. Politically effective managers understand that influence is about relationships.[96]

Managers can develop political competence, and they can learn to use a wide variety of influence tactics depending on their own position as well as the specific situation. Some tactics rely on the use of "hard power," which is power that stems largely from a person's position of authority. This is the kind of power that enables a supervisor to influence subordinates with the use of rewards and punishments, allows a manager to issue orders and expect them to be obeyed, or lets a domineering CEO force through his or her own decisions without regard for what anyone else thinks. However, effective managers more often use "soft power," which is based on personal characteristics and building relationships.[97] Jeff Immelt, CEO of General Electric, considers himself a failure if he exercises his formal authority more than seven or eight times a year. The rest of the time, Immelt is using softer means to persuade and influence others and to resolve conflicting ideas and opinions.[98]

HOW DO YOU FIT THE DESIGN?

POLITICAL SKILLS

How good are you at influencing people across an organization? To learn something about your political skills, answer the questions that follow. Please answer whether each item is Mostly True or Mostly False for you.

		Mostly True	Mostly False
1.	I am able to communicate easily and effectively with others.	___	___
2.	I spend a lot of time at work developing connections with people outside my area.	___	___
3.	I instinctively know the right thing to say or do to influence others.	___	___
4.	I am good at using my connections outside my area to get things done at work.	___	___
5.	When communicating with others, I am absolutely genuine in what I say and do.	___	___
6.	It is easy for me to reach out to new people.	___	___
7.	I make strangers feel comfortable and at ease around me.	___	___
8.	I am good at sensing the motivations and hidden agendas of others.	___	___

Scoring: Give yourself one point for each item marked as Mostly True.

Interpretation: Having some basic political skill helps a manager gain broad support and influence. Political skills help a manager build personal and organizational relationships that enhance your team's outcomes. A score of 6 or higher suggests active political skills and a good start for your career, especially in an organization in which things get done politically. If you scored three or less, you may want to focus more on building collegial and supportive relationships as you progress in your career. If not, perhaps join an organization in which decisions and actions are undertaken by rational procedures rather than by support of key coalitions.

Source: Adapted from Gerald R. Ferris, Darren C. Treadway, Robert W. Kolodinsky, Wayne A. Hochwarter, Charles J. Kacmer, Ceasar Douglas, and Dwight D. Frink, "Development and Validation of the Political Skill Inventory," *Journal of Management* 31 (February 2005), 126–152.

Even the U.S. military is talking about the importance of building relationships rather than using brute force. Former defense secretary Robert Gates, for instance, says that in the battle for hearts and minds abroad, the United States has to be "good at listening to others" rather than just good at kicking down doors, and the Army's new stability operations field manual openly talks about the value of soft power.[99] Wesley Clark, former supreme commander of NATO who led the mission against Serb president Slobodan Milosevic, suggests that, for leaders in businesses as well as nations, building a community of shared interests should be the first choice, rather than using threats, intimidation, and raw power.[100] The effectiveness of soft power is revealed in a study of 49 professional negotiators over a nine-year period of time. Researchers found that the most effective negotiators spent 400 percent more time than their less-effective counterparts looking for areas of mutual benefit and shared interest, rather than just trying to force their own agenda.[101]

The following sections summarize various tactics that managers can use to increase their own or their department's power base, and the political tactics they can use to achieve desired outcomes. Most of these tactics, summarized in Exhibit 13.9, rely on the use of soft rather than hard power.

EXHIBIT 13.9
Power and Political
Tactics in Organizations

Tactics for Increasing the Power Base	Political Tactics for Using Power
1. Enter areas of high uncertainty.	1. Build coalitions and expand networks.
2. Create dependencies.	2. Assign loyal people to key positions.
3. Provide scarce resources.	3. Control decision premises.
4. Satisfy strategic contingencies.	4. Enhance legitimacy and expertise.
5. Make a direct appeal.	5. Create superordinate goals.

Tactics for Increasing Power

Four **tactics for increasing power** are as follows:

1. *Enter areas of high uncertainty.* One source of individual or departmental power is to identify key uncertainties and take steps to remove those uncertainties.[102] Uncertainties could arise from stoppages on an assembly line, from the quality demanded of a new product, or from the inability to predict a demand for new services. Once an uncertainty is identified, the department can take action to cope with it. By their very nature, uncertain tasks will not be solved immediately. Trial and error will be needed, which is to the advantage of the department. The trial-and-error process provides experience and expertise that cannot easily be duplicated by other departments.

2. *Create dependencies.* Dependencies are another source of power.[103] When the organization depends on a department or individual for information, materials, knowledge, or skills, that department or individual will hold power over others. A somewhat amusing example comes from Evan Steingart's consumer products company. A low-level inventory-transfer clerk in the shipping department had to sign off on the shipment of all goods. Salespeople were dependent on the clerk for his signature. Those who wanted their orders shipped quickly learned to cozy up to the clerk. Arrogant ones who treated him badly would find themselves at a disadvantage, as the clerk would have a long list of things to do before he could get to their shipping order, and the salespeople had no recourse but to wait.[104] An equally effective and related strategy is to reduce dependency on other departments by acquiring necessary information or skills when possible, so that your department isn't in a dependent position. For example, the sales manager might seek signing authority to eliminate salespeople's dependence on the inventory clerk and the shipping department.

3. *Provide scarce resources.* Resources are always important to organizational survival. Departments that accumulate resources and provide them to an organization in the form of money, information, or facilities will be powerful. An earlier example described how university departments with the greatest power are those that obtain external research funds for contributions to university overhead. Likewise, sales departments are powerful in most firms because they bring in financial resources.

4. *Satisfy strategic contingencies.* The theory of strategic contingencies says that some elements in the external environment and within the organization are especially important for organizational success. A contingency could be a critical event, a task for which there are no substitutes, or a central task that is interdependent with many others in the organization. An analysis of the organization and its changing environment will reveal strategic contingencies. To the extent that contingencies are new or are not being satisfied, there is room for a department to move into those critical areas and increase its importance and power.

In summary, the allocation of power in an organization is not random. Power is the result of organizational processes that can be understood and predicted. The abilities to reduce uncertainty, increase dependency on one's own department, obtain resources, and cope with strategic contingencies all enhance a department's power. Once power is available, the next challenge is to use it to attain desired outcomes.

Political Tactics for Using Power

The use of power in organizations requires both skill and willingness. Many decisions are made through political processes because rational decision processes do not fit. Uncertainty or disagreement is too high. **Political tactics for using power** to influence decision outcomes include the following:

1. *Build coalitions and expand networks.* Effective managers develop positive relationships throughout the organization, and they spend time talking with others to learn about their views and build mutually beneficial alliances and coalitions.[105] Most important decisions are made outside of formal meetings. Managers discuss issues with each other and reach agreement. Effective managers are those who huddle, meeting in groups of twos and threes to resolve key issues.[106] They also make sure their networks cross hierarchical, functional, and even organizational boundaries. One research project found that the ability to build networks has a positive impact on both employees' perception of a manager's effectiveness and the ability of the manager to influence performance.[107] Networks can be expanded by (1) reaching out to establish contact with additional managers and (2) co-opting dissenters. Establishing contact with additional managers means building good interpersonal relationships based on liking, trust, and respect. Reliability and the motivation to work with rather than exploit others are part of both networking and coalition building.[108] The second approach to expanding networks, cooptation, is the act of bringing a dissenter into one's network. One example of cooptation involved a university committee whose membership was based on promotion and tenure. Several professors who were critical of the tenure and promotion process were appointed to the committee. Once a part of the administrative process, they could see the administrative point of view. Cooptation effectively brought them into the administrative network.[109]

2. *Assign loyal people to key positions.* Another political tactic is to assign trusted and loyal people to key positions in the organization or department. Top managers as well as department heads often use the hiring, transfer, and promotion processes to place in key positions people who are sympathetic to the outcomes of the department, thus helping to achieve departmental goals.[110] Top leaders frequently use this tactic, as we discussed earlier. Look at what is happening with Pope Francis at the Vatican.

IN PRACTICE

The Vatican

Less than a year into his papacy, Pope Francis had significantly reshaped the way the Catholic Church is run by changing who is running it. Francis has been steadily bringing his own people to positions of power to help him achieve his goal of creating a more inclusive and relevant church for this century.

Conservative cardinals such as Raymond L. Burke, one of the highest-ranking Americans at the Vatican, who had tremendous influence in selecting new bishops in the United States, and Mauro Piacenza, who ran the powerful Congregation for the Clergy, have been demoted or had their power diluted. Francis is replacing these traditionalists put in place by his predecessor with more moderate leaders who are in tune with his mission for transforming the church. Guido Pozzo, another conservative who was elevated to the rank of archbishop and appointed to run the church's charity office by Benedict, has also been sent back to his former post by Francis.

Similar changes are going on in other areas. Shortly before he resigned, Benedict approved new five-year terms for the existing five-man committee that oversees the Vatican Bank. Francis has replaced all but one of those committee members with his own picks. He also appointed a separate special commission to examine the bank's activities and improve control and oversight. "It's a strong signal of change in the management of the pontifical finances," said journalist Carlo Marroni, an expert on Vatican financial affairs.

Many of the changes Francis has made have been criticized as "upending the career ladder that many prelates have spent their lives climbing." Moreover, many once-powerful officials feel out of the loop. Francis believes too many within the church have "succumbed to worldly temptations" and that breaking down the power circles is a way to reverse that trend.[111]

Like other top leaders, Pope Francis is using the hiring, promotion, and transfer processes to put loyal and trusted people in positions where they can help him achieve his mission and goals for the organization.

3. *Use reciprocity.* There is much research indicating that most people feel a sense of obligation to give something back in return for favors others do for them.[112] This *principle of reciprocity* is one of the key factors affecting influence relationships in organizations. When a manager does a favor for a colleague, the colleague feels obliged to return the favor in the future. "We're given serious persuasive powers immediately after someone thanks us," says Robert Cialdini, a leading social scientist in the field of influence. Cialdini says managers should take advantage of that to remind others that it's a reciprocal relationship by saying something like, "Of course, it's what partners do for each other."[113] The "unwritten rule of reciprocity" is one reason organizations like Northrup Grumman, Kraft Foods, and Pfizer make donations to the favorite charities of House and Senate members. Leaders attempt to curry favor with lawmakers whose decisions can significantly affect their business.[114] As with other political tactics, managers sometimes use reciprocity for self-serving purposes that can harm the organization and its stakeholders. For instance, investigators have questioned whether a "culture of complicity" that involves nuclear industry officials, power company managers, politicians, and regulators doing favors for one another played a role in the accident at the Fukushima Daiichi power plant.[115]

The pattern of favors revealed by investigations into Japan's nuclear industry reflects the significant role reciprocity plays in influence relationships. Some researchers argue that the concept of exchange—trading something of value for what you want—is the basis of all other influence tactics. For example, rational persuasion works because the other person sees a benefit from going along with the plan, and making people like you is successful because the other person receives liking and attention in return.[116] This chapter's BookMark further discusses reciprocity and other basic influence principles.

4. *Enhance legitimacy and expertise.* Managers can exert the greatest influence in areas in which they have recognized legitimacy and expertise. This tactic is highly effective with the younger generation of managers and employees. Today's young workers define power based on an individual's knowledge and skills rather than a position of authority over people. Indeed, many people don't appreciate the strong use of politics and expect people to rely on their knowledge and credibility to influence others.[117] When managers make a request that is within the task domain of a department and is consistent with the department's vested interest, other departments will tend to comply. Members can also identify external consultants or other experts within the organization to support their cause.[118]

BOOKMARK 13.0 HAVE YOU READ THIS BOOK?

Influence: Science and Practice
By Robert B. Cialdini

Managers use a variety of political tactics to influence others and bring about desired outcomes. In his book *Influence: Science and Practice,* Robert Cialdini examines the social and psychological pressures that cause people to respond favorably to these various tactics. Over years of study, Cialdini, Regents' Professor of Psychology at Arizona State University, has identified some basic *influence principles,* "those that work in a variety of situations, for a variety of practitioners, on a variety of topics, for a variety of prospects."

INFLUENCE PRINCIPLES

Having a working knowledge of the basic set of persuasion tools can help managers predict and influence human behavior, which is valuable for interacting with colleagues, employees, customers, partners, and even friends. Some basic psychological principles that govern successful influence tactics are as follows:

- *Reciprocity.* The principle of reciprocity refers to the sense of obligation people feel to give back in kind what they have received. For example, a manager who does favors for others creates in them a sense of obligation to return the favors in the future. Smart managers find ways to be helpful to others, whether it be helping a colleague finish an unpleasant job or offering compassion and concern for a subordinate's personal problems.
- *Liking.* People say *yes* more often to those they like. Companies such as Tupperware or Pampered Chef have long understood that familiar faces and congenial characteristics sell products. In-home parties allow customers to buy from a friend instead of an unknown salesperson. Salespeople in all kinds of companies often try to capitalize on

this principle by finding interests they share with customers as a way to establish rapport. In general, managers who are pleasant, generous with praise, cooperative, and considerate of others' feelings find that they have greater influence.

- *Credible authority.* Legitimate authorities are particularly influential sources. However, research has discovered that the key to successful use of authority is to be knowledgeable, credible, and trustworthy. Managers who become known for their expertise, who are honest and straightforward with others, and who inspire trust can exert greater influence than those who rely on formal position alone.
- *Social validation.* One of the primary ways people decide what to do in any given situation is to consider what others are doing. That is, people examine the actions of others to validate correct choices. For instance, when homeowners were shown a list of neighbors who had donated to a local charity during a fundraiser, the frequency of contributions increased dramatically. By demonstrating, or even implying, that others have already complied with a request, managers gain greater cooperation.

THE PROCESS OF SOCIAL INFLUENCE

Because life as a manager is all about influencing others, learning to be genuinely persuasive is a valuable management skill. Cialdini's book helps managers understand the basic psychological rules of persuasion—how and why people are motivated to change their attitudes and behaviors. When managers use this understanding in an honest and ethical manner, they improve their effectiveness and the success of their organizations.

Influence: Science and Practice (4th edition), by Robert B. Cialdini, is published by Allyn & Bacon.

5. *Make a direct appeal.* If managers do not ask, they seldom receive. An example of direct appeal comes from Drugstore.com, where Jessica Morrison used direct appeal to get a new title and a salary increase. Morrison researched pay scales on PayScale.com and approached her boss armed with that and other pertinent information. Her direct appeal, backed up with research, won her the promotion.[119] Political activity is effective only when goals and needs are made explicit so the organization can respond. An assertive proposal may be accepted because other managers have no better alternatives. Moreover, an explicit proposal will often receive favorable treatment because other alternatives are ambiguous and less well defined. Effective political behavior requires sufficient forcefulness and risk-taking to at least ask for what you need to achieve desired outcomes.

Managers can use an understanding of these tactics to assert influence and get things done within the organization. When managers ignore soft power and political tactics, they may find themselves failing without understanding why. For example, at the World Bank, Paul Wolfowitz tried to wield hard power without building the necessary relationships he needed to assert influence.

IN PRACTICE
World Bank

After former deputy secretary of defense Paul Wolfowitz lost his bids to become defense secretary or national security advisor in the Bush administration, he jumped at the chance to be the new president of World Bank. But Wolfowitz doomed his career at World Bank from the start by failing to develop relationships and build alliances.

Most World Bank leaders had been in their positions for many years when Wolfowitz arrived, and they were accustomed to "promoting each other's interests and scratching each other's backs," as one board member put it. Wolfowitz came in and tried to assert his own ideas, goals, and formal authority without considering the interests, ideas, and goals of others. He quickly alienated much of the World Bank leadership team and board by adopting a single-minded position on key issues and refusing to consider alternative views. Rather than attempting to persuade others to his way of thinking, Wolfowitz issued directives to senior bank officers, either personally or through his handpicked managers. Several high-level officers resigned following disputes with the new president.

Eventually, the board asked for Wolfowitz's resignation. "What Paul didn't understand is that the World Bank presidency is not inherently a powerful job," said one former colleague. "A bank president is successful only if he can form alliances with the bank's many fiefdoms. Wolfowitz didn't ally with those fiefdoms. He alienated them."[120]

Wolfowitz realized too late that he needed to use a political, soft-power approach rather than trying to force his own agenda. Even when a manager has a great deal of power, the use of power should not be obvious.[121] If a manager formally draws on her power base in a meeting by saying, "My department has more power, so the rest of you have to do it my way," her power will be diminished. Power works best when it is used quietly. To call attention to power is to lose it. People know who has power. Explicit claims to power are not necessary and can even harm the manager's or department's cause.

Also, when using any of the preceding tactics, recall that most people think self-serving behavior hurts rather than helps an organization. If managers are perceived to be throwing their weight around or pursuing goals that are self-serving rather than beneficial to the organization, they will lose respect. On the other hand, managers must recognize the relational and political aspect of their work. It is not sufficient to be rational and technically competent. Developing and using political skill is an important part of being a good manager.

Design Essentials

- The central message of this chapter is that conflict, power, and politics are natural outcomes of organizing. Differences in goals, backgrounds, and tasks are necessary for organizational excellence, but these differences can throw groups into conflict. Managers use power and politics to manage and resolve conflict.

- Two views of organization were presented. The rational model of organization assumes that organizations have specific goals and that problems can be logically solved. The other view, the political model of organization, is the basis for much of the chapter. This view assumes that the goals of an organization are not specific or agreed upon. Departments have different values and interests, so managers come into conflict. Decisions are made on the basis of power and political influence. Bargaining, negotiation, persuasion, and coalition building decide outcomes.

■ Although conflict and political behavior are natural and can be used for beneficial purposes, managers also strive to enhance collaboration so that conflict between groups does not become too strong. Tactics for enhancing collaboration include integration devices, confrontation and negotiation, intergroup consultation, member rotation, and shared mission and superordinate goals.

■ The chapter also discussed the vertical and horizontal sources of power. Vertical sources of power include formal position, resources, control of information, and network centrality. In general, managers at the top of the organizational hierarchy have more power than people at lower levels. However, positions all along the hierarchy can be designed to increase the power of employees. As organizations face increased competition and environmental uncertainty, top executives are finding that increasing the power of middle managers and lower-level employees can help the organization be more competitive. Empowerment is a popular trend. Empowering employees means giving them three key elements: information and resources, necessary knowledge and skills, and the power to make substantive decisions.

■ Research into horizontal power processes has revealed that certain characteristics make some departments more powerful than others. Differences in power can be understood using the concept of strategic contingencies. Departments responsible for dealing with key resource issues and dependencies are more powerful. Such factors as dependency, resources, nonsubstitutability, and dealing with uncertainty determine the influence of departments.

■ Managers need political skills to exercise soft power. Many people distrust political behavior, fearing that it will be used for selfish ends that benefit the individual but not the organization. However, politics is often needed to achieve the legitimate goals of a department or organization. Three areas in which political behavior often plays a role are structural change, management succession, and resource allocation because these are areas of high uncertainty. Managers use political tactics, including building coalitions, expanding networks, using reciprocity, enhancing legitimacy, and making a direct appeal, to help their departments achieve desired outcomes.

❯ KEY CONCEPTS

authority	intergroup conflict	power
centrality	labor-management teams	power sources
collective bargaining	negotiation	rational model
competition	network centrality	sources of intergroup conflict
confrontation	nonsubstitutability	strategic contingencies
dependency	organizational politics	tactics for enhancing collaboration
domains of political activity	political model	tactics for increasing power
empowerment	political tactics for using power	

DISCUSSION QUESTIONS

1. Give an example from your personal experience of how differences in tasks, personal background, and training lead to conflict among groups. How might task interdependence have influenced that conflict?

2. Consumer products giant Procter & Gamble and Internet leader Google have entered into a marketing partnership. What organizational and environmental factors might determine which organization will have more power in the relationship?

3. In a rapidly changing organization, are decisions more likely to be made using the rational or political model of organization? Discuss.

4. What is the difference between power and authority? Is it possible for a person to have formal authority but no real power? Discuss.

5. Discuss ways in which a department at a health insurance company might help the organization cope with the increased power of large hospital systems such as Carilion by obtaining prior information, prevention, or absorption.

6. State University X receives 90 percent of its financial resources from the state and because tuition is cheap is overcrowded with students. The admissions office is overwhelmed with applications, and the university is trying to pass regulations to limit student enrollment. Private University Y receives 90 percent of its income from student tuition and has barely enough students to make ends meet. The admissions office is actively recruiting students for next year. Using the strategic contingencies notion of power, in which university will the admissions office have greater power? What implications will this have for professors and administrators? Discuss.

7. A financial analyst at Merrill Lynch tried for several months to expose the risks of investments in subprime mortgages, but he couldn't get anyone to pay attention to his claims. How would you evaluate this employee's power? What might he have done to increase his power and call notice to the impending problems at the firm?

8. The engineering college at a major university brings in three times as many government research dollars as does the rest of the university combined. Engineering appears wealthy and has many professors on full-time research status. Yet, when internal research funds are allocated, engineering gets a larger share of the money, even though it already has substantial external research funds. Why would this happen?

9. Some researchers argue that the concept of exchange underlying the principle of reciprocity (trading something of value to another for what you want) is the basis of *all* influence. Do you agree? Discuss. To what extent do you feel obligated to return a favor that is done for you?

CHAPTER 13 WORKSHOP   How Do You Handle Conflict?

Think about how you typically handle a dispute with a team member, friend, or co-worker and then answer the following statements based on whether they are True or False for you. There are no right or wrong answers, so answer honestly.

	Mostly True	Mostly False
1. I feel that differences are not worth arguing about.	____	____
2. I would avoid a person who wants to discuss a disagreement.	____	____
3. I would rather keep my views to myself than argue.	____	____
4. I typically avoid taking positions that create a dispute.	____	____
5. I try hard to win my position.	____	____
6. I strongly assert my opinion in a disagreement.	____	____
7. I raise my voice to get other people to accept my position.	____	____
8. I stand firm in expressing my viewpoint.	____	____
9. I give in a little if other people do the same.	____	____
10. I will split the difference to reach an agreement.	____	____
11. I offer tradeoffs to reach a solution.	____	____
12. I give up some points in exchange for others.	____	____
13. I don't want to hurt others' feelings.	____	____
14. I am quick to agree when someone I am arguing with makes a good point.	____	____
15. I try to smooth over disagreements by minimizing their seriousness.	____	____
16. I want to be considerate of other people's emotions.	____	____

17. I suggest a solution that includes the other person's point of view. _____ _____
18. I combine arguments into a new solution from ideas raised in the dispute. _____ _____
19. I try to include the other person's ideas to create a solution they will accept. _____ _____
20. I assess the merits of other viewpoints as equal to my own. _____ _____

Scoring and Interpretation: Five categories of conflict-handling strategies are measured by these 20 questions: avoiding, dominating, bargaining, accommodating, and collaborating. These five strategies reflect different levels of personal desire for *assertiveness* or *cooperation.* The higher your score for a strategy, the more likely that is your preferred conflict-handling approach. A lower score suggests you probably do not use that approach.

Dominating Style (my way) reflects a high degree of assertiveness to get one's own way and fulfill one's self-interest. Sum one point for each Mostly True for items 5–8: _____.

Accommodating Style (your way) reflects a high degree of cooperativeness and a desire to oblige or help others as most important. Sum one point for each Mostly True for items 13–16: _____.

Avoiding Style (no way) reflects neither assertiveness nor cooperativeness, which means that conflict is avoided whenever possible. Sum one point for each Mostly True for items 1–4: _____.

Bargaining Style (half way) reflects a tendency to meet half way by using a moderate amount of both assertiveness and cooperativeness. Sum one point for each Mostly True for items 9–12: _____.

Collaborating Style (our way) reflects a high degree of both assertiveness and cooperativeness to meet the needs of both parties. Sum one point for each Mostly True for items 17–20: _____.

Questions

1. Which strategy do you find easiest to use? Most difficult?
2. How would your answers change if the other party to the conflict was a friend, family member, or co-worker?
3. How do you feel about your approach to handling conflict? What changes would you like to make?

CASE FOR ANALYSIS | The Daily Tribune[122]

The *Daily Tribune* is the only daily newspaper serving a six-county region of eastern Tennessee. Even though its staff is small and it serves a region of mostly small towns and rural areas, the *Tribune* has won numerous awards for news coverage and photojournalism from the Tennessee Press Association and other organizations.

Rick Arnold became news editor almost 20 years ago. He has spent his entire career with the *Tribune* and feels a great sense of pride that it has been recognized for its journalistic integrity and balanced coverage of issues and events. The paper has been able to attract bright, talented young writers and photographers thanks largely to Rick's commitment and his support of the news staff. In his early years, the newsroom was a dynamic, exciting place to work—reporters thrived on the fast pace and the chance to occasionally scoop the major daily paper in Knoxville.

But times have changed at the *Daily Tribune.* Over the past five years or so, the advertising department has continued to grow, in terms of both staff and budget, while the news department has begun to shrink. "Advertising pays the bills," publisher John Freeman reminded everyone at this month's managers' meeting. "Today, advertisers can go to direct mail, cable television, even the Internet, if they don't like what we're doing for them."

Rick has regularly clashed with the advertising department regarding news stories that are critical of major advertisers, but the conflicts have increased dramatically over the past few years. Now, Freeman is encouraging greater "horizontal collaboration," as he calls it, asking that managers in the news department and the ad department consult with one another regarding issues or stories that involve the paper's major advertisers. The move was prompted in part by a growing number of complaints from advertisers about stories they deemed unfair. "We print the news," Freeman said, "and I understand that sometimes we've got to print things that some people won't like. But we've got to find ways to be more advertiser-friendly. If we work together, we can develop strategies that both present good news coverage and serve to attract more advertisers."

Rick left the meeting fuming, and he didn't fail to make his contempt for the new "advertiser-friendly" approach known to all, including the advertising manager, Fred Thomas, as he headed down the hallway back to the newsroom. Lisa Lawrence, his managing editor, quietly agreed but pointed out that advertisers were readers too, and the newspaper had to listen to all its constituencies. "If we don't handle this carefully, we'll have Freeman and Thomas in here dictating to us what we can write and what we can't."

Lawrence has worked with Rick since he first came to the paper, and even though the two have had their share of conflicts, the relationship is primarily one of mutual respect and trust. "Let's just be careful," she emphasized. "Read the stories about big advertisers a little more carefully, make sure we can defend whatever we print, and it will all work out. I know this blurring of the line between advertising and editorial rubs you the wrong way, but Thomas is a reasonable man. We just need to keep him in the loop."

Late that afternoon, Rick received a story from one of his corresponding reporters that had been in the works for a couple of days. East Tennessee Healthcorp (ETH), which operated a string of health clinics throughout the region, was closing three of its rural clinics because of mounting financial woes. The reporter, Elisabeth Fraley, lived in one of the communities and had learned about the closings from her neighbor, who worked as an accountant for ETH, before the announcement had been made just this afternoon. Fraley had written a compelling human-interest story about how the closings would leave people in two counties with essentially no access to healthcare, while clinics in larger towns that didn't really need them were being kept open. She had carefully interviewed both former patients of the clinics and ETH employees, including the director of one of the clinics and two high-level managers at the corporate office, and she had carefully documented her sources. After this morning's meeting, Rick knew he should consult with Lisa Lawrence, since East Tennessee Healthcorp was one of the *Tribune's* biggest advertisers, but Lawrence had left for the day. And he simply couldn't bring himself to consult with the advertising department—that political nonsense was for Lawrence to handle. If he held the

story for Lawrence's approval, it wouldn't make the Sunday edition. His only other option was to write a brief story simply reporting the closings and leaving out the human-interest aspect. Rick was sure the major papers from Knoxville and other nearby cities would have the report in their Sunday papers, but none of them would have the time to develop as comprehensive and interesting an account as Fraley had presented. With a few quick keystrokes to make some minor editorial changes, Rick sent the story to production.

When he arrived at work the next day, Rick was called immediately to the publisher's office. He knew it was bad news for Freeman to be in on a Sunday. After some general yelling and screaming, Rick learned that tens of thousands of copies of the Sunday paper had been destroyed and a new edition printed. The advertising manager had called Freeman at home in the wee hours of Sunday morning and informed him of the ETH story, which was appearing the same day the corporation was running a full-page ad touting its service to the small towns and rural communities of East Tennessee.

"The story's accurate, and I assumed you'd want to take advantage of a chance to scoop the big papers," Rick began, but Freeman cut his argument short. "You could have just reported the basic facts without implying that the company doesn't care about the people of this region. The next time something like this happens, you'll find yourself and your reporters standing in the unemployment line!"

Rick had heard it before, but somehow this time he almost believed it. "What happened to the days when the primary purpose of a newspaper was to present the news?" Rick mumbled. "Now, it seems we have to dance to the tune played by the ad department."

CASE FOR ANALYSIS | The New Haven Initiative

When Burton Lee took over as plant manager for the New Haven division of a large manufacturing company, he saw the opportunity to transform the lowest performing unit as a pathway to his promotion into top management.

Burton was aware of his reputation within the company as an intellectual, which he credited, in part, to an undergraduate minor in philosophy. Fifteen years after obtaining his MBA, he retained a passion for reading the classics—Homer, Tacitus, Plato, Herodotus, and Cicero—in the original Greek and Latin. Like Thomas Jefferson, he carried a pocket-size Greek grammar with him. Co-workers admiringly and grudgingly accustomed themselves to his familiar phrases, "*When you look at this logically . . .*" or "*it should be obvious that . . . .*"

It was obvious to Burton that changes had to be made at New Haven. The division's reputation as the weak link in the company, with excessive machine downtime, backlogs, and complaints about quality, negatively affected employee morale. In a down economy, rumors often circulated that the New Haven plant might be closed.

"My academic background taught me that there is a logical way to approach and solve problems. Manufacturing is often stuck in the past—*the way it has always been done.*

Over and over in manufacturing you find that individuals in management have come up through the ranks and are reluctant to change—often even in the face of overwhelming evidence. Because they are stuck in this mindset, they are reluctant to explore ideas, to stay on top of manufacturing trends, or to see the bigger picture. I believe that innovation in thinking, in technology, in streamlining processes and empowering employees is crucial to success at New Haven.

"When I came here to take over New Haven, the plant was a mess, to put it bluntly. We were awash in paper. We were stuck on the traditional assembly line. When I talked to line supervisors, I felt like they were channeling Henry Ford. We needed a new paradigm, a new culture that was not stuck in the past. We had to end the backlogs, move product faster, and improve the quality. I can't do that. The workers in the plant have to do that. But they need the tools to work with. What was it that Churchill told FDR in World War II? 'Give us the tools and we'll finish the job.' That was the culture I wanted here in New Haven.

"I explored everything, talked to everyone, and investigated what was working in other industries. I knew we'd have to take these individual tasks and build a system to coordinate them into complex, but not complicated, interactions with specific targets that raise overall equipment effectiveness. The question was how could we do that?

"When you look at this logically, when you venture outside of your comfort zone and see what other industries have done, you discover a number of models and you find that there are resources in the form of technology and software out there that can help. I somehow managed to convince top management to invest in a pilot project with software that enabled us to create a virtual plant to look at every aspect of the operation—plant layout, material flow, machinery, everything. Initially, my on-site management team really got into this. With this software, we could simulate various problems and do some 'what-if' analysis. The idea was to create lean manufacturing clusters that could serve as a benchmark for the rest of the company.

"On the line, we moved toward dividing the assembly line into cells of self-managed teams. The idea is to empower and motivate the workers to make real-time decisions. Employees seemed enthusiastic and eager to have more control over the day-to-day operations. Supervisors were the first to balk, worried that they were losing prestige and that seniority was being shoved aside, as one long-time supervisor claimed, so that 'Joe Blow, who's only been on the line for ten months, can start making decisions.' Likewise, there were some line workers who balked. You would think that the opportunity to change from being essentially a cog in the wheel to becoming part of a dynamic, self-managed team would be appealing to everyone.

But I guess some are afraid of decision-making and feel a need for constant guidance. For some workers the mention of self-managed teams produced a 'deer in the headlights' reaction.

"It should be obvious that these steps would bring improvement, but in order for this whole process to work, we needed worker cooperation and full management support. We had started making some progress and seeing some improvement in production and quality, when suddenly it was as if top management put on the brakes. We need resources and time to make the changes. Managers at other plants complained of preferential treatment for New Haven and argued that they were expected to produce and deliver while we were sitting around 'playing video games' and 'holding hands'—a reference, I'm certain, to the new software and the self-managed teams. Corporate repeatedly delayed funding for the new equipment and training that could transform this plant into a 21st century manufacturing division.

"I admit that I am shocked and disappointed that so many people in this organization fail to see the rationale here, which is obvious to anyone with eyes and a brain, and that they are failing to support our efforts. I'm showing them data that supports everything we're attempting here at New Haven. We're getting knee-jerk reactions when we need enlightened leadership. Now I'm wondering, what is the next step to go forward? A major success is being taken from me. And I heard informally that I am not a candidate for promotion."

NOTES

1. David Gelles, "At Odds, Omnicom and Publicis End Merger," Dealbook column, *The New York Times*, May 8, 2014, http://dealbook.nytimes.com/2014/05/08/ad-agency-giants-said-to-call-off-35-billion-merger/?_php=true&_type=blogs&_r=0 (accessed June 5, 2014); and Suzanne Vranica and Ruth Bender, "Clashes over Power Threaten $35 Billion Ad Agency Merger," *The Wall Street Journal Online*, April 25, 2014, http://online.wsj.com/news/articles/SB10001424052702304788404579524030560224554 (accessed June 5, 2014).

2. Phred Dvorak, Suzanne Vranica, and Spencer E. Ante, "BlackBerry Maker's Issue: Gadgets for Work or Play?" *The Wall Street Journal Online*, September 30, 2011, http://online.wsj.com/article/SB10001424052970204422404576597061591715344.html (accessed September 30, 2011).

3. Lee G. Bolman and Terrence E. Deal, *Reframing Organizations: Artistry, Choice, and Leadership* (San Francisco: Jossey-Bass, 1991).

4. Paul M. Terry, "Conflict Management," *The Journal of Leadership Studies* 3, no. 2 (1996), 3–21; Kathleen M. Eisenhardt, Jean L. Kahwajy, and L. J. Bourgeois III, "How Management Teams Can Have a Good Fight," *Harvard Business Review*, July–August 1997, 77–85; and Patrick Lencioni, "How to Foster Good Conflict," *The Wall Street Journal Online*, November 13, 2008, http://online.wsj.com/article/SB122661642852326187.html (accessed November 18, 2008).

5. Clayton T. Alderfer and Ken K. Smith, "Studying Intergroup Relations Imbedded in Organizations," *Administrative Science Quarterly* 27 (1982), 35–65.

6. Muzafer Sherif, "Experiments in Group Conflict," *Scientific American* 195 (1956), 54–58; and Edgar H. Schein, *Organizational Psychology*, 3rd ed. (Englewood Cliffs, NJ: Prentice-Hall, 1980).

7. M. Afzalur Rahim, "A Strategy for Managing Conflict in Complex Organizations," *Human Relations* 38 (1985), 81–89; Kenneth Thomas, "Conflict and Conflict Management," in M. D. Dunnette, ed., *Handbook of Industrial and Organizational Psychology* (Chicago: Rand McNally, 1976); and Stuart M. Schmidt and Thomas A. Kochan, "Conflict: Toward Conceptual Clarity," *Administrative Science Quarterly* 13 (1972), 359–370.

8. L. David Brown, "Managing Conflict Among Groups," in David A. Kolb, Irwin M. Rubin, and James M. McIntyre, eds., *Organizational Psychology: A Book of Readings* (Englewood Cliffs, NJ: Prentice-Hall, 1979), 377–389; and Robert W. Ruekert and Orville C. Walker, Jr., "Interactions Between Marketing and R&D Departments in Implementing Different Business Strategies," *Strategic Management Journal* 8 (1987), 233–248.

9. Amy Barrett, "Indigestion at Taco Bell," *BusinessWeek*, December 14, 1994, 66–67; and Greg Burns, "Fast-Food Fight," *BusinessWeek*, June 2, 1997, 34–36.

10. Susanne Craig, "Morgan Stanley Strives to Coordinate 2 Departments Often at Odds," *The New York Times*, February 19, 2013, B1.

11. George Westerman, "IT Is from Venus, Non-IT Is from Mars," *The Wall Street Journal*, April 2, 2012, R2.

12. Victoria L. Crittenden, Lorraine R. Gardiner, and Antonie Stam, "Reducing Conflict Between Marketing and

Manufacturing," *Industrial Marketing Management* 22 (1993), 299–309; and Benson S. Shapiro, "Can Marketing and Manufacturing Coexist?" *Harvard Business Review* 55, September–October 1977, 104–114.

13. Thomas A. Kochan, George P. Huber, and L. L. Cummings, "Determinants of Intraorganizational Conflict in Collective Bargaining in the Public Sector," *Administrative Science Quarterly* 20 (1975), 10–23.

14. Eric H. Neilsen, "Understanding and Managing Intergroup Conflict," in Jay W. Lorsch and Paul R. Lawrence, eds., *Managing Group and Intergroup Relations* (Homewood, IL: Irwin and Dorsey, 1972), 329–343; and Richard E. Walton and John M. Dutton, "The Management of Interdepartmental Conflict: A Model and Review," *Administrative Science Quarterly* 14 (1969), 73–84.

15. Jay W. Lorsch, "Introduction to the Structural Design of Organizations," in Gene W. Dalton, Paul R. Lawrence, and Jay W. Lorsch, eds., *Organization Structure and Design* (Homewood, IL: Irwin and Dorsey, 1970), 5.

16. James D. Thompson, *Organizations in Action* (New York: McGraw-Hill, 1967), 54–56.

17. Walton and Dutton, "The Management of Interdepartmental Conflict."

18. Joseph McCann and Jay R. Galbraith, "Interdepartmental Relations," in Paul C. Nystrom and William H. Starbuck, eds., *Handbook of Organizational Design*, vol. 2 (New York: Oxford University Press, 1981), 60–84.

19. Roderick M. Cramer, "Intergroup Relations and Organizational Dilemmas: The Role of Categorization Processes," in L. L. Cummings and Barry M. Staw, eds., *Research in Organizational Behavior*, vol. 13 (New York: JAI Press, 1991), 191–228; Neilsen, "Understanding and Managing Intergroup Conflict"; and Louis R. Pondy, "Organizational Conflict: Concepts and Models," *Administrative Science Quarterly* 12 (1968), 296–320.

20. Julian E. Barnes, "Branches of Military Battle over Shrinking War Chest," *The Wall Street Journal*, July 31, 2013, http://online.wsj.com/news/articles/SB10001424127887324260204578583513940889092 (accessed June 5, 2014).

21. Jeffrey Pfeffer, *Power in Organizations* (Marshfield, MA: Pitman, 1981).

22. Amy Barrett, "Marc Cinque Hired a Corporate Pro to Upgrade His Sausage Company. Will the Move Pay Off?" *Inc.*, December 2010–January 2011, 74–77.

23. Clinton O. Longenecker and Mitchell Neubert, "Barriers and Gateways to Management Cooperation and Teamwork," *Business Horizons*, November–December 2000, 37–44.

24. Amanuel G. Tekleab, Narda R. Quigley, and Paul E. Tesluk, "A Longitudinal Study of Team Conflict, Conflict Management, Cohesion, and Team Effectiveness," *Group and Organization Management* 34, no. 2, April 2009, 170–205.

25. Robert R. Blake and Jane S. Mouton, "Overcoming Group Warfare," *Harvard Business Review*, November–December 1984, 98–108.

26. Blake and Mouton, "Overcoming Group Warfare"; and Paul R. Lawrence and Jay W. Lorsch, "New Management Job: The Integrator," *Harvard Business Review* 45, November–December 1967, 142–151.

27. Jill Jusko, "Nature vs. Nurture," *Industry Week*, July 2003, 40–46.

28. Neal E. Boudette and Jeff Bennett, "UAW Boss Makes Nice, Touts End of Us vs. Them," *The Wall Street Journal*, August 4, 2011, B1.

29. Robert R. Blake, Herbert A. Shepard, and Jane S. Mouton, *Managing Intergroup Conflict in Industry* (Houston: Gulf Publishing, 1964); and Doug Stewart, "Expand the Pie Before You Divvy It Up," *Smithsonian*, November 1997, 78–90.

30. Patrick S. Nugent, "Managing Conflict: Third-Party Interventions for Managers," *Academy of Management Executive* 16, no. 1 (2002), 139–155.

31. Blake and Mouton, "Overcoming Group Warfare"; Schein, *Organizational Psychology*; Blake, Shepard, and Mouton, "Managing Intergroup Conflict in Industry"; and Richard E. Walton, *Interpersonal Peacemaking: Confrontation and Third-Party Consultations* (Reading, MA: Addison-Wesley, 1969).

32. Neilsen, "Understanding and Managing Intergroup Conflict"; and McCann and Galbraith, "Interdepartmental Relations."

33. Ben Horowitz, "The *Freaky Friday* Management Technique," Ben's Blog, Andreessen Horowitz Website, January 19, 2012, http://www.bhorowitz.com/the_freaky_friday_management_technique (accessed June 5, 2014). This story is also told in Horowitz, *The Hard Thing About Hard Things: Building a Business When There Are No Easy Answers* (New York: HarperBusiness, 2014).

34. Neilsen, "Understanding and Managing Intergroup Conflict"; and McCann and Galbraith, "Interdepartmental Relations."

35. Dean Tjosvold, Valerie Dann, and Choy Wong, "Managing Conflict Between Departments to Serve Customers," *Human Relations* 45 (1992), 1035–1054.

36. Robert A. Dahl, "The Concept of Power," *Behavioral Science* 2 (1957), 201–215.

37. W. Graham Astley and Paramjit S. Sachdeva, "Structural Sources of Intraorganizational Power: A Theoretical Synthesis," *Academy of Management Review* 9 (1984), 104–113; and Abraham Kaplan, "Power in Perspective," in Robert L. Kahn and Elise Boulding, eds., *Power and Conflict in Organizations* (London: Tavistock, 1964), 11–32.

38. Gerald R. Salancik and Jeffrey Pfeffer, "The Bases and Use of Power in Organizational Decision-Making: The Case of the University," *Administrative Science Quarterly* 19 (1974), 453–473.

39. Rosabeth Moss Kanter, "Power Failure in Management Circuits," *Harvard Business Review*, July–August 1979, 65–75.

40. Richard M. Emerson, "Power-Dependence Relations," *American Sociological Review* 27 (1962), 31–41.

41. Brian Stelter, "Creator of 'Mad Men' Agrees to Deliver Multiple Seasons," *The New York Times*, April 1, 2011, B2; Lauren A. E. Schuker, "'Mad Men' Put on Ice; AMC's Hit Drama Postponed to 2012 Amid Contract Talks," *The Wall Street Journal*, March 30, 2011, B8; and "Count on AMC to Make it a 'Mad,' 'Mad,' 'Mad,' 'Mad,' 'Mad' World," *The Washington Post*, March 30, 2011, C1.

42. Anthony D'Allessandro, "'Mad Men' Cast and Matthew Weiner Reflect on Half Season and Bert Cooper's Final Dance Number," *Deadline Hollywood*, June 4, 2014, http://www.deadline.com/2014/06/mad-men-cast-season-finale-deadline-screening/#more-740191 (accessed June 6, 2014).

43. Examples are Robert Greene and Joost Elffers, *The 48 Laws of Power* (New York: Viking, 1999); and Jeffrey J. Fox, *How to Become CEO* (New York: Hyperion, 1999).

44. John R. P. French, Jr., and Bertram Raven, "The Bases of Social Power," in D. Cartwright and A. F. Zander, eds., *Group Dynamics* (Evanston, IL: Row Peterson, 1960), 607–623.

45. Ran Lachman, "Power from What? A Reexamination of Its Relationships with Structural Conditions," *Administrative Science Quarterly* 34 (1989), 231–251; and Daniel J. Brass, "Being in the Right Place: A Structural Analysis of Individual Influence in an Organization," *Administrative Science Quarterly* 29 (1984), 518–539.

46. Rachel Feintzeig, "The Most Powerful Person in the Office: Executive Assistant Jobs May Be Thankless, but They Also Offer Big Impact," *The Wall Street Journal*, October 29, 2013, http://online.wsj.com/news/articles/SB1000142405270230447050457916414266342 5498 (accessed June 6, 2014).

47. Michael Warshaw, "The Good Guy's Guide to Office Politics," *Fast Company*, April–May 1998, 157–178.

48. A. J. Grimes, "Authority, Power, Influence, and Social Control: A Theoretical Synthesis," *Academy of Management Review* 3 (1978), 724–735.

49. Astley and Sachdeva, "Structural Sources of Intraorganizational Power."

50. Jean-Louis Barsoux and Cyril Bouquet, "How to Overcome a Power Deficit," *MIT Sloan Management Review*, Summer 2013, 45–53.

51. Jeffrey Pfeffer, *Managing with Power: Politics and Influence in Organizations* (Boston: Harvard Business School Press, 1992).

52. Monica Langley, "Columbia Tells Doctors at Hospital to End Their Outside Practice," *The Wall Street Journal*, May 2, 1997, A1, A6.

53. Richard S. Blackburn, "Lower Participant Power: Toward a Conceptual Integration," *Academy of Management Review* 6 (1981), 127–131.

54. Feintzeig, "The Most Powerful Person in the Office."

55. Kanter, "Power Failure in Management Circuits," 70.

56. Erik W. Larson and Jonathan B. King, "The Systemic Distortion of Information: An Ongoing Challenge to Management," *Organizational Dynamics* 24, no. 3 (Winter 1996), 49–61; and Thomas H. Davenport, Robert G. Eccles, and Laurence Prusak, "Information Politics," *Sloan Management Review*, Fall 1992, 53–65.

57. Based on Perry Buffett, "Using Influence to Get Things Done," *Strategy + Business*, Spring 2011, http://www.strategy-business.com/article/11104?pg=all (accessed June 9, 2014); and Andrew M. Pettigrew, *The Politics of Organizational Decision-Making* (London: Tavistock, 1973).

58. Nancy F. Koehn, "Lincoln's School of Management," *The New York Times*, January 26, 2013; Hitendra Wadhwa, "Lessons in Leadership: How Lincoln Became America's Greatest President," Inc.com, February 12, 2012, http://www.inc.com/hitendra-wadhwa/lessons-in-leadership-how-abraham-lincoln-became-americas-greatest-president.html (accessed March 4, 2013); and Gil Troy and Karl Moore, "Leading from the Centre: What CEOs Can Learn from U.S. Presidents," *Ivey Business Journal*, September–October, 2010, http://www.iveybusinessjournal.com/topics/leadership/leading-from-the-centre-what-ceos-can-learn-from-u-s-presidents (accessed May 21, 2013).

59. Scott Wilson, "Obama, the Loner President," *Washington Post*, October 7, 2011, http://articles.washingtonpost.com/2011-10-07/opinions/35280751_1_president-obama-politics-obama-administration (accessed October 8, 2011); and Peter Nicholas, "Obama's Insular White House Worries His Allies," *Los Angeles Times*, December 24, 2010, http://articles.latimes.com/2010/dec/24/nation/la-na-obama-insular-presidency-20101225 (accessed December 25, 2010).

60. Astley and Sachdeva, "Structural Sources of Intraorganizational Power"; and Noel M. Tichy and Charles Fombrun, "Network Analysis in Organizational Settings," *Human Relations* 32 (1979), 923–965.

61. Jeffrey Pfeffer, "Power Play," *Harvard Business Review*, July–August 2010, 84–92.

62. Edwin P. Hollander and Lynn R. Offermann, "Power and Leadership in Organizations," *American Psychologist* 45, February 1990, 179–189.

63. Quoted in D. Keith Denton, "Enhancing Power," *Industrial Management*, July–August 2011, 12–17.

64. Jay A. Conger and Rabindra N. Kanungo, "The Empowerment Process: Integrating Theory and Practice," *Academy of Management Review* 13 (1988), 471–482.

65. David E. Bowen and Edward E. Lawler III, "The Empowerment of Service Workers: What, Why, How, and When," *Sloan Management Review*, Spring 1992, 31–39; and Ray W. Coye and James A. Belohav, "An Exploratory Analysis of Employee Participation," *Group and Organization Management* 20, no. 1 (March 1995), 4–17.

66. Robert C. Ford and Myron D. Fottler, "Empowerment: A Matter of Degree," *Academy of Management Executive* 9, no. 3 (1995), 21–31.

67. Doug Kirkpatrick, "Self-Management's Success at Morning Star," *T+D*, October 2012, 25–27; and Gary Hamel, "First, Let's Fire All the Managers," *Harvard Business Review*, December 2011, 48–60.

68. Charles Perrow, "Departmental Power and Perspective in Industrial Firms," in Mayer N. Zald, ed., *Power in Organizations* (Nashville, TN: Vanderbilt University Press, 1970), 59–89.

69. Susan Miller, David Hickson, and David Wilson, "From Strategy to Action: Involvement and Influence in Top Level Decisions," *Long Range Planning* 41 (2008), 606–628.

70. Deborah Solomon, "Bair's Legacy: An FDIC with Teeth," *The Wall Street Journal*, July 7, 2011, C1.

71. D. J. Hickson, C. R. Hinings, C. A. Lee, R. E. Schneck, and J. M. Pennings, "A Strategic Contingencies Theory of Intraorganizational Power," *Administrative Science Quarterly* 16 (1971), 216–229; and Gerald R. Salancik and Jeffrey Pfeffer, "Who Gets Power—and How They Hold onto It: A Strategic-Contingency Model of Power," *Organizational Dynamics*, Winter 1977, 3–21.

72. William C. Rhoden, "The N.F.L. Backed Down for All the World to See," *The New York Times*, December 30, 2007, Sunday Sports section, 1, 3.

73. Pfeffer, *Managing with Power*; Salancik and Pfeffer, "Who Gets Power"; C. R. Hinings, D. J. Hickson, J. M. Pennings, and R. E. Schneck, "Structural Conditions of Intraorganizational Power," *Administrative Science Quarterly* 19 (1974), 22–44.

74. Also see Carol Stoak Saunders, "The Strategic Contingencies Theory of Power: Multiple Perspectives," *Journal of Management Studies* 27 (1990), 1–18; Warren Boeker, "The Development and Institutionalization of Sub-Unit Power in Organizations," *Administrative Science Quarterly* 34 (1989), 388–510; and Irit Cohen and Ran Lachman, "The Generality of the Strategic Contingencies Approach to Sub-Unit Power," *Organizational Studies* 9 (1988), 371–391.

75. Lorne Manly and Michael Cooper, "Hey Stars, Be Nice to the Stagehands. You Might Need a Loan," *The New York Times*, December 27, 2013, http://www.nytimes.com/2013/12/28/arts/hey-stars-be-nice-to-the-stagehands-you-might-need-a-loan.html?_r=0 (accessed June 5, 2014).

76. Emerson, "Power-Dependence Relations."

77. Jeffrey Pfeffer and Gerald Salancik, "Organizational Decision-Making as a Political Process: The Case of a University Budget," *Administrative Science Quarterly* (1974), 135–151.

78. Salancik and Pfeffer, "Bases and Use of Power in Organizational Decision-Making," 470.

79. Hickson et al., "A Strategic Contingencies Theory."

80. Pettigrew, *The Politics of Organizational Decision-Making*.

81. Robert Levine, "For Some Music, It Has to Be Wal-Mart and Nowhere Else," *The New York Times*, June 9, 2008, C1.

82. Hickson et al., "A Strategic Contingencies Theory."

83. Ibid.

84. Jennifer Smith, "Lawyers' In-House Roles Grow with New Regulation," *The Wall Street Journal*, November 5, 2012, http://online.wsj.com/news/articles/SB1000142405297020475540457809910023566338 (accessed June 6, 2014).

85. John Carreyrou, "Nonprofit Hospitals Flex Pricing Power—In Roanoke, Va., Carilion's Fees Exceed Those of Competitors," *The Wall Street Journal*, August 28, 2008, A1.

86. Jeffrey Gantz and Victor V. Murray, "Experience of Workplace Politics," *Academy of Management Journal* 23 (1980), 237–251; and Dan L. Madison, Robert W. Allen, Lyman W. Porter, Patricia A. Renwick, and Bronston T. Mayes, "Organizational Politics: An Exploration of Managers' Perceptions," *Human Relations* 33 (1980), 79–100.

87. Gerald R. Ferris and K. Michele Kacmar, "Perceptions of Organizational Politics," *Journal of Management* 18 (1992), 93–116; Parmod Kumar and Rehana Ghadially, "Organizational Politics and Its Effects on Members of Organizations," *Human Relations* 42 (1989), 305–314; Donald J. Vredenburgh and John G. Maurer, "A Process Framework of Organizational Politics," *Human Relations* 37 (1984), 47–66; and Gerald R. Ferris, Dwight D. Frink, Maria Carmen Galang, Jing Zhou, Michele Kacmar, and Jack L. Howard, "Perceptions of Organizational Politics: Prediction, Stress-Related Implications, and Outcomes," *Human Relations* 49, no. 2 (1996), 233–266.

88. Ferris et al., "Perceptions of Organizational Politics: Prediction, Stress-Related Implications, and Outcomes"; John J. Voyer, "Coercive Organizational Politics and Organizational Outcomes: An Interpretive Study," *Organization Science* 5, no. 1, February 1994, 72–85; and James W. Dean, Jr. and Mark P. Sharfman, "Does Decision Process Matter? A Study of Strategic Decision-Making Effectiveness," *Academy of Management Journal* 39, no. 2 (1996), 368–396.

89. Jeffrey Pfeffer, *Managing with Power: Politics and Influence in Organizations* (Boston: Harvard Business School Press, 1992); and Pfeffer, "Power Play."

90. Amos Drory and Tsilia Romm, "The Definition of Organizational Politics: A Review," *Human Relations* 43 (1990), 1133–1154; Vredenburgh and Maurer, "A Process Framework of Organizational Politics"; and Lafe Low, "It's Politics, As Usual," *CIO*, April 1, 2004, 87–90.

91. Pfeffer, *Power in Organizations*, 70.

92. Madison et al., "Organizational Politics"; and Jay R. Galbraith, *Organizational Design* (Reading, MA: Addison-Wesley, 1977).

93. Gantz and Murray, "Experience of Workplace Politics"; and Pfeffer, *Power in Organizations*.

94. Daniel J. Brass and Marlene E. Burkhardt, "Potential Power and Power Use: An Investigation of Structure and Behavior," *Academy of Management Journal* 38 (1993), 441–470.

95. Pfeffer, "Power Play."

96. Robyn L. Brouer et al., "Leader Political Skill, Relationship Quality, and Leadership Effectiveness: A Two-Study Model Test and Constructive Replication," *Journal of Leadership and Organizational Studies* 20, no. 2 (2013), 185–198; Gerald R. Ferris et al., "Political Skill in Organizations," *Journal of Management*, June 2007, 290–320; "Questioning Authority; Mario Moussa Wants You to Win Your Next Argument" (Mario Moussa interviewed by Vadim Liberman), *The Conference Board Review* (November–December 2007), 25–26; and Samuel B. Bacharach, "Politically Proactive," *Fast Company*, May 2005, 93.

97. Joseph S. Nye, Jr., *Bound to Lead: The Changing Nature of American Power* (New York: Basic Books, 1990); and Diane Coutu, "Smart Power: A Conversation with Leadership Expert Joseph S. Nye, Jr.," *Harvard Business Review*, November 2008, 55–59.

98. Reported in Liberman, "Questioning Authority; Mario Moussa Wants You to Win Your Next Argument."

99. Anna Mulrine, "Harnessing the Brute Force of Soft Power," *US News & World Report*, December 1–December 8, 2008, 47.

100. Wesley Clark, "The Potency of Persuasion," *Fortune*, November 12, 2007, 48.

101. Study reported in Robert Cialdini, "The Language of Persuasion," *Harvard Management Update*, September 2004, 10–11.

102. Hickson et al., "A Strategic Contingencies Theory."

103. Pfeffer, *Power in Organizations*.

104. Jared Sandberg, "How Office Tyrants in Critical Positions Get Others to Grovel," *The Wall Street Journal*, August 21, 2007, B1.

105. Ferris et al., "Political Skill in Organizations"; and Pfeffer, *Power in Organizations*.

106. V. Dallas Merrell, *Huddling: The Informal Way to Management Success* (New York: AMACON, 1979).

107. Ceasar Douglas and Anthony P. Ammeter, "An Examination of Leader Political Skill and Its Effect on Ratings of Leader Effectiveness," *The Leadership Quarterly* 15 (2004), 537–550.

108. Vredenburgh and Maurer, "A Process Framework of Organizational Politics."

109. Pfeffer, *Power in Organizations*.

110. Ibid.

111. Jason Horowitz and Jim Yardley, "Pope with the Humble Touch Is Firm in Reshaping the Vatican," *The New York Times*, January 14, 2014, A1; and Jim Yardley and Gaia Pianigiani, "Pope Names Cardinals to Oversee Troubled Vatican Bank," *The New York Times*, January 16, 2014, A7.

112. Robert B. Cialdini, *Influence: Science and Practice*, 4th ed. (Boston: Allyn & Bacon, 2001); R. B. Cialdini, "Harnessing the Science of Persuasion," *Harvard Business Review*, October 2001, 72–79; Allan R. Cohen and David L. Bradford, "The Influence Model: Using Reciprocity and Exchange to Get What You Need," *Journal of Organizational Excellence*, Winter 2005, 57–80; and Jared Sandberg, "People Can't Resist Doing a Big Favor—Or Asking for One" (Cubicle Culture column), *The Wall Street Journal*, December 18, 2007, B1.

113. The Uses (and Abuses) of Influence" (an interview with Robert Cialdini), *Harvard Business Review*, July–August 2013, 76–81.

114. Raymond Hernandez and David W. Chen, "Keeping Lawmakers Happy Through Gifts to Pet Charities," *The New York Times*, October 19, 2008, A1.

115. Norimitsu Onishi and Ken Belson, "Culture of Complicity Tied to Stricken Nuclear Plant," *The New York Times*, April 27, 2011, A1.

116. Cohen and Bradford, "The Influence Model."

117. Marilyn Moats Kennedy, "The Death of Office Politics," *The Conference Board Review*, September–October 2008, 18–23.

118. Pfeffer, *Power in Organizations*.

119. Damon Darlin, "Using the Web to Get the Boss to Pay More," *The New York Times*, March 3, 2007, C1.

120. Steven R. Weisman, "How Battles at Bank Ended 'Second Chance' at a Career," *The New York Times*, May 18, 2007, A14.

121. Kanter, "Power Failure in Management Circuits"; and Pfeffer, *Power in Organizations*.

122. This case was inspired by G. Pascal Zachary, "Many Journalists See a Growing Reluctance to Criticize Advertisers," *The Wall Street Journal*, February 6, 1992, A1, A9; and G. Bruce Knecht, "Retail Chains Emerge as Advance Arbiters of Magazine Content," *The Wall Street Journal*, October 22, 1997, A1, A13.

INTEGRATIVE CASE 1.0
W. L. Gore—Culture of Innovation*

Why ... couldn't an entire company be designed as a bureaucracy-free zone?[1]

This was the thought that enthralled Wilbert ("Bill") L. Gore, a chemical engineer at E. I. du Pont de Nemours and Company (DuPont). This thought led him to break out of the traditional management practices and create a company that would cherish human imagination and freedom.

W. L. Gore & Associates, Inc. (referred to as W. L. Gore, or just Gore, in what follows) was founded in 1958. It was a privately held company headquartered in the suburbs of Newark, Delaware. In 2011, it was ranked for the 14th consecutive year among the "100 Best Companies to Work For" by *Fortune* magazine. Also, for several years in a row, it was named one of the best workplaces in the United Kingdom, Germany, France, and Italy. In recent years, it had appeared in the Sweden and Spain lists as well.[2]

The voluntary turnover rate at Gore was around 5 percent—one-third the average rate in its industry (durable goods) and one-fifth that for private firms of similar size.[3] In 2012, it had "more than 9,500 employees, called associates, located in 30 countries worldwide, with manufacturing facilities in the United States, Germany, Scotland, Japan, and China, and sales offices around the world."[4]

Though the company did not publish its financials, it had reportedly been profitable every year since its inception, and its revenues were approximately $3 billion.[5]

When Bill Gore embarked on his dream to create an innovative enterprise over a half century ago, he had a lot of questions:

Could you build a company with no hierarchy—where everyone was free to talk with everyone else? How about a company where there were no bosses, no supervisors, and no vice presidents? Could you let people choose what they wanted to work on, rather than assigning them tasks? Could you create a company with no "core" business, where people would put as much energy into finding the next big thing as they did into milking the last big thing? And could you do all of this while still delivering consistent growth and profitability?[6]

Background and Brief History

In April 1938, Dr. Roy J. Plunkett, a research chemist at DuPont, discovered PTFE (polytetrafluoroethylene resin), which was trademarked under the brand name Teflon.[7] Bill Gore, during his 17-year career at DuPont, was assigned several times to small R&D task forces, the last one of which was responsible for finding a meaningful commercial use for Teflon. While they were working on this assignment, another group at DuPont came up with a way to make thermoplastics out of Teflon. Hence, DuPont felt no need for Gore's group to continue. Gore observed, "Du Pont felt that [the thermoplastic version of Teflon] was good enough, and our group was dissolved."[8]

Gore believed that DuPont was largely underestimating the potential of this "slick, waxy fluoropolymer,"[9] so he continued to work on it in his spare time. Gore

*This case was prepared by Jay Rao, Professor of Technology Operations and Information Management at Babson College, based on published sources. It was developed as a basis for class discussion rather than to illustrate effective or ineffective handling of an administrative situation. It is not intended to serve as an endorsement, source of primary data, or illustration of effective or ineffective management.

Copyright © 2012 Babson College and licensed for publication to European Case Clearing House (ECCH). All rights reserved. No part of this publication can be reproduced, stored or transmitted in any form or by any means without prior written permission of Babson College.

[1]Gary Hamel with Bill Breen, *The Future of Management* (Boston: Harvard Business School Press, 2007), p. 85.

[2]W. L. Gore & Associates, Inc., "Working in Our Unique Culture," W. L. Gore & Associates website, http://www.gore.com/en_xx/careers/whoweare/ourculture/gore-company-culture.html (accessed March 10, 2012).

[3]Rebecca Serwer, "Creating Competitive Advantage in Today's Labor Market: Lessons Learned from Three Model Companies." Master of Professional Studies thesis, University of Denver University College, 2008, p. 54.

[4]W. L. Gore & Associates, Inc., "Gore Locations Worldwide," W. L. Gore & Associates website, http://www.gore.com/en_xx/aboutus/locations/index.html (accessed March 19, 2012).

[5]W. L. Gore & Associates, Inc., "About Gore," W. L. Gore & Associates website, http://www.gore.com/en_xx/aboutus/index.html (accessed March 9, 2012).

[6]Hamel, p. 86.

[7]"Dr. Roy J. Plunkett, Discoverer of Fluoropolymers," obituary, *The Fluoropolymers Division Newsletter*, Summer 1994, p. 1, available at http://www.fluoropolymers.org/news/PlunkArt94.pdf (accessed March 10, 2012).

[8]Alan G. Robinson and Sam Stern, *Corporate Creativity: How Innovation and Improvement Actually Happen* (San Francisco: Berrett-Koehler, 1998), p. 177.

[9]Hamel, p. 85.

EXHIBIT 1
A Few Notable Events in W. L. Gore's History

Year	Event
1958	The enterprise's first product was Multi-Tet insulated wire and cable. Early associates were paid in part with awards of Gore stock, establishing a tradition of associate ownership through shareholding.
1960	The company issued its first profit share to associates.
1963	The company earned its first patent. U.S. Patent 3,082,292 was issued to Bob Gore for the "Multiconductor Wiring Strip" known as Multi-Tet cable.
1972	Gore's annual sales reached $10 million.
1981	Gore fibers were used in space suits in the inaugural space shuttle mission.
1986	Bill Gore died while hiking in Wyoming at age 74. Bob Gore became CEO.
1992	Glide dental floss was introduced nationally.
1997	Elixir guitar strings were introduced.
2000	Chuck Carroll became president and CEO.
2005	Vieve Gore passed away at age 91. Terri Kelly succeeded Chuck Carroll as president and CEO.
2007	Gore hit the $2 billion sales mark.

Source: Case writer's extracts from "50 Years of Gore History Online," W. L. Gore & Associates website, http://www.gore.com/timeline/ (accessed March 11, 2012).

knew Teflon's unique properties as an electrical insulator and was trying to coat wire with it. Finally, in the fall of 1957, with help from his son Bob, he succeeded in producing a good ribbon cable by sandwiching wire between Teflon tapes. DuPont, with its traditional business of supplying raw materials, didn't want to enter the wire business. Nonetheless, it granted Bill Gore permission to start his own company and agreed to provide the required supply of Teflon.[10]

In 1958, Bill and his wife, Genevieve ("Vieve"), both 45 years old, invested their life savings to form W. L. Gore & Associates, which operated from the basement of their home in the suburbs outside of Newark, Delaware. The company's first product was the Multi-Tet insulated wire and cable. In 1960, Gore received its first major order, for 7.5 miles of insulated ribbon cabling from the Denver Water Company. This required increased manufacturing capacity and prompted the company's move from the family basement into its first manufacturing plant nearby.[11]

In 1969, Bob Gore discovered that rapidly stretching PTFE did not break the material but made it strong, highly porous, and extremely versatile. This new polymer, expanded polytetrafluoroethylene (ePTFE), was the first step toward Gore-Tex, the waterproof and breathable fabric that made the company famous. This polymer found its way into shoes, gloves, head gear, and other outdoor adventure wear that was used in expeditions to the North

and South Poles and Mount Everest.[12] In 1981, the spacesuits worn by NASA astronauts on the space shuttle *Columbia* were made with Gore-Tex fabric.[13]

By 2011, Gore held more than 2,000 patents worldwide in fields ranging from fabrics, electronics, medical devices (implant biomaterials), consumer products, pharmaceuticals, and polymer processing.[14] More than 25 million people around the world had Gore's medical implants. Gore also supplied the most technologically advanced portfolio of membrane electrode assemblies (MEA products) for the fuel-cell industry.[15] Refer to Exhibit 1 for some other notable events in the history of the company.

---

[10]Robinson and Stern, pp. 177–178.

[11]W. L. Gore & Associates, Inc., "Our History," W. L. Gore & Associates website, http://www.gore.com/timeline/ (accessed March 10, 2012).

[12]Hamel, p. 85.

[13]W. L. Gore & Associates, Inc., "Our History," W. L. Gore & Associates website, http://www.gore.com/timeline/ (accessed March 10, 2012).

[14]Ibid.

[15]W. L. Gore & Associates, Inc., "About Gore," W. L. Gore & Associates website, http://www.gore.com/en_xx/aboutus/index.html (accessed March 10, 2012).

EXHIBIT 2
The Mission

Nurture a vibrant **Culture** that engages talented **Associates** who deliver innovative **Products** that create extraordinary value for all of our stakeholders

Culture	Associates	Products
Believes in individuals and the power of small teams	Live the culture	We are proud of
Encourages the entrepreneurial spirit	Act with the utmost integrity	Build upon our deep knowledge
Instills ownership for the success of the Enterprise	Offer divers perspectives	Leverage core technology and other competencies
Takes a global, long term view	Are passionate about what they do	Do what we say they will do

Source: Case writer, adapted from Terri Kelly, "Nurturing a Vibrant Culture to Drive Innovation," talk given on December 9, 2008, at Wong Auditorium, MIT Sloan School of Management, Cambridge, MA, available from MIT World video collection, http://mitworld.mit.edu/video/643.

Lattice Enterprise, No Hierarchies

I spend a significant amount of time focusing on the environment at Gore. I'm a firm believer that if you get the environment right, the business stuff is easy."

Terri Kelly, CEO, Gore[16]

Gore's mission statement put the culture of the firm ahead of its employees and its products (Exhibit 2).

While at DuPont, although Bill Gore was part of a much bigger organization, the small, focused teams that he used to work in had innate passion, initiative, and courage. The freewheeling spirit and operational autonomy that drove these small teams energized Gore, and he knew they invigorated his colleagues, too.[17] Further, Bill Gore's philosophy of management was deeply inspired by two sets of management theory: Abraham Maslow's hierarchy of needs, published in 1943, and Douglas McGregor's 1960 bestseller, *The Human Side of Enterprise*.[18]

Maslow suggested that there are five human needs—physiological, safety, belonging, esteem, and self-actualization—and these needs are in a hierarchical order in the shape of a pyramid. At the base of the pyramid are the most basic physiological needs—food, water, shelter, and clothing. At the next level of the need pyramid is safety, that is, security in one's person, finances, and health. At the next level is belonging, which is about friendship, intimacy, and family. Esteem needs include achievement, confidence, and respect. Finally, at the top of the pyramid is self-actualization, which includes creativity, morality, and problem solving.[19]

McGregor challenged the prevailing management beliefs of his time, which he labeled Theory X. According to him, Theory X assumes that the average human being has an inherent dislike of work and will avoid it if possible. Most people need to be forced to put in effort adequate to attain organizational success. By contrast, Theory Y assumes that the average human being finds work a source of satisfaction and will exercise self-direction and self-control in achieving the objectives he or she is committed to.[20]

These beliefs have been at the core of Gore's culture since its founding (Exhibit 3). Bill Gore deliberately set up his fledgling firm with the notion that an entire company can be designed to be bureaucracy free:

The simplicity and order of an authoritarian organization make it an almost irresistible temptation. Yet it is counter to the principles of individual freedom and smothers the creative growth of man. Freedom requires orderly restraint. The restraints imposed by the need for cooperation are minimized with a lattice organization.[21]

A lattice organization is one that involves direct transactions, self-commitment, natural leadership, and lacks assigned or assumed authority. Every successful organization has a lattice organization that underlies the façade of authoritarian hierarchy. It is through these lattice

[16]Terri Kelly, "Nurturing a Vibrant Culture to Drive Innovation," Talk given on December 9, 2008, at Wong Auditorium, MIT Sloan School of Management, Cambridge, MA, available from MIT World video collection, http://mitworld.mit.edu/video/643 (accessed March 9, 2012).

[17]Hamel, p. 85.

[18]Ibid., p. 86.

[19]Abraham Maslow, "A Theory of Human Motivation," *Psychological Review* 50, 376–390.

[20]Douglas McGregor, *The Human Side of Enterprise* (New York: McGraw-Hill, 1960).

[21]"The Lattice Organization," Slide presentation, Newark, DE: W. L. Gore & Associates, Inc., n.d., p. 13, available at http://www.boozersclass.org/Gore_lattice.pdf (accessed April 10, 2011).

EXHIBIT 3
Gore Culture

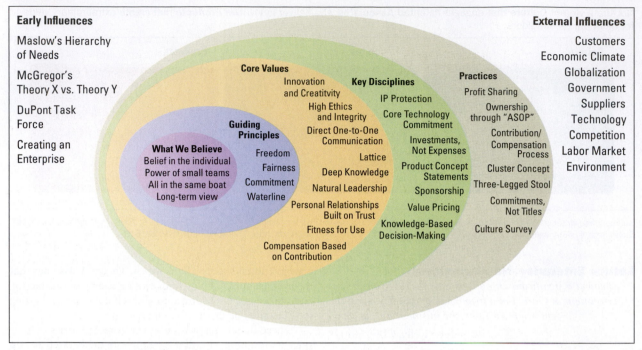

Early Influences

Maslow's Hierarchy
of Needs

McGregor's
Theory X vs. Theory Y

DuPont Task
Force

Creating an
Enterprise

Core Values
Innovation
and Creativity
High Ethics
and Integrity
Direct One-to-One
Communication
Lattice
Deep Knowledge
Natural Leadership
Personal Relationships
Built on Trust
Fitness for Use
Compensation Based
on Contribution

**Guiding
Principles**
Freedom
Fairness
Commitment
Waterline

What We Believe
Belief in the individual
Power of small teams
All in the same boat
Long-term view

Key Disciplines
IP Protection
Core Technology
Commitment
Investments,
Not Expenses
Product Concept
Statements
Sponsorship
Value Pricing
Knowledge-Based
Decision-Making

Practices
Profit Sharing
Ownership
through "ASOP"
Contribution/
Compensation
Process
Cluster Concept
Three-Legged Stool
Commitments,
Not Titles
Culture Survey

External Influences

Customers
Economic Climate
Globalization
Government
Suppliers
Technology
Competition
Labor Market
Environment

Source: Case writer, adapted from Kelly.

organizations that things get done, and most of us delight in going around the formal procedures and doing things the straightforward and easy way.[22]

While W. L. Gore & Associates seemingly had a divisional structure, underneath it was a very flat lattice organization: "no traditional organizational charts, no chains of command, nor pre-determined channels of communication."[23] Each person in the lattice could interact with every other person without an intermediary. All employees were known by the same title, "Associate." There was no hierarchy of communication. Associates were free to go directly to whoever they believed had an answer.

The lack of a formal organizational chart meant that the associates had to build their own network through personal relationships. It was their personal responsibility to connect and build their own lattice on their own initiative. This heavy emphasis on relationships extended beyond associates to customers, vendors, and surrounding communities. Direct face-to-face communication and phone calls were found to work best in collaborating, building, and maintaining long-term relationships.[24] So, co-location of facilities and plants was very important for Gore. For instance, there were 15 sites clustered around their headquarters, in Delaware, and 10 plants around Flagstaff, Arizona. This density enhanced both cross-functional and cross-team communication and collaboration.[25] Further,

most of Gore's buildings were very un-corporate-like: unassuming, bland, boring, and unimpressive.[26]

The company had four major divisions: fabrics, electronic products, medical products, and industrial products. It had small, product-focused business units, with all the company-wide support functions to ensure smooth day-to-day operation. No business unit was allowed to grow beyond a certain size and, with only a few exceptions, facility and manufacturing sites were limited to no more than 250 associates. Bill Gore believed that the firm had "to divide so that you can multiply."[27] A cluster of small plants in proximity

[22]Ibid., p. 2.

[23]W. L. Gore & Associates, Inc., "Our Culture," W. L. Gore & Associates website, http://www.gore.com/en_xx/aboutus/culture/index.html (accessed March 10, 2012).

[24]W. L. Gore & Associates, Inc., "Working in Our Unique Culture," W. L. Gore & Associates website, http://www.gore.com/en_xx/careers/whoweare/ourculture/gore-company-culture.html (accessed March 19, 2012).

[25]Hamel, p. 93.

[26]Alan Deutschman, "The Fabric of Creativity," *Fast Company*, December 19, 2007, http://www.fastcompany.com/magazine/89/open_gore.html?page=0%2C1 (accessed March 12, 2012).

[27]Simon Caulkin, "Gore-Tex Gets Made Without Managers," *The Observer*, November 2, 2008, http://www.guardian.co.uk/business/2008/nov/02/gore-tex-textiles-terri-kelly (accessed March 10, 2012).

allowed for everyone to know everyone else, have a sense of "ownership and identity,"[28] as well as accountability for their decisions. This closeness also helped associates to move easily between projects.

Bill Gore was not in favor of manuals or bureaucratic rules for prescribing a fixed solution in any given situation. So, according to Terri Kelly, president and CEO, policy manuals were quite useless, since every situation was different, and they took judgment away from individuals.[29] Gore's associates had the freedom to analyze and come up with their own conclusion as to the best way to deal with different situations. Rather than providing a playbook, the firm used a set of four guiding principles, originally articulated by Bill Gore, to help associates with their decisions and behaviors:

- **Freedom**: The company was designed to be an organization in which associates can achieve their own goals best by directing their efforts toward the success of the corporation; action is prized; ideas are encouraged; and making mistakes is viewed as part of the creative process. We define freedom as being empowered to encourage each other to grow in knowledge, skill, scope of responsibility, and range of activities. We believe that associates will exceed expectations when given the freedom to do so.
- **Fairness**: Everyone at Gore sincerely tries to be fair with each other, our suppliers, our customers, and anyone else with whom we do business.
- **Commitment**: We are not assigned tasks; rather, we each make our own commitments and keep them.
- **Waterline**: Everyone at Gore consults with other associates before taking actions that might be "below the waterline"—causing serious damage to the company.[30]

At Gore, a governing metaphor was "the Gore Ship": every ship has a "waterline." If you make one bad decision and that makes a hole in the ship above the waterline, the ship may be damaged, but it will survive and not sink. You can learn from that experience and move on. But if you make a hole below the waterline, the ship could sink.

At most firms, guiding principles tended to be nice displays in entrances and in hallways or brochures. At Gore, the associates had to live them every day, since there were no job descriptions or direct reports.

Leaders, Sponsors, and Associates: No Titles or Bosses

"[Gore] is a tough place to lead."[31]

There were no fixed or assigned authorities at Gore. Even the CEO did not have direct reports.[32] Leaders at Gore focused on decentralization, made working groups cross-functional, and allocated resources. Leaders could not make commitments for others. Extreme freedom and autonomy meant that all associates had to understand their own capabilities and limits, set their own agendas, and make commitments to deliver results. Results were evaluated by their peers.

Hiring was considered a "waterline" decision, so candidates were interviewed by a broad and diverse team. The hiring process was heavily weighted toward a candidate's fit with the values and the culture, rather than merely a technical fit. Gore hired fiercely motivated people who were able to take initiative, felt free to pursue ideas on their own, communicated effectively, built their own networks, and collaborated to create innovative products. Gore cherished the notion of "natural leadership."[33]

Natural leadership was defined by followership. It was not possible to be a leader at Gore unless you had followers. No one started as a leader at Gore. Leadership was earned over time. Most often, leaders emerged naturally by demonstrating special knowledge, skill, or experience that advanced business objectives. A leader had to keep re-earning the respect at every step, because teams had the liberty to fire their chief at any time. "We vote with our feet," [said] Rich Buckingham, a manufacturing leader in Gore's technical fabrics group. "If you call a meeting, and people show up, you're a leader."[34] A leader who had repeatedly earned such a label was free to use the word "leader" on his or her business card.[35]

Leadership was defined by one's ability to influence followers: leadership without authority. Influence was cultivated by building credibility. This required a great deal of preparation, validation, and people skills to marshal the resources, rather than dictation based on authority. This lack of authority also meant that leaders were often required to explain their decisions and actions. As Steve Young, a consumer-marketing expert hired from Vlasic Foods, quickly discovered, "If you tell anybody what to do here, they'll never work for you again."[36]

[28]Ibid.

[29]Kelly, "Nurturing a Vibrant Culture."

[30]W. L. Gore & Associates, Inc., "What We Believe," W. L. Gore & Associates website, http://www.gore.com/en_xx/careers/whoweare/whatwebelieve/gore-culture.html (accessed March 10, 2012).

[31]Kelly, "Nurturing a Vibrant Culture."

[32]Jeffrey Hollender, "Inventing the Future of Management: Part IV," Jeffrey Hollender Partners: The Next Generation of Business, http://www.jeffreyhollender.com/?p=309 (accessed March 10, 2012).

[33]Deutschman, "The Fabric of Creativity," p. C2.

[34]Hamel, p. 88.

[35]Ibid.

[36]Ibid., p. 92.

Kelly's path to becoming CEO, one of the very few titles at Gore, reflects the company's overall approach to leadership.[37] In 1983, Kelly joined Gore as a process engineer. During her early years at Gore, she focused on gaining experience as a product specialist with the then-small military fabrics business unit. She later led the unit and helped it grow into a leading producer of protective products for the armed forces globally. In 1998, Kelly gained recognition as part of the leadership team for the global Fabrics Division and helped establish Gore's first Asian fabrics manufacturing plant, in Shenzhen, China. Concurrently serving on the Enterprise Operations Committee, she also contributed to guiding the company's strategic direction.[38] In 2005, when Chuck Carroll retired as CEO, the management asked associates to choose someone they would be willing to follow. They weren't given a predefined list of names and were free to choose anyone. As Kelly recalled, "To my surprise, it was me."[39]

Every associate had a personal sponsor, someone who had voluntarily made a commitment to the associate's development, maximizing his or her contribution to the organization.[40] All understood that their job was to make everyone else successful.[41] The sponsors helped newcomers with their commitments and in fulfilling what it would take to deliver on them. They guided new recruits in finding a good fit between their skills and the needs of a particular team. During the first few months, a new associate was likely to experience different teams and be audited for a role. As the associates' commitments and needs changed, they or their sponsors were free to determine whether changes were needed, or even a new sponsor. Similarly, teams could choose whether they wanted to adopt a new member.[42] So, if an associate had difficulties finding a sponsor or a team, it was a strong indication that the associate would not be a good fit at Gore.[43]

One of the primary responsibilities of a sponsor, as a positive advocate, was to collect 360-degree information and feedback regarding the associate's personal development. This information, gathered from peers and leaders, was then shared with the appropriate compensation committee. Most sponsors were responsible for about five to seven associates. Leaders at Gore had four overarching requirements, centered on "living the culture" (see also Exhibit 4).

Leading Self—Be introspective, determine your capabilities, how your actions could impact the enterprise.

Getting it done—Be capable of doing the work, influencing others to get the necessary work done in an appropriate amount of time.

Shaping the vision—This differentiates a "Leader" and "Associate," the ability to shape or define the vision.

Leading others—One cannot go it alone and then have the ability to influence others to complete the tasks.

Living the culture—Did the leader uphold the values of culture in the process of getting their work done?[44]

EXHIBIT 4
Leadership Expectations

Source: Case writer, adapted from Kelly.

While these requirements described what was expected, certain behaviors did not fit with the culture. Self-promotion, being a "know-it-all," declaring, "I am an expert," and displaying a lone ranger[45] type of behavior were disdained at Gore. It would be evident when an associate did not exhibit the behaviors consistent with the culture. When this happened, the associate's sponsors and mentors would try to work with the individual to create an action plan to correct these behaviors; otherwise, the parties would look at other options—including voluntary or involuntary termination.

Only Commitments, No Assignments

Associates were responsible for managing their own workload and would be accountable to others on their team. Only the associate could make a commitment to do something—a task, a project, or a new role. Once the commitment was made, the associate was expected to meet it. New associates

[37]Hamel, p. 88.

[38]Kelly, "Nurturing a Vibrant Culture."

[39]Hamel, p. 89.

[40]Ibid.

[41]Kelly, "Nurturing a Vibrant Culture."

[42]Hamel, p. 89.

[43]Kelly, "Nurturing a Vibrant Culture."

[44]Paraphrased from Kelly, "Nurturing a Vibrant Culture."

[45]Business jargon for going it alone on decisions rather than consulting and including others in setting priorities and objectives. The term is based on a fictional character of radio and television shows, although the business connotation is a reductionist version of the character's ethic. See http://en.wikipedia.org/wiki/Lone_Ranger.

EXHIBIT 5
Setup for Success

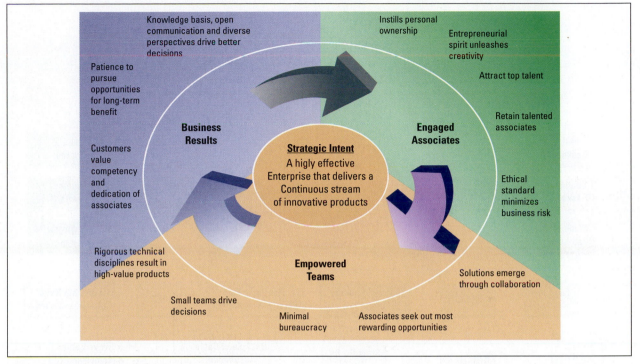

Source: Case writer, adapted from Kelly.

were regularly cautioned against overextending themselves, and associates could reject any request. But once someone said, "I will do this," it was considered a near-sacred oath.

Projects and teams were not formed by assignment; rather, a product or project concept was usually formed by an individual, who garnered support to move forward. As the project progressed, project founders—not managers—had to sell their idea to other associates who they felt had the necessary technical, market, and organizational skills to advance the project.

Objectives were set by those who made them happen. This strategy was based on the belief that associates who were allowed to choose which projects to sponsor—by committing their resources—would more likely be motivated, because they would choose projects they believed in and felt they had an ownership stake in their success. Further, small teams with highly motivated associates supporting a project or product concept were more likely to succeed, because they believed in what they were doing. Exhibit 5 highlights this link between associate engagement, autonomous teams, and business success.

Teams were usually quite diverse, consisting of mathematicians, engineers, accountants, machinists, and chemists. All these small, multidisciplinary, and boundary-crossing teams were freewheeling R&D groups who shared two common goals: to make money and have fun. Project teams were usually one-of-a-kind teams. They did not regroup

over and over for subsequent projects. The composition of teams was opportunity driven—each one required different types of people with different kinds of expertise.

Anyone Can Be an Innovator: Nerds Are Mavericks

All associates were given free dabble time. They could spend up to 10 percent of their work hours in pursuing their own purpose.[46] When associates joined Gore, they wouldn't have endless freedom; rather, the dabble time had to be earned.[47] Associates competed for the discretionary time of other talented individuals who were keen to work on something new and exciting and be part of promising projects. Assembling a self-motivated team to work on a new idea was, according to Kelly, "a process of giving away ownership of the idea to people who want to contribute. The project won't go anywhere if you don't let people run with it."[48]

As an instance, Dave Myers, an engineer who was principally developing cardiac implants for Gore's medical products division, used the Gore-Tex polymer to coat his mountain-bike cables as a grit repellent. That dabbling went on to become Gore's Ride-On line of bike cables.

[46]Deutschman, p. C2.

[47]Kelly, "Nurturing a Vibrant Culture."

[48]Hamel, p. 91.

EXHIBIT 6

Product Mix: Core Technology as a Common Link

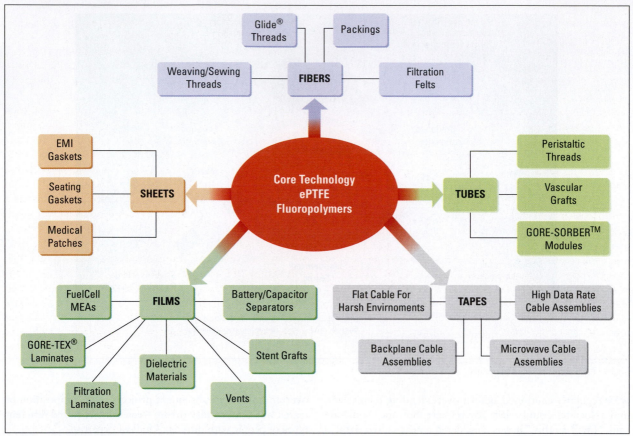

Source: Case writer, adapted from Kelly.

That in turn led to improving the strings that controlled large puppets at Walt Disney World theme parks and Chuck E. Cheese's restaurants.[49] Impressed with the results, Myers continued his experimentation with the concept. He thought that such a coating could be ideal for guitar strings, as it would prevent skin oil buildup on the string and help retain its tonal qualities. Gore's absence from the music industry and Myers's lack of expertise with guitars did not prevent Myers from spending his dabble time working on the guitar project. Instead, he sought volunteers with knowledge of guitars to help with the R&D.[50]

He was joined by Chuck Hebestreit, an engineer and a guitarist, and later by John Spencer, a musician himself. Together, they convinced six other associates to help with the project.[51] After three years of informal experimentation, the team thought they had hit a home run with a guitar string that could hold the tone three times longer than traditional ones did. But merchants refused to carry Gore's $15 Elixir guitar strings. Elixir was priced nearly four times more than the most expensive string on the market in 1996. So, Gore went directly to the backstage—the shows and subscriber lists of guitar magazines—and gave away 20,000 samples in the first

year.[52] The artists were hooked and Elixir quickly became the leading brand of acoustic guitar strings in the United States.[53]

At any given time, Gore had hundreds of projects at various stages of development.[54] While this proliferation could be perceived as chaotic, there was discipline behind it. First, most of the opportunities were clearly rooted in Gore's deep knowledge and mastery in ePTFE. Applications and adjacencies were explored and filtered using this technology boundary. Almost all of Gore's thousands of products were based on just that one very versatile polymer (Exhibit 6).

[49]Deutschman, p. C2.

[50]Hamel, p. 90.

[51]Deutschman, p. C2.

[52]Deutschman, p. C3.

[53]Ann Harrington, "Who's Afraid of a New Product? Not W. L. Gore. It Has Mastered the Art of Storming Completely Different Businesses," *Fortune*, November 10, 2003, available at http://money.cnn.com/magazines /fortune/fortune_archive/2003/11/10/352851/index.htm (accessed March 18, 2012).

[54]Ibid.

Second, ideas died if associates didn't sign up for projects. Product champions gave the gift of a new opportunity, and in return other associates donated their talent, experience, and commitment. So Gore could be considered as a "gift economy."[55] Associates had to "gift" their dabble time and get involved in their colleagues' projects.

"Real, Win, Worth"[56]

Gore did not care for me-too products. They pursued opportunities that were "unique and valuable."[57] Gore aimed for quantum improvements that gave them a highly differentiated positioning in the market place.

The belief at Gore was that it was tough to plan for innovation, but it was possible to organize for it.[58] "We have a methodical way of how we do innovation."[59]

At Gore, the journey from dabbling to profitability was guided by three "reality checks." According to Gore's former president, Chuck Carroll, "We go through an exercise called Real, Win, Worth. . . . Is the opportunity real? Is there really somebody out there that will buy this? Can we win? What do the economics look like? Can we make money doing this? Is it unique and valuable? Can we have a sustained advantage [such as a patent]?"[60] Each post-dabble project was scrutinized with periodic cross-functional reviews that required the project to survive these checks.[61]

Early on, the product champions identified critical hypotheses and tested fundamental assumptions in low-cost ways. The company never invested big until all the key uncertainties were resolved. Associates had a lot of latitude and discretionary time to experiment and test their ideas. But to take the project beyond the dabble stage, the team needed to show that the product opportunity was real. The team had to demonstrate that the opportunity solved a genuine customer problem for which the customer would be willing to pay—usually a premium. This step was crucial in order to attract resources to the project.[62] "It starts with the consumer. If we have a new technology but if it is not matching a consumer need, then it won't go far," said Christy Haywood, product manager from Gore's fabric division.[63]

As a project evolved from dabble-time experiment to one that sought formal support, the team prepared to participate in a series of peer reviews in which they were pressed on the fitness of the project. First, did the opportunity create a unique and differentiated product? Did the company get a technological advantage that it could defend? And did Gore have the resources and capabilities to make sure the product would do what the team said it would do?

Purpose, Passion, Persistence, Patience

"Gore has immense patience about the time it takes to get it right and get it to market," says Bob Doak, who leads a Gore plant in Dundee, Scotland. "If there's a glimmer of hope, you're encouraged to keep a project going and see if it could become a big thing."[64]

Project teams self-organized or coalesced around passionate champions. Promising projects got nurtured for as long as they continued to pique the interest of a few associates and were not "burning through too much cash."[65] Concepts were given ample time, sometimes even years, to take form, and there were no cut-throat timelines or calendar marks. However, the company often knew when to pull the plug on a project, whether it was a new initiative or a successful business.

For instance, the origin of Glide dental floss dated back to 1971, when Bill Gore tried to use a Gore-Tex fabric ribbon to floss his teeth. For about 20 years, the company wasn't able to take the product to market, as it could not get health care product companies to adopt its technology or local drug stores to put the product on their shelves. In 1991, John Spencer came up with the idea of promoting the floss as a medical technology product instead of a normal consumer product. He gave away free samples of the floss to dentists, who were impressed with its shred resistance and helped build a strong followership among dental hygienists.[66] By 2003, when it sold the dental floss business to Procter & Gamble, Gore had reached dental floss sales of over $45 million in the U.S. market. Chuck Carroll commented on why Gore sold its successful Glide business to P&G: "To stay in that market long-term, you really need a whole family of health-care products. The Wal-Marts don't want to buy floss from one guy and toothpaste from another."[67]

Freedom to Experiment: No Fear of Failure

Ideas were encouraged, action was prized, and making mistakes was viewed as part of the creative process. There were very low barriers to experimentation, as there was always ready access to equipment and materials. A project failure did not necessarily mean the team failed. Associates were

[55]Hamel, p. 91.

[56]Harrington.

[57]Ibid.

[58]Hamel, p. 96.

[59]Kelly, "Nurturing a Vibrant Culture."

[60]Harrington.

[61]Ibid.

[62]Hamel, p. 95.

[63]Emily Walzer, "Ingredients for Innovation," *Textile Insight*, May/June 2010, p. 18, available at http://www.gore.com/MungoBlobs/861/698/TextileInsightW_L_Gore.pdf (accessed March 18, 2012).

[64]Deutschman, p. C4.

[65]Hamel, p. 95.

[66]Lindsay Hunt, "W. L. Gore, MarketBuster," p. 2, available at http://www.marketbusting.com/casestudies/WL%20Gore.pdf (accessed March 18, 2012).

[67]Harrington.

ultimately judged by the success of the entire organization, and the individual's contribution to the enterprise was evaluated by a thorough 360-degree review process to score and rank the individuals in a team. When a project failed, there was a postmortem: Was the concept flawed? Were there poor decisions made along the way? Was it a flawed approach to the solution, or was it simply poorly executed? The goal of this postmortem was to learn from the experiment and to leverage it in other parts of the enterprise. When an initiative was killed, they "celebrated" with beer and champagne.[68]

Compensation for associates was based on contribution. It was determined by a committee of leaders with expertise in the functional area. The committee reviewed and rank-ordered the associates on the basis of input from the leaders as well as the associate's peer group regarding his or her impact and effectiveness.[69] Even if projects failed or couldn't hit targets, contribution was judged on the basis of the associate's overall impact on the enterprise. For instance, coaching new hires was considered as a significant contribution. To ensure fairness and competitiveness externally, Gore continually compared compensation packages with similar firms and rewarded associates accordingly. They were also compensated through stock and profit-sharing programs.[70] "We are all in the same boat."[71]

After one year of employment, all associates were eligible to be owners in the firm. Employees owned nearly 25 percent of the firm.[72] Both risks and rewards were shared, with a commitment to long-term success. Investment decisions were based on long-term payoff. The costs and resources associated with experimentation and research were not looked upon as "expenses" but rather as "investments."[73] Associates were encouraged to treat investments as if they were using their own money.

Freedom with Discipline

While there was very little bureaucracy within Gore, it was not as though there was endless freedom. It was not a free-for-all environment. Knowing that distributed leadership could very quickly devolve into chaos, Gore had several sources of "key disciplines" (Exhibit 3). Gore had very methodical ways of describing opportunities, leveraging core technologies, evaluating opportunities in terms of business results, demanding peer-review processes, giving associates discretion

to explore (earned over time), pursuing rigorous patent protection of its intellectual property, and ensuring sponsors' personal commitment to the success of associates.[74]

Culture across Cultures

In 2012, Gore was operating in 30 countries. One would have expected that a strong culture like Gore's would be quite a challenge to implement in certain countries, especially in Asia. Gore had made sure that there was room for adaptation. For instance, in Korea, it was inconceivable not to have business cards with clearly labeled titles. It was critical for communication with customers and business partners, as well as for the associates' families. So, Korean associates had all kinds of fancy titles on their business cards. Yet they very well knew that these titles didn't mean anything internally and having them didn't mean they could behave differently.[75]

While subcultures existed within Gore around the world with subtle differences, some of the fundamental beliefs of Gore were held sacrosanct. According to Kelly, "The values are the same in Asia. Who doesn't want to be believed in? Who doesn't want to feel they can make a huge contribution? Most people want to be part of a team."[76]

Fifty years after its founding, a majority of the core tenets of Bill Gore's management philosophy were still thriving at W. L. Gore & Associates—not just in the U.S. operations but in several of its divisions around the world.

[68]Deutschman, p. C3.

[69]Hamel, p. 92.

[70]Dawn Anfuso, "1999 Optimas Award Profile W. L. Gore and Associates Inc.," *Workforce*, March 1, 1999, available at http://www.workforce.com/article/19990301/NEWS02/303019952 (accessed March 18, 2012).

[71]Kelly, "Nurturing a Vibrant Culture."

[72]Anfuso.

[73]Kelly, "Nurturing a Vibrant Culture."

[74]Ibid.

[75]Kelly, "Nurturing a Vibrant Culture."

[76]Tina Nielsen, "WL Gore (Company Profile)," *Director*, February 2, 2010, http://www.director.co.uk/magazine/2010/2_Feb/WLGore_63_06.html (accessed April 4, 2012).

INTEGRATIVE CASE 2.0
Rondell Data Corporation*

"Damn it, he's done it again!" Frank Forbus threw the stack of prints and specifications down on his desk in disgust. The Model 802 wide-band modulator, released for production the previous Thursday, had just come back to Frank's Engineering Services Department with a caustic note that began, "This one can't be produced either. . . ." It was the fourth time production had kicked the design back.

Frank Forbus, director of engineering for Rondell Data Corporation, was normally a quiet man. But the Model 802 was stretching his patience; it was beginning to look just like other new products that had hit delays and problems in the transition from design to production during the eight months Frank had worked for Rondell. These problems were nothing new at the sprawling old Rondell factory; Frank's predecessor in the engineering job had run afoul of them, too, and had finally been fired for protesting too vehemently about the other departments. But the Model 802 should have been different. Frank had met two months before (July 3, 1998) with the firm's president, Bill Hunt, and with the factory superintendent, Dave Schwab, to smooth the way for the new modulator design. He thought back to the meeting. . . .

"Now we all know there's a tight deadline on the 802," Bill Hunt said, "and Frank's done well to ask us to talk about its introduction. I'm counting on both of you to find any snags in the system and to work together to get that first production run out by October 2nd. Can you do it?"

"We can do it in production if we get a clean design two weeks from now, as scheduled," answered Dave Schwab, the grizzled factory superintendent. "Frank and I have already talked about that, of course. I'm setting aside time in the machine shop, and we'll be ready. If the design goes over schedule, though, I'll have to fill in with other runs, and it will cost us a bundle to break in for the 802. How does it look in engineering, Frank?"

"I've just reviewed the design for the second time," Frank replied. "If Ron Porter can keep the salesmen out of our hair and avoid any more last-minute changes, we've got a shot. I've pulled the draftsmen off three other overdue jobs to get this one out. But, Dave, that means we can't spring engineers loose to confer with your production people on manufacturing problems."

"Well, Frank, most of those problems are caused by the engineers, and we need them to resolve the difficulties. We've all agreed that production bugs come from both of us bowing to sales pressure, and putting equipment into production before the designs are really ready. That's just what we're trying to avoid on the 802. But I can't have 500 people sitting on their hands waiting for an answer from your people. We'll have to have some engineering support."

Bill Hunt broke in. "So long as you two can talk calmly about the problem I'm confident you can resolve it. What a relief it is, Frank, to hear the way you're approaching this. With Kilmann (the previous director of engineering) this conversation would have been a shouting match. Right, Dave?" Dave nodded and smiled.

"Now there's one other thing you should both be aware of," Hunt continued. "Doc Reeves and I talked last night about a new filtering technique, one that might improve the signal-to-noise ratio of the 802 by a factor of two. There's a chance Doc can come up with it before the 802 reaches production, and if it's possible, I'd like to use the new filters. That would give us a real jump on the competition."

Four days after that meeting, Frank found that two of his key people on the 802 design had been called to production for emergency consultation on a bug found in final assembly: two halves of a new data transmission interface wouldn't fit together because recent changes in the front end required a different chassis design for the back end.

Another week later, Doc Reeves walked into Frank's office, proud as a new parent, with the new filter design. "This won't affect the other modules of the 802 much," Doc had said. "Look, it takes a few connectors, some changes in the wiring harness, and some new shielding, and that's all."

Frank had tried to resist the last-minute design changes, but Bill Hunt had stood firm. With a lot of overtime by the engineers and draftsmen, engineering services should still be able to finish the prints in time.

Two engineers and three draftsmen went onto 12-hour days to get the 802 ready, but the prints were still five days late reaching Dave Schwab. Two days later, the prints came back to Frank, heavily annotated in red. Schwab had worked all day Saturday to review the job and had found more than a dozen discrepancies in the prints—most of them caused by the new filter

*John A. Seeger, Professor of Management, Bentley College. Reprinted with permission.

design and insufficient checking time before release. Correction of those design faults had brought on a new generation of discrepancies; Schwab's cover note on the second return of the prints indicated he'd had to release the machine capacity he'd been holding for the 802. On the third iteration, Schwab committed his photo and plating capacity to another rush job. The 802 would be at least one month late getting into production. Ron Porter, vice president for sales, was furious. His customer needed 100 units NOW, he said. Rondell was the customer's only late supplier.

"Here we go again," thought Frank Forbus.

Company History

Rondell Data Corporation traced its lineage through several generations of electronics technology. Its original founder, Bob Rondell, had set the firm up in 1939 as "Rondell Equipment Company" to manufacture several electrical testing devices he had invented as an engineering faculty member at a large university. The firm branched into radio broadcasting equipment in 1947 and into data transmission equipment in the late 1960s. A well-established corps of direct salespeople, mostly engineers, called on industrial, scientific, and government accounts but concentrated heavily on original equipment manufacturers. In this market, Rondell had a long-standing reputation as a source of high-quality, innovative designs. The firm's salespeople fed a continual stream of challenging problems into the Engineering Department, where the creative genius of Ed "Doc" Reeves and several dozen other engineers "converted problems to solutions" (as the sales brochure bragged). Product design formed the spearhead of Rondell's growth.

By 1998, Rondell offered a wide range of products in its two major lines. Broadcast and telecommunications equipment sales now accounted for more than half of company sales. In the field of data transmission, an increasing number of orders called for unique specifications, ranging from specialized display panels to entirely untried designs.

The company had grown from a few dozen employees in the early years to over 800 in 1998. (Exhibit 1 shows the 1998 organization chart of key employees.) Bill Hunt, who had been with the company since 1972, had presided over much of that growth, and he took great pride in preserving the "family spirit" of the old organization. Informal relationships between Rondell's veteran employees formed the backbone of the firm's day-to-day operations; all the managers relied on personal contact, and Hunt often insisted that the absence of bureaucratic red tape was a key factor in recruiting outstanding engineering talent. The personal management approach extended throughout the factory. All exempt employees were paid on a straight salary plus a share of the profits. Rondell boasted an extremely loyal group of senior employees and very low turnover in nearly all areas of the company.

The highest turnover job in the firm was Frank Forbus's. Frank had joined Rondell in January 1998, replacing Jim Kilmann, who had been director of engineering for only 10 months. Kilmann, in turn, had replaced Tom MacLeod, a talented engineer who had made a promising start but had taken to drink after a year in the job. MacLeod's predecessor had been a genial old-timer who retired at 70 after 30 years in charge of engineering. (Doc Reeves had refused the directorship in each of the recent changes, saying, "Hell, that's no promotion for a bench man like me. I'm no administrator.")

For several years, the firm had experienced a steadily increasing number of disputes between research, engineering, sales, and production people—disputes generally centered on the problem of new product introduction. Quarrels between departments became more numerous under MacLeod, Kilmann, and Forbus. Some managers associated those disputes with the company's recent decline in profitability—a decline that, in spite of higher sales and gross revenues, was beginning to bother people in 1998. President Bill Hunt commented:

Better cooperation, I'm sure, could increase our output by 5–10 percent. I'd hoped Kilmann could solve the problems, but pretty obviously he was too young, too arrogant. People like him—conflict type of personality—bother me. I don't like strife, and with him it seemed I spent all my time smoothing out arguments. Kilmann tried to tell everyone else how to run their departments, without having his own house in order. That approach just wouldn't work here at Rondell. Frank Forbus, now, seems much more in tune with our style of organization. I'm really hopeful now.

Still, we have just as many problems now as we did last year. Maybe even more. I hope Frank can get a handle on engineering services soon. . . .

The Engineering Department: Research

According to the organization chart (see Exhibit 1), Frank Forbus was in charge of both research (really the product development function) and engineering services (which provided engineering support). To Forbus, however, the relationship with research was not so clear-cut:

Doc Reeves is one of the world's unique people, and none of us would have it any other way. He's a creative genius. Sure, the chart says he works for me, but we all know Doc does his own thing. He's not the least bit interested in management routines, and I can't count on him to take any responsibility in scheduling projects, or checking budgets, or what-have-you. But as long as Doc is director of research, you can bet this company will keep on leading the field. He has more ideas per hour than most people have per year, and he keeps the whole engineering staff fired up. Everybody loves Doc—and you can count me in on that, too. In a way, he works for me, sure. But that's not what's important.

Rondell Data Corporation 1998 Organization Chart

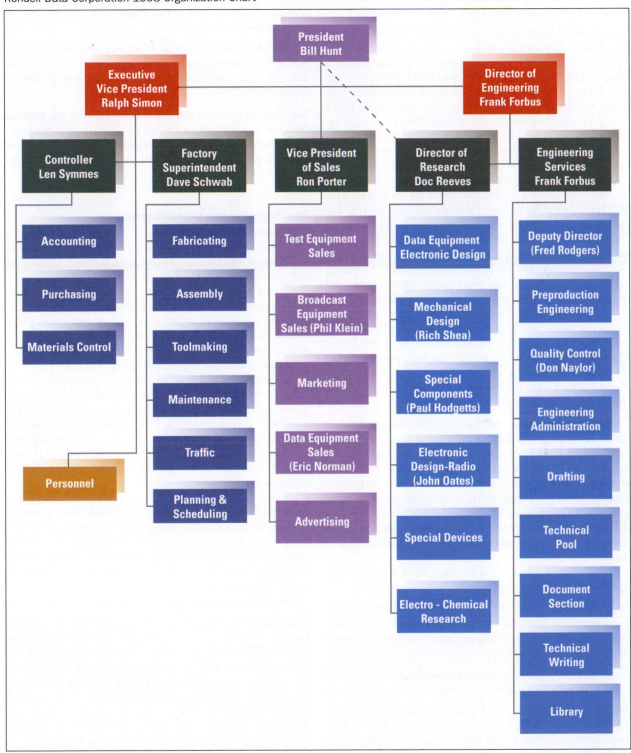

Doc Reeves—unhurried, contemplative, casual, and candid—tipped his stool back against the wall of his research cubicle and talked about what was important:

Development engineering. That's where the company's future rests. Either we have it there, or we don't have it.

There's no kidding ourselves that we're anything but a bunch of Rube Goldbergs here. But that's where the biggest kicks come from—from solving development problems, and dreaming up new ways of doing things. That's why I so look forward to the special contracts we get involved in. We accept them not for the revenue they represent, but because they subsidize the basic development work which goes into all our basic products.

This is a fantastic place to work. I have a great crew and they can really deliver when the chips are down. Why, Bill Hunt and I (he gestured toward the neighboring cubicle, where the president's name hung over the door) are likely to find as many people here at work at 10:00 P.M. as at 3:00 in the afternoon. The important thing here is the relationships between people; they're based on mutual respect, not on policies and procedures. Administrative red tape is a pain. It takes away from development time.

Problems? Sure, there are problems now and then. There are power interests in production, where they sometimes resist change. But I'm not a fighting man, you know. I suppose if I were I might go in there and push my weight around a little. But I'm an engineer and can do more for Rondell sitting right here or working with my own people. That's what brings results.

Other members of the Research Department echoed Doc's views and added some additional sources of satisfaction with their work. They were proud of the personal contacts they built up with customers' technical staffs—contacts that increasingly involved travel to the customers' sites to serve as expert advisers in the preparation of overall system design specifications. The engineers were also delighted with the department's encouragement of their personal development, continuing education, and independence on the job.

But there were problems, too. Rick Shea, of the mechanical design section, noted:

In the old days I really enjoyed the work—and the people I worked with. But now there's a lot of irritation. I don't like someone breathing down my neck. You can be hurried into jeopardizing the design.

John Oates, head of the electronic design section, was another designer with definite views:

Production engineering is almost nonexistent in this company. Very little is done by the preproduction section in engineering services. Frank Forbus has been trying to get preproduction into the picture, but he won't succeed because you can't start from such an ambiguous position.

There have been three directors of engineering in three years. Frank can't hold his own against the others in the company. Kilmann was too aggressive. Perhaps no amount of tact would have succeeded.

Paul Hodgetts was head of special components in the research and development department. Like the rest of the department, he valued bench work. But he complained of engineering services:

The services don't do things we want them to do. Instead, they tell us what they're going to do. I should probably go to Frank, but I don't get any decisions there. I know I should go through Frank, but this holds things up, so I often go direct.

The Engineering Department: Engineering Services

The Engineering Services Department provided ancillary services to R & D and served as liaison between engineering and the other Rondell departments. Among its main functions were drafting; management of the central technicians' pool; scheduling and expediting engineering products; documentation and publication of parts lists and engineering orders; preproduction engineering (consisting of the final integration of individual design components into mechanically compatible packages); and quality control (which included inspection of incoming parts and materials and final inspection of subassemblies and finished equipment). Top management's description of the department included the line, "ESD is responsible for maintaining cooperation with other departments, providing services to the development engineers, and freeing more valuable people in R & D from essential activities that are diversions from and beneath their main competence."

Many of Frank Forbus's 75 employees were located in other departments. Quality control people were scattered through the manufacturing and receiving areas, and technicians worked primarily in the research area or the prototype fabrication room. The remaining ESD personnel were assigned to leftover nooks and crannies near production or engineering sections.

Frank Forbus described his position:

My biggest problem is getting acceptance from the people I work with. I've moved slowly rather than risk antagonism. I saw what happened to Kilmann, and I want to avoid that. But although his precipitate action had won over a few of the younger R & D people, he certainly didn't have the department's backing. Of course, it was the resentment of other departments that eventually caused his discharge. People have been slow accepting me here. There's nothing really overt, but I get a negative reaction to my ideas.

My role in the company has never been well defined really. It's complicated by Doc's unique position, of course, and also by the fact that ESD sort of grew by itself over the years, as the design engineers concentrated more and more on the creative parts of product development. I wish I could be more involved in the technical side. That's been my training, and it's a lot of fun. But in our setup, the technical side is the least necessary for me to be involved in.

Schwab (production head) is hard to get along with. Before I came and after Kilmann left, there were six months intervening when no one was really doing any scheduling. No work loads were figured, and unrealistic promises were made about releases. This puts us in an awkward position. We've been scheduling way beyond our capacity to manufacture or engineer.

Certain people within R & D—for instance, John Oates, head of the electronic design section—understand scheduling well and meet project deadlines, but this is not generally true of the rest of the R & D department, especially the mechanical engineers who won't commit themselves. Most of the complaints come from sales and production department heads because items—like the 802—are going to production before they are fully developed, under pressure from sales to get out the unit, and this snags the whole process. Somehow, engineering services should be able to intervene and resolve these complaints, but I haven't made much headway so far. I should be able to go to Hunt for help, but he's too busy most of the time, and his major interest is the design side of engineering, where he got his own start. Sometimes he talks as though he's the engineering director as well as president. I have to put my foot down; there are problems here that the front office just doesn't understand.

Salespeople were often observed taking their problems directly to designers, while production frequently threw designs back at R & D, claiming they could not be produced and demanding the prompt attention of particular design engineers. The latter were frequently observed in conference with production supervisors on the assembly floor. Frank went on:

The designers seem to feel they're losing something when one of us tries to help. They feel it's a reflection on them to have someone take over what they've been doing. They seem to want to carry a project right through to the final stages, particularly the mechanical people. Consequently, engineering services people are used below their capacity to contribute and our department is denied functions it should be performing. There's not as much use made of engineering services as there should be.

Frank Forbus's technician supervisor added his comments:

Production picks out the engineer who'll be the "bum of the month." They pick on every little detail instead of using their heads and making the minor changes that have to be made. The 15-to-20-year people shouldn't have to prove their ability any more, but they spend four hours defending themselves and four hours getting the job done. I have no one to go to when I need help. Frank Forbus is afraid. I'm trying to help him but he can't help me at this time. I'm responsible for fifty people and I've got to support them.

Fred Rodgers, whom Frank had brought with him to the company as an assistant, gave another view of the situation:

I try to get our people in preproduction to take responsibility, but they're not used to it and people in other departments don't usually see them as best qualified to solve the problem. There's a real barrier for a newcomer here. Gaining people's confidence is hard. More and more, I'm wondering whether there really is a job for me here.

(Rodgers left Rondell a month later.) Another of Forbus's subordinates gave his view:

If Doc gets a new product idea, you can't argue. But he's too optimistic. He judges that others can do what he does—but there's only one Doc Reeves. We've had 900 production change orders this year—they changed 2,500 drawings. If I were in Frank's shoes I'd put my foot down on all this new development. I'd look at the reworking we're doing and get production set up the way I wanted it. Kilmann was fired when he was doing a good job. He was getting some system in the company's operations. Of course, it hurt some people. There is no denying that Doc is the most important person in the company. What gets overlooked is that Hunt is a close second, not just politically but in terms of what he contributes technically and in customer relations.

This subordinate explained that he sometimes went out into the production department but Schwab, the production head, resented this. Personnel in production said that Kilmann had failed to show respect for old-timers and was always meddling in other departments' business. This was why he had been fired, they contended.

Don Taylor was in charge of quality control. He commented:

I am now much more concerned with administration and less with work. It is one of the evils you get into. There is tremendous detail in this job. I listen to everyone's opinion. Everybody is important. There shouldn't be distinctions—distinctions between people. I'm not sure whether Frank has to be a fireball like Kilmann. I think the real question is whether Frank is getting the job done. I know my job is essential. I want to supply service to the more talented people and give them information so they can do their jobs better.

The Sales Department

Ron Porter was angry. His job was supposed to be selling, he said, but instead it had turned into settling disputes inside the plant and making excuses to waiting customers. He jabbed a finger toward his desk:

You see that telephone? I'm actually afraid nowadays to hear it ring. Three times out of five, it will be a customer who's hurting because we've failed to deliver on schedule. The other two calls will be from production or ESD, telling me some schedule has slipped again.

The Model 802 is typical. Absolutely typical. We padded the delivery date by six weeks, to allow for contingencies. Within two months, the slack had evaporated. Now it looks like we'll be lucky to ship it before Christmas. (It was now November 28.) We're ruining our reputation in the market. Why, just last week one of our best customers—people we've worked with for 15 years—tried to hang a penalty clause on their latest order.

We shouldn't have to be after the engineers all the time. They should be able to see what problems they create without our telling them.

Phil Klein, head of broadcast sales under Porter, noted that many sales decisions were made by top management. Sales was understaffed, he thought, and had never really been able to get on top of the job.

We have grown further and further away from engineering. The director of engineering does not pass on the information that we give him. We need better relationships there. It is very difficult for us to talk to customers about development problems without technical help. We need each other. The whole of engineering is now too isolated from the outside world. The morale of ESD is very low. They're in a bad spot—they're not well organized.

People don't take much to outsiders here. Much of this is because the expectation is built up by top management that jobs will be filled from the bottom. So it's really tough when an outsider like Frank comes in.

Eric Norman, order and pricing coordinator for data equipment, talked about his own relationship with the Production Department:

Actually, I get along with them fairly well. Oh, things could be better of course, if they were more cooperative generally. They always seem to say, "It's my bat and ball, and we're playing by my rules." People are afraid to make production mad; there's a lot of power in there. But you've got to understand that production has its own set of problems. And nobody in Rondell is working any harder than Dave Schwab to try to straighten things out.

The Production Department

Dave Schwab had joined Rondell just after the Vietnam War, in which he had seen combat duty as well as intelligence duty. Both experiences had been useful in his first year of civilian employment at Rondell. The factory superintendent and several middle managers had been, apparently, indulging in highly questionable side deals with Rondell's suppliers. Dave Schwab had gathered evidence, revealed the

situation to Bill Hunt, and stood by the president in the ensuing unsavory situation. Seven months after joining the company, Dave was named factory superintendent.

His first move had been to replace the fallen managers with a new team from outside. This group did not share the traditional Rondell emphasis on informality and friendly personal relationships and had worked long and hard to install systematic manufacturing methods and procedures. Before the reorganization, production had controlled purchasing, stock control, and final quality control (where final assembly of products in cabinets was accomplished). Because of the wartime events, management decided on a checks-and-balance system of organization and removed these three departments from production jurisdiction. The new production managers felt they had been unjustly penalized by this organization, particularly since they had uncovered the behavior that was detrimental to the company in the first place.

By 1998, the production department had grown to 500 employees, 60 percent of whom worked in the assembly area—an unusually pleasant environment that had been commended by *Factory* magazine for its colorful decoration, cleanliness, and low noise level. An additional 30 percent of the work force, mostly skilled machinists, staffed the finishing and fabrication department. About 60 others performed scheduling, supervisory, and maintenance duties. Production workers were nonunion, hourly-paid, and participated in both the liberal profit-sharing program and the stock purchase plan. Morale in production was traditionally high, and turnover was extremely low.

Dave Schwab commented:

To be efficient, production has to be a self-contained department. We have to control what comes into the department and what goes out. That's why purchasing, inventory control, and quality ought to run out of this office. We'd eliminate a lot of problems with better control there. Why, even Don Taylor in QC would rather work for me than for ESD; he's said so himself. We understand his problems better.

The other departments should be self-contained too. That's why I always avoid the underlings and go straight to the department heads with any questions. I always go down the line.

I have to protect my people from outside disturbances. Look what would happen if I let unfinished, half-baked designs in here—there'd be chaos. The bugs have to be found before the drawings go into the shop, and it seems I'm the one who has to find them. Look at the 802, for example. (Dave had spent most of Thanksgiving red-penciling the latest set of prints.) ESD should have found every one of those discrepancies. They just don't check drawings properly. They change most of the things I flag, but then they fail to trace through the impact of those changes on the rest of the design. I shouldn't have to do that. And those engineers are tolerance crazy. They want everything to a millionth of an inch. I'm the only one in the company who's had any experience with actually machining things to a millionth of an inch. We make sure that the things that engineers say on their drawings actually have to be that way and whether they're obtainable from the kind of raw material we buy.

That shouldn't be production's responsibility, but I have to do it. Accepting bad prints wouldn't let us ship the order any quicker. We'd only make a lot of junk that had to be reworked. And that would take even longer.

This way, I get to be known as the bad guy, but I guess that's just part of the job. (He paused with a wry smile.) Of course, what really gets them is that I don't even have a degree.

Dave had fewer bones to pick with the Sales Department because, he said, they trusted him.

When we give Ron Porter a shipping date, he knows the equipment will be shipped then.

You've got to recognize, though, that all of our new-product problems stem from sales making absurd commitments on equipment that hasn't been fully developed. That always means trouble. Unfortunately, Hunt always backs sales up, even when they're wrong. He always favors them over us.

Ralph Simon, age 65, executive vice president of the company, had direct responsibility for Rondell's production department. He said:

There shouldn't really be a dividing of departments among top management in the company. The president should be czar over all. The production people ask me to do something for them, and I really can't do it. It creates bad feelings between engineering and production, this special attention that they [R & D] get from Bill. But then Hunt likes to dabble in design. Schwab feels that production is treated like a poor relation.

The Executive Committee

At the executive committee meeting on December 6, it was duly recorded that Dave Schwab had accepted the prints and specifications for the Model 802 modulator and had set Friday, December 29, as the shipping date for the first 10 pieces. Bill Hunt, in the chairperson's role, shook his head and changed the subject quickly when Frank tried to open the agenda to a discussion of interdepartmental coordination.

The executive committee itself was a brainchild of Rondell's controller, Len Symmes, who was well aware of the disputes that plagued the company. Symmes had convinced Bill Hunt and Ralph Simon to meet every two weeks with their department heads, and the meetings were formalized with Hunt, Simon, Ron Porter, Dave Schwab, Frank Forbus, Doc Reeves, Symmes, and the personnel director attending. Symmes explained his intent and the results:

Doing things collectively and informally just doesn't work as well as it used to. Things have been gradually getting worse for at least two years now. We had to start thinking in terms of formal organization relationships. I did the first organization chart, and the executive committee was my idea too—but neither idea is contributing much help, I'm afraid. It takes top management to make an organization click. The rest of us can't act much differently until the top people see the need for us to change.

I had hoped the committee especially would help get the department managers into a constructive planning process. It hasn't worked out that way because Mr. Hunt really doesn't see the need for it. He uses the meetings as a place to pass on routine information.

Merry Christmas

"Frank, I didn't know whether to tell you now, or after the holiday." It was Friday, December 22, and Frank Forbus was standing awkwardly in front of Bill Hunt's desk.

"But, I figured you'd work right through Christmas Day if we didn't have this talk, and that just wouldn't have been fair to you. I can't understand why we have such poor luck in the engineering director's job lately. And I don't think it's entirely your fault. But. . . ."

Frank only heard half of Hunt's words and said nothing in response. He'd be paid through February 28. . . . He should use the time for searching. . . . Hunt would help all he could. . . . Jim Kilmann was supposed to be doing well at his own new job and might need more help. . . .

Frank cleaned out his desk and numbly started home. The electronic carillon near his house was playing a Christmas carol. Frank thought again of Hunt's rationale: Conflict still plagued Rondell—and Frank had not made it go away. Maybe somebody else could do it.

"And what did Santa Claus bring you, Frankie?" he asked himself.

"The sack. Only the empty sack."

INTEGRATIVE CASE 3.0
IKEA: Scandinavian Style

"Behind the mountain there are people too." Old Swedish Proverb

As one of the world's most successful businessmen, Ingvar Kamprad never forgot the dreams, aspirations, and hard work of rural people or their ability to find solutions to difficult problems. Growing up on the farmland of southern Sweden, Kamprad embodied many of the traits of the hearty men and women who surrounded him and, as an ambitious working boy, revealed the business traits that contributed to his later success and reputation. As a child, Kamprad learned the concept of serving the needs of ordinary people by purchasing matches in bulk, which he then sold to rural customers at a profit. While still in his teens, he expanded his retail operation to sell everything from pencils to Christmas cards and upgraded the efficiency of his distribution by using the regional milk-delivery system.

Beginnings

In 1943, at age 17, Kamprad formed IKEA with initials representing his first and last names, along with that of the family farm (Elmtaryd) and the nearby village (Agunnaryd). Anticipating the rising consumerism amid the rebuilding boom that followed the war, IKEA moved quickly to provide families with low-cost furniture designs through the convenience of catalog sales. With the opening of the company's first showroom in 1953, Kamprad created a model of vertical integration, uniting a variety of suppliers under the IKEA umbrella, coordinating long-run production schedules, and controlling distribution. That model expanded in 1964 with the introduction of the first warehouse store, eliminating an entire step in product distribution by allowing warehouse container pick-up by customers.

The business lessons Kamprad mastered as a boy entrepreneur were evidenced at the corporate level in many ways. For example, the bulk purchasing of matches in his youth was a forerunner to the bulk purchase of fabric that expanded upholstery choices for consumers and made the luxury of fabric options, formerly limited to the wealthy, available to all customers. Likewise, IKEA used imaginative distribution and delivery options, such as when an IKEA employee cleverly discovered the company's "flat-box" approach in 1955. While attempting to load a table into a customer's automobile, an employee simply removed the table legs, enabling a new vision of selling furniture unassembled. Practical solutions wedded to a low-cost promise created a new IKEA formula of "knock down" furniture, flat-box storage and shipping, and assembly by consumers armed with IKEA-developed assembly tools and visual instructions. This formula revolutionized the home-furnishings industry.

A major strength of IKEA lies in its pioneering distribution created through unique corporate–supplier relationships. In the earliest days of the company, Swedish fine furniture manufacturers attempted to boycott IKEA and drive it out of business for selling furniture at such low cost. Kamprad outmaneuvered them by forging new partnerships with other Scandinavian manufacturers, providing assurances of long production runs. Moreover, top managers learned that affordable furniture can be provided without the necessity of owning the factories. IKEA is something of a "hollow" or virtual corporation because nearly all of its manufacturing is outsourced. IKEA uses normal short-term purchasing contracts with suppliers, which means it can quickly adjust orders to changes in demand and not be saddled with huge unsold inventory. Suppliers also are in competition with one another to keep costs low. IKEA has indirect control over suppliers because it often purchases 90 to 100 percent of a supplier's production. Aware of the importance of supplier relationships, IKEA maintains a constant vigilance in working with suppliers to find ways to cut costs while keeping quality standards high, occasionally even agreeing to underwrite supplier technical assistance. That can-do attitude with suppliers has served IKEA well over time.

Supplier Relationships

Today, with 1,300 suppliers in 53 countries, IKEA's integrated design, production, and distribution faces new problems. The sheer numbers can weaken long production runs and disperse supply lines. Global reach also means that domestic requirements vary from one region to another or that certain areas, such as Eastern Europe, have few suppliers capable of high-quality, low-cost production. In addition, furniture competitors have not been idly sitting by but have garnered lessons from the furniture giant. In the face of these challenges, IKEA continues to believe in the power of its ingenuity. Design teams work with suppliers in imaginative ways. For example, the need for expertise in bent-wood design for a popular armchair resulted in a partnership with ski-makers. Likewise, the need throughout Scandinavia for affordable housing resulted in IKEA's expansion into manufactured homes, built on supplier factory floors and delivered to construction sites, ready to be filled with IKEA furnishings, conveniently assisted through $500 in IKEA gift certificates to the homeowner.

From the outset, IKEA represented more than catch phrases such as low price and convenience. Looking out for the families of modest incomes leads to IKEA's constant adherence to frugality, which is reflected in a cultural abhorrence for corporate office perks such as special parking or dining facilities. IKEA executives are expected to fly "coach." In his effort to bring "a little bit of Sweden to the world," Kamprad created a lifestyle model that would mold consumer habits and attitudes. True to the rural values of his homeland, Kamprad nurtured the ideal of the *IKEA family*, referring to employees as *co-workers* and bestowing the name *Tillsammans* (Swedish for "Together") on the corporate center.

Mission and Culture

The higher cultural purpose of IKEA was reaffirmed in 1976 with the publication of Kamprad's *Testament of a Furniture Dealer,* which states explicitly that IKEA is about "creating a better everyday life for the majority of people." He went on, "In our line of business, for instance, too many new and beautifully designed products can be afforded by only a small group of better-off people. IKEA's aim is to change this situation." The purpose of providing fine-looking furniture to the masses was to be met via an internal culture that Kamprad described with words such as the following: "informal, cost conscious, humbleness, down to earth, simplicity, will-power, making do, honesty, common sense, facing reality, and enthusiasm." Achieving this purpose meant employees had to have direct personal experience with the needs of the customer majority.

Visualizing the constantly changing needs of a customer base comprised of farmers and college students, young professionals, and on-the-go families, Kamprad defined IKEA's business mission as "*to offer a wide variety of home furnishing items of good design and function at prices so low that the majority of people can afford to buy them.*" This is "place-holder" furniture, filling the constantly changing needs in the lives of individuals and families. But the company would go further than merely providing the solution to a consumer's immediate needs. From furniture design to catalog layout or the arrangement of warehouse showrooms, Kamprad and his co-workers gently imprinted Swedish style and cultural values of home, frugality, and practicality. As CEO Anders Dahlvig explained in a 2005 interview for *Business Week*, "IKEA isn't just about furniture. It's a lifestyle."

That lifestyle is reflected in the consumer shopping experience. The convenience of helpful touches—providing tape measures and pencils, a playroom that frees parents for leisurely shopping, and a restaurant midway through the building to provide a shopping break—is a key part of the IKEA experience. Also familiar is the gray pathway, guiding the shopper along wide aisles through the 300,000-square-foot store. A veritable labyrinth, the route provides the charm of surprise as shoppers venture past the showrooms or leads to total confusion for those who venture off the intended path. Everything is carefully orchestrated; price tags are draped always to the left of the object, large bins lure with the promise of practical and inexpensive "must-haves," and room arrangements include special touches that spark vision and stimulate add-on purchases.

IKEA's attention to detail is honed through a variety of strategies that link management and co-workers at all levels to their customers. *Antibureaucracy week* places executives on stock-room and selling floors, tending registers, answering customer queries, or unloading merchandise from trucks. IKEA's *Loyalty Program* and *Home Visits Program* allow company researchers entrance to consumer homes in order to better determine individual and community needs for furniture designs. The results of such efforts can be practical, such as specially designed storage units for urban apartment dwellers or deeper drawers to meet the wardrobe needs of Americans. They can also help in detecting or anticipating cultural shifts. IKEA was the first retailer to acknowledge through its advertising the broadening definition of family to include multiracial, multigenerational, and single-sex family arrangements and to promote its openness to "all families."

Challenges

Over the decades, efforts at strengthening IKEA and consumer family ties and encouraging repeat business as customers moved from one phase of life into another produced a unique global brand famous for innovation. The company's devotion to lifestyle solutions led to rapid movement on two fronts, the expansion of product lines (now over 9,500 products) and the expansion of global markets. By 2010, there were 332 IKEA stores in 41 countries. Global economic woes of recent years—including slumps in world stock markets, rising unemployment, and personal financial insecurity—increased sales and profits for IKEA. As consumers searched for ways to trim overall expenses and cut home-furnishing costs, the company continued experiencing steady growth with a sales increase of 7.7 percent to 23.1 billion Euros.

However, the company's rapid global expansion and the rise of imitators in providing low-cost, quality home furnishings led some critics to believe IKEA had abandoned its maverick methods and relinquished its innovative edge. They detected a loosening of the company's strict core values, established more than half a century ago and reinforced in the training of co-workers in the *IKEA Way*.

Other critics take the opposite view and claim that IKEA is provincial. The problems from this viewpoint are the result of those strict core values, monitored on a regular basis through *Commercial Reviews*, measuring how closely the various stores adhere to the IKEA Way. IKEA repeatedly surveys customers, visitors, suppliers, and co-workers about their satisfaction with the IKEA relationship. Repeating the surveys provides clear feedback and even measures important trends, especially if the results venture from the expected 5s toward the dreaded 1s. The critics would argue that the constant pressure for Kamprad's "little bit of Sweden" creates a culture that scorns strategic planning, is slow to react to cultural nuance in new locations, and offers limited opportunity for professional growth or advancement for non-Swedes. They could point out that the notion of *people behind the mountain* should work both ways.

Globalization

Global expansion into non-European markets, including the United States, Japan, and China, magnified the problems and the need for flexibility. Examples abound. The focus on standardization rather than adaptation poses problems for an industry giant such as IKEA, particularly as it enters Asian markets that are culturally different. IKEA's dependence on standardization for everything from store layout to the Swedish names of all products presented translation problems when informing Asian consumers about shopping and shipping procedures. Addressing cultural differences (women are the prime decision makers and purchasers for the home), store and product specifications (e.g., lowering store shelves and adjusting the length of beds), or consumer purchasing power (a worker may need up to a year and a half to purchase a product) was critical to company success in China. Furthermore, IKEA managers realized the need to shift focus from selling furniture to providing home decorating advice when they discovered that many skilled consumers could use the convenient tape measures and pencils to sketch pieces that they could then build for themselves at home.

In the U.S. market, IKEA was slow to make allowances, such as a shift from measuring in meters to feet and inches. While consumers embraced low pricing and the convenience of break-down furniture, the company's delay in bed size designation to the familiar king, queen, and twin drove U. S. customers bonkers because "160 centimeters" meant nothing to them. Co-worker issues also arose. Angry American workers in locations such as Danville, Virginia, moved to unionize amid complaints of discrepancies in pay ($8.00 per hour compared to the $19.00 per hour for workers in Sweden), vacation (12 days annually for U.S. workers compared to five weeks for their counterparts in Sweden), and the constant demands by strict managers in requiring, for example, mandatory overtime.

Officials with IKEA admit they "almost blew it" in America and that they are committed to being both global and local. They insist they are responsive to issues and people. The company points to a history of standing against corruption and to its own quick response when a subcontractor's bribery efforts brought the hint of scandal to IKEA's door. CEO Mikael Ohlsson proudly points to the company's recent record in looking out for the needs of ordinary people through charitable projects such as IKEA Social Initiatives, benefiting over 100 million children. Service to people "behind the mountain" also requires acknowledgement of the mountain. IKEA places a priority on sustainability, working to improve company energy efficiency as reflective of its commitment to thrift, the wise use of natural resources, and a family-level regard for stewardship of the earth. From the elimination of wood pallets and the ban on use of plastic bags to the installation of solar panels and the phasing out of sales on incandescent light bulbs, IKEA leads consumers and competitors by example and demonstration of its core values.

Behind the Curtain

Despite the concerns of critics, those values established by Kamprad remain intact through the combination of co-worker training in the IKEA Way and a carefully crafted organization structure that leaves little room for cultural or corporate change. Although retired (since 1986), Kamprad remains senior advisor on a board dominated by fellow Swedes. Organization structure resembles the IKEA flat box, with only four layers separating the CEO and the cashier on the sales floor. And the culture is in good hands with current CEO Mikael Ohlsson, who says bluntly, "we hate waste," as he points with pride at a sofa that his engineers found a way to ship in one-half the container space, thus shaving €100 from the price—and sharply reducing carbon-dioxide emissions while transporting it.

Historically, financial details about IKEA have been kept tight and neat and, until recently, secretive. The full public disclosure of information such as sales, profits, assets, and liabilities appeared for the first time in 2010 on the heels of a Swedish documentary. The ability to maintain such an opaque organization dates back 30 years. The year 1982 marked the transfer of IKEA ownership to Ingka Holding, held by Stichting INGKA Foundation (a Dutch nonprofit). Kamprad chairs the foundation's five-member executive committee. The IKEA trademark is owned by IKEA Systems, another private Dutch company whose parent, IKEA Holding, is registered in Luxembourg and owned by Interogo, a Liechtenstein foundation controlled by the Kamprad family. This complex organizational setup enables IKEA to minimize taxes, avoid disclosure, and through strict guidelines protect Kamprad's vision while minimizing the potential for takeover.

The Future

The vision remains, but with global expansion IKEA's corporate culture ventured into ways to use technology to bond loyal IKEA customers while tapping into their ideas and valuable feedback. The company expanded its e-commerce sales and initiated the *IKEA Family Club* in order to strengthen ties with existing customers and build long-term relationships. Family club members assist in sharing values and ideas and providing co-creating value for everything from product development to improvements in stores and service. Members are encouraged to increase their visits to stores, on-site "experience rooms," and the website to familiarize themselves with products and to build ties of shared-development in finding real-life solutions to the home-furnishings challenges they encounter at various stages of their lives. This latest development in the long history of IKEA reinforces the decades-old goal of the founder to continue to look behind the mountain to meet the needs of ordinary people.

Sources

Laura Collins, "House Perfect: Is the IKEA Ethos Comfy or Creepy?" *The New Yorker*, October 3, 2011, 54–66.

Colleen Lief, "IKEA: Past, Present & Future," *IMD International*, June 18, 2008, http://www.denisonconsulting.com/Libraries/Resources/-IMD-IKEA.sflb.ashx (accessed January 4, 2012).

Kerry Capell, "IKEA: How the Swedish Retailer Became a Global Cult Brand," *BusinessWeek*, November 14, 2005, 96–106.

Bo Edvardsson and Bo Enquist, " 'The IKEA Saga': How Service Culture Drives Service Strategy," *The Services Industry Journal* 22, no. 4 (October 2002), 153–186.

Katarina Kling and Ingela Goteman, "IKEA CEO Anders Dahlvig on International Growth and IKEA's Unique Corporate Culture and Brand Identity," *Academy of Management Executive* 17, no. 1(2003), 31–37.

Anonymous, "The Secret of IKEA's Success: Lean Operations, Shrewd Tax Planning, and Tight Control," *The Economist*, February 26, 2011, 57–58.

"IKEA: Creativity Key to Growth," *Marketing Week*, July 19, 2007, 30.

Gareth Jones, "IKEA Takes Online Gamble," *Marketing*, May 25, 2007, 14.

Bob Trebilcock, "IKEA Thinks Global, Acts Local," *Modern Material Handling* 63 no. 2 (February 2008), 22.

Anonymous, "IKEA Focuses on Sustainability," *Professional Services Close-Up*, September 26, 2011.

D. Howell, "IKEA 'LEEDS' the Way," *Chain Store Age* special issue, 2006, 97–98.

Ulf Johansson and Asa Thelander, "A Standardized Approach to the World," *International Journal of Quality & Service Sciences* 1, no. 2 (2009), 199–219.

Anonymous, "IKEA Aims to Have 15 Stores in China by 2015," *Asia Pulse*, June 24, 2011.

Mei Fong, "IKEA Hits Home in China: The Swedish Design Giant, Unlike Other Retailers, Slashes Prices for the Chinese," *The Wall Street Journal*, March 3, 2006, B.1.

Ali Yakhlef, "The Trinity of International Strategy: Adaptation, Standardization, and Transformation," *Asian Business & Management* 19, no. 1 (November 2009), 47–65.

M. Roger, P. Grol, and C. Schoch, "IKEA: Culture as Competitive Advantage," *ECCH Collection*, 1998, available for purchase at http://www.ecch.com/educators/products/view?id=22574 (Case reference # 398-173-1).

INTEGRATIVE CASE 4.0
Engro Chemical Pakistan Limited—Restructuring the Marketing Division*

In November 2008, Khalid Mir, General Manager Marketing at Engro Chemical, a fertilizer company in Pakistan, was looking at the results of an internal survey to ascertain how well the newly implemented sales structure was functioning. The company had undertaken a restructuring of the marketing division to retain mid-level employees and to become more customer focused.

Feedback from multiple sources about the new structure had flagged a number of issues, which included (1) the need for development of new competencies and further revision of standard operating procedures to prepare employees to handle changes in their tasks; (2) the fear and anxiety of employees losing their authority and power; (3) the confusion resulting from new reporting relationships, especially relating to the support functions; (4) the Tier IV syndrome, which referred to the uncertainty and dissatisfaction among Tier IV officers regarding their upward mobility; and (5) the lack of coordination with other divisions of the company about the restructuring of the marketing division.

Now, Mir was contemplating his next steps. Should he fine-tune the new structure or was another round of restructuring imperative? What other steps were essential to realize the full potential of the marketing division?

Company Background

Engro Chemical Pakistan Limited was established in 1965 under the name Esso Chemical Pakistan Limited, which was later changed to Exxon Chemical Pakistan Limited in 1978 and eventually Engro[1] Chemical Pakistan Limited (ECPL) in 1991, when Exxon divested its fertilizer business worldwide. (Exhibit 1 details Engro's historical timeline.) Engro Chemical Pakistan Limited was a major competitor in Pakistan's fertilizer market and the second largest producer of urea in Pakistan with a total production capacity of 975,000 tons per annum, approximately 19 percent of the total domestic production capacity. It was also a market leader in blended fertilizers (NPK), with an annual production capacity of 160,000 tons and was involved in imported phosphate fertilizers. Engro had also successfully diversified into various other sectors through new projects, joint ventures, acquisitions, and mergers (see Exhibit 2 for a list of Engro's subsidiaries).

ECPL's main production facility was located at Daharki in upper Sindh, near the Mari gas fields. This plant had increased its production capacity nearly sixfold since its inception. The latest expansion plan, which would be operative in the year 2009, would increase production by another 1.3 million tons. This $1 billion project was estimated to bring Engro's share of total domestic production capacity up to 32 percent.

Culture

Engro Chemical was committed to supporting its culture through policies and administrative frameworks that promoted open communication, maintained employee and partner privacy, and assured employee health and safety. Over 700 employees brought their expertise and dedication to the workplace.

According to Mir:

All employees are valued and their inputs and views are given significance, which builds a friendly environment within the organization, independent of any barriers in communication.

Such an open environment had a positive impact on employee morale and their willingness to continue working in the organization. Engro's safety, health, and environmental responsibilities extended beyond protection and enhancement of its own facilities and included the distribution, use, and disposal of its products as well.[2]

A significant change could be seen in the culture since 1991 when Exxon divested its fertilizer operations and the company was named Engro Chemical Pakistan Limited.

*This case study was written by Professor Anwar Khurshid at Lahore University of Management Sciences and Muddassir Shafique Chaudary to serve as a basis for class discussion rather than to illustrate either effective or ineffective handling of an administrative situation. Research assistance was provided by Mehwish Ibrahim and Salman Humayoun. This material may not be quoted, photocopied, or reproduced in any form without the prior written consent of the Lahore University of Management Sciences.

Originally published in Asian Journal of Management Cases, Vol. 7 No.2 Copyright © 2010 Lahore University of Management Sciences, Lahore. All rights reserved. Reproduced with the permission of the copyright holders and the publishers, Sage Publications India Pvt. Ltd, New Delhi.

[1]Engro is an acronym for Energy for Growth.

[2]For more information about Engro visit www.engro.com.

EXHIBIT 1

Historical Timeline up to 2003

- **1957** Search for oil by Pak Stanvac, an Esso/Mobil joint venture, led to the discovery of Mari gas field situated near Daharki, a small town in upper Sindh province. Esso was the first to study this development in detail and propose the establishment of a urea plant in that area.

- **1964–1965** The proposal was approved by the government and led to a fertilizer plant agreement signed in December 1964. The Esso Pakistan Fertilizer Company Limited was incorporated, with 75 percent of the shares owned by Esso and 25 percent by the general public of Pakistan. Soon, a land area of 500 acres was selected for the plant site at Daharki.

- **1966** The construction of a urea plant was started with the annual capacity of 173,000 tons.

- **1968** The construction of a urea plant was completed and commissioned at a cost of US$ 43 million. A full-fledged marketing organization was established and given the important task of effective marketing and commencing agronomic programs to educate the farmers of Pakistan. As a result of these efforts, not only did the consumption of fertilizers greatly increase in Pakistan but also the company launched its own branded urea, Engro.

- **1978** As part of an international name change program, Esso became Exxon and the company was renamed Exxon Chemical Pakistan Limited. The company continued to prosper as it relentlessly pursued productivity gains and strived to attain professional excellence.

- **1990** The plant capacity was expanded in low cost steps to 268,000 tons.

- **1991** Exxon divested its fertilizer businesses worldwide deciding to sell a 75 percent share of the company's equity. The company underwent an employee-led buy-out, the first in the corporate history of Pakistan. Engro came into existence in 1991.

- **1993** The Pakven Project was launched, to increase the company's capacity by more than double, that is, 600,000 tons. This also helped to relocate urea/ammonia plants from the United Kingdom and the United States, with an investment of US$ 130 million. The prime minister of Pakistan inaugurated the expansion. The company celebrated the silver jubilee of its operation.

- **1995** Plant capacity was further increased to 750,000 tons per annum with an investment of US$ 23 million. Engro entered into its first 50/50 joint venture, with Royal Vopak of Netherlands, to form and build a fully integrated state-of-the-art jetty and bulk liquid chemical and LPG storage facility at a cost of US$ 65 million.

- **1996** The company successfully engineered and implemented an expansion program that gave a major boost to the urea production and its capacity increased to 850,000 tons per annum.

- **1997** On October 10, Engro entered into its second 50/50 joint venture, called Engro Asahi Polymer & Chemical Limited (EAPCL) Company, in collaboration with Asahi Glass Company and Mitsubishi Corporation of Japan to build the first world-scale PVC resin manufacturing facility at a cost of US$ 80 million.

- **1998** Another innovative and modernization project, called Energy Conservation and Expansion Strep (ECES-850), was successfully implemented. The project was constructed at a cost of US$ 72 million and had increased Engro's annual urea production capacity from 750,000 to 850,000 tons. On May 2, the prime minister of Pakistan formally inaugurated Engro Vopak Terminal Limited (EVTL).

- **1999** On March 9, the prime minister of Pakistan formally inaugurated the 850 KT expansion project at the Daharki urea plant. Workshops of the Daharki urea plant received ISO 9002 certification.

- **2000** On February 9, General Pervez Musharraf, the chief executive of Pakistan, inaugurated Engro Asahi Polymer & Chemical's PVC resin manufacturing plant at Port Qasim.

- **2001** On July 26, Engro mourned the death of its chairman, Shaukat Raza Mirza.

- **2002** On August 9, Engro's NPK fertilizer plant at Port Qasim was inaugurated by two federal ministers. On October 9, Engro signed an MoU with Oman Oil Company to build an ammonia urea fertilizer complex in Oman.

- **2003** On April 28, Engro acquired controlling interest in the Automation & Control Division of Innovative Private Limited (INET) (www.innovative-pk.com/automation), a Lahore-based technology company. The new company is called Innovative Automation & Engineering (Private) Limited, headquartered in Lahore.

Source: Company documents.

Subsidiaries of Engro

Over the years, Engro has successfully diversified its business into various related fields as well as a recent venture into a FMCG line:

- Engro Vopak Terminal Limited (EVTL)
- Engro Polymer & Chemical Limited (EPCL)
- AVANCEON (formerly Engro Innovative Automation & Engineering [Private] Limited)
- Engro Foods Limited (EFL)
- Engro Energy Limited (EEL)

Source: Company documents.

Nasir Iqbal, National Sales Manager (NSM) in 2008, recalled:

From a bureaucratic and rigid structure, the company has moved on to become a work place where challenges to the status quo are encouraged and new ideas are generated, nurtured and developed, something which was lacking under the Exxon management.

Moreover, the dignity and self-esteem of the people were highly valued. Everyone in the workplace was consistently treated with respect and a joint effort was observed to create an organizational environment in which individuals were encouraged and empowered to contribute, grow, and develop themselves and their colleagues.

Need for Restructuring

Toward the beginning of 2008, Mir discovered through internal feedback from the sales teams and field offices that Engro Chemical had begun to face major problems relating to employee turnover, inventory control, low market development, and suboptimal merchandising efforts in its original marketing-division structure. Hence, in March 2008, Mir took it upon himself to convince the upper management about the dire need for Engro Chemical to undertake a restructuring initiative of its entire marketing division in order to work on these areas. The major focus of this restructuring was personnel and customer driven—a majority of the previous Tier III[3] sales force were promoted to area marketing managers, new Tier IV level sales personnel were hired, and the number of personnel working on market development and merchandising efforts was increased.

Original Structure of the Marketing Division

Originally, Engro Chemical had divided Pakistan into six sales regions with one regional manager (RM) responsible for each region. Exhibit 3 presents the original structure of the marketing division. The regional managers reported directly to the national sales manager who in turn reported directly to the general manager agribusiness. The regions were further divided into various districts; each district had one sales officer (SO), and there was one technical services officer (TSO) for every two or three districts. Each region also had one distribution officer (DO) and several warehouse in-charge officers.[4]

At ECPL, the criterion for selection of sales officers was an MBA from a respected institution for the various positions in the field. The graduate was then gradually promoted over a stretch of five years, after which the designation of senior sales officer was received. Based on the level of performance, a senior sales officer was eventually promoted to one of the regional manager positions in approximately four to six years.

The sales officer was responsible for meeting sales objectives, cost controls, and profit maximization through collaboration with the technical services officer and distribution officer. The latter in turn was responsible for inventory control and warehousing in the entire region and ensured a smooth flow of supply to meet regional demand. The TSO was responsible for conducting market development activities through meetings with farmers and educating them on agronomic information and fertilizer usage.

Problems with the Original Setup

When Mir sat down with Nasir Iqbal in an informal meeting to discuss the restructuring process, they realized that there were three main reasons why the original structure needed to be changed.

High Employee Turnover

When the company evaluated current and previous employees through surveys and face-to-face interviews, it was discovered that there was a low level of job satisfaction in Tier III of the organizational structure, specifically among MBA sales officers. The main cause for this was a

[3]Engro's marketing division is structured according to different hierarchical levels called *tiers*, where each of its five tiers comes with a different status, responsibility, and compensation within the organization.

[4]The officers were a mix of MBAs and agriculture graduates, with the majority of the workforce comprising the latter.

EXHIBIT 3
Original Structure of the Marketing Division

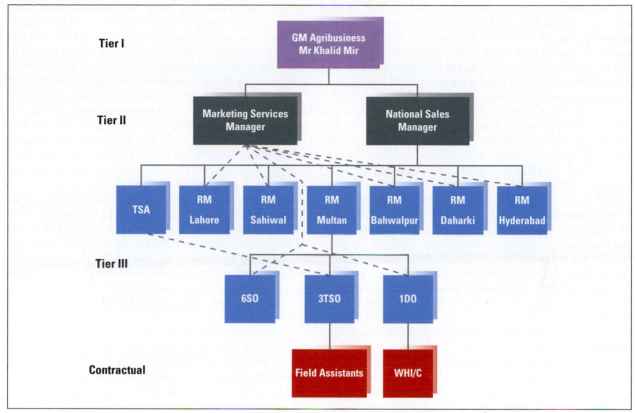

Source: Company documents.

mismatch between the job content and employee skill levels. The sales job required long hours of travelling and relocation to distant rural areas of Pakistan; there was no supervisory role and very little managerial application. Furthermore, the promotions in the first five years were solely salary based; there was no improvement in fringe benefits and no addition to job content.

In contrast, the MBA graduates being hired were highly ambitious individuals, with a high need for achievement.

Mir realized that

Employees would lose motivation in three years or less and there was a general feeling of underemployment, which naturally led to dissatisfaction and high turnover.

An additional external factor that contributed to the high turnover rate was the better opportunities that existed in the FMCG (Fast Moving Consumer Goods) and financial sectors of the country's urban areas.

Weak Market Development
The limited number of TSOs for each region resulted in long travel times for TSOs. Some TSOs reported spending almost 50 percent of their time travelling; as a result, their efforts in market development activities and activity-to-

time ratios were significantly lower than optimal. This meant that the tasks that were envisioned for the TSOs were not being carried out in all districts.

Inventory Control
The distribution officer's primary responsibility included physical audit of warehouses' inventory. Taking the example of the Multan region, it was seen that one distribution officer had to visit 16 warehouses spread throughout the region per month; this translated into each warehouse being visited only once a month or less. As a result, inventory control was not as efficient as it should have been.

The Change Process
Faced with such difficulties like low morale, high employee turnover, and ineffective market development of new products, there was a general realization by the management that something needed to be done. After conducting a few exit interviews with MBAs leaving the organization, Mir realized that the old structure needed to be changed. One of the sales officers he interviewed claimed that, "in FMCG companies, young MBA graduates like me are given more opportunity in terms of job scope and job status. This is something that is lacking in the current Sales Officer position at Engro."

Mir began to consult experts and held several meetings to discuss his ideas about ways to tackle these problems. He met with Nasir Iqbal, National Sales Manager at the time, and they both agreed that the matter was critical in nature because the dearth of MBAs in the organizational hierarchy meant that there was a diminishing pool for future senior management. Also, the Zarkhez Rejuvenation Study[5] that was conducted during this period highlighted the need for Engro to better connect with its customers. One of the consultants that Mir met during the change process advised him to adopt an eight-step model[6] to lead the change initiative at Engro. Mir decided to move fast by creating a sense of urgency for bringing about this change.

He held meetings with RMs, the marketing services manager (MSM), and the NSM to form powerful guiding coalitions. He shared his vision of "revamping the rigid fertilizer sales structure to make it more flexible and capable of meeting the needs of its employees and customers" with the top management and sought their feedback. It was found that everyone was in favor of the restructuring. Buy-in from other employees was gained through a series of meetings. Mir held a meeting in each region and shared with the employees his vision of the new structure. In addition, regular notifications and announcements were sent out to the field offices to keep them updated with the changes.

The initial plans were drafted and presented in all the regions to all permanent employees. In the plan, Mir communicated his vision and discussed the benefits of the new structure and addressed any reservations people might have toward the restructuring. It was also the desire and objective of the management that no employee would be laid off during the change process and that a smooth transition would take place into the new structure. These intentions were clearly communicated to all the employees.

Once the management's vision was conveyed to the regions, it was necessary to ensure that all employees were onboard with the decision and that little resistance would be met during the change process. In collaboration with the other support divisions, including accounting, finance, and IT, a special task force consisting of senior employees was set up to develop new processes according to the revised structure and roles. A Limits of Authority manual was also prepared in conjunction with the zonal offices and the head office, which outlined the basic changes in reporting lines and authority of all members.

Implementation

In March 2008, Engro Chemical went ahead with the restructuring of the marketing division. The first step was the dissolution of the previous sales regions and the formation of three zones; Lahore and Sahiwal regions became the North Zone, Multan and Bahawalpur regions became the Central Zone, and Daharki and Hyderabad regions became the South Zone. (See Exhibit 4 for a map of Engro's territories.) The sales districts were then grouped into 23 areas based on sales volumes; smaller districts were merged into one area, whereas large districts became areas of the same name. For example, small sales districts like Multan and Muzaffargarh became the Multan Area and large sales districts like Dera Ghazi Khan became the Dera Ghazi Khan Area. Area offices were designed to be located in the sales districts with greater sales volume so as to allow the area marketing managers (AMMs) to effectively address their sales responsibilities. (Exhibit 5 shows the new structure for the marketing division.) It was anticipated that this new structure would be able to compete better against Engro's main and biggest competitor, Fauji Fertilizer (FFC). Exhibit 6 presents FFC's probable sales structure based on market intelligence and can be used for comparison to Engro's structure.

In terms of manpower, a zonal marketing manager (ZMM) was in charge of each zone. The hierarchical level for this designation was equivalent to the NSM in the old organizational structure. The three ZMMs reported directly to the GM marketing. The ZMMs consisted of the previous NSM and the two experienced regional managers from the previous setup. New positions for the remaining regional managers were created at the head office in Karachi.

The top performing SOs and TSOs from the previous structure were promoted to area marketing managers. Each of the new areas was headed by an AMM who was responsible for meeting sales targets and market development and distribution in their area. Effectively, their role was equivalent to that of the regional managers from the previous setup but with a smaller geographical and market spread. Each district had one sales officer and one market development officer (MDO) (replacement of the technical services officer).[7] In addition, each area had one distribution and merchandising officer (D&MO) (replacement of the distribution officer). Quantitatively, this meant that there were approximately 87 percent more man-hours on market development and 110 percent more on distribution and warehousing.

The D&MO was also responsible for merchandising activities in his area. In the previous setup, there was no specific officer assigned for monitoring and carrying out merchandising activities. As a result, most material was left at dealer stores without proper display or follow-up. The D&MO's responsibilities also included visiting dealer

[5]The Zarkhez Rejuvenation Study was conducted for one of Engro's leading NPK brands, Zarkhez, to gauge how well the brand was performing. Zarkhez is used in Urdu, the national language of Pakistan, to mean "fertile."

[6]John P. Kotter, "Leading Change—Why Transformation Efforts Fail," *Harvard Business Review*, March–April 1995.

[7]In a few districts where sales volume was very low, only a sales & market development officer (S&MDO) was employed. They were usually agronomists with experience in sales and marketing as well. In the previous setup, they were referred to as STOs, that is, sales and technical officers.

EXHIBIT 4

Map of Engro's Territories in Pakistan

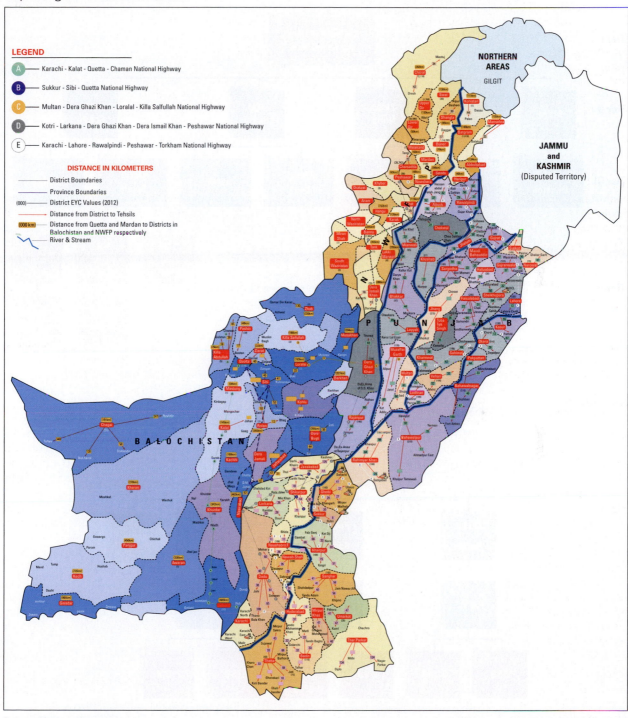

EXHIBIT 5
Restructured Marketing Division

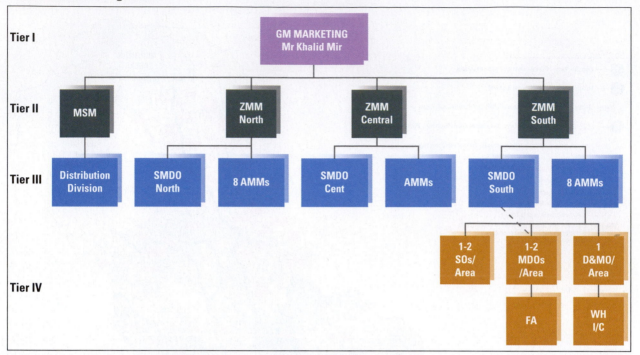

Source: Company documents.

EXHIBIT 6
Leading Competitor's Sales Force Structure

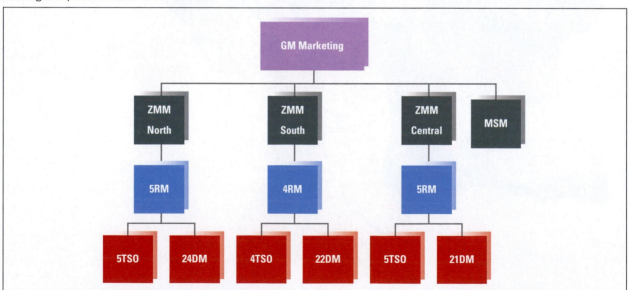

Source: Company documents.

outlets and providing them with merchandising material at the correct time as well as ensuring proper display of the material and products.

Another replacement was the designation of a senior market development officer (SMDO)[8] equivalent to the technical services advisor (TSA) of the previous setup. Each zone had one SMDO who, in the absence of the ZMM, was in charge of their respective zones. The SMDO was also responsible for the overall strategy development and execution of market development activities in areas in collaboration with AMMs and MDOs. Each zone had one SMDO who reported to the ZMM.

AMMs, under the new structure, were responsible for handling key accounts per the 80:20 principle, where the top 20 percent of the customers that resulted in 80 percent of Engro's sales were given the utmost priority. It was the top management's vision to incorporate this principle into the new structure, thus improving customer relations. This had helped to improve the company's reputation in the market.

In the months following March, monthly marketing meetings (MMM) were held in order to ensure that the restructuring proceeded per schedule. ZMMs, MSM, HSE coordinator, and marketing coordinator were the core members of this meeting under the chairmanship of GM marketing. Critical issues and areas of improvement were highlighted during these meetings and matters such as hiring of personnel and funding issues were discussed. The role of HSE under the new structure was examined and it was made sure that it was given precedence. Moreover, people were at the heart of all initiatives at Engro, so management was extremely concerned about whether or not they were adjusting into the new structure and this matter was discussed at length during these meetings.

In order to measure the success of the new structure, some performance indicators were identified. The Zarkhez Tracking System was established to measure the improvement in sales for one of Engro's leading brands, Zarkhez. Through this system, farmer sales were tracked and monitored to assess their satisfaction with the newly launched product. Follow-up interviews were conducted to determine whether or not farmers were content with the product and this helped build loyalty for Zarkhez in the market.

Following restructuring, Annual Zonal Conferences were established for the first time to acknowledge top performing Tier IV officers. All zonal employees of Tier II, III, and IV attended this conference apart from head office delegates. This conference provided them with an opportunity to meet the marketing management at least once a year. The first International Marketing Conference (MARCON) was held in Bangkok. Previously, MARCON was held within the country, so having it at a foreign location improved the prestige of all those attending it, including the newly promoted AMMs. The theme of the conference was "Engaging the Leader in You" and it was held with the specific intent of giving importance to the newly promoted AMMs and their role in helping to achieve Engro's sales objectives.

Improvements

Mir assembled a functional team of four individuals under the leadership of a marketing coordinator to conduct an audit to analyze how well the new structure was operating. Some marked improvements could be seen as a result of the restructuring.

Increased Communication Among Employees

Dealers and employees both commented on the ease with which they could resolve their grievances after the restructuring. In the previous structure, there was one regional manager for each of the six regions (Hyderabad, Daharki, Bahawalpur, Multan, Sahiwal, and Lahore) who was accountable for administrating sales in all the areas pertaining to his/her region. In this way, a regional manager in Daharki would also have to deal with the sales officers and dealers in Quetta, which resulted in a communication gap between the regional managers and the field representatives. In the new structure, a new managerial seat of an AMM was added, and these AMMs were designated to all 23 areas of the sales districts. Having a managerial representative in each area eliminated the delay in resolving grievances between the customers, field force, and top management.

Efficient Inventory Control

There was one DO for each region in the previous setup, who was responsible for all the inventory checks and audits pertaining to that region.

As Mir revealed:

It was impossible for one distribution officer to cover all the districts and warehouses and the inefficiency had become apparent to all through quarterly inventory audits that were conducted within the company.

To counter this, the DOs were replaced by D&MOs in every area, who were now able to visit and audit a warehouse more often, marking a significant increase in efficiency of inventory audits. Similarly, the safety audits also tended to become more efficient in the new sales force setup as there was now one AMM for each area responsible for the safety audits in the warehouses of that particular area.

---

[8]Not to be confused with S&MDO, sales & market development officer.

Greater Market Penetration and Exposure

Further efforts were effectively being put into market development and merchandising. With one MDO in every district and one D&MO in every area, greater market penetration in terms of market development and merchandising was ensured. The registered results of these activities included a significant rise in farmer awareness, trial purchases, and dealer satisfaction with merchandising display since the change in the marketing structure.

Greater Job Satisfaction of Tier III Employees in Their New Role as AMMs

The MBA graduates hired as AMMs seemed to be more satisfied with the new setup and the overall restructuring effort. In the previous structure, a newly graduated MBA would be hired as an SO and after gathering an average experience of about four to five years in the field, he or she would be promoted to a management position in the regional office as a RM. However, in the new structure, a newly graduated MBA was hired as an AMM and after two years in the field, he or she could be promoted to a management-oriented job at the head office. This change in the structure was observed to provide greater job satisfaction among the Tier III MBA employees.[9]

Quantitative Analysis

The audit team that was initially sanctioned by Mir conducted a quantitative analysis of the restructuring, which revealed that in terms of the change in manpower, there had been a significant increase in the efforts of the company in market development and distribution activities. (Detailed information on the quantitative changes in manning is presented in Exhibits 7 and 8.)

There had been a 44 percent increase in total man-hours, which would go up to 58 percent when all positions would be filled per management's original plan. This translated into an increase of 248 and 328 hours, respectively. Among the four main functions, man-hours in market development had increased by 116 hours and in distribution by 72 hours. In the new structure, it was seen that at least 74 hours were dedicated to merchandising activities.

Management was quick to realize, however, that this analysis was simplistic in nature since it assumed an eight-hour workday for employees, whereas in reality, field staff spent a variable amount per day, which also included travelling time. Additionally, overtime had not been accounted for. Another imperfection in this analysis was that it did not account for follow-up sales calls conducted by MDOs after a market development activity or by D&MOs after setting up merchandising material. Furthermore, per the discretion of the AMM, employees were engaged in different functions at different times. The AMM was at liberty to utilize his entire area team for sales activities one day and for market development the next. Thus, the figures presenting the analysis in Exhibit 7 were an approximation, albeit one that was determined through interviews with relevant personnel.

Concerns and Challenges

Although there were numerous concerns identified related to the restructuring, the management believed that a lot of these were interrelated. After conducting feedback interviews with employees who were a part of the restructuring process and reviewing the restructuring audit report, Mir identified certain areas for improvement.

In the previous structure, all officials were aware of the procedures pertaining to their job or tasks. For instance, a sales officer was handed out a ready manual of standard operating procedures (SOPs) on the first day of his job. With the restructuring of the marketing division and a fresh flow of newly graduated, inexperienced officials being employed, it was observed that the SOPs needed to be revised keeping in view the change in employees' responsibilities and tasks. By the end of 2008, SOPs in relation to sales had been revised, whereas SOPs in relation to market development, merchandising, and distribution were still in the process of being revised.

Likewise, with the reorganization of tasks and jobs among the employees, it was observed that people were relatively unaware of or confused about the reporting lines, specifically with regard to support functions. For instance, when an SO in the old structure had to report a delay in the distribution of materials or goods, he could report it to the DO. However, in the new structure, the AMM, who replaced the SO, initially found it hard to determine whom to report to in terms of issues concerning distribution.

An AMM, who had only been involved in sales in the past, needed some exposure to the specifics of distribution, merchandising, and market development. Moreover, the lack of resources, knowledge, and training of the new SOs at Tier IV resulted in a delayed response to fulfill dealer requests. This resulted in the reduced standard of SOs in terms of etiquette and confidence, while the delayed response to dealers' statement requests disrupted the flow of information, especially the Engro product dealer transfer price. Hence, market development and distribution network needed to be improved further. These responses were a result of the inadequate training and orientation of officers as compared to the previous structure and the breakdown of communication with officers in the field.

It was also seen that during restructuring, there was little effort made to deal with the anxiety and disorientation of people losing their authority and power in the new

---

[9] It should be noted that this aspect had also drawn critique from very senior members of the company who felt that early and rapid promotions would not prepare a person adequately for the top management slots.

EXHIBIT 7
Quantitative Changes in Manning

Note: S&MDOs are individuals performing both SO and MDO responsibilities in smaller areas.

	Designation	NUMBER OF PERSONNEL	NUMBER OF MAN HOURS	Sales	Market development	Distribution	Merchandising	NUMBER OF PERSONNEL	NUMBER OF MAN HOURS
				ACTIVITY (% OF TIME SPENT)				**TIER WISE CHANGES**	
OLD STRUCTURE TIER II	NSM	1	8	100%	0%	0%	0%	2	16
	TSA	1	8	0%	100%	0%	0%		
TIER III	RM	6	48	70%	15%	15%	0%	69	552
	SO	30	240	100%	0%	0%	0%		
	TSO	18	144	0%	100%	0%	0%		
	DO	7	56	0%	0%	100%	0%		
	STO	8	64	50%	50%	0%	0%		
TIER IV	N/A							N/A	N/A
TOTAL MAN HOURS			568	313.6	191.2	63.2	0		
NEW STRUCTURE TIER II	ZMM	3	24	40%	40%	20%	0%	3	24
	SMDO	3	24	10%	75%	10%	5%		
TIER III	AMM	23	184	65%	25%	10%	0%	40	320
	SO	5	40	100%	0%	0%	0%		
	MDO	7	56	0%	100%	0%	0%		
	DMO	1	8	0%	0%	60%	40%		
	S&MDO	1	8	50%	50%	0%	0%		
TIER IV	SO	14	112	100%	0%	0%	0%	69	552
	MDO	22	176	0%	100%	0%	0%		
	DMO	22	176	0%	0%	60%	40%		
	S&MDO	11	88	50%	50%	0%	0%		
TOTAL MAN HOURS			896	331.6	353.6	136	74.8		
ACTUAL CHANGE			328	18	162.4	72.8	74.8		
% CHANGE			58%	6%	85%	115%	N/A		

Source: Company Documents.

Man-hours Spent on Different Activities

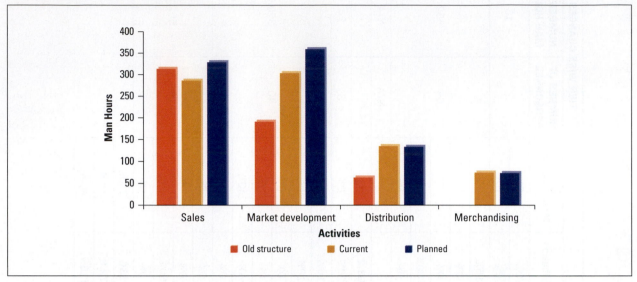

Source: Company documents.

structure. For instance, the future roles of the existing national sales manager, regional managers, or Tier III (non-AMM) officers were not properly defined. Mir realized that senior management should have recognized each individual's contribution in the organization so far and highlighted the need for the change in structure. There was also a slight feeling of annoyance observed among the Tier III employees who did not make their mark to the AMM position at being equivalent in designation to Tier IV personnel, that is, a fresh-graduate Tier IV hire was an SO, a D&MO, or an MDO and a Tier III non-AMM employee of five years' experience was also an SO, a D&MO, or an MDO.

An AMM shared his experience:

One person who was working with me as a fellow SO in the old structure started reporting to me in the new structure when I became an AMM and he did not. For the first month, I faced strong resistance from him. It became worse when I was invited to the marketing conference and he was not invited. In the past, both of us used to go together to the marketing conference.

Emphasis on Tier IV had a negative connotation attached to it as employees believed they belonged to the bottom-most rung of the ladder. This feeling had led to the Tier IV syndrome, which referred to the uncertainty and dissatisfaction among Tier IV officers regarding their jobs and promotions. Moreover, the company had hired a third party agency to aid in the hiring of Tier IV personnel, which resulted in several problems. Employees believed that they had been misinformed and cheated during the hiring

process by the recruitment agency regarding the offered salaries. Most new Tier IV employees felt that the terms of employment should have been more explicitly stated by the third party recruiting agency.

As one AMM stated:

Tier IV SOs are unable to deliver the kind of professionalism and quality of work that is required.

According to one manager:

Dealers don't give importance to Tier IV SOs as they know that the main authority is AMM, whereas in the old structure the SO was the king of his area. Now your front-line people enjoy little autonomy/respect at dealers' level.

One major reason of restructuring was to motivate Tier III employees through a supervisory role and job enrichment. An AMM was responsible for five functional areas: sales; market development; distribution & merchandising; health, safety, & environment; and Six Sigma projects for process improvements. Without adequate support staff and infrastructure, some AMMs were feeling over-stretched.

According to an AMM:

All these five functions are required by the management to be managed from the one room office of an AMM through only his laptop, with no support staff. He even has to make his own tea.

AMMs felt that they needed adequate staff and infrastructure support in order to be effective. They also wanted to have better-quality Tier IV employees working on their teams.

One AMM suggested:

We need to improve the quality of Tier-IV employees either through training them or through attracting more talented personnel by increasing Tier-IV salaries and incentives.

Some AMMs thought that the management could have done more to prepare AMMs and SOs in advance for their new roles and expectations.

An AMM shared his feelings:

It seemed to me as if I was thrown into the pool along with my SOs in my area without adequate preparation about our new roles and what to expect. We learnt as we moved along.

While a sense of urgency was created and overall communication within the marketing division had increased after the restructuring of the sales structure, efforts seemed to be lacking in bringing about synergy within all other divisions regarding the newly implemented changes. Other divisions included Manufacturing, Finance and Planning, Human Resource and Public Affairs, and Corporate Services. Although the restructuring idea was thoroughly discussed throughout the marketing division, Mir felt that other divisions were somewhat isolated from the discussion and they were simply informed through e-mail about the implemented changes.

As one manager noted, there was lack of sufficient IT support in the new structure. In the previous structure, all IT-related information in the Management Information and Dealer Accounting System (MIDAS) was at the authority of the zonal office and solely available to the ZMMs. Indirect link to MIDAS resulted in longer response time to customers' queries and orders and required constant communication and reporting with the head office and zonal office. Hence, when the instructions and requests finally came through to the AMM, there was a delayed response to customers. Moreover, the SO had access to a personal desktop and e-mail ID in the previous structure,

but after restructuring such facilities were lacking. This meant that hard copies of e-mails, reports, queries, and so on from an SO had to be entered in the laptop by the AMM concerned to be communicated to ZMMs or other relevant interfaces. Several AMMs felt this to be merely a clerical task that contributed to delays in communication. According to one AMM, "communications were usually late and incomplete."

Khalid Mir was contemplating his next steps. How successful had the restructuring effort been? Should he continue with the new structure or was another round of restructuring imperative? How could Engro reap maximum benefits out of this newly implemented structure? What lessons could be learnt regarding change management that might be helpful in future restructuring efforts? These questions still remained to be answered.

List of Acronyms Used

AMM	Area Marketing Manager
D&MO	Distribution & Merchandising Officer
DM	District Manager
DO	Distribution Officer
FMCG	Fast Moving Consumer Goods
GM	General Manager
HSE	Health, Safety, & Environment
HO	Head Office
MBA	Masters in Business Administration
MDO	Market Development Officer
NSM	National Sales Manager
RM	Regional Manager
S&MDO	Sales & Market Development Officer
SMDO	Senior Market Development Officer
SO	Sales Officer
SOP	Standard Operating Procedures
STO	Sales and Technical Officer
TSO	Technical Services Officer
ZMM	Zonal Marketing Manager
ZO	Zonal Office

INTEGRATIVE CASE 5.0
First Union: An Office Without Walls*

Meg Rabb was a self-made woman. Having started her full-time career at 18, she was at the pinnacle of her career as vice president of training for First Union Federal, a large (fictitious name) savings and loan association located in the eastern United States. Meg's division was responsible for both employee training and management development, and the services that her staff provided were very visible in the organization. Her unit was known as a "staff" one in the organization; that is, the training and development division served the needs of other units that were directly tied to serving consumers. These later "line" divisions were closer to final customers and, therefore, enjoyed high status in the organization.

Having recently survived several years of financial crisis and regulatory scrutiny, First Union was embarking on a new customer focus that it took very seriously. Significant amounts of financial resources were directed to employee training. All branch delivery mechanisms and systems were aimed at the achievement of a single service target: meeting consumers' changing financial needs. New approaches to service focused on customers' convenience needs and on the delivery of consistently high-quality personal service. At the same time, attention to cost containment was necessary to avoid further financial crisis and to please the board of directors; the organization spent resources available for internal programs very carefully. In sum, then, the fact that the training and development division was getting a big slice of the available resources gave it some stature in the organization as well as the clout that went with it, even though the division was still a staff function and not involved in direct customer interactions or service delivery.

Meg's achievements were financially rewarding and personally satisfying. She was very good at both the design and implementation phases of the training process, and the 12 trainers and management development specialists under her charge were highly qualified and respectful of her developmental and caring leadership style. Vice president titles at First Union Federal were hard to get, and Meg had only recently been promoted to the position of vice president. Five years ago, when she had been hired at the level of assistant vice president, not a single woman enjoyed the VP rank and title and only a handful of men were VPs, out of a total work force of 1,700 employees. After five years of hard work and measurable success in her job, Meg was promoted to the level of vice president. One week after the announcement of her promotion, her boss, Dan Cummings, told her that she would receive a new office and that new furniture would be available to her should she be interested in replacing her existing desk and other fixtures, lamps, and equipment.

The Office as an Incentive

Being a VP at First Union brought certain perquisites, or nonfinancial rewards. An office, a travel allowance, a larger share of human and other departmental financial resources, and a parking space in the corporate lot—all of these traditionally accompanied an assistant vice president in the trip up the corporate ladder to vice president.

Meg looked forward to the privacy that her new office would afford. That, above all other nonfinancial perquisites, was to be cherished in her very busy office. The office was characteristically noisy, with lots of people shuffling in and out of the office area all day long to attend training sessions or to schedule programs.

The physical office layout in her department was uncomplicated. Each employee, in a total staff of 12, had his or her own section, a partitioned area walled off with movable screens. Employees had variable quality office furniture within their areas, depending on their level in the organizational hierarchy. All areas had desks; however, the lowest-level employees received cheaper-quality furniture of the hand-me-down variety, a desk chair, and possibly a guest chair. Lower-level employees typically had just enough room to move around in their space and often had to share space within screened-off areas with other employees. Meg herself had been seated within a screened-off area located in the corner of the work area; this space had two floor-to-ceiling glass walls that overlooked the expansive city, 10 stories below. Her plan was to make this same space her office.

---

*This case was written by Susan Stites-Doe and Melissa Waite, SUNY College/at Brockport, and Rajnandini Pillai, California State University at San Marcos. Used with permission. Originally published in the *Journal of Private Enterprise*.

The Walls Came Down

The construction of the office was completed quickly, within three weeks of her promotion. The office was simply decorated, with grey carpet and sparse decorations that included some tasteful (but inexpensive) modern prints, a desk lamp of modern design (selected from an office supply catalog), and utilitarian desk accessories of simple design. Meg planned on using her existing office furniture in order to economize. The old furniture suited the décor of the new office, and she felt good about saving money for First Union. Her own preference was for modern décor—a stark contrast to the other executives' offices, which were decorated in conservative colonial décor. She occupied her new office space comfortably for one day.

Upon arriving at work the following morning, she was summoned into her boss's office. Dan Cummings was the senior vice president of human resources. He was well liked and was very accurately "tuned in" to the political rules of the game; his influence in the organization seemed to blossom after he organized the first annual "Dan Cummings Golf Invitational," now in its fourth year of operation. Golfers from the old guard at First Union, those VPs and assistant VPs close to the senior management group, always felt honored by their invitations. Invitations denoted status in the organization. Meg had taken golf lessons this past summer in hopes of being included in next year's tournament, despite the fact that no female employees had ever received an invitation to the tournament. Even though her boss knew about her golf lessons, she had not been invited that year, and she'd never voiced her disappointment over not being included to anyone.

Upon entering Dan's office, Meg was perfunctorily informed that the president of First Union had expressed concern over the size of Meg's office. A close friend of the building manager, the president had strolled down to the construction site two days ago to meet the manager for lunch. The bottom line was this: the president had ruled that the office was too large. Meg was told that the existing office would have to be modified to conform to new building regulations set in place just that week. The plan was to tear down her office walls and to rebuild them using the proper 10 feet by 10 feet specifications detailed in the new regulations. Her office, unfortunately, had been built using 12 feet by 12 feet specifications deemed by the building manager to be appropriate.

Meg's immediate reaction to this troubling news was one of anger. She masked her true feelings behind a demeanor of cooperative resistance. She was very concerned about what this decision would mean to her employees— how they would take the news and how she could present it to them to mitigate damage to her department's normally healthy morale. She had other concerns, too. She worried that this event would cause her to lose power and esteem among her peers. Meg questioned the building manager later that morning to try to get a handle on how and why such an expensive mistake had been made. He told her that the 12 feet by 12 feet specifications that had been used for her office were set in place by him personally to take advantage of the view and to make the best use of the surrounding building structure. Other contacts told her that the former building regulations that were more lax than the current ones, yet were similar to the existing ones, had been frequently ignored to suit individual employees' tastes. She couldn't help but feel sorry for the building manager. He had used his skills in office design to try to match form with function, and his friendship with the president had apparently not been enough to shield him from personal repercussions. The tone of his voice and his eagerness to end their telephone conversation suggested that he was annoyed about the entire affair. Her empathy for him was joined with confusion. Had he not taken risks in the past by deviating from strict adherence to the regulations? Had he not already considered these risks? And, why was she the first person to fall victim to strict adherence to this regulation?

The Culture and Power Base at First Union

The overall culture of the bank was marked by conservatism. As one might expect when money is involved, cautiousness and conservatism were valued, as was care in retaining tight financial control over depositors' money. Power and influence at First Union were clustered primarily in the line units and at the executive levels of the organization. The mortgage division was particularly powerful. First Union had only recently remodeled the floor on which the mortgage division was located. As the "bread and butter" arm of the organization, the mortgage division enjoyed substantial power because of the revenues it generated and its contribution to the bottom line. Visitors to the newly remodeled offices never failed to remark on the beauty of the mortgage offices and on their distinctiveness from the rest of the bank. Rumor had it that the president of the bank was disturbed about the cost of the renovations but failed to act on the matter due to the high share of profits that the division generated.

In terms of power distribution across genders, First Union had no ranking female executives at or above the level of vice president prior to Meg's promotion. This fact prompted intervention from the Equal Employment Opportunity Commission, which encouraged First Union to seek out qualified female managers for promotion to executive status. The EEOC's scrutiny was public information, and Meg often felt awkward about being the first female to pave the way. Meg did not have a mentor at a higher rank than she was in the organization.

Her philosophy had always been that hard work pays off, and she was not particularly sensitive to social and political cues in the environment. Her male counterparts were very active and visible across the political terrain at First Union, as her boss's golf tournament activities attested. Friendships mattered a lot in the organization, and many of her male counterparts in other divisions were socially connected with their superiors outside of work.

Some of the artwork at First Union seemed to be very telling of values held to be near and dear to the organization. One lithograph was particularly indicative of the gender values in the organization. It featured a series of free-floating female breasts arranged in a decorative manner. The print was located in the president's conference room and was visible to board members, outside clients, and internal staff members who attended regular meetings in the room. One lower-level female manager who visited the room perhaps 15 times had never deciphered the objects in the lithograph. A higher-ranking male colleague proudly pointed out the identity of the shapes to her, laughing as he said, "Hey, did you see what this print is made up of?" She was embarrassed by his remark but joined in his laughter to get past the moment.

What Should She Do?

Meg sat down and made notes about how she would proceed. One thing was sure: If she was going to survive at First Union, she would have to learn how to play ball. As a VP in a staff unit, she had to do what she could to elevate her political status in the organization. Her worst fear was that she might lose her job; her very survival might depend on developing more political savvy. She had no one to turn to in the organization for advice and felt that she couldn't afford to make even a single mistake. Meg resolved to supplement her golf lessons with a crash course in organizational politics.

INTEGRATIVE CASE 6.0
Lean Initiatives and Growth at Orlando Metering Company*

It was late August 2002 and Ed Cucinelli, vice president of Orlando Metering Company (OMC), sat in his office on a late Saturday morning. He had come in to prepare for some strategic planning meetings that were scheduled for the upcoming week. As he noticed the uncommon silence in the building, Ed contemplated the current situation in his organization.

The Orlando Metering Company was one of several facilities owned by a leading manufacturer of water meters for the worldwide utility industry. The facility specialized in the assembly, testing, and repair of water meters used to measure the amount of water consumed by private homes, organizations, and large cities. In 1999, OMC started the process of moving from a traditional manufacturing to a lean manufacturing organization with a fully empowered workforce. Due to the tremendous success the organization achieved, the corporate headquarters decided to transfer four new product lines to the Orlando facility in 2001. This transfer resulted in considerable expansion of the business, doubling the number of employees and shifts needed at the plant and quadrupling the revenues of the organization. As Ed looked through some old pictures on his desk, he reflected on how proud he was of everything that his leadership team and employees had been able to accomplish in the short year-and-a-half time frame that was given to them by the headquarters.

However, the organization was currently experiencing some very tough challenges due to the recent change and expansion. Although OMC successfully brought in the new business, Ed and his management team made some mistakes in the transition. When he walked through the production floor, Ed could feel that the energy and commitment of the employees were at an all-time low. He knew that his current 108 employees were stressed and unhappy. Turnover and absenteeism were at an all-time high, and productivity and quality were suffering. The organization had lost a lot of the momentum it had gained in its implementation of lean manufacturing. Just last week, Ed had received a call from his supervisor at corporate, expressing concerns about the current situation at OMC. The corporate headquarters had given Ed and his leadership team three months to turn things around and show some improvements.

Ed knew that it was time to take some serious action. He knew that the process side of planning the inventory and physically assembling the meters according to the principles of lean manufacturing were working efficiently in his facility. However, the company had lost the team-based, lean manufacturing culture in which the employees took ownership and worked together as a team to solve problems and run their own work cells. He knew that to truly take advantage of the potential of the lean layout and processes operating in his plant, the company needed to have the culture to support it. Ed knew that it was the right decision to keep the lean production process in the operation, inventory planning, and assembling meters. However, he needed to decide whether to refocus the organization on reestablishing the *team-based, lean culture and thinking* that it had lost or return to the traditional top-down management methods of the past.

Background

Fresh out of college, Ed began his career at OMC in 1993 as a mechanical engineer. The company was originally founded in Orlando, Florida in 1974. The PMG group, OMC's parent company based in Europe, was seeking growth opportunities and saw the United States as a great opportunity given the size of the market and the fact that OMC's product offered a new technology compared to those available at that time. There were many styles of water meters for different applications, and OMC's new product at that time provided a solution to issues within the market, mainly suspended solids (i.e., sand) in the water. Traditional meters would slow down and stop due to suspended solids, thus reducing a water utility's revenues. This new meter allowed the suspended solids to pass through and provided better accuracy for measuring water use, thus increasing revenues. Therefore, the meter quickly gained acceptance in many markets and the company had grown since the new meter's introduction.

As sales continued to increase, so did the number of employees and the need for more space. Ed was in charge of designing and overseeing the construction of

*This case was prepared by Wanda Chaves from Ringling College of Art and Design and Ed Cucinelli from Crummer Business School. The views presented here are those of the case authors and do not necessarily reflect the views of the Society for Case Research. The authors' views are based on their own professional judgments.

CASE
6.0

a new facility. Having no prior experience working within a lean enterprise, Ed designed the new facility as a larger model of the old. Adding more space and more equipment did not create a more efficient workplace, but with the right people, the company still accomplished the job. As he sat in his office, Ed remembered the long nights working side by side with maintenance, quality, and production personnel, all trying to insure that the new facility move would be successful. The power of teamwork was evident as the employees completed the project in a timely fashion and production efficiencies remained stable. At this time, many of the employees at OMC had been with the company for nearly 10 years. Employees knew each other and each other's families, and they felt a sense of responsibility to one another. Even though OMC did not have the best tools, offered a compensation package that did not exceed the market average, and ran without air-conditioning, the employees felt that they belonged to something special.

The Decision to Go Lean

In 1998, OMC's parent company was purchased by a much larger competitor. Soon after, the board of directors came to Orlando for a board meeting. The board decided to pursue a lean manufacturing culture within the organization. At that time, however, none of the company's facilities operated in a lean manner. As a test and learning experience, the board decided to challenge the Orlando plant, and it gave the facility an aggressive nine-week time frame within which to implement the reconstruction of the production floor and change the manufacturing process to lean.

At this point, Ed accepted the position of Lean Champion, where he became responsible for implementing the lean changes and initiatives. Ed knew that all of the employees at OMC would need to be involved if the

organization was to successfully achieve this nine-week goal. Immediately, the leaders of the plant held a plant-wide meeting and outlined the goals. Everyone quickly realized that the small Orlando facility would be closed and relocated to one of the large sister facilities if the change was not successful. Ed organized the employees into teams, conducted lean training, and provided constant management of the project and deadlines. All employees responded, and through long hours, many weekends, and a lot of sweat, all production lines and half of the office processes were converted to utilize the lean concepts. Exhibit 1 details the specific timeline that was developed and accomplished.

Background on Lean Manufacturing

The goals of implementing lean manufacturing at the OMC facility included improving material handling, inventory, quality, scheduling, personnel, and customer satisfaction. In general, the key objectives of the lean facility's layout and flow were to deliver high-quality, low-cost products quickly while maintaining a safe and pleasant working environment (Henderson & Larco, 1999). By implementing just-in-time (JIT) production, one-piece flow, self-directed work teams, and cellular manufacturing, the leaders expected the following improvements to occur as part of the new lean environment:

1. A decrease in the cost of space, inventory, and capital equipment
2. A reduction in throughput time, cycle time, or lead time
3. An increase in capacity utilization
4. A reduction in lost-time accidents

Exhibit 2 details the strategic advantages of implementing lean manufacturing.

EXHIBIT 1
Nine-Week Project Timeline

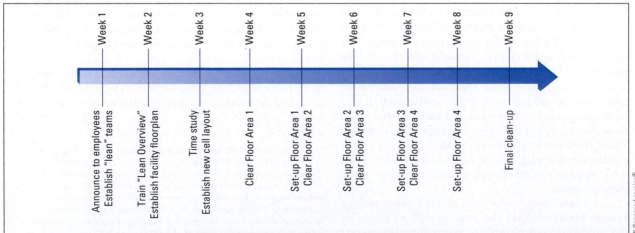

© Cengage Learning®

Lean is not only a production system of tools and processes to continually improve, but it also involves implementing a culture and atmosphere in which the systems and tools can be best utilized. Without the culture and support of all the people, the benefits cannot be maximized. Exhibit 3 illustrates the principal components of lean production, and Exhibit 4 provides details on lean management and the key elements needed to sustain a lean manufacturing culture.

Strategic Advantages of Lean Manufacturing

Manufacturing lead time	Reduced by one day
Delivered quality	3 parts per million (PPM)
Delivery performance	99+ percent
Inventory turns	Greater than 50
Conversion cost (materials to finished goods)	25 to 40 percent less than mass producers
Manufacturing space	35 to 50 percent less than mass producers
New product development	Less than six months

Source: B. A. Henderson and J. L. Larco, *Lean Transformation: How to Change Your Business into a Lean Enterprise* (Richmond, VA: The Oaklea Press, 1999), 42.

Principal Components of Lean Production

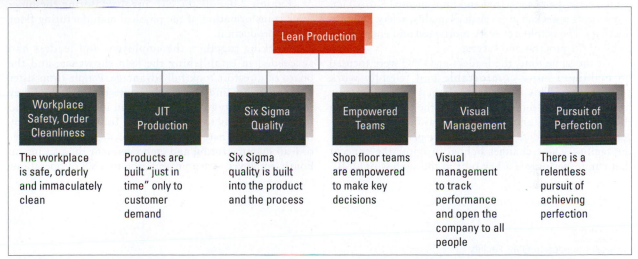

Source: B. A. Henderson and J. L. Larco, *Lean Transformation: How to Change Your Business into a Lean Enterprise* (Richmond, VA: The Oaklea Press, 1999), 46.

Principal Elements of Lean Management

Element	Key Characteristics
Leader standard work	Daily checklists for line production leaders—team leaders, supervisors, and value stream managers—that state explicit expectations for what it means to focus on the process
Visual controls	Tracking charts and other visual tools that reflect actual performance compared with expected performance of virtually any process in a lean operation, production and nonproduction alike
Daily accountability process	Brief, structured, tiered meetings that are focused on performance with visual action assignments and follow-up to close gaps between actual results versus expected performance
Discipline	Leaders themselves consistently following and following up on others' adherence to the processes that define the first three elements

Source: D. Mann, *Creating a Lean Culture: Tools to Sustain Lean Conversions* (New York: Productivity Press, 2005), vi.

Becoming the Lean Showcase

Next, the employees and leaders needed to work together to transform the company into a lean showcase. Ed knew that simply making changes to the production processes would not create the lean showcase that the board expected. Although employees were supportive and dedicated, the management team provided most of the direction and led the change. As discussed above, one of the critical elements to the successful implementation of a lean environment is the development and maintenance of a self-directed, empowered workforce (Henderson and Larco, 1999). Ed realized that the time had come to transition to team-based production lines. Over the next few months Ed and the OMC leadership team, with the help of a trainer, began an intensive team-based training program. The employees went through team skills training, including sessions on feedback and communication, problem solving, meeting skills, team dynamics, and an informal session on company financials. The teams began to see the results of the training and hard work. They began to run their own team meetings and suggested and implemented 8 to 10 improvements a week in areas such as quality, safety, and productivity. The employees were motivated and encouraged by all of the progress and success.

At the same time, the leaders at OMC were focused on making a more comfortable and friendly work environment. This was accomplished by adding new lighting that tripled the brightness of the facility; painting the floor, walls, and equipment; and installing air-conditioning. Leaders even placed live plants throughout the facility. These changes helped promote the concept that employees played a key part in the success of OMC.

The facility looked clean and beautiful. Exhibit 5 provides before and after pictures of the facility.

After an 18-month implementation cycle (which included the physical changes to the manufacturing floor as well as the implementation of lean manufacturing production and administrative processes), the organization was able to achieve the following benefits:

- The managers and employees were able to reduce inventory by 50 percent and completely eliminate finished goods.
- Quality control changes resulted in the conversion to 100 percent testing of all products without adding any additional employees or equipment.
- The plant was able to cut total production cycle times from days to minutes (typically one to two days to process reduced to 5 to 15 minutes).
- Total floor space was reduced by 41 percent (so much that a basketball court was added within the facility), as displayed in Exhibit 6.

Exhibit 7 details the cost involved during the nine-week transformation of the physical manufacturing floor to lean production.

Working together, the employees and leaders had succeeded in establishing the lean showcase, and the board of directors took full advantage. People from sister companies around the world came to Orlando. They toured the facility to learn about lean manufacturing and the best methods to implement it. Tours were given by the employees. There was no better evidence of the power of lean manufacturing and empowerment than seeing an hourly employee give a presentation to a VP of operations

EXHIBIT 5
Physical Changes to OMC Facility

Source B. A. Henderson and J. L. Larco, *Lean Transformation: How to Change Your Business into a Lean Enterprise* (Richmond, VA: The Oaklea Press, 1999).

EXHIBIT 6
Reduction of Floor Space at OMC

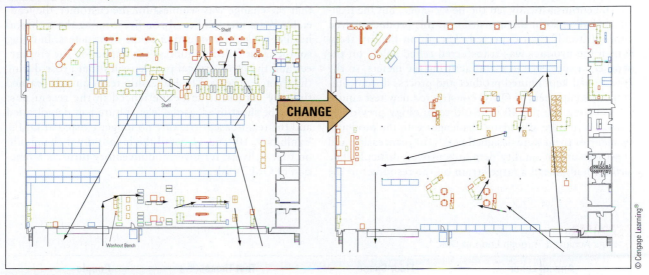

EXHIBIT 7
Project Costs

"Nine-Week" Phase Costs		"Showcase" Phase Costs	
Equipment & tools	$15,000	Air conditioning	$250,000
Lost productivity	$10,000	Floor coating	$120,000
Lighting	$10,000	Equipment & tools	$45,000
Training	$6,000	Painting	$33,000
Supplies	$4,000	Training	$12,000
	$45,000	Supplies	$10,000
			$470,000

of another facility. Morale was at its highest point ever. There were no obstacles that this Orlando facility could not overcome. At this point, Ed and the leadership team knew that the OMC facility was being underutilized. They needed more business.

Over the next year, the Orlando facility continued to be the "showcase." Performance continued to improve. The rapid success of OMC captured the attention of OMC's customers as well as other corporate officers. In 2001, the board decided to relocate four new product lines from a sister facility to OMC. Although OMC had installed new production lines in the past, this change represented a much larger scale. It would require doubling the workforce, quadrupling sales, and converting the existing production lines to utilize the lean concepts, all within 18 months.

Rapid Growth at OMC

Ed was the project manager responsible for the transition of the new business into the Orlando facility. However, nine months into this project the current VP of operations was promoted and Ed became the VP of operations, in charge of the entire Orlando facility.

Although slightly behind schedule, Ed and his leadership team and employees completed the project in 20 months, and they exceeded the projected savings. Lean manufacturing again provided significant benefits to the OMC operations. Through the change, OMC achieved significant savings in labor costs, floor space, and process times, as exhibited in Exhibit 8.

Ed enthusiastically led the new change, but the technical challenges in the transition of this product proved more difficult than expected. The union facility from which the product was transferred relied solely on the worker's experience in manufacturing the meters, so the facility had kept limited product and process documentation. The engineers at OMC constructed new test equipment to replace the 40-year-old technology previously used. There were also many challenges with the products, as many of them were designed nearly 50 years earlier and meeting current quality demands proved difficult. The project had placed a large strain on the resources in the Orlando facility, and many sacrifices were made. In order to ensure that the project was completed on time and that the change was seamless for the customer, the leadership team focused heavily on overcoming the technical hurdles with the production of the new meters. In doing so, the team failed to address the impact on the employees and the other critical people issues that arose during the change process. The leadership team quickly learned that the success it had experienced in the recent past would be short-lived, as the lean culture had deteriorated and the team-based structure no longer existed at OMC. Exhibits 9, 10, and 11 detail the longitudinal changes in on-time delivery, turnover, and inventory turns as a function of OMC's sales.

EXHIBIT 8
Savings Achieved Through Lean at OMC

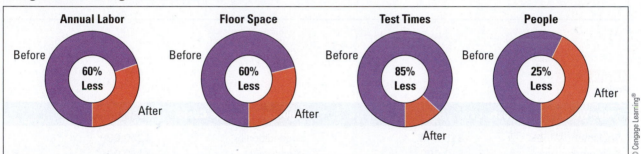

EXHIBIT 9
Changes in On-Time Delivery

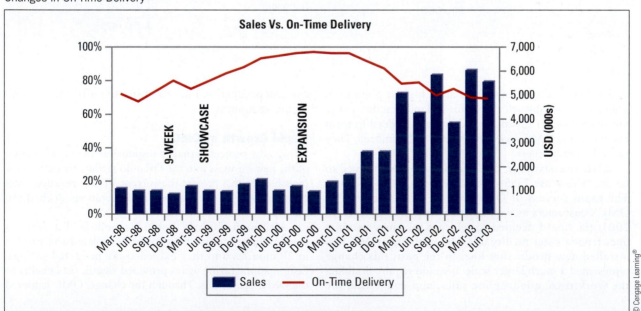

© Cengage Learning®

EXHIBIT 10
Changes in Turnover

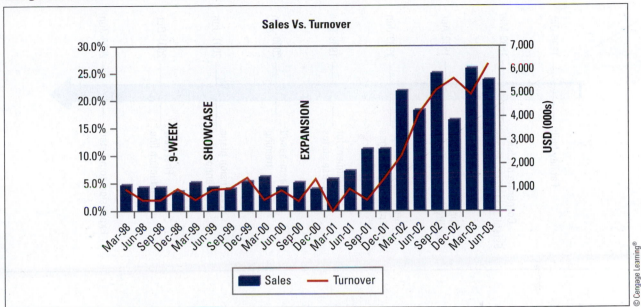

EXHIBIT 11
Changes in Inventory Turns

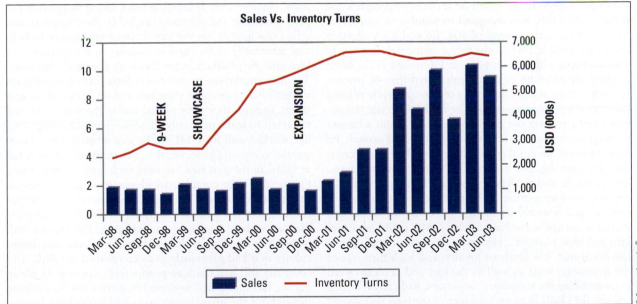

© Cengage Learning®

EXHIBIT 12
Overall Timeline for OMC Changes

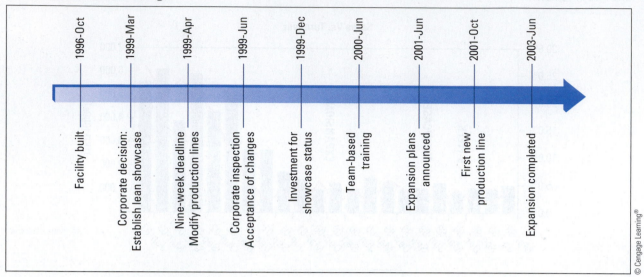

| 1996-Oct | 1999-Mar | 1999-Apr | 1999-Jun | 1999-Dec | 2000-Jun | 2001-Jun | 2001-Oct | 2003-Jun |

Facility built — Corporate decision: Establish lean showcase — Nine-week deadline Modify production lines — Corporate inspection Acceptance of changes — Investment for showcase status — Team-based training — Expansion plans announced — First new production line — Expansion completed

© Cengage Learning®

Exhibit 12 summarizes the overall timeline of the changes that have occurred at OMC since the facility was built in 1996.

Current State at OMC

Ed now sat in his office contemplating the current state of the organization. It had taken 20 months to complete the project, and OMC had increased its number of employees from 50 to its current total of 108. Ed and his leadership team had relied heavily on the use of temporary agencies to provide them with new employees. Ed looked at the latest staffing sheets on his desk and calculated that 40 percent of OMC's current employees were temporary workers hired through the staffing agencies. The decision to use temporary employees was not Ed's preference. Without a human resource department to accommodate the rapid growth, Ed lacked enough qualified staff to help with the rapid recruiting, interviewing, and hiring of 58 additional employees. Therefore, he and the leadership team had resorted to the use of temporary agencies. His hope had been that the temporary agency would do the pre-screening for OMC and recruit qualified individuals whom OMC could later hire into full-time positions. However, the lack of appropriate qualifications, low levels of loyalty, and high turnover of the temporary staff, as well as the fees and costs involved in maintaining the temporary employees, had caused a large setback for OMC in its maintenance of the lean, team-based culture that had started to develop when the organization was much smaller.

Ed also reevaluated the decision made by him and the leadership team regarding the training and integration of the new employees into the workforce. Ed and his team had decided to disperse the existing employees throughout the various production lines, both new and old.

The intent was to provide a solid base of experienced and self-directed employees within each cell, lean-thinking employees in each new production area, as well as to retain some experience in the already existing production lines. However, the leadership team failed to provide the proper training and attention needed by the employees and relied too heavily on the experienced employees to help and informally share their knowledge and experience on lean and the production process with the new employees. The new employees received very little formal training on the technical aspects of their job and on lean culture and teams. Instead, they were placed within the work cells and expected to learn primarily by observing and doing. This had worked well for OMC in the past when it was a much smaller company; however, the changes that had occurred at OMC in the past had not been such large-scale changes that needed to be completed within a very tight timeframe. In hindsight, Ed now realized the importance of formal training and the constant support needed by employees through such a large, accelerated change. The lack of both had now resulted in the dismantling of the lean, team-based culture that had previously been established at OMC. The company still had the lean production processes in place, but the fact that it had neglected to sustain the lean culture throughout the growth processes had caused the serious problems that OMC now faced.

The culture of the organization changed drastically due to the tremendous growth that OMC had undergone. The organization moved from a small, one-shift, family-oriented organization to a midsized, two-shift organization in which many of the employees did not know each other's names or each other's jobs. At this time, 60 percent of the workforce had been with OMC for less than one year, including most of the management team. This was an especially difficult change for those employees who had been with the organization for 10 or more years and had seen the organization's culture change so significantly. The constant flux of new employees, the lack of effective training, and limited communications had challenged, frustrated, and stressed the employees on all the teams in the facility on a daily basis. Ed thought back to just a short year and a half ago when OMC was the lean showcase. At that time, the teams were so successful and confident that the teams and the leaders felt that there was nothing the teams could not accomplish. Today, he thought in dismay, every team in the facility was faltering.

Even members of the management team had lost focus on the lean culture as day-to-day activities consumed all their efforts. With more than half of the management team arriving after the lean transformation, the personal commitment and management styles varied. The manufacturing manager had been at OMC for one year. He was experienced in team-based organizations and slowly won the support of the production employees. His preference was a high level of team-based management. The engineering manager had worked at the company for seven years. He was a major contributor to the success in growth and development of new equipment and had excellent technical and design abilities. His preference was for top-down management and tight control of the engineering and maintenance department. OMC's finance manager was in her sixth year with the organization. She was very experienced and understood business in general and saw the financial impact of the lean implementation and culture. Her preference was for a team-based approach to management.

The materials manager had been with OMC for one year and was very experienced in materials and processing. However, he struggled with lack of information from OMC's outdated business systems. He supported team-based management functions within a salaried workforce; however, he did not believe hourly workers would perform at optimal levels without direct supervision. The quality manager was in his sixth month at OMC. His prior experience was within tightly controlled industries where teams existed, but strict controls limited the ability of these teams to make significant changes. Given his experience, he preferred team-based operations with a limited scope on teams' abilities. Finally, the human resources manager was in his first month at OMC and had strong prior experience in recruitment and personnel development; however, he

had limited experience in lean manufacturing. His focus was to rely heavily on the policies, procedures, and benefits provided by the corporate office. Overall, Ed felt that the management team had the technical skills necessary to move the organization to the next level of lean in terms of production. Yet he had struggled in bringing the team together in terms of their understanding and support for the lean, team-based culture that he was trying to maintain within his organization.

Ed once again examined the staffing data on his desk and reviewed the turnover and absenteeism figures he had been tracking. Turnover in the organization had risen to alarming numbers, with an average of one new temporary or full-time employee leaving every day for the first six months after the change. Ed cringed at the thought of the costs that OMC was incurring due to the turnover and the temporary agency fees the company was still paying. Absenteeism rates were also very high, averaging nearly 50 individual absences each month.

The instability in the workforce had also elevated labor costs, which, in turn, increased manufacturing costs to a point where corporate had started to show concern and demanded immediate improvements. Productivity dropped 25 percent in comparison to the past performance of the organization. This instability had also impacted the quality of the product and on-time deliveries, and as a result there had been an increase in the number of customer complaints.

Ed had received a phone call last week from corporate. The expectations were that the organization needed to improve results within three months; otherwise, corporate would dictate future changes to the people in Orlando. Ed now stood by the window in his office and reflected on just how quickly success and performance can diminish and disappear. He was confident that OMC would meet the goal set by headquarters, as it had done in the past. This time, however, the situation was different given the current levels of low morale and instability in the workforce. He needed to take immediate action. The question was, should he try to reimplement the lean manufacturing culture and lean thinking in the new organization or should he abandon this goal and instead focus on reestablishing the traditional management methods of the past?

Sources

B. A. Henderson and J. L. Larco, *Lean Transformation: How to Change Your Business into a Lean Enterprise* (Richmond, VA: The Oaklea Press, 1999).

D. Mann, *Creating a Lean Culture: Tools to Sustain Lean Conversions* (New York: Productivity Press, 2005).

INTEGRATIVE CASE 7.0
Sometimes a Simple Change Isn't So Simple*

Introduction

On Monday, Kate Cohen was excited because the day for implementing the new computerized medical administration record had finally arrived. The medication administration record (MAR) was a chart of all of the medications administered to a patient by the hospital staff at Central Hospital. Kate, a programmer/analyst in the Management Information Systems department, led a team to computerize the MAR. The team had been working diligently on the pilot project for a year and hoped for a smooth execution. The computerized MAR was launched and immediately failed. By 10:00 A.M., floor nurses and staff pharmacists complained that the system did not work and was too complicated. After hearing nurses' complaints, physicians expressed concern about patient safety. At 1:30 P.M., the computer system crashed, and the MAR project was suspended. Late in the afternoon, Kate assembled the project team to study the project failure.

On Tuesday, Kate Cohen arrived at work early feeling very worried and anxious. At 2:00 P.M., Kate will make a presentation to Central Hospital's management group on the MAR project failure. As Kate began to prepare for the meeting, she thought back over the evolution of the MAR project.

Background

Central Hospital was a community hospital affiliated with Integrated Health, a large, private, nonprofit health care system in Tempe, Arizona. Integrated Health consisted of four community hospitals located within a 75-mile radius, three long-term care facilities, a heart institute, a cancer treatment center, two graduated care retirement facilities, a hospital services company, and a health maintenance organization. Integrated's Board of Directors decided to implement the MAR in stages. In the first stage, the MAR system would be developed and implemented at Central Hospital. After the problems were worked out, the MAR would be implemented throughout other facilities of Integrated Health. Responsibility for the MAR project was delegated to the MIS department at Central, and today it seemed to rest squarely on Kate's shoulders.

The Rationale

Regulatory and competitive changes in the health care industry resulted in a more complex and dynamic environment. According to the National Coalition on Healthcare, the United States spent $1.9 trillion on health care per year, of which $450 billion were administrative costs. At Integrated Health, administrative costs rose at an annual rate of 6 percent, and the board's strategy to reduce administrative costs began with the MAR.

As the trend in insurance coverage shifted from indemnity plans to managed care and capitation, insurers required that health care providers document services in a timely, accurate manner. Paper charts or records were the traditional method of reporting information. The need to deliver more information in shorter time periods resulted in paper reporting not being an efficient or effective method of delivering this data to insurers. For use within the health care system, paper charts must be physically transferred from one department to another as patients move from department to department. In the industry, specialists reported that patients referred to them ended up without a paper file 30 percent of the time. Moreover, it was reported that lost paperwork or illegible handwriting resulted in 10 to 15 percent of patients' medical tests being repeated unnecessarily.

Integrated's management learned that private insurance companies, Medicare, and Medicaid would soon require electronic transfer of patient information on treatment, medication, surgical procedure reports, and billing information. This information would be collected in a centralized database and then uploaded to the computers of the insurers. Computerized records were retrievable by those who need access to patient information in order to provide services or to process requests for payment. Electronic transfer of all information was expected to become a requirement in the future. One aspect of patient information that lends itself to computerization from both clinical and data collection perspectives was medication charting.

Like most other health care systems, Integrated was trying to adjust and position itself for the changes and challenges that managed health care would bring.

*Edward Jernigan, University of North Carolina at Charlotte; Joyce M. Beggs, University of North Carolina at Charlotte. "Sometimes a Simple Change Isn't So Simple," *Journal of the International Academy for Case Studies* 17, no. 3 (2011), 41–48.

Integrated's management viewed the move to a system such as MAR as one of many business process changes necessary if the system was going to be competitive in the long term. For example, if the MAR project was successful, most billing functions could be completed on the day of service. Therefore, the hospital could receive payment more quickly with the utilization of fewer resources. Ultimately, the MAR could eliminate the need for most of the manual billing and allow for staff reductions.

For years, Integrated Health invested little money in information technology. Instead of utilizing the power of technology, the company had relied on old-fashioned paper records held in rows of filing cabinets. Central's computer system was still primarily a mainframe system that some staff considered antiquated, and hardware limitations resulted in cumbersome applications for several clinical departments.

The Project Team

Art Baxter, the chief information officer at Central Hospital, decided to computerize the MAR over a 1-year period. Art heard rumors of a management shakeup at Central Hospital but thought MIS would not be affected. Completing the MAR in such a short period of time would definitely improve Art's image. Art, a former plumbing supply salesperson, lacked a technical background in MIS and was known to boast about not knowing how to turn on a computer. Art's cousin was a member of Central's Board of Directors.

Art assigned Kate Cohen as project leader of the MAR. Kate was known as one of the better programmer/analysts at Central, and she was given day-to-day operational responsibility for the MAR project. Art told Kate that except for monthly executive updates and critical decisions he would not be involved with the project.

Kate assembled a project management team consisting of Guy Smith, pharmacy operations coordinator and MIS liaison; Lauren Hill, nurse trainer and MIS liaison; and Ben Hoffman from Internal Audit. Kate developed good working relationships with Guy and Lauren, who represented two departments critical to the success of this project. Guy Smith had experience developing and implementing the computerized order entry system used in Pharmacy Services for 4 years. Guy personally developed most of the user applications for the order entry system. Kate felt he would be an asset in developing MAR user applications. Lauren Hill was often referred to as "Super Trainer" because of her ability to train even the most difficult employee. Ben Hoffman was an expert on accounting information systems; he had been at Central Hospital for a short time, and the computerized MAR was his first major project. Additional representatives from MIS, Nursing Services, Pharmacy, Internal Audit, Accounting, and other areas of the hospital served on the team on an as needed basis.

For Kate Cohen and other MIS employees, the MAR project was a chance to create a good impression. Therefore, the attitude of the MIS staff was generally positive. If the MAR was successfully developed and implemented at Central, Kate might be asked to lead the MAR project across Integrated Health. The MIS staff viewed the MAR project as an opportunity to demonstrate their importance to Integrated Health. With the pressure on health care providers to hold down costs, the MIS staff thought that the project was a chance to prove their value to the organization and protect them from a layoff.

MAR Project Development

When the MAR implementation target date was 12 months away, the team assembled and developed an action plan. Software preparation began in earnest; and after about 3 months, Kate and Guy finished the coding work on roughly one-third of the user screens. In the fourth month, several demonstrations of the software and available reports were offered to physicians. However, physician turnout to the demonstrations was poor. At first, Kate thought low turnout indicated a low level of interest. Later Kate concluded that the low turnout was not necessarily a bad sign for the team, given physicians' busy schedules.

The team members worked well with each other. In the early stages of the project, the team met at least twice every month to review progress and make new assignments. Communication flowed freely between the team and two of the ultimate end users—the pharmacy and the billing department. However, not much information seemed to pass between the team and other end users of the MAR such as nursing.

Jane Ritchie, the director of nursing, did not support the change to the MAR system. Jane was more comfortable with doing work the traditional way, and she rarely accepted change without noticeable resistance. Jane felt that the nurses had only limited information about the MAR project and that the benefits of the MAR were unclear. Furthermore, an undercurrent of antagonism surfaced between Jane and Art because of the nurses' frustration over the MAR project.

The nursing staff at Central was considered critical to the success of the MAR project. Nurses would be responsible for entering over 50 percent of the data, and the MAR project would create a significant addition to their heavy workload. Occasionally, during development, the nurses were asked for their input. Approximately half of their suggestions and requests could not be accommodated due to coding issues or to limits on computer capability. Generally, the nurses felt their suggestions and recommendations were rejected without full explanation. Members of the nursing staff and MIS met several times to assess whether or not implementing the computerized MAR in 12 months was achievable.

The pharmacists saw the MAR as the logical extension of the computerized order entry function that they had been using for 4 years. In the entry function, the pharmacist reads the physician's order for a specific patient and enters it into the computer. Pharmacists anticipated some initial problems but knew from experience that most issues could be solved. Pharmacists equated the MAR development and implementation process to growing pains, while nurses saw it as unnecessary. To the pharmacists, the computerized MAR was a tool to reduce work, errors, and time spent entering orders. This time could be better spent on more rewarding clinical and professional activities. In general, pharmacists saw computerization as the only option, and most were used to change. The profession had evolved from compounding and dispensing drugs to patient education, drug information services, and pharmacokinetics consultations. New drugs emerged weekly, especially biotech and genetically engineered drugs, so change was expected.

Guy Smith, who developed the pharmacy subsystem, was asked about the feasibility of the implementation date. After reviewing the screens and hearing the concerns of the nurses, Guy thought that the target date was too ambitious. Lauren Hill, the nurse trainer, thought that the nurses would not be ready to use the system in 12 months. She just did not see how she could train Central's 400-member nursing staff in the time available. Kate Cohen thought the screen modifications and programming changes requested by the nurses could take between 9 and 12 months. However, Art Baxter rejected the advice of Guy, Lauren, and Kate and refused to change the implementation date.

Testing

Kate and Guy tested the MAR at every phase of development. During testing, only a few users were on the system at one time. As many scenarios as possible were tried during each test. However, because of the large number of possible combinations, everything did not come up for review. Corrections were made as soon as glitches were identified. As a follow-up, Ben Hoffman, the internal auditor, conducted a test of the full system a month before the scheduled implementation date.

Training

User training for nurses began about 3 months before the target implementation date for the MAR. Lauren Hill, the nurse trainer, was responsible for teaching 400 nurses everything they needed to know about online MAR charting. She thought the training had gone well and had patterned

the nurses' training after the training for the pharmacy department's computerized entry function. The training plan included a pretest, an online demonstration, and a posttest. In order to accommodate all the nurses in such a short timeframe, the class sizes were large. The class size for the pharmacists had been small since there were only 20 pharmacists.

During the training, the nurses complained that the screens were too cluttered, and they became more and more frustrated with the user-unfriendly screens. Another frequent complaint expressed by nurses was that the screens were difficult to read. There was nothing on the screens that stood out to direct the eye to a specific function. In order to complete a transaction, multiple screens were required, and frequently the system response time to move from one screen to another seemed too slow. There were times when the information from the nursing subsystem did not synchronize with the pharmacy subsystem. Another frequently voiced concern was the lack of available computer terminals on which to enter the data and the distances from the patient's room.

Reorganization

About 4 months after Kate and her team had begun work on the MAR project, reorganization at Central Hospital was announced (See Exhibits 1 and Exhibit 2). Greg Korensky, vice president of operations, was moved into a newly created position of executive vice president. Greg would have responsibility for coordinating operations across the Integrated Health system rather than just at Central Hospital. In another important change, Food and Nutrition and Pharmacy Services would become part of the Nursing division. The jobs of the chief operating officer, the director of nursing, and the hospital operations administrator were eliminated as part of the restructuring. The positions held by the director of nursing and the hospital operations administrator were combined into a single position of vice president of patient care services.

After a 6-month search, Sharon Green joined Central Hospital as the vice president of patient care services. She quickly became an enthusiastic supporter of the MAR project. However, Sharon was out of town on the day the MAR was implemented, due to being on vacation.

Implementation

On Monday, the MAR was implemented and immediately failed. Floor nurses and staff pharmacists complained that the MAR was too complicated, then physicians expressed concern about patient safety, and next the computer system crashed. Therefore, the MAR project was suspended, and Kate's team assembled late yesterday afternoon to review the failure. On Tuesday, at 2:00 P.M., Kate would present to the hospital's management. Kate wondered what she was going to say.

EXHIBIT 1
Partial Organization Chart for Central Hospital before the Reorganization

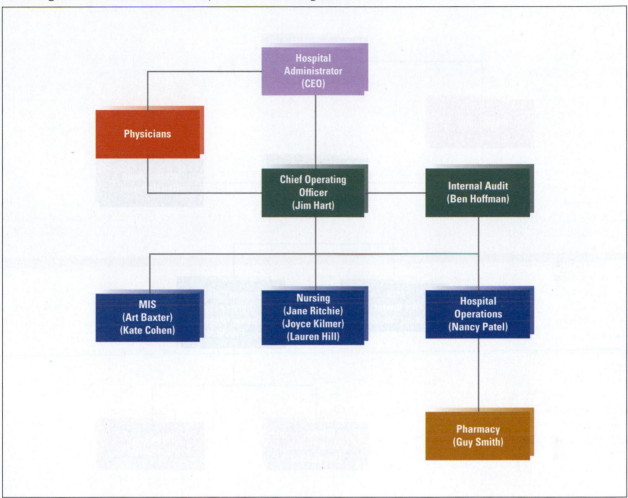

EXHIBIT 2
Partial Organization Chart for Central Hospital after the Reorganization

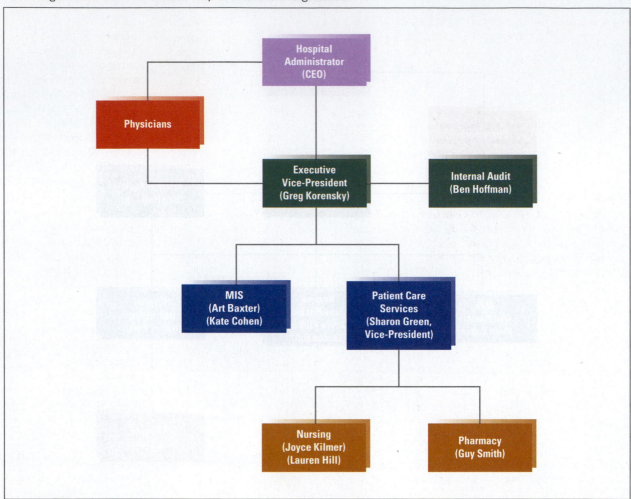

INTEGRATIVE CASE 8.0
Costco: Join the Club

Following high school, James Sinegal worked for discount warehouse Fed Mart unloading mattresses. Then, in the 1970s as an employee of California-based Price Club, he absorbed every detail of the high-volume, low-cost warehouse club formula pioneered by Sol Price.

Armed with knowledge and ideas, Sinegal partnered with Jeffrey Brotman to establish Costco Wholesale Corporation. The duo opened their first store in Seattle in 1983. Today, after more than 30 years in business, Sinegal's vision and success not only eclipsed those of his mentor but led to the merger of Costco and Price Club.

No Frills
With its reputation for rock-bottom pricing and razor-thin profit margins, Costco is the nation's second-largest retailer (behind Walmart) and the number-one membership warehouse retailer with 663 stores (468 in the United States), 185,000 employees, and 71 million members. Between 2009 and early 2013, sales zoomed 39 percent. For fiscal year 2013, sales reached $105 billion, reflecting, in part, a consumer tendency in a poor economy to focus on value but more significantly a unique corporate culture that gives not only lip-service to the value of employees but also maintains a reputation for honoring that value.

The no-frills warehouse-club concept exemplifies the much-maligned "big box" store—merchandise stacked floor to ceiling on wooden pallets, housed in 150,000 square footage of bare concrete, and illuminated by fluorescent lighting. Customers flash member cards and push oversized carts or flatbeds down wide aisles unadorned by advertising or display. Costco reflects industry standards and consumer expectations for providing limited selection, volume buying, and low pricing.

Valuing People
Costco's current CEO, Craig Jelinek, who took over the top job in 2012, has vowed to continue Sinegal's philosophy. The owners believe the secret to Costco's success lies in the many ways the company ventures from the norm by overturning conventional wisdom. Because the owners view people as the organization's "competitive edge," labor and benefits comprise 70 percent of Costco's operating costs. Despite Wall Street criticism, the company maintains its devotion to a well-compensated workforce and scoffs at the notion of sacrificing the well-being of employees for the sake of profits. The 2010 Annual Report declares, "With respect to expenses relating to the compensation of our employees, our philosophy is not to seek to minimize the wages and benefits they earn. Rather, we believe that achieving our longer-term objectives of reducing turnover and enhancing employee satisfaction requires maintaining compensation levels that are better than the industry average." The report admits Costco's willingness to "absorb costs" of higher wages that other retailers routinely squeeze from their workforce. As a result, what the company lacks in margin per item, management believes it makes up in volume, in maintaining "pricing authority" by "consistently providing the most competitive values," and in purchased loyalty memberships, which, as Sinegal once pointed out, "locks them into shopping with you."

Jelinek, like Sinegal before him, is a no-nonsense CEO whose annual salary is a fraction of the traditional pay for large corporate executives and reflects an organizational culture that attempts to minimize disparity between management and workers. Luxury corporate offices are out of the question. Almost 70 percent of warehouse managers started out ringing cash registers or pushing warehouse carts. Even top managers dress in casual attire, wear nametags, answer their own phones, and spend a significant amount of time on the warehouse sales floor.

This unorthodox employer–employee relationship is in sharp contrast to the industry norm, with employees in most companies feeling the added stress of infrequent site visits by suited corporate executives. During an interview for ABC's news magazine "20/20" in 2006, Sinegal provided a simple explanation for the frequency of warehouse visits. "The employees know that I want to say hello to them, because I like them." Indeed, Costco employees marveled at the former CEO's ability to remember names and to connect with them as individuals. It is that "in the trenches together" mind-set that defines Costco's corporate culture, contributing to a level of mutual support, teamwork, empowerment, and rapid response that can be activated for confronting any situation. A dramatic example occurred when employees instantly created a Costco emergency brigade, armed with forklifts and fire extinguishers, whose members organized themselves and rushed to offer first aid and rescue trapped passengers following the wreck of a commuter train behind a California warehouse store.

CASE
8.0

Costco's benevolent and motivational management approach manifests itself most dramatically in wages and benefits. Employees sign a one-page employment contract and then join co-workers as part of the best-compensated workforce in retail. Average hourly wages of $21.00 smash those of competitors ($10 to $11.50 per hour). Rewards and bonuses for implementation of time-saving ideas submitted by an individual employee can provide up to 150 shares of company stock. In addition, employees receive a generous benefits package including health care (82 percent of premiums are paid by the company) as well as retirement plans.

Costco's generosity to employees flies in the face of industry and Wall Street conventional wisdom whereby companies attempt to improve profits and shareholder earnings by keeping wages and benefits low. Yet Sinegal insisted that the investment in human capital is good business. "You get what you pay for," he asserted, and Jelinek agrees. "If you treat consumers with respect and treat employees with respect, good things are going to happen to you," Jelinek says. As a result, Costco enjoys the reputation of a loyal, highly productive workforce, and store openings attract thousands of quality applicants.

By turning over inventory rather than people, Costco can boast an annual employee turnover of only 5 percent, compared to retail's dismal 50 percent average. Taking into account the cost of worker replacement (1.5 to 2.5 times the individual's annual salary), the higher wages and benefits package pays off in the bigger picture with higher retention levels, a top-quality workforce, low shrinkage from theft (0.2 percent), and greater sales per employee. The combination results in increased operating profit per hour. Whether used for attracting customers or employees, the need for PR or advertising is nonexistent. Sinegal told ABC that the company doesn't spend a dime on advertising, as it already has over 140,000 enthusiastic ambassadors scattered through Costco's warehouses (today, that number of enthusiastic employees is around 185,000).

Design to Fit

Equal care has been given to organization design. Sinegal's belief in a "flat, fast, and flexible" organization encouraged de-facto CEO designation for local warehouse managers. Local managers have the freedom and authority to make quick, independent decisions that suit the local needs of customers and employees. The only requirement is that any decision must fit into the organization's five-point code of ethics. Decisions must be lawful, serve the best interests of customers and employees, respect suppliers, and reward shareholders. Likewise, employee training places a high priority on coaching and empowerment over command and control.

All of this fits together in a culture and structure in which the focus on meeting customer needs goes beyond rock-bottom pricing. Costco's new store location efforts seek "fit" between the organization and the community it serves. Typical suburban locations emphasize the bulk shopping needs of families and small businesses, and Costco has extended its own private label, Kirkland Signature. While other companies downsize or sell their private labels, Costco works to develop Kirkland, which now accounts for approximately 400 of Costco's 4,000 in-stock items. The private label provides additional savings of up to 20 percent off of products produced by top manufacturers, such as tires made by Michelin specifically for the Kirkland label. Additional efforts to better meet the needs of customers contributed to Costco's decision to run selected stores as test labs. Over the past decade, selected Costco stores paved the way for launching a variety of ancillary businesses, including pharmacies, optical services, and small business services to better serve the one-stop-shopping needs of the company's suburban customers.

Meanwhile, urban Costco locations acknowledge the customer's desire to purchase in bulk while also serving the upscale shopping desires of condo-dwellers. In these locations, the urgency to "purchase before it's gone" tempts consumers into treasure hunts with special deals on luxury items such as Dom Perignon Champagne, Waterford crystal, or Prada watches.

The rapid growth of Costco from one store in Seattle to America's warehouse club leader and global retailer has come with a share of growing pains as the organization attempts to adapt to its various environments. The merger with Price Club brought an infusion of unionized workers, forcing owners and management officials to push Costco's "superior" wages and benefits as a way to negate the need for unionization.

New Issues

Costco's own reputation for high ethical standards and self-regulation has, in the face of rapid expansion, come up against myriad new problems ranging from complaints about a lack of notification for management job openings to persistent complaints of a glass-ceiling that provides few opportunities for the advancement of women within the organization. In response, the company instituted online job postings, automated recruiting, the use of an outside vendor for hiring, and a recommitment to equity in promotion.

International issues are often more complex and often run up against local needs and perceptions. For example, efforts to expand into Cuernavaca, Mexico, were viewed from the company perspective as a win-win situation, opening a new market and providing jobs and high-quality, low-priced items for area shoppers. When the site of a dilapidated casino became available, Costco moved quickly but suddenly found itself facing charges of cultural insensitivity in Mexico. Accusations in Cuernavaca that Costco was locating a parking lot over an area with significance in artistic and national heritage led to negotiations under which Costco set aside millions of dollars to preserve landscape, restore murals, and work alongside city planners and representatives of the Mexican Institute of Fine Arts & Literature in the building of a state-of-the-art cultural center and museum.

The story illustrates the emphasis on moral leadership that has come to characterize Costco and its senior management. Business decisions based strictly on financial terms take a back seat to success based on broader criteria: Are we creating greater value for the customer? Are we doing the right thing for employees and other stakeholders? Management believes that the answers to these broader questions help keep the company relevant to the issues and trends shaping the future of business.

Indications are bright for Costco's future, but questions loom on the horizon. Everyone from Wall Street pundits to customers, shareholders, and employees is still wondering how the organization might change now that Sinegal has stepped down. So far, things look good, but will future leaders be willing to maintain the modest levels of compensation for top management and maintain the company's above-average wages and benefits for employees? And how will increased globalization alter the strong corporate culture?

Sources

Richard L. Daft, "Costco Wholesale Corporation, Parts One-Six," in *Management*, 8th ed. (Mason, OH: Southwestern, 2008).

"Table of Contents, Item 7—Management's Discussion and Analysis of Financial Conditions," *Costco 2010 Annual Report*.

Wayne F. Cascio, "The High Cost of Low Wages," *Harvard Business Review* 84, no. 2 (December 2006).

Brad Stone, "Costco CEO Craig Jelinek Leads the Cheapest, Happiest Company in the World," *Bloomberg Businessweek* (June 6, 2013), http://www.businessweek.com/articles/2013-06-06/costco-ceo-craig-jelinek-leads-the-cheapest-happiest-company-in-the-world (accessed August 26, 2013).

Sharon Edelson, "Costco Keeps Formula as It Expands," *Women's Wear Daily*, Issue 19 (January 30, 2012), 1.

Costco Wholesale Investor Relations: Company Profile, http://phx.corporate-ir.net/phoenix.zhtml?c=83830&p=irol-homeprofile (accessed October 30, 2014).

Alan B. Goldberg and Bill Ritter, "Costco CEO Finds Pro-Worker Means Profitability," ABC News 20/20, August 2, 2006, http://abcnews.go.com/2020/Business/story?id=1362779 (accessed January 4, 2012).

Doug Desjardins, "Culture of Inclusion: Where Top Executives Lead by Example and Honesty and Frugality Are Valued Virtues," *DSN Retailing Today*, December 2005.

Michelle V. Rafter, "Welcome to the Club," *Workforce Management* 84, no. 4 (April 2005), 40–46.

INTEGRATIVE CASE 9.0
The Donor Services Department*

Joanna Reed was walking home through fallen tree blossoms in Guatemala City. Today, however, her mind was more on her work than the natural beauty surrounding her. She unlocked the gate to her colonial home and sat down on the porch, surrounded by riotous toddlers, pets, and plants, to ponder the recommendations she would make to Sam Wilson. The key decisions she needed to make about his Donor Services Department concerned who should run the department and how the work should be structured.

Joanna had worked for a sponsorship agency engaged in international development work with poor people for six years. She and her husband moved from country to country setting up new agencies. In each country, they had to design how the work should be done, given the local labor market and work conditions.

After a year in Guatemala, Joanna, happily pregnant with her third child, had finished setting up the Donor Services Department for the agency and was working only part-time on a research project. A friend who ran a "competing" development agency approached her to do a consulting project for him. Sam Wilson, an American, was the national representative of a U.S.-based agency that had offices all over the world. Sam wanted Joanna to analyze his Donor Services Department, because he'd received complaints from headquarters about its efficiency. Since he'd been told that his office needed to double in size in the coming year, he wanted to get all the bugs worked out beforehand. Joanna agreed to spend a month gathering information and compiling a report on this department.

Sponsorship agencies, with multimillion-dollar budgets, are funded by individuals and groups in developed countries who contribute to development programs in less-developed countries (LDCs). Donors contribute approximately $20.00 per month plus optional special gifts. The agencies use this money to fund education, health, community development, and income-producing projects for poor people affiliated with their agency in various communities. In the eyes of most donors, the specific benefit provided by sponsorship agencies is the personal relationship between a donor and a child and his or her family in the LDC. The donors and children write back and forth, and the agency sends photos of the child and family to the donors. Some donors never write the family they sponsor; others write weekly and visit the family on their vacations. The efficiency of a Donor Services Department and the quality of their translations are key ingredients to keeping donors and attracting new ones. Good departments also never lose sight of the fact that sponsorship agencies serve a dual constituency—the local people they are trying to help develop and the sponsors who make that help possible through their donations.

What Is a Donor Services Department in a Sponsorship Agency Anyway?

The work of a Donor Services Department consists of more than translating letters, preparing annual progress reports on the families, and answering donor questions directed to the agency. It also handles the extensive, seemingly endless paperwork associated with enrolling new families and assigning them to donors, reassignments when either the donor or the family stops participating, and the special gifts of money sent (and thank you notes for them). Having accurate enrollment figures is crucial because the money the agency receives from headquarters is based upon these figures and affects planning.

The Department Head

Joanna tackled the challenge of analyzing the department by speaking first with the department head (see the organizational chart in Exhibit 1). José Barriga, a charismatic, dynamic man in his 40s, was head of both Donor Services and Community Services. In reality, he spent virtually no time in the Donor Services Department and was not bilingual. "My biggest pleasure is working with the community leaders and coming up with programs that will be successful. I much prefer being in the field, driving from village to village talking with people, to supervising paperwork. I'm not sure exactly what goes on in Donor Services, but Elena, the supervisor, is very responsible. I make it a point to walk through the department once a week and say hello to everyone, and I check their daily production figures."

The Cast of Characters in the Department

Like José, Sam was also more interested in working with the communities on projects than in immersing himself in the details of the more administrative departments. In part, Sam had contracted Joanna because he rightfully worried that Donor Services did not receive the attention it deserved from José, who was very articulate and personable but seldom had time to look at anything

*Joyce S. Osland, San Jose State University.

beyond case histories. José never involved himself in the internal affairs of the department. Even though he was not considered much of a resource to them, he was well liked and respected by the staff of Donor Services, and they never complained about him.

The Supervisor

This was not the case with the supervisor José had promoted from within. Elena had the title of departmental supervisor, but she exercised very little authority. A slight, single woman in her 30s, Elena had worked for the organization since its establishment ten years earlier. She was organized, meticulous, dependable, and hard working. But she was a quiet, nonassertive, nervous woman who was anything but proactive. When asked what changes she would make if she were the head of the department, she sidestepped the question by responding, "It is difficult to have an opinion on this subject. I think that the boss can see the necessary changes with greater clarity."

Elena did not enjoy her role as supervisor, which was partly due to the opposition she encountered from a small clique of long-time translators. In the opinion of this subgroup, Elena had three strikes against her. One, unlike her subordinates, she was not bilingual. "How can she be the supervisor when she doesn't even know English well? One of us would make a better supervisor." Bilingual secretaries in status-conscious Guatemala see themselves as a cut above ordinary secretaries. This group looked down on Elena as being less skilled and educated than they were, even though she was an excellent employee. Second, Elena belonged to a different religion than the organization itself and almost all the other employees. This made no difference to Sam and José but seemed important to the clique who could be heard making occasional derogatory comments about Elena's religion.

The third strike against Elena was her lack of authority. No one had ever clarified how much authority she really possessed, and she herself made no effort to assume

Organizational Chart—Donor Services Department

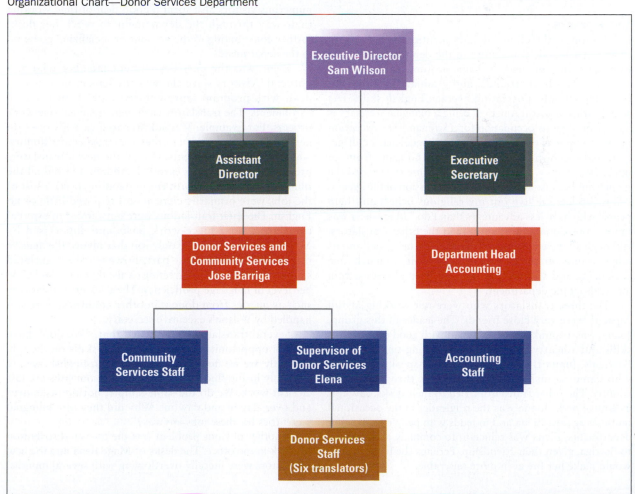

control of the department. "My instructions are to inform Don José Barriga of infractions in my daily production memo. I'm not supposed to confront people directly when infractions occur, although it might be easier to correct things if I did." ("Don" is a Latin American honorific used before the first name to denote respect.)

This subgroup showed their disdain and lack of respect for Elena by treating her with varying degrees of rudeness and ignoring her requests. They saw her as a watchdog, an attitude furthered by José who sometimes announced, "We (senior management) are not going to be here tomorrow, so be good because Elena will be watching you." When Sam and José left the office, the clique often stopped working to socialize. They'd watch Elena smolder out of the corners of their eyes, knowing she would not reprimand them. "I liked my job better before I became supervisor," said Elena. "Ever since, some of the girls have resented me, and I'm not comfortable trying to keep them in line. Why don't they just do their work without needing me to be the policeman? The only thing that keeps me from quitting is the loyalty I feel for the agency and Don José."

The Workers

In addition to the clique already mentioned, there were three other female translators in the department. All the translators but one had the same profile: in their 20s, of working-class backgrounds, and graduates of bilingual secretary schools, possessing average English skills. (As stated earlier, in Latin America, being a bilingual secretary is a fairly prestigious occupation for a woman.) The exception in this group was the best translator, Magdalena, a college-educated recent hire in her late 30s who came from an upper-class family. She worked not because she needed the money but because she believed in the mission of the agency. "This job lets me live out my religious beliefs and help people who have less advantages than I do." Magdalena was more professional and mature than the other translators. Although all the employees were proud of the agency and its religious mission, the clique members spent too much time socializing and skirmishing with other employees within and without the department.

The three translators who were not working at full capacity were very close friends. The leader of this group, Juana, was a spunky, bright woman with good oral English skills and a hearty sense of humor. A long-time friend of Barriga's, Juana translated for English-speaking visitors who came to visit the program sites throughout the country. The other translators, tied to their desks, saw this as a huge perk. Juana was the ringleader in the occasional mutinies against Elena and in feuds with people from other departments. Elena was reluctant to complain about Juana to Barriga, given their friendship. Perhaps she feared Juana would make her life even more miserable.

Juana's two buddies (*compañeras*) in the department also had many years with the agency. They'd gotten into the habit of helping each other on the infrequent occasions when they had excessive amounts of work. When they were idle or simply wanted to relieve the boredom of their jobs, they socialized and gossiped. Juana in particular was noted for lethal sarcasm and pointed jokes about people she didn't like. This clique was not very welcoming to the newer members of the department. Magdalena simply smiled at them but kept her distance, and the two younger translators kept a low profile to avoid incurring their disfavor. As one of them remarked, "It doesn't pay to get on Juana's bad side."

Like many small offices in Latin America, the agency was located in a spacious former private home. The Donor Services Department was housed in the 40 × 30-foot living room area. The women's desks were set up in two rows, with Elena's desk in the back corner. Since the offices of both Wilson and Barriga were in former back bedrooms, everyone who visited them walked through the department, greeting and stopping to chat with the long-time employees (Elena, Juana, and her two friends). Elena's numerous visitors also spent a good deal of time working their way through the department to reach her desk, further contributing to the amount of socializing going on in the department.

Elena was the only department member who had "official" visitors since she was the liaison person who dealt with program representatives and kept track of enrollments. The translators each were assigned one work process. For example, Marisol prepared case histories on new children and their families for prospective donors, while Juana processed gifts. One of the newer translators prepared files for newly enrolled children and did all the filing for the entire department (a daunting task). Most of the jobs were primarily clerical and required little or no English. The letter translations were outsourced to external translators on a piece-work basis and supervised by Magdalena. Hers was the only job that involved extensive translation; for the most part, however, she translated simple messages (such as greeting cards) that were far below her level of language proficiency. The trickier translations, such as queries from donors in other countries, were still handled by Wilson's executive secretary.

Several translators complained that, "We don't have enough opportunity to use our English skills on the job. Not only are we not getting any better in English, we are probably losing fluency because most of our jobs are just clerical work. We do the same simple, boring tasks over and over, day in and day out. Why did they hire bilingual secretaries for these jobs anyway?"

Another obvious problem was the uneven distribution of work in the office. The desks of Magdalena and the new translators were literally overflowing with several months' backlog of work, while Juana and her two friends had time to kill. Nobody, including Elena, made any efforts to even out the work assignments or help out those who were buried. The subject had never been broached.

The agency was growing at a rapid pace, and there were piles of paperwork sitting around waiting to be processed. Joanna spent three weeks having each department member explain her job (in mind-numbing detail), drawing up flow charts of how each type of paperwork was handled, and poking around in their files. She found many unnecessary steps that resulted in slow turnaround times for various processes. There were daily output reports submitted to Barriga, but no statistics were kept on the length of time it took to respond to requests for information or process paperwork. No data were shared with the translators, so they had no idea how the department was faring and little sense of urgency about their work. The only goal was to meet the monthly quota of case histories, which only affected Marisol. Trying to keep up with what came across their desks summed up the entire focus of the employees.

Joanna found many instances of errors and poor quality, not so much from carelessness as lack of training and supervision. Both Barriga and Wilson revised the case histories, but Joanna was amazed to discover that no one ever looked at any other work done by the department. Joanna found that the employees were very accommodating when asked to explain their jobs and very conscientious about their work (if not the hours devoted to it). She also found, however, the employees were seldom able to explain why things were done in a certain way, because they had received little training for their jobs and only understood their small part of the department. Morale was obviously low, and all the employees seemed frustrated with the situation in the department. With the exception of Magdalena who had experience in other offices, they had few ideas for Joanna about how the department could be improved.

INTEGRATIVE CASE 10.0
Cisco Systems: Evolution of Structure

The evolution of Cisco from a university campus computer networking solution devised by the husband/wife Stanford team of Len Bosack and Sandy Lerner to a global technology leader has been a dynamic process. The speed of technological innovation means that managers are already talking about the "next new thing" during the launch of each new product or service. Parallel with the rapid technological evolution at Cisco have been the changes in organizational structure necessary to meet the management and decision-making needs of the corporate giant.

Growth

Faced with the challenge of devising a system allowing Stanford computer networks to talk to each other, Bosack and Lerner created a multiprotocol router to break through the communication barriers. The perceived need by many organizations for increasingly sophisticated routers and related products led to the founding of the Silicon Valley hi-tech powerhouse Cisco in 1984. As a start-up company, Cisco had a vision, eight employees, and a host of financial challenges. The early days were financed by credit cards, home mortgages, and periods when payrolls were delayed, but in 1986, Cisco shipped its first router. The company turned to a venture capitalist, Sequoia Capital, which moved Cisco toward financial stability, but founders Bosack and Lerner were forced out and replaced with new management. Cisco quickly became established as a viable business and, armed with a growing reputation in the industry, went public in 1990.

A leader in the development of routers, Cisco faced new challenges with the emergence of competitors for rapid, less-expensive technology. Facing the threat of losing high-profile customers and industry leadership, Cisco management took a bold move in its innovation strategy through the acquisition of small innovative companies such as Crescendo Communication, a company that had attracted the attention of major customers including Boeing.

Cisco was selective in its acquisitions, focusing on small start-up companies that were working on a great product that could be moved from development into production within 6 to 12 months. The company's goal was to *purchase the future* by acquiring the engineers who were working on the *next generation* of products

and services. Therefore, the retention of employees was critical to a successful acquisition. For its part of the deal, Cisco could offer the start-up the power of Cisco's financial resources, manufacturing, and distribution channels. Cisco's reputation for finding and bringing into the fold the best of the smaller companies reminded admirers and critics alike of *the Borg*, the notorious alien being from Star Trek fame that absorbed species as it expanded across the universe.

As Cisco expanded into wireless devices for home (Linksys) and business, data center switching systems, networking equipment, communications gear, and network security apparatus, visionary John Chambers was brought in as CEO. One of a generation of gurus who championed the power and practical solutions of technology, Chambers expanded the company into advanced technologies including digital voice and data, web-conferencing, and more diverse security products. By 2000, Cisco had attained a brief designation as the world's most valuable company.

Cisco 1

During the early period that would later become designated as Cisco 1, the organization had created a three-division organization structure. The three self-contained product divisions were each focused on a distinct customer segment: Service Products (such as AT&T), Enterprises (usually multinational corporations), and Small to Mid-Size Commercial Companies. Each of the three divisions had its own engineering, manufacturing, and marketing functions. Goals were established by each division's managers to develop products and services customized to address the specific and changing needs within that customer group.

With corporate headquarters in San Jose and a dominance of U.S. sales, Cisco found that it could minimize costs with a move toward outsourcing manufacturing to contract manufacturers from within each of the divisions. Cisco had, in effect, a structure wherein managers were rewarded for the performance of their own division. Flexibility and coordination occurred across the functional departments within each division, but there was little collaboration across the three divisions. This decentralized structure seemed to work fine in a prosperous and rapidly growing company.

What a difference a year can make. In 2001, one year after a brief designation as the world's most valuable company, a sharp economic downturn hit Cisco and other companies in the high-tech industry. The techno bubble of the 1990s had burst. Across Silicon Valley, tech stocks tumbled, layoffs proliferated, and companies struggled to adjust and survive. At the same time, increasing product complexity and technical advancement within the field pushed management at Cisco to reconsider whether the existing divisional organizational structure was sufficient to carry the company into the future.

Cisco 2

Reviewing the three-division structure, Chambers and his management team detected serious overlap in the work of functional departments across the product divisions. One glaring example was the overlap of engineering groups in each of the three divisions who were all working on similar products without knowing it. This was a huge excess of engineering talent focused on relatively straightforward new products. The lack of communication across the three divisions created a lack of awareness and cooperation necessary for finding shared solutions, avoiding repetition, and speeding the process time required to introduce a new product. Likewise, the complete independence and separation of each division resulted in a glut of separate vendors and suppliers for the divisions in addition to the duplication of employees working on similar projects—all of which added to company costs.

In order to address the need for efficient use of resources while trying to meet the need for new products and geographic expansion, the company moved toward a functional structure. Changes came swiftly in the move to streamline operations and bring costs down. Between 2001 and 2006, the company moved through the reorganization, designated Cisco 2, cutting the work force by 8,000 employees, reducing the number of vendors (1,500 to 200) and suppliers (600 to 95), and trimming outsourced manufacturing from 13 major plants to 4. The company's costs as well as overlap were further cut as the major functions of sales, accounting, and engineering were combined into single large centralized groups that reported to headquarters. The three separate and autonomous divisions were gone. The huge engineering staff was broken down into 11 functional groups that reflected the core technologies on which they worked, resulting in added efficiency and reduced overlap.

Cisco 2 provided senior management of each function much vertical control over the work of their engineers, sales people, etc. Top managers could set goals and expect to achieve those goals, along with performance bonuses, because of direct control over their functional departments and the projects on which employees worked. Cisco became much more efficient with fewer people needed within each function, but it was also becoming more hierarchical and encountered new coordination problems because each functional department became more like a separate silo, with people focused on their own function's goals and projects with little concern for the needs of other groups.

Cisco 3

By 2006, expanded globalization and product lines and the continued need and movement toward horizontal collaboration brought further structural evolution, called Cisco 3. The new structure added 12 business councils at the senior level, one for each key customer segment. Each council was composed of approximately 14 executive VPs and senior VPs—roughly one from each major function. The intention of the new structure was to instill a culture of collaboration that would provide better horizontal coordination across functions. The business councils worked at the policy level, involving representatives from each function to select and coordinate new programs and speed products to market in their segment.

Beneath the business council level, 47 boards were created, to align cross-functional teams below the vice president level. Each board consisted of about 14 people and included one VP or senior VP. Board members would collaborate across functions to implement the new product decisions from the councils.

Beneath the boards, temporary working groups were created of up to 10 people each as needed to execute the details of new product and project implementation in the short term. Having three levels of matrix-type horizontal relationships built into Cisco's structure was viewed as a better way to address a complex environment characterized by uncertainty and rapid change by providing the internal teamwork, coordination, and information-sharing needed for continuous innovation.

The 21st century tech giant's structural evolution brought difficult cultural adjustments. While growth and performance targets remained, emphasis was now placed on collaboration to find solutions for customer needs by involving people from other functions. Executive compensation changed from achieving one's own department's goals to achieving cooperation with other departments, and bonuses for some senior executives, as Chambers admits, "went poof." With managers no longer dependent solely on hitting targets within a tightly controlled function, the organization experienced initial executive resistance to giving up control, to sharing information and resources, and to joint decision making. The new focus for performance evaluation was on peer review ratings based on successful teamwork. Chambers estimated a loss of approximately 20 percent of top management who "couldn't make the transition" to collaborative work, including the development chief, the senior VP for routers and service provider networks, and the mergers and acquisitions chief. But the new structure eventually fell into place as its benefits became apparent, and Cisco successfully rode out the loss of key managers.

The structure continued to evolve and streamline as Cisco evolved. Five years later, in 2011, the number of business councils had been reduced to 3 and the number of boards to 15. This was sufficient to make collaborative decisions on key new products for customer segments. Over time Cisco's top management saw the need to reduce the number of business councils from 12 to 9 and then to 3. Cisco also slashed the number of internal boards and working groups because managers grumbled about the staggering number of boards and council meetings taking up their time.

Simultaneously, Cisco planned to further strengthen the coordination across functions and departments by tapping into social media. Since 2006, the company execs have utilized TelePresence, a system of lifelike videoconferencing to connect customers and colleagues around the globe. Today, with the introduction of *Ciscopedia*, the organization is allowing a greater level of information sharing and consultation between employees and among members of the remaining business councils and boards. Employees use social media, blogs, video, and bookmarking to post ideas, coordinate teams, share information, and avoid duplication across departments, product lines, and geographic areas.

Further Developments

Despite the constant structural evolution, by early 2011, Cisco was suffering through a fourth consecutive quarter of shrinking profits, with its stock price down 35 percent over a four-year period. Nervous investors watched Hewlett Packard's rapid rise to number 2 in global shared networking and grumbled as they also watched a three-year drop in Cisco's core areas (10 percent in routers and 11 percent in edge connecting markets). They pointed consistently to what they saw as Cisco's "reckless ventures" and complained that the boards were proving to be little more than "rubber stamps" for the CEO's wishes.

In April 2011, Chambers released an internal memo, admitting mistakes resulting in "employee confusion, disappointment among investors, and the loss of credibility in the market place." He called for a refocus on the core networking business, insisting Cisco's strategy was "sound." The problems, he said, were with "operational execution," with lack of accountability, slow decision making, and the inability to react to surprises. "We know we have to change," Chambers said.

With yet another structural change, five board committees covering Acquisitions, Audits, Compensation and Management Development, Finances, and Nominations/Governance were created. The problem of accountability was also addressed by a Code of Conduct, monitored by the ethics office. The goal was to become the customers' *most trusted* business and technology advisor. But flexibility and the *need for speed* in anticipating and capturing market transitions was equally important. The implementation of 29 performance measures was seen as a way to clarify department and team goals and keep teams focused and on track. With vision and strategy clarified, functional leaders were empowered to implement additional changes.

In October 2012, Cisco was expanding the roles and responsibilities of a number of key executives including Gary B. Moore, who was promoted to president and COO and heralded Cisco's latest moves as proof that the changes made were successfully advancing both accountability and operational discipline.

But with rapid, looming changes in networking software, by May 2014, Chambers was warning of a "brutal, brutal consolidation of the IT industry," predicting that when the smoke cleared, only two or three of the major players would remain standing." With all of its structural changes, will Cisco be one of those? Does Cisco have it right this time?

Sources

Don Clark and Shara Tibkin, "Corporate News: Cisco to Reduce Its Bureaucracy," *The Wall Street Journal* (Eastern Division), New York, May 6, 2011, B.4.

"Cisco Systems, Inc.: Collaborating on New Product Introduction," Stanford Graduate School of Business; Case: GS-66, June 5, 2009.

Matt Rosoff, "Cisco's Crazy Management Structure Wasn't Working, So Chambers Is Changing It," *Business Insider*, May 5, 2011, http://www.businessinsider.com/ciscos-crazy-management-structure-wasnt-working-so-chambers-is-changing-it-2011-5 (accessed October 31, 2014).

Craig Matsumoto, "Cisco Cuts Down on Councils," *News Analysis, LightReading.com*, May 5, 2011, http://www.lightreading.com/ethernet-ip/cisco-cuts-down-on-councils/d/d-id/686486 (accessed October 31, 2014).

Ranjay Galuti, "Cisco Business Councils (2007): Unifying a Functional Enterprise with an Internal Governance System," Harvard Business School, Case 409-062, June 11, 2010.

Brad Reese, "Cisco's Restructuring Embeds Operating Committee, Councils, Boards, and Working Groups Deeper into Cisco's New Management Structure," BradReese.com, May 5, 2011, http://www.bradreese.com/blog/5-5-2011.htm (accessed October 31, 2014).

Mina Kimes, "Cisco Systems Layers It On," *Fortune*, December 8, 2008.

Rik Kirkland, "Cisco's Display of Strength," *Fortune*, October 31, 2007, http://archive.fortune .com/2007/10/30/magazines/fortune/cisco_strength .fortune/index.htm (accessed October 31, 2014).

Jay Galbraith, "How Do You Manage in a Downturn?" *Talent Management Magazine*, August 2009, 44–46.

Nir Breuiller and Laurence Capron, "Cisco Systems: New Millennium—New Acquisitions Strategy?" INSEAD, The Business School for the World, March 2010, http://www.insead.edu/facultyresearch/faculty /personal/lcapron/teaching/documents/CiscoIronPort .pdf (accessed January 4, 2012).

Cisco: The Network (Cisco's Technology News Site), March 7, 2013, http://newsroom.cisco.com/press -release (accessed June 8, 2014).

Julie Bort, "Cisco CEO: 'Brutal' Times Are Coming for the Tech Industry," *Business Insider*, May 20, 2014, http://www.businessinsider.in/Cisco-CEO -Brutal-Times-Are-Coming-For-The-Tech-Industry /articleshow/35399890.cms (accessed June 8, 2014).

Cisco: The Network (Cisco's Technology News Site), "Cisco Announces New, Expanded Roles for Key Executives," October 4, 2012, http://newsroom .cisco.com/release/1048448/Cisco-Announces-New -Expanded-Roles-for-Key-Executives (accessed June 8, 2014).

INTEGRATIVE CASE 11.0
Hartland Memorial Hospital (A): An Inbox Exercise*

Introduction

Hartland Memorial Hospital, established 85 years ago when wealthy benefactor Sir Reginald Hartland left an estate valued at more than $2 million, is a 285-bed, free-standing community general hospital located in Westfield, a ski resort community of 85,000 people. Ridgeview Hospital is the only other hospital in the area, situated some 18 miles away in the village of Easton. Hartland Memorial is a fully accredited institution that provides a full range of medical and surgical services. It has an excellent reputation for delivering high-quality medical care for the citizens of Westfield and the surrounding area.

You and the Hospital

You are Elizabeth Parsons, BSN, MSN, PhD, vice president for Nursing Services at Hartland Memorial. You accepted this position 17 months ago and have been instrumental in introducing a number of innovations in nursing practice and management. In particular, these innovations have included the establishment of job sharing, self-scheduling, and a compressed workweek for all general-duty nurses. In addition, you have developed a new performance appraisal system and are contemplating using it to create a merit pay system for the nursing staff.

Your administrative assistant is Wilma Smith, who handles your correspondence, as well as scheduling meetings and conferences. Each morning she opens whatever hard-copy mail and memos you have received and puts them on your desk. She also places hard-copy phone messages on your desk from those people who did not want to be routed to your voicemail. Although she has access to your e-mail, voice mail, and electronic calendar, she does not routinely monitor them. Wilma is only moderately comfortable with the new modes of communicating, generally preferring the ways of the "pre-electronic" era.

Your second in command is Anne Armstrong, who is assistant director for Nursing Services. Anne has worked at Hartland Memorial for seven years and is very competent. She has only recently returned to work, however, after spending some time in the hospital recovering from the suicide of her husband. A list of the key personnel at Hartland Memorial is presented in Exhibit 1 and selected biographical sketches can be found in Exhibit 2.

EXHIBIT 1
List of Key Personnel at Hartland Hospital

Name	Position
Allan Reid	President and CEO
Scott Little	Assistant to the president
Elizabeth Parsons	Vice president—nursing services
Anne Armstrong	Assistant director—nursing services
Cynthia Nichols	Vice president—human resources
Clement Westaway, MD	President—medical staff
Janet Trist	Nursing supervisor—3 East
Sylvia Godfrey	Weekend supervisor
Jane Sawchuck	Clinical nurse specialist
Norm Sutter	Vice president—finance
Marion Simpson	Auditing clerk
Fran Nixon	Staff relations officer
George Cross	Nurses union representative
Bernard Stevens	Chairman of the board
Wilma Smith	Administrative assistant

The Situation

You have just returned from a greatly needed long weekend off. At your husband's insistence, the two of you left Thursday evening for a mountain resort and just got back last night. Long hours, high stress, and constantly being accessible by cell phone, voice mail, and e-mail have been taking their toll—you seem to have been "on-call" continuously for months now. Compounding these "curses-of-the-modern-job" have been meeting

---

*This case was written by Kent V. Rondeau, University of Alberta, Edmonton, John E. Paul, University of North Carolina at Chapel Hill, and Jonathon S. Rakich, Indiana University Southeast, New Albany. The case is intended solely as a vehicle for classroom discussion and is not intended to illustrate either effective or ineffective handling of the situation described.

Brief Biographical Sketches of Key Players at Hartland

Elizabeth Parsons	A professionally trained and degreed registered nurse (BSN, MSN, PhD). Age 45, with 20 years of progressive management and nursing experience. Married, two children, 10 and 12.
Allan Reid	CEO at Hartland Hospital for 2 years. Age 35, with 6 years experience as an assistant administrator at a 100-bed rural hospital. MHA degree. Married, two children.
Bernard Stevens	Colonel, U.S. Army Infantry (retired). Chairman of the board for Hartland Hospital for the past 12 years. Age 70. Widower, four grown children.
Clement Westaway, MD	Medical degree from the University of Pennsylvania. Internist. Member of the Hartland medical staff for 30 years and president of medical staff for the past 10 years. Age 64. Divorced, two grown children.
Anne Armstrong	Assistant director of Nursing Services at Hartland for the past five years. Has MSN degree. Age 35. Recently widowed, two children.
Janet Trist	Nursing supervisor. Interrupted career at age 26 to raise her children. Resumed working two years ago. RN (diploma program). Age 41. Married.
Wilma Smith	Administrative assistant in her present position for the past 15 years. Has worked at Hartland for 28 years. Age 50. Single, no children.

the needs ("being there") for your school-age kids and, a recent development, the demands of addressing your parents' needs as they age. In particular, your mom seems increasingly incapable of taking care of your dad, for whom some other living arrangements may have to be found. Caught between responsibilities with kids and parents (to say nothing about spouse) you are truly in the "sandwich" generation.

The weekend away, however, was wonderful. You were out of cell phone coverage, and the inn did not make its computer generally available to guests. In any case, your husband would have probably left you if you'd logged on or called in. Sunday night after getting home you had planned on logging on and assessing the situation facing you at work, after four blessed days out of touch. The kids, however, needed attention, the dog needed walking, and Mom called and talked for over an hour about what to do about Dad. You never got to your voice mail, either.

It is now 7:45 A.M. on Monday morning, and you have just a little over one hour until your first meeting of the day with Norm Sutter, vice president for Finance. You really have to get through your e-mail, voice mail, and the hard-copy items Wilma left on your desk—letters, phone messages, and so on—and take some action before meeting with Norm. You know the rest of the day will be a blur, and you'll have no further opportunities to get caught up. Moreover, new stuff will be coming in and piling up constantly. The refreshed feeling you had after the weekend out of town is rapidly slipping away. . . . A hard-copy schedule of your appointments for the day left on Friday by Wilma is shown in Exhibit 3. You know that it will likely be changing.

What Needs to Be Done

This case includes the various e-mails, voice mails, and hard-copy letters and messages that Elizabeth finds awaiting her. Since Wilma doesn't arrive until 8:30 A.M., Elizabeth has the office by herself. Note that the Hartland Hospital IT system does a fairly good job of filtering out spam and junk mail. The occasional item does make it through, which Elizabeth immediately deletes. Additionally, however, there are the e-newsletters from The Kaiser Family Foundation, the Commonwealth Fund, ACHE, and so on, to which Elizabeth subscribes, but which she rarely has time to read. She tends to let these pile up in her inbox, sometimes making it hard to find the critical material there. The newsletters that came in over her mini holiday are not included.

For each item, indicate the course of action you think Elizabeth should pursue. You can choose from one of the following action alternatives. Because you may not have all the information needed to make a decision, please make notes that explain your assumptions, thinking, and justification for that item. Be prepared to defend your underlying rationale. If delegating a task, identify who should be responsible for each item. *Work sequentially through each item.*

Action Alternatives
_Call immediately
_Note to call within 2–3 days
_E-mail immediately
_E-mail within a day
_Meet with ASAP
_Forward to: _____
_Note to meet within 2–3 days
_Other (Specify: _____)
_No response needed

Schedule of Appointments, Monday, October 7 (as of 7:45 A.M.;
left on your desk by Wilma, Friday afternoon at 5 P.M.)

8:00 A.M.	
8:30	
9:00	Meeting with Norm Sutter
9:30	
10:00	Reg. Monday morning meeting with nursing supervisors
10:30	
11:00	Meeting with Clement Westaway
11:30	
12:00 P.M.	Lunch with Anne Armstrong
12:30	
1:00	Orientation talk to new nursing recruits
1:30	
2:00	
2:30	Meeting of infection control committee
3:00	
3:30	
4:00	Meeting with Allan Reid
4:30	
5:00	
5:30	

Elizabeth Parson's "Inbox" Monday, October 7

ITEM 1: E-mail

To: Elizabeth Parsons, VP—Nursing Services
From: Scott Little, Assistant to the President
Date: October 4, 8:00 A.M.
Subject: Wandering patients—IMPORTANT!

On Thursday evening, Mrs. Grace O'Brien, a patient with diabetes and Alzheimer's disease, was missing
from her room when her daughter came to visit her. It took the staff more than 3 hours to finally locate
her. She was found naked and unconscious in the basement washroom of the Stuart Annex. Her daughter
is extremely upset and is threatening to sue the hospital.
We don't need another lawsuit!!!
—Scott

ITEM 2: Letter

September 26
President, Hartland Hospital

Eliz—Please note what actions are needed! ~A.

Dear Sir,

I have been a patient in your hospital on three different occasions over the last 4 years. In the past I have been very satisfied with the nursing care that I have received; however, my last stay there has left much to be desired. For the most part I have found that many of your nurses are very rude and arrogant. On a number of times when I asked these people for assistance, they would either refuse to help me, tell me they were too busy, or ignore me altogether.

I have great respect for Hartland Hospital and I trust that you would want to correct this problem. My late husband, Horace, was once a trustee at your hospital and would never have allowed this to happen.

Sincerely,
Mable Coleman Westfield

ITEM 3: Voice Mail

(Voice message left at 7:30 A.M. on office phone—you forgot to turn on your cell phone driving into work.)

"Elizabeth, this is Mom. I tried to get you before you left home this morning, but just missed you—Dad got up today upset and saying that he was 'a burden.' He's gone back to sleep now. What should I do? Please call when you get a chance!"

ITEM 4: E-mail

To: Elizabeth Parsons, VP—Nursing Services
From: Allan Reid, President/CEO
Date: October 4
Time: 2:10 P.M.
Subject: EOM

I have heard that a number of other hospitals have been very successful at motivating their staff by implementing employee recognition programs. These programs can go a long way toward increasing employee commitment and morale. I would like to institute an "Employee-of-the-Month" award here at Hartland. I have a few ideas and would like to discuss them with you.   A.

ITEM 5: E-mail

To: Elizabeth Parsons, VP—Nursing Services
From: Sylvia Godfrey, R.N., Weekend Supervisor
Date: October 6
Time: 9:07 P.M.
Subject: Insufficient staffing

Again this weekend we had a number of nurses call in sick and we were subsequently short staffed. I had to call in nurses from the "availability list" that was provided by the Temp Placement Agency. I don't really think these nurses are any good because they are poorly trained and make too many errors. I am sick and tired of having to go through this hassle every week!
Sylvia

ITEM 6: E-mail

To: Elizabeth Parsons, VP—Nursing Services
From: Janet Trist, R.N., Supervisor—3 East
Date: October 4
Time: 1:23 P.M.
Subject: Scheduling problems

    I am really having a problem with this new self-scheduling system that we adopted last month. A number of my senior nurses are refusing to go along with it and are threatening to quit unless we go back to the old system. It's affecting the morale on my unit and making my life miserable. We need to discuss this right away.
    Janet

ITEM 7: Letter

WESTFIELD HIGH SCHOOL

September 28
Elizabeth Parsons
Vice President—Nursing Services
Hartland Hospital Westfield

Dear Mrs. Parsons;
    The Future Careers Club of Westfield High School would like to invite you to be the guest speaker at our November meeting. The meeting will be held on November 14 at 8:00 P.M. in the school auditorium. We would like you to discuss "The Changing Role of the Professional Nurse."
    We believe that your presentation will be quite informative for us because several of our students are interested in pursuing a nursing career.
    We hope that you will be able to accept this invitation. Please call our sponsor, Mrs. Bonnie Tartabull, to confirm at your earliest convenience. Thank you.

Sincerely,
Kathy Muller
President, Westfield High Future Careers Club

ITEM 8: E-mail

To: Elizabeth Parsons, VP—Nursing Services
From: Marion Simpson, Auditing
Date: October 4
Time: 9:45 A.M.
Subject: Hours of work for part-time nurses

Once again, many part-time nurses are working between 25 and 30 hours per week. If we permit this to continue, under the terms of the collective agreement, we must give full-time benefits to those involved. The agreement states that full-time benefits must be given to those working in excess of 25 hours per week.
The actual number of hours worked per week for part-timers averaged 24.5 hours for the month of September.
Marion Simpson

ITEM 9: Written note from Wilma

To: Elizabeth Parsons
From: Scott Little, Assistant to the President
Time: 10:20
Mr. Little called, but did not leave a message.

ITEM 10: E-mail

To: Elizabeth Parsons, Vice President—Nursing Services
From: Cynthia Nichols, Vice President—Human Resources
Date: October 2
Time: 4:45 P.M.
Subject: Sexual harassment charges

STRICTLY CONFIDENTIAL
We have just received a notification from a nurse employed here at Hartland alleging sexual harassment
by one of our physicians on staff. The charges, if verified, are extremely serious. I would like to appoint
you, along with Fran Nixon, from our staff relations department, and George Cross, union representative
for the nurses association, to form a committee to investigate these charges. I have been told that the
individual claiming harassment has already begun legal action, so we need to proceed with haste.

Cynthia Nichols, Vice President

ITEM 11: Hard Copy

MEMO
To: Elizabeth Parsons, Vice President—Nursing Services
From: Marion Simpson, Auditing
Date: October 3
Subject: Reimbursement for travel

   Further to your request for travel reimbursement for your upcoming conference, I regret to inform you
that you have already used up this year's travel budget allocation and therefore will not be reimbursed
from this account.
   Marion Simpson

ITEM 12: Written note from Wilma

Telephone Message
To: Elizabeth Parsons
From: Norm Sutter
Date: October 4
Time: 3:05 P.M.

Mr. Sutter called and asked if the next year's budget projections for nursing have been finished. He
needs these figures by Monday.   Wilma

ITEM 13: Hard Copy

MEMO
To: Elizabeth Parsons, VP—Nursing Services
From: Scott Little, Assistant to the President
Date: October 3
Subject: United Way Campaign

This is a follow-up to our discussion of last week concerning the appointment of someone from your department to serve as a representative for our hospital's annual United Way Campaign. I need to have the name of your representative by Friday, October 4th.   —Scott

ITEM 14: Written note from Wilma

To: Betty Parsons
Date: October 4
Time: 2:12 P.M.

Mr. Stevens dropped in and was looking for you. He seemed quite upset and was muttering something about a lawsuit. He wants you to call him as soon as you get back from your trip.
Wilma

ITEM 15: E-Mail

October 4
4:45 P.M.

Ms. Parsons Can you "please" bring the snacks for the team for Jimmy's tee-ball game Monday night? Several other moms have already said they couldn't! Please confirm if this is OK.
Thanks so much!! You're the true "Super-Mom"! Regards, Coach Bailey

ITEM 16: E-Mail

To: Elizabeth Parsons, VP—Nursing Services
From: Jane Sawchuck, Clinical Nurse Specialist
Date: October 3
Subject: Nosocomial Infections

It has come to my attention that, again last month, we have recorded high levels of Staphylococcus and Pseudomonas in operating rooms B and C. It is becoming apparent that we need to review our standard procedures in this area before an epidemic breaks out.
Jane

ITEM 17: E-Mail

To: Betty Parsons
From: Allan Reid
Date: October 3

My niece, Jennifer, just graduated from nursing school and will be in town just one day Monday, October 7. She is looking for a job in her field and I have asked her to talk to you. She is a delightful girl. Would you please see her?   Allan

ITEM 18: E-Mail

To: Elizabeth Parsons, VP—Nursing Services
From: Scott Little, Assistant to the President
Date: October 4
Subject: Nurse working illegally

Carmen Espinoza, the woman I talked to you about, was working illegally for us. She was using a stolen Social Security number. The Immigration and Naturalization Services (INS) contacted me yesterday and a representative will be coming Monday afternoon to inquire about the matter.
Please give me a call right away.   Scott

ITEM 19: Telephone Message

(Wilma intercepted the call and took a message; put note in front of you)

To: Elizabeth Parsons, Vice President—Nursing Services
From: Bernard Stevens, Chairman of the Board
Date: October 7
Time: 8:55 A.M.

Mr. Stevens just called and says that he needs to meet with you and Allan Reid this morning at 10:00 A.M.

ITEM 20: E-Mail

To: Elizabeth Parsons, Vice President—Nursing Services
From: Dr. Clement Westaway, President—Medical Staff
Date: October 2
Subject: Nurse–physician relations

Further to our discussion last week concerning the pressing need to improve communication between physicians and nurses at Hartland Memorial, I am hoping that the suggestions that I gave you will be successfully implemented by your staff. Remember, we are all trying to provide the best possible medical care for our patients.   *C.W., MD*

ITEM 21: E-Mail

To: Elizabeth Parsons, Vice President—Nursing Services
From: Cynthia Nichols, VP—Human Resources
Date: October 3
Subject: Firing Ms. Jean White, R.N.

As we discussed yesterday, it is important to conduct the termination interview of nurse Jean White as soon as possible. Her last day of work at Hartland will be October 18 and, according to our collective agreement, she requires 2 weeks' notice. Please call me when the deed is done.
Cynthia Nichols, VP—HR

STOP!!

Do not proceed to the next page until you have responded to all previous items.

ITEM 22: Telephone Call (**LIVE**)

Time: 9:45 A.M., Monday, October 7

Allan Reid just calls, and tells you that Mrs. Grace O'Brien, the patient with diabetes and Alzheimer's disease, is again missing from her room, apparently since late last night. He advises you that he was just informed of this by a local newspaper reporter who had gotten wind of the story. He instructs you to call Mrs. O'Brien's daughter to tell her of this recent development before she hears or reads it in the media. Reid gives you no opportunity to respond, saying, "I have the reporter on the other line and have to go." He then hangs up the telephone.

Exhibit 4 is a partial diagram of the formal organization structure at Hartland Memorial Hospital.

After completing your action alternatives and justifications for each inbox item, use your knowledge of relationships to construct an informal organization chart, or *sociogram*, for the hospital. Use the organization chart in Exhibit 4 to draw lines between Elizabeth Parsons and other people. Portray positive/neutral/negative relationships with lines of different colors or thickness. Also indicate power relationships, the level of trust, frequency of communication, and criticality of relationships for her successful performance. Include all players about whom you have information. What does your diagram reveal about what is going on that day?

EXHIBIT 4
Hartland Memorial Hospital (Partial Organization Chart)

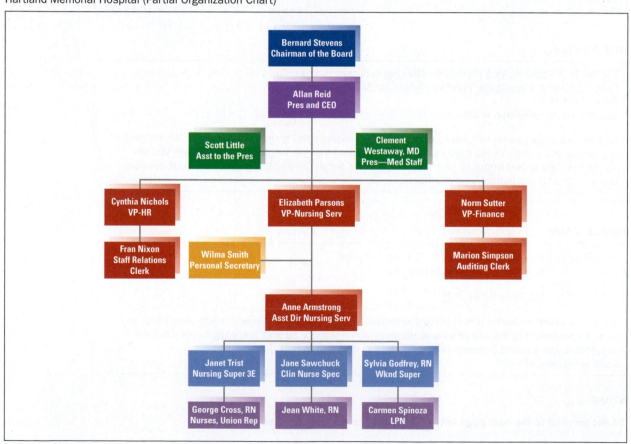

INTEGRATIVE CASE 12.0

Disorganization at Semco: Human Resource Practices as a Strategic Advantage*

"There is no contest between the company that buys the grudging compliance of its workforce and the company that enjoys the enterprising participation of its employees."[1]

-Ricardo Semler, CEO, Semco, in 1989

"For the past thirty years, this company owner has essentially blocked a "real" CEO from ruining his company by holding the position himself and refusing to rule. Instead, his employees rule, in what is one of the few truly democratic workplaces in all the world."[2]

-Ted Coine, Author and Speaker, in May 2011

Semco, based in São Paolo, Brazil, was considered by experts as one of the most innovative democratic workplaces in the world. Ricardo Semler, the majority stockholder of the privately-owned company, had essentially handed over total control of the company to the company's workforce. The company actively promoted the principles of democracy, transparent communications, constructive dissent, creativity, and employee growth.[3] The outcome was noteworthy—Semco's revenue, margins, employee strength, and business segments had expanded significantly.[4] The fact that the company had an inspired workforce was reflected in its low attrition rates. As of 2003, Semco's businesses comprised the production of industrial mixers, manufacturing of cooling towers for commercial estates, property and facility management services, environmental consulting, e-businesses, and inventory management. In 2007, Semco was also getting its hospitality business started and was dabbling in hospital and airport ventures.[5] Several observers were especially startled by the cultural metamorphosis that Semco had achieved, given the fact that, to begin with, it was a top-down driven autocratic set-up. But experts wondered if the transformations at Semco would work in other organizations.

Background Note

Semco was established in 1953 in São Paulo, Brazil, by Antonio Curt Semler (Antonio), an immigrant from Austria. The company was most popular for the marine pumps that it manufactured. Nine-tenths of these pumps were supplied to Brazil's shipbuilders.[6] Semco was a strictly hierarchy-based company, which had regulations and policies governing every issue. Fear was the overriding maxim of the company at that time. Guards scouted the shop floor, regulated workers' visits to the washroom, and checked workers when they exited the factory premises.[7]

In 1982, Antonio's son, Ricardo Semler (Semler), aged 24, took charge of Semco. At the time of Semler's entry, the company was financially in dire straits. Semler started his stint as the new CEO by dismissing around 66 percent of the company's executives, many of them his father's confidants.[8] Initially, he focused on ensuring that the company remained solvent. After the company's financial condition improved, he moved to purchase other companies and explore new businesses.[9] To begin with, Semler too followed authoritarian practices, appointed managers who pushed the employees hard, and put in long hours himself. Despite Semco's speedy expansion, the overwhelming stress on output and on reaching stiff expansion targets exhausted the organization and had negative repercussions on management's

*This case was written by **Tangirala Vijay Kumar,** under the direction of **Debapratim Purkayastha,** IBS Hyderabad. It was compiled from published sources and is intended to be used as a basis for class discussion rather than to illustrate either effective or ineffective handling of a management situation.

© 2012 IBS Center for Management Research

[1]Ricardo Semler, "Managing without Managers," *Harvard Business Review*, September-October 1989.

[2]Ted Coine, "The UnCEO: 6 Unconventional Leaders to Know," http://sustainablebusinessforum.com, May 16, 2011.

[3]Gary A. Yukl and Wendy S. Becker, "Effective Empowerment in Organizations," *Organization Management Journal*, Vol. 3, No. 3, 2006.

[4]"How Mavericks Manage in the Downturn," www.ariadne-associates.co.uk, January 11, 2011.

[5]Dominique Haijtema, "The Boss Who Breaks All the Rules," http://odewire.com, January 21, 2007.

[6]Ekaterina Zakomurnaya, "Semco SA: Brazilian Miracle Where Employees Set Their Salaries and Sleep in Hammocks," www.good2work.com, August 8, 2007.

[7]Jaclyn Fierman and Therese Eiben, "Winning Ideas from Maverick Managers; Unconventional Leaders Share an Ability to Stun the Competition with Their Personal Brand of Can-Doism . . .," http://money.cnn.com, February 6, 1995.

[8]"The Journeys of 2nd Tier Leaders over Time," http://integralleader-hipreview.com, March 2008.

[9]Darrell Mann, "Ideality and 'Self-X,' " http://www.triz-journal.com/archives/2003/04/f/06.pdf.

CASE
12.0

relations with employees.[10] The hectic schedule also took its toll on Semler. On a particular day, while touring a pump factory near New York, he fainted on the shop floor. The doctor declared that he was essentially healthy but more mentally strained than any person aged 25 years that he had previously encountered.[11] After that incident, Semler resolved to harmonize his office and personal life better and to refashion his employees' lives similarly. Primarily, this entailed their enjoying their work lives.

At Semco, Semler started by clipping what he termed "corporate oppression." Sign-ins and sign-outs, attire rules, security checks, hierarchically reserved work areas, and allowances were all removed. The posts of receptionists and personal assistants/aides were done away with. All the employees had to receive their visitors themselves, fax their messages themselves, and prepare their own coffee.[12] The number of administrative staff was reduced by three-fourths. The top management was no longer entitled to exclusive dining halls or reserved parking lots.[13] Semler also allowed all his office employees to work flexible hours. To his pleasant surprise, he realized that the greater the autonomy that was bestowed upon Semco's employees, the greater was the adaptability, output, and trustworthiness that they displayed and the more efficient Semco became.[14] Semler pushed further to democratize Semco and, according to experts, finally created an organization where employees were free to decide when, where, and how they worked and how they got paid for it.

Organizational Strategy

At Semco, there was no vision/mission statement or regulations manual. It also had no official organizational chart. When it was critical to portray the architecture of the organization, it was only drawn with pencil and was disposed of immediately.[15] The company's course was almost completely reliant on the zeal and creativity of its employees.[16]

Every business division of Semco had complete autonomy to expend its allocated finance as it deemed fit. Each of these business divisions had only a few hundred employees. Within each of these divisions, the practice was to form self-run teams, comprising 10 to 12 individuals, which manufactured a complete product and not merely an individual part. These teams themselves decided their strategies, courses of action, and outcomes and were answerable for them.[17] The small team sizes ensured that employees knew their coworkers well.

Since 1981, Semco had not budgeted for a period exceeding six months. Assessing the status of its business on a half-yearly basis enabled the company to keep up with the changing business scenario.[18] By means of a thorough budgeting and planning mechanism, each business was required to substantiate its continuation. The questions taken into account would be whether a business, assuming that it were not in existence, would be considered worthy of being floated and whether shutting a business would have a negative impact on Semco's relations with its key clients. If the answers were negative, both the financial and human resources were shifted to other businesses.[19] Analysts felt that Semco's businesses owed their resilience to these regular litmus tests to which they were subjected. Also, every six months, each of Semco's divisions estimated the number of employees it needed for the subsequent six months. This exercise also entailed every employee justifying his/her reappointment. Also, since the company did not plan for a period exceeding six months, it did not strategize the new businesses it intended to get into. Rather, Semco experimented with new businesses in a small way. Also, every Semco employee, through his/her vote, had a say in determining whether or not to purchase a new company.[20]

Semco goaded each team to consider itself as a tiny business unit. If a new business proposition that a team put forth was approved, it was the team's responsibility to conduct that business and it was allowed to retain a predetermined percentage, occasionally nearly 50 percent, of the ensuing profits. Consequently, Semco expanded from a small plant manufacturing marine and industrial machinery to an alliance of 16 enterprises, also comprising 10 online businesses, all funded by the respective

[10]Lawrence M. Fisher, "Ricardo Semler Won't Take Control," www.strategy-business.com, November 29, 2005.

[11]Jaclyn Fierman and Therese Eiben, "Winning Ideas from Maverick Managers; Unconventional Leaders Share an Ability to Stun the Competition with Their Personal Brand of Can-Doism . . .," http://money.cnn.com, February 6, 1995.

[12]Charles Handy, "The Handy Guide to the Gurus of Management: Programme 11—Ricardo Semler," http://downloads.bbc.co.uk/worldservice/learningenglish/handy/semler.pdf.

[13]Ricardo Semler, *Maverick*, (Arrow Books, 1999).

[14]Brad Wieners, "Ricardo Semler: Set Them Free," www.cioinsight.com, April 1, 2004.

[15]Peter A. Maresco and Christopher C. York, "Ricardo Semler: Creating Organizational Change through Employee Empowered Leadership," http://www.newunionism.net/library/workplace%20democracy/SEMCO%20-%20Creating%20Organizational%20Change%20through%20Employee-Powered%20Leadership%20-%202005.pdf

[16]Simon Caulkin, "Stone Age Bosses Aren't All That Bad," www.guardian.co.uk, January 14, 2001.

[17]Kevin Herring, "Management in Real Life," www.hr.com, October 7, 2005.

[18]Fred Roed, "Brazilian Legend Ricardo Semler Challenges South Africans to 'Find a Better Way,'" www.ideate.co.za, September 21, 2011.

[19]Ricardo Semler, "How We Went Digital without a Strategy," http://hbr.org/2000/09/how-we-went-digital-without-a-strategy/ar/1?conversationId=2310899.

[20]Martin Simon, "Radical Works: A Different Kind of Employee Incentive," www.forburypeople.com, September 2009.

businesses.[21] Also at Semco, any new business proposals that employees came up with were vetted speedily and transparently. Each proposal was presented to an executive committee comprising emissaries from key business divisions. Any employee could be present at these meetings. Each proposal was required to fulfill the two conditions of operating in the premium segment and of the product or service being intricate, entailing engineering processes, and being difficult to get into. These conditions were even otherwise used to judge any new business that Semco was contemplating entering.[22]

Unlike most CEOs, Semler was not concerned about putting down in black and white the business segments that Semco operated in. According to him, he was neither aware of the business segments that Semco operated in nor keen to know them, as that would curtail employees' innovation, confine their thinking, and discourage them from exploring new avenues. This openness, according to experts, was the reason for Semco expanding from traditional production to services and further to cutting-edge Internet ventures.

Organizational Structure

Semler's efforts to change Semco's DNA partly included his tinkering with its organizational structure. Semco's initial structure was a functional one. This was a traditional pyramidal structure where the power was concentrated at the top and where it was difficult for employees to move up the ladder. Employees of each functional area such as manufacturing, sales, and accounts reported to the respective functional heads at the head office. Semler found that Semco's expansion was being slowed down by the bureaucracies and interdepartmental frictions inherent in a functional system. Semco briefly experimented with the matrix structure but found it ineffective. In 1986, Semco adopted a structure comprising independent business divisions, each headed by a general manager. It then decided to revert to the functional structure.[23]

After 1998, Semco designed for itself a radical organizational architecture comprising three concentric circles—a small one in the middle and two relatively bigger ones. The tiny circle in the middle comprised six individuals including Semler, akin to the vice presidential and higher cadres in traditional organizations. They were responsible for aligning Semco's overall plans and strategies and were referred to as Counselors. The second circle comprised the leaders of each of Semco's business divisions, referred to as Partners.[24] The biggest and outermost circle comprised all other Semco employees. The majority of them were referred to as Associates, and they were engaged in research, design, sales, and production jobs. This associate category comprised both permanent and temporary employees and the task heads who were specifically referred to as Coordinators. Coordinators included the sales, marketing, and manufacturing supervisors and foremen, who had elementary managerial responsibilities in the previous structure.

These coordinators headed teams of associates.[25] None of the coordinators reported to the other coordinators, which effectively cut down the hierarchy. The number of organizational tiers was truncated from 12 to 3.[26]

Each of the six Counselors in the company assumed the CEO post on a half-yearly basis. This ensured that the financial/business performance of the company was not the responsibility of a single individual. According to experts, if the financial/business health of a company were to be a single individual's headache, all the others could afford to take it easy. But at Semco, each of the Counselors could hand over the CEO's post to others but had to reassume the position two and a half years down the line and deal with the situation prevailing then.[27]

Human Resources Practices—The Essence of Semco

Autonomy

All Semco employees were free to do what they desired. They individually determined their respective salaries/ wages, their respective work timings, and their respective attires. Employees were not evaluated on the basis of the number of work hours that they clocked but on the basis of their meeting the set output targets. Clovis Bojikian, Semco's director of human resources as of 2003, explained, "We don't know how many hours any of our employees work weekly. Not even if they work at all. As long as you're getting the job done for yourself and the company, you're free to manage your own time."[28] According to Semler, Semco had been allowing its employees to work from home since 1981.[29] Employees were even encouraged to relax on Monday morning at the beach in case they had to stay back in the office on Saturday afternoon for work.

[21]Charles Handy, "The Doughnut Dimension," www.guardian.org.uk, January 16, 2005.

[22]Ricardo Semler, "How We Went Digital without a Strategy," http://hbr.org/2000/09/how-we-went-digital-without-a-strategy/ar/l?conversationId=2310899.

[23]Ricardo Semler, *Maverick*, (Arrow Books, 1999).

[24]Ibid.

[25]Ibid.

[26]Peter A. Maresco and Christopher C. York, "Ricardo Semler: Creating Organizational Change through Employee Empowered Leadership," http://www.newunionism.net/library/workplace%20democracy/SEMCO%20-%20Creating%20Organizational%20Change%20through%20Employee-Powered%20Leadership%20-%202005.pdf.

[27]Joan Lancourt and Charles Savage, "Organizational Transformation and the Changing Role of the Human Resource Function," *Compensation & Benefits Management*, Vol. 11, No.4, 1995.

[28]Roberto Guimaraes and John Southerst, "Semco: Work + Space = Freedom," www.oneworkplace.com, November 3, 2003.

[29]Sharon Shinn, "The Maverick CEO," www.aacsb.edu, April 25, 2012.

Some experts appreciated Semco for providing hammocks in its gardens where employees could relax whenever they wanted.

Semco's principal policy was not to have any written policies and regulations, except for a short "Survival Manual" produced in comic-book style that got fresh recruits acquainted with its unconventional methods.[30] No one at Semco had a permanent workstation; rather, they had to make their reservation on a daily basis. On a specific day, a top executive might be seated next to an intern.[31] The total operations at Semco revolved around the doctrine that employees needed to take their own decisions in the course of accomplishing their tasks. Penal rules were substituted by the common sense principle and by individual decision-making underlined by accountability for which employees were mentored.[32] For instance, Semco did not institute any travel-related regulations on those who needed to travel on work. Employees were free to take their own decisions regarding the mode of their travel. Being empowered in this aspect, employees did not have to waste time fulfilling micro aspects stipulated by a company's typical travel policy.[33] According to experts, autonomy and self-interest were vital elements of all activities carried out at Semco. Free of policies, procedures, and regulations, Semco's employees were answerable only to themselves. Semler explained, "People who are motivated by self-interest will find solutions that no one can envision. They see the world in their unique way—one that others often overlook."[34]

The main objective of equipping Semco's employees with workplace autonomies was to spur their creative thought processes. Semler explained, "People perform very badly when you assume they must be under control."[35] He felt that approximately 30 percent of productive time at organizations was devoted to petty issues such as dealing with employees who arrived late to the office, ensuring everyone attended meetings, making employees stay back late, etc. This resulted in the subordinates losing their initiative and accomplishing the minimum required to survive the scrutiny.[36]

The way human resources were treated at Semco had two underpinning beliefs. One was faith in grown-up behavior—the fundamental human urge to be productive, to strive for a better tomorrow, and to contribute to an endeavor of significance. The second was that each individual's functioning was distinct with regard to the time, place, and mode of delivering their best output.[37]

Doing Only What Was Needed

There was no compulsion for the employees to attend any of the meetings—if no one attended a meeting, it was an indication that its agenda for the meeting was worthless. Two positions at the board meeting were kept vacant for all the employees, to be filled up on a first come-first serve basis. Also at meetings, employees were vigorously prodded

to raise queries, to leave a meeting if they lost interest, and to attend any meeting whose agenda they were keen on. The ultimate objective was to focus on what really mattered and make productive use of time.[38] One of the company norms was that the employees had to restrict all circulars, reports, letters, and minutes to a single page. This forced them to focus on putting down only what was necessary.[39]

Bottom-Up Approach

The employees themselves nominated the corporate executives and triggered many of Semco's entries into new business arenas and its exit from existing ones. They could veto even the CEO's decisions.[40] Though Semler was the major shareholder at Semco, he had a single vote just like other company employees. One day, when Semler arrived at work, he realized that his personal cabin had been removed. His team decided that he did not require it and that the area could instead be utilized for another activity that could further business prospects.[41,42]

Joao Vendramin, who was heading the durable goods unit and was one of the CEOs, said, "Ricardo will say, 'If you want to know my opinion, I can give it to you now or later. But it's just another opinion.' "[43] Semler did not agree

[30]"The Journeys of 2nd Tier Leaders over Time," http://integralleader-hipreview.com, March 2008.

[31]Roberto Guimaraes and John Southerst, "Semco: Work + Space = Freedom," www.oneworkplace.com, November 3, 2003.

[32]Sudam Chandima Kaluarachchi, "Is Management a Dream without Managers?" www.ft.lk, October 19, 2010.

[33] Langdon Morris, "Top-Down Innovation: Leaders Define Innovative Culture," http://www.realinnovation.com/content/c070528a.asp.

[34]Ricardo Semler, *The Seven-Day Weekend*, (Arrow Books, 2004).

[35]Stephen Moss, " 'Idleness Is Good'," www.guardian.co.uk, April 17, 2003.

[36]"Brazil—The Caring Capitalist," www.journeyman.tv, July 4, 2005.

[37]Polly LaBarre, "Forget Empowerment—Aim for Exhilaration," www.managementexchange.com, April 25, 2012.

[38]Ibid.

[39]Martin Simon, "Radical Works: A Different Kind of Employee Incentive," www.forburypeople.com, September 2009.

[40]Greg Ferenstein, "How Brazil Is Blazing a Trail for Electronic Democracy," http://mashable.com, September 14, 2010.

[41]Colin Emerson, "Business: How Do You Become One of the Most Outstanding Leaders Ever in Your World?" www.ecademy.com, February 7, 2012.

[42]Ted Coine, Richard McGill Murphy, Marc Gunther, Edward E. Lawler III, Charles Erlcson, Aad Boot, and Simon Herrlott, *Return on Culture: New Perspectives on Corporate Governance*, http://sustainablebusinessforum.com/sites/sustainablebusinessforum.com/files/Return_on_Culture_Ebook.pdf.

[43]Jaclyn Fierman and Therese Eiben, "Winning Ideas from Maverick Managers; Unconventional Leaders Share an Ability to Stun the Competition with Their Personal Brand of Can-Doism . . .," http://money.cnn.com, February 6, 1995.

EXHIBIT 1

Recruitment Procedure Followed at Semco

At Semco, if any team felt the need to recruit a new employee, the requirement was mentioned on the company's intranet, along with the date and time at which the selection criteria would be finalized. Any Semco employee was free to attend and aid the recruitment process. On the specified day, the interested employees would sit together and arrive at the selection criteria and advertise accordingly. If, for instance, 200 resumes had been received, they would be distributed for screening among the employees participating in the recruitment process. This procedure, by allowing employees themselves to screen the resumes, enabled the spotting of candidates who might not fit the immediate profile but might be suitable for other jobs in the organization. Also, the company employees, occasionally in dozens, jointly interviewed potential recruits. These candidates were free to come back to Semco any number of times to get clarifications on any concerns they had, which would help them in deciding whether or not to join the organization. This largely ensured that new employees fitted into Semco's culture, which was based on trust.

Sources: Brad Wieners, "Ricardo Semler: Set Them Free," www.cioinsight.com, April 1, 2004; Sharon Shinn, "The Maverick CEO," www.aacsb.edu, April 25, 2012.

at all times with the decisions taken by the employees. However, at Semco, this was considered beneficial. It was felt that the more the autonomy and less the focus on a single person, the greater would be the robustness. A particular choice might even prove incorrect, but it was considered to be evidence of the autonomy and consistency that employees enjoyed and, hence, was viewed as being beneficial for the company's long-term health.[44]

At Semco, there were almost no official designations. All employees, including workers, chose their managers by vote. Even managers recruited from the outside were interviewed by the related team members. Explaining the idea behind employees themselves selecting their managers, Semler said, "We think it's better business when the boss is not simply imposed on people. If you're not involved in the choice of your boss, you are also free from commitment. When you ask, 'Do you like this boss or do you want that one?' the mindset changes dramatically."[45]

Leadership Earned

Leadership positions were considered to be vital and one needed to have followers to lay claim to a leadership role. Eligibility for leadership/managerial roles was periodically vetted by taking the approval of the managed. Every Semco manager was appraised on a half-yearly basis by his/her team members through 36 multiple choice questions. These questions were chiefly aimed at gauging the ability of the managers to motivate their team members and their capacity to accept their feedback.[46] And the appraisal results were displayed on the company's intranet. According to experts, the 36 questions proved that Semler expected managers to be calm, just, affable, capable of delegation, dependable, and efficient. Those rated low had to better their performance, failing which they were demoted.

Semco's personnel department was done away with as the leaders were expected to have the competence to deal with employees appropriately.[47] Only two individuals from the department were retained in the company to inform everyone about the developments in human resources practices elsewhere. As there was no personnel department, employees had to themselves determine whether they required a new team member and recruit one (refer to Exhibit 1 for the innovative recruitment procedure followed at Semco).

Transparency

Semco also maintained complete financial transparency. There was no information that could be categorized as confidential within the company.[48] All employees of the company were given the company's financials. Training sessions were conducted to enable all employees, including workers and cleaners, to comprehend the company's financial statements. Semco held a meeting every month where all employees participated in evaluating the company's finances. They could gauge what the company's turnover and payroll were, the reasons that set them apart from their rivals, and the reasons for the profits increasing or decreasing.[49]

All employees determined their respective salaries, which could be viewed by all on the company's intranet.[50] Explaining the rationale for providing unrestricted access

[44]Simon Caulkin, "Who's in Charge Here? No One," www.guardian.co.uk, April 27, 2003.

[45]David Creelman, "Thought Leaders: Ricardo Semler on a New Form of Management," www.hr.com, May 4, 2005.

[46]Robert Heller, "Business Leadership: To Be a Good Manager, You Have to Lead," www.thinkingmanagers.com, April 8, 2005.

[47]"When Happiness Is Your Driving Force in Business," http://health2organisations.com, March 3, 2010.

[48]Adrian Gaskell, "Should Your Salary Be Public Knowledge?," www.managers.org.uk, July 16, 2009.

[49]Ricardo Semler, *The Seven-Day Weekend*, (Arrow Books, 2004).

[50]Nick Easen, "Democracy in the Workplace," http://edition.cnn.com, May 20, 2004.

Semco's Compensation Options

1. Fixed salary
2. Bonuses
3. Profit sharing
4. Commission
5. Royalties on sales
6. Royalties on profits
7. Commission on gross margin
8. Stock or stock options
9. Initial Public Offering (IPO) or sale (could be availed of only when a specific business division went for an IPO or the division was sold)
10. Self-set yearly appraisal/compensation (wherein an employee was paid for achieving self-determined targets)
11. Value added, a percentage of the difference between the present and the future, three-year worth of the company

Source: Ricardo Semler, *The Seven-Day Weekend* (Arrow Books, 2004).

to the salary details of all the employees, Semler said, "If you are embarrassed about the size of your salary you're probably not earning it."[51] Semco offered its employees a list of 11 diverse compensation payment choices that they could combine in any proportion (refer to Exhibit 2 for the different compensation options).[52] Some of these payment alternatives were fixed pay, allotment of company's shares, and commission on sales. Several of the employees opted for a portion of their salaries to be given in the form of profit apportioning plans, an indication of their confidence that their employer would offer them a better return on their money than compensation in hard cash.[53]

Individual Driven

Semco emphasized that employees strive for personal challenges and gratification before working toward the organization's goals.[54] He believed that if the employees of an organization led balanced lives, the entity would remain healthy. And, according to him, the balance could be attained when employees were given room to figure out their strengths and likings and align their individual ambitions with organizational objectives. Once they were stimulated and energized, their endeavors would automatically lead to fruitful organizational development. Job rotation was actively promoted across the organization as Semler was of the view that many of the employees were the products of an education system that forced them to decide on their career paths early in their lives when they had insignificant knowledge and no clue about occupations. The company's employees were given the freedom to search for jobs in which they were interested. They could opt to be a part of any team subject to there being a vacancy, their skill sets being the required ones,

and the team members being open to their inclusion.[55] According to commentators, every Semco employee was in charge of his/her individual career. Semco funded the training programs that each was interested in, irrespective of the area of learning, subject to a budget.

Semco did not have an information technology department. Each Semco employee was free to buy information technology infrastructure of his/her choice. This ensured that he/she took the advice of many individuals and purchased a device that was the latest and the most updated. This minimized the risk of technological obsolescence. If an employee bought an exorbitantly priced device, his performance was expected to match up to the bill that the organization had to foot for the device.[56] Also, according to Semler, by avoiding centralized purchase of information technology requirements, Semco did away with the procedure followed by conventional companies of collating the requirements of all the departments and inviting tenders and then realizing that the devices that they had bought were inferior to speedier and more efficient new launches.

[51]Wayne Visser, "The Age of Responsibility: CSR 2.0 and the New DNA of Business," *Journal of Business Systems, Governance and Ethics*, Vol. 5, No. 3, http://www.jbsge.vu.edu.au/issues/vol05no3/Visser.pdf.

[52]Simon Caulkin, "Few Options Left for Meg, Jeff and Tim," www.guardian.org.uk, March 18, 2001.

[53]Ricardo Semler, *The Seven-Day Weekend*, (Arrow Books, 2004).

[54]Gary A. Yukl and Wendy S. Becker, "Effective Empowerment in Organizations," *Organization Management Journal*, Vol. 3, No. 3, 2006.

[55]Kevin Herring, "Management in Real Life," www.hr.com, October 7, 2005.

[56]Brad Wieners, "Ricardo Semler: Set Them Free," www.cioinsight.com, April 1, 2004.

A Balanced Approach

The freedom bestowed upon employees was tempered by certain measures. One such measure was peer group scrutiny of employee activities. This discouraged employees from taking advantage of the system by, for instance, unnecessarily traveling in business class, as their counterparts would evaluate their expenses. One more of Semler's important techniques was the rewarding of employees with variable compensation. Their compensation—23 percent of each business unit was apportioned among that division's employees—was directly related to the company's performance, motivating every one of them to consistently work at their best.[57,58] Semco also created certain conditions to ensure that employees set their individual salaries appropriately. It provided employees with the details of salaries that employees in other companies received. The salary details of every employee in the company, in any case, were known to every other employee, and the financial condition of the company could be gauged from its financials.[59] Moreover, all work was accomplished in small teams where work was apportioned in such a manner that each employee had a clear idea of how he/she contributed to the company. Hence, according to an expert, employees could determine their salary in a fair manner as they had access to three crucial details: they were aware of their market worth, they were aware of how their output fitted into the team's output, and they were aware of the company's financial condition.[60] Also, the salary of each employee was subject to perusal by others.[61] If an employee set his/her salary unusually high and his/her performance did not match up to it, that individual ran the risk of not being selected by any of the teams when they were formed anew after six months.

Production Staff—Brothers in Partnership

At Semco, the worker committees administered the factories.[62] These committees regularly held parleys with the executives of each plant. The committees had a say in expense reductions, in making significant alterations to product lines, and, during difficult times, in choosing the employees who would face the axe.[63] Workers, of their own volition, performed multiple tasks. On a typical day, depending upon the output goals, a lathe operator might opt to concurrently handle a grinder or steer a forklift.[64]

According to experts, one of the distinctive aspects of Semco's work culture was the company's production staff determining their respective work hours. Generally, they jointly decided the time at which they should be at work. In the 1980s when Semco was to introduce flexible work timings for workers in the manufacturing line, the production executives were up-in-arms against the initiative as they felt that it would infringe on the

elementary assumption that for a manufacturing set-up to function, each of the individuals involved had to work during the same hours. Semler's response was that if the workers were not operating at a particular time, the manufacturing line would come to a standstill. As grown-ups, even the workers were aware of this and also of the fact that they would be jobless if there was no output. And, according to Semler, if the workers still did not care about the company's productivity, it would be more ominous for the company in the long run. Also, it would be in the best interests of the company to be aware of this fact early. The day before the flexible hour policy was implemented, the production workforce came together and agreed on their work timings.[65]

Single-Minded Focus on Performance

The Semco employees who contributed little did not remain unscathed. To remain in the organization, an individual had to be required by any of the teams for the subsequent six months, which could not be achieved by indulging in politics. Semler explained, "It's as free market as we can make it. People bring their talents and we rely on their self-interest to use the company to develop themselves in any way they see fit. In return, they must have the self-discipline to perform."[66]

It was not lost on some observers that the freedom given to employees to determine their respective work hours ultimately enhanced the organizational productivity. Semler elaborated, ". . . if you wake up in a bad mood on Monday morning, you don't have to come to work. We

[57]Mark Hillary, "Brazil IT Management Needs Transparency," http://itdecs.com, April 6, 2012.

[58]Dave Gray, "A Business within the Business," www.dachisgroup.com, November 28, 2011.

[59]David Creelman, "Thought Leaders: Ricardo Semler on a New Form of Management," www.hr.com, May 4, 2005.

[60]Balaji Pasumarthy, "Do You Want to Decide Your Own Salary?" http://wealth.moneycontrol.com, November 6, 2008.

[61]Tammy Erickson, "Should Your Coworkers Know How Much You Make?" http://blogs.hbr.com, April 25, 2009.

[62]Nick Easen, "Democracy in the Workplace," http://edition.cnn.com, May 20, 2004.

[63]Martin Simon, "Radical Works: A Different Kind of Employee Incentive," www.forburypeople.com, September 2009.

[64]Lawrence M. Fisher, "Ricardo Semler Won't Take Control," www.strategy-business.com, November 29, 2005.

[65]Francisco Trindade, "Focus on the Right Point," http://blog.franktrindade.com, August 12, 2008.

[66]Simon Caulkin, "Who's in Charge Here? No One," www.guardian.co.uk, April 27, 2003.

don't even want you to come because you simply don't feel like it and will therefore not make a contribution. We want employees who are ready and willing to work. If that means they only come twice a week, that's okay. It's about results."[67]

The overwhelming stress on objectivity also led to the company's head office being dismantled and replaced by satellite offices akin to the airport lounges scattered across São Paulo. Employees were deprived of not only permanent workstations but also of permanent offices. According to Semler, "They thought it was about location. In fact, it's about eliminating control. If you don't even know where people are, you can't possibly keep an eye on them. All that's left to judge on is performance."[68] Another objective of closing the head office was to cut down the time employees spent battling São Paulo's traffic to reach the office. Semco calculated that one million hours per annum were devoted to travelling to and fro. Hence, it was decided that Semco's employees would work in smaller settings closer home.

Semco encouraged its employees to take afternoon naps—something looked down upon in conventional companies—in the hammocks. Semler believed short spurts of sleep in the afternoon were a part of the natural body rhythm and helped in reenergizing employees.

Semco adhered to a six-month strategy rather than a one year one that most other companies adopted as the management did not want its employees to emulate their counterparts in other companies who got things moving only in the second half of the financial year.

Lessons in Surviving Economic Crises

According to observers, Semco's robustness was in full display during the 1990s when the Brazilian economy was in the doldrums. At a time when Brazil's gross industrial product declined by 14 percent, 11 percent, and 9 percent in 1990, 1991, and 1992, respectively, when the country's capital equipment production contracted to the 1977 position, and when 28 percent of its capital equipment producers went bust, Semco managed to maintain its revenue and profit momentum. This was made possible by certain radical shifts implemented by Semco and, more importantly, its employees. In 1990, Semco too had frequently been staring at nil monthly sales and employee retrenchment had become imminent. At that stage, Semco's workers took the initiative and proposed to take a 30 percent reduction in wages, subject to their slice of profits being enhanced to 39 percent, management pay being reduced by 40 percent, and their being entitled to vet every expense. They also themselves executed several tasks that had previously been outsourced like preparing meals, cleaning, guarding the plants, delivering the end products to the customers, and hawking the replaced

components.[69] The changes brought about during that period resulted in a 65 percent decline in inventories, a significant compression of product delivery times, and a product defect percentage of below 1 percent.[70] As the economic situation became better, Semco's financial outlook stabilized.

Despite Semco's financial health being restored, the company's management felt that, given the fragility of the Brazilian economy, Semco's operational and financial efficiencies could only be sustained by reducing its permanent workforce and outsourcing some of the operations. Semco's management preferred assigning the work to employees who might get the axe to outsourcing the jobs to outsiders.[71] These employees were encouraged to exit Semco and set up their respective satellite firms and, to begin with, get subcontracts from Semco. These subcontractors were allowed to lease Semco's machinery and could further operate from Semco's factories. They could get orders from other companies and still execute them deploying Semco's machines. Initially, they did not have to pay lease charges for using Semco's machinery and its other infrastructure. Semco benefited in terms of reduced expenses, both salaries and inventory, and by getting the work executed by individuals who knew its requirements inside out.[72] Making entrepreneurs out of Semco's employees took their commitment, which was already robust, to the next level. As of 1998, nearly 66 percent of Semco's new products were produced by these satellite firms, and 66 percent of its workforce operated through these units.

Impact

Semco was a privately held company that did not disclose its financials. Its turnover had increased from U.S. $4 million in 1982 to more than U.S. $1 billion by 2007[73,74]

---

[67]Dominique Haijtema, "The Boss Who Breaks All the Rules," http://odewire.com, January 21, 2007.

[68]Simon Caulkin, "Who's in Charge Here? No One," www.guardian.co.uk, April 27, 2003.

[69]Ricardo Semler, "Why My Former Employees Still Work for Me," *Harvard Business Review*, January 1994.

[70]"BRIC is Next," http://sephisemagazine.org/contemporary-south/bric-is -next.html.

[71]Ricardo Semler, "Why My Former Employees Still Work for Me," *Harvard Business Review*, January 1994.

[72]Kelly Killian, Francisco Perez, and Caren Siehl, "Ricardo Semler and Semco S.A.," http://www.thunderbird.edu/knowledge_network/case _series/1998/_98-0024.htm.

[73]https://socialimprints.com/pages/empowering-the-community.

[74]Kerry O'Brien, "Interview with Semco's Business Guru," www.abc.net.au, June 3, 2007.

EXHIBIT 3

Annual Revenues of Semco (US$ million)

1980	4
1994	35
2001	160
2003	212
2007	>1000

Sources: https://socialimprints.com/pages/empowering-the-community; Ricardo Semler, *The Seven-Day Weekend* (Arrow Books, 2004); A.J. Vogl, "The Anti-CEO," *The Conference Board Review*, May/June 2004; Kerry O'Brien, "Interview with Semco's Business Guru," www.abc.net.au, June 3, 2007.

(refer to Exhibit 3 for the increase in Semco's revenues over the years). And, according to Semler, Semco was clocking average yearly revenue and bottom-line growth of 40 percent.[75] Semco's success could also be gauged from the fact that an investment of U.S. $100,000 in 1985 would have yielded an additional U.S. $5.3 million by 2005.[76] Its employee strength had increased from 90 in 1982 to 5000 by 2007.[77, 78] And, according to experts, the fact that repeat clients accounted for nearly four-fifths of Semco's yearly turnover of 2003 indicated the company's client retention abilities.

According to observers, Semco earned significant goodwill because of the freedom it gave its employees (refer to Exhibit 4 for some of Semco's innovative employee programs). At Semco, at times, there would be gaps of up to fourteen months before an employee resigned from his/her job. At any point in time, the company had to process at least 2,000 job applicants, with several of the applicants being prepared to take up any work offered to them at Semco.[79] Also, according to Semler, the yearly attrition rate at Semco had been below 2 percent since 1981.

Some experts felt that the true impact of the employees being at the helm of affairs in the organization was felt in the resilience that Semco developed. This became clear when, in February 2005, Semler met with a near-fatal accident and had to be in the intensive care unit for an extended period of time, recovering from the multiple operations he had to undergo. During this time, Semco operated smoothly—targets were reached and agreements sealed, and there was no disruption to business.[80] Semco had reached a stage where it was not dependent on a single individual, not even Semler. At least for 10 years since 1993, Semler had not taken

EXHIBIT 4

Some of the Innovative Employee Programs at Semco

Retire-A-Little (RAL): This program was based on the premise that employees in their 30s and 40s might not be able to pursue their hobbies and interests due to financial constraints. However, when they were in a financially comfortable position in their 60s, they did not have the physical wherewithal to pursue their interests. Under RAL, an employee could take time out, possibly for half a day in a week, to engage in his/her personal pursuits, which would also entail a slight deduction in the monthly salary. After retirement, he/she could redeem from Semco the deducted salary by working the corresponding number of hours.

Lost In Space (LIS): Under LIS, for one year, every young entrant into Semco was free to do whatever he/she desired, work in any of Semco's business divisions, or hop across any number of divisions he/she wanted to. However, after the completion of a year, if none of the divisions where an entrant worked came up with a job offer or if the entrant did not find anything interesting, he/she had to quit. LIS was based on the premise that under the prevailing education system, adolescents were pressured by their parents to choose a particular career path, which might ultimately not fully unlock their potential.

Up'n Down Pay (UDP): Under this program, employees had the flexibility to adjust their compensations based on certain situations in life. An individual could reduce the number of his/her working hours or responsibilities due to factors such as taking care of infant children. There would be a corresponding reduction in pay.

Work'n Stop (WSP): Under WSP, employees could take extended breaks of up to three years to pursue studies or their interests or to introspect on where they were headed.

Rush Hour MBA (RHM): The RHM program, conducted once every week for 2 hours starting at 6:00 P.M., was devised to enable Semco's employees to avoid São Paolo's heavy traffic and simultaneously make productive use of their time. Any of Semco's employees could volunteer to lecture to the employees on a subject of his/her interest or to tell them about an interesting article he/she had read recently. The 2 hours spent allowed employees to not only enrich themselves but also to reach home faster upon completion.

Source: Ricardo Semler, *The Seven-Day Weekend* (Arrow Books, 2004).

[75]Polly LaBarre, "What Does Fulfillment at Work Really Look Like?," http://management.fortune.cnn.com, May 1, 2012.

[76]Lawrence M. Fisher, "Ricardo Semler Won't Take Control," www.strategy-business.com, November 29, 2005.

[77]"BRIC is Next," http://sephisemagazine.org/contemporary-south/bric-is-next.html.

[78]Kerry O'Brien, "Interview with Semco's Business Guru," www.abc.net.au, June 3, 2007.

[79]J. Patrick Murphy, "We Want the Best," http://las.depaul.edu, September 26, 2008.

[80]Lawrence M. Fisher, "Ricardo Semler Won't Take Control," www.strategy-business.com, November 29, 2005.

a single decision at Semco.[81] He had no role in initiating businesses that contributed to three-fifths of Semco's turnover as of 2006.[82]

A result of Semco's steadfast adherence to placing faith in employee choices regarding the time when they worked, how much they were paid, deciding themselves whether or not to skip meetings, and purchasing their own information technology infrastructure was an intensely faithful and productive workforce.[83] According to a long-serving Semco employee who had started small and had worked her way up Semco's ladder, "In all these years, Semco never discounted a minute's worth of salary, even when I was late or absent. I take a reciprocity position. When Semco needs me I am there. When my brother got sick, I was gone for four days and Semco didn't discount a penny from my cheque. In turn, I haven't claimed overtime for the weekends I worked . . . There's a virtuous circle in place that requires no overt declaration."[84]

Constraints to Replication?

Though Semco's radical management practices had indicated that they could result in profitable and sustainable growth, experts were skeptical about the extent to which these tenets could result in similar successes in other companies, genuine though their efforts might be. Their skepticism had its roots in the deliberate strategy chosen by Semco of being present only in businesses that entailed significant levels of engineering/complexity (this ensured

that the barriers to entry for other aspirants in terms of technological competence required were high); of being only a premium player in each of its product/service segments; and of carving out a distinct niche in each product/service segment, which ensured that Semco was a prominent player in the concerned industry.[85] Experts wondered whether a company operating in a product/service segment that was easy for others to enter, which was not present in a premium or a niche segment—this meant that economies of scale could not be ignored—could afford to bestow similar freedoms upon its employees. Some commentators also observed that Semler, being the majority shareholder in a privately held company, had the luxury of trying out his radical ideas. Would it be within the realm of possibility, they wondered, for a large public company with diffused ownership to embark on such a journey? So, would relinquishing control, described by Semler as Semco's competitive advantage, be limited to just one company?

[81]Simon Caulkin, "Who's in Charge Here? No One," www.guardian.co.uk, April 27, 2003.

[82]Dominique Haijtema, "The Boss Who Breaks All the Rules," http://odewire.com, January 21, 2007.

[83]Edward H. Baker, "Editorial: April 2004," www.cioinsight.com, April 1, 2004.

[84]Ricardo Semler, *The Seven-Day Weekend*, (Arrow Books, 2004).

[85]Ibid.

A

adaptability culture a culture characterized by strategic focus on the external environment through flexibility and change to meet customer needs.

administrative principles a management perspective that focuses on the design and functioning of the organization as a whole.

ambidextrous approach a design approach that incorporates structures and management processes that are appropriate to both the creation and the implementation of innovation.

analyzability a dimension of technology in which work can be reduced to mechanical steps and participants can follow an objective, computational procedure to solve problems.

analyzer the analyzer tries to maintain a stable business while innovating on the periphery.

authority a force for achieving desired outcomes that is prescribed by the formal hierarchy and reporting relationships.

B

balanced scorecard a comprehensive management control system that balances traditional financial measures with operational measures relating to a company's critical success factors.

behavior control managers' direct observation and supervision of employee actions to see whether the individual follows rules and policies and performs tasks as instructed.

big data refers to any massive data set that exceeds the boundaries and conventional processing capabilities of IT.

big data analytics refers to the process of examining these large data sets to uncover hidden patterns, correlations, and other useful information and make better decisions.

boundary-spanning roles activities that link and coordinate an organization with key elements in the external environment.

bounded rationality perspective a perspective that describes how decisions actually have to be made under severe time and resource constraints.

buffering roles activities that absorb uncertainty from the environment.

bureaucracy an organizational framework marked by rules and procedures, specialization and division of labor, hierarchy of authority, emphasis on technically qualified personnel, and written communications and records.

bureaucratic control the use of rules, policies, hierarchy of authority, written documentation, standardization, and other bureaucratic mechanisms to standardize behavior and assess performance.

bureaucratic culture a culture with an internal focus and a consistency orientation for a stable environment.

bureaucratic organizations organizations that emphasize designing and managing on an impersonal, rational basis through such elements as clearly defined authority and responsibility, formal recordkeeping, and uniform application of standard rules.

business intelligence high-tech analysis of large amounts of internal and external data to spot patterns and relationships that might be significant.

C

Carnegie model organizational decision making that involves many managers making a final choice based on a coalition among those managers.

centrality reflects a department's role in the primary activity of an organization and is a source of horizontal power.

centralization refers to the level of hierarchy with authority to make decisions.

change process the way in which changes occur in an organization.

charismatic authority is based on devotion to the exemplary character or to the heroism of an individual person and the order defined by him or her.

clan control the use of social characteristics, such as shared cultural values, commitment, traditions, and beliefs, to control behavior.

clan culture a culture with a primary focus on the involvement and participation of the organization's members and on rapidly changing expectations from the external environment.

coalition an alliance among several managers who agree about organizational goals and problem priorities.

code of ethics a formal statement of the organization's values concerning ethics and social responsibility.

codified knowledge formal, systematic knowledge that can be articulated, written down, and passed on to others in documents, rules, or general instructions.

coercive forces the external pressures exerted on an organization to adopt structures, techniques, or behaviors similar to other organizations.

cognitive biases severe errors in judgment that all humans are prone to and that typically lead to bad choices.

collaboration a joint effort between people from two or more departments to produce outcomes that meet a common goal or shared purpose and that are typically greater than what any of the individuals or departments could achieve working alone.

collaborative-network perspective an emerging perspective whereby organizations join together to become more competitive and to share scarce resources.

collective bargaining the negotiation used to resolve disagreement between workers and management.

collectivity stage the life cycle stage in which employees identify with the mission of the organization and spend long hours helping the organization succeed. Members feel part of a collective.

competitive advantage refers to what sets the organization apart from others and provides it with a distinctive edge for meeting customer or client needs in the market place.

competition rivalry among groups in the pursuit of a common prize.

competing values model a model that tries to balance a concern with various parts of the organization rather than focusing on one part.

complexity refers to heterogeneity, or the number and dissimilarity of external elements that affect an organization's operations.

compliance officer a high-level company executive who oversees all aspects of ethics, including establishing and broadly communicating ethical standards and advising managers on the ethical aspects of corporate decisions.

confrontation a situation in which parties in conflict directly engage one another and try to work out their differences.

conscious capitalism refers to organizational policies and practices that both enhance the economic success of a company and advance the economic and social conditions of the communities in which the company operates; also referred to as a shared value approach.

contingency theory meaning that one thing depends on other things.

contingency decision-making framework a perspective that brings together the two dimensions of problem consensus and technical knowledge about solutions.

contingency factors larger elements that influence structural dimensions, including the organization's size, technology, environment, culture, and goals.

continuous-process production a completely mechanized manufacturing process in which there is no starting or stopping.

cooptation occurs when leaders from important sectors in the environment are made part of an organization.

core competence something the organization does especially well in comparison to its competitors.

core technology the work process that is directly related to the organization's mission.

corporate social responsibility (CSR) refers to management's obligation to make choices and take action so that the organization contributes to the welfare and interest of all organizational stakeholders.

craft technologies are characterized by a fairly stable stream of activities, but the conversion process is not analyzable or well understood.

creative departments departments that initiate change, such as research and development, engineering, design, and systems analysis.

creativity the generation of novel ideas that may meet perceived needs or respond to opportunities.

crowdsourcing an approach to open innovation that solicits ideas, services, or information from a large number of volunteers, usually via social media and the Internet.

culture the set of values, norms, guiding beliefs, and understandings that is shared by members of an organization and taught to new members as the correct way to think, feel, and behave.

culture innovations changes in the values, attitudes, expectations, beliefs, abilities, and behavior of employees.

culture strength the degree of agreement among members of an organization about the importance of specific values.

D

data intermediaries firms that collect data from multiple organizations and analyze the combined data for outsourcing partners.

data warehousing the use of huge databases that combine all of a company's data and allow users to access the data directly, create reports, and obtain responses to what-if questions.

decentralization means that decision-making authority is pushed down to lower organizational levels.

decentralized control uses rules and procedures only when necessary and relies on shared goals and values to guide behavior.

decision learning a process of recognizing and admitting mistakes that allows managers to acquire sufficient experience and knowledge to perform more effectively in the future.

defender a business strategy that is concerned with stability or even retrenchment.

departmental grouping a grouping in which employees share a common supervisor and common resources, are jointly responsible for performance, and tend to identify and collaborate with one another.

dependency an aspect of horizontal power, in which one department is dependent on another and the latter is in a position of greater power.

devil's advocate the role of challenging the assumptions and assertions made by the group.

differentiation the differences in cognitive and emotional orientations among managers in various functional departments and the differences in formal structure among these departments.

differentiation strategy a business strategy that attempts to distinguish an organization's products or services from others in the industry.

direct interlock occurs when one individual is the link between two companies, such as when a member of one company's board also sits on the board of another company.

disruptive innovation refers to innovations that typically start small and end up completely replacing an existing product or service technology for producers and consumers.

divisional grouping a grouping in which employees are organized according to what the organization produces.

divisional structure a structure in which separate divisions can be organized with responsibility for individual products, services, product groups, major projects or programs, divisions, businesses, or profit centers; sometimes called a *product structure* or *strategic business units*.

domain the chosen environmental field of action; the territory an organization stakes out for itself with respect to products, services, and markets served.

domains of political activity areas in which politics plays a role. Three domains in organizations are structural change, management succession, and resource allocation.

domestic stage the first stage of international development in which a company is domestically oriented while managers are aware of the global environment and may want to consider initial foreign involvement to expand production volume and realize economies of scale.

downsizing intentionally reducing the size of a company's workforce.

dual-core approach an organizational change perspective that compares management and technical innovation.

dynamism refers to whether the environment in which the organization operates is stable or unstable.

E

economies of scale achieving lower costs through large volume production; often made possible by global expansion.

economies of scope achieving economies by having a number and variety of products and services or by operating in a number and variety of regions, countries, and markets.

effectiveness the degree to which an organization achieves its goals.

efficiency the amount of resources used to achieve an organization's goals; based on the quantity of raw materials, money, and employees necessary to produce a given level of output.

elaboration stage a mature stage of the life cycle in which a red tape crisis is resolved through the development of a new sense of teamwork and collaboration.

empowerment the delegation of power or authority to subordinates in an organization, also known as *power sharing*.

engineering technologies tend to be complex because there is substantial variety in the tasks performed, but the various activities are usually handled on the basis of established formulas, procedures, and techniques.

entrepreneurial stage the life cycle stage in which an organization is born and its emphasis is on creating a product and surviving in the marketplace.

escalating commitment persisting to invest time and money in a solution despite strong evidence that it is not working.

ethical dilemma arises in a situation concerning right and wrong in which each alternative choice seems undesirable because of potentially negative ethical consequences.

ethics the code of moral principles and values that governs the behaviors of a person or group with respect to what is right or wrong.

ethics committee a cross-functional group of executives who oversee company ethics.

ethics hotlines telephone numbers employees can call to seek guidance as well as report questionable behavior.

evidence-based management a commitment to make more informed and intelligent decisions based on the best available facts and evidence.

expert locator system systems that identify and catalog experts in a searchable database so people can quickly identify who has knowledge they can use.

external adaptation refers to how the organization meets goals and deals with outsiders.

F

factors of production resources necessary for production, such as land, raw materials, and labor.

feedback control model a control cycle that involves setting strategic goals for departments or the organization as a whole, establishing metrics and standards of performance, comparing metrics of actual performance to standards, and correcting or changing activities as needed.

focus a value dimension that states whether dominant values concern issues that are *internal* or *external* to the firm.

formalization the degree to which an organization has rules, procedures, and written documentation.

formalization stage the life cycle stage that involves the installation and use of rules, procedures, and control systems.

functional grouping a grouping that places together employees who perform similar functions or work processes or who bring similar knowledge and skills to bear.

functional matrix type of matrix structure in which the functional bosses have primary authority and the project or product managers simply coordinate product activities.

functional structure organization structure in which activities are grouped together by common function from the bottom to the top of the organization.

G

garbage can model decision-making model that describes the pattern or flow of multiple decisions within an organization.

general environment those sectors that might not have a direct impact on the daily operations of a firm but will indirectly influence it.

generalist an organization with a wide niche or domain that offers a broad range of products or services or serves a broad market.

global companies companies that no longer think of themselves as having a single home country; sometimes called *stateless corporations*.

global geographic structure structure that divides the world into geographic regions, with each geographic division reporting to the CEO.

global matrix structure a form of horizontal linkage for an international organization in which both product and geographical structures are implemented simultaneously.

global product structure structure in which the product divisions take responsibility for global operations in their specific product area.

global stage the stage of international development in which the company transcends any single country.

global teams cross-border work groups made up of multiskilled, multinational members whose activities span multiple countries; also called *transnational teams*.

globalization strategy the standardization of product design, manufacturing, and marketing strategy throughout the world.

goal approach an approach to effectiveness that is concerned with an organization's output goals and assessing how well the organization has attained those goals.

groupthink the tendency of people in groups to suppress contrary opinions.

H

Hawthorne Studies a series of experiments on worker productivity begun in 1924 at the Hawthorne plant of Western Electric Company in Illinois; attributed employees' increased output to managers' better treatment of them during the study.

heroes organization members who serve as models or ideals for upholding cultural norms and values.

hierarchical control involves monitoring and influencing employee behavior through extensive use of rules, policies, and hierarchy of authority, written documentation, reward systems, and other formal mechanisms.

high-velocity environments industries in which competitive and technological change is so extreme that market data is either unavailable or obsolete, strategic windows open and shut quickly, and decisions must be made quickly with limited information.

horizontal coordination model a model of the three components of organization design needed to achieve new product innovation: departmental specialization, boundary spanning, and horizontal coordination.

horizontal grouping a grouping in which employees are organized around core work processes, the end-to-end work, information, and material flows that provide value directly to customers.

horizontal linkage refers to communication and coordination horizontally across organizational departments.

horizontal structure organization structure that organizes employees around core processes.

human relations emphasis incorporates the values of an internal focus and a flexible structure.

hybrid organization an organization that mixes value systems and behaviors that represent two different sectors of society, which leads to tensions and conflict within the organization over goals and priorities.

hybrid structure a structure that combines characteristics of various approaches tailored to specific strategic needs.

I

idea champions organization members who provide the time and energy to make change happen; sometimes called *advocates, intrapreneurs,* and *change agents.*

idea incubator a safe harbor in which ideas from employees throughout the organization can be developed without interference from company bureaucracy or politics.

imitation the act of adopting a decision tried elsewhere in the hope that it will work in this situation.

incremental decision model decision-making model that describes the structured sequence of activities undertaken from the discovery of a problem to its solution.

indirect interlock occurs when a director of company A and a director of company B are both directors of company C.

inspiration refers to an innovative, creative solution that is not reached by logical means.

institutional environment norms, values, and expectations from stakeholders (e.g., customers, investors, boards, government, and the community).

institutional perspective the view of how organizations survive and succeed through congruence between an organization and the expectations from its institutional environment.

institutional similarity the emergence of a common structure and approach among organizations in the same field; called *institutional isomorphism* in the academic literature.

integration the quality of collaboration among departments.

integrator a position or department created solely to coordinate several departments.

intellectual capital the sum of an organization's knowledge, experience, understanding, relationships, processes, innovations, and discoveries.

intelligence team cross-functional group of managers and employees, usually led by a competitive intelligence professional, who work together to gain a deep understanding of a specific business issue.

intensive technologies provide a variety of products or services in combination to a client.

interdependence the extent to which departments depend on each other for information, resources, or materials to accomplish their tasks.

intergroup conflict the behavior that occurs among organizational groups when participants identify with one group and perceive that other groups may block their group's goal achievement or expectations.

interlocking directorate formal linkage that occurs when a member of the board of directors of one company sits on the board of directors of another company.

internal integration a state in which members develop a collective identity and know how to work together effectively.

internal process approach in the internal process approach, effectiveness is measured by assessing internal organizational health and efficiency.

internal process emphasis reflects values of internal focus and structural control.

international division a division organized to handle business in other countries.

international stage the second stage of international development, in which the company takes exports seriously and begins to think multidomestically.

interorganizational relationships the relatively enduring resource transactions, flows, and linkages that occur among two or more organizations.

intranet a private, companywide information system that uses the communications protocols and standards of the Internet but is accessible only to people within the company.

intuitive decision making experience and judgment rather than sequential logic or explicit reasoning are used to make decisions.

J

joint optimization the goal of the sociotechnical systems approach, which means that an organization functions best when the social and technical systems are designed to fit the needs of one another.

joint venture a new and distinct organizational entity set up by two or more organizations to jointly develop an innovative product or shared technology.

K

knowledge management the efforts to systematically find, organize, and make available a company's intellectual capital and to foster a culture of continuous learning and knowledge sharing.

L

labor-management teams a cooperative approach designed to increase worker participation and provide a cooperative model for union-management problems.

large group intervention an approach that brings together participants from all parts of the organization, often including key stakeholders from outside the organization as well, in an off-site setting to discuss problems or opportunities and plan for change.

large-batch production a manufacturing process characterized by long production runs of standardized parts.

lean manufacturing a process that uses highly trained employees at every stage of the production process, who take a painstaking approach to squeeze out all waste to improve value to the customer.

legends stories of historic events that may have been embellished with fictional details.

legitimacy the general perception that an organization's actions are desirable, proper, and appropriate within the environment's system of norms, values, and beliefs.

level of analysis in systems theory, the subsystem on which the primary focus is placed; four levels of analysis normally characterize organizations.

liaison role a role in which a person is located in one department but has the responsibility for communicating and achieving coordination with another department.

life cycle the concept that organizations are born, grow older, and eventually die.

long-linked technology the combination in one organization of successive stages of production, with each stage of production using as its inputs the production of the preceding stage and producing inputs for the following stage.

low-cost leadership strategy a strategy that tries to increase market share by keeping costs low compared to competitors.

M

management innovation the adoption and implementation of a management practice, process, structure, strategy, or technique that is new to the organization and is intended to further organizational goals.

management science approach organization decision making that uses mathematical models and statistical techniques to analyze numerous variables and arrive at the best solution; the analog to the rational approach by individual managers.

managerial ethics principles that guide the decisions and behaviors of managers with regard to whether they are right or wrong.

market control the use of price competition to evaluate the output and productivity of an organization or its major departments and divisions.

mass customization using mass-production technology to quickly and cost-effectively assemble goods that are uniquely designed to fit the demands of individual customers.

matrix structure an organization structure that is multifocused in that both product and function or geography and function are emphasized at the same time.

mechanistic an organization system marked by rules, procedures, a clear hierarchy of authority, and centralized decision making.

mediating technology provides products or services that mediate or link clients from the external environment and allows each department to work independently.

mimetic forces the pressure to copy or model other organizations that are generally regarded as successful.

mission the organization's reason for existence; describes the organization's shared values and beliefs and its reason for being.

mission culture a culture characterized by emphasis on a clear vision of the organization's purpose and on the achievement of goals, such as sales growth, profitability, or market share, to help achieve the purpose.

multidomestic means competitive issues in each country are independent of other countries; the company deals with each country individually.

multidomestic strategy strategy in which competition in each country is handled independently of competition in other countries.

multifocused grouping a grouping in which the organization embraces two or more structural grouping alternatives simultaneously, often called *matrix* or *hybrid*.

multinational stage the stage of international development in which a company has extensive experience in a number of international markets and has established marketing, manufacturing, or research and development (R&D) facilities in several foreign countries.

N

negotiation the bargaining process that often occurs during confrontation and that enables the parties to systematically reach a solution.

network centrality a source of power based on being centrally located in the organization and having access to information and people that are critical to the company's success.

new-venture fund a fund that provides financial resources for employees to develop new ideas, products, or businesses.

niche a domain of unique environmental resources and needs.

noncore technology a department work process that is important to the organization but is not directly related to its primary mission.

nonprogrammed decisions novel and poorly defined, and no procedure exists for solving a problem.

nonroutine technologies technologies characterized by high task variety, and the conversion process is not analyzable or well understood.

nonsubstitutability a source of horizontal power when a department's function cannot be performed by other readily available resources.

normative forces pressures to achieve standards of professionalism and to adopt techniques that are considered by the professional community to be up to date and effective.

O

official goals formally stated definition of business scope and outcomes the organization is trying to achieve.

open innovation an approach that extends the search for and commercialization of new products beyond the boundaries of the organization.

open system a system, such as an organization, that must interact with the environment to survive.

open systems emphasis an approach that is shaped by a combination of external focus and flexible structure

operating goals designate the ends sought through the actual operating procedures of the organization and explain what the organization is trying to do.

organic an organization characterized by free-flowing, adaptive processes, an unclear hierarchy or authority, and decentralized decision making.

organization development focuses on the human and social aspects of the organization as a way to improve the organization's ability to adapt and solve problems.

organization structure designates formal reporting relationships, including the number of levels in the hierarchy and the span of control of managers and supervisors; identifies the grouping together of individuals into departments and of departments into the total organization; and includes the design of systems to ensure effective communication, coordination, and integration of efforts across departments.

organization theory and design is a macro examination of organizations analyzing the whole organization as a unit.

organizational behavior a micro approach to organizations that focuses on the individuals within organizations as the relevant units of analysis.

organizational change the adoption of a new idea or behavior by an organization.

organizational decision making the process of identifying and solving problems.

organizational decline a condition in which a substantial, absolute decrease in an organization's resource base occurs over time.

organizational ecosystem a system formed by the interaction of a community of organizations and their environment.

organizational environment everything that exists outside the boundary of the organization and has the potential to affect all or part of the organization.

organizational form an organization's specific technology, structure, products, goals, and personnel, which can be selected or rejected by the environment.

organizational goal a desired state of affairs that the organization attempts to reach.

organizational innovation the adoption of an idea or behavior that is new to the organization's industry, market, or general environment.

organizational politics the activities of acquiring, developing, and using power and other resources to influence others and obtain the preferred outcome when there is uncertainty or disagreement about choices.

organizations social entities that are goal-directed, designed as deliberately structured and coordinated activity systems, and are linked to the external environment.

organized anarchy extremely organic organizations characterized by highly uncertain conditions.

outcome control management control based on monitoring and rewarding results rather than on how those results are obtained.

outsourcing contracting out certain tasks or functions, such as manufacturing or credit processing, to other companies.

P

personnel ratios the proportions of administrative, clerical, and professional support staff.

point–counterpoint a decision-making technique that divides decision makers into two groups and assigns them different, often competing, responsibilities.

political model a definition of an organization as being made up of groups that have separate interests, goals, and values in which power and influence are needed to reach decisions.

political tactics for using power these include building coalitions, expanding networks, assigning loyal people to key positions, using reciprocity, enhancing legitimacy and expertise, and making a direct appeal.

pooled interdependence the lowest form of interdependence among departments, in which work does not flow between units.

population a set of organizations engaged in similar activities with similar patterns of resource utilization and outcomes.

population-ecology perspective focuses on organizational diversity and adaptation within a population of organizations.

power the ability of one person (or department) to influence other people (or departments) to carry out orders or to do something they would not otherwise have done.

power sources the five sources of horizontal power in organizations are dependency, financial resources, centrality, nonsubstitutability, and the ability to cope with uncertainty.

problem consensus the level of agreement among managers about the nature of a problem or opportunity and about which goals and outcomes to pursue.

problem identification the decision-making stage during which information about environmental and organizational conditions is monitored to determine if performance is satisfactory and to diagnose the cause of shortcomings.

problem solution the decision-making stage during which alternative courses of action are considered and one alternative is selected and implemented.

problemistic search search that occurs when managers look around the immediate environment for a solution to quickly resolve a problem.

process an organized group of related tasks and activities that work together to transform inputs into outputs that create value for customers.

product and service innovations pertain to the product or service outputs of an organization.

product matrix type of matrix structure in which the project or product managers have primary authority and functional managers simply assign technical personnel to projects and provide advisory expertise as needed.

programmed decisions repetitive and well defined, these decisions are used when procedures exist for resolving the problem.

prospect theory theory that suggests that the threat of a loss has a greater impact on a decision than the possibility of an equivalent gain.

prospector a business strategy of innovating, taking risks, seeking out new opportunities, and growing.

Q

quasirationality a decision-making trend that involves a combination of intuitive and analytical thought.

R

rational approach decision-making process based on systematic analysis of a problem followed by choice and implementation in a logical sequence.

rational goal emphasis represents management values of structural control and external focus.

rational model a model of organization characterized by rational decision processes, clear goals and choices, centralized power and control, an efficiency orientation, and little conflict among groups.

rational–legal authority is based on employees' belief in the legality of rules and the right of those elevated to positions of authority to issue commands.

reactor a response to environmental threats and opportunities in an ad hoc fashion.

reciprocal interdependence the highest level of interdependence, in which the output of operation A is the input to operation B, and the output of operation B is the input back again to operation A.

reengineering the redesign of a vertical organization along its horizontal workflows and processes.

relational coordination refers to frequent, timely, problem-solving communication carried out through relationships of shared goals, shared knowledge, and mutual respect.

resource dependence a situation in which organizations depend on the environment but strive to acquire control over resources to minimize their dependence.

resource-based approach assesses organizational effectiveness based on how successfully the organization obtains and manages valued resources.

resource-dependence theory describes rational ways organizations try to minimize their dependence on other organizations and influence the environment to make resources available.

retention the preservation and institutionalization of selected organizational forms.

rites and ceremonies the elaborate, planned activities that make up a special event and are often conducted for the benefit of an audience.

role a part in a dynamic social system that allows an employee to use his or her discretion and ability to achieve an outcome or meet a goal.

routine technologies are characterized by little task variety and the use of objective, computational procedures.

rule of law that which arises from a set of codified principles and regulations that describe how people are required to act, that are generally accepted in society, and that are enforceable in the courts.

S

satisficing the acceptance of a satisfactory rather than a maximum level of performance, enabling an organization to achieve several goals simultaneously.

sayings mottoes or mantras that encapsulate key cultural values

scientific management emphasizes scientifically determined jobs and management practices as the way to improve efficiency and labor productivity.

sectors subdivisions of the external environment that contain similar elements.

selection the process by which a new organizational form is suited to the environment and can survive, or is "selected out" and fails.

sequential interdependence a serial form of interdependence with parts produced in one department becoming inputs to another department.

service technology is characterized by simultaneous production and consumption, customized output, customer participation, intangible output, and being labor intensive.

skunkworks a separate, small, informal, highly autonomous, and often secretive group that focuses on breakthrough ideas for the business.

small-batch production a manufacturing process that relies heavily on the human operator and is not highly mechanized.

smart factories link manufacturing components that previously stood alone and are also referred to as digital factories, computer-integrated manufacturing, flexible manufacturing systems, advanced manufacturing technology, or agile manufacturing.

social business refers to using social media technologies such as blogs, social networks, or Twitter for interacting with and facilitating communication and collaboration among employees, customers, and other stakeholders.

social capital the quality of interactions among people and the degree to which they share a common perspective.

social construct created and defined by an individual or group rather than existing independently in the external world.

social media include company online community pages and forums, blogs and wikis for virtual collaboration, social media sites such as Facebook or LinkedIn, video channels such as YouTube, and microblogging platforms such as Twitter and China's Sina Weibo.

social media command center a dedicated office where a company can monitor what is being said about the company on social media platforms.

social network analysis a valuable technique enabled by IT, which can help managers learn about informal relationships and network structures within an organization.

social networking a peer-to-peer communication channel, where people interact in an online community, share personal data and photos, and produce and share a variety of information and opinions.

sociotechnical systems approach recognizes the interaction of technical and human needs in effective job design, combining the needs of people with the organization's need for technical efficiency.

sources of intergroup conflict factors that generate conflict, including goal incompatibility, differentiation, task interdependence, and limited resources.

specialist an organization that provides a narrower range of goods or services or that serves a narrower market.

stakeholder any group within or outside of an organization that has a stake in the organization's performance.

stakeholder approach integrates diverse organizational activities by looking at various organizational stakeholders and what they want from the organization.

standardization policies that ensure all branches of the company at all locations operate in the same way.

stories narratives based on true events that are frequently shared among employees and told to new employees to inform them about an organization.

strategic alliance an alliance that is less formal and binding than a joint venture.

strategic constituents approach an approach that measures effectiveness by focusing on the satisfaction of key stakeholders, those who are critical to the organization's ability to survive and thrive.

strategic contingencies events and activities both inside and outside an organization that are essential for attaining organizational goals.

strategic intent means that all the organization's energies and resources are directed toward a focused, unifying, and compelling overall goal.

strategy a plan for interacting with the competitive environment to achieve organizational goals.

strategy and structure innovations pertain to the administrative domain in an organization.

strategy map a visual representation of the key drivers of an organization's success that shows how specific outcomes in each area are linked.

structural dimensions provide labels to describe the internal characteristics of an organization, and create a basis for measuring and comparing organizations.

structure a value dimension that pertains to organization structure and whether stability or flexibility is the dominant structural consideration.

struggle for existence the concept that organizations and populations of organizations are engaged in a competitive struggle over resources, and each organizational form is fighting to survive.

subcultures cultures that develop to reflect the common problems, goals, and experiences that members of a team, department, or other unit share.

sustainability economic development that generates wealth and meets the needs of the current generation while saving the environment so future generations can meet their needs as well.

switching structures an organization creates an organic structure when such a structure is needed for the initiation of new ideas and reverts to a more mechanistic structure to implement the ideas.

symbol something that represents another thing.

symptoms of structural deficiency signs that the organization structure is out of alignment, including absence of collaboration among units, delayed or poor quality decision making, failure to respond innovatively to environmental changes, a decline in employee performance, and the failure to meet goals.

T

tacit knowledge knowledge based on personal experience, rules of thumb, intuition, and judgment that is difficult to communicate and pass on to others.

tactics for enhancing collaboration these include techniques such as integration devices, confrontation and negotiation, intergroup consultation, member rotation, and shared mission and superordinate goals that enable groups to overcome differences and work together.

tactics for increasing power these include entering areas of high uncertainty, creating dependencies, providing scarce resources, and satisfying strategic contingencies.

task a narrowly defined piece of work assigned to a person.

task environment sectors with which the organization interacts directly and that have a direct impact on the organization's ability to achieve its goals.

task force a temporary committee composed of representatives from each organizational unit affected by a problem.

team building activities that promote the idea that people who work together can work as a team.

teams permanent task forces, often used in conjunction with a full-time integrator.

technical complexity the extent of mechanization of the manufacturing process.

technical knowledge the understanding and agreement about how to solve problems and reach organizational goals.

technology the work processes, techniques, machines, and actions used to transform organizational inputs (materials, information, ideas) into outputs (products and services).

technology innovations are changes in an organization's production process, including its knowledge and skill base, that enable distinctive competence.

trade associations groups that allow organizations in the same industry to meet, share information, and monitor one another's activities.

traditional authority is based on a belief in traditions and in the legitimacy of the status of people exercising authority through those traditions.

transaction processing systems systems that automate the organization's routine, day-to-day business transactions.

transnational model a form of organization that has multiple centers, subsidiary managers who initiate strategy and innovations for the company as a whole, and unity and coordination achieved through shared vision and values.

U

uncertainty condition that exists when decision makers do not have sufficient information about environmental factors, and they have a difficult time predicting external changes.

V

values-based leadership a relationship between a leader and followers that is based on shared, strongly internalized values that are advocated and acted upon by the leader.

variation the appearance of new, diverse forms in a population of organizations.

variety in terms of tasks, the frequency of unexpected and novel events that occur in the conversion process.

venture teams a technique used to foster creativity within organizations by setting up small teams as their own companies to pursue innovations.

vertical information system a strategy for increasing vertical information capacity.

vertical linkages are used to coordinate activities between the top and bottom of an organization and are designed primarily for control of the organization.

virtual network grouping with this grouping the organization is a loosely connected cluster of separate components that are electronically connected for the sharing of information and completion of tasks.

virtual network structure the firm subcontracts many or most of its major processes to separate companies and coordinates their activities from a small headquarters organization; sometimes called a *modular structure*.

virtual team a team made up of organizationally or geographically dispersed members who are linked primarily through advanced information and communications technologies.

W

whistle-blowing employee disclosure of illegal, immoral, or illegitimate practices on the part of the organization.

Name Index

Page numbers followed by the letter n indicate the note in which the entry is located.

Corporate Name Index

Note: Page numbers in *italic* type indicate exhibits.